Commentary
ON THE GOSPEL OF
St. Matthew

St. Thomas Aquinas

Translated by Rev. Paul M. Kimball

DOLOROSA PRESS
MMXII

COMMENTARY ON THE GOSPEL
OF SAINT MATTHEW

From the original Latin by St. Thomas Aquinas.

Translation in English,
Copyright © 2012 by Paul M. Kimball
All rights reserved.

Cover art and layout design
Copyright © 2011 by Wesley Talley
(artisforgod@yahoo.com)
All rights reserved.

No part of this book may be reproduced or transmitted in any form or by any means, electronic or mechanical, including information and retrieval systems, without permission in writing from the copyright holder, except by a reviewer who may quote brief passages in a review.

ISBN: 978-0-615-44040-8

ACKNOWLEDGEMENTS

I am grateful to Fr. Timothy Bellamah, OP for sending me a copy of the Basel manuscript, to Dr. Hans Kraml, professor at the University of Innsbruck for deciphering and transcribing the Basel manuscript, to Mrs. Klara Worley for her translation of Fr. Pelster's article in German, to Mr. Stephen McNulty for his translation of Fr. Shooner's and Fr. Renard's articles in French, to Mrs. Patricia Petersen for her indefatigable labors of proofreading the text countless times, to Mrs. Cheryl Hadley for proofreading the entire text as well, to Mr. Wesley Talley, who showed unlimited patience in arranging and rearranging the layout, proofreading and using his extraordinary artistic ability to draw the portrait of St. Thomas on the cover, and finally to my own good mother, whose patient labors and loving support of any work that her priestly son might choose to do for the glory of God and the good of His holy Church can only be rewarded by the One who gave to mankind His last and most precious gift on the Cross when He said, "Behold thy Mother."

PREFACE

The following commentary by the Angelic Doctor on the Gospel of St. Matthew is unlike his more famous works, such as the *Summa Theologica* or his *Catena Aurea*, which is his "Golden chain" linking the interpretations of the Church Fathers on each verse of the four Gospels. This Commentary, however, is very typical of his day-to-day work of teaching Sacred Scripture, which he used as the basis of his theological works. Hence, Fr. J.-P. Torrell, O.P., wrote:

> Though long overlooked in favor of the *Sentences* or the *Summa*, this kind of Biblical teaching was nevertheless Thomas' ordinary labor. And it was in this way that he commented on a little more than half of the New Testament and several books of the Old. If we wish, therefore, to get a slightly less one-sided idea of the whole theologian and his method, it is imperative to read and use in a much deeper fashion these Biblical commentaries in parallel with the great systematic works.[1]

Scholastic theology is sometimes viewed as too speculative and not founded upon Scripture, considered by some to be the only "pure source" of revelation. But those who have studied the Biblical commentaries of St. Thomas can see clearly that his systematic summaries of reasoned theology are solidly grounded upon his comprehensive study of Scripture and the Church Fathers, who in the fervent days of the Early Church breathed out citations from Scripture in practically every line of their sermons. In this commentary, as in his others, one finds not merely one holy and learned doctor of the Church passing down the interpretations gleaned from the Apostles and the Fathers, and their own pious meditations, but an encyclopedia or synthesis of all their best insights in words clearer than their own, but having the same meaning. "By the reverent use of the Fathers, St. Thomas—as Cajetan has observed in a famous passage[2]—has in some way captured the spirit of them all."[3] So Pope John XII could conclude: "He (Thomas Aquinas) enlightened the Church more than all the

---

[1]. Jean-Pierre Torrell, O.P., *Saint Thomas Aquinas* (Washington D.C.: The Catholic University of America Press, 1993), p. 55.
[2]. "Unde patet fundamentum authoris esse solidum, peripateticum, et consonum non solum sibi, sed sacris doctoribus, quos quia summe veneratus est author, ideo intellectus omnium quodamodo fortitus est." "Hence it is evident that the foundation of the author is solid, peripatetic, and consonant not only with itself, but with the sacred doctors, whom because the author highly venerates, and therefore the understanding of them all is as it were strengthened."(Thomas Cajetan, Commentary on II-II q. 148, a. 4 ad 1um).
[3]. Walz, O.P., Father Angelus, *Saint Thomas Aquinas* (Westminster, Maryland, The Newman Press, 1951), p. 174.

other Doctors together; a man can derive more profit from his books in one year than from a lifetime spent in pondering the philosophy of others."[4] St. Pius V confirmed this opinion when he ordered the feast of St. Thomas as Doctor to be kept by the universal Church, saying: "But inasmuch as, by the providence of Almighty God, the power and truth of the philosophy of the Angelic Doctor, ever since his enrollment amongst the citizens of Heaven, have confounded, refuted and routed many subsequent heresies, as was so often clearly seen in the past and was lately apparent in the sacred decrees of the Council of Trent, We order that the memory of the Doctor by whose valor the world is daily delivered from pestilential errors be cultivated more than ever before with feelings of pious and grateful devotion."[5]

The authority of this Prince of theologians can hardly be overestimated. Less than fifty years after his death, Tolomeo of Lucca wrote: "This man is supreme among modern teachers of philosophy and theology, and indeed in every subject. And such is the common view and opinion, so that nowadays in the University of Paris they call him the *Doctor Communis* because of the outstanding clarity of his teaching."[6] Jacques Maritain gives a list of 66 Popes who have praised St. Thomas Aquinas, from Pope Alexander IV during the saint's lifetime to Pope Pius XI in 1923, who wrote his Encyclical *Studiorum Ducem* for the sixth centenary of St. Thomas. Now in modern times, when Modernism is currently wreaking havoc within the Church, Pope St. Pius X gave the study of St. Thomas' scholastic philosophy as the first remedy of Modernism.[7] Modernists firstly attacked the Church by undermining her foundation of the orthodox interpretation of Sacred Scripture, and so Pope Pius X countered this attack by founding the Biblical Institute of Rome in 1909. "As the study of the Bible is both the most important and the most dangerous study in theology, Pius X wished to found at Rome a center for these studies, to give assurance at once of unquestioned orthodoxy and scientific worth; and so, with the assistance of the whole Catholic world, there was established at Rome the Biblical Institute, under the direction of the Jesuits."[8]

Pope Pius XII, in his allocution to the professors and students of the *Angelicum* on January 14, 1958, highlighted in particular the special importance of St. Thomas' commentaries on Sacred Scripture:

4. Consistorial address of 1318.
5. Bull *Mirabilis Deus* of April 11, 1567.
6. *Historia Eccles.* xxiii, c. 9.
7. Pascendi Dominici Gregis, n. 45.
8. "Pope Pius X," The Catholic Encyclopedia (1911 ed.), vol. 12, p. 138.

To the theologian this is also a rule, that, keeping the example of Aquinas before his eyes, he diligently study and assiduously handle Sacred Scripture, which ought also to be esteemed of incomparable importance by students of the religious disciplines: for, this same most holy Doctor bearing witness, '(Sacred doctrine) uses the authority of the canonical Scriptures as an incontrovertible proof... For our faith rests upon the revelation made to the Apostles and Prophets who wrote the canonical books, and not on the revelations (if any such there are) made to other doctors.' (I q. 1, a. 8 ad 2um). As he taught, so he always acted. For the commentaries made by him on the Old and New Testaments, especially on the Epistles of St. Paul, in the opinion of those having the most expert judgment, shine with such solidity, subtlety, and precision, that they can be numbered among his greatest theological works, and as such are to be deemed a Biblical complement of great importance. Wherefore, if anyone should neglect them, he is scarcely to be said to fully and entirely (*plane et plene*) enjoy a familiarity and knowledge of the holy Angelic Doctor.[9]

Among St. Thomas' works, his lectures on the Gospel of St. Matthew may be classified as a minor work, but coming from such a master of theology, it is worthy of our attention. As an introduction to this particular commentary on the Gospel of St. Matthew, let us firstly read part of a short study on this commentary that was only recognized for its worth many years after it was written. Fr. I. T. Eschmann, O.P., of the Pontifical Institute of Mediaeval Studies, commends its author as follows:

Fr. F. Pelster, S.J., whose recent death is deplored by all lovers of St. Thomas, observed, in 1923,[10] that the documentation of the *Lectura super Matthaeum* closely resembled, and probably followed, the documentation of the *Glossa continua in Matthaeum*. Its date therefore should be set at "after 1264." When Mandonnet brought forth his theory about the Parisian origin, Pelster's observation appeared to be irrelevant.[11] It may, after closer examination of the facts, turn out to be the most pertinent dating, in modern literature, of the *Lectura super Matthaeum*.[12]

Here, then, follows Fr. Pelster's analysis of both the authenticity and date of these lectures:

9. AAS 50 (1958), 151-152.
10. "*Echtheitsfragen bei den exegetischen Schriften des hi. Thomas v. A. II, 2: Die Lectura in Evangelium Matthaei*"; Biblica, IV (1923), 300-307.
11. "Grabmann supported Pelster's opinion in *Enciclopedia Italianit.*

XXXIII (1937), p. 1014. *In Die Werke...* (1949), p. 264, he agrees with the common opinion.
12. I. T. Eschmann, "The Quotations of Aristotle's Politics in St. Thomas' *Lectura Super Matthaeum*," Mediaeval Studies, 18 (1956), p. 240.

As a proof of the authenticity of the printed Commentary, the circumstantial evidence does not suffice, at least according to contemporary levels of our knowledge. Which manuscript may have served the first editor Bartholomew Spina, O.P., (who in 1527 published the Commentary on Matthew together with the Expositions on Isaias, Jeremias and the Lamentations, published in Venice by Octavian Scotus) as the basis, we do not know.

Firstly, let us point out the close connection between the *Catena Aurea* and the Commentary. Again and again especially those quotations of the Fathers are used which are cited by the *Catena*. Often the name of the Father is given, but at times it is not disclosed. Let us compare the beginning of the first chapter to start with.

CATENA CH. 16	COMMENTARY CH. 16
CHRYS; He adds 'of Philip,' to distinguish it from the other Cesarea, of Strato. And He asks this question in the former place, leading His disciples far out of the way of the Jews, that being set free from all fear, they might say freely what was in their mind. JEROME; This Philip was the brother of Herod, the tetrarch of Ituraea, and the region of Trachonitis, who gave to the city, which is now called Paneas, the name of Cesarea in honor of Tiberius Cæsar...	He added Philippi, because there were two Cesareas, namely, Cesarea Trachonitis(!), where Peter was sent to Cornelius; another Cesarea is this one which is otherwise called Paneas. The first was established in honor of Cæsar Augustus, and Philip constructed the latter in honor of Tiberius Cæsar... this city was located beyond the borders of the Jews; for that reason, before He chose to question them concerning their faith, He brought them away from the Jews.
ORIGEN; Christ puts this question to His disciples, that from their answer we may learn that there were at that time among the Jews various opinions concerning Christ; and to the end that we should always investigate what opinion men may form of us; that if any ill be said of us, we may cut off the occasions of it.	When a wise man asks, he teaches, as Jerome says.[13] Hence, we are instructed in many things, so that we may be mindful of what is said about ourselves: so that if any ill is said about us, we are careful to correct it.
JEROME; Beautifully is the question put, *Whom do men say that the Son of Man is?* For they	Likewise, those who know His divinity are called gods... but those who know His humanity

---

[13]. Here by oversight, a mistake has been made; because after Origen follows Jerome in the *Catena*, who offers a different explanation though, which follows straightaway.

who speak of the Son of Man, are men: but they who understood His divine nature are called not men but Gods.

HILARY; By asking, *Whom do men say that the Son of Man is?* He implied that something ought to be thought respecting Him beyond what appeared, for He was the Son of Man.

are called men; hence, it is said: *Whom do men say that the Son of man is?*

But, as Hilary says, Christ seemed to be merely a man: for that reason, He wanted them to know that He is more than just a simple man.

So much should follow already from these few cited texts: The author of the Matthew Commentary had the *Catena Aurea* in view. Otherwise it would be unexplainable that he, out of a great number of the writings of the Fathers, should choose exactly those that are being quoted in the *Catena Aurea* and generally in the same sequence, too, as they appear there. The reverse case is impossible as Thomas, in the *Catena*, according to his own testimony, avails himself directly of the original sources; moreover, as there the connection is much closer; and finally, in some cases the Commentary only refers to the meaning without the name, while the *Catena* gives the name as well.

Yet on those grounds an important conclusion for the date of composition is drawn: The Commentary cannot have come into being during 1256-59, as assumed by Fr. Madonnet.[14] It was written, at the earliest, between 1264-1265, and probably even a good deal later than that, as Thomas reasonably will have commented next on the three last Gospels, too, in *Catena* form. It is likely though, that these were completed in 1265 or later.

["Known as the *Catena Aurea*, this work was undertaken by Thomas at the request of Urban IV towards the end of 1262 or the beginning of 1263. The speed of Thomas's work has something surprising about it, since the volume on Matthew was offered to the pope before his death on October 2, 1264"—Torrell, p. 136]

But is Thomas the author or has someone else, with help of the *Catena*, written the Commentary?

There is a second inner criterion: the conformity of doctrine. Only a few examples are here given: In Mt. 1, 23- the author distinguishes the prophecy of predestination, of foreknowledge, and of denunciation. This same grouping we meet in the *Summa Theol.* II II, q. 174, a. 1. In the same passage the explanation of the conditional future is explained through the gazing into a mirror of eternity. In Mt. 4, 10, he develops, over the latreutic worship that is owed to God as the Highest Lord and the last end, the very same thoughts as in the *Summa* II II, q. 84, a. 1 and in the *Summa Contra Gentiles* bk. 3, ch. 120. In the same way, the explanation of the Beatitudes and their relation to the Gifts corresponds throughout with the grouping

---

14. *Revue des Sciences Philos. Et Théol.* IX (1920), p. 142.

and explanation which Thomas gives in the *Summa* I II, q. 69, a. 3. In Mt. 16, 19 & 26, is developed the Thomastic teaching of instrumental efficacy of the Sacraments. In Mt. 17, 2, the author rejects— as he does in the *Summa* III, q. 65, a. 2 – the statement, that Christ had received the gift of clarity on Mount Thabor; this, Thomas says, would be specific to the time after the Resurrection.

Lastly, the authenticity shows itself, too, in the form and construction of his thoughts, occasionally a marked similarity to other writings of his, assuredly authentic ones where, though, there does not exist that dependency which is found with a plagiarist. Two examples will be sufficient here. In Mt. 2, 2, subsequent to the star of the Magi, the teaching about fate is discussed. The same question Thomas has dealt with in the *Summa Contra Gentiles* bk. 3, chap. 93, and in the *Quodlibet* 12, a. 4.

Matthew 2, 2	C. Gent. 3, 93	Quodl. 12, a. 4
Note, therefore, that we see many things in human affairs that happen accidentally and by chance... Some said that these chance events could not be attributed to another higher, controlling cause. And so they denied the existence of fate... And this was, according to Augustine, the opinion of Cicero. But we say that these chance events are to be attributed to a higher controlling cause. But also, since the word 'fate' is so-called from the verb *for, fari*, meaning, as it were, 'something proclaimed' and 'spoken out.' There is a difference of opinions about the source of this ordina-	Indeed, men observe that many things happen by accident in this world if their particular causes be considered, and some men have maintained that they are not even ordered by higher causes. To these people it has appeared that there is no fate at all. But others have attempted to reduce these events to certain higher causes from which they result in an orderly way, in accord with a definite plan. These people have asserted that there is fate in the sense that things observed to happen by chance are "pre-fated," that is, foretold and pre-ordained to happen... Some of these people, then, have	Now we see that many things happen by accident. And so in past times there was a doubt whether these things which happen variably and without order, are reduced to some ordaining cause. And they who deny this, say that fate is nothing, as Cicero says. Others say that they are ordained by some higher cause; and these men name fate, from *for, faris*, as though all these things were "pre-fated" by some higher cause. Others reduce these things to some higher cause, namely, to the heavenly bodies; hence, they say that fate is nothing other than the power of the position of the stars...

tion. For some said that it comes from the power of celestial bodies. Whence, they say that fate is nothing other than the arrangement of the stars. Others attribute these chance events to Divine Providence.	tried to reduce all contingent events which occur by chance, here below, to causes among the celestial bodies... Some men have desired to reduce to the control of divine providence all things...	Others reduce all things to Divine Providence.

In these passages it is proven that the celestial bodies cannot bring about fate, as they cannot directly influence our spiritual faculties, and that furthermore any worship of the Divine and any facilitation of government would be destroyed and finally human wickedness would be attributed to God. The first reason, and in slightly different form, the last as well, can be found again in *Quodlibet*. Similarly, a quotation from Augustine can be found again in *Quodlibet*. The same quotation and a second one from Gregory are contained in the *Summa Contra Gentiles*.

From the comparison of those three passages it should follow that the same author is speaking throughout: We find the same ideas, essentially the same order, the same etymology..., the same quotations. On the other hand, that slavish dependency, which one frequently finds with a copyist, does not exist; on the contrary, we are convinced by seeing how an independent mind treats the same object in a similar yet constantly reforming and improving way.

Comparing the sequence of the writings supplies a second result, especially when comparing the whole text of the question: it can be safely assumed that the passage in the Commentary on Matthew was written after the *Summa Contra Gentiles*, because with regard to the contents it takes them in some respects further than in the *Summa Contra Gentiles*, for instance, when it mentions Cicero; when it specifically introduces the verb, *for*; when it represents the proof, that the celestial bodies do not directly influence the higher spiritual and intellectual faculties...

The result of the study so far should be that Thomas is the author of the entire Commentary on Matthew. Examples of proof have been taken from various parts, and, if drawn from the entire writing, many more could be found. Moreover, it follows, from the comparison with the *Summa Contra Gentiles* and especially from those comparisons with the *Catena Aurea*, that the explanation was written after those works, that is, at the earliest after 1264.[15]

---

15. Fr. Pelster S.J., "Echtheitsfragen Bei Exegetischen Schriften des Hl. Thomas von Aquin," Biblica: Commentarii editi a Pontificio Instituto Biblico, IV (Rome, 1923), p.300-306.

Are we dealing with an exposition or a reportation? Everything points to the latter. An edited text surely would have found a wider circulation; it would have been included in the Paris *Exemplaria*. An exposition surely would have found a wider circulation; it would have had a prologue. Reading it carefully one discovers some clear signs of an oral lecture, signs which, as a rule, are missing in Thomas' writings. In connection with this, there is the unusually frequent usage of the questioning form, untypical for Thomas, which is evident everywhere. Indicative, also, of oral delivery is the repeated use of the vivid *Notate* ("Observe that...") instead of the related but abstract, *Notandum* ("It ought to be observed..."). Occasionally, too, the form is not as lucid and distinct as we are used to from Thomas. Here and there parts of the construction are announced and then not followed up. Several times the impression is given that here the thought is only outlined and not developed.

But if the Commentary on Matthew is truly a reportation, then we have without a doubt the *"Lecturam super Matthaeum; idem frater Petrus [de Andria] quondam scholaris Parisiensis [recollegit] quae defectiva est"*[16] in front of us, which Bartholomew of Capua speaks about in his publications. The solution would be given by Nicholas Trivet. He writes, *"Item Lectura super Matthaeum incompleta, quam partim idem frater [Petrus de Andria], partim saecularis quidam recollegit ejus studio delectatus."*[17] According to Bartholomew, the copy originates from Peter of Andria, and, according to Nicholas, from a secular cleric as well. The copy which was in the possession of Bartholomew, or was made available to him, and which also was known to the author of the Stamser Catalog, would have only comprised the first fifteen chapters, while Nicholas Trivet knew the second part as well. Therefore, the reading *'completa'* instead of *'incompleta'* by Echard, should definitely be considered. As against his available material, perhaps Trivet wanted to stress that there existed a complete copy. Another indication can be found by the fact that an irregularity occurred at the end of the chapter 15 in our text. While normally verse after verse is explained, the explanation of the last verse is missing.

In brief, let us sum up the result. The printed Matthew commentary is an authentic work of Aquinas. The commentary, though, does not belong to the *–Expositio ad Litteram-* of the four Gospels, but is the *–Lectura super Matthaeum-* which comes under the *Reportata*, and which was copied by the Dominican Peter of Andria and another pupil. Chronologically, the commentary belongs to the period after 1264. Yes, the *'quondam scholaris Parisiensis'* of the Logothete [Bartholomew of Capua] seems to point to the Parisian

---

16. i.e. "The lecture on Matthew, Brother Peter [of Andria] a Parisian scholar compiled, which is defective" (Bartholomew of Capua's list: *Naples* 85, p. 389).

17. "Likewise the Lecture on Matthew is incomplete, which in part the same brother [Peter of Andria], in part a certain secular cleric compiled who delighted in the study of it" (cf. the study by Shooner in 'La *Lectura in Matthæum* de S. Thomas (Deux fragments inédits et la *Reportatio* de Pierre d'Andria),' *Angelicum*, 33 (1956), pp. 134-135).

residence. The depth of the perceptions, the maturity and universality of the explanation would fit such a late time rather well. This document is of a special charm, too, because it reveals the living teacher to us more than do other works."[18]

This date has been made more precise in recent times:

> Two arguments push the date most probably into the second Paris regency (1268-72). A case can be made that Peter of Andria revised his notes from the lectures on Matthew after the year 1273, and it does not seem likely that he would have waited many years after the lectures were given to revise his notes for publication. Finally, Thomas echoes several arguments which had arisen in a dispute with Gerard of Abbeville in 1270 over the state of perfection; in particular in his commentary on Mt. 19, 21, he echoes a phrase which Gerard had brought into the discussion from a text by Chrysostom, according to which a bishop is in a higher state of perfection than any monk, 'be it Elias himself.'
>
> The date of the lectures' production is foundational for understanding Thomas' accomplishment. He commented on the Gospel of Matthew toward the end of his life, after he had composed the *Catena Aurea* on Matthew (1263), and during the same general period as he was researching and writing the later parts of the *Summa Theologiae*; he probably began his lectures at some point during the composition of the *Secunda Pars* and completed them some time before writing the *Tertia Pars*.[19] Hence, the Aquinas who undertook to comment on Mattthew's Gospel was Aquinas at the height of his powers, with the entire Patristic tradition at his fingertips and a complete command of scholastic theology. This fact will be the key to the production of the *Lectura in Matthœum*.[20]

After considering the authenticity of the text and its date of composition, let us now turn our attention to the manuscripts that are the records of this lecture, as this will give an appreciation of why the part of the text for the Sermon on the Mount in Chapters Five and Six will not be derived in this new English edition from the previously Latin edition published by Marietti, which is only partly authentic. Dr. Jeremy Holmes, a Senior Fellow of the St. Paul Center for Biblical Theology, who has published a concise summary of this question, has kindly given permission for his words below to be quoted here at length:

18. Pelster, pp. 306-307.
19. Jean-Pierre Torell, *Saint Thomas Aquinas*, vol. I *The Person and His Work* (trans. Robert Royal; Washington DC: The Catholic University of America Press, 1996), pp. 146-47.

20. Jeremy Holmes, "Aquinas' *Lectura in Matthaeum*," in Aquinas on Scripture: An Introduction to his Biblical Commentaries, ed. by Thomas G. Weinandy, OFM, Cap., Daniel A. Keating, and John P. Yocum (New York, T&T International, 2005), p. 76.

Our access to Thomas' actual comments on the Gospel of Matthew is much more limited than might be implied by a casual reference to 'St. Thomas' commentary on St. Matthew.' St. Thomas himself never wrote out his lectures for publication. The term *lectura* denotes commentary delivered orally rather than committed directly to writing; a commentary written by St. Thomas himself would be called an *expositio*. The *lectura* comes down to us through *reportationes*, that is, notes taken down by a person in the audience and later filled out from memory or other sources to look more like the actual transcript of a lecture. Thomas never looked over the resulting document to check its faithfulness to his intention.

Two individuals took down *reportationes*, namely, Peter of Andria[21] (who was responsible for preserving others of St. Thomas' works as well) and one Leodegar of Bensançon, a secular professor at the university.[22] Neither *reportatio* is complete. Peter seems to have written down comments on chapters 1-12 of St. Matthew,[23] while Leodegar recorded the lectures from 6.9 through the end of the Gospel.[24] The result is unusual: from 6.9 through the end of the chapter 12 we have two divergent yet equally authentic texts of the *Lectura in Matthæum*.[25]

Only four manuscripts survive of the lectures on Matthew.[26] In three of these manuscripts, Leodegar's report of 6.9 through the end of the Gospel has been completed by borrowing the earlier chapters from Peter's transcript. Unfortunately, all three of these manuscripts have lacunae from 5.11-6.8 and from 6.14-19. When in 1517 Bartholomew of Spina brought out the first printed edition of the lectures on Matthew, he based his text on a manuscript of this hybrid type, but filled in the gaps in his manuscript source with borrowed material from a commentary by Peter of Scala, a Dominican of the thirteenth century.[27] Bartholomew's printed text became the basis of the later printed versions, with the result that even today the Marietti text of

---

21. Peter of Andria was most probably a student of St. Thomas and a Dominican. (Walz, p. 133). He later became the first Provincial of Naples and the bishop of Vico-Equense, near Sorrento, Italy and died in 1316.
22. We don't know much about Leodegar, but far more about Peter.
23. This manuscript [Naples, Naz. VII.B.21] refers, among other works of St. Thomas to "non-attributed fragments of a commentary on chapters 22, 23, 28 and of St. Matthew which could be also parts of the written record of Peter of Andria in the parts which have not come down to us (Guyot, *Bulletin Thomiste* 11 (1960-62), p. 12)." (Fr. J. P. Renard, *La Lectura super Matthaeum V, 20-48 de Thomas d'Aquin* (Édition d'après le MS. Bâle, Univ. Bibl. B. V. 12). *Recherches de Théologie Ancienne et Médiévale*, 50 (1983), p. 148).
24. These complicated inter-relationships were only clarified by the discovery of the Basel manuscript and its subsequent analysis by H.-V. Shooner, in 'La *Lectura in Matthæum* de S. Thomas (Deux fragments inédits et la *Reportatio* de Pierre d'Andria),' *Angelicum*, 33 (1956), pp. 121-142.
25. Louis-Jacques Bataillon offers a very helpful overview of the issues surrounding the manuscripts of Thomas' many works in 'La Diffusion Manoscritta e Stampata dei Commenti Biblici de San Tommaso d'Aquino,' *Angelicum*, 71 (1994), pp. 579-90. Regarding the *Lectura in Matthæum*, see especially pp. 587-88.
26. Compare this with the 38 surviving manuscripts on the lectures on John, and 60 of the commentary on Job!
27. This 'fraud' was first exposed by Roger Guindon, 'La `Lectura super Matthæum incomplete de saint Thomas,' *Revue de l'Université d'Ottawa*, 25

the *Lectura in Matthœum* is spurious from paragraph numbers 444-582 and from 603-610.

The fourth manuscript was only discovered in 1955, at the university library in Basel.[28] It has been marked as 'anonymous' and had lain unrecognized probably since the end of the thirteenth century, because the text begins at Mt. 1.22. It appears to be the *reportatio* of Peter of Andria. This manuscript not only gives us Peter's divergent report of the lectures on 6.9 through the end of 12, but also fills in the lacunae in the previously known manuscripts.[29]

Fr. H.-V. Shooner, O.P., discovered the authentic text of Thomas in the library of the University of Basel and recalled how the insertion of foreign text was noticed by a student of Bartholomew of Spina, but thereafter ignored before its discovery:

A recent study of P.R. Guindon points out, indeed, that the three manuscripts omit two important sections of the commentary, that of V^{11} to VI^8 and VI^{14-19} in the Sermon on the Mount.

The same study has also revealed that, in our editions, the texts corresponding to these missing parts are not those of St. Thomas, but ones inserted by the zeal of the first editor, Bartholomew of Spina, who was concerned, by his own admission, to correct and complete the manuscript that he was using and which belonged without doubt to the same group as ours. This pious fraud did not pass entirely unnoticed: already by the XVI Century Jerome Vielmius, the pupil of Bartholomew of Spina of the Convent of St. Anastasia of Verona, asserted that he had noticed that one part, *aliquot quaterniones*, of the text edited by his master coincided with the *Postilla* of St. Matthew written by the Dominican Peter of Scala (d.1295), of which the Convent of Verona possessed one copy; and, continues Vielmius:

A little later, as though he were guilty of possessing what ought to be returned, I admonished our teacher and my very dear instructor, Brother Bartholomew of Spina, who had been the first of all to print that work in Latin, that he had not indicated what he had done to the reader.[30]

(1955), pp. 213-219. "MS Vat. Urb. lat. 25, to which Bartholomew of Spina had access, has a scribal note in chap. 5: 'At this point the major part of the fifth chapter is missing and a third part of the sixth, namely to the words "Sic orabitis, etc." as in the original" (James A. Weisheipl O.P., Friar Thomas D'Aquino: His Life, Thought & Works (Washington D.C, The Catholic University of America Press, 1983), p. 427).

28. The manuscript comes from the ancient Convent of the Dominicans of Basel and is now preserved in the University library of that town under the title, "B.V. 12."

29. Holmes, pp. 74-75.

30. "*Paulo post, veluti repetundarum reum, admonui magistrum nostrum et praeceptorem meum clarissimum, fratrem Bartholomaeum Spinam, qui id opus omnium primus typis in vulgus dederat, quod lectori factum non indicasset.*" H. Vielmii, O.P., *De divi Thomae Aquinatis doctrina et scriptis*, Brescia, 1748, p. 102. (The first Edition was published in Padua in 1564). H.-V. Shooner O. P., "La *Lectura in Matthœum* de S. Thomas (Deux fragments inédits de la Reportatio de Pierre d'Andria), Angelicum, 33 1956), pp. 123.

A surprising consequence of Bartholomew's insertion of extraneous text is noted by Fr. J. Weisheipl, O.P.,: "It is ironic that when the Dominican feast, the Patronage of Saint Thomas, was first introduced in the Dominican calendar in the 1920's, the homily for the third lesson was taken from the unsuspected spurious part of the *lectura* commenting on '*Vos estis sal terrae*.' This feast was established on the thirteenth of November to allow festivities outside of Lent, since the original feast of Thomas, which had always been celebrated on March 7, the date of his death, invariably fell in Lent. The November 13 feast has been abolished, and Thomas' feast has now been transferred to January 29."[31]

Although the complete Basel manuscript has yet to be published as a whole, H.-V. Schooner has published the comments on 5.13-16, Fr. J.-P. Renard made available the comments on 5.20-48. Lastly, R. Busa published the comments on 5.3-7 and 6.3.[32] These transcriptions of the Basel manuscript have been utilized and translated in this edition of the Commentary, along with a new transcription generously and well made especially for this publication by Dr. Hans Kraml of the University of Innsbruck. So, for the first time in any language, the complete Commentary, entirely composed of authentic text, is being published.[33] Note that Leodegar of Bensançon's reportation of chapter VI, verses 19-34, has been replaced by the corresponding but superior reportation of Peter of Andria.[34] For, as Fr. Eschmann wrote, "A comparison of the above texts will easily show that Peter's transcript, at least in these places, is superior to that of his classmate."[35] There are six more chapters of Peter of Andria's reportation which have yet

---

31. Weisheipl, p. 122.
32. *Super Mt.*, cap. 6, v. 10-15 S. Thomae Aquinatis *Opera omnia ut sunt in Indice thomistico additis 61 scriptis ex aliis Medii Aevi auctoribus*, t. 6, codex 087, n. 2: Ex lectura super Matth. [Reportatio Petri de Andria]. Ed. R. BUSA (Frommann-Hoolzbog, Stuttgart-Bad Cannstadt, 1980) p. 364-365. Super Mt., cap. 6, v. 9 H. V. SHOONER, *La Lectura in Matthaeum de S. Thomas (Deux fragments inédits et la Reportatio de Pierre d'Andria)*, Angelicum 33 (1956) 156. [Reportatio Petri de Andria]. Super Mt., cap. 5, v. 10 ("unde...")-12, 17-19 S. Thomae Aquinatis *Opera omnia ut sunt in Indice thomistico additis 61 scriptis ex aliis Medii Aevi auctoribus*, t. 6, codex 087, n. 1: *Ex lectura super Matth.* [Reportatio Petri de Andria]. Ed. R. BUSA (Frommann-Hoolzbog, Stuttgart-Bad Cannstadt, 1980) p. 360-362. Super Mt., cap. 5, v. 13-16 H. V. SHOONER, *La Lectura in Matthaeum de S. Thomas (Deux fragments inédits et la Reportatio de Pierre d'Andria)*, Angelicum 33 (1956) 138-142. Super Mt., cap. 5, v. 20-48 Fr. J. P. RENARD, *La Lectura super Matthaeum V, 20-48 de Thomas d'Aquin* (Édition d'après le MS. Bâle, Univ. Bibl. B. V. 12). *Recherches de Théologie Ancienne et Médiévale*, 50 (1983) 153-189. [Reportatio Petri de Andria].
33. The newly transcribed text is accompanied by full citations of the writings of the Church Fathers from which he drew so as to clarify and support the new transcription.
34. The Latin transcription of the newly transcribed text may be found in the Appendix.
35. Eschmann, p. 236.

to be both transcribed and published, which would certainly enhance this Commentary if combined with that of Leodegar's reportation. It can be supposed that the Leonine Commission would make use of this new manuscript when making their expected critical edition which is currently underway. But as this will not be done in the foreseeable future, the present edition will make this unique text available at least unofficially until then.

Regarding the place where these lectures were given, Paris is commonly supposed but this is far from certain. Fr. S. Tugwell, O.P., for example, wrote, "The presence of Léger, together with some references to Paris in the text, make it probable that the lectures were given in Paris, in which case they must be dated to the second regency [1269-72]."[36] Likewise, Fr. J. Weisheipl maintained, "This lecture is almost certainly of Parisian origin." But the evidence to support this may merely be circumstantial, for only in the reportation of Leodegar is there reference to Paris. The corresponding parts of the two reportations are given below:

MATTHEW CHAPTER 9, LECTURE 1

Leodegar of Bensançon

But there is a question: Why do Mark and Luke say that this happened in Capharnaum; while here it is maintained that this happened in His own city, which was Nazareth? It ought to be said that a certain city was Christ's by reason of His birth; and this was Bethlehem: a certain city was Christ's by reason of His education; and this was Nazareth: and a certain city was Christ's by reason of His social intercourse and of working miracles; and in this way, Capharnaum was His city: for this reason, it is well said, 'Into his own city.' Hence, it is said: "As great things as we have heard done

Peter of Andria

But it is inquired why in Luke 5 and Mark 2 it is also said that this miracle happened in Capharnaum, but here is it said that it happened in Nazareth, for He was brought up there, on account of which it is called His city because this can be upheld in three ways. Chrysostom[37] says that it can be understood of three cities when it is said, 'His own city,' because a city is 'His own' either by reason of His birth, and so Bethlehem is said to be 'His city,' or by reason of His education and so Nazareth is 'His city,' or by reason of His frequenting and performance of miracles, and in this way Capharnaum is 'His city'; "As

---

36. S. Tugwell O.P., *Albert & Thomas: Selected Writings* (Mahwah, N.J, Paulist Press, 1988), p. 247.
37. *Hom.* (30) *in Matthaeum;* PG 57, 357. Cf. *Glossa continua,* in h. l.

in Capharnaum, do also here in thy own country" (Lk. 4, 23). Augustine solves the question differently, because, among the other cities, Capharnaum was the most famous: hence, it was, as it were, a metropolis. And it is just as if someone were from some village near Paris, it might be said that he was from Paris on account of the notoriety of the place; in this way, the Lord, because He was from the surroundings of Capharnaum, was said to be from there. Or it can be explained otherwise, that the other Evangelists omitted something, whence, something can be added, namely, that He passed through Nazareth, and He came into Capharnaum.

great things as we have heard done in Capharnaum, do also here in thy own country" (Lk. 4, 23). And so Augustine[38] says that Capharnaum is called 'His city' because it was, as it were, the metropolis of all Galilee to which all Galileans were coming often from their villages, and Nazareth was a village subject to it. The third explanation is also Augustine's,[39] namely, that the Evangelists frequently...

From this divergence Fr. Eschmann warns, "... the omission, in Peter's transcript, of the example of Paris and its surroundings is worthy of note: it should make us cautious in drawing a chronological conclusion from texts which may be nothing but embellishing additions of Master Leodegar, *secularis Parisiensis*, who, according to Nicolas Trivet, was much delighted by St. Thomas' lectures on St. Matthew."[40] Likewise, "Fr. Synave, in order to show the French coloring of the *Lectura super Matthœum*, pointed to a text found in chapter 26, i.e., the part of which we have no report of Peter de Andria."[41]

On the other hand, one could make a similar argument that the lectures were given in Naples since in the reportation of Peter of Andria on Mt. 5, 21-22, but not in Leodegar's edited reportation, there are two long digressions, the first of approximately 250 words and the second of approximately 400 words. The first is on "three errors" about the fifth precept of the Decalogue, "Thou

---

38. *De consensu evangelistarum* II, 25 (PL 34, 1105 f); *Glossa continua* in h. 1.
39. "...just as the writers do in many instances, leaving unnoticed much that intervenes, and, without any express indication of the omissions they are making..." (*De consensu evangelistarum*; l.c.; *Glossa continua*, in h. l.).
40. Eschmann, p. 240.

41. ibid. The passage referred to here is, "Jerome resolves this question, saying, that in the same language there are often different manners of speaking, as it appears in France, there are different manners of speaking in Picardy and in Burgundy, and, nevertheless, there is one language. So the Galileans have a different manner of speaking from the Jerusalemites" (Mt. 26, lect. 7).

shalt not kill," and soon afterwards, a second is on whether "all anger is contrary to virtue." Wording very similar to these passages is found in St. Thomas' *On the Two Laws of Charity and the Ten Commandments* (article 7). Fr. Eschmann speaks of the first of these two quotations:

> The first quotation *(In Mt. v, 21)* was brought to my attention by Fr. Shooner. When I saw it, it looked familiar to me. It is indeed identical with a text from the *Collationes de decem praeceptis.* The reading of the Basel *MS* made it evident at once that not only the small passage containing the Aristotelian quotation but a much longer development in the same *Opusculum* corresponds most exactly to Peter of Andria's transcript of the *Lectura* of St. Thomas. The whole passage in the *Collatio de quinto praecepto*,[42] ed. Taurin, 1954, nn. 1259 *(Circa quod praeceptum ...)* 1260, 1261 (*... sicut dicitur de Samsone.)* is in all relevant details the same as the passage MS Basel B.V. 12, fol. 36rb *(Notandum quod in isto praecepto ...)* and fol. 36va (*... et ita excusat Samsonem.).* I am not prepared at the moment to see in this parallelism anything but a confirmation of Fr. Shooner's hypothesis, according to which the *Reportatio* of Basel is due to Peter of Andria; for it is this same Peter whom tradition credits with the *Reportatio* of those *Collationes* which are said to have been, originally, Aquinas' sermons, preached in the vernacular, in Lent 1273, to the students and the people in Naples. I am aware that (at least) the passage of these *Collationes* to which I referred above is not part of the Neapolitan Lenten-Cycle. But the history of St. Thomas' *Opuscula* collections, and the part which their posthumous first editors played in their constitution, are other problems.[43]

Perhaps future studies of the yet to be published part of Peter of Andria's reportation on chapters 7-12 would yield more conclusive evidence for the place of composition, and, as a result, a more precise date of composition.

Finally, let the reader remember that the reportation which follows is a transcription of the lectures of St. Thomas and so it has the format of notes taken hurriedly, though surprisingly well. Such are typical of this time. "The system of transcribing lectures was practiced throughout the twelfth and thirteenth centuries. No pretence at style was made; quotations were usually abruptly recorded without introduction and the references were normally left for the master to fill in later. University statutes required that a master correct the reports personally before they were published."[44] Still the Com-

---

42. On this chapter-heading see J. Destrez, *Bulletin thomiste,* I (1926), 66.
43. Eschmann, p. 234.

44. Matthew L. Lamb, O.C.S.O, Commentary on Saint Paul's Epistle to the Ephesians (Albany, N.Y.: Magi Books, 1966), intro.

mentary has a more flowing and vivacious style than is found in the *Catena Aurea on Matthew*, as it is a more rounded discourse of a masterly teacher. The literal sense of the Gospel consistently serves throughout as the basis of "mystical," or spiritual, meanings, which are of three kinds: the allegorical, anagogical, and moral senses, as the Angelic Doctor says below on Chapter 2, 11.[45]

Such an exposition is far different from the dry, merely internal and often skeptical criticisms of modern exegesis. Here instead one finds a feast of knowledge that satisfies both the mind and soul at one and the same time. Priests will find in these lectures abundant material for their personal meditation and for fruitful preaching to the faithful, as it draws from the best of Patristic interpretations, which are needed to plumb the deep well of God's words to men. Of all the Gospels, St. Matthew's Gospel is the catechist's Gospel, meant to serve as the first instruction to a pagan world about the life and teachings of the Savior of mankind; hence the importance of it being understood well by priests and faithful alike.

Bartholomew of Spina wrote in a letter to the Dominican Grimanus the following woeful lamentation: "With nearly infinite vigils, and not without the help of God, I have edited the Commentaries of Saint Thomas *On Matthew, Isaias, Jeremias, Lamentations of the same Jeremias*; or (so that I might speak more correctly) I became mutilated and crippled through the injury of time through recomposing his discourses."[46] Such too has been the work of the feeble translation of sentences completable only by inference, and quotations begging correction from their Patristic sources. If errors be found, or the clear resonance of Common Doctor's voice be unrecognized in this first English translation of the "delightful" commentary on St. Matthew's Gospel by the Prince of Theologians, may the reader be indulgent, or far better, summon a more skillful hand willing to bravely rework the unwieldy word, so that, as anon, priests equipped and well versed in the Divine Word may once again set the world aflame with the aid of the *Doctor Communis*, the irrefutable "hound of the Lord," singularly sent by God "to praise, bless and preach."

---

45. "With regard to contemplation, however, by these three things can be signified either, three senses of Sacred Scripture, namely the literal sense, under which is included the allegorical, anagogical, and moral senses" (Commentary on St. Mattthew's Gospel, lecture 3).

46. Fr. Giovanni Francesco Bernardo Maria De Rossi O.P., "*Admonitios Praevia*," in *Evangelia S. Matthaei et S. Joannis Commentaria* (Turin, Marietti, 1925), p. iii.

PROLOGUE

Matthew, from Judea, just as his Gospel is placed first in order, so he wrote the Gospel first in Judea. His calling to God was from publican activities. He presumed in the genealogy of Christ the beginnings of two things, the first of which was circumcision in the flesh, the other of which was election according to the heart, and by both of which Christ was in the fathers. And, the number having thus been put down as three fourteens, he shows by extending the beginning from the faith of the believer unto the time of election, and directing it from the election to the day of the deportation, and defining it from the deportation up to Christ that the generation of the advent of the Lord had been reached, so that, in making satisfaction both in number and in time, and in showing itself for what it was, and in demonstrating that the work of God in itself was still in these whose race he established, the time, order, number, economy, or reason of all of these matters might not deny the testimony, which is necessary for faith, of Christ, who was working from the beginning. God is Christ, who was made from a woman, who was made under the law, who was born from a virgin, who suffered in the flesh, who fixed all things on the Cross so that, triumphing over them for eternity, rising in the body, He might restore both the name of the Father to the Son in the fathers and the name of the Son to the Father in the sons, without beginning, without end, showing that He is one with the Father, because He is one. In this gospel it is useful for those desiring God to know the first things, the medial things and the perfect things, so that, reading of the calling of the Apostle and the work of the gospel and the choosing of God, born into the universe in the flesh, they might understand and recognize it in Him, in whom they have been apprehended and seek to apprehend. It was certainly possible in this study of the subject matter for us to both convey the fidelity of what was done and not be silent that the economy of God at work must be diligently understood by those seeking to do so.[1]

---

1. This prologue was translated by Ben C. Smith with the help of Stephen C. Carlson. cf. *http://www.textexcavation.com/latinprologues.html*.

COMMENTARY OF ST. THOMAS
ON THE ABOVE PROLOGUE

Matthew is from Judea, etc. Before Matthew's Gospel, Jerome inserts a prologue in which he does three things: firstly, he describes the author; secondly he discloses the mysteries of the Gospel, where it is said, *He emphasizes in the genealogy of Christ two important things*; and thirdly he shows his intention, where it is said, *For it was our aim in this discourse*.

Now he describes the author by four things: firstly, by his name, when he says, *Matthew*; secondly by his origin, when he says, *from Judea*; thirdly by the placement of his writing, where he says, *And just as his Gospel is placed first in order*; and fourthly, by his calling, where he says, *His calling to the Lord*, meaning to Christ, etc. Concerning this, it is written in Matthew[2] and Luke.[3] And observe that there is an interlinear gloss,[4] which says: "*first*, meaning there was no Gospel written before this one," etc. This seems to suggest that the other Evangelists after Matthew wrote in Judea, which is not true: for only Matthew wrote in Judea, Mark in Italy, Luke in Achaia, and John in Asia. Afterwards he discloses the mysteries of the Gospel itself. And firstly, he discloses the mysteries at the beginning of the Gospel; secondly, he shows that the same mysteries are to be sought also both in the middle and at the end of the Gospel, etc.

Now in the beginning of the Gospel two things are mentioned. Firstly, is related a quasi-title, when it is said, "The book of the generation"; secondly, the lineage of a particular genealogy is traced, when it is said, *Abraham begot Isaac*, etc. Therefore, he firstly relates the mysteries of the title, or the things that are mentioned in the title; secondly, he mentions the mysteries of Christ's genealogy, where it is said, *So all the generations*

---

2. "And when Jesus passed on from thence, he saw a man sitting in the custom house, named Matthew; and he saith to him: Follow me. And he arose up and followed him" (9, 9).
3. "And after these things, he went forth and saw a publican named Levi, sitting at the receipt of custom: and he said to him: Follow me" (5, 27).
4. Interlinear glosses were Scriptural commentaries "written over the words in the text of the Vulgate. It was the work of Anselm of Laon (†1117), who had some acquaintance with Hebrew and Greek." Ordinary glosses were written by Walafrid Strabo (†849), who "had some knowledge of Greek and made extracts chiefly from the Latin Fathers and from the writings of his master, Rabanus Maurus, for the purpose of illustrating the various senses—principally the literal sense—of all the books of Holy Writ." ("Glosses, Scriptural" *Catholic Encyclopedia* (1907 ed.), vol. 6, p. 588).

from Abraham to David, are fourteen generations. Now in the title it is said, "The book of the generation of Jesus Christ"; wherein two important persons are mentioned, namely, David and Abraham. And this is because to Abraham was firstly given the command of circumcision; "And [Abraham] received the sign of circumcision, a seal of the justice of the faith which he had, being uncircumcised: that he might be the father of all them that believe" (Rom. 4, 11). David, on the other hand, was chosen by the Lord; "I have found a man according to my heart." (I Kings 13, 14). Hence, on account of these men, two things are inferred, for it is signified that Christ drew His origin from a circumcised father and from a chosen father. And the meaning is, His origin was from two men, or two important ancestors, namely David and Abraham.

Afterwards, Jerome mentions the mysteries which are mentioned in the genealogy. And firstly, he mentions the mysteries of the Gospel itself, or of the Evangelist; and secondly, he mentions the mysteries of Christ Himself, where it is said, *of all these generations*, etc. And it is a mystery that the Evangelist distinguishes three groups of fourteen generations: of which the first is from Abraham until David; the second is from David to the transmigration; and the third is from the transmigration until Christ: and he does this to show that Christ was from a circumcised father, and from a chosen father, and from those fathers who transmigrated. And this is by having related the aforementioned genealogy in three groups, meaning by a triple repetition of fourteen fathers, *from the faith of a believer*, meaning from Abraham, who was an exemplary model of a believer, *unto the time of an election*, meaning leading to David, *from that election*, meaning from David, *unto the time of the transmigration; and finishing the genealogy with the time from the transmigration until Christ*, meaning having mentioned briefly and cursorily Christ's genealogy, he shows the birth of the Lord having been reached, it fulfills the number of generations and time of His birth. This is evident.

Of all these generations, etc. Notice that in the series of generations four things are mentioned: the time, number, order and selection or reason; because *from Abraham until David*, etc.[5] All these things show nothing else besides the fact that *Christ is God*: for Christ intended these things according to His choice and allegorical reasons, because He is God. *Which tes-*

---

5. Mt. 1, 17.

timony is necessary for faith, namely, the belief that ***Christ is God***, meaning among all the truths of the faith, none is more necessary than the truth that Christ is God. ***Who was born of a virgin***, etc. Notice, explain, and remember these truths. ***Who fastened all things to the Cross***, meaning all sins, "He hath taken the same out of the way, fastening it to the cross" (Col. 2, 14). And what is more, Christ, in that He is God and man, who is all things, according to that which is written: "And I, if I be lifted up from the earth, will draw all things to myself" (Jn. 12, 32); and: "That in the name of Jesus every knee should bow, of those that are in heaven, on earth, and under the earth" (Phil. 2, 10). ***So that triumphing over all things in Himself***, by the triumph of the Cross, He subjected all things to Himself, and He triumphed over everything. ***Both the name of the Father to the Son in the fathers***.

Now, as proof of this it ought to be noticed that in the series of generations some fathers and some sons are listed, as can be seen in the genealogy. Likewise, there is listed in it a certain father without a father, like Adam: and there is a son without a son, namely, Jesus. Similarly, some fathers are listed who are both fathers and sons, namely, all the intermediary fathers. Now by this it is mystically signified that in the Trinity there is the Father and the Son, as in this genealogy there are some fathers and some sons. Likewise, by the fact that the first father does not have a father in this series, nor the last son have a son, it is shown that the Father and Son are eternal. Moreover, by the fact that a father and a son are one and the same person in relation to different persons, it is inferred that these are one, not indeed in person, but in nature.

And this is what He says, ***He restored both the name of the Father to the Son in the fathers***, meaning that the Son has a Father; ***in the fathers***, meaning that the Son has a Father by the fact that some fathers are listed there. And ***He restored the name of the Father***, meaning that the Father has a Son, ***in the sons***, meaning by the fact that some sons are listed there without a beginning and without an end: because the first father does not have a father, nor the last son have a son. ***Showing that He is one being with the Father***, meaning He is one in nature with the Father, because each is an individual person, namely, the fathers and their sons are individual persons, though related to different persons in the aforesaid genealogy. Note the interlinear gloss, which says: ***Christ is one being***; because nothing was said [about this].

Afterwards he shows similar mysteries are to be sought in the aforesaid Gospel, not only in the beginning but also in the middle and at the end: and *In this Gospel*, namely Matthew's, *it is useful for those desiring God in this way*, meaning in the same way as we have said, *to know the first things,* meaning the *beginning*, and the *intermediate and the perfect things*, meaning their end and completion; *so that, reading through all the words about the calling of the apostle*, etc. It is written: "But I follow after, if I may by any means apprehend" (Phil. 3, 12). *For it was our aim*. Now here he makes known his intention, namely, that he intends that the things which are said here are historically true, and nevertheless are to be understood spiritually. *For it was our aim*, meaning this is our intention, *in this discourse*, meaning this prologue.

CHAPTER ONE

1. The book of the generation of Jesus Christ, the son of David, the son of Abraham:

Among the Evangelists, Matthew is especially concerned with Christ's humanity: hence, according to Gregory, He is denoted by a man in the figure of the four animals. By means of His humanity, Christ entered into the world, He went forth, and departed. And therefore, the whole Gospel is divided into three parts. For the Evangelist firstly treats concerning the entrance of Christ's humanity into the world; secondly, of His course of life; and thirdly, of His departure. The second part begins at chapter 3, verse 1, where it is said, *And in those days cometh John the Baptist preaching in the desert of Judea.* The third part begins at chapter 21, verse 1, where it is said, *And when they drew nigh to Jerusalem and were come to Bethphage, unto mount Olivet.* In the first part he does two things; Firstly, Christ's generation is described; secondly, the manifestation of His generation is added, where it is said, *When Jesus therefore was born in Bethlehem of Juda, in the days of king Herod* (chapter 2). In the first part he does three things; For firstly, a sort of title of the whole book is placed at the beginning, when it is said, *The book of the generation of Jesus Christ*; secondly, the lineage of His ancestors is traced, *Abraham begot Isaac*; and thirdly, when it is said, *Now the generation of Christ was in this wise*, Christ's generation is described in particular. Now the title which is presented at the beginning is the following: *The book of the generation of Jesus Christ.*

However, it seems to be imperfect speech. For the title is put in the nominative case without a verb; but it is not imperfect speech. For Matthew wrote the Gospel in Hebrew; and for that reason, in his writing he kept the style of the Jews. Now it was customary for the Hebrews to speak in this way, just as when it is said: "The vision of Isaias the son of Amos," it is understood, 'This is': and is it not necessary to add these words; so here when it is said, *The book of the generation*, it is understood, 'This is.' And this manner of speaking is also customary for us; for if we wish to entitle some book, it is called *Priscianus Major* and *Priscianus Minor*;[1] nor is it necessary to add, 'This is,' or 'Begins.'

---

[1]. Priscian, a Latin grammarian (491-518) who taught at Constantinple, is chiefly known for his 18 books of the *Institutiones Grammaticae*, the most important work of grammatical antiquity. The first 16 (*Priscianus Major*), treat of forms; the last 2 (*Priscianus Minor*) of syntax. St. Thomas elsewhere calls him the "Father of Grammar" (cf. *Postilla in Genesis*, ch. 4).

Likewise, it is inquired, since a small portion of this book is about Christ's generation, why he entitled his book as he did. And it ought to be maintained that Matthew, who wrote for the Hebrews, in his writing kept the manner of Hebrews. Now it was customary for the Hebrews to entitle their books from their beginning, just as Genesis is so called, because therein is treated about Generation or Creation; hence: "This is the book of the generation of Adam" (Gen. 5, 1). And the book of Exodus is so called, because in the first part is treated concerning the exodus of the children of Israel from Egypt.

But it is sought, why is *of Jesus Christ* added? And it ought to be maintained that, according to the Apostle, "As in Adam all die, so also in Christ all shall be made alive" (I Cor. 15, 22). Now Matthew had seen the first book of the Old Testament, in which it is said in chapter 5: "This is the book of the generation of Adam." Therefore, in order that the New Testament, in which it is treated about the regeneration and restoration, might correspond to it by opposition, he says, **The book of the generation of Jesus Christ**, so that it might be shown that the Author of both is the same.

Herein, however, it is inquired about the fact that here it is said, **The book of the generation of Jesus Christ**. For the contrary is found in Isaias 53, 8, where it is said, "Who shall declare his generation?" But the sense is, according to Jerome, that in Christ there is a twofold generation. Namely, there is the divine generation, which cannot be declared: because even if in some way we describe the Begotten Son, nevertheless, the manner by which He is begotten, neither man nor angel is able to comprehend. The other, however, is the human generation, concerning which it is treated in this Gospel; but, nevertheless, even in this generation, there are many difficult things. And for that reason, according to Remigius, there are very few who can declare it.

Likewise, it is inquired about the fact that he says, **Generation**, since many generations are traced here. But it ought to be said that although many generations are enumerated, nevertheless, all are brought forward for the sake of the one, namely, Christ's generation, concerning which it is said below: **The generation of Christ was in this wise** (this chapter).

Now He, whose generation is traced, is described firstly by His name, when it is said, **Jesus**; secondly, from His office, when it is said, **Christ**; and thirdly, from His origin, when it is said, **The son of David, the son of Abraham**. Although there will have been others who were also called "Jesus," such as Jesus the son of Nave, about whom it is written; "Valiant in war was

Jesus the son of Nave, who was successor of Moses among the prophets" (Eccli. 46, 1); and another lived about the time of the building of the Temple, about whom it is written in Zacharias 3.[2] These men were Jesus nominally and figuratively, insofar as they were prefiguring him. The former Jesus[3] led the people of Israel into the promised land; but this Jesus, who is our Savior, did not lead us into a carnal land, but into a heavenly land: For we have the author and finisher in His Blood, etc., (Heb. 12, 2). And He is rightly called *Jesus*, because the name agrees with Him according to both natures, namely, the divine and the human. Indeed, according to His human nature, He suffered in His flesh, and completed the mystery of our redemption: and since that suffering would not have efficacy except by virtue of the divine nature joined to it, on account of this it is said below: **His name shall be called Jesus: for he shall save his people from their sins** (this chapter).

But it is inquired why he says, **Christ**. Did not *Jesus* suffice? I reply that this was done, because, as it has been said, others also were called Jesus.

Now he describes Him when he says, **Christ**, that is 'anointed.' Observe, however, that there were three anointings in the Old Law. For Aaron was anointed as a priest (Lev. 8). Saul was anointed by Samuel as a king in I Kings 10. And David was so-anointed in I Kings 16. Eliseus was anointed as a prophet in III Kings 19. Therefore, because Christ was a true priest, as it is said in Psalm 109, verse 4: "Thou art a priest for ever according to the order of Melchisedech," etc., and a king and a prophet: for that reason He is rightly called **Christ**, on account of the three offices which He exercised.

The son of David, the son of Abraham. Here there is a twofold question, namely, concerning their number and order.

As to the first question, why he named these two, this was done on account of the reason stated in the prologue, namely, because Abraham was a prophet. In Genesis 20, 7 the Lord said to Abimelech, the king of Gerara: "Restore the man his wife, for he is a prophet." Likewise, Abraham was a priest (Gen. 15, 9), since he fulfilled the office of a priest, namely, by offering a victim to the Lord; "Take me," He said, "a cow of three years old," etc. And now David was a prophet, as it is evident in Acts 2, 20.[4] He was

---

2. "And the Lord shewed me Jesus the high priest standing before the angel of the Lord" (verse 1).
3. Josue.

4. "Whereas therefore he was a prophet and knew that God hath sworn to him with an oath, that of the fruit of his loins one should sit upon his throne."

also a king, as it is evident in II Kings 2, 4.[5] Because, therefore, Christ was a king, and a prophet, and a priest; for that reason, it is rightly said that he was the Son of these men. For if he had named only Abraham, it would not be signified that Christ was a king. Likewise, if he had named only David, the priestly dignity in Christ would not be denoted; and therefore he put down both.

As to the second question, namely, why he wrote the names in such an order, it ought to be said that, according to Jerome, David is put first, and the order is interchanged on account of the necessity of tracing the genealogy; for if he were firstly to say, *The son of Abraham*; and secondly, *The son of David*, he would need to repeat Abraham a second time so that the order of the genealogy might be preserved. According to Ambrose, however, one should say that David is put first by reason of dignity; for to David was made the promise about the Head Himself, when it is said: "Of the fruit of thy womb I will set upon thy throne" (Ps. 131, 11). But to Abraham was made the promise about the members, namely, of the Church; hence: "In thy seed shall all the nations of the earth be blessed" (Gen. 22, 11).

Here it ought to be observed that there were many errors concerning Christ. For some men erred about His divinity, such as Paul of Samosata, Photinus, and Sabellius; some men erred about His humanity; and some erred about both. Others, however, erred about His person. About His humanity, the first to have erred was Manes,[6] who said that He did not have a true body, but had received an imaginary one. Against this is that which the Lord says: "Handle, and see: for a spirit hath not flesh and bones, as you see me to have" (Lk. 24, 39). After him, secondly erred Valentine, who said He brought down a heavenly body with Him, and He did not assume a body from the Virgin, but passed through her like water through a channel. Now this error is contrary to what is said: "Who was made to him of the seed of David, according to the flesh" (Rom. 1, 3). The third error was that of Apollinaris, who said He only took a body, and not a soul, but in the place of the soul He had the divinity. But it is contrary to what is frequently said in Scripture: "Now is my soul troubled" (Jn. 12, 27). But on account of this passage, this same man changed his opinion, and said Christ had a vegetative and sensible soul, yet not a rational soul, but the divinity in its place. But then something unfitting would follow, that Christ was no more a man than

---

5. "And the men of Juda came, and anointed David there, to be king over the house of Juda."
6. Founder of the Manichaeans.

an animal. The Evangelists, however, divided these errors unto themselves as though by a kind of casting of lots. For Mark and John chiefly destroyed those errors which are about His divinity; hence, John said immediately at the beginning of His Gospel: "In the beginning was the Word." And Mark began his Gospel thus: "The beginning of the gospel of Jesus Christ, the Son of God" and he did not say, 'The son of Abraham.' Matthew, however, and Luke destroyed in the beginning of their Gospels those errors that are about His humanity. Hence, observe that in this which is said, *The son of David, the son of Abraham*, all the errors which were about Christ's humanity are excluded. For someone is not said to be the son of someone, unless though univocal generation, which is according to a likeness of species. For however much something is generated by man, unless he shares the same nature by species, it is never said to be a son, as is evident concerning little lice and the like. If, therefore, Christ is the son of David, and of Abraham, it is necessary that He have the same nature by reason of the same species; however, He would not have the same nature by reason of the same species, if he would not have a true and natural body, nor if He had brought it from heaven; nor also if He lacked a sensitive or rational soul. Hence, the exclusion of every error is evident.

2. Abraham begot Isaac. And Isaac begot Jacob. And Jacob begot Juda and his brethren.
3. And Juda begot Phares and Zara of Thamar. And Phares begot Esron. And Esron begot Aram.
4. And Aram begot Aminadab. And Aminadab begot Naasson. And Naasson begot Salmon.
5. And Salmon begot Booz of Rahab. And Booz begot Obed of Ruth. And Obed begot Jesse.
6a. And Jesse begot David the king.

Having set forth the title, here His genealogical lineage is traced: and it is divided into three parts, according to the three series of fourteen by which the said genealogical lineage is traced. The first series of fourteen is from Abraham until David, which proceeds through the Patriarchs. The second series proceeds from David until the Babylonian Captivity, which proceeds through the kings. The third series is from the Babylonian Captivity until Christ, which begins with the leaders, and proceeds though private persons. The second is where it is said, *And David the king begot Solomon*. The third is where it is said, *And after the transmigration of Babylon*, etc. The first is divided into three parts. For firstly, the ancestors are set forth who were before the entrance into Egypt; secondly are set forth they who were in the going out itself,[7] and the entrance into the promised land; thirdly are set forth they who were after the entrance into the promised land. He says, therefore, firstly, **Abraham begot Isaac**.

Here it ought to be considered, before we proceed further, that two Evangelists describe Christ's generation according to the flesh in detail, namely, Luke and Matthew; but they describe it differently. And this difference is observed in regard to five things. For, firstly, they differ so far as regards the position; secondly, they differ as regards the order; thirdly, they differ as regards the manner; fourthly, they differ as regards the terminus; fifthly, they differ as regards the persons enumerated. Firstly, I say that they differ regarding the position: because Matthew starts to trace Christ's generation in the beginning of the Gospel; Luke, however, starts to trace Christ's generation not in the beginning, but after His baptism: and the reason is, according to Augustine, that Matthew received the obligation of describing Christ's carnal generation; and, for that reason, he ought to put it immediately at the beginning; Luke, however, especially intended to praise the priestly person in Christ; now to the priest pertains the expiation of sins. And, for that reason, after the baptism, in which the expiation of sins occurs, Christ's generation is conveniently placed by Luke. Now, secondly, Luke and Matthew in tracing Christ's genealogy differ regarding the order: because Matthew traces Christ's generation by beginning from Abraham, and descending all the way to Christ; Luke, however, begins from Christ, and, by ascending, proceeds all the way to Abraham and even further. And the reason is that, according to the Apostle (Rom. 4, 25),[8] in Christ there were two things, namely, His humility in accepting the defects of our nature, and the power of His divinity and grace, through which He made atonement for us from these defects; "God sent his own Son in the likeness of sinful flesh" (on account of the first), "and of sin, hath condemned sin in the flesh" (on account of the second)" (Rom. 8, 3). Matthew, therefore, who stressed Christ's carnal generation, through which He descended even to the assumption of our infirmity, fittingly wrote out His generation by descending. But Luke, who commended the priestly dignity in Him, through which we are reconciled to God

---

7. Included here, too, are those who were born in Egypt.
8. "Who was delivered up for our sins and rose again for our justification."

and united to Christ, fittingly proceeds by ascending. Thirdly, they differ regarding the manner: because in the detailed exposition of the genealogy, Matthew uses the word **begot**, but Luke uses the word "was": and this is because Matthew, in his whole detailed exposition, gives the ancestors according only to the flesh; but Luke gives many ancestors according to the Law, or by adoption. For it was commanded in the Law that if someone were to die without children, that his brother would take his wife, and beget sons unto him: hence, those sons did not belong to him who begot them; but through a kind of adoption they were imputed to the former. Hence, Luke, who gives many sons begotten through adoption, does not say **begot**, but "was"; because although they had not begotten them, nevertheless, they were theirs through a kind of adoption. Matthew, however, who gives only the ancestors according to the flesh, says, **begot**. However, the reason for this is that, as it was said, Matthew's aim is chiefly directed towards Christ's humanity. And because He was born from the ancestors according to the flesh, for that reason, in Matthew's genealogy no one is set down who will not have been an ancestor according to the flesh. Luke, however, chiefly commends the priestly dignity in Christ, through which we are adopted as sons of God; and therefore, he set down not only the ancestors according to the flesh, but also the legal ancestors. Fourthly, they differ regarding the terminus, because Matthew starts his parentage from Abraham, and it is continued even unto Christ; Luke, however, starts from Christ, and his parentage is continued not only unto Abraham, but even unto God. The reason for this can be taken from the fact that Matthew wrote for the Hebrews; now the Hebrews were especially taking pride in Abraham; "We are the seed of Abraham" (Jn. 8, 33), who was the first principle of believing; and therefore Matthew started from Abraham. Luke, however, wrote for the Greeks, who knew nothing about Abraham, except in reference to Christ: for if Christ had not existed, they would have never known anything about Abraham; and therefore, Luke began from Christ and ended not only with Abraham, but with God. Fifthly, they differ regarding the persons enumerated: because in Luke's entire genealogical lineage there is absolutely no mention of a woman; in Matthew's, however, some women are interspersed. The reason for this is, according to Ambrose, that Luke, as it was said, especially commended the priestly dignity; in a priest, however, purity is especially required. Matthew, however, traced His generation according to the flesh: and therefore some women are placed therein.

Nevertheless, one ought to observe that in Matthew's entire genealogy only sinful women are put down, or rather women who were known to have been in some sin, such as Thamar, who was an fornicator (Gen. 38); and Ruth, who was an idolatress, because she was a Gentile: and the wife of Urias, who was an adulteress (II Kings 11). And this was for the purpose of signifying, according to Jerome, that He, whose genealogy is traced, came into this world for the sake of redeeming sinners. Another reason is mentioned by Ambrose, namely, the sinful women were included so that the Church's embarrassment might be taken away. For if Christ willed to be born of sinners, then infidels ought not to mock, if sinners come into the Church. Another reason can be assigned, I believe it is according to Chrysostom, that the imperfection of the Law might be shown: and that Christ came to fulfill the Law. For by the fact that certain sinful women are mentioned, it is denoted that they, who were greatest in relation to the Law, were sinners; such as David and Juda; and in this he indicates the imperfection of the others. For if these were sinners, much more others were sinners also; "All have sinned and do need the glory of God" (Rom. 3, 23). And, therefore, these are put down in Christ's generation, so that it might be signified that He had fulfilled the Law. Observe, nevertheless, that these women, although they all were sinners, nevertheless, were not sinners at the time when their genealogy is traced; but had been by then cleansed by penance.

He says, therefore, **Abraham begot Isaac.** Firstly, it ought to be noted, that here there are two things to be considered according to the letter of the text, or literal sense: firstly, that Christ is signified by these ancestors, and secondly, that these things are also recalled, and can be recalled for our instruction. He says, therefore, **Abraham begot Isaac.** And this is recorded in Genesis 21. **And Isaac begot Jacob** (Gen. 25). **And Jacob begot Juda and his brethren.**

Here it is inquired, since Abraham had a son other than Isaac, namely, Ismael, and similarly Isaac had another son, why no mention is made of them, just it is said here, **Juda and his brethren.** Likewise, it is inquired why Juda is given more prominence by being named rather than the others.

The reason is that Juda and his brethren remained in the worship of the one God: and, for that reason, mention is made of them in Christ's generation. This was not true for the other sets of brothers: Isaac and Ismael, nor Jacob and Esau. In answer to the second question, this was so that it might be shown that the prophecy of Jacob was fulfilled in Christ: "The sceptre shall

not be taken away from Juda, nor a ruler from his thigh, till he come that is to be sent, and he shall be the expectation of nations" (Gen. 49, 10); "For it is evident that our Lord sprung out of Juda" (Rom. 7, 14); and therefore, more mention is made of him than of the others.
And Juda begot Phares and Zara of Thamar. Here it is inquired, since the Lord was not born of Zara, but of Phares, why mention is made of him. Likewise, why he is mentioned by name? For previously he said, *his brethren*; why, therefore, did he mention the name of Zara?

And it ought to be replied, according to Ambrose, that this was done in accordance with a mystery. For the proof of which, observe the historical account which is found in Genesis 38, that in Thamar's giving birth, Zara appeared first, on whose hand the midwife tied a scarlet thread, saying: "This shall come forth the first, and therefore she called his name Zara.[9] But he drawing back his hand, the other came forth: and the woman said: "Why is the partition divided for thee?" Now Zara, who appeared first, signifies the Jewish people, on whose hand the midwife tied a scarlet thread, which signifies circumcision, which took place with a flow of blood. But he drawing back his hand, etc., the other went out: because "blindness in part has happened in Israel, until the fullness of the Gentiles should come in" (Rom. 11, 25). For thus did the divided Gentile nations enter into the light of the faith, going out from the womb of ignorance and infidelity.

Secondly, it ought to be observed, that by the ancestors listed in Christ's generation, Christ is signified by reason either of the name, or of a deed, or of something else, as is apparent in each instance. For Abraham is interpreted 'the father of many nations,' and he signifies Christ, of whom it is written: "Who had brought many children into glory" (Rom. 2, 10). Likewise, Abraham, by the Lord's command, went out from his own land (Gen. 12, 1). And Christ is signified, who said, "I have forsaken my house, I have left my inheritance," etc., (Jer. 12, 7). Similarly, it is Abraham who laughed, saying, "God hath made a laughter for me" (21, 6).[10] And Christ is signified, at whose birth a cause of joy is announced not only to one person, but to the whole world; "Behold, I bring you good tidings of great joy that shall be to all the people: for, this day is born to you a Saviour, who is Christ

---

9. 'Zara' means "Orient or rising"; 'Phares' means "a breach or division."
10. cf. Gen. 17, 17: "Abraham fell upon his face, and laughed, saying in his heart: Shall a son, thinkest thou, be born to him that is a hundred years old?"

the Lord" (Lk. 2, 10). Similarly, He is signified by Jacob,[11] both by reason of the meaning of his name, and by reason of his deed, as is evident in this, that he put a rock, that is, the hardness of the Cross, under his head. Similarly, He is signified by Juda, and also Phares, which means 'division': for he will divide the sheep from the goats (below 25, 32).[12]

Morally, however, in these generations the state of our justification is denoted, according to the six things which are required for justification, namely, faith is denoted by Abraham who was justified by the justice of faith; "That he might be the father of all them that believe, being uncircumcised" (Rom. 4, 11). By Isaac, hope is denoted, because his name is interpreted 'laughter'; "Rejoicing in hope" (Rom. 12, 12). Charity is denoted by Jacob, who married two wives, namely, Lia, which means 'laboring,' and Rachel. They denote the two lives which are in charity, according to the two precepts of charity: for the contemplative life is delighted in God; and it is the active life, however, through which our neighbor is helped. By Juda, 'confession' is denoted, which is twofold: there is the confession of faith; "With the heart, we believe unto justice: but, with the mouth, confession is made unto salvation" (Rom. 10, 10): and there is the confession of one's sins: "Confess therefore your sins one to another" (James 5, 16). Now, from this follows a twofold effect, namely, the destruction of vices, which is denoted by Phares, and the beginning of the virtues, which is signified by Zara. And these things originate from Thamar, which means 'bitterness'; "I will recount to thee all my years in the bitterness of my soul" (Is. 38, 15).

And Phares begot Esron. Here is set forth the genealogical lineage of the ancestors who were born in Egypt, or in the exodus from there: for just as Christ is signified by Phares, which means 'division'; "He shall separate the sheep from the goats" (below 25, 32); so He is signified by Esron, which means 'arrow,' or 'courtyard.' For He is called an arrow on account of the efficacy of His preaching, by which it penetrated the hearts of His listeners; "Thy arrows are sharp: under thee shall people fall, into the hearts of the king's enemies" (Ps. 44, 6). Now He is a 'courtyard' on account of His breadth of charity, by which He loved not only His friends,

---

11. "REMIG: Jacob is interpreted 'supplanter,' and it is said of Christ, You have cast down beneath Me them that rose up against Me" (*Catena Aurea* on *St. Matthew*, ch. 1, lec. 2).
12. cf. Gen. 30, 32: "Go round through all thy flocks, and separate all the sheep of divers colors, and speck- led; and all that is brown and spotted, and of divers colors, as well among the sheep as among the goats, shall be my wages."
[Note that where "above" and "below" are used in the references, this refers to Scriptural references in the Gospel of St. Matthew.]

but also His enemies; "When we were enemies, we were reconciled to God by the death of his Son" (Rom. 5, 10); "He hath prayed for the transgressors" (Is. 53, 12). And again: "Father, forgive them, for they know not what they do" (Lk. 23, 34).

And Esron begot Aram. Now Aram is interpreted 'elect' or 'elevated': "Behold my servant, He is elevated above all men" (Is. 42, 1);[13] "He set him above all principality" (Eph. 1, 20-21).

And Aram begot Aminadab, which means 'willing.' It is He in whose person the Psalmist says: "I will freely[14] sacrifice to thee, and will give praise, O Lord, to thy name: because it is good" (Ps. 53, 8); and "He was offered because it was his own will, and he opened not his mouth" (Is. 53, 7); "I came down from heaven, not to do my own will but the will of him that sent me" (Jn. 6, 38).

And Aminadab begot Naasson, which means 'augury' or 'like a serpent': because Christ not only knew the present, but also the past and the future; "All things are naked and open to his eyes" (Heb. 4, 13). Likewise, He is 'like a serpent' on account of His prudence; for prudence is attributed to a serpent; "Be ye wise as serpents" (below 10, 16); "He knoweth both the deceivers, and him that is deceived" (Job 12, 16). Note that this Naasson lived in the time of Moses, and went out with him from Egypt, and was a prince in the tribe of Juda in the desert, as it is stated in Numbers 1, 7. But it ought to be observed that in Exodus 13, 18, where our text reads: "The children of Israel went up armed out of the land of Egypt," Aquila[15] translated the word 'armed' as 'equipped,' on account of an equivocation; the Septuagint text, however, is better: "The children of Israel in the fifth generation went out of Egypt."

But on the contrary, this Naasson was not the fifth from Jacob, but the seventh, as is evident by counting Jacob, Juda, etc., down to Naasson. Therefore, this happened not in the fifth,

13. Isa. 42, 1 in the Douay translation reads: "Behold my servant, I will uphold him: my elect." "There is some difference in the text of Isaias, whence this is taken. The apostles and evangelists did not confine themselves to cite the very words of the text, but only the sense" (*Bible de Vence*). St. Thomas explains the difference between these texts when commenting on Mt. 12, 8. He says below: "It ought to be known that some Apostles recite the passages according to the Hebrew original, others according to the exposition of the Septuagint, and others were merely expressing the sense of the words."
14. or willingly.

15. "Aquila, a proselyte from Sinope in Pontus, completed about 128 A.D. a Greek translation of the protocanonical books. It was slavishly literal, and was condemned by Christians for its textual corruptions and incomprehensible Greek. Yet, it was held in the highest esteem by the Jews for four centuries. When, in 553 A.D., Emperor Justinian ordered the Jews throughout the Byzantine Empire to study the original Hebrew text, the version of Aquila lost its authority. The version was taken by Origen in his Hexapla, and fragments survive in Hexaplaric MSS" (John F. Steinmueller, *A Companion to Scripture Studies*, (New York, Joseph F. Wagner, Inc., 1952), vol. 1, p. 163).

but in the seventh generation. But it is replied that one ought not to count through the tribe of Juda, but through the tribe of Levi, under whose leadership the children of Israel went out from Egypt; "Thou hast conducted thy people like sheep, by the hand of Moses and Aaron" (Ps. 76, 21). And it is clear that there were only five generations through the tribe of Levi. For Jacob begot Levi, and Levi begot Caath, Caath begot Amram, Amram begot Moses and Aaron, as is evident in Exodus 2; and under Moses they went out from Egypt.

Observe here that the tribe of Juda was the most multiplied among all the tribes: and this was because from it the kings were to come, who were obliged to fight. The least multiplied among all the tribes was the tribe of Levi: and this was because it had been preordained to the divine service, and the priesthood, for which fewer men sufficed. And, for that reason, He willed that by likewise counting through the tribe of Juda, it would be true what is said in Genesis 15, 16: "In the fourth generation they shall return hither."[16] Therefore, Jerome says that what is said there ought to be understood by counting through the tribe of Levi; what is said here however, ought to be understood by counting through the tribe of Juda. For Phares himself with Jacob his father entered into Egypt. And, for that reason, these generations are not to be counted from Jacob, but from Phares. Similarly, Levi himself entered into Egypt with his father, Jacob. And for that reason, the generations are to be counted from Levi, and not from Jacob. Now it is clear that Moses was the fourth from Levi.

And Naasson begot Salmon. Salmon is interpreted 'sensible': and he signifies Christ, in whom are hidden all the treasures of wisdom and knowledge.[17]

Morally, here it ought to be noted, that just as in the first set of generations the order of our justification is signified as regards the

---

16. "How is Gen. 15, 16, 'in the fourth generation they shall come hither again,' to be reconciled with Ex. xiii. 18, Ex. xiii LXX, 'in the fifth generation the children of Israel went up out of the land of Egypt'? "(Letter XXXV. From Pope Damasus). "The words rendered by the LXX. 'in the fifth generation' more probably mean 'harnessed'" (St. Jerome, Letter XXXVI to Pope Damasus).

17. "**And Naason begot Salmon.** Salmon is interpreted to mean 'sensible.' Christ is sensible, Who said to the woman touching His garments from behind: 'Somebody hath touched me; for I know that virtue is gone out from me': Who knows all things before they happen, Who knew all past, present, and future events. We also ought to be sensible in the Lord, and only possess those things which are good, and may we be perfect in sense, but children in malice, so that we may all with one voice honor the Lord, and Father of the Lord Jesus Christ, and having been instructed in the senses of Sacred Scripture, we may be made docile according to the prophecy of Isaias who said: 'And they shall all be taught of God' (John 6, 45). (Walafrid Strabo, *Homily of the Beginning of St. Matthew's Gospel*, PL 114, 853). cf. "All thy children shall be taught of the Lord" (Isa. 54, 13).

state of beginners; so in this second set of generations, which similarly contains five men; the progress of the advanced is signified. For the first thing which follows from the fact that a man is justified from sin, is that he has a zeal for souls. And, for that reason, it is appropriate that Phares begot Esron, which means 'arrow' on account of the efficacy of the preaching by which the hearts of the listeners are penetrated; "He hath made me as a chosen arrow" (Is. 49, 2). And the other names apply in this way.

And Salmon begot Booz, etc. Here are set forth the ancestors who were born after the entrance into the Promised Land. For Salmon was born in the desert, and entered with Josue into the Promised Land, and married Rahab the harlot, of whom he begot Booz. Booz is interpreted 'strong'; "O Lord, my might, and my strength" (Jer. 16, 19). Now Rahab is interpreted 'hunger' or 'breadth': and she signifies the Church, because to it pertains the beatitude: "Blessed are they that hunger and thirst after justice: for they shall have their fill," etc., (below 5, 6). Her name is also interpreted 'breadth,' because the Church has been spread throughout the whole world; "Enlarge the place of thy tent, and stretch out the skins of thy tabernacles," etc., (Is. 54, 2). Likewise, her name is interpreted 'might,' because by the might of Christ's preaching He converted kings and philosophers. Likewise, she signifies the Church by reason of her deed. Rahab let out a scarlet cord in a window, by which she was freed from the overthrow of Jericho (Jos. 2, 21). Our window is our mouth: therefore, the cord in the window is the confession of Christ's Passion, through which the Church was freed from death. Again, she signifies the Church by reason of her marriage, because just as Rahab was joined in matrimony to Salmon, who was the prince in the tribe of Juda, so Christ espoused Himself to the Church; "I have espoused you to one husband, that I may present you as a chaste virgin to Christ" (II Cor. 11, 2).

But here it is sought: According to the passage, since Rahab was a harlot, how was she espoused to so great a prince, who was greater than the others?

And one ought to reply that Rahab did something very great, because, having despised her people and her native religion, she chose the worship of God. And, for that reason, she was given to the noblest prince as a very great honor.

And Booz begot Obed of Ruth. This is stated in the last chapter of Ruth. Obed is interpreted 'a servant' or 'servitude' and he signifies Christ, concerning whom it is said by the prophet: "Thou hast made me to serve with thy sins" (Is. 43, 24). Now Ruth signifies the Church born of the Gentiles by reason of her place of birth;

for she was a Moabitess. Moab is interpreted 'of his father'; "You are of your father the devil" (Jn. 8, 44); and again she signifies the Church by reason of her marriage, as is evident in the Gloss.

But it is sought, why these women are named here, since they were sinners.

Jerome points out the reason concerning Ruth, namely, it was so that she might fulfill the prophecy: "Send forth, O Lord, the lamb, the ruler of the earth, from Petra of the desert" (Is. 16, 1). Petra of the desert is certainly an evil place,[18] and by it Ruth the Moabitess is signified. Now Ambrose indicates the reason saying: "For it was to come to pass that the Church would be gathered together from the infidel Gentiles; and for that reason she would have been ashamed and confounded, unless they saw that Christ also was born from sinners." Hence, to take away their shame and confusion, they are named here.

But it is inquired: In Deuteronomy 23, 3 it is said: "The Ammonite and the Moabite shall not enter into the church"; therefore, since Ruth was a Moabitess, how was she received into the Church?

But one ought to answer from the words of the Apostle in Galatians 5, 18, that they who are led by the spirit are not under the law: for the intention of the legislator ought to be better observed than the words of the law: for what was the reason why the Lord forbade that they enter the Church? It was because, to wit, He found idolatry among them, and so He made this law lest they draw away the Jews into idolatry. Hence, this woman, who was already converted, was not an idolatress; and for that reason she was not subject to the prohibition.

And Obed begot Jesse (Ruth 4, 17). Now Jesse is interpreted 'sacrifice' or 'fire; and he signifies Him who offered Himself as a victim to God in the odor of sweetness.

But it is sought, since this man is called by another name, Isai, as is evidenced in I Kings in many places, and that name was more solemn, why did the Evangelist not name him thus?

And it ought to be said that this was so that it might be shown that which was said by the prophet Isaias (11, 1) was fulfilled in Christ: "There shall come forth a rod out of the root of Jesse."

And Jesse begot David the king. David is interpreted 'of a strong hand' and 'of a desirable appearance'; all these things are seemly to Christ, as is evident; for He is strong who conquered the devil; "But if a stronger than he come upon him and over-

---

18. This was the capital city of Arabia Petra, where Ruth is supposed to have lived, (Tostat) being, according to Challoner and others, the daughter of Eglon, king of Moab (Haydock's Introduction to Ruth).

come him, he will take away all his armor wherein he trusted and will distribute his spoils" (Lk. 11, 22). Likewise, He is "beautiful above the sons of men" (Ps. 44, 3).

But here it is sought: since many others were kings, why only he is called 'king'?

And it is replied that he was the first king in the tribe of Juda, from which the Lord descended: for although Saul was a king, nevertheless, he was of the tribe of Benjamin. A second reason is that the others reigned on account of the merits of David himself; "And I will make his seed to endure for evermore: and his throne as the days of heaven" (Ps. 88, 30). A third reason is to show the fulfillment of the prophecy in Jeremias 23, 5: "I will raise up to David a just branch: and a king shall reign, and shall be wise: and shall execute judgment and justice in the earth"; "He shall sit upon the throne of David, and upon his kingdom" (Is. 9, 7).

Morally, however, in this generation, the fruit of the perfect is designated, just as in the other generations the fruit of the beginners and of the advanced are designated. For the first thing which is required in a perfect man is that he himself be strong in going against adversities, such that he be not retarded on account of some difficulty: and this is signified by Booz; for his name is interpreted 'strong'; "They that hope in the Lord shall renew their strength, they shall take wings as eagles, they shall run and not be weary, they shall walk and not faint" (Is. 40, 31); "Who shall find a valiant woman?" etc., (Prov. 31, 10). The second thing is the humility of a servant, so that the greater he actually is, so much the more he humbles himself in all things; and this is signified by Obed, whose own name is interpreted 'a servant' or 'servitude'; "He that is the greater among you, let him become as he that serveth" (Lk. 22, 26). The third thing is fervor of charity, which is signified by Jesse, which means 'burnt' or 'fire'; "Let my prayer be directed as incense in thy sight," etc., (Ps. 140, 2). And from this, one reaches the kingdom and glory: because Jesse begot David the king; "He hath made us to our God a kingdom and priests to God His Father" (Apoc. 5,10); "You are a chosen generation, a kingly priesthood, a holy nation, a purchased people" (I Pet. 2, 9).

6b. *And David the king begot Solomon, of her that had been the wife of Urias.*
7. And Solomon begot Roboam. And Roboam begot Abia. And Abia begot Asa.
8. And Asa begot Josaphat. And Josaphat begot Joram. And Joram begot Ozias.

**9. And Ozias begot Joatham. And Joatham begot Achaz. And Achaz begot Ezechias.
10. And Ezechias begot Manasses. And Manasses begot Amon. And Amon begot Josias.
11. And Josias begot Jechonias and his brethren in the transmigration of Babylon.**

Having set forth the genealogical lineage of the ancestors, which ran through the Patriarchs, here the Evangelist sets forth the lineage of the fathers, which proceeds through the kings: and it is divided in two parts. In the first is set forth the kings who were born of Israel without mixture of a foreign race; in the second are set forth the kings who followed the joining of foreign blood, where it is said, **And Joram begot Ozias.**

Here there is a twofold question. For Luke, in computing Christ's generation, ascends through Nathan; Matthew, however, proceeds by descending from David to Christ through Solomon: hence, there seems to be some opposition.

But it ought to be answered, just as it has been said. Luke, in Christ's genealogy, lists many ancestors who were not ancestors of carnal origin through propagation, but through legal adoption; Matthew, however, lists no one who was not a carnal ancestor. And it is true that, according to the flesh, the Lord descended from David through Solomon and not through Nathan; and nevertheless, according to Augustine, it is not without mystery that Matthew descends from David through Solomon to Christ; Luke however ascends from Christ to David through Nathan. For Matthew had received the obligation of describing Christ's carnal generation, according to which Christ descended even unto the likeness of sinful flesh: and, for that reason, Matthew rightly descends in His generation from David through Solomon, since David himself sinned with Christ's fore-mother; Luke, however, who especially intended to commend the priestly dignity in Christ, through which was the expiation of sins, rightly ascends through Nathan, who was a holy man.

Note, nevertheless, that according to the same Augustine in his book, *Retractions*, one ought not to think that Nathan the prophet, who reprehended David, was the same as his son whom he begot: but they were merely similar in name.

Secondly it is sought why Bersabee is not mentioned by name, as were Thamar, Rahab, and Ruth.

And it ought to be said that the others, although they were sinners at one time, nevertheless, afterwards were converted and penitent; this woman, however, disgracefully sinned by the crime of adultery and in consenting to homicide: and thus, on account of the shamefulness of these crimes, her name is not added.

Observe, nevertheless, that in Scripture the sins of great men are told, for example of David and of others; and this is because the devil overthrew not only small and lowly men, but also great men; for he is our adversary. And, for that reason, they are told as a safeguard, so that he who stands may take heed lest he fall. Another reason is, lest someone deem them to be something more than men. For if someone were to consider only the perfection in them, he might be deceived through idolatry; but when he sees them to have fallen through sin, he does not imagine them to be anything more than men.

Note also this, according to Gregory, that sometimes an actual deed is evil, but something good is signified; however, sometimes a deed is good, and something evil is signified. For Urias was a good and just man, and he was not reprehended in Scripture about anything; but, nevertheless, he signifies the devil. Bersabee, however, was a sinful woman; and, nevertheless, she signifies a good thing, namely, the Church, as the Gloss on II Kings 12 indicates, and as the Gloss, which interprets the figure in an allegorical sense, also indicates. Urias is interpreted 'God is my light,' and he signifies the devil, who inordinately desired the light of the divinity; "I will be like the most High" (Is. 14, 14). Bersabee is interpreted 'well of the seven' or 'well of the alliance';[19] and it signifies the Church of the Gentiles, by reason of the sevenfold baptismal grace. The devil had espoused this Church to himself; but David, that is, Christ, took it away from him, joined it to Himself, and killed the devil. Otherwise, Bersabee signifies the Law, through the ways of which the people were led, and signifies those who do not wish to enter into the house through spiritual understanding, and for that reason, it carries the edict of its own death, because "The letter killeth" (II Cor. 3, 6). But David, that is Christ, took the Law away from the Jews, when He taught that it, i.e. the law, is to be understood spiritually.

And Solomon begot Roboam, etc. Now, just as David is interpreted 'of a strong hand' and 'of a desirable appearance,' so

---

19. "And Abraham set apart seven ewelambs of the flock. And Abimelech said to him: What mean these seven ewelambs which thou hast set apart? But he said: Thou shalt take seven ewelambs at my hand: that they may be a testimony for me, that I dug this well. Therefore that place was called Bersabee; because there both of them did swear" (Gen. 28, 31) Bersabee... That is, 'the well of oath.' *Ber* means 'well'; *saba* means 'lambs' or 'sheep,' or also 'oath' according to St. Jerome. (cf. *Postilla in Librum Geneseos*, p. 21)

Solomon is interpreted 'peace-maker': and this is fitting, because peace of conscience proceeds from the strength of good deeds; "Much peace have they that love thy law" (Ps. 118, 165). Now it happens that from peace of conscience a man wants others to come to what is good. Hence, Solomon begot Roboam, which means 'might': because one having peace of conscience is motivated to spread the name of Christ by the might of preaching; as it is read concerning the Apostles: "When they shall rush in unto Jacob, Israel shall blossom and bud, and they shall fill the face of the world with seed" (Is. 27, 6). Now both signify Christ, because He is peace. Likewise, He is Roboam, who converted people by the might of preaching.

And Roboam begot Abia, which means 'God the Father': because from the fact that a man is zealous for the spiritual benefit of others, or their corporal benefit through works of mercy, he is made worthy of God's paternity, as it is written: "Do good to them that hate you, that you may be the children of your Father who is in heaven," etc., (above 5, 44). And in Luke 6, 36 it is written: "Be ye merciful" (Lk. 6, 36). This belongs to Christ, of whom it is said: "I will be to him a Father, and he shall be to me a Son" (Heb. 1, 5).

And Abia begot Asa, which means 'lifting up': because sometimes a man, from the fact that he is made a father or a superior of others, becomes guilty of a certain carefree negligence; and for that reason, *Abia begot Asa*, namely, so that man may be in continual advancement, and may always lift himself up to greater things. This also belongs to Christ, who is called 'lifting up,' that is, growing; "And the child grew" (Lk. 2, 40). Or 'lifting up,' because He took away the sins of the world.

And Asa begot Josaphat, which means 'judging,' because from the fact that the spiritual man grows, he is made one who judges; "The spiritual man judgeth all things" (I Cor. 2, 15). And this belongs to Christ, because "The Father hath given all judgment to the Son" (Jn. 5, 22).

And Josaphat begot Joram, which means 'one dwelling on high'; for he who is constituted a judge, ought to dwell on high; "He shall dwell on high" (Is. 33, 16). Now the Apostle says how this may be: "Our conversation is in heaven" (Phil. 3, 20). And this belongs to Christ, because "He is high above all nations" (Ps. 112, 4).

And Joram begot Ozias. Here there is a literal question. For in I Paralipomenon 3, 11, it is said that Joram begot Ochozias. Ochozias, however, begot Joas.[20] And Joas begot Amasias, who is

---

20. The text seems to erroneously put Joram as the son of Ochozias.

also called Azarias. And Amasias begot Ozias. Therefore, it seems that the Evangelist erred in two points in his genealogical lineage. Firstly, he erred because Joram did not beget Ozias, but Amasias; and secondly, he erred because he omitted three generations. And it ought to be said, in regard to the first point, that to generate some other person can be understood in two ways, mediately and immediately: immediately, as, for instance, a carnal father immediately had generated a son: and in this way Joram did not generate Ozias. Or this may be understood in the other way, namely, mediately, as, for instance, we are said to be sons of Adam; and in this way a son can be said to be begotten by his grandfather, or his great-grandfather, because he descended from him through a mediate generation. Now three reasons are assigned for why he omitted the three generations. The first is by Jerome, who says (just as it is written in Ex. 20, 5): "The Lord visits the iniquity of the fathers upon the children, unto the third and fourth generation, to those who are made imitators of the crimes of their fathers." Now Joram married the daughter of Jezebel, namely, Athalia, who drew him into idolatry. Ochozias also was more given to idolatry than his father. And, similarly, Joram imitated the crimes of his fathers, who in addition to the crime of idolatry, also killed Zacharias, the son of Joiada: and, for that reason, these three men, as though unworthy, are excluded from Christ's generation. Chrysostom assigns another reason. For the Lord commanded Jehu (IV Kings 9), the son of Namsi, that he himself eradicate the house of Achab, who was diligent in the execution of the precept, and, nevertheless, did not withdraw from the worship of many gods: for he adored the molten calves. And because he diligently accomplished the Lord's command by destroying the house of Achab, it was said to him that his sons would sit upon the throne of the house of Israel unto the fourth generation. Hence, just as Jehu merited the kingdom of Israel unto the third or fourth generation, so, by opposition, Joram, who married Gentile women, and transferred the iniquity of the of house of Israel to the house of Juda, should lose the names of his posterity in the genealogy of Christ unto the fourth generation, when the expiation had been made. Augustine, in his *On Questions of the New and Old Testament*, assigns another reason. For he says that some ancestors were good and happened to have good parents, such as Isaac and Jacob: some were evil, and, nevertheless, happened to have good parents, as, for instance, Solomon, who was a sinner, and, nevertheless, had a just and holy man, David, for his father: some ancestors were neither good nor had good parents, as these three were, as is evident from what was said previously. Joram sinned, and his sin continued all the way to Ozias, who did almost nothing evil, except that he burned incense; the continuation of sin is the cause and reason of destruction. And, for that reason, these three, who persisted in the sin of idolatry, are excluded from Christ's genealogy. A mystical reason, however, is assigned on account of the three series of fourteen generations, by which Matthew intends to describe Christ's genealogy. Now Ozias is interpreted 'the strong One of the Lord'; and he signifies Christ, about whom it is written: "The Lord is my strength and my praise: and he is become my salvation," etc., (Ps. 117, 14). Mystically, however, *Joram begot Ozias*, because those who dwell on high, ought to perform deeds of strength.

Note that under this Ozias, Isaias prophesied, as appears in Isaias 1.[21] For on account of the leading men, the kings and also the people, God took away prophecy and teaching; hence, under a good king the outpouring of prophecy began again.

And Ozias begot Joatham, which means 'perfected'; and he signifies Christ, through whom the Church grows daily in perfection. And so it is fitting that Ozias begot Joatham because those who perform deeds of strength, continually advance in perfection; "They shall go from virtue to virtue" (Ps. 83, 8).

And Joatham begot Achaz, which means 'comprehending'; because through continual growth in the perfection of the virtues one comes to the knowledge of God; "By thy commandments I have had understanding: therefore have I hated every way of iniquity" (Ps. 118, 104); "They declared the works of God (by showing them forth in their works), and understood his doings" (Ps. 63, 10). On account of which Paul wrote: "I follow after, if I may by any means apprehend (*comprehendam*), wherein I am also apprehended by Christ Jesus" (Phil. 3, 12). And this belongs to Christ, who alone perfectly comprehends the divinity; "No one knoweth the Father but the Son" (Lk. 10, 22).

And Achaz begot Ezechias, that is 'the strong Lord': because such a man has strength from God; "The Lord is my courage, and my strength" (II Kings 22, 2). And this belongs to Christ, who is strong in battle.

And Ezechias begot Manasses, and his name is interpreted 'forgetfulness': because he who now perfectly knows God, is forgetful of temporal things; "Forget thy people and thy father's

---

21. "The vision of Isaias the Son of Amos, which he saw concerning Juda and Jerusalem in the days of Ozias, Joathan, Achaz, and Ezechias, kings of Juda" (verse 1).

house" (Ps. 44, 11); "The Lord God hath made me to forget all my labours" (Gen. 41, 51). And this belongs to Christ, concerning whom it is said, "If the wicked doeth penance for all his sins which he hath committed, I will not remember all his iniquities that he hath done" (Ez. 18, 21).

And Manasses begot Amon, that is, 'faithful' and 'fostering': because he is truly faithful who despises temporal things. For, according to Gregory, deceit is the daughter of avarice: and, for that reason, he who perfectly despises temporal things, has no inclination to be unfaithful with the goods of others.[22] Hence, it is rightly said that *Manasses begot Amon*. This name is also interpreted 'fostering': because he who despises temporal things, ought thenceforth to foster the poor through mercy; "If thou wilt be perfect, go sell what thou hast," behold the despising, "and give to the poor," behold the fostering; now this belongs to Christ, who is truly faithful; "The Lord is faithful in all his words" (Ps. 144, 13); and again, He is a foster father; "I who was a foster father to Ephraim, carried them in my arms: and they knew not that I healed them" (Osee 11, 3); "How often would I have gathered together thy children, as the hen doth gather her chickens under her wings, and thou wouldst not?" (below 23, 37).

And Amon begot Josias, which means 'the salvation of the Lord,' or 'incense'; because from this it follows that a man obtains salvation, that he is even now forgetful of temporal things and bestows, or distributes them. Or it is interpreted incense, and this belongs to Christ; "He hath wrought salvation in the midst of the earth" (Ps. 73, 12): "And He hath delivered himself a sacrifice to God for an odour of sweetness" (Eph. 5, 2).

And Josias begot Jechonias and his brethren, which means 'preparation of the Lord' or 'resurrection'; and he signifies Christ, who prepared a place for us (Jn. 14) and who says, "I am the resurrection and the life" (Jn. 11, 25), and by passing through this life we come to the resurrection.

Here, however, there are three literal questions. Firstly, it is asked in what way is Josias said to have begotten Jechonias; and, nevertheless, he did not beget him, but his father Joakim begot him.

And there is a twofold answer to this. For, according to Chrysostom, with whom Augustine agrees, Joakim's name is completely omitted; and this is because he did not reign by divine ordinance,

---

22. "...Amon, that is 'faithful,' for whoso despises all temporal things defrauds no man of his goods" (*Catena Aurea on St. Matthew*, chap. 1, lect. 3)
23. He is also called "Johanan." He was two years older than Joakim.

but by Pharaoh's might, who set him on the throne, having imprisoned his firstborn brother Joachaz,[23] who had reigned before him. And with respect to this, note the history in IV Kings 23 and II Paralipomenon 36. Josias, in fact, had three sons: Joachaz, Joakim, who is also Eliacim, and Sedecias. For if, as Augustine says, those three kings were excluded from the genealogy, because they were corrupted by idolatry, how much more he, who neither by God, nor by a prophet, but by the placement of a Gentile man was set on the throne? It is the opinion, but not the words, of Jerome, with whom Ambrose maintains and agrees, that both he who is placed at the end of these fourteen generations, and he who is placed at the beginning of the third, were called Joakim, and, moreover, that Jechonias and Joakim are the same person. Hence, it ought to be observed that Josias had three sons: Joakim, who is also called Eliacim, Joachaz, and Sedecias. Now when Josias died, Joachaz, namely, his middle son, reigned in his place; who was thereafter captured and imprisoned by Pharaoh, king of Egypt, who then appointed as king, Joakim, the firstborn son of Josias, imposing tribute upon him; afterwards, Nabuchodonosor, king of Babylon, having conquered the king of Egypt, besieged Jerusalem and took away Joakim, whom he sent back to Jerusalem under tribute. Afterwards, however, when Joakim, relying upon the help of the king of Egypt, wanted to rebel against the king of Babylon, Nabuchodonosor went up to Jerusalem, captured it, and put Joakim's son, Joachin, in his place, whom he also named Jechonias, the name of his father.[24] Which having been done, Nabuchodonosor, fearing that this man, remembering his father's death, would ally with the King of Egypt, returned to Jerusalem, and besieged it. And Jechonias, or this Joachim, namely, the son of the other one, by the counsel of Jeremias handed himself, his wife, and his children over to king Nabuchodonosor. And these persons are properly said to have been carried away in the transmigration. But Nabuchodonosor appointed Sedecias, the brother of his father, king in his place, and led Joachim himself into Babylon; and he is of whom it is said afterwards, *And after the transmigration.*

But why is he named Jechonias, since his name was Joachim? And it ought to be answered that this name was imposed by a prophet, namely, Jeremias; "Thus saith the Lord, if Jechonias the son of Joakim the king of Juda were a ring on my right hand, I

---

24. "JEROME. We may consider the first Jechonias to be the same as Joakim, and the second to be the son not the father, the one being spelled with *k* and *m*, the second by *ch* and *n*. This distinction has been confounded both by Greeks and Latins, by the fault of writers and the lapse of time" (*Catena Aurea on St. Matthew, ibid.*).

would pluck him thence" (Jer. 22, 24). And afterwards it is said, "Is this man Jechonias an earthen and a broken vessel?" (v. 28). And for that reason he is rather named with this kind of name to show that the Evangelist is in accord with the Prophet.

Note also that although the name is the same, nevertheless, it is written in different ways. For the name of the first Joakim is written with a 'k', and he seems to be called Joakim; but the name of the second is written with the letter 'ghimel',[25] hence, it is pronounced Joachim: and, for that reason, it has various interpretations. For the first name it is interpreted 'resurrection'; but second name is interpreted 'preparation of the Lord.'

Secondly, it is sought why it is said, *Jechonias and his brethren*. For there were many of the kings who had brothers; but never is mention made of their brothers.

And it ought to be answered, according to Ambrose, that wherever there is mention of brothers, as for instance when it is said: *Juda and his brethren*, and *Phares and Zara of Thamar*, this signifies that they were equal in sanctity, or equal in malice. Now all these three were evil.[26] Alternatively, it can be said it was because it is not certain which one of these men reigned, as it is clear from the things that have been said; it was not so, however, in regard to the brothers of the other kings.

Thirdly, it is inquired about the fact that it is said *in the transmigration*. This seems false because Josias never was carried away.

And it is replied that this ought to be taken according to the Divine foreknowledge, according to which it had been ordained that those whom he begot would be carried away. Or it is replied that *in the transmigration* is almost the same as near to the transmigration, or it was then imminent.

12. And after the transmigration of Babylon, Jechonias begot Salathiel. And Salathiel begot Zorobabel.
13. And Zorobabel begot Abiud. And Abiud begot Eliacim. And Eliacim begot Azor.
14. And Azor begot Sadoc. And Sadoc begot Achim. And Achim begot Eliud.
15. And Eliud begot Eleazar. And Eleazar begot Mathan. And Mathan begot Jacob.
16. And Jacob begot Joseph the husband of Mary, of whom was born Jesus, who is called Christ.

25. i.e. *ch*.
26. i.e. Joachaz, Joakim and Sedecias.

17. So all the generations from Abraham to David, are fourteen generations. And from David to the transmigration of Babylon, are fourteen generations: and from the transmigration of Babylon to Christ are fourteen generations.
18. Now the generation of Christ was in this wise. When as his mother Mary was espoused to Joseph, before they came together, she was found with child, of the Holy Ghost.
19. Whereupon Joseph her husband, being a just man, and not willing publicly to expose her, was minded to put her away privately.
20. But while he thought on these things, behold the angel of the Lord appeared to him in his sleep, saying: Joseph, son of David, fear not to take unto thee Mary thy wife, for that which is conceived in her, is of the Holy Ghost.
21. And she shall bring forth a son: and thou shalt call his name Jesus. For he shall save his people from their sins.

Here is related the third series of fourteen in Christ's generation, which proceeds through private persons. About this Jechonias, as it was said above, there were two opinions. For Jerome and Ambrose held that one Jechonias was he who is put at the end of the first fourteen generations, and was called Joakim; but there was another Jechonias who was called Joachim. But according to Augustine, it was as was said above.[27] For this transmigration of the children of Israel signifies the translation of the faith to the Gentiles; "To you it behooved us first to speak the word of God" (Acts 13, 46). In that transmigration there was made a sort of bending back of the Jews toward the Gentiles. Hence, what one might call a sort of corner was established; and, for that reason, this Jechonias signifies Christ, who was made the cornerstone, joining both peoples of the Jews and the Gentiles in Himself; "The stone which the builders rejected; the same is become the head of the corner" (Ps. 117, 22).

But here a question is asked. In Jeremias 22, 30 it is said, "Write this man (Sedecias) barren, a man that shall not prosper

---

27. St. Augustine held that the same Jechonias was named both at the end of the second fourteen generations and the beginning of the third set of fourteen. The reason he gives for this is that Joakim was not a valid king since Pharaoh put him on the throne. "From Abraham then to David are fourteen generations: after that, the enumeration begins with Solomon, for David begot Solomon; the enumeration, I say, begins with Solomon, and reaches to Jechonias, during whose life the carrying away into Babylon took place; and so are there other fourteen generations, by reckoning in Solomon at the head of the second division, and Jechonias also, with whom that enumeration closes to fill up the number fourteen; and the third division begins with this same Jechonias. (St. Augustine, *Sermon I on the New Testament*, n. 12)

in his days: for there shall not be a man of his seed that shall sit upon the throne of David." How, therefore, is it said that Christ descended from David through Sedecias, since Isaias wrote concerning Christ as follows, "He shall sit upon the throne of David, and upon his kingdom," (9, 7)? And it is replied, according to Ambrose, that when Christ is said to sit upon a throne, it is understood of a spiritual and not corporeal kingdom, except insofar as by David's corporeal kingdom a spiritual kingdom is signified.

And Salathiel begot Zorobabel. Against this it is said in I Paralipomenon 3 that the sons of Jechonias were Asir, Salathiel, Melchiram, and Phadaia. And Phadaia had sons, Zorobabel and Semei. Concerning Abiud, however, there is completely no mention there. Therefore, it seems that the Evangelist spoke wrongly, saying that Salathiel begot Zorobabel, and that Zorobabel begot Abiud.

Regarding this, it is answered in three ways in the Gloss. One answer is that, in the book of Paralipomenon, many things have been corrupted through the errors of transcribers, especially concerning those things that pertain to numbers and to names. Hence, the Apostle forbids giving heed to these corrupted generations, which lead to more questions than real utility (I Tim. 1, 4).[28] Another answer is that Salathiel had two different names. For he is called Salathiel and Phadaia;[29] and for that reason the book of Paralipomenon names Zorobabel the son of Phadaia, but the Evangelist names him the son of Salathiel. There is, therefore, no opposition. There is a third answer, and it is truer, that Salathiel and Phadaia were brothers, as the book of Paralipomenon relates. Phadaia however begot a son whom he called by the same name, namely, Zorobabel, and this man begot Abiud.[30] Also, it ought to be said that the book of Paralipomenon recounts the genealogy of Phadaia himself; but the Evangelist recounts the generation of Salathiel, because Christ was born of him.

It ought to be observed, however, that regarding these men who were from Abiud all the way until Joseph, there is no mention of them in Sacred Scripture, but these things were taken from the

---

28. "Not to give heed to fables and endless genealogies, which furnish questions rather than the edification of God which is in faith."
29. The text reads, "Caphadara" and later "Capha" instead of Phadaia. Phadaia however seems to fit the context better. Perhaps this was a second spelling or name of Phadaia. cf. "Or it may be said, that Salathiel and Phadaias are the same man under two different names" (*Catena Aurea on St. Matthew*, chap. 1, lect. 6) "Of Phadaia were born Zorobabel and Semei" (I Par. 3, 19).
30. "Or that Salathiel anti Phadaias were brothers, and both had sons of the same name" (ibid).

annals of the Hebrews, which Herod in large part caused to be burned, so that the ignobility of his lineage might be hidden.

Note, therefore, that in this part of the genealogy there are set forth three ranks. The first is the rank of the doctors, and it contains four generations: for before prayer preparation is required, according to that which is said, "Before prayer prepare thy soul" (Eccli. 18, 23). And, for that reason, after Jechonias, which means 'preparation of the Lord,' follows Salathiel, which means 'my petition'; and they signify Christ, who in all his prayers "was heard for his reverence" (Heb. 5, 7). Now, prayer ought to precede teaching, according to that passage, "Pray that speech may be given me in the opening of my mouth" (Eph. 6, 19); and, for that reason, after Salathiel follows Zorobabel, that is, 'the master of Babylon,' which means 'of confusion.' This is because, through the teaching and preaching of the Apostles, the Gentiles were called back to the true God, and this was unto the confusion of idolatry. And this pertains mainly to Christ, who says, "You call me Master and Lord. And you say well" (Jn. 13, 13). Now, through teaching and preaching, a man acquires the dignity of a father; hence, they are called the fathers of those whom are spiritually instructed; "For if you have ten thousand instructors in Christ, yet not many fathers. For in Christ Jesus, by the gospel, we are children" (I Cor. 4, 15); and, for that reason, there follows, **And Zorobabel begot Abiud**, which means 'he is my father'; and this belongs to Christ; "He shall cry out to me: Thou art my father" (Ps. 88, 27).

And Abiud begot Eliacim. Here is indicated the rank of the beginners, namely, the hearers. Now the first thing that occurs in the hearer by preaching, and which a preacher ought to intend, is that the hearer rise from his vices to the virtues, according to that which is said, "Rise, thou that sleepest" (Eph. 5, 14). And, for that reason, **Abiud begot Eliacim**, which means 'resurrection'; and this belongs to Christ who says, "Every one that believeth in me has eternal life" (Jn. 11, 26). Now one who rises is not able to arrive at the state of justice except through God's help. And, for that reason, after he will have risen, a man needs God's help, according to that which is said, "My help is from the Lord" (Ps. 120, 2); and, for that reason, it continues, **And Eliacim begot Azor**, which means 'aided.' And this also belongs to Christ, of whom it is said in Psalm 26, 9: "Be thou my helper, O Lord." And through this help one arrives at justice. Hence, **Azor begot Sadoc**, which means 'the just'; "The justice of God, by faith of Jesus Christ, unto all, and upon all them that believe in him" (Rom. 3, 22). Now the consummation or the end of justice is charity; "The end of justice is Christ, the end of the commandment is charity" (I Tim. 1, 5). There are only two precepts, namely, the love of God and the love of neighbor; "And this commandment we have from God, that he who loveth God love also his brother" (I Jn. 4, 21). And, for that reason, **Sadoc** is followed by **Achim**, and **Achim** is followed by **Eliud**. Achim is interpreted 'my brother.' Hence, it signifies love of neighbor; "Behold how good and how pleasant it is for brethren to dwell together in unity!" (Ps. 132, 1). This belongs to Christ, who is our flesh and our brother. And because love of neighbor cannot be without love of God, it continues: **And Achim begot Eliud**. Eliud is interpreted 'my God'; "Thou art my God" (Ps. 30, 15).

And Eliud begot Eleazar. Here is designated the rank of the advanced. Now one cannot advance without divine help; and, for that reason, **Eliud** is rightly followed by **Eleazar**, which means 'God is my helper'; "Blessed is the man whose help is from thee" (Ps. 83, 6). But because God can help towards salvation in many ways, such as by removing obstacles and by giving opportunities, there is very powerful help through the gift of His grace; "By the grace of God, I am what I am" (I Cor. 15, 10). And, for that reason, **Eleazar**, that is to say, God's help, is followed by **Mathan**, which means 'gift,' namely, of divine grace. And this belongs to Christ, who is also one who gives; "For God so loved the world, as to give his only begotten Son" (Jn. 3, 16); "He gave gifts to men" (Heb. 4, 8). But because man might merely rely upon the gift of grace, because he falls into negligence by not cooperating with grace by his free will, therefore **Jacob** follows, which means 'wrestler'; on account of this it is said, "By the grace of God, I am what I am" (I Cor. 15, 10). And it continues, "And his grace in me hath not been void"; "We do exhort you that you receive not the grace of God in vain" (II Cor. 6, 1). And now **Joseph** follows, meaning 'increase,' because through grace and the effort of free will man comes to an increase; "The path of the just, as a shining light, goeth forwards, and increaseth even to perfect day" (Prov. 4, 18). Hence, **Jacob begot Joseph the husband of Mary**.

But here there are two questions. For firstly it is inquired about the contrariety which seems to exist between Luke and Matthew. For Luke says that Joseph was of Heli, who was of Mathat. Matthew, however, says that he was of Jacob. Therefore, there seems to be a contrariety between them.[31]

---

31. Please refer to the chart of the Genealogy of Our Lord Jesus Christ on the following page.

GENEALOGY OF
OUR LORD JESUS CHRIST

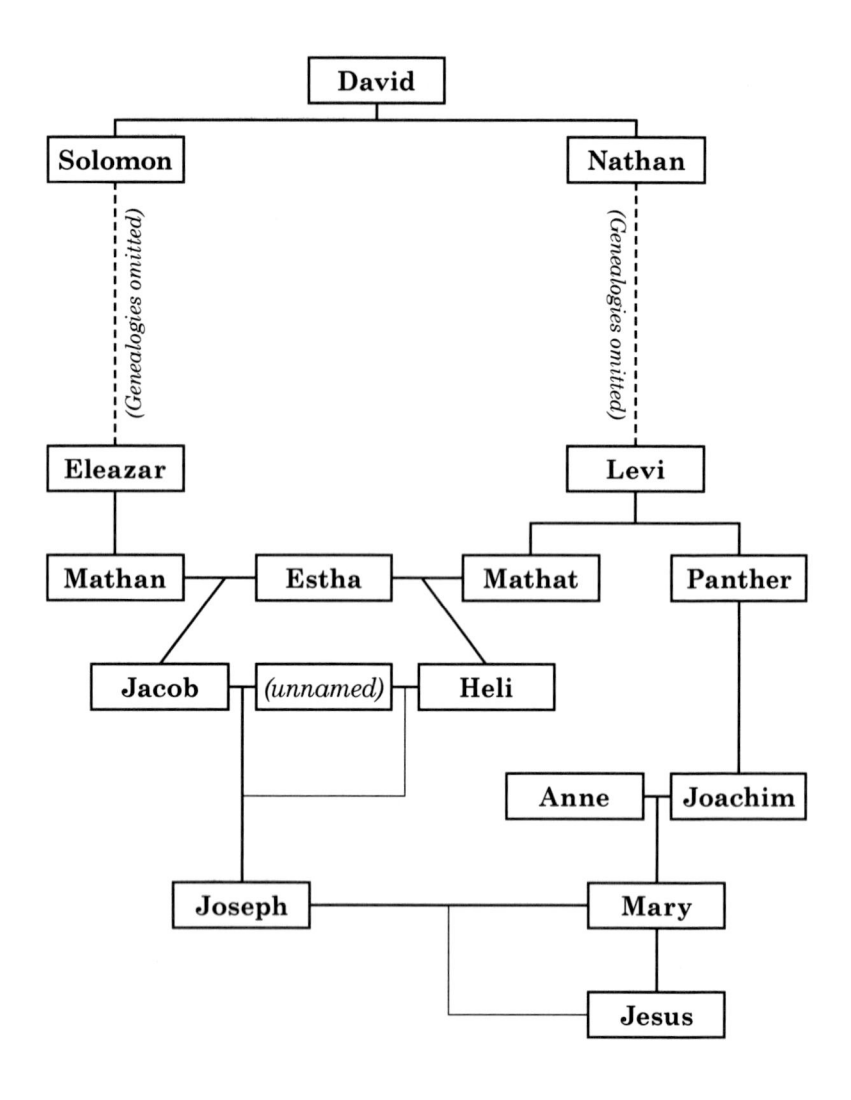

```
                         David
              ┌────────────┴────────────┐
           Solomon                    Nathan
              │                         │
     (Genealogies omitted)      (Genealogies omitted)
              │                         │
           Eleazar                     Levi
              │                ┌────────┴────────┐
           Mathan ── Estha ── Mathat           Panther
              │        │        │                 │
            Jacob ─(unnamed)─ Heli                │
              │                              Anne ── Joachim
              │                                      │
            Joseph ──────────────── Mary
                                     │
                                   Jesus
```

But it ought to be said regarding this that the two were of the same stock but not of the same family, namely, Mathan and Mathat. For they were of the stock of David; but one descended from the stock of David through Solomon, namely, Mathan; the other descended from David through Nathan, namely, Mathat. Therefore Mathan took a wife by the name of Estha, of whom he begot Jacob. Now when Mathan died, because the Law did not forbid a widow to marry, she married his brother, Mathat, who begot of her Heli. Hence, Jacob and Heli were brothers of the same mother, but not of the same father. Now Heli took a wife and died without children; whence Jacob, to raise up seed to his brother, took the same wife and begot Joseph. Hence, Joseph was the son of Jacob according to the flesh, but the son of Heli according to adoption. And, for that reason, Matthew, who gives only Christ's ancestors according to the flesh, says that Joseph was the son of Jacob; Luke, however, who gives many ancestors who were not ancestors according to the flesh, says he was the son of Heli. The reason for this diversity was stated above.

It ought to be observed, however, when a brother took his brother's wife, to raise up his name, it ought not to be understood that the son who was begotten, was called by the name of the deceased brother. For Booz who took Ruth, to raise up seed to Elimelech, begot a son whom he did not call Elimelech, but Obed; but in this sense he is said to raise up his name, because that son was ascribed to him according to the Law. Nor is this unfitting, because, as it is said in ecclesiastical history, the Apostles and the Evangelists themselves were instructed by Christ's nearer ancestors about Christ's genealogy, who were keeping this in their hearts partly by memory and partly from the aforesaid books of Paralipomenon.

There is a second question. Matthew intends to write Christ's generation. Since, therefore, Christ was not the son of Joseph, only of Mary, why was it necessary to trace Christ's generation from Abraham to Joseph?

To which it is responded that it was the custom of the Jews, and is still so till this day, to take a wife from one's own tribe. Hence, in Numbers 36, 7, it is said that every man ought to take a wife from his tribe and kindred. And though this was not necessarily observed, nevertheless, the custom was observed. Hence, Joseph took Mary for his wife, as she was very closely related to him. And, for that reason, since they were of the same tribe, by the fact that it is shown that Joseph descended from David, it is also shown that Mary and Christ were of the seed of David. But whence can it be held that Joseph and Mary were of the same family? It is evident from what is stated in Luke 2, 4, that when a census had been due to occur, Joseph and Mary themselves went up to the city of David, which is Bethlehem. Hence, by the fact that he brought her with him, it is evident that they were of the same family.

But it is inquired why he does not show Christ's generation from David through Mary. It is replied that it was not the custom among the Hebrews, nor even among the Gentiles, to trace a genealogy through women. Hence, Christ, who had come for the salvation of men, willed to be imitated in this, namely, to observe the customs of men; and so His genealogy is not traced through women, particularly since without danger to the truth His genealogy could be known through men.

The husband of Mary. Jerome says, "When you hear this word 'husband,' let not the suspicion of wedlock arise."

On the contrary, was there not a true marriage? It is replied that it was indeed, because there were present the three goods of matrimony: offspring, namely, God Himself; faith, since there was no adultery; and sacrament, since it was an indivisible union of minds. What, therefore, is to be said? This denial of Jerome must be understood in respect to the consummation of marriage, which is through carnal intercourse. Now, for that reason, as Augustine says, he is called Mary's husband, so that it might be shown that the marriage was between spouses equally bound by a vow of continence.[32]

But how was this a marriage? For a vow impedes contracting marriage, and annuls the contract. Therefore, since the Blessed Virgin vowed her virginity, it seems there was no marriage. Furthermore, she would have agreed to carnal intercourse, if it was a marriage.

But it ought to be replied that the Blessed Virgin was straitened between two things: for on one side, she was straitened by the curse of the Law, to which a sterile person was subject; on the other side, she was straitened on account of her intention to observe chastity. And, for that reason, she resolved to practice virginity, unless the Lord would ordain otherwise. As to what is asserted, that she consented to carnal intercourse, it ought to be replied that she did not. She did, in fact, consent directly to marriage; however, she would have consented somewhat implicitly to carnal intercourse, if God had willed this.

---

32. "Afterwards, however, having taken a husband, according as the custom of the time required, together with him Mary took a vow of virginity" (II II, q. 28, a. 4).

33. *De qua* is translated "Of whom." *Qua* is feminine while *quo* is masculine. Hence, the text could be read, "of her."

34. "Of them," in the plural.

Of whom was born Jesus, who is called Christ. Here a twofold error is excluded. One error asserts that Christ was the son of Joseph. And this is excluded by that which is said, *De qua*.[33] For if He were the son of Joseph, the Evangelist would have said, *De quo*; or at least he would have said *De quibus*.[34] Another error is excluded, namely, of Valentine, who says that Christ did not take a body of the Blessed Virgin; instead, He brought it from heaven and passed through the Blessed Virgin as through a channel. What is said, ***Of whom***, is opposed to this. For if it were as he says, the Evangelist would not have said, ***Of whom***, but instead 'through whom,' or 'by whom,' or 'from whom,' or something similar. For this preposition *of* always indicates consubstantiality; the preposition 'from', however, does not. Hence, it can be said: 'From morning comes the day" and that 'The chest comes from the craftsman.' But it is never said, 'The chest is made out of the craftsman.' Hence, by the fact that he says ***of***, he indicates that Christ's body was formed out of the body of the Blessed Virgin; "God sent his Son, made of a woman, made under the law" (Gal. 4, 4). Here the error of Nestorius, who asserted that there were two persons in Christ, is guarded against; and, for that reason, he did not admit that God was born or suffered. Nor would he attribute to a man other things that belong to God, such as to exist from eternity, or to have created the stars. Hence, in some of his letters he interpreted this passage as a confirmation of his error. ***Of whom was born Jesus***; he does not say God, but Jesus, which is the name of a man, as is also ***Christ***. But according to this, there would not have been any union in Christ, nor could Christ be said to be one.

Hence, observe that in Christ, because a union of the two natures occurs in one Person, a communication of idioms occurs, such that those things which belong to God may be attributed to a man, and vice versa. And any kind of example can be given of two accidents in one substance, as, for instance, an apple is said to be white and savory. And inasmuch as it is savory, it is said to be white, by reason of the fact that an apple is white, and vice versa.

Who is called Christ. Note: He is simply called Christ without any additional name, to indicate that He was anointed with invisible oil, unlike the kings and prophets in the Law who were anointed with material oil; "Thy God, hath anointed thee with the oil of gladness above thy fellows" (Ps. 44, 8).

So all the generations. Having related Christ's generation, here he ends the number of generations. And he divides them into three series of fourteen. The first series of fourteen is from Abraham to David inclusively, i.e. such that David is named in that first series of fourteen; and this is what is said, *So all the generations.* The second series of fourteen extends from David exclusively, such that David is not numbered, but rather it starts from Solomon and ends at the Babylonian Captivity; and this is what is said, *And from David to the transmigration of Babylon, are fourteen generations.* The third begins from the Babylonian Captivity and ends at Christ, such that Christ is the fourteenth generation.

Chrysostom assigns the reason: that, in these three series of fourteen, some change of the people of Israel was always made. For in the first fourteen they were under the leaders; in the second they were under the kings; and in the third they were under the priests. And Christ was a leader, king and priest; "The Lord is our judge, the Lord is our lawgiver, the Lord is our king" (Is. 33, 22). And about His priesthood it is said, "Thou art a priest forever according to the order of Melchisedech" (Ps. 109, 4). He assigns another reason, namely, that the necessity of Christ's coming might be shown. For in the first fourteen they asked for a king against God's will, and they transgressed the Law. Now in the second they were led into captivity on account of their sins. But in the third we are freed from all guilt, misery, and spiritual slavery of sin. Jerome assigns a third reason, namely, that by these men are signified the three times, in which the lives of all mankind are led. For by the first fourteen is signified the time before the Law, because in it are listed some fathers who were before the Law. By the second, the time under the Law is signified, because all those fathers who are listed were under the Law. Now by the third, the time of grace is signified, because it ends at Christ, i.e. by whom "grace and truth came" (Jn. 1, 17). This division also corresponds to a mystery, because fourteen is a number composed of four and ten. By ten therefore the Old Testament is understood, which was given in ten Commandments. By four, however, the Gospel is understood, because it is divided into four books. Now the three groups of fourteen designate faith in the Trinity. Hence, by the fact that Matthew divides the genealogy into three groups of fourteen, it is indicated that through the New and Old Testament, in faith of the Trinity, one comes to Christ. Now, concerning the number of generations, there are two opinions. For according to Jerome, who says, because there is a different Jechonias at the end of the first fourteen and at the beginning of the second, there are forty-two generations; for they make a total of three series of fourteen. But according to Augustine, there are only forty-one; and by the fact that Christ is the last one, this also corresponds to a mystery. For the number forty is the product of four and ten, or conversely. According to the Platonists, four is the number of bodies: for a body is composed of the four elements; ten, however, is the number which is the sum of the lineal numbers: for one, two, three and four make ten. And because Matthew intends to declare how Christ descended lineally to us, for that reason Christ came to us by forty generations. Luke, however, who intends to commend in Christ His priestly dignity, to which belongs the expiation of sins; "I say not to thee, till seven times; but till seventy times seven times," etc., (below 18, 22), lists seventy-seven generations: for this number is the product of seven and eleven: for seven times eleven are seventy-seven. By eleven, therefore, the transgression of the Decalogue is understood; by seven, however, is understood the sevenfold grace, through which the sins are forgiven. Now because, according to Jerome, there are forty-two generations, this is also not without a mystery, because by those two is understood the two precepts of charity; or the two Testaments are understood, the New and the Old.

Now the generation of Christ was in this wise. Having set forth Christ's generation in general, here His generation is described in detail; and it is divided into three parts. Firstly, he sets forth a sort of title; secondly, the Evangelist describes the mode of generation, where it is said, *When as his mother Mary was espoused to Joseph*; and thirdly, he proves the mode of generation, where it is said, *Whereupon Joseph her husband*. He says, therefore, *Now the generation of Christ*. This can be read in two ways: for according to Chrysostom it is a kind of prologue of the things to be said; but according to Remigius it is a type of epilogue of the things which were said. It is read in the first way as follows: Thus, it has been said concerning Christ's genealogy, how Abraham begot Isaac, etc., through carnal admixture. *But the generation of Christ was in this wise*; supply the words, 'as it will be said in what follows.' In the second way it is read thus, as though it were an epilogue of what preceded: as it is said, Abraham, etc., to Christ. *Now the generation of Christ was in this wise*; supply the words, 'namely, that it extended from Abraham through David and the others unto Christ.' Afterwards, he describes the mode of the generation; and firstly, he describes the person generating, when he says, *When as his mother Mary was espoused*; secondly, he describes the actual generating of Christ, when he says, *Before they came together, she was found with child*; thirdly, he describes the author of the generation, when he says, *of the Holy Ghost*. He describes the person generating by three things. Firstly, he describes her by her condition, when he says, *espoused to Joseph*; secondly, he describes her by her dignity, when he says, *His mother*; and thirdly, he describes her by her proper name, when he says, *Mary*. He says, therefore, *When as Mary the mother of Jesus was espoused to Joseph*.

But here there immediately arises a question. Since Christ willed to be born of a virgin, why did He will that His mother be espoused?

A threefold reason, according to Jerome, is assigned. The first is so that the testimony of her virginity would be more credible: for if she had not been espoused, and said she was a virgin, when she was with child, it would seem that she asserted this for no other reason than to hide the crime of adultery. But since she had been espoused, she had no need to lie. And, for that reason, she would have been believed more easily; "Thy testimonies are become exceedingly credible" (92, 5). Another reason is so that she would have a man's protection, either when she fled to Egypt, or when she returned from thence. The third reason was so that His birth might be hidden from the devil, lest, to wit, if he knew, he might impede His Passion, and the fruit of our redemption; "For if they had known it, they would never have crucified the Lord of glory" (I Cor. 2, 8); and this is expounded of the devil, meaning the devil would not have permitted Him to be have been crucified.

But it seems it was the contrary. Did the devil never learn that she was a virgin? For her virginity was in her uncorrupted flesh. Therefore, the devil could have known that she was a virgin.

But it ought to be replied, according to Ambrose, who also assigns this reason, that the devils can know some things by some subtlety of their nature, nevertheless there are certain things which they cannot know except by divine permission. Hence, the devil might have known her virginity if he had not been divinely prevented from making a careful investigation. Three reasons are assigned by Ambrose. The first is that it was for the sake of preserving the honor of the mother of the Lord: "The Lord preferred men to doubt of His origin, rather than of His mother's purity. And, for that reason, He willed that she be espoused, so that the suspicion of adultery might be taken away: for He had come to fulfill the Law, not to destroy it; "I am not come to destroy, but to fulfill" (below 5, 17); "Honour thy father and thy mother" (Ex. 20, 12). Another reason is that an excuse for virgins' ill-fame for adultery might be taken away: for if the mother of the Lord had not been espoused, and nevertheless was with child, they might excuse themselves through her; "Incline not my heart to evil

words; to make excuses in sins" (Ps. 140, 4). The third reason is that Christ espoused Himself to the Church, which is a virgin; "For I have espoused you" (II Cor. 11, 2). And, for that reason, He willed to be born of an espoused virgin as a sign that He espoused Himself to the Church.
 When as his mother Mary was espoused. But to whom? To Joseph. According to Chrysostom, Joseph was a carpenter; and he signifies Christ, who through the wood of the Cross restored all things heavenly, etc. *His mother*, that is to say, God's mother. Here, her dignity is shown: for this was not granted to any other creature, neither man nor angel, to have been the father or mother of God; on the contrary, this was a singular grace, that she would become the mother not of a mere man but of God; and, for that reason, it is said in the Apocalypse, "A woman clothed with the sun" (12, 1), as though she were completely filled with the divinity. This is what Nestorius denied; and he denied this, saying that the divinity was not received by the Virgin. Against whom Ignatius Martyr uses a beautiful example to show that she was the Mother of God. "It is clear," he says, "that in the generation of men in general, a woman is called one's mother; and, nevertheless, the woman does not give the rational soul, which is from God, but furnishes the substance for the formation of the body. In this way, therefore, a woman is called the mother of the whole man, because that which is taken from her, is united to a rational soul. Similarly, when Christ's humanity was taken from the blessed Virgin, on account of the union to the divinity she is called not only the mother of a man, but also the Mother of God; although the divinity was not taken from her; just as in other men the soul is not taken from the mother." *Mary*, her proper name, is interpreted 'Star of the sea,' or 'Enlightener,' or in her own language it is interpreted, 'Mistress': hence, in the Apocalypse (12, 1) she is described with the moon under her feet. *Before they came together*, etc.
 Here Helvidius objects: If it is said 'before they came together,' therefore, at some time, they came together; hence, he denied the virginity of Christ's mother: not before the birth, nor during the birth, but after the birth he says that she was known by man.
 Jerome responds that, without a doubt, this word which is said, *Before*, always implies a relationship to the future. But this can be in two ways; either according to reason, or according to the acceptation of the intellect. For if it be said: 'Before I ate in the port of Rome, I sailed to Africa,' it must not be understood that I ate after I sailed to Africa; it is understood that I had intended to eat, and, having been prevented by the voyage, I did not eat; so it

is here: it is not to be so understood that afterwards they really came together, just as that impious man says; but it is understood from the very fact that she had become espoused according to the common opinion, it was lawful for them to come together at some time, although they never came together. Remigius expounds this otherwise, namely, that it may be understood of the solemn celebration of the nuptials; for the espousal was beforehand, and the espousal took place for some days, and, meanwhile, the spouse was under the guardianship of her husband; afterwards, however, the solemn celebration took place, and then she was led to the house of the husband. Of these espousals, the Evangelist speaks here. And, according to this, the objection of Helvidius has no basis. Note the propriety of the word: for that thing is properly said to be 'found,' about which it was not hoped, nor thought; and Joseph had such a great opinion of Mary's purity, that it was beyond his estimation that he found her with child.

She was found with child, supply the words, 'by Joseph himself,' who, as Jerome says, "was investigating nearly all her secrets as being her espoused husband." *Of the Holy Ghost*. Here is treated the performer of the conception. This, however, is to be read separately from that which preceded: for it is not to be read or understood that Joseph found her with child of the Holy Ghost; but only that he found her with child. And lest the suspicion of adultery might arise in the meantime to the hearers, the Evangelist added, *Of the Holy Ghost*, that is, of the power of the Holy Ghost, not of His substance, lest He be believed to be the Son of the Holy Ghost. **The Holy Ghost shall come upon thee, and the power of the most High shall overshadow thee** (Lk. 1, 35). Although, however, according to Augustine, the works of the Trinity are indivisible, and therefore, that conception was worked not only by the Holy Ghost but also by the Father and Son; nevertheless, by a certain appropriation, it is attributed to the Holy Ghost; and this is for three reasons. The first reason is, because the Holy Ghost is love. And this was the sign of the greatest love, that God willed His Son to be incarnated; "God so loved the world, as to give His only begotten Son" (Jn. 3, 16). The second reason is that to the Holy Ghost is attributed grace; "There are diversities of graces, but the same Spirit" (I Cor. 12, 4); and this was the greatest grace.[35] The third reason is assigned in the acts of the Council of Nicea, which is; that in us there is a twofold word: the word of the heart and the word of the voice. The word

---

35. Grace here means 'a free gift.'

VER. 12-21   ACCORDING TO ST. MATTHEW   43

of the heart is that conception of the intellect, which is hidden from men, except inasmuch as it is expressed by the voice or the word of the voice. To the word of the heart is compared the eternal Word before the Incarnation, when He was with the Father, and hidden from us; but to the word of the voice is compared the Incarnate Word which now has appeared to us and is manifest. But the word of the heart is not joined to the voice except by means of the breath;[36] and thus, rightly, the Incarnation of the Word, through which He visibly appeared to us, was made by means of the Holy Ghost.

Note here the four reasons why Christ willed to be born of a virgin. The first of which was, because original sin is contracted in the offspring from the marital union. Whence, if Christ was born of sexual intercourse, He would have contracted original sin. But this was not fitting since He came into the world to take away our sins. Hence, He ought not to be infected with the contagion of sin. The second is that Christ was the chief teacher of chastity; "There are eunuchs, who have made themselves eunuchs for the kingdom of heaven" (below 19, 12). The third is for the sake of purity and cleanliness. "Wisdom will not enter into a malicious soul" (Wis. 1, 4). Whence, it was fitting that the womb of His mother be not polluted by any corruption. The fourth is on account of the characteristic of a word, namely, that as a word comes forth from the heart without corrupting the heart, so Christ willed and ought to have been born without corrupting the Virgin.

Whereupon Joseph her husband being a just man. After setting down the manner of the generation, here he confirms it by testimony. For since the Evangelist said above that the mother of Jesus was found with child, and that this was of the Holy Ghost, someone might believe that the Evangelist reckons this because of his devotion to the Master; therefore, the Evangelist here confirms the aforesaid manner of generation. And this is firstly confirmed by the angelic revelation, where it is said, *And Joseph rising*; and secondly, by the prophetic prediction, *Now this was done*. In the first part there are three elements. Firstly, the person is introduced, to whom the revelation was made; secondly, the person revealing, where it is said, *But while he thought upon these things, behold the angel of the Lord appeared*; thirdly, the words of the revelation are set forth, where it is said, *Joseph, son of David*. Now, the person to whom the revelation was made, is rendered acceptable from two things, namely, from that he is

36. *Spiritus.*

just, and thus, he would not lie; secondly, from the fact that he is her spouse, or husband; "The jealousy and rage of the husband will not spare in the day of revenge," (Prov. 6, 34). Therefore, it reads thus, *She was found* by Joseph *with child. Whereupon Joseph her husband, being a just man, and not willing publicly to expose her.* Here there are two opinions of the Saints, namely, of Ambrose and Augustine. For Augustine holds that Joseph, who was not present when the angelic annunciation was made, returning and finding her with child, had the suspicion of adultery.

But then immediately the question arises: How was he just if he was not willing to expose, that is, to make public, the crime of her whom he was suspecting of adultery? For in this he would seem to be consenting to the sin, as it says in Rom. 1, 32 that "not only they that do them, but they also that consent to them that do them are worthy of death."

But to this there is a threefold response. The first is according to John Chrysostom, that justice is twofold: for one is the justice which is the cardinal virtue, which is called special justice, the other is legal justice, which includes every virtue: piety, clemency, and suchlike. Therefore, when it is said that Joseph was just, it is to be understood of general justice, just as justice may be taken for piety. Whence, because he was just, that is to say pious, he was not willing to expose her. A second response is that of Augustine, who says that sin is twofold, namely, hidden sin and manifest sin: for a hidden sin is not to be publicly accused, but in a different way is a remedy to be applied to it. Therefore, the suspicion of adultery, which Joseph had, was the suspicion of a hidden sin, and not of a manifest one, because he alone knew of it; and, therefore, if others knew her to be with child, they could only think that it was his; and thus her crime ought not to have been made public. The third response, in fact, is of Rabanus, that indeed Joseph was just and pious: for in that he was pious, he wished not to make public her crime; but in that he willed to put her away, he appeared just: for he knew that "He that keepeth an adulteress, is foolish and wicked," as says Proverbs 18, 22. But, according to Jerome and Origen, he did not suspect adultery: for Joseph knew Mary's chastity; he read in Scripture that a virgin would conceive: "And there shall come forth a rod (virga) out of the root of Jesse, and a flower shall rise up out of his root," etc., (Isaias 7, 14 & 11, 1). He also knew that Mary had descended of the line of David. Hence, he more easily believed this to be fulfilled in her, than for her to have been ravished. And therefore, considering himself to be unworthy to dwell with one of so great holiness, he wanted to put her away privately, as Peter said: "Depart from me, O Lord, for I am a sinful man," Luke 5, 8. Whence, he was not willing to take her, that is to lead her home to himself, and accept her as a spouse, thinking himself to be unworthy. Or, according to the opinion of others, being unaware of the purpose, he did so lest he be held guilty if he concealed the matter, and kept her with himself.

But while he thought upon these things. Here the person revealing is introduced: and three things are mentioned: For firstly, the time is mentioned; secondly, the person revealing is introduced, *Behold the angel*; thirdly, the manner of revelation is expressed, *Appeared to Joseph in his sleep*. Therefore, he says, *But while he thought upon these things*, that is, while he was turning over these things in his mind within himself, *behold the angel of the Lord appeared*. Note that two things are here commended about Joseph, namely, his wisdom and clemency: his wisdom indeed in that he before he acted, he deliberated; "Let thy eyelids go before thy steps" (Prov. 4, 25): that is, do nothing without judgment and thoughtful deliberation. Likewise, his clemency or piety in that he did not manifest or make public her deed, unlike many men who immediately will to exteriorly publicise the thing which they have in their heart; "As a city that lieth open and is not compassed with walls, so is a man that cannot refrain his own spirit in speaking" (Prov. 25, 28). And thus, he merited to be instructed, or consoled; whence it follows: *Behold the angel of the Lord appeared*: as if to say, the help of God were at hand; "A helper in due time in tribulation" (Ps. 53, 6); "For behold God is my helper: and the Lord is the protector of my soul" (Ps. 9, 10). *The angel of the Lord*: nothing indeed is better able to free from blame, than he who was aware of her preserved virginity. Hence, it is believed that the same angel who was sent to Mary (Luke 1) was sent to Joseph; "The angel of the Lord shall encamp round about them that fear him" (Ps. 23, 8), actually, to Mary and Joseph, that he might deliver her from disgrace, and not leave Joseph in confusion.

But here it is sought, why was not the revelation made to Joseph in the beginning, before he was troubled? Likewise, why didn't Mary make known to him the angelic annunciation, which was made to her?

Now to the first is to be answered that the angel did this so that Joseph's testimony might be more believable. For just as the Lord permitted the Apostle Thomas to doubt His Resurrection, so that doubting he would touch His wounds, and touching might believe, and believing might remove the wound of infidelity in us;

so also the Lord permitted Joseph to doubt concerning the chastity of Mary, that doubting he might receive the angelic revelation, and by receiving, might believe more firmly. To the second question it may be answered that if Mary had told him, he would not have believed.

Appeared to him in his sleep: behold the manner of revelation. Note that, strictly speaking, to appear is a characteristic of those things, which of their nature are invisible, yet they possess the power to become visible: such as God, or an angel: for those things which are already visible by their nature, are not properly said to appear: whence, it is called a divine or angelic apparition: hence, it is properly said, **Appeared to him in his sleep**.

But here is inquired, why in his sleep? The reason is given in the Gloss, that Joseph was in some way doubting: whence, he was in some way sleeping: and therefore it is rightly said that the angel appeared to him *in his sleep*. Another reason can be better assigned. For as the Apostle says in I Corinthians 14, 22 "Prophecy is given to believers, but signs to unbelievers." And a revelation, which is called prophetic, properly occurs in sleep: "If there be among you a prophet of the Lord, I will appear to him in a vision, or I will speak to him in a dream" (Num. 12, 6); and so, because Joseph was just and faithful, to him, as one faithful, it was fitting that there be an apparition which is suitable for believers, namely, a somewhat prophetic revelation. However, because a corporeal apparition is miraculous, such a type of apparition was not becoming to him, since he believed and was faithful.

But then it is inquired why a visible apparition was made to Mary, since she was the most faithful?

And it must be said that the mystery of the Incarnation was revealed to Mary at the beginning, when it was more difficult to be believed; and, therefore, it was fitting that a visible apparition be made to her; but to Joseph it was not revealed at the beginning, but instead when it was by then mostly completed, since he already saw her stomach enlarged, whence, he was more easily able to believe: and thus that apparition was sufficient for him which occurred in his sleep.

Joseph, son of David. Here the words of the revelation are related: and they are divided into three parts according to the three things which the angel did. For firstly, he prohibits a divorce for Mary and Joseph; secondly, he makes known the mystery of the Incarnation when he says, **That which is conceived in her, is of the Holy Ghost**; he foretells the future service of Joseph, which in fact he would show to the Child, where it is said,

And she shall bring forth a son. And so he says, *Joseph.* He calls him to make him attentive to listening, and that he might subject him to himself. This is common in Scripture, namely, that when an apparition is first bestowed, which is of a superior being, there is required in the hearer some lifting of the mind and attention; "Son of man, stand upon thy feet, and I will speak to thee" (Ez. 2, 1). And further, "O son of man, hear all that I say to thee: and do not provoke me" (verse 8). "I will stand upon my watch" (Hab. 2, 1). *Son of David*; thus his lineage is expressed to advert to that which is said in Isaias 7, 13: "Hear ye therefore, O house of David: Is it a small thing for you to be grievous to men, that you are grievous to my God also?" etc.[37] For this sign was not given to one person, but to the whole tribe or house: hence, because the angel was obliged to instruct Joseph about this, he is bidden by the expression of his lineage to recall to mind the prediction of the Prophet.[38] *Fear not.* Every apparition inspires some fear, whether it be of a good or bad angel: and this is because such an apparition is unfamiliar and somewhat strange to human nature; and so it makes a man to be somewhat besides himself. But there is this difference, that the apparition of a bad angel incites terror, and leaves a man in this terror; so that, namely, he might more easily lure the man put out of himself into sin. But the apparition of a good angel, although it inspires some terror, nevertheless this terror is immediately curtailed and followed by consolation, so that the man might return to himself and heed what things are said to him. Whence, in Luke 1, where it is said that an angel appeared to Zachary, immediately follows (v. 13) the words: "Fear not, Zachary," and likewise in the same place (v. 80): "Fear not, Mary." Hence, after the apparition occurred, consolation is immediately bestowed upon Joseph. He had a twofold fear: namely, of God and also of sin, lest he should sin by dwelling with Mary, as one conscious of a sin, and so, *Fear not*, is added, namely, from fear of sin, *to take Mary for thy wife.* Note that she is called his wife, not on account of their matrimony, but on account of their espousal: for it is the custom of Scripture to call espoused those who are spouses and spouses those who are espoused.

But it is inquired, why does the angel command him to take her, when he had not yet put her away? And it is to be said that although he had not put her away corporeally, nevertheless he did put her away in thought: and so he is commanded to take

---

[37]. The following verse of Isaias is: "Therefore the Lord Himself shall give you a sign. Behold a virgin shall conceive, and bear a son, and his name shall be called Emmanuel."
[38]. i.e. Isaias.

her. Or, *fear not to take*, refers to the solemnization or celebration of the nuptials.

For that which is conceived in her, is of the Holy Ghost. Here he makes plain the mystery of the Incarnation. Note that although there were three elements on that occasion, namely, the Virgin herself conceiving, the Son of God conceived, and the active power of the Holy Ghost; the angel indicates two of them well: namely, the one conceiving, and the author of the conception; but the third, the very one conceived, the Son of God, is not indicated except vaguely: ***For that which***, he said, ***is born in her***: and this is to show that He is ineffable and incomprehensible, not only to man, but also to the angels. For that which, he says, is born in her: he does not say, 'Of her,' because to be conceived of a mother is to go forth into the light: to be born in a mother is the same thing as to be conceived; ***is of the Holy Ghost***. This, therefore, is the angelic testimony, which the Evangelist cites to prove that which he said above, ***She was found with child, of the Holy Ghost***.

Note that in the conception of other women, in the seed of man is a formative power, whose subject is the seed, and by this power the fetus is formed, and is nourished in the body of the woman. But the power of the Holy Ghost supplied for this: and thus it is sometimes found to have been said by the Saints, that the Holy Ghost was there as the seed: yet, sometimes it is said that there was no seed there. And this is because in the man's seed are two things, namely, the corruptible substance itself, which descends from the body of a man, and the formative power itself. Therefore, it must be said that the Holy Ghost was there as the seed, as to the formative power; but He was not there as the seed, as to its corpulent substance, because neither the body of Christ nor His conception was made of the substance of the Holy Ghost. And so it is clear, that the Holy Ghost cannot be called the father of Christ, neither according to His divine nature, nor according to His human nature. Indeed, not according to His divine nature, because although Christ shares the same glory with the Holy Ghost, nevertheless the Son according to His divine nature receives nothing from the Holy Ghost; and so He cannot be called His Son: for a son receives something from his father. Likewise, neither according to His human nature, because a father and a son ought to coincide in substance; but Christ, although He was conceived by the power of the Holy Ghost; yet He was not of the substance of the Holy Ghost.

But on the contrary, this, which is said, ***Of the Holy Ghost***, is what is said in Proverbs 9, 1, that "Wisdom hath built herself a house." Therefore, it seems that the divine Wisdom Itself, that is the Son of God, united a human nature to Himself, and so it was not done by the power of the Holy Ghost.

But according to Augustine there is a twofold response. The first is that the expression written in Proverbs 9 is to be understood of the Church, which Christ founded by His Blood. The second is that the operations of the Trinity are indivisible: and so that which the Son does, the Holy Ghost does as well; but nevertheless, by a certain appropriation, it is attributed to the Holy Ghost: and the reason of this was said above.

And she shall bring forth a son. Here he foretells the service that Joseph will show to the child soon-to-be-born; he also does three things; For firstly, he foretells the offspring of the Virgin; secondly, he makes known the service to be shown to the child by Joseph himself, when he says, **And thou shalt call his name**; thirdly, he manifests the name imposed upon that child, when he says, **Jesus**. He says, therefore: **She shall bring forth**, thus, she indeed conceived of the Holy Ghost first, but **she shall bring forth a son**: he does not say, 'To thee,' because he did not beget the child. In Luke 1, 13 it is said to Zachary: "Thy wife shall bear thee a son," because Zachary begot him. Or therefore, he does not say, 'To thee,' that it might be shown that He was born for all men: not only for thee, nor for herself does she bring forth her son, but for the whole world; "Behold, I bring you good tidings of great joy, (that shall be to all the people): for this day, is born to you a Saviour, who is Christ the Lord, in the city of David", etc. (Lk. 2, 10). But because Joseph would be able to say: 'Thus she conceived of the Holy Ghost, and will bring forth a son, what therefore is this to me? In nothing am I necessary for him?' And so, he adds the service of Joseph himself, **Thou shalt call his name**. It was the custom among the Hebrews, and still is today, that on the eighth day they circumcise the child, and then they impose upon him his name; and this was done by Joseph; whence, in this work, he was the minister. Whence, it is said to him, **Thou shalt call**: he does not say, 'Thou shalt impose,' because it was already imposed upon him; "Thou shalt be called by a new name, which the mouth of the Lord shall name" (Is. 62, 2). **Jesus**, this is the name imposed by God; and he gives the reason, **For he shall save his people**, which He acquired unto Himself by His blood, this is His people. In Daniel 9, 26 it is said: "The people that shall deny him shall not be his"; whence to be the people of the Lord is through faith; "You are a chosen generation, a kingly priesthood, a purchased people" (I Pet. 2, 9). **From their sins**; In the book of

Judges it is frequently said that such-or-such a one saved Israel; but from whom? It was from their carnal enemies; but here it is *from their sins*, by remitting sins, which belongs to God alone (to do); "But that you may know that the Son of man hath power on earth to remit sins" (Lk. 5, 24).

Note that here Nestorius is confounded, who was saying that the things which belong to God, to be from eternity, to be omnipotent, or suchlike, do not fittingly belong to this man. Behold, it is this very same man, who was born of the Virgin, who is called Jesus. *He shall save his people from their sins.* Whence, since no one is able to remit sins but God alone, one is correct in saying that this man is God, and that those things which belong to God, most truly are applicable to him.

22. Now all this was done that it might be fulfilled which the Lord spoke by the prophet, saying:

23. Behold a virgin shall be with child, and bring forth a son, and they shall call his name Emmanuel, which being interpreted is, God with us.

The Evangelist had said before that the mother of God was found with child of the Holy Ghost, and he proved this above by the angelic revelation: here he proves this by the prediction of the prophet. Whence, he says, *All this was done that it might be fulfilled which the Lord spoke by the prophet.* And one should realize that this small passage can be introduced in two different ways. For Chrysostom favors that the angel said all this, and thus introduced the prophecy. And the reason is that, in order that what he announced might not appear to be a new thing, he immediately wished to show that it was foretold of old; "Who now has done what was to come to pass," (Is. 48, 3) according to another translation. Others say, and I believe more correctly, that this phrase, namely, *All this was done*, etc., are the words of the Evangelist: for the words of the angel are completed where it is said, *For he shall save his people*, etc. And the Evangelist introduces those words on account of three things. Firstly, that he might show that the Old Testament pertains to Christ; "To him all the prophets give testimony, that by his name all receive remission of sins, who believe in him" (Acts 10, 43). Secondly, that they[39] might more easily believe in Christ; "For if you did believe Moses, you would perhaps believe me also; for he wrote of me" (Jn. 5, 46). Thirdly, to show the conformity of the Old and New

---

39. i.e. the Jews.

Testament; "Which are a shadow of things to come, but the body is of Christ" (Col. 2, 17). But, in order to know what is contained in this prophecy, one needs to know that the angel announces three things. For firstly he says, *That which is conceived in her*, etc., secondly, *She shall bring forth a son*; thirdly, *Thou shalt call his name Jesus*. These are contained in the prophecy in order. And he proves the first when he says, *Behold a virgin*; secondly, *And she shall bring forth*; and thirdly, *And he shall be called*. Therefore, He was of the Holy Ghost, because He was conceived through virginity. And this is what is said in the prophecy, *Behold a virgin shall be with child*. "It shall bud forth and blossom, and shall rejoice with joy and praise," etc., (Is. 35, 2). Likewise, *A virgin shall be with child*, because in giving birth, her virginity was in no way harmed; "And there shall come forth a rod out of the root of Jesse, and a flower shall rise up out of his root" (Is. 11, 1). Indeed, Christ is the flower. Therefore, in nothing is her virginity harmed.

It follows, *And his name shall be called Emmanuel*. But it is inquired, why does this not agree with the words of the angel saying, *And He shall be called Jesus*?

It is to be pointed out that this promise was made to the Jews, who were to have salvation from the coming of Christ. And Jesus is interpreted 'Savior,' which has the same meaning as 'Emmanuel', or *God with us*. For God is with us in four ways: by the assumption of our nature; "The Word was made flesh" (Jn. 1, 14); by the conformity of nature, because He is similar to us in all things; "In the likeness of men, and habit found as a man" (Phil. 2, 7); by His corporeal presence; "Afterwards he was seen upon earth, and conversed with men" (Bar. 3, 38); and by His spiritual presence; "Behold I am with you all days, even to the consummation of the world" (below 28, 20).

Yet it is sought about the literal sense, why did not the Evangelist use the same words as the prophet, but instead uses the name of Jesus?

But it ought to be pointed out that it was spoken by the same Spirit. Nevertheless, Jerome says the reason why the Evangelist spoke thus, *She shall be with child*,[40] is because he was speaking of what was already accomplished.

---

40. "St. Jerome: For that which Matthew the Evangelist says, *Shall have in her womb*, the Prophet who is foretelling something future, writes, *shall receive*. The Evangelist, not foretelling the future but describing the past, changes *shall receive* into *shall have*; but he who has, cannot after receive what he has. He says, *Lo, a Virgin shall have in her womb, and shall bear a Son*" (*Catena Aurea on St. Matthew*, chap. 1 lect. 13).

Likewise, it is asked, why in Isaias is it said, "And he will be called" (7, 14); but here it is said, *And they will call*. To this Jerome says, that here it is said *They will call*, because what the angel first called by announcing (Lk. 2) afterwards the Apostles called by preaching and magnifying, "That in the name of Jesus every knee should bow," etc., (Phil. 2, 10).

Which being interpreted is, God with us. But it is asked, who added this interpretation of the prophecy, *God with us*, the prophet or the Evangelist? And it seems that it was not the Evangelist, because this was not needed, since he wrote in Hebrew.

But it can be replied in one way, that Emmanuel is a composed name, and so the Evangelist also interpreted it in the Hebrew. Or it can be said that the one, who first translated the Gospel from the Hebrew, interpreted it.

And it is to be noted that in the Gloss there are three types of prophecy, namely, of predestination, of foreknowledge, and of threatening; and these differ. For a prophecy is called a foretelling of things which are far off, that is, of future events; now certain future events are what only God does; certain other things, however, even if God does them, nevertheless, they happen through us and also through other creatures; and there are certain things, however, which in no way does God do them, such as evil things. The foretelling of those things which only God does is called a prophecy of predestination, such as the conception of the Virgin; whence the prophecy in Isaias 7, 14: "Behold a virgin shall conceive," is a prophecy of predestination. But those things which occur from secondary causes can be doubly considered. Firstly, inasmuch as they are in the foreknowledge of God, for example concerning Lazarus: for if someone considered the natural causes, he might say that he would never rise, and he would say a true thing: although, nevertheless, he was due to be brought back to life according to the order of divine foreknowledge. Therefore, when a prophecy is a prediction, according to it being in the divine foreknowledge, it is always fulfilled; but when it is according to the order of inferior causes, it is not always fulfilled, as appears in Isaias 38, 1, when Isaias said to Ezechias: "Take order with thy house, for thou shalt die, and not live."[41]

But does a prophecy never impose a necessity to His foreknowledge? And I reply that it does not; because a prophecy is what one might call a sign of the divine foreknowledge, which

---

41. Ezechias was actually spared an imminent death due to his prayer for a longer life. "Thus saith the Lord the God of David thy father: I have heard thy prayer, and I have seen thy tears: behold I will add to thy days fifteen years" (verse 5).

does not impose a necessity to the foreknown things, because it considers future events in their presentiality: for whatsoever is done, is present to God, because His gaze does not impose a necessity, as when I see someone sit down. And it is in this way that we understand these prophecies, which are cited in this book. For it is to be considered that there were three errors. One was of the Manichaeans, saying that in the whole Old Testament there is not found any prophecy concerning Christ: and whatever is cited in the New Testament from the Old Testament, is all from a corruption of the text. Opposed to this is the passage: "Paul, a servant of Jesus Christ, called to be an apostle, separate unto the gospel of God, which he had promised before, by his prophets," etc., (Rom. 1, 1). And what may be said of the Jewish prophets is said further on: "Whose are the fathers, and of whom is Christ, according to the flesh," etc., (Rom. 9, 5). Another error was Theodore's,[42] saying that none of those passages that are cited from the Old Testament literally concern Christ, but are adapted to Him. It is as when they cite that saying of Virgil, 'Remembering he was considering such things, and immovable he persists in his opinions';[43] for this was adapted to Christ. And then that saying, **That it might be fulfilled**, ought to be expounded thus. It is as if the Evangelist said, 'And this can be adapted to Christ.' Opposed to this is Luke 24, 44: "All things must needs be fulfilled, which are written in the law of Moses, and in the prophets, and in the psalms, concerning me." And if anyone asserts a different literal sense, he is a heretic, and his heresy is condemned. But because not only the words of the Old Testament, but also the deeds signify something concerning Christ; sometimes certain things are said of certain other things in their literal sense. But they refer to Christ, inasmuch as they bear the figure of Christ, as concerning Solomon it is said: "And he shall rule from sea to sea," etc., (Ps. 71, 8); for this was not fulfilled in him. The third error was the error of the Jews.

And it is to be known that the Jews especially object to this passage, because in the Hebrew there is not the word "Virgin" but "*Alma*," which is the same as 'a young maiden.' Whence, these things are not literally said about Christ, but about Emmanuel, or about some son of Isaias, according to others.

But Jerome points out, in opposition to these things, that this word cannot be said to refer to the son of Isaias as is proved by the fact that he was already born when this was said. Likewise,

---
42. i.e. Theodore of Mopsuestia, teacher of Nestorius.
43. "Talia pendebat memorans, fixusque manebat."

no famous person may be found to have lived at that time who was called Emmanuel. Again, it is not a sign that a maiden gives birth. Hence, Jerome says that "Alma" is equivocal, and signifies sometimes a period of life, and other times signifies a girl who has been hidden, and then it means a carefully preserved virgin; and such is its meaning here.

Again, the Jews object that the expression was to be a sign (Is. 7, 3 ff.), that two kings would come against Achaz and he promised that they would be freed from these things by giving this sign to Achaz.

But it is to be replied that he gave this sign not only to Achaz, but also to the house of David, because he says, "Hear ye, therefore, O house of David." It is as though the prophet were to say: the Lord will help you against this king, because he will do far greater things, for there will not only be a liberation of him, but of the whole world. But let us return to the text itself. *Now all this was done.*

But it is to be stated in one way, according to Rabanus, that *All this was done*, etc., refers to the things done in the past, that the angel appeared to the Virgin, and said these words, *All this was done*, for the preservation of the Virgin, so that the word *that* may be taken causatively. Or it refers to those things that he had foretold, and it can be said that all this was done by means of a prophecy of predestination. Or it can be said that the Evangelist was writing when all was accomplished; and thus he refers to it. Whence, the word, *that*, is taken consequently, because God did not will to take flesh for the sake of the fact that the prophecy might be fulfilled, as if the Old Testament were worthier than the New; but the fact that Christ became incarnate happened according to the prophecy.

24. And Joseph rising up from sleep, did as the angel of the Lord had commanded him, and took unto him his wife.

25. And he knew her not till she brought forth her first born son: and he called his name Jesus.

Above, the Evangelist proved that the Mother of God conceived of the Holy Ghost, from two things, namely, from the revelation of the angel, and from the foretelling of the prophet. He likewise intends to show this from the obedience of Joseph, who would not have acquiesced to the words of the angel, that he would take Mary as his spouse, unless he had known that she was with child of the Holy Ghost. And he did two things concerning this. Firstly, the obedience of this spouse to the angel is set forth; and secondly, the manner of the obedience is described, where it is said, *And he took unto him.* And note that because through the disobedience of the first man we are fallen into sin; "By the disobedience of one man, many were made sinners" (Rom. 5, 19); wherefore obedience is placed in the beginning of our reparation.

And we can note four things, which are necessary for obedience. The first quality is that it be ordered. And I say "ordered" because, firstly, vices are to be forsaken, and afterwards, one must follow the practice of the virtues; "Break up anew your fallow ground, and sow not upon thorns," (Jer. 4, 3), etc. And so here it is said, that Joseph, *rising from sleep*, that is from the sleep of sluggishness and doubtfulness. Concerning this sleep, it is said in Ephesians 5, 14: "Rise thou that sleepest, and arise from the dead." The second, in fact, is that it ought to be quick: and this is what is said in Ecclesiasticus 5, 8: "Delay not to be converted to the Lord, and defer it not from day to day. For his wrath shall come on a sudden." And so here it is said, that immediately *He did as he had commanded him*; and the Gloss reads, "Whoever are advised by God ought to give up delays, rise from sleep, do what he is enjoined." The third, in fact, is that it ought to be perfect, that not only what is commanded be done, but that it be done in the same manner that it is enjoined, and in the same manner it is commanded. Whence, here where it is said, *As he had commanded*, the Gloss reads, "This is perfect obedience." "Children obey your parents in all things" (Col. 3, 20). The fourth quality is that it ought to be discerning, that one obey him who is to be obeyed, and in what matters he is to be obeyed, so that nothing happens which is opposed to God. When he says that *he did as the angel had commanded him*, the angel is not a bad angel, but the Lord's angel; "Believe not every spirit, but try the spirits if they be of God: because many false prophets are gone out into the world," etc., (I Jn. 4, 1).

And he took unto him. Here is shown in what things he obeyed: and three things are set forth. Firstly, the obedience which he showed to the angel; secondly, the reverence which he showed to the Mother; and thirdly, the guardianship which he showed to Christ having been born. The angel ordered Joseph, *Fear not to take unto thee Mary thy wife*, and Joseph did as he ordered, etc. Whereupon, it is clear that he gained a good woman.

But did he ever not have her in his house? Why, therefore, does he say, *Rising... he took unto him*?

Chrysostom replies: "It is because he had not cast her out from his house, but from his heart." Or it is because first she was married, and afterwards the nuptials were to be celebrated and then it is affirmed, she is also his wife. And lest anyone suspect that carnal intercourse occurred, it is added, **And he knew her not.**

In this place it should be known that this verb "to know" is taken in two senses in Sacred Scripture. Sometimes it is taken for knowledge; "Henceforth you shall know him, and you have seen him" (Jn. 14, 7). Sometimes it is taken for carnal intercourse, as in Genesis 4, 1: "And Adam knew Eve, his wife", etc., that is, carnally.

But it is objected, why does it not say simply, **he knew her not**, etc., instead of, **till she brought forth her son**. From this it would seem to follow that he knew her afterwards. Whence, Helvidius likewise said, "Although a Virgin conceived Christ, nevertheless, afterwards she had other children of Joseph."

And so Jerome says, that *until* sometimes means something limited and determinate, as if I would say, 'I will not come until I eat, because I signify that I am about to come afterwards.' At other times it means something unlimited and indeterminate, for example in I Corinthians 15, 25: "For he must reign, until he hath put all his enemies under his feet." Will He not reign forever afterwards? He will indeed. But Scripture uses such manner of speaking, because it intends to remove that which could be doubted. For it could have been doubted whether He would reign when He had not put His enemies under His feet. Likewise, it could have been doubted, when the blessed Virgin had given birth, whether before the birth she had been known by Joseph. But from the start, we cannot possibly doubt; namely, because the angels sang: "Glory to God in the highest; and on earth peace to men of good will" (Lk. 2, 14). And thus, the Evangelist intends to say this. And so, Jerome argues against Helvidius: "You say, O Helvidius, that, before they came together, Joseph did not know her, because he was warned in his sleep by an angel. If, therefore, a warning in sleep was influential enough that he would not unite himself to Mary, how much more the knowledge of the angels, and the adoration of the shepherds and wise men?"[44] Chrysostom, however, takes knowledge for an intellectual knowing. So when it is said **He**

---

44. "JEROME. Lastly, I would ask, Why then did Joseph abstain at all up to the day of birth? He will surely answer, Because of the angel's words, That which is born in her, &c. He then who gave so much heed to a vision as not to dare to touch his wife, would he, after he had heard the shepherds, seen the Magi, and known so many miracles, dare to approach the temple of God, the seat of the Holy Ghost, the Mother of his Lord?" (*Catena Aurea on St. Matthew*, chap. 1 lect. 14).

knew her not, one ought to understand, namely, that he did not understand that she was of such great dignity; but after she gave birth, he knew this. Others say that it is to be taken for sensible knowledge; and their opinion is indeed sufficiently probable. For they say that Moses, from his conversing with the Lord, had so great glory in his face, that the children of Israel could not behold it (II Cor. 3, 7). Therefore, if Moses had this from his association with God, much more did this blessed Virgin, who carried Him in her womb, have so great glory in her countenance that Joseph did not know her. But the first exposition is more literal.

Likewise, Helvidius says this because the text says, ***Till she brought forth her firstborn son***. He is said to be the first with respect to a subsequent child. Therefore, she had other children.

Jerome replies that it is customary in Sacred Scripture that they are called firstborn, whom other children do not precede. In Exodus 13, it is said that the firstborn of the Jews are to be offered to the Lord. Jerome asks, 'Was it fitting then to wait because they are not to be offered until a second child was born?' Therefore, those who do not precede other children are also called firstborn; and so it is understood here.

The guardianship follows. Luke described this more fully (chapter 2), while Matthew briefly touches upon it. For thus the Holy Ghost wills, that what things one has said, the other passed over in silence. ***He called His name Jesus***. This name indeed was well known and desired by the ancients; "I will look for thy salvation, O Lord" (Gen.49, 18). And: "But I will rejoice in the Lord; and I will joy in God my Jesus" (Hab.3, 18).

CHAPTER TWO

1. When Jesus therefore was born in Bethlehem of Juda, in the days of king Herod, behold, there came wise men from the East to Jerusalem,
2. Saying: Where is he that is born king of the Jews? For we have seen his star in the East, and are come to adore him.

Above, the Evangelist treated of Christ's genealogy: here he intends to show forth his birth. And firstly, by the testimony of the Innocents, where it begins, **And after they departed**. About the first, three things are set forth. For firstly, Christ's birth is announced; secondly, the place is examined; and thirdly, the person is examined. The second begins where it is said, **And king Herod hearing this**. The third begins where it is said, **Then Herod**. About the first he does three things. For firstly, Christ's birth is set forth, to which testimony is cited; secondly, witnesses are introduced; and thirdly, the testimony is given. The second begins where it is said, **Behold there came wise men**. The third begins where it is said, **Where is he that is born?** About the first verse, four things are touched upon: the birth, the name of the one born, the place and the time. The first begins where it is said, **When Jesus therefore was born**. And it is to be noted that Luke more fully describes the birth, while, on the contrary, Matthew more fully describes the adoration of the Wise Men than Luke does. The name is treated where it is said, **Jesus**. The place is treated where it is said, **In Bethlehem of Juda**. And note, it is not Bethlehem of *Judea*, because Judea is the name given to the whole region of the Israelite people. On the contrary, it is said, **of Juda**; this is that land which had come to the lot of Juda. It is called Bethlehem of Juda to differentiate it from the other Bethlehem, which is in the tribe of Zabulon, about which it is written in Josue 19.[1] And note that these three phrases, **When Jesus therefore was born in Bethlehem of Juda, in the days of king Herod**, are suitably expressed. For Bethlehem represents the Church, in which Jesus was born, who is the true bread, of Whom it is said in John 6, 35: "I am the bread of life who descended from heaven." Salvation comes forth to no one, unless he is in the house of the Lord. Christ the Savior was born at this place and time; "Salvation shall possess thy walls, and praise thy gates," etc., (Is. 60, 18). And he added, **king**, to differenti-

---

[1] "And Cateth and Naalol and Semeron and Jedala and Bethlehem: twelve cities and their villages" (verse 15).

ate another Herod: for he was surnamed Ascalonite, under whom Christ was born; but the other who killed John, was the son of this Herod, and was not a king.

But it is inquired why Scripture makes mention of this time.[2] And it ought to be replied that it is on account of three reasons; Firstly, to show that the prophecy of Jacob was fulfilled, "The sceptre shall not be taken away from Juda, nor a ruler from his thigh, till he come that is to be sent, and he shall be the expectation of nations" (Gen. 49, 10). Herod was, in fact, the first foreigner who reigned in Judea. The second reason is that a greater sickness requires a greater and better doctor. Now the people of Israel were then in very great distress under Gentile domination, and so they were in need of a very great consoler; for, in their other afflictions, the prophets were sent to them. But now, on account of the magnitude of the affliction, the Lord of the prophets was sent to them; "According to the multitude of my sorrows in my heart, thy comforts have given joy to my soul" (Ps. 93, 19).

Next, the witnesses are related, where it is said, **Behold, there came wise men**. And these are described in three ways: by their profession, by their homeland, and by the place where they bore witness. Concerning the first, he says, **Behold Magi**; who, according to the common manner of speaking, are called sorcerers; but in the Persian language, philosophers and wise men are called 'Magi.' These men indeed came to Jesus, because they recognized that the glory of the wisdom which they possessed came from Christ. And they are, in fact, the first fruits of the Gentiles, because they were the first Gentiles to come to Christ. And so that which is written in Isaias is fulfilled, according to Augustine, by the coming of these men; "For before the child knew to call his father and his mother, the strength of Damascus, and the spoils of Samaria shall be taken away before the king of the Assyrians" (Is. 8, 4). For even before Christ spoke, He took away the strength of Damascus, and the riches and spoils of Samaria, that is to say, idolatry. For these men cast away idolatry and offered gifts.

Moreover, it should be considered that some men came from the Jews to Christ, namely, the shepherds; and some from the Gentiles, namely, the Magi, came to Christ. For Christ Himself is the cornerstone, which made both to be one. And why did the Magi and the shepherds come to Christ? It was because shepherds are simpler, and the former are greater sinners. And so it was to show that Christ received both.

2. In ancient times, time was specified through reference to kings.

How many those Wise Men were, the Evangelist does not say. It seems, however, judging from their gifts, that there were three kings, although many other men are symbolized by these men; "And the Gentiles shall walk in thy light" (Is. 60, 3).

Concerning the second point, namely, their homeland, he says, *from the East*. And it is to be noted that certain persons explain *from the East* to refer to the territories of the East; but then how did they come in so few days? And it is answered, as certain persons say, that they came miraculously; others say that they had dromedaries. Chrysostom, nevertheless, says that the star appeared to them for two years before His birth, and that, during this time, they prepared themselves, and came to Jerusalem in two years and thirteen days. It can be otherwise explained, however, in that *From the East* refers to a certain region which was near Jerusalem on the East side. For these men are said to have been of the followers of Balaam, who said in Numbers 24, 17: "A star shall rise out of Jacob"; and that Balaam dwelt near the Promised Land on the East side.

Next, we hear of the place, *They came to Jerusalem*. But why did they come to Jerusalem? There are two reasons: The first is that it was the royal city; hence, they were seeking the king of the Jews in the royal city. Similarly, this was done by Divine Providence, so that testimony to Christ might be given firstly in Jerusalem, that the prophecy in Isaias 2, 3 might be fulfilled: "The law shall come forth from Sion and the word of the Lord from Jerusalem." Their testimony is set forth after this, where it is said, *Where is he that is born?* In which place, three things are said: Firstly, they announce the birth of the king; secondly, they bring forth the sign of the birth, where it is said, *We have seen his star*; thirdly, they profess a pious intention, where it is said, *And we are come to adore*. Therefore, they say, *Where is he?* Now it must be considered that these Wise Men are the first fruits of the Gentiles, and they prefigure in themselves our state. For these men suppose something, namely, the birth of Christ; and they seek something, namely, the place. And we indeed hold Christ by faith; but we seek something, namely, by hope; for we will see Him face to face; "For we walk by faith, and not by sight" (II Cor. 5, 7).

But there is a question. Since they heard that a king was in Jerusalem, why were they saying these things? For everyone who publicly declares another king in the city of a king, exposes himself to danger. But they were certainly doing this with the zeal of the faith. Whence, in them is announced that intrepid faith, which is written, "Fear ye not them that kill the body" (below 10, 28).

Thereupon, they propose a sign of this birth, saying, **We have seen.** And note that in these words was an occasion for two errors. Certain men, such as the Priscillianists, said all the actions of men are done and ruled by fate. And they support their view by this reference, **For we have seen his star.** Therefore, he was born under a star. Another error is the Manichaeans', who reject fate, and consequently, reject this Gospel; for they were saying that Matthew inserted fate into this Gospel. But both of their errors are excluded.

But before we proceed to the literal explanation, firstly it is necessary to see what is fate, and how and why these things ought not to be believed. Note, therefore, that we see many things in human affairs that happen accidentally and by chance. And so it happens that something is by chance and fortuitous in reference to a lower cause, but in reference to a higher cause, it is not fortuitous. It is just as if some master sends three persons to find someone, and each one does not know of the other. And if they happen to meet each other, it is fortuitous to them. But if these things are referred to the intention of the master, it is not fortuitous. But in accordance to this, there were two opinions about fate. Some said that these chance events could not be attributed to another higher, controlling cause. And so they denied the existence of fate, and furthermore, they denied the whole of Divine Providence. And this was, according to Augustine, the opinion of Cicero. But we say that these chance events are to be attributed to a higher controlling cause. But also, since the word 'fate' is so-called from the verb *for, fari*,[3] meaning, as it were, 'something proclaimed' and 'spoken out.' There is a difference of opinions about the source of this ordination. For some said that it comes from the power of celestial bodies. Whence, they say that fate is nothing other than the arrangement of the stars. Others attribute these chance events to Divine Providence. But one must deny that fate exists in the first way. For human acts are not governed by the arrangement of celestial bodies, which is well-known at the present time, since there are many convincing reasons for this. Firstly, it is impossible that a corporeal power could act in a way above an incorporeal power, because nothing that is lower in the order of nature affects a superior nature. Now, in the soul, there are certain powers elevated above the body. There are also certain powers attached to organs, namely, the sensitive and nutritive powers. And although celestial bodies indeed directly affect lower bodies

---

3. For, *fari* means 'to speak.'

and modify them in themselves, nevertheless, they accidentally affect the powers attached to the organs. In powers not attached to organs, however, they in no way affect them by necessitating, but only by inclining them. For we say this man is hot-tempered, that is, prone to anger, and this is from celestial causes, but his choice as such is directly in his will. Whence, there can never be so strong a disposition in the human body, that it actually overwhelms the judgment of free will. Hence, whoever would say that free will is subjected to the celestial bodies from necessity, might as well also claim that the senses do not differ from the intellect in any way. Secondly, it would follow that all divine worship is worthless, because everything happens then out of necessity. And thus, the ruling of the state government would then also be destroyed, because neither would it be fitting to take counsel, nor to foresee anything, and the like. Thirdly, it would follow that we could attribute men's evil behavior to God, which would dishonor Him, Who is the Creator of the stars. Therefore, it is clear that to say this is completely contrary to the faith. And thus, Gregory says, "Far be it from the hearts of the faithful that fate be said to be a real thing." If, however, you wish Divine Providence to be called fate, then it is a real thing. But, as Augustine says, because we ought to have nothing in common with the infidels, we should not impose this name to it. Whence, he says, "Correct the expression, keep the opinion." Therefore, it cannot be said, **We have seen the star,** i.e. on which His whole life depends. For, according to Augustine, the star would then not follow the One born, because then Christ would rather be said to be the fate of the star, rather than the contrary.

It should be noted also that this star was not one of those that were first made, which is evident from four things. Firstly, this is evident from its motion, because no star is moved from north to south. But the region of the Persians, from which these Wise Men came, is located to the north. Moreover, other stars never stay still; but this one was not continually moving. Thirdly, this is evident from its time, because no star shines during the day; but this one was shedding light during the day for the Wise Men. Fourthly, this is evident from its position, because it was not in the firmament, which is clear, because, by means of it, these men precisely identified the house. Therefore, it must be said that this star was specially created for the service of Christ; and so he says, **We have seen his star**, that is, the one made for His service.

Now some say that this star was the Holy Ghost, who, just as He appeared above Him, who was baptized, in the form of a dove, so also now does He appear in the form of a star. Others say that it was an angel. But it must be said that it was a true star. And He chose to be made known under the sign of a star, firstly, because it was fitting for Him. For He is the king of the heavens, and, for that reason, He chose to be manifested by a heavenly sign; "The heavens show forth the glory of God and the firmament declareth the work of his hands" (Ps. 18, 1). Christ was made known to the Jews indeed by angels, through whom they had received the Law; "The law was given by angels" (Gal. 3, 19). But He was made known to the Gentiles by a star, because they came to the knowledge of God through created things; "The invisible things of God, by the things that are made, are clearly seen" (Rom. 1, 20). Secondly, this is because it was appropriate for those to whom it was being shown, namely, the Gentiles, whose calling was promised to Abraham in the likeness of the stars; "Look up to heaven and number the stars, if thou canst," etc., (Gen. 15, 5). Whence, both in the Nativity and in the Passion a sign occurred in the sky, because this made Christ known to all the Gentiles. Likewise, it was appropriate for all men, because He is the Savior of all men. But he says, ***In the East***, which is explained in two ways. According to Rabanus, it is thus; A star existing in Judea appeared to those Gentiles who were in the East. Or, we saw a star in the East. The latter is better said. Whence, ***Behold the star which they had seen in the East, went before them*** (this chapter, v. 9). Likewise, it is evident from this that this star, by its position, was near to the earth, because otherwise it would not have identified the place. Therefore, it could not have been seen from such a remote region.

Afterwards, their pious intention is set forth, where it is said, ***And we came to adore Him.***

Here there are two questions. For Augustine says, "Were not these men curious, because whensoever there would be a sign through some star, they would seek a king who was born?" For this is foolishness.

But it is to be replied that they did not render homage to an earthly king, but to a heavenly king, in whom Divine power is shown to have been present. Otherwise, if they had sought an earthly king, they would have lost all their devotion when they found Him wrapped in swaddling clothes.

But Augustine again inquires how were they able to know from the star that the God-man was born. And he replies that this was by means of an angel revealing. For He who showed the star to them, sent an angel who would reveal this. Pope Leo says, that "just as their eyes were exteriorly being filled with the light of that star, so a divine ray was interiorly revealing."

A third explanation for this is that these men were of the stock of Balaam, who said, "A star shall rise out of Jacob" (Num. 14, 17). Whence, they possessed knowledge about the star from his prophecy. And, for that reason, by seeing the star's very great brightness, they suspected that the heavenly king was born. And, therefore, they were seeking him. And this passage is, *We are come to adore him.* In this, that which was written is fulfilled, "And all kings of the earth shall adore him: all nations shall serve him" (Ps. 71, 11).

3. And king Herod hearing this, was troubled, and all Jerusalem with him.

4. And assembling together all the chief priests and the scribes of the people, he inquired of them where Christ should be born.

5. But they said to him: In Bethlehem of Juda. For so it is written by the prophet:

6. And thou Bethlehem the land of Juda art not the least among the princes of Juda: for out of thee shall come forth the captain that shall rule my people Israel.

7. Then Herod, privately calling the wise men learned diligently of them the time of the star which appeared to them;

8. And sending them into Bethlehem, said: Go and diligently inquire after the child, and when you have found him, bring me word again, that I also may come and adore him.

9a. Who having heard the king, went their way.

Christ's birth having been announced by the Wise Men, here King Herod inquires concerning the place of the birth. And three things are set forth. Firstly, the motive for inquiring is given; secondly, the inquiry is adjoined; and thirdly, the discovery of the truth is related. The second is where it is said, *And assembling.* The third is where it is said, *But they said to him: In Bethlehem of Juda.* The motive was the troubling of Herod. Whence, it begins, *And king Herod hearing.* And he significantly calls Herod a king, to show him to be a different king from the King whom they were seeking. Now there were three causes of the troubling. The first came from the ambition that he had about the keeping of his own kingdom, principally because he was a foreigner. For he knew or had heard that passage of Daniel 2, 44: "In the days of the kingdoms of Israel the God of heaven will set up a kingdom that shall not be delivered up to another people" etc., But in this he was being deceived, because that kingdom was spiritual; "My kingdom is not of this world" (Jn. 18, 36). Whence, Herod was troubled, fearing the loss of his own kingdom, but the devil was more troubled, fearing the total destruction of his own kingdom; "Now shall the prince of this world be cast out" (Jn. 12, 31).

And note that men positioned in high places, as Chrysostom says, are troubled from a light word brought forth against them; "I being exalted have been humbled and troubled" (Ps. 87, 6); the humble, however, never fear.

The second cause proceeds from fear of the Roman Empire; for it had been decreed by the Roman Empire that no one might be called a god or a king without their consent; whence, he was fearful. But this fear was worldly, which is prohibited; "Who art thou, that thou shouldst be afraid of a mortal man, and of the son of a man, who shall wither away like grass?" (Is 51, 12). The third cause is from the blush of disgrace. For he was disgraced before the people that someone else would be called a king. In this he was like Saul, who said, "I have sinned: yet honor me now before the ancients of my people, and before Israel," etc., (I Kings 15, 30). But the passage that follows is surprising, **And all Jerusalem with him**. For it seemed that they should have rejoiced. But it should be known that they had three causes of trouble. The first was their wickedness. For they were wicked men, to whom social intercourse with the just is always detestable; "Fools hate them that flee from evil things" (Prov. 13, 19). The second was in order to please Herod; "As the judge of the people is himself, so also are his ministers" (Eccli. 10, 2). The third was that they feared that, when Herod had heard this, he might more furiously rage against the nation of the Jews.

In this, however, it is mystically indicated that he was worldly. Gregory says, "The king of the land was troubled when the king of heaven was born, because the earthly height is of course confounded, when the heavenly expanses are displayed." "And the moon shall blush, and the sun shall be ashamed, when the Lord of hosts shall reign in mount Sion, and in Jerusalem" (Is 24, 23). And it ought to be noted that, as Augustine says, "What, on the other hand, will the tribunal of the one judging be, when the cradle of the infant terrified proud kings? Let the kings be frightened before the one sitting at the right hand of the Father, whom the impious king feared, lapping the breasts of his mother."

And assembling together. Here is set forth the inquiry. And, as it has been said, Herod had been anxious to inquire, both on account of his kingdom and on account of his fear of the Romans. Whence, he sought the truth. But to have certitude about something, those who are inquiring seek after three things. For a man believes a multitude of people, those having authority, and experts. Whence, he assembled together many men, both having authority and being experts. And this is what he says, **Assembling together all**, which pertains to the first; "The multitude of the wise is the welfare of the whole world" (Wis. 6, 26). **The chief priests** pertains to the second; "The lips of the priest shall keep knowledge, and they shall seek the law at his mouth" (Mal. 2, 7). **And the scribes**, pertains to the third. They are called scribes not only because they functioned as writers,[4] but also as interpreters of the Writings[5] of the Law. By means of these men, he indeed wished to investigate the truth; "In the company of great men take not upon thee: and when the ancients are present, speak not much" (Eccli. 32, 13). **He inquired of them where Christ should be born.** The Wise Men said 'king,' but they were looking for the Christ. For they became aware from speaking with the Jews that the legitimate king of the Jews would be anointed.

But it is asked: Either he believed the prophecy or he did not. If he believed in it, then he knew that Christ could not be prevented from reigning. Why, then, did he slay the children? If he did not believe, then why was he looking for Him?

But it is answered that he did not believe perfectly, because he was ambitious; and ambition makes a man blind.

But they said to him: In Bethlehem of Juda. Herein the truth is found. Firstly, the truth is declared; and secondly, it is confirmed by its prophecy, where it is said, **And thou Bethlehem the land of Juda.**

And it should be known that Christ wished to be born in Bethlehem for three reasons. Firstly, it was to avoid glory. For on account of this, He chose two places: He chose one in which He wished to be born, namely, Bethlehem; He chose another place in which He suffered, namely, Jerusalem. And this is opposed to those who seek glory, who wish to be born in eminent places, and do not wish to suffer in a place of honor; "I seek not my own glory" (Jn. 8, 50). Secondly, this place was chosen to confirm His doctrine, and to show His truthfulness. For if He had been born in some great city, the power of His doctrine could have been ascribed to a human power; "You know the grace of our Lord Jesus Christ" (II Cor 8, 9). Thirdly, it was to show that He was of the

---

4. i.e. *Scriptors.*   5. i.e. *Scriptura.*

lineage of David; "Joseph and Mary went to Bethlehem to be enrolled there because they were of the house and family of David" (Luke 2, 3). It coincides also to a mystery, because Bethlehem is interpreted 'house of bread'; and Christ is that "living bread which came down from heaven" (Jn 6, 51).

Afterwards, the truth is confirmed. Whence it reads, *And thou Bethlehem*, etc. From this prophecy, we can consider two things; for the Wise Men were announcing something, and they were seeking something. And both are shown from this prophecy; because regarding the first, he says, *And thou, Bethlehem*; and regarding the second, he says, *For out of thee shall come forth the captain*. And thus Christ's birth is confirmed by double testimony, namely, of the star and of the prophecy, because what is in the mouth of two or three witnesses is the truth; "In the mouth of two or three witnesses every word shall stand" (Deut 19, 15).

And note that at the time when men were all unbelievers, they were given corporeal signs. But when they later were believers, a prophecy was given to them; "Wherefore tongues are for a sign, not to believers, but to unbelievers; but prophecies not to unbelievers, but to believers" (I Cor 14, 22).

And it ought to be known that the Jews doubly erred in their citation of the prophecy. Because it is said there (Mic. 5, 2), "And thou, Bethlehem Ephrata." And they again erred because it is not said there, *art not the least*. And two reasons can be given why they changed this passage. It can be explained in one way that they did this out of ignorance. It can be explained in another way that they knowingly used different words to recite the passage. The reason is, since Herod was a foreigner, he did not recognize the passage of the prophet, and so they said that which was understandable to Herod. Whence, they say, *Land of Juda* and *Thou art not the least*, that is, thou art not the least among the thousands of men of Juda; or, *among the princes of Juda*, that is, among the principal cities of Juda. *For out of thee shall come forth the captain that shall rule my people Israel*. Reference is made to this captain[6] in Dan 9, 25, "Until Christ the prince"; and in Psalm 30, 5, "Thou wilt be a leader to me." For He governs the people of Israel, not only carnally, but also spiritually; "Hath God cast away his people?" etc., (Rom. 11, 1); "Give ear, O thou that rulest Israel: thou that leadest Joseph like a sheep" (Ps. 79, 2). And note that they truncate the rest of the passage pertaining to His importance, namely, "And his going forth is from the beginning, from the days

---

6. The Latin word used for all the words "leader," "captain" and "prince" is *dux*.

of eternity." By these words, it is insinuated that He was not going to be an earthly king, but a heavenly king. But if Herod had known this, he would not have been cruel. Hence, they were responsible for causing the death of those infants.[7] Similarly, from that ending of the passage it is also clearly shown that the interpretation of the Jews, who expound it as pertaining to Zorobabel, is false. For what is written does not apply to him: "And his going forth is from the beginning, from the days of eternity." Likewise, he was born, not in Judea, but in Babylon.

Afterwards, it is inquired concerning the Person born, when he says, **Then Herod privately calling the wise men, learned diligently of them the time of the star which appeared to them**. And firstly, the inquiry is set forth; secondly, the finding of the one sought is related, where it says, **They found him**, etc.; thirdly, the veneration of Him who was found is related, where it says, **And falling down they adored him**. They were motivated to seek the Person born from two things: from Herod's persuasion and from the star's guidance. Whence, regarding the first, Herod's exhortation is related; secondly, the Wise Men's investigation upon the star's alteration is related, where it says, **Who having heard the king, went their way**. Regarding the first, three things are related. For firstly, Herod asks about the time of the star's appearance; secondly, he makes known the place, where it says, **And sending them into Bethlehem**; thirdly, he imposes upon them the duty of investigating, where it says, **Go and diligently inquire after the child**. Therefore, the Evangelist says, **Then Herod**. At this point it should be considered that the Jews knew the place, but not the time, of Christ's coming. Whence, they are confuted by the Lord, "Because thou hast not known the time of thy visitation" (Lk. 19, 44), and, "The ox knoweth his owner, and the ass his master's crib: but Israel hath not known me, and my people hath not understood" (Is. 1, 3). Therefore, the time of the star's appearance is sought. And Chrysostom says that the star appeared to these men for two years previously. Others, however, say that it appeared on the very day of the Nativity. He announces the place, where it is said, **And sending**. He enjoins the duty upon them of investigating, where it is said, **Go, and inquire**, etc. And so he urges two things. And in order that they fulfill his wishes, he promises a third thing. Regarding the first, he says, **Go**, etc. And he seeks the Child deceitfully in order to kill Him, just like those men to whom it is said, "You shall seek

---

7. i.e. the Holy Innocents.

me, and shall not find me" (Jn. 7, 34). Regarding the second, he speaks thus, *And when you have found him, bring me word again.* And he was saying this for an evil purpose also; "By much talk he will sift thee" (Eccli. 13, 14). Regarding the third, he says, *That I also may come and adore him*; and he is, in fact, deceitfully promising worship of God; "Their tongue is a piercing arrow, it hath spoken deceit" (Jer. 9, 8); "Who speak peace with their neighbor, but evils are in their hearts" (Ps. 27, 3).

And note that although the Wise Men were publicly declaring Christ to be a king, Herod calls Him a child, because out of the fullness of the heart the mouth speaks. Note also, he asks the Jews where Christ would be born, wishing to try them, and to find out whether they would rejoice.

Afterwards, the investigation of the Wise Men is related. He had enjoined two things: that they would seek after the Child and that they would return. But the Wise Men did only one of these two things; whence, it reads, *Who having heard the king, went their way.* The other thing, they did not do. Hearers ought to be such as these men, that they would add the good things to their knowledge, but leave behind the evil things; "Whatsoever they say do, but according to their works do ye not," etc., (below 23, 3).

9b. And behold the star which they had seen in the East, went before them, until it came and stood over where the child was.
10. And seeing the star they rejoiced with exceeding great joy.
11. And entering into the house, they found the child with Mary his mother, and falling down they adored him: and opening their treasures, they offered him gifts; gold, frankincense, and myrrh.
12. And having received an answer in sleep that they should not return to Herod, they went back another way into their country.

Above, the Evangelist set forth one motive of the Wise Men, namely, Herod's persuasion. Here he gives another motive of the Wise Men for seeking Christ, namely, the star's guidance; and concerning this he does two things. For firstly, he relates the star's guidance; secondly, he relates the effect of joy from this guidance, where it is said, *And seeing the star they rejoiced with exceeding great joy.* And note that the star firstly accomplishes its role by its movement, because it was leading the Wise Men directly to

Christ; likewise, by its standing still, it showed clearly the location of the Child, where it is said, *Until it came and stood over where the child was.* Wherefore, so far as concerns the first, he said, *It went before them.* From this, however, that he says, *Behold the star, which they had seen in the east, went before them,* it is given to be understood that when the Wise Men turned aside into Jerusalem, the star disappeared; but when they were withdrawing from Herod, it appeared. Now it disappeared on account of three reasons: firstly, this happened to put the Jews to shame, who although they had been instructed in the Law, and the Gentiles had not been instructed, nevertheless, the Gentiles seek Christ and the Jews despise Him. Whence, is fulfilled that saying in Isaias 55, 5: "The nations that knew not thee shall run to thee." Secondly, this happened for the instruction of the Wise Men; for the Lord wished to manifest Himself to them not only by means of the star, but also by means of the Law, so that knowledge of the Law might be added to the knowledge of creatures; "In the mouth of two or three witnesses every word shall stand"; "To the law rather, and to the testimony" (Is. 8, 20). Thirdly, this happened for our instruction; and we are instructed about two things, according to the Gloss. Firstly, we are taught thereby that they who seek human help, are abandoned by divine help; for it is not allowed to seek human help, not seeking the divine help; "Woe to them that go down to Egypt for help, trusting in horses, and putting their confidence in chariots, because they are many: and in horsemen, because they are very strong: and have not trusted in the Holy One of Israel, and have not sought after the Lord" (Is. 31, 1). Secondly, we are instructed as far as this, that we, who are the faithful, ought not to seek signs as those men, who *seeing the star rejoiced*, etc.; but we ought to be content with the teachings of the Prophets, because "signs are given to the infidels."[8] In this also there is a twofold mystery. For the star represents Christ; "I am the root of David, the bright and morning star" (Apoc. 12, 16). Whence we can understand this star to signify God's grace, which we lose when we approach Herod, that is, the devil; "You were heretofore darkness, but now light in the Lord" (Eph. 5, 8). Likewise, when we withdraw from Herod, that is, the devil, we find the star, that is, the grace of Christ: a similar occurrence is in Exodus 13, 21, where it is said that the Lord went before Israel, when they left Egypt, in the form of fire, etc. Here, however, He was going before in the form of a star.

---

8. "Wherefore tongues are for a sign, not to believers but to unbelievers: but prophecies, not to unbelievers but to believers" (I Cor. 14, 22).

Until it came and stood over where the child was. Here we perceive two things. One is that this star was not very high, because otherwise they could not have distinguished the house of the Child. Another is that the star, having completed its task, was returned to its original material. *Where the child was.* The Evangelist frequently says, *Child,* so that you might know that He was the one about whom it is said in Isaias 9, 6: "A child is born to us." Afterwards, is set forth the effect of the guidance of this star with respect to the Wise Men: whence, *And seeing the star they rejoiced,* etc. They rejoiced on account of the hope which they recovered. For they were fearing, that having come from far off regions, they might lose what they were hoping to find; "Rejoicing in hope"; (Rom. 12, 12). Moreover, he adds, *With joy;* for some men rejoice, yet they do not rejoice, because human gladness is not perfect joy; "Mourning taketh hold of the end of joy" (Prov. 14, 13). But the true and perfect joy is from God; "I will greatly rejoice in the Lord, and my soul shall be joyful in my God" (Is. 61, 10). Thirdly, he adds, *Great,* because these men were already knowing great things about God, that God was made flesh and is very merciful; "Rejoice, and praise, O thou habitation of Sion: for great is he that is in the midst of thee, the Holy One of Israel," (Is. 12, 6). Fourthly, he adds, *Very,* because they were rejoicing intensely; for they had recovered what they had lost; "There shall be joy before the angels of God," (Lk. 15, 10). Afterwards, it is treated concerning the finding of the Child. Whence, *And entering the house, they found the child with Mary, his mother.* And he touches upon three things: *The house,* concerning which, if one were to ask what was it like, it is shown in Luke 2. Again, if one were to ask what the Child was like, he was in no way differing from others, as the Saints say. Regarding His appearance: He was not speaking, He seemed weak, etc. Likewise, if one were to ask what His mother was like, it may be answered, she has the qualities of a carpenter's wife. And thus I say this, that if these men had sought an earthly king, by seeing these things they would have been scandalized; but seeing common things and considering the highest things, they were moved to admiration, and so they adored Him. And this is what is written, *And falling down they adored him.*

But why is there no mention of Joseph? It ought to be said that this happened by a divine dispensation that he was not present, lest a suspicion of an incorrect opinion be given to these men who were the first fruits of the Gentiles.

Afterwards is mentioned the reverence which they showed to the Child, where it is said, *And falling down.* And they showed reverence to the Child in three ways: by adoring, offering and obeying Him. He says therefore: *And falling down they adored him*, as God hiding in a man; "Before him the Ethiopians shall fall down," (Ps 71, 9). Likewise, by offering, they showed reverence; whence, *And opening their treasures*. For it was the custom among the Persians, that they always adored with a gift; and this is said, *And opening their treasures, they offered him gifts; gold, frankincense, and myrrh*; "The kings of Tharsis and the islands shall offer presents: the kings of the Arabians and of Saba shall bring gifts" (Ps. 52, 10); "All they from Saba shall come bringing gold and frankincense: and showing forth praise to the Lord" (Is. 60, 6).

Mystically, it ought to be considered that these men, not on the way, but only when they came to Christ, firstly opened their treasure: likewise, we ought not to display our goods on our way to heaven. Whence, this fault is reproved with regard to the virgins in chapter 25 below; and in chapter 13, verse 44, it is said, "The kingdom of heaven is like unto a treasure hidden in a field, which a man having found, hid it, and for joy thereof goeth, and selleth all that he hath, and buyeth that field."

They offered him gifts, etc. Some assign a literal reason of these gifts; and these say that the Wise Men found three things: a shabby house, a weak Child, and a poor mother. And thus they offered gold for the support of the mother, myrrh for the sustenance of the Child's limbs, and frankincense to remove the stench. But it ought to be said that here something is mystically put forward, and these three things rather refer to three things which we ought to offer, namely, faith, action and contemplation. They pertain to faith in two ways: firstly, they pertain to those things which coincide in Christ, namely, royal dignity, "A king shall reign, and shall be wise" (Jer. 23, 5), and thus they offered *gold* in tribute. Priesthood was in Christ as well, and thus they offered *frankincense* in sacrifice. And human mortality was in Christ, and thus they offered *myrrh*. Likewise, they pertain to faith in the Trinity, because the Persons of the Trinity are represented to us. Secondly, they can refer to our action. For wisdom can be signified by the gold; "If thou shalt dig for her as for a treasure: then shalt thou understand the fear of the Lord" (Prov. 2, 5). Prayer can be signified by the frankincense; "Let my prayer be directed as incense in thy sight," etc., (Ps. 140, 2). Mortification of the flesh can be signified by the myrrh; "Mortify therefore your members which are upon earth" (Col. 3, 5); "My hands dropped with myrrh" (Cant. 5, 5). With regard to contemplation, however, by these three things can be signified, either three senses of Sacred Scripture, namely, the literal sense, under which is included the allegorical, anagogical, and moral senses; or three parts of philosophy, namely, ethics, logic and physics. For we ought to use all these things for the service of God.

Afterwards, it is related how they showed reverence in obeying; whence, it is said, *And having received an answer in sleep that they should not return to Herod, they went back another way into their country.* But why did they, who did not ask, receive a response? But it can be said that the Lord will sometimes respond to one who asks mentally, and these men were inwardly seeking what might please God regarding their return; "Why criest thou to me?" (Ex. 14, 15). But are revelations from God directly? Dionysius proves they are not given except by means of the angels. Why, therefore, does he not name the angel? But it can be answered that whenever Scripture makes mention of God, and not of an angel, this occurs from some excellence of that manifestation; "The law was ordained by an angel in the hand of a mediator" (Gal. 3, 19); "This is that Moses who said to the children of Israel: A prophet shall God raise up to you of your own brethren, as myself: him shall you hear," etc., (Acts 7, 37). Whence, what the Gloss says, that this was directly from God, refers to Scripture's manner of speaking.

They went back another way into their own country. In this is shown that we arrive at paradise, our own country from which we were expelled, by obedience; "For the Lord knoweth the ways that are on the right hand: but those are perverse which are on the left hand" (Prov. 4, 27). Chrysostom here says, that when these men returned to their own country they led a holy life, and, afterwards, were made helpers of St. Thomas the Apostle; nevertheless, nothing about them is found written in Sacred Scripture after their departure.

13. And after they were departed, behold an angel of the Lord appeared in sleep to Joseph, saying: Arise, and take the child and his mother, and fly into Egypt: and be there until I shall tell thee. For it will come to pass that Herod will seek the child to destroy him.

14. Who arose, and took the child and his mother by night, and retired into Egypt: and he was there until the death of Herod:

15. That it might be fulfilled which the Lord spoke by the prophet, saying: Out of Egypt have I called my son.

16. Then Herod perceiving that he was deluded by the wise men, was exceeding angry: and sending, killed all the menchildren that were in Bethlehem, and in all the borders thereof, from two years old and under, according to the time which he had diligently inquired of the wise men.
17. Then was fulfilled that which was spoken by Jeremias the prophet, saying:
18. A voice in Rama was heard, lamentation and great mourning; Rachel bewailing her children, and would not be comforted, because they are not.
19. But when Herod was dead, behold an angel of the Lord appeared in sleep to Joseph in Egypt,
20. Saying: Arise, and take the child and his mother, and go into the land of Israel. For they are dead that sought the life of the child.
21. Who arose, and took the child and his mother, and came into the land of Israel.
22. But hearing that Archelaus reigned in Judea in the room of Herod his father, he was afraid to go thither: and being warned in sleep retired into the quarters of Galilee.
23. And coming he dwelt in a city called Nazareth: that it might be fulfilled which was said by the prophets: That he shall be called a Nazarene.

It was treated above how the Wise Men bore witness to Christ being born; now, however, is treated how the Holy Innocents bear witness, not by speaking, but by dying; and about this the Evangelist does three things. For firstly, Christ's hiding is related; secondly, the killing of the children is related, where it is said, **Then Herod**; thirdly, the return of Christ Himself is related, where it is said, **Herod being dead**. Concerning the first, he does three things. For firstly, the angel's warning is set forth; secondly, Joseph's obedience is shown; and thirdly, the fulfillment of the prophecy is set forth. The second thing is where it is said, **Who arose, and took the child and his mother by night**. The third thing is where it is said, **That it might be fulfilled**.[9] Concerning the first, three things are mentioned. Firstly, the time of the apparition is related; secondly, the apparition itself, and the manner of the apparition, are described where it is said, **Behold an angel**; thirdly, the warning itself made by the angel

---

9. The text here seems to be mistaken as it reads, "The second point is where it is said, **That it might be fulfilled**, and the third point was omitted. The text has been corrected and the missing point has been supplied from the context.

is related, where it is said, ***Arise, and take the child.*** The time is described, where it is said, ***And when they were departed.*** And it is to be understood that this apparition did not immediately occur after the Wise Men's departure, because everything which is related in Luke 2, 6 ought to be inserted, namely, about the purification: *After her days were accomplished*, etc. For Herod did not immediately plan to kill the children. Whence, when he says: ***And when they were departed***, the whole history of the purification ought to be inserted. Afterwards, the apparition itself is set forth; whence, it reads: ***Behold an angel appeared in sleep***, etc. It is said that he appeared in sleep, because then men cease from exterior actions, and to suchlike men does a revelation by angels happen; "In peace in the self same I will sleep, and I will rest" (Ps. 4, 9); "Thou shalt rest, and thy sleep shall be sweet" (Prov. 3, 24). In this warning, three things are related. For firstly, the angel persuades him to flee; secondly, he prescribes a period of time; and thirdly, he ascribes the cause. Therefore he says, ***Arise.***

And note that, as Hilary says, the Blessed Virgin is named spouse by the angel before the nativity (above 1, 5), but after the nativity she is not so-named. And this is for two reasons. Firstly, it is unto the praise of the Virgin. For just as the Virgin conceived, so the Virgin gave birth; secondly, it is on account of her dignity. For she was the Mother of God, the greatest of all dignities; and titles are given for one's greater worthiness. Likewise, note that, as Chrysostom says, the Child had not come for the sake of the mother, but rather the contrary is true; and so he says, ***Take the child and his mother***, etc.

But why is it said, ***Fly into Egypt***? Does not Psalm 18, 15 say, "O Lord, my helper, and my redeemer"?

But it should be known that He fled for three reasons. Firstly, it was for manifesting His humanity; for just as His divinity became visible in the star, so His humanity became visible in His flight; "Being made in the likeness of men" (Phil. 2, 7). Secondly, it was as an example. For He showed by example that which He taught by word; "And when they shall persecute you in this city, flee into another" (below 10, 23). Thirdly, it was for the sake of a mystery. For just as He chose to die, that He might call us back from death, so He chose to flee, that He might call back those who were fleeing from His face on account of sin; "Whither shall I go from thy spirit?" (Ps. 38, 7).

And be there. But why go to Egypt rather than elsewhere into another country?

It can be said for two reasons. The first is that it is proper to God that He be mindful of mercy in His anger.[10] For the Lord was angry against the Egyptians for persecuting the children of Israel, because the children of Israel were the first-born of God. And thus, it was given to Egypt to aid the Only-Begotten; "Behold the Lord will ascend upon a swiftcloud, and will enter into Egypt," etc., (Is. 19, 1); "The people that walked in darkness, have seen a great light: to them that dwelt in the region of the shadow of death, light is risen" (ibid. 9, 2); "We saw his glory, the glory as it were of the only begotten of the Father, full of grace and truth" (Jn. 1, 14). The second reason is that, because He Himself caused darkness to appear in Egypt, and so He willed to firstly enlighten it. And so He correctly fled there; "The people that walked in darkness have seen a great light: to them that dwelt in the region of the shadow of death, light is risen" (Is. 9, 2).[11]

Note that when someone wishes to flee sin, he ought firstly to shake off laziness; "Rise thou that sleepest, and arise from the dead: and Christ shall enlighten thee" (Eph. 5, 14). Secondly, he ought to take confidence from the Mother and Son, namely, Christ; "In me is all hope of life and of virtue" (Eccli. 24, 25). Thirdly, he ought to flee from sin, helped by the assistance of the Mother and Child; "Lo, I have gone far off flying away; and I abode in the wilderness" (Ps. 54, 8).

He adds the cause of this flight: *For it will come to pass that Herod will seek the child to destroy him.* Herod was deceived, because he wished to destroy Him who had come to share His kingdom; "And I dispose to you, as my Father hath disposed to me, a kingdom" (Lk. 22, 29). Secondly, he was deceived because he wished to destroy Him who was not seeking worldly glory; "Who having joy set before him, endured the cross" (Hebr. 12, 2). *Who arose.* Here is related the execution of the angel's command, and he relates it so far as concerns the flight and so far as concerns the period of time. Whence, it is said, *Who arose and took the child and his mother.* And mention is made of the time. Whence, he says, *by night,* on account of fear and affliction, according to that which is written in Isaias 26, 9, "My soul hath desired thee in the night," that is, in affliction; for in times

---

10. "When thou art angry, thou wilt remember mercy" (Habac. 3, 2).
11. "Persecuted Jews had ever sought refuge in Egypt. About the time of Christ, Jewish colonists were especially numerous. According to Philo, they numbered at least a million. In Leontopolis the Jews had a temple (160 B.C.-73 A.D.) which rivaled in splendor the temple of Jerusalem. The Holy Family might therefore expect to find in Egypt a certain amount of help and protection" ("Virgin," *Catholic Encyclopedia* (1907 ed.), vol. 15, p. 465).

of affliction one has recourse to God; "In their affliction they will rise early to me" (Osee 6, 1). *Who arose.* Then was fulfilled that which is written in Isaias 19, 1, "Behold the Lord will ascend upon a swift cloud, and will enter into Egypt." And this was literally fulfilled. *And he was there.* It is said that he was there seven years, and dwelt in the city of Heliopolis.

So far as concerns the mystery, however, by Joseph, preachers are signified, that is, the Apostles, who are placed to expel the darkness by doctrine, who, withdrawing from the Jews, turned towards the Gentiles; "To you it behoved us first to speak the word of God: but because you reject it, and judge yourselves unworthy of eternal life, behold we turn to the Gentiles" (Acts 13, 46). *And be there until I shall tell thee*, that is, until the Jews' infidelity is finished; "Blindness in part has happened in Israel" (Rom. 11, 25).

Afterwards, he brings forth the testimony of the prophecy; whence, he says, *That it might be fulfilled which the Lord spoke by the prophet.* This passage, according to Jerome's translation, is, "Out of Egypt have I called my son," (Osee 11, 1). In the Septuagint translation, however, it is not so, but instead, "Out of Egypt I have called his son."

There seems to be a question here. Because this passage does not seem to pertain to the matter at hand, for this saying is preceded by the words, "Because Israel was a child," etc., and so he seems to speak of the calling of Israel from Egypt.

But it can be said that in all the passages, which in the Gospels or in the Epistles are related about Christ, a certain distinction is to be noted. Because certain things are said specially about Christ, as that in Isaias 53, 7, "He shall be led as a sheep to the slaughter." On the other hand, certain things are said in relation to certain other things, because they form a figure of Christ. And such is this passage. For these men were not children of Israel, except in so far as they bore the likeness of the only begotten Son; and this what is said, "Out of Egypt have I called my son," namely, the special one.

Then Herod. Here is treated concerning the killing of the children; and about this he does three things. Firstly, the occasion of the killing is related; secondly, the killing itself is related, where it is said, *And sending, killed all the menchildren*; and thirdly, a prophecy is cited, where it is said, *Then was fulfilled*, etc. The occasion was Herod's anger; whence, *Then Herod was angry*; "The anger of man worketh not the justice of God" (James 1, 20). And it is to be observed that when a king dreads the loss of his kingdom, he is quickly angered and is enraged. *Perceiving that he was de-*

luded by the Wise Men, he was exceedingly angry on account of two things. For when someone is angry, he is mightily enraged for any little reason; whence, because he was dreading the loss of his kingdom and having been deluded by the Wise Men, *he was exceedingly angry*; "Of one spark cometh a great fire" (Eccli. 11, 34). *And sending*. In this anger there was cruelty with regard to three things: as to the multitude of people, as to the place, and as to the time. As to the multitude of people, there was cruelty because in order to get one person, he killed many; whence, it is said, *And sending, killed all the menchildren*. And note what Augustine says, "He never had gained so great obsequiousness, as he gained hate."

But it is asked: Since the children did not have free will, how can it be said that they died for Christ?

But, as it is said, "God sent not his Son into the world, to judge the world, but that the world may be saved by him" (Jn. 3,17). For God never would have permitted them to be killed, unless it were useful for them. Whence, Augustine says, that it is the same to doubt whether this killing benefited them, as it is to doubt whether baptism benefits children: for they suffered as martyrs; and, by dying, they confessed Christ, although not by speaking; "I saw under the altar the souls of them that were slain for the word of God" (Apoc. 6, 9).

The second cruelty is that he killed *in all the borders*; for he feared that Christ would flee, actually to some city. And it happened to him as to a wounded beast which does not care whom it ought to wound; "As a roaring lion, and a hungry bear, so is a wicked prince over the poor" (Prov. 28, 15). The third regards the time; whence, *From two years old*, that is, the children who were two years old.

And note what Augustine says, that the Innocents were killed in the same year in which Christ was born. But then why does he say, *From two years and under*? Some say that the star appeared during two years before, whence, Herod was doubting whether He had been born since the time of the star; and thus he says, *According to the time which he had diligently inquired of the Wise Men*. Others, however, say that these children were not killed in the same year, but after two years.

But why did he wait so long? Three reasons can be related from different persons. One is that, at first, he thought the Wise Men had been deluded, and that they had found nothing; but after he heard many things about Christ from Zachary, Simeon, and Anna, then he was prompted to seek. Others say that he did this out of caution: for he feared that the parents had hid the Child whom he was seeking. Whence, he first wanted to put them off guard. Others say that he was impeded by being busy, because he sent men after the Wise Men as far as to Tharsus of Cilicia, and made their ships to be burned. Again, he was busy, because he was summoned to Rome having been accused by his sons. And so, after coming back, he began to be brutal. And he says, *And under*, etc., because Herod thought Christ had such great power, that He could change His appearance.

By this killing is signified the killing of martyrs, because they are children through their humility and innocence; "Suffer the little children, and forbid them not to come to me" (below 19, 14); again it is said, "Unless you be converted and become as little children, you shall not enter into the kingdom of heaven" (below 18, 3). *In Bethlehem and in all the borders thereof*; because martyrs are killed throughout the whole world; "You shall be witnesses unto me" (Acts 1, 8), namely, by dying. The two years are the twofold charity, love of God and of neighbor, because "faith without works is dead" (James 2, 20).

And observe that, after Christ is born, immediately persecution rages, because immediately when someone is converted to Christ, he begins to be tempted; "Son, when thou comest to the service of God, stand in justice and fear, and prepare thy soul for temptation" (Eccli. 2, 1).

Then was fulfilled that which was spoken by Jeremias the prophet. Having related the killing of the children, here the Evangelist, according to his custom, sets forth the prophecy which foretold this event, which is, "A voice in Rama was heard of lamentation, of mourning and weeping, of Rachel weeping for her children, and refusing to be comforted for them, because they are not" (Jer. 31, 15).

And it is to be observed that, as Jerome says, wherever some passage of the Old Testament is cited by the Apostles and the Evangelists, it need not be quoted always word for word, but as the Holy Ghost gave to them to write, and sometimes the meaning is accommodated to our understanding. Thus we have, "A voice was heard on high of lamentation, of mourning and weeping, of Rachel weeping for her children, and refusing to be comforted for them, because they are not" (Jer. 31, 15). And the meaning is the same.

And it is to be considered to what this passage refers. This is one of those passages which is quoted in the Gospel, which although it has a literal sense, it is a figure of that which happened in the New Testament. Whence, for the understanding of it, some history must be considered, which is read in Judges 21, where it is said that, on account of a sin committed in regard to the wife of a Levite, nearly the whole tribe of Benjamin was exterminated. And it is said that in that place there was great wailing, such that it was heard from Gabaa as far as Rama at a distance from Bethlehem of twelve milestones.[12] In this it is said that Rachel wept, because she was the mother of Benjamin; and it is figurative speech, namely, to express the greatness of her sorrow. But this is a prophecy concerning a past event. In another way, it is a prophecy of a future event in two ways. Because in one way it can be referred to the captivity of Israel, who, when they were being led into captivity, are said to have wept on the road close to Bethlehem; and then it is said that Rachel wept, because she was buried there.[13] And this is said in the same manner of speech by means of which a place is said to weep for the evil deeds that happen in the place. Therefore, the Prophet wishes to say that just as there was sorrow and mourning when the tribe of Benjamin was exterminated, so there is to be another very great sorrow in the time of the captivity. In a third way it is explained thus; the Evangelist takes the fact of the killing of the Innocents, and expands upon this sorrow in four ways. He expands upon how the sorrow was widespread in many places, how the sorrows were numerous, the reason for the sorrow, and the sorrow's inconsolability. Therefore, he says, **A voice in Rama**. Rama is a certain city in the tribe of Benjamin (Josue 18), and can be taken for the city of Lia. Here, however, it is taken for a place on high; and it can be explained in two ways. Firstly, it is as follows: **A voice** brought forth on high **was heard**, because a voice that is in a high place goes far and wide; "Get thee up upon a high mountain, thou that bringest good tidings to Sion: lift up thy voice with strength" (Is 40, 9). Or "it was heard on high" means in heaven before God; "The prayer of him that humbleth himself shall pierce the clouds: and till it come nigh he will not be comforted: and he will not depart till the most High behold" (Eccli. 35, 21). And again, "Do not the widow's tears run down the cheek, and her cry against him that causeth them to fall?" (ibid., verse 18). **Lamentation**; this can be referred to the crying of the infants killed. **And great mourning**; this can be referred to the mothers' lamentation; or both can be referred to the children: there was **lamentation** because the soldiers lifted them up; there was **mourning** because their throats were cut. The grief of the mothers was greater than the multitude of the children. Moreover, the mothers' grief was continually present, but the children's was brief.

---

12. i.e. a little more than 11 miles away
13. So Rachel died, and was buried in the highway that leadeth to Ephrata, this is Bethlehem" (Gen. 35:19).

On account of which it says in Zacharias 12, 10, "They shall mourn for him as one mourneth for an only son, and they shall grieve over him, as the manner is to grieve for the death of the firstborn." Likewise, he expands upon the reason for the sorrow, namely, the death of the children. Whence, Rachel weeps.

But it is objected that Bethlehem was not in the tribe of Benjamin, but in the tribe of Juda, who was the son of Lia.

And this is solved in three ways. Firstly, it can be answered that Rachel was buried near Bethlehem (Gen. 35, 15). And so she wept for her children in that way by which some place is said to weep; "Be astonished, O ye heavens at this, and ye gates thereof, be ye desolate, saith the Lord" (Jer. 2, 12). Or it may be solved otherwise. It was related above that Herod killed the children in Bethlehem and in the entire surrounding regions, etc. But Bethlehem was in the frontier of two tribes, namely, of Juda and of Benjamin; whence, those who were killed were of the tribe of Benjamin: and thus the objection ceases, as Jerome expounds. Augustine, however, explains this differently, and says that it is usual that when some favorable things succeed for someone, he, when adversities come, grieves more. Now Lia and Rachel were sisters, and those who were killed were Lia's children. And thus they were killed bodily, lest they be punished eternally, as in the event at Gabaa.[14] Therefore, it is said she wept from seeing her own children killed and damned. Or, by Rachel, the Church is signified, because Rachel means 'seeing God,' and the Church sees by faith. The Church weeps for her children, not because they were killed, but because through them she could have acquired other children.[15] Or she does not weep for those killed, but for those killing.

The inconsolability of the sorrow follows: *And she would not be comforted.* This phrase can be explained in multiple ways. Firstly, it can be explained as referring to the people who lived at that time. For comfort ought to be present as long as some remedy can be expected. But when one cannot be expected, there is no comfort, as is evident in the hopelessly sick; and thus, he says, as referring to the belief of the mothers, *Because they are not*, because, in fact, they do not appear; "The boy doth not appear" (Gen. 37, 30). Or, *she would not be comforted, because they are not*, meaning as though they were not. For comfort is not due except for evils. Whence, according to this view, this phrase refers to the Church's belief, which maintains that they are reigning in heaven. Whence,

---

14. cf. Judges 20.
15. Other children, presumably, who would see God.

she rejoices concerning them as ones reigning; "And we will not have you ignorant brethren, concerning them that are asleep, that you be not sorrowful, even as others who have no hope" (I Thess. 4, 12). Or, **she would not be comforted** about the present, but she expects comfort in the future; "Blessed are they that mourn: for they shall be comforted" (below 5, 5).

Afterwards, is treated about the recalling of Christ; whence, **But when Herod was dead, behold an angel of the Lord appeared in sleep to Joseph.** And firstly, the angel's apparition is set forth; secondly, the angel's command; and thirdly, the execution of the angel's command. About the first, three things are related. Firstly, the time is described; secondly, the person is described; and thirdly, the manner of the apparition is described. He says, therefore, **Herod was dead**: he is not the same Herod, who lived at the time of Christ's death, for that Herod was that Herod's son. **Behold an angel appeared.**

It should be observed that every disturbance of the Church, according to a mystery, is ended by the persecutors' death; because "when the wicked perish there shall be praise" (Prov. 11, 10). Note, likewise, that when the Jews' infidelity is finished, Christ will return to us. "And so all Israel shall be saved" (Rom. 11, 26).

Behold he appeared. It is to be observed that such is the ordination of angels and men that divine illuminations do not happen to us except through angels; "They are all ministering spirits, sent to minister for them, who shall receive the inheritance of salvation" (Heb. 1, 14). Whence, also Christ, as man, willed to be heralded by angels. The manner is where it is said, **in sleep to Joseph in Egypt.** The command is where it is said, **Arise and take the child.** He does not say, "son," nor "wife," but **the child**, in order that the Child's dignity and the mother's virginal integrity might be indicated. In this is signified that Joseph was not given to her for carnal intercourse, but for service and guardianship. Afterwards, he gives the reason for the command, **For they are dead that sought the life of the child.**

But it may be asked, why does he say, **they are**? For only Herod was dead.

This is solved in two ways. Firstly, it was because he had done so many evil deeds that the Jews were rejoicing over his death. He, foreseeing this, commanded his sister, while he was still living, that she would kill the more noble men of the Jews at his own death; and these men had sought the Child's life with Herod; and so it reads, **they are dead that sought the life of the child.** Or it can be solved otherwise. It is the custom of Sacred Scripture to use the plural for the singular; whence, *they are dead*, means he is dead, etc. Note that from the passage, *that sought the soul of the child*,[16] Apollinarius' error is destroyed, who said that the divinity was in Christ in place of His soul.

The execution of this command is related, *Who arose and took the child and his mother*; and regarding this, the Evangelist does three things. Firstly, he shows how Joseph returned into the land of Israel; secondly, he shows what part he avoided; and thirdly, he shows in what part he dwelt, where it is said, *And being warned in sleep, retired into the quarters of Galilee.* He says, therefore, *Who arose*. It should be observed that the angel did not say, "Go into the land of Juda," or "Into Jerusalem," but generally, *Into the land of Israel*, in which designation Galilee can also be understood. Whence, it can be said that Joseph entered the borders of the land where Juda dwelt. Afterwards, it is told which area he avoided, where it is said, *But hearing that Archelaus reigned in Juda.*

And at this point, the history of Herod should be noted; this Herod had six sons and, before his death, he killed Alexander and Aristobolus.[17] But soon, before his own death, he commanded that Antipater be killed. Whence, three remained, among which Archelaus was the firstborn, and he acquired the kingdom for himself; but at length, having been accused by the Jews before Caesar Augustus, his kingdom was taken away from him and it was divided into four parts. Archelaus had two, and the two other parts other men divided unto themselves, so that Herod Antipas had one tetrarchy, and Philip had another, as is stated in Luke 3. This Archelaus was sent into exile after nine years of his reign.[18]

---

16. *Animus* in Latin means "life" or "soul."

17. "JOSEPHUS; Herod had nine wives, by seven of whom he had a numerous issue. By Josida, his first born Antipater - by Mariamine, Alexander and Aristobulus - by Mathuca, a Samaritan woman, Archelaus - by Cleopatra of Jerusalem, Herod, who was afterwards tetrarch, and Philip. The three first were put to death by Herod, and after his death Archelaus seized the throne by occasion of his father's will, and the question of the succession was carried before Augustus Caesar. After some delay, he made a distribution of the whole of Herod's dominions in accordance with the Senate's advice. To Archelaus he assigned one half, consisting of Idumea and Judea, with the title of tetrarch, and a promise of that of king if he showed himself deserving of it. The rest he divided into two tetrarchates, giving Galilee to Herod the tetrarch, Ituraea and Trachonitis to Philip. Thus Archelaus was after his father's death a duarch, which kind of sovereignty is here called a kingdom" (*Catena Aurea on St. Matthew*, chap. 2, lect. 11).

18. Archelaus was succeeded by Herod Agrippa I, who was made king by the emperor Caius. (See Jos. vi 18. Antiq. a. viii and L xix. a. 5). It was Agrippa who put to death St. James the greater, brother to St. John. Agrippa was also brother to the famous Herodias, who was the cause of St. John the Baptist's decollation, and grandson of Herod the Great, by his father Aristobulus. His son, Herod Agrippa II judged St. Paul (Acts. 25, 26).

And being warned in sleep. The angel had firstly said that he should go into the land of Israel; but because Joseph had not yet understood, therefore the angel, who before has revealed indeterminately, now does so determinately; and this is expressed, *And being warned... retired into the quarters of Galilee.*

But there is an objection. Just as Archelaus was reigning in Judea, so Herod was reigning in Galilee. But one must say that this was immediately after Herod's death, when Archelaus possessed the whole kingdom, because the division was made afterwards.

But then it is also inquired, why did he not fear Archelaus? The answer is that the seat of the kingdom was in Jerusalem; whence, he was almost always residing there.

But it is inquired, why is it said in Luke 2, 41, that every year they were bringing the Child to Jerusalem? And Augustine resolves the question saying that they were safely bringing Him with a large crowd that was going up at that time; but He would have been danger if He had stayed there a long time.

Likewise, it is asked, why did the Evangelist intimate that Joseph came to Nazareth almost unexpectedly, but in Luke 2, 39, it is said that he had his own house in Nazareth? But the answer is that the angel had said to him that he go into the land of Israel, which, taken strictly, did not include Galilee, nor Nazareth; and in this way did Joseph understand the angel's words; and, therefore, he was not planning to go to Nazareth.

That it might be fulfilled which was said by the prophets: That he shall be called a Nazarene. This is not found written, but it can be said that it is gathered from many places. Accordingly, the word Nazarene is interpreted 'saint,' and Christ is called the Saint; "Until the saint may be anointed" (Dan. 9, 24); thus it is distinctly said, *By the prophet.* Or it can be said that by *Nazarene* is meant 'flowery'; and this meaning is used in Isaias 11, 1: "And there shall come forth a rod out of the root of Jesse, and a flower shall rise out of his root," etc.; and this agrees with that which is said in Canticles 2, 1: "I am the flower of the field, and the lily of the valleys."

CHAPTER THREE

1. And in those days cometh John the Baptist preaching in the desert of Judea.
2. And saying: Do penance: for the kingdom of heaven is at hand.
3. For this is he that was spoken of by Isaias the prophet, saying: A voice of one crying in the desert, Prepare ye the way of the Lord, make straight his paths.
4. And the same John had his garment of camel's hair, and a leathern girdle about his loins: and his meat was locusts and wild honey.
5. Then went out to him Jerusalem and all Judea, and all the country about Jordan:
6. And were baptized by him in the Jordan, confessing their sins.
7. And seeing many of the Pharisees and Sadducees coming to his baptism, he said to them: Ye brood of vipers, who hath shewed you to flee from the wrath to come?
8. Bring forth therefore fruit worthy of penance.
9. And think not to say within yourselves, We have Abraham for our father. For I tell you that God is able of these stones to raise up children to Abraham.
10. For now the axe is laid to the root of the trees. Every tree therefore that doth not yield good fruit, shall be cut down, and cast into the fire.
11. I indeed baptize you in water unto penance, but he that shall come after me, is mightier than I, whose shoes I am not worthy to bear: he shall baptize you in the Holy Ghost and fire.
12. Whose fan is in his hand, and he will thoroughly cleanse his floor and gather his wheat into the barn; but the chaff he will burn with unquenchable fire.

Above, the Evangelist treated about Christ's entrance into the world; now, however, he treats of the course of His life, which is, in fact, considered according to the spreading of His teaching; for unto this He came (Jn. 18, 37).[1] Now, in reference to His teaching, two things are observed. For firstly, the preparation for His teaching is related; secondly, the teaching itself is related (chap. 5). Now two things are required for a teacher of Gospel-teaching. Firstly, it is required that he be robed with sacred mysteries,

---

[1] "For this came I into the world; that I should give testimony to the truth."

and secondly, that he be tested in his virtues. And so, two things precede His teaching, namely, His baptism and His temptation (chap. 4). Regarding the first, he does two things. Firstly, John's baptism is presented, where it is said, **Went out to him Jerusalem**; secondly, the instruction of those baptized, where it is said, **And seeing many**. John invited them in two ways, namely, by word and by example. The latter is where it is said, **And the same John had his garment of camel's hair**, etc. Regarding John's teaching, he does or mentions three things: Firstly, the person of the teacher is presented; secondly, the doctrine is related; and thirdly, the confirmation is related. The second is where it is said, **Do penance**; and the third is where it is said, **For this is he that was spoken of**. Regarding the person, five things are related, namely, the time, the person himself, his ministry, his life's purpose, and the place. The first is where it is said, **In those days**, etc. And this ought not to be referred to the days about which mention has been made, namely, the days of Christ's infancy; for it is not to be understood that this happened during the days in which Christ returned from Egypt. But this is so-stated because Christ continually dwelt in Nazareth after He returned from Egypt; "And the child grew, and waxed strong, full of wisdom; and the grace of God was in him" (Lk. 2, 40). Secondly, the person is presented, where it is said, **Cometh John**; he cometh, that is, he appeared, who firstly had been hidden; he is the man of whom it is said, "This man came for a witness, to give testimony of the light" (Jn. 1, 7).

But why did Christ want his testimony when He would have the testimony of His own works?

The answer is that this was on account of three things. Firstly, on account of us, who are brought to the knowledge of spiritual things through things which are familiar to us; "This man came for a witness, to give testimony to the light" (Jn. 1,7). But why did he give testimony to the light? "That all men might believe through him" (ibid). Secondly, this was on account of the Jews' malice, because Christ was not alone giving testimony to Himself, according to that which they were saying; "Thou givest testimony of thyself" (Jn. 8,13). But also, another person gave testimony to Him; "You sent to John, and he gave testimony to the truth" (Jn. 5, 33). Finally, this was to show the equality of Christ to the Father, because as the Father had forerunners, namely, the prophets, so Christ would also have the same. "And thou, child, shalt be called the prophet of the Highest for thou shalt go before the face of the Lord to prepare his ways" (Lk. 1, 76).

Thirdly, his ministry of baptizing is related. This was his special ministry, he was the first who baptized, and his baptism was preparatory for Christ's baptism: because if Christ had enjoined a new rite, men might have been immediately scandalized. And so John came before in order that he might prepare men for baptism; "That he may be made manifest in Israel" (Jn. 1, 31). Fourthly, his life's purpose is related, for *he cometh* to preach diligently, and so it is said, *Preaching baptism*. Christ indeed was about to baptize and enjoined it to be done, "Go, teach ye all nations; baptizing them in the name of the Father, and of the Son, and of the Holy Ghost" (below 28, 19). John, however, prepared the way for both Christ's and the Apostles' baptizing.

And observe that John was thirty years old when he did this, at which age David was made king and Joseph received the rule of the kingdom of Egypt.[2] By which it is given to be understood that one ought not to be elevated to any ministry before the perfect age.

Fifthly, the place is presented. *In the desert*. Now he preached in the desert for four reasons. Firstly, he was in the desert so that men might listen to him more tranquilly. For in the city many curious men were impeding his discourses, but in the desert only zealous men were going out to hear him. "The words of the wise are as goads, and as nails deeply fastened in, which by the counsel of masters are given from one shepherd" (Eccli. 12, 11). Secondly, he was in the desert because it was in accord with his preaching, for he was preaching penance. Now a place of penance ought to be suchlike, either corporeally or mentally;[3] "Lo, I have gone far off flying away; and I abode in the wilderness" (Ps. 54, 8). Thirdly, this was to show the condition of the Church, which is signified by the desert. For it is given to be understood that the preaching of salvation is not in the synagogue but in the Church. "Give praise, O thou barren, that bearest not sing forth praise, and make a joyful noise, thou that didst not travail with child for many are the children of the desolate more than of her that hath a husband, saith the Lord" (Is. 54,1). Fourthly, this was to designate the condition of the Jews, who were already being abandoned by God; "Behold, your house shall be left to you desolate" (below 23, 38).

He continues, *Do penance*, etc. John announces a certain new life, as Augustine says in his book *De Poenitentia*, "No man who has the use of free-will, can begin the new life, unless he firstly re-

---

[2]. "Now [Joseph] was thirty years old when he stood before king Pharao, and he went round all the countries of Egypt" (Gen. 41, 46).

[3]. "The religious state is a most fitting place for penance" (II II, q. 186, a. 1 ad 4um).

pent of his former life."[4] See the Gloss. And thus, he firstly advises penance; and secondly, he announces salvation, where it is said, *For the kingdom of heaven is at hand.* Likewise, *Do penance*, by which is the remission of sin. Chrysostom says, "Once the Son of God was born, God sent His herald into the world."

And observe that it is one thing to do penance and another to repent. A man repents who weeps for his sins, and by weeping does not commit them again. And know that the whole matter refers to the mind's resolution, so that it might be truly said, 'And by weeping he does not commit them,' that is to say, he resolves not to commit them, for repentance requires this. To do penance however means to satisfy for one's sins; "Bring forth fruits worthy of penance" (Lk. 3, 8).

And here a question arises. Since all sins are forgiven in baptism, why does John, when foretelling Christ's baptism, begin with penance?

And it is answered in the Gloss, that penance is threefold, namely, before baptism, because one ought to have sorrow for one's sins when one approaches the sacrament; secondly, after baptism, one ought to have sorrow for mortal sins; and thirdly, one ought to have sorrow for venial sins. Here is treated about the penance, which is after baptism; whence, Peter said, "Do penance" (Acts 2, 38), namely, that you may be able to attain salvation.

Is at hand. And observe that the promised kingdom of heaven is nowhere found in the books of the Old Testament; but John is the first to announce it, which pertains to his dignity. Now the kingdom of heaven, in Sacred Scripture, can be understood in four different ways. For, sometimes, this is said as meaning Christ Himself dwelling in us by grace; "The kingdom of God is within you" (Lk. 17, 21). And this is said to be the kingdom of God because, by the indwelling of grace, the way to the heavenly kingdom is begun in us. Secondly, it sometimes means Sacred Scripture; "The kingdom of God shall be taken from you" (below 21, 43), that is to say, Sacred Scripture. And Scripture is said to be a kingdom because its law leads to a kingdom. Thirdly, it sometimes means the Church militant on earth; "The kingdom of heaven is like to a net cast into the sea, and gathering together of all kind of fishes," etc., (below 13, 47). And this is called the kingdom of heaven because it was founded to be like the heav-

---

4. "Every man who has the use of free-will, when he approachs the sacraments of the faithful, cannot begin the new life unless he repent of the old. Only infants when they are baptized are exempt from this kind of repentance; for they cannot yet use free will." (Sermon 351).

enly Church. Fourthly, the heavenly court is sometimes called the kingdom of heaven; "They shall come from the east and the west, and shall sit down with Abraham, and Isaac, and Jacob in the kingdom of heaven" (below 8, 11). Before John's time, however, the kingdom of heaven was not mentioned, but only the kingdom of the Jebusites;[5] but now the kingdom of heaven is promised to His Church. Afterwards, the confirmation of this preaching is related, *This is he that was spoken of by Isaias the prophet*, etc. And, as Augustine says, this passage can be explained in two ways. Firstly, the words of the Evangelist could be rephrased, 'This is he who was written about'; and then the meaning is clearer. Secondly, Matthew inserts this statement, as being the words of John, discoursing on penance. Whence, *This is he*, that is to say, 'I am he.' And so he speaks of himself as being a different person, just as in John 1 the author speaks of himself as being a different person; but though the words do not indicate this meaning, they have the same sense. *For this is he of whom it was written*, "The voice of one crying in the desert: Prepare ye the way of the Lord, make straight in the wilderness the paths of our God" (Is. 40, 3). Three things are set forth, by which the three things preached are confirmed. Firstly, the place of John's preaching is confirmed, because it reads, *The voice of one crying in the desert*; secondly, the coming of the kingdom of heaven is confirmed; whence, it reads, *Prepare ye the way*; thirdly, penitence is confirmed, where it is said, *Make straight his paths*.

He says, therefore, *A voice of one crying in the desert*. And he says, *A voice*, for three reasons. Firstly, it is because, as Gregory says, "The voice precedes the word and John precedes Christ." "He shall go before him in the spirit and power of Elias" (Lk. 1,17). Secondly, it is because through the voice the word is known; so John makes Christ known; "That he may be made manifest in Israel, therefore am I come baptizing with water" (Jn. 1, 31). Thirdly, it is because a voice without a word does not give certitude of the mind; "For if the trumpet give an uncertain sound, who shall prepare himself to the battle?" (I Cor. 14, 8). And the revelation of divine mysteries was not made through John except so far as he announced Christ, and through Christ the word was revealed; "The only begotten Son who is in the bosom of the Father, he hath declared him"

---

5. The Jebusites were the former inhabitants of Jerusalem, which was anciently inhabited by the Jebusites. "And I have said the word to bring you forth out of the affliction of Egypt, into the land of the Chanaanite, and Hethite, and Amorrhite, and Pherezite, and Hevite, and Jebusite, to a land that floweth with milk and honey" (Ex. 3, 17).

(Jn. 1, 18). As was said above, *a voice of one crying*; and this can be understood in two ways. Firstly, it can be understood of the crying of Christ, who was speaking in John; "Do you seek a proof of Christ that speaketh in me?" (II Cor. 13, 3). In like manner, He cried in all the prophets. Whence, it is always said, "The word of the Lord came to Jeremias," or "The word of the Lord came to Isaias," etc. And, nevertheless, none of these are called a voice, because they did not immediately precede Christ; "Behold I send my angel, and he shall prepare the way before my face. And presently the Lord, whom you seek, and the angel of the testament, whom you desire" (Mal. 3, 1). Or, *a voice crying*, is referring to John shouting. One ought to know that shouting is made to the deaf, and such were the Jews; "Hear, ye deaf, and, ye blind, behold that you may see. Who is blind, but he to whom I have sent my messengers?" (Is. 42, 18). Secondly, shouting is made out of indignation; "The Lord was exceedingly angry with his people: and he abhorred his inheritance" (Ps. 105, 40). Thirdly, shouting is made to those far away, and these people were withdrawn from God.

Prepare ye the way of the Lord. And it seems it would have been more suitable that he would have said, 'Prepare your way' for receiving the Lord. And it ought to be known that we were so weak, that we could not have drawn near to the Lord, unless He came to us. And thus John said above, "The kingdom of God is at hand": and so it is said, **Prepare ye.** But what is this way? It is faith, which is by hearing; "That Christ may dwell by faith in your hearts" (Eph. 3, 17). Gregory says, "Faith's way is devout hearing"; "Be prepared to meet thy God, O Israel" (Amos 4, 12).

Make straight. Faith is universal, and so it is one; but it directs diverse works. And thus he says, **make straight.** Now, ways of these works are straight, only when they are not out of harmony with the divine law, which is the measure of all human acts, just as the measure of the goodness of a clay vessel is according to the potter's purpose, as can be gathered from Jer. 18. Or this saying, namely, **prepare ye**, pertains to charity, which is necessary for salvation: "This is the way, walk in it: and go not aside neither to the right hand, nor to the left" (Is. 30, 21). Therefore, by **the way** is understood all that which pertains to salvation in general; "I will show unto you yet a more excellent way" (I Cor. 12, 31). But the paths are the observances of the counsels: which paths are said to be straight, because they ought not to be made out of vainglory. "Do not your justice before men, to be seen by them" (below 6, 1); "Her ways are beautiful ways, and all her paths are peaceable" (Prov. 3, 17).

Afterwards is shown how John bore witness to Christ by his life, where it is said, *And the same John.* But who bore witness to John, who now bears witness to Christ? And the answer is that his life bore witness to himself. This is because, as Chrysostom says, no one is a worthy witness of another, unless he is his own witness, and this is by a good life. "The attire of the body, and the laughter of the teeth, and the gait of the man, show what he is" (Eccli. 19, 27).

Whence, here is described his austerity in his life and food: and the passage is, *And he was clothed with camel's hair*, etc. Other men had garments of wool, but John of hair. For he reckoned a woolen garment to be a luxury, which is not fitting for a preacher. Likewise, *a leathern girdle.* That can be explained in two ways. Jerome says that at that time the Jews used to wear a belt of wool; but John, reckoning this to be a luxury, made his belt out of skins in imitation of Elias; as is said in IV Kings 1. Rabanus explains it otherwise, and he says that John was wearing raw skins, not treated, and was using them to refrain concupiscence: and so it is said, *And a girdle.* Whether it be explained in one way or the other, in both ways, nevertheless, the austerity of his life is understood. *And his meat was locusts and wild honey.* This food was not prepared, but was what nature was providing; and there are certain species of locusts fit for eating. *And wild honey.* This can be understood in two ways. For, properly, that honey, which is said to be wild, is not found in man-made beehives, but in the forests, in some trees. And others say that it is sugar cane and the kind of "honey" which is found inside of the reed is very sweet. Nevertheless, in all these explanations, nothing else is surmised except that he was content with simple things; "Having food, and wherewith to be covered, with these we are content" (Tim. 6, 8).

Afterwards, it is treated about his baptism, whence, it is said, *Then went out*: and three things are mentioned. Firstly, it is said how the crowds were visiting him; secondly, how the crowds were baptized; and thirdly, how they were confessing their sins. And regarding the first, it ought to be known that there were three things that were drawing men to go out to John. Firstly, his preaching was new, in that they had never heard mention be made concerning the kingdom of heaven; "Dost thou know the order of heaven, and canst thou set down the reason thereof on the earth?" (Job 38, 33). John was the first to teach that the concept of the kingdom of heaven was not to be understood as being primarily based upon earth. Secondly, they were invited by his manner of life; whence, he says, *Then went out*, namely, those seeing his life; "Show me thy faith without works; and I will show thee, by works, my faith," etc., (James 2, 18). Thirdly, they were drawn to go out because Judea was deprived of the instruction of the Prophets; "Our signs we have not seen, there is now no prophet" (Ps. 73, 9). And thus, *they were going out* from Judea to see; and the passage is, *Then they were going out, and were baptized by him in the Jordan.*

But why was he baptizing in the Jordan? It was because baptism was firstly prefigured in the Jordan in IV Kings 2, where it is said that Eliseus passed over the Jordan, and Elias was taken up into heaven. Again, it was there that Naaman the leper was cleansed, which signifies the cleansing from sins in baptism. Likewise, it is because its very meaning is in accord with baptism; for 'Jordan' means 'descent'; and it signifies the humility which a man ought to have in baptism; "As newborn babes, desire the rational milk without guile" (I Pet. 2, 2).

The third point regarding his baptism is related where he says, *Confessing their sins.* The reason why confession was introduced was given above, namely, that it is necessary for salvation; "Confess your sins one to another" (James 5, 16). And the Gloss says that it was introduced so that man might have shame. But it ought to be known that shame is an incidental reason, but the main reason why confession was introduced is on account of the power of the keys. For no one could bind or loosen unless he knew what were to be bound or loosened. Whence, just as no one can eliminate the necessity of the keys, so also no one could eliminate vocal confession.

But it is asked, whether one approaching baptism is bound to confess. It seems that he would not need the power of the keys, since all sins are forgiven in baptism.

But it is to be answered that one is held to confess at least in general; and one does this when he renounces Satan, and all his pomps. For in doing this, a man declares he was under the dominion of Satan.

And seeing many. After having indicated that John was baptizing many, here he treats of their instruction; and, regarding this, he does two things. Firstly, it is related who they are who may be instructed; and secondly, their instruction is related, where he says, *Who hath showed you to flee from the wrath to come?* Therefore, he says, *And seeing many of the Pharisees and Sadducees.* It ought to be known that among the Jews there are some sects, and among them, these were the principal ones. Now a Pharisee is one who is set apart, as it were, from common life, on account of his observances. These men were speaking well on many points; nevertheless, they were erring in that, as it is said, they maintained that everything happens out of necessity. Other men, namely, the Sadducees, were saying that they were just men on account of certain special observances of the Law. These same men were not receiving the Prophets, nor were they affirming that after the corruption of the body the soul would be raised again, nor the existence of anything spiritual. And both sects were being identified by the very names, because 'Phares' means 'division,' which is opposed to charity. And these men were completely separated from other men, as if they were to have a superabundance of the Holy Ghost. For this would be something good. Others also, namely, the Sadducees, were usurping justice for themselves; against whom it is written: "For they, not knowing the justice of God, and seeking to establish their own, have not submitted themselves to the justice of God" (Rom. 10, 3). And even though they appeared to be more just, they were coming to John as to a teacher; "Kings shall see, and princes shall rise up, and adore, for the Lord's sake, because he is faithful, and for the holy One of Israel, who hath chosen thee" (Is 49, 7). Therefore, these men were here being fittingly instructed; whence, it is said, **Who hath showed you to flee from the wrath to come?** And observe, that instruction ought to be varied according to the condition of the hearers. For it suffices to speak briefly about those things which pertain to salvation to simple men; but the detailed points ought to be explained to the wise; the Apostle intimates this, "And I could not speak to you as unto spiritual, but as to carnal" (I Cor. 3, 1). John acted in this manner. He briefly admonished the crowds concerning penance, and he proclaimed the kingdom of heaven. He explained each of these two things to the Pharisees. Whence, he firstly exhorts to penance; and secondly, he announced the drawing near of the kingdom of heaven, where it is said, *I indeed baptize you*, etc. In regard to the first, he does two things. Firstly, he gives an incentive for doing penance; and secondly, he removes those things that might withdraw a man from doing penance, where it is said, **And do not think to say within yourselves, We have Abraham for our father**. Regarding the first, he does two things. Firstly, he gives the incentive for doing penance; and secondly, he sets forth the manner of doing perfect penance, where it is said, **Bring forth therefore fruit worthy of penance**. Now there are two things that incline one to do penance: the consideration of one's own sins, "Show my people their wicked doings" (Is. 58, 1). The second is the fear of divine judgment. John proclaimed these two things. Whence, he says, **Ye brood of vipers**.

And note that a man is said to be the son of him whom he imitates. "Your father an Amorrite" (Ez. 16, 45). "You are of your father the devil, and the desires of your father you will do" (Jn. 8, 44). These men were similar to vipers, and so he says, **Ye brood of vipers.**[6] And they are like vipers in three ways, according to Chrysostom. For its nature is to hasten back to water when it poisons someone; and if it finds it, it does not die, otherwise it dies. Whence, John, considering their intention, why they were coming to the water of baptism, said, **Ye brood of vipers.** But why were those who were poisoned coming for baptism? It was because John was promising them the remission of their sins. Hence, he was making those laying aside their evil will to enter the water, and so he says, **Do penance.** And he was baptizing them. A second, natural, characteristic of a viper is that by being born it kills its parents; whence, it is said, as it were, "giving birth violently"; and these men do likewise; "Which of the prophets have you not killed?" (Acts, 7, 52). The third reason is because a viper is beautiful exteriorly, but interiorly having venom: these men also are exteriorly beautiful, having simulated a certain justice, but interiorly having sins. "Woe to you scribes and Pharisees, hypocrites; because you are like to whited sepulchres, which outwardly appear to men beautiful, but within are full of dead men's bones, and of all filthiness" (below 23, 27). And according to this, **brood of vipers** stands for something evil. Ambrose explains this otherwise, and he says that prudence is ascribed to serpents; "Be ye wise as serpents" (below 10, 16). Whence, John commending them for their prudence, because they were coming for baptism, says, **Ye brood of vipers.** The first thing, therefore, that leads one to do penance is the consideration of one's own sins; the second is fear of the divine judgment; "By the fear of the Lord every one declineth from evil" (Prov. 15, 27); "Know ye that there is a judgment" (Job 19, 29). And this is just what he says, **Who hath showed you to flee from the wrath to come?** And it is to be known that Ambrose and Chrysostom explain this as referring to past events, but Rabanus explains it as referring to future events; whence, he says, "Who will show you?" And according to Ambrose it is thus, **Ye brood of vipers, who hath showed you to flee from the wrath to come?** as if he were to say: no one, except God. "Show us, O Lord, thy mercy; and grant us thy salvation" (Ps. 84, 8). According to Chrysostom, it is thus, **Ye brood of vipers** is said because they retain their willingness

6. Or 'offspring of vipers.'

to sin, and *who hath showed you to flee*, when you will such as you do? Not so, because Isaias said "Wash yourselves, be clean, take away the evil of your devices from my eyes" (Is. 1, 16). Not so, because David said: "Wash me yet more from my iniquity, and cleanse me from my sin" (Psalm 50, 4); and afterwards it continues, "A sacrifice to God is an afflicted spirit: a contrite and humbled heart, O God, thou wilt not despise" (Ps. 50, 19). Rabanus explains this of the future, thus; it is as if he were to say, 'It is good that you would do penance, because otherwise, *who will show you?* "Whither shall I go from thy spirit? or whither shall I flee from thy face?" (Ps. 138, 7). Anger, for God, is not to be taken to mean a mood of the mind, but rather as standing for its effect: whence, His anger is revenge.

After having given two reasons for doing penance, the Evangelist afterwards concludes, *Bring forth therefore fruit worthy of penance*. Now in a tree the fruits come after the flowers: and if the flowers are not followed by fruits, then that tree is good for nothing. For the flower of penance indeed appears in contrition, but the fruit of penance is in its execution. "My flowers are the fruit of honor and riches" (Eccli. 24, 23).

And note that one is the fruit of justice and another is that of penance: for more is required of a penitent than of one who has not sinned. Now there are three fruits worthy of penance. The first is that one punish himself for that which one has committed, and this is done according to the judgment of a priest. "For after thou didst convert me, I did penance: and after thou didst shew unto me, I struck my thigh" (Jer. 31, 19). That is, 'I afflicted my flesh.' The second is that one flee from sins and the occasions of sin; hence, it is said that one is said to satisfy if one cuts off the causes of sin; "My son, hast thou sinned? Do so no more: but for thy former sins pray that they may be forgiven thee... as from the face of a serpent" (Eccli. 21, 1). The third is that one strive as much to do well as one had striven to sin; "I speak an human thing, because of the infirmity of your flesh. For as you have yielded your members to serve uncleanness and iniquity, unto iniquity: so now yield your members to serve justice, unto sanctification" (Rom. 6, 19).

Afterwards, he removes the obstacles to doing penance, when he says, *And think not to say within yourselves, We have Abraham*. There are two obstacles to doing penance: presumption regarding oneself, and despair of a divine judgment. Initially, he removes the first; and next, he removes the second, where it is said, *For now the axe is laid to the root of the trees*.

Firstly, he proscribes the impediment; and secondly, he gives the explanation, where it is said, *For I tell you*. He says, therefore, *And think not to say within yourselves, We have Abraham for our father*. These men were descendants of Abraham according to the flesh. Whence, they could think that however much they might sin, God would be merciful to them for the sake of Abraham; "Why, O Lord, is thy indignation enkindled?"(Ex.23, 11) and afterwards it is said, "Remember Abraham, Isaac, and Israel, thy servants." And so John proscribes this, *And think not to say*. And such is a manner of speaking, as though he were to say, 'You should not say this, because it will not be of no avail to you.' "Not they that are the children of the flesh are the children of God: but they that are the children of the promise are accounted for the seed," etc., (Rom. 9, 8). For these men were glorifying very much in being children of Abraham, but the Lord says, "If you be the children of Abraham, do the works of Abraham" (John 8, 39). Against such persons, Chrysostom says, "What does an illustrious parentage avail him whom morals defile?" And this is also true in spiritual affairs. Afterwards, he gives the explanation, *For I tell you* (for it is greater to imitate a father than to be born of him): *God is able of these stones to raise up children to Abraham*. It is read in Josue 4, that when the people of Israel passed over the Jordan without getting their feet wet, in memory of the miracle Josue commanded that twelve stones be drawn from the bottom of the river and be placed on the edge of the river and twelve stones from the edge of the river be put into the river. Now, when John was baptizing in that place, he pointed to these rocks.[7] Now this can be understood in two ways. Firstly, it can be understood in regard to its literal sense, for the first foundation of faith is to believe in the omnipotence of God; "I know that thou canst do all things, and no thought is hid from thee" (Job 42, 2). Or we can understand of the rocks to be the Gentiles, who are called 'rocks' for two reasons. The first is that they adore rocks, and the second is on account of their hardness. Although rocks are hard, nevertheless, they retain an impression for a long time: and although a building made out of them is built slowly, nevertheless, it is strong and durable. Whence, the Gentiles, although they were hard to receiving the faith of Christ, nevertheless, they held it strongly. This is signified in Ezechiel 36, 26: "I will take

---

7. "REMIG. There is a tradition, that John preached at that place of the Jordan, where the twelve stones taken from the bed of the river had been set up by command of God. He might then be pointing to these, when he said, Of these stones" (*Catena Aurea on St. Matthew*, chap. 3, lect. 4).

away the stony heart out of your flesh, and will give you a heart of flesh, and I will put my spirit in the midst of you." But, according to St. Jerome, these words seem to recall to mind the prophecy in Isaias 51, 2, "Look unto Abraham your father, and to Sara that bore you," etc. For he calls Abraham a rock on account of his impotency in generating, and Sarah, likewise, because of her sterility; as though he were to say, 'God who made Abraham potent and Sarah fecund, *is able of these stones to raise up children to Abraham.*'

For now the axe is laid to the root of the trees. For they might be able to say, 'We do not believe that any punishment will come upon us.' And so he removes this impediment, saying, *For now.* Hence, he sets forth the judgment, and secondly, he sets forth the sentence of the judgment. He says, therefore, *For now,* etc. For some men refuse to repent for two reasons. The first arises from despair of a judgment, because they do not believe there will be a judgment; "Say not I have enough to live on" (Eccli. 5, 1); "Flee then from the face of the sword, for the sword is the revenger of iniquities: and know ye that there is a judgment" (Job 19, 29). Others, however, refuse to repent from the delay of the judgment; "The Lord delayeth not his promise, as some imagine, but dealeth patiently for your sake, not willing that any should perish, but that all should return to penance" (II Pet. 3, 9). But John proscribes both errors. Firstly, he proscribes the first error when he says, *For now the axe,* and secondly, he proscribes the second error when he says, *Is laid*; as if he were to say, "It will not delay." And this can be understood in three ways. Chrysostom says that by the axe is understood the strictness of divine judgment, which sometimes is designated by an axe, sometimes by a bow, and sometimes by a sword; "Except you will be converted, he will brandish his sword; he hath bent his bow, and made it ready" (Ps. 7, 13). St. Jerome says, "By the axe is understood the preaching of the Gospel, because, by the teaching of the Gospel, some are led to life, and, similarly, scorners are led to death. "Are not my words as a fire, saith the Lord: and as a hammer that breaketh the rock in pieces?" (Jer. 23, 29). "Behold this child is set for the fall and for the resurrection of many in Israel and for a sign which shall be contradicted" (Lk. 2, 34); as if he were to say, "It is ready to come." According to Gregory, by the axe our Redeemer is understood, which, as it were, by its handle and blade, corresponds to His humanity and divinity; the humanity of whom patiently waits, as though it were held: the divinity, as though it were a blade, cuts. Therefore, the axe is laid to the root because judgment occurs by God and man. And he says, *to the root*, for two reasons, because a universal cutting off occurs at the root, even of that part which is in the branches. Again, that which is cut at the root does not germinate; it is as though he were to say, 'There will be universal uprooting of evils.' He continues accordingly; and he firstly relates the universality, saying, *Every tree*; as though he were to say, 'Both the Jews and the Gentiles'; "There is no respect of persons with God" (Rom. 2, 11). Likewise, he relates the guilt that it does not bear fruit, for a punishment occurs due to a mere omission; "For I was hungry and you gave me not to eat" (below 25, 42). Thirdly, he relates the double punishment: namely, a temporal one, *Shall be cut down*, that is to say, out of this life; "Behold, for these three years I come seeking fruit on this fig tree and I find none. Cut it down therefore" (Luke 13, 7). And afterwards, "Why cumbereth it the ground?" And this is to say, *Shall be cut down*, with its earthly prosperity. Moreover, he relates the eternal punishment, hence, it is said, *shall be cast into the fire*; "Their worm shall not die, and their fire shall not be quenched" (Is. 66, 24); and, "Depart from me, you cursed, into everlasting fire" (below 25, 41). *I indeed baptize*. Above John exhorted to fully perform penance, now he endeavors to do what he frequently had said he would do, namely, announce the kingdom of heaven: and about this he does two things. Firstly, the preparation for the kingdom is set forth; and secondly, it is treated about the foretelling of the kingdom, where it is said, *But he that shall come after me*. That kingdom is Christ, of whom it is said, "The kingdom of God is within you" (Lk. 17, 21). The preparation is indeed baptism; whence, *I indeed*, which is startling to you, *baptize* in water only, that is to say, because I am simply a man. Whence, he could only wash the body and could not give the Holy Ghost, since the price for sin had not yet been paid; "for without shedding of blood there is no remission" (Heb. 9, 22). Moreover, the Holy Ghost had not yet descended, nor had Christ yet sanctified the water by touch of His flesh. Why then was he baptizing? This was for three reasons. Firstly, he was baptizing to prepare for Christ; "Thou shalt go before the face of the Lord to prepare His ways" (Lk. 1, 76). Secondly, he was baptizing in order that, having gathered men together, he might have an opportunity of preaching about Christ; "That he may be made manifest in Israel, therefore am I come baptizing with water" (Jn. 1, 31). Thirdly, he was baptizing to prepare for Christ's baptism. Whence, it is the custom in the Church that those who are to be baptized firstly become catechumens, that is to say, that there be some preparation that they may show some indication, by which they are deemed worthy: and this is what he says, *I baptize*, namely, in order that you may know that you are well disposed, you who intend to be baptized by Christ.

Note that the Master[8] in his *Sentences, Book IV* says that those baptized by John were not baptized by Christ, except those who were placing hope in John. But this is false; hence, John says, *He shall baptize you.*

Again note that Augustine raises a question. If they were rebaptized after John's baptism, why are they not rebaptized after the baptism of heretics?

It ought to be stated that John was baptizing in his own person; heretics baptize in the person of Christ; hence, it is reckoned to be Christ's baptism.

Afterwards, it is treated about the kingdom. And firstly, he shows its dignity; and secondly, he shows its function, where it is said, *He shall baptize you.* He says, therefore, *He that comes after me*, by being born, by baptizing, by preaching, by dying, and by descending into hell. But here he only speaks about two things, namely, about preaching and baptism; whence, he says, *He that comes after me*, to baptize and to teach; "He shall go before him in the spirit and power of Elias" (Lk. 1, 17). *He is mightier than I*, and His baptism is stronger; "There is none strong like our God" (I Kings 2, 2); "If strength be demanded, he is most strong"(Job 9, 19). And lest it be so- believed that there is a resemblance between them, he says, *Whose shoes I am not worthy to bear*; as though he were to say, 'He is incomparably more worthy than me,' as Chrysostom expounds, 'such that I ought not render him a ministration.'

But it ought to be known that in the other three Gospels it is not thus: because there it said, "loose," but here it is said, *bear*. Whence, Augustine says that John willed to show how great was his lowliness and Christ's excellence, and then the same meaning is expressed in all the Gospels. Hence, he says this was by the inspiration of the Holy Ghost, that in such matters the Evangelists disagree in words, so that we may accept the teaching, because we do not lie if we express the same meaning as others do, although we do not say the same words. But if he intended to indicate something mystical, then there is a difference in the words of Matthew and the others: and so two things can be signified in the latchet of the shoe, because by the shoe

---

8. Peter Lombard.

humanity is signified; "Into Edom will I stretch out my shoe" (Ps. 59, 10). The latchet is the union by which the humanity is joined to the divinity. And because he was not considering himself to be competent to explaining the mystery of the union, thus he says, ***Whose shoes I am not worthy to bear.*** Or there was a custom among the Jews (Deut. 25), that if someone refused to take his own brother's wife, his shoe ought to be loosed from him by the one who would take the wife. Christ's spouse is the Church. Consequently, therefore, John was considering himself to be unworthy to take Christ's spouse. Or according to Hilary it is otherwise: the proclaimers of Christ's humanity throughout the world truly carry the shoe, which privilege was reserved to the Apostles; "How beautiful upon the mountains are the feet of him that bringeth good tidings, and that preacheth peace: of him that sheweth forth good, that preacheth salvation" (Is. 52, 9). Therefore, John says that he himself is not worthy to carry the shoe that was reserved to the Apostles: for it is a greater ministry to preach than to baptize; "Christ sent me not to baptize, but to preach the gospel" (I Cor. 1, 17).

Were the Apostles, therefore, greater than John was? Not by merit, but by ministry of the New Testament. And according to this sense it is said below, "He that is the lesser in the kingdom of heaven is greater than he" (below 11, 11).

Or it is otherwise, according to Chrysostom. The feet are the Apostles, and his other servants, among whom was John. The shoe is their infirmity: because as the beauty of the feet is not known as long as they are covered by a shoe, so the beauty of the Apostles likewise; "Gladly will I glory in my infirmities, that the power of Christ may dwell in me" (II Cor. 12, 9). ***Whose shoes I am not worthy to bear***: this is said because neither he nor the Apostles considered themselves to be worthy to be ministers of Christ's Gospel; "And such confidence we have, through Christ, towards God. Not that we are sufficient to think any thing of ourselves, as of ourselves: but our sufficiency is from God" (II Cor. 3,4).

If, therefore, these two expressions[9] signify different things according to the mystic sense, which of these did John say?

I answer, saying, according to Augustine, that if John's words refer to diverse things, then he said both. Or it can be answered that John, preaching to the crowds, sometimes said one thing and sometimes another.

---

9. i.e. 'to bear' and 'to loose.'

Afterwards, he treats about Christ's ministry. And firstly, he treats about His ministry of baptizing; and secondly, he treats of His ministry of judging, where it is said, *Whose fan is in his hand.* He says, therefore, *He shall baptize you in the Holy Ghost and fire.* Many manuscripts have 'and fire.'[10] But these are written according to the custom of the Greeks who lack the ablative case. And he says, *Holy Ghost and fire*: in which it is given to be understood that Christ's baptism produces more than John's baptism, because it adds to it that Christ is in the water and the spirit; "Unless a man be born again of water and the Holy Ghost, he cannot enter into the kingdom of God" (Jn. 3, 5).

But note that, when he says, that *He shall baptize you in the Holy Ghost*, he insinuates that there has to be an abundance of the Holy Ghost, which completely washes those possessing it; "you shall be baptized with the Holy Ghost" (Acts 1, 5). He also insinuates an easy transformation.[11]

And fire. This phrase is explained in many different ways. Jerome says that the same thing is designated by the Holy Ghost and fire; "I am come to cast fire on the earth. And what will I, but that it be kindled?" (Lk. 12, 49) that is to say, the Holy Ghost. And thus he also appeared in the form of fire; "And there appeared to them parted tongues, as it were of fire" (Acts 2, 3). According to Chrysostom, fire signifies the present tribulation, which purges sins; "The furnace trieth the potter's vessels, and the trial of affliction just men" (Eccli. 27, 6). But one ought to know that he says this baptism is necessary, because the baptism of the Holy Ghost includes the goal of not being overcome by temptations; but it does not take away the sprouts of the flesh: and so tribulation is necessary, because, only when the flesh has been worn down, will it not sprout concupiscence. Or by fire is understood the future purgation in Purgatory; "The fire shall try every man's work, of what sort it is" (I Cor. 3, 13). Hilary, however, explains this of this fire of hell, and says that the Evangelist asserts two things when he says, *He shall baptize you in the Holy Ghost and fire*, namely, the welfare which it effects in the present time and in the future. In the future, it will purify by the fire of hell, insofar as it will attract evil men; and this agrees with that which follows, *But the chaff he will burn with unquenchable fire.*

Afterwards, it is treated of his judiciary power, *Whose fan is in his hand.* And so firstly, he touches upon His judiciary

---

10. *Et ignis* meaning, 'and fire,' instead of *Et ingi* meaning 'and (in) fire' as in the Vulgate.
11. Of becoming a son of God.

power, secondly, the effect of the judgment, and thirdly, the manner of judgment. He says, therefore, **Whose fan,** and he uses a similitude. The threshing floor is the Church; the grains are the faithful, who will be gathered by the angels; "Pray ye therefore the Lord of the harvest that he send laborers into his harvest" (Lk. 10, 2); "Who sent me, that I may perfect his work" (Jn. 4, 34). The fan is Christ's judiciary power, which distinguishes the wheat from the chaff; "The Father gave all judgment to the Son" (Jn. 5, 27); "It is he who was appointed by God to be judge of the living and of the dead" (Acts 10, 42). **Will thoroughly cleanse,** that is to say, He will cleanse perfectly. Firstly, He will cleanse by tribulations that are, as it were, a kind of wind, which if it were not present, the chaff would be mixed with the wheat. In this way also, the good are not distinguished from the wicked as long as they remain in the Church. And just as the fine chaff are driven away by a light wind and the coarse chaff by a strong wind, so also those who seem to be staunch in the Church fall if tribulation increases; "They believe for a while and in time of temptation they fall away" (Lk. 8, 13). Secondly, He cleanses through the judgments of the prelates, namely, when they are excommunicated; "Put away the evil one from among yourselves" (I Cor. 5,13). Thirdly, He will cleanse on judgment day, when the good will be separated from the wicked; **He will gather into the barn,** namely, paradise, **his wheat,** that is to say, his elect; "Save us, O Lord, our God: and gather us from among the nations" (Ps. 105, 47). **But the chaff he will burn.** And note the difference between the chaff and the cockle: for one is the seed of the chaff and another of the cockle, because the seed of the chaff is identical with wheat. Hence, by the cockle we can perceive the schismatics, who do not communicate with us in the sacraments; by the chaff, we can perceive the faithful, albeit the wicked ones. But both will be burned with fire. **Unquenchable fire;** "Their fire shall not be quenched" (Is 66, 24); and he says, **Unquenchable,** to differentiate the fire of Purgatory. Concerning this unquenchable fire, he says below, "Depart, you cursed, into everlasting fire," etc., (25, 41).

13. Then cometh Jesus from Galilee to the Jordan, unto John, to be baptized by him.
14. But John stayed him, saying: I ought to be baptized by thee, and comest thou to me?
15. And Jesus answering, said to him: Suffer it to be so now. For so it becometh us to fulfill all justice. Then he suffered him.

**16. And Jesus being baptized, forthwith came out of the water: and lo, the heavens were opened to him: and he saw the Spirit of God descending as a dove, and coming upon him.
17. And behold a voice from heaven saying: This is my beloved Son, in whom I am well pleased.**

Above, the Evangelist introduced John baptizing; now he introduces Christ coming to John's baptism: and regarding this, he does two things. Firstly, he sets forth those things which preceded baptism; and secondly, the consequences of baptism, where it is said, **And Jesus being baptized**. Regarding the first, he relates four things: firstly, Christ's humility; secondly, John's admiration of His humility; thirdly, Christ's giving satisfaction to his admiration; and fourthly, John consents to this satisfaction. The second is where he says, **But John stayed him**; the third is where he says, **And Jesus answering**; and the fourth is where he says, **Then he suffered him**. Concerning the first, four things are related: the time, the persons, the places, and the ministry. He relates the time, where he says, **Then**, namely, when John had his own light. For just as the sun rises when the morning star still appears, so Christ comes when John is preaching and baptizing (Lk. 1). "Canst thou bring forth the day star in its time, and make the evening star to rise upon the ends of the earth?" (Job 38, 32). Or, **then** was when Christ was in His thirtieth year (Lk. 3), in order to indicate that a man ought not to take up the ministry of preaching and of governing before the perfect age. Or, **then** was when He could have committed many sins in that course of time as other men had done. Hence, He did not want to be baptized immediately, but instead, observed the Law for a long time, as though he were subject to the Law, and, moreover, in order that the Jews would not have a cause of scandal, for he did not "come to destroy the law" (below, chap. 5). But it might seem to someone that Christ had abolished the Law because He could not fulfill the Law; and for that reason he was not quickly baptized. The persons are related, where it is said, **Jesus cometh unto John**, the Lord to the servant, and the Creator to the creature; "Learn of me, because I am meek, and humble of heart" (below 11, 29). Then the places are related, firstly by the words, **From Galilee**. These words mystically accord with those who have been baptized, because Galilee signifies 'a passing': for those who have been baptized ought to pass from vices to virtues; "Wherefore laying away all malice and all guile and dissimulations and envies and all detractions" (I Pet.

2, 1). Likewise, he says, **To the Jordan**. *Jordan* is interpreted 'a descent' and signifies humility, which ought to be present in the one being baptized in order that he receive grace; "God giveth grace to the humble" (James 4, 6). The ministry is related, where he says, **To be baptized**. God willed to be baptized by John for four reasons. Firstly, this was so that John's baptism would be retained, because some men were detracting it (below chap. 21).[12] Secondly, this was so that He might consecrate all water by His touch; and thus baptism is said to be performed from the fountains of the Savior; "Thou shall draw waters with joy out of the saviour's fountains" (Is. 12, 3). Thirdly, this was so that He might illustrate in Himself the condition of man, because as He was in the likeness of sinful flesh (Rom. 8, 3), so He willed to be cleansed as though He were a sinner. Fourthly, this was so that He might impose upon others the obligation of being baptized: for He wished to observe beforehand what He imposed; "Jesus began to do and to teach" (Acts 1, 1), contrary to those of whom it is said below, "For they bind heavy and insupportable burdens and lay them on men's shoulders: but with a finger of their own they will not move them" (23, 41). Afterwards, the admiration is related.

And note three things. For firstly, John refuses the honor offered to him; secondly, he confesses his lowliness; and thirdly, he confesses his feebleness. The second is where he says, **But John stayed him**; "Seek not of the Lord a preeminence, nor of the king the seat of honour" (Eccli. 7,4). The third is where he says, **I ought to be baptized by thee**. For he knew that He would baptize interiorly; and therefore he says, **to be baptized**, that is, to be cleansed from original sin: so says the Gloss.

But it was on the contrary, for he was sanctified in the womb. But I answer, saying that, before the coming of Christ, some men were cleansed in a certain way so far as concerns the stain of the person through circumcision and suchlike; but so far as concerns the guilt and stain of the whole race, no one was cleansed before Christ's Passion.

And comest thou to me? "Thy knowledge is become wonderful to me: it is high, and I cannot reach to it" (Ps. 138, 6). Afterwards, Christ's giving satisfaction is related. Note that John had done one thing, in that he was staying Him; and he had said two things: **I ought to be baptized by thee, and comest thou to me?** And, nevertheless, Christ does not respond to the one,

---

12. "The baptism of John, whence was it? From heaven or from men? ... And answering, they said: We know not" (verses 25 & 27)

namely, *I by thee*; but He responds to this that he was staying Him; hence, He says, *Suffer it to be so now*. And He says now, because according to Chrysostom, John was afterwards baptized by Christ, not only with the baptism of desire, but also of water. Or, *Suffer it to be so now*, that I be baptized with the baptism of water, because I have to be baptized with another baptism, namely, with the baptism of the Passion; "And I have a baptism wherewith I am to be baptized. And how am I straitened until it be accomplished?" (Lk. 12,50) And John was also baptized by this baptism, insofar as he died for justice, which is the same as to die for Christ. Or, *Suffer it to be so now*, when I take a servile form, to allow me a role of humility: because when I will appear glorious, then I will baptize you with the baptism of glory. Afterwards, Christ responds to John's admiration, and says, *For so it becometh us to fulfill all justice*. This is explained in three ways. Firstly, *For so it becometh us to fulfill all justice* is explained by baptism: for it was to be that Christ would fulfill all justice, both of the Law and of nature; but He willed to fulfill it in this way, because without baptism it would not be fulfilled; "Unless a man be born again, he cannot see the kingdom of God" (Jn. 3, 3). Remigius expounds *For so it becometh us to fulfill all justice* as follows: 'It behooves me to give an example of receiving this sacrament, in which the plentitude of all justice is given, because the fullness of grace and of the other virtues is given'; "The river of God is filled with water" (Ps. 64,10), that is to say, of graces. Or it is thus: *For so it becometh*, etc., that is, it becometh me to possess perfect humility. The first degree is not to prefer oneself to an equal, and to subject oneself to one who is greater, which indeed is necessary. The second is when one subjects oneself to an equal. Perfect humility, however, is when a superior subjects himself to an inferior: and thus it is said, *For so it becometh*, etc., that is, to fulfill perfect humility. But although there was such an altercation between them, Christ triumphed: hence, *Then he suffered him*, etc., that is, Christ permitted that He would be baptized by him. The Gloss reads, "It is true humility which does not relinquish obedience: for to resist pertinaciously, is a sign of pride." It is "like the crime of idolatry, to refuse to obey" (I Kings 15, 23): for thus Jeremias and Moses are praised because they at length consented.[13]

Afterwards, four consequences of His baptism are related when he says, *And Jesus being baptized, forthwith came out*

---

13. To be sent by God on their missions.

of the water. And know that just as Christ gave an example of being baptized to others, so also in the consequences of His baptism He gave to be understood what we may affect. Now, there are four consequences, namely, Christ's rising, the opening of heaven, the Holy Ghost's apparition, and the Father's bearing witness. The first is where it is said, *And Jesus being baptized, forthwith came out of the water.* And with regard to the literal sense, he says this because the river was containing deep channels. Nevertheless, by this is signified that they who are baptized rise by good works. And he says, *forthwith*, because those who are baptized immediately put on Christ; "For as many of you as have been baptized in Christ have put on Christ" (Gal. 3, 27). Again, they acquire a heavenly inheritance; "He hath regenerated us unto a lively hope, by the resurrection of Jesus Christ from the dead unto an incorruptible inheritance" (I Pet. 1,3): in other words, *The heavens were opened.* This is not to be understood corporeally, but as an imaginary vision. *The heavens were opened to him.* And this signifies that heaven had been closed to the human race by sin; "And he placed before the paradise of pleasure Cherubims, and a flaming sword, turning every way, to keep the way of the tree of life" (Gen. 3, 24). It is said that He stationed Cherubim,[14] but it was also opened by Christ.

But it is inquired: Why were the heavens opened to Him, since they were always open to Him?

And I answer, saying that, according to Chrysostom, the Evangelist speaks according to the common manner of speech, because, by the merit of His baptism, the heavens were opened to us: it is just as a king says to his friend asking a favor, "I grant this to you."

And one ought to know that there are three kinds of men who immediately fly to heaven after death: the baptized, as shown here; martyrs; hence, "Behold, I see the heavens opened and the Son of man standing on the right hand of God" (Acts 7, 55); and those who have completely performed penance; in Acts 10, 19 it is said that "When Peter was praying heaven was opened" (Acts 10, 11).

Afterwards, the apparition of the Holy Ghost is related; hence: *And he saw the Spirit of God descending as a dove, and coming upon him.* And this befits those who are baptized, who receive the Holy Ghost in themselves; "That which is born of the Spirit is spirit" (Jn. 3, 6), that is to say, he is spiritual. *And*

---

14. The text erroneously has 'Seraphim' for 'Cherubim.' cf. Gen. 3, 24.

he saw, not by an imaginary vision; otherwise he alone would have seen *the Spirit of God*, that is, a dove. And one ought to know that nothing corporeal can be attributed to God according to His substance, but instead it can be attributed to God by an imaginary vision; "I saw the Lord sitting upon a throne high and elevated" (Is. 6, 1); or by signification; "And the rock was Christ" (I Cor. 10, 4); or by assumption unto the unity of a person; "And the Word was made flesh" (Jn. 1, 14). In none of these ways, however, is the Holy Ghost said to be the dove. It is clear that it was not an imaginary vision because it was commonly seen by all. It was not by signification because it had not previously existed. It was not by assumption unto the unity of a person. And thus, there is a fourth way, which is when some outward appearance is newly formed for the representation of divine effects, just as in Exodus 3, 2, when the Lord appeared in the burning bush; and, likewise, He appeared at the time of the framing of the Law in the lightning and thunder (Ex. 19). Hence, the dove existed to represent the influence of the Holy Ghost: and the passage is, *And he saw the Spirit of God descending*. Now He appeared in the form of a dove for four reasons. Firstly, this was on account of its charity; for it is a loving animal. Chrysostom says: "A servant of the devil possesses other gifts in a falsely assumed appearance, which gifts the servant of God possesses in truth: only the charity of the Holy Ghost can the unclean spirit not imitate." "Open to me, my sister, my love, my dove, my undefiled" (Cant. 5, 2). Secondly, this was on account of its innocence and simplicity: "Be ye wise as serpents and simple as doves" (below 10, 16). Thirdly, this was because it has a mourning for its singing; and the man sanctified by the Holy Ghost ought to mourn for his sins; "And her bondwomen were led away mourning as doves" (Nahum 2, 7). Fourthly, this was on account of its fecundity. Whence, it was also commanded in the Law that they offer a dove: and this is suitable for the baptized, because, as He says in John 3, 6: "That which is born of the Spirit is spirit."[15] The emanation of divine gifts in whatsoever creature from God is always by a descent, because a creature cannot receive them except through a condescension unto it; "Every best gift and every perfect gift is from above, coming down from the Father of lights" (James 1, 17). *And coming upon him.*

Note this. A visible mission is always a sign of an invisible mission: and it signifies either newly received grace or an in-

---

15. The Holy Ghost is fruitful by giving a share of Himself to men.

crease of grace: as when the Holy Ghost appeared in the tongues, it signified an increase of grace in the Apostles. Likewise, such a mission either signifies grace bestowed at that time or previously bestowed. And so in Christ it did not signify a new effect, because from the moment of His conception He was full of grace and truth; moreover, the grace which was previously conferred upon Him was possessed insofar as He is a man, not insofar as He is God.

Afterwards, when he says, **And behold a voice from heaven saying**, the Father's bearing witness is related, **This is my beloved Son**. Note that Baptism not only makes men spiritual, but even sons of God; "He gave them power to be made the sons of God" (Jn. 1, 12). And know that this voice, in a way, expresses that which the dove signified. He is **beloved**, not as other creatures (Wis. 2), but as His natural Son: "For the Father loveth the Son and sheweth him all things which himself doth: and greater works than these will he shew him, that you may wonder" (Jn. 5, 20). "The Lord hath said to me: Thou art my son, this day have I begotten thee" (Ps. 2, 7). But because holy men are also loved by Him, He adds, **Son**, by which He distinguishes His Son, according to one meaning, from the others. **In whom I am well pleased**. For in whatever the good of someone shines forth, in that is a thing pleasing to oneself; just as a worker is well pleased in the beauty of his own work, or just as if a man were to see his own beautiful appearance in a mirror. The Divine goodness is in every single creature; but it is never completely perfect except in the Son and the Holy Ghost; and thus the whole world does not please Him, save in the Son, who possesses as much goodness as the Father: and so the phrase is, **In whom**, that is, I am well pleased in Him; "The Father loveth the Son: and he hath given all things into his hand" (Jn. 3, 35).

But note that there seems to be a contradiction between this Evangelist and other Evangelists, because Mark (Chap. 1) and Luke (Chap. 3) say, "Thou art my beloved Son"; but Matthew says, **This is my beloved Son**: and "In thee."[16] But the meaning is the same, because what is said is, "Thou art"; and this was being perceived to be said to Christ; but it was said for the sake of others, because Christ was sure of His Father's love. And thus Matthew expresses the intention of the one speaking, and he says, **This is**, etc. Hence, he presents the phrase as if it were said to others; so Augustine stated.

---

16. cf. "Thou art my beloved Son. In thee I am well pleased" (Lk. 3, 22).

Likewise, it is sought why Matthew and Mark say, *In whom I am*, but Luke says, "In thee." Augustine says that the Father pleases Himself in the Son and in men. Therefore, on account of this it is said, *In whom*, and it signifies that in men He is well pleased. Hence, 'He is pleased with others for My sake,' that is, for My honor, because some seeing the Son have glorified the Father. Or, according to both meanings: *In whom I am well pleased*, that is, 'My pleasure was to accomplish the salvation of men': and this is expressed, "In thee," that is to say, through thee.

And note that in this baptism, not only the purpose and the fruit are represented, but also the form of baptism, which is, "in the name of the Father and of the Son and of the Holy Ghost," etc., (below 28, 19). For the Son was in the flesh, the Father in the voice, and the Holy Ghost in the form of a dove. And note that the fact that they were separated does not pertain to a division of operations of the Persons of the Trinity, since just as there is a common essence, so there is a common operation; but this is related on account of a certain appropriation, because the entire Trinity created the voice, dove, and flesh; but these things are referred to diverse Persons.

CHAPTER FOUR

1. Then Jesus was led by the spirit into the desert, to be tempted by the devil.
2. And when he had fasted forty days and forty nights, afterwards he was hungry.
3. And the tempter coming said to him: If thou be the Son of God, command that these stones be made bread.
4. Who answered and said: It is written, Not in bread alone doth man live, but in every word that proceedeth from the mouth of God.
5. Then the devil took him up into the holy city, and set him upon the pinnacle of the temple,
6. And said to him: If thou be the Son of God, cast thyself down, for it is written: That he hath given his angels charge over thee, and in their hands shall they bear thee up, lest perhaps thou dash thy foot against a stone.
7. Jesus said to him: It is written again: Thou shalt not tempt the Lord thy God.
8. Again the devil took him up into a very high mountain, and shewed him all the kingdoms of the world, and the glory of them,
9. And said to him: All these will I give thee, if falling down thou wilt adore me.
10. Then Jesus saith to him: Begone, Satan: for it is written: The Lord thy God shalt thou adore, and him only shalt thou serve.
11. Then the devil left him; and behold angels came and ministered to him.

It was shown above that Christ prepared Himself for teaching by receiving baptism; now, however, He prepares Himself by overcoming temptation. About this the Evangelist does two things. Firstly, the victory, which Christ had over temptation, is set forth; secondly, how He called His disciples to hear the teaching is set forth, where it is said, **And Jesus walking by the sea of Galilee**. Concerning the first he does three things. Firstly, he premises a sort of preamble about the temptation; secondly, the assault of the temptation is related, where it is said, **And the tempter coming said**; and thirdly, Christ's victory over temptation is related, where it is said, **Then the devil left him**. Now three preambles are set forth, namely, the place, His fasting, and His experience of hunger. Regarding the first preamble, four points are touched upon: the time, the place, the leader, and the purpose of this leading. The time is indicated when he says, **Then**, namely, after it had been declared by the voice of the Father that He was the Son of God. In this he gives to be understood that temptation menaces those who are made sons of God by baptism; "Son, when thou comest to the service of God, stand in justice and in fear, and prepare thy soul for temptation" (Eccli. 2, 1). This desert was between Jerusalem and Jericho, where many were being killed, about which it is said, "A certain man went down from Jerusalem to Jericho and fell among robbers, who also stripped him and having wounded him went away, leaving him half dead" (Lk. 10, 30).

And note the five reasons why someone is tempted after having received a spiritual grace. The first is so that he may receive a trial of his own justice; "What doth he know, that hath not been tried?" (Eccli. 34, 9). Secondly, it is to repress pride; "And lest the greatness of the revelations should exalt me, there was given me a sting of my flesh, an angel of Satan, to buffet me" (II Cor. 12, 7). Thirdly, it is to confound the devil, that he may know how great is Christ's power, so that he may not be able to take pride. An example of this is had in Job 1, 8: "Hast thou considered my servant, Job?" Fourthly, it is so that one may be made stronger, just as soldiers are made stronger though exercise; "Why did He chose to leave the enemy with the children of Israel?" (Judges 3).[1] Fifthly, it is so that someone may know his own dignity: because when the devil approaches someone, he bestows an honor, for the devil approaches Saints; "His food is grass... and he trusteth that the Jordan may run into his mouth" (Job 40, 10).

The passage continues concerning the place, **Then Jesus was led into the desert**. This agrees with the events that preceded and with the events that follow: because it was fitting that after His baptism He would enter the desert. This is signified in the Israelite people, who after crossing the Red Sea, which was a figure of Baptism, came into the promised land through a desert and wilderness: so the baptized ought to seek a solitary and quiet life, by leaving the world with their body or with their mind; "I will lead her into the wilderness: and I will speak to her heart" (Osee 2, 14). "Lo, I have gone far off flying away; and I abode in the wilderness" (Ps. 54, 8). For it was fitting that He would go out into the desert, as if to a single-combat with the devil. Chrysostom says: "He goes out into the desert, who goes out beyond the intentions (that is the

---

1. This is not a direct quotation but it is understood from the context of Judges 3. The Lord chose to leave the Gentiles in the midst of Israel that they might by strengthened by their continual combats.

will) of the flesh and the world, where there is no place for temptation. For how is one tempted concerning lust, who is the whole day with his wife?" But those who do not go out from the will of the flesh and the world, are not sons of God, but sons of the devil, who even having their own wife, desire another; but the sons of God, possessing the Holy Ghost, are led into the desert in order to be tempted with Christ, concerning whom it follows: **He was led by the spirit**, and take this to mean the Holy Ghost.

But he who leads is greater than he who is led. Therefore, the Holy Ghost seems to be greater than Christ.

It is to be replied: If this be referred to Jesus insofar as He is the Son of God, in this way He is equal to the Holy Ghost: and someone can lead another either by a command, and then he is greater: or by exhortation, and then he is equal; Andrew led Peter to Jesus by exhortation (Jn. 1); and in such a way was Jesus led. Hilary refers this to Christ insofar as He is a man: namely, the Holy Ghost exposed the man whom He had filled to temptation. For men are then led by the Holy Ghost, when they are moved by charity, such that they are not moved by their own initiative, but by another, because they follow the impulse of charity; "The charity of God presseth us" (II Cor. 5, 14). And the sons of God are driven by the Holy Ghost so that they may pass through the time of this life, which is full of temptations ("The life of man upon earth is a temptation" Job 7, 1), with victory through Christ's power. For He willed to be tempted so that, just as by His death He conquered ours, so by His temptation He might overcome all our temptations; "We have not a high priest who cannot have compassion on our infirmities: but one tempted in all things like as we are, without sin" (Heb. 4, 15). Gregory says that there are three stages of temptation, namely, by suggestion, pleasure and consent. The first is from without, and can be without sin; the second is from within, in which it begins to be a sin, and which indeed is completed by consent. The first stage could have been in Christ, but not the others. And observe that the devil had not dared approach to tempt Christ, until Christ had firstly approached him.

Afterwards, the second preamble is set forth, namely, the fasting, **And when he had fasted**, etc., which agrees with the preceding and future events: it agrees with the preceding, because a man fittingly fasts after Baptism. Since after Baptism one ought not to spend time in idleness, but to exercise oneself in good works; "For you, brethren, have been called unto liberty" (Gal. 5, 13); true liberty, however, is not to be used for a carnal life. Likewise, it agrees with the future events, in that He would fast, whom the devil was about to tempt, because "This kind is not cast out but by prayer and fasting" (below 17, 20). *Forty days.* This is to be understood literally. And he adds, *And nights*, lest some might believe that it might be allowed to eat at night, as the Saracens do. And it ought to be known that this number is prefigured in the Old Testament by Moses and Elias (Ex. 24 & III Kings 19). A mystery lies hidden in this number, because such a number arises from ten multiplied by four. Ten signifies the Law, because the entire Law is contained in ten precepts. Four signifies the composition of the flesh, because the flesh is composed out of the four elements. Therefore, because we transgress the Divine law through the suggestion of the flesh, it is just that we afflict our flesh for forty days. According to Gregory, however, this number was established by the Church, because by this number we pay tithes of the whole year: for from the first Sunday[2] to Easter there are thirty-six fasting days, which are a tenth part of the year itself, six days excepted. And for this reason a half-day[3] was added by certain persons, who were fasting until midnight of Holy Saturday.

A third preamble is added, for the Evangelist says, *Afterwards he was hungry*. This is not read of Moses and Elias (i.e. that they were hungry), although they were men; but Christ chose to hunger, in order to demonstrate His humanity; because otherwise the devil would not have dared to tempt Him; "Being made in the likeness of men, and in habit found as a man" (Phil. 2, 7). Afterwards, the devil's assault is set forth; and it is threefold. The first is of gluttony; the second is of vainglory; and the third is of ambition. The second is where it is said, *Then the devil took him up into the holy city*. The third is where it is said, *Again the devil took him up into a very high mountain*. About the first, he does two things. Firstly, he sets forth the devil's assault; and secondly, how Christ responds, where it is said, *Who answered*, etc. *And the tempter coming said.* This certainly could have been brought about, inasmuch as he might approach to Jesus in some corporeal form. And temptation is threefold, because God tempts in order to instruct, "God tempted Abraham" (Gen. 22, 1). Sometimes a man tempts in order to add knowledge, just as the queen of Saba tempted Solomon (III Kings, 10, 1), where it is said of her, "And the queen of Saba having heard of the fame of Solomon in the name of the Lord, came to try him with hard questions." And the devil tempts in order to deceive; "Lest perhaps he

---
   2. He is referring to the first Sunday of Lent.
   3. A half-day was added to the thirty-six to be one tenth of the three hundred sixty-five days of the year.

that tempteth should have tempted you" (I Thess. 3, 5). Whoever wills to tempt on account of knowledge, firstly tempts about common things. Now among the common vices of the entire human race is especially gluttony. Likewise, he who wishes to besiege a fortress begins from the weaker side; now a man has two sides, carnal and spiritual. The devil always tempts from the weaker side; hence, he firstly tempts regarding carnal vices, as is clear in the first parent, whom he firstly tempted regarding gluttony. His astonishing craftiness in tempting ought to be noted, *If thou be the Son of God*: for in this way he directly tempted regarding one thing, although obliquely regarding another. Whence, he was persuading the first man to eat from the tree, which directly pertains to a carnal sin, namely, gluttony; but he was hiddenly inducing to pride and avarice, which are spiritual sins; whence, he said, "And you shall be as Gods" (Gen. 3, 5). He was persuading Christ in the same way; for he had heard that Christ was to come into the world, and this man seemed to be the Son of God; but he had fallen into doubt whether this man was He about whom it had been prophesied, because he was perceiving nothing in Him;[4] "For the prince of this world cometh, and in me he hath not anything" (Jn. 14, 30). Hence, he was suggesting what is delightful to a hungry man. Likewise, he was inducing him to desire those things that belong to God; and the passage is: *If thou be the Son of God, command that these stones be made bread.* "His word is full of power" (Eccle. 8, 4); "By the word of the Lord the heavens were established; and all the power of them by the spirit of his mouth" (Ps. 34, 6). And so a rock could be changed by His word. Therefore, the devil wanted to influence Christ to do this, so that if He performed this, the devil would know that He is the Son of God; if not, he was inclining Him to arrogance. And one should note there are many men who consent to carnal sins, thinking that they would not lose the spiritual life. But if a man, consenting in this thing towards which he is tempted, were not to lose his spiritual life, then the temptation was light. Just as the devil willed to tempt the woman, he also did to Christ, promising spiritual things. *Who answered and said: It is written, Not in bread alone doth man live.* In this response, He gives three instructions which ought to be followed by the one who has been tempted. Firstly, that one ought to have recourse to the medicine of Scripture; "Thy words have I hidden in my heart, that I may not sin against thee" (Ps. 118, 11). Hence, He said, *It is written.*

---

4. That is, nothing extraordinary in him yet.

The second instruction is that man ought to do nothing at the devil's choice. Vegetius[5] said, "A wise leader ought to do nothing at the choice of his enemy, even if it seem to be good." And thus, although the Lord would have been able to change the rocks into bread without sin, He was not willing to do so because the devil was suggesting it. The third is that one ought not to do anything without utility, and for the display of one's power, because this is vanity. *Who answered and said: It is written, Not in bread alone doth man live.* It ought to be observed that the devil was trying to do two things. Firstly, he was trying to induce an inclination to carnal things, and also to presumption. Christ, however, being opposed to both, firstly avoids boasting; it is as though He were to say, 'You call me the Son of God, I name Myself a man'; whence, *Not in bread alone doth man live.* Likewise, the devil motivates a desire for carnal things, *Command that these stones be made bread*; Christ motivates Himself to desire spiritual things, *But in every word that proceedeth from the mouth of God*; it is as though He were to say, 'Corporeal life is not to be desired as much as spiritual life, which is preserved by spiritual food'; *But in every word that proceedeth from the mouth of God.* "Lord, to whom shall we go? Thou hast the words of eternal life" (Jn. 6, 69); "Thy justifications I will never forget: for by them thou hast given me life" (Ps. 118, 93). And He says, *In every word*, because all spiritual doctrine is from God, whether it is said by man or by God. And again, *From the mouth*; because the preacher is a mouth of God; "If thou wilt separate the precious from the vile, thou shalt be as my mouth" (Jer. 15, 19). Or it is otherwise. *Not in bread alone*, that is, man does not only live by bread, but also by God's word, that is, by His command, can a man be preserved without food. *Then the devil took him up into the holy city.* Having set forth the first temptation, in regard to which the devil was conquered; now the second is set forth, namely, in regard to vainglory. And the order is fitting, in that, after the devil saw himself conquered in regard to carnal vice, he tempted in regard to vainglory or pride: because as St. Augustine says in his rule, "Pride lies in wait for good works, so that they may perish." Therefore, regarding this temptation, the Evangelist does three things. Firstly, the place of the temptation is related; secondly, the assault, or the attempt of temptation is related, where it is said, *If thou be the Son of God, cast thyself*

---

5. Flavius Renatus Vegetius was an author who wrote *de re Militari*, in the latter part of the fourth century.

down; and thirdly, Christ's resistance, where it is said, ***Jesus said to him***. But it ought to be known that Luke relates the third temptation in reverse order from what is given here;[6] but there is no difference in meaning, according to Augustine: for everything which is narrated here is also narrated in Luke nor is it related in Luke either that this was the first or the second temptation. But Rabanus says that Luke observes the order of history; and thus he ordered the account according to which it happened. On the other hand, Matthew followed the nature of the temptations, because after the temptation of gluttony and of vainglory follows the temptation of ambition: for thus was Adam tempted, since firstly he was tempted regarding gluttony, whence: "In what day soever thou shalt eat of it, thou shalt die the death" (Gen. 2, 17); secondly, regarding glory: "You shall be as Gods" (Gen. 3, 5); and thirdly, regarding avarice or ambition, "Knowing good and evil."

But why does he say, ***Then he took him up***? For the word, taking, implies violence.

And Jerome replies that the Evangelist says this in accordance with the devil's opinion, for what Christ virtuously permitted the devil to do, the devil assumed that he did by his own power.

He says ***holy*** place, either because holy things were done there, namely, temporal sacrifices and suchlike, or he says this on account of the holiness of their Fathers who were there. Hence, from an old custom he calls the place holy, although it ceased to be such; "How is the faithful city, that was full of judgment, become a harlot?" (Is. 1, 21) But afterwards he says, "Thou shalt be called the city of the just, a faithful city," etc.

But it ought to be known that in Mark 1, 13, it is said, "He was in the desert forty days and forty nights, and was tempted by Satan." From this it seems that all the temptations were in the desert. Therefore, what is said, ***Then the devil took him up***, does not seem to be true.

And here there is a twofold response. Some say that all the temptations were in the desert, and that they were according to the manner of an imaginary vision, namely, that Christ was given to imagine these things, and He furthermore permitted this. Others say that they were according to the manner of a corporeal vision: and that the devil appeared to him in a corporeal form. This seems to be implied, because he says that ***He took him up into the holy city***. Some say that the reason of this is that it pertains to a desert, because Jerusalem had been deserted by God. But it

---

6. St. Luke relates the third temptation of St. Matthew before the second.

ought to be better said that the former passage, which is said in Mark 1, 13, is not to be understood such that all the temptations would have been in the desert, and furthermore he does not say this; but only that he was tempted by Satan. And thus it should be known that the first temptation was in the desert; the other two were outside the desert.

But it is inquired, how did he take Him? Some say that he carried Him upon himself. Others say (and indeed better), that by exhorting he induced Him that He go to this place; and Christ from the ordinance of His wisdom, went into Jerusalem. *And set him upon the pinnacle of the temple*, etc. It ought to be known that it is read in III Kings 6 that Solomon made three stories to the temple with a flat roof, and also a certain pinnacle[7] near the temple, by which men had been able to ascend: and concerning this it is said here, *and set him upon the pinnacle of the temple*. Now whether He went to the first, second, or third story, it is not said here; but it is certain that He ascended.

But were not men looking when the devil was carrying Christ?

It must be said, according to those who say that he was carrying Him, that Christ was effecting that he could not be seen. Or it must be said that the devil was in the figure of a man; and it was usual that men would ascend in this manner.

And said to him: If thou be the Son of God, cast thyself down. The devil always strikes with two arrows: for, on one hand he induces vainglory, on the other hand, murder; and this is what he says, *If thou be the Son of God, cast thyself down.* But this inference is certainly not fitting to Christ, because it befits Him to rise upwards; "And no man hath ascended into heaven, but he that descended from heaven, the Son of man who is in heaven," etc., (Jn. 3, 13). And he says, *Cast*, because his intention is always to throw down headlong, just as he was thrown down headlong; "The dragon's tail drew the third part of the stars of heaven and cast them to the earth" (Apoc. 12, 4). The devil is also aware of his own weakness, because no one, except one who is willing, is conquered by him; whence, he says, *Cast*, and he does not throw down headlong; "Bow down, that we may go over" (Is. 51, 23).

But why did he set Him upon a pinnacle? The Gloss says: "Because they were teaching in that place." Hence, it signifies that the devil tempts great men concerning vainglory. Against which the Apostle says: "Nor sought we glory of men, neither of you, nor

---

7. In Palestine, all buildings had a flat roof, with a balustrade or a parapet. It was probably upon the parapet that the devil conveyed Jesus.

of others" (I Thess. 2, 6). And he says, **Cast thyself down**, etc., because men who seek glory cast themselves down, and they can only persuade inasmuch as they manifest God's humble sonship in many things; and thus, as Cicero says in *de Officiis*: "We must beware of the desire for glory: for it deprives us of the liberty that is the prize for which all great men struggle."[8]

Afterwards, the devil cites Scripture, saying, **It is written**: and he uses it not to teach, but to deceive; this argumentation is used, because just as he transfigures himself into an angel of light, so also do his ministers use the authority of Sacred Scripture to deceive the simple; "The unlearned and unstable wrest the Scriptures to their own destruction" (II Pet. 3, 16). Hence, the devil was prefiguring this in himself as in their head. **That he hath given his angels charge over thee.**

Observe that a man can wrest the authority of Sacred Scripture in three ways: sometimes as when what is said of one thing, is interpreted of another: it is just as if what is said concerning a just man, is interpreted concerning Christ; for example, "He that could have transgressed, and hath not transgressed" (Eccli. 31, 10). Likewise, "The Father is greater than I" (Jn. 14, 28), and this is said concerning Christ, according as He is man. Hence, if it is interpreted concerning Him according as He is the Son of God, the passage is wrested. Thus, here the devil says, **angels**, because Psalm 90 says this concerning Christ's members, who need the angels' guardianship, which is evident from what follows, **lest perhaps thou dash**: for this cannot be said concerning Christ, because He would not have been able to dash by an occasion of some sin. One wrests Scripture in a second way, when someone cites a passage for something, to which the passage does not pertain; such as that passage, "If thy enemy be hungry, give him to eat: if he thirst, give him water to drink," etc. For if one does something to someone so that he may be punished by God, he does this contrary to the meaning of the passage.[9] The devil spoke in this manner, because the Scripture means that a just man is thus guarded by

---

8. Literally, "The desire for glory must be guarded against: for it snatches away the soul's liberty, for which in great men every effort ought to be."

9. "If the enemy be hungry, give him to eat; if he thirst, give him to drink. For, doing this, thou shalt heap coals of fire upon his head" (Rom. 12, 20). "Firstly [St. Paul] gives the teaching that we ought to help our enemies in a case of necessity, because this is the fulfillment of a precept, as it was said above. And this is what he says, namely **"If the enemy be hungry, give him to eat; if he thirst, give him to drink.** 'Do good to them that hate you' (below 5, 44). Secondly he gives the reason, by saying that in doing this one heaps coals of fire upon his head. Which in fact can be understood in a bad way, such that the sense would be: 'If you do good to him, it will turn into something

angels, so that he may not fall into danger; "A helper in due time in tribulation," etc., (Ps. 9, 10). The devil, however, interprets this passage to mean that a man may put himself into danger, which is to tempt God. One wrests Scripture in a third way, when one accepts from a passage that part which is favorable to oneself and rejects the other part which is contrary to oneself, which is the custom of heretics: so the devil did here, because he rejected the part that follows, which was contrary to him, namely: "Thou shalt walk upon the asp and the basilisk: and thou shalt trample underfoot the lion and the dragon" (Ps. 90, 13). Whence, he has become the model of all those wresting the Scriptures.

The Lord said to him. He does not defend Himself with violence, but with wisdom: "No evil can overcome wisdom" (Wis. 7, 30). And so He cites a passage against the passage, which explains the aforesaid; it is as though He were to say, 'You say that I may cast forth myself, in order that I may see whether God would deliver me; but Scripture forbids this; hence, **Thou shalt not tempt the Lord thy God** (Deut. 6, 16).' Or otherwise, 'You tempt me, and by tempting me you act contrary to Scripture; and one who acts contrary to Scripture ought not to make use of the authority of Scripture. And the Scripture says, **Thou shalt not tempt**, etc. But you tempt the Lord thy God, whom I Am; "You call me Master and Lord. And you say well: for so I am," etc., (Jn. 13, 13).' Nevertheless, the first interpretation is more literal. Afterwards, the third temptation is set forth, namely, of ambition, or of avarice; hence, **Then the devil took him up into a very high mountain.** And thus the assault of the temptation is related; and secondly, Christ's resistance, where it is said, **Then Jesus saith to him: Begone, Satan.** Now the devil tempts in two ways, by deed and by word; hence, **All these will I give thee**, etc. In the deed, two things are to be considered. For firstly, he took Him into a mountain; and secondly, he showed Him all the kingdoms of the world. He says, therefore, **Then he took.** Regarding the taking, it is discussed above; but this saying, namely,

---

bad for him, for from this he incurs the burning of eternal fire through his ingratitude.' But this meaning is repugnant to charity, against which one would be acting who were to help someone so that it would result in something bad for him. And thus it must be expounded in a good sense, such that the meaning of **For doing this**, etc., would be, **thou shalt heap upon his head,** meaning 'upon his mind,' by helping one in need, **coals of fire**, that is to say the love of charity about which it is spoken in Canticles 8, 6: 'the lamps thereof are fire and flames.' For as Augustine says in his Book *De Catechizandis Rudibus* (iv), 'Nothing will incite another more to love you than that you love him first: for he must have a hard heart indeed, who not only refuses to love, but declines to return love already given'" (*Commentary on Romans*, chap. 12, lect. 3).

Into a mountain, can be explained in two ways. Rabanus says that this mountain was in the desert, because, according to him, all the temptations took place in the desert. Now it is said to be very high in comparison to the others which were surrounding it. Chrysostom, however, says that he led Him to the highest mountain in the world; and this seems to agree with the text, since it is said, ***Very high***. Now in this it is signified that the devil always lifts up to pride, just as he is proud; "Before your feet stumble upon the dark mountains" (Jer. 13, 16). Whence, also, he is called a mountain; "For behold I will call together all the families of the kingdoms of the north" (Jer. 1, 15). ***And shewed him all the kingdoms of the world.***

It ought to be known that *the kingdom of the world* is understood in two ways. Firstly, spiritually: and in this way the devil is said to reign in it; "Now is the judgment of the world: now shall the prince of this world be cast out" (Jn. 12, 31). Secondly, the kingdom of the world is said literally, according to which one man rules over another. Now that which is said here, seems to some to be what may be said about the devil's kingdom; hence, ***He shewed him all the kingdoms of the world***, namely, over which he was ruling, *and the glory of them*, etc., because when he fully rules over men, he also makes them exult; "They are glad when they have done evil, and rejoice in the most wicked things" (Prov. 2, 14); "Why dost thou glory in malice?" (Ps. 51, 3). Others expound this of physical kingdoms.

But then it is asked, how could he show all kingdoms of the world? Remigius says that it was done miraculously: because he showed all the kingdoms in the blink of an eye, just as it is also read concerning St. Benedict, that the whole world was shown to him in one glance. But it ought to be known that these two do not seem to be good explanations, because it would not be appropriate to say that ***He took him up into a very high mountain***: because all this could have happened in a valley. Whence, Chrysostom says otherwise: ***He showed him***, not that he showed him every single kingdom, but only some part of each kingdom; and not only this, but ***shewed the glory of them***; this is to say, that he represented to him the world's temporal glory; "I will change their glory into shame" (Osee 4, 7); "Whose glory is in their shame: who mind earthly things" (Phil. 3, 19). ***And said to him: All these will I give thee***. In these words he does two things: he promises one thing and he seeks after another: and there is a lie in the promise, pride in the seeking. The devil, in the first temptation, tested whether Christ was the Son of God; and now, believing that he had found out that He was not, he says, ***All these will I give thee***, etc.; this is where the lie is, because these were not in his power; "By me kings reign, and lawgivers decree just things" (Prov. 8, 15). "Till the living know, that the most High ruleth in the kingdom of men: and he will give it to whomsoever it shall please him" (Dan. 4, 14); for no evil man reigns except by divine permission; "Who maketh a man that is a hypocrite to reign for the sins of the people" (Job. 34, 30).

Observe three things. Firstly, that the devil always persists towards that for which he strove in the beginning; "I will ascend into heaven, I will exalt my throne above the stars of God, I will sit in the mountain of the covenant, in the sides of the north. I will ascend above the height of the clouds, I will be like the most High" (Is. 14, 13). And accordingly he induces men into idolatry, wishing to usurp for himself that which belongs to God. Likewise, observe that no one adores the devil unless he fall, just as he fell; "Falling down they adored the golden statue" (Dan. 3, 7). And thus he says, ***If falling down thou wilt adore me***. Thirdly, observe that there is avarice here. Wherefore he promises a kingdom, in which is understood an abundance of riches, and a preeminence of honors. And he asks him to fall down: because the ambitious always humble themselves more than is due. Whence, Ambrose says: "Ambition harbors yet another danger within itself: it will bow in submission that it may be crowned with honor: and while it aims to be high, it becomes debased."

Afterwards the catching of the enemy is related; hence, ***Then Jesus saith to him***: and about this He does two things. Firstly, He curbs the temptation; and secondly, He cites a passage, where it is said, ***It is written***, etc. The Evangelist says, therefore, ***Then Jesus saith to him***.

Observe that Christ had heard many insults, but He did not take notice. But this saying, ***If falling down thou wilt adore me***, He did not endure: because the first ones were resulting in the injury of Himself; but this one unto the injury of God. Hence, Chrysostom says: "An injury to oneself ought to be endured: to ignore an injury to God is exceedingly impious." And thus He says, ***Begone, Satan***. "With zeal have I been zealous for the Lord God of hosts: for the children of Israel have forsaken thy covenant" (III Kings 19, 10); "The zeal of thy house hath eaten me up" (Ps. 68, 10). Observe, likewise, that it is not in the devil's power to tempt as much as he wills, but only as much as God permits; hence, He says, ***Begone***; as though He were to say: 'I do not allow that you tempt Me further'; "Let no temptation take hold on you, but such as is human. And God is faithful, who will not suffer you to be tempted above that which you are able: but will make also with temptation issue, that you may be able to bear it" (I Cor. 10, 13); "Hitherto thou shalt come, and shalt go no further, and here thou shalt break thy swelling waves" (Job 38, 11). And one should observe that the Lord said almost the same words to Peter (below, chap. 16). But there He said "Behind." And so the meaning differs here and there: for Satan is interpreted 'adversary.' Therefore, the Lord wanted Peter to get behind Him, because he was wishing to impede the Passion; but here He says, **Begone**, only; because the devil could not follow Him; and thus He says, **Begone**, namely, to hell; "Depart from me, you cursed, into everlasting fire, which was prepared for the devil and his angels" (below 25, 41). *It is written*; namely, it is in Deut. 6, 16. And He frequently cites such passages from Deuteronomy, to indicate that the New Testament's doctrine is signified throughout Deuteronomy. What follows, **The Lord God**, can be understood in two different ways; it is as if He were to say, 'You devil, you say that falling down I can adore thee; but the Law says, **The Lord thy God shalt thou adore**.' Hence, it can be inferred that a mere man should not be adored; or it can be understood that He speaks of Himself as God. **The Lord thy God shalt thou adore**, etc.; as though He were to say, 'Rather you ought to adore Me, than conversely: because *it is written*, etc.' The first interpretation, however, is more literal.

And note that He says two things, namely, **shalt thou adore** and **shalt thou serve**; and there is a difference between these two things. For a man ought to be oriented towards God in two ways: for he ought to be subject to Him; and he ought to elevate himself up to Him as unto his ultimate end. So far as concerns the first, we owe to Him all obedience; "We ought to obey God rather than men" (Acts 5, 29). For we are subject to Him only when we do His entire will. We are elevated up to God, however, in two ways; for sometimes we draw ourselves to Him; "Come ye to him and be enlightened: and your faces shall not be confounded" (Ps. 33, 6), and sometimes we draw others to Him; "For we are God's coadjutors" (I Cor. 3, 9). We show both of these sensibly; for when we prostrate ourselves, we admonish ourselves that we ought to be subject to God; and thus He says, **The Lord God**; "All nations shall serve him" (Ps. 71, 11). Likewise, in this, that we offer sacrifices and praises, we signify that we ought to elevate our mind to Him: and to this pertains worship; and the passage is, **And him only shalt thou serve**. Now worship is twofold; there is a certain kind which is due to God alone; and in Greek it is called *latria*: and this is twofold. For a certain kind is adoration which is due to God alone, so that He be worshipped above all things; another worship due to God is that we tend to Him as unto the ultimate end. There is also a second kind of worship that is due to superiors, which in Greek is called *dulia*: for there is a certain adoration or worship which belongs only to subjects, as when inferiors heed superiors; "Let every soul be subject to higher powers" (Rom. 13, 1). But one should not obey them above all things, because one never ought to obey them contrary to God. Similarly, no creature ought to be regarded as the ultimate end; "Put not your trust in princes: in the children of men, in whom there is no salvation" (Ps. 145, 3); "Cursed be the man that trusteth in man" (Jer. 17, 5).

Afterwards, Christ's victory is related, and it is indicated by two things. It is indicated by the devil's withdrawal; **Then the devil left him.** "Resist the devil: and he will fly from you" (James 4, 7). And also it was the custom among the ancients, that when some men had a victory that they were honored; and so here Christ's triumph is celebrated by the angels. Whence, **And behold angels came and ministered to him.** He does not say, 'They descended': because they were always with Him, even if by His will they withdrew for a time so that the devil might have an opportunity to tempt Him: for they were performing services in exterior things, namely, in the miracles and in other corporeal matters which occur by the mediating angels: but in interior things He did not need them. In this passage it is signified that men who conquer the devil merit the angels' ministration; "It came to pass that the beggar died and was carried by the angels into Abraham's bosom" (Lk. 16, 22). And it ought to be known that the devil left Christ until a certain time: because later he used the Jews as his members to attack Christ, etc.

12. And when Jesus had heard that John was delivered up, he retired into Galilee:
13. And leaving the city Nazareth, he came and dwelt in Capharnaum on the sea coast, in the borders of Zabulon and of Nephthalim;
14. That it might be fulfilled which was said by Isaias the prophet:
15. Land of Zabulon and land of Nephthalim, the way of the sea beyond the Jordan, Galilee of the Gentiles:
16. The people that sat in darkness, hath seen great light: and to them that sat in the region of the shadow of death, light is sprung up.

17. From that time Jesus began to preach, and to say: Do penance, for the kingdom of heaven is at hand.

18. And Jesus walking by the sea of Galilee, saw two brethren, Simon who is called Peter, and Andrew his brother, casting a net into the sea (for they were fishers).

19. And he saith to them: Come ye after me, and I will make you to be fishers of men.

20. And they immediately leaving their nets, followed him.

21. And going on from thence, he saw other two brethren, James the son of Zebedee, and John his brother, in a ship with Zebedee their father, mending their nets: and he called them.

22. And they forthwith left their nets and father, and followed him.

Above, the Evangelist showed how Christ was tried and approved, namely, by conquering the devil; here he shows how Christ began to teach: and about this he does three things. For firstly, the place in which He teaches is described; secondly, he shows how He chose the ministers of His preaching, where he says, **And Jesus walking by the sea of Galilee, saw two brethren**; and thirdly, he shows how He drew the crowd to hear Him, where he says, **And Jesus went about all Galilee.** About the first, he describes the time, place and manner of preaching; the second is where he says, **He retired into Galilee**, etc.; and the third is where he says, **From that time Jesus began to preach.** This time of Christ's public preaching[10] was after John's imprisonment; hence, he says, **And when Jesus had heard that John was delivered up**, by God, that is, because He permitted it.

And this passage ought to be considered for understanding the Evangelists, because here there seems to be some discrepancy between John and the other three Evangelists: because the latter say that Christ went down to Capharnaum after John's imprisonment; but John says that He went down to Capharnaum before John's imprisonment: which, nevertheless, was in Galilee. It is responded that John, who was the final Evangelist, supplied those things which were omitted by the others.

But why did they omit them? It must be said that, although Christ did some things in the first two years, nevertheless, He had done few in comparison with those things which were done

---

10. Here Christ's public preaching refers only to the third year of His public ministry as is explained just below.

in the last year. Therefore, it ought to be said that John speaks concerning the former things which He did in the first and second years, and some things from the third year: but the others speak concerning what things were done in the last year.

Again, it is inquired how many years Christ preached. Some say that it was for two-and-a-half years, so that the half is calculated from Epiphany until the Pasch, even though it is not a complete half year: for John only made mention of three Paschs: because after the baptism he says that He went to Jerusalem.[11] Afterwards he makes mention of the Pasch, when the miracle of the five loaves was performed, and it was one year until the Passion. But this opinion does not seem to be true thus far, because it does not agree with the Church's opinion, that three miracles happened on the day of the Epiphany, namely, of the adoration of the Wise Men, of the baptism, and of the conversion of water into wine. Therefore, one ought to say that from the baptism to the conversion of water into wine was one year. Hence, it seems that Christ preached for three years, because until the miracle of the wine was one year: and thence to the Pasch was another half year: another year was from the purification[12] until the Passion: for thus reckons the Church. And according to this it must be said that John says little about the first year; of the second he says something, namely, how He went down to Capharnaum: and about the question of the purification between John's disciples and the Jews.[13]

And it should also be known that John was killed about the time of the Pasch: because it is read in John 6 that when the miracle of the five loaves was worked, that the Pasch was near; and in Matthew 14 it is said that Christ, having heard of John's death, retired into Galilee. Therefore, it is clear that John was beheaded near the time of the Pasch: and Christ did not preach publicly for one year.

Then it is treated concerning the place, when it is said, *He retired into Galilee.* And firstly, the Evangelist treats of the place of the province; and secondly, of the city. He says, therefore, *He retired*; this retiring was not the first, of which John speaks; but this was after one or two years, because the other Evangelists pass over this in silence. Now He retired for two reasons. Firstly, it was that He might delay His Passion; "My time is not yet come" (Jn. 7, 6). Secondly, it was for our example, namely, that we may flee

---

[11]. "And the Pasch of the Jews was at hand: and Jesus went up to Jerusalem" (Jn. 2, 13).

[12]. The second purification of the Temple (Jn. 2, 13-22)

[13]. The text seems to erroneously state, "between Christ Himself and the Jews." But this has been corrected according to John 3, 25.

persecutions; "If they have persecuted me, they will also persecute you" (Jn 15, 20). But, mystically, he declares that Christ's preaching had been about to pass over to the Gentiles: because the Jews were persecuting God's grace; "To you it behoved us first to speak the word of God: but because you reject it and judge yourselves unworthy of eternal life, behold we turn to the Gentiles" (Acts 13, 46). Now coming into Galilee He came firstly into Nazareth, as Luke says: and there He entered into the synagogue, and taught (chap. 4, 18): "The spirit of the Lord is upon me." And from thence the Jews led Him to the brow of the hill, and they wanted to cast Him down headlong, and after this Christ fled, and He came into Capharnaum, and there He immediately cured the demoniac, concerning which is in Mark 1. But this Matthew omits. Now Nazareth is interpreted 'flower.' By this is understood the teachers of the Law, who do not come to maturity. Capharnaum is interpreted 'beautiful village' and signifies the Church; "Thou art beautiful, O my love," etc., (Cant. 6, 3). Capharnaum is a sea village on the shore, because it is beside a freshwater lake. For the Jews called every body of water a sea: and, mystically, because the Church is placed near the tribulations of the world. ***In the borders of Zabulon and of Nephthalim.*** For Galilee was divided, so that one part was in Zabulon and another in Nephthalim. Now after that, the princes of the Church were chosen, namely, the Apostles. ***That it might be fulfilled which was said by Isaias the prophet.*** Observe that this is not said exactly as it is written in Isaias 9, 1; but only the meaning is related. Isaias wrote as follows: "At the first time the land of Zabulon, and the land of Nephtali was lightly touched:[14] and at the last the way of the sea beyond the Jordan of the Galilee of the Gentiles was heavily loaded. The people that walked in darkness, have seen a great light," etc. And this is expounded in three ways, according to Jerome. Firstly, it is as follows. "At the first time" it was unburdened of their sins through Christ's preaching, and "at the last time" the way, which is next to the sea of Galilee, was burdened with the burden of their sins, because after Christ's preaching they persecuted the Apostles. Or it can be explained otherwise. "At the first time." He touches upon history: because the king of the Assyrians, Teglatphalassar, who firstly came upon the land of the Jews, firstly led those tribes into captivity. And so it is written "At the first time it was lightly touched:" because then the sinners were firstly led into captivity. "And at the last," etc., because afterwards the whole nation was led into captivity.

---

14. Literally "made light or unburdened."

But what has this to do with the matter at hand? One must answer that where persecution firstly began, there the Lord first willed to give consolation.

Or it may be explained otherwise. "At the first time," that is, at the time of Christ's preaching, "it was lightly touched," etc., that is, it was unburdened from the burden of their sins through Christ's preaching: "and at the last it was heavily loaded," that is, Christ' preaching was condensed, and multiplied by Paul, who preached there. For the Evangelist only relates the sense in the construction: *Land of Zabulon and land of Nephthalim, the way of the sea beyond the Jordan*, that is, next to the sea. And he says, *Land*, that is, the people, so that all might be named. And he says, *Galilee of the Gentiles*, because Galilee was divided into two parts: one belonging to the Gentiles and one belonging to the Jews: and it was divided according to what is said in III Kings 9, because Solomon, on account of the timber which the king of Tyre sent to him for the building of the temple, gave to him twenty cities: who, since he was a Gentile, placed Gentiles to dwell there; and thus it is called *Galilee of the Gentiles*: and it was in the tribe of Nephthalim; "beyond the Jordan of the Galilee," that is, in comparison to Galilee. But the first exposition is better.

"The people that walked in darkness, have seen a great light."[15] It (S. Scripture) says two things, "That walked" and *That sat*: for he, who from the beginning is in darkness which is not very thick, is not bewildered by it, and goes forth; most especially when he hopes to find light: but when he is bewildered by the darkness, he stands still. This is the difference between the Jews and the Gentiles: because the Jews, although they were in darkness, nevertheless were not totally oppressed by it, because they were not all worshipping idols, but were hoping that Christ was about to come, and thus they were walking; "Who hath walked in darkness, and hath no light? let him hope in the name of the Lord," etc., (Is. 50, 10). But the Gentiles were not waiting; and there was not hope for light. And again, they were oppressed with darkness, because they were worshipping idols; for, according to Psalm 75, 2, "In Judea God is known"; and thus they were standing. And this is what is said, *The people that sat in darkness, hath seen great light*. The light of the Jews was not great: "And we have the more firm prophetical word: whereunto you do well to attend, as to a light that shineth in a dark place" (II Peter 1, 19); but this light is great even like the light of the sun; "But unto

---

15. Isaias 9, 1 cited above.

you that fear my name, the Sun of justice shall arise" (Mal. 4, 2). *And to them that sat*, that is, the Gentiles, *in the region of the shadow of death*. Death is damnation in hell; "Death shall feed upon them" (Psalm 48, 15). The shadow of death is a likeness of the future damnation, which is found in sinners. Now the great pain of those who are in hell is separation from God. And because sinners are already separated from God, thus they possess a likeness of the future damnation, as also the just possess a likeness of the future beatitude; "But we all, beholding the glory of the Lord with open face, are transformed into the same image from glory to glory" (II Cor. 3, 18). And observe that a light sprung up, because they did not go to the light, but the light came to them; "The light is come into the world" (Jn. 3, 19). *Is sprung up to them*. And that land is in the confines of the Jews and of the Gentiles, so that He might show that He called both; "It is a small thing that thou shouldst be my servant to raise up the tribes of Jacob, and to convert the dregs of Israel." And afterwards: "Behold, I have given thee to be the light of the Gentiles, that thou mayst be my salvation even to the farthest part of the earth" (Is. 49, 6). *From that time Jesus began to preach*. Having set forth the place where Christ first began to preach, here is set forth the manner of preaching. *From that time*, namely, after the conquering of gluttony, vainglory and ambition, or avarice, *He began to preach*: for suchlike men can suitably preach. And in this way is fulfilled that passage of Acts 1, 1: "Jesus began to do and to teach." Or, *from that time*, that is, after John's imprisonment, He began to preach publicly: for previously He preached secretly and to certain men (Jn. 1, 38 ff.), namely, to Peter, Andrew, Philip, and Nathaniel, but here publicly. Now He did not at first wish to preach publicly, to give place to John's preaching: otherwise it would have been of no avail, just as the light of the stars is obscured by the light of the sun. Now it is signified by this that when the figures of the Law had ceased, Christ's preaching began; "But when that which is perfect is come, that which is in part shall be done away" (I Cor. 13, 10). For by John the Law is signified; "The prophets and the law were until John" (below 11, 13). *Do penance*.

It is to be observed that Christ here says the same words that John said, on account of two reasons. For firstly, He admonishes us concerning humility, so that, namely, no one disdain to preach the words of others, since the very Source of ecclesiastical science preached the same words. Secondly, it is because John is the voice; but He is the Word. Now the same thing is indicated by the voice and the word, only because the word is expressive of the voice.

Now about this, He does two things. He admonishes one thing and He promises another. The first is where it is said, **Do penance**; and the second is where it is said, **for the kingdom of heaven is at hand.**

But why did He not admonish concerning justice at the beginning of His preaching, rather than to do penance? It must be answered that the reason was, because He had already admonished concerning justice through the Natural Law and Scripture's Law; but they had been transgressed; "They have transgressed the laws, they have changed the ordinance, they have broken the everlasting covenant" (Is. 24, 5). For in this He gives to understand that He finds all to be sinners; "Christ Jesus came into the world to save sinners" (I Tim. 1, 15); "For all have sinned and do need the glory of God" (Rom. 3, 23). And so the passage is, **Do penance**. He promises, on the other hand, something else; hence, **For the kingdom of heaven is at hand.** This promise differs in two points from the promise of the Old Testament; because therein temporal things were promised, but here heavenly and eternal things are promised; "If you will hearken to me, you shall eat the good things of the land" (Is. 1, 19). Again, there He promised the kingdom of the Canaanites and Jebusites; here He promises the kingdom of heaven; hence, **the kingdom of heaven is at hand**, that is, unto you. And thus Christ's doctrine is called the New Testament: because therein was made a new pact between us and God about the kingdom of heaven; "I will make a new covenant with the house of Israel, and with the house of Juda" (Jer. 31, 31). Secondly, because the Old Law contained a threat along with a promise; "If you be willing, and will hearken to me, you shall eat the good things of the land. But if you will not, and will provoke me to wrath: the sword shall devour you" (Is. 1, 19). And in Deut. 28, the same thing is found: wherein many blessings are promised to those who will have kept the Law, and Moses threatened many curses to the transgressors of the Law. And, therefore, for that reason, the Old Law was a law of fear, but the New Law was a law of love. As Augustine says: "The brief difference is love and fear." "For you are not come to a mountain that might be touched and a burning fire and a whirlwind and darkness and storm, and the sound of a trumpet and the voice of words, which they that had excused themselves, that the word might not be spoken to them" (Heb. 12, 18). **The kingdom of heaven is at hand**, that is to say, eternal beatitude. And he says **is at hand**[16] because He who was bestowing descended to us, because we had not been able to ascend to God.

---

16. Literally, "will draw near."

And He was walking, etc. After He began to preach, He wanted to have ministers of His preaching: hence, here He calls them to Himself: and about this He does two things, in that He calls two pairs of ministers. For, firstly, He called Peter and Andrew; and secondly, He called James and John. About the first, the Evangelist does four things. For firstly, the place of the calling is described; secondly, the condition of the ones called is set forth, where it is said, *For they were fishers*; thirdly, the calling, where it is said, *And he saith to them*; and fourthly, their perfect obedience, where it is said, *And they immediately leaving their nets, followed him*. Therefore, he says, *walking by the sea of Galilee*. The place is fitting: because, as it says in the Gloss, 'He was about to call fishers, and so He walked by the sea.'

So far as concerns the mystery, however, it ought to be known that, to stand, signifies God's eternity and immobility; but His walking signifies His temporal birth. By the fact, therefore, that, while walking, He called His disciples, it is signified that through the mystery of His Incarnation He calls us to Himself; "Arise, O Lord, my God, in the precept which thou hast commanded," which Thou has decreed to be fulfilled, "And a congregation of people shall surround thee" (Ps. 7, 7). "Christ had the likeness of a sinner; God, sent his own Son in the likeness of sinful flesh," etc., (Rom. 8, 3). Afterwards, the condition of those called is described. And firstly, regarding the number; secondly, regarding the names; thirdly, regarding their activity; and fourthly, regarding their occupation. He says, therefore, *He saw two*, not merely with the eye of the body, but also of the mind: for His glance is a regard of mercy; whence, in Exodus 3, 7: "Seeing I have seen the affliction of my people in Egypt," etc. And observe that the same thing is indicated by *two* and *brethren*: for both pertain to charity, which consists in the love of God and of neighbor. And therefore He chose them two by two, and He sent them two by two to preach: and He wanted spiritual charity to be signified by this, because charity is more strengthened when it is founded upon nature; "Behold how good and how pleasant it is for brethren to dwell together in unity" (Ps. 132, 1). *Simon who is called Peter*, actually, now, but not then: because Christ afterwards imposed this name upon him, but firstly He promised to do so; "Thou shalt be called Cephas" (John 1, 42), but He imposed it when He said, "Thou art Peter" (below 16, 18). *And Andrew*. Every preacher ought to have these names. For Simon is interpreted 'obedient,' Peter means 'knowing,' and Andrew means 'fortitude.' And a preacher ought to be obedient, so that he can summon others to do this; "An obedient man shall speak of victory" (Prov. 21, 28); he ought to be knowledgeable, so that he may know how to instruct others: "I had rather speak five words with my understanding, that I may instruct others also" (I Cor. 14, 19): he also ought to be strong, so that he may not be terrified by threats; "I have made thee this day a fortified city, and a pillar of iron, and a wall of brass" (Jer. 1, 18); "Behold I have made thy face stronger than their faces: and thy forehead harder than their foreheads. I have made thy face like an adamant and like flint" (Ez. 3, 8). It continues, *Casting a net into the sea.*

Chrysostom asks why the Lord chose this particular moment. And he says it was so that an example might be given that we never ought to omit God's service due to occupations. Or thus, because by this activity is prefigured the action of future preachers, because men are drawn by the preachers' words as it were by nets.

Their occupation is related thus, *For they were fishers.* And it ought to be known that among all men, fishermen are the most simple; and the Lord willed to have men from the most simple state, and so He chose them, so that that which was accomplished through them might not be attributed to human wisdom; "For see your vocation, brethren, that there are not many wise according to the flesh, not many mighty, not many noble. But the foolish things of the world hath God chosen, that he may confound the wise: and the weak things of the world hath God chosen, that he may confound the strong" (I Cor. 1, 26). And therefore He did not choose Augustine, or Cyprian the orator, but Peter the fisherman: and from a fisherman was gained a commander-in-chief and an orator. *And he saith.* Here the calling is set forth, about which three things are to be considered. For firstly, He invites; secondly, He promises guidance; and thirdly, He promises a reward. He says, therefore, *Come ye.* This is solely from the divine bounty, that He draws men to Himself; "Come over to me, all ye that desire me, and be filled with my fruits" (Eccli. 24, 26); "Come to me all you that labor and are burdened, and I will refresh you" (below 11, 28). *After me*, as though He were to say, 'I go, and come ye after Me, because I will be your leader'; "I will shew thee the way of wisdom, I will lead thee by the paths of equity: which when thou shalt have entered, thy steps shall not be straitened, and when thou runnest, thou shalt not meet a stumblingblock" (Prov. 4, 11); "But to me thy friends, O God, are made exceedingly honourable: their principality is exceedingly strengthened" (Psalms 138, 17). *I will make*, as it were, 'I will exchange your occupation into a greater one.' Concerning these men it is said: "Behold I will send many fishers, saith the Lord, and they shall fish them," etc., (Jer,

16, 16). And He says, *I will make*, because one preaching exteriorly labors in vain, unless the Redeemer's grace is interiorly present: for they were not drawing men by their own power, but by Christ's operation. And thus He says, *I will make*. This is indeed a very great dignity; whence, Dionysius says: "Nothing is of greater dignity in men's occupation than to become a cooperator with God." For dignity consists in one's own solitary splendor. Now those who are so-illuminated such that they may illuminate others approach more closely to that dignity; and although they who follow Christ illumine men and do great things as far as justice; they still assert Christ's dignity as the solitary splendor; for the preachers' lives assert Christ's dignity only as a reflected brightness; "They that instruct many to justice, shall shine as stars for all eternity" (Dan. 12, 3). Their obedience is set forth, *And they immediately leaving their nets, followed him*. And the Evangelist shows their obedience regarding three things. Firstly, regarding promptitude, because they did not delay: hence, *And they*. Such is opposed to those of whom it is written: "Delay not to be converted to the Lord, and defer it not from day to day" (Eccli. 5, 8); "But when it pleased him who separated me from my mother's womb and called me by his grace, to reveal his Son in me, that I might preach him among the Gentiles: immediately I condescended not to flesh and blood" (Gal. 1, 15). "The Lord God hath opened my ear, and I do not resist: I have not gone back" (Is. 50, 5). Secondly, regarding the removal of obstacles, because they left them behind; for the wealth is not to be measured, but rather the affection for it; because a man leaves all things who leaves whatever he could have.

But what is the necessity for leaving all things? Chrysostom says: "No one can possess riches and perfectly come to the kingdom of heaven; for they are an impediment to virtue, because they diminish forethought for eternal things: on account of which a man cannot completely cling to riches." And thus they are to be relinquished; "Every one that striveth for the mastery refraineth himself from all things," etc., (I Cor. 9, 25).

Thirdly, regarding the execution, because they followed Him: for it is not very great to leave all things, but perfection consists in the following of Him, which is through charity; "And if I should distribute all my goods to feed the poor, and if I should deliver my body to be burned, and have not charity, it profiteth me nothing" (I Cor. 13, 3). For perfection does not in itself consist in exterior things, namely, poverty, virginity, and suchlike, unless these things are instruments with respect to charity; and thus he says, *And they followed him*. Afterwards, it is treated concerning another calling:

And going on from thence, he saw other two brethren, James the son of Zebedee, and John his brother. And firstly, those called are described; secondly, the calling is set forth, where it is said, *And he called*, etc.; and thirdly, the obedience of those called, where it is said, *And they left their nets and father, and followed him.* Those called are described in four ways. They are described regarding their number, names, piety, and poverty. He says, therefore, *And going on from thence, he saw other two brethren.* Note that at the beginning He called brothers: and although He called many others, nevertheless, mention is specially made of these, because they were outstanding, and because He called them by pairs: for the New Law is founded in charity: whence, also in the Old Law, He called two brothers, Aaron and Moses, because even then the commandment of charity was given. And because the New Law is more perfect, thus at the beginning a double number of brothers is called, *James the son of Zebedee, and John his brother.* By these four men the four Gospels' doctrine, or four virtues, is signified: because by Peter, which is interpreted 'knowing,' the virtue of prudence is signified; by Andrew, which is interpreted 'virile' or 'very strong,' the virtue of fortitude is signified; by James, which is interpreted 'supplanter,' the virtue of justice is signified; and by John, on account of his virginity, the virtue of temperance is signified. Their piety is set forth, because they were with their father, Zebedee. Chrysostom says: "Their piety is to be admired, because the poor seek bread by the piscatorial art, nevertheless, they do not abandon their aged father." "He that feareth the Lord, honoureth his parents" (Eccli. 3, 8). Their poverty is denoted in this, because they were mending their nets. Nonetheless, by those who were casting nets is signified they who in their early years do business in the world; by those who have already cast their nets, and were mending them, is signified they who have long done business in the world; and are now absorbed by sin, and are called to Christ. "It is good for a man, when he hath borne the yoke from his youth" (Lam. 3, 27). *And he called them*, interiorly and exteriorly; "Whom he predestinated, them he also called" (Rom. 8, 30). Observe the previous two only left their boat, but these left their nets, boat, and father: in which it is signified that for Christ's sake we ought to lay aside all temporal occupations, which is designated by the net; "No man, being a soldier to God, entangleth himself with secular businesses" (II Tim. 2, 4); riches, or possessions, which is designated by the ship; "If thou wilt be perfect, go sell what thou hast, and give to the poor, and thou shalt have treasure in heaven: and come, follow me" (below 19, 21); and carnal affection, which is designated by the father; "forget thy people and thy father's house" (Ps. 44, 11). Mystically, however, the world is signified by Zebedee, which is interpreted 'violent flow.'

But here there is a question: for it seems that these sinned by abandoning their poor and old father, since children are bound to aid their parents. And, in general, it is asked whether it is allowed for someone, by entering religion, to abandon their parents in their extreme need.

It ought to be answered that a counsel never supersedes a precept; and this obligation, namely, "Honour thy father and thy mother" (Ex. 20, 12), is a precept; and thus, if a father can in nowise live except he be helped by his son, the son ought not to enter religion. But this was not the case for Zebedee, because he was able to help himself, and he had the things he needed.

Likewise, there is a literal question. For Matthew seems here to be contrary to John and Luke: for John, in chapter 1, says that He called them near the Jordan; but here Matthew says that it was near the Sea of Galilee. Similarly, Luke, in chapter 5, says that He simultaneously called Peter and Andrew, James and John, though he does not mention the other two, because it is believed that they were there. Again, there it is said that all were called together, but here it is said that they were called separately.

But it should be known that there was a threefold calling of the Apostles. For they were firstly called to Christ's acquaintance, and that is said in John 1, and this was during the first year of Christ's preaching. Nor does this conflict with what is said afterwards: "Jesus and his disciples went up to Cana of Galilee" (Jn. 2, 2), because, according to Augustine, they were not then disciples, but were about to become His disciples: as if it were said that Paul the Apostle was born in Tarsus of Cilicia, when he was not then an Apostle. Or it can be said that the Evangelist speaks of other disciples who are called, meaning, all those who believe in Christ. Secondly, they were called to the discipleship; and about this it is written in Luke 6.[17] The third calling was so that they might firmly adhere to Christ; and about this calling is spoken here; which is evident, according to Augustine, because this is found in Luke 5,

---

17. The original text actually references Luke 5 but this seems to be a misprint since Lk. 5 contains the calling of the four Apostles, which would be the third calling of which St. Thomas speaks here. Rather the second calling was in Luke 6 which immediately preceded the Sermon on the Mount, though St. Matthew's Gospel would then not be chronological in placing this Sermon after the final call of the Apostles. But this is typical of St. Matthew's Gospel which was not written as chronologically as St. Luke's Gospel. St. Matthew may have preferred to simplify the two callings by only relating the final calling just before the beatitudes.

11, "And having brought their ships to land"; therefore, they possessed a ship and were taking care of it, as if they would return to it; but here it is said, "But they leaving all things," etc. And thus it must be said that he speaks here about the final following.

23. And Jesus went about all Galilee, teaching in their synagogues, and preaching the gospel of the kingdom: and healing all manner of sickness and every infirmity, among the people.

24. And his fame went throughout all Syria, and they presented to him all sick people that were taken with divers diseases and torments, and such as were possessed by devils, and lunatics, and those that had the palsy, and he cured them:

25. And much people followed him from Galilee, and from Decapolis, and from Jerusalem, and from Judea, and from beyond the Jordan.

It is the custom among kings, that when they have gathered an army they go forth to war: so Christ, having gathered an army of Apostles, goes forth to fight against the devil through their office of preaching, in order to expel him from the world. Whence, here is treated concerning Christ's teaching and preaching. And firstly, Christ's preaching is related; and secondly, the effect of the preaching, where it is said, **His fame went throughout all Syria**, etc. About the first, he touches upon three things. Firstly, he touches upon the diligence of the one teaching and His manner of teaching, and upon the confirmation of the proposed doctrine. And His diligence is shown in two things, in that He was not seeking His own ease; hence, **He went about**; "In carefulness not slothful" (Rom. 12, 11). Secondly, it is shown in that He was not an acceptor of persons, of lands, or of towns, but, **He went about all Galilee**, without distinction; "Let us go into the neighbouring towns and cities, that I may preach there also" (Mk. 1, 38); "in every place of his dominion" (Ps. 102, 22). His manner is touched upon, where it is said, **teaching in their synagogues**. He says two different things, **teaching** and **preaching**; He was teaching what is to be done at present, and preaching concerning the future: or, He was teaching those things which pertain to the instruction of morals; "I am the Lord thy God that teach thee profitable things" (Is. 48, 17); and He was preaching concerning future things; "How beautiful upon the mountains are the feet of him that bringeth good tidings, and that preacheth peace: of him that sheweth forth good, that preacheth salvation!" (Is. 52, 7). Or, He was teaching natural justices; for there are certain truths which are passed on in theology which natural reason dictates, namely, justice and suchlike; and, as to this, the Evangelist says, *teaching*; but there are certain things which exceed reason, such as the mystery of the Trinity, and suchlike: and, as to this, he says, *preaching*.

But it is objected concerning this, because the Gloss says that He taught natural justifications, such as chastity, and humility, and suchlike: for natural virtues do not seem to be capable of being called virtues, because virtues are by grace.

And it ought to be answered that the inclination and the beginning is natural; but the perfection, by which a man is rendered pleasing, is from grace, civic virtue, and from custom.

In their synagogues. Observe two things. The first is that He was seeking a multitude, so that His preaching might profit in a higher degree; "I will give thanks to thee in a great church" (Ps. 34, 18). Likewise observe that He was preaching only to the Jews; "To you it behoved us first to speak the word of God" (Acts 13, 46). *And preaching the gospel of the kingdom*: not fables and curiosities, but things that pertain to the kingdom of God, and those things which might be profitable to men. Afterwards the preaching is confirmed by miracles; "But they going forth preached everywhere: the Lord working withal, and confirming the word with signs that followed" (Mk. 16, 20). Hence, He was *healing*. Sickness can be referred to corporeal infirmities, infirmities can be referred to the soul's infirmity: for the infirmities of the soul are not less than those of the body. Or, by sicknesses is meant severe and long-lasting infirmities; by infirmities is meant whatever else; "who healeth all thy diseases" (Ps. 102, 3); "The physician cutteth off a short sickness" (Eccli. 10, 12). In this it is also given to be understood that preachers ought to confirm their teaching by works: and if this is not done by miracles, then by a holy life; "For I dare not to speak of any of those things which Christ worketh not by me, for the obedience of the Gentiles, by word and deed, by the virtue of signs and wonders, in the power of the Holy Ghost" (Rom. 15, 18). *And his fame went throughout all Syria.* Here is set forth the effect of His preaching: and it is threefold, namely, the fame of His example, the confidence which men had in Him, and the devotion by which men followed Him. He says, therefore, *And his fame went throughout all Syria.* Syria is the region from Capharnaum all the way to the Great Sea:[18] hence, His fame was spread forth in

---

18. So the Mediterranean Sea was called by the ancient Greeks and Romans.

the land of the Gentiles. This also pertains to preachers, that they have a good reputation; "Take care of a good name" (Eccli. 41, 15); "But carefully study to present thyself approved unto God, a workman that needeth not to be ashamed, rightly handling the word of truth" (II Tim. 2, 15). By Syria, however, the world's pride can be understood, because it is so-interpreted: and Christ's fame is diffused throughout the whole world. Men's confidence in Him is demonstrated where it is said, *And they presented to him all sick people that were taken with divers diseases*; for they knew that He had the power to heal; "Heal me, O Lord, and I shall be healed: save me, and I shall be saved" (Jer. 17, 14). And he says, firstly, *And his fame went throughout*, etc., and afterwards, *They presented to him*, etc., because when someone has a reputation for sanctity, men more readily uncover their wounds of conscience to him. *That were taken with divers diseases and torments*. By these grave infirmities, spiritual infirmities are designated. By diseases, long-lasting infirmities can be understood, and a long persistent infirmity is signified; "A long sickness is troublesome to the physician" (Eccli. 10, 11). And because some men were burdened with infirmity, but others by the acuteness of pain, this is signified when he says, *taken with torments*: and those are signified, who have a heavy tormented conscience; "The sorrows of death surrounded me: and the torrents of iniquity troubled me" (Ps. 17, 5). *And such as were possessed by devils*; and this is what is also said in Luke 6, 18: "And they that were troubled with unclean spirits were cured." By these men is understood those who were worshiping idols; "All the gods of the Gentiles are devils" (Ps. 95, 5); "I would not that you should be made partakers with devils" (I Cor. 10, 20). They are properly called lunatics, who suffer the infirmity of a certain madness in the eclipse of the moon: and then they are seized by devils. And the devil afflicts more then because of two reasons. Jerome assigns one and it is so that he may disgrace a creature of God; and this also happens in the effects of the magical art, by which devils are invoked under certain constellations, and devils come for the purpose that they may extol the creature, and lead men into idolatry. The second reason is better, namely, that the devil cannot do anything, except by a body's powers. Now there is no doubt that the inferior bodies are changed by the changes of the superior bodies. And thus, the devil, having been invoked willingly, comes when he sees the superior bodies operate for that effect for which he is invoked. Now at the time of an eclipse of the moon, as is evident, fluids diffuse; and thus the eclipse of the moon brings on such an infirmity, when the earth does not abound with moisture; and for that reason the devil agitates more: and so it is said, *And lunatics*. By these men we can also understand the inconstant (Eccli. 27, 12: "A holy man continueth in wisdom as the sun: but a fool is changed as the moon"), who have the intention of living chastely, but are chained by the passions, according to that passage in Romans 7, 15: "For I do not that good which I will: but the evil which I hate, that I do." *And those that had the palsy*. Those are properly said to have the palsy, who have paralyzed members, so that they are unable to have the use of their members. By these are signified the ignorant: and all these are cured by Christ; whence, it is said, *And he cured them*, that is to say, perfectly. Afterwards, the third effect is related, namely, the devotion of the followers; hence, *And much people followed him*; "Arise, O Lord, my God, in the precept which thou hast commanded, and a congregation of people shall surround thee" (Ps. 7, 8). Now it ought to be known that men were following Him in divers manners, for some men were following from a zeal for well-being, that is to say, their spiritual well-being, more precisely, the Apostles; whence, it is written above (in this chapter): "having left all things they followed him"; "Behold we have left all things, and have followed thee" (below 19, 27). Certain men were following Him from zeal for bodily well-being; "A very great multitude of people from all Judea and Jerusalem and the sea coast, both of Tyre and Sidon, who were come to hear him and to be healed of their diseases" (Lk. 6, 17). Certain men followed Him only out of curiosity for seeing miracles; "And a great multitude followed him, because they saw the miracles which he did on them that were diseased" (Jn. 6, 2). Others were following Him to ensnare Him, such as the Pharisees and the Scribes; "For I heard the reproaches of many, and terror on every side" (Jer. 20, 10). *From Galilee*. This is the province in which Christ principally preached, and is interpreted 'a passing.' By this is signified those who ought to pass from vices to virtues. *And from Decapolis*. In this region there are ten villages; and those are signified who strive to observe the ten commandments. *And from Jerusalem*. Jerusalem is interpreted 'vision of peace'; and it signifies those who, from their desire for peace, come to Christ; "Much peace have they that love thy law" (Ps. 188, 165). *And from Judea*. Judea is interpreted 'confession'; and it signifies those who, through the remission of their sins, come to Christ; "Judea was made his sanctuary" (Ps. 113, 2). *And from beyond the Jordan*; and those are signified who through baptism come to Christ: for baptism was figured in the Jordan.

CHAPTER FIVE

1. And seeing the multitudes, he went up into a mountain, and when he was set down, his disciples came unto him.
2. And opening his mouth he taught them, saying:

And seeing the multitudes. Here the Lord presents His doctrine: and it is divided into three sections. In the first section, Christ's doctrine is related; in the second, the doctrine's power is related; and in the third, the goal to which He leads is related. The second section begins in chapter 13; the third section begins in chapter 17. The first section is divided into three parts. In the second part, the ministers of His doctrine are instructed; and in the third part, His adversaries are confounded. The second part begins in chapter 10; and the third begins in chapter 11. The first part is divided into two parts. Firstly, Christ's doctrine is set forth; and secondly, it is confirmed by miracles. In the first part, what one might call a kind of preamble to His doctrine is premised; and in the second part, the doctrine itself is explained, where it is said, **Blessed are the poor in spirit**. About the first the Evangelist does three things. Firstly, he describes the place where Christ's doctrine was proposed; secondly, he describes the hearers of the doctrine; and thirdly, he relates His manner of teaching. The second is where it is said, *And when he was set down*; and the third is where it is said, *And opening his mouth he taught them*. He says, therefore, 'I spoke because many men have followed Me,' etc. *And Jesus seeing the multitudes.* This phrase can be understood in two different ways. Firstly, it is as follows. **He went up** to teach the multitudes, that is to say, not avoiding them. Whence, Chrysostom says, that just as a craftsman, when he sees the material prepared, is delighted to work, so a priest is delighted to preach when he sees the people gathered together; and therefore, **He went up**; "I will give thanks to thee in a great church" (Ps. 34, 18). Or it is otherwise: **He went up**, that is to say, avoiding the multitudes, so that He might more freely teach His disciples; "The words of the wise are heard in silence" (Eccles. 9, 17).

And it should be noted that Christ is said to have had three refuges; for sometimes He fled to a mountain, as said here; and it is written in John 8, 1: "And Jesus went unto mount Olivet." Sometimes He fled to a boat; "When the multitudes pressed upon him... going into one of the ships that was Simon's... sitting he taught" (Lk. 5). And thirdly, sometimes He fled into the desert; "Come apart into a desert place" (Mk. 6, 31). And this was fitting enough; for in three things can a man have a refuge in relation to God: in the protection of the divine loftiness; "They that trust in the Lord shall be as mount Sion" (Ps. 124, 1): in ecclesiastical society, which is designated by the ship; "Jerusalem, which is built as a city, which is compact together" (Ps. 121, 3): and in the solitude of religious life, which is connoted by the desert, though the contempt of temporal things; "I will lead her into the wilderness: and I will speak to her heart" (Osee 2, 8); "Lo, I have gone far off flying away; and I abode in the wilderness" (Ps. 54, 8). Now He went up into the mountain for five reasons. The first was to manifest His excellence: for He is the mountain, about which it is said in Psalm 67, 16: "The mountain of God is a fat mountain." The second was to show that a teacher of this doctrine ought to ascend to an eminence of life; "Get thee up upon a high mountain, thou that bringest good tidings to Sion" (Is. 40, 9). Chrysostom says: "No one can stay standing in a valley and speak of heaven," etc. The third reason was to show the sublimity of the Church to whom the doctrine is proposed; "The mountain of the house of the Lord shall be on the top of mountains, and it shall be exalted above the hills" (Is. 2, 2). Fourthly, this was to manifest the perfection of this doctrine, in that it is most perfect; "Thy justice is as the mountains of God" (Is. 35, 7). Fifthly, this was so that this doctrine might correspond to the old legislation which was given upon a mountain (Ex. 19 & 24).

Afterwards, the hearers are related, *And when he was set down, his disciples came unto him.* Two things can be noted in His sitting. The first is His humbling of Himself; "Thou hast known my sitting down" (Ps. 138, 2). When He was in the loftiness of His majesty, His doctrine could not be received; but then men began to receive it, when He humbled Himself. Or this pertains to a teacher's dignity; "The scribes and the Pharisees have sitten on the chair of Moses" (below 23, 2). For the study of wisdom requires repose. *His disciples came unto him*, etc., not only by means of their bodies, but also by means of their souls; "Come ye to him and be enlightened" (Ps. 33, 6); "They that approach to his feet, shall receive of his doctrine" (Deut. 33, 3). And observe that when the Lord preached to the multitudes, He stood; "And coming down with them, he stood in a plain place" (Lk. 6, 17); but here, when He preached to His disciples, He sat. From this the custom evolved that one preaches to the multitudes standing, but to religious sitting. *And opening his mouth he taught them.* Here His manner of teaching is related. In this that he says, *Opening*, it is indicated that He had been silent previously for a long time. And it shows that He was about to make a great and long sermon, as Augustine says. Or it shows that He was about to speak great and profound things; "After this, Job opened his mouth, and cursed his day" (Job 3, 1). And he says, *His*: for previously He had opened the mouths of the prophets; "For wisdom opened the mouth of the dumb, and made the tongues of infants eloquent" (Wis. 10, 21): for He is the Father's wisdom.

But here there is a question: for this sermon relates many of the same things found in Luke 6. But discrepancies seem to exist here and there, as is evident in the text.

And so Augustine gives two solutions. One is that this sermon is a different sermon from the other one: for, firstly, He went up into the mountain, and He gave this sermon to His disciples: and afterwards, coming down, He found the crowd gathered, to which He preached the same thing, and He recapitulated many things: and of this it is related in Lk 6. Or it can be explained otherwise, that there was one mountain, and it had a level spot on its side: a higher peak was rising above that level spot. Hence, the Lord went up into the mountain, meaning that he went up into a level spot of that mountain. And, firstly, He went up higher, and called together the disciples, and there He chose the twelve Apostles, just as it is related in Luke: and afterwards, coming down, He found the crowd gathered together, and when His disciples came He sat down, and gave this sermon to the crowds and disciples. And this seems to be more true: because Matthew relates in the end of the sermon (chap. 7, 28) that "the people were in admiration at his doctrine."

3. Blessed are the poor in spirit: for theirs is the kingdom of heaven.
4. Blessed are the meek: for they shall possess the land.
5. Blessed are they that mourn: for they shall be comforted.
6. Blessed are they that hunger and thirst after justice: for they shall have their fill.
7. Blessed are the merciful: for they shall obtain mercy.
8. Blessed are the clean of heart: for they shall see God.
9. Blessed are the peacemakers: for they shall be called the children of God.
10. Blessed are they that suffer persecution for justice' sake: for theirs is the kingdom of heaven.

The Evangelist, above, set forth a kind of brief preamble to Christ's teaching; now he relates the teaching itself and its effect, namely, the admiration of the multitudes. Now it ought to be considered that, according to Augustine, the whole perfection of our life is contained in this sermon. And he proves that the height of perfection, to which Christ leads, is contained in this sermon by the words that the Lord adds, namel,y a particular promise.[1] Now that which man desires most of all is happiness. Hence, the Lord does three things here. Firstly, He promises a reward which is gained by those who receive this doctrine; secondly, He relates the precepts, where it is said, **Do not think that I am come to destroy the law**; and thirdly, He teaches how a man can come to observe these things, where it is said, **Ask, and it shall be given you**. About the first, He does two things, for some are only observers of this doctrine; and others are ministers of it. Firstly, He describes the happiness of the observers, and secondly, of the ministers, where it is said, **Blessed are ye when they shall revile you**.

Now one should note that many things are here related about the beatitudes; but never could anyone speak so skillfully about the Lord's words, that he could attain to the Lord's full purpose. Yet it should be known that in these words every complete happiness is included: for all men desire happiness; but they differ in judging about happiness; and thus some desire this and others desire that. Now, we find four opinions about beatitude. For some believe that it consists only in exterior things, namely, in an abundance of these temporal things; "They have called the people happy, that hath these things" (Ps. 134, 15). Others believe that perfect beatitude consists in this, that man satisfies his own will; hence, we say happy is he who lives as he wishes; "And I have known that there was no better thing than to rejoice" (Eccles. 3, 12). Others

---

[1] "If anyone will piously and soberly consider the sermon which our Lord Jesus Christ spoke on the mount, as we read it in the Gospel according to Matthew, I think that he will find in it, so far as regards the highest morals, a perfect standard of the Christian life: and this we do not rashly venture to promise, but gather it from the very words of the Lord Himself. For the sermon itself is brought to a close in such a way, that it is clear there are in it all the precepts which go to mold the life. For thus He speaks: 'Therefore, whosoever heareth these words of mine, and doeth them, I will liken him unto a wise man, which built his house upon a rock: and the rain descended, and the floods came, and the winds blew, and beat upon that house; and it fell not: for it was founded upon a rock. And every one that heareth these words of mine, and doeth them not, I will liken unto a foolish man, which built his house upon the sand: and the rain descended, and the floods came, and the winds blew, and beat upon that house; and it fell: and great was the fall of it.' Since, therefore, He has not simply said, 'Whosoever heareth my words,' but has made an addition, saying, 'Whosoever heareth these words of mine,' He has sufficiently indicated, as I think, that these sayings which He uttered on the mount so perfectly guide the life of those who may be willing to live according to them, that they may justly be compared to one building upon a rock. I have said this merely that it may be clear that the sermon before us is perfect in all the precepts by which the Christian life is molded; for as regards this particular section a more careful treatment will be given in its own place" (Augustine, *Our Lord's Sermon on the Mount*, bk. 1, chap. 1, n. 1).

say that perfect beatitude consists in the virtues of the active life. Others say that it consists in the virtues of the contemplative life, namely, of divine and intelligible things, as Aristotle supposed. All these opinions, however, are false, although not in the same way. Whence, the Lord reproves all these opinions. He reproves the opinion of those who said that it consists in an abundance of exterior things: hence, He says, **Blessed are the poor**, as though He were to say, the rich are not happy. He reproves the opinion of those who were placing beatitude in the satisfaction of their appetite when He says, **Blessed are the merciful**. But it should be known that the appetite is threefold in man: the irascible, which desires revenge of one's enemies: and He reproves this when He says, **Blessed are the meek**; the concupiscible, whose good is to rejoice and enjoy: He reproves this when He says, **Blessed are they that mourn**; the will's appetite, which is twofold, according to the two things that it seeks. Firstly, it seeks that its will be not coerced by any higher law; and secondly, that that it restrain others as subjects: hence, it desires to preside and not to be subject. The Lord, however, shows the contrary to be true in regard to both opinions. And regarding the first, He says, **Blessed are they that hunger and thirst after justice**. And regarding the second, He says, **Blessed are the merciful**. Therefore, both they who place their beatitude in exterior wealth, and those who place their beatitude in the satisfaction of desire, err. Those, however, who place their beatitude in actions of the active life, namely, in moral practices, err; but they err less, because that is the means to beatitude. Hence, the Lord does not reprove it as evil, but He shows it to be something ordered to beatitude: because either the virtues are ordered to oneself, such as temperance and the like; and their end is cleanliness of heart, because they enable one to conquer the passions: or they are ordered to others; and so their end is peace, and the like. For the work of justice is peace. And thus these virtues are means to beatitude, and not beatitude itself; and so the passage is, **Blessed are the clean of heart: for they shall see God**. He does not say, 'They see God,' because this would be beatitude itself. And, likewise, **Blessed are the peacemakers**, not because they are peacemakers, but because they aim at something else, **for they shall be called the children of God**. Now, the Lord reproves the opinion of those who say that beatitude consists in the contemplation of divine things, as to its time, for otherwise it is true, for ultimate happiness consists in the contemplation of the most intelligible thing, namely, God: wherefore He says, **They shall see**.

And it ought to be observed that, according to the Philosopher, in order that contemplative actions make one to be happy, two things are required: one thing is substantially required, namely, that it be an actuation by the highest intelligible being, who is God; the other is formally required, namely, love and delight. For delight perfects happiness, just as beauty perfects youth. And thus the Lord states two things, ***They shall see God***, and, ***They shall be called the children of God***: for this pertains to a union of love: "Behold what manner of charity the Father hath bestowed upon us, that we should be called and should be the sons of God" (I Jn. 3, 1).

Again, it should be noted that in these beatitudes certain things are set forth as merits, and certain things are set forth as rewards: and this one by one. ***Blessed are the poor in spirit:*** see the merit; ***for theirs is the kingdom of heaven***: see the reward, and so forth in the others.

And something should also be observed about the merits in general, and about the rewards in general. Regarding the merits, it ought to be known that the Philosopher distinguishes two kinds of virtue: one is common, which perfects man in a human manner. For when a strong man fears when he ought to fear, this is a virtue. But if he were not to fear, this would be a vice. If, however, he would never fear, having trusted in God's help, this virtue would be above the human manner: and these virtues are called divine. These acts, therefore, are perfect, and a virtue, also according to the Philosopher, is a perfect operation. Therefore, these merits either are acts of the gifts, or acts of the virtues, to the extent that they are perfected by the gifts. Again, observe that acts of the virtues are those concerning which the Law prescribes; now, the merits of the beatitudes are acts of the virtues; and thus everything which is prescribed, or is included within what is prescribed, are related to these beatitudes. Hence, just as Moses firstly presented the precepts, and afterwards He said many things which were related to the presented precepts: so Christ in his teaching firstly premised these beatitudes, to which all the other teachings are reduced. Now concerning the first, it ought to be noted that God is the reward of them who serve Him; "The Lord is my portion, said my soul: therefore will I wait for him" (Lam. 3, 24); "The Lord is the portion of my inheritance and of my cup" (Ps. 15, 5); "I am the Lord who brought thee out from Ur of the Chaldees, to give thee this land, and that thou mightest possess it" (Gen. 15, 7). Augustine says, in *II Confessions*, "When the soul withdraws from Thee, it seeks goods outside of Thee." Now men seek after various things; but all that could be found in whatever kind of way of life, the Lord in return promises all in God. For some men place the highest good to be an abundance of riches, by which they can arrive at the greatest dignities; the Lord promises a kingdom which encompasses both; but to arrive at this kingdom, He says, is by way of poverty, not by way of riches. Wherefore, He says, **Blessed are the poor**. Others strive to arrive at these honors through wars; the Lord, however, says, **Blessed are the meek**, etc. Some seek consolations through pleasures; and so the Lords says, **Blessed are they that mourn**. Some others do not wish to be subjected, and so the Lord says, **Blessed are they that hunger and thirst after justice**. Some others wish to avoid hardship by oppressing their subordinates, and so the Lord says, **Blessed are the merciful**. Others suppose the vision of God to be in the contemplation of truth on earth; the Lord, however, promises it to be in Heaven; wherefore, **Blessed are the clean of heart**, etc. And it ought to be observed that these rewards, which the Lord touches upon here, can be possessed in two ways, namely, perfectly, and by way of a completion, and in this way they exist in heaven only: and these rewards can be possessed by way of a beginning, and imperfectly, and in this way they exist on earth. Whence, the Saints have some beginning of that beatitude. And because these things cannot be explained in this life just as they will be in heaven; thus Augustine expounds them in such a way as they are in this life. **Blessed are the poor in spirit**: not only by the happiness which consists in hope, but also by the happiness attained in reality. "The kingdom of God is within you" (Lk. 17, 21). Wherefore, these things having been prefaced, let us proceed to the text.

In these beatitudes, the Evangelist does two things. Firstly, the beatitudes themselves are set forth; and secondly, their clarification is set forth, where it is said, **Blessed are they that suffer persecution for justice' sake: for theirs is the kingdom of heaven**; for this is explanatory of all the beatitudes. Now virtue does three things: for it withdraws from evil, it does good works and makes good works to be done, and it disposes to that which is best. Firstly, He prescribes about the first, where it is said, **Blessed are the poor**; He prescribes about the second, where it is said, **Blessed are they that hunger**; and He prescribes about the third, where it is said, **Blessed are the clean of heart**. Now virtue withdraws from three evils: the evil of cupidity, the evil of cruelty or inquietude, and the evil of harmful pleasure. The first is indicated, where it is said, **Blessed are the poor**; the second is indicated, where it is said, **Blessed are the merciful**; and the third is indicated, where it is said, **Blessed are they that mourn**. He says, therefore, **Blessed are the poor**. This can be read in two ways. Firstly, it is as follows: **Blessed are the poor**, that is to say, the humble, who esteem themselves poor: for they are truly humble, who esteem themselves poor, not only in exterior things but also in interior things; "But I am a beggar and poor" (Ps. 39, 18), as opposed to that which is written in Apocalypse 3, 17: "Because thou sayest: I am rich and made wealthy and have need of nothing: and knowest not that thou art wretched and miserable and poor and blind and naked," etc. And then, that which He says, **In spirit**, can be read in three ways. For man's pride is sometimes called a spirit; "Cease ye therefore from the man, whose breath (*spiritus*) is in his nostrils, for he is reputed high" (Is. 2, 22); "the blast (*spiritus*) of the mighty is like a whirlwind beating against a wall" (Is. 25, 4). And pride is called a spirit because just as bags are inflated by blowing so men are inflated by pride; "Puffed up by the sense of his flesh" (Col. 2, 18). Therefore, **blessed are the poor**, namely, those who possess little of the spirit of pride. Or a spirit can be taken for man's will. For some men are humble through necessity, and these are not blessed, but are those who affect humility. Thirdly, a spirit can be taken for the Holy Ghost (*Spiritus*); hence, **Blessed are the poor in spirit**, who are humble through the Holy Ghost; "To whom shall I have respect, but to him that is poor and little, and of a contrite spirit, and that trembleth at my words?" (Is. 66, 2). To these poor is promised in return, a kingdom, by which is understood the highest excellence. And given that this will be granted in return to any virtue, nevertheless, it is especially given to humility, because "whosoever shall humble himself shall be exalted" (below 23, 12). And: "Glory shall uphold the humble of spirit" (Prov. 39, 23). Or it is otherwise, according to Jerome. **The poor in spirit**, is to be understood literally, in the disowning of temporal things. And He says, **In spirit**: because some men are poor by necessity, but the beatitude is not due to them, but to those who are poor by choice. And these are called poor in two ways; because even if some have riches, nevertheless, they do not have them in their hearts; "If riches abound, set not your heart upon them" (Ps. 61, 11). Others neither have, nor desire riches, and this is safer because the mind is drawn away from spiritual things by riches. And these are properly called poor in spirit, because the acts of the gifts, which are above the human manner, belong to a blessed man: and that a man would cast away all riches, so that he also does not desire them in any way, this is above the human manner.

Now to these men the kingdom of heaven is promised in return, in which is indicated not only a height of honor, but also an abundance of riches; "Hath not God chosen the poor in this world, rich in faith?" (James 2, 5)

And observe that Moses firstly promised riches; "The Lord thy God will make thee higher than all the nations that are on the earth" (Deut. 28, 1); and further on: "Blessed shalt thou be in the city, and blessed in the field" (v. 3). And thus, in order that the Lord might distinguish the Old Law from the New, He firstly places beatitude in the contempt of riches.

Likewise, according to Augustine, note that this beatitude pertains to the gift of fear: because fear, especially filial fear, causes one to have reverence towards God; and from this a man despises riches. Isaias sets forth the beatitudes by descending; "And there shall come forth a rod out of the root of Jesse, and a flower shall rise up out of his root. And the spirit of the Lord shall rest upon him: the spirit of wisdom, and of understanding, the spirit of counsel, and of fortitude, the spirit of knowledge, and of godliness. And he shall be filled with the spirit of the fear of the Lord" (Is. 11, 1). Christ, on the contrary, sets them forth starting from the gift of fear, namely, from poverty, because Isaias foretold Christ's coming to earth; Christ, however, was drawing from the earth upwards.

Blessed are the meek. This is the second beatitude; but lest someone might say that poverty suffices for beatitude, He shows that it does not suffice: nay, rather meekness is also required, which moderates movements of anger, while temperance moderates movements of concupiscence: for he is meek who is also not irritated. Now this can be done through virtue, namely, so that you are not angered except from a just cause; but if you were even to have a just cause, and you are not provoked, this is above a human manner; and therefore He says, **Blessed are the meek.** For fighting is for the sake of an abundance of exterior things; and thus there would never be a disturbance if a man would not desire riches; and thus those who are not meek, are not poor in spirit. And for that reason, He immediately adds, **Blessed are the meek.** And observe that this consists in two things. Firstly, it consists in that a man is not angered; and secondly, it consists in that, if he is angered, that He tempers his anger. Accordingly, Ambrose says: "It belongs to a prudent man to moderate the movements of anger, and it is not said to be less of a virtue to be angered temperately, than it is to be not angered at all: and I think that the latter is very much less than the former", etc. Chrysostom says:

"Amidst many eternal promises He sets forth one that is earthly." Hence, literally, the meek possess this land. For many quarrel so that they may acquire possessions, but frequently they destroy their life and all their possessions, and frequently the meek possess it all; "The meek shall inherit the land" (Ps. 36, 11). But it is better expounded as referring to the future. And it can then be expounded in many ways. Hilary expounds it as follows: *They shall possess the land*, that is, Christ's glorified body, because they will be conformed in their body to that glory; "His eyes shall see the king in his beauty, they shall see the land far off" (Is. 33, 17); "He will reform the body of our lowness, made like to the body of his glory" (Phil. 3, 21). Or, in a different way, this land is now the land of the dead, because it is subjected to corruption, but it shall be freed from corruption, according to the Apostle (Rom. 8, 21). Therefore, this land, when it shall be glorified and freed from the servitude of corruption, will be called the land of the living. Or, by the land is understood the empyreal heaven, in which the blessed are: and they are called the land, because just as the land is related to heaven, so heaven is to the heaven of the Holy Trinity. Or, *they shall possess the land*, that is, their own glorified bodies. Augustine expounds this metaphorically: and he says that by this is to be understood a sort of solidity of the Saints in the knowledge of the first truth; "I believe to see the good things of the Lord in the land of the living" (Ps. 36, 13).

This second beatitude is suited to the gift of piety: because those are particularly angered who are not content with the divine ordination.

Blessed are they that mourn, etc. Two beatitudes have been set forth, through which we are drawn away from the evils of cupidity and cruelty; here a third is set forth, by which we are drawn away from the evil of harmful pleasure, or of delight: and the passage is, *Blessed are they that mourn.* In the Old Testament He was promising earthly things and earthly delight; "They shall flow together to the good things of the Lord, for the corn, and wine, and oil" (Jer. 31, 12); and afterwards: "The virgin shall rejoice in the dance, the young men and old men together" (v. 13). But on the contrary, the Lord places beatitude in mourning. It ought to be observed, however, that not any lamentation can be called mourning; but that by which a person laments someone beloved to oneself who has died: for the Lord speaks here by way of an excess. Just as above it is said, *Blessed are the poor*; so here He makes mention of a very great mourning; for just as these men who lament the dead accept no consolation, so the Lord wants our life to be in mourning; "Make thee mourning as for an only son, a bitter lamentation," etc., (Jer. 6, 26). And this mourning can be explained in three ways. Firstly, mourning can be not only for one's own sins but also for others' sins; because if we lament those who have carnally died, much more should we lament those who have died spiritually; "How long wilt thou mourn for Saul," etc., (I Kings 16, 1); "Who will give water to my head, and a fountain of tears to my eyes? and I will weep day and night for the slain of the daughter of my people" (Jer. 9, 1). Now this beatitude is, fittingly enough, related after the previous one; for someone could say, 'It suffices not to do evil': and this is true at first, before sin; but after sin has been committed, it does not suffice except you make satisfaction. Secondly, it can be understood of the mourning for the sojourning of the present misery; "Woe is me, that my sojourning is prolonged" (Ps. 119, 5). This is a watering above and below, of which it is written in Josue 15, 19: "Weep for your sins and for the sojourning of the heavenly home"[2] Thirdly, according to Augustine, it can be for the mourning which men have for the joys of the present time, which they forsake by coming to Christ: for men die to some worldly life, and worldly life dies to them; "By whom the world is crucified to me, and I to the world" (Gal. 6, 14). Now just as we ourselves mourn for the dead, so they mourn: because it cannot be that in abandoning, one would not feel some sorrow. Now to this triple mourning corresponds a triple consolation: because to the mourning for sins is given the remission of sins, which David was requesting saying: "Restore unto me the joy of thy salvation" (Ps. 50, 14). To the love of the heavenly home, and to the sojourning of the present misery, corresponds the consolation of eternal life about which it is written: "I will turn their mourning into joy, and will comfort them, and make them joyful after their sorrow" (Jer. 31, 13); and: "You shall be comforted in Jerusalem" (Is. 66, 13). To the third mourning corresponds the consolation of divine love: for when someone is sorrowful about the loss of a loved thing, he receives consolation if he acquires another thing loved more. Hence, men are consoled, when in place of temporal things, they receive spiritual and eternal things, which is to receive the Holy Ghost; for this reason He is called the Paraclete[3] (Jn. 15, 26). For through the Holy Ghost, who is divine love, men rejoice; "Your sorrow shall be turned into joy" (Jn. 16, 20).

---

2. Josue 15, 19 is actually as follows: "Give me a blessing: thou hast given me a southern and dry land, give me also a land that is watered. And Caleb gave her the upper and the nether watery ground."
3. Paraclete means a comforter.

And it ought to be noted that this beatitude is ascribed to the gift of knowledge, because those men mourn who know the miseries of others: whence, it is said about certain men not having such knowledge: "Whereas they lived in a great war of ignorance, they call so many and so great evils peace" (Wis. 14, 22); on the other hand: "He that addeth knowledge, addeth also labour" (Eccles. 1, 18).

And it ought to be observed that these rewards are so-ordered that the subsequent one always adds something to the preceding one. For firstly He said, *Blessed are the poor in spirit: for theirs is the kingdom of heaven*; and afterwards, *For they shall possess the land*: for it is greater to possess than merely to have. Again afterwards, *For they shall be comforted*: for it is greater to be consoled than to possess: for some possess these things, but they do not delight in them.

Subsequently, having set forth the beatitudes which pertain to the removal of evil, here is set forth the beatitude which pertains to the performance of good. Now there is a twofold performance of good, namely, of justice and of mercy. And thus He sets forth two things. As to the first, He says: *Blessed are they that hunger and thirst after justice*. Justice is understood in three ways, according to Chrysostom and the Philosopher. For sometimes it is taken for every virtue: and so every virtue is called legal justice, which commands about the acts of the virtues. Hence, so far as a man obeys the law, he fulfills the work of all virtues. In another way, such that it is a special virtue, it is one of the four cardinal virtues, which is opposed to avarice, or injustice, and is concerned with buying, selling, and renting. Therefore, what He says here, *that hunger and thirst after justice*, can be understood generally or specifically. If it is understood in the general sense, He says this for two reasons. The first reason is Jerome's, who says that it does not suffice that a man perform a work of justice, unless he acts willingly; "I will freely sacrifice to thee," etc., (Ps. 53, 8); "My soul panteth after God the fountain of water," etc., (Ps. 41, 2). "I will send forth a famine into the land: not a famine of bread, nor a thirst of water, but of hearing the word of the Lord" (Amos 8, 11). Therefore, there is hunger when one acts willingly. There is a second reason. Justice is twofold, perfect and imperfect: we cannot have perfect justice in this world, because "If we say that we have no sin, we deceive ourselves and the truth is not in us" (I Jn. 1, 8). And it is written in Isaias 64, 6: "All our justices [are] as the rag of a menstruous woman"; and in Isaias 60, 21: "And thy people shall be all just, they shall inherit the land for ever." But we can here possess the desire for justice: and thus He says, *Blessed are*

they that hunger and thirst after justice, etc. And it is similar to that which Pythagoras did: for in the time of Pythagoras, those who were studying were called *sophi*, that is, the wise men; Pythagoras, however, did not wish to be called *sophos*, that is, a wise man, but *Philosophos*, which means a lover of wisdom: so also the Lord wished that His own followers be, and be called, lovers of justice. If, however, it be understood as special justice, namely, that a man render to everyone what is his due, it is fittingly said, **Blessed are they that hunger**, etc; because hunger and thirst properly belong to avaricious men, for they are never satiated who desire to unjustly possess others' possessions: hence, this hunger, about which the Lord speaks, is opposed to this one, namely, of the avaricious. And the Lord wills that we long for this justice, because we can never, as it were, be satiated in this life, just as an avaricious man is never satiated. **Blessed are they that hunger and thirst after justice: for they shall have their fill.** A suitable reward is related, **Shall have their fill**, and, firstly, such will be in the eternal vision, for they shall see God through His essence; "I shall be satisfied when thy glory shall appear" (Ps. 16, 15): for in the eternal vision nothing will be left to desire; "Who satisfieth thy desire with good things" (Ps. 102, 5); "To the just their desire shall be given" (Prov. 24, 10). Secondly, they will be filled in the present time. And this is twofold. One way is in spiritual goods, that is, in the fulfillment of God's commandments; "My meat is to do the will of him that sent me, that I may perfect his work" (Jn. 4, 34): and Augustine explains this meaning. It is taken in another way as referring to a fullness of temporal goods. Unjust men are never filled, but men who have justice itself as their limit, pass no further; "The just eateth and filleth his soul" (Prov. 13, 25).

This beatitude, according to Augustine, is related to the gift of fortitude: because what a man performs justly with labor, pertains to fortitude. Likewise, it adds in addition something above the reward stipulated, because to be filled is to totally fulfill a desire.

Similarly, observe that He says, firstly, **Blessed are they that mourn**: for a man, when he is sick, does not wish to eat; but from the time when he begins to be healed, then he begins to desire to eat: and so it is in spiritual matters, because when men are in sin they do not feel spiritual hunger; but when they abandon sins, then they feel hunger; and thus, He immediately adds, **Blessed are the merciful**: for justice without mercy is cruelty; mercy without justice is dissolution. And thus it is fitting that both are joined together, according to the passage: "Let not mercy and truth leave thee" (Prov. 3, 3). "Mercy and truth have met each other" (Ps. 84, 11).

Blessed are the merciful: for they shall obtain mercy. Mercy is to have a sorrowful heart in respect to others' misery: now, we have mercy concerning others' misery at the moment when we consider it to be in a certain way our own. Now, we feel pain about our own misery, and so we strive to repel it. There is, however, a twofold misery of our neighbor. The first is in these temporal things; and in regard to this we ought to have a sorrowful heart; "He that hath the substance of this world and shall see his brother in need and shall shut up his bowels from him: how doth the charity of God abide in him?" (I Jn. 3, 17). The second is the misery by which, through sin, a man is made miserable: because just as beatitude is in the works of the virtues, so one's own misery is in the vices; "Sin maketh nations miserable" (Prov. 14, 34). And thus, when we admonish those falling into sin that they return to virtue, we are merciful; "And seeing the multitudes, Jesus had compassion on them" (below 9, 36). These merciful persons, therefore, are blessed. And why? *For they shall obtain mercy.* And it ought to be known that God's gifts always exceed our merits; "For the Lord maketh recompense, and will give thee seven times as much" (Eccli. 35, 13). Therefore, much greater is the mercy which God grants to us, than that which we grant to our neighbor. This mercy begins in this life in two ways. In the first place, it is begun because sins are remitted; "Who forgiveth all thy iniquities" (Ps. 102, 3). In the second place, it is begun because He relieves our temporal needs, such that He makes His sun to rise; this will be completed in the future, when all miseries, guilt, and punishments will be eliminated; "O Lord, thy mercy is in heaven" (Ps. 35, 6). And so the passage is, *For they shall obtain mercy.*

This beatitude is related to the gift of counsel: for this is a unique counsel, such that, amidst the dangers of this world, we may attain mercy; "Godliness is profitable to all things" (I Tim. 4, 8); and: "Let my counsel be acceptable to the king" (Dan. 4, 24).[4]

In this way, therefore, are set forth the acts of the virtues, by which we are withdrawn from evil and perform the good. Now are set forth the acts by which we are disposed to the best; hence, *Blessed are the clean of heart,* etc. These beatitudes consist in two things: in the vision of God and in the love of neighbor: whence, firstly, He relates the beatitude which pertains to the vi-

---

[4]. The full quotation of Daniel 4, 24 clearly pertains to mercy and is as follows: "Wherefore, O king, let my counsel be acceptable to thee, and redeem thou thy sins with alms, and thy iniquities with works of mercy to the poor: perhaps he will forgive thy offences."

sion of God; and secondly, He relates the beatitude which pertains to love of neighbor, where it is said, ***Blessed are the peacemakers***, etc. He says, therefore: ***Blessed are the clean of heart: for they shall see God.***

There is, firstly, here a literal question. For we hold that God cannot be seen; "No man hath seen God at any time" (I Jn. 4, 12). And lest someone might say that, although no one may see God in the present, one will see Him in the future, the Apostle eliminates this possibility in I Tim. 6, 16: "He inhabiteth light inaccessible: whom no man hath seen, nor can see."

But it ought to be known that there are various opinions concerning this. For some maintained that God may never be seen in His essence, but only in some reflection of His glory; but this is reproved by the Gloss upon the passage of Exodus 33, 20: "Man shall not see me, and live" for two reasons. In the first place, it is because this opposes the authority of Scripture, I Jn. 3, 2: "We shall see him as he is." Likewise, it is opposed to I Corinthians 13, 12: "We see now through a glass in a dark manner: but then face to face." Moreover, it is opposed to reason, because man's beatitude is the ultimate good of man, in which his desire is quieted. Now it is a natural desire that a man, seeing effects, inquires about the cause: hence, the wonderment of the philosophers was the origin of philosophy, because seeing effects they wondered, and they sought the cause. Therefore, this desire will not be quieted until it arrives at the first cause, which is God, and, more precisely, at the divine essence itself. Therefore, He will be seen in His essence. Others erred more by maintaining the contrary: because they said that we will not only see the essence of God with the eye of the mind, but also with the eyes of the body: and that Christ sees the divine essence with His corporeal eyes. But this is not suitable: and it is evident from the passage which is set forth here, for it would not say, ***Blessed are the clean of heart***, but rather 'Blessed are they who have clean and pure eyes.' Therefore, He gives to understand that He is not seen except by the heart, that is to say, by the intellect: for in such a way is the heart understood here, just as it is also understood in Ephesians 1, 18: "The eyes of your heart having been enlightened." Secondly, it is not suitable, because the sense of the eye cannot function except on its own object; if, however, it be said that then it will have greater power, it must be said that it would not then be corporeal vision, because the corporeal eye does not see unless it sees colors; it sees the essence indirectly [*per accidens*], according to Augustine, in the last book of *The City of God*, chapter 19. Just as when I see a living thing, we can say that

I see life, inasmuch as I see some indications by which its life is indicated to me; so it will be in the divine vision, because so great will be the refulgence in the new heaven, in the new earth, and in the glorified bodies, that through these things we will be said to see God, as it were, with the corporeal eyes. Therefore, **Blessed are the clean of heart**, etc.

That passage, "No man hath seen God," can truly be explained in three ways. Firstly, it can be explained that it is not by a comprehensive vision; secondly, it is not by the corporeal eyes; and thirdly, it is not in this life: because if it were given to someone that he will have seen God in this life, this was because he was totally separated and elevated above the corporeal senses: and thus it is said, **Blessed are the clean of heart**: because just as it is suitable that an eye seeing color be purified, so the mind seeing God also; "Seek him in simplicity of heart: For he is found by them that tempt him not: and he sheweth himself to them that have faith in him" (Wis. 1, 1): for by faith the heart is purified; "Purifying their hearts by faith" (Acts 15, 9). And because vision succeeds faith, therefore it is said, **For they shall see God**. **Blessed are the clean of heart**, namely, who have complete cleanliness from foreign thoughts, through which their hearts are holy temples of God, in which they see God contemplated: for 'temple' seems to be named from 'contemplating'. Indeed, specially **Blessed are the clean of heart**, that is to say, who have purity of the flesh: for nothing so impedes spiritual contemplation as uncleanness of the flesh. "Follow peace with all men and holiness: without which no man shall see God" (Heb. 12, 14). And so, some say that the moral virtues, and especially chastity, are conducive to the contemplative life. And according to this, **Blessed are the clean of heart**, can be understood of the vision of the present life: for the Saints, who have their hearts filled with justice, see more excellently than others who see through corporeal effects: for as much as the effects are nearer, so much more is God known by them. Hence, the Saints who have justice, charity, and effects of this kind, which are very similar to God, know more than others; "O taste, and see that the Lord is sweet" (Ps. 33, 9).

Blessed are the peacemakers: for they shall be called the children of God. Here is related the seventh beatitude: and, as it was said, the virtues, disposing to the best, dispose to two things, namely, to the vision and love of God. And just as cleanliness of heart disposes to the vision of God, so peace disposes to love of God, by which we are named, and are, sons of God; and in this way it disposes to love of neighbor, because, as it is said in I

John 4, 20: "He that loveth not his brother whom he seeth, how can he love God whom he seeth not?" And it ought to be observed that actually two rewards of the beatitudes are set forth here: ***Blessed are the peacemakers*** and ***Blessed are they that suffer persecution for justice' sake.*** And all the preceding ones are reduced to these two, and they are effects of all the preceding ones. For what is accomplished through poverty of spirit, through mourning, through meekness, except that a clean heart be possessed? What is accomplished through justice and mercy, except that we have peace? "And the work of justice shall be peace, and the service of justice quietness, and security for ever" (Is. 32, 17). Therefore, ***Blessed are the peacemakers.*** But it ought to be seen what peace is, and how we can attain it. Peace is the tranquility of order. Now order disposes things equal and unequal in their proper place.[5] Hence, man's mind ought to, firstly, be subject to God. Secondly, the movements and inferior powers, which are common to us and to beasts, ought to be subject to man: for by reason man has dominion over the animals; "Let us make man to our image and likeness: and let him have dominion over the fishes of the sea, and the fowls of the air, and the beasts, and the whole earth, and every creeping creature that moveth upon the earth" (Gen. 1, 26). Thirdly, man ought to have peace with other men, because in this way he will be completely ordered. This orderly arrangement, however, can only be in holy men; "Much peace have they that love thy law, and to them there is no stumbling block" (Ps. 118, 165); "There is no peace to the wicked" (Is. 48, 22): for they are unable to have interior peace; "Whereas they lived in a great war of ignorance, they call so many and so great evils peace" (Wis. 14, 22). The world is not able to give such peace; "Not as the world giveth, do I give unto you" (Jn. 14, 27). Moreover, all this does not suffice, but they ought to make peace between discordant men; "Joy followeth them that take counsels of peace" (Prov. 12, 20). Nevertheless, it ought to be known that this peace begins here, but it is not perfected here, because no one can have the animal movements completely subject to reason; "I see another law in my members, fighting against the law of my mind and captivating me in the law of sin that is in my members" (Rom. 7, 23). Hence, true peace will be in eternal life; "In peace in the self same I will sleep, and I will rest" (Ps. 4, 9); "The peace of God, which surpasseth all understanding" (Phil. 4, 7). ***For they shall be called the children of God***, for three reasons. The first is because they will

---

5. This definition is taken from St. Augustine in *De Civitate Dei* xix, 13. cf. I, q. 96, 3 s. c.

have the function of the Son of God: for unto this purpose the Son is said to have come into this world, to gather the dispersed; "For he is our peace" (Eph. 2, 14); "making peace through the blood of his cross, both as to the things that are on earth and the things that are in heaven" (Col. 1, 20). Secondly, this is because through peace, together with charity, one attains to the eternal kingdom, in which all are called children of God; "Behold, how they are numbered among the children of God, and their lot is among the saints" (Wis. 5, 5). "Careful to keep the unity of the Spirit in the bond of peace" (Eph. 4, 3). Thirdly, this is because by this peace man is likened to God, because where there is peace, there is not any resistance; and no one can resist God; "Who hath resisted him, and hath had peace? (Job 9, 4).

And it ought to be observed that each of these beatitudes mutually add something in addition to the rest: for it is greater to obtain mercy than to be filled: for to have one's fill is to be filled in that amount which is proportionate to itself, but mercy superabounds this amount. Likewise, not all who receive mercy are admitted by the king to seeing the king. Likewise, it is greater to be the son of the king, than to see the king. And, nevertheless, it ought to be known that by all these things one reward is designated.

But why did the Lord will to so-portray it by many things? It must be answered that all things which are divided into lower things, are gathered together in the higher things. And because in human affairs these things are found dispersed, and we are led by the hand through sensible things; for that reason the Lord portrayed that eternal reward through many things.

Now this seventh beatitude relates to the gift of wisdom: for wisdom makes us to be sons of God. Likewise, it should be observed, in the seventh beatitude peace is set forth, just as in the seventh day there was rest (Gen. 2).

Subsequently, the eighth beatitude is set forth, which designates the perfection of all the preceding ones: for a man is perfected in all those things at the time when he will lack nothing on account of tribulations; "The furnace trieth the potter's vessels, and the trial of affliction just men," etc., (Eccli. 27, 6).

But perhaps someone hearing, **Blessed are the peacemakers**, will say these men are not blessed on account of persecution: because persecution disturbs peace, or totally takes it away; but certainly it does not take away the interior, but the exterior peace; "Much peace have they that love thy law" (Ps. 118, 165).

Now persecution itself does not make one blessed, but it is its cause: hence, He says, *for justice' sake,* they are **blessed**.

Chrysostom says: "He does not say from the pagans, and for the sake of the faith, but on account of justice:"[6] "Strive for justice for thy soul, and even unto death fight for justice, and God will overthrow thy enemies for thee" (Eccli. 4, 33).[7]

11. Blessed are ye when they shall revile you, and persecute you, and speak all that is evil against you, untruly, for my sake:
12. Be glad and rejoice for your reward is very great in heaven. For so they persecuted the prophets that were before you.

The prophets were killed because they did not deny the faith, but instead proclaimed the truth; John the Baptist was killed and was a martyr because he was proclaiming the truth.

And it ought to be observed that this beatitude is put in the eighth place, just as circumcision was performed on the eighth day, in which a kind of general circumcision of the martyrs is foretold.

For theirs is the kingdom of heaven. These words seem to be taken from words that are related in the first beatitude; hence, it is expounded in various ways by the Saints. For some say that this is the same as that which is said: "Blessed are the poor in spirit: for theirs is the kingdom of heaven" (above, verse 3), and this is to designate the perfection of patience; "And patience hath a perfect work: that you may be perfect and entire, failing in nothing" (James 1, 4). Now, patience is designated by the fact that it returns to its origin, as appears in a circle. Likewise, he who suffers persecution, is a poor man for justice' sake and all other things ought to be given to him, because "Blessed are the meek: for they shall possess the land" (above, verse 4), and, "Blessed are the merciful: for they shall obtain mercy" (above, verse 7), and so forth for the other beatitudes.

6. "PSEUDO-CHRYS. He said not, Blessed are they who suffer persecution of the Gentiles; that we may not suppose the blessing pronounced on those only who are persecuted for refusing to sacrifice to idols; yea, whoever suffers persecution of heretics because he will not forsake the truth is likewise blessed, seeing he suffers for righteousness. Moreover, if any of the great ones, who seem to be Christians, being corrected by you on account of his sins, shall persecute you, you are blessed with John the Baptist. For if the Prophets are truly martyrs when they are killed by their own countrymen, without a doubt he who suffers in the cause of God has the reward of martyrdom though he suffers from his own people. Scripture, therefore, does not mention the persons of the persecutors, but only the cause of the persecution, that you may learn to look, not by whom but why you suffer" (*Catena Aurea on St. Matthew*, chap. 5, lect. 8).

7. From this point onward, until the end of chapter 6, begins the restored, original Commentary of St. Thomas, which had been, for many years, replaced by material borrowed from Peter of Scala in other, previous editions of this Commentary.

Hence, Ambrose says that the kingdom of heaven is set forth in relation to the glory of the soul and of the heart: for the kingdom of heaven corresponds to the virtues of the soul, but the beatitude which consists in the glorification of the bodies corresponds to martyrdom, on account of the afflictions which they suffered. Or it is otherwise: the kingdom of heaven is promised in hope to the poor, because they do not immediately fly upwards to heaven, but it is promised to the martyrs in reality because they immediately fly upwards to heaven.

Blessed are ye when they shall revile you, etc. Here He touches upon the dignity of those who ought to teach the very doctrine of the Apostles. And it should be known that all the beatitudes pertain to three things, for the first three are for removing evil, namely: "Blessed are the poor," "Blessed are the meek," and "Blessed are they that mourn"; the other four are for doing good; the last beatitude, however, pertains to patiently suffering evil. Now these three things ought to be in the teacher of Sacred Scripture by way of excellence, because in enduring evils, not only ought he to patiently bear them, but he ought to rejoice in them; likewise, he ought to remove evils from others; moreover, thirdly, he ought to enlighten others for the purpose of doing good. Hence, in these three things Christ commends the apostolic dignity in order, and He starts from persecution, because, by this, the perfection of all the others is designated, and it signifies that no one ought to assume the office of preaching unless he be perfect; "The learning of a man is known by patience" (Prov. 19, 11); and: "They shall suffer well, that they may preach" (Ps. 91, 15).[8] About this He does three things: firstly, He enumerates the evils that they are about to suffer; secondly, He teaches the manner of suffering them, where it is said, **Be glad and rejoice**; and thirdly, He assigns the reason for rejoicing, where it is said, **for your reward is very great in heaven**. Now evils are either present or absent; likewise, the present evils happen either by word or by deed. Hence, He sets forth every kind of evil. He says, therefore: **Blessed are ye**.

Now, here Augustine raises a question, in that He firstly says: **when they shall revile you**, and afterwards He says: **when they shall speak all that is evil against you**, for it seems to be the same thing. But it should be known that they **revile**, who give an affront to those who are present, but they **speak all**

---

[8]. *Bene patientes erunt ut adnuntient* is translated in the Douay Bible as, "They shall be well treated, that they may shew."

that is evil, who detract those who are absent. For they revile those to whom many reproaches are made; "All curse me" (Jer. 15, 10), and, "Who, when he was cursed, did not curse" (I Pet. 2, 23). ***Blessed are ye when they shall revile you,*** meaning when they shall offend you by word and deed. Chrysostom says: "The merit of eternal life consists in two things: in doing good and in bearing evil, and just as every good deed, however small, is not without merit, so every injury has a reward." ***And persecute you,*** meaning by driving you out from city to city; "We are reviled: and we bless. We are persecuted: and we suffer it" (I Cor. 4, 12), "Behold I send to you prophets and wise men and scribes: and some of them you will persecute from city to city" (below 23, 34), and, "If you be reproached for the name of Christ, you shall be blessed" (I Pet. 4, 14). But it ought to be known that not everyone about whom bad things are said is reviled, but it is required, firstly, that it be said mendaciously, and secondly, that it be said for Christ's sake, hence, He says: ***untruly, for my sake,*** and these words, *for my sake,* refer to all the aforesaid evils. Likewise, note that what He says: *for my sake* and *for justice' sake*[9] (above, verse 10), are the same thing.

Be glad and rejoice. Here He teaches the manner, namely, of how evils are to be endured. Above, when he was speaking of all men, He said: ***Blessed are they that suffer persecution,*** meaning who do not become indignant; but in the Apostles this does not suffice, nay, it is needful that they rejoice; "Count it all joy, when you shall fall into divers temptations" (James 1, 2); and, "The Apostles went from the presence of the council, rejoicing that they were accounted worthy to suffer reproach for the name of Jesus" (Acts 5, 41).

But on the contrary, Augustine says, "You command them to be endured, not to be loved."[10] I answer, saying that one need not rejoice concerning the tribulations, but concerning the hope that they produce in enduring them; just as he who takes medicine does not rejoice concerning the bitterness of the medicine but concerning the hope of health.

And He says: ***Rejoice and exult,***[11] where it ought to be known that to delight, to exalt, to rejoice, and to be glad are the same as regards the thing signified, but differ logically from one another.

---

9. The text here reads "for Christ's sake," but as this phrase is nowhere to be found in this Gospel, "for justice' sake" has been substituted as best fitting the context. The full verse from which this phrase was taken reads, "Blessed are they that suffer persecution for justice' sake: for theirs is the kingdom of heaven."
10. *Confessions* bk. 10, chap. 28.
11. The Douay version, however, reads, ***Be glad and rejoice.***

For delight, properly speaking, is from the conjunction of the loved and suitable thing itself; joy is not only in the conjunction but in the apprehension; interior gladness and exaltation are the effects following joy and delight, because from the latter the heart is firstly dilated: hence, gladness (*laetitia*) is a certain dilation (*latitia*) of the heart; likewise, not only is the heart inwardly dilated, but when it is expressed, it appears outwardly, and then it is called exaltation as though appearing outwardly (*extra apparens*).

Now one ought to rejoice concerning tribulation, because it will be for the confusion of unbelievers and for the joy of the faithful; so blessed Laurence rejoiced on the gridiron, as it is read of him. And there is a twofold cause of joy: firstly, the reward is a cause of joy, hence, **your reward is very great in heaven**, namely, the empyrean heaven,[12] hence: "We shall be taken up in the clouds to meet Christ, into the air: and so shall we be always with the Lord" (I Thess. 4, 16). Augustine says, "By the fact that He says, **in heaven**, He names the object and substance of beatitude, which will not be in corporeal, but in spiritual things," more precisely, in the enjoyment of God; and these spiritual things are designated by the heavens on account of their solidity and firmness. And He says, **very great**, on account of the superabundant reward of the Apostles; "Give: and it shall be given to you: good measure and pressed down and shaken together and running over shall they give into your bosom" (Lk. 6, 38), and, "I am thy reward exceeding great" (Gen. 15, 1). The second cause why one ought to rejoice concerning tribulation is the example of the prophets. Hence, **For so they persecuted the prophets that were before you**. For it is a great comfort when some men are likened to the great fathers who preceded them; "Which of the prophets have not your fathers persecuted?" (Acts 7, 52), and, "Take, my brethren, for example of suffering evil, of labor and patience, the prophets who spoke in the name of the Lord. Behold, we account them blessed who have endured" (James 5, 10-11). And observe that, in these words, Christ's dignity is indicated, because He has His prophets suffering for Him in the Old Testament, and, also, the dignity of the Apostles is indicated, who are assimilated to the prophets.

---

12. "The empyrean heaven rests only on the authority of Strabus and Bede, and also of Basil; all of whom agree in one respect, namely, in holding it to be the place of the blessed.... It was fitting that even from the beginning, there should be made some beginning of bodily glory in something corporeal, free at the very outset from the servitude of corruption and change, and wholly luminous, even as the whole bodily creation, after the Resurrection, is expected to be. So, then, that heaven is called the empyrean, i.e. fiery, not from its heat, but from its brightness" (I, q. 66, a. 3).

*13. You are the salt of the earth. But if the salt lose its savour, wherewith shall it be salted? It is good for nothing anymore but to be cast out, and to be trodden on by men.
14a. You are the light of the world.*

You are the salt of the earth. Above, the Lord showed the Apostles' dignity as to the fact that in tribulations they ought not only to be patient but joyful; now, however, He speaks of their excellence in that they ought to restrain others from evil, and therefore He compares them to salt: **You are the salt of the earth.** And about this He does two things: for firstly, He describes their duty of keeping others from evil; and secondly, He shows how they ought to keep themselves from evil, where it is said: **But if the salt lose its savour.**

He says, therefore: **You are the salt.** He compares them to salt on account of four reasons. The first reason is on account of the production of salt, which comes from both the wind and the sun's heat: for spiritual generation is from the water of Baptism and the power of the Holy Ghost; "Unless a man be born again of water and the Holy Ghost, he cannot enter into the kingdom of God" (Jn. 3, 5). And the production of salt comes from the heat of the sun, meaning from the fervor of love which is from the Holy Ghost; "The charity of God is poured forth in our hearts, by the Holy Ghost who is given to us" (Rom. 5, 5). Secondly, it is on account of the utilities of salt, of which the first is its use, that all things are seasoned with salt: hence, it signifies the wisdom which apostolic men ought to have; "The wisdom of doctrine is according to her name, and she is not manifest unto many, but with them to whom she is known, she continueth even to the sight of God" (Eccli. 6, 23), and, "Walk with wisdom towards them that are without, redeeming the time" (Col. 4, 5). The second use[13] was that in every sacrifice salt was added (Lev. 2, 13),[14] because apostolic teaching ought to be reflected in our every deed. The third use is that it absorbs excess moisture and by this preserves from putrefaction. In this way the Apostles were restraining carnal concupiscences by their teaching; "The time past is sufficient to have fulfilled the will of the Gentiles, for them who have walked in riotousness, lusts, excess of wine, revellings, banquetings and unlawful

---

13. Here the text has "the second reason" but the context seems to imply that "the second use" is rather meant here.

14. "Whatsoever sacrifice thou offerest, thou shalt season it with salt: neither shalt thou take away the salt of the covenant of thy God from thy sacrifice. In all thy oblations thou shalt offer salt."

worshipping of idols" (I Pet. 4, 3), and, "Let us walk honestly, as in the day: not in rioting and drunkenness, not in chambering and impurities, not in contention and envy" (Rom. 13, 13). The fourth effect of salt is that it makes the ground sterile. Hence, it is said that some conquerors oversowed salt outside a city which they captured so that nothing would grow. In like manner, also the Gospel teaching makes the ground sterile, namely, so that earthly works do not spring up in us; "And have no fellowship with the unfruitful works of darkness: but rather reprove them" (Eph. 5, 11). Therefore, the Apostles are called **salt** because they have pungency for withdrawing from sins; "Have salt in you: and have peace among you" (Mk. 9, 49).

But someone could say, 'It suffices that I have salt.' But on the contrary, it is necessary that the power of salt keep you from sin, and for this He cites four reasons. The first is taken from its incorrigibility, and hence it is said, **But if the salt lose its savor, wherewith shall it be salted?** Those things properly lose their savor that lose their strength: just as strong wine sometimes loses its strength, so salt sometimes loses its pungency; "But if the salt become unsavoury, wherewith will you season it?" (Mk. 9, 49). Hence, one then loses his savor when he is guilty of sin; "They became vain in their thoughts. And their foolish heart was darkened" (Rom. 1, 21). If, therefore, on account of tribulations or some other reason you withdraw from virtue, in what shall you be salted, meaning in what other thing will you be salted with salt? For if the people sin they can be corrected, but if a prelate sins, no one can reform him; "How long will they be incapable of being cleansed?" (Os. 8, 5). And it ought to be observed that in Luke 14, 34, it is said: "But if the salt shall become tasteless (*infatuatum*)":[15] For it is great foolishness (*fatuitas*) to relinquish eternal things for temporal things.

The second reason is taken from its utility, hence, it is said: **It is good for nothing**, and He explains this in Luke 14, 35, where it is said: "Neither profitable for the land nor for the dunghill," because it makes the land sterile and does not fertilize it. So spiritual men, when they sin, are able to do nothing, because they are not able to do secular business as soldiers or men of this kind are able to do; "Son of man, what shall be made of the wood of the vine...? Shall wood be taken of it, to do any work, or shall a

---

15. Luke is here quoted in a pre-Jerome version of the Bible. The same is true for the following citation. cf. *Novum Testamentum latine*, Wordsworth-White edition, I, p. 415. *Infatuatum* is found in the *Itala*, the Old Latin version of this verse, in many manuscripts. It means both "foolish" and "tasteless."

pin be made of it for any vessel to hang thereon? Behold it is cast into the fire for fuel... shall it be useful for any work?" (Ez. 15, 2-4), and, "They are all gone aside, they are become unprofitable together" (Ps. 13, 3). The third reason is taken from the imminent danger, and it has two branches according to two dangers. The first is expulsion, hence: *but to be cast out*, namely, from the Church; "Without are dogs and sorcerers and unchaste and murderers and servers of idols and every one that loveth and maketh a lie" (Apoc. 22, 15). Likewise, the dignity of priestly teaching is taken away from him; "Because thou hast rejected knowledge, I will reject thee, that thou shalt not do the office of priesthood to me" (Osee 4, 6), and, "Therefore I say to you that the kingdom of God shall be taken from you and shall be given to a nation yielding the fruits thereof" (below 21, 43), and so it is said, *but to be cast out*. The second danger is being made worthless, because they who firstly live supernaturally and fail, become contemptible, and so it is said: *and to be trodden on by men*; "This man began to build and was not able to finish" (Lk. 14, 30), and, "You have departed out of the way, and have caused many to stumble at the law: you have made void the covenant of Levi, saith the Lord of hosts. Therefore have I also made you contemptible, and base before all people, as you have not kept my ways" (Mal. 2, 8-9). And it ought to be observed, according to Augustine,[16] that if some holy men are made worthless, as it is said above, "And they shall speak all that is evil against you, untruly, for my sake" (5, 11), still they can never be trodden on, because they always have their hearts in heaven, and they are properly trodden on who lie on the earth.

You are the light of the world. Here the third dignity of the Apostles is set forth. For, just as they ought to keep others away from evils, so they also ought to enlighten them. And about this He does two things: firstly, He shows their dignity, and secondly, He removes their pusillanimity, where it is said, *A city seated on a mountain cannot be hid.*

He says, therefore: *You are the light of the world*, as though not only are they the light of Judea or of Galilee, but also of the whole world; "For so the Lord hath commanded us: I have set thee to be the light of the Gentiles: that thou mayest be for salvation unto the utmost part of the earth" (Acts 13, 47). And this was marvelous, that their light was hardly known in their own land and yet it went out into the whole world. But it is objected that it

---

16. *De Sermone Domini in monte*, Lib. I, cap. 6, n. 16 (PL 34, 1237).

seems that this word that He says, *light*, applies only to Christ; "[John the Baptist] was not the light, but was to give testimony of the light," and afterwards it is said that "[Christ] was the true light" (Jn. 1, 8-9). I answer, saying that only Christ is the light essentially, but the Apostles are called illuminated lights, namely, by participation, just as the eye is an illuminating light and yet it is illuminated.[17]

And observe that these three things, namely: *Blessed are ye when they shall revile you*, *You are the salt of the earth*, and *You are the light of the world*, seem to pertain to the three last beatitudes, namely, the first to "Blessed are they that suffer persecution for justice' sake," the second to "Blessed are the peacemakers," meaning they pacify themselves and others, and the third to "Blessed are the clean of heart." For if the Apostles were outstanding in these three beatitudes, all the more were they outstanding in the previous beatitudes.

The Lord had said, "Blessed are ye when they shall revile you," and, "Blessed are they that suffer persecution for justice' sake"; therefore, they might say, 'If we ourselves will endure so many persecutions, then we want to hide ourselves.' And for that reason the Lord afterwards takes away their pusillanimity, and hence it is said, *A city seated on a mountain cannot be hid*. And firstly, He forbids their hiding, and secondly, He shows the manner how they ought to show themselves, where it is said, *So let your light shine before men*. He proves that they ought not to hide themselves for two reasons. Firstly, that they could not hide themselves even if they wanted to do so, and this is what is said, *A city seated on a mountain cannot be hid*; and secondly, that they ought not to hide themselves, and this is what is said: *Neither do men light a candle and put it under a bushel*.

14b. A city seated on a mountain cannot be hid.
15. Neither do men light a candle and put it under a bushel, but upon a candlestick, that it may shine to all that are in the house.
16. So let your light shine before men, that they may see your good works, and glorify your Father who is in heaven.

[17]. "And although the apostles are called light – 'You are the light of the world' (Mt 5:14) - they are not light in the same way as Christ. For they are a light whose light has been given to them, even though in some way they also give light, that is, in their ministry" (*Comm. On St. John's Gospel*, chap. 12, lect. 8). "*That was the true Light*. AUG. Wherefore is there added, true? Because man enlightened is called light, but the true Light is that which lightens. For our eyes are called lights, and yet, without a lamp at night, or the sun by day, these lights are open to no purpose" (*Catena Aurea on St. John*, chap. 1, lect. 11).

A city seated on a mountain cannot be hid. The *city* is the congregation of the faithful, namely, the very assembly of the Apostles; "Glorious things are said of thee, O city of God" (Ps. 86, 3). Now, it is located *on a mountain*, namely Christ; "The mountain of the house of the Lord shall be prepared in the top of the mountains" (Mic. 4, 1), and, "A stone was cut out of a mountain without hands" (Dan. 2, 34). Or, *on a mountain*, in the perfection of justice; "Thy justice is as the mountains of God" (Ps. 35, 7). A city on a mountain, however, cannot hide itself, so the Apostles cannot hide themselves, as Chrysostom says.[18] If men who are standing at the bottom of the mountain of justice commit sin, they can hide themselves, but if they are standing at the top, they cannot hide themselves; "My lord, O king, the eyes of all Israel are upon thee" (III Kings 1, 20). Hilary[19] expounds this passage otherwise, and the meaning is almost the same: *A city seated on a mountain* is Christ, because on the part of His human nature, which He shares with us, He is a city; "I have made thee this day a fortified city" (Jer. 1, 18); He is *on a mountain*, because He is a mountain in His divinity, which is a mountain; "The mountain of God is a fat mountain" (Ps. 67, 16). And thus, Christ could not hide; and therefore, 'You, Apostles, are unable to hide Me.'

The second reason He gives why they cannot hide themselves is where it is said, *Neither do men light a lamp.*[20] It is as though He were to say, 'Let us suppose that you could hide yourselves, nevertheless, you ought not to do so. For no one receiving a benefit ought to do something with it contrary to the intention of its donor. God gave you knowledge so that you would share it with others; "As every man hath received grace, ministering the same one to another" (I Pet. 4, 10). And so these words are said, *Neither do they light a lamp*, namely, men, or the Father, Son, and Holy Ghost. By *lamp* one can firstly understand this to mean the Gospel teaching; "Thy word is a lamp to my feet, and a light to my paths" (Ps. 118, 105). For a lamp has a light incorporated in it; the light of truth is placed in Sacred Scripture, and it is lighted by the Father, Son and Holy Ghost. Or, by *lamp*, can be understood the Apostles insofar as the light of grace was imparted to them; "He was a burning and a shining light" (Jn. 5, 35), and, "I have prepared a lamp for my anointed" (Ps. 131, 17). Or, by *lamp*, Christ is signified, because just as a lamp is a light

---

18. *Opus Imperf. in Mt.*, Hom. X (PG 56, 685).
19. *In Mt.*, super V[15] (PL 9, 935).

20. The word used here is *lucerna* which can mean either a "candle," as stated in the Douay Rheims translation, or "lamp," which is the more literal meaning used here by St. Thomas.

in an earthen vessel, so Christ's divinity is in His humanity; "For thou art my lamp O Lord" (II Kings 2, 29).

After *a lamp* having been understood in this way, by *a bushel* we can understand three things. Firstly, according to Augustine,[21] corporeal things are understood, on account of two reasons. The first reason is that a bushel is a measure; "Thou shalt have a just and a true weight, and thy bushel shall be equal and true" (Deut. 25, 15). Now that which we do in the body will be recompensed to us; "For we must all be manifested before the judgment seat of Christ, that every one may receive the proper things of the body, according as he hath done" (II Cor. 5, 10);[22] or another reason is that all corporeal things are measured, divine things, however, are unlimited because they are beyond measure. Therefore, they put the lamp *under a bushel*, who compare His teaching with temporal gain, whereas the former is more precious; "For neither have we used at any time the speech of flattery, as you know: nor taken an occasion of covetousness" (I Thess. 2, 5). In a second way, according to Chrysostom,[23] worldly men are called a bushel, because they are empty above and solid below: they have, in fact, madness above, because they perceive nothing of the Holy Ghost; "The sensual man perceiveth not these things that are of the Spirit of God" (I Cor. 2, 14). But below, in worldly affairs, meaning in business matters, they are wise; "For the children of this world are wiser in their generation than the children of light" (Lk. 16, 8). And this is a rather literal exposition. Then, therefore, according to this way of exposition, a lamp is put *under a bushel* when doctrine is hidden due to worldly fear; "Who art thou, that thou shouldst be afraid of a mortal man" (Is. 51, 12), and, "I labor even unto bands, as an evildoer. But the word of God is not bound" (II Tim. 2, 9). If, however, the Gospel teaching, or Christ, be understood by the lamp, it would be hidden under Judea, but in order that it would be manifested to the whole world; "Behold, I have given thee to be the light of the Gentiles, that thou mayst be my salvation even to the farthest part of the earth" (Is. 49, 6).

But upon a candlestick. These words can be expounded in three ways, for one's body can be signified by *a candlestick*, and the Gospel teaching by the lamp; hence, the same things said above are signified by the bushel and the candlestick, as though

---

21. *De sermone Domini in monte*, Lib. I, cap. 6, n. 17 (PL 34, 1237).

22. In the Latin text a similar quotation is also cited here, namely, "We shall all stand before the judgment seat of Christ" (Rom. 14, 10), which is the one actually found in the writings of St. Augustine when commenting on this verse, e. g. *Enchridion*, cap. CX (PL 40, 283).

23. *Opus imperf. in Mt.*, hom. X (PG 56, 686).

He were to say: 'The Gospel teaching ought not to be submitted to temporal things, but all things ought to minister to it; hence, when you give things, your body or even your life unto death, for love of Christ, then you put the lamp *upon a candlestick.*' Or, by *a candlestick,* the Church is understood, because they who are lamps are put in a higher place; "As the lamp shining upon the holy candlestick, so is the beauty of the face in a ripe age" (Eccli. 26, 22). If, however, the candlestick be understood of Christ, then, by the *candlestick,* the Cross is understood; "And through him to reconcile all things unto himself, making peace through the blood of his cross, both as to the things that are on earth and the things that are in heaven" (Col. 1, 20).

That it may shine to all that are in the house. This passage can be expounded in three ways.[24] By *the house,* the Church can be understood; "That thou mayest know how thou oughtest to behave thyself in the house of God, which is the church of the living God" (I Tim. 3, 15). Or, by *the house,* the whole world is understood; "For every house is built by some man: but he that created all things is God," etc., (Heb. 3, 4)

Afterwards the manner in which they ought to manifest themselves to the world is related, and firstly, He relates the manner of how they ought to manifest themselves, because they ought to shine *before men,* by enlightening them; "To me, the least of all the saints, is given this grace, to preach among the Gentiles the unsearchable riches of Christ and to enlighten all men" (Eph. 3, 8-9). Secondly, He relates the order of how they ought to manifest themselves, where it is said, *That they may see your good works.* Thirdly, He relates of the purpose of manifesting themselves, namely, not for their own glory; "For we are not as many, adulterating the word of God: but with sincerity: but as from God, before God, in Christ we speak" (II Cor. 2, 17). And this is where it is said, *and glorify your Father who is in heaven.* For, on account of God's glory, we ought to perform good works so that God may be glorified by our good life; "Therefore, whether you eat or drink, or whatsoever else you do, do all to the glory of God," etc., (I Cor. 10, 31).

Do not think that I am come to destroy the law, or the prophets. I am not come to destroy, but to fulfil. Observe here that the Lord fulfilled the Law in five ways. Firstly, He fulfilled the Law because He fulfilled those things which were prefigured in the Law; "For I say to you that this that is written must yet

---

24. One of these three expositions is missing.

be fulfilled in me" (Lk. 22, 37).[25] Secondly, He fulfilled the Law by observing its legal prescriptions; "But when the fulness of the time was come, God sent his Son, made of a woman, made under the law" (Gal. 4, 4). Thirdly, He did this by doing works through grace, namely, by sanctifying through the Holy Ghost, which the Law was unable to do; "For what the law could not do, in that it was weak through the flesh, God, sending his own Son... that the justification of the law might be fulfilled in us who walk not according to the flesh, but according to the spirit" (Rom. 8, 3-4). Fourthly, He did this by satisfying for the sins by which we were transgressors of the Law. Hence, when the transgressions were taken away, He fulfilled the Law; "Whom God hath proposed to be a propitiation, through faith in his blood, to the shewing of his justice, for the remission of former sins" (Rom. 3, 25). Fifthly, He did this by applying certain perfections to the Law, which were either about the understanding of the Law, or for a greater perfection of justice. Observe that the Law is destroyed in three ways: by totally denying it, or by expounding it badly, or by not fulfilling its moral precepts.

17. Do not think that I am come to destroy the law, or the prophets. I am not come to destroy, but to fulfill.
18. For amen I say unto you, till heaven and earth pass, one jot, or one tittle shall not pass of the law, till all be fulfilled.
19. He therefore that shall break one of these least commandments, and shall so teach men shall be called the least in the kingdom of heaven. But he that shall do and teach, he shall be called great in the kingdom of heaven.

Do not think that I am come to destroy the law. After having set forth the beatitudes to which Christ's doctrine pertains, here He begins to promulgate His own doctrine, and firstly He makes known His intention, and secondly, He puts forth the rule and precepts of His doctrine, where it is said, *For I tell you*. About the first part, He does two things: firstly, He rejects what was assumed to be his intention, and secondly, He adds His true intention, where it is said, *I am not come to destroy, but to fulfil.*

The Lord had said, above, to the Apostles: "Blessed are ye when they shall revile you," etc., (verse 11); hence, the Apostles could have suspected such a teaching was, as it were, betraying the Law,

---

25. The text here also has an added reference here to Lk. 24, 44, "All things must needs be fulfilled which are written in the law of Moses and in the prophets and in the psalms, concerning me."

for which reason they needed to go into hiding, as though Christ were saying something contrary to the Law; and therefore the Lord rejects this opinion, saying: *Do not think that I am come to destroy the law*, etc. And likewise, because it might have been said that no other prophet, after Moses who gave Law, fulfilled the Law, wherefore, the Lord says that He is going to do more than the other prophets. Hence, He says, *but to fulfil*; for no prophet fulfilled the Law. And note that these words are very effective against those who condemn the Law as if it were from the devil; "For this purpose the Son of God appeared, that he might destroy the works of the devil" (1 Jn. 3, 8). But He declares: *I am not come to destroy, but to fulfil*; wherefore the Law is not the work of the devil. By this argument a certain man was converted to the faith and was a Friar Preacher.[26] Hence, the Manicheans very much abhor this chapter; hence, Faustus[27] objects multiple times to this passage, according to Augustine, and all his objections are reduced to three. Firstly, he objects to the authority of the Law, for it is said, "A word shall not be added to what I speak to you, neither shall you take away from it" (Deut. 4, 2); but Christ added to it; therefore He acted contrary to the Law. Likewise, it is said, "In saying a new, he hath made the former old" (Heb. 8, 13); but Christ said that He was the institutor of the New Law, "This is my blood of the new testament" (below 26, 28); therefore, He destroyed the Old Law. Thirdly, it is said, "I have given you an example, that as I have done to you, so you do also" (Jn. 13, 15); wherefore every action of Christ is a true instruction; thus, if He fulfilled the Old Law, then we ought also to fulfill it; therefore, we ought to be circumcised and to keep all the prescriptions of the Law; and this opinion is shared also by the Nazarenes and the Manicheans. Therefore, Faustus was saying that either Christ did not say these words, but Matthew said them, who was not present at the Sermon on the Mount, while John, who was present, did not say them; or if Christ said them and Matthew wrote them, the Gospel is expounded otherwise. For in Sacred Scripture 'law' is expounded in three ways; for there is the law of Moses ("We are

---

26. This refers to the conversion of an unknown Cathar. "The Dominicans who had come from Catharism were quite numerous in the 13th Century. One of the best known, Raynier Sacconi, was converted under the influence of St. Peter Martyr and he became the collaborator of the latter, publishing a *Summa de Catharis* in 1250 against his former co-religionists." (H. V. SHOONER, *La Lectura in Matthaeum de S. Thomas (Two previously unpublished fragments and Reportation of Peter of Andria)*, *Angelicum*, 33 (1956), p. 129).

27. "Faustus [Manichaean bishop of Mileve, (350-400 A.D.)] was an African by race, a citizen of Mileum; he was eloquent and clever, but had adopted the shocking tenets of the Manichaean heresy. He is mentioned in my *Confessions*, where there is an account of my acquaintance with him" (Augustine, *Contra Faustum Manichaeum*, lib. 1, n. 1). cf. *Confessions*, v. 3, 6.

loosed from the law of death" (Rom. 7, 6) in God's law), the law of nature ("When the Gentiles, who have not the law, do by nature those things that are of the law; these, having not the law, are a law to themselves" (Rom. 2, 14)), and the law of truth ("The law of the spirit of life, in Christ Jesus, hath delivered me from the law of sin and of death" (Rom. 8, 2)). Accordingly, therefore, this matter is examined by Faustus in three ways, namely, the question of the Old Law, the question of the law of nature ("One of them a prophet of their own, said: The Cretans are always liars, evil beasts, slothful bellies" (Tit. 1, 12)), and the question of the law of truth ("Therefore behold I send to you prophets and wise men and scribes" (below 23, 34)). Therefore, according to Faustus, what He says here: *I am not come to destroy, but to fulfil*, etc., ought to be understood of the law of nature and of the law of truth, which fulfillment also occurred in certain patriarchs of old; and a sign of this is that the Lord, when He was speaking about the precepts, some He seemed to approve, while others He did not approve, namely, those which were proper to the Mosaic law, namely, that which is said: "An eye for an eye, and a tooth for a tooth" (above 5, 38) and other precepts of this kind.

But, against this, Augustine objects as follows. Firstly, he objects that whoever denies one thing in the Gospel, with equal reason denies everything else in the Gospel, and so destroys Scripture; but a believer ought to believe everything that is in Scripture. Likewise, that which Faustus says, 'He is speaking about another law and about the prophets,' is false, because in the whole New Testament everywhere that mention is made of the Law, it is understood of the Mosaic law; "Who are Israelites: to whom belongeth the adoption as of children and the glory and the testament and the giving of the law and the service of God and the promises" (Rom. 9, 4); therefore, the Lord also is speaking about the Mosaic law when He speaks about these precepts.

Hence, it ought to be seen, firstly, how Christ came to fulfill the Law, and afterwards we will solve the objections. Therefore, it ought to be known that Christ fulfilled the Law of the prophets in five ways. Firstly, He did this because He fulfilled those things which were prefigured in the Law and the prophets by His actions; "All things must needs be fulfilled which are written in the law of Moses and in the prophets and in the psalms, concerning me" (Lk. 24, 44). Secondly, He fulfilled the Law by observing its prescriptions to the letter; "When the fulness of the time was come, God sent his Son, made of a woman, made under the law" (Gal. 4, 4). Thirdly, He fulfilled the Law by giving grace through His works, which the law of nature could not do; for every law exists so that we men may be made just; but Christ did this by the Holy Ghost; "For what the law could not do, in that it was weak through the flesh, God, sending his own Son... that the justification of the law might be fulfilled in us" (Rom. 8, 3-4). Fourthly, according to Augustine, He did this by satisfying for our sins by which we were made transgressors of the Law; hence, having taken away the transgression it is said that He fulfilled the Law; "Whom God hath proposed to be a propitiation, through faith in his blood, to the shewing of his justice, for the remission of former sins," etc., (Rom. 3, 25). Fifthly, He did this by adding perfections to the Law which were either concerning the understanding of the Law or for the greater perfection of justice; "For the law brought nothing to perfection: but a bringing in of a better hope, by which we draw nigh to God" (Heb. 7, 19); and this seems to be Christ's intention because, when He made mention of all the prescriptions of the Law, He added, "Be you therefore perfect, as also your heavenly Father is perfect" (below 5, 48). Accordingly we solve the objections of Faustus as Augustine solved them.

In regard to that which is said, "A word shall not be added" (Deut. 4, 2), I reply, saying that Christ did not add to the Law, but explained it; for they were thinking of the act of murder, when the Law said: "Thou shalt not kill" (below 5, 21); Christ expounded that it also forbade hatred and anger. Likewise, in regard to that which is said, "In saying a new, he hath made the former old" (Heb. 8, 13), I reply, saying that the New Testament is the same as the Old Testament, in that the former testament was a figure and the latter testament is the fulfillment of its figures. In regard to which Testament we ought to observe, I reply, saying that something can be signified by speech and figure, and what is signified in both Testaments does not differ in any way. Hence, concerning Christ, before He was born it could be said, 'Christ will be born and will die,' but now it is said, 'Christ has been born,' and so forth. And nevertheless, by this it is shown that by different words the same thing either as done or to be done is expressed. Hence, what was signified by figures as a future event, now that the event has occurred, is signified as being present by new figures, namely, the sacraments of the New Law. Hence, although Christ fulfilled the figures, nevertheless, now that the truth has come, whoever would observe these figures would do an injury to the truth. In this way, therefore, the words are understood, *I am not come to destroy, but to fulfil.*

For amen I say unto you. Here the reason for Christ's fulfillment of the Law is related, and He seems to assign three reasons: firstly, He fulfilled it because of the immobility of the Law, secondly, this was because of the punishment for those violating the Law, and thirdly, this was because of the reward of those fulfilling the Law. The second point is where it is said, **He therefore that shall break one of these least commandments**; and the third point is where it is said, **But he that shall do and teach**. He says, therefore, **For amen I say unto you**, and it ought to be known that in the Old Law all of Christ's mysteries were prefigured, but, as it is said: "The Lord God doth nothing without revealing his secret to his servants the prophets" (Amos 3, 7); therefore, Christ's mysteries will last until very end of time; "And behold I am with you all days, even to the consummation of the world" (below 28, 20). Hence, not all the mysteries of the prophets were fulfilled at Christ's first coming, nay, they will not be fulfilled until the end of the world. And that which He said cannot be changed; "Hath the Lord said, and will he not do?" (Num. 23, 19). Therefore, if the Law predicted those things which are to come, and so it is necessary that they must happen, He thence says, **Amen I say unto you, till heaven and earth pass... till all be fulfilled**, meaning all things will be successively fulfilled until the end of the world.

It ought to be known that **Amen** is a Hebrew word, and no translator, out of reverence for this word, because the Lord frequently used it, dared to change it; and it is sometimes used as a noun, hence, **Amen** is taken to mean 'a true thing'; sometimes it is used as an adverb, meaning 'truly,' and so it is used here; sometimes it is used to mean 'so be it,' and hence, in Psalms where we have in English, 'so be it,' in Hebrew it is rendered 'Amen'; wherefore a Hebrew expression is said here, and instead of 'true,' 'truly,' and 'so be it,' **Amen** is said. Hence, the Lord here draws attention to listening.

Till heaven and earth pass, not according to their substance, but according to their arrangement; "For the fashion (*figura*) of this world passeth away" (I Cor. 7, 31), and, "The heavens being on fire shall be dissolved, and the elements shall melt with the burning heat" (II Pet. 3, 11). **Till heaven and earth pass**, which means, until the end of the world.

One jot (*iota*). An *iota* among the Greeks is a letter which we call a small 'i'; among the Hebrews, however, it is called *jod*, and *iota* among the Greeks stands for 'y' and it is a new letter (for every letter stands for some number), hence, it pertains to the perfection of the Decalogue,[28] and perhaps for this reason the

---

[28]. "RABAN. He fitly mentions the Greek iota, and not the Hebrew jot, because the iota stands in Greek for the number ten, and so there is an allusion to the Decalogue of which the Gospel is the point and perfection" (*Catena Aurea on St. Matthew*, chap. 5, lect. 12).

Evangelist put *jot* (*iota*) rather than *jod*, according to what holy men say. The *tittle* of a letter is put above the letters both in Hebrew and in Greek, but for different reasons, because among the Hebrews a *tittle* sometimes has the sound of the letter 'a' and at other times the letter 'e,' and this *tittle* is known by certain dots and they are called 'tittles'; likewise, among the Greeks certain signs are put above the letters to distinguish the aspiration and the accents, and these are called 'diacritics' among the Greeks. Therefore, the Lord wishes to say that nothing is so small that it ought not to be fulfilled.

He therefore that shall break one of these least commandments. Here the second reason is related and it is taken from the punishment of those breaking the commandments. It is as though He were to say, 'Whoever shall break one of these commandments will incur a punishment as if he were a transgressor of a divine precept.' Now the *least commandments*, according to Chrysostom, are Christ's commandments; hence, *Whoever shall break one of these least commandments* which I am about to say. And the argumentation can be connected as follows. Since the Law cannot be broken, and from the fact that I do not break it, it follows that whoever shall break these will incur a punishment.' And they are called *least commandments* on account of Christ's humility, just as He also called Himself a child; "Unless you be converted, and become as little children, you shall not enter into the kingdom of heaven" (below 18, 3). Or they are called *least commandments* in regard to their transgression, because one who breaks Christ's commandments sins less; but the commandments which Christ commanded are greater than those of the Law, as regards their observance, because the Law commanded, "Thou shalt not kill," whereas Christ commanded men not to be angry. Augustine and Jerome speak otherwise as follows. He speaks of the least commandments in the Law in a literal sense, because He said, *One jot, or one tittle shall not pass of the law, till all be fulfilled.* And they are called *least commandments*, because the principle commandments are: "Thou shalt love the Lord thy God" (Deut. 6, 5), and, "Thou shalt love thy neighbour as thyself" (Lev. 19, 18). Hence, some observances are called least commandments, as for example, there are many observances in Leviticus 19. And He says this to revile the Pharisees, because the Pharisees, on account of their observances, were transgressing many commandments; "And he shall not honour his father or his mother: and you have made void the commandment of God for your tradition" (below 15, 16). Now the Law is broken in three ways: firstly, by completely denying it, secondly, by badly interpreting it, and thirdly, by not fulfilling its moral precepts.

And shall so teach men. He acts badly who does evil deeds, but worse is he who teaches others to do evil deeds; "Thou hast there them that hold the doctrine of Balaam who taught Balac to cast a stumblingblock before the children of Israel" (Apoc. 2, 14). And therefore He says, **He therefore that shall break one of these least commandments, and shall so teach men**, namely, to break the commandments, **shall be called the least in the kingdom of heaven**. And according to this it seems that he who breaks the commandments will be in the kingdom of heaven. But it ought to be known that, according to Augustine, the kingdom of heaven here is taken for eternal life, and the Lord wanted to make it understood that no one will be there who **shall break one of these least commandments, and shall so teach men**, because in that place there will only be great men; "Whom he predestinated, them he also called. And whom he called, them he also justified. And whom he justified, them he also glorified" (Rom. 8, 30). Hence, those who are too small will never be able to enter. Secondly, according to Rabanus, it is as follows. Men seek fame before men, because in the present life it is a certain glory that a man be reputed great in the kingdom of men. But **He that shall break one of these least commandments, shall be called the least in the kingdom of heaven** by not being there. For, there, one is deemed a small man, who transgresses the commandments, and is deemed the least, who teaches that they ought to be transgressed. Chrysostom expounds this otherwise. Scripture sometimes calls the Last Judgment the kingdom of heaven, as the Psalm says, "The Lord hath reigned, let the earth rejoice: let many islands be glad. Clouds and darkness are round about him: justice and judgment are the establishment of his throne" (96, 1-2). And there will be different orders there, but he shall be the least who teaches that the commandments are to be broken, because to the kingdom of heaven, in this sense, pertains also those who are in hell. Gregory expounds this verse as follows. The kingdom of heaven stands for the Church, hence, **he shall be called the least** in the Church, "because he whose life is despicable, it remains that his preaching be also despised."[29]

---

29. Gregory the Great, *Homiliae in Evangelia*, 1, *Homilia* XII (ML 76, n. 1476).

But he that shall do and teach. He is great who does well, but greater is he who does and teaches; hence, he will have great glory; "Every one therefore that shall confess me before men, I will also confess him before my Father who is in heaven" (below 10, 32), and, "In all things thou didst magnify thy people, O Lord, and didst honor them" (Wis. 19, 20).

20. For I tell you, that unless your justice abound more than that of the scribes and Pharisees, you shall not enter into the kingdom of heaven.
21. You have heard that it was said to them of old: Thou shalt not kill. And whosoever shall kill, shall be in danger of the judgment.
22. But I say to you, that whosoever is angry with his brother, shall be in danger of the judgment. And whosoever shall say to his brother, Raca, shall be in danger of the council. And whosoever shall say, Thou fool, shall be in danger of hell fire.
23. If therefore thou offer thy gift at the altar, and there thou remember that thy brother hath anything against thee;
24. Leave there thy offering before the altar, and go first to be reconciled to thy brother, and then coming thou shalt offer thy gift.
25. Be at agreement with thy adversary betimes, whilst thou art in the way with him: lest perhaps the adversary deliver thee to the judge, and the judge deliver thee to the officer, and thou be cast into prison.
26. Amen I say to thee, thou shalt not go out from thence till thou repay the last farthing.

For I tell you, that unless your justice abound more than that of the scribes and Pharisees. Above, the Lord showed that it was not His intention to destroy the Law but to fulfill it, wherefore, here He begins to fulfill it. In the Law there were four things: namely, moral precepts, judicial precepts, figurative precepts, and promises. Three of these the Lord fulfilled by His words, namely, the moral precepts, the promises, and the judicial precepts, meaning that He teaches us to fulfill these things; on the other hand, He fulfilled the figurative precepts by a deed, namely, by His Passion. Hence, this part is divided into three sections. In the first section, He fulfills the Law insofar as the moral precepts, in the second section, insofar as the promises, and in the third section, insofar as the judicial precepts.

The moral precepts are of two kinds: some are prohibitive and others are permissive. Firstly, He fulfills the precepts of the first kind, and secondly, He fulfills the precepts of the second kind, where it is said, *And it hath been said, Whosoever shall put away his wife*. About the first kind, He does two things. Firstly, He forbids murder, and secondly, He forbids adultery, where it is said, *You have heard that it was said to them of old: Thou shalt not commit adultery*, etc. About the first thing, He does two things: firstly, He relates the necessity, and secondly, He relates His fulfillment of the precept, where it is said, *You have heard that it was said to them of old: Thou shalt not kill.*

He says, therefore, *For I tell you, that unless your justice abound more than that of the scribes and Pharisees*. Notice that justice is understood in two ways. For sometimes justice is a special virtue, one of the four cardinal virtues, and it has a determinate matter, namely, exchangeable goods which serve the use of human life; but other times justice is said to be a general virtue, which is a common virtue that the Philosopher[30] calls legal justice, which pertains to the fulfillment of the law. And in this way it is taken here.

And *unless your justice abound more than that of the scribes and Pharisees*. He says, *scribes and Pharisees*, because they were more excellent in legal justice, because they even were adding certain observances. Therefore, in order to indicate the excellence of the New Testament, He shows that it even transcends the justice of those men. Wherefore, it is said that "he that is the lesser in the kingdom of heaven," meaning in the Church, "is greater than he" (below 11, 11). Thus, the meaning is, *Unless your justice abound more*, meaning unless it be more perfect, *than that of the scribes and Pharisees, you shall not enter into the kingdom of heaven*.

And it ought to be known that the state of the Gospel is the middle between the state of the Law and the state of glory,[31] and this is evident, because the Apostle compares the state of the Law to a child and the state of the Gospel to perfect age,

---

30. Aristotle, *Ethica Nicomachea* V, 3 (1129b 26-30), in *Arist.* lat. XXVI, 1-3, fasc. 3.

31. "As Dionysius says (*De Ecclesiastica Hierarchia* v), there is a threefold state of mankind; the first was under the Old Law; the second is that of the New Law; the third will take place not in this life, but in heaven. But as the first state is figurative and imperfect in comparison with the state of the Gospel; so is the present state figurative and imperfect in comparison with the heavenly state, with the advent of which the present state will be done away as expressed in that very passage (1 Corinthians 13:12), 'We see now through a glass in a dark manner; but then face to face.'" (I II, q. 106, a. 4 ad 1um).

and so he says in Galatians 4, "So we also, as long as we were children,[32] were serving under the elements of the world," etc., (verse 3) and this is after "Wherefore the law was our pedagogue in Christ" (3, 24), etc., and, "When I was a child, I spoke as a child, I understood as a child," etc., (I Cor. 13, 11). Therefore, there is a middle state, and this is natural, because no one can reach the end unless he starts at the beginning: for no one can arrive at old age unless he pass through childhood; so the Lord says that no one can arrive at the state of the kingdom of heaven unless he also pass through the other states.

Likewise, a greater reward is acquired by greater labor; "He who soweth sparingly shall also reap sparingly: and he who soweth in blessings shall also reap blessings" (II Cor. 9, 6). Now, in the Law temporal and earthly rewards were promised; "If you be willing, and will hearken to me, you shall eat the good things of the land" (Is. 1, 19). But here, heavenly things are promised. Therefore, justice ought to abound in us because a greater reward is expected.

But it is objected against this that the Lord says, *Unless your justice abound more than that of the scribes and Pharisees*, because the justice of the Law consists in fulfilling the Decalogue; but he who fulfills the precepts of the Decalogue will have eternal life; "If thou wilt enter into life, keep the commandments" (below 19, 17). And the objection is solved as follows. It is universally said, firstly, that the observers of the Decalogue never could enter eternal life unless in faith and through the redemption of Christ's blood; "For if justice be by the law, then Christ died in vain" (Gal. 2, 21). And therefore it must be said that the passage, "If thou wilt enter into life, keep the commandments," should be understood with faith having been presupposed. The scribes and Pharisees, however, did not have faith; "Israel, by following after the law of justice, is not come unto the law of justice. Why so? Because they sought it not by faith," etc., (Rom. 9, 31-32). And this solution is good enough.

Another solution of that of Augustine,[33] who says that all these fulfillments which Christ did are contained in the Old Law, because there anger is also forbidden; "Thou shalt not hate thy brother in thy heart" (Lev. 19, 17). Therefore, why did the Lord give his prohibition in addition to these? I answer, saying that He added a prohibition in that He added to their little understanding,

---

32. The Vulgate here reads, "cum essem parvulus," meaning, "when I was a child."

33. *Contra Faustum* 19, 28 and 23.

namely, of the scribes and Pharisees, because they believed that in the precept, ***Thou shalt not kill***, they were not forbidden to be angry except from fear of an act, namely, the act of murder. Hence, the Lord expounded this precept, and thus He does not simply say, 'Unless your justice abound more than the Law,' but, ***Unless your justice abound more than that of the scribes and Pharisees***.

A second solution of Augustine is as follows. For Christ had said, ***He that shall do and teach***, etc., and, ***He that shall break one of these least commandments***, etc.; Now, the Pharisees and scribes do not do and teach; "For they say, and do not," etc., (below 23, 3). Therefore, ***Unless your justice abound more than that of the scribes and Pharisees***, etc., meaning that 'you say and you ought also to do. Therefore, you shall not enter into the kingdom of heaven.'[34]

But there remains another question, because the Lord said, ***He therefore that shall break one of these least commandments... shall be called the least in the kingdom of heaven***, and he who does not abound in justice will not enter the kingdom of heaven; therefore, he who breaks the commandments will be in the kingdom of heaven. And so Chrysostom[35] solved this objection, saying that it is one thing to be in a kingdom of heaven and another to enter it. For they properly enter who partake in the ownership of a kingdom, but they are in a kingdom who reside anywhere in the kingdom; hence, they who are detained in prison are said to be in the kingdom. So also in the kingdom of heaven, because those brought to punishment are in the kingdom of heaven, but they do not partake of the kingdom. Augustine[36] solved this differently, and he says that from these words we can understand that the kingdom of heaven is twofold: one kingdom of heaven is that into which they do not enter who do not have justice, and this is eternal life; another is that into which those breaking the commandments enter, and this is the present Church.

You have heard that it was said to them of old. Here the fulfillment of the precepts is related, and about this He does three things. Firstly, He relates the precepts, secondly, He fulfills them, and thirdly, He admonishes the observance of their fulfillment. The second thing is where it is said, ***But I say to you***; and the third thing is where it is said, ***If therefore thou offer thy gift***. About the first point, He does two things. Firstly, He relates

---

34. *City of God*, bk. 20, chap. 9.
35. *Op. imp. In Mt.*, hom. 11 (PG 56, 689).
36. *City of God*, bk. 20, chap. 9.

the precepts prohibiting murder; and secondly, He relates the punishment for murder.

He says, therefore, **You have heard that it was said to them of old: Thou shalt not kill.** This passage is found in Exodus 20, 13, and in Deuteronomy 5, 17. And He says, **to them of old**, because, according to Chrysostom,[37] it is just as if a teacher were to say to one of his students, 'I have taught you the basic elements long enough; it is time that you learn greater things,' so the Lord does likewise; "For whereas for the time you ought to be masters, you have need to be taught again what are the first elements of the words of God," etc., (Heb. 5, 12).

And it ought to be observed that regarding this precept three errors are made. For some men said that it was unlawful to kill even the least animals. But this is false, because it is not a sin to use those things which are subject to man's power. For it is the natural order that there be plants for the nourishment of animals and certain animals for the nourishment of other animals; and all animals are for man's nourishment; "And every thing that moveth, and liveth shall be meat for you: even as the green herbs have I delivered them all to you" (Gen. 9, 3). And the Philosopher[38] also, in his *Politics*, says that hunting is like a just war.

The second error is the error of certain men who said, **Thou shalt not kill**, namely man, hence, they call murderers all secular judges,[39] who condemn according to certain laws. Against which error, Augustine[40] says that God did not deprive Himself of the power of killing, hence it is said, "I will kill and I will make to live: I will strike, and I will heal, and there is none that can deliver out of my hand" (Deut. 32, 39). Therefore, it is lawful for those secular judges to kill because they kill by God's command, for then God is doing this. For every law is a commandment of God; "By me kings reign, and lawgivers decree just things" (Prov. 8, 15), and, "For he beareth not the sword in vain. For he is God's minister: an avenger to execute wrath upon him that doth evil" (Rom. 13, 4). Therefore, **Thou shalt not kill** ought to be understood to mean that one ought not to kill on one's own authority.

The third error is that some men supposed **Thou shalt not kill** another man, but it is lawful to kill oneself, because this is found concerning Samson[41] and Cato[42] and of certain virgins

---

37. *In Mt.* Hom. 16 (PG 57, 245).
38. *Politics* 1, 8 (1256b 23-26), in *Arist. lat.* XXIX, I.
39. "Secular" judges are opposed to ecclesiastical judges. Cf. II II, q. 33, a. 7 ad 5um.
40. *City of God*, bk. 1, chap. 21.
41. cf. Judges 16, 30.
42. Marcus Porcius Cato Uticensis, commonly known as Cato the Younger (*Cato Minor*), committed suicide in 46 B.C.

who cast themselves into a river,[43] according to what Augustine recounts.[44] But Augustine[45] replies, that he who kills himself kills a man, because one ought not to kill another man, except by God's authority, nor oneself except by God's will or an instinct of the Holy Ghost, and in this way he excuses Samson.

And whosoever shall kill. Here the punishment for murder is related, namely, ***shall be in danger of the judgment***, meaning the punishment which the Law will adjudicate; "He that striketh a man with a will to kill him, shall be put to death" (Ex. 21, 12).

He continues: ***But I say to you***, etc. Having related the precept of the Old Law, here the Lord fulfills it, and this fulfillment does not empty out the Law, rather it conduces to a greater fulfillment, because he who gets angry is prone to commit murder, but sometimes he who gets angry does not commit murder. This anger is in some way contained in this commandment, because this law was given by God, and there is a difference between man's law and God's law, namely, that man is the judge of exterior actions, but God is the judge of interior actions; "For men seeth those things that appear, but the Lord beholdeth the heart" (I Kings 16, 7). Hence, in these words, ***Thou shalt not kill***, is also included the impulse to kill. But there is a twofold impulse to injure one's neighbor, namely, of anger and of hatred; and hatred is not the same thing as an inveterate anger,[46] but is the causal predication, because hatred comes from inveterate anger. Therefore, there is a difference, because anger does not desire evil to one's neighbor except insofar as it wants revenge. Hence, once revenge has been made, it rests; in hatred, however, the same injury is wanted in itself and the desire of injuring one's neighbor never rests. Therefore, the impulse of hatred is more grievous than that of anger. God, however, not only forbids the impulse of hatred but also that of anger, which is less grievous; "But he that hateth his brother is in darkness and walketh in darkness and knoweth not whither he goeth: because the darkness hath blinded his eyes" (I Jn. 2, 11).

Now He sets forth three degrees of anger. The first degree is of anger hidden in the heart; the second degree is of anger

---

43. The text here reads "cast themselves into a fire," but since St. Augustine uses the word "river" (*fluvium*) and not "fire" (*flammam*) as found in the text, this must be an error of the copyist and so has been corrected here. cf. *City of God*, bk. 1, chap. 26.

44. "But, they say, in the time of persecution some holy women escaped those who menaced them with outrage, by casting themselves into rivers which they knew would drown them; and having died in this manner, they are venerated in the Catholic Church as martyrs" (*City of God*, bk. 1, chap. 26).

45. *City of God*, bk. 1, chap. 20-21.

46. Cicero says (*De Quaestionibus Tusculanis* iv, 9) that "hatred is inveterate anger." cf. II II, q. 46, a. 3 ad 2um.

appearing outwardly; and the third degree is of anger breaking forth into injuring. The first is where it is said, ***But I say to you***, and Augustine[47] says that the reading ought to be, 'without cause,' because he who without cause gets angry ***shall be in danger of the judgment***. Jerome,[48] however, says that 'without cause' is not in the text, because then a place would have been left to anger; the Lord however left no place to anger.

But is all anger contrary to virtue? It ought to be known that, as Augustine[49] says, there were two opinions of the philosophers about this. The Stoics said that the wise man is free from all passions; even more, they maintained that true virtue consisted in perfect quiet of soul.[50] The Peripatetics, on the other hand, held that the wise man is subject to anger, but in a moderate degree. This is the more accurate opinion. It is proved both from authority, since in the Gospels we find these passions in some way attributed to Christ in whom was the fullness of wisdom; and from reason, because if all passions were contrary to virtue, there would be some powers of the soul[51] whose service is harmful, because they would not have some suitable acts, and then the irascible and concupiscible powers would have been given in vain to man. And therefore it ought to be said that anger is sometimes a virtue, but other times it is not.

Now anger can be taken in three ways. Firstly, it is taken as it exists solely in the judgment of reason without any perturbation of soul; this, however, is not called anger but judgment. For in this way the Lord, when punishing the wicked, is said to be angry;[52] "I will bear the anger of the Lord" (Mich. 7, 9).

Secondly, it is taken as being a passion. This is in the sensitive appetite and is twofold. Sometimes it is ordained by reason, and it is restrained within proper limits by reason, as when one gets angry as much as he ought, to whom he ought, and suchlike, and then it is an act of virtue and it is called zealous anger. Hence, the Philosopher[53] also says that meekness does not consist in never

---

47. *De serm. Dom.* I, 9, 25.
48. *Comm. in Mt.*, I.
49. *City of God*, bk. 9, chap. 4.
50. cf. St. Thomas Aquinas, *De Duobus Praeceptis Charitatis* (*On the Two Laws of Charity and the Ten Commandments*), a. 7.
51. "Powers of the soul" has been added from the parallel text in *De Duobus Praeceptis Charitatis*, a. 7, namely, "If all the passions were opposed to virtue, then there would be some *powers of the soul* which would be without good purpose; indeed, they would be positively harmful to man, since they would have no acts in keeping with them."
52. The text reads *iratus apparet*, meaning "He appears angered," but based on the parallel text in the *De Duobus Praeceptis Charitatis, iratus dicitur*, meaning "He is said to be angry," has been substituted as it is more accurate, as God is not directly observed by us.
53. Aristotle, *Ethica Nicomachea* IV, 12 (1125b 26s.) in *Arist. lat.* XXVI, 1-3, fasc. 3.

getting angry in any way. And so Chrysostom[54] says that if anger were entirely taken away, discipline would also be taken away, etc. Therefore this kind of anger is not a sin.

There is a third anger, which overthrows[55] the judgment of reason, and this is always a sin, but sometimes it is a venial sin, and other times it is a mortal sin, and it will be deemed the latter when it comes from a very bad impulse to injure one's neighbor. For something is a mortal or venial sin in two ways: from its genus or from its circumstances, or in other words, by its act or from the consent to the act. For example, murder is an act of a mortal sin by reason of its genus because it is directly opposed to a divine precept, and therefore consent to murder is a mortal sin. This is because if an action is a mortal sin, then consent to that action is also a mortal sin. Likewise, if action were a venial sin, then consent to the action would be a venial sin, and so forth. Sometimes, however, a sin is mortal by reason of its genus, but nevertheless, the impulse is not a mortal sin, because it is without consent. For example, if an impulse of concupiscence arises for fornication and if there is no consent, then it is not a mortal sin. Similarly, anger is an impulse to avenge a wrong done. For this is anger properly speaking. If, therefore, this impulse, for example to commit murder, comes solely from the state of passion so that reason is also led astray, then it is a mortal sin; if, however, reason is not perverted, then it is a venial sin. If, however, an impulse is not by reason of its genus a mortal sin, then if consent is given, it is not a mortal sin.

Therefore, that which the Lord says, **Whosoever is angry with his brother, shall be in danger of the judgment**, is to be understood concerning an impulse tending to do injury and coming solely from the state of passion, and if there be consent to this impulse, it is a mortal sin; "And all things that serve,[56] God will bring into judgment for every error, whether it be good or evil" (Eccle. 12, 14). And this is the meaning of **But I say to you, that whosoever is angry with his brother, shall be in danger of the judgment**.

And observe that no prophet speaking of the Law of Moses spoke in this way, **But I say to you**, etc., but instead they were only inducing men to observe the Law of Moses. From which it is evident

---

54. *Op. imp. in Mt..*, hom. XI (PG 56, 690).

55. The word used here in the Latin text is *effugit*, meaning "flees." But in a parallel text found in the *De Duobus Praeceptis Charitatis* (a. 7), *refugit*, meaning "overthrows," is used in this context, and since this word gives a clearer meaning and is more precise, it has been substituted here.

56. This verse slightly varies from the Vulgate in that *seviunt*, meaning "serve," replaces *fiunt*, meaning "are done." It probably is taken from an Old Latin version.

that the Lord shows that He has authority, and He shows that He is the Legislator of the Law, when He says, *But I say to you*, etc.

Afterwards the second degree of anger is related, namely, when it appears outwardly without any infliction of an injury.

Raca, according to certain men, is a word not signifying any determinate concept, but is an interjection of someone getting angry. According to Augustine,[57] it is like 'heu,' an interjection of someone in pain, and it signifies a certain emotion; hence, the anger has already broken forth outwardly, nevertheless it has not broken forth into an injury. According to Chrysostom,[58] it is an interjection of someone despising, and denotes contempt. Now both of these things are forbidden, namely, both to show bitterness to one's brother, as the Apostle says: "Let all bitterness and anger and indignation and clamour and blasphemy be put away from you, with all malice" (Eph. 4, 31), and to despise him; "Why then doth every one of us despise his brother, violating the covenant of our fathers?" (Mal. 2, 10).

According to others, *raca* is a word signifying a determinate concept, and according to this there are two opinions, for according to Augustine,[59] it means the same thing as 'ragged' (*pannosus*), coming from [the Greek ῥάκος, meaning] 'a rag,'[60] and this agrees with the opinion of Chrysostom;[61] according to Jerome,[62] *raca* signifies 'empty,' hence, *raca* signifies, as it were, 'without a brain,' and this is a great injury, nay, it is an injury to the Holy Ghost when one calls a wise brother full of the Holy Ghost 'empty-headed,' etc.

But Chrysostom[63] asks if 'empty' is the same as 'fool,' because the Lord says afterwards, *And whosoever shall say, Thou fool.* And he said that there are words in every idiom which do not[64] signify an insult, but from their usage and custom of speech, have become an insult. For although *raca* means the same thing as *fool*, nevertheless they do not have the same usage, because *raca* is said familiarly; and it is a sin when it is said in anger.

He shall be in danger of the council. Augustine[65] says that it is a worse thing before God to be in danger of the council than to be in danger of the judgment, because before the judgment, when

---

57. *De serm. Dom.* I, 9, 23-24.
58. *In Mt. Hom.* XVI (PG 57, 248).
59. *De serm. Dom.* I, 9, 23.
60. "AUG. Some seek the interpretation of this word in the Greek, and think that *Raca* means 'ragged' [*pannosus* in Latin], from the Greek *pannus*, 'a rag'" (*Catena Aurea on St. Matthew*, chap. 5, lect. 13).
61. *In Mt. Hom.* XVI (PG 57, 248).
62. *Com. In Mt.,* I.
63. *Op. imp. in Mt..,* hom. XI (PG 56, 690-1).
64. "Not" has been added here as it seems needed by the context.
65. *De sermone Domini in monte,* Lib. I, cap. 9, n. 22 & 24 (PL 34, 1240).

the accused is still being judged and it is doubted whether one be guilty, [there is yet opportunity for defense];[66] "I charge thee... that thou observe these things without prejudice, doing nothing by declining to either side" (I Tim. 5, 21). But after the accused has been convicted of a crime, the accused is no longer being judged, but instead the judges draw him to the Council for the punishment to be inflicted. Hilary[67] says that the accused *shall be in danger of the council* of the Saints, because he who does an injury to the Holy Ghost deserves to be condemned by the Saints. Chrysostom says that the Apostles[68] expounded this verse as follows: *He shall be in danger of the council*, meaning that he would be numbered among those who came into Council against Christ.

And whosoever shall say, Thou fool. Here the third degree of anger is related, which is when one inflicts an injury with one's words. And just as he who calls his brother *Raca* inflicts an injury to the Holy Ghost, so he who says, *Thou fool*, inflicts an injury to the Son of God, who "is made unto us wisdom and justice and sanctification and redemption" (I Cor. 1, 30).

He shall be in danger of hell fire. This is the first place where mention is made of hell, *Gehenna*, as no one ever used this word before. "Near Jerusalem there was a certain deserted[69] valley which is called the valley of Topheth or the valley of the sons of Ennom;[70] in it, however, the children of Israel worshipped idols and God threatened them through Jeremias that in it their carcasses deserved to be thrown down to the ground. Hence, it is said, "Behold the days come, saith the Lord, that this place shall no more be called Topheth, nor the valley of the son of Ennom, but

---

66. These words are supplied from a parallel passage in the *Catena Aurea on St. Matthew* (chap. 5, lect. 13).
67. *Com. in Mt.* hom. XI (PL 9, 937C).
68. cf. "PSEUDO-CHRYS. In danger of the council; that is (according to the interpretation given by the Apostles in their Constitutions), in danger of being one of that Council which condemned Christ" (*Catena Aurea on St. Matthew* chap. 5, lect. 13). Note that this remark is not found in the *Constitutions of the Holy Apostles* as we now have them. cf. Ps. Chrys., *Op. imp. in Mt.*, hom. XI (PG 56, 690).
69. The text here reads, *delicata*, meaning "charming," but *derelicta* meaning "deserted" might fit the context better here.
70. "Tophet, the valley of the sons of Ennom, is called 'Gehenna,' because fire was kept there for the sacrifice in the rocks of Tophet. The same is the valley of Gethsemani, in which the army of Sennacherib was destroyed. Or hell is signified by it. Hence, the Jews conjecture that hell is there, because in between two palm trees which are there, smoke is always emitted" (*Expositio super Isaiam ad litteram*, chap. 30). "There are two palm trees in the Valley of Ben Hinnom and between them smoke arises... and this is the gate of Gehenna?" (*Babylonian Talmud*, Erubin, 19a). Calmet says that the valley of Tophet is where Nehemias hid sacred fire used for the sacrifices and that this hiding place mentioned in II Machabees was still shown in his day. "For when our fathers were led into Persia, the priests that then were worshippers of God, took privately the fire from the altar, and hid it in a valley where there was a deep pit without water, and there they kept it safe" (1, 19).

the valley of slaughter. And I will defeat the counsel of Juda and of Jerusalem in this place: and I will destroy them with the sword in the sight of their enemies, and by the hands of them that seek their lives: and I will give their carcasses to be meat for the fowls of the air, and for the beasts of the earth" (Jer. 19, 6).

Gehenna, according to the Hebrews, is the same place as the valley of Ennom. And so, because when they were going down from Jerusalem many were thrown down to the ground and killed by Nabuchodonosor in it, therefore He calls the place of hell, **Gehenna**. For, just as He changed the earthly promises in the Old Law into heavenly and eternal goods, so He changed the temporal punishments which the Old Law was inflicting into eternal punishments. Now, just as the guilts are also related to each other, because it is worse to show exterior anger than to hold interior anger, and worse still to inflict an injury, so in the first place is judgment, in the second place is the council, and in the third place are specific punishments; and all these things, namely, judgment, the council, and Gehenna, signify the pain of hell. And He says many things, because He shows in this diversity of punishments, that they will be punished more, who inflict harm

But then there is a question: Did he who said to his brother, **Raca**, sin mortally? Some say that **he shall be in danger of the council** is said hyperbolically in order to frighten, but this is false, because Christ's teaching is a teaching full of truth. Hence, it ought to be known that the third sin includes the second, and the second includes the first. In the first, the sin of anger is understood, which is a mortal sin. And if from that anger one breaks forth into injurious words or inflicts an injury, one sins mortally. Similarly, he who said, **Raca**, broke forth into injurious words, and there is anger which is a mortal sin. But it was necessary for the Apostle to have done this, who said the words, "O senseless Galatians, who hath bewitched you that you should not obey the truth" (Gal. 3, 1). I reply, saying that he was not speaking out of anger, but out of the necessity of justice, and for the same reason scourging is not a sin. And therefore Augustine[71] says that when He said, **whosoever is angry**, He added the phrase "without cause," and in the second and third statements he also says that there was the phrase "without cause." Yet, according to him, the meaning is also the same even if the phrase "without cause" is not included.[72]

---

71. *De Sermone Domini in monte*, Lib. I, cap. 9, n. 25 (PL 34, 1241).
72. cf. In *Retract.* I. xix. 4 where St. Augustine also helps us to understand how the word εἰκῆ (*without cause*) in the preceding clause crept into some of the Mss. when he writes, "The Greek codices do not have 'without cause,' as it is set forth here [in Mt. 5, 22], although the meaning is the same."

Afterwards, when He says, *If therefore thou offer thy gift*, having set forth the fulfillment of the precept, *Thou shalt not kill*, He shows how it ought to be observed. And firstly, He shows how a man ought to treat the one whom he has injured; secondly, He shows how a man ought to treat one who has harmed him, where it is said, *Be at agreement with thy adversary betimes*. About the first part, He does three things. Firstly, He sets forth good advice; secondly, He sets forth the obstacles to carrying out His advice; and thirdly, He sets forth a remedy to these obstacles. The second part is where it is said, *And there thou remember that thy brother hath anything against thee*; and the third part is where it is said, *Leave there thy offering before the altar*.

He says, therefore, *If therefore thou offer thy gift at the altar*. It is as though He were to say, 'Because you ought not to offend anyone, *if therefore thou offer thy gift at the altar, and there thou remember that thy brother hath anything against thee*, etc.' By this *gift*, we honor God in that we recognize that all things are given to us by God; "All things are thine: and we have given thee what we received of thy hand," etc., (I Par. 29, 14). Likewise, we honor the Church, because from such gifts the poor are supported by the Church; "Honour the Lord with thy substance, and give him of the first of all thy fruits" (Prov. 3, 9). "Honour the Lord with thy substance," (Prov. 3, 9), and not with thy neighbor's substance. "For I am the Lord that love judgment, and hate robbery in a holocaust" (Is. 61, 8).[73] *If therefore thou offer thy gift at the altar*, not to idolaters;[74] "Beware lest thou offer thy holocausts in every place that thou shalt see, but in the place which the Lord shall choose" (Deut. 12, 13-14).

An offense to one's neighbor is obstructive [to offering gifts to God], hence He says, *And there thou remember that thy brother hath anything against thee*. Observe that sometimes you have something against your brother, and other times your brother has something against you, namely, when you offend him or he offends you. But you ought to spare him. For the Apostle says, "Bearing with one another and forgiving one another, if any have a complaint against another" (Col. 3, 13). And because the one who is offended is not said to ask pardon of him who offended him, but vice versa, wherefore He says, *And there thou remember that*

---

73. The reference here is "Isaias xli: *Ego Dominus habens*," but as all these words are not to be found in one verse of this chapter, Isaias lxi, 8: *Ego Dominus diligens iudicium odio habens*, etc., seems more correct and the Roman numerals may have been accidentally reversed by the copiest.

74. The text here seems mistaken as it has *ioculatoribus*, meaning 'jesters,' instead of *idololatris*, meaning 'idolaters.'

thy brother hath anything against thee, etc. When, according to Chrysostom,[75] you do more than this, it is more perfect. "With them that hated peace I was peaceable: when I spoke to them they fought against me without cause" (Ps. 119, 7).

And He says, *there thou remember*, because perhaps before you did not remember; wherefore He gives three counsels. Firstly, *Leave there thy offering*. The Lord never wants that a good deed be completely abandoned on account of an evil deed, since one is offering a good thing, but He wants one to stop offering it on account of the evil deed; "But a beast that may be sacrificed to the Lord, if any one shall vow, shall be holy and cannot be changed: that is to say, neither a better for a worse, nor a worse for a better," etc., (Lev. 27, 9-10). And therefore He says, *Leave there thy offering*, and not 'stop thy offering,' meaning, keep the intention and remove the impediment, and this is the meaning of the words, *and go first to be reconciled*.

But here Augustine objects that if the Lord means this literally, then something unfitting follows, since one's brother can be on the other side of the sea. But it ought to be understood that if one does not have the opportunity of finding him, one ought to go with one's heart. You ought to also understand that by *the altar*, faith is signified; without which "it is impossible to please God" (Heb. 11, 6). Augustine also says that if a mortal sin is remembered before the altar, and one wishes to offer a gift, if one does not have an opportunity for confessing, one can offer with contrition and the intention of confessing; therefore, *go first to be reconciled to thy brother*, at least in one's heart, *and then coming thou shalt offer thy gift*; "The most High approveth not the gifts of the wicked: neither hath he respect to the oblations of the unjust, nor will he be pacified for sins by the multitude of their sacrifices" (Eccli. 34, 23).

And afterwards He says, *And then coming thou shalt offer thy gift*, in which it is noted that by the exercise of charity towards one's neighbor, we come to the charity of God; "If any man say: I love God, and hateth his brother; he is a liar," etc., (I Jn. 4, 20).

Be at agreement with thy adversary betimes. Above, the Lord premised one useful teaching for putting the fulfillment into practice, now He puts forward another. And this teaching can

---

75. Psuedo-Chrysostom, *Op. imp. in Mt.*, hom. XI (PG 56, 692): "For if you injured him, and therefore you asked pardon, the Lord will spare you that you harmed, because you asked first; nevertheless, you have no reward if you asked pardon only when you were found guilty. If, however, he will have injured you, and you shall have asked pardon first, you will have a great reward. Therefore make haste to precede your enemy."

be connected with the preceding ones in two ways. Firstly, it is as follows. The Lord determined above how you ought to behave with him whom you have injured, now He teaches how you ought to behave with someone who has injured you, and this is what is said here, *Be at agreement*, etc. Or it is otherwise, such that *adversary* is taken in a broad sense, either as he who injured you, or him whom you have injured.

Thus the Lord teaches that you ought to be reconciled with your brother. But someone could say, 'I will be reconciled, but not so quickly.' Wherefore the Lord says, *betimes*; "Let not the sun go down upon your anger" (Eph. 4, 26). And it ought to be observed that as Jerome[76] says, *at agreement* is the translation of a certain Greek word which means "benevolent" or "clement."

But it is asked, who is this *adversary*? And it ought to be known that there are five adversaries with whom we ought to be at agreement, namely, the man [who injured you], the devil, the flesh, God, and God's word.[77] Concerning the first adversary, it is written, "Give heed to me, O Lord, and hear the voice of my adversaries" (Jer. 18, 19). Concerning the second adversary, it is written, "Let my enemy be as the ungodly, and my adversary as the wicked one" (Job 27, 7). Concerning the third adversary, it is written, "The flesh lusteth against the spirit: and the spirit against the flesh: For these are contrary one to another" (Gal. 5, 17), and, "I see another law in my members, fighting against the law of my mind" (Rom. 7, 23). Concerning the fourth adversary, namely God, who is opposed to those sinning, both when He punishes and also when He commands contrary precepts, it is written, "Thou art changed to be cruel toward me, and in the hardness of thy hand thou art against me" (Job 30, 21).[78] Concerning the fifth adversary, it is written, "Deliver me, O my God, out of the hand of the sinner, and out of the hand of the transgressor of the law and of the unjust" (Ps. 70, 4), and, "How very unpleasant is wisdom to the unlearned, and the unwise will not continue with her" (Eccli. 6, 21). Therefore, this is the reason why Augustine[79] asks: Which of these adversaries is understood in this passage? It is not understood

---

76. *Com. in Mt.*, I.
77. The first and third adversary in this list were exchanged to be consonant with the explanations that follow.
78. "As Augustine says (*Contra Faustum Manichaeum* xix,26), those precepts of Our Lord are not contrary to the precepts of the Old Law. For what Our Lord commanded about a man not putting away his wife, is not contrary to what the Law prescribed... The same applies to the prohibition about swearing, as stated above. The same is also clear with respect to the prohibition of retaliation" (I II, q. 107, a. 2 ad 2um).
79. *De Sermone Domini in monte*, Lib. I, cap. 11, n. 31-32 (PL 34, 1244-1245).

concerning the man [who injured you], for two reasons. Firstly, on account of that which follows: *lest perhaps the adversary deliver thee to the judge*; for how could a man deliver you to Christ who will judge you both at the same time? Secondly, it is not understood concerning the man [whom you injured] because if he die, would not hope of pardon be ended? Therefore, it cannot be understood of a man. Thirdly, it cannot be understood of the devil. For God would not want this, since by the fact that a man previously consented to him, man fell into misery. Although some other exegetes, according to Jerome,[80] expound *the adversary* as referring to the devil, and they say that we are *at agreement* with the devil when we keep the pact that we made with him at our baptism, for instance we said the words, "I renounce Satan"; but this exposition is distorted. Fourthly, it cannot be understood of the flesh.[81] Fifthly, it cannot be understood of God, since He says, *Be at agreement with thy adversary betimes, whilst thou art in the way with him.* For, although God is with every man, nevertheless not every man is with God. Hence, Augustine[82] says that it is understood of God's words and laws, which laws are opposed to us insofar as we sin. Nevertheless, the exposition of Jerome[83] and of Chrysostom[84] is more literal, who say, *Be at agreement with thy adversary*, meaning make peace with the man who injured you or whom you injured, and do this *betimes*; "Delay not to be converted to the Lord, and defer it not from day to day" (Eccli. 5, 8), *in the way*, meaning in this life.

Afterwards He assigns the reason for His advice, based on the troubles that would follow from not following it, which are four. He states the first trouble, where it is said, *Lest perhaps the adversary deliver thee to the judge*. If *the adversary* be understood of God's words, the literal meaning is clear. Christ is here taken as the judge; "The Father hath given all judgment to the Son" (Jn. 5, 22), and, "It is he who was appointed by God to be judge of the living and of the dead" (Acts 10, 42). Hence, God's words deliver us to Christ in that they accuse us of sin which we committed against God's laws. Hence, "The word that I have spoken, the same shall judge him in the last day" (Jn. 12, 48). If, however, *the adversary* be understood of the man [who injured

---

80. *Com. in Mt.*, I.
81. St. Augustine, *De Sermone Domini in monte*, Lib. I, cap. 11, n. 31 (PL 34, 1245): "But much less do I see how we are enjoined to bear goodwill towards, or to agree with, or to yield to, the flesh. For it is sinners rather who love their flesh, and agree with it, and yield to it; but those who bring it into subjection are not the parties who yield to it, but rather they compel it to yield to them."
82. *De Sermone Domini in monte*, Lib. I, cap.11, n. 32 (PL 34, 1245).
83. *Com. in Mt.*, I.
84. *Op. imp. in Mt.*, hom. XI (PG 56, 693).

you], then he would ***deliver*** you causally or occasionally, because discord is the reason why you would be delivered to the judge, and from that sin you are made a criminal to the judge. And He says, ***perhaps***, because if he should die, and you remain in this life, a place of repentance will not be taken from you, because God, whom you should have loved, suffices [for a reconciliation];[85] nevertheless, if He were ***the adversary***, the reconciliation is easier.[86]

He states the second trouble, where it is said, ***And the judge deliver thee to the officer***, etc. Here, ***the officer***, according to Augustine,[87] is the good angels; "Bless the Lord, all ye his angels: you that are mighty in strength, and execute his word, hearkening to the voice of his orders. Bless the Lord, all ye his hosts: you ministers of his that do his will." (Ps. 102, 21-22). Nor is there any doubt that the angels will come with Christ to the Judgment and will be the executors of the things that are done there; "And when the Son of man shall come in his majesty, and all the angels with him, then shall he sit upon the seat of his majesty" (below 25, 31). Chrysostom[88] understands ***the officer*** of the bad angels, as if the punishment were under the devil's power. But is the devil said to be God's minister? I reply, saying that someone can be said to be another person's minister in two ways: as to the deed, meaning that he does another's will, or as to the intention; and in this second way the devil is not God's minister, because he does not serve on account of God's justice, but on account of his hatred of men, whom he punishes. Hence, only in the first way is he said to be God's minister, and something similar is stated in Jeremias 27: "I have given all the lands of the earth into the hand of Nabuchodonosor king of Babylon my servant" (verse 6).[89]

He states the third trouble, where it is said, ***and thou be cast into prison***. Here the ***prison*** is understood of the prison of hell, concerning which it is said, "Behold, the devil will cast some of you

---

85. "And this for the additional reason, that if any one has injured a man by killing him, there will be no time now in which to agree with him; for he is not now in the way with him, i.e. in this life: and yet a remedy will not on that account be excluded, if one repents and flees for refuge with the sacrifice of a broken heart to the mercy of Him who forgives the sins of those who turn to Him, and who rejoices more over one penitent than over ninety-nine just persons" (*De Sermone Domini in monte*, Lib. I, cap. 11, n. 31 (PL 34, 1244-1245)).

86. "The apostle says, 'For if, when we were enemies, we were reconciled to God by the death of His Son, much more, being reconciled, we shall be saved by His life' (Rom. 5, 10). And from this it may be perceived that no nature [as being] bad is an enemy to God, inasmuch as the very parties who were enemies are being reconciled" (Ibid.)

87. *De Sermone Domini in monte*, Lib. I, cap. 11, n. 29 (PL 34, 1243).

88. *Op. imp. in Mt.*, hom. XI (PG 56, 693).

89. The text in the Vulgate reads, "all these lands" instead of "all the lands of the earth."

into prison," etc., (Apoc. 2, 10).[90] And hell is said to be a *prison* by reason of a similitude, because they who are there have their free will bound, in that they are obstinate in evil. Nevertheless, if *the officer* be understood of the good angels, it ought to be known that they sometimes punish; according to Dionysius,[91] they never punish the good but the wicked, for example, they struck the army of Sennacherib. (IV Kings 19, 35-36).

He states the fourth trouble, where it is said, **Amen I say to thee, thou shalt not go out from thence till thou repay the last farthing.** A *farthing* is a certain small Roman coin which contains two mites, and it is called a *farthing* because it was a fourth part of a larger coin.[92] Therefore, the Lord wishes to say, **Thou shalt not go out from thence till** you pay the punishments and satisfy for even the least venial sins. Hence, the similitude of the *farthing* is adopted on account of its smallness. Or, according to Augustine, the metaphor can be adopted on account of its number.[93] Hence, it can signify sins which are committed from love of earthly things, and earth is the fourth element.[94]

But why did He say, **Thou shalt not go out till**, wherefore going out happens? I reply, saying that the word *till* sometimes designates a limited time, and other times an unlimited time, as that passage reads, "For he must reign, until he hath put all his enemies under his feet" (I Cor. 15, 25). Does it follow that He will cease to reign afterwards? Far be it. Hence, the word is used limitlessly in that passage, and so it is used here, where it is said, **Thou shalt not go out till**, meaning one will never go out, because one will never pay the *last farthing*. And for this reason, Hilary[95] expounds this passage as follows. Doubtlessly no sin is forgiven except through charity; "Charity covereth all sins" (Prov. 10, 12). Therefore, he who dies with discord, dies without charity, and so will never be purged from his sins. And observe in these words that men are punished eternally in hell not only for mortal sins but also for venial sins, *from thence till thou repay the last farthing.*

---

90. The manuscript is obscure here and so the quotation might instead be, "The devil, who seduced them, was cast into the pool of fire and brimstone" (Apoc. 20, 9).

91. Dionysius Ps. Areopagita, *De divinis nominibus* IV, 22 (PG 3, 723).

92. I.e. the "as," which was one sixteenth of a denarius.

93. *De Sermone Domini in monte,* Lib. I, cap. 11, n. 30 (PL 34, 1243-1244):

"For as a fourth part of the separate component parts of this world, and in fact as the last, the earth is found; so that you begin with the heavens, you reckon the air the second, water the third, the earth the fourth."

94. "These four bodies are fire, air, water, earth. Fire occupies the highest place among them all, earth the lowest" (Aristotle, *Meteorology,* Bk. 1, Pt. 2).

95. *Com. in Mt.*, IV (PL 9, 938BC).

On account of this difficulty from the word *till*, other expositions are put forth. Hence, *into prison*, meaning into the prison of the tribulations of the present life; "Behold, the devil will cast some of you into prison, that you may be tried: and you shall have tribulation ten days" (Apoc. 2, 10). Sometimes when God punishes someone in the present life for his sins, He does not relent unless he be completely purged. Chrysostom,[96] since he says that the whole passage can be expounded in relation to the present life, says, *be reconciled* as quickly as possible, not only due to the fact that eternal punishment is imminent, but also because temporal harm in this life is imminent, wherefore he expounds *lest perhaps*, etc., literally. And Christ says, *perhaps*, because this does not always happen, because the Gospel promises are concerning eternal goods; nevertheless, the Lord sets forth temporal promises and eternal punishments, and this is what is said, *Amen I say to thee*, etc.

27. You have heard that it was said to them of old: Thou shalt not commit adultery.
28. But I say to you, that whosoever shall look on a woman to lust after her, hath already committed adultery with her in his heart.
29. And if thy right eye scandalize thee, pluck it out and cast it from thee. For it is expedient for thee that one of thy members should perish, rather than thy whole body be cast into hell.
30. And if thy right hand scandalize thee, cut it off, and cast it from thee: for it is expedient for thee that one of thy members should perish, rather than that thy whole body go into hell.

You have heard that it was said to them of old: Thou shalt not commit adultery. Above, the Lord fulfilled the Law as to the prohibitive precept concerning murder, now He fulfills it as to the prohibitive precept concerning adultery. And about this He does three things. Firstly, He sets forth the precept; secondly, He sets forth the fulfillment of the precept; and thirdly, He teaches how it can be observed. The second part is where it is said, *But I say to you, that whosoever shall look on a woman*; and the third part is where it is said, *And if thy right eye scandalize thee*. And fittingly, after the prohibitive precept concerning murder, the prohibitive precept concerning adultery is related,

---

96. Ps. Chrys., *Op. imp. in Mt.*, hom. XI (PG 56, 693).

because adultery holds the second place after murder. For murder is opposed to the life of an already existing man, but adultery is opposed to the life of a man to be begotten; for it takes away the certitude of the offspring and consequently its education.[97]

Thou shalt not commit adultery (*moechaberis*). *Moechia*[98] is adultery properly speaking. This precept is found in Exodus 20, 14,[99] and Deuteronomy 5, 18.[100]

And it ought to be known that, because in the precepts of the Decalogue simple fornication is not prohibited but only adultery, some men supposed that simple fornication is not a mortal sin, because it is not against the Law since it is not in the precepts of the Decalogue. Firstly, it is said in Leviticus, "If a man carnally lie with a woman... they both shall be scourged: and they shall not be put to death," etc., (19, 20). Therefore, simple fornication is a venial sin. Furthermore, "All iniquity is sin. And there is a sin unto death" (I Jn. 5, 16-17). But he who commits simple fornication, commits iniquity to no one: not to oneself, because he fulfills his will, nor to another person, nor to God, because it is not directly opposed to Him as are blasphemy and idolatry and the like. Therefore it is not a mortal sin.

I answer that it ought to be most certain in the eyes of the faithful that all simple fornication is a mortal sin, and, briefly, all use of the genital members outside the use of marriage; "For fornicators and adulterers God will judge" (Heb. 13, 4) and He gave these sins as distinct from one another, because as He will judge adulterers, so He will judge fornicators; "Take heed to keep thyself, my son, from all fornication, and beside thy wife never endure to know a crime" (Tob. 4, 13), and, "There shall be no whore among the daughters of Israel" (Deut. 23, 17). It is evident, therefore, by authority from the Old and New Testaments, that it is a mortal sin. And the reason for this is that marriage is natural not only according to our faith but even to pagans, because it is natural that a man be joined together matrimonially not to anyone indeterminately but to one person

---

97. "There is in men a certain natural solicitude to know their offspring. This is necessary for this reason: the child requires the father's direction for a long time. So, whenever there are obstacles to the ascertaining of offspring, they are opposed to the natural instinct of the human species. But if a husband could put away his wife, or a wife her husband, and have sexual relations with another person, certitude as to offspring would be precluded, for the wife would be united first with one man and later with another." (*Summa Contra Gentiles*, bk. 3, chap. 123, n. 5).

98. "It is often asked whether fornication is also comprised by the name of *moechia*. For this is a Greek word, which Scripture in fact uses in place of the Latin word" (St. Augustine, *Quaestionum In Heptateuchum Libri Septem*, lib. II, 71, 4).

99. *Non moechaberis*, i.e. "Thou shalt not commit adultery."

100. *Neque moechaberis*, i.e. "Neither shalt thou commit adultery."

and determinately, and it does not matter with what celebration it takes place insofar as the intention of nature. What, however, is from the natural law? Marriage is perverted in those who lack the use of reason. For the joining of a man and a woman is ordained to generation and education of children. In some animals the female alone suffices for the education of the offspring, and in such animals the father never involves himself with the education of the offspring; and thus the certitude of the offspring is not necessary, and accordingly such animals have intercourse with any other, as appears in the case of dogs. In other animals, however, we see that in any of these animals the female is not able by herself to educate the offspring, and so in this case the male and female remain together until the offspring is educated. Therefore, it is apparent that since sexual intercourse is for the sake of education, all sexual intercourse from which the due education does not follow is against nature. Wherefore, since a newborn child needs many things from the father's care, it is necessary that the man have a determinate woman, and this is marriage. Now, whether a man may have many women is another question. Therefore, fornication will be opposed to this education. Therefore, it is against nature and a mortal sin. Now Moses spoke to the Jews, as a teacher of ignorant hearers, the most basic principles. The Decalogue is the beginning of the Law, and thus it expresses therein only those principles which are the most evident. Hence, some men say that God Himself spoke the Decalogue, leaving all other things to be explained by others. Hence, in these words, **Thou shalt not commit adultery**, every other sin is understood which is from the use of the genital members outside of marriage. Likewise, the fornicator sins against himself; "He that committeth fornication sinneth against his own body" (I Cor. 6, 18), because acts of this kind ought not to be done except on account of the generation of another. Likewise, in the Law, certain sins were not punished by death, such as theft and many other sins; therefore, that which is objected from Leviticus[101] proves nothing. Therefore, it is evident that fornication is a mortal sin.

But I say to you, that whosoever shall look on a woman to lust after her. Here the Lord fulfills the Law as to the prohibitive precept concerning adultery. For the Pharisees and scribes understood this precept, **Thou shalt not commit adultery**, only insofar as the act of adultery. Now the Lord also forbids concupiscence. But here Augustine objects that the prohibition of concupiscence is a precept of the Decalogue: "Thou

---

101. i.e. Lev. 19, 20 quoted above.

shalt not covet thy neighbor's wife: nor his house, nor his field, nor his manservant, nor his maidservant, nor his ox, nor his ass, nor any thing that is his" (Deut. 5, 21).[102] Therefore the Lord did not fulfill this precept of the Law. And he replies that the Lord understands "Thou shalt not covet thy neighbor's wife" as taking away [all related sins];[103] hence, He puts *Thou shalt not commit adultery* together with "Thou shalt not covet thy neighbor's wife... nor his maidservant."

And observe that He does not say, 'He who looks and lusts,' but who *shall look on a woman to lust after her*. And it is expounded in two ways. Firstly, it is expounded as follows. He who *shall look on a woman to lust after her*, meaning in order that may he lust, so that there is concomitance. There are two kinds of concupiscence: one which is a propassion and the other is a passion. Something is called a propassion, as it were, an imperfect passion, when the movement exists merely in the sensible appetite without the consent of reason. Something is called a passion when the reason consents to the movement in the sensible appetite, and then there is a mortal sin. And thus, He says, *He hath already committed adultery with her in his heart,* because God is the searcher of hearts, and such a man does not forego the act except due to an obstacle.

Or, the word *to*, according to Augustine,[104] conveys an end, meaning, he who *shall look on a woman to lust after her*, that is to say, for the very end that he may lust. But the rule is that whatever a man does for the sake of a mortal sin, is all a mortal sin, and whatever he does for the sake of a meritorious end, is all

---

102. "It is likewise inquired, how does what is said, 'Thou shalt not commit adultery,' differ from that which is said a little afterwards, 'Thou shalt not covet thy neighbor's wife'? 'Thou shalt not covet' could also have been understood to be that former precept. Unless perhaps in these two precepts, of not committing adultery and of not stealing, the same deeds are denoted, but in the latter precepts, concupiscence itself is denoted: which precepts differ very much, for example sometimes someone may commit adultery, who does not covet his neighbor's wife, when he have intercourse with her for another reason, other times however someone may covet his neighbor's wife, and not have intercourse with her, fearing the punishment: and perhaps this is what the Law wanted to show, that both are sins" (*Quaestionum In Heptateuchum Libri Septem*, lib. II, 71, 3).
103. The words "all (*totum*) related sins" have been supplied here based on two parallel texts: "[The Lord] wanted the whole (*totum*) to be understood from the part; and in fact by the name of adultery all illicit intercourse, and unlawful use of those members ought to be understood to be forbidden" (*Quaestionum In Heptateuchum Libri Septem*, lib. II, 71, 4), and, "Christ's law alone brought mankind 'to perfection' (Hebrews 7:19) by bringing man back to the state of the newness of nature. Wherefore neither Mosaic nor human laws could remove all (*totum*) that was contrary to the law of nature, for this was reserved exclusively to 'the law of the spirit of life' (Romans 8:2)" (Supp. q. 67, a. 1 ad 1ᵘᵐ).
104. *De Sermone Domini in monte*, Lib. I, cap. 12, n. 33 (PL 34, 1246).

meritorious, as is evident in the case of a man who goes out to church or goes out to steal: whatever happens in the mean time, all is either meritorious or a sin. Now there are two kinds of consent. One is consent to the act, as when reason proceeds in that it wants to do the act for the sake of a final end. The other is consent to pleasure, as when one stirs up shameful pleasures in order to enjoy them. Although one does not consent in the first manner, it is a mortal sin when a man looks upon woman for the purpose of taking shameful pleasure, and therefore he has consented, *already having committed adultery in his heart* insofar as God is concerned; "I made a covenant with my eyes, that I would not so much as think upon a virgin" (Job. 31, 1), and, "Gaze not upon a maiden, lest her beauty be a stumblingblock to thee" (Eccli. 9, 5). Chrysostom[105] also says that women who adorn themselves for the purpose of being lusted after, sin mortally; "If a man open a pit, and dig one, and cover it not, and an ox or an ass fall into it, the owner of the pit shall pay the price of the beasts" (Ex. 21, 33). And if no one lusts after her, nonetheless it ought to be said that she sins mortally, just as she also, who prepares poison. For although it be not taken by him for whom it is prepared, nevertheless, she, by preparing it, sins mortally, because insofar as it is in her power, she has killed.

And if thy right eye scandalize thee. Here the Lord shows how this precept can be easily observed, namely as follows: by avoiding occasions of sin. Now occasions of sin are designated by the eye and the hand for four reasons. Firstly, the eye and the hand are corporeal, and so *cut it off* ought to be understood corporeally. According to Chrysostom,[106] this exposition cannot stand, because there is no member of the body which may not scandalize; "For I know that there dwelleth not in me, that is to say, in my flesh, that which is good" (Rom. 7, 18). Hence, all the members of the body would need to be cut off. Therefore, this is not the meaning here. Or it is otherwise. For the body is said to be killed in two ways: as regards the life of its nature and by guilt; "Our old man is crucified with him, that the body of sin may be destroyed, to the end that we may serve sin no longer" (Rom. 6, 6). And so, *cut off thy right eye* to sin. But the left eye would not then be innocent. Therefore, this is not the meaning here.[107]

---

105. *In Mt.*, hom. XVIII (PG 57, 257).
106. Ps. Chrys., *Op. imp. in Mt.*, hom. XII (PG 56, 695).
107. "PSEUDO-CHRYS. As the whole man when he is turned to God is dead to sin, so likewise the eye when it has ceased to look evil is cut off from sin. But this explanation will not suit the whole; for when He says, your right eye offends you, what does the left eye do? Does it contradict the right eye, and it is preserved innocent?" (*Catena Aurea on St. Matthew*, chap. 5, lect. 17).

I reply, therefore, saying that by the eye sometimes a neighbor who is a help to you is understood; for the function of the eye is to direct you on the way. Hence, your counselor in worldly matters is your left eye, and your counselor in divine matters is your right eye. The function of the hand is that it helps you. Hence, a neighbor who does business in temporal matters is your left hand, and in spiritual matters, your right hand; "I was an eye to the blind, and a foot to the lame" (Job 29, 15). Therefore, by understanding this passage according to this meaning, the eye or hand may scandalize you in two ways. Because if some counselor in worldly or divine matters scandalize you, *cut it off*, etc. He does not mention the left one, because if the right one ought to be cut off, all the more *cut off*, etc., the left one. Or it is otherwise. The Lord wants that you not only guard purity in yourself, but also in your family; hence, if an unclean person lives in your family, *cut off*, etc., that person; "He that worketh pride shall not dwell in the midst of my house" (Ps. 100, 7).

Or we can understand the eye or the hand of the interior man; "Though our outward man is corrupted, yet the inward man is renewed day by day" (II Cor. 4, 16), because as the exterior, so the interior; "May God give unto you enlightened eyes of your heart" (Eph. 1, 17-18). Now in the passage, the motive power is called the hand and intellectual power is called the eye, and according to this, the passage can be expounded in two ways. Firstly, it is as follows. From the fact that man's interior eye, which is in his intellectual part which has free will, is on his right side, and his exterior eye [which is in his sensible part which does not have free will] is on his left, the Lord does not say that you cast cut off your left part, because it is not in the power of free will that the exterior members be not moved, but that the interior members be not moved badly and not look badly.[108] He says, therefore, ***And if thy right eye scandalize thee***, to thinking badly, remove this understanding; likewise, if the will is bad, remove it.

Or it is otherwise. The eye designates a good intention, and the hand designates a good desire; if from these scandal were to follow, or an occasion of concupiscence, remove it, etc. For example, if one has a good desire in visiting poor women, if from this an occasion of concupiscence were to follow, *cut it off*.

---

108. "But the parts of the soul are called right, for the soul was created both with free will and under the law of righteousness, that it might both see and do rightly. But the members of the body, being not with free will but under the law of sin, are called the left" (ibid.). Cf. Psuedo-Chrysostom, *Op. imp. in Mt.*, hom. XII.

Fourthly, by the eye, the contemplative life can be signified; by the hands, the active life can be signified. These things sometimes scandalize, because sometimes from excessive contemplation error is incurred. Likewise, someone, because he is not apt, does not fulfill the work of contemplation, but degenerates into laziness; "The enemies have seen her, and have mocked at her sabbaths" (Lam. 1, 7); therefore, *cut it off* and go to a practice of labor. Or, in the active life sometimes they become troubled and run into occasions of sin; hence, one ought to pass into a different state.

Therefore, the first manner of expounding ought to be excluded, the second manner is concerning one's neighbor, the third manner is concerning the interior man, the fourth manner is concerning a good intention and a good work, and in the fifth manner the passage is expounded concerning the active and contemplative life, where they make an exposition on the passage, *For it is expedient for thee that one of thy members should perish,* etc.[109]

31. And it hath been said, Whosoever shall put away his wife, let him give her a bill of divorce.

32. But I say to you, that whosoever shall put away his wife, excepting the cause of fornication, maketh her to commit adultery: and he that shall marry her that is put away, committeth adultery.

And it hath been said, Whosoever shall put away his wife, let him give her a bill of divorce. After having fulfilled the prohibitive precepts of the Law, the Lord now fulfills the permissive precepts of the Law. And this part is divided into two parts. Firstly, He fulfills the Law as to the permissive precepts, which pertain to God, and secondly, He fulfills those which pertain to one's neighbor, where it is said, *You have heard that it hath been said: An eye for an eye.* The first part is divided into two sections. In the first section, He fulfills the permissive precept concerning the bill of divorce, and in the second section, another which is concerning an oath, where it is said, *Again you have heard that it was said to them of old, thou shalt not*

---

[109] cf. Ps. Chrys., *Op. imp. in Mt.*, hom. XII (PG 56, 696): "Nevertheless, in general, every good thing, which scandalizes either ourselves or others, we ought to cut off from us. For what sort of good thing is that from which something evil is born? For it is better that we be saved without one good intention or one good work, than that while we wanted to do all good works, we perish with them all."

forswear thyself. In the first section He does two things: firstly, He relates the words of the Law, and secondly, He relates their fulfillment, where it is said, *But I say to you, that whosoever shall put away his wife*, etc.

He says, therefore, *It hath been said, Whosoever shall put away his wife,* etc. This precept is found in Deut. 24, 1. Here there is a question. If someone *shall put away his wife, let him give her a bill of divorce.* This is the precept, but there is a permission to put away one's wife. Certainly Moses permitted this, but he did not command it. Now permission is multiple, namely: permission of concession, when lawful things are allowed, as for example, a monk is allowed by his abbot to visit his father; permission of dispensation, when things which are not lawful become lawful through a dispensation, as for example, a monk is permitted by dispensation to eat meat with others; permission of indulgence, when something lawful is permitted whose opposite is better, as for example, the permission of the Apostle for second marriages and yet continence of widowhood is better (and according to this you resolve what is said in the Gloss,[110] namely, that the Apostles commanded second marriages, meaning that they permitted them: or it is a command if you do not wish to be continent, otherwise it would not oblige as a precept); permission of forbearance, as when God permits some evils to occur, although He always produces some good; and permission of tolerance, when some evil tolerated, lest it become worse, as is the case here.[111]

Whosoever shall put away his wife. Is not the inseparability of marriage from the law of nature? But is this, also, what was in the Mosaic law through dispensation: *let him give her a bill of divorce,* in which the reasons for the divorce were written? Or [the reason for the bill] is otherwise, according to Josephus.[112]

---

110. "For this reason the Apostles commanded second marriages on account of men's incontinence. [Moses] permitted [divorce], he did not command it. Being unwilling, we command what we permit: because we are unable to fully forbid men's bad wills" (*Biblia cum Glossa Ordinaria,* vol. V (Antwerp 1617), p. 113A).
111. cf. footnote n. 44 below.
112. "He that desires to be divorced from his wife for any cause whatsoever, (and many such causes happen among men), let him in writing give assurance that he will never have her as his wife any more; for by this means she may be at liberty to marry another husband, although before this bill of divorce be given, she is not to be permitted so to do: but if she be misused by him also, or if, when he is dead, her first husband would marry her again, it shall not be lawful for her to return to him" (*Antiquities of the Jews,* bk. IV, chap. 8, §23). "The causes for divorce were not particularized in the bill, but were indicated in a general way, so as to prove the justice of the divorce. According to Josephus (*Jewish Antiquities* iv, 6) this was in order that the woman, having the written bill of divorce, might take another husband, else she would not have been believed. Wherefore according to him, it was written in this wise: 'I promise never to have thee with me again.'" (Suppl. q. 67, a. 7).

Or it is thus according to Augustine,[113] namely, that the reason why the bill was written was in order to cause a delay, so that the husband might be dissuaded by the counsel of the notaries to refrain from his purpose of divorce. According to Jerome[114] on this passage, the reason for permission being given for divorcing a wife was the avoidance of wife-murder.

But was it lawful for the divorced wife to remarry? *But I say to you, that whosoever shall put away his wife, excepting the cause of fornication, maketh her to commit adultery.* But there is a question: Is it lawful for a man to put away his wife for the cause of fornication? And it seems that it is not lawful, because evil ought not to be returned for evil. I answer, saying that the Lord allowed a man to put away his wife on account of fornication as a punishment for the one who was unfaithful. But is one bound by the precept to do this?[115] I answer that the putting away of a wife guilty of fornication was prescribed in order that the wife's crime might be corrected. But can a man put her away on his own judgment?[116] *And he that shall marry her that is put away, committeth adultery*, because the man that shall marry her is supervenient to marriage.[117]

33. Again you have heard that it was said to them of old, thou shalt not forswear thyself: but thou shalt perform thy oaths to the Lord.

34. But I say to you not to swear at all, neither by heaven for it is the throne of God:

35. Nor by the earth, for it is his footstool: nor by Jerusalem, for it is the city of the great king:

---

113. *Contra Faustum* 19, 26.
114. "In a later passage, the Lord explains this more fully, that Moses commanded that a bill of divorce be given on account of the hardness of heart of the husbands, not granting divorce, but taking away murder" (*Com. in Mt.*, I); Ps. Chrys., *Op. imp. in Mt.*, hom. XII (PG 56, 696). "It is the general opinion of holy men, that the reason for permission being given to divorce a wife was the avoidance of wife-murder" (Supp. q. 67, a. 6).
115. cf. Supp. q. 62, a. 2.
116. "A husband can put away his wife in two ways. First as to bed only, and thus he may put her away on his own judgment, as soon as he has evidence of her fornication: nor is he bound to pay her the marriage debt at her demand, unless he be compelled by the Church, and by paying it thus he nowise prejudices his own case. Secondly, as to bed and board, and in this way she cannot be put away except at the judgment of the Church; and if she has been put away otherwise, he must be compelled to cohabit with her unless the husband can at once prove the wife's fornication. Now this putting away is called a divorce: and consequently it must be admitted that a divorce cannot be pronounced except at the judgment of the Church" (Supp. q. 62, a. 3).
117. "Nothing supervenient to marriage can dissolve it: wherefore adultery does not make a marriage cease to be valid. For, according to Augustine (*De Nuptiis et Concupiscentia* i,10), 'as long as they live they are bound by the marriage tie, which neither divorce nor union with another can destroy.' Therefore, it is unlawful for one, while the other lives, to marry again" (Supp. q. 62, a. 5).

36. Neither shalt thou swear by thy head, because thou canst not make one hair white or black.

37. But let your speech be yea, yea: no, no: and that which is over and above these, is of evil.

Again you have heard that it was said to them of old, thou shalt not forswear thyself. Above, the Lord fulfilled one permissive precept, namely, concerning the bill of divorce. Here, He fulfills another permissive precept, namely, concerning oaths. And about this He does three things. For firstly, He cites the words of the Law; secondly, He fulfills the precept; and thirdly, He answers a question. The second part is where it is said, *But I say to you not to swear at all*; and the third part is where it is said, *But let your speech be yea, yea: no, no.*

Now it ought to be considered that two [kinds of moral precepts] are contained in the words of the Law, of which one was simply prohibitive, and the other permissive. There was a prohibitive precept regarding forswearing, namely, *You have heard that it was said to them of old, thou shalt not forswear thyself,* etc. "Thou shalt not swear falsely by my name, nor profane the name of thy God. I am the Lord" (Lev. 19, 12), and with almost the same meaning, "Thou shalt not take the name of the Lord thy God in vain," etc., (Ex. 20, 7). Regarding swearing, there was a permissive precept, namely, *Thou shalt perform thy oaths to the Lord*, meaning, when you have occasion to swear, you will not swear by creatures, but by God; as it is written "Thou shalt fear the Lord thy God, and shalt serve him only, and thou shalt swear by his name" (Deut. 6, 13). And according to this, it seems that this sacrament,[118] namely, to swear by God, is not a sin, but that the Law permitted this because the Jews were prone to idolatry, not as though this thing were right, but so that something worse might be avoided, namely, idolatry. [119]

But it remains, however, that to show reverence to God is good in itself. To swear by God is to show reverence to God,

---

118. "Even an oath has a certain relation to sacred things, insofar as it consists in calling a sacred thing to witness. And in this sense it is called a sacrament: not in the sense in which we speak of sacraments now; the word sacrament being thus used not equivocally but analogically, i.e. by reason of a different relation to the one thing, viz. something sacred" (III, q. 60, a. 1 ad 3um).

119. St. Jerome *(Com. in Mt.,* I), where this quotation continues: "The Gospel truth, however, does not receive an oath, since every word of the faithful takes the place of swearing." "As Augustine says *(ad Publicam, Sermone* 47), 'though we are forbidden to swear, I do not remember ever to have read in the Holy Scriptures that we must not accept oaths from others.' Hence, he that accepts an oath does not sin, except perchance when of his own accord he forces another to swear, knowing that he will swear falsely" (II II, q. 98, a. 4 ad 2um).

because everyone [swears by his god][120] and "For men swear by one greater than themselves: and an oath for confirmation is the end of all their controversy" (Heb. 6, 16). Therefore, to swear by God is good in itself. Furthermore, to swear by God is to invoke God as a witness. But this is good in itself. Therefore, to swear is good in itself.

And it ought to be known that in itself swearing is not something ordered, nay, in itself it implies a disorder. To swear by God is nothing other than to invoke God as a witness to a human assertion; now this happens in two ways. It is either because the divine witness is adduced to confirm a human assertion, or because divine judgment is sought, as though it were said: 'If it be not so, may the swearer be condemned by God.' Among men's deeds, however, nothing is so fragile as their words; "If any man offend not in word, the same is a perfect man" (Jam. 3, 2). Hence, to call upon God as a witness in these deeds in which man is so fragile, is to contemn God's judgment; "A man that sweareth much, shall be filled with iniquity" (Eccli. 23, 12).

The Lord, however, afterwards fulfills this precept here. Hence, He says, **But I say to you not to swear at all**, etc. Thus, an oath in itself is unlawful. Therefore, when judges compel men to swear in their lawsuits, it seems that they act contrary to this precept, and this is the opinion of certain heretics, saying that no one is allowed to swear. And Jerome[121] replies that the Lord here forbids a man to swear by creatures, and He does this on account of the Jews, who were prone to idolatry. Hence, He does not simply forbid oaths. But this does not seem to be a good exposition, because then the Lord would have added nothing to the words of the Law, which says, **Thou shalt perform thy oaths to the Lord**. And therefore, it ought to be said, according to Augustine, that the Lord forbids men to swear by God and by creatures.

But then there remains a twofold question. The first is that our Lord would have destroyed the Law, which says, **Thou shalt perform thy oaths**; and the second is that according to this, it seems that an oath would be unlawful. And Augustine replies that just as a bill of divorce was not intended by the Law, but was permitted on account of the cruelty of the Jews, and the Lord fulfilled it because He in no wise wanted it to be given; similarly, here the Law commanded that they would not swear, but if they swore, they would swear not by creatures but by God; but the

---

120. The text here gives a reference to a Gloss which is unknown. Hence, this sentence has been completed based on a similar passage from St. Thomas' commentary *In Isaiam*, chap. 45.
121. *Comm. in Mt.*, I.

Lord fulfilled this when He said, **Not to swear at all**, etc. And just as he who is silent is in no wise a liar, so he who in no wise swears is further removed from perjury. [122]

Regarding that which is said, namely, that an oath is unlawful, I answer, according to Augustine,[123] that the same Holy Ghost is He who spoke in Sacred Scriptures and who also worked in the saints. Hence, what is the meaning of Scriptures appears in the sayings of the saints. Paul was moved by the Holy Ghost and yet he swore twice, for he swore with an oath of simple attestation; "For God is my witness, whom I serve in my spirit in the gospel of his Son, that without ceasing I make a commemoration of you" (Rom. 1, 9). And he swore with an oath of execration, which is when someone pledges their salvation or their soul to God; "I call God to witness upon my soul that to spare you, I came not any more to Corinth" (II Cor. 1, 23). And if it be said that this is not an oath, this is absurd, because to swear "by God" and "upon my soul" are the same; "I die daily, I protest by your glory, brethren, which I have in Christ Jesus our Lord" (I Cor. 15, 31), and in Greek, the word "by" is so understood that one is swearing.[124] Therefore, if Paul swore, it seems that the Lord did not intend to forbid swearing, but rather swearing easily. And Augustine shows that an oath is not something to be desired in itself, but on the contrary, only on account of the need of swearer. And therefore he says that Paul never swore except in writing, because it ought not to be done except with great caution and deliberation and on account of a need, that is to say, unless the good of others calls for it.[125]

But someone could say that to swear by God is evil, but not by something less than God. And the Lord excludes this; hence, it is said, **Neither by heaven for it is the throne of God**, etc.

---

122. "It is also written, 'But I say unto you, Swear not at all.' But the Apostle himself has used oaths in his Epistles (Rom. 9, 1; Phil. 1, 8; and Gal. 1, 20). And so he shows how that is to be taken, which is said, 'I say unto you, Swear not at all': that is, lest by swearing one come to a facility in swearing, from facility to a custom, and so from a custom there be a downfall into perjury." (St. Augustine, *On Lying* chap. 15, n. 28).

123. "The things that in the New Testament were done by the saints, where there is a most evident com-mending of morals to be imitated, avail as examples for the understanding of the Scriptures, which are digested in the precepts" (*On Lying* chap. 15, n. 26).

124. St. Augustine, *De serm. Dom.* I, 17, 51; "AUG. It is ridiculous to make such a distinction; yet the Apostle has used even this form, 'I die daily, by your glory.' That this does not mean, 'your glory has caused my dying daily,' but is an oath, is clear from the Greek texts, in which what is written: *ni tin kauchisin himeteran*, meaning, 'by your glory,' is only said by one who is swearing" (*Catena Aurea on St. Matthew*, chap. 5, lect. 19).

125. "And therefore he is not found to have sworn except in writing, where there is more wary forethought, and no precipitate tongue withal." (*On Lying* chap. 15, n. 28).

To swear by creatures can be either from idolatry or without idolatry. For if judgment is attributed to those things, namely, by entreating judgment from creatures, then this is idolatry; just as the ancients did, who were saying that the heavens are a God.[126] In another way, swearing by creatures can be without sin and idolatry in two ways. Firstly, insofar as a creature be pledged to God by entreating justice upon it, as for example, when men swear by their heads;[127] secondly, insofar as in a creature there appears a reflection of the Divine Majesty, as for example, when an oath is sworn by heaven, Whose power and potentiality is shown in the heavens. Hence, here He sets forth superior creatures by which someone might swear.

And this superiority is shown in three things, namely, in two elements, heaven and earth, and under which all other things are contained as means between extremes. And in regard to this, He says, **Neither by heaven**; "Thus saith the Lord: Heaven is my throne, and the earth my footstool," etc., (Is. 66, 1). Chrysostom[128] says that He does not say, **not to swear at all, neither by heaven**, because it is a great body, **nor by the earth**, which is the mother of all things,[129] but He shows the excellence of these things in comparison with God.

But does God have limbs and posture and the like? Hence, this passage is expounded in two ways. Firstly, it is expounded literally. For that is called a seat where someone rests, and one rests where he abides perfectly. Therefore, because among corporeal creatures the heavens share the most in the divine goodness, and the earth the least, heaven is called God's seat and earth His **footstool**. Likewise, men are accustomed to sit

---

126. "Since the heaven is such as to have been called 'God' by the ancients, not indeed because it is the supreme God, but because its body is something divine by virtue of being ungenerated and indestructible, as was previously explained; consequently it possesses a circular body in order that it may be moved forever and in a circular way" (*De coelo et mundo*, bk. 2, lect. 4, n. 5).

127. "The other way of swearing is by cursing, and in this kind of oath a creature is adduced that the judgment of God may be wrought therein. Thus, a man is wont to swear by his head, or by his son, or by some other thing that he loves, even as the Apostle swore (2 Corinthians 1:23), saying: 'I call God to witness upon my soul'" (II II, q. 89, a. 6).

128. *In Mt. hom.* XVII (PG 57, 260-261): "But mark, I pray thee, on what ground He magnifies the elements; not from their own nature, but from God's relation to them, such as it had been in condescension declared. For because the tyranny of idolatry was great, that the elements might not be thought worthy of honor for their own sake, He hath assigned this cause, which we have mentioned, which again would pass on to the glory of God. For He neither said, 'because Heaven is beautiful and great,' nor, 'because earth is profitable'; but 'because the one is God's throne, the other His footstool'; on every side urging them on towards their Lord."

129. "Earth, the mother of all" (Hesiod, *Works and Days*). "The power of the earth takes the place of a mother, as the Philosopher says" (*In II Sent.* dist. 14, q. 1, a. 4 ad 5um).

for judging, and because the Lord sometimes judges by means of those things which come from the heavens; "And lighten with his light from above, he shall cover also the ends of the sea. For by these he judgeth people, and giveth food to many mortals" (Job 36, 30-31), namely, by means of lightning and the like, and so *heaven* is called His seat.

Mystically, however, by *heaven*, holy men are understood, whose conversation is in heaven; "But our conversation is in heaven" (Phil. 3, 20). God judges in these men; "But the spiritual man judgeth all things" (I Cor. 2, 15). By *the earth*, sinners are understood, on account of their affection for earthly things; "They are enemies of the cross of Christ... who mind earthly things" (Phil. 3, 18-20). And [God's feet are] upon this *footstool*, because if men do not fulfill the laws to which they are subject, they will be punished.[130]

In human society men establish cities, and Jerusalem excels among other cities because God was worshipped there, and so these words are said, *nor by Jerusalem*; "Glorious things are said of thee, O city of God" (Ps. 86, 3), and, "Jerusalem, which is built as a city, which is compact together. For thither did the tribes go up, the tribes of the Lord: the testimony of Israel, to praise the name of the Lord" (Ps. 121, 3-4).

And then the Lord speaks concerning bodily members. But since it could be said that we ought not to swear by these greater things, but by lesser things, He says, *Neither shalt thou swear by thy head*. For anyone can do what he wishes with that which is his, but man does not have power over his head as to smallest matters. Therefore, one ought not to swear by that member and this is what is said, *because thou canst not make one hair white or black*, naturally speaking, namely, "And which of you by taking thought, can add to his stature one cubit?" (below 6, 27).

But it could be said: How then will we speak? He replies, and firstly, He answers the question; and secondly, He gives the reason. He says, therefore, *But let your speech be yea, yea: no, no*. And it can be expounded in three ways. Firstly, it is expounded as follows. If someone were to ask, 'Is it so?' *let your speech be yea, yea: no, no*. Secondly, it is expounded as follows. Let not your mouth say one thing, and your heart feel another thing, and your deed show yet another thing. "With the workers of iniquity

---

130. "The enemies of Christ are now under His power, but in two ways: either because they are converted by Him, as Paul, whom he caused to fall on the ground" (Acts 9, 3); or inasmuch as Christ does His own will, even in regard to those who act here against Christ's will. So He puts His enemies under his feet by punishing them; but in the future He will put them under His feet, i.e., under Christ's humanity" (Comm. on I Cor., chap. 15, lect. 3).

destroy me not: Who speak peace with their neighbor, but evils are in their hearts" (Ps. 27, 3). Thirdly, it is expounded as follows, and it is more literal. *Let your speech be yea, yea: no, no,* as though He were to say: 'May you say both simply.' For this is the definition of truth,[131] namely, everything that is, is said to be; and what is not, is said not to be. This is Hilary's exposition;[132] "For the Son of God, Jesus Christ... was not: *It is* and *It is not*. But, *It is,* was in him" (II Cor. 1, 19).

And that which is over and above these, is of evil. He does not say, 'is evil,' but, 'is of evil,' and it is not from your evil but from another's evil, because you are forced to swear, although nevertheless it would be beneficial for him to believe your oath; and the Apostle swore in this way. Or it is expounded, according to Chrysostom, as follows. *And that which is over and above these, is of evil.*[133] By this it appears that in the Old Law one oath was prohibitive, namely, to perjure; it permitted another, namely, to swear out of necessity; it rejected a third oath, namely, a superstitious oath, which is when reverence is shown to a creature which is owed to God.

38. You have heard that it hath been said: An eye for an eye, and a tooth for a tooth.

39. But I say to you not to resist evil: but if one strike thee on thy right cheek, turn to him also the other:

40. And if a man will contend with thee in judgment, and take away thy coat, let go thy cloak also unto him.

41. And whosoever will force thee one mile, go with him other two.

42. Give to him that asketh of thee, and from him that would borrow of thee turn not away.

You have heard that it hath been said: An eye for an eye. Above, the Lord fulfilled the Law as to permissive precepts which pertain to God. Now He fulfills them as to those things which pertain to one's neighbor, and He does this in respect to two things: as to actions and as to affections. The second is where

---

131. "The Philosopher says that in defining truth we say that truth is had when one affirms that 'to be which is, and that not to be which is not'" (*De Veritate,* q. 1, a. 1).
132. *Com. in Mt.,* IV (PL 9, 940B).
133. "CHRYS. Or, *of evil,* that is, from their weakness to whom the Law permitted the use of an oath. Not that by this the Old Law is signified to be from the devil, but He leads us from the old imperfection to the new abundance" (*Catena Aurea on St. Matthew,* chap. 5, lect. 19): cf. St. John Chrysostom stitious oath, which is when aor us. Perhaps Fr. Summers would like to offer the Mass, as I think I will need to offer a Mass , *In Mt. hom.* XVII (PG 57, 262).

it is said, ***Thou shalt love thy neighbour.*** About the first part, He does two things. Firstly, He cites the command of the Law, and secondly, He fulfills it.

He says, therefore, ***You have heard that it hath been said:*** you ought to exact ***an eye for an eye***; "Eye for eye, tooth for tooth, hand for hand, foot for foot" (Ex. 21, 24), and, "Thou shalt not pity him, but shalt require life for life, eye for eye, tooth for tooth, hand for hand, foot for foot" (Deut. 19, 21). In these words of the Law, however, there was a wider intention to fix the manner of judging justly in regard to the judges, namely, so that they would inflict a determined punishment; the Jews, however, supposed that everyone might take revenge for injuries inflicted upon oneself, which is contrary to the Law; "Seek not revenge, nor be mindful of the injury of thy citizens" (Lev. 19, 18).

Therefore, the Lord fulfills this precept in relation to their bad interpretation. Hence, He says, ***But I say to you not to resist evil.*** And about this, He does two things, for He fulfills the precept in two ways. Firstly, He fulfills it as to the fact that revenge is not demanded by the precept; and secondly, He fulfills it as to the fact that one may do good to someone who inflicts an injury to oneself, where it is said, ***Give to him that asketh of thee.*** About the first part, He does two things. Firstly, He fulfills the precept in general, and secondly, He fulfills it in particular, where it is said, ***But if one strike thee on thy right cheek, turn to him also the other.***

Regarding the surface meaning of the text, it seems that that this new precept is a bad law from its being contrary to the old precept. But according to Augustine,[134] the Lord did not destroy but to fulfill. For the intention of this law was to curb men from excessive and immoderate revenge. The Lord, however, completely forbade revenge. Hence, if the Law had said, 'Thou shalt not seek revenge beyond what is due,' and the Lord had said, 'Thou may not seek revenge in any way,' then He would have fulfilled the command of the Law.

And according to Augustine, there are here five stages [in fulfilling this precept].[135] The first stage is of him who inflicted an injury, and this stage is the greatest in wickedness; the second stage is of him who, after having been offended, inflicts an equal injury: this level of iniquity is lower; the third stage is of him who returns an injury but less than that which he received; the fourth stage is of him who returns no injury; and the fifth stage

---

134. *Contra Faustinum* 19, 25.   **135.** *De serm. Dom.* I, 19, 56-57.

is of him who does not return the injury, but also does not impede that another evil be inflicted upon himself, and the Lord teaches this stage. Hence, ***But I say to you not to resist evil***, etc.; and it is understood of an evil certainly not of guilt, but of punishment or of injury; "Revenge not yourselves, my dearly beloved; but give place unto wrath, for it is written: Revenge is mine, I will repay, saith the Lord" (Rom. 12, 19). And this precept agrees sufficiently with the aforesaid one.

But someone could say, 'I do not wish to revenge myself so that the one who offended me might be slain in revenge, but so that I may not be offended again'; but the Lord also rejects this, saying, ***But I say to you not to resist evil.***

But it ought to be seen how this declaration of the Lord is to be understood. For objections are made in two ways according to two errors. The first error is that of the pagans, as Augustine says in his letter against Marcellinus,[136] who so argue that without revenge no state would be able to be safeguarded; in this way enemies are resisted and thieves punished, which if this did not happen, the state would completely perish. Therefore, the Gospel law destroys human society, wherefore it ought to be rejected. On the other hand, heretics say that the Gospels support revenge and they do not wish to remove those things which pertain to society by taking away revenge. Hence, I reply that these men proceed from a false understanding of this teaching. For someone can resist evil in two ways: from love of the public good and from the love of his private good. Now God did not intend to forbid that evil be not resisted for the common good, but that one burn to take revenge for one's private good. For nothing so much safeguards human society than that a man not have the power of doing evil privately.

But moreover, it seems that God would not intend to forbid this, because it is a natural inclination of everything that it resist an evil corrupting its good. Therefore, this precept cannot be kept. But I reply that it is a natural inclination that everything repel its own harm, and similarly, it is a natural inclination that everything expose itself to its own loss so that it may avoid a common loss, just as a hand exposes itself to danger for the sake of the body, and any other member for the whole body. Hence, it is natural that a man endure an evil for the good of the state, and to this pertains political virtues such as fortitude and suchlike.

---

136. *Epist.* 138, II, 9; *Epist.* 136, 2 (ibid., 95).

But Augustine says that these words, *not to resist evil*, etc., ought to be understood according to the preparation of the soul, because a man, for the good of his neighbor, ought to be prepared to withstand or suffer all evils, and he give an example.[137] If a man were to care for an insane person, and this person were to strike him or do something of this kind, if the man have goodwill toward this person, he ought to be prepared also to suffer other evils for this person's welfare; and in such manner we ought to act for the good of the Church.

And it ought to be observed that these words which Our Lord says are in one way a precept and in another way a counsel. It is a precept, if someone were to let go those things regarding which he is bound to do out of fear of some temporal inconvenience, as for example, a bishop who watches over his flock ought to be prepared in his own mind to endure all losses before he let go those things regarding which he is bound to do. It is a counsel, if someone does not put aside those things regarding which he is not bound to do; as for example, if someone, on account of his entrance into religion, endures many kinds of harm from his parents, it is a counsel that he not put aside what is better.

Afterwards the Lord explains in detail what He had said in general, where it is said, *But if one strike thee on thy right cheek, turn to him also the other.* A man can inflict a threefold harm to another: by injuring his body, by taking away his possessions, and by forcing him to do labors. And He gives an example of these three things.

He says, therefore, *But if one strike thee on thy right cheek, turn to him also the other*; "He shall give his cheek to him that striketh him, he shall be filled with reproaches" (Lam. 3, 30), and, "He shall give his cheek to him that striketh him, he shall be filled with reproaches" (Is. 50, 6). It ought to be considered how these words ought to be understood from the deeds of the holy men. For the Lord began to do and to teach, and He did not fulfill this [in His deeds]; "Jesus answered him: If I have spoken evil, give testimony of the evil; but if well, why strikest thou me?" (Jn. 18, 23), and the Apostle did not fulfill this; "Then Paul said to him: God shall strike thee, thou whited wall. For, sittest thou to judge me according to the law and, contrary to

---

137. *De serm. Dom.* I, 19, 57: "As regards compassion, they feel it most who minister to those whom they greatly love as if they were their children, or some very dear friends in sickness, or little children, or insane persons, at whose hands they often endure many things; and if their welfare demand it, they even show themselves ready to endure more, until the weakness either of age or of disease pass away."

the law, commandest me to be struck?" (Acts 23, 3). From these passages, Augustine concludes that through the deeds of holy men we know how Scripture ought to be understood. Hence, he says that this precept ought to be understood such that the mind ought to be prepared to fulfill it.[138]

This text can also be understood mystically. Yet it ought to be known that he strikes you in the face, who insults you publicly; "For you suffer... if a man strike you on the face" (II Cor. 11, 20). The right cheek pertains to spiritual things, the left to temporal things. Therefore, He wishes to say that if you withstand an injury in spiritual things, then you ought to withstand an injury in temporal matters much more than what some prelates do, who withstand loss of churches but not the loss of their relatives.

And if a man will contend with thee in judgment. This happens in two ways: if a man contend with you so that he may get his own things back, then it is not a great deed if you yield to him; but if someone contend with you so that he may take away your things, this belongs to perfection if you yield, and this is what He says, **and take away thy coat**, meaning any temporal thing, **let go thy cloak also unto him**, meaning any other thing. And this is also in readiness of mind, because if someone calumniates you, nevertheless, you ought not to relinquish the charity that you have towards him; "Already indeed there is plainly a fault among you, that you have law suits one with another" (I Cor. 6, 7).

This judgment ought to be avoided for two reasons. One reason is that if he is a cleric, by submitting himself to a secular judge he diminishes his own dignity; the other reason is that although he does not intend some calumny, nevertheless if he sees the cause of his contention calumniated, an occasion is given to him of doing similar things and therefore to contend in judgment is dangerous.

Likewise, to begin legal proceedings can happen in two ways: lawfully and unlawfully. It is unlawful to make a legal claim in a court of unbelievers. Likewise, it is required that one not make a legal claim with contention; for contention is an assault upon the truth, accompanied by the confidence of shouting;[139] "It is an honor for a man to separate himself from contentions" (Prov. 20, 3).[140] It is lawful to make a legal claim, nay, almost desirable, in two cases: when there are the goods of the poor or of the Church

---

138. "For these precepts are to be taken as binding 'the mind to be prepared to fulfill them,' as Augustine says (*De Sermone Domini in Monte*, Lib. I, cap. 19 (PL 34, 1239))" (I II, q. 108, a. 3 ad 2um).

139. cf. Ambrose (*Glossa Ordinaria* in Rom. 1:29) quoted in II II, q. 38, a. 1.

140. The Douay translation here is "... from quarrels."

involved, hence, if a prelate does not make a legal claim, he sins; the other case is when he who takes away is made more insolent and more demanding unless he be resisted. It is charity, because then his soul is freed from death; when, however, there is a private good and correction is not expected, then a legal claim ought not to be made. Yet all these things are to be understood in regard to readiness of mind.

And whosoever will force thee one mile. To force [*angariare*], properly speaking, is to mancipate in regard to servile works without justice.[141] **Go with him other two**, namely miles; "For you suffer if a man bring you into bondage, if a man devour you, if a man take from you, if a man be lifted up, if a man strike you on the face" (II Cor. 11, 20).

And it ought to be noted that the Lord proceeds in a certain order. Firstly, He said not to resist evil, afterwards He said that a man ought to be prepared not only not to resist but to endure equal punishment, but now He says more, because He goes all the way up to double.

Give to him that asketh of thee. Here He says that we ought to do well in two ways to one who is doing evil: by way of a simple gift and by way of a loan. In regard to the first, He says, **Give to him that asketh of thee**; "If thou have much give abundantly: if thou have little, take care even so to bestow willingly a little" (Tob. 4, 9), and, "If I have denied to the poor what they desired, and have made the eyes of the widow wait" (Job 31, 16). But it is objected that the poor are unable to do this; likewise, the rich are unable to do this, because if they were always to give, nothing would be left for themselves. And Augustine[142] solves this in two ways. Firstly, he solves it as follows, saying that you ought not to give everything that he asks, because you ought not to give what is wicked, nor what is unjust or unreasonable, nor that which you need more. And this is a precept if you are bound to give, and a counsel if you are not bound. Jerome,[143] nevertheless, says that it is understood of a spiritual good, because such cannot be harmful to anyone.

And from him that would borrow of thee turn not away. This word, *borrow*, can be understood in two ways. The first way is that whoever does good to another, even if he gives simply, expects repayment; "He that hath mercy on the poor, lendeth to the Lord: and he will repay him" (Prov. 19, 17), and, "Cast thy bread upon

---

141. "CHRYS. The word here used signifies to drag unjustly, without cause, and with insult" (*Catena Aurea on St. Matthew*, chap. 5, lect. 20).

142. *De Sermone Domini in monte*, Lib. I, cap. 20, n. 67 (PL 34, 1263-1263).

143. *Com. in Mt.*, I.

the running waters: for after a long time thou shalt find it again" (Eccle. 11, 1). Or it can be understood otherwise. *From him that would borrow* something so that he may repay, *turn not away*. And it might seem to someone that God would not recompense his possession that he expects from man, and thus he might be more motivated to giving rather than loaning, so that he might receive from God; but the Lord says that he [who lends] will also receive from God. Or He says, *turn not away*, because they sometimes fear to be defrauded and thus they do not loan; "Many have refused to lend, not out of wickedness, but they were afraid to be defrauded without cause," etc., (Eccli. 29, 10) and afterwards it is said, "Lose thy money for thy brother and thy friend" (verse 13). And it ought to be observed that this can be a precept and a counsel according to the different conditions, which is evident from what was said.

43. You have heard that it hath been said, Thou shalt love thy neighbour, and hate thy enemy.

44. But I say to you, Love your enemies: do good to them that hate you: and pray for them that persecute and calumniate you:

45. That you may be the children of your Father who is in heaven, who maketh his sun to rise upon the good, and bad, and raineth upon the just and the unjust.

46. For if you love them that love you, what reward shall you have? do not even the publicans this?

47. And if you salute your brethren only, what do you more? do not also the heathens this?

48. Be you therefore perfect, as also your heavenly Father is perfect.

You have heard that it hath been said, Thou shalt love thy neighbour. Above, the Lord fulfilled the Law as to permissive acts, and here He fulfills the Law as to the affection of hatred according to that which was seen. And this is the last fulfillment. And these things befit the fulfillment of the Law in respect to the love of neighbor;[144] "Love therefore is the fulfilling of the law" (Rom. 13, 10). About this He does two things. Firstly, He sets forth those things which pertain to the Law, and secondly, He fulfills them, where it is said, *But I say to you, Love your enemies*. In these words He touches upon two things, namely, *Thou shalt love* and *thou shalt hate*.

---

[144]. "The whole fulfillment of the Law depends on love of neighbor" (*Super Ep. in Rom.*, chap 13, lect. 2).

About the first point, it ought to be considered that some men understood that only an intimate friend or relative is said to be a neighbor, but in fact, every man is called a neighbor, and even the angels, because it is said in Luke 10[145] that he who shewed mercy to the half-dead man is said to be a neighbor. From which passage we can understand that he is called a neighbor from whom we receive mercy, such as the angels, or to whom we owe mercy, such as a man. This precept is in Leviticus 19.[146]

And the Lord wished to use this word, **neighbour**, because by this word the reason of the love is given to be understood. For every friendship is founded upon some likeness or nearness;[147] "Every beast loveth its like: so also every man him that is nearest to himself" (Eccli. 13, 19). Now there is a certain natural likeness according to which all men belong to the same species; hence, just as it is natural that every animal loves what is similar to itself, so it is natural that every man loves what is similar to himself. Another likeness is a political likeness, because a man ought to love someone insofar as he is his fellow citizen, and this is political friendship. There is also a likeness of grace, and this is broader, because it extends to all who have an ordination to beatitude, namely, the angels and men, and this is the precept of charity, which is founded upon this union. Therefore, that which He says, **Thou shalt love thy neighbour**, ought not to be understood only as regarding origin of blood or of friendship, but as regarding the ordination to beatitude.

And thou shalt hate thy enemy. These words are nowhere written in the Law, but can be assumed based on certain passages. For example, in Exodus 23, where the Lord said that they may not enter into league with other men, etc.,[148] and in Deuteronomy 7, He commands that they utterly destroy them.[149] From these passages, they assumed that they were to hate their enemies, and due to this interpretation, He says, **Thou shalt hate thy enemy**. Now heretics say the opposite, namely, the Law says *hate thy enemy*, etc. But hatred is a sin, and therefore, the Law commands a sin. And Augustine[150] replies that the Lord commands us to love our enemies. I prove this from the fact that He does good both to the good and to the wicked; therefore, inasmuch as we are made like God by doing this, we ought to love our enemies. But

---

145. Verse 37.
146. "Thou shalt love thy friend as thyself. I am the Lord" (verse 18).
147. "... the word neighbor (*proximus*) denotes a kind of nighness (*propinquitas*)" (II II, q. 44, a. 7 arg. 1ᵘᵐ).
148. "Thou shalt not enter into league with [the inhabitants of the land], nor with their gods" (verse 32).
149. "Thou shalt utterly destroy them" (verse 2).
150. *Contra Faustum* 19, 24.

God hates some men; "Detractors, hateful to God" (Rom. 1, 30), and yet God loves all things; "For thou lovest all things that are" (Wis. 11, 25). Hence, I reply that God loves the nature, but hates the guilt. And, likewise, the Law wanted this.

Hence, the Lord fulfills this precept in respect to the misinterpretation of the scribes and Pharisees, who were distorting it into hatred in itself, which, nevertheless, was contrary to the Law; "Thou shalt not hate thy brother in thy heart" (Lev. 19, 17), but they were understanding a brother to be one of the Jews. Yet all men were created by God, and are ordained for one beatitude. Therefore, the Lord fulfills this precept when He says, **But I say to you, Love your enemies: do good to them that hate you**, etc. And about this He does three things. Firstly, the fulfillment is related; secondly, the reason proving the fulfillment is related; and thirdly, He concludes to His main proposition. The second part is where it is said, **That you may be the children of your Father**, and the third part is where it is said, **Be you therefore perfect**. Now He fulfills this precept in respect to three things, namely, as to the affections of the heart, the role of deeds in doing good, and the role of the mouth in praying. The second part is where it is said, **Do good to them that hate you**, and the third part is where it is said, **Pray for them that persecute and calumniate you**.

He says, therefore, **Love your enemies**. But it seems that this is unfitting. For it is clear that nothing can take away a natural movement. But here there is a natural movement, namely, to hate an enemy. Hence, everything is opposed to its contrary, just as a sheep flees from a wolf, and even in those things lacking knowledge, for fire pursues water.[151] Therefore, why does the Lord say, **Love your enemies**?

But it ought to be known that, as Chrysostom[152] says, love is twofold and hate is twofold, namely, of the flesh and of reason. The Lord did not give this precept to the flesh, but to reason. Therefore, when you feel a movement of hatred arise in yourself, and you suppress it so that you do not do harm, then it is hatred of the flesh only.

But ought we also to love our enemies according to our reason? I reply that, according to Augustine,[153] it is so as to their nature, but it is not so as to their guilt. Hence, in that which our adversary is similar to us, he ought to be loved, as also it is evident in natural things, because white is opposed to black

---

151. "Fire pursues water... because fire and water are always enemies" (Isidore of Seville, *Etymologies* xvii, 55).

152. Ps. Chyys., *Op. imp. in Mt.*, hom. XIII (PG 56, 702).

153. *Contra Faustum* 19, 24.

insofar as it is dissimilar, for insofar it is black it is dissimilar and not insofar as it is a color. Hence, we ought to destroy hatred, meaning the fact that he is our enemy ought to displease us, and also we ought to destroy this [hatred] for him.

But again there is a question: Are all bound to do this? It seems that they are not, because Augustine, in his *Enchiridion*,[154] says that to love one's enemies belongs to perfection and can hardly belong to so great a multitude as we believe are heard when they use this petition, "Forgive us our trespasses, as we forgive those who trespass against us," etc., (Mt. 6, 12). Therefore, God forgives someone his trespasses, who does not love his enemy. But no one is forgiven a trespass unless he be in charity. Therefore, to love one's enemy is not necessary for salvation.

But it ought to be known that Augustine[155] says that we can speak of this enemy in two ways: in one way before he ask pardon, and in another way after he asks. Now after he asks pardon, he ought to no longer be deemed an enemy. And the Lord does not remit trespasses except to one asking pardon. Therefore, He does not command that you forgive except to one asking pardon. Therefore, if he does not ask, he will remain in hatred.

I reply, saying that to love an enemy not asking pardon is in a certain way a precept and in another way a counsel. For every friendship is founded upon some union. Now a union which is between two things is either general or special. A special union is the union of that from which I have received many good things, and with which I always have familiarity and things of this kind; and we have a general union insofar as we are citizens of the heavenly Jerusalem. And according to this love, it is not necessary that I bear a special affection towards anyone of that multitude [of the citizens of the heavenly Jerusalem], yet I ought to want that all men be as myself and be saved. And according to this, we are not bound to love an enemy with a special affection, but we are bound not to exclude him from the general love. Hence, it would be against the precept if I were to desire all men to be saved except my enemy. Now, that I bear special love for him, this belongs to perfection and is a counsel. And Augustine says this: "It suffices not to hate," meaning that you do not exclude someone from your general love.

And it ought to be known that to love someone is to want good for him. Now there is a twofold good: the good of eternal life, and charity intends this because I am bound to love my neighbor, in relation to eternal life, as myself; the other is the temporal good,

---
154. XIX, 73.
155. *De Sermone Domini in monte,* Lib. II, cap. 8, n. 29 (PL 34, 1282).

and in this I am not bound to love my neighbor except insofar as these things are ordained to obtaining eternal life. Hence, without a violation of charity I can choose some temporal evil for my neighbor, insofar as there be given by this evil an occasion of doing good and of arriving at eternal life. Hence, Gregory says in his *Moralia*[156] that there is a sign that you do not love your neighbor when you rejoice upon his ruin; but I can rejoice in the ruin of his temporal affairs, insofar as it is ordained unto good of him or of others, and also of the multitude.[157]

But because "Love is proved by deeds,"[158] and it is said, "My little children, let us not love in word nor in tongue, but in deed and in truth" (I Jn. 3, 18), wherefore the Lord adds, **Do good to them that hate you**, etc.; "If thy enemy be hungry, give him to eat: if he thirst, give him water to drink," and, "If thou see the ass of him that hateth thee lie underneath his burden, thou shalt not pass by, but shalt lift him up with him" (Ex. 23, 5). And in certain cases this is a precept, and in other cases it is a counsel. It is a precept in the cases in which you are bound to do good to all men, even to an enemy, meaning, even to an enemy who is in extreme need. It is a counsel, however, if you give alms. I do not speak of common alms,[159] because from it an enemy ought not to be excluded, but if you give special alms and you do not exclude your enemy from it, this is also a counsel of perfection.

And pray for them that persecute and calumniate you. For someone could say, 'I cannot *do good* because I am poor'; wherefore He says, **Pray for them that persecute and calumniate you**. They are called persecutors, who openly persecute, and they are called calumniators, who harm by frauds and subterfuges. "My people went down into Egypt at the beginning to sojourn there: and the Assyrian hath oppressed them without any cause at all" (Is. 52, 4). And we have an example, namely, that the Lord prayed for those who crucified Him; "And Jesus said: Father, forgive them, for they know not what they do" (Lk. 23, 34). And Stephen did likewise; "And falling on his knees, he cried with a loud voice,

---

156. Gregory the Great, *Morals on the Book of Job* XXII, XI.
157. "But herein it is needful to know that it very often happens that without charity being lost, both the destruction of an enemy rejoices us, and again his glory without any sin of envy saddens us, both when he falling to ruin, we believe that there are persons rightly set up, and he being advanced, we dread very many being unjustly borne down... But for preserving these things, a scrutiny of the exactest discrimination is absolutely requisite, lest when we are carrying out our own hatred, we be deceived under the appearance of the utility to another" (Gregory the Great, *loc. cit.*)
158. Gregory the Great, Hom. 30 *In Evangelia.*
159. i.e. small alms. cf. IV Sent. q. 2, a. 5 where St. Thomas says that a wife is able to give "common and small alms" without the permission of her husband.

saying: Lord, lay not this sin to their charge" (Acts 7, 59). And this is a precept insofar as such a person ought not to be excluded from the public prayers of the Church. It is a counsel, however, if men make special prayers for him, because you certainly are not bound to do this for every living being.

But there are more serious questions, for we find many prophets who prayed against their enemies; "May his children be fatherless, and his wife a widow" (Ps. 108, 9); and many similar passages are found. And I reply, saying that these words are not said from a desire for revenge, but from a spirit of prophecy, and not from a desire of the wisher, but from the spirit of prediction. Hence, when it is said, "his wife be a widow," the meaning is, 'I will see her to be a widow.' Or it ought to be said that the saints will rejoice when they will see revenge;[160] so the saints, because they are perfect in God's justice, earnestly want divine justice to be fulfilled.

Another question is that it is said, "He that knoweth his brother to sin a sin which is not to death," and yet afterwards it is said, "There is a sin unto death. For that I say not that any man ask," etc., (I Jn. 5, 16). Thus, among brothers there are sins unto death; wherefore, if we ought not to pray for them, all the more we ought not to pray for persecutors. And Augustine[161] explains that not every mortal sin is said to be unto death, but only a sin against the Holy Ghost, which, properly, is final impenitence. And this suffices for the present, because an explanation of this will be found below in chapter 12. Nor must one believe that there is some sin which could not be pardoned, because no sin is so great, because there is a passage in which Cain said, "My iniquity is greater than that I may deserve pardon," etc., (Gen. 4, 13). But just as God, on account of some preceding sins, forsakes men of His grace, and on account of this men fall into sins, hence, they are also said to be hardened and blinded; "God gave them up to the desires of their heart, unto uncleanness" (Rom. 1, 24). In this way, on account of the enormity of some sin, God does not give His grace so that the sinner may repent, and this sin is when man knows the good and persecutes it.[162] Hence, "a sin unto death" is not so named as though no men repent of it, but because, in and of itself, they do not merit that grace be conferred. Hence,

---

160. "The just shall rejoice when he shall see the revenge" (Ps. 57, 11).
161. *Sermo* LXXI, c. 12, 20 (PL 38, 455).
162. "Blessed Gregory says, 'There are some then in the Church, who so far from doing good, even persecute it, and who even detest in others what they neglect to do themselves. The sin of these persons, not committed from infirmity or ignorance, but of intention alone,' is a sin against the Holy Ghost" (Sermons of St. Thomas Aquinas, n. 11, part 2).

because it is hard to repent of it, and it is done with difficulty, it follows that it is called "a sin unto death." And because prayers are not made for sinners except so that they might be converted, it follows that [if they do not convert] it is made in vain for them. Hence, when the Lord said, "Father, forgive them, for they know not what they do" (Lk. 23, 34), He did not pray for all persecutors, but for those who had been predestined. And He knew who they were who were due to be converted; but because we do not know who are the predestined, and who are in sin unto death, it follows that we ought to pray for all men.

The third question is, and it is found in the Gloss,[163] that it seems that it is not fitting to pray for persecutors, because in the Apocalypse it is said, "Revenge the blood of the saints."[164] Therefore, we ourselves can also ask for revenge. And this question is solved by Augustine in two ways. One solution is that when it is said, "Revenge the blood," it can be understood in two ways: "Revenge the blood" of wicked men or of the kingdom of wickedness.[165] For someone is said to revenge in one way, in that the wickedness of him, who offends you through his wickedness, be destroyed, and this is the best revenge. In this way Stephen was revenged of Paul. And someone is said to revenge in another way, in that a punishment be inflicted, not because they desire the revenge, but from zeal of justice. Or "revenge" ought not to be understood as though they eagerly desire revenge, but they are said to cry out insofar as an unjust death itself calls for vengeance from God, as it is said, "The voice of thy brother Abel's blood crieth to me from the earth" (Gen. 4, 10).

Afterwards the Lord gives the supporting reasons. And there are two: one taken from a divine example, and the other from the end [of loving one's neighbor].

As to the first point, He says, *That you may be the children of your Father.* But here nothing seems to be said. For a man becomes a son of God by grace, therefore it is not from works.

---

163. "Augustine: But we read in the Apocalypse that the martyrs pray that they be revenged" (*Biblia cum Glossa Ordinaria*, vol. V (Antwerp 1617), p. 119C).
164. "And they cried with a loud voice, saying: How long, O Lord... dost thou not judge and revenge our blood on them that dwell on the earth?" (Apoc. 6, 10); cf. Apoc. 19, 2: "And [God] hath revenged the blood of his servants, at her hands."
165. The text here has "wicked king," but the following words of St. Augustine, which refer to "dominion of sin," elucidate the meaning here: "For who would venture to affirm, in regard to those white-robed saints, when they pleaded that they should be avenged, whether they pleaded against the men themselves or against the dominion of sin?... But the dominion of sin is destroyed and overthrown, partly by the amendment of men... partly by the condemnation of those who persevere in sin" (*De serm. Dom.* I, 22, 77).

The Lord, however, seems to suggest that a man ought to act well in order to acquire grace. But it ought to be known that this sonship is not a natural sonship, but one of likeness; "For whom he foreknew, he also predestinated to be made conformable to the image of his Son" (Rom. 8, 29). Hence, someone grows in the Divine likeness inasmuch as he grows in Divine sonship. The beginning of the Divine likeness is from faith; now, no one believes unless he be willing to believe. Hence, free will operates there; "He gave them power to be made the sons of God, to them that believe in his name" (Jn. 1, 12). And now this likeness grows from charity, and it grows more through works, but especially when it will obtain glory; "Behold, how they are numbered among the children of God, and their lot is among the saints" (Wis. 5, 5), and then "When he shall appear we shall be like to him: because we shall see him as he is" (I Jn. 3, 2). Therefore, *That you may be the children of your Father*, by imitation of His works in hope, but in reality by glory in eternal life.

Who is in heaven, because He presides in heaven watching over corporeal and spiritual affairs.

Who maketh his sun to rise. This can be understood literally of the sun and material rain. And according to this sense, observe two things. The first is that, if He gives the good things that He created, why will you not give them? You, who dispense *upon the good*, meaning your friends, *and bad*, meaning your enemies; and He says, *upon the good and bad*, because He gives in one way to the good and another way to the bad. For He grants things to the good for their benefit, because they are neither exalted in prosperity nor cast down in adversity, but to the wicked unto their detriment. Observe another thing, that temporal goods ought not to be desired, nor temporal evils feared, due to the fact that sometimes bad things are given to the good, and many times good things are given to the bad.

Or, *who maketh his sun to rise* can be expounded of the spiritual sun and of spiritual rain.[166] But it is objected that it is written, "Therefore we have erred from the way of truth, and the light of justice hath not shined unto us, and the sun of understanding hath not risen upon us" (Wis. 5, 6), and, "And now I will shew you what I will do to my vineyard... and I will command the clouds to rain no rain upon it. For the vineyard of

---

166. "... that spiritual sun does not rise except on the good and holy; for it is this very thing which the wicked bewail in that book which is called the Wisdom of Solomon, 'And the sun rose not upon us' and 'that spiritual rain does not water any except the good" (St. Augustine, *De serm. Dom.* I, 23, 78).

the Lord of hosts is the house of Israel" (5, 5-7). But it ought to be said that to the good and to the bad He gives these things, as to their sufficiency, but as to their efficacy, He gives them only to the good, just as Christ's teaching is efficacious for the good, but not for the bad. Or by these two things is understood baptism,[167] and so the fervor of the Holy Ghost is to be understood by the sun, and the water of baptism is to be understood by the rain.

Do not even the publicans this. They are called publicans because they were in charge of the public tributes, and it is said that they were instituted by Publius, a Roman Consul, and these men were reputed as usurers are now, on account of the frauds which they used to do; "A merchant is hardly free from negligence" (Eccli. 26, 28).

And if you salute your brethren only, etc., **do not also the heathens**, who are gentiles without charity, do **this?**; for the word **heathen** (*ethnos*) in Greek[168] is translated as *gens* (Gentile) in Latin.

Afterwards the Lord concludes everything that He said in this chapter, saying, **Be you therefore perfect, as also your heavenly Father is perfect**; "Walk before me, and be perfect" (Gen. 17, 1), and, "Leaving the word of the beginning of Christ, let us go on to things more perfect" (Heb. 6, 1). But the question is whether this is a precept or a counsel: If it is a precept, then we are all bound to perfection; and if it is a counsel, since all are sons of the Father, then all ought to imitate the Father.

But I answer, saying that as [the Divine] nature is distinct [from others], so perfection is threefold: simply, in respect to its nature and in respect to time. Regarding the first perfection, only God is perfect. There is perfection in respect to nature, when someone has those things which his nature requires. There is perfection in respect to time, as for example, a boy is said to be perfect. Therefore, when we speak of perfect love, we then likewise speak of perfection: God is loved as much as He ought to be loved, and this is only in God; for no creature can love Him as much as He ought to be loved; for He is loved due to His goodness which is infinite. And thus it ought to be said that the word **as** implies a likeness of imitation.

There is another perfection of love possible for a creature, namely, that the creature love God according to his totality. And there are three degrees of this perfection. And one is not possible

---

167. "HILARY; Or, the sun and rain have reference to the baptism with water and Spirit" (*Catena Aurea on St. Matthew*, chap. 5, lect. 21).
168. i.e. θυος.

in this life, and the other two are possible. Regarding the first of these, all are bound, because this totality can be referred to the act of love, and such is the perfection of heaven; for in this life, because of its many occupations, this perfection is not possible.

There is also a totality in the way [to heaven] which pertains to one's intention, namely, such that you have God in all your actions as your final end, after having thought nothing against Him. And this is a precept; for all are bound to ordain themselves and their actions to God.[169]

Another is a middle perfection. And this belongs to the religious. For inasmuch as a man is exempted from the affairs of the world, to that degree he thinks of God in his actions and rises closer to those things which are in heaven.[170] And accordingly, the Apostles wanted to be poor, not for the sake of poverty, but so that they might give themselves to contemplation. And thus virginity or continence belongs to the perfection of a counsel; because the married think upon those things which pertain to the world, and consequently they are not brought as much to the contemplation of God.

Therefore, it is evident that one is the love that is perfection simply, another is that which is possible for a creature, and there is another in between as it was said.

---

[169]. cf. II II q. 44, a. 4 ad 2um.   [170]. cf. II II q. 44, a. 4 ad 3um.

CHAPTER SIX

1. Take heed that you do not your justice before men, to be seen by them: otherwise you shall not have a reward of your Father who is in heaven.

2. Therefore when thou dost an alms-deed, sound not a trumpet before thee, as the hypocrites do in the synagogues and in the streets, that they may be honored by men. Amen I say to you, they have received their reward.

3. But when thou dost alms, let not thy left hand know what thy right hand doth.

4. That thy alms may be in secret, and thy Father who seeth in secret will repay thee.

Take heed that you do not your justice before men. Above, the Lord fulfilled the Law as to the precepts, now He begins to fulfill it as to its promises. For in the Old Law temporal things were promised, as Augustine says,[1] and these were the two most desirable temporal things, namely, worldly glory and an abundance of riches;[2] "Now if thou wilt hear the voice of all his commandments, which I command thee this day, the Lord thy God will make thee higher than all the nations that are on the earth. And all these blessings shall come upon thee and overtake thee," etc., (Deut. 28, 1-2). Now in this chapter the Lord teaches not to do the works of justice on account of temporal goods, nor on account of the glory of the world, nor on account of an abundance of riches. Now this chapter is divided into two parts. In the first part, He teaches that the works of justice ought not to be done on account of the glory of the world; and in the second part, He teaches that they ought not to be done on account of riches, where it is said, ***Lay not up to yourselves treasures on earth.*** About the first part, He does two things. Firstly, He sets forth His teaching in general; and secondly, He proceeds by parts, where it is said, ***Therefore***

---

1. "No one doubts that promises of temporal things are contained in the Old Testament, for which reason it is called the Old Testament; or that the kingdom of heaven and the promise of eternal life belong to the New Testament" (*Contra Faustum Manichaeum* iv, 2 (PL 42, 217)).

2. "All worldly goods may be reduced to three – honors, riches, and pleasures; according to I John 2, 16: 'All that is in the world is the concupiscence of the flesh,' which refers to pleasures of the flesh, 'and the concupiscence of the eyes,' which refers to riches, 'and the pride of life,' which refers to ambition for renown and honor. Now the Law did not promise an abundance of carnal pleasures; on the contrary, it forbade them. But it did promise exalted honors and abundant riches; for it is written in reference to the former (Deut. 28, 1): 'If thou wilt hear the voice of the Lord thy God... He will make thee higher than all the nations'; and in reference to the latter, we read a little further on (Deut. 28, 11): 'He will make thee abound with all goods'" (I II, q. 108, a. 3 ad 4um).

when thou dost an alms-deed. About the first point, He does two things. Firstly, He sets forth the teaching, and secondly, He gives the reason for the teaching, where it is said, **Otherwise you shall not have a reward.** He says, therefore, **Take heed that you do not your justice before men.**

He says pointedly, **Take heed**, on account of three reasons. Firstly, attention is needed wherever something is subtlety implied. This is the case regarding the desire for human praise. Hence, Chrysostom says, "It enters in secretly, and carries off insensibly all that is within";[3] "Of the arrow that flieth in the day" (Ps. 90, 6).[4] Secondly, attention is needed regarding those things that are hard to resist. As Augustine says in a *Letter to Aurelius*, "Men do not easily know what power the desire for human glory has upon their wills, except those who shall have declared war upon these powers. Because even if human glory is easily not sought when it is denied [to them], nevertheless it is relinquished with difficulty, when it is offered";[5] "Therefore they could not believe" (Jn. 12, 39). Thirdly, attention is needed because the greater are the works, the less can man be on his guard. Chrysostom says that every evil vexes the sons of the devil, but this evil vexes the sons of God;[6] "Satan stood on his right hand to be his adversary" (Zach. 3, 1), that is, the devil laying snares by good works.

And He did not say **Take heed** except after He eliminated the soul's anger, concupiscence, and hate. For a soul subject to passions cannot take heed to what is happening in the heart; "With all watchfulness keep thy heart, because life issueth out from it" (Prov. 4, 23), and afterwards it is said, "Let thy eyes look straight on, and let thy eyelids go before thy steps" (verse 25).

That you do not your justice before men, meaning a work of justice. Justice sometimes denotes a fault, namely, when

---

3. "The evil beast comes in upon us secretly, and without noise puffs all away, and unobservedly carries out all that is within" (hom. xix, 1 (PG 57, 273)).

4. "Having overcome this temptation to despair, we have next to arm ourselves against human praise, which is evoked especially by holiness of life. Otherwise we shall run the risk of being wounded by the 'arrow that flieth in the day,' that is to say, by vainglory. For, in a sense, good fame may truly be said to fly. And it flies in the day, because it springs from the works of light" (Bernard, *Sermon on the Canticle of Canticles*, serm. 33,12 (PL 183, 957D)).

5. "For the man who has not declared war against this enemy has no idea of its power; for if it be comparatively easy to dispense with praise so long as it is denied to him, it is difficult to forbear from being captivated with praise when it is offered" (Ep. 22, ii, 8 (PL 33, 93)); this quotation is cited in II II, q. 132, a. 3 obj. 3.

6. "But a desire of vainglory assails not only the servants of the devil, but even the servants of God and faithful people; in fact, it assails the servants of God more than the servants of the devil. For wherever a glorious matter is being carried out, there an opportunity for boasting more readily finds room." (*Op. imp. in Mt.*, hom. iii (PG 56, 704)).

it is presumed by one's own powers; "For they, not knowing the justice of God and seeking to establish their own," etc., (Rom. 10, 3). Other times it denotes a virtue, as here when it is said, ***Do not your justice before men***, which, in fact, is required of us. For the Lord had said, "Unless your justice abound more than that of the scribes and Pharisees, you shall not enter into the kingdom of heaven" (above 5, 20); and He specifies how justice could be practiced, and if it were entirely referred to the praise of men, it would not be justice; wherefore a right intention is necessary, and this is the meaning of the words, ***Do not your justice before men***, etc.

But Chrysostom asks: What if I take a poor man aside? He answers, saying that if a man were to have vainglory in his heart, and were to have the intention of glorying, taking the poor man aside would not suffice.[7] And so Gregory says, a work ought to be so done in public that the intention remain secret,[8] and this is the meaning of the words, ***Do not your justice before men, to be seen by them***.

But do we not always seek glory when we want to be seen by men? Augustine says that something is sought in two ways, in one way as the ultimate end, and in another way as necessary for the end. We seek something in a proper sense which we want as the ultimate end; on the other hand, we do not properly seek something else which we want as necessary for the end, as, for example, someone seeks a ship so that he may go to a country. He does not properly seek the boat but the country.[9] Therefore, it follows that if you wish to be seen by men so that you may give them an example, and on account of God's glory, you would not be forbidden, because He said above, "So let your light shine before men, that they may see your good works, and glorify your Father who is in heaven" (above 5, 16). On the other hand, it is forbidden

---

[7] "Shall we seek a secret place apart where there are no people? But how does it help if people were not in a place but a vain thought was in your heart? Therefore it is better that a vain thought not be present in your heart than that there be no people in a place" (Ibid.)

[8] "I do not say this, however, that our neighbors may not see our good works, since it is written, 'That they may see your good works, and glorify your Father who is in heaven,' (Mt. 5, 16), but that we may not seek praise from outside for what we do. And so it is necessary that our works that we do in public remain hidden insofar as our intention, so that we may also give an example to our neighbors by the good work, and yet regarding the intention, whereby we seek to please God, let us prefer to keep it secret" (*Homiliarum in Evangelia Libri Duo*, lib. 1, hom. xi, 1 (PL 76, 1115B)).

[9] "As, therefore, that man would not speak absurdly who should say, *In this work of seeking a ship, it is not a ship, but my native country, that I seek*: so the Apostle also might fitly say, *In this work of pleasing men, it is not men, but God, that I please; because I do not aim at pleasing men, but have it as my object, that those whom I wish to be saved may imitate me*" (Augustine, *De serm. Dom.* II, i, 3 (PL 34, 1271)).

that one's intention be directed [to pleasing men] as the last end, and this what He says, *that you may be seen by them* only; that is, as also pleasing men is sometimes reproached: "If I yet pleased men, I should not be the servant of Christ" (Gal. 1, 10); and sometimes is praised: "As I also in all things please all men, not seeking that which is profitable to myself but to many: that they may be saved" (I Cor. 10, 33).

Afterwards He assigns the reason for His teaching, wherefore He says, *Otherwise you shall not have a reward.* No one merits something from another to whom he gives nothing.[10] Hence, he who does something for men's sake, and not for God's sake, is said to give nothing. Chrysostom says: What wisdom is it to give alms and to lose God's reward?[11] Concerning this reward it is said, "I am thy reward exceeding great" (Gen. 15, 1), and, "Your reward is very great in heaven" (above 5, 12).

Afterwards He proceeds by parts, when He says, *Therefore when thou dost an alms-deed.* And He relates these three things, according to Chrysostom, [because] the Lord wanted to instruct against those things by which they may be tempted, namely, concerning gluttony, avarice, and vainglory, as is evident from what was said above in chapter four; and fasting is opposed to gluttony, almsdeeds are opposed to avarice, and prayer is opposed to vainglory. For nothing [besides prayer] is able to conquer vainglory, since it is also increased by good works.[12]

It ought to be considered that these three things are parts of justice in two ways. For justice is satisfactory, so that he who sins may satisfy [by these three things]. Now sin is threefold. It is either against God, or against oneself, or against one's neighbor. One sins against God through pride, and the humility of prayer is opposed to this; "The prayer of him that humbleth himself, shall pierce the clouds" (Eccli. 35, 21). One sins against one's neighbor through avarice, and therefore one satisfies by almsdeeds. One sins against oneself through concupiscence of

---

10. "What will you who have given nothing to God receive from God? For whatever is given for God's sake is given to God and received from Him. But whatever is done for people's sake is scattered to the winds and hoped for by nobody. What else is the praise of people than the sound of winds passing by?" (Pseudo-Chrysostom, *Op. imp. in Mt.*, hom. xiii (PG 56, 706)).

11. "But what wisdom is it, to bestow our goods, to reap empty words, and to have despised the reward of God that would remain forever in heaven and to choose the fleeting words of people?" (Ibid.).

12. "The more good you do, while wishing to restrain vainglory, the more you stir it up. And the reason is that every vice arises from evil, but only vainglory proceeds out of a good deed... Therefore there is no remedy against vainglory except prayer alone, and even prayer itself can produce vanity, unless you look carefully to see if you are praying well" (Pseudo-Chrysostom, *Op. imp. in Mt.*, hom. xv (PG 56, 715)).

the flesh, and therefore one satisfies by fasting.[13] Jerome says that by prayer the plague of every mind is healed, by fasting the plague of the body is healed.[14] Likewise, these three things are parts of justice, which is a proper act of the virtue of religion. For religious men ought to offer sacrifice to God. Now there is a threefold good [of religious men]: their exterior goods, namely, their property, and their interior goods, namely, their body and soul. By almsdeeds, therefore, they offer their exterior goods; "And do not forget to do good and to impart: for by such sacrifices God's favor is obtained" (Heb. 13, 16). By prayer, they offer their soul to God, for prayer is "the raising up of the soul to God";[15] "Let my prayer be directed as incense in thy sight; the lifting up of my hands, as evening sacrifice" (Ps. 140, 2).[16]

Therefore, regarding almsdeeds, which is the first, He does two things. He excludes an undue manner, and secondly, He sets forth the due manner [of almsgiving], where it is said, *But when thou dost alms*. About the first point, He excludes the undue manner, and secondly, He assigns the reason, where it is said, *Amen I say to you, they have received their reward*. He excludes the undue manner resulting from three things: resulting from the signal, the place, and the end [of almsgiving].

As to the first, He says, *Therefore when thou dost an alms-deed*. This is a continuation of the words, *Take heed that you do not your justice before men*, etc. Hence, since almsdeeds are a part of justice, *when thou dost an alms-deed, sound not a trumpet before thee*. It was a custom of the Jews that when they gave alms in public, they would sound trumpets so

---

13. "Satisfaction should be of such a nature as to involve something taken away from us for the honor of God. Now we have but three kinds of goods, bodily, spiritual, and goods of fortune, or external goods" (Suppl., q. 15, a. 3).

14. "PSEUDO-JEROME; Or else, the folly which is connected with the softness of the flesh, is healed by fasting; anger and laziness are healed by prayer. Each wound has its own medicine, which must be applied to it; that which is used for the heel will not cure the eye; by fasting, the passions of the body, by prayer, the plagues of the soul, are healed" (*Catena Aurea on St. Mark*, chap. 9, lect. 3).

15. "Prayer is the raising up of the mind to God or a petitioning of God for what is fitting" (Damascene, *De Fide Orthodoxa*, iii, 24 (PG 94, 1090D)); cf. III, q. 21, a. 1, Obj. 3.

16. "Man's good is threefold. There is first his soul's good which is offered to God in a certain inward sacrifice by devotion, prayer and other like interior acts: and this is the principal sacrifice. The second is his body's good, which is, so to speak, offered to God in martyrdom, and abstinence or continency. The third is the good which consists of external things: and of these we offer a sacrifice to God, directly when we offer our possession to God immediately, and indirectly when we share them with our neighbor for God's sake" (II II, q. 85, a. 3 ad 2um). The missing quotation to support the third point may be supplied from II II, q. 88, a. 2 ad 3um where the mortification of the body by fasting and vigils is discussed: "Present your bodies a living sacrifice, holy, pleasing unto God" (Rom. 12, 1).

that the poor would gather together. This, therefore, which was introduced due to a certain necessity, men's malice perverted to vainglory. And so the Lord forbids this, and, according to Chrysostom, it is alike to a sounding trumpet when you desire to appear for any good deed, even if it would be done in secret;[17] "Lift up thy voice with strength, thou that bringest good tidings to Jerusalem" (Is. 40, 9).

As the hypocrites. Here it is related for the first time concerning hypocrites. Hence, it ought to be seen what this name, 'hypocrite,' precisely means. It was derived and produced from the representations which were being made in theatrical plays where they were bringing in men having masked faces in order to represent men, by which they were representing their deeds. Hence, the word 'hypocrite' was being said from *hypo,* which means 'under,' and *krisio,* which means 'judgment.'[18] For a man was one thing and he appeared to be another, and such is the hypocrite, who outwardly has the appearance of holiness, but inwardly he does not fulfill what he shows. Gregory says that one is not a hypocrite if sometimes one falls due to weakness, for they are properly hypocrites who have the appearance of holiness so that they may be seen.[19]

Afterwards He excludes the undue manner of almsgiving as to the place, and this also is to be reprehended if it should happen by pretense, but not if it would happen for the sake of an example.

In the synagogues [is said] as now in the Church [is said], *and in the streets* is as now in a public place. *That they may*

---

17. "The trumpet is every act or deed through which boasting about the deed is made known. Think of one who gives alms whenever he sees someone present but does not do so otherwise. This is a trumpet because his boast is proclaimed through this. Again, he who gives alms when someone intercedes but does not do so when there is no intercessor— this behavior is a wicked trumpet. Moreover, whoever gives alms if he sees a more trustworthy individual who can report the matter (even if he gives alms secretly) and gives nothing to a pauper who is bound in his passions— this too is a trumpet. Even if it took place in secret, it nonetheless was with the intention that he might seem praiseworthy: first because he did it; second, because he hid it; the very act of hiding it is the trumpet of his alms" (Pseudo-Chrysostom, *Op. imp. in Mt.,* hom. xiii (PG 56, 707)).

18. "Isidore says (*Etymologiarum* x ad litt. H (ML 82, 379)): 'Hypocrite is a Greek word corresponding to the Latin *simulator,* for whereas he is evil within,' he 'shows himself outwardly as being good; the Greek word *hypo* denoting falsehood, and the Greek word *krisis,* judgment'" (II II, q. 111, a. 2 sc.)

19. "But we must not believe that these persons fall into the numbers of hypocrites, for it is one thing to sin from infirmity, and another from wickedness. There is, therefore, this difference between these persons and hypocrites, that these, conscious of their own infirmity, prefer being reproved by all for their faults, to being praised for pretended sanctity. But those are both sure that they are doing wrong, and yet in the judgments of men are puffed up with the name of sanctity" (*Moralia,* xxxi, 13, 5 (PL 75, 586 C-D)).

be seen and this is what He said above, *that they may be* publicly *honored*, etc.; "How can you believe, who receive glory one from another: and the glory which is from God alone, you do not seek?" (Jn. 5, 44).

Afterwards He assigns the reason [for excluding the undue manner of almsgiving], saying, *Amen I say to you, they have received their reward*. For a reward is that on account of which someone works; "Didst thou not agree with me for a penny?" (below 20, 13).

Next He assigns the due and fitting manner [of almsgiving], and thereafter He gives the reason, where it is said, *That thy alms may be in secret*. He says, therefore, *But when thou dost alms, let not thy left hand know what thy right hand doth*. This can be expounded in multiple ways. For Chrysostom says that in the book of *The Canons of the Apostles* it is expounded such that by the *left hand* the unbelievers are signified, and by the *right hand* the faithful are signified.[20] Hence, He wants that nothing happen in the presence of infidels.

Against this, Augustine says that either someone gives alms for the sake of glory, and then this also ought not to be seen by the faithful, or it is for the sake of utility, and then it ought to be done in the presence of unbelievers;[21] [and this] is especially [useful] "that seeing your good works, they many glorify your Father who is in heaven" (above 5, 16).

Others, however, expound this passage such that by the *left hand* one understands a wife who is accustomed to sometimes impede her husband from works of mercy. Hence, the husband also does not want his wife to know, and it is likewise understood regarding anyone else. And Augustine similarly objects, because

---

20. "PSEUDO-CHRYS. The Apostles in the book of the Constitutions interpret thus: The right hand is the Christian people which is at Christ's right hand; the left hand is all the people who are on His left hand. He means then, that when a Christian does alms, the unbeliever should not see it" (*Catena Aurea on St. Matthew*, chap. 6, lect. 2); Pseudo-Chrysostom, *Op. imp. in Mt.*, hom. xiii (PG 56, 707). *The Apostolic Constitutions* are a fourth-century pseudo-Apostolic collection, in eight books, of independent, though closely related, treatises on Christian discipline, worship, and doctrine, intended to serve as a manual of guidance for the clergy, and to some extent for the laity.

21. "But when thou doest alms, let not thy left hand know what thy right hand doeth. If you should understand unbelievers to be meant by the left hand, then it will seem to be no fault to wish to please believers; while nevertheless we are altogether prohibited from placing the fruit and end of our good deed in the praise of any men whatever. But as regards this point, that those who have been pleased with your good deeds should imitate you, we are to act before the eyes not only of believers, but also of unbelievers, so that by our good works, which are to be praised, they may honour God, and may come to salvation" (*De serm. Dom.*, II, 6 (PL 34, 1272)).

this precept is also given to everyone, and therefore one would be bound to say, 'Let not thy right hand know,' etc.[22]

Hence, Augustine, and also Chrysostom,[23] expound this otherwise, and it comes to almost the same [meaning]. They say that in Scripture, by the ***left hand*** temporal goods are understood, by the ***right hand*** spiritual goods are understood;[24] "Length of days is in her right hand, and in her left hand riches and glory" (Prov. 3, 16). Wherefore the Lord wanted that almsdeeds would not occur for earthly glory.[25] Or it is expounded otherwise, and it comes to almost the same meaning. By the ***right hand*** the works of virtue are sometimes understood, and by the ***left hand*** sins are understood, as though when a work of virtue is done it may not be done without some sin.[26] Chrysostom, nevertheless, relates the literal meaning and says that the Lord speaks by excess, as though someone were to say, as if it could happen, 'I do not want my foot to know this.'[27]

The reason [for this fitting manner of almsgiving] is related, where it is said, ***That thy alms may be in secret***, and in your conscience, which is hidden;[28] "Our glory is this: the testimony of

---

22. "By the expression left hand a wife is meant; so that, inasmuch as in family affairs women are wont to be more tenacious of money, it is to be kept hid from them when their husbands compassionately spend anything upon the needy, for fear of domestic quarrels. As if, forsooth, men alone were Christians, and this precept were not addressed to women also! From what left hand, then, is a woman enjoined to conceal her deed of mercy? Is a husband also the left hand of his wife? A statement most absurd" (*De serm. Dom.*, II, 7 (PL 34, 1272)).

23. "But as we have said above, the right hand is the will of the soul, always striving for good. The left hand is the will of the flesh, always opposed to God. Therefore let the left hand (the will of the flesh) not know what the will of the soul is" (*Op. imp. in Mt.*, hom. xiii (PG 56, 707)).

24. "The right hand is the love of heavenly goods, while the left hand is the love of temporal goods, namely, of praise and the like" (*Glossa interlinearis* (ML 162, 1304B)).

25. "And therefore the left hand seems to have no more suitable meaning than just this delight in praise. But the right hand means the intention of fulfilling the divine commands. When, therefore, with the consciousness of him who does alms is mixed up the desire of man's praise, the left hand becomes conscious of the work of the right hand: 'Let not, therefore, thy left hand know what thy right hand doeth'; i.e. let there not be mixed up in thy consciousness the desire of man's praise, when in doing alms thou art striving to fulfil a divine command" ((*De serm. Dom.*, II, 2, 8 (PL 34, 1273)).

26. "*Let not the left hand know*, etc. The left hand is the vices, and the right hand is the virtues. Therefore what virtue does, let not elation or vainglory know, or any of the vices, but may the light of performing the deed rightly put to flight the darkness of sin" (*Glossa Ordinaria* (PL 114, 99A)).

27. "Here again His enigmatical meaning is not of the hands, but He hath put the thing hyperbolically. As thus: 'If it can be,' saith He, 'for thyself not to know it, let this be the object of thine endeavor; that, if it were possible, it may be concealed from the very hands that minister.'" (Hom. xix, 2 (PG 57, 275)).

28. "*In secret*, that is to say, in a good conscience, where man does not see. One ought to seek nothing outwardly, but it ought to be hidden, such that your life may be hidden with Christ" (*Glossa Interlinearis, Bibliorum Sacrorum cum Glossa Ordinaria* (1603), p. 123)).

our conscience, that in simplicity of heart and sincerity of God" (II Cor. 1, 12). For thus is interpreted that which is written, "For it is not he is a Jew, who is so outwardly... But he is a Jew that is one inwardly" (Rom. 2, 28-29).

And thy Father who seeth in secret will repay thee. "All things are naked and open to his eyes" (Heb. 4, 13). "The heart of man is perverse above all things, and unsearchable, who can know it? I am the Lord who search the heart" (Jer. 17, 9-10).[29] Augustine says that in some texts is found, *will repay thee* 'openly,'[30] because just as the devil tries to open and make public deeds that are on the conscience so that he might give scandal, so God, for greater benefit and also to counter the examples of evil deeds, brings forth good deeds. Hence, also many saints are unable to hide;[31] "And he will bring forth thy justice as the light, and thy judgment as the noonday" (Ps. 36, 6) which you were keeping secret. This word, ['openly'] nevertheless, does not seem to belong to the text.

5. And when ye pray, you shall not be as the hypocrites, that love to stand and pray in the synagogues and corners of the streets, that they may be seen by men: Amen I say to you, they have received their reward.

6. But thou when thou shalt pray, enter into thy chamber, and having shut the door, pray to thy Father in secret, and thy father who seeth in secret will repay thee.

7. And when you are praying, speak not much, as the heathens. For they think that in their much speaking they may be heard.

8. Be not you therefore like to them for your Father knoweth what is needful for you, before you ask him.

---

29. The Vulgate reads "The heart is perverse above all things" (*pravum est cor omnium*), etc., but St. Thomas typically quotes "The heart of man" (*cor hominis*) in place of "The heart above all" (*cor omnium*), e.g. I, q. 57, a. 4 sc.; III, q. 59, a. 2 obj. 3; *De Veritate* q. 8, a. 4 sc. 8. Presumably this variant wording is derived from the Vulgate as edited by Alcuin in 800 AD which was the quasi-official text for lectures in the University of Paris at the time of St. Thomas.

30. "Many Latin copies have it thus, 'And thy Father who seeth in secret shall reward thee openly'; but because we have not found the word 'openly' in the Greek copies, which are earlier, we have not thought that anything was to be said about it" (*De serm. Dom.* II, 2, 9 (PL 34, 1274)).

31. "PSEUDO-CHRYS. For it is impossible that God should leave in obscurity any good work of man; but He makes it manifest in this world, and glorifies it in the next world, because it is the glory of God, as likewise the Devil manifests evil, in which is shown the strength of his great wickedness. But God properly makes public every good deed only in that world, the goods of which are not common to the righteous and the wicked; therefore to whomever God shall there show favor, it will be manifest that it was as reward of his righteousness" (*Catena Aurea on St. Matthew*, chap. 6, lect. 2); *Op. imp. in Mt.*, hom. xiii (PG 56, 708)).

And when ye pray. Above, regarding the work of almsdeeds, the Lord showed that it ought not to be done for human glory. Here He shows that same thing regarding prayer, and about this He does two things. Firstly, He teaches the manner of prayer, and secondly, He teaches what ought to be asked for in prayer, where it is said, *Thus therefore shall you pray.* About the first point, He does two things. Firstly, He teaches men to avoid the vanities of hypocrites, and secondly, to avoid the vanity of the Gentiles, where it is said, *And when you are praying, speak not much.* About the first thing, He excludes an unsuitable manner of praying, and secondly, He gives the suitable manner, where it is said, *But thou when thou shalt pray.* He excludes the unsuitable manner of praying by way of the example of the hypocrites. Hence, He firstly excludes this example, secondly, He explains this example, and thirdly, He gives the reason. The second part is where it is said, *That love to stand and pray*, and the third part is where it is said, *Amen I say to you.*

It is very fitting that after almsgiving He here treats about prayer, because, as it is said, "Before prayer prepare thy soul," etc., (Eccli. 18, 23). For by good works, among which the first is almsdeeds, the soul is prepared for prayer;[32] "Let us lift up our hearts with our hands to the Lord in the heavens" (Lam. 3, 41), which happens when good works accord [with prayers].

And it ought to be observed that the Lord does not bid one to pray, but He teaches the manner of praying,[33] and this is when He says, *When ye pray, you shall not be as the hypocrites, that love to stand and pray in the synagogues and corners.* By *hypocrites* is understood dissemblers, who do all for human praise, and although this is a fault to be avoided in every work, nevertheless it ought to especially be avoided in prayer, according to Chrysostom, because prayer is a sacrifice which we offer to God from our inmost hearts;[34] "Let my prayer be directed as incense in thy sight; the lifting up of my hands, as evening sacrifice" (Ps.

32."PSEUDO-CHRYS. Solomon says, 'Before prayer, prepare your soul' (Eccli. 18, 23). This he does who comes to prayer doing alms; for good works stir up the faith of the heart, and give the soul confidence in prayer to God. Alms, then, are a preparation for prayer, and therefore the Lord after speaking of alms proceeds accordingly to instruct us concerning prayer" (*Catena Aurea on St. Matthew*, chap. 6, lect. 3); *Op. imp. in Mt.*, hom. xv (PG 56, 715).

33. "Here at the present stage the admonition is not that we should pray, but as to how we should pray" (Augustine, *De serm. Dom.* II, 3, 11 (PL 34, 1274)).

34. "PSEUDO-CHRYS. Prayer is, as it were, a spiritual tribute which the soul offers of its own bowels. Wherefore the more glorious it is, the more watchfully ought we to guard that it is not made vile by being done to be seen of men." (*Catena Aurea on St. Matthew*, chap. 6, lect. 2); *Op. imp. in Mt.*, hom. xiii (PG 56, 708 ff.).

140, 2). It is not allowed that sacrifice be offered except to God, but it is offered to men if it is done on account of human glory. Hence, such men are idolaters.

Now, hypocrites are described insofar as their affecting every place above and below themselves. As to the first affectation, He says, **Who love to stand and pray in the synagogues and corners of the streets**. For some touch of vainglory sometimes occurs in holy men, but they are not on this account to be numbered among the hypocrites unless they do this of set purpose; "A wild ass accustomed to the wilderness in the desire of his heart, snuffed up the wind of his love" (Jer. 2, 24).

And note that there are two kinds of hypocrites who clearly seek human glory, namely, they who pray in public places [and they who pray in private places]. Hence, He says, **in the synagogues**, where there was a congregation of people; "And a congregation of people shall surround thee" (Ps. 7, 8). Others pray in private places and they seek human glory from the very avoidance of glory.[35] For they want to seem to seek concealment when nevertheless they love public places, and this is what He says, **in the synagogues and corners of the streets**. For if they truly seek concealment, let them seek not the corners of the streets, but an enclosed place. Or we can say that they seek a public place in the open. But there are two kinds of public places, one is deputed to prayer, namely, **the synagogue**, and another is not deputed to prayer, namely, a **corner of the streets**, and a corner is properly where two lines intersect each other.[36] Hence, **corners of the streets** are two streets crossing over each other such that a intersection is made there and this place is very public and is not deputed to prayer; "The stones of the sanctuary are scattered in the top of every street" (Lam. 4, 1).

It also ought to be observed that one of the useful things for prayer is humility; "The prayer of the humble and the meek hath always pleased thee" (Jud. 9, 16), and, "Thou hast regarded my humility, thou hast saved my soul out of distresses" (Ps. 30, 8), but these [hypocrites] stand like proud men.

But it seems that in no place is it forbidden to pray; "I will therefore that men pray in every place" (I Tim. 2, 8), and, "In the churches bless ye God the Lord" (Ps. 67, 27). But I answer that it is not a sin [**to pray in corners of the streets**] except on account of this intention, **that they may be seen by men**. And,

---

35. "Even if thou shouldest enter into thy closet, and having shut the door, shouldest do it for display, the doors will do thee no good" (John Chrysostom, *In Mt.*, hom. xix, 3 (PG 57, 276).

36. "GLOSS. Or, *the corners of the streets*, are the places where one way crosses another, and makes four crossways." (*Catena Aurea on St. Matthew*, chap. 6, lect. 3).

as Chrysostom says, although to want to be seen by men harms in other works, nevertheless this especially harms in prayer, because it harms both in respect to the end and in respect to the substance of the work, because even if prayer would be made with a good intention, man is scarcely able to keep his mind from being distracted by many things; all the more, therefore, when prayer is made on account of the glory of men,[37] and this is what is said, *that they may be seen by men.*

Therefore, ought one never to pray in a public place? It ought to be known that God intends to forbid the manner of praying, by which [prohibition] vainglory is taken away, which is never sought except on account of something singular, because when there are many who keep one manner of praying, then glory is not sought from another. Hence, the Lord takes away the singular manner of praying, namely, so that no one would pray in a place not deputed to prayer, unless there be someone of such authority that also he bids others to pray.[38] Hence, according to Chrysostom, these words which He says, *in the corners of the streets*, are to be referred to everything whereby you may seem to be set apart from others with whom you associate.[39]

Amen I say to you, they have received their reward. Here He comes to the reason, and He says two things, *reward* and *their.* The reward of everyone is that by which one is fed from his work.[40] Hence, when we do something on account of the glory of men, the glory of men is our reward, when nevertheless we ought to wait for the true glory of God, and this is what is said, *they have received their reward*, with good reason, because they have usurped it;[41] "For what things a man shall sow, those also shall he reap" (Gal. 6, 8).

37. "In everything it is good to be freed from vainglory, so most especially in prayer. For if even without this, we wander and are distracted, when shall we attend unto the things which we are saying, should we enter in having this disease also? And if we who pray and beseech attend not, how do we expect God to attend?" (*In Mt.*, hom. xix, 3 (PG 57, 276)).

38. "PSEUDO-CHRYS. He forbids us to pray in an assembly with the intent of being seen of that assembly, as He adds, *that they may be seen of men.* He that prays, therefore, should do nothing singular that might attract notice; as crying out, striking his breast, or reaching forth his hands" (*Catena Aurea on St. Matthew*, chap. 6, lect. 3"; *Op. imp. in Mt.*, hom. xiii (PG 56, 709)).

39. "PSEUDO-CHRYS. In the corners of the streets, namely, that they may seem to be praying retiredly and thus earn a twofold praise: that they pray, and that they pray in retirement" (Ibid.).

40. "PSEUDO-CHRYS. Verily I say to you, they have received their reward, for every man where he sows, there he reaps, therefore they who pray because of men, not because of God, receive praise of men, not of God" (Ibid.).

41. "JEROME; A reward not of God, but of themselves, for they receive praise of men, for the sake of which it was that they practiced their virtues" ((*Catena Aurea on St. Matthew*, chap. 6, lect. 2); *Comm. in Mt.*, I (PL 26, 42B)).

But thou when thou shalt pray. Here He relates the due manner of praying, and firstly, He relates the manner of praying, and secondly, He gives the reason for this manner, where it is said, ***And thy father who seeth in secret will repay thee.*** He says, therefore, ***But thou when thou shalt pray***, meaning, 'when you shall be disposed to pray,'[42] ***enter into thy chamber.*** This is expounded in three ways. It is understood firstly in a literal sense of a separate room. But do not they do the contrary, who go to a church?[43] But it ought to be said that He is speaking about private prayer, which only ought to be made in a private place and this is for three reasons. Firstly, it is because it is consonant with the faith, because you then confess that God is present everywhere;[44] "Lord, all my desire is before thee, and my groaning is not hidden from thee" (Ps. 37, 10), and, "Shall a man be hid in secret places, and I not see him, saith the Lord? do not I fill heaven and earth, saith the Lord?" (Jer. 23, 24). Secondly, it is because although prayer which is made in public is impeded by many things, prayer which is made in private is quiet;[45] "I will lead her into the wilderness: and I will speak to her heart" (Osee 2, 14). Thirdly, it is because vainglory is avoided;[46] "And going in, [Eliseus] shut the door upon him, and upon the child, and prayed to the Lord" (IV Kings 4, 33). Nevertheless, it ought to be said that prayer ought to be made in a private place so that one may pray before the Lord, alone, namely, ***and having shut the door*** literally, you may also exclude the possibility of [anyone] approaching [you].[47]

42. *"But thou when thou shalt pray.* That is, you who wish to be heard and not to be seen, you who wish to be truly praiseworthy and not merely appear to be so, you who speak in the ears of God, not in the eyes of the people" (Pseudo-Chrysostom, *Op. imp. in Mt.*, hom. xiv (PG 56, 709)).

43. "'What then,' it may be said, 'ought we not to pray in church?' Indeed we ought by all means, but in such a spirit as this. Because everywhere God seeks the intention of all that is done. Since even if thou shouldest enter into thy closet, and having shut the door, shouldest do it for display, the doors will do thee no good" (*In Mt.*, hom. xix, 3 (PG 57, 276)).

44. "In His teaching the Lord bade us to pray in secret, in hidden and remote places, in our very bed-chambers, because it is more befitting our faith to realize that God is everywhere present, that He hears and sees all, and by the plenitude of His majesty penetrates also hidden and secret places" (Cyprian, *On the Lord's Prayer*, iv (PL 4, 521C)).

45. "Hence the door is to be shut, i.e. the fleshly sense is to be resisted, so that spiritual prayer may be directed to the Father, which is done in the inmost heart, where prayer which is in secret is offered to the Father" (Augustine, *De serm. Dom.* II, 3, 11 (PL 34, 1274)).

46. "JEROME; This, if taken in its plain sense, teaches the hearer to shun all desire of vain honor in praying" (*Catena Aurea on St. Matthew*, chap. 6, lect. 3); *Comm. in Mt.*, I (PL 26, 42B).

47. *"Go into your room and shut the door.* This is so that there will be nobody there except you who pray and He to Whom you pray, and so there will not be another person with you except for Him Whom you need. A witness burdens one who prays and does not help him, because God is not compelled by prayers as much as He is pleased by them. I am speaking of another person who has a different heart. But wherever they are of the same heart, even if there were many people who were praying, they are one because one spirit prays in

Secondly, by *chamber* can be understood the interior secret of the heart;[48] "The things you say in your hearts, be sorry for them upon your beds" (Ps. 4, 5). *Having shut the door*; "Hedge in thy ears with thorns, hear not a wicked tongue, and make doors and bars to thy mouth" (Eccli. 28, 28), as though He were to say, 'Pray silently,' and He says this for three reasons. Firstly, it is because [the truths] of the faith are [thereby] attested, because then you confess that God knows the thoughts of hearts;[49] "Man seeth those things that appear, but the Lord beholdeth the heart" (I Kings 16, 7). Secondly, it is because it is unfitting that others would know your petitions;[50] "My secret to myself, my secret to myself" (Is. 24, 16). Thirdly, it is because if you would speak with your voice you would impede others [from praying];[51] "Hammer and axe were not heard in the house when it was in building" (III Kings 6, 7).

But what shall we say about public prayer? It ought to be said that the Lord is speaking about private prayer in which the good of one person is sought. But, likewise, in public prayer the good of the multitude is sought, and by acclamations of this kind some men are stimulated to devotion, wherefore chants were instituted. Hence, Augustine in his *Confessions* says that blessed Athanasius, lest he enjoy too much in singing, wanted that everything be read quietly. But because chants of this kind profited Augustine much before he was converted, he dared not to speak against them but instead approved them.[52]

---

all of them" (Pseudo-Chrysostom, *Op. imp. in Mt.*, hom. xiv (PG 56, 709)).

48. "*Enter into thy chamber*, that is to say, the secrets of the heart" (*Glossa Ordinaria* (PL 114, 875D)).

49. "For many evils arise out of loud prayer, especially these three. First, whoever prays loudly does not believe that God is everywhere and can hear in hidden places, as indeed He does. For God must not be beaten down with a loud voice but rather pleased by a clean conscience, since He does not listen to the voice but to the heart" (Pseudo-Chrysostom, *Op. imp. in Mt.*, hom. xiv (PG 56, 710)).

50. "The second evil is that you entrust the secrets of your petition, which perhaps nobody ought to know except for you and God, to the ears of good and evil people alike... you are moreover laughed at by those people to whom you have revealed your secrets" (Ibid.).

51. "Now the third evil is that you do not allow anyone else to pray next to you when you pray loudly. By your voice you draw his attention to your words, and so not only are you not heard because you are praying badly, but furthermore you heap up more sin as you do not allow others to pray" (Ibid.).

52. "And safer it seems to me what I remember once was related to me concerning Athanasius, bishop of Alexandria, who required the readers of the psalm to use so slight an inflection of the voice that it was more like speaking than singing. However, when I call to mind the tears I shed at the songs of thy Church at the outset of my recovered faith, and how even now I am moved, not by the singing but by what is sung (when they are sung with a clear and skillfully modulated voice), I then come to acknowledge the great utility of this custom. Thus I vacillate between dangerous pleasure and healthful exercise. I am inclined—though I pronounce no irrevocable opinion on the subject— to approve of the use of singing in the church, so that by the delights of the ear the weaker minds may be stimulated to a devotional mood" (*Confessiones* x, 33, 50 (PL 32, 800)).

But the question is whether someone praying in a private place ought to say words or not. But a distinction ought to be made here, because sometimes words come forth intentionally, and other times from an impulse of the heart, as it is said, "Who can withhold the words he hath conceived?" (Job 4, 2).

Now words can be considered in two ways, either as owed and then they ought to be recited;[53] "I cried to the Lord with my voice: with my voice I made supplication to the Lord" (Ps. 141, 2); or they can be considered as useful for praying, and then it ought to be distinguished regarding the beginning and end, because "Better is the end of a prayer than the beginning" (Eccle. 7, 9), [meaning, the prayers] of the Church. For if in the beginning of prayer affections for praying devotedly are aroused by the words, then it is useful to express words, when, however, the affections are not aroused by the words, then words ought not to be expressed and [the affections] ought to be enclosed, because just as what is hot is diminished by evaporating, so the affections are emptied out by words, as it also is evident from a sorrow expressed to others; "My heart grew hot within me: and in my meditation a fire shall flame out" (Ps. 38, 4), and, "I said: I will not make mention of him, nor speak any more in his name: and there came in my heart as a burning fire" (Jer. 20, 9). Augustine[54] expounds the passage in this way.

But Augustine expounds *having shut the door* in a third way such that by *chamber* the heart is understood, and by *the door* the outward senses and also the imagination are understood, as it were, because such a man ought to enter his heart and close his senses and imagination so that nothing enters within except what pertains to prayer.[55] And Cyprian assigns two reasons. The first reason is that it is reprehensible that you do not pay attention to

---

53. "The voice is used in praying as though to pay a debt, so that man may serve God with all that he has from God, that is to say, not only with his mind, but also with his body: and this applies to prayer considered especially as satisfactory" (II II, q. 83, a. 12).

54. The text here has "Chrysostom" but this quotation does not appear to be in his writings but instead something similar is found in the writings of St. Augustine as quoted in the *Summa* as follows: "Augustine says (*ad Probam.* Ep. 130, ix, 18 (PL 33, 501) that 'by means of words and other signs we arouse ourselves more effectively to an increase of holy desires.' Hence, then alone should we use words and such like signs when they help to excite the mind internally. But if they distract or in any way impede the mind we should abstain from them; and this happens chiefly to those whose mind is sufficiently prepared for devotion without having recourse to those signs" (ibid.)

55. "It is a small matter to enter into our bed-chambers if the door stand open to the unmannerly, through which the things that are outside profanely rush in and assail our inner man. Now we have said that outside are all temporal and visible things, which make their way through the door, i.e. through the fleshly sense into our thoughts, and clamorously interrupt those who are praying by a crowd of vain phantoms" (*De serm. Dom.* II, 1, 11 (PL 34, 1274)).

what you say when you speak with a king.[56] The second reason is that, why should God pay attention to you if you do not pay attention to yourself?[57] This is *the door*, concerning which it is said, "Behold, I stand at the gate and knock. If any man shall hear my voice and open to me the door, I will come in to him and will sup with him: and he with me" (Apoc. 3, 20).

And thy father who seeth. Here He gives the reason for the due manner of praying. For no one prays except to Him who sees him. Now God see all things;[58] "All things are naked and open to his eyes, to whom our speech is" (Heb. 4, 13). ***In secret***, [referring to] either [the secrecy] of the heart[59] or of the place, ***will repay thee.***

And when you are praying, etc. Here He teaches to avoid a second fault [in praying], namely, the many words of the Gentiles, and about this He does three things. Firstly, He teaches us to avoid the example of the Gentiles, and secondly, He relates their intention, and thirdly, He gives the reason [for His teaching]. The second part is where it is said, ***For they think that in their much speaking they may be heard***; and the third part is where it is said, ***Be not you therefore like to them***. He says, therefore, ***And when you are praying, speak not much***, and notice that He does not say, 'Do not pray much,' because this would be contrary to that which is said, "Instant in prayer" (Rom. 12, 12), and, "Being in an agony, he prayed the longer" (Lk. 22, 43).

He was praying "the whole night in the prayer of God" (Lk. 6, 12), but He says, ***Speak not much***. Augustine says in his *Letter to Proba*, "There may not be much speaking, but much entreaty"[60] if a fervent intention is not lacking. But many and few, much and little, are relative,[61] for ***much*** can be said in two ways in comparison to prayer, which is "the raising up [of the mind] to God."[62] Or ***they speak much*** when their words exceed their prayer and this happens in two ways, namely, if the words are concerning unlawful

---

56. "This is altogether to make no provision against the enemy; that is when praying to God, to offend God's majesty by the neglectfulness of your prayer." (*On the Lord's Prayer*, iv (PL 4, 539C)).
57. "How can you claim of God to attend to you, when you do not attend to yourself? Shall God remember you in your supplications, when you are forgetful of yourself?" (Ibid.).
58. "REMIG. Let it be enough for you that He alone know your petitions, who knows the secrets of all hearts; for He Who sees all things, the same shall listen to you" (*Catena Aurea on St. Matthew*, chap. 6, lect. 3).
59. "*In secret*: In the inmost heart" (*Interlinear Gloss*).
60. "Let prayer then be without much speaking, but not without much entreaty" (*Ad Probam, de orando Deum*, Ep. 130, x, 20 (PL 33, 502)).
61. "Large and small, many and few, according to the Philosopher, are said relatively" (Quodlibeta IV, q. 12. a. 1. ad 9[um]).
62. Damascene, *De Fide Orth*. iii, 24 (PG 94, 1089C).

things and this is harmful, and when devotion is not present, and then man is made weary and praying is made odious, and wherefore Augustine says that the monks in Egypt had frequent but short prayers.[63] For they saw that devotion was necessary for the one praying, which is emptied out through a multitude of words, and wherefore in the Church it is appointed that various prayers be said at various hours of the day; "Speak not any thing rashly, and let not thy heart be hasty to utter a word before God" (Eccle. 5, 1). Augustine says, "This business, namely prayer, is frequently done with groans rather than with words, etc."[64]

As the heathens. The Gentiles worshipped devils as gods;[65] "All the gods of the Gentiles are devils" (Ps. 95, 5). Regarding the devils, it surely ought to be considered, namely, that they do not know the future[66] or the secrets of hearts except insofar as it is revealed to them.[67] Hence, it was necessary for the Gentiles that they would say everything through words;[68] "Cry with a louder voice: for he is a god; and perhaps he is talking," etc., (III Kings 18, 27).

Likewise, the devils have changeable affections. Hence, they can be changed by words. Hence, Augustine says said that Plato said that the devils were changed by words.[69] God, however, knows

---

63. "Wherefore Augustine says (*ad Probam*, Ep. 130, x, 20 (PL 33, 501)): 'It is said that the brethren in Egypt make frequent but very short prayers, rapid ejaculations, as it were, lest that vigilant and erect attention which is so necessary in prayer slacken and languish, through the strain being prolonged. By so doing they make it sufficiently clear not only that this attention must not be forced if we are unable to keep it up, but also that if we are able to continue, it should not be broken off too soon'" (II II, q. 83, a. 14).
64. "Further on [Augustine *ad Probam*, Ep. 130, x, 20 (PL 33, 502)] says: '... Indeed this business is frequently done with groans rather than with words, with tears rather than with speech.'" (Ibid.).
65. "But the Gentiles, who were serving devils and adoring idols, were praying by trusting in many words" (*Gloss Ordinaria*).
66. "Of the future both the angels of God and the demons are alike ignorant" (Damascene, *De Fide Orthodoxa*, ii, 4 (PG 94, 878B)) cited in *De malo*, q. 16 a. 7 s.c. 1.
67. "As Augustine says, the demons can know the secrets of hearts only in so far as these become known from movements of the body" (*Qu. Disp. de Veritate*, q. 18, a. 4, arg. 14). "Hence Augustine says (*De Divinis Daemon*. v, 9 (PL 40, 586)) that demons 'sometimes with the greatest faculty learn man's dispositions, not only when expressed by speech, but even when conceived in thought, when the soul expresses them by certain signs in the body'; although (*Retractationum* ii, 30 (PL 32, 643)) he says 'it cannot be asserted how this is done'" (I q. 57, 4).
68. "Gloss. ord.: What He condemns is many words in praying that come of want of faith; as the heathens do. For a multitude of words were needful for the heathens, seeing the demons could not know for what they petitioned, until instructed by them; they think they shall be heard for their much speaking" (*Catena Aurea on St. Matthew*, chap. 6, lect. 2).
69. "The same Platonist, when speaking concerning the manners of demons, said that they are agitated with the same perturbations of mind as men; that they are provoked by injuries, propitiated by services and by gifts, rejoice in honors, are delighted with a variety of sacred rites, and are annoyed if any of them be neglected...The demons are flattered by honors; but the true religion commands us by no means to be moved by such things" (*De Civitate Dei*, bk. 8, xvi& xvii (PL 41, 241-242).

all things and is not persuaded by words; "For I am the Lord, and I change not" (Mal. 3, 6); "God is not a man, that he should lie, nor is the son of man, that he should be changed" (Num. 23, 19); and, "Behold among his saints none is unchangeable, and the heavens are not pure in his sight" (Job 15, 15). "I will not spare them, nor their mighty words, and framed to make supplication" (Job 41, 3).[70]

For they think that in their much speaking they may be heard. And why is this? Jerome answers that we do not ask with words so that we may make known, but so that we may request.[71] And again it could be asked: Why do we utter words? Augustine replies that it is one thing which we do in speech to a man and another thing to God, because regarding a man, many words avail in that we persuade him, but in regard to God, many words avail in that we lift up our hearts to Him;[72] and wherefore Augustine says that although affection ought always to be had to God, nevertheless it is sometimes necessary to pray with words so that our affection does not fail.[73] And as Chrysostom says,

---

70. "Although from the words being said to be mighty, and framed for entreaty, the emptiness of their prayer is plainly pointed out. For truly to pray is to utter bitter groans in compunction, and not well arranged words" (Gregory, *Moralia*, xxxiii, 23 (PL 76, 701)).

71. "A heresy has arisen based upon this passage and also upon a perverse doctrine of philosophers, who say: If God knows what we should pray for and is aware of what we need even before we ask for it, then we are speaking in vain to the one who knows. One can respond briefly to these people by saying that [in prayer] we are not narrators but askers. For it is one thing to narrate to one who is ignorant; it is something else to make a request from one who knows. In the former there is the giving of information; in the latter there is obedience. In the former we faithfully inform; in the latter we pitifully implore" (*Comm. in Mt.*, I [PL 26, 42C]).

72. "Every kind of much speaking comes from the Gentiles, who make it their endeavor to exercise the tongue rather than to cleanse the heart. And this kind of useless exertion they endeavor to transfer even to the influencing of God by prayer, supposing that the Judge, just like man, is brought over by words to a certain way of thinking. 'Be not ye, therefore, like unto them,' says the only true Master. 'For your Father knoweth what is needful for you, before you ask him" (Mt. 6, 32). For if many words are made use of with the intent that one who is ignorant may be instructed and taught, what need is there of them for Him who knows all things, to whom all things which exist, by the very fact of their existence, speak, and show themselves as having been brought into existence; and those things which are future do not remain concealed from His knowledge and wisdom, in which both those things which are past, and those things which will yet come to pass, are all present and cannot pass away?" (*De serm. Dom.* II, 3, 12 [PL 34, 1274-1275]).

73. "But again, it may be asked (whether we are to pray in ideas or in words) what need there is for prayer itself, if God already knows what is necessary for us; unless it be that the very effort involved in prayer calms and purifies our heart, and makes it more capacious for receiving the divine gifts, which are poured into us spiritually. For it is not on account of the urgency of our prayers that God hears us, who is always ready to give us His light, not of a material kind, but that which is intellectual and spiritual: but we are not always ready to receive, since we are inclined towards other things, and are involved in darkness through our desire for temporal things" (*De serm. Dom.* II, 3, 14 [PL 34, 1275]).

from frequent prayer it comes that man is rendered intimate with God and God with him;[74] "And when he was gone into the tabernacle of the covenant, the pillar of the cloud came down, and stood at the door, and [the Lord] spoke with Moses," etc., (Ex. 33, 9). Likewise, from this humility proceeds, because God's sublimity and one's own weakness are considered;[75] "I will speak to my Lord, whereas I am dust and ashes" (Gen. 18, 27). Moreover, from this he is directed in his actions and he asks for help from God;[76] "I have lifted up my eyes to the mountains, from whence help shall come to me," etc., (Ps. 120, 1), and, "All whatsoever you do in word or in work, do all in the name of the Lord Jesus Christ, giving thanks to God and the Father by him" (Col. 3, 17).

9. Thus therefore shall you pray: Our Father who art in heaven, hallowed be thy name.
10. Thy kingdom come. Thy will be done on earth as it is in heaven.
11. Give us this day our supersubstantial bread.
12. And forgive us our debts, as we also forgive our debtors.
13. And lead us not into temptation. But deliver us from evil. Amen.
14. For if you will forgive men their offences, your heavenly Father will forgive you also your offences.
15. But if you will not forgive men, neither will your Father forgive you your offences.

Thus therefore shall you pray. Above, the Lord taught the manner of praying, namely, that we avoid both the vanity of hypocrites and the many words of the Gentiles; here He teaches what we ought to ask in prayer, and about this He does two things: firstly, the title of the prayer is related, and secondly, the prayer is put forth. Now He continues what was previously said, as follows: 'I said, "When you are praying, speak not much," etc.;

---

74. "*For He knoweth,* saith He, *what things ye have need of.* And if He know, one may say, what we have need of, wherefore must we pray? Not to instruct Him, but to prevail with Him; to be made intimate with Him, by continuance in supplication; to be humbled; to be reminded of thy sins" (*In Mt.* hom. xix, 5 (PL 57, 278)).

75. "Do thou also therefore, entering as into a palace,–not that on the earth, but what is far more awful than it, that which is in heaven,–show forth great seemliness" (*In Mt.* hom. xix, 4 [PL 57, 277]).

76. "With these then mingle thyself, when thou art praying, and emulate their mystical order. For not unto men art thou praying, but to God, who is everywhere present, who hears even before the voice [speaks], who knows the secrets of the mind. If thou so pray, great is the reward thou shalt receive" (Ibid.).

therefore, in order that you may speak[77] with few words, ***thus shall you pray.*** And observe that the Lord does not say, 'you shall pray,' but, ***thus shall you pray***, for He does not forbid us to pray with other words, but rather He is teaching the manner of praying. And as Augustine says in his *Letter to Proba* concerning prayer, no one prays as he ought unless he ask one of those things that are contained in the Lord's Prayer.[78] Now it is fitting that we pray in these words because, as Cyprian says in his book, *On the Lord's Prayer*, "It is a loving and friendly prayer to beseech God with His own words" and he gives an example that such is customary with lawyers who put words into the mouths of people which they ought to say in court.[79] Hence, this prayer is most trustworthy, as they are words formulated by our Advocate, who is the most wise; "In whom are hid all the treasures of wisdom and knowledge" (Col. 2, 3). Hence, Cyprian says, "And since we have Him as an advocate with the Father for our sins, let us, when as sinners we petition on behalf of our sins, put forward the words of our advocate";[80] "We have an advocate with the Father, Jesus Christ the just" (I Jn. 2, 1). Wherefore it is said, "Let us go therefore with confidence to the throne of grace," etc., (Heb. 4, 16) and, "But let him ask in faith, nothing wavering" (Jam. 1, 6).

And this prayer has three qualities: brevity, perfection and efficacy. It is brief for two reasons. Firstly, it is brief so that all, both the great and the lowly, may easily learn it, because "The same is Lord over all, rich unto all that call upon him" (Rom. 10, 12),[81] and, "The Lord God of hosts shall make a consumption, and an abridgment in the midst of all the land" (Is. 10, 23);[82] and secondly,

---

77. The imperfect tense of "speak" in the text (*loquebaris*) has been changed to the subjunctive tense (*loquaris*) to fit the context. The script in the manuscript itself is somewhat ambiguous as to the form here.
78. *Ad Probam, de orando Deum*, Ep. 130, chap. 12, n. 22 (PL 33, 502). Proba was a wealthy Roman widow and mother of three consuls.
79. Chap. 3; PL 4, 521.
80. "And since we have Him as an Advocate with the Father for our sins, let us, when as sinners we petition on behalf of our sins, put forward the words of our Advocate. For since He says that 'whatsoever we shall ask of the Father in His name, He will give us' (Jn. 16, 23), how much more effectually do we obtain what we ask in Christ's name, if we ask for it in His own prayer!" (Ibid.) Cf. St. Thomas, *In Orationem Dominicam*, prologue.

81. "For when the Word of God, our Lord Jesus Christ, came unto all, and gathering alike the learned and unlearned, published to every sex and every age the precepts of salvation, He made a large compendium of His precepts, that the memory of the scholars might not be burdened in the celestial learning, but might quickly learn what was necessary to a simple faith" (Cyprian, *On the Lord's Prayer*, 28 (ML 4, 538B). More alike to this quotation, the reportation of Leodegar of Besançon has "the learned and the unlearned" instead of "the great and the lowly."
82. The text here has "a short word" (*verbum abbreviatum*) for "abridgment (*adbreviationem*)." Cf. Rom. 9, 28, which has *verbum breviatum*. The quotation has been moved here from following "It is also perfect" according to the context and its placement in the reportation of Leodegar of Besançon.

it is brief so that it may give confidence of more easily obtaining the object of one's prayer.[83] It is also perfect, hence, as Augustine says, whatever can be contained in other prayers, all is contained in this one. Hence, he says, "If we pray rightly, and as becomes our wants, we say nothing but what is already contained in the Lord's Prayer";[84] "The works of God are perfect" (Deut. 32, 4). It is efficacious, because, according to Damascene, prayer is "to ask becoming things of God";[85] "You ask and receive not: because you ask amiss" (James 4, 3). Now to know what ought to be asked is very difficult, as also to know what is to be desired; "For, we know not what we should pray for as we ought: but the Spirit himself asketh for us with unspeakable groanings" (Rom. 8, 26). And because God taught this prayer, it follows that it is most efficacious, and so it is said, "Lord, teach us to pray" (Lk. 11, 1).

Now the Lord does two things in this prayer. Firstly, He sets forth the prayer, and secondly, He assigns an explanation, where it is said, *For if you will forgive men their offences*.

It ought to be known that in every speech, even of rhetoricians, before a petition benevolence is won.[86] Hence, as it happens in a speech (*oratio*) which is made to men, so likewise it ought to be done in a prayer (*oratio*) which is made to God, but the intention differs, because in man benevolence is won inasmuch as we bend his soul,[87] but in God it is inasmuch as we lift up our soul to Him. Therefore the Lord sets forth two phrases for winning benevolence, which are necessary for the one praying. For it is necessary that he believe Him from Whom he asks, and that He from Whom he asks be willing and able to give. And therefore He puts forth the words, *Father*, and, *who art in heaven*.[88] Now the fact that He

---

83. "[The Lord] composed the prayer with brief words so that we might become confident of quickly obtaining a nod of assent, because He wishes to be asked briefly" (*Bibliorum Sacrorum cum Glossa Ordinaria (1603)*, p. 127B).
84. *Ad Probam, de orando Deum*, Ep. 130, chap. 12, n. 22 *Ad Probam* (PL 33, 502).
85. *De Fide Orthodoxa* iii, 24.
86. This "winning of benevolence" is called in Latin a *captatio benevolentiae*. "Seeing that in all prayer we have to conciliate the goodwill of him to whom we pray, then to say what we pray for; goodwill is usually conciliated by our offering praise to him to whom the prayer is directed, and this is usually put in the beginning of the prayer: and in this particular our Lord has bidden us say nothing else but 'Our Father who art in heaven'" (Augustine, *De serm. Dom.*, Lib. II, cap. 4, n. 15 (PL 34, 1275)). "But before coming to the petitions, a captivation of good will is put first into the mouth of the one praying, namely the words, 'Our Father' (St. Bernard of Clairveax, *Expositio in Orationem Domiinicam*, 1 (PL 184, 813B).
87. "By prayer we bend the mind (*anima*) of the person to whom we pray, so that he may do what is asked of him" (II II, q. 83, a. 2 arg. 2). N.B. Mind and soul are the same word in Latin, i.e. *anima*.
88. "And to show that He is willing, He says, *Father*: for if He is a father, He wants the good of His children. He shows that He is able, adding, *Who art in heaven*: for if He is in heaven, He is able to do what He wishes to do" (taken from the reportation of Leodegar of Besançon).

says *Father* serves five purposes. Firstly, it serves for instruction regarding the Faith; for faith is necessary for the one praying.

Now there were three errors by which prayer was excluded: the first two were nearly destroying prayer and the third was giving to prayer more than it was due; and they are excluded by the fact that He says, *Our Father*. For some men said that God does not care about human affairs; "The Lord hath forsaken the earth, and the Lord seeth not" (Ez. 9, 9). Hence, according to this error, it is vain that something be asked of God. Others said that God does not have providence, but providence itself[89] imposes a necessity upon things. The third error was giving more to prayer than it was due, because it asserted that God disposes all things by His providence, but by prayer the Divine disposition is changed.[90]

Now, He eliminates all these errors when He says, *Our Father who art in heaven*, because if He is *our Father*, then He has providence; "But thy providence, O Father, governeth it: for thou hast made a way even in the sea, and a most sure path among the waves" (Wis. 14, 3). Likewise, the second error is eliminated, for a man is called a father by relation to his son, and a man is called a master by relation to his servant.[91] Thus by the fact that we say, *Father*, we call ourselves His children. For we scarcely ever find in Sacred Scripture that God is called the father of insensible creatures, though there is an exception where it is said, "Who is the father of rain? or who begot the drops of dew?" (Job 38, 28). Therefore, He is called a father by relation to His sons, and by this fact we call ourselves His children. For a son has the notion of liberty; wherefore necessity is not imposed upon us.[92]

By the fact that He says, *in heaven*, a changeable disposition [in God] is excluded. Now prayer avails for this, as we may believe that God so disposes all things according to what befits the natures of things. For it is from His providence that man by his actions obtains his end; hence, prayer neither changes providence nor is outside of providence, but falls within it. Firstly, this prayer avails for the instruction of our faith. Secondly, it avails for the support of our hope. For if He is a *Father*, then He wishes to

---

89. The text reads *illa*, meaning "that," but it more likely should be *ipsa*, "itself," here based on a parallel passage in I, q. 103, a. 6.
90. cf. II II, q. 83, a. 2.
91. "'Master' and 'servant' is the classical example of the kind of relative term described by Aristotle in *Cat.* 7 (6b28-33), that is, terms which are mutually dependent (if there is no servant there can be no master and vice versa)." (Simon Tugwell, *Albert & Thomas: selected writings*, p. 457).
92. "Just as this fear produces servitude, so the love of charity produces the liberty of sons. For it makes a man to perform voluntary deeds for God's honor, which belongs properly to sons" (*Super Ep. ad Romanos*, chap. 8, lect. 3).

give, because, as it is written below, "If you then being evil, know how to give good gifts to your children: how much more will your Father who is in heaven, give good things to them that ask him?" (7, 11).[93] Thirdly, it avails for stirring up charity.[94] For it is natural that a father loves his son and vice versa. "Be ye therefore followers of God, as most dear children" (Eph. 5, 1). Wherefore by this word we are provoked to imitate Him. For a son ought to imitate his father as much as he can; "Thou shalt call me father and shalt not cease to walk after me" (Jer. 3, 19). Fourthly, by this word we are provoked to humility; "If then I be a father, where is my honour?" (Mal. 1, 6). Fifthly, by this word our affections are directed to our neighbor, since if there is one Father of all men, someone ought not to scorn his neighbor by reason of his race;[95] "Have we not all one father? hath not one God created us? why then doth every one of us despise his brother?" (Mal. 2, 10).

But why do we not say, 'My father'? The reason is twofold. Firstly, it is because Christ wanted to reserve this expression for Himself, because He is His Son by nature, but we are sons through adoption, which is common to all men; "I ascend to my Father and to your Father, to my God and to your God" (Jn. 20, 17), because in one way He is Mine, and in another way He is yours.[96] Secondly, it is because, according to Chrysostom, the Lord teaches us not to make private prayers but to pray commonly for the whole people, which prayer is in fact more acceptable to God.[97] Hence, Chrysostom says, "Necessity binds us to pray for ourselves, fraternal charity urges us to pray for others: and the prayer that fraternal charity proffers is sweeter to God than that which is the outcome of necessity," etc.[98] "Pray one for another, that you may be saved. For the continual prayer of a just man availeth much," etc., (James 5, 16).

A second phrase which pertains to winning benevolence is, **Who art in heaven**. Which phrase can be expounded in two

---

93. "For what would He not now give to sons when they ask, when He has already granted this very thing, namely, that they might be sons?" (Augustine, *De serm. Dom.*, Lib. II, cap. 4, n. 16 (PL 34, 1276)).

94. "We put this very same grace in the beginning of our prayer, when we say 'Our Father.' And by that appellation both love is stirred up--for what ought to be dearer to sons than a father?" (Ibid.)

95. This last phrase, "since... race," is taken from the reportation of Leodegar of Besançon.

96. This last phrase, "because... yours," is taken from Leodegar of Besançon.

97. "He teaches, moreover, to make our prayer common, on behalf of our brethren also. For He saith not, 'my Father, which art in Heaven,' but, 'our Father,' offering up his supplications for the body in common, and nowhere looking to his own, but everywhere to his neighbor's good" (Hom. xix, n. 5 (PG 56, 711)).

98. Psuedo-Chrysostom, *Op. imp. in Mt.*, Hom. xiv.

ways. Firstly, it can be expounded literally, so that we understand *heaven* to be the corporeal heavens; but we do not understand that He is contained therein, because it is written, "Do not I fill heaven and earth, saith the Lord?" (Jer. 23, 24). But *Who art in heaven* is said on account of the eminence of this creature according to that which is written, "Heaven is my throne" (Is. 66, 1). Likewise, by this phrase they are instructed who are unable to be elevated above corporeal things,[99] and thus Augustine says that this is the reason why we adore towards the East, because from the East the heavens arise; and just as heaven is above our body, so God is above our spirit. Hence, it is given to be understood that our spirit ought to be turned towards God Himself, just as our body is turned towards that part of heaven when praying.[100] Now He says, *Who art in heaven*, to lift up your intention from earthly things;[101] "Unto an inheritance, incorruptible, and undefiled and that cannot fade, reserved in heaven for you" (I Pet. 1, 4).

Or, by the heavens, the saints are understood,[102] according to that which is said, "Hear, O ye heavens, and give ear, O earth, for the Lord hath spoken" (Is. 1, 2), and, "But thou dwellest in the holy place, the praise of Israel" (Ps. 21, 4). And He says this for greater confidence of impetrating, because He is not far from us; "But thou, O Lord, art among us, and thy name is called upon by us, forsake us not" (Jer. 14, 9).

Hallowed be thy name. Here, having won benevolence,[103] the petitions are related, and let us discuss them firstly in general, and afterwards in detail. In these petitions we ought to consider three things. For a petition serves a desire: for we ask for those things which we wish to have. Now in this prayer is contained everything whatsoever that we can desire. Secondly, the order in which we ought to desire is contained. A third point is that these petitions correspond to the gifts and the beatitudes.[104]

Now, it ought to be known that man naturally desires two things, namely, to obtain what is good and avoid what is evil. Now,

---

99. "And therefore, as regards those who as yet are taken up with the beauties that are seen, and cannot think of anything incorporeal, inasmuch as they must necessarily prefer heaven to earth, their opinion is more tolerable, if they believe God, whom as yet they think of after a corporeal fashion, to be in heaven rather than upon earth" (Augustine, *De serm. Dom.* II, 5, 18 (PL 34, 1277)).
100. ibid.
101. "But when He saith, 'in Heaven,' He speaks not this as shutting up God there, but as withdrawing him who is praying from earth, and fixing him in the high places, and in the dwellings above" (Chrysostom, *Hom.* xix, 5).
102. "Let the new people, therefore, who are called to an eternal inheritance, use the word of the New Testament, and say, 'Our Father who art in heaven,' i.e., in the holy and the just" (Augustine, *De serm. Dom.* 5, 17 (PL 34, 1276)).
103. This clause is taken from the reportation of Leodegar of Besançon.
104. cf. *De serm. Dom.* II, 11, 38 (PL 34, 1286).

four goods are set forth here to be desired. Now, a desire tends to the end before tending to those things which are ordained to the end.[105] Now, the ultimate end of all things is God. Hence, the first thing to be desired is God; "Do all to the glory of God" (I Cor. 10, 31). And we ask for this here, *Hallowed be thy name*. Among those things which pertain to us, the last end is eternal life; and we ask for this when we say, *Thy kingdom come*. The third thing which we ought to ask is about those things which are ordained to the end, namely, that we have virtue and good works, and this is where it is said, *Thy will be done on earth as it is in heaven*. And what we ask regarding the virtues is nothing else but this. Therefore, our beatitude is ordained to God, and our virtues are ordained to our beatitude. But it is necessary to have help, be it temporal or spiritual, such as the sacraments of the Church, and we ask for this where it is said, *Give us this day our supersubstantial bread*, meaning our exterior or sacramental bread. In these four things every good is contained. Man avoids evil insofar as it is impeditive to good. Now the first good, namely, the Divine honor, cannot be impeded, because if justice occurs then God is honored, and if evil occurs, God is likewise honored insofar as He punishes it, although He would not be honored as to the evil in the one sinning. Now sin impedes beatitude, and thus He firstly eliminates this when He says, *And forgive us our debts*. Temptation is contrary to the good of the virtues, and therefore we ask, *And lead us not into temptation*. Any deficiency is contrary to the needs of life, and so it is said, *But deliver us from evil*. Therefore it is evident that whatever things are desired, the Lord's Prayer contains them all.

And it ought to be known that the gifts of the Holy Ghost can be associated with these petitions, but in different ways, because they can be associated by ascending and descending, such that the first petition is associated with fear, which produces poverty of spirit and makes one seek God's honor, and therefore we say, *Hallowed be thy name*, (by descending, so that we may say that the last gift, namely, wisdom which makes us sons of God, may be associated to this petition. But this ought to be seen [when it will be treated] concerning this petition, *Hallowed be thy name*).

Now this word, *hallowed*, seems to be unfitting, for God's name is always holy; why, therefore, do we request it?[106] And it

---

105. "Thus it is evident that the first thing to be the object of our desire is the end, and afterwards whatever is directed to the end." (II II, q. 83, a. 9).

106. This last clause is taken from the reportation of Leodegar of Besançon.

ought to be known that this word is expounded by the Saints in multiple ways. Firstly, it is expounded by Augustine as follows, and I believe that his exposition is more literal. **Hallowed be thy name**, meaning, may the name which is always holy appear holy among men.[107] And this is to honor God. For as a result of this, glory does not increase for God, but the knowledge of that glory increases for us; "For as thou hast been sanctified in us in their sight, so thou shalt be magnified among them in our presence," etc., (Eccli. 36, 4). And it is quite appropriate that after, **Our Father who art in heaven**, He says, **Hallowed be thy name**, because nothing else so proves that we are sons of God. For a good son shows the father's honor.[108] According to Chrysostom, it is said, **Hallowed be thy name**, meaning through our works, as though we were to say, 'Make us live in such a way that from our works Thy name may appear holy';[109] "Sanctify the Lord Christ in your hearts" (I Pet. 3, 15). Or, according to Cyprian, when it is said, **Hallowed be thy name**, the meaning is, 'sanctify us in Thy name';[110] "And he shall be a sanctification to you" (Is. 8, 14).

And it ought to be known that **Hallowed** is firstly understood such that they who are not holy become holy. For this prayer is made for all mankind; secondly, when it is said, **Hallowed**, the meaning is, may they persevere in holiness; and thirdly, when it is said, **Hallowed**, the meaning is that if something is admixed in our holiness, may it be removed. For we are in want of holiness every day on account of our daily sins.

Thy kingdom come. This petition corresponds either to the gift of understanding, which cleanses the heart,[111] or to the gift of piety.[112] **Thy kingdom come**. According to Chrysostom and Augustine, the kingdom of God is eternal life, and I believe that this is the literal exposition; therefore we ask that God's

---

107. "'Hallowed be Thy name.' And this is prayed for, not as if the name of God were not holy already, but that it may be held holy by men; i.e., that God may so become known to them, that they shall reckon nothing more holy, and which they are more afraid of offending" (*De serm. Dom.* II, 5, 19 (PL 34, 1277)).

108. "The name of a father is shown in his sons by their life and morals" (*Glossa ordinaria*, Patrologiae Cursus Completus, 100D).

109. "For 'hallowed' is glorified. For His own glory He hath complete, and ever continuing the same, but He commands him who prays to seek that He may be glorified also by our life" (Hom. xix, n. 7).

110. "After this we say, 'Hallowed be Thy name'; not that we wish for God that He may be hallowed by our prayers, but that we beseech of Him that His name may be hallowed in us" (*On the Lord's prayer*, xii; PL 4, 526).

111. "Here the spirit of understanding is requested, by which the heart is cleansed so that God may be seen" (*Glossa Ordinaria (1603)*, p. 130E).

112. "If it is piety through which the meek are blessed, inasmuch as they shall inherit the earth; let us ask that His kingdom may come" (Augustine, *De serm. Dom.* II, 11, 38 (PL 34, 1286)).

kingdom *come*, that is to say, make us arrive at and share in eternal beatitude;[113] "Come, ye blessed of my Father, possess you the kingdom prepared for you from the foundation of the world" (below 25, 34), and, "And I dispose to you, as my Father hath disposed to me, a kingdom" (Lk. 22, 29).

Or it may be expounded otherwise, also according to Augustine. *Thy kingdom come*. He began to reign from the time when He redeemed the world;[114] "Now is the judgment of the world: now shall the prince of this world be cast out. And I, if I be lifted up from the earth, will draw all things to myself" (Jn. 12, 31-32),[115] and, "All power is given to me in heaven and in earth" (Mt. 28, 18). Therefore, *Thy kingdom come*, meaning, 'May the consummation of Thy kingdom come.'[116] And this will be when He puts all His enemies under His feet.[117] Hence, *come*, meaning, 'Lord, may Thou come to judgment so that Thy kingdom may appear'; "But when these things begin to come to pass, look up and lift up your heads, because your redemption is at hand," etc., (Lk. 21, 28). And the Saints desire Christ's coming, because then they will possess perfect glory;[118] "There is laid up for me a crown of justice which the Lord the just judge will render to me in that day: and not only to me, but to them also that love his coming" (II Tim. 4, 8).

But on the contrary, it is said, "Woe to them that desire the day of the Lord: to what end is it for you? the day of the Lord

---

113. "The kingdom of God is said to be the reward or suffering that the just receive as a reward for their righteousness or sinners for the fault of their sins" (Pseudo-Chrysostom, *Op. Imp. in Mt.* 14, (PG 56, 711). "When we say: 'Thy kingdom come,' which shall certainly come whether we wish it or not, we do by these words stir up our own desires for that kingdom, that it may come to us, and that we may be found worthy to reign in it." (Augustine, *Ep.* 130, chap. 11, n. 21 (PL 33, 502)).

114. "'The Lord hath reigned, let the people be angry.' For our Lord Jesus Christ began to reign, [meaning] He began to be preached, after He rose from the dead and ascended into heaven, after He filled His disciples with the confidence of the Holy Ghost, so that they would not fear death, which He now had killed in Himself." (Augustine, *Ennaratio in Psalmum 98*, 2 (PL 37, 1258)).

115. The only reference here is to "John," so this citation may not be correct here.

116. "'Thy kingdom come.' Come it surely will, whether we ask or no. Indeed, God hath an eternal kingdom. For when did He not reign? When did He begin to reign? For His kingdom hath no beginning, neither shall it have any end. But that we may know that in this prayer also we pray for ourselves, and not for God (for we do not say, 'Thy kingdom come,' as though we were asking that God may reign); we shall be ourselves His kingdom, if believing in Him we make progress in this faith. All the faithful, redeemed by the Blood of His Only Son, will be His kingdom. And this His kingdom will come, when the resurrection of the dead shall have taken place; for then He will come Himself." (*Sermons on the New Testament*, Serm. 7 [LVII. Ben.], n. 5).

117. "For he must reign, until he hath put all his enemies under his feet" (I Cor. 15, 25).

118. "Then will the blessed life in all its parts be perfected in the saints unto eternity" (Augustine, *De serm. Dom.* II, 6, 20 (PL 34, 1278)).

is darkness, and not light" (Amos 5, 18),[119] because it belongs only, according to Jerome, to the secure conscience not to fear the Judge.[120]

Or, ***Thy kingdom come***, meaning may the kingdom of sin be destroyed, and Thou, O Lord, reign over us. For when we serve justice, God reigns; when, however, we serve sin, the devil reigns; "Let not sin therefore reign in your mortal body" (Rom. 6, 12), and, "For they have not rejected thee, but me, that I should not reign over them" (I Kings 8, 7).[121]

And observe that they were very justly asking ***Thy kingdom come***, who had proven themselves to be sons by saying, ***Our Father***, etc.[122] For an inheritance is due to sons; but this kingdom is in heaven, hence, you cannot go there unless you are made heavenly. And therefore He afterwards adds, ***Thy will be done on earth as it is in heaven***, that is to say, 'Make us to be imitators of heavenly things'; "Therefore, as we have borne the image of the earthly, let us bear also the image of the heavenly" (I Cor. 15, 49).

And observe that He does not say, ***Thy will be done***, as though He were to say, 'May God do our will.' But it is as though He were to say, 'May God fulfill His will through us,' which is, "Who will have all men to be saved and to come to the knowledge of the truth" (I Tim. 2, 4), "For this is the will of God, your sanctification" (I Thess. 4, 3), and, "Teach me to do thy will, for thou art my God. Thy good spirit shall lead me into the right land" (Ps. 142, 10). Hence, we ask that God's will be executed by us; and this would be frustrated, except that it was from God; and therefore it is said: ***Thy will be done***, because God works in

---

119. "The confidence of the proud is struck down at the same time, who, in order that they may appear just before men, are accustomed to wait for the Judgment Day, and say, 'O, that the Lord may come; O, that it may be granted to us to be dissolved and to be with Christ' (Phil. 1, 23), imitating the Pharisee who was saying in the Gospel, 'O God, I give thee thanks that I am not as the rest of men'... For from the very fact that they desire the day of the Lord, and they are not terrified, they are judged deserving of punishment, because no one among men is without sin, and 'the stars are not pure in his sight' (Job 25, 5)... Certainly if their own conscience would not also vex them, they would have imitated Paul saying, 'Who is weak, and I am not weak? Who is scandalized, and I am not on fire?' (II Cor. 11, 29)" (*Comm. in Amos Prophetam Libri Tres*, (PL 25, 1052B)).

120. "And at the same time it must be observed that it would be proper to great audacity and to a pure conscience to ask for the kingdom of God and not to fear the Judgment" (*Comm. in Mt.*, I (PL 26, 43A)).

121. "*Thy kingdom come*. Or He asks in general for the kingdom of the whole world, that the devil would cease to reign in the world, or that God would reign in everyone, and sin would not reign in the mortal body of man (Rom. 6)" (Ibid.).

122. "GLOSS. It follows suitably, that after our adoption as sons, we should ask a kingdom which is due to sons" (*Catena Aurea on St. Matthew*, chap. 6, lect. 6).

us.[123] In which words the error of Pelagius[124] is destroyed, who was saying that we do not need Divine help.

As it is in heaven. These words are expounded by Augustine in multiple ways. Firstly, it is as follows. *As it is in heaven*, meaning, 'As the Angels in heaven do Thy will, so may we fulfill Thy will on earth';[125] concerning the Angels it is said, "Bless the Lord, all ye his hosts: you ministers of his that do his will" (Ps. 102, 21). In which words the error of Origen is destroyed, who asserted that an angel is able to sin.[126]

Or it may be expounded otherwise. *Thy will be done on earth as it is in heaven*, meaning as it is done in Christ, so may it be done in the Church.[127] For the earth is fertilized by heaven. Hence, the pagans were also saying that the gods of the heavens were male and the gods of the earth were female; "I came down from heaven, not to do my own will but the will of him that sent me" (Jn. 6, 38).

Or, by the heavens is understood the saints, whose "conversation is in heaven" (Phil. 3, 20). Now as the relationship is of heaven to earth, so the relationship is of saints to sinners. It is as though it were said, 'Lord, convert sinners to doing Thy will.'[128]

---

123. This sentence is taken from the reportation of Leodegar of Besançon. "We also say in addition: 'Thy will be done in heaven as it is on earth,' not that God may do what He wishes, but that we may be able to do what God wishes... we pray and petition that God's will be done in us." (Cyprian, *On the Lord's Prayer*, 14 (PL .4, 528C)).
124. Pelagius (c. 360-420) denied original sin as well as the necessity of grace. Consequently he held that man's free will without grace is sufficient for salvation. Pelagianism was condemned by the Council of Ephesus in 431. Cf. Augustine: "The beginning of faith also is God's gift, since the holy Church prays not only for believers, that faith may be increased or may continue in them, but, moreover, for unbelievers, that they may begin to have what they have not had at all, and against which, besides, they were indulging hostile feelings" (*On the Gift of Perseverance*, chap. 3, n. 6 (PL 45, 997) and quoted in *Catena Aurea on St. Matthew*, chap. 6, lect. 6).
125. *De serm. Dom.* II, 6, 21 (PL 34, 1278).
126. "'Thy will be done, on earth as it is in heaven.' In the same way that the angels serve Thee guiltlessly in heaven, so may men serve Thee on earth. Let them be ashamed from this sentence, they who lie saying that downfalls occur daily in heaven, as though there is also sin in heaven" (Jerome, *In Mt.* I (PL 26, 43B).
127. "'Thy will be done as in heaven so in earth,' as in our Lord Jesus Christ Himself, so also in the Church: as if one were to say, 'As in the man who fulfilled the will of the Father, so also in the woman who is betrothed to him.' For heaven and earth are suitably understood as if they were man and wife; since the earth is fruitful from the heaven fertilizing it" (*De serm. Dom.* II, 6, 24 (PL 34, 1279)).
128. "If God dwells in His temple, and the saints are His temple, the expression 'which art in heaven' is rightly used in the sense, which art in the saints. And most suitable is such a similitude, so that spiritually there may be seen to be as great a difference between the righteous and sinners, as there is materially between heaven and earth... so that it is said, 'Thy will be done as in heaven so on earth,' –as if the meaning were, 'As the righteous do Thy will, in like manner let sinners also do it, so that they may be converted unto Thee'" (*De serm. Dom.* II, 5, 17 & 6, 22 (PL 34, 1277 & 1279)).

Or, ***Thy will be done***, etc. For as heaven is compared in the world[129] to the earth, so the spirit is compared to the flesh in man; the spirit, in and of itself, does God's will, but the flesh resists God's will;[130] "But I see another law in my members, fighting against the law of my mind and captivating me in the law of sin that is in my members" (Rom. 7, 23), and, "Create a clean heart in me, O God: and renew a right spirit within my bowels" (Ps. 50, 12). All these petitions are partly begun now, but will be fulfilled in the life to come.[131]

Chrysostom, however, says that these words, namely, ***as it is in heaven***, refer to all the preceding words. Hence, ***Thy kingdom come, as it is in heaven*** and in like manner as regards the other petitions.[132] Likewise, according to Chrysostom, observe that He did not say, 'let us hallow,' nor 'sanctify,' but spoke in a middle form of speech. Nor did He say, 'let us go to the kingdom,' but ***Thy kingdom come***. So in all the forms of speech He held the middle place, and He did this because two things are required for our salvation: God's grace and free will. Hence, if He had said, 'hallow,' there would have been no place for free will; on the other hand, if He had said, 'let us do Thy will,' He would have given all place to free will, but He spoke in a middle form of speech and so here it is said, ***Thy will be done***, and so forth.[133]

Give us this day our supersubstantial bread. After He taught to ask for God's glory, eternal life and the practice of the virtue by which we merit eternal life, here He teaches all the things that are necessary for the present life. Now these words, ***Give us this day our supersubstantial bread***, can be expounded in four ways. In the first way, it is expounded concerning the bread which is Christ;[134] "I am the bread of life," etc., (Jn. 6, 35 & 6, 48),

---

129. "World" (κόσμος) was a synonym for the "universe" and also "the cosmos" among the ancient Greek philosophers. So it is used elsewhere by St. Thomas, e.g. "... the immobility of the earth in the middle of the world" (I II, q. 13, a. 6).

130. "We are to take heaven and earth in the sense of spirit and flesh... Let the will of God be done on earth, as it is in heaven; i.e., in such a way that, in like manner as the spirit does not resist God, but follows and does His will, so the body also may not resist the spirit or soul" (*De serm. Dom.* II, 6, 23 (PL 34, 1279)).

131. "Although the three first petitions begin to be answered in this life... those three things will remain consummated and thoroughly completed in that life which is promised us" (Augustine, *De serm. Dom.* II, 10, 36 (PL 34, 1285)).

132. "PSEUDO-CHRYS. These words, *As in heaven so on earth*, must be taken as common to all three preceding petitions" (*Catena Aurea on St. Matthew*, chap. 6, lect. 6 (PG 56, 712)).

133. "PSEUDO-CHRYS. He used a middle form of speech, and the impersonal verb; for as man can do nothing good without God's aid, so neither does God work good in man unless man wills it." (ibid.)

134. "'Give us this day'... is put for the sacrament of the body of Christ, which we daily receive" (Augustine, *De serm. Dom.* II, 7, 25 (PL 34, 1280)). The *Glossa Ordinaria* here quotes Tertullian and the referred quotation is, "We may

who is especially the bread according to which He is contained in the Sacrament of the altar; "The bread that I will give is my flesh, for the life of the world" (Jn. 6, 52), and again in the same place it is said, "For my flesh is meat indeed" (verse 56).

And He says, *Our*, because it does not belong to anyone at all but to the faithful;[135] "For a child is given to us" (Is. 9, 6). For from the fact that someone becomes a member of Christ in Baptism, he can share this bread. And therefore in no way ought it to be given to unbaptized infidels.

Supersubstantial bread. Jerome says that in Greek the word is *epiousion* (ἐπιούσιον), and Symmachus[136] translates this word as 'chief' or 'excellent.' The old translation,[137] however, has the word *daily*. Now what would be **supersubstantial**, meaning above all substances, is clear; "Which he wrought in Christ... setting him on his right hand in the heavenly places" (Eph. 1, 20). He says *daily* because it ought to be received daily, but not by everyone. Hence, it is said in the book *De Ecclesiasticis Dogmatibus*, "I neither praise nor blame [daily reception of the Eucharist]."[138]

But the Eucharist ought to be received daily in the Church; or it ought to be spiritually received by the faithful daily by faith.

rather understand, 'Give us this day our daily bread,' spiritually. For Christ is our Bread; because Christ is Life, and bread is life" (Tertullian, *On Prayer*, Chap. 6 (PL 1, 1262B-1263A).

135. Cyprian, *On the Lord's Prayer*, 18 (PL .4, 532A).

136. According to Epiphanius, Symmachus (fl. late 2nd century) was a Samaritan. He was the author of one of the Greek versions of the Old Testament included by Origen in his *Hexapla* and *Tetrapla*. He was admired by Jerome for his excellent Greek, who used his work in composing the Vulgate.

137. "JEROME; in the Gospel, entitled *The Gospel according to the Hebrews, supersubstantialis* is rendered *mohar*, that is, 'tomorrow's'; so that the sense would be, 'Give us today tomorrow's bread'—i.e., for the time to come" (*Catena Aurea on St. Matthew*, chap. 6, lect. 7). Cf. *Comm. in Mt.*, I (PL 26, 43B). It is disputed whether the Gospel according to the Hebrews is an original Hebrew version of St. Matthew's Gospel. Though Eusebius rejects this, St. Jerome asserts this. "And among these some have placed also the Gospel according to the Hebrews, with which those of the Hebrews that have accepted Christ are especially delighted. And all these may be reckoned among the disputed books" (Eusebius, *Church History*, bk. III, chap. 25, n. 5). "In the Gospel according to the Hebrews, which is written in the Chaldee and Syrian language, but in Hebrew characters, and is used by the Nazarenes to this day (I mean the Gospel according to the Apostles, or, as is generally maintained, the Gospel according to Matthew, a copy of which is in the library at Caesarea)..." (*Against Pelagius* 3, 2; PL 23, 597B).

138. "Daily communion I neither praise nor blame, but I exhort all to receive every Sunday. But if the mind is set on sin, it will be dragged down by receiving the Eucharist rather than purified. Therefore, although someone is remorseful for sin, if his will is turned away from sin, and he satisfies for it by tears and prayers, trusting in the Lord's mercy, he may approach the Eucharist with confidence and security. But I am speaking of someone who is not guilty of mortal sins" (Gennadius of Massilia, *De Eccl. Dogm.*, Chap. LIII. (PL 58, 994B)). This passage was selected by St. Thomas as part of the third lesson of Matins for the third day of the Octave of Corpus Christi (*Officium Sacerdos*, octav. 1 dies 3, lect. 3).

In the Eastern Church, however, it is not received daily in the Church, because Mass is not celebrated daily, in fact, it is only celebrated once a week.[139] But because the Church permits this, it suffices that they receive spiritually and not sacramentally.

Give us. If this bread is ours, why does He say, *Give us?* Cyprian replies, *Give us,* meaning make us so live that we can receive this bread for our profit. Hence, he who asks this, asks for nothing other than for perseverance in good, that is to say, so that there may be nothing opposed to sanctity in him;[140] "For he that eateth and drinketh unworthily eateth and drinketh judgment to himself," etc., (I Cor. 11, 29).

Here Augustine objects that this prayer is said at any hour of the day, even at the last hour of the day; therefore are we asking that He give us this bread then, at that time?[141] But I reply, saying that *this day* is taken in two ways. For sometimes it signifies a determinate day, and other times it signifies the whole present life; "Wherefore, as the Holy Ghost saith: To-day if you shall hear his voice" (Heb. 3, 7) is referring to a determinate day. Hence, the meaning is, 'Give us that in the present life we may be able to partake of this bread.'

And He says with reason, *Give us this day our supersubstantial bread,* because this sacramental bread is very necessary in this life. For when we will see Him as He is, we will not need sacraments and signs. Hence, this unique and special bread is very necessary in the present life; and now we receive it at certain times, but then continually. Secondly, by **bread,** God is understood, more precisely His divinity;[142] "Blessed is he that shall eat bread in the kingdom of God" (Lk. 14, 15), and, "Man ate the bread of angels: he sent them provisions in abundance" (Ps. 77, 25). Therefore, *Give us this day our supersubstantial*

---

139. Augustine, *De serm. Dom.* II, 7, 26 (PL 34, 1280).
140. "We ask that this bread be given daily, lest we, who are in Christ and receive the Eucharist daily as food of salvation, with the intervention of some more weighty sin, while we are shut off and as non-communicants are kept from the heavenly bread... And so we petition that our bread, that is Christ, be given us daily, so that we, who abide and live in Christ, may not withdraw from His sanctification and body" (*Treatise on the Lord's Prayer,* xviii (PL 4, 531A)).
141. "And since this is the case, who is there who would venture to say that we ought only once to use the Lord's Prayer, or at least that, even if we have used it a second or a third time before the hour at which we partake of the Lord's body, afterwards we are assuredly not so to pray during the remaining hours of the day? For we shall no longer be able to say, 'Give us this day,' respecting what we have already received; or every one will be able to compel us to celebrate that sacrament at the very last hour of the day" (*De serm. Dom.* II, 7, 26 (PL 34, 1280)).
142. "We can also understand *supersubstantial bread* otherwise, [that is to say, it is He] who is above all substances, and is above all creatures" (Jerome, *Comm. in Mt.,* I (PL 26, 43C)).

bread, namely, so that according to the manner of the present life we can enjoy Him. Thirdly, by ***bread*** can be understood God's precepts, which are the bread of wisdom; "Come, eat my bread, and drink the wine which I have mingled for you. Forsake childishness, and live, and walk by the ways of prudence" (Prov. 9, 5-6). For he eats bread, who keeps the precepts of wisdom; "My meat is to do the will of him that sent me" (Jn. 4, 34). These divine precepts are now bread, because they are ground with a certain difficulty by considering and working, but afterwards they will be a drink, because they will refresh without difficulty.[143] Fourthly, by ***bread***, corporeal bread is literally understood.[144] For the Lord had said, ***Thy will be done***, and He wanted us to be heavenly in fulfilling the Divine will; but mindful of our fragility, He teaches us to ask also for temporal things which are necessary for our livelihood. Hence, He does not teach us to ask for magnificent or superfluous things, but for necessary things; "But having food and wherewith to be covered, with these we are content" (I Tim. 6, 8). So also Jacob asked for necessary things; "And he made a vow, saying: If God shall be with me, and shall keep me in the way, by which I walk, and shall give me bread to eat, and raiment to put on, and I shall return prosperously to my father's house: the Lord shall be my God" (Gen. 28, 20-21).

Now He says ***Our*** for two reasons. He says that no one may appropriate temporal things for himself, according to Chrysostom, firstly, because no one ought to eat bread from robbery, but from one's own labor; secondly, because we so ought to receive temporal goods, which are given on account of necessity, that we share them with others; "If I have eaten my morsel alone, and the fatherless hath not eaten thereof" (Job 31, 17).[145]

143. "For perhaps for this reason also it is called bread, not drink, because bread is converted into aliment by breaking and masticating it, just as the Scriptures feed the soul by being opened up and made the subject of discourse; but drink, when prepared, passes as it is into the body: so that at present the truth is bread, when it is called daily bread; but then it will be drink, when there will be no need of the labour of discussing and discoursing, as it were of breaking and masticating, but merely of drinking unmingled and transparent truth" (Augustine, *De serm. Dom.* II, 10, 37 (PL 34, 1285)).

144. "Others simply think [that the meaning is that], according to the words of the Apostle saying, 'But having food and wherewith to be covered, with these we are content,' the saints only take care about food for the present [day]. Hence, in the following words is the precept, 'Be not therefore solicitous for to morrow' (verse 34)"(Jerome, *Comm. in Mt.*, I (PL 26, 43C)).

145. "PSEUDO-CHRYS. He says *Our* for two reasons. First, because all things that God gives us He gives through us to others, that of what we receive of Him we may impart to the helpless. Whoever, then, of what he gains by his own toil, bestows nothing on others, eats not his own bread only, but others' bread also. Secondly, he who eats bread got righteously, eats his own bread; but he who eats bread got with sin, eats others' bread" (*Catena Aurea on St. Matthew*, chap. 6, lect. 7).

But what is the reason that He says, *Supersubstantial*? And Augustine says, that from the fact that bread is excellent and principal among all the various things that we need for our support, it follows that bread signifies the whole of these things.[146] For bread is the most necessary thing for man; "The chief thing for man's life is water and bread, and clothing, and a house to cover shame" (Eccli. 29, 27). And for this reason it is called, *supersubstantial*, because it principally pertains to necessary things.

Now if you say, *Daily*, then it has a twofold meaning, according to Cyprian. Firstly, it means that you ought not to seek temporal things for a long time, because otherwise you would contradict yourself. For you said, *Thy kingdom come*, and by asking for a long life, you contract yourself.[147] Or He says *daily* against prodigal men, who spend excessively and do not use daily bread, which suffices for the sustenance of one day.[148]

But if the bread is ours, why does He say, *Give us*? It is on account of two reasons, according to Chrysostom. Firstly, it because temporal goods are given to the good and the wicked, but in a different way respectively. For they are given to the good for their benefit, but to the wicked for their harm, because they use them badly; hence, temporal goods are not given to the wicked because they abuse them, and this happens not by God but by the devil. And he says something similar, namely, that it is as if someone offers bread to a priest so that he may bless it and afterwards asks for it back. He could say, 'Give me the bread that is mine by ownership,' or 'Give me the bread as a blessing.'[149]

He says, *This day*, because He does not want us to ask for bread for a long time. But Augustine raises a question, that the

---

146. "When we say, *Give us this day our daily bread*; by the word that is said, *daily*, it is signified 'in the present time,' wherein we ask for that sufficiency which is signified from a part that is foremost, meaning by the name of bread we signify all things" (*Ad Probam, de orando Deum*, Ep. 130, chap. 11, n. 21 (PL 33, 502)).

147. "Worthily then does the disciple of Christ, who is forbidden to think of the tomorrow, ask for his sustenance unto the day, because it becomes contrary and repugnant to Him that we seek to live long in the world, who seek that the kingdom of God come quickly. Thus also the blessed Apostle advises, establishing and sustaining the firmness of our hope and faith." (*On the Lord's Prayer*, xix; PL 4, 533A).

148. ibid. xx (PL 4, 533B).

149. "PSEUDO-CHRYS. We pray, *Give us this day our daily bread*, not only that we may have what to eat, which is common to both righteous and sinners, but that what we eat we may receive at the hand of God, which belongs only to the saints. For to him God gives bread, who earns it by righteous means; but to him who earns it by sin, the Devil is that gives. Or that inasmuch as it is given by God, it is received sanctified; and therefore He adds *our*, that is, such bread as we have prepared for us, that do You give us, that by Your giving it may be sanctified. Like as the Priest taking bread of the laic, sanctifies it, and then offers it to him, the bread indeed is his that brought it in offering, but that it is sanctified is the benefit from the Priest" (*Catena Aurea on St. Matthew*, chap. 6, lect. 7).

Lord afterwards teaches us not to have solicitude for temporal things: "Be not solicitous therefore, saying: What shall we eat: or what shall we drink, or wherewith shall we be clothed, etc.?" (below verse 31). Therefore, it seems that we ought not to pray for temporal things. Here, however, He teaches us to ask for them.[150] And he replies that we can lawfully pray for every desirable thing, because we expect to receive desirable things from God, and so we can ask for what we expect to receive from God;[151] and this is true not only in extreme necessity but also when we ask for what is befitting to one's state, because many more things are necessary for a king than for a servant: hence, it is lawful to ask for these things.[152] Now it is one thing to desire, and it is another thing to be solicitous about something as though it were one's last end, because the Lord forbids this as it will be said below.

But again it is inquired about these words, **Give us this day**, because it seems that we ought not to desire except for one day; therefore all who desire otherwise sin, and then human life will perish because no one will gather the harvest in the summer so that he may eat in the winter.[153] And I reply, saying that the Lord does not intend to forbid that someone would think of the future, but He forbids solicitude because one ought not to usurp solicitude to oneself in advance. For if now solicitude is a duty then one ought to exercise this solicitude, but one ought not to exercise in advance that solicitude about what might become a duty.

And forgive us our debts. Here He begins to set forth the petitions which pertain to the removal of evil, and firstly, He sets forth that petition by which the principal evil is removed, namely, the evil of guilt. Hence, He says, **And forgive us our debts.** It is repugnant that man who lives from God's things would live opposed to God. **Debts** are sins, because for our sins we are made liable to God by a debt: for if you receive something unjustly from another, you are bound to restitution. And because when you sin you usurp what belongs to God, since it belongs to God that every will be regulated according to God's will, therefore you take away what is God's and you are bound to restitution. Now you pay back for sin when you endure

---

150. This sentence is supplied from the reportation of Leodegar of Besançon. "For perhaps some one may wonder why we should pray that we may obtain the things which are necessary for this life,--such, for instance, as food and clothing,--when the Lord Himself says, 'Be not anxious what ye shall eat, or what ye shall put on' (Augustine, *De serm. Dom.* II, 7, 25 (PL 34, 1280)).

151. *Ad Probam, de orando Deum*, Ep. 130, chap. 12, n. 22 (PL 33, 502).
152. These last phrases, "because... things," are taken from the reportation of Leodegar of Besançon.
153. "For every time has its own fitting proper solicitude; thus solicitude about the crops belongs to the summer time, and solicitude about the vintage to the time of autumn" (II II, q. 55, a. 7).

something against your will according to God's will; "I forgave thee all the debt, because thou besoughtest me" (below 18, 32). Therefore, ***Forgive us our debts***, meaning our sins; "O forgive me, that I may be refreshed, before I go hence, and be no more" (Ps. 38, 14).

From these words two heresies are confuted, namely, the heresies of Pelagius and of Novatian.[154] Pelagius said that some perfect men in this life were able to live without sin and to fulfill that which is written, "That he might present it to himself, a glorious church, not having spot or wrinkle or any such thing; but that it should be holy and without blemish" (Eph. 5, 27). But if there were so, then we would not say, ***Forgive us our debts***; "A just man shall fall seven times" (Prov. 24, 16), and, "If we say that we have no sin, we deceive ourselves and the truth is not in us" (I Jn. 1, 8). Novatian said that a man who sins mortally after Baptism cannot do penance. But if this were so, then in vain would we say, ***Forgive us our debts***; "But as many as received him, he gave them power to be made the sons of God, to them that believe in his name" (Jn. 1, 12), namely, by being adopted through grace, which would not come about unless sins were forgiven.[155]

As we also forgive our debtors. Now men can be debtors in two ways, either because they sinned against us, or because they owe us money. Now He does not advise us that we forgive this second kind of debt, but any sin whatsoever, and also in regard to the taking away of our temporal goods. For it would be unworthy to ask pardon from God and not to grant pardon to a fellow servant; "Man to man reserveth anger, and doth he seek remedy of God?" (Eccli. 28, 3), and, "Forgive thy neighbor if he hath hurt thee: and then shall thy sins be forgiven to thee when thou prayest" (Eccli. 28, 2).[156]

But what ought to be said about those who do not wish to forgive and yet they say the ***Our Father***? It seems that they never ought to say it, because they are lying. Hence, it is said that certain men were omitting this clause, ***As we also forgive our debtors***. But this is disproved by Chrysostom in two ways: firstly, because they do not keep the form of the Church in praying, and secondly, because their prayer is not accepted by God since that which Christ dictated they do not keep.[157] Hence, it ought to be said

---

154. Novatian was an antipope of the third century.
155. This clause is taken from the reportation of Leodegar of Besançon.
156. The text here has *dimitte proximo* ("forgive thy neighbor") with the reference of Eccli. 29, 2, which has *fenera proximum* ("lend to thy neighbor"), but *relinque proximo* ("forgive thy neighbor") in Eccli. 28, 2, is more likely.
157. "PSEUDO-CHRYS. With what hope then does he pray, who cherishes hatred against another by whom he

that one does not sin by saying the **Our Father**, no matter how much one be in rancor and in grave sin, because such men ought to do whatever good they can, as for example, almsdeeds, prayers and suchlike things, which are dispositive for recuperating grace. Nor does one lie, because this prayer is not founded on one's own person but belongs to the whole Church, and it is evident that the Church forgives debts to all who are in the Church. Now such men lose the fruit [of this prayer] because only they who forgive obtain the fruit.

On the contrary, it seems that not only they who forgive offenses obtain the fruit. But it ought to be known that Augustine, in fact, resolves this objection insofar as it pertains to the present life, because it was said above concerning the love of one's enemies that God, as a condition, wants us to forgive offenses, whereupon He forgives us our faults.[158] Now He does not forgive anyone except those who ask for pardon. And therefore, whoever is so disposed that he is prepared to ask pardon, this man does not lose the fruit as long as in general he does not hate anyone, as it was said above.[159]

And lead us not into temptation. Here He sets forth another petition [which pertains to the removal of evil]. A second reading has, 'And bring (*inferas*) us not,' and another has, 'And permit (*sinas*) us not,' and the latter is the exposition of the former.[160] For God tempts no one, although He permits us to be tempted. And

has been wronged? As he prays with a falsehood on his lips, when he says, *I forgive*, and does not forgive, so he asks indulgence of God, but no indulgence is granted him. There are many who, being unwilling to forgive those that trespass against them, will not use this prayer. How foolish! First, because he who does not pray in the manner Christ taught, is not Christ's disciple; and secondly, because the Father does not readily hear any prayer which the Son has not dictated; for the Father knows the intention and the words of the Son, nor will He entertain such petitions as human presumption has suggested, but only those which Christ's wisdom has set forth" (*Catena Aurea on St. Matthew*, chap. 6, lect. 8 (PG 56, 714)).

158. "For in no other sentence do we pray in such a way that we, as it were, enter into a compact with God: for we say, 'Forgive us, as we also forgive.' And if we lie in that compact, the whole prayer is fruitless" (*De serm. Dom.*, Lib. II, cap. 11, n. 39 (PL 34, 1287)).

159. *De serm. Dom.* II, 8, 29 (PL 34, 1282). Cf. *Enchiridion* 19, 73-4.

160. "When, therefore, we say to God, 'Bring (*inferas*) us not into temptation,' what do we say but, 'Permit (*sinas*) us not to be led'? Whence some pray in this manner, and it is read in many codices, and the most blessed Cyprian thus uses it: 'Do not suffer (*patiaris*) us to be led into temptation.' In the Greek gospel, however, I have never found it otherwise than, 'Bring (*inferas*) us not into temptation.'" (*On the Gift of Perseverance*, chap. 6, n. 12 (PL 45, 1000)). "The sixth petition is, 'And bring (*inferas*) us not into temptation.' Some manuscripts have the word 'lead (*inducas*),' which is, I judge, equivalent in meaning: for both translations have arisen from the one Greek word (εἰσενέγκῃς) which is used. But many parties in prayer express themselves thus, 'Suffer us not to be led (*patiaris induci*) into temptation'; that is to say, explaining in what sense the word 'lead (*inducas*)' is used." (*De serm. Dom.*, Lib. II, cap. 9, n. 30 (PL 34, 1282)).

He does not say, 'Do not let us be tempted,' because temptation is useful, and one is tempted so that what is known to God may be known to oneself and to others; "What doth he know, that hath not been tried?" (Eccli. 34, 9). But instead He says, **And lead us not**, meaning 'Do not allow us to succumb to temptation,' as though someone were to say, 'I want to be warmed by the fire, but not burned';[161] "God is faithful, who will not suffer you to be tempted above that which you are able" (I Cor. 10, 13).

In this narration the error of Pelagius is refuted as to two things. For he said that man is able to persevere by his free will without God's help, which is nothing other than not to succumb to temptation. Likewise, he said that it does not pertain to God to change men's wills. But it is in His power to change or not to change the will; "For it is God who worketh in you, both to will and to accomplish, according to his good will" (Phil. 2, 13).

But deliver us from evil. This is the last petition. **Deliver us from** past, present and future evil,[162] of guilt, of punishment and from every evil. Augustine says, every Christian in whatever necessity pours out his tears and makes his groans into these words;[163] "Deliver me from my enemies, O my God; and defend me from them that rise up against me" (Ps. 58, 2), and, "I myself will comfort you: who art thou, that thou shouldst be afraid of a mortal man" (Is. 51, 12).

Amen, meaning 'So be it done' in Hebrew.[164] Out of reverence, no one has wanted to translate this word, since the Lord used it frequently. In this word surety of impetrating is given, as long as the things that have been said are kept.

It ought to be known that in the Greek[165] three words are added, which Chrysostom expounds. The first is, "For Thine is the kingdom," and afterwards, "And the power and the glory. Amen." And they seem to correspond to three previous petitions.

---

161. "Here, therefore, the prayer is not that we should not be tempted, but that we should not be brought into temptation: as if, were it necessary that any one should be examined by fire, he should pray, not that he should not be touched by the fire, but that he should not be consumed" (*De serm. Dom.*, Lib. II, cap. 9, n. 32 (PL 34, 1283)).

162. "Deliver us, we beseech Thee, O Lord, from all evils, past, present and to come" (Embolism of the Tridentine Mass).

163. "And the fact that this petition is placed last in the Lord's Prayer shows plainly that the Christian man, beset by any kind of trouble, utters his groans by means of it, pours out his tears in it, begins, continues, and ends his prayer by it" (*Ad Probam, de orando Deum*, Ep. 130, chap. 11, n. 21 (PL 33, 502)).

164. "In Hebrew" is taken from the reportation of Leodegar of Besançon.

165. The text here has "Hebrew" but the reportation of Leodegar of Besançon has "Greek." Also, the first document recording the devotional use of this doxology at the end of the Our Father is the *Didache* written in Greek, though in Palestine. Hence, "Greek" has here been substituted for "Hebrew."

"Thine is the kingdom" corresponds to *Thy kingdom come*; "the power" corresponds to *Thy will be done*; "the glory" corresponds with *Our Father* and to all the other things which are for God's glory.[166] Or it is otherwise. 'Thou art able to do these other things because Thou art a king, and therefore no one else can do them'; 'Thine is the power,' and thus Thou can give the kingdom; and 'Thine is the glory,' wherefore it is said, "Not to us, O Lord, not to us; but to thy name give glory" (Ps. 113, 9).[167]

For if you will forgive men their offences. The Lord had put a certain condition in this prayer, namely, *Forgive us our debts, as we also forgive our debtors.* Now, as this condition said there might seem to someone to be hard, wherefore He shows its reason, and about this He does two things. Firstly, He shows that this condition is useful, and secondly, He shows that it is necessary. It is useful, because by it we obtain the remission of our sins, and this is where it is said, *For if you will forgive men their offences*, which they sinned against you, *your heavenly Father will forgive you also your offences*, which you sinned against Him; "Forgive thy neighbor if he hath hurt thee: and then shall thy sins be forgiven to thee when thou prayest" (Eccli. 28, 2).

But observe that He says, *For if you will forgive men*, for men, as long as they are innocent, are gods; when however they sin, they fall into the human condition; "I have said: You are gods and all of you the sons of the most High," etc., (Ps. 81, 6), and afterwards it is said, "But you like men shall die, etc.," (verse 7). Therefore, you who are gods and are spiritual, *forgive men*, that is to say, sinners.[168]

Likewise, observe that He says, *Your heavenly Father*, etc. For offenses which happen in relation to men, happen on account of something earthly. On the other hand, heavenly men who have

---

166. "PSEUDO-CHRYS. This is also connected with the foregoing. 'Thine is the kingdom' has reference to 'Thy kingdom come,' that none should therefore say, God has no kingdom on earth. 'The power,' answers to 'Thy will be done,' as in earth so in heaven, that none should say thereon that God cannot perform whatever He would. 'And the glory,' answers to all that follows, in which God's glory is shown forth" (*Catena Aurea on St. Matthew*, chap. 6, lect. 10).

167. "Doth it not then follow, that if His be the kingdom, we should fear no one, since there can be none to withstand, and divide the empire with him... 'And the power,' saith He. Therefore, manifold as thy weakness may be, thou mayest of right be confident, having such a one to reign over thee, who is able fully to accomplish all, and that with ease, even by thee. 'And the glory, for ever. Amen.'" (Hom. xix, n. 10). Leodegar of Besançon's reportation of this lecture ends here.

168. "But if this which is written, 'I have said: You are gods and all of you the sons of the most High: but you like men shall die' (Ps. 81, 6-7), is said to those who for their sins deserve to become men instead of gods, then they to whom sins are forgiven are rightly called men" (Jerome, *Comm. in Mt.*, I (PL 26, 43D)).

a Father in heaven ought to have nothing to do with discord on account of earthly things; "Be ye therefore merciful, as your Father also is merciful" (Lk. 6, 36).

This condition is also necessary, because without it no remission of sin occurs, and hence it is said, *But if you will not forgive men, neither will your Father forgive you your offences.* And it is not surprising, because a sin is never forgiven without charity; "Charity covereth all sins" (Prov. 10, 12). For he who has hatred towards one man is not in charity, and therefore his sin is not forgiven him; "Man to man reserveth anger, and doth he seek remedy of God?" (Eccli. 28, 3), and, "For judgment without mercy to him that hath not done mercy" (James 2, 13).

But someone might suppose that from the fact that so it is that sins ought to be forgiven, therefore the Church sins when she does not forgive. I answer that if a sinner asks pardon, one would sin if he would not forgive; if, however, the sinner does not ask pardon, then one does not forgive, either on account of hatred, and in such a way one sins, or on account of the good of the sinner or of others, namely, so that the evil would not be done often, and in such a way one does not sin.

16. And when you fast, be not as the hypocrites, sad. For they disfigure their faces, that they may appear unto men to fast. Amen I say to you, they have received their reward.

17. But thou, when thou fastest anoint thy head, and wash thy face;

18. That thou appear not to men to fast, but to thy Father who is in secret: and thy Father who seeth in secret, will repay thee.

And when you fast, be not as the hypocrites, sad. After having specified the manner of praying and of giving alms, here He specifies the manner of fasting, and firstly, He excludes the unsuitable manner of fasting, and secondly, He gives the right manner of fasting, where it is said, *But thou, when thou fastest.* About the first point, He does three things. Firstly, He teaches to avoid the manner of the example of the hypocrites, secondly, He shows their example, and thirdly, He gives the reason for His teaching. The second part is where it is said, *For they disfigure their faces,* and the third part is where it is said, *Amen I say to you, they have received their reward.*

It is very fitting that after prayer He treats about fasting, because prayer is slender which is not accompanied with fasting, and though prayer is "the raising up of the mind to God,"[169] the more the flesh is strengthened on the other hand, the more prayer is weakened; "Prayer is good with fasting and alms more than to lay up treasures of gold" (Tob. 12, 8). And everywhere it is read that when some solemn prayer took place, there is mention of fasting;[170] "And I set my face to the Lord, my God, to pray and make supplication with fasting, and sackcloth, and ashes" (Dan. 9, 3), and, "Blow the trumpet in Sion, sanctify a fast, call a solemn assembly" (Joel 2, 15).

He says, therefore, **And when you fast**. Chrysostom says that He does not say 'Do not be [sad]' because it is impossible that those who fast do not fall into the passions of sorrow, just as on the other hand, they who fast are made joyful from eating and drinking.[171] But He says, **Become not sad** (*Nolite fieri*), meaning that you ought not to make an effort to become outwardly sad, instead of inwardly sorrowing for your sins; "For the sorrow that is according to God worketh penance, steadfast unto salvation: but the sorrow of the world worketh death" (II Cor. 7, 10), and, "Give not up thy soul to sadness, and afflict not thyself in thy own counsel" (Eccli. 30, 22).

As the hypocrites, meaning [do not fast] with the same intention [as the hypocrites have]. Simulators who simulate the person of a just man are called **hypocrites** as was explained above.[172] Since, however, they become sad, He adds, **They disfigure their faces**. Jerome says that these words, namely, **they disfigure** (*exterminant*), are improperly put metaphorically, because 'to disfigure' (*exterminare*) properly means 'to put outside the borders.' Hence, it is derived from exiles (*exulibus*) of a State. Hence, it is said, 'Saul had put away all the magicians and

---

169. Damascene, *De Fide Orth.* iii, 24 (PG 94, 1089C).

170. "Fasting is an aid to prayer because prayer without fasting is slender and weak. For that prayer is strong that takes place in a humble spirit and a troubled heart, as also the prophet says, 'A sacrifice to God is an afflicted spirit: a contrite and humbled heart, O God, thou wilt not despise' (Ps. 50, 19). But a spirit that eats and drinks and enjoys delicacies cannot have a humble and contrite heart, because bread strengthens the heart and wine gladdens it (cf. Ps. 103, 15). The strength that comes from bread does not allow the spirit of the flesh to be humble, and the pleasure that comes from wine does not allow the heart to be contrite. So whenever the saints wished to pray to God for some necessity, they joined a fast with their prayers, as Daniel and others did. Therefore, because the power of prayer is fasting, they should never be separated from one another, but always put together" (Pseudo-Chrysostom, *Op. imp. in Mt.*, hom. xv (PG 56, 715-716)).

171. "Can it happen that the person who fasts does not feel it? But it is better that your fast shows you rather than you show your fast. Because the Lord knows that the one who fasts cannot happen to be joyful, so He does not say, 'Do not be sad,' but 'Do not become sad.' It is one thing to be sad and quite another to become sad" (Pseudo-Chrysostom, *Op. imp. in Mt.*, hom. xv (PG 56, 716-717)).

172. See lecture 1 above on verse 2.

soothsayers out of the land' (I Kings 28, 3 & 9). Here, however, is properly put that 'they destroy' (*demoliuntur*) [their faces].[173] Or it can be expounded saying that *they disfigure their faces* by putting forth [a manner] outside of the ordinary manner.[174] *That they may appear unto men to fast.* This is their prayer; "A man is known by his look, and a wise man, when thou meetest him, is known by his countenance" (Eccli. 19, 26).

Observe here, according to Augustine, that not only glory is sought from the ostentatious display of clothing but also from the coarseness of clothing, and according to him this is more dangerous, because the fact that some men deceive by their display of clothing and suchlike, cannot harm since it may be known, but when glory is sought from squalor of the body it can be a danger because if he is not a spiritual man he can easily lead [others] into error. Nevertheless, Augustine says that such a man can be discerned from other actions, because if on one hand he follows the abandonment of the world and on the other hand he acquires riches, he is a simulator. But due to the fact that some hypocrites usurp to themselves coarseness of clothing to hide their malice, should they who do this for God's sake abandon [coarse clothing]? I answer that they should not, because, as the Gloss says,[175] a sheep ought not to abandon its own skin even though a wolf sometimes covers himself with it.[176]

---

173. "JEROME; The word *exterminare*, so often used in the ecclesiastical Scriptures through a blunder of the translators, has a quite different meaning from that in which it is commonly understood. It is properly said of exiles, who are sent beyond the boundary of their country. Instead of this word, it would seem better to use the word *demoliri*, 'to destroy,' in translating the Greek *aphanizousi*. The hypocrite destroys his face, in order that he may feign sorrow, and with a heart full of joy wears sorrow in his countenance" (*Catena Aurea on St. Matthew*, chap. 6, lect. 12); *Comm. in Mt.*, I (PL 26, 44A). Note here that the Greek has a play on words, *aphanizousi...phanosi* ('they mar their appearance, that they may make an appearance'). "'Moreover, when ye fast,' says He, 'be not, as the hypocrites, of a sad countenance: for they disfigure their faces (*vultum*), that they may appear (*videantur*) unto men to fast'" (Augustine, *De serm. Dom.* II, xii, 40 (PL 34, 1287)).

174. "The Philosopher says (*Ethica Nicomachea* iv, 7) that it is 'the practice of boasters both to make overmuch of themselves, and to make very little of themselves': and for the same reason it is related of Augustine (Possidius, *Vita S. August.* C. 22 (ML 32, 51)) that he was unwilling to possess clothes that were either too costly or too shabby, because by both do men seek glory. An excess and an immoderate deficiency in externals seem to pertain to boasting precisely because a certain singularity in a man is displayed in the case of each" (II II, q. 113, 2 ad 2um). Cf. *Sent. Libri Ethicorum*, iv, lect. 15, n. 17.

175. "Note that sheep ought not to put aside their skins but to be clothed, even if sometimes wolves cover themselves with them [sheep's skin]" (*Glossa Ordinaria* (ML 114, 103C)).

176. "But in this section it is chiefly to be noticed, that there may be ostentatious display not merely in the splendour and pomp of things pertaining to the body, but also in doleful squalor itself; and the more dangerous on this account, that it deceives under the name of serving God. And therefore, he who is very

Amen I say to you, they have received their reward. Here He gives the reason for His teaching. For it is foolishness to lose an eternal reward for human praise;[177] "I am thy reward exceeding great" (Gen. 15, 1).

But thou, when thou fastest anoint thy head, and wash thy face. Here is set forth the suitable manner of fasting, and about this He does three things. Firstly, He sets forth the suitable manner, secondly, He gives its reason, and thirdly, He sets forth its usefulness. He says, therefore, *But thou, when thou fastest*; something similar is written, "At all times let thy garments be white, and let not oil depart from thy head" (Eccli. 9, 8), and here Augustine raises the question, that although it is the custom among many persons that they wash their face daily, nevertheless that they anoint their head is deemed as lasciviousness. Therefore, does the Lord want this?[178] Likewise, Chrysostom says that fasting ought to be done hiddenly. But whenever we see someone anointed we will say that he is fasting.[179]

They answer these objections in three ways. Jerome therefore says, and I believe that it is the most literal [exposition], that there was a custom among the Palestinians at that time that men daily anointed their heads with oil and washed their faces. Hence,

---

conspicuous by immoderate attention to the body, and by the splendour of his clothing or other things, is easily convicted by the things themselves of being a follower of the pomps of the world, and misleads no one by a cunning semblance of sanctity; but in regard to him, who under a profession of Christianity, fixes the eyes of men upon himself by unusual squalor and filth, when he does it voluntarily, and not under the pressure of necessity, it may be conjectured from the rest of his actions whether he does this from contempt of superfluous attention to the body, or from a certain ambition: for the Lord has enjoined us to beware of wolves under a sheep's skin; but 'By their fruits,' says He, 'you shall know them.' For when by temptations of any kind those very things begin to be withdrawn from them or refused to them, which under that veil they either have obtained or desire to obtain, then of necessity it appears whether it is a wolf in a sheep's skin or a sheep in its own. For a Christian ought not to delight the eyes of men by superfluous ornament on this account, because pretenders also too often assume that frugal and merely necessary dress, that they may deceive those who are not on their guard: for those sheep also ought not to lay aside their own skins, if at any time wolves cover themselves there with" (*De serm. Dom.* II, xii, 41 (PL 34, 1287)). Cf. II II, q. 187, a. 6 ad 1um.

177. "The pleasure of praise is enjoyed as long as it is heard, but as soon as it has passed through one's ears, so the pleasure of praise passes away" (Pseudo-Chrysostom, *Op. imp. in Mt.*, hom. xv (PG 56, 718)).

178. "For it would not be right in any one to teach (although we may wash our face according to daily custom) that we ought also to have our heads anointed when we fast. If, then, all admit this to be most unseemly, we must understand this precept with respect to anointing the head and washing the face as referring to the inner man" (*De serm. Dom.* II, xii, 42 (PL 34, 1288)).

179. "It is truly vain if we pour oil on our head whenever we fast, even if we wash our face with water. And who goes about with an unwashed face? If we do this, we publicize all the more that we are fasting through these signs of washing and anointing." (Pseudo-Chrysostom, *Op. imp. in Mt.*, hom. xv (PG 56, 718)).

that woman said in IV Kings, "I, thy handmaid, have nothing in my house but a little oil, to anoint me" (4, 2). Hence, this custom was considered necessary. Therefore the Lord wishes to say that He who fasts ought not to change his manner of living, which is that he anoint his head and wash his face.[180] Or, according to Chrysostom, the Lord speaks by hyperbole as He also said above, "But when thou dost alms, let not thy left hand know what thy right hand doth" (verse 3) wherefore [the meaning is], 'If it be suitable, you ought to do the typical actions of hypocrites.'[181] Thirdly, according to Augustine and also Chrysostom, the Lord speaks by way of a similitude, and this exposition is mystical. By the *head* two things are understood; "The head of every man is Christ" (I Cor. 11, 3). Wherefore you anoint your Head when you show mercy to your neighbor;[182] "What you have done to one of these My least brethren," etc., (below 25, 40).[183] Or the head of man is either the reason or the spirit, according to Augustine, which is the man,[184] as though He were to say, 'You ought to afflict the flesh in this manner so that the inner spirit is refrained through devotion';[185] "Though our outward man is corrupted, yet the inward man is renewed day by day" (II Cor. 4, 16). "Our man," that is, our flesh, "which is outward," that is, exposed to evils,

---

180. "JEROME; But He speaks in accordance with the manners of the province of Palestine, where it is the custom on festival days to anoint the head. What He enjoins, then, is that when we are fasting we should wear the appearance of joy and gladness" (*Catena Aurea on St. Matthew*, chap. 6, lect. 13); *Comm. in Mt.*, I (PL 26, 44B).

181. "The simple interpretation of this passage is this, that those things must be understood through hyperbole, as were the rest of the things previously said. It is as if He were to say, 'You ought to keep yourself from showing off your fast, so that if it can be, you do not do even that which is not fitting, namely, those things that seem to be indications of a variety of luxury and fasting'" (Pseudo-Chrysostom, *Op. imp. in Mt.*, hom. xv (PG 56, 718)).

182. "Moreover, your head is Christ. Give the thirsty something to drink, feed the hungry, clothe him who is cold, and so you have anointed your head, that is, Christ, with the most precious myrrh, that is, the oil of mercy, as Christ proclaims in the Gospel, saying, 'What you have done to one of these My least brethren, you have done to Me' (below 25, 40)" (Pseudo-Chrysostom, *Op. imp. in Mt.*, hom. xv (PG 56, 718)).

183. St. Thomas typically used a variant wording of this verse. Cf. II II q. 188, a. 2: "Mt. 25, 40, 'What you have done [*Vulg.*: 'As long as you did it'] to one of these My least brethren, you did it to Me.'"

184. "According to the Philosopher, in *Ethics* 9.9, and according to the way we speak, each thing is said to be that which is most important in it... In truth the most important thing in man is the mind. Hence, according to the judgment of spiritual men, the mind is called the inward man." (*Super II ad Cor.*, chap. 4, lect. 5).

185. "We must understand this precept with respect to anointing the head and washing the face as referring to the inner man. Hence, to anoint the head refers to joy; to wash the face, on the other hand, refers to purity: and therefore, that man anoints his head who rejoices inwardly in his mind and reason. For we rightly understand that as being the head which has the preeminence in the soul, and by which it is evident that the other parts of man are ruled and governed. And this is done by him who does not seek his joy from without, so as to draw his delight

"is corrupted, yet the inward man," that is, the soul fortified with hope of a future [reward],[186] to which human fury does not approach, "is renewed day by day," that is, he is continually made purer through the fire of tribulation (II Cor. 11);[187] "Though our outward man is corrupted" (II Cor. 4, 16).

Now He says, **Wash thy face**, meaning one's conscience. For just as someone is made pleasing to men on account of a comely face, so by a pure conscience one is made pleasing to God;[188] "He that loveth cleanness of heart" (Prov. 22, 11), and, "Is not this rather the fast that I have chosen?" (Is. 58, 6). And He says, **anoint thy head**, and not, 'wash [thy head],' because Christ does not need washing, but our conscience does.[189]

That thou appear not to men to fast. Here is the reason [for the suitable manner of fasting]. [This reason] ought to be understood of individual fasting and not of common fasting. **But to thy Father**

---

in a fleshly way from the praises of men. For the flesh, which ought to be subject, is in no way the head of the whole nature of man. 'No man,' indeed, 'ever yet hated his own flesh,' as the Apostle says, when giving the precept as to loving one's wife (Eph. 5, 25-33); but the man is the head of the woman, and Christ is the head of the man (I Cor. 11, 3). Let him, therefore, rejoice inwardly in his fasting in this very circumstance, that by his fasting he so turns away from the pleasure of the world as to be subject to Christ, who according to this precept desires to have the head anointed" (*De serm. Dom.* II, xii, 42 (PL 34, 1288)).

186. "Therefore, it is according to this manner that the Apostle is speaking here when he says, 'Though our outer man,' i.e., the body with its sentient nature, 'is corrupted,' in tribulations, fasts, abstinences and watchings: 'Our old man is crucified with him' (Rom. 6, 6); 'Let rottenness enter into my bones' (Hab. 3:16), 'yet the inward man,' namely, the mind or reason fortified with hope and strengthened with the safeguard of faith, 'is renewed'" (*Super II ad Cor.*, chap. 4, lect. 5).

187. "*For which cause*, namely, so that we may be imitated, I do not say that *we faint* in tribulations only for the life of Jesus, *but though our man*, meaning our flesh, *which is outward*, namely, *is corrupted* having been exposed to evils, *yet the inward man*, meaning the soul fortified with the hope of a future [reward], to which human fury does not approach, meaning God's image, *is renewed*, in the knowledge of God, *from day to day*, meaning it is continually purified from vices through the fire of tribulation." (Peter Lombard, *Collectanea in Epist. D. Pauli-in Ep. II Cor.* (PL 192, 34D)). The original source however is St. Ambrose: "*Though our outward man is corrupted, but the inward man is renewed day by day.* The flesh *is corrupted* by distresses, stripes, hunger, thirst, cold, and nakedness, but the soul by the hope of a future reward *is renewed*, because it is purified by continual tribulations. For [the soul] benefits in distress, it does not perish, so that by the approaching trials it daily acquires merit; and also this corruption advances the flesh toward immortality by the soul's merit" (*In Epistolam Beati Pauli ad Corinthios Secundam* (PL 17, 309A-B)). Cf. Glossa Interlinearis, *Bibliorum Sacrorum cum Glossa Ordinaria* (1603), p. 388D.

188. "The face of the soul is called the conscience. For just as a comely face is made pleasing in the sight of men, so also a pure conscience is beautiful in the eyes of God" (Pseudo-Chrysostom, *Op. imp. in Mt.*, hom. xv (PG 56, 717)).

189. "And how rightly He said to wash the face, and not to wash the head, but to anoint it. As long as we are in the body, our conscience is always filthy with sins. But our Head, Christ, does not need any washing, but only anointing, because 'He hath done no iniquity, neither was there deceit in his mouth' (Is. 53, 9)" (Pseudo-Chrysostom, *Op. imp. in Mt.*, hom. xv (PG 56, 718)).

who is in the *secret* of eternity; "He is hid from the eyes of all living" (Job 28, 21). Or [He is] in the secret of our conscience,[190] because God "dwells in us by faith" (Eph. 3, 17).[191]

Will repay thee; "Who will render to every man according to his works" (Rom. 2, 6), and, "The searcher of hearts and reins is God" (Ps. 7, 10).[192]

19. Lay not up to yourselves treasures on earth: where the rust, and moth consume, and where thieves break through, and steal.

20. But lay up to yourselves treasures in heaven: where neither the rust nor moth doth consume, and where thieves do not break through, nor steal.

21. For where thy treasure is, there is thy heart also.

22. The light of thy body is thy eye. If thy eye be single, thy whole body shall be lightsome.

23. But if thy eye be evil thy whole body shall be darksome. If then the light that is in thee, be darkness: the darkness itself how great shall it be!

24. No man can serve two masters. For either he will hate the one, and love the other: or he will sustain the one, and despise the other. You cannot serve God and mammon.

25. Therefore I say to you, be not solicitous for your life, what you shall eat, nor for your body, what you shall put on. Is not the life more than the meat: and the body more than the raiment?

26. Behold the birds of the air, for they neither sow, nor do they reap, nor gather into barns: and your heavenly Father feedeth them. Are not you of much more value than they?

27. And which of you by taking thought, can add to his stature one cubit?

28. And for raiment why are you solicitous? Consider the lilies of the field, how they grow: they labour not, neither do they spin.

29. But I say to you, that not even Solomon in all his glory was arrayed as one of these.

---

190. "*In secret*: He is in your conscience" (Glossa Interlinearis, *Bibliorum Sacrorum cum Glossa Ordinaria* (1603), p. 135A).

191. "GLOSS. That is, to your heavenly Father, who is unseen, or who dwells in the heart through faith" (*Catena Aurea on St. Matthew*, chap. 6, lect. 13). Note that this variant wording of this verse, "dwells in us by faith" [*Vulg.*: "may dwell by faith in your hearts" (Eph. 3, 17], is also found in III, q. 62, a. 5.

192. "REMIG. For it is enough for you that He who sees your conscience should be your rewarder" (*Catena Aurea on St. Matthew*, chap. 6, lect. 13).

30. And if the grass of the field, which is today, and tomorrow is cast into the oven, God doth so clothe: how much more you, O ye of little faith?

31. Be not solicitous therefore, saying: What shall we eat: or what shall we drink, or wherewith shall we be clothed?

32. For after all these things do the heathens seek. For your Father knoweth that you have need of all these things.

33. Seek ye therefore first the kingdom of God, and his justice, and all these things shall be added unto you.

34. Be not therefore solicitous for tomorrow; for the morrow will be solicitous for itself. Sufficient for the day is the evil thereof.

Lay not up to yourselves treasures on earth. Above, the Lord prescribed that we do not do works for the sake of [human] glory. Here, He teaches that we ought not to put riches as our end in [doing] good works. For there are two evils which follow upon each other: covetousness and vainglory. For many seek riches, not out of necessity, but for ostentation.[193] Or the argument may be connected as follows: Above, the Lord did not teach nor suggest that we give alms or say prayers, but He taught the manner of doing these things. Now He wishes to encourage us to do these things, and so, firstly, He encourages almsdeeds,[194] secondly, He encourages prayers, where it is said, **Ask, and it shall be given you**, and thirdly, He encourages fasting, where it is said, **Strait is the way that leadeth to life**.[195] Or it may be connected otherwise. Above, He taught that we ought

---

[193]. "*Lay not up for yourselves treasures upon earth.* Thus, after He hath cast out the disease of vainglory, and not before, He seasonably introduces His discourse of voluntary poverty. For nothing so trains men to be fond of riches as the fondness for glory. This, for instance, is why men devise those herds of slaves, and that swarm of eunuchs, and their horses with trappings of gold, and their silver tables, and all the rest of it, yet more ridiculous; not to satisfy any wants, nor to enjoy any pleasure, but that they may make a show before the multitude" (John Chrysostom, *In Matth*, hom. xx, 2 (PG 57, 288-289)).

[194]. "This present passage does not seem to follow logically from the preceding passage because that passage spoke about fasting, but this passage speaks about alms. What does this mean then? If we remember, the Lord taught nothing about alms or prayer or fasting above, but only restrained their counterfeits so that they may neither do those things before others in order to be seen by them, not because it is possible to do them in such a way that others do not see them (as we said above), but He makes a person consider how much he is striving to do those things so as not to be seen, so that that very good work, as far as a Christian is concerned, might take place in the disposition as in the deed... Therefore, just as we stated, because Christ had not taught anything about those things, now He introduced three consequences of His teaching in accordance with the three aforementioned forms of justice (almsgiving, prayer and fasting)" (Pseudo-Chrysostom, *Op. imp. in Mt.*, hom. xv (PG 56, 718-719)).

[195]. "The third consequence pertains to the third justice of fasting, and is a part of the teaching given concerning fasting so that the discourse can be arranged as follows: '*But thou, when thou fastest, anoint your head and wash your face,* that your fasting may not be

not to do almsdeeds and fasting on account of human glory. Here, He wishes to show, furthermore, that *No man can serve two masters.*[196] But the first [exposition] is the most in accord with the literal sense, and it is Chrysostom's. Therefore, according to this meaning, because all [of these interpretations] are nearly the same, He does two things. Firstly, He teaches to avoid excessive care for riches, and secondly, He teaches to avoid solicitude for necessary things, where it is said, *Therefore I say to you, be not solicitous for your life.* About the first part, He does two things. Firstly, He advises not to gather excessive riches and He proves this by reason of their instability, and secondly, He proves this from the harm that comes therefrom, where it is said, *For where thy treasure is, there is thy heart also.* About the first point, He does two things. Firstly, He sets forth the instability of earthly riches, and secondly, He sets forth the stability of heavenly riches which we ought to gather, where it is said, *But lay up to yourselves treasures in heaven.* Therefore, He firstly speaks thus: 'I say that we ought not to do good works on account of earthly glory but also not to gather riches,' and this is where it is said, *Lay not up to yourselves treasures on earth. On earth*, meaning in any earthly thing.

But according to this it seems that kings and bishops act contrary to this precept. But it ought to be said that in treasures one can understand two things, namely, two kinds of abundance, more precisely, a necessary and a superfluous abundance. For it is superfluous for a private man to gather regal riches, while on the other hand, it is not superfluous for a king to do so because he needs an abundance of riches for the protection and defense of his kingdom.[197] Hence, this is forbidden, namely, to accumulate riches

---

seen by men but by *your Father who is in secret; and your Father who sees in secret will repay you* in secret. *Enter ye in by the narrow gate.*' This is because every entrance of justice into eternal life is *narrow* for the person living in the flesh because of the adversity of the fleshly nature. But it is not as *narrow* and laborious as fasts undertaken sincerely" (Pseudo-Chrysostom, *Op. imp. in Mt.*, hom. xviii (PG 56, 733)).

196. "AUG. For if any does a work with the mind of gaining thereby an earthly good, how will his heart be pure while it is thus walking on earth? For anything that is mingled with an inferior nature is polluted therewith, though that inferior be in its own kind pure. Thus gold is alloyed when mixed with pure silver; and in like manner our mind is defiled by lust of earthly things, though earth is in its own kind pure" (*Catena Aurea* on St. Matthew, chap. 6, lect. 14); *De serm. Dom.* II, xiii, 44 (PL 34, 1288-1289).

197. "It ought to be noted that in fortuitous goods there is some good, because by them a wise man is more unhindered to carry out his office of governing his subjects. For those who exceed others by their power and fame are more suited to governing the state, because they are more suited to relieving the oppressed, and to crushing evils, to protecting the good, to fighting against enemies: and so for a wise man who deals with the affairs of the state, power and an abundance of riches are needed. But for the wise man who gives his time to contemplation, riches are burdensome, because from thence he assumes too much anxious care" (*In Boethii de Consol. Philos.*, bk. 4, chap. 9).

beyond the needs of the person or office. The other thing that is understood by *treasures* is the confidence which is had in them, and this is also forbidden, and this is what He says, **Lay not up to yourselves treasures**; "Charge the rich of this world not to be highminded nor to trust in the uncertainty of riches, but in the living God" (I Tim. 6, 17), and, "That hoard up silver and gold, wherein men trust" (Bar. 3, 18).

Afterwards He shows their instability, where it is said, **Where the rust, and moth consume, and where thieves break through and steal**, and He relates three kinds of things by which riches are literally destroyed. For riches are either possessed in metals, or in clothes, or in stones and the like. Metals are consumed by rust, clothes by moths, but thieves carry away stones.[198] Or it can be expounded otherwise. Another text reads, "Where moths consume and banquetings clear away,"[199] meaning they are eaten, and Chrysostom expounds this passage as follows. Temporal goods are destroyed in three ways: they are destroyed as regards the things, for from clothing comes forth *the moth*; they are destroyed by the luxury of their owner, hence He says, *they are eaten*; and they are destroyed by strangers, hence He says, *thieves break through and steal.*[200] But someone could say that this does not always happen, and Chrysostom says that even if it does not always happen, nevertheless it frequently happens, and if it does not frequently happen, nevertheless it could happen, and the Lord wishes this to be proven because He teaches us to put our hope in lasting and stable things;[201] "That which the palmerworm hath left, the locust hath eaten" (Joel 1, 4). Mystically, **rust** is

198. "RABAN. Here are three precepts according to the three different kinds of wealth. Metals are destroyed by rust, clothes by moth; but as there are other things which fear neither rust nor moth, as precious stones, He therefore names a common damage, that by thieves, who may rob wealth of all kinds" (*Catena Aurea on St. Matthew*, chap. 6, lect. 14; cf. *Comm. in Mt. Libri Octo*, bk. 2 (PL 107, 834)).
199. Chrysostom, Augustine and Cyprian use this variant text, *ubi neque tinea neque comestura exterminant*, instead of the Vulgate wording, *ubi neque erugo neque tinea demolitur* (Augustine, *De serm. Dom.* II, xliv, (PL 34, 1288); Cyprian, *Testimoniorum Libri Tres Adversus Judaeos*, bk. 3 (PL 4, 730B)).
200. "A threefold destruction destroys all the goods of the world. Either they grow old by themselves and become moth-ridden, like clothes, or they are eaten by their owners who are living luxuriously, like other provisions, or they are snatched away by others either by trickery or force or calumny or some other unjust method. This is because all people who hasten to make someone else's property their own are called thieves" (Pseudo-Chrysostom, *Op. imp. in Mt.*, hom. xv (PG 56, 719)).
201. "But you say, 'Do all who have these things lose them? I show off my garment, and it does not grow mothridden. I am thrifty, and my provisions are not eaten; I guard my property, and it is not taken by thieves.' Meanwhile, let me say that many people lose their property, even if everybody does not. What can we conclude? Is it better to store up treasure on earth where the outcome of attempts to preserve them is uncertain, or is it better to do so in heaven, where their preservation is certain?" (ibid.).

visible, but *the moth* hides. Hence, by *rust* carnal sins can be understood, and by *the moth* spiritual sins can be understood. For some sins are committed against oneself, and these are understood by *rust and the moth*; and other sins are committed unto the scandal of another, and this is understood by *thieves*. Or it may be expounded otherwise. *Rust* tarnishes beauty, wherefore pride can be understood, which lays in wait for good works so that they perish; "As a brass pot his wickedness rusteth" (Eccli. 12, 10), so the moth corrodes clothing, which are the exterior works that are consumed through envy; "As a moth doth by a garment, and a worm by the wood: so the sadness of a man consumeth the heart" (Prov. 25, 20). Now the demons, when they are unable to deceive by stealth, draw men to vainglory, and this is what is said, *where thieves break through and steal*. Having set forth earthly instability, He sets forth the stability of heavenly treasures.

And it ought to be noted, according to Augustine, that these words ought not to be understood of the corporeal heaven, because we ought not to fix our heart in evil corporeal things nor have our treasure there. Hence, *in heaven*, ought to be understood to mean in spiritual goods, that is to say, in God Himself; "The heaven of heaven is the Lord's: but the earth he has given to the children of men" (Ps. 113, 24).[202] And He says, *treasure*, because if a carnal man wants to gather more and more on earth, it ought not to suffice for [a spiritual man] that he have whatsoever place in the kingdom of heaven, but that he may have a greater reward; and therefore He says, *treasure*, meaning they abound with rewards [in heaven], and He says, *to yourselves*, because, as it is said, "If thou do justly, what shalt thou give him, or what shall he receive of thy hand?" (Job 35, 7). Then He shows how one ought to lay up treasure; "Sell all whatever thou hast and give to the poor: and thou shalt have treasure in heaven" (Lk. 18, 22), and, "If thou wilt be perfect, go sell what thou hast, and give to the poor, and thou shalt have treasure in heaven" (below 19, 21). Therefore, by almsgiving treasure is laid up, and thus Chrysostom says that He is here encouraging almsgiving.[203] This

---

202. "But we would not understand heaven in this passage as anything corporeal, because everything cor-poreal is to be reckoned as earth. For he who lays up treasure for himself in heaven ought to despise the whole world. Hence, it is in that heaven of which it is said, 'The heaven of heavens is the Lord's' (Ps. 113, 24), i.e., in the spiritual firmament: for it is not in that which is to pass away that we ought to fix and place our treasure and our heart, but in that which ever abideth; but 'heaven and earth shall pass away' (below 24, 35)" (*De serm. Dom.* II, xiii, 44 (PL 44, 1289)).

203. "PSEUDO-CHRYS. He now teaches the benefit of almsgiving. He who places his treasure on earth has nothing to look for in Heaven; for why should he look up to Heaven where he has nothing laid up for himself? Thus he doubly sins; first, because he gathers together things evil; secondly, because he has his heart in earth; and so on the contrary he does

treasure is incorruptible because it does not have corruption of itself, because neither moth [nor rust consumes it] as regards the body; "This corruptible will put on incorruption" (I Cor. 15, 53), nor as regards the soul; "And thy people shall be all just, they shall inherit the land for ever" (Is. 60, 21), nor [corruption] from outward things, meaning by those lying in wait, that is to say, the demons, and this is what is said, *where thieves break through and steal*, neither secretly nor openly; "They shall not hurt, nor shall they kill in all my holy mountain" (Is. 11, 9).

Where thy treasure is, there is thy heart also. Here He intends to show that we ought [to lay up treasure] in heaven and not [on earth] primarily because of the harm which thenceforth arises, and it is twofold. The first is distraction of heart, and the second is alienation from God,[204] where it is said, *No man can serve two masters*. About the first part, He does two things. Firstly, He relates the harm of the distraction of heart; secondly, He shows the magnitude of this harm, where it is said, *The light of thy body is thy eye*. He says, therefore, I said that *thieves break through*, etc., but something else unfitting remains. Hence, *For where thy treasure is, there is thy heart also*. For "Wherever love is, there the eye is also";[205] and, "While we look not at the things which are seen, but at the things which are not seen. For the things which are seen are temporal: but the things which are not seen, are eternal" (II Cor. 4, 18), but these men do the opposite; "The eyes of fools are in the ends of the earth" (Prov. 17, 24).

And because few consider this harm, namely, distraction of heart, wherefore the Lord shows how great this danger is by an example. Hence, *The light of thy body is thy eye*, and He instructs through sensible things about intellectual things, and these words can be read in two ways. Firstly, that the Lord is making a comparison with the corporeal heaven, and afterwards adapts the comparison to spiritual things, where it is said, *If then the light that is in thee, be darkness*, and this exposition is clear. And about this He does three things. Firstly, He shows the role of the eye; secondly, He shows the benefit of a good eye; and thirdly, He shows the harm of a hidden evil.

right in a twofold manner who lays up his treasure in Heaven" (*Catena Aurea on St. Matthew*, chap. 6, lect. 14; Pseudo-Chrysostom, *Op. imp. in Mt.*, hom. xv (PG 56, 720)).

204. "For there is no greater or worse death than when death never dies. But because the soul from its very nature, being created immortal, cannot be without some kind of life, its utmost death is alienation from the life of God in an eternity of punishment" (Augustine, *City of God*, bk. 6, chap. 12 (PL 41, 194)).

205. Richard of St. Victor, *De Praeparatione Animi Ad Contemplationem Liber Dictus Benjamin Minor* (PL 196:10A).

He says, therefore, ***The light of thy body is thy*** corporeal ***eye***, which as a light directs [the body]; ***If thy eye be single***, meaning powerful for seeing, according to Jerome,[206] otherwise it could not be understood of the corporeal eye. Hence, it is ***single***, meaning powerful for seeing. For when a man has weak eyes, one thing is seen as two. Hence, if the eyes can be fixed in one thing on account of its strength, ***thy whole body shall be lightsome***, for by the light of the eye daylight is captured for directing all the members in their acts. ***But if thy eye be evil***, meaning troubled, more precisely blear-eyed, likewise ***thy whole body shall be darksome***, meaning all the members so act as though they were in darkness.

Afterwards He applies the comparison. ***If then the light that is in thee be darkness***, namely, the light of reason: ***the darkness itself how great shall it be!*** Concerning this light, it is written, "The light of thy countenance, O Lord, is signed upon us: thou hast given gladness in my heart" (Ps. 4, 7). Therefore, He wishes to say that if the heart, which is the eye of the soul, be darkened by applying itself to earthly things, the other eyes, which according to their natures are darkness because they can only know corporeal things, will be very dark. Hence, if reason, which can be directed to spiritual things, be directed to earthly things, then all the senses are directed to earthly things, and this is what is said, ***If then the light that is in thee***, etc. Or it is expounded otherwise. The Lord wishes here to speak about the spiritual eye and He wishes to use these words, ***If then the light that is in thee***, etc., to prove the aforesaid by an argument from a less important case, and [the rest] is as said before.

He says, therefore, ***The light of thy body is thy eye***. Here the ***eye*** can be expounded in four ways, namely, the eye of reason as it was said, and this is the exposition according to Chrysostom and Hilary. For as by a lamp things are illuminated to be seen, so by reason things are enlightened for acting; "The spirit of a man is the lamp of the Lord" (Prov. 20, 27).

If thy eye be single, meaning if your whole mind is directed to one thing, namely to God, ***thy whole body shall be lightsome***. And ***if thy eye be evil***, meaning it is applied to earthly things, ***thy whole body shall be darksome***. And this can be understood in two ways. For the body will be ***lightsome*** or ***darksome*** as to present works. It will be ***lightsome*** if all the exterior members

---

206. "Sore eyes customarily see numerous lamps. A single and pure eye looks at simple and pure things. All this transfers to the senses. For just as the body, if there are no eyes, is totally in darkness, so if the soul loses its principal splendor, all the senses die with it in an obscure darkness" (*Comm. in Mt.*, I (PL 26, 44C-D)).

operate for God's sake, and when this happens, reason will be directed to God, because then the members are kept pure from sin, since sin does not come forth except from the consent of the mind. *But if thy eye be evil thy whole body shall be darksome.* If reason is occupied with earthly things, [then *thy whole body shall be darksome*] because then the members will be occupied with dark works; "Cast off the works of darkness and put on the armor of light" (Rom. 13, 12).[207]

Or it is expounded otherwise, according to Hilary. *If thy eye be single*, meaning if reason is simply directed to God, *thy whole body shall be lightsome*, because from the clarity of the soul redounds the clarity of the body. And so it is said, "The just shall shine as the sun, in the kingdom of their Father" (below 13, 43). *But if thy eye be evil*, etc.[208] Or it can be expounded otherwise, according to Augustine. By the eye, the intention is understood. For man firstly considers the distance to the destination, and afterwards goes forth. So in doing works, he firstly determines the end [of the works] and from the end, the intention proceeds to doing the works, wherefore the eye directs [the deeds]; "Her lamp shall not be put out in the night. She hath put out her hand to strong things" (Prov. 31, 18-19).[209] Hence, if the intention shall have been pure, the work or an accumulation of works proceeding from that intention will be pure, and this ought to be understood

---

207. "Or; The eye He speaks of is not the external but the internal eye. The light is the understanding, through which the soul sees God. He whose heart is turned to God has an eye full of light; that is, his understanding is pure, not distorted by the influence of worldly desires. The darkness in us is our bodily senses, which always desire the things that pertain to darkness. Whoso then has a pure eye, that is, a spiritual understanding, preserves his body in light, that is, without sin; for though the flesh desires evil, yet by the might of divine fear the soul resists it. But whoever has an eye, that is, an understanding, either darkened by the influence of the malignant passions, or fouled by evil lusts, possesses his body in darkness; he does not resist the flesh when it desires evil things, because he has no hope in Heaven, which hope alone gives us the strength to resist desire" (*Catena Aurea on St. Matthew*, chap. 6, lect. 15; Cf. Pseudo-Chrysostom, *Op. imp. in Mt.*, hom. xv (PG 56, 720-721)).

208. "HILARY; Otherwise; from the office of the light of the eye, He calls it the light of the heart; which if it continue single and brilliant, will confer on the body the brightness of the eternal light, and pour again into the corrupted flesh the splendor of its origin, that is, in time resurrection. But if it be obscured by sin, and evil in will, the bodily nature will yet abide subject to all the evils of the understanding" (*Catena Aurea on St. Matthew*, chap. 6, lect. 15; *In Evangelium Matthaei Commentarius*, v, 4 (PL 9, 944A)).

209. "And this passage we are to understand in such a way as to learn from it that all our works are pure and well-pleasing in the sight of God when they are done with a single heart, i.e. with a heavenly intent, having that end of love in view; for love is also the fulfilling of the law (Rom. 13, 10). Hence, we ought to here take the eye in the sense of the intent itself, wherewith we do whatever we are doing; and if this be pure and right, and looking at that which ought to be looked at, all our works which we perform in accordance therewith are necessarily good" (Augustine, *De serm. Dom.* II, xiii, 45 (PL 34, 1289)).

of those [works] which are in themselves good, because, as it is said, "The damnation is just of those who said, Let us do evil that there may come good" (Rom. 3, 8). If, however, the intention shall have been perverse, the whole working is rendered darkness, nor ought it to be seen strange if by works the body is signified, because, as it is said, "Mortify therefore your members which are upon the earth," etc., (Col. 3, 5). Thirdly, [Chromatius] sets forth [another exposition]: The eye of the soul is faith, which directs every work;[210] "Thy word is a lamp to my feet, and a light to my paths" (Ps. 118, 105). "A lamp to my feet" is simple when it does not vacillate. But "Faith works through charity" (Gal. 5, 6). If, however, the faith becomes depraved, the whole body, [meaning] one's works, is darksome; "All that is not of faith is sin" (Rom. 14, 23). Or it is expounded otherwise. The eye signifies prelates, who are among those able to see, according to what is said, "David's men said: Thou shalt go no more out with us to battle, lest thou put out the lamp of Israel" (II Kings 21, 17), and, "As the judge of the people is himself, so also are his ministers" (Eccli. 10, 2).[211] Now that which He says, *If then the light that is in thee, be darkness*, according to the first exposition, He is syllogizing from the preceding propositions, and according to these propositions He is proving the preceding proposition, as though you were to say, *If thy eye be single, thy whole body shall be lightsome*, etc., and the proof is, *If then the light that is in thee, be darkness*, about which less is seen, *the darkness itself how great shall it be*; if the light of reason be dark, the deed will also be dark, and in this respect the exposition is not changed, but it is related to other things such that, as Augustine says, anyone can know the kind [of a deed] from one's intention, but one cannot know what

---

210. "By the light of the body, the intelligence of the mind and the faith of the heart are understood: which if it is pure and lightsome in us, without doubt it enlightens our whole body. Now for this reason light is put in comparison with faith, because just as light enlightens the steps of those walking at night, lest while walking they run either into pits or any obstacle: so in the night of this world the splendor of faith enlightens all the steps of our life, going before with the light of truth; lest we fall into the pits of sins or into the obstacles of the devil. This is therefore what the Lord says, *The light of thy body is thy eye. If thy eye be single, thy whole body shall be lightsome. But if thy eye be evil thy whole body shall be darksome, because if this faith of ours, which is signified* by the light or eye of the body, is blinded in us by the darkness of sins or by the obscurity of disbelief; without doubt, our whole body is rendered obscure and dark." (Chromatius of Aquileia, *In Evangelium Sancti Matthaei*, tract. xvii (PL 20, 366C)); Cf. *Glossa Interlinearis, Bibliorum Sacrorum cum Glossa Ordinaria* (1603), p. 137.

211. "GREG NAZ. The light and eye of the Church is the Bishop. It is necessary, then, that as the body is rightly directed as long as the eye keeps itself pure, but goes wrong when it becomes corrupt, so also with respect to the Prelate, according to what his state may be, must the Church in like manner suffer shipwreck, or be saved" (*Catena Aurea on St. Luke*, chap. 11, lect. 10).

kind of result one's deed may have. Hence, the intention is *light*, but the deed is *darkness*;[212] "For all that is made manifest is light" (Eph. 5, 13).

Or it is otherwise, according to Augustine, who says that there are two kinds of works: works of light and works of darkness; "Let us, therefore cast off the works of darkness and put on the armor of light" (Rom. 13, 12).[213] *If then the light*, a work of justice, *that is in you be darkness*, meaning, it is done due to a bad intention, *the darkness itself*, meaning the bad actions, *how great shall it be*.[214]

Or it is otherwise. If one's faith be bad, everything directed by faith is bad, and similarly if a prelate be bad, all the more will his subjects be bad.[215]

212. "It is not, therefore, what one does, but the intent with which he does it, that is to be considered. For this is the light in us, because it is a thing manifest to ourselves that we do with a good intent what we are doing; 'For all that is made manifest is light' (Eph. 5, 13). For the deeds themselves, which go forth from us to human society, have an uncertain issue; and therefore He has called them darkness. For I do not know, when I present money to a poor man who asks it, either what he is to do with it, or what he is to suffer from it; and it may happen that he does some evil with it, or suffers some evil on account of it, a thing I did not wish to happen when I gave it to him, nor would I have given it with such an intention. If, therefore, I did it with a good intention,--a thing which was known to me when I was doing it, and is therefore called light,--my deed also is lighted up, whatever issue it shall have; but that issue, inasmuch as it is uncertain and unknown, is called darkness. But if I have done it with a bad intent, the light itself even is darkness. For it is spoken of as light, because every one knows with what intent he acts, even when he acts with a bad intent; but the light itself is darkness, because the aim is not directed singly to things above, but is turned downwards to things beneath, and makes, as it were, a shadow by means of a double heart. *If, therefore, the light that is in thee be darkness, how great is that darkness!* i.e., if the very intent of the heart with which you do what you are doing (which is known to you) is polluted by the hunger after earthly and temporal things, and blinded, how much more is the deed itself, whose issue is uncertain, polluted and full of darkness! Because, although what you do with an intent which is neither upright nor pure, may turn out for some one's good, it is the way in which you have done it, not how it has turned out for him, that is reckoned to you" (*De serm. Dom.* II, xiii, 46 (PL 34, 1289-1290)).

213. St. John Chrysostom is cited here, but the following words of St. Augustine seem to be cited instead: "AUG. But acts which are known to be in themselves sins, are not to be done as with a good purpose; but such works only as are either good or bad, according as the motives from which they are done are either good or bad, and are not in themselves sins; as to give food to the poor is good if it be done from merciful motives, but evil if it be done from ostentation. But such works as are in themselves sins, who will say that they are to be done with good motives, or that they are not sins? Who would say, Let us rob the rich, that we may have to give to the poor?" (*Catena Aurea on St. Matthew*, chap. 6, lect. 15; cf. *Contra Mendacium Ad Consentium* vii, 18 (PL 40, 528-529)).

214. "GREG. Otherwise; if the light that is in you, that is, if what we have begun to do well, we overcloud with evil purpose, when we do things which we know to be in themselves evil, how great is the darkness!" (*Catena Aurea on St. Matthew*, chap. 6, lect. 15; cf. *Moralia* xxviii, chap. 11, n. 30 (PL 76, 465 C)).

215. "REMIG. Otherwise; faith is likened to a light, because by it the goings of the inner man, that is, action, are lightened that he should not stumble, according to that, *Your word is a light to my feet*. If that, then, be pure and single, the whole body is

No man can serve two masters. Above, the Lord put forth one teaching that we ought not to accumulate treasures on earth because the heart is distracted by this. Now He puts forth another, because, in fact, accumulating treasures makes one a stranger in respect to God, and this is what He says, *No man can serve two masters.* Or it can be continued otherwise. Above, He warned us not to accumulate treasures on earth, but in heaven, but someone could say, 'I want to gather treasures in heaven and on earth,' and so here the Lord shows this to be impossible, saying, *No man can serve two masters.*[216] But the first continuation is better and it is Chrysostom's.[217]

This passage can be read in two ways, firstly so that these words, *No man can serve two masters*, are understood as a conclusion or inference, and then the Lord, according to the exposition of Chrysostom[218] and Jerome,[219] goes on to common opinions to illustrate His point. In another way, it can be understood to be read such that the Lord firstly states what He wants [to say] and afterwards He goes on [to different points], and this is according to Augustine.[220] Now let us follow both through.

light; but if defiled, the whole body will be dark. Yet otherwise; by the light may be understood the ruler of the Church, who may be well called the eye, as he it is that ought to see that wholesome things be provided for the people under him, which are understood by the body. If then the ruler of the Church err, how much more will the people subject to him err?" (*Catena Aurea on St. Matthew*, chap. 6, lect. 15).

216. "GLOSS. Otherwise; it had been declared above, that good things become evil, when done with a worldly purpose. It might therefore have been said by someone, *I will do good works from worldly and heavenly motives at once.* Against this the Lord says, *No man can serve two masters*" (*Catena Aurea on St. Matthew*, chap. 6, lect. 16).

217. "Thus, 'wealth,' saith He, 'hurts you not in this only, that it arms robbers against you, nor in that it darkens your mind in the most intense degree, but also in that it casts you out of God's service, making you captive of lifeless riches, and in both ways doing you harm, on the one hand, by causing you to be slaves of what you ought to command; on the other, by casting you out of God's service, whom, above all things, it is indispensable for you to serve'" (*In Mt.*, Hom. xxi, 1 (PG 57, 295)).

218. "Let us see, first, how the present words follow the preceding things that have been spoken. Earlier He commanded to give alms, saying, *Lay up to yourselves treasures in heaven*, because whoever stores up treasures for himself in heaven has his heart in heaven and his hope in God: he has a sound eye of the soul, that is, a pure and spiritual mind, one that also always meditates not on earthly things, but on heavenly matters. But whoever has a pure and spiritual mind can keep his body clear, that is, without sin. But whoever does not give alms does not have his heart in heaven or his hope in God, nor does he have a pure and spiritual mind, nor can he keep his body clear, that is, without sin, because *No man can serve two masters, God and mammon*—that is, wealth" (*Op. imp. in Mt.*, hom. xvi (PG 56, 722)).

219. "JEROME: Let the covetous man who is called by the Christian name hear this, that he cannot serve both Christ and riches. Yet He said not, he who has riches, but, he who is the servant of riches. For he who is the slave of money, guards his money as a slave; but he who has thrown off the yoke of his slavery, dispenses them as a master" (*Catena Aurea on St. Matthew*, chap. 6, lect. 16; *Comm. in Mt.*, I (PL 26, 45A)).

220. "Because, although what you do with an intent which is neither upright nor pure, may turn out for some one's good, it is the way in which you have

Therefore, according to the first exposition, He does two things. Firstly, He relates the common opinion and custom of men, and secondly, He gives the reason, where it is said, *For either he will hate the one, and love the other.* He says, therefore, *No man can serve two masters.* Now the reason for this will appear if we properly understand what a slave is and what a master is. For the notion of a slave consists in the fact that he belongs to another, namely, to his master. Hence, his end is his master. Now it is impossible that one thing be directed toward two things as toward two final ends. If, therefore, it belongs to his being a slave that he order his actions to his master as to his final end, it is impossible that he serve two masters; "The bed is straitened, so that one must fall out, and a short covering cannot cover both" (Is. 28, 20). Yet a slave can have two masters, of which one is under the other, as one end can be under another end, or according to the Gloss, *No man can serve two* contrary *masters*, because if they consent, they are one master.[221]

He gives the reason [for this opinion of men, where it is said], *Either he will hate the one, and love the other.* And it ought to be known that rulership is twofold. For some men rule in this way, because they are loved by their subjects, and this is royal rulership. Other men rule such that they are feared, and this is the rulership of tyrants.[222] Therefore, if a slave serves his master with love, then it befits him to hate an opposing master. If, however, the slave serves his master with fear, then it is befitting that 'you sustain the one,' meaning that you tolerate the one, 'and you despise the other,' and this is what He says, *Or he will sustain the one, and despise the other.*[223] Concerning this rulership that ought more to be sustained than loved, it is written, "When

done it, not how it has turned out for him, that is reckoned to you. Then, further, the statement which follows, *No man can serve two masters*, is to be referred to this very intent, as He goes on to explain, saying: *For either he will hate the one, and love the other; or else he will submit to the one, and despise the other*" (De serm. Dom. II, xiii-xiv, 46-47 (PL 34, 1290)).

221. "*No man can serve two masters*, which is understood when they are opposed, dissimilar, and not placed one under the other" (Nicholas of Lyra, *Glossa Interlinearis, Bibliorum Sacrorum cum Glossa Ordinaria* (1603), p. 137).

222. "The rule of a father over his children is royal, for he rules by virtue both of love and of the respect due to age, exercising a kind of royal power" (Aristotle, *Politics*, bk. 1, part 12). "A natural difference distinguishes kingly rule from political rule, which is by nature between equals. And love distinguishes kingly rule from that of a tyrant, who rules for his own convenience, not because of love that he has for his subjects" (*Commentary on Aristotle's Politics*, I, x, 3).

223. "GLOSS. Or; He seems to allude to two different kinds of servants; one kind who serve freely for love, another who serve servilely from fear. If then one serve two masters of contrary character from love, it must be that he hate the one; if from fear, while he trembles before the one, he must despise the other" (*Catena Aurea on St. Matthew*, chap. 6, lect. 16).

the wicked shall" feign "to bear rule, the people shall mourn" (Prov. 29, 2), meaning *he will sustain* patiently by tolerating. *No man can serve two masters*, but God and the devil are opposing masters, because they are inclining to opposite things, therefore, *You cannot serve God and mammon. Mammon* means riches in the Persian language, according to Jerome.[224]

Nevertheless it ought to be known that it is one thing to abound with riches and another thing to serve them. For some men abound with riches and [use them] for their ordained good [end], and these men do not serve riches. Others have riches and they take neither corporeal nor spiritual benefit [from them], and these men serve their riches, because they afflict themselves in order to acquire riches; "There is also another evil, which I have seen under the sun, and that frequent among men: A man to whom God hath given riches, and substance, and honour, and his soul wanteth nothing of all that he desireth: yet God doth not give him power to eat thereof, but a stranger shall eat it up. This is vanity and a great misery" (Eccles. 6, 1-2). For in whatever thing a man places his last end, that thing is his god; "Whose God is their belly" (Phil. 3, 19), or by *mammon* the devil is understood, who is in charge of riches; not that he is able to give them but because he uses them to deceive. For some spirit is in charge of every vice. Hence, the spirit appointed to avarice allures men to sinning. This is one exposition of this passage.

No man can serve two masters [can also be expounded] such that it is read illatively and generally. Now Augustine understands this passage spiritually, namely, of God and the devil, who are opposed; "What concord hath Christ with Belial?" (II Cor. 6, 15) and He is saying that you are unable to be partakers [of them both] at the same time; "How long do you halt between two sides? If the Lord be God, follow him: but if Baal, then follow him" (III Kings 18, 21). *For either he will hate the one*, meaning the devil, *and love the other*, meaning God. And notice that He did not say the converse, but He said, *or he will sustain the one*, because every creature is naturally disposed to love God. But the devil, because he has a depraved nature, is immediately abhorred since no one loves evil, and so He said, *or he will sustain the one*, because the devil is endured as an oppressing tyrant; just as someone endures the master of a handmaid to whom he is joined by affection, not because he loves the master but on account of the handmaid. So cupidity endures

---

224. "In the Syriac language, riches are called *mammon*" (*Comm. in Mt.*, I (PL 26, 44D)).

the devil on account of the cupidity, which is the handmaid of the devil. Hence, when someone wants to take pleasure in any sin, in that he enjoys it, he suffers the slavery of the devil, and this is what is said, *or he will sustain the one*; and insofar as he endures [the slavery of the devil] he withdraws from God's commandments, and by withdrawing he despises [God], and this is what is said, *and despise the other.*[225]

But here it is objected concerning this which is said [by Augustine above], namely, that God is not hated, that the Psalm says, "The pride of them that hate thee ascendeth continually" (73, 23), therefore, someone has hatred towards God. On account of this passage, Augustine, in his book *Retractions*,[226] retracts what he had said before, namely, that goodness itself cannot be hated; and yet both are true, because if it be considered what God is, namely, goodness itself, He cannot be hated, because a good thing is always loved in itself; however, He can be hated as to an effect which is contrary to the will.[227] So then it is evident that one cannot serve two masters; "Woe to the sinner that goeth on the earth two ways" (Eccli. 2, 14).

Therefore I say to you, be not solicitous. After the Lord showed that we ought not to place our end in earthly and superfluous treasures, He wishes also to show that [we ought not to be solicitous] in acquiring the necessaries of life, and this is what He says, *Therefore I say to you, be not solicitous for your life.* And about this He does two things. Firstly, He forbids solicitude for necessaries of life as to present things, and secondly, as to future things, where it is said, *Be not solicitous therefore, saying: What shall we eat.* About the first point, He does two things. Firstly, He proposes what He intends, and secondly, He proves the proposition, where it is said, *Is not the life more than the meat.* He says, therefore, *Therefore I say to you, be not solicitous*, as though He were to say, 'Because you cannot serve

---

225. "But he who serves mammon certainly serves him who, as being set over those earthly things in virtue of his perversity, is called by our Lord "the prince of this world" (Jn. 12, 31 and 14, 30). A man will therefore *either hate the one, and love the other*, i.e. God; *or he will sustain the one, and despise the other*. For whoever serves mammon submits to a hard and ruinous master: for, being entangled by his own lust, he becomes a subject of the devil, and he does not love him; for who is there who loves the devil? But yet he submits to him; as in any large house, he who is connected with another man's maid servant submits to hard bondage on account of his passion, even though he does not love him whose maid-servant he loves" (*De serm. Dom.* II, xiv, 47 (PL 34, 1290)).

226. "Likewise, that which I said, 'For almost no one's conscience can hate God' (*De serm. Dom.* II, xiv, 48 (PL 34, 1290)), I do not see that it should have been said; for there are many of whom it is written, 'The pride of them that hate thee ascendeth continual' (Ps. 73, 23)" (*Retractationum* I, xix, 8 (PL 32, 617)).

227. cf. III, q. 95, a. 5.

God and mammon, therefore you ought not to serve riches so that you may serve God.'

Neither for your life (*animae*)***, what you shall eat***. But it seems that the soul (*anima*) does not need food. But I reply that although it does not need food of itself, yet it needs food insofar as it is joined to a body, because without life it could not be there or otherwise be called a soul in that instance; "He that loveth his life shall lose it and he that hateth his life in this world keepeth it unto life eternal" (Jn. 12, 25).

Nor for your body. Observe that from this passage heresies took their origin. For, according to Augustine, there were some men saying that it was not lawful for a contemplative man to work,[228] and against these men Augustine made a book, *On the Work of Monks*. But how these words that the Lord says ought to be understood, we ought to investigate from the saints. Note that it is said, "If any man will not work, neither let him eat" (II Thess. 3, 10), and one will understand of these words the work of the hands, as is evident from the preceding words. Hence also, as an example, the Apostle himself worked with his hands.[229]

But are all bound to do this? If all are bound, then either it is a precept or a counsel. If it is a precept, no one ought to be exempt; if it is a counsel, then to whom is it given? It is certain that it was a precept for the people of his time because then there were no religious. To a counsel, however, no one is bound except from a vow, wherefore all can desist [from doing this]. I reply that this is a precept and all are bound to this, because it was given to all men. For the Apostle is speaking to the whole Church.[230] But something is a precept in two ways, on account of itself and on account of

---

228. "AUG. There are certain heretics called Euchitae, who hold that a monk may not do any work even for his support; who embrace this profession that they may be freed from necessity of daily labor" (*Catena Aurea on St. Matthew*, chap. 6, lect. 17; *De Haeresibus*, 57 (PL 42, 41)); The Euchites, who were so called from their profession of prayer, were properly fanatical monks of the fourth and following centuries, but their name is often taken as synonymous with Mystics. They were of oriental origin, and disparaged, if not denied, the efficacy of Baptism.

229. "AUG. For they say the Apostle did not speak of personal labor, such as that of husbandmen or craftsmen, when he said, *If any man will not work, neither let him eat*. For he could not be so contrary to the Gospel, where it is said, *Therefore I say to you, be not solicitous*." (*Catena Aurea on St. Matthew*, chap. 6, lect. 17; *De Opere Monachorum* chap. 1, n. 2 (PL 40, 549)).

230. "Now this [precept] does not apply to religious any more than to seculars, which is evident for two reasons. First, on account of the way in which the Apostle expresses himself, by saying: 'That you withdraw yourselves from every brother walking disorderly.' For he calls all Christians brothers, since at that time religious orders were not as yet founded. Secondly, because religious have no other obligations than what seculars have, except as required by the rule they profess: wherefore if their rule contain nothing about manual labor, religious are not otherwise bound to manual labor than seculars are" (II II, q. 183, a. 2 ad 2um).

something else. For example, if you take the cross to go across the sea,[231] it is a precept that one go and the precept is on account of itself; but that you would seek a ship, this is a precept not on account of itself but on account of something else, because whoever is bound to some end is also bound to everything which is for the end. Now everyone is bound to conservation of his life by the natural law, and thus they are bound to everything else by which life is preserved. If, therefore, someone has the wherewithal by which he can live, he is not bound to labor with his hands, and therefore the Apostle does not say, 'with one's hands,' but, "If any man will not work," etc., as though he were to say, 'You are bound to labor in that manner by which [you are able] to eat.' Now who are bound to labor with their hands, this matter may be put aside for time being.

Now in that He says, *solicitous*, it ought to be known that solicitude pertains to foresight, but not every foresight is solicitude. But *solicitous* in its proper sense means foresight with diligence, which is the vehement application of the mind. Hence, here solicitude implies a vehement application of the mind. Now in this vehement application there can be sin in four ways. Firstly, there is sin when there is solicitude for temporal things as the ultimate end, and according to this way it is reprehended; "The expectation of the solicitous shall perish" (Prov. 11, 7). Secondly, there is sin when someone cares too much about acquiring temporal things, and in this way the following words are understood: "To the sinner God hath given vexation, and superfluous care, to heap up and to gather together," and afterwards it is said, "But this also is vanity, and a fruitless solicitude of the mind" (Eccles. 2, 26). Thirdly, it is a sin when a soul occupies itself excessively about thoughts of temporal things. Hence Jerome says, "The toil is to be undergone, the anxiety put away";[232] and in this way is understood the words, "But he that is with a wife is solicitous for the things of the world: how he may please his wife. And he is divided" (I Cor. 7, 33), because his heart is drawn apart to diverse things. Fourthly, it is a sin when foresight is with a certain fear and desperation. For it seems to some men that they can never acquire so much that it can suffice for them. And all these things He forbids here, as is evident from His following words, and so in regard to this last way the words are understood, "be not solicitous" to seek after the asses (I Kings 9, 20), meaning, do not despair of finding them.

---

231. A cross made of cloth was worn as a badge on the outer garment of those who took part in the Crusades. "Medieval writers used the term *crux* (*pro cruce transmarina*, Charter of 1284, cited by Du Cange s. v. *crux*)" ("Crusades," *Catholic Encyclopedia*, (1908 ed.), vol. 4, p. 543).

232. *Comm. in Mt.*, I (PL 26, 45B).

Is not the life more than the meat. Above, the Lord taught that we ought not to be solicitous for the necessaries of life, here He adduces the reason for His admonition, and He puts forward three reasons. The first reason is taken from the greater [to the less], the second reason is taken from the less [to the greater], and the third reason is taken from the opposite. The second reason is where it is said, ***Behold the birds of the air.*** The third reason is where it is said, ***Be not solicitous therefore.***

The first of these reasons is as follows. He who gave the greater will give the less. But the Lord gave the soul and the body; therefore, He will give the food. And this is what is said, ***Is not the soul*** (*anima*) ***more than the meat***, meaning, the life (*vita*), for we do not live in order to eat, but vice versa. For food is ordained to life, wherefore life is better [than food], just as the end is better than those things which are for the end; and similarly, clothing is for the sake of the body, and not vice versa. Now, that God gave the soul and body, it is stated when firstly "God formed" matter for the body (Gen. 2, 7), "He breathed into" the matter for the soul. But He who gave [life] will preserve it by giving those things which are necessary [to preserve life];[233] "He created all things that they might be" (Wis. 1, 14). Hilary expounds this otherwise, for he says, "Since solicitude implies a certain doubting, the Lord wanted to remove doubting concerning the future resurrection of the soul."[234] ***Be not solicitous for your life***, meaning, 'You do not want to disbelieve concerning the resurrection, because He who will reform the body in the resurrection will preserve [your life] without clothing and food.' But this is not a literal exposition.

Afterwards, the second reason is from the less, and it is the following. He who provides for lesser things, things which one cares little about, will also provide for the greater things.[235] But

---

233. "PSEUDO-CHRYS. For had He not willed that, that which was should be preserved, He had not created it; but what He so created that it should be preserved by food, it is necessary that He give it food, as long as He would have it to be preserved" (*Catena Aurea on St. Matthew*, chap. 6, lect. 17; *Op. imp. in Mt.*, hom. xvi (PG 56, 723)).

234. "HILARY; Otherwise; Because the thoughts of the unbelievers were ill-employed respecting care of things future, caviling concerning what is to be the appearance of our bodies in the resurrection, what the food in the eternal life, therefore He continues, *Is not the life more than food?* He will not endure that our hope should hang in care for the meat and drink and clothing that is to be in the resurrection, lest there should be affront given to Him who has given us the more precious things, in our being anxious that He should also give us the less" (*Catena Aurea on St. Matthew*, chap. 6, lect. 17; *In Evangelium Matthaei Commentarius*, v, 8 (PL 9, 946A)).

235. "PSEUDO-CHRYS. Having confirmed our hope by this arguing from the greater to the less, He next confirms it by an argument from less to greater, *Behold the fowls of the air, they sow not, neither do they reap*" (*Catena Aurea on St. Matthew*, chap. 6, lect. 18; *Op. imp. in Mt.*, hom. xvi (PG 56, 723)).

God provides for the plants and the birds, etc. And about this He does two things. Firstly, He deduces the reason as to food, and secondly, as to clothing, where it is said, *And for raiment why are you solicitous?* About the first point, He does two things. Firstly, He teaches to cast away solicitude by the example of the animals; secondly, on account of its inefficacy, where it is said, *And which of you by taking thought, can add to his stature one cubit?* About the first part, He does four things. Firstly, He proposes for consideration the brute animals; secondly, He points out the lack [of solicitude] accompanying these things; thirdly, He points out Divine providence; and fourthly, it is argued from the latter. Therefore, **Behold the birds of the air**, meaning, 'consider [them]'; "Ask now the beasts, and they shall teach thee: and the birds of the air, and they shall tell thee" (Job 12, 7). For from the consideration of these things man sometimes learns; "Go to the ant, O sluggard, and consider her ways, and learn wisdom" (Prov. 6, 6). **For they neither sow.**

Man's food is his daily bread. For its acquisition, it is obtained by a threefold work: by sowing, by reaping, and by storing. Hence, He excludes these three things from birds, **For they neither sow**, etc. Now there is also a sowing of spiritual doctrine; "Behold the sower went forth to sow" (below 13, 3), [meaning the sowing] of good works; "To him that soweth justice, there is a faithful reward. Clemency prepareth life" (Prov. 11, 18-19), and, "He who soweth sparingly shall also reap sparingly: and he who soweth in blessings shall also reap blessings" (II Cor. 9, 6). And there is also a bad sowing of carnal sins; "He that soweth in his flesh of the flesh also shall reap corruption" (Gal. 6, 8), [and there is a bad sowing] of spiritual sins; "On the contrary, I have seen those who work iniquity, and sow sorrows, and reap them" (Job 4, 8). Now the holy preachers reap when they bear away some men to the faith; "I have sent you to reap that in which you did not labor" (Jn. 4, 38).

Afterwards, the help of Divine Providence is related, and He says, **and your heavenly Father**. He is not the Father of those things, because properly God is the Father of rational creatures which are [made] "to His image" (Gen. 1, 25). He also says, **heavenly**, because we have something for attaining heaven, namely, our soul which pertains to a likeness of substances. Hence, [if] our Father feeds those things of which He is only their God, all the more He [will feed] us of whom He is our Father; "Who giveth to beasts their food: and to the young ravens that call upon him" (Ps. 146, 9). Afterwards it is argued, **Are not you more**, meaning of greater value by ordination, namely, "Let him have dominion over the fishes of the sea, and the fowls of the air, and the beasts, and the whole earth, and every creeping creature that moveth upon the earth" (Gen. 1, 26). For sometimes a horse is sold for more than a man, because the valuation of a thing is twofold. The valuation is either in respect to the order of nature, and in this way man is better than other things, or it is in respect to a valuation or perhaps to the pleasure, and in this way sometimes an animal is sold for more. About this passage, it ought to be considered that some men, I believe it was Origen, expounded it otherwise and they say that by *birds* is understood the holy angels, who do not exercise bodily labors and yet God feeds them with spiritual food, concerning which it is said, "the bread of angels" (Ps. 77, 25).[236] But as Jerome says, this cannot stand because God adds, *Are not you of much more value than they?*[237] Hilary, however, by the birds understands the devils, and so the *birds of the air* that are fed, insofar as they are preserved in the being of their nature, [are the devils]. And men *are more than they*, because the Lord adduces as a proof that if they who are predestined to death are sustained by God, much more will we be sustained by Him.[238] But according to Augustine, these things that our Lord says are not to be taken allegorically, because the Lord wishes to draw an argument from these sensible things to show the proposition.[239]

But it ought to be known that here there was an error of certain men, saying that it is not lawful for spiritual men to labor corporeally

---

236. "Since the angels also are nourished on the wisdom of God and receive strength to accomplish their own proper works from the contemplation of truth and wisdom, so in the Psalms we find it written that the angels also take food" (*De Oratione*, n. 27 (PL 11, 514B)).
237. "JEROME; There be some who, seeking to go beyond the limits of their fathers, and to soar into the air, sink into the deep and are drowned. These will have the birds of the air to mean the Angels, and the other powers in the ministry of God, who without any care of their own are fed by God's providence. But if this be indeed as they would have it, how follows it, said to men, *Are not you of much more value than they?* It must be taken then in the plain sense; If birds that today are, and tomorrow are not, be nourished by God's providence, without thought or toil of their own, how much more men to whom eternity is promised!" (*Catena Aurea on St. Matthew*, chap. 6, lect. 18; *Comm. in Mt.*, I (PL 26, 45C)).
238. "Hilary: It may be said, that under the name of birds, He exhorts us by the example of the unclean spirits, to whom, without any trouble of their own in seeking and collecting it, provision of life is given by the power of the Eternal Wisdom. And to lead us to refer this to the unclean spirits, He suitably adds, *Are not ye of much more value than they?* Thus showing the great interval between piety and wickedness" (*Catena Aurea on St. Matthew*, chap. 6, lect. 18; *In Evangelium Matthaei Commentarius*, v, 9 (PL 9, 947A)).
239. "But these examples are not to be treated as allegories, so that we should inquire what the fowls of heaven or the lilies of the field mean: for they stand here, in order that from smaller matters we may be persuaded respecting greater ones" (*De serm. Dom.* II, xv, 52 (PL 34, 1291-1292)).

on account of this similitude of the birds, against whom Augustine, in his book *On the Work of Monks*, says that it is impossible that men imitate the life of birds in everything. Hence, some perfect men went into the desert and they rarely went to the city, hence, it behooved them to gather many of their victuals; on the other hand, the Apostles worked with their hands; hence, not to labor does not pertain to perfection, and Augustine gives the example that God frees those who are hoping in Him, as it is evident concerning Daniel and the boys in the furnace. Therefore, ought one placed in trials to do nothing so that he might be freed? On the contrary, because the Lord said, "When they shall persecute you in this city, flee into another" (below 10, 23),[240] and therefore I reply, saying that the Lord wishes that in all things man would do what he can while hoping in God. God will give to him what He shall see to be expedient, because, on the other hand, if he were to do otherwise, He would be a tempter and foolish. Therefore, God has providence concerning man's actions, yet so that He provides for everyone according to their manner [of being], because He provides in one way for men and another way for birds, because He did not give the power of reason to the birds by which one can procure things necessary for oneself. But all is endowed to them by their nature, but to man He gave the power of reason by which he may procure things necessary for himself. Hence, He gave all things to man by giving him the power of reason, and wherefore if we do what is in us, He will do what is in Himself.

And which of you by taking thought, can add to his stature one cubit? Here He draws forth an argument from experience. For it is evident that as God provides for the animals in the works of nature, so He provides for man. For in man there is a certain part which is subject to reason, such as the parts consisting of the motive and appetitive powers, and there are others which are not subject to reason, such as the nutritive and augmentative powers. But man, in regard to those things which are subject to reason, differs from brute animals and thus he is provided for differently, because he is provided for through his reason, but others through their nature. But as to those things in which he shares equally

---

240. "For neither does it follow that because the Lord hath said, 'Call upon me in the day of trouble: I will deliver thee, and thou shalt glorify me' (Ps. 49, 15), therefore the Apostle ought not to have fled, and to be let down by the wall in a basket that he might escape the hands of a pursuer (Acts 9, 25), but should rather have waited to be taken, that, like the three children from the midst of the fires (Dan. 3, 50), the Lord might deliver him... Or, because they say that they imitate the Gospel birds, do they fear to be, as it were, plucked, lest they be not able to fly?" (*De Opere Monachorum* chap. 26-30, n. 35-39. (PL 40, 574-578)).

with the brute animals, all are provided for equally. For all things are grown through the work of nature, and because the growth of the body is from Divine providence, we ought not, in view of the least solicitude for temporal things, to put aside spiritual works; "He made the little and the great, and he hath equally care of all" (Wis. 6, 8), and this is what He says, *And which of you by taking thought, can add to his stature one cubit?*

Hilary expounds this passage of the state of the future resurrection, and he says that in the resurrection all will be equal in quantity, and wherefore to some men quantity will be added, and this is the meaning of *And which of you by taking thought, can add to his stature one cubit?*[241] But Augustine disproves this in his book, *City of God*, and I believe that he speaks better. For it is said that "He will reform the body of our lowness, made like to the body of his glory" (Phil. 3, 21), therefore, we ought to hope that those things which appeared in Christ when rising, and were shown to the disciples, will be in us. But Christ rose in the same quantity in which He was before, therefore nothing accrued to Him, nor likewise is anything taken away from anyone, because the Lord says, a hair of our head shall not perish (Lk. 21, 18).[242] Hence, he replies that in the resurrection all men will conformed to Christ as to their age, and everyone will rise in the quantity in which he would have had at that age. Now what is from a defect of nature in dwarfs will be taken away. Hence, they will rise in such quantity and quality as they would have attained if nature had not failed to have reached that age, namely, Christ's age.[243]

---

241. "HILARY; Otherwise; As by the example of the spirits He had fixed our faith in the supply of food for our lives, so now by a decision of common understanding He cuts off all anxiety about supply of clothing. Seeing that He it is who shall raise in one perfect man every various kind of body that ever drew breath, and is alone able to add one or two or three cubits to each man's stature; surely in being anxious concerning clothing, that is, concerning the appearance of our bodies, we offer affront to Him who will add so much to each man's stature as shall bring all to an equality" (*Catena Aurea on St. Matthew*, chap. 6, lect. 18; *In Evangelium Matthaei Commentarius*, v, 10 (PL 9, 947B-C)).

242. "And if the saying of the apostle, that we are all to come to the measure of the age of the fullness of Christ, (Ephesians 4,13) or that other saying, Whom He predestinated to be conformed to the image of His Son, (Romans 8,29) is to be understood to mean that the stature and size of Christ's body shall be the measure of the bodies of all those who shall be in His kingdom, then, say they, the size and height of many must be diminished; and if so much of the bodily frame itself be lost, what becomes of the saying, Not a hair of your head shall perish? Besides, it might be asked regarding the hair itself, whether all that the barber has cut off shall be restored? And if it is to be restored, who would not shrink from such deformity?" (*City of God*, bk. 22, chap. 12, n. 1 (PL 41, 775)).

243. "It may also be understood thus, that as He was conformed to us by assuming mortality, we shall be conformed to Him by immortality; and this indeed is connected with the resurrection of the body. But if we are also taught in these words what form our bodies shall rise in, as the

And for raiment why are you solicitous? Here He deduces a reason as to clothing, and firstly He states His intention; secondly, He makes a comparison; and thirdly, He argues from these points. The second part is where it is said, **Consider the lilies of the field**, and the third part is where it is said, **And if the grass of the field**. After solicitude for food and drink, He suitably treats concerning solicitude for clothing, because just as food and drink come to be necessities of life, so also clothing; "Having food and wherewith to be covered, with these we are content" (I Tim. 6, 8). And Jacob said, "If God shall be with me, and shall keep me in the way, by which I walk, and shall give me bread to eat, and raiment to put on and I shall return prosperously to my father's house: the Lord shall be my God" (Gen. 28, 20-21).

Consider the lilies of the field. He adduces an example and He puts forward two things, a comparison and the help of a Divine promise, where it is said, **But I say to you**. He says, therefore, **Consider the lilies of the field.** Now the consideration of the Divine works avails in that the soul breaks forth into praise of the Creator; "And I will meditate on all thy works: and will be employed in thy inventions. Thy way, O God, is in the holy place: who is the great God like our God?" (Ps. 76, 13-14). **How they grow**; "But God gave the increase" (I Cor. 3, 6). **They labor not**. For clothing the work of men and women is needed, and this is what is said, **They labor not, neither do they spin**. Or **they labor not** to dye, **neither do they spin** to prepare [the clothing], hence, they labor neither on account of the color nor on account of the substance of the clothing.

But I say to you. Here the benefit of the Divine promise is related. For He provides in such a way that all human efforts cannot be equated to His, because the things that occur according to art cannot be equated to those things that occur according to nature, and this is what He says, **that not even Solomon in all his glory was arrayed as one of these**, who was more glorious than all the kings known by the Jews; "Solomon the son of David was strengthened in his kingdom, and the Lord his God was with him, and magnified him to a high degree" (II Par. 1, 1). And He says, **in all his glory**, because he could not have for one day clothing as the flowers have, and this is the exposition of

---

measure we spoke of before, so also this conformity is to be understood not of size, but of age. Accordingly all shall rise in the stature they either had attained or would have attained had they lived to their prime, although it will be no great disadvantage even if the form of the body be infantine or aged, while no infirmity shall remain in the mind nor in the body itself" (*City of God*, bk. 22, chap. 16 (PL 41, 778)).

Chrysostom and is the literal meaning.[244] Or, *not even Solomon*, etc., can be expounded otherwise, namely, that these corporeal things have clothing without solicitude, which Solomon did not have.[245] Hilary says, anagogically, by the lilies the holy angels are signified; "My beloved to me, and I to him who feedeth among the lilies" (Cant. 2, 16), and the Lord wishes to eliminate solicitude concerning clothing in the resurrection. For just as the angels are clothed with brightness, so also will our bodies be clothed.[246]

And if the grass of the field which is to day, and to morrow is cast into the oven, God doth so clothe, etc. Here He argues from an example. Above, the Lord had made mention of the lilies, here He changes *the lilies* to *the grass of the field*, because He intends to argue from the less. Hence, on one hand He points out a defect [of grass] to show man's preeminence, whence on the other hand He shows man's preeminence as to his dignity of substance, because we are men but a flower is *the grass of the field*; "The grass is withered, and the flower is fallen, because the spirit of the Lord hath blown upon it" (Is. 40, 7). He shows man's preeminence as to his duration, because we are perpetual as to our soul, but a flower is, as it were, momentary, because it *is to day, and to morrow is cast into the oven*. And He uses the indeterminate future for the determinate future, as it is said, "My justice shall answer for me tomorrow" (Gen. 30, 33), and, "Let them be as grass upon the tops of houses: which withereth before it be plucked up" (Ps. 128, 6). He shows man's preeminence as to his end, because man is made for the sake of beatitude, however, the end of things of this kind is so that they may come into man's use; "Who maketh

---

244. "But if Solomon was surpassed by their beauty, and that not once nor twice, but throughout all his reign: for neither can one say, that at one time he was clothed with such apparel, but after that he was so no more; rather not so much as on one day did he array himself so beautifully: for this Christ declared by saying, *in all his reign* and if it was not that he was surpassed by this flower, but vied with that, but he gave place to all alike (wherefore He also said, *as one of these*: for such as between the truth and the counterfeit, so great is the interval between those robes and these flowers)" (*In Mt.*, hom. xxii, 1 (PG 57, 300)).
245. "PSEUDO-CHRYS: Or the meaning may be that Solomon, though he toiled not for his own raiment, yet he gave command for the making of it. But where command is, there is often found both offence of them that minister, and wrath of him that commands. When, then, any are without these things, then they are arrayed as are the lilies" (*Catena Aurea on St. Matthew*, chap. 6, lect. 19); cf. *Op. imp. in Mt.*, hom. xvi (PG 56, 723-724).
246. "HILARY; Or; By the lilies are to be understood the eminence of the heavenly angels, to whom a surpassing radiance of whiteness is communicated by God. They toil not, neither do they spin, because the angelic powers received in the very first allotment of their existence such a nature, that as they were made so they should ever continue to be; and when in the resurrection men shall be like to angels, He would have them look for a covering of angelic glory by this example of angelic excellence" (*Catena Aurea on St. Matthew*, chap. 6, lect. 18; *In Evangelium Matthaei Commentarius*, v, 11 (PL 9, 948B)).

grass to grow on the mountains, and herbs for the service of men" (Ps. 146, 8). Or therefore He said above, *lilies*, and afterwards, *grass*, because flowers are to grass, as clothing is to men. For it is the use of clothing, namely, for protecting and covering, and if God provides for the lesser things as to their adornment, all the more will He provide for the greater things as to their necessities of life, and this is what is said, *And if the grass of the field which is to day, and to morrow is cast into the oven, God doth so clothe: how much more you, O ye of little faith*, who have not hoped for the least things from God; "O thou of little faith, why didst thou doubt?" (below 14, 31). Hilary, however, does not continue with the previous exposition, but says that just as by *the lilies* the holy angels are understood, so by *the grass of the field* unbelievers are understood; "Indeed the people is grass" (Is. 40, 7); because if God provides for unbelievers, foreknown to eternal punishment, how much more for us who are foreknown to eternal life.[247]

Be not solicitous therefore, saying: What shall we eat: or what shall we drink, or wherewith shall we be clothed? Here [His proposition] is argued, and about this He does two things. Firstly, He infers one conclusion, and secondly, He infers another, where it is said, *For after all these things do the heathens seek*. Above, He treats separately concerning solicitude about food and drink, and about clothing. Here, He concludes concerning both. Hence, He says, *Be not solicitous therefore*. And those words which He said above ought to be recalled, namely, that solicitude for temporal things is forbidden as to four things, namely, that we may not put the end in them, that we ought not to seek them excessively, that we ought not to occupy our mind with them too much, and that we ought not to despair of God's providence. Here, certain other things are related, and He sets forth one other meaning. Hence, He says, *Be not solicitous therefore*, etc., meaning, when you live in some society, now you are solicitous to have something special in food, drink, and clothing; "Be among them as one of them" (Eccli. 32, 1).[248] *For after all these things do the heathens seek*, as though the unbelievers ought not to do this, hence the unbelievers are rebuked; but the heathens are rebuked concerning this, therefore, etc. And firstly, He relates the error of the unbelievers;

---

247. "HILARY; Or, under the signification of grass, the Gentiles are pointed to. If then an eternal existence is only therefore granted to the Gentiles, that they may soon be handed over to the judgment fires; how impious it is that the saints should doubt of attaining to eternal glory, when the wicked have eternity bestowed on them for their punishment" ((*Catena Aurea on St. Matthew*, chap. 6, lect. 19; *In Evangelium Matthaei Com-mentarius*, v, 11 (PL 9, 949B)).
248. "RABAN. It should be observed that He does not say, 'Do not you seek, or be thoughtful for, food, drink, and

secondly, He disproves it; and thirdly, He shows what ought to be done by the believers. The second part is where it is said, *For your Father knoweth that you have need of all these things*, and the third part is where it is said, *Seek ye therefore first the kingdom of God*. He speaks, therefore, as follows, 'I say that you ought not to be solicitous about this because you ought not to be "conformed to this world" (Rom. 12, 2).'

For after all these things do the heathens seek, and He says this for two reasons, according to which to seek can be taken in two ways, because it can chiefly imply the notion of an end, and in this way the heathens, who do not believe in eternal things, seek after these things as their end, or if they do not seek them as their ultimate end, nevertheless they seek everything with solicitude, because they do not believe in Divine providence, and consequently they also do not believe in God; "Like the Gentiles that know not God" (I Thess. 4, 5).

Afterwards, He defends Divine providence, and it ought to be known that providence presupposes two things, namely, knowledge and will, and therefore He shows both. For providence is nothing other than the ordination of some things to their end, namely, the end having been predetermined, to choose the means by which one may arrive at the end. Hence, firstly, it is necessary that one know and will the end; secondly, that one know the order of importance of the things directed to the end, just as a builder knows the order of the stones to be put into a house. Hence, for this it is necessary that God have providence concerning human affairs, it is required that He know and understand those things, and He will to direct [those things] to their end, and wherefore He says, *For your Father knoweth that you have need of all these things*; "For all things were known to the Lord God, before they were created: so also after they were perfected he beholdeth all things" (Eccli. 23, 29), and, "All things are naked and open to his eyes" (Heb. 4, 13). *Your Father*, therefore, wishes to administer [human affairs]; "But thy providence, O Father, governeth it" (Wis. 14, 3). For He would not be a father unless He was a provider; "If you then being evil, know how to give good gifts to your children: how much more will your Father who is in heaven, give good things to them that ask him?" (below 7, 11).

---

raiment,' but *what you shall eat, what you shall drink, or wherewith you shall be clothed*. Wherein they seem to me to be convicted, who, using themselves the usual food and clothing, require of those with whom they live either greater sumptuousness, or greater austerity in both"(*Catena Aurea on St. Matthew*, chap. 6, lect. 20; *Commentariorum In Matthaeum Libri Octo*, bk. II, (PL 107, 838C)).

Seek ye therefore first the kingdom of God, and his justice, and all these things shall be added unto you. Here He points out three things. [Firstly,] He points out the kingdom of God as the end, because in ***the kingdom*** (*regnum*) ***of God*** is understood eternal beatitude. For then something is properly ruled (*regitur*) when it is submitted to the rulership (*regulae*) of the one governing. But in this life men are not completely submitted to God, because we are not without sins, and this [submission] will be in glory where we will perfectly do the Divine will; "Blessed is he that shall eat bread in the kingdom of God" (Lk. 14, 15). Secondly, He points out the correct means. For in ***the kingdom of God*** one advances by justice. Hence, if you wish to go to ***the kingdom of God*** it is needful that you keep the justice of the kingdom. And He says, ***justice***, not simply, but ***his***, because justice is twofold: man's justice, by which man presumes by his own strength to be able to fulfill God's commandments, and God's justice, by which, with the help of grace, man believes that he can be saved; "They, not knowing the justice of God and seeking to establish their own, have not submitted themselves to the justice of God" (Rom. 10, 3). The third thing that He points out is, ***and all these things shall be added unto you.*** A generous seller of his possessions gives and adds something, and we have agreed with God for a penny a day (below 20, 2), which is eternal life.[249] Hence, whatever He adds besides, all is a certain addition and there is no computation, and this is what is said, ***and all these things shall be added unto you.*** He does not say, 'shall be given';[250] "The Lord will not afflict the soul of the just with famine" (Prov. 10, 3), and, "Give me neither beggary, nor riches: give me only the necessaries of life" (Prov. 30, 8).

And notice that ***Seek ye first*** can be understood in two ways, as an end or reward, and in this way He says, ***Seek ye first the kingdom of God***, and not temporal things. For we ought not to preach the Gospel so that we may eat, but vice versa.[251] If you do not firstly seek the kingdom of God, you pervert the order.

---

249. "PSEUDO-CHRYS; For what is our hiring, and the wages of that hiring? The promise of eternal life; for the Gentiles knew neither God, nor God's promises" (*Catena Aurea on St. Matthew*, chap. 20, lect. 1; *Op. imp. in Mt.*, hom. xxxiv (PG 56, 819)).
250. "CHRYS. And He said not, 'shall be given,' but, 'shall be added,' that you may learn that the things that are now, are nothing to the greatness of the things that shall be" (*Catena Aurea on St. Matthew*, chap. 20, lect. 1; hom. xxii, 1 (PG 57, 303)).

251. "For neither ought we, for example, to preach the Gospel with this object, that we may eat; but to eat with this object, that we may preach the Gospel: for if we preach the Gospel for this cause, that we may eat, we reckon the Gospel of less value than food; and in that case our good will be in eating, but that which is necessary for us is preaching the Gospel. And this the apostle also forbids, when he says it is lawful for himself even, and permitted by the Lord, that *they who preach the gospel should live by the gospel* (I Cor. 9,

And it ought to be known that the Lord likewise teaches in His prayer, where the seven petitions are set forth, that firstly we ought to seek God's good itself, namely, His glory, [hence it is said, "Hallowed by thy name"]. In other petitions, however, we ought to seek firstly God's kingdom [hence, "Thy kingdom come"], secondly, His justice [hence, "Thy will be done"], and thirdly, [we ought to seek virtues and merits, hence,] "Thy will be done," [fourthly, we ought to seek the necessaries of life,] which are to be *added [unto you*, hence], "Give us this day our supersubstantial bread," etc.[252]

But contrary to these words, **And all these things shall be added unto you**, Augustine objects that the Apostle says, "Even unto this hour we both hunger and thirst and are naked and are buffeted and have no fixed abode" (I Cor. 4, 11), and, "I have labored in hunger and thirst, in fastings often, in cold and nakedness" (II Cor. 11, 27). And he answers that God, as a wise doctor, knows what is expedient. Hence, as a doctor sometimes withdraws food on account of the health of the body, so God, on account of the health of the soul, withdraws temporal things because it is for our good, namely, so that past sins are punished and we may be on our guard against future sins, and for the good of others, so that by seeing our patience they may advance towards the good.[253]

---

14), i.e. should have from the Gospel the necessaries of this life; but yet that he has not made use of this power. For there were many who were desirous of having an occasion for getting and selling the Gospel, from whom the apostle wished to cut off this occasion, and therefore he submitted to a way of living by his own hands (Acts 20, 34)" (*De serm. Dom.* II, xvi, 54 (PL 34, 1292)).

252. "By way of brief summary, it should be known that the Lord's Prayer contains all that we ought to desire and all that we ought to avoid. Now, of all desirable things, that must be most desired which is most loved, and that is God. Therefore, you seek, first of all, the glory of God when you say: *Hallowed be Thy name.* You should desire three things from God, and they concern yourself. The first is that you may arrive at eternal life. And you pray for this when you say: *Thy kingdom come.* The second is that you will do the will of God and His justice. You pray for this in the words: *Thy will be done on earth as it is in heaven.* The third is that you may have the necessaries of life. And thus you pray: *Give us this day our daily bread.* Concerning all these things the Lord says: 'Seek ye first the kingdom of God,' which complies with the second, 'and all these things shall be added unto you,' (Mt. 6, 33) as in accord with the third" (*In Oratione Dominica*, art. 7).

253. "But when we read this, let us not imagine that the promises of God have wavered, so that the Apostle suffered hunger and thirst and nakedness while seeking the kingdom and righteousness of God, although it is said to us, *Seek ye first the kingdom of God and His righteousness; and all these things shall be added unto you* : since what that Physician, to whom we have once for all entrusted ourselves wholly, and from whom we have the promise of life present and future, knows such things just as helps, when He sets them before us, when He takes them away, just as He judges it expedient for us; whom He rules and directs as parties who require both to be comforted and exercised in this life, and after this life to be established and confirmed in perpetual rest. For man also, when he frequently takes away the fodder from his beast of burden, is not depriving it of his care, but rather does what he is doing in the exercise of care" (*De serm. Dom.* II, xvii, 58 (PL 34, 1296)).

Be not therefore solicitous for to morrow. Here He forbids solicitude for future things, and firstly, He sets forth His admonition, and secondly, He explains it, where it is said, *For the morrow will be solicitous for itself.* He says, therefore, *Be not therefore solicitous for to morrow.*

And observe that the Lord also does not intend to forbid that a man be somewhat solicitous concerning what he ought to eat tomorrow. For He does not teach men to observe a greater perfection than the Apostles themselves observed, but He had a purse, as it is said in John concerning Judas, who was carrying the Lord's money.[254] Hence, He did not teach what He did not do, who "began to do and to teach" (Acts 1, 1), and again, the Apostles gathered victuals, as it is said in Acts (11, 28-30).[255] Hence, here four expositions are set forth, of which the last is the most literal. The first is Augustine's, who says the following: *Be not therefore solicitous for to morrow*, meaning for temporal things. *Tomorrow*, however, is put for the future in Scripture, temporal things, however, are altered through yesterday and tomorrow; "While we look not at the things which are seen, but at the things which are not seen. For the things which are seen are temporal: but the things which are not seen, are eternal" (II Cor. 4, 18). But these temporal things, which pertain to time, have their own annexed solicitude, and wherefore He says, *for the morrow will be solicitous for itself. Sufficient for the day*, meaning for the present life, *is the evil thereof*, meaning the necessity by which we are forced to provide concerning temporal

---

254. "Now he said this not because he cared for the poor; but because he was a thief and, having the purse, carried the things that were put therein" (Jn. 12, 6).

255. "As Augustine says, 'When we see a servant of God taking thought lest he lack these needful things, we must not judge him to be solicitous for the morrow, since even Our Lord deigned for our example to have a purse, and we read in the Acts of the Apostles that they procured the necessary means of livelihood in view of the future on account of a threatened famine. Hence, Our Lord does not condemn those who, according to human custom, provide themselves with such things, but those who oppose themselves to God for the sake of these things'" (II II, q. 55, a. 7 ad 3um; cf. *De serm. Dom.* II, xvii, 56 (PL 34, 1294-1295)). "Our Lord's words (Matthew 6, 34), *Be not solicitous for to morrow*, do not mean that we are to keep nothing for the morrow... And, as Augustine says (*De Opere Monachorum*, xxiii), 'If this saying of our Lord, *Be not solicitous for to morrow*, means that we are to lay nothing by for the morrow, those who shut themselves up for many days from the sight of men, and apply their whole mind to a life of prayer, will be unable to provide themselves with these things.' Again he adds afterwards: 'Are we to suppose that the more holy they are, the less do they resemble the birds?' And further on (*De Opere Monachorum*, xxiv): 'For if it be argued from the Gospel that they should lay nothing by, they answer rightly: Why then did our Lord have a purse, wherein He kept the money that was collected? Why, in days long gone by, when famine was imminent, was grain sent to the holy fathers? Why did the Apostles thus provide for the needs of the saints?'" (II II, q. 188, a. 7 ad 2um).

things. And *the evil thereof* is said, because it is derived from the fault of the first parent.²⁵⁶

Chrysostom expounds the passage as follows. Things that are accumulated are always accumulated so that they may suffice for a long time. Hence, **Be not solicitous**, meaning, for accumulating superfluous things. ***For the morrow will be solicitous for itself***, meaning, a superfluity of temporal things finds for itself solicitude because men are solicitous how they may snatch away these riches for themselves. **Sufficient for the day**, meaning, it suffices that you accept the necessities of life.²⁵⁷

Hilary²⁵⁸ expounds the passage as follows. In any action two things are to be considered, namely, the action itself and the result of the action. For the fact that man sows this thing is a certain action, but what he ought to gain, this indeed is the outcome. Therefore, the Lord wishes that concerning those things which do not depend upon us, we ought not to be solicitous, and this is a more literal and subtler exposition.²⁵⁹ The fourth exposition

---

256. "For tomorrow is not spoken of except in time, where the future succeeds the past. Therefore, when we do anything good, let us not think of what is temporal, but of what is eternal; then will that be a good and perfect work. *For the morrow*, says He, *will be solicitous for itself*; i.e., so that, when you ought, you will take food, or drink, or clothing, that is to say, when necessity itself begins to urge you. For these things will be within reach, because our Father knoweth that we have need of all these things. For *sufficient for the day*, says He, *is the evil thereof*; i.e. it is sufficient that necessity itself will urge us to take such things. And for this reason, I suppose, it is called *evil*, because for us it is penal: for it belongs to this frailty and mortality which we have earned by sinning." (*De serm. Dom.* II, xvii, 56 (PL 34, 1294)).

257. "Pseudo-Chrys: Otherwise; By *today* are signified such things as are needful for us in this present life; *Tomorrow* denotes those things that are superfluous. *Be not ye therefore solicitous for the morrow*, thus means, 'Seek not to have aught beyond that which is necessary for your daily life, for that which is over and above, i.e. Tomorrow, shall care for itself.' *Tomorrow will be solicitous for itself*, is as much as to say, 'When you have heaped up superfluities, they shall care for themselves, you shall not enjoy them, but they shall find many lords who shall care for them. Why then should you be anxious about those things, the property of which you must part with?' *Sufficient for the day is the evil thereof*, as much as to say, 'The toil you undergo for necessaries is enough, do not toil for things superfluous'" (*Catena Aurea on St. Matthew*, chap. 21 ;Cf. *Op. imp. in Mt.*, hom. xvi (PG 56, 724)).

258. St. Jerome is cited here in the text, but St. Hilary seems to be more likely who says, "We are commanded not to be careful about the future, because sufficient for our life is the evil of the days wherein we live, that is to say, the sins, that all our thought and pains be occupied in cleansing this away. And if our care be slack, yet will the future be careful for itself, in that there is held out to us a harvest of eternal love to be provided by God" (*In Evangelium Matthaei Commentarius*, v, 13 (PL 9, 950A)).

259. "But since, in spite of our having the power to act, we do not have the power to guarantee the success of our actions in attaining their proper end, because of impediments which may occur, this success that may come to each man from his action lies within the disposition of Divine providence. Therefore, the Lord commands us not to be solicitous concerning what pertains to God, namely, the outcome of our actions. But He has not forbidden us

is Jerome's, and is straightforward. ***Be not solicitous*** is not to be understood concerning a future time, but He wants that solicitude which ought to apply to the future be not in the present. For in the time of harvesting there are harvesters, and not at the time of gathering grapes, and not vice versa, and this exposition is consonant with the literal meaning. ***The morrow***, meaning a future time, will have its own cares. ***Sufficient for the day is the evil thereof***, meaning, affliction and hardship are in this way said [to be ***evil***]; "The affliction of an hour maketh one forget great delights" (Eccli. 11, 29).[260]

---

to be concerned about what pertains to us, namely, our own work. So, he who is solicitous about things that he can do does not act against the Lord's precept. Rather, he does who is solicitous concerning the things which can result, even if he carries out his own actions, so that he omits the actions that are required to avoid these eventualities, against which we must rather place our hope in God's providence, by which even the birds and the flowers are supported. To have solicitude of this kind seems to pertain to the error of the Gentiles who deny divine providence. This is why the Lord concludes that we must not be "solicitous for tomorrow." He did not forbid us, by this injunction, from taking care in time of the things necessary for the future, but, rather, from being concerned about future events in despair of divine help" (Mat. 6:34)" (*Contra Gentiles*, bk. III, chap. 135, n. 24).

260. "Jerome: *Tomorrow* in Scripture signifies the future time, as Jacob in Genesis says, 'And my justice shall answer for me tomorrow before thee' (Gen 30, 33). And in the phantasm of Samuel, the Pythoness says to Saul, 'To morrow thou shall be with me' (I Kings 28, 19). He yields, therefore, unto them that they should care for things present, though He forbids them to take thought for things to come. For sufficient for us are the thoughts concerning the present time; let us leave to God the future which is uncertain. And this is that He says, *The morrow will be solicitous for itself*; that is, it shall bring its own anxiety with it. For *sufficient for the day is the evil thereof.* By *evil* He means here not that which is contrary to virtue, but toil, and affliction, and the hardships of life" (*Catena Aurea on St. Matthew*, chap. 21;Cf. *Comm. in Mt.*, I (PL 26, 46B)).

CHAPTER SEVEN

1. Judge not, that you may not be judged.

2. For with what judgment you judge, you shall be judged: and with what measure you mete, it shall be measured to you again.

3. And why seest thou the mote that is in thy brother's eye; and seest not the beam that is in thy own eye?

4. Or how sayest thou to thy brother: Let me cast the mote out of thy eye; and behold a beam is in thy own eye?

5. Thou hypocrite, cast out first the beam out of thy own eye, and then shalt thou see to cast out the mote out of thy brother's eye.

6. Give not that which is holy to dogs; neither cast ye your pearls before swine, lest perhaps they trample them under their feet, and turning upon you, they tear you.

7. Ask, and it shall be given you: seek, and you shall find: knock, and it shall be opened to you.

8. For every one that asketh, receiveth: and he that seeketh, findeth: and to him that knocketh, it shall be opened.

9. Or what man is there among you, of whom if his son shall ask bread, will he reach him a stone?

10. Or if he shall ask him a fish, will he reach him a serpent?

11. If you then being evil, know how to give good gifts to your children: how much more will your Father who is in heaven, give good things to them that ask him?

12. All things therefore whatsoever you would that men should do to you, do you also to them. For this is the law and the prophets.

13. Enter ye in at the narrow gate: for wide is the gate, and broad is the way that leadeth to destruction, and many there are who go in thereat.

14. How narrow is the gate, and strait is the way that leadeth to life: and few there are that find it!

Christ fulfilled the Law as to its precepts and as to its promises, now He fulfills the Law as to its judgments. Firstly, therefore, He directs that judgment not be temerarious, and He says, **Judge not**, etc., that is, from the bitterness of hate; "You have turned judgment into bitterness" (Amos 6, 13). Or it is thus. **Judge not**, insofar as regards those things which are not committed to our judgment. Judgment is the Lord's, He has committed to us the judgment about exterior things, but He has retained judgment about interior things to Himself. Do not, therefore, judge concerning these; "Judge not before the time" (I Cor. 4, 5); "The heart is perverse above all things, and unsearchable, who can know it?" (Jer. 17, 9). For no one ought to judge about another that he is a bad man: for doubtful things are to be interpreted according to the better part. Likewise, judgment ought to be congruous as far as concerns the person of the one judging. Hence, if you are in the same sin, or greater sin, you ought not to judge; "For wherein thou judgest another, thou condemnest thyself" (Rom. 2, 1). Likewise, judgment is not prohibited to superiors but to subjects: hence, they ought to judge only their subjects. But Chrysostom says: "Do not judge yourselves by taking revenge. Hence, if you forgive, you will not be judged hereafter; nay, by reason of this mercy you will obtain mercy." The reason follows, **For with what judgment you judge, you shall be judged**; "His iniquity shall come down upon his head," etc., (Ps. 7, 17). And: "He that takes the sword shall perish with the sword" (below 26, 52). Or it is thus. They ought to fear, who judge, lest the Lord allow them to be punished with this judgment, as it is said in Isaias: "Woe to thee that spoilest, shalt not thou thyself also be spoiled?" (33, 1)

With what measure, etc. Here, He sets forth the reason under the similitude of a judgment: for the judge is like a living measuring stick: for when you wish to make two things equal, and refer to the measuring stick, what superabounds from one you cut off: in this way, if someone were to possesses from another more than he ought to possess, he cuts it off, and gives back to each one what is his, that is, according to this measure, **it shall be measured to you again**.

But an objection is made. Someone sins for a time, and hereafter is punished eternally; it seems that it is not an equal judgment.

I say that in sin two things are to be considered: the duration and the offense; and in the offence, there are two things, namely, a turning away from something and a turning towards something. On the part of that towards which one turns, the guilt is finite; on the part of that from which one turns, the guilt is infinite, because one is turned away from God, who is infinite. Therefore, since one turns oneself from the Infinite, one ought to be punished infinitely. Likewise, on the part of the duration, two things are to be considered, namely, the act and the stain. The act is momentary, the stain is infinite, that is, eternal; thus, infinitely, that is, eternally, one ought to be punished. Hence, if the stain could be severed from the demons, they could be freed from the guilt and the punishment. Similarly, on the part of the punishment there is severity, and this is finite. Likewise, there is the duration, and this is infinite.

And why seest thou the mote that is in thy brother's eye; and seest not the beam that is in thy own eye? Here, He says that there ought not to be inordinate judgment: for it is inordinate when it begins by someone who has not fully examined the case, or the gravity of the sin: for in judging, two things are necessary: knowledge of the case and a trial. Concerning the first, it is written: "The cause which I knew not, I searched out most diligently" (Job 29, 16). ***And why seest thou the mote***, a light sin, ***in the eye***, that is in your brother's conscience: ***but sest not the beam***, that is, the grave sin, ***that is in thy own eye?*** By means of the beam and the mote He teaches us to consider the greatness of the sins: for often, those who commit grave sins reprove those who commit light sins, as happens in judging religious, since some men, who commit grave sins, judge the light things which they see in religious to be grave; but those things are absorbed like a drop of water in a large amount of wine. Likewise, it happens that someone, out of weakness, sins lightly, and some bad judge, who wishes to punish him out of hatred, observes the mote in his eye, but not the beam in his own eye. ***Or how***, that is, with what effrontery, are you able to say: ***Let me cast the mote out of thy eye***? You ought to be ashamed. Chrysostom says: "With what purpose does a man love another more than himself?" For, if you correct him with the purpose of correction, you will firstly correct yourself; but you do this with hate, or vainglory; therefore, etc.

But it is sought whether one, who is in mortal sin, can correct another? I say that either at some time he was in sin, or he was not: if he was never in sin, he ought to fear lest he fall, for this reason he ought to correct unwillingly. And perhaps for that reason the Lord permitted Peter to fall, so that he might be more mild with sinners; and, concerning Christ, Paul says: "We have not a high priest who cannot have compassion on our infirmities: but one tempted in all things like as we are, without sin" (Heb. 4, 15). If, however, he is subject to the sin, either it is public or hidden: if it is hidden, either it is from weakness, because it displeases him that he sins; and in that case he can correct, because what he corrects in another, he corrects in himself; but if he sins out of malice, he ought never to correct. If, however, the sin is public, he ought not to correct with severity, but to mildly join himself to him. Hence, one must not upbraid against sinners with harshness.

It continues, **Thou hypocrite, cast out first the beam out of thy own eye.** The Lord begins rebuking, just as He does below (18, 32) against the wicked servant, etc. Augustine says: "He shows that He intends to reprehend him, who assumes authority which is not his own": "But to the sinner God hath said: Why dost thou declare my justices, and take my covenant in thy mouth? But thou hast hated discipline," etc., (Ps. 49, 16). **Cast out first**, by fasting and by praying, **the beam out of thy own eye**; and then you shall be able to see the mote in the eye of your brother. It continues: **Give not that which is holy to dogs.** In which He shows that judgment ought to be differentiating.

It ought to be observed, therefore, what is signified by 'holy' and what is signified by 'pearl.' Augustine says: "Holy things are kept inviolate and immaculate; and precious pearls ought not to be despised." By 'dogs,' which tear with their teeth, heretics are signified; by 'swine,' which trample with their feet, the unclean are signified. Therefore, to give holy things to dogs is to administer holy things to heretics. Likewise, if something spiritual is consecrated, and this is despised, it is given to swine. Or, by 'holy things,' the ecclesiastical sacraments are signified; by 'pearls,' the mysteries of truth are signified. A dog is an entirely unclean animal;[1] a pig is partly unclean, and partly not unclean. By 'dogs,' the infidels are signified; by 'swine,' the bad faithful are signified. Therefore, **Give not that which is holy to dogs**, that is, do not give the sacraments to infidels. The 'pearls,' that is, the spiritual interpretations, ought not to be given to swine; "The sensual man perceiveth not these things that are of the Spirit of God" (I Cor. 2, 14), that is, lest they despise them; "A soul that is full shall tread upon the honeycomb" (Prov. 27, 7). Hence, **turning**, to sins, **they tear**, because they despise, or they raise objections.

But why? Did not Christ say many things to the infidels, and they were trampling upon His words? I say that He did this for the sake of the good men who were with the bad men, who thereafter were profiting.

Ask, and it shall be given you. He gave His doctrine, which is complete and perfect; here, He teaches how it can be fulfilled; for this, however, prayer and diligent attention are necessary. Firstly, therefore, He teaches to ask; secondly, He gives assurance of obtaining requests, where it is said, **Or what man is there among you,**

---

[1] "The dog and the swine are unclean animals; the dog indeed in every respect, as he neither chews the cud, nor divides the hoof; but the swine in one respect only, seeing they divide the hoof, though they do not chew the cud" (*Catena Aurea on the Gospel of St. Matthew*, chap. 7, lect. 3).

etc. He says, therefore, ***Ask***. And in this see that two false opinions are rejected. The first, namely, belongs to proud men, who think they can fulfill the precepts by their own powers. But He says that it is necessary to ask this of God. "What hast thou that thou hast not received?" (I Cor. 4, 7). Likewise, He rejects the opinion of many who say that God does not care about prayers, and that they would not obtain their requests if they would ask; therefore, He adds, ***And you shall receive***. Likewise, He adds, ***Seek, and you shall find***. And this is explained, firstly, that in these two sayings, nothing is added, only the manner is expressed. For careful attention is required for asking; likewise, fervent devotion is required: and He suggests these two things when He says, ***Seek***, that is, pray. Or, ***Ask***, just like those, who seek after something, place therein their whole attention. Hence, to that pertains what the spouse says in Canticles 3, 1: "I sought him whom my soul loveth." ***And you shall find***; "One thing I have asked of the Lord, this will I seek after" (Ps. 26, 4). Likewise, ***seek***, after the manner of one knocking: because one who shouts at the gate, if he be not heard, knocks loudly. "Come, my beloved, let us go forth into the field, let us abide in the villages" (Cant. 7, 11). Secondly, it is explained, according to Augustine, by referring to those things which Christ says about Himself: "I am the way, and the truth, and the life" (Jn. 14, 6): if you wish to go by this way, ***ask*** from Him, that He may direct your ways, saying with the Psalmist: "Shew, O Lord, thy ways to me, and teach me thy path" (Ps. 24, 4). If you wish to know the truth, ***seek, and you will find***; but it is not sufficient to know the way and the truth, unless we come to the life, that is, in order that you may enter into it, ***knock***; hence: "Thou shalt bring them in, and plant them in the mountain of thy inheritance" (Ex. 15, 17). But according to the same authority, it is far better that all these things be recited as a most earnest petition. Likewise, it is otherwise expounded by referring to various actions. ***Ask***, by praying; ***seek***, by striving; ***knock***, by doing. ***Everyone who asks receives***, etc.

Someone will say, 'You say that we may ask. I believe that this is said to holy men, but I am not among the number of these'; therefore, He says, ***Everyone that asketh, receiveth***, etc. But it seems to be false, because it is written: "We know that God doth not hear sinners" (Jn. 9, 31).

And Augustine solves this objection. If God does not hear sinners, how is it said concerning the Publican that he was saying: "O God, be merciful to me a sinner" (Lk. 18, 13).[2] But it ought to be

---

2. "Wherefore God hears sinners; for if He do not hear sinners, the Publican said in vain, *Lord, be merciful to me a sinner*" (*Catena Aurea on the Gospel of St. Matthew*, chap. 7, lect. 4).

known that prayer is meritorious and impetrative; and it can be meritorious even if it be not impetrative.

But what is it that He says, that *Everyone that asketh, receiveth*? It seems to be false, because what is asked is not always received.

I say that in four cases a man asks and is not heard. It is because either he asks for what is not expedient; "You know not what you ask" (below 20, 22); therefore, things necessary for salvation ought to be asked. Or likewise, secondly, it is because one does not ask well; "You ask and receive not: because you ask amiss" (James 4, 3); therefore, one ought ask piously, that is, with faith. In like manner, one ought to ask humbly: hence, "He hath regarded the humility of his handmaid" (Lk. 1, 48). Moreover, one ought to ask piously, that is, devoutly. Likewise, one is sometimes not heard when one prays for another whose demerits gainsay the prayer; "If Moses and Samuel shall stand before me, my soul is not towards this people" (Jer. 15, 1). Likewise, it is not heard, because one had not persevered; "Because we ought always to pray" (Lk. 18, 1), and perseveringly; because God wants prayers to multiply. Also, it happens that the Lord hears; but it does not seem so, because the Lord gives what is useful, not what is wanted, as happened to Paul. Augustine says: "The good Lord often does not grant what we ask, so that He may give what we will prefer: and because we ourselves call Him Father, He gives to us what a father gives to his son." For that reason, He adds, *What man is there among you, of whom if his son shall ask bread, will he reach him a stone?* By bread is understood Christ; "I am the living bread which came down from heaven," etc., (Jn. 6, 51). Similarly, bread is sacred doctrine; "I shall feed him with the bread of life and understanding" (Eccli. 15, 3). Likewise, it is charity; "The bread of the land shall be most plentiful, and fat" (Is. 30, 23). On the other hand, the stone is the devil; "His heart shall be as hard as a stone" (Job. 41, 15). Likewise, hardness of heart is called a stone; hence, it is said: "I will take away the stony heart out of you, and will give you a heart of flesh" (Ez. 36, 26). Also, false doctrine is called a stone; "The flood divideth the stone that is in the dark and the shadow of death," etc., (Job 28, 3). Hence, if someone asks from God, as from a father, bread, that is, Christ, He will not give the devil. It is in like manner *if he shall ask him a fish*. A fish lives in the water, and by water is signified the understanding of revealed doctrines; "He that shall drink of the water that I will give him shall no longer thirst" (Jn. 4, 13). And: "It will be a fountain of water, springing up into life everlasting" (Ibid. 4, 14). Also, by water, tribulations are signified:

hence, by fish are signified those living in the waters of tribulations. Or, faith is called a fish, which hides under the water, that is, the protection of the spirit; but by the serpent is signified the doctrine of heretics. He says, therefore, *And if he shall ask him a fish, will he reach him a serpent?* Another Evangelist sets forth a third thing,[3] namely, an egg. So that by bread, charity is signified; by a fish, faith is signified; and by an egg, hope is signified. He concludes: *If you then being evil, know how to give good gifts to your children: how much more will your Father who is in heaven, give good things to them that ask him?*

But someone will say: 'He said this to the Apostles, who were not evil men.' And Chrysostom solves the matter, saying: "That on the contrary they were evil men in comparison with the divine goodness." "All our justices [are] as the rag of a menstruous woman" (Is. 64, 6). Jerome says: "And if all are not evil according to their actions, nevertheless, they are evil according to their proneness to evil." Hence, it is stated: "That all the thought of the human heart was bent upon evil at all times" (Gen. 6, 5). "Behold every one of you walketh after the perverseness of his evil heart" (Jer. 16, 12). Augustine says: "*If you then being evil*: it is not said, 'You are evil,' but, *you then being (sitis) evil*, give to your temporal children temporal goods which you reckon to be good things; much more, therefore, will your Father do so, who is the Highest Good." And this is what follows: *How much more will your Father who is in heaven, give good things to them that ask him*, if you wish to receive them? *All things therefore whatsoever you would that men should do to you*; that is, forgive others, if you wish to be forgiven. Some have added 'All good things'; but one ought not to do so, because He says, *You would*. Now good things belong to the will, but evil things belong to cupidity; for that reason it is not necessary to add, 'good.' Hence, what you wish to happen to you, do to others. *For this is the law and the prophets*; and He does not say: 'The entire Law and the prophets,' as when He spoke on the first Commandments: "On these two commandments dependeth the whole law and the prophets" (below 22, 40). *Enter ye in at the narrow gate.* Lest perhaps someone believe that because He had said, *Ask and you shall receive*, that man might have everything from God without good works; for that reason He teaches that this also happens through good works. Firstly, therefore, He sets forth an admonition; and secondly, the reason for the admonition. He says, there-

---

3. Lk. 11, 12: "Or if he shall ask an egg, will he reach him a scorpion?"

fore, ***Enter ye***, that is to say, strive to enter. Augustine expounds this in two ways. Christ is the gate; "I am the gate" (Jn. 10, 9), because without Him one cannot enter into the kingdom. This gate is narrow through humility, because He humbled Himself unto death. Hence, "The Lord God of hosts shall make an abridgment in the land" (Is. 14, 2). Hence, ***Enter ye in at the narrow gate***, that is, through the humility of Christ; "For Christ ought to have suffered these things, and so to enter into his glory" (Lk. 24, 26); and we ought to enter in the same way. Hence, it behooves us to enter the kingdom of God through many tribulations. Likewise, this gate is said to be charity; "This is the gate of the Lord, the just shall enter into it" (Ps. 117, 20). This gate is made narrow by the divine law; and through this gate we ought to enter, by keeping the law and the precepts. Next, He assigns the reason for the admonition: ***For wide is the gate, and broad is the way that leadeth to destruction***. And He describes two gates, one wide and the other narrow. One is described as being wide, because the wide one is the devil, and wide is the presumption of pride; "The gates of hell shall not prevail against it" (below 16, 18). This gate is wide, because something wide is what receives all: for there is nothing that may fill it. Likewise, this gate is said to be iniquity, or vice: and this is wide, because it occurs in many ways. For what is named a virtue belongs to one way of acting, but what is named a vice belongs to numerous ways; "Cursing, and lying, and killing, and theft, and adultery, have overflowed, and blood hath touched blood" (Osee 4, 2). Likewise, wide is the way, and this is, or signifies, sinful works: "What hast thou to do in the way of Egypt" (Jer. 2, 18). Again, this way is broad, because in its beginning it seems to be wide, but afterwards it is straitened,[4] because it ultimately leads to perdition, for, "The wages of sin is death" (Rom. 6, 23). ***And many there are who go in thereat***. Here He touches upon the number, because in the literal sense, "The number of fools is infinite" (Eccl. 1, 15). ***Narrow is the gate, and strait is the way that leadeth to life***. This is the contrary to the preceding; and this way is strait, because it is straitened according to the rule of the law; and it is a way contrary to the other way; "For the Lord knoweth the ways that are on the right hand; but those are perverse which are on the left hand," etc., (Prov. 4, 27).

But it can be inquired why the way of charity is strait, because it seems that it is wide; "I will lead thee by the paths of equity, which when thou shalt have entered, thy steps shall not be

---

[4] That is to say, made narrow so that one is put into difficult circumstance from which he cannot easily escape.

straitened" (Prov. 4, 11). The way of sinners, however, is narrow; hence, "We have walked through hard ways" (Prov. 5, 7).

It ought to be said that there is a way of the flesh and a way of reason. The way of charity in the way of the flesh is the strait way, in the way of reason it is the contrary. Take, for example, a teacher: for the more he loves a child, the more he straitens his way. Hence, the ways of charity in the way of the flesh are straitened, in the way of reason it is the contrary; "Pierce thou my flesh with thy fear" (Ps. 118, 120).

And few there are that find it! Here, He makes mention of the difficult and rare discovery of the way of the spirit: and of the way of the flesh it is not so. And the reason is that the way of the flesh is pleasure, and this way is manifest; but the way of the spirit is hidden; hence, "O how great is the multitude of thy sweetness, O Lord, which thou hast hidden for them that fear thee!" (Ps. 30, 20). For, because it is hidden, on that account there are also few that find it. But there are also some who find it and turn back, concerning whom it is said: "No man putting his hand to the plough and looking back is fit for the kingdom of God" (Lk. 9, 62).

15. Beware of false prophets, who come to you in the clothing of sheep, but inwardly they are ravening wolves.
16. By their fruits you shall know them. Do men gather grapes of thorns, or figs of thistles?
17. Even so every good tree bringeth forth good fruit, and the evil tree bringeth forth evil fruit.
18. A good tree cannot bring forth evil fruit, neither can an evil tree bring forth good fruit.
19. Every tree that bringeth not forth good fruit, shall be cut down, and shall be cast into the fire.
20. Wherefore by their fruits you shall know them.
21. Not every one that saith to me, Lord, Lord, shall enter into the kingdom of heaven: but he that doth the will of my Father who is in heaven, he shall enter into the kingdom of heaven.
22. Many will say to me in that day: Lord, Lord, have not we prophesied in thy name, and cast out devils in thy name, and done many miracles in thy name?
23. And then will I profess unto them, I never knew you: depart from me, you that work iniquity.
24. Every one therefore that heareth these my words, and doth them, shall be likened to a wise man that built his house upon a rock,

25. And the rain fell, and the floods came, and the winds blew, and they beat upon that house, and it fell not, for it was founded on a rock.

26. And every one that heareth these my words and doth them not, shall be like a foolish man that built his house upon the sand,

27. And the rain fell, and the floods came, and the winds blew, and they beat upon that house, and it fell, and great was the fall thereof.

28. And it came to pass when Jesus had fully ended these words, the people were in admiration at his doctrine.

29. For he was teaching them as one having power, and not as the scribes and Pharisees.

He gives precautions concerning those whom one ought to be on one's guard against. Now, they are described from their profession, that they are prophets.

But it can be inquired, of which prophets does He speak, because the Law and the prophets were until John; hence, at that time there were no prophets in regard to Christ, because they came to an end in Him. Therefore, it ought to be said that the prophets are the teachers in the Church and the prelates.

But what is this that He says: **False**? They are called false who are not sent. About such men it is said: "I did not send prophets, yet they ran" (Jer. 23, 21). Likewise, they are called false who speak a lie; hence, "The prophets prophesied in Baal" (Jer. 2, 8). In this way, also, there were many pseudo-prophets in the nation: just as also there will be lying teachers among us.

Beware, that is, be attentively on guard, because they are hidden, and one must be on guard against their snares. Hence, their malice hides inwardly. He says, therefore, **who come to you in the clothing of sheep**, etc. The sheep are the faithful: "We are his people and the sheep of his pasture" (Ps. 99, 3). Now, their clothing is the fasting and almsgiving by which they cover themselves: "Having an appearance indeed of godliness but denying the power thereof" (II Tim. 3, 5). But it ought to be known that if the wolves cover themselves with the skins of sheep, nevertheless, not on account of this does a sheep discard its skin: although those evil men may cover themselves in this way, nevertheless, good men profit much by the doing of such works. **But inwardly they are ravening wolves**. This is principally expounded as concerning heretics, and, in consequence, of bad prelates. Hence, it is said on the passage: "I am the good shepherd" (Jn. 10, 11), "Someone is said to be a pastor, who governs and who rules; and someone is said to be a wolf, who intends destruction; and someone is said to be a mercenary, who seeks his own profit. Hence, a pastor is to be loved, a wolf fled, and a mercenary tolerated."[5] Therefore, that which is said, that *inwardly they are ravening wolves*, is understood of those who have the intention of perverting the people, and so are to be called wolves. Likewise, they are said to be mercenaries, namely, bad Christians, who scatter the flock by their bad example, and who lead a bad life; so far as regards their effect, they have the manner of a wolf; "I know that after my departure ravening wolves will enter in among you, not sparing the flock," etc., (Acts 20, 29). And He says, *Inwardly*, because they have the bad intention of killing the people. *By their fruits you shall know them*, etc. *By their fruits*, that is, by their actions.

But it seems to be the contrary, because they have the clothing of sheep; and clothing is the works. Chrysostom says: "The fruit is the confession of faith." Hence, if one confesses the faith, he is not a heretic. "For the fruit of the light is in all goodness and justice and truth," etc., (Eph. 5, 9). If, however, it is explained of dissimulators, then it is explained in this way, that by the clothing, exterior works are signified. Hence, "But the fruit of the Spirit is, charity, joy, peace," etc., (Gal. 5, 22).

But you will inquire: How can they be known? It ought to be said that scarcely can some hypocrite be so composed that something of his malice, either by word or by deed, does not appear; "As the faces of them that look therein, shine in the water, so the hearts of men are laid open to the wise" (Prov. 27, 19). And Seneca says: "No one can maintain a fictitious personality for a long time." Now in two things they are especially manifested. This happens in those things which are to be done suddenly, because in those things which someone does with deliberation, one takes heed of himself. Likewise, they are manifested in tribulations; "There is a friend for his own occasion, and he will not abide in the day of thy trouble" (Eccli. 6, 8). Moreover, they are manifested when they cannot get what they want, or when they have already gotten what they want. Hence, lordship shows the man.

Do men gather grapes of thorns, or figs of thistles? By grapes, from which wine is made, is understood spiritual joy: because, "Wine may cheer the heart of man" (Ps. 103, 15). By figs, the sweetness of ecclesiastical peace is understood, which is charity. These cannot spring forth of thistles, that is to say, of sinners,

---

5. cf. *Glossa Ordinaria* by Walafrid Strabo, (MPL 114, p. 397).

because, "Thorns and thistles shall it bring forth to thee" (Gen. 3, 18). And He proves this by an example: *Every good tree bringeth forth good fruit, and the evil tree bringeth forth evil fruit.* From this passage the Manichaeans assumed there to be two natures, namely, the good and the bad. But this is not true: because we see from a bad creature good fruit, and conversely bad fruit from a good creature. Hence, in regard to this you ought to understand that a tree is the origin of the fruit. But an origin is twofold. There is the origin of nature, and the origin of behavior. The origin of nature is the soul: and whatever naturally proceeds from thence is something entirely good. The origin, however, of a behavior is the will; for that reason, if the will shall have been good, there shall also be a good deed, since one has a good will with a good intention; because if one would want to steal for the sake of giving alms, even if the will is good, nevertheless the intention is not upright. But what will become of the bad tree? *Every tree that bringeth not forth fruit, shall be cut down*: because if it does not bring forth, or if it omits to produce when it can do so, it shall be cut down; hence, "If any one abide not in me, he shall be cast forth as a branch and shall wither: and they shall gather him up and cast him into the fire: and he burneth" (Jn. 15, 6). Hence, in Luke 13, 7, it is said concerning the fig tree, namely, that the Lord commanded it to be cut down and taken away: "Let the wicked be taken away, that he should not behold the glory of God."[6] He concludes: *Wherefore by their fruits you shall know them. Not everyone that saith to me, Lord, Lord*, etc. Having set forth the doctrine, He shows that one ought to observe it, because nothing else suffices for salvation. And about the commandments, or the doctrine of God, four things are necessary or praiseworthy: that we confess it with the mouth, that it be confirmed by miracles, moreover, that the word of God be heard, and executed by deed. Concerning the first, it is written: "With the heart, we believe unto justice: but, with the mouth, confession is made unto salvation" (Rom. 10, 10). Concerning the second, it is written: "The Lord working withal, and confirming the word with signs that followed" (Mk. 16, 20). Likewise, concerning the third point, that it be heard: "He that is of God heareth the words of God" (Jn. 8, 47). Likewise, fourthly, it is required that one do what is taught: "Be ye doers of the word and not hearers only" (James 1, 22). Hence, He wishes to show that three things without the fourth do not profit; hence, He says: *Not everyone that saith to me, Lord, Lord*, etc.

6. This is taken from the Septuagint version of Is. 26, 10. (cf. Marginal note in *Catena Aurea on the Gospel of St. Luke*, p. 318).

But this seems to be contrary to the Apostle saying: "No man can say The Lord Jesus, but by the Holy Ghost" (I Cor. 12, 3). But he, who has the Holy Ghost, enters the kingdom of heaven.

Augustine solves that objection, saying, that 'to say' is said in various ways: commonly, and strictly, as well as properly. Now, 'to say,' strictly, is nothing other than to show one's desire and will; and so it is said by the Apostle: "No man can say The Lord Jesus, but by the Holy Ghost," etc., (loc. cit.). And this is nothing other than to believe and obey the Lord. Likewise, the word 'say' is said commonly, that is, to declare with the mouth in whatsoever way; concerning which it is said: "This people honors me with their lips, but their heart is far from me" (Is. 29, 13). Or it is as follows. *Not everyone that saith to me, Lord, Lord*, etc. He repeats this word, *Lord, Lord*, to signify that confession is twofold, namely, of the voice and of praise, neither of which suffices. For that reason it is written: "This people honors me with their lips, but their heart is far from me." Who, therefore, will enter? Not he who says, *Lord, Lord, shall enter into the kingdom of heaven: but he that doth the will of my Father*, etc. "No man hath ascended into heaven, but he that descended from heaven" (Jn. 3, 13). Hence, no man can ascend, unless he descend as Christ did, concerning whom it is said: "I came down from heaven, not to do my own will but the will of him that sent me" (Jn. 6, 38). Hence, one ought to do the will of God; "For this is the will of God, your sanctification" (I Thess. 4, 3). Hence, David was saying: "Teach me to do thy will" (Ps. 142, 10). And also, as the Lord taught us to pray, "Thy kingdom come" (above 6, 10). But it ought to be observed, that by this word which He said, *Kingdom*, eternal remuneration is touched upon; hence, He says, *Shall enter*. For that kingdom consists in spiritual goods, not in exterior goods; for that reason, He says, *Shall enter*. On that account, it is written: "The king hath brought me into his storerooms" (Cant. 1, 3). Likewise, He says, *Of heaven*, because, although someone may have riches or honors in this world, all the latter [material goods] is for the sake of the former [spiritual goods]. Hence, the remuneration will be in sublime things. But someone could say that to perform miracles suffices for salvation. He excludes this, in that He says, *many will say to me in that day: Lord, Lord, have not we prophesied in thy name*, etc.? And He says, *Many*, signifying those who withdraw from unity, because they are amongst the multitude to be condemned: because "The number of fools is infinite" (Eccl. 1, 15). Likewise, He brings this forth to explain what He had said earlier, that *every tree that bringeth not forth good fruit, shall be cut down*. For He had not said by whom it would be cut down; and, for that reason, He says, *To me*, as it were, to an appointed judge; because "The Father hath given all judgment to the Son" (Jn. 5, 22). Likewise, He says, *In that day.* He uses the term day, but it is not according to the quality of time; because Judgment Day is sometimes called a night. Now, it is sometimes called a day, and sometimes a night, because it is uncertain when it shall come. Hence, it is said: "At midnight there was a cry made: Behold the bridegroom cometh. Go ye forth to meet him" (below 25, 6). The Apostle calls it a day, in I Corinthians 4, 3.[7] And in Psalm 26, 6, it is written: "And he will bring forth thy justice as the light, and thy judgment as the noonday" (Ps. 36, 6). *Lord, Lord.* He multiplies the word to signify greater confusion and fear; "They shall be troubled with terrible fear" (Wis. 5, 2). *Have not we prophesied in thy name?* This is a supernatural power; "There is no power upon earth that is worthy be compared with this (namely, the power of the devil)" (Job 41, 24).

But then it is inquired how they, who cast out devils, become reprobates. Chrysostom replies, that these men are lying. Another response is that at a certain time they were good, and they performed miracles; afterwards, they became wicked. But this cannot stand, because the Lord says, *I never knew you.* One ought to reply in a different manner, because they say, *In thy name*, not in the name of the Holy Ghost. For certain men cast out devils by the power of the Holy Ghost, and certain men do not. For, as it is related in Jeremias 2, 8,[8] certain men prophesied in the name of Baal. Likewise, certain men prophesied by means of magical arts.

But it is inquired in what way the demons perform miracles. I say that they cannot do so; but they perform some things which seem to be miracles, and, nevertheless, are not miracles. The former are called miracles, when the effects appear, and the causes are hidden. Hence, something can be marvelous in the presence of some less knowledgeable men, which are not so in the presence of wise men, as is evident concerning an eclipse. Hence, since demons may know natural things in a truer manner, they can do things which seem to us to be miracles. It is expounded otherwise by Jerome. Because, according to what he says, among the gifts of the Holy Ghost there are certain ones which are given freely:[9] it is charity alone which distinguishes between the sons of God and the sons of the devil; "The manifestation of the Spirit is given to every man unto profit" (I Cor. 12, 7), or, for the advancement of

---

7. "To me it is a very small thing to be judged by you or by man's day" (I Cor. 4, 3).

8. "The prophets prophesied in Baal, and followed idols" (Jer. 2, 8).

9. That is, *gratiae gratis datae*.

His goodness, or of the Church, so that the faith which it preaches may be manifested. And in this way, also, sometimes a prelate living badly is able to perform miracles.

And then will I profess unto them, I never knew you, that is, I did not approve of you, not even when you were performing miracles; "The Lord knoweth who are his" (II Tim. 2, 19). He says, *I never knew you*, since He says, *Depart from me*, because you were never approved. *Every one therefore that heareth*, etc. He shows that without works nothing suffices, not even the hearing of God's word; because hearing is ordered to faith. "Faith then cometh by hearing" (Rom. 10, 17). For hearing does not suffice. And this He makes clear in two ways, because He proposes, under a similitude, the outcome of him who hears and does, and of him who hears and does not. And firstly, He does three things. Firstly, He sets forth, for our consideration, a building; and secondly, the flooding of the house, where it is said, *And the rain fell*, etc.; and thirdly, the immutability of the building, where it is said, *And it fell not*, etc. He says, therefore, that hearing does not suffice; though hearing is necessary; "Because he that is of God heareth the words of God" (Jn. 8, 47). But it does not suffice; "For not the hearers of the word, but the doers shall be justified" (Rom. 2, 13). Likewise, He says well: *These my words*: because whatever pertains to salvation is contained therein. Hence, *he that heareth these my words, and doth them, shall be likened to a wise man*. And He does not say that 'he is wise,' but, *Shall be likened to a wise man*. And this likeness can be understood of a corporeal builder: and in such a way the literal meaning is clear. Or it can be understood spiritually: and in this way this man is Christ. "One man among a thousand I have found" (Eccle. 7, 29). The house of Christ is the Church: for He knows how He ought to build. Hence, it is said of Him: "Wisdom hath built herself a house" (Prov. 9, 1). And, "A wise woman buildeth her house" (Prov. 14, 1). *Upon a rock*; "And the rock was Christ" (I Cor. 10, 4). Hence, Christ builds upon Himself: for He is the foundation; hence, "Other foundation no man can lay, but that which is laid: which is Christ Jesus" (I Cor. 3, 11). For this is the foundation of eternal truth. Now this is completely immovable; "They that trust in the Lord shall be as mount Sion" (Ps. 124, 1). The flooding of this house follows, *And the rain fell*. By rain, doctrine is understood: there is both good and bad rain. Therefore, that which beats upon, is bad doctrine; "The Lord rained upon Sodom and Gomorrha brimstone and fire" (Gen. 19, 24). Likewise, there are good rivers, and not good ones; "Whose land the rivers have spoiled" (Is. 18, 2); and by this are signified the wise men who deem themselves to be wise. These rivers are produced from the rains. By the winds, the demons are signified. Hence, in the canonical Epistle of Jude, it is written: "Clouds without water, which are carried about by winds" (v. 12). *And they beat upon that house*, that is, the Church, *and it fell not*. "Neither shall any of the cords thereof be burst forever" (Is. 33, 20). And why? *It was founded on a rock*, that is, Christ. Afterwards, He sets forth a similitude relating to the outcome of the one who hears and does not do: and about this, He firstly sets forth the building; secondly, the flooding, where it is said, *And the rain fell*, etc.; and thirdly, the destruction, where it is said, *and it fell*, etc. He says: *And every one that heareth these my words and doth them not, shall be like a foolish man*, who fell away from the light of wisdom. Hence: "Better is a wise servant than a foolish old man" (Eccle. 4, 13).[10] Likewise, the devil is foolish. The house which he builds is the assembly of the infidels: hence, it is written: "The earth has been filled with dwellings of iniquity" (Ps. 73, 20). And this man builds *upon the sand*. By sand are signified the infidels who are unfruitful. Likewise, the infidels are so signified on account of their numerousness: "The number of fools is infinite" (Eccl. 1, 15). Likewise, sand does not adhere to anything, so these men are always in strife. Therefore, he founds upon sand, that is, his end, which is, as it were, his foundation; namely, he fixes his intention upon temporal goods. *The rain fell*, that is, the good doctrine, *the floods came*, that is, the sacred doctors, and *the winds blew*, that is, the angels; "Who makest thy angels spirits" (Ps. 103, 4). "Babylon is fallen, is fallen" (Apoc. 14, 8), namely, through preaching. *And great was the fall thereof.* If we wish to adjust the similitude, it ought to be stated in this manner, that a man ought to build as Christ did. And the Apostle teaches this: "Let every man take heed how he buildeth thereupon" (I Cor. 3, 10). For some build a dwelling of God; certain men, on the contrary, do not build a dwelling of God, as is stated further on; and as it is said in I Cor. 3, 7, certain men build upon stubble. For a foundation is that upon which someone places their intention. For certain men hear in order that they may know, and these build upon the intellect: and this is a building upon sand; hence, "He who hears, and does not do, he shall be compared to a man beholding his own countenance in a glass" (James 1, 23). Hence, they build upon something changeable. On the other hand, a certain man hears in order that he may do and love; and this man builds

---

10. The actual verse is: "Better is a child that is poor and wise, than a king that is old and foolish" (Eccle. 4, 13).

upon rock, because he builds upon something firm and stable; "A young man according to his way, even when he is old, he will not depart from it" (Prov. 22, 6). For such a foundation is upon charity. The Apostle says: "Who then shall separate us from the love of Christ?" (Rom. 8, 35).

But here it can be inquired why a foundation upon the intellect is unstable and not firm, but only the one which is in the affections. The reason is that to the intellect pertains universals: for it cannot know many things except in a universal concept; for this reason, by wandering around a universal, there is no stability; but actions and affections are about particular things, and about good habits; for that reason, if temptation comes, the affections adhere to that to which it is accustomed, namely, to the good action: and for that reason, it resists the temptation.[11]

But then it is sought what one may understand by the rain. For that reason, it ought to be stated that the devil never firstly tempts in greater things, but firstly in lesser things, and then proceeds to greater things. Hence, by the rain is understood wicked thoughts. Therefore, he tempts in a wicked thought; and if one consents, he tempts afterwards in something greater, and in this way, afterwards, it is augmented. And from these things the floods come to be: and afterwards the devil beats upon him with all his strength, and necessarily he falls; "He that contemneth small things, shall fall by little and little" (Eccle. 19, 1). Or it is as follows. ***The rain*** is the temptations of the flesh; ***the floods*** are the temptations of the world, ***the winds*** are the temptations of the devil. Or, according to Augustine, ***the rain*** is superstitious doctrines, one adhering to which falls gravely, and great destruction comes to pass; but the destruction is not great when one wavers, but does not fall, because when temptation occurs, such a one fears and laments. But some fall completely; "Rase it, rase it, even to the foundation thereof" (Ps. 136, 7). Or, the destruction is said to be great because the heart is impenitent; "They spend their days in wealth, and in a moment they go down to hell" (Job 21, 13). ***And it came to pass when Jesus had fully ended these words, the people were in admiration***. The effect is related. For there were three types of men who were following the Lord Jesus. For certain men were marveling and were scandalized, such as the Pharisees, concerning whom see below (chap. 15). Certain men were marveling and were not being scandalized, such as the people. But certain men, such as the perfect, were not marveling.

---

11. "Pleasure is more voluntary in particular cases than in general" (Aristotle, 3 *Ethics* quoted in *The Religious State*).

But it ought to be inquired about this that he says, *The people*, because the people were not there. And it can be said that the sermon was also made both to the people and to the disciples; but on the mountain, below the peak of the mountain, there was some level ground. Therefore, the disciples were on the peak with Christ; but the people were on the level ground. Or it can be said that firstly He preached to the disciples, and afterwards to the people. Or it can be said: a crowd of disciples followed Him.

But what was the reason for the admiration? It was because He was *teaching them as one having power*. Hence, in Him was fulfilled that which was said: "His word is full of power" (Eccle. 8, 4). Hence, *as one having power*, because He was speaking as a ruler or as a legislator. Or, *He was teaching them as one having power*, with power of penetrating the heart. Hence, it is said: "He will give to his voice the voice of power" (Ps. 67, 34). Or, He was teaching with the power of performing miracles: because what He was saying, He was confirming with miracles.

Augustine says that all the things which are said in this sermon ought to be reduced to the seven gifts,[12] and to the beatitudes; because, firstly, it is said, *Thou shalt not kill*, this pertains to the gift of fear, and to the beatitude of poverty. Now that which follows, *Be at agreement with thy adversary*, pertains to the gift of piety, through which meekness is fulfilled. Now that passage, *Thou shalt not commit adultery*, etc., pertains to the gift of knowledge, through which the beatitude of mourning is fulfilled. That passage about withstanding evil,[13] is related to the gift of fortitude, whereby it is fulfilled and it pertains to the beatitude, *Blessed are they that hunger and thirst after justice*, etc. Now that which is said, *Love your enemies*, pertains to the gift of counsel, by which is fulfilled the beatitude of mercy. But, by means of that which follows in chapter six, about not having solicitude, up until, *Enter ye in at the narrow gate*, He intends to cleanse the heart: hence, it pertains to the gift of understanding, and to the beatitude which is cleanliness of heart; hence: *Blessed are the clean of heart: they shall see God*. All that follows pertains to the gift of wisdom.[14]

---

[12]. The order of the gifts of the Holy Ghost here is the reverse order of the enumeration of the gifts in Isaias 11, 2.

[13]. Namely, "Not to resist evil" etc. (above 5, 39 ff.).

[14]. The beatitude which corresponds with the gift of wisdom is "Blessed are the peacemakers" (cf. II II, q. 45, a. 6).

CHAPTER EIGHT

1. And when he was come down from the mountain, great multitudes followed him:
2. And behold a leper came and adored him, saying: Lord, if thou wilt, thou canst make me clean.
3. And Jesus stretching forth his hand, touched him, saying: I will, be thou made clean. And forthwith his leprosy was cleansed.
4. And Jesus saith to him: See thou tell no man: but go, shew thyself to the priest, and offer the gift which Moses commanded, for a testimony unto them.

It could appear that the Lord was speaking out of boastfulness; for that reason, He commends His authority by signs. Firstly, therefore, signs are set forth by which men are freed from bodily dangers; secondly, signs are set forth by which men are freed from spiritual ones (Chap. 9). About the first, the Evangelist does two things. Firstly, he sets forth the signs by which men are freed from bodily dangers proceeding from intrinsic causes; secondly, from extrinsic ones, such as the tempest, where it is said, ***And when he entered into the boat***. He commends His authority, because He performed signs instantly, because He performed signs being absent, because He performed signs perfectly, and because He performed signs upon many men. That He performed signs instantly, is demonstrated in the leper; that He performed signs being absent, is demonstrated in the servant of the centurion; that He performed signs perfectly, is demonstrated in Peter's mother-in-law; that He performed signs upon many men, is demonstrated in the many other men.

About the first, there are three things: Firstly, the witnesses of the miracle are introduced; secondly, the sick man is presented, where it is said, ***And behold a leper***; and, thirdly, help is given, where it is said, ***And Jesus stretching forth his hand, touched him, saying: I will, be thou made clean***. He says, therefore: ***And when he was come down from the mountain***, etc. This mountain is heaven; "A mountain in which God is well pleased to dwell" (Ps. 67, 17). Hence, after He descended from heaven, ***great multitudes followed him***; "He emptied himself, taking the form of a servant, and in habit found as a man," etc., (Phil. 2, 7). Or, by the mountain, the loftiness of His doctrine is signified; "Thy justice is as the mountains of God" (Ps. 35, 7). When He was on the mountain, that is, when He led a lofty life, His disciples followed Him. ***And*** *when he was come down, great multitudes followed him*; "I could not speak to you as unto spiritual" (I Cor. 3, 1). Secondly, the person of the sick man is introduced: and two things are related. Firstly, his sickness is shown; and secondly, care is given. There is sickness, because he is a leper; and, by this, he signifies spiritual infirmities. For there are some infirmities hiding within, such as fevers; on the other hand, some, even if they are within, their effects, nevertheless, appear outwardly, such as leprosy. Therefore, he is a leper, whose evil will is shown through an evil action; "We have thought him as it were a leper" (Is. 53, 4).

But there is a question, because in Luke it is said that when He came to Capharnaum, He healed the leper.[1] It ought to be said that Matthew follows the historical order of events, because when He was going to Capharnaum, on the way, a leper appeared to Him.

His care follows, because, firstly, the leper came; and secondly, he adored; hence, the Evangelist says, **Behold a leper.** In this manner, the sinner comes through faith, but he adores through humility; "God will save the humble of spirit" (Ps. 33, 19). Likewise, he confesses Christ's power, when he says, **Lord, if thou wilt, thou canst make me clean.** Similarly, he calls him Lord. If He is the Lord, He is able to save. In Ps. 99, 3, it is written: "Know ye that the Lord he is God." Likewise, he confides in God's mercy. One ought not to request mercy, but only to show one's neediness to Him: and so this man says: **Lord, if thou wilt, thou canst make me clean.** Hence, "Lord, all my desire is before thee, and my groaning is not hidden from thee" (Ps. 37, 10). Likewise, he shows forth Christ's wisdom: because he does not seek anything except His will: because Christ knows better what is necessary for you than you yourself know. For this reason, he leaves all to Christ's wisdom. Next, the Evangelist mentions the help. Firstly, Christ heals: and secondly, He instructs. Firstly, the Evangelist mentions the deed; and, secondly, he mentions the effect, where it is said, **And forthwith his leprosy was cleansed.** Christ does three things by curing. He extends His hand, whence He imparts assistance; "Put forth thy hand from on high, take me out, and deliver me" (Ps. 143, 7). Sometimes, He extends His hand, but does not touch; "I have spread forth my hands all the day to an

---

1. "And it came to pass, when he was in a certain city, behold a man full of leprosy" (Lk. 5, 12). St. Augustine is quoted in the *Catena Aurea on St. Matthew* saying, "Luke has mentioned the cleansing of this leper, though not in the same order of events, but as his manner is to recollect things omitted, and to put first things that were done later, as they were divinely suggested; so that what they had known before, they afterwards set down in writing when they were recalled to their minds" (chap. 8, lect. 1).

unbelieving people," etc., (Is. 65, 2). Sometimes, He touches; and this is when He transforms, as it is said in Psalm 143, 5: "Touch the mountains, and they shall smoke," through compunction.

But why does He touch him, since it is forbidden in the Law? He did this to show that He is above the Law. It is read about Eliseus, that he did not touch Naaman, but he sent him to the Jordan. Hence, this Man, Who touched, seems to destroy the Law. But, according to the truth, He does not destroy the Law, because it was forbidden to touch lepers on account of contagion. And since He could not be infected, He could touch him. Likewise, He touched him in order that He might show His humanity; because it does not suffice for a sinner to be subject to God as far as concerns His divinity, but also as far as concerns His humanity.

I will, be thou made clean. Jerome says that some men expound this badly. For they maintain that the word *mundare* is in the form of an infinitive; but this is not true; on the contrary, because the leper had said, *If thou wilt*, Christ says, *I will*; and the word *mundare* is in the imperative mood. Hence, He who spoke, commanded, and it was done.

Likewise, **He touched**, in order that He might give an instruction on the power which is in the sacraments, because not only is touching required, but words also. Because when the word is added to the element, this becomes a sacrament.[2] And by this, when He touched, three errors are excluded. For He shows His true body, against the Manichaeans. Because He says, *I will*, He speaks against Apollinaris.[3] By this word, namely, *be thou made clean*, He shows that He is true God, against Photinus.[4]

And the effect follows, *And forthwith his leprosy was cleansed*, and he was cured. Chrysostom says that it happened more quickly than He could say this word, *be thou made clean*: because this word is said in time, but that the time of being cured is in an instant. *And he saith to him*. Here He instructs him: for it would have been a small thing to heal him if He did not also instruct him; "I will give thee understanding, and I will instruct thee" (Ps. 31, 8). Firstly, He prescribes silence upon him, *See thou tell no man*. Chrysostom says: "Because He knew that the Jews were calumniating about His deeds, for that reason He said: *See thou tell no man*." Or it is otherwise. Such can be expounded

---

2. St. Augustine on *St. John's Gospel*, quoted in III, q. 60, a. 4, Sed Contra.
3. Apollinaris the Elder (c.315-c.390) of Laodicea in Syria taught that Christ was nothing more than the Divine Nature united Itself to a mere human body and that He possessed the Divine Logos in place of the human mind and will.
4. Photinus (d. 376) taught that Christ was firstly a mere man and later merited to become an adopted son of God.

that He said this for an example. For it was because, earlier, He had taught to hide good deeds; for that reason, He gives an example, because no one ought to boast about good deeds. He continues: *but go, shew thyself to the priests*. And why does He say this? It is because He had touched a leper, and so He says this so that He might not seem to be a complete breaker of the Law. He is sent to the priests, as is said in Leviticus 14. *And offer the gift*, etc. Why? It is because there was a precept of the Law that a man cleansed from leprosy would offer two young turtle-doves.

But, according to this, it seems that, since the Lord commanded this, it ought to still be done today. It should to be said that figures ought not to cease, until the truth is completely manifested. This, however, did not happen until after the Resurrection.

For a testimony unto them: and this is expounded in two ways. *Moses commanded for a testimony unto them*. And, by this saying, He teaches that the commands of Moses were for a testimony of Christ, as is said in John 5, 46: "If you did believe Moses, you would perhaps believe me also." Or it is otherwise. *For a testimony unto them*, that is, against them, who saw miracles and did not believe. Or, *for a testimony unto them*, namely, of your being cured. Because, when they will have received your offering, they will not be able to deny the miracle.

Likewise, according to a mystical understanding of this event, three things are prescribed by Christ. He prescribed that one be ashamed of sin; against those about whom it is said, "They have proclaimed abroad their sin as Sodom, and they have not hid it" (Is. 3, 9). Hence, it is said: "There is a shame that bringeth sin, and there is a shame that bringeth glory and grace" (Eccli. 4, 25). Similarly, one ought to show oneself to the priest by confessing. "Confess therefore your sins one to another" (James 5, 16). And here it seems that the Lord has prescribed confession. And he was healed: instantly, because in the contrition itself, when one laments and intends to confess and to abstain from the sin, the sin is remitted, according to that which is written: "I will confess against myself my injustice to the Lord: and thou hast forgiven the wickedness of my sin" (Ps. 31, 5). Likewise, satisfaction is prescribed, when He says: *Offer thy gift*. Moreover, He teaches us to keep the commandments, when He says, *As Moses commanded*.

5. *And when he had entered into Capharnaum, there came to him a centurion, beseeching him,*

6. *And saying, Lord, my servant lieth at home sick of the palsy, and is grievously tormented.*

7. And Jesus saith to him: I will come and heal him.

8. And the centurion, making answer, said: Lord, I am not worthy that thou shouldst enter under my roof; but only say the word, and my servant shall be healed.

9. For I also am a man subject to authority, having under me soldiers; and I say to this, Go, and he goeth, and to another Come, and he cometh, and to my servant, Do this, and he doeth it.

10. And Jesus hearing this, marvelled; and said to them that followed him. Amen I say to you, I have not found so great faith in Israel.

11. And I say to you that many shall come from the east and the west, and shall sit down with Abraham, and Isaac and Jacob in the kingdom of heaven:

12. But the children of the kingdom shall be cast out into the exterior darkness: there shall be weeping and gnashing of teeth.

13. And Jesus said to the centurion: Go, and as thou hast believed, so be it done to thee. And the servant was healed at the same hour.

And when he had entered into Capharnaum. Here, Christ's power is shown from His absence. And firstly, the centurion's piety with faith is commended; and secondly, his humility is commended, where it is said, *And the centurion, making answer*, etc. About the first, two things are to be noted: firstly, that the centurion's piety is indicated; and secondly, Christ's goodness is shown. And about the first, there are three things: firstly, the place is set forth; secondly, the speech is described, where it is said, *Lord, my servant lieth at home sick of the palsy*; and thirdly, the hearkening to the request is set forth, where it is said, *And Jesus saith to him*. The place is firstly set forth: *When he had entered into Capharnaum*, which is interpreted 'the town of fatness,' actually, a town of the Gentiles, which was overflowing with the fatness of devotion. "Let my soul be filled as with marrow and fatness" (Ps. 62, 6). Then, *a centurion came to Him*.

But here it can be inquired: Why is it that Luke asserts that he sent priests? Augustine says that he did not personally come, but because it is said that he came, all is referred to his intention: because someone does something if it happens by his authority. Chrysostom expounds this otherwise, because he says that this man was placed over a hundred soldiers, and for that reason he was a ruler. Hence, the Jews, being willing to flatter him for the sake of keeping his good favor, said to him: 'Master, we ourselves will go, and plead for you.' Then, in order to satisfy them, he permitted them to go; but afterwards he himself followed them.

This miracle differs from the first in three things. For the first was done for a Jew, the second for a Gentile; by which it is given to be understood, that Christ came not only for the Jews, but also for the Gentiles. Similarly, in the first, the Jew approached by himself, this man did not. And this is because the Lord has mercy upon some through their own devotion, and upon others through the intercession of others. Likewise, this centurion can be understood to be some angel in that place in charge of the salvation of the Gentiles, or of the firstfruits of the Gentiles. Again, he was a leper, in whom uncleanness remains at rest. Paralytics, however, are they who cannot move their members. Lepers are the intemperate, and the paralytics are the incontinent. And they are paralytics, who sin out of weakness; they are lepers, who sin out of determined malice. By the centurion can be understood the mind. "Be renewed in spirit of your mind" (Eph. 4, 23). And this man says: *Lord, my servant* (*puer*), i.e. boy that is my servant (*servus meus*). And in this is shown the goodness of the centurion, because he entreats in this way for his servant; hence, he does that which is said in Ecclesiasticus 33, 31: "If thou have a faithful servant, let him be to thee as thy own soul." And this servant is said to be the lower part of the soul. He says, therefore, that *he lieth and is grievously tormented*; and he speaks out of affection, because when someone loves another, he considers a small sickness to be very great. The lower part of the soul lies down, therefore, when it is unable to lift itself up; "The flesh lusteth against the spirit" (Gal. 5, 17): and it is tormented. Lascivious men rejoice: "For they are glad when they have done evil, and rejoice in the most wicked things" (Prov. 2, 14). But these men are tormented, because they sin out of weakness, and when they will have fallen, they lament. And so they are tormented out of sorrow. *And Jesus saith to him: I will come and heal him*; that is, I will not just speak and he would be healed. Hence, observe that no one would dare to ask so much as the Lord says He is willing to give: *I will come and heal him*, because Christ's presence is the cause of salvation.

But it ought to be observed that He did not wish to go to the son of a ruler,[5] but He did go to a servant; which is opposed to many men, who wish to visit only great men, contrary to that passage: "Make thyself affable to the congregation of the poor" (Eccli. 4, 7).

5. Jn. 4, 46-50.

It continues, *And the centurion, making answer.* The centurion's goodness, together with his faith, were related; now his humility, together with his faith, are set forth. Firstly, therefore, his humility and faith are set forth; and secondly, Christ's goodness is set forth, where it is said, *And Jesus hearing this, marvelled.* About the first, the centurion does three things. Firstly, he confesses his unworthiness, where it is said, *But only say the word;* secondly, he confesses Christ's power; and then he introduces a similitude, where it is said, *For I also am a man subject to authority.* The Lord had shown Himself to be favorable. But because this man was a Gentile, he considered himself to be unworthy, saying: *Lord, I am not worthy*, etc. In this manner, Peter likewise said, "Depart from me, for I am a sinful man" (Lk. 5, 8). And Augustine says, "By confessing himself unworthy, he rendered himself worthy." And just as this man speaks, so we also ought to say: 'I am not worthy that Thou shouldst enter my body.' Then the faith of the centurion, confessing Christ's power, is indicated: *But only say the word, and my servant shall be healed*, because, as it is said: "It was neither herb, nor mollifying plaster, that healed them, but thy word, O Lord, which healeth them" (Wis. 16, 12). And in Psalm 106, 20: "He sent his word, and healed them." Then he introduces a similitude, and proves from the lesser. Firstly, he describes his chain of command; and secondly, his power, when he says, *For I also am a man subject to authority*, etc. And the chain of command is treated: because some men are superiors, such that they do not have a superior; and some men are superiors, such that they have a superior to themselves; but some men are inferiors, who do not have inferiors to themselves; therefore, some men are in the middle; and of these men was this man, because he was under a tribune, but was having soldiers under himself. For he was having under himself certain men whose governor he was, and these were the soldiers; hence, he says, *And I say to this, Go, and he goeth, and to another Come, and he cometh*; in which saying, obedience is commended to us. "Obey your prelates and be subject to them" (Heb. 13, 17). Likewise, he was having servants by whom he was being supplied with food. "Fodder, and a wand, and a burden are for an ass: bread, and correction, and work for a slave" (Eccli. 33, 25). *And I say to my servant, Do this, and he doeth it*; hence, he wishes to argue from the lesser: because, 'If I, who am constituted in power, can do these things, how much more can the Lord of lords, etc.?'

But it ought to be seen that rational creatures are free, and they are like soldiers; "Is there any numbering of his soldiers?"

(Job. 25, 3) And therefore, He is called the Lord of armies.[6] But the irrational creature has a servile subjection, because he does not have the faculty of free will. Therefore, he wishes to say: 'Because Nature obeys you, speak to Nature, and it will obey you, because your will is full of judgment.' It ought to be seen that this twofold dominion is found in the soul: for the soul directs the body; but reason directs the irascible and concupiscible powers. The first is a dominative power, because the body is moved at the command of the soul; the second directs the other powers by a sort of a commanding, dominative or royal power: hence, it has something of its own motion. And these are, as it were, its soldiers; "From whence are wars and contentions among you? Are they not hence, from your concupiscences, which war in your members?" (James 4, 1). "We exhort you, as strangers and pilgrims, to refrain yourselves from carnal desires which war against the soul" (I Pet. 2, 11). Hence, we ought to say to the latter, *Go*, that is, to the bad morals; *and Come*, namely, to the good morals, and *to* this *servant, Do this*. Hence, we ought to apply the body to work, in order that, "As you have yielded your members to serve uncleanness and iniquity, unto iniquity: so now yield your members to serve justice, unto sanctification" (Rom. 6, 19).

And Jesus hearing this, marvelled, etc. Here, Christ's goodness is mentioned. But what is it that he says, *He marvelled*? Because admiration does not happen to God; because it does not occur except out of ignorance of the cause, which cannot be in God. Similarly, it is the apprehension of the greatness of an effect, which arises from the imagination and appearance of some great effect, and so it also cannot happen in Christ: hence, when it is said that He marvelled, the meaning is that He considered the centurion's faith to be great, and He showed this to the crowds following Him. And He commended him: hence, He said to those following Him: *I have not found so great faith in Israel*.

But what is this? Was there not greater faith in Abraham, Isaac and Jacob? It must be said that there was indeed; but what is said here is understood according to that time.

But then there is the same question concerning the Apostles, and Martha, and Mary. And it ought to said that this man had greater faith, because he had seen nothing preceding, in comparison to those men who had seen miracles. Likewise, Peter came at the word of Andrew, and Andrew at the word of John. Likewise, there was some uncertainty in the words of Martha, because she

---

6. Or 'Lord of hosts'.

said, "Lord, if thou hadst been here, my brother had not died" (Jn. 11, 21); as if, while He was absent, He could not prevent death. Chrysostom expounds this passage otherwise. He says that something is said to be great or small, not absolutely, but in comparison, just as a number of people are called many in a house, and few in a theater. Hence, *I have not found so great faith in Israel*, actually, in comparison with that Gentile. "The stranger that liveth with thee in the land, shall rise up over thee, and shall be higher" (Deut. 28, 43).

And I say to you. By occasion of this, He gives a comparison of the Jews and the Gentiles; firstly, concerning the calling of the Gentiles; and secondly, concerning the reprobation of the Jews. *I say that many shall come from the east and the west*, etc. And this is said in comparison, because "Many are called, but few chosen" (below 20, 16). *From the east and the west*, so that, by this, the whole world is understood. Or, *from the east*, in the time of prosperity is understood: *and the west*, in the time of adversity. Or, *from the east*, in the time of youth is understood; *and the west*, the time of old age. *And they shall sit down*. This sitting is the opulence of spiritual things, namely, in contemplation. "And I dispose to you, as my Father hath disposed to me, a kingdom, that you may eat and drink at my table, in my kingdom" (Lk. 22, 29). And: "Behold my servants shall eat, and you shall be hungry: behold my servants shall drink, and you shall be thirsty," etc., (Is. 65, 13).

But why *with Abraham, and Isaac and Jacob*? Because the Gentiles are justified through faith, just like the Jews, as is found in Romans 4 and Genesis 12.[7] Similarly, the promise was made to these men, that "In thy seed shall all the nations be blessed" (Gen. 22, 18). For this reason, these men shall sit down with their fathers

It continues, *But the children of the kingdom shall be cast out into the exterior darkness*. Here He shows the reprobation of the Jews, and He describes the punishment of damnation, because they will lose good things, and they will incur evils. He says, however, *The children of the kingdom*, because God was reigning in them; "In Judea God is known: his name is great in Israel" (Ps. 75, 2). Moreover, by the figures of the Law, they were His servants. Likewise, the promise was made to them, as said in Romans 4. *They shall be cast out into the exterior darkness*. And this is the punishment of damnation. Consequently,

---

7. Abraham was justified by faith before he was circumcised.

He enumerates the evils which they shall incur: that anyone who has at first incurred interior darkness with regard to the intellect, will be afterwards cast out into the exterior darkness, because then they will be completely alienated from God, who is true light. And this is what is said in Tobias 4, 11: "Alms deliver from all sin, and from death, and will not suffer the soul to go into darkness." Similarly, so far as concerns the effect, *there shall be weeping*. Weeping proclaims the sorrow of the reprobate, "Behold my servants shall rejoice, and you shall be confounded" (Is. 65, 14). Likewise, the suffering of the body is shown, because He says, *gnashing of teeth*: for they will possess their bodies in the resurrection; "Judgments are prepared for scorners: and striking hammers for the bodies of fools" (Prov. 19, 29): which penalty of sorrow pertains to the concupiscible appetite, but the gnashing pertains to the irascible appetite. Or, according to Jerome, both pertain to bodily punishment, because the resurrection will not only be in the soul but in the body: because there will be both much heat, and much cold; "They will pass from the snow waters to excessive heat" (Job 24, 19).

God's goodness is shown, when He says, *Go, and as thou hast believed, so be it done to thee*. But also the effect follows, *And the servant was healed*, because His word is full of power (Eccle. 8, 4).

14. And when Jesus was come into Peter's house, he saw his wife's mother lying, and sick of a fever;
15. And he touched her hand, and the fever left her, and she arose and ministered to them.
16. And when evening was come, they brought to him many that were possessed with devils: and he cast out the spirits with his word: and all that were sick he healed:
17. That it might be fulfilled, which was spoken by the prophet Isaias, saying: He took our infirmities, and bore our diseases.
18. And Jesus seeing great multitudes about him, gave orders to pass over the water.
19. And a certain scribe came and said to him: Master, I will follow thee whithersoever thou shalt go.
20. And Jesus saith to him: The foxes have holes, and the birds of the air nests; but the Son of man hath not where to lay his head.
21. And another of his disciples said to him: Lord, suffer me first to go and bury my father.

22. But Jesus said to him: Follow me, and let the dead bury their dead.

23. And when he entered into the boat, his disciples followed him:

24. And behold a great tempest arose in the sea, so that the boat was covered with waves, but he was asleep.

25. And they came to him, and awaked him, saying: Lord, save us, we perish.

26. And Jesus saith to them: Why are you fearful, O ye of little faith? Then rising up, he commanded the winds, and the sea, and there came a great calm.

27. But the men wondered, saying: What manner of man is this, for the winds and the sea obey him?

And when Jesus was come into Simon Peter's house, etc. Christ's power is commended in the cure of the leper, it is commended also in the sudden cure of the centurion's servant; here, it is commended in the complete cure of the mother of Peter's wife. Firstly, therefore, the Evangelist describes the place of the cure; secondly, he describes the type of sickness; thirdly, he declares Christ's help; and fourthly, he declares the effect of the cure. He says, therefore, **When He was come**, etc. The Evangelist does not mention when this was done; but both Luke and Mark pass over what has already been written by Matthew to other facts.

But it should be known that where the Evangelists relate the circumstance, or something pertaining to the order of events, it is a sign that it pertains to the continuation of history; but where they do not, it is a sign that the narration of a particular event pertains to the continuation of memory. Hence, what they were recalling, they were writing.

Jesus came into Peter's house. And we can consider three things. We can consider the honor which He renders to His disciples, because He did not want to go to the centurion's house; nevertheless, He went to the house of a poor fisherman; whence, "Thy friends, O God, are made exceedingly honorable" (Ps. 138, 17). Likewise, He built upon humility, because nothing else is so pleasing to the Lord. "With meekness receive the ingrafted word, which is able to save your souls," etc., (James 1, 21). Thirdly, in this, the respect is shown which the Lord had for Peter, because He offered Himself to go, although Peter did not ask. *He saw his wife's mother*; *He saw*, namely, with the mind's eye; "I have seen the affliction of my people in Egypt" (Ex. 3, 7). *Peter's wife's mother*. By this can be understood the synagogue.

"He who wrought in Peter to the apostleship of the circumcision (that is to say, to the Jews) wrought in me also among the Gentiles" (Gal. 2, 8). This woman, that is to say, the synagogue, had a fever, namely, the fever of envy. Or, by this mother-in-law, the soul burning with the fire concupiscence is understood. *And he touched her hand.* Here he mentions the curing.

Chrysostom inquires, 'Why did He cure the centurion's servant by only a word, but this woman by a touch?' And he answers, 'It is on account of the close acquaintance; and in this He was also showing more His humility': and, for that reason, He gave help with a touch; "Thou hast held me by my right hand" (Ps. 72, 24). It continues, *And she arose.* It is the experience of those having a fever, that when they begin to be healed, they are weaker then they were in the sickness, but the Lord's healing was not in this manner; on the contrary, He restored complete health; because "The works of God are perfect" (Deut. 32, 4). For the Lord cures in one way and Nature in another. For that reason, it continues, *And she ministered. And when evening was come.* Here, God's power is confirmed through the multiplicity of cures. Firstly, therefore, the Evangelist mentions the multiplicity; and secondly, he adjoins the authority of Scripture, where it is said, *That it might be fulfilled, which was spoken by the prophet Isaias.* He says, therefore, that He cured the demoniacs and the sick. And by the demoniacs can be understood those sinning out of malice; and by the sick, those sinning out of ignorance. Hence, he says, *And when evening was come*; observe for what cause this did not happen on the day of the Sabbath, on which day the Jews regarded it to be unfitting to cure; but in the evening the Sabbath was finished, and so *they brought to him many that were possessed.* Or it is said, *in the evening*, because our Savior came in the evening. "The sun riseth, and goeth down" (Eccle. 1, 5), namely, Christ. *He cast out*, by a mere rebuke: hence, at His voice alone, the demons were fleeing. Likewise, *the sick*, so that that which is said in Acts 10, 38 is applicable to Him: "He delivered all that were oppressed by the devil." Hence, it ought to be observed that the Evangelists did not relate all the miracles of Christ, but rather those spread among the people. And because it might seem marvelous that He would cure so many people, for this reason, the Evangelist confirms his words with the passage which is contained in Isaias 53, 4: "He hath borne our infirmities and carried our sorrows." And although the quotation is not exactly in context, we may explain it according as it is found. *He took our infirmities*, that is, He took them away; such that infirmities may be taken for light sins. *And bore our diseases* (that is, our greater sins), that is, He carried them away: or, since He Himself is God's power and wisdom, *He took away our infirmities*, namely, of suffering and death. Hence, He accepted passibility[8] for the sake of taking away our infirmity and sickness, etc. "Who his own self bore our sins in his body upon the tree: that we, being dead to sins, should live to justice" (I Pet. 2, 24).

But since Isaias spoke about sins, it is asked why this is said concerning bodily infirmities. And this is because, frequently, bodily sicknesses are caused by spiritual sins.

And Jesus seeing the multitudes. Because the miracles opposed to interior sins were related, here he sets forth miracles opposed to exterior sins: namely, a miracle opposed to a storm. Firstly, he relates the event preliminary to the miracle, namely, the entrance into the boat; then he relates the miracle, where it is said, *Then rising up, he commanded the winds, and the sea*; and thirdly, he relates the effect of the miracle, where it is said, *And there came a great calm*. About the first, he initially relates the precept; and then the fulfillment of the command. About the first, Christ does three things. Firstly, He orders that they follow; secondly, He repels the man obtruding himself; and thirdly, He rebukes another disciple. He says, therefore, *And Jesus seeing the multitudes*.

But why did He enter the boat? He did this for two reasons. Firstly, He entered the boat so that He might show the weakness of human nature; and secondly, it was so that He might please the disciples; hence, sometimes He went up into a mountain with the disciples, sometimes into the desert, and sometimes into a boat. Likewise, it was so that He might give an example to us, that we ought not to seek the favor of men. Moreover, He did this for the sake of taking away the Jews' envy; "The smoking flax he shall not quench" (Is. 42, 3).

The repulsion follows, *And a certain scribe came*: and it seems that this man approached very devotedly. And so why did He repel him? Jerome says: "Because he was not possessing good faith." And this is evident: because he only called Him 'Master'; but the true disciples were calling Him 'Lord.' Hence, it is said in John 13, 13: "You call me Master and Lord." Likewise, he wanted to follow Him out of a bad intention; because he was hearing that a miraculous sign had been performed, he wanted to follow so that he might perform miraculous signs, just as it is said about

---

8. Passibility is the ability to suffer.

Simon the Magician (Acts, 8). Similarly, Chrysostom says that he sinned in another way, namely, by pride, because he was placing himself apart from other men. Hence, he was accounting himself more worthy than other men. Hilary reads this passage interrogatively: 'Master, will I follow thee?' This man is deserving blame, because what was certain, he questioned, and what he needed to do, he placed in doubt. It continues, *The foxes have holes*. Jerome expounds this literally, that God is responding to the intention, which He often does. He was willing to follow, but he was intending to profit: and against this the Lord relates His own poverty; for that reason, He says, *The foxes have holes, and the birds of the air nests; but the Son of man hath not where to lay his head*; just as it is said in II Corinthians 8, 9: "Who being rich he became poor." According to Augustine, He reproves him concerning three faults. In regard to the fault of deceitfulness, because he was having sweetness in his mouth and poison in his heart, as is stated in Psalm 13, 3.[9] Again, He reproved Him concerning pride, since He said, *The birds of the air*, by which pride is understood. Or, *the birds*, are understood to be demons, as is stated below (13, 4), where it is said, "And the birds of the air came and ate them up." Moreover, He reproached him concerning infidelity, because he was not in charity, which dwells in us through faith. It continues, *And another of his disciples said to him*. The first obtruded himself, but the second excused himself. And the reproof of the one excusing, is where it is said, *But Jesus said to him*, etc. *Lord, suffer me first to go and bury my father*. And there is a great difference between this and the preceding man. This man called Him 'Lord,' the former called him 'Master.' Likewise, the former alleged a deceitful thing, the latter alleged a pious thing, because there was a precept about honoring one's father: hence, he asked for a delay. A similar thing is related concerning Eliseus (III Kings 19).[10] The reprehension of this man follows, *Follow me*: because he who wishes to follow Christ, ought not to cease to follow on account of some temporal business; hence, it is said: "Forget thy people and thy father's house" (Ps. 44, 11). Moreover, He commanded this to him because there were others who were able to bury his father.

---

9. "Their throat is an open sepulchre; with their tongues they acted deceitfully: the poison of asps is under their lips."

10. "And he forthwith left the oxen, and run after Elias, and said: Let me, I pray thee, kiss my father and my mother, and then I will follow thee. And he said to him: Go, and return back: for that which was my part, I have done to thee" (III Kings 19, 20).

For that reason, He said: ***Let the dead bury their dead***. Similarly, He did this because, as often happens, that he who is impeded by some business, when he takes on one thing, quickly falls into another; so if this man had gone to bury his father, he might have afterwards had thought about his father's inheritance, and in this way, he perhaps might have become completely withdrawn. "Woe to you that draw iniquity with cords of vanity" (Is. 5, 18). Hence, this was not cruelty.[11] It is as if we were to see some excessive affection concerning the death of a man's father, and he is held back from the funeral on account of his danger, as is found in Eccli. 30, 25: "Sadness hath killed many." But He says, ***the dead*** (*mortuos*), in the plural, because he had died a double death, namely, the death of infidelity and bodily death. Hence, he had died in his body and in his soul. Hence, He gives four teachings. The first is, namely, that he who is called to the state of perfection may not know his carnal father through inordinate affection; "One is your father, who is in heaven" (below 23, 9). The second is that the affection of family ties pulls men between being faithful or infidels. Hence: "If any man come to me, and hate not his father and mother and wife and children and brethren and sisters, yea and his own life also, he cannot be my disciple" (Lk. 14, 26). And this is true where father and mother draw one away from God. The third is that a remembrance of infidels ought not to be made among the Saints. The fourth is that everyone who lives outside of Christ is dead, because He is the Life, according to Gregory. ***And when he entered into the boat.*** The Lord's command about crossing the sea having been related; here is related the execution of the command. Because there were evident miracles on land, He wishes to make known His miracles on the water, so that He might show Himself to be master of land and sea. By this ship is understood the Church, or Christ's Cross; hence, concerning this ship, that passage can be said to refer: "Men trust their lives even to a little wood (Wis. 14, 5). The Lord's disciples follow Him in the Church though the observance of the Commandments. Likewise, they follow Him ascending upon the Cross. "By whom the world is crucified to me, and I to the world" (Gal. 6, 14). Thereupon, the miracle is subjoined. And, firstly, the imminent danger is related; secondly, the disciples' appeal is related, where it is said, ***And they came***; and thirdly, the hearkening to them, where it is said, ***And Jesus saith to them***. The danger is

---

11. "It is rather the reverse of cruelty. And it is a much greater evil to draw one away from spiritual discourse; especially when there were who should perform the rites" (*Catena Aurea on St. Matthew*, chap. 8, lect. 6).

touched upon by way of the tempest, and Christ's sleeping. ***And behold a great tempest.*** As the Saints say, the tempest did not occur due to the air's inclemency, but it came to pass by divine ordinance. And this happened for several reasons: firstly, it was so that the disciples, who were specially loved and called, might be humble and not exalt themselves; and also, this symbolized the future danger, which was due to come at the time of the Passion. And the dangers that were to come thereafter are also symbolized, as Paul the Apostle says: "We were pressed out of measure above our strength, so that we were weary even of life" (II Cor. 1, 8). Moreover, it was so that they might know how to live among dangers and overcome them, as it is said: "In all these things we overcome, because of him that hath loved us" (Rom. 8, 37). Similarly, Chrysostom explains that these men were about to preach the things which they had seen concerning Christ; for that reason, in order that they would have experienced miracles pertaining to themselves, and would be more certain about them, the Lord wanted them to suffer. Hence, it is said in Psalm 65, 16: "Come, and I will tell you the works of the Lord." For they could more easily remember things that happened to themselves. ***But he was asleep***: and this occurred in order to show that He was a true man; for He acted in this way in everything which He did, so that, whenever He wanted to show His divinity, He always showed His humanity. He was sleeping, because He was "in habit found as a man" (Phil. 2, 7). Likewise, He was sleeping, so that they might be established between fear and hope. Again, it was in order that He might show singularity, because He was remaining secure amidst so great a storm; "When he established the sky above, and poised the fountains of waters, and when he set a law to the waters" (Prov. 8, 28-29). The appeal of the disciples follows, ***The disciples came***, etc. For the wind was so great, that it was necessary to awaken Him: and all this was predicted in the figure of Jonas, because Jonas was sleeping in a boat: and the sailors awakened him for questioning, but these disciples awakened Christ to save themselves; hence, they say, ***Lord, save us, we perish***. And, firstly, they confess His power, when they say, ***Lord***; "Thou rulest the power of the sea: and appeasest the motion of the waves thereof" (Ps. 88, 10). Similarly, they ask for His help, because they knew that He is the Savior; "He himself will come and will save you" (Ps. 35, 4). Likewise, they were expressing the perishability of earthly things. And herein Christ's death is signified, in the sleeping of Him who also was stirred up by the Resurrection. Or, He is said to sleep in the tribulations and temptations of the Saints; and then He awakens through the prayers of the Saints: hence, it is said: "Arise, why sleepest thou, O Lord?" (Ps. 43, 23) Again, He sleeps in the slothful; hence, He ought to be aroused, as Paul admonishes: "Rise, thou that sleepest, and arise from the dead: and Christ shall enlighten thee" (Eph. 5, 14). How He assists the disciples follows, *Why are you fearful, O ye of little faith?* It seems that they were not of little faith, because they were saying, *Save us*; but they truly were of little faith, because they were not believing that He could save them even while sleeping. Or, they were *of little faith*, because if they had great faith, they themselves would have been able to command the sea. *Then rising up, he commanded the winds*: for a storm arises from the winds as from the efficient cause, from the waters as from the material cause: and so He commanded both; hence, "He said the word, and a storm of wind ceased" (Ps. 106, 25).[12] And this is just what is said, *And there came a great calm*. But it is usual that when a storm occurs, the sea is not completely calm for two days. For that reason, a great calm immediately came so that the miracle would appear perfect, for, "The works of God are perfect" (Deut. 32, 4). *But the men wondered*, etc. Here the effect is related, namely, the admiration of the crowds. What he says, namely, the word *men*, ought not to be understood of the Apostles, because the Apostles are never named in this manner; but by men understand that it was the sailors. Or, according to Jerome, even if you understand 'men' as meaning the Apostles, it can be that they were able to doubt like men, saying, *What manner of man is this?* Here Chrysostom adds, they say, *man*, for it is because they had seen Him sleeping, they call Him a 'man'; because they had seen a sign of His divinity, for that reason, they were doubting. *For the winds and the sea obey him*; because every creature obeys its Creator; "Fire, hail, snow, ice, stormy winds, which fulfill his word," etc., (Ps. 148, 8). This is not because they have a rational soul, but because they are constituted in the manner of someone obeying. Just as the hand and the members of the body obey the soul, for they are immediately moved at its command, in this fashion all things obey God.

28. And when he was come on the other side of the water, into the country of the Gerasens, there met him two that were possessed with devils, coming out of the sepulchres, exceeding fierce, so that none could pass by that way.

---

12. *Dixit et stetit spiritus procellae.* The Douay translation however is, "He said the word, and there arose a storm of wind".

29. And behold they cried out, saying: What have we to do with thee, Jesus Son of God? art thou come hither to torment us before the time?
30. And there was, not far from them, a herd of many swine feeding.
31. And the devils besought him, saying: If thou cast us out hence, send us into the herd of swine.
32. And he said to them: Go. But they going out went into the swine, and behold the whole herd ran violently down a steep place into the sea: and they perished in the waters.
33. And they that kept them fled: and coming into the city, told everything, and concerning them that had been possessed by the devils.
34. And behold the whole city went out to meet Jesus, and when they saw him, they besought him that he would depart from their coast.

And when he was come on the other side of the water. Because the miracles have been treated by which the Lord freed many men from exterior dangers, here are related the miracles by which occurred a liberation from interior, or spiritual, dangers. And firstly, a miracle is related; secondly, the effect is related, where it is said, ***But they going out went into the swine***. And about the first, the demons' malice is shown, firstly, as far as concerns the fierceness which they exercise upon men; secondly, as far as their unwillingness to suffer, where it is said, ***And behold they cried out***, etc.; and thirdly, as far as their wickedness, where it is said, ***And the devils besought him***, etc. About the first, to begin with, the place is described; and next, the demons' fierceness is declared. There was a certain region which was called the region of the ***Gerasens***: Gerasa is interpreted 'casting out the farmer,' or 'approaching foreigner,' because it was near the Gentiles. ***There met him two that were possessed with devils.*** Their fierceness is shown, firstly, because they were oppressing them, i.e. the two men; and secondly, because they were striving to deceive men.

But it is asked why the other Evangelists only make mention of one man and this Evangelist mentions two. It ought to be said that without a doubt there were two; but one was more famous. And they were fierce, because they were harming, not only corporeally, but also spiritually. Hence, they were dwelling in the sepulchres so that they might frighten men. Hence, there was an error which certain men maintained, that the demons could lead back some soul into a dead body, as is read concerning Simon the Magician;[13] but this was nothing real, but, in fact, the demons were feigning this to deceive men. Hence, Porphyrius[14] says that the whole group of demons is deceptive. Hence, these magicians especially use the bodies of the dead: wherefore, the demons were dwelling in the sepulchres; "That dwell in sepulchres, and sleep in the temple of idols" (Is. 65, 4). For they were so fierce that no one could pass by that way: because, "In this way wherein I walked, the proud have hidden a snare for me" (Ps. 141, 4), and by the proud are understood the demons. But their unwillingness to suffer is shown, because they were not enduring Christ's presence; whence, it is said, *They cried out*: and in this their unwillingness to suffer is shown; "You shall cry for sorrow of heart, and shall howl for grief of spirit" (Is. 65, 12). They confess God's power, saying, *What have we to do with thee, Jesus Son of God?* In fact, they had nothing to do with Him, because there is no concordance of Christ with Belial.[15] But why were they saying this? It was because they were punishing men severely, and they had heard that Christ was due to take away the power from them. Wherefore, they wished to say: 'And if we harmed others, we did not harm you, for which reason you ought not to oppress us.' Likewise, they were confessing Him to be the Son of God. And in this, the Arians are confounded, because if they do not believe the Saints, at least they may believe the demons.

But it is on the contrary, because it seems that the demons did not know Him; because, "If they had known it, they would never have crucified the Lord of glory," etc., (II Cor. 2, 8). But it ought to said that when the Lord wished, He showed His humanity in such a way that He was hiding Himself from them.

For which reason art thou come to torment us before the time? The demons know that on Judgment Day the demons are due to receive greater torment when it shall be said: "Depart from me, you cursed, into everlasting fire" (below 25, 41). Moreover, some believe that the demons do not suffer the pain of sense until Judgment Day, but only the pain of damnation: and this opinion is based upon this passage, *art thou come before the time*. But against this is what Damascene says: "What death is

---

13. Hippolytus of Rome related that "in order to give his scholars there [at his native town Gitta in Samaria] a proof of his higher nature [as he claimed to be a god] and divine mission and thus regain his authority, he had a grave dug and permitted himself to be buried in it, after previously prophesying that after three days he would rise alive from it. But the promised resurrection did not take place; Simon died in the grave." Taken from *The Catholic Encyclopedia*, (1912 ed.), vol. 13, p. 798.

14. Saint Porphyrius (347-420) was a bishop of Gaza in Palestine.

15. II Corinthians 6, 15.

to men, the fall was to the angels." But men, when they die, immediately receive the pain of sense, in like manner, the angels who fell received it also. Certain men say that they always carry their fire with them.

But how can that be, because this fire is corporeal? It ought to be said that although this fire is corporeal, nevertheless, it has something spiritual: hence, it torments by means of a certain binding: for a spirit surpasses the nature of a body, but God binds the spirits to bodies; just as when the soul is bound to the body, He grants to the body that it may be moved according to the will of the soul: just as if some prelature is given to someone in a certain church, the one to whom it is given is not himself in that church; in this way, although this fire is corporeal, by reason of its spirituality it can act upon the demons here on earth.

To torment us, etc. They reckon it to be a great torment that they would be unable to harm men. But if they were in hell, they could not harm in this way; and in this way it is a great torment for them to enter into hell. **And there was, not far from them, a herd of many swine feeding.** Here their malice is touched upon, because they not only harm men, but even the beasts. **Herd of swine**: hence, it is apparent that this event was not in Judea, because the Jews do not make use of swine. **If thou cast us out hence, send us into the herd of swine.**

But why did they not ask that He would send them into men? It was because they themselves were seeing Him to be solicitous concerning the care of men. But why did they ask to be sent into a herd of swine? It was because they were nearer than any other animals. Similarly, it was because it is a very unclean animal. Hence, to indicate their uncleanness, He permitted them to enter into the swine: and this seems to be signified in Job 40, 22: "Will he make many supplications to thee, or speak soft words to thee?"

Christ's concession follows, **And he said to them: Go**, etc. But it seems that the Lord gave heed to devils. It ought to be said that He did not heed them; but from His own wisdom He permitted it to happen in this way, and He ordained that the malice of the demons be shown, because unless the Lord would restrain them, so would they fall upon men, just as they fell upon the swine. But when the Lord permits some things to the demons, He does not completely permit them to do all they would wish to do, but He imposes a restraint unto them, as in the case of Job. Hence, to indicate this, He permitted them to fall upon the swine. Likewise, He permitted this to indicate that they can do nothing except by God's permission. Moreover, He permitted this so that men might know their dignity, since, for the well-being of one man, He would permit so many thousands of swine to be killed.

The execution of His command follows, *And the whole herd ran violently down a steep place into the sea*; in which is denoted that no one can be completely destroyed by the devil, unless he show himself to be a swine, that is, entirely unclean. Hence, it is written: "With such violence as this, shall Babylon be thrown down" (Apoc. 18, 21); "These men, as irrational beasts, shall perish in their corruption, receiving the reward of their injustice," etc., (II Pet. 12-14). The admiration of the shepherds follows; hence, *They that kept them fled... and told everything*. Those having profited from the swine announced something sad and something joyful: sad, concerning their swine; but joyful, concerning the cured demoniac. By these shepherds is signified the leaders of the Synagogue, who, on account of temporal things, whenever they can, contradict Christ. Afterwards, the admiration of the whole people follows, *And behold the whole city went out to meet Jesus, and when they saw him, they besought him that he would depart from their coast*. And why? It was because He had caused great losses to them, wherefore they feared that if He were to stay longer He would cause them many more losses. In this way, some men, on account of temporal harm, fear to be with Christ, as it is found in Isaias: "Turn away the path from me, let the Holy One of Israel cease from before us" (Is. 30, 11). Or it is otherwise. They did this, not out of malice, but out of devotion, because they were considering themselves to be unworthy. Peter said something similar: "Depart from me, for I am a sinful man, O Lord" (Lk. 5, 8).

CHAPTER NINE

1. And entering into a boat, he passed over the water and came into his own city.

2. And behold they brought to him one sick of the palsy lying in a bed. And Jesus, seeing their faith, said to the man sick of the palsy: Be of good heart, son, thy sins are forgiven thee.

3. And behold some of the scribes said within themselves: He blasphemeth.

4. And Jesus seeing their thoughts, said: Why do you think evil in your hearts?

5. Whether is easier, to say, Thy sins are forgiven thee: or to say, Arise, and walk?

6. But that you may know that the Son of man hath power on earth to forgive sins, (then said he to the man sick of the palsy,) Arise, take up thy bed, and go into thy house.

7. And he arose, and went into his house.

8. And the multitude seeing it, feared, and glorified God that gave such power to men.

Above, the Evangelist set forth miracles opposed to bodily dangers; here, he sets forth miracles opposed to spiritual dangers: and, according to this, he does two things. Firstly, he shows how Christ aids those coming to Him; and how He seeks after those whom He may save, where it is said, **And Jesus went about all the cities and towns.** About the first, Christ begins by setting forth a remedy against sin; and, secondly, He sets forth a remedy against death, where it is said, **As he was speaking these things unto them**, etc. About the first, He initially sets forth the remedy against sin by forgiving; and secondly, He sets forth the remedy by drawing sinners to Himself, where it is said, **And it came to pass as he was sitting at meat in the house**, etc. First, the Evangelist sets forth a kind of preamble to the good deed; and secondly, he sets forth the good deed itself, where it is said, **But that you may know**, etc. And firstly, he relates the place; and secondly, the devotion of those bringing the sick man, where it is said, **And behold they brought to him one sick of the palsy.** He says, therefore, **And entering into a boat, he passed over the water.** And this part is continued from the last chapter, because they were beseeching Him to depart from them, wherefore He entered the boat. Hence, He gives us to understand that if some men were to say, "Depart from us, we desire not the knowledge of thy ways" (Job

21, 14), He immediately departs; for that reason, He entered into a boat. This boat signifies the Cross or the Church. ***He came into his own city***, namely, into a city of the Gentiles, who were given to Him. Hence, in Psalm 2, 8, it is said: "Ask of me, and I will give thee the Gentiles for thy inheritance."

But there is a question: Why do Mark and Luke say that this happened in Capharnaum; while here it is maintained that this happened in His own city, which was Nazareth?

It ought to be said that a certain city was Christ's by reason of His birth; and this was Bethlehem: a certain city was Christ's by reason of His education; and this was Nazareth: and a certain city was Christ's by reason of His social intercourse and of working miracles; and in this way, Capharnaum was His city: for this reason, it is well said, ***Into his own city***. Hence, it is said: "As great things as we have heard done in Capharnaum, do also here in thy own country" (Lk. 4, 23). Augustine solves the question differently, because, among the other cities, Capharnaum was the most famous: hence, it was, as it were, a metropolis. And it is just as if someone were from some village near Paris, it might be said that he was from Paris on account of the notoriety of the place; in this way, the Lord, because He was from the surroundings of Capharnaum, was said to be from there. Or it can be explained otherwise, that the other Evangelists omitted something, whence, something can be added, namely, that He passed through Nazareth, and He came into Capharnaum: and then they brought to Him the one sick of the palsy.

And behold they brought to him one sick of the palsy. Here the devotion of those bringing the sick man is mentioned: hence, in Mark it is mentioned that, because they had not been able to get through the multitude in the house, they set him down through the roof tiles. This paralytic signifies a sinner lying in sin; hence, just as a paralytic cannot move himself, so neither can a sinner. Those, however, who carry the paralytic, are they who carry the sinner to God by their admonitions. ***And Jesus, seeing their faith***, etc. He relates the good deed: wherein we can see three things. Firstly, we see what moves Jesus to act; secondly, we see what it is that is required; and thirdly, we see the dispute opposing the good deed. The Lord sometimes cures someone on account of his faith, sometimes on account of his prayers or the prayers of others. ***Jesus therefore, seeing their faith, said.*** Hence, it is said: "Whatsoever you ask when ye pray, believe that you shall receive, and it shall be done unto you" (Mk. 11, 24). ***Be of good heart, son***. What, therefore, is required? Faith; "They that trust in the Lord shall be as mount Sion: he shall not be moved for ever that dwelleth in Jerusalem" (Ps. 124, 1). And: "Purifying their hearts by faith" (Acts 15, 9). *Thy sins are forgiven thee.* Here the good deed is mentioned. But why is it that this man was asking for the health of the body, and the Lord gives health of the soul? The reason is that sin was the cause of the sickness, as it is written in Psalm 15, 4: "On account of their sins their infirmities were multiplied."[1] Hence, the Lord acted like a good doctor, who cures the cause of the sickness. Then the Evangelist relates the dispute opposing the good deed, where it is said, *And Jesus knowing their thoughts*, etc. He says, therefore: *And behold some of the scribes said within themselves: He blasphemeth.* And why were they marveling? Because they were seeing a man, and they were not seeing God; for it belongs to God alone to forgive sins: for that reason, they were saying He was blasphemous, according to that passage in Job 34, 18: "Who saith to the king: Thou art an apostate: who calleth rulers ungodly," etc. *And Jesus seeing their thoughts, said: Why do you think evil in your hearts?* Here He confounds them in three ways: by His thought, word, and deed, because just as it pertains to God alone to forgive sins, so also to know the secrets of the heart; "The searcher of hearts and reins is God" (Ps. 7, 10). *And Jesus seeing*, because only He knows men's thoughts. And firstly, He depicts their wickedness, *Why do you think evil in your hearts?* because they were saying within themselves that He was blasphemous; "Take away the evils from your thoughts" (Is. 1, 16).[2] *Whether is easier, to say*, etc. Here he sets forth the refutation. But it seems that the Lord argues badly, because He argues by affirming from the lesser: for it seems easier to heal the body than to heal the soul. But Jerome expounds this passage in this way: it is easier to say than to do; it is true, so far as concerns the deed, that it is more mighty to heal the soul than to heal the body; but so far as concerns the power, the power is the same for both. But, referring to what was said, we see that liars quickly lie whenever they cannot be detected: for in such things which appear, they can be detected, but not in those things which are concealed. Hence, in such things which appear, they speak audaciously, wherein they cannot be detected. It is easier to say something, therefore, if you are not able to know if it is true or

---

1. "Their infirmities were multiplied: afterwards they made haste. I will not gather together their meetings for blood offerings: nor will I be mindful of their names by my lips" is the actual verse. St. Thomas follows more the sense of the passage than the actual words for the sake of clarity.

2. The literal verse is: "Take away the evil of your devices from my eyes."

not. For that reason, He says, ***But that you may know that the Son of man hath power on earth to forgive sins***. He shows the truthfulness of His words by a deed. And firstly, the end of the work is related; secondly, the manner is related; and thirdly, His efficient power is related; hence, He says: on account of this, *that you may know that the Son of man hath power on earth to forgive sins, (then said he to the man sick of the palsy,) Arise, take up thy bed, and go into thy house*. By this, He shows Himself to be God. "For it is he who shall save his people from their sins" (above 1, 21). He says, ***That the Son of man***, and also He says, ***On earth***, and He crushes a twofold error, namely, of Nestorius and of Photinus. Nestorius said that the Son of man and the Son of God were two supposits: nor could it be said of one what is said of the other; wherefore, it could not be said: 'This Child created the stars.' For that reason, Christ says, *of man*; because it belongs to God to forgive sins. Likewise, He is speaking against Photinus, who was saying that Christ had received His beginning of existence from the Virgin Mary: and by merit He acquired His divinity: and he was relying upon that passage: "All power is given to me in heaven and in earth" (below 28, 18); and for that reason, Christ says, ***On earth***. Hence, in Baruch 3, 38, it is said: "Afterwards he was seen upon earth, and conversed with men." ***Hath power***.

It seems that it cannot be proved from this, because the Apostles themselves also had this power. But it ought to be affirmed that these men had this power by way of its administration, not by way of its source. This, however, which is said, ***That you may know***, etc., can be read in two ways: either as being the words of the Evangelist, and in this way it was a narration: or they are the words of Christ saying, ***That you may know***, etc., and in this way the speech is incomplete, because these men were doubting: and, for that reason, so that you may know that I have the power of forgiving sins, ***he said to the man sick of the palsy: Arise***, etc. Hence, He cured by a word, which is proper to God, according to that passage in Psalm 32, 9: "He spoke and they were made."

The sick man had to endure three things: he was lying in a bed, he was being carried by others, and could not move himself. Therefore, because he was lying down, Christ said, ***Arise***; because he was being carried, Christ commanded that he, the sick man, would carry, saying, ***Take up thy bed***; and because he could not move himself, Christ said, ***And walk***; "The works of God are perfect" (Deut. 32. 4). Likewise, it is said to the sinner lying in his sins, ***Arise***, from sin through contrition; ***Take up*** *thy bed*, through satisfaction, "I will bear (*portabo*)³ the wrath of the Lord, because I have sinned against him" (Mic. 7, 9). *And go into thy house*, into the house of eternity, or into one's own conscience;⁴ "When I go into my house, I shall repose myself with her" (Wis. 8, 16). The execution follows, *And he arose, and went into his house. And the multitude seeing it*, not the scribes, because they were unworthy, *feared*; "O Lord, I have heard thy hearing, and was afraid" (Hab. 3, 2). But why were they fearful? They were fearful because they **glorified God**, because all things redound unto God: "Not to us, O Lord, not to us; but to thy name give glory" (Ps. 113, 1). *That gave such power to men*. Hence, these men do not scorn, as the scribes do; but because it is said, *to men*, for that reason Hilary expounds this passage: "*That gave such power to men* of being made sons of God," as it is said in John 1, 12: "He gave them power to be made the sons of God."

9. And when Jesus passed on from thence, he saw a man sitting in the custom house, named Matthew; and he saith to him: Follow me. And he arose up and followed him.

10. And it came to pass as he was sitting at meat in the house, behold many publicans and sinners came, and sat down with Jesus and his disciples.

11. And the Pharisees seeing it, said to his disciples: Why doth your master eat with publicans and sinners?

12. But Jesus hearing it, said: They that are in health need not a physician, but they that are ill.

13. Go then and learn what this meaneth, I will have mercy and not sacrifice. For I am not come to call the just, but sinners.

Here, the conversion of sinners is firstly related; and secondly, the dispute of the Pharisees is related, where it is said, *And the Pharisees seeing it, said to his disciples*. And firstly, the Evangelist says how Christ called certain men to discipleship; and secondly, how He called many men to His fellowship, where it is said, *And it came to pass as he was sitting at meat in the house*, etc. He says, therefore, *When Jesus passed on from thence*. Why did He pass on? It was because they were laying snares for Him, as it is said, "Kindle not the coals of sinners" (Eccli. 8, 13). *He saw a man*. He was truly a man, because

---

3. Literally, "I will carry..."
4. "Rabanus: His rising up is the drawing off the soul from carnal lusts; his taking up his bed is the raising the flesh from earthly desires to spiritual pleasures; and his going to his house is his returning to Paradise, or to internal watchfulness of himself against sin" (*Catena Aurea on St. Matthew*, p. 335).

he was a sinner; "But you like men shall die: and shall fall like one of the princes" (Ps. 81, 7). ***Sitting in the custom house***. A custom house pertains to taxes. Therefore, it was a place where taxes were received; hence, he was in a particular station in life wherein a man can scarcely live without sin. ***Named Matthew***. The other Evangelists call him Levi, to preserve his reputation, so that it might not be known that he was a sinner; but he calls himself Matthew, because a just man in the beginning of his speech is an accuser of himself, thereby giving us to understand that the Lord is not an acceptor of persons. ***And he saith to him: Follow me***. Hence, he could say that which is written in Job 23, 11: "My foot hath followed his steps, I have kept his way, and have not declined from it."

But it is objected that it could not be that at one word this man followed him. And it ought to be said that Jesus' fame was so widespread that one who followed Him already considered himself blessed; for that reason, at one word, this man followed Him. Hence, his obedience is shown, because he followed Him immediately.

But why did He not immediately call him from the beginning? It ought to be said that this man was wise with the world's wisdom. Now, the Lord delayed to call him until the miracles would rouse him. Or it can be said that this was said by way of repetition, because he was present at the Lord's preaching on the mount.

But why then does Matthew set forth the events in this way? I say it is by reason of his humility: for it is because he considered his calling a miracle, for that reason, he recalled this event among the miracles.

But why is there greater mention of the calling of Peter, and of Andrew, as well as of Matthew, than of the others? It ought to be said that fishermen were among lowlier men. And among fishermen especially, those who were receiving taxes were still lowlier. And, for that reason, mention is specially made of these men, that it be known that God is not an acceptor of persons.

It continues: ***And it came to pass as he was sitting at meat in the house, behold many publicans and sinners came, and sat down with Jesus and his disciples***. Here it is mentioned how He called many to His fellowship; hence, the Evangelist says, ***And it came to pass***, etc. The other Evangelists say that Matthew made the banquet; but this Evangelist passes over that fact in silence. And it is true that he made the banquet; hence, he invited many so that they might be drawn to God, because one curtain draws another curtain (Ex. 26, 3).[5] Hence, it is a sign that someone has firmly converted to the Lord, when he draws others, whom he loves more. Hence, he says, that **Many publicans and sinners came, and sat down with Jesus**, because "If any man shall hear my voice and open to me the door, I will come in to him and will sup with him: and he with me" (Apoc. 3, 20). **And the Pharisees seeing it**, etc. It has been said how the Lord invites sinners to follow Him, and how He receives them at a banquet; here is related the dispute: firstly, concerning His association with sinners; and secondly, concerning the banquet, where it is said, **Then came to him the disciples of John**. About the first, to begin with, the question is set forth; and secondly, the response is set forth, where it is said, **Jesus said**, etc. He says, therefore, **And the Pharisees seeing it, said to his disciples**. It ought to be observed that these Pharisees were malicious; hence, they wanted to create a division between the disciples and Jesus; wherefore they were criticizing Jesus to the disciples, and the disciples to Jesus. Hence, being willing to criticize Jesus to His disciples, they say: **Why doth your master eat with publicans and sinners?** These men belong to the number of those about whom it is said: "Six things there are, which the Lord hateth, and the seventh his soul detesteth" (Prov. 6, 16), namely, "him that soweth discord among brethren" (verse 19).

But it is inquired why Luke says that this was spoken in reference to the disciples.[6] And Augustine replies that the sense of both passages is the same, albeit the words differ, because they were attributing the whole matter to the Master's teaching: hence, Luke refers to the words, but Matthew to the sense.

But it seems that these Pharisees were arguing correctly, because associations with sinners should be avoided. But it ought to be observed that sometimes associations with sinners are avoided on account of pride and contempt, such as these men were doing, as it is written: "Come not near me, because thou art unclean" (Is. 65, 5). But others avoid such associations on account of the utility of the sinners, in order that they may be ashamed, and in this way may be converted; and in this manner Paul says: "I speak to your shame. Is it so that there is not among you any one wise man?" (I Cor. 6, 5). Likewise, someone avoids associations with sinners as a safeguard to his own safety, fearing that he may be

---

5. "Five curtains shall be joined one to another, and the other five shall be coupled together in like manner." St. Thomas quotes the sense but not the words.

6. "Why do the disciples of John fast often and make prayers, and the disciples of the Pharisees in like manner; but thine eat and drink?" (Lk. 5, 33)

perverted; "He that toucheth pitch, shall be defiled with it" (Eccli. 13, 1). And it is written in Psalm 17, 27: "With the perverse thou wilt be perverted." On the contrary, some men dwell with sinners for the purpose of proving themselves: hence, the temptation is a proof of themselves, as it is stated in Ecclesiasticus 27, 6.[7] And, "For in sight and hearing he was just, dwelling among them" (II Pet. 2, 8). And, "As the lily among thorns, so is my love among the daughters" (Cant. 2, 2). And thereupon, the Gloss says: "He was not good, who could not tolerate evil men." Moreover, some men stay among evil men for the sake of their conversion, as Paul says: "I became all things to all men, that I might save all" (I Cor. 9, 22). But the difference is that one ought not to communicate with persisting sinners, and ones unwilling to repent; but concerning those about whom it is hoped that they would repent, one must distinguish in regard to him who is dwelling with them, whether he be strong or weak: if he is weak, he ought not to dwell with them; if he is strong, it is appropriate that he dwell with them, so that he may convert them to God. Just so, Jesus was a steadfast doctor; for that reason, although He was with them, he was not fearing danger; therefore, etc.

Jesus' reply follows. And He sets forth three reasons: Firstly, He speaks according to a similitude: *But Jesus hearing it, said: They that are in health need not a physician*. And the Lord calls Himself a doctor and He says well; "Who healeth all thy diseases" (Ps. 102, 3), namely, both of soul and of body; for that reason, He mentions the diseases both of soul and of body; hence, He says, *They that are in health need not a physician*, etc. They are called healthy, who, out of pride, consider themselves to be in good health, concerning whom it is said: "Thou sayest: I am rich and made wealthy and have need of nothing: and knowest not that thou art wretched and miserable and poor and blind and naked" (Apoc. 3, 17). And such men need not a physician, *but they that are ill*, that is, those admitting their fault: just as David said: "I know my iniquity" (Ps. 50, 5). Secondly, He invokes the authority of Scripture saying, *Go then and learn what this meaneth*; as though He were to say: 'You do not understand the Scriptures, but go, and learn what this means,' *I will have mercy and not sacrifice*. This is written in Osee 6, 6. And it is expounded in two ways. Firstly, it is expounded such that one thing is preferred to the other, because I will have more mercy than justice: hence, sacrifice is preferred to sacrifice. A lamb is

---

7. "The furnace trieth the potter's vessels, and the trial of affliction just men."

a sacrifice, and mercy is also: for, by means of such victims, God has mercy. Which one of these is better? "To do mercy and judgment, pleaseth the Lord more than victims" (Prov. 21, 3). Or, it is expounded such that one is approved but the rest reproved; I want mercy, but not the sacrifices, which you perform. Hence, I will not have holocausts, because "your hands are full of blood" (Is. 1, 15). Or, *I will have mercy and not sacrifice* may be expounded otherwise. For someone is said to want that which he wants on account of itself, and not on account of something else, just as if a doctor were to say: 'I want health'; and in this way, among the works which we offer to God, we offer certain ones on account of themselves, such as loving God and our neighbor; but others on account of these things; "I will shew thee, O man, what is good, and what the Lord requireth of thee: Verily to do judgment, and to love mercy" (Mic. 6, 8). Thirdly, the Lord brings forth another reason as a consequence of His own office, that if some representative had been sent, and uses his office; if he is forbidden by another, he would say: 'You are foolish, because you forbid what belongs to me.' The Lord had come to save sinners; hence, it was said: "And thou shalt call his name Jesus. For he shall save his people from their sins" (above 1, 21). And, for that reason, He says: *I am not come to call the just, but sinners*. Luke adds, 'to penance.'[8] And this addition is justified, because He did not come to call sinners in order that they might remain in their sins, but in order that they might be withdrawn from them.

But it can be inquired concerning *the just*, because no one is just, except God alone, because we are all sinners. Likewise, what He says seems false, because John was just, Simeon was just, and Zacharias was just; and, nevertheless, He called them.

It ought to be said that, concerning justice, one needs to distinguish; because someone is said to be just who is not guilty of sin; and in this way no one is just, because all men are guilty of either mortal, venial, or original sin, at least as far as concerns the debt; and this He completely blotted out, because "He came that they may have life" (Jn. 10, 10). Hence, He did not come to call the just, insofar as they are just, but insofar as they are sinners. Likewise, one is said to be just who is not guilty of mortal sin: hence, 'I am not come to call the just to repentance, but to greater justice.' Or, it may be expounded thus: *I am not come to call the just*, that is, those who trust in their own justice, *but sinners*, who repent, taking no notice of their own justice.

---

8. Luke 5, 32.

14. Then came to him the disciples of John, saying: Why do we and the Pharisees, fast often, but thy disciples do not fast?

15. And Jesus said to them: Can the children of the bridegroom mourn, as long as the bridegroom is with them? But the days will come, when the bridegroom shall be taken away from them, and then they shall fast.

16. And nobody putteth a piece of raw cloth unto an old garment. For it taketh away the fulness thereof from the garment, and there is made a greater rent.

17. Neither do they put new wine into old bottles. Otherwise the bottles break, and the wine runneth out, and the bottles perish. But new wine they put into new bottles: and both are preserved.

Here a question concerning eating is related; and the response follows, where it is said, *And Jesus said.*

But then there is here a literal question, why in Mark 2, 18, and Luke 6, 33, it seems that the question was made by some other men: in which place it is said: "Why do the disciples of John and of the Pharisees fast; but thy disciples do not fast?" (Mk. 2, 18). Therefore, the disciples of John did not speak. Augustine resolves the question. So it was that the Pharisees were lying in wait for Christ: hence, sometimes they drew the Herodians with themselves, but now they take to themselves John's disciples. Hence, He could have been asked this question both by other men and by John's disciples.

But why was it that they were fasting? On this particular point it is replied that it was from their traditions, or from the Law, as, for instance, it is stated in the Law that on the day of propitiation they were held to fast. And also it is written: "The fast of the fourth month, and the fast of the fifth, and the fast of the seventh, and the fast of the tenth shall be to the house of Juda, joy, and gladness, and great solemnities" (Zach. 8, 19). Likewise, John's disciples were fasting by reason of their master's example, who was a man of great austerity; but Christ's disciples were not fasting.

And Jesus said to them. Here Jesus responds, and He responds subtly. Firstly, He indicates the reason in regard to Himself, and then in regard to His disciples. About the first He does two things. Firstly, He determines the time of eating; secondly, He determines the time of fasting, where it is said, *But the days will come, when the bridegroom shall be taken away from them, and then they shall fast.* He says, therefore, *Can the children of the bridegroom mourn, as long as the bridegroom is with them?* Where this Evangelist says, 'mourn,' another Evangelist[9] says, 'fast'; for although fasting has a certain spiritual joy, nevertheless, as it is stated in Holy Writ: "All chastisement for the present indeed seemeth not to bring with it joy, but sorrow" (Heb. 12, 11). Hence, there is a fasting of spiritual joy, as it is said: "I set my face to the Lord, my God, to pray and make supplication with fasting, and sackcloth, and ashes" (Dan. 9, 3). Likewise, there is a mournful fasting, and a fasting of affliction, as when it is done on account of sorrows. The Lord replies concerning both fastings. The bridegroom is Christ: for he who has the spouse is the bridegroom. For He is the spouse of the whole Church, and is its origin. The Old Law has one origin, the New Law another; for the Old Law had its origin in fear; but the New Law in love; hence, "For you have not received the spirit of bondage again in fear: but you have received the spirit of adoption of sons of God" (Rom. 8, 15). And, "You are come to mount Sion and to the city of the living God, the heavenly Jerusalem" (Heb. 12, 22). Because, therefore, the origin of the New Law was in love, for that reason, He should have nourished His disciples in a kind of love: for that reason, He calls Himself a spouse, and His disciples, sons, because these are names of love. 'Hence, it is a good thing that I keep them; and for that reason I do not want to impose anything burdensome upon them lest they abhor it, and in this way go back.' And, therefore, they who are new in religious orders, are not to be burdened. Hence, Ambrose, in the book, *De Similitudinibus*, reprehends those who heavily burden novices; and this is what Christ says: **Can the children of the bridegroom mourn**, etc.?; as though He were to say: 'It is not fitting that they fast, but rather to live in a certain sweetness and love; so that in this way they may receive My law in love,' as it is written: "As Christ is risen from the dead by the glory of the Father, so we also may walk in newness of life" (Rom. 6, 4). Hence, from Easter until Pentecost, fasting does not take place, because then the Church recalls the newness of the law. **But the days will come**, etc. And this is said literally. **The days will come**, namely, when you are governing the Church, **the bridegroom shall be taken away from them, and then they shall fast**. And He foretold this to them, saying, "You shall lament and weep, but the world shall rejoice" (Jn. 16, 20). For they who were before Christ, desired Christ's presence, such as Abraham, and Isaias, and the other prophets. Likewise, after His death, His presence was desired by the Apostles: hence, Peter was, as it were, in continual sorrow on account of Christ's absence; and Paul

---

9. Actually, Mark and Luke both use the word 'fast.' cf. Mk. 2, 19 & Lk. 5, 34.

was saying, "I desire to be dissolved and to be with Christ" (Phil. 1, 23). Hence, then was the time of fasting. Another reason why they were not bound to fast in His presence was because fasting ought to be opted inasmuch as it chastises the body, lest the body prevail against spirit; but when He was present, He was keeping them from excess; therefore, it was not necessary for them to fast; hence, it is written in John 17, 12: "Father, while I was with them, I kept them." But John the Baptist did not have this power, for that reason his disciples were obliged to fast. But when Christ was taken away, it was necessary for Christ's disciples to fast. Hence, Paul says: "I chastise my body and bring it into subjection," etc., (I Cor. 9, 27). *And nobody putteth a piece of raw cloth unto an old garment.* Here, He proposes another reason in regard to the disciples, and He proposes two examples. One interpretation is according to Augustine, and another according to Jerome. Hence, according to Augustine, He wishes to say: 'It was said that the disciples ought not to fast, neither in Christ's presence, nor also by reason of their condition, because burdensome things ought not to be imposed upon the imperfect. Therefore, since these men are imperfect, fasting ought not to be imposed upon them.[10] In order to show this, therefore, He speaks of it under the metaphors of cloth and wine. Because justice consists in exterior works, and in the newness of affection, therefore, He cites two examples. He says, therefore, *Nobody putteth*, etc., so that if someone wished to join together new cloth, he does not put *a piece*, that is, a patch,[11] *of raw cloth*, that is, new cloth, *unto an old garment*, because it would take away its beauty; so if someone, being imperfect, has his own way of life, if you wish to impose upon him another yoke, he withdraws from that to which he had been accustomed, *and there is made a greater rent. Neither do they put new wine into old bottles.* He sets forth here another example concerning wine; it is as if He were to say: 'My disciples are like old bottles.' The new wine is the New Law by reason of its newness: hence, when they had received the Holy Ghost, men said that they were drunk with wine (Acts 2, 13). Hence: *Neither do they put new wine into old bottles. Otherwise the bottles break.* Hence, if upon an old man, who for a time has a particular way of life, you impose a new manner of living, his heart is broken through the unbearableness. Moreover, *the wine runneth out*, that is, it is not preserved, *and*

---

10. cf. *De Quaest. Evang.*, Bk. 2, n. 18.
11. Lit. *depetiaturam*. This seems to be a vulgarization close to the modern Italian *pezzatura*. *Depetiatura* would indicate more clearly than *commissura* the idea of repairing a hole by sewing in a small piece of cloth. A piece of cloth or paper is *pezzo* in modern Italian.

the bottles perish: because they trampled upon God's Commandments; and, for that reason, they perish. *But new wine they put into new bottles*, making the spiritual doctrine new through their affection, as the Apostle says: "Comparing spiritual things with spiritual" (I Cor. 2, 13). "If wisdom shall enter into thy heart, and knowledge please thy soul: counsel shall keep thee, and prudence shall preserve thee, that thou mayst be delivered from the evil way, and from the man that speaketh perverse things," etc., (Prov. 2, 10-12). Jerome expounds these examples otherwise: wherefore, he calls the Pharisees' rules of conduct an old garment, and he calls the Gospel teaching a new garment; it is as if He were to say, 'It is not good that they would keep your teachings, because thus they would make the old rents'; and so they would not be able to receive the new teaching, just as we see that one more easily receives His doctrine, who is not imbued with contrary doctrines, than he who is imbued. And, therefore, 'It is not good that they be imbued with your doctrines.'

18. As he was speaking these things unto them, behold a certain ruler came up, and adored him, saying: Lord, my daughter is even now dead; but come, lay thy hand upon her, and she shall live.
19. And Jesus rising up followed him, with his disciples.
20. And behold a woman who was troubled with an issue of blood twelve years, came behind him, and touched the hem of his garment.
21. For she said within herself: If I shall touch only his garment, I shall be healed.
22. But Jesus turning and seeing her, said: Be of good heart, daughter, thy faith hath made thee whole. And the woman was made whole from that hour.
23. And when Jesus was come into the house of the ruler, and saw the minstrels and the multitude making a rout,
24. He said: Give place, for the girl is not dead, but sleepeth. And they laughed him to scorn.
25. And when the multitude was put forth, he went in, and took her by the hand. And the maid arose.
26. And the fame hereof went abroad into all that country.

The Evangelist has related the miracles by which remedies were applied against the dangers of sin; here, he relates those miracles by which remedies are applied against the dangers of death. And it is divided into two parts: wherefore, firstly, he recounts how Christ restored life; and secondly, he recounts how

Christ restored vital operations, where it is said, *And as Jesus passed from thence*. About the first, to begin with, the invitation to accomplish the miracle is related; secondly, evidence of His power to perform miracles is related, where it is said, *And behold a woman*, etc.; and thirdly, the preparation of the miracle is related, where it is said, *And when the multitude was put forth*. About the first, he does four things. Firstly, he describes the time of the invitation; secondly, the person inviting; thirdly, the invitation; and fourthly, the acceptance of the invitation. He says, therefore, *As he was speaking these things*, that is to say, in Matthew's house.

But there is an objection: it is that Mark and Luke relate the events in a different order, namely, that this man approached Jesus after He had crossed over the sea. Augustine resolves this by saying that when something is mentioned by the Evangelists pertaining to time, then the historical order is represented; and therefore, when it is said here, *As he was speaking*, the historical order is designated; but in Mark and Luke the events are related according to the order of their memory. Or, it can be said that there was some middle place where this occurred. For sometimes they do not say whether something happened immediately, later, or at what time.

It continues, *Behold a certain ruler*. Here is set forth the person inviting, namely, a ruler of the synagogue, and he is named Jairus,[12] meaning 'illuminating' or 'illuminated.' In Genesis 23, 6, it is written: "Thou art a prince of God among us." Firstly, he showed reverence, because he *came up* personally. Moreover, he *adored*. He also confessed Christ's power, because he says, *Lord*. This ruler represents the Fathers of old, because they came up through their desire, and believing, they adored Christ still to come; "We will adore in the place where his feet stood" (Ps. 131, 7); "Know ye that the Lord he is God" (Ps. 99, 3).

The danger follows: *Lord, my daughter is even now dead*. The opposite is stated in Luke and Mark: because there (Mark 5, 23) it is said: "My daughter is at the point of death. And when He was on the way his servants came to him," etc.[13]

Augustine resolves this objection as follows: he says that when this Jairus departed from his home, she was already at the point of death, and he was supposing that he would not find her alive when he would return; for that reason, he was asking Him to come and

---

12. cf. Mark 5, 22 & Luke 8, 41.

13. The second part of this quotation is taken from the context of the passage cited.

restore her to life, rather than that He cure her: hence, he says, *My daughter is even now dead*, etc., as though he were to say: 'I suppose that she is already dead': the other Evangelists, therefore, spoke according to what happened. Therefore, Augustine gives a good teaching, that it is not necessary that the very same words be recorded; but it suffices that only the meaning be declared.

But why did the servants say: "Do not trouble the master" (Mk. 5, 35)? This seems to have been spoken out of disbelief. It ought to be said that this would be true if this would have been spoken in conformity with their master's intent; but they themselves did not know his intent. Chrysostom expounds this passage as follows: It is the custom of some persons, when they wish to move others to compassion, that they exaggerate the evil; therefore, so that he might move Him more to compassion, he said, *My daughter is dead*.

This daughter is the Synagogue, which is the daughter of the ruler, namely, Moses, which is dead through its infidelity; "But now they are hidden from thy eyes," etc., (Lk. 19, 42). But it seems that in this ruler his faith is mixed with infidelity, because he believed that Christ could restore life, and this was belonging to faith; but because he believed that when absent He could not, this was belonging to infidelity. Hence, he was similar to Namaan, who said: "I thought he would have come out to me, and standing, would have invoked the name of the Lord his God, and touched with his hand the place of the leprosy, and healed me" (IV Kings, 5, 11).

But come, lay thy hand upon her, and she shall live. Mystically, here is signified the desire of the Patriarchs for Christ's coming; hence, they were saying: *Come, lay thy hand*, that is to say, Christ, as it is written in Psalm 143, 7: "Send forth thy hand from on high." *And Jesus rising up followed him. Rising up*, namely, from the dinner. Herein is contained an example of Christ's mercy, because, at the request of that man, He went immediately as it is stated: "As soon as he shall hear, the Lord will answer thee" (Is. 30, 19). Likewise, He gives an example to prelates about solicitude, that they be careful to immediately aid those with sins. Likewise, He gives an example of obedience, because He drew His disciples with Him, as it is stated: "Obey your prelates" (Heb. 13, 17). But He did not draw Matthew, because he was still weak. *And behold a woman*. He gives an example of power: and the Evangelist does three things. Firstly, her sickness is described; secondly, the praise of the woman is described, where it is said, *She said within herself*, etc.; and thirdly, the goodness of Christ's healing is described, where it is said, *But*

Jesus turning, etc. He says, therefore, **And behold a woman.** And it is stated in Leviticus 12, that a woman who was troubled with an issue of blood was unclean, and did not dwell with men; for that reason, she did not approach Him in the house, but on the road. And she signifies the heathen nations, which entered into the fullness of the Jews, as is stated: "Blindness in part has happened in Israel, until the fullness of the Gentiles should come in" (Rom. 11, 25). She, namely, the Synagogue, has an issue of blood, namely, the error of sacrificial blood. Or, it can be applied to the sins of the flesh; hence, "Flesh and blood cannot possess the kingdom of God" (I Cor. 15, 50). This woman was **troubled twelve years**, and the ruler's daughter was twelve years old;[14] hence, she began to be troubled when the ruler's daughter was born. **She came behind him, and touched the hem of his garment.** Here is related the praise of the woman herself from her own humility, and from her faith, which is very important for entreating. **She came, and touched the hem of his garment** from behind. Why from behind? It is because she was considered unclean; hence, whatever she touched was unclean according to the Law, and for that reason, she dared to touch only the hem. It was commanded in the Law that in the four corners of clothing they wear tassels, and there they wore timbrels for a remembrance of God's commandments, and in order that they would thus be distinguished from others; and Christ was wearing this clothing. Mystically, the woman signifies the heathen nations, which came near by faith. But from behind, because they came not while He was living. Likewise, they touched His garment, namely, His humanity, and only the hem, because they touched only through the Apostles. **For she said within herself: If I shall touch only his garment, I shall be healed.** Hilary says: "Great is Christ's power, because it not only overflows into His soul, but from His soul into His body, and from His body into His clothing." And thus we ought to hold in reverence everything that has touched Christ's body; "Like the precious ointment on the head, that ran down upon the beard, the beard of Aaron, which ran down to the skirt of his garment," etc., (Ps. 132, 2). "That ran down upon the beard," that is, the divinity into the flesh: and, "to the skirt of the garment," that is, to the Apostles. **I shall be healed.** If we act in this manner, and adhere to Him, we shall be healed. "Every one that shall call upon the name of the Lord, shall be saved" (Joel 2, 32). **But Jesus turning and seeing her, said: Be of good**

---

14. "He had an only daughter, almost twelve years old" (Lk. 8, 42).

heart, daughter. Here, Christ's goodness is set forth. Firstly, it is shown by an action, because He turned towards her. And why? It was lest she lack confidence: for because she had approached stealthily, she did not imagine that He would turn towards her. Likewise, He did this so that the faith of this woman might be held up as an example. Similarly, it was so that He might show Himself to be God: hence, He turned with the turning of mercy, and He saw her with the eye of pity; "Turn ye to me, and I will turn to you" (Zach. 1, 3). Moreover, His goodness is shown, when He says, **Be of good heart**: because she approached fearfully, for that reason He spoke to her soothingly; "If you return and be quiet, you shall be saved" (Is. 30, 15). Again, He calls her, ***daughter***, lest she be timid; "He gave them power to be made the sons of God" (Jn. 1, 12). Likewise, He gives hope, ***Thy faith hath made thee whole***. Hence, "our salvation is by faith" as is stated in Romans 3.[15] And the effect follows, ***And the woman was made whole from that hour***; and not from the moment when Christ spoke, but from the moment when she touched. ***And when Jesus was come into the house of the ruler, and saw the minstrels***, etc. Here the restoration to life is related: and he does four things. Firstly, the signs of death are related; secondly, hope is given, where it is said, ***Give place***, etc.; thirdly, the restoration to life is related; and fourthly, the effect is related. He says, therefore, ***when He was come... and saw***, etc. And why did the minstrels come? The crowd came just as it usually happens now for the dead; but the minstrels came, because it was the custom that minstrels would come and sing dirges, in order that they might excite others to weeping, as it is stated in Jeremias 9, 17: "Consider ye, and call for the mourning women, and let them come." These minstrels are the false teachers: "Their tongue, and their devices are against the Lord, to provoke the eyes of his majesty" (Is. 3, 8). The crowd, however, is the Jewish people: "Thou shalt not follow the multitude to do evil" (Ex. 23, 2). The Lord raised this girl to life in the house; for the Lord raised three persons to life: the young girl in the house, the young man in the gate, and Lazarus in the tomb. For some men die from sin; but they are not carried outside, and this is by consenting to sin; but they do not go outside by deeds. Some men, however, are carried outside as a result of an action; and this is signified by him whom He raised to life in the gate. But some men, from their habit of sinning, lie in the tomb, who are signified by Lazarus. This girl,

---

15. "We account a man to be justified by faith" (Rom. 3, 28).

therefore, signifies a sinner who is in a hidden sin, namely, in the mind. The minstrels are they who encourage him in the sin; "The sinner is praised in the desires of his soul" (Ps. 9, 3). The crowd is the thoughts: and this the Lord heals; hence, He says, *Give place, for she is not dead.* Here He gives hope. *She is not dead*, namely, to Him; *but sleepeth*, because it is just as easy for Him to raise to life as it is for anyone to raise someone from sleep. Something similar is said in John 11, 11: "Lazarus our friend sleepeth." *She is not dead.* And why did He speak in this fashion? This seems unfitting, because they laughed him to scorn. And why did He want to be ridiculed? This was so that they could not speak against the miracle. Hence, firstly, He made His adversaries confess, so that afterwards they could not contradict. *And when the multitude was put forth.* And why was the crowd put forth? It was because it was not worthy to see. The crowd of the Jews is they who are not converted. And, morally, in order for the soul to be raised to life, it is fitting that the crowd of the thoughts be expelled; and then the Lord enters. *He went in, and took her by the hand*, etc. "The right hand of the Lord hath wrought strength" (Ps. 117, 16). He holds the hand of the sinner, when He gives him help. *And the maid arose*, namely, to life; in this way, we arise to life through God's help. The spreading abroad of His fame into all the country consequently followed.

27. And as Jesus passed from thence, there followed him two blind men crying out and saying, Have mercy on us, O Son of David.

28. And when he was come to the house, the blind men came to him. And Jesus saith to them, Do you believe, that I can do this unto you? They say to him, Yea, Lord.

29. Then he touched their eyes, saying, According to your faith, be it done unto you.

30. And their eyes were opened, and Jesus strictly charged them, saying, See that no man know this.

31. But they going out, spread his fame abroad in all that country.

32. And when they were gone out, behold they brought him a dumb man, possessed with a devil.

33. And after the devil was cast out, the dumb man spoke, and the multitudes wondered, saying, Never was the like seen in Israel.

34. But the Pharisees said, By the prince of devils he casteth out devils.

Above, it was shown how He restored life; here is mentioned how He gave vital functions. And, firstly, it is mentioned how He restored sight; and secondly, is mentioned how He restored speech, where it is said, *And when they were gone out*, etc. And firstly, the Evangelist does four things. Firstly, the petition of the blind men is related; secondly, the examination of these believers is related, where it is said, *And Jesus saith to them*, etc.; thirdly, the granting of their request is related, where it is said, *Then he touched their eyes*; and fourthly, the instruction to the men given sight is related, where it is said, *And He strictly charged them*. About the petition of these men, we can observe five things, which make their petition worthy of being heard. Firstly, their petition was worthy of being heard because they chose a suitable time for asking, because they asked *as He passed*; and in this is signified the time of the Incarnation, which is a time to have mercy. Hence, in Psalm 101, 12, it is said: "For it is time to have mercy on it." And for that reason they were more readily heard, as is stated in Hebrews 5, 7: "He was heard for his reverence." Likewise, their petition was worthy of being heard because, to obtain their request, *they followed him*: for those who do not follow God by obeying, do not obtain their request. *Two blind men*. These two blind men are two peoples, namely, the Jews and the Gentiles: for they are blind, who do not have faith; concerning such persons it is said: "We have groped like blind men for the wall" (Is. 49, 10). Likewise, their petition was worthy of being heard because fervor of devotion is required, and their fervor is shown when it is said, *Crying out*, as it is stated in Psalm 119, 1: "In my trouble I cried to the Lord: and he heard me." Again, humility of the petitioners is required, and their humility is shown when it is said, *Saying, Have mercy on us, O Son of David*, as it is stated, "O our God, hear the supplication of thy servant" (Dan. 9, 17). Similarly, their faith is mentioned, because they call Him the *Son of David*, and this is necessary, as it is stated: "Let him ask in faith, nothing wavering" (James 1, 6). Then He examines the men asking. Firstly, He examines them by an action, by deferring to grant their petition: for then faith is shown to be firm, when one's request is not immediately obtained; "If it make any delay, wait for it: for it shall surely come" (Hab. 2, 3). Hence, He led them to the house. *And when he was come to the house*, etc. By this house, the Church is understood, because this is the house of God: or heaven may be understood by this house; "The heaven of heaven is the Lord's" (Ps. 113, 16). Likewise, He examined them by word, *Do you believe, that I can do this unto you?* And He asks this not as though He were unknowing, but in order that their merit might be increased; "With the heart, we believe unto justice: but, with the mouth, confession is made unto salvation" (Rom. 10, 10). Moreover, He asks in order that their faith might be shown to others, so that others might know that He gave sight to them justly. Likewise, He asks in order to prod them forward to greater things: for they had confessed something great, that He is the Son of David. But this was not sufficient, therefore, He asks more from them. ***Do you believe, that I can do this unto you?*** Namely, by His own power, which belongs to God alone. ***They say to him, Yea, Lord.*** Hence, now they call Him Lord, which is proper to God alone. The granting of their petition follows. And, firstly, the act of healing is related; then secondly, the effect of the act of healing is related, where it is said, ***And their eyes were opened.*** The act of healing is related when it is said, ***he touched their eyes, saying***; hence, He touched and He spoke. Either was sufficient; nevertheless, He did both, so that it might be signified that blindness is illuminated though the incarnate Word; "And the Word was made flesh and dwelt among us and we saw his glory" (Jn. 1, 14). Hence, He says, ***According to your faith, be it done unto you***, because by the merit of faith men are given sight, who without faith are blind. The effect follows, ***And their eyes were opened.*** Firstly, therefore, He gives light; and thus is fulfilled the passage: "And the life was the light of men" (Jn. 1, 4). "He himself will come and will save us" (Is. 35, 4). The instruction follows; hence, the Evangelist says, ***and Jesus strictly charged.***

And why was this? For elsewhere it is said: "Go thou to your own and preach the kingdom of God" (Lk. 9, 60). Chrysostom says: "In our goods we ought to reckon that we possess two things: what is God's and what is ours: what is ours, we ought to hide, what is God's we ought to make known, as Paul said: "Not seeking the things that are their own, but the things that are Jesus Christ's" (Phil. 2, 21). "That they may see your good works, and glorify your Father who is in heaven" (below 5, 16). Hence, He says, ***See that no man know this***, in order to teach that vainglory ought to be avoided. ***But they going out***, not being unmindful of the benefits received, ***spread his fame abroad***, as it is stated: "I will remember the tender mercies of the Lord" (Is. 63, 7).

But did not these men sin, because they acted contrary to the Lord's command? I say that they did not, because they acted in good faith, and they acted thus in order that they might make manifest how much holiness the Lord displayed.

When they were gone out, behold they brought him a dumb man. Above, the Lord restored sight to the blind; now He restores speech to the mute. And these are adequately joined together, because speech is a sign of one's interior vision; "He himself will come and will save you. Then shall the eyes of the blind be opened, and the ears of the deaf shall be unstopped" (Is. 35, 4-5). And in this the Evangelist does three things. Firstly, the sick man is described; secondly, the healing is touched upon, where it is said, *And after the devil was cast out, the dumb man spoke*; and thirdly, the effect of the healing is touched upon, where it is said, *and the multitudes wondered.* He says, therefore, *And when they were gone out*, etc. From this man faith is not sought, as from the preceding men, because this man was obsessed by the devil; for that reason, he was not sane: and, therefore, He did not inquire about his faith. And this man signifies the Gentile world, which was mute as regards praise; "Pour out thy wrath upon the nations that have not known thee" (Ps. 78, 6). Likewise, they have a devil, because they sacrifice to demons; "All the gods of the Gentiles are devils" (Ps. 95, 5). Firstly, therefore, as a good doctor, He cured the cause; secondly, He cured the malady, because He firstly cast out the devil, and so *after the devil was cast out, the dumb man spoke.* So when the Gentile world was freed from the slavery of idols, *the dumb man spoke*, namely, the praise of God; the Gentile world was freed "that every tongue should confess that the Lord Jesus Christ is in the glory of God the Father" (Phil. 2, 11). The effect follows, *And the multitudes wondered.* Hence, they were wondering about these things which they were seeing. And because they were wondering, therefore they were saying, *Never was the like seen in Israel.* It is true that Moses performed miracles, and others also; but there had never been such a one, that is to say, who did so many. Likewise, there never had been such a one who cured only by touching. Furthermore, there never had been such a one who cured immediately; such that the following is applicable to Him: "Who is like to thee, among the strong, O Lord? who is like to thee?" as it is stated in Exodus 15, 11; and, "The works that I do give testimony of me" (Jn. 10, 25). Moreover, He cures through faith, which the Law had not been able to do, as is stated in Romans 8, 2: "For the law of the spirit of life, in Christ Jesus, hath delivered me from the law of sin and of death, which the law could not do." *But the Pharisees said.* Pharisees, that is, the separated,[16] spoke against Christ, because

---

16. i.e. separated from other men. cf. above, chapter 3, verse 10.

they were interpreting perversely, as it is written: "They turneth good into evil" (Eccli. 11, 33). Hence, they were saying, *By the prince of devils he casteth out devils.*

Here Augustine says that it should be observed that Christ performed the same miracle twice. And this is evident, because the Evangelists speak in a different manner.[17] Hence, since we find, as it were, contrary things, we can refer to one or the other miracle, by saying it is a different miracle.

35. And Jesus went about all the cities and towns, teaching in their synagogues, and preaching the gospel of the kingdom, and healing every disease, and every infirmity.

36. And seeing the multitudes, he had compassion on them: because they were distressed, and lying like sheep that have no shepherd.

37. Then he saith to his disciples, The harvest indeed is great, but the labourers are few.

38. Pray ye therefore the Lord of the harvest, that he send forth labourers into his harvest.

It has been shown how Christ had helped those coming to Him; here the Evangelist mentions that Christ was going to them: and here he mentions two things. Firstly, he mentions how He bestows an effect to certain men; and secondly, he mentions how He bestows His affection, where it is said, *And seeing the multitudes, he had compassion on them.* And about the former, he firstly shows where He bestowed help; secondly, he shows what He taught; and thirdly, he shows what He did. He says, therefore, *And Jesus went about all the cities and towns.* In so-doing, an example is given to preachers, that they be not content to preach in one place only; "I have appointed you, that you should go and should bring forth fruit," etc., (Jn. 15, 16). *All the cities and towns.* And that passage is well-ordered with the preceding ones. Because the Pharisees had said that by the prince of devils He was casting out devils; for that reason, He shows Himself not to have a devil, in order that the passage may be applicable to Him: "With them that hated peace I was peaceable: when I spoke to them they fought against me without cause" (Ps. 119, 7). What He was announcing follows; indeed, He was doing two things, because in the synagogues He was *teaching and preaching.* He was *teaching* matters pertaining to faith, and *preaching* matters pertaining to morals. Likewise, He was teaching and preaching in the presence of many men, be-

---

17. cf. Matthew 12, 22; Mark 7, 32; Mark 9, 24.

cause He was teaching and preaching in the synagogues; in Psalm 39, 10, it is written: "I have declared thy justice in a great church": in which, also, He differs from the teaching of the heretics, which is in secret. Christ's teaching was otherwise; "In secret I have spoken nothing" (Jn. 18, 20). Likewise, the Evangelist mentions what Christ teaches, for he says, **The gospel of the kingdom**; "For this was I born, and for this came I into the world; that I should give testimony to the truth," etc., (Jn. 18, 37). Hence, He was teaching heavenly things; "I am the Lord thy God that teach thee profitable things" (Is. 48, 17). Afterwards, it is shown by His deeds what He did, **Healing every disease, and every infirmity. Diseases**, is said with respect to serious sicknesses; **infirmities** is said with respect to less serious sicknesses; in Psalms 102, 3, it is written: "Who forgiveth all thy iniquities: who healeth all thy diseases." And why did He do this? It is so that He might confirm by miracles what He was saying with words, as it is said in Mark 16, 20: "The Lord working withal, and confirming the word with signs that followed." Likewise, this was to show an example to preachers, that they might do and teach; "Jesus began to do and to teach" (Acts 1, 1). **And Jesus seeing the multitudes, he had compassion on them**. Here he shows how the Lord bestowed His affection upon certain men; and this is opposed to certain men; for their opinion was that no affection sufficed, but an effect was required; but here he says, **Jesus seeing the multitudes, he had compassion on them**. And firstly, he mentions how He was having compassion; then, secondly, he sets forth His example. And firstly, he sets forth Christ's mercy; and secondly, he sets forth the cause. He says, therefore, **Seeing**, etc., namely, by loving consideration, **he had compassion on them**, for it is proper to Him to have mercy; "His tender mercies are over all his works" (Ps. 144, 9). David was desiring this glance, saying: "Look thou upon me, and have mercy on me" (Ps. 44, 16). And then he mentions upon whom Christ had mercy, for he says, **the distressed**, by demons, likewise, those **lying**, namely, those prostrate from their infirmities. Or, they are **the distressed**, due to their errors, and **lying**, due to their sins, **like sheep that have no shepherd**. Hence: "Where there is no governor, the people shall fall," etc. And: "My sheep were scattered, because there was no shepherd" (Ez. 34, 5); and in the same place it is said: "Woe to the shepherds of Israel, that fed themselves" (verse 2). As it is written: "O shepherd, and idol, that forsaketh the flock" (Zach. 11, 17).[18] **Then he saith to his disciples**. Here He induces

---

18. The Hebrew text reads, "Shepherd of nothing."

certain men to have pity, and firstly, He points out the motives; secondly, He induces them to the effect, where it is said, ***Pray ye therefore the Lord of the harvest, that he send forth labourers into his harvest.*** And He sets forth two motives. Firstly, He sets forth the great number of those tending to good; and secondly, He sets forth the scarcity of teachers, where it is said, ***the labourers are few.*** Many men had gathered; for that reason He says, ***The harvest indeed is great.*** It is not called the harvest when the corn blossoms, or when it is in the ear, but only when it is actually ready to be gathered; in this way, men had already been disposed to believe through the effect of preachers: something similar is stated in John 4, 35: "Lift up your eyes, and see the countries. For they are white already to harvest." ***But the laborers are few***, namely, good ones; hence, the Apostle wrote: "For we are God's coadjutors." Bestow, therefore, of what is yours. And what is this? ***Pray ye therefore the Lord of the harvest, that he send forth labourers into his harvest.*** When we have a need, we ought to have recourse to God, since the office of preaching is not obtained except through prayers: for He, who sends the laborers, is the Lord; hence, it is said: "I have sent you" (Jn. 4, 38); and He asks that He be asked, so that He may increase our merit when we pray for the salvation of others. Likewise, He established an order, that the sanctity of some would benefit others, as it is said: "As every man hath received grace, ministering the same one to another: as good stewards of the manifold grace of God," etc., (I Pet. 4, 10). Hence, He wishes that whatever they have received of grace and sanctity, they bestow upon others, and He, when asked, hears our petitions. For He asks to be asked to send them; "How shall they preach unless they be sent" (Rom. 10, 15); for their authority was received;[19] likewise, their grace is received: hence, "The charity of Christ presseth us" (II Cor. 5, 14). ***Pray ye therefore the Lord of the harvest, that he send forth labourers***, not profit seekers who destroy by their bad example, ***into his harvest***, namely, into God's harvest. For profit seekers are not sent into God's harvest, but into their own harvest, because they do not seek God's glory, but their own benefit.

---

19. Lit. 'acquired,' meaning they did not have it of themselves.

CHAPTER TEN

1. And having called his twelve disciples together, he gave them power over unclean spirits, to cast them out, and to heal all manner of diseases, and all manner of infirmities.
2. And the names of the twelve Apostles are these: The first, Simon who is called Peter, and Andrew his brother,
3. James the son of Zebedee, and John his brother, Philip and Bartholomew, Thomas and Matthew the publican, and James the son of Alpheus, and Thaddeus,
4. Simon the Cananean, and Judas Iscariot, who also betrayed him.
5. These twelve Jesus sent: commanding them, saying: Go ye not into the way of the Gentiles, and into the city of the Samaritans enter ye not.
6. But go ye rather to the lost sheep of the house of Israel.
7. And going, preach, saying: The kingdom of heaven is at hand.
8. Heal the sick, raise the dead, cleanse the lepers, cast out devils: freely have you received, freely give.
9. Do not possess gold, nor silver, nor money in your purses:
10. Nor scrip for your journey, nor two coats, nor shoes, nor a staff; for the workman is worthy of his meat.
11. And into whatsoever city or town you shall enter, inquire who <u>in</u> it is worthy, and there abide till you go thence.
12. And when you come into the house, salute it, saying: Peace be to this house.
13. And if that house be worthy, your peace shall come upon it; but if it be not worthy, your peace shall return to you.
14. And whosoever shall not receive you, nor hear your words: going forth out of that house or city shake off the dust from your feet.
15. Amen I say to you, it shall be more tolerable for the land of Sodom and Gomorrha in the day of judgment, than for that city.

Above, He had presented His doctrine, here, He appoints His ministers. And they are described by their number, their power, and the listing of their names. They are described by their number; hence, the Evangelist says, **And having called the twelve.** And why does He appoint twelve? It is in order that the conformity of the Old and New Testaments may be shown, because in the Old

Testament there were twelve patriarchs. The second reason is so that their power, and what will be effected through them, may be shown: for this number is composed of its multiplied parts three and four, that is to say, four times three or three times four. By the number three, the Trinity is designated: by the number four, the world is designated. Therefore, it is signified that their preaching ought to be extended unto whole world; hence, the Lord says: "Go ye into the whole world and preach the gospel to every creature," etc., (Mk. 16, 15). Likewise, the number twelve is used to signify perfection, because the number twelve is formed from the doubling[1] of the number six: for six is a perfect number, because it is derived from all its aliquot parts;[2] for it is the product of the numbers one, two and three, and these numbers added together equal six: hence, He called such a number of men in order to signify perfection. "Be you therefore perfect, as also your heavenly Father is perfect" (above 5, 48). He continues, concerning their power: hence, **he gave them power**, etc., namely, that they may themselves do, or may be able to do, as He Himself did. And not only what things He did, but even greater things (Jn. 14, 12).[3] For it is not written that sick men were cured by the shadow of Christ, as, indeed, it is written that many were cured by the shadow of Peter (Acts 5, 15). **Over unclean spirits, to cast them out**. Hence, He did not wish that they would themselves cast out unclean spirits, as He did Himself; on the contrary, He cast them out by His own word; but they would cast them out in Christ's name: hence, "In my name they shall cast out devils," etc., (Mk. 16, 17). And not only did He give them the power to cast out devils, but also **to heal all manner of diseases**, etc., as it is stated: "They shall lay their hand upon the sick: and they shall recover" (Mk. 16, 18).

But if you were to ask why this power is not now given to preachers; Augustine responds, because a very great miracle is now before everyone's eyes, namely, that the whole world has been converted. Therefore, either many miracles have been performed, and thus I have proved what I proposed to prove; if not, this is the greatest miracle: that the whole world was converted by twelve most abject fishermen.[4]

1. "And this doubling seems to have some reference to the two precepts of charity, or to the Testaments" (*Catena Aurea on St. Matthew*, chap. 10, lect. 1).
2. An *aliquot part* is another name for a *proper divisor*, i.e. any divisor of a given number other than the number itself. A prime number has only one aliquot part – the number 1. 1, 2, 3, 4, and 6 are all aliquot parts of 12.
3. "Amen, amen, I say to you, he that believeth in me, the works that I do, he also shall do: and greater than these shall he do."
4. cf. *Saint Thomas' Commentary on I Corinthians* 15, lecture 1 where St. Augustine's argument is as follows: "To believe those things which are of faith, either there are miracles or there are not. If miracles were performed, I

The listing of their names follows. And why? It is lest some false prophet would come, who would say that he was an Apostle, and he would be believed; and for this reason, the *Epistola Fundamenti*,[5] namely, of the Manichaeans, is reproved.

And it ought to be observed that this Evangelist always joins two names of the Apostles together. And why is this? It is because the number two is the number of charity. Likewise, wherever he puts down someone who is called by two names, he puts down something by which he may be differentiated from another bearing the same name. Likewise, it ought to be known that he does not keep the order of dignity; nevertheless, Peter is always placed first, who also is called Simon, that is, 'obedient'; hence, it is said: "An obedient man shall speak of victory" (Prov. 21, 28). **Peter** is named from *petra*[6] on account of his firmness; and 'Cephas', is his Syriac,[7] and not his Hebrew, name. **Andrew** is interpreted, 'manly'; hence, it is said: "Do manfully, and let thy heart take courage" (Ps. 26, 14). Likewise, **Philip** is interpreted, 'The mouth of a lamp'; such a one ought to be a preacher. "Thy word is exceedingly on fire"[8] (Ps. 118, 140). **Bartholomew** is interpreted, 'The son of him that raiseth waters'; and Christ is called this, about whom it is written: "He bindeth up the waters in his clouds" (Job 26, 8).[9] Again, **James the son of Zebedee** is listed, who was killed by Herod, and who is named 'The supplanter.'[10] And **John**, who is named 'grace';[11] "By the grace of God, I am what I am" (I Cor. 15, 10). This Evangelist does not follow the order of dignity, as Mark does. Likewise, **Thomas and Matthew** are listed. The other Evangelists do not put 'the Publican'; but he himself puts 'the

---

have proved what I proposed to prove, namely, that to believe matters of faith is most worthy and certain. If they were not performed, this is the greatest of all miracles, that an infinite multitude of men were converted to the faith through some few men; rich men were converted through poor men preaching poverty; wise men and philosophers were converted by uneducated persons, preaching things which exceed reason."

5. *The Fundamental Epistle*, which is probably the same as the *Treatise of the Two Elements* seems to have been a sort of hand-book for Manichaean catechumens or Auditors. It is extensively quoted in Saint Augustine's refutation of Manachaeism and was well-known to Latin writers. Mani claimed to be an "Apostle of the true God."

6. i.e. rock. Rock in Greek is *petra* and being feminine, the name became in that language *Petros*, in Latin *Petrus*, it being contrary to custom to give a feminine name to a man.

7. An Aramaic language.

8. The Douay version, however, reads, "exceedingly refined."

9. "Christ raises the hearts of His preachers from earthly to heavenly things, and hangs them there, that the more they penetrate heavenly things, the more they should steep and inebriate the hearts of their hearers with the droppings of holy preaching" (*Catena Aurea on St. Matthew*, ibid.)

10. He is called 'The supplanter' because "he not only supplanted the vices of the flesh, but even contemned the same flesh when Herod put him to death" (ibid).

11. "John is interpreted 'The grace of God,' because he deserved before all to be loved by the Lord; whence also in the favor of His especial love, he leaned in the Lord's bosom" (ibid).

publican' for the sake of humility. Similarly, the others put Matthew before Thomas: but he, on the contrary, puts Thomas first in the pair of names. ***Thomas*** is named, 'an abyss,' on account of his profundity of faith. ***Matthew*** is named, 'given,'(*donatus*)[12] as it is stated in Ephesians chapter 4, 32: "Forgiving (*donates*) one another, even as Christ hath forgiven you." ***James the son of Alpheus*** is so-called to differentiate him from the other James, i.e. the son of Zebedee. He is called the Lord's brother, because he is His cousin.[13] And he lists ***Thaddeus***, the brother of James. He is also called the Judas[14] who he wrote the epistle, and his surname, ***Thaddeus,*** is interpreted, 'heart';[15] "With all watchfulness keep thy heart" (Prov. 4, 23). Again, ***Simon the Cananean*** is surnamed from the village of Cana. ***And Judas Iscariot*** is so-named to differentiate him from the other Judas; and he is called, ***Iscariot,*** either from his village or from the tribe of Issachar; and he is named, 'death.'[16] ***Who also betrayed him***. And why did he add this? It was to give a lesson, that dignity of state does not sanctify a man. Likewise, there is another reason, for noting that it scarcely ever happens that there is not some evil person in a large group of men; and, for that reason, it is so-added, to show that good men are sometimes not without evil men; "As the lily among thorns, so is my love among the daughters" (Cant. 2, 2). And Augustine says: "My house is not better than the Lord's house." God chose ***these twelve***, and he made them spreaders of sacred Scripture among the people. ***Commanding them, saying***, etc. Here he relates their instruction. And firstly, He instructs them by word; secondly, He does so by example, where it is said: "And it came to pass, when Jesus had made an end of commanding his twelve disciples," etc., (below 11, 1). He instructs them by word in three ways. Firstly, He instructs them about their office; secondly, He instructs them about things received from the faithful; and thirdly, He instructs them about their dangers. He instructs them about the second point, where it is said, ***Do not possess gold, nor silver***; and He instructs them about third point,

---

12. "Matthew is interpreted 'given,' because by the Lord's bounty he was made an Evangelist of a Publican" (ibid)
13. James and John are the sons of Mary, the sister of the Lord's Mother. "John the Evangelist calls her *Mary the wife of Cleophas*, probably because Cleophas and Alpheus were the same person. Or Mary herself on the death of Alpheus after the birth of James married Cleophas" (ibid)
14. Or more commonly 'Jude'.
15. "There follows, *And Thaddaeus, that is 'corculum,'* which means 'he who guards the heart,' one who keeps his heart in all watchfulness" (*Catena Aurea on St. Mark*, chap. 3, lect. 3).
16. "And Iscariot, 'the memory of death.' But many are the proud and vain-glorious confessors in the Church, as Simon Magus and Arius, and other heretics, whose deathlike memory is celebrated in the Church, that it may be avoided" (ibid)

where it is said, ***Behold I send you as sheep in the midst of wolves***. About their office He commands four things. Firstly, He commands whither they may go; secondly, He commands what they may say, where it is said, ***And going, preach***, etc.; thirdly, He commands what they may do, where it is said, ***Heal the sick***, etc.; and fourthly, He commands for what end they are to fulfill their office, where it is said, ***Freely have you received, freely give***. And firstly, He says whither they may not go; secondly, He says whither they may go, where it is said, ***But go ye rather to the lost sheep of the house of Israel***. And about the first, He says two things. Firstly, ***Go ye not into the way of the Gentiles, and into the city of the Samaritans enter ye not***. The latter held a middle position between the Jews and the Gentiles, about whom it is written in IV Kings 27, and they partly retained the ceremonies of the Jews and partly the ceremonies of the Gentiles, and they were very opposed to the Jews. Hence, He forbids them go to the pure Gentiles or to these middlemost men.

But it seems that He has said the contrary: "Go, teach ye all nations" (below 28, 19); and, "All flesh together shall see, that the mouth of the Lord hath spoken" (Is. 40, 5). Therefore, why does He say, ***Go ye not into the way of the Gentiles***?

It ought to be replied that they were sent to both: but order needed to be observed. The order was that they go firstly to the Jews. And one reason is, that what justice demands ought to happen firstly, rather than what proceeds from mercy; but it was just that they preach firstly to the Jews: because they possessed that prerogative by promise, as it is stated: "I say that Christ Jesus was minister of the circumcision for the truth of God, to confirm the promises made unto the fathers" (Rom. 15, 8). To the Gentiles, He was bound by mercy; for as it is stated in Romans 11, 17, the Gentiles are the wild olives received by the olive tree, namely, by the faith of the Patriarchs of old: hence, it is said in that place, "And thou, being a wild olive, art ingrafted in them and art made partaker of the root and of the fatness of the olive tree." Firstly, therefore, the olive tree had to be nourished, so that He might receive something from it, afterwards the wild olive needed to be ingrafted (Rom. 11). Likewise, wishing to lead the faithful into the faith of the Patriarchs, He willed that the faith be preached firstly to the Jews. The second reason was that the Lord infuses into all men that to which they are disposed; but many of the Jews were already disposed through faith. And just as fire acts firstly upon those things which are near, so the Lord willed, out of charity, that the faith be preached to those who were near. Hence, it is said: "They will come to announce peace to those who are near, and peace to those who are far off" (Is. 57, 19).[17] Moreover, if He had firstly gone to the Gentiles, the Jews, who greatly hated the Gentiles, would have reproved Him out of indignation; for that reason, it is written in Acts 13, 46: "To you it behooved us first to speak the word of God." Hence, He says, *Go ye not into the way of the Gentiles*, that is, you may not approach the way that leads to the Gentiles, so that they may not talk about you. But He does not say, 'You may go into the way of the Samaritans.' And, mystically, they who are the Lord's disciples, ought not to go into the way of the Gentiles, nor of the heretics; hence: "What hast thou to do in the way of Egypt, to drink the troubled water?" (Jer. 2, 18).

But go ye rather to the lost sheep of the house of Israel. And why are they to go to the sheep? It is because they perished more from the errors of the Pharisees than from their own fault. Hence: "We are his people and the sheep of his pasture" (Ps. 99, 3). And: "You were as sheep going astray: but you are now converted to the shepherd and bishop," etc., (I Pet. 2, 25). But what will they, going here and there, do? *And going, preach.* "I have appointed you, that you should go and should bring forth fruit; and your fruit should remain" (Jn. 15, 16). And He sent them, just as He Himself was sent, namely, to preach. Hence, *preach, saying*, etc. He had begun His preaching saying, "Do penance, for the kingdom of heaven is at hand" (above 4, 17); "Salvation is far from sinners" (Ps. 118, 155); but now it is near through Christ's Passion; "By his own blood, entered once into the Holies, having obtained eternal redemption" (Heb. 9, 12). Hence, He says: *The kingdom of heaven is at hand*, namely, through My Passion: hence, it is established in them through the participation of grace: "For the whole kingdom of God is within you" (Lk. 17, 21). But they could say: How will we confirm the things that we will say? They will do so, undoubtedly, by miracles, just as He did. Hence, He says, *Heal the sick*, etc.

But if someone were to say: 'Why does the Church not perform miracles now?' One ought reply, that miracles were performed to prove the faith; but now the faith has been proved. And for that reason, just as he who makes a demonstration to prove some conclusion would not need to make another proof, and so it is here. Hence, a very great miracle is the conversion of the whole world: for that reason, it is not necessary that other miracles take place: and just as

---

17. St. Thomas give rather the sense of this verse which in the Douay version is as follows: "I created the fruit of the lips, peace, peace to him that is far off, and to him that is near, said the Lord, and I healed him."

other corporeal miracles were performed, so spiritual miracles happen daily, because the spiritually sick are cured. For the sick are those troubled by sin, and who are inclined to sin; "Now him that is weak in faith, take unto you" (Rom. 14, 1): and these men are cured by the Lord. Those, however, who consent to sin, are dead, because they are separated from God: and these are raised back to life by the Lord: "Rise, thou that sleepest, and arise from the dead" (Eph. 5, 14). Likewise, the lepers are cleansed: for they are called lepers, who are infectious to others, because leprosy is a contagious disease: and these men sometimes are cured. In IV Kings 5 it is said that the leprosy of Naaman adhered to Giezi. Similarly, demons are cast out: for they are demons, whose sin has already been carried into effect, about whom it is said: "They are glad when they have done evil, and rejoice in the most wicked things" (Prov. 2, 14). And, as it is related concerning Judas (Jn. 13, 27), that "Satan entered into him," etc. And these are sometimes cured.

And because the Apostles might say: 'Now we will be rich; if we perform miracles, we will possess many things,' and from this motive Simon the Magician wanted to perform miracles, the Lord excludes this motive saying: ***Freely have you received, freely give***. It is a great thing to perform miracles, but to live virtuously is greater. Hence, He rids them of pride, because pride can come about in two ways; either from one's cupidity, or from one's merits. It is a very great pride when someone attributes to himself the good which he possesses. For that reason, He excludes such pride in that He says, ***you have received***; "What hast thou that thou hast not received?" (I Cor. 4, 7). Likewise, you ought not to be proud, because you have received, not on account of your merits, but ***freely***. For he who receives on account of his merits, does not receive freely. Similarly, He excludes cupidity saying, ***freely give***, that is, not for the sake of some temporal good. For the price of a thing is either greater or equal to the thing traded. For that which you trade for a price is not so highly valued in your heart as the price which you receive. Nothing, however, is greater than or equal to God's gift; "I did not compare unto her any precious stone: for all gold, in comparison of her, is as a little sand; and silver, in respect to her, shall be counted as clay" (Wis. 7, 9). ***Do not possess gold***, etc. Because they could say: 'From what means of support, therefore, shall we live?' For that reason, He instructs them concerning things received. And firstly, He forbids them to carry provisions; and secondly, He teaches from whom they may accept their necessities, where it is said, ***And into whatsoever city or town you shall enter***, etc. He says, therefore: ***Do not possess gold***.

And the words which follow ought to be noted, because He says: *Nor shoes*; yet Mark says: "Be shod with sandals" (6, 9). Likewise, He says, *Nor a staff*; but Mark says, "He commanded them that they should take a staff": for that reason, these words give rise to some doubt and difficulty. For what He says, *Do not*, etc., is either a precept or it is a counsel. But it is sure that this is a precept, because it is said thus: *Jesus commanding them*, etc. But the Apostles both were Apostles and were faithful. Therefore, either it was a precept for them, insofar as they were faithful, or insofar as they were Apostles. If it was insofar as they were faithful, then all the faithful are bound to this precept; and this was a certain heresy, as Augustine says, which maintained that no one could be saved unless they possessed nothing; and this was the heresy of the Apostolici.[18] Likewise, another heresy was that no one can be saved unless they go about bare-footed: and these were heresies, not because they prescribed something evil; but because they precluded those who did not observe their prescriptions from the way of salvation. If, however, it was commanded to them insofar as they were Apostles, then all prelates, who are the successors of the Apostles, are bound to these things. But assuming that these men did not act badly, did not Paul, who was carrying such things and was accepting such things from some men to give them to others, act badly? For that reason, these words have a difficulty. And so it ought to be said, that according to Jerome there was a correct way of understanding this command by expounding it literally, that He commanded something on account of their office of the apostleship and not because it was simply necessary, but it was necessary for that time. Hence, before the Passion He command them to carry nothing. At the Passion, however, He says, "When I sent you without purse and scrip and shoes, did you want anything?" (Lk. 22, 35). And He continues, "But now he that hath a purse, let him likewise buy a scrip. And he that hath not, let him sell his coat and buy a sword." Hence, before the Passion they were sent to the Jews; now, among the Jews, there was a custom that they ought to provide for their teachers. For that reason, He commanded them to carry nothing when He sent them to the Jews. But this was not the custom among the Gentiles; for which reason, when they were sent to the Gentiles, permission was given to them of carrying provisions. Therefore, they carried

---

18. The Apostolici were heretics of the third century in Syria and Asia Minor who claimed to lead the life of the Apostles but rigoristically proscribed marriage and property-holding as evil things. They lapsed into Novatianism and finally became Manichaeans. ("Apostolici," *The Catholic Encyclopedia* (1907 ed.), vol. 1, p. 647).

these things when they preached to men other than the Jews. And it ought to be observed that some things are of necessity, and other things are the means by which necessaries are bought: and this is what is said, that certain things are artificial riches,[19] such as clothes and shoes; and for that reason, He forbids both. He says, therefore, **Do not**, etc. Because all money either is made of gold, or of silver, or of copper; for that reason, He forbids them to possess gold or silver; hence, Peter was saying: "Silver and gold I have none; but what I have, I give thee" (Acts 3, 6). And why did God command this? One reason is that the Lord was sending poor men to preach; therefore, someone might believe that they preached merely for the sake of gain. Therefore, in order that this suspicion might be eliminated, He commanded them to carry nothing. Likewise, He commanded this to remove solicitude: for if they had been excessively solicitous about this, God's word would be impeded. Likewise, He forbids riches, which render aid in necessity. And because they could say: 'We do not carry gold or silver, but instead we carry eggs and bread, which are necessaries for living'; He forbids this also, saying, **Nor scrip for your journey**. And why does He forbid this? Chrysostom says that it was to show them His power: because He could send them without these things; hence, He says in Luke 22, 35, "When I sent you without purse and scrip and shoes, did you want anything?" Therefore, He did this to show His power. Likewise, so far as concerns clothing, He says, **Nor two coats**: it was not that they could only wear one coat, but that they could not own two sets of clothing; such that they would put away one set, and wear the other. Hence, by the name of one coat, He understands one suit of clothes; "He that hath two coats, let him give to him that hath none" (Lk. 3, 11). **Nor shoes**. And why does he prohibit them? The reason is twofold, namely, for the same reasons He forbade gold and silver. The Lord was sending them barefooted, so that amidst all men they would be deemed poor. Hence, the Apostle says, "Not many mighty hath God chosen" (I Cor. 1, 26). For that reason, He willed that they be lowly: for the poor in the Eastern parts of the world go forth bare-footed: nevertheless, they use those shoes which are called sandals, and they make them out of straw. Another reason was because, just as Plato taught that men ought not to cover their feet or their head frequently; so, likewise, to strengthen them so that they might be strong in enduring, He commanded them to go barefooted. But why does He say, **nor a staff**? For some men use

---

19. i.e. man-made goods, as for example, money. Artificial riches are opposed to natural riches.

horses; but others are supported by a staff: for that reason, He also forbids that very small thing, so that they might completely trust in Him, according to the passage in Psalm 22, 4: "Thy rod and thy staff, they have comforted me." Hence, because He says elsewhere that they may carry a staff, it was not a precept to be observed, except in certain places and at certain times. Augustine takes a different line of thought, saying that these are neither precepts, nor counsels, but are permissions, so that it is rather a counsel to abstain than to fulfill them. Hence, the sense is, *Do not*, etc., that is, it is not a matter of great importance that you do not possess other shoes besides these, which you are wearing. *Nor a staff*, that is, nothing, as it is said, 'Not a speck.' And why? *For the workman is worthy of his meat*, etc. Because you have the right of receiving from others yourselves; and, for that reason, you do not need to carry these things. Hence, when something is permitted, if it does not happen, it is not a sin; however, whatever happens over and above, is supererogatory. Hence, Paul also, although he could have received from others, accepted nothing, and this was a supererogation, according to Augustine, because not to use permitted things is supererogatory. Hence, Paul says: "It is good for me to die rather than make my glory void" (I Cor. 9, 15). And why? Because he was not using that which was permitted: *For the workman is worthy of his meat*.

But what is that which He says elsewhere, that they may carry a staff? Augustine says that it is not unseemly that sometimes certain things be said mystically, and at other times literally. Hence, what Matthew says here, he says literally, that they ought not to carry a staff: but what Mark says, is understood mystically, namely, that they may not carry temporal things, but they have the right of receiving from others. Hence, *For the workman is worthy of his meat*. This word 'for' is not there by accident. These workmen are they about whom it was said above: "Pray ye the Lord of the harvest, that he send forth laborers into his harvest" (above 9, 38). A third exposition is, *Do not possess gold*, that is, worldly wisdom; *nor silver*, that is, worldly eloquence; *nor purse*, that is, excessive solicitude; *nor two coats*, that is, duplicity; *nor shoes*, that is, earthly affections; for shoes are made from the skins of dead animals.

Into whatsoever city or town you shall enter, etc. Above, the Lord ordained that the Apostles should not carry the things they need with them: and gave a reason, namely, that *the workman is worthy of his meat*: now He prescribes the manner in which they ought to accept what they need; and firstly, He gives the manner, that they ought to accept what they need from those willing to give; and secondly, what happens to those who are willing to give. About the first, He does three things. Firstly, He teaches them to select their host; secondly, He forbids them to change their lodging; and thirdly, He commands that their host be greeted. He says, therefore: It has been said that *the workman is worthy of his meat*. In order that you may know from whom you ought to accept what they need, lest you think that you are permitted to stay at anyone's house; for that reason, He says, *into whatsoever city or town you shall enter, inquire who in it is worthy*. And He says this lest on account of the host's bad reputation your preaching be despised, as it is stated in I Timothy 3, 7: "He must have a good testimony of them who are without." The second reason is that if someone would be a good man, he will more easily supply your necessities. And in saying this He provides for them. The third reason is so that the suspicion of profit-seeking may be excluded: because when men see such poor men accepting only from good men, it was a sign to them that they were not preaching for the sake of profit. Chrysostom puts forth the last two expositions; Jerome puts forth the first. And the Apostle says same, "For neither have we used at any time the speech of flattery, nor taken an occasion of covetousness" (I Thess. 2, 5). Likewise, He says: *Who in it is worthy*, and this because it is reputed a great thing to him, who receives such guests. Hence, to Abraham it was reputed a great thing that he received guests, as is stated in Hebrews 13, 2: "Hospitality do not forget: for by this some, being not aware of it, have entertained angels." *And there abide*. Here He speaks about stability in their lodging. *There abide*, that is, do not pass from lodging to lodging. And why? The reason is, lest your host be made sad; and if he is worthy, he will receive you willingly, and so he will send you away with sadness; "Shall evil be rendered for good?" The second reason is, lest they incur a reputation of levity, which is not befitting to a preacher. "I will praise thee in a serious minded people" (Ps. 34, 18).[20] Likewise, it was so that they might avoid the reputation of gluttony, because if they would leave a bad host for a good one, it might be ascribed to gluttony. For that reason, the Lord says that before they enter, they ask who was worthy in that place. *And when you come into the house, salute it*. Here the greeting of the host is noted. And firstly, He sets forth the salutation; and secondly, He sets forth

20. "In populo gravi laudabo te" which is translated in the Douay version as, "I will praise thee in a strong people."

the effect, where it is said, ***And if that house be worthy, your peace shall come upon it.*** For it is fitting that, to them who were supplying temporal things, they would supply spiritual things, and not only spiritual things, but those things which are necessary for salvation, by saying, ***Peace be to this house***, etc. And this was a suitable manner of greeting, because the world was at war; the world, however, has been reconciled in Christ: for these men were the Lord's legates, and for what purpose? Certainly for peace; for that reason this greeting was suitable. The effect follows with respect to the good, and with respect to the evil. ***And if that house be worthy***, etc. We can say that that house will thence have some power of a blessing. Hence, the Apostles, or bishops, in the first turning towards the people say, *Pax vobis*.[21] Hence, it is said: "They shall invoke my name upon the children of Israel, and I will bless them" (Num. 6, 27). ...***but if it be not worthy, your peace shall return to you***. But what is this that He says? Had He not said that firstly they ought to inquire who was worthy? For that reason, He shows that in such inquiries men can be deceived: "For man seeth those things that appear, but the Lord beholdeth the heart," as it is stated in I Kings 16, 7. For they were not yet so perfect that they could know who was worthy. ***Your peace shall return to you***; and this is because someone sometimes prays and labors for the salvation of another, and, nevertheless, the effect is not attained; and, nevertheless, what he does, he does not lose, but it returns unto himself. Hence, ***shall return to you***, that is, the fruit is given back to you. ***And whosoever shall not receive you***. Here is treated concerning those who do not receive them. And firstly, He teaches them what they ought to do; and secondly, He teaches them what they shall receive from God. He says, therefore, ***And whosoever shall not receive you***. And He sets forth two faults. One is that they had not received them; and the other is that, as the Apostles had been sent to preach, those who did not receive them were not listening to the Word of God. Therefore, ***going forth out of that house or city***, because sometimes they were received in the city, but not in a house; but other times they were neither received in a house nor in the city; just as it is related in the Acts of the Apostles. What, therefore, ought to be done? ***Shake off the dust from your feet.*** And it is read that Paul and Barnabas did this literally, as is stated in Acts 14, 51. And why did the Lord command this? Dust, of course, adheres to

---

21. i.e. at a Pontifical Mass.

the feet. Hence, He ordered this to show that they had made the labor of their journey in vain. And this was as a punishment to those who had not received them; as though He were to say: 'For which sake you are worthy of condemnation'; nevertheless, the Apostle says: "I have not labored in vain" (Phil. 2, 16). Likewise, another reason is that the least thing that can be possessed is dust; for that reason, He willed that they shake off the dust from their feet as a sign that they possess nothing from them. A third reason is that by dust, temporal things are signified, and by their feet the affections are signified, to indicate that nothing temporal ought to remain in their affections. A fourth cause is mystical. The feet are their affections: for howsoever much preachers are holy, it is necessary that their affections be moved by some dust, or from some vainglory, etc., as is stated in John 13, where it is said that the Lord washed the feet of the disciples, and said: "He that is clean needeth not but to wash his feet, but is clean wholly" (verse 10). Hence, they needed a washing in regard to sellable goods. And why did the Lord command this? It was to show that a preacher chooses a dangerous course. Wherefore, if they do not believe him, this reverts unto their condemnation. But what is this? Will they be worse off? Nay, *I say to you, it shall be more tolerable for the land of Sodom and Gomorrha in the day of judgment, than for that city*. Because as it is written: "If I had not come and spoken to them, they would not have sin" (Jn. 15, 22). For they who hear and do not, fulfill sin more than those who have never heard. Therefore, perhaps, because these Sodomites did not hear, for that reason it will be more tolerable for them. Likewise, although these men were unclean, nevertheless they were hospitable. Hence, in regard to this it will be more tolerable for them.

But the contrary is stated in Genesis 19, that the sin of the Sodomites is the gravest sin, as appears from its punishment. And one ought to reply, that in the category of sins of the flesh that sin is the gravest. That sin, however, which is immediately opposed to God, such as idolatry, is graver than it. Or it ought to be answered that He is not comparing one sin to another, but He is comparing in regard to a circumstance; because these men were sinning, to whom the Gospel had been preached, but it had not been preached to the others. Likewise, He is reproving certain heretics who were saying that all sins, and all punishments, and all merits, and all rewards were equal. For that reason, He excludes this, when He says, *it shall be more tolerable*, etc., for some sins there will be a worse punishment.

16. Behold I send you as sheep in the midst of wolves. Be ye therefore wise as serpents and simple as doves.

17. But beware of men. For they will deliver you up in councils, and they will scourge you in their synagogues.

18. And you shall be brought before governors, and before kings for my sake, for a testimony to them and to the Gentiles:

19. But when they shall deliver you up, take no thought how or what to speak: for it shall be given you in that hour what to speak:

20. For it is not you that speak, but the spirit of your Father that speaketh in you.

21. The brother also shall deliver up the brother to death, and the father the son; and the children shall rise up against their parents, and shall put them to death.

22. And you shall be hated by all men for my name's sake: but he that shall persevere unto the end, he shall be saved.

23. And when they shall persecute you in this city, flee into another. Amen I say to you, you shall not finish all the cities of Israel, till the Son of man come.

24. The disciple is not above the master, nor the servant above his lord.

25. It is enough for the disciple that he be as his master, and the servant as his lord. If they have called the good man of the house Beelzebub, how much more them of his household?

26. Therefore fear them not. For nothing is covered that shall not be revealed: nor hid, that shall not be known.

27. That which I tell you in the dark, speak ye in the light: and that which you hear in the ear, preach ye upon the housetops.

28. And fear ye not them that kill the body, and are not able to kill the soul: but rather fear him that can destroy both soul and body in hell.

29. Are not two sparrows sold for a farthing? and not one of them shall fall on the ground without your Father.

30. But the very hairs of your head are all numbered.

31. Fear not therefore: better are you than many sparrows.

32. Every one therefore that shall confess me before men, I will also confess him before my Father who is in heaven.

33. But he that shall deny me before men, I will also deny him before my Father who is in heaven.

34. *Do not think that I came to send peace upon earth: I came not to send peace, but the sword.*

35. *For I came to set a man at variance against his father, and the daughter against her mother, and the daughter in law against her mother in law.*

36. *And a man's enemies shall be they of his own household.*

37. *He that loveth father or mother more than me, is not worthy of me; and he that loveth son or daughter more than me, is not worthy of me.*

38. *And he that taketh not up his cross, and followeth me, is not worthy of me.*

39. *He that findeth his life, shall lose it: and he that shall lose his life for me, shall find it.*

40. *He that receiveth you, receiveth me: and he that receiveth me, receiveth him that sent me.*

41. *He that receiveth a prophet in the name of a prophet, shall receive the reward of a prophet: and he that receiveth a just man in the name of a just man, shall receive the reward of a just man.*

42. *And whosoever shall give to drink to one of these little ones a cup of cold water only in the name of a disciple, amen I say to you he shall not lose his reward.*

Above, the Lord instructed the Apostles concerning their office, and concerning their necessary means of livelihood; but now He instructs them concerning their imminent dangers: and about this He does two things. Firstly, He sets forth their instruction in a figure; and secondly, He expounds that figure, where it reads, *But beware of men*. About the former, He firstly foretells the dangers; and secondly, He instructs how they ought to conduct themselves in dangers, where it is said, *Be ye therefore wise as serpents and simple as doves*. He says, therefore, *Behold I send you*. Because He had said, *Into whatsoever city or town you shall enter*, etc., and then, that *the workman is worthy of his meat*: they might believe that everyone is bound to receive them; for that reason He excludes this; as though He were to say, 'It will not be so.' *Behold I send you as sheep in the midst of wolves*, hence, I send you into dangers. And He says this on account of two things, lest it be imputed to His ignorance, or His inability, in that He was unable to protect them. Likewise, He said this to them, lest they think themselves to have been deceived; and He compares them to sheep on account of their gentleness, but He compares their persecutors to wolves on account of their greediness; for Christ Himself was a sheep, about whom it is written: "As a sheep to the slaughter" (Is. 53, 7). And His disciples were sheep; "We are his people and his sheep of his pasture" (Ps. 94, 7). But lest you believe that this was not from my will, *I send you in the midst of wolves*; "As the Father hath sent me, I also send you" (Jn. 20, 21). And why did God so will to send them into dangers? This was for the manifestation of His power, because, if He had sent some men armed, that would be ascribed to His violence, not to God's power; for that reason, He sent poor men. For it was a great thing that by poor, despised, and unarmed men so many men were converted to the Lord, as the Apostle says: "Not many wise according to the flesh, not many mighty, not many noble God hath chosen; but the foolish things of the world hath God chosen," etc., (I Cor. 1, 26-27). *Be ye therefore wise as serpents and simple as doves.* Here He shows how they ought to conduct themselves. And because two evils could have happened to them: namely, that if the Apostles had consented to them, some harm could have befallen them; if they had contradicted, similarly some harm could have befallen them; for that reason He admonishes them regarding two things, namely, regarding prudence and simplicity. He admonishes them regarding prudence, so that they might avoid the evils inflicted upon them. Hence, because I send you, *Be ye wise.*[22] The prudence of a serpent consists in that it always wishes to defend its head. The head is Christ, whom He commands them to serve. Hence: "I have fought a good fight: I have finished my course: I have kept the faith" (II Tim. 4, 7). Likewise, they ought to guard the Head, because it is the principle of the whole (I Cor. 11, 3);[23] "With all watchfulness keep thy heart" (Prov. 4, 23). Likewise, there is another prudence of a serpent, that when it grows old, it passes through a narrow hole and sheds its vesture, or skin; so we ourselves ought to do in relation to our manner of living. And the Apostles says: "Stripping yourselves of the old man with his deeds," etc., (Col. 3, 9). Moreover, we ought to have a serpent's prudence in preaching, because, as it is stated in Gen. 3, on account of the serpent's shrewdness, the human race was cast down, because he attacked the weaker sex. Likewise, he showed her a tree. So preachers ought to convert sinners through the most apt means. Similarly, they ought to exhort concerning the tree of the Cross, so that just as the devil derived benefit from a tree for an evil end, so these men ought to derive benefit from the tree of the Cross for a good end. *And simple as doves.* He had

---

22. *Estote prudens*, i.e., "Be ye prudent" according to a different translation.
23. "But I would have you know that the head of every man is Christ."

compared them to a sheep, because it does not murmur back, likewise it does not harm; here He compares them to a dove, because it does not have anger in its heart. Likewise, they ought to be simple facing deceitfulness, which carries one thing in the heart and another thing in the mouth, according to the passage: "Who speak peace with their neighbor, but evils are in their hearts" (Ps. 27, 3). Facing torments, they ought to have patience and simplicity. "The simplicity of the just shall guide them" (Prov. 11, 3). Afterwards, He exposes the dangers they will face, saying, **But beware of men**, etc. And firstly, He does this in general; secondly, He does this in particular. Because these men are simple, they might think that He was sending them into the middle of wolves, so that they might think He was speaking literally; for that reason He expounds His words, **Beware of men**. For everything ought to be named by that which is principally in it. Hence, it should be seen what more principally sets a man in motion. If it is reason, he is a man; if it is anger, he is a bear, or a lion; if it is concupiscence, then he is not a man, but rather a pig, or a dog. Hence, although they are men by nature, nevertheless, they are wolves by their affections; in Psalm 48, 13, it is said: "And man when he was in honour did not understand; he is compared to senseless beasts, and is become like to them," etc. And elsewhere it is said: "Do not become like the horse and the mule, who have no understanding" (Ps. 31, 9). **For they will deliver you up**, etc. Firstly, He touches upon to whom they shall be delivered up; and secondly, by whom they shall be delivered up, where it is said, **The brother also shall deliver up the brother**, etc. And firstly, He makes plain what was said;[24] and secondly, He comforts them, where it is said, **But when they shall deliver you up**, etc. And firstly, He says to whom they shall be delivered up; and secondly, what follows from this delivering up, where it says, **And they will scourge you in their synagogues**. About the first, it is as follows. Such was the custom among the Jews, that if someone were to say or do something a first time against the Law, the first time he was called before the Council and reprehended; but if it happened a second time, he was reprimanded and scourged; but if it happened a third time, either he was killed, when this power belonged to them, or he was delivered up to him to whom the power belonged. And this actually happened, as it is said in Acts 3 and 5; for there it is said that the Apostles, after they had spoken to the people, were threatened by the rulers; and after this, since they were still speaking to the

---

24. Namely, "I send you in the midst of wolves."

people, they were scourged, in order that they would not speak to the people; and thirdly, the Jews stoned Stephen and delivered up James to Herod: for that reason, beware, because *they will deliver you up in their councils*; "I have not sat with the council of vanity: neither will I go in with the doers of unjust things" (Ps. 25, 4). *And you shall be brought before governors, and before kings*, as, for example, to Herod and to many others. But you ought to have great consolation, because it is *for my sake*, whom you love. Augustine says: "Love makes everything to be, as it were, empty, to be nothing." Likewise, "Blessed are they that suffer persecution for justice' sake" (above 5, 10). And what follows therefrom? This will be *for a testimony to them*, that is to say, unfavorable to them, by whom are meant the Jews and the Gentiles. For, because they will deliver you up in councils, for that reason, it will be for a testimony unfavorable to them. Likewise, because you shall be brought before kings and governors, this, similarly, shall be unfavorable to them. Hence: "Behold I send to you prophets and wise men and scribes: and some of them you will put to death and crucify: and some you will scourge in your synagogues," etc., (below 23, 34). Or it is thus: *For a testimony to them*, namely, to the Jews, *and to the Gentiles*, because I send you to them, witnesses of My faith to the Jews and to the Gentiles; hence, a martyr is the same thing as a witness; because by your suffering[25] you will be witnesses of My Passion; "And you shall be witnesses unto me in Jerusalem, and in all Judea, and Samaria, and even to the uttermost part of the earth," etc., (Acts 1, 8). *But when they shall deliver you up, take no thought how or what to speak*, etc. The Apostles would be able to say: 'We are ignorant fishermen, and so we will be made speechless.' And it is not surprising, because Moses, who was instructed in the Law, when the Lord commanded him to go before Pharaoh, said, "I have more impediment of tongue" (Ex. 4, 10). For that reason, to exclude this, He says, *But when they shall deliver you up*, etc. And He does three things. Firstly, He excludes speechlessness; secondly, He promises the gift of wisdom, where it is said, *for it shall be given you in that hour what to speak*; and thirdly, He relates the author of the gift, where it is said, *For it is not you that speak, but the spirit of your Father that speaketh in you*. Therefore, do not think about this. And He excludes two things: He excludes so far as concerns that which is said, and so far as concerns the manner of speaking. The first pertains to wisdom, the second to eloquence.

---

25. *Passionem.*

But what the Apostle Peter says in his first epistle seems to be opposed to this: "Being ready always to satisfy everyone that asketh you a reason of that hope which is in you" (I Pet. 3, 15). Chrysostom solves the difficulty, saying that when someone has the necessity of responding, and has the time of deliberating, he ought not to expect divine help; but the Apostles, when they were in tribulation, did not have time, for which reason they were obliged to commit themselves to the Son of God: it is in this way, too, that when someone has the opportunity, he ought to do what he can; but certainly if one does not have time, he ought to commit himself to the Son of God, but if he has time to think, he ought not to tempt God. For that reason the Lord did not only say, **take no thought**, but He said, **when they shall deliver you up... take no thought**, etc. And it follows from that promise, **it shall be given you in that hour**; because "in God's hand are all our words" (Wis. 7, 16). And, "I will be in thy mouth; and I will teach thee what thou shalt speak" (Ex. 4, 12). And: "I will give you a mouth and wisdom" (Lk. 21, 15).

And who is the author? Certainly it is the Holy Ghost. **For it is not you that speak, but the spirit of your Father that speaketh in you.** Something similar is stated in II Corinthians 13, 3: "Do you seek a proof of Christ that speaketh in me?"

But how is it that these men seem possessed? It ought to be observed that every action which is caused by two things, of which one is the principle agent, but the second, in fact, is the instrumental agent, ought to be named from the more principle agent. These men were the agents instrumentally, the Holy Ghost was the agent principally; for that reason, the whole action ought to be named by the Holy Ghost. But it ought to be considered that sometimes the Spirit moves by disturbing the mind, and sometimes He moves by comforting the mind. Hence, there is this difference between the movement of the devil and of the Holy Ghost. For man is not a master except by his power of reason, by which he is free; hence, when man is not moved according to his power of reason, then there is the movement of one possessed. When man is moved with his power of reason, then it is said to be a movement by the Holy Ghost. For the motion of the devil disturbs man's power of reason. These men, however, although they were speaking by the agency of the Holy Ghost, nevertheless, the power of reason was remaining in them; and, for that reason, they were also speaking by the agency of themselves, unlike possessed men. Hence, He brings them to know prophetic truth, as it is stated: "And we have the more firm prophetical word" (II Pet. 1, 19).

But the Apostles would be able to say: 'Who will deliver us up? We do not have enmities.' Firstly, therefore, He shows by whom they will be delivered up; and secondly, He gives a consolation, where it is said, ***But he that shall persevere unto the end, he shall be saved.*** Someone could guard badly against a persecution foretold to him only in general; for that reason, He foretells the persecution in particular. And He says two things regarding the first. ***The brother also shall deliver up the brother.*** This literally happened that a father delivered up his son, and on the other hand, a brother also delivered up his brother, either on account of fear or on account of hatred; because so great is the power of faith, that between men who are not of the same faith there can scarcely be firm friendship. And this is what He says, ***The brother also shall deliver up the brother***, etc. Hence, it is said also in Jeremias 9, 4: "Let every man not trust in any brother of his" (Jer. 9, 4). And, because of this, it is necessary that they be on their guard, both on account of the injury which a man suffers, and on account of the loss of friendship; it is written in Psalm 54, 13: "If my enemy had reviled me, I would verily have borne with it." Again, it is more necessary that you be on your guard, because you will not go to persons known to you, but to strangers. And this will not be strong enough, because "The hour cometh, that whosoever killeth you will think that he doth a service to God" (Jn. 16, 2). But did this ever really happen? Were there not many men who received them? Therefore, He was speaking about men who lived like men. But others, who were of God, were receiving them. But the cause of this is assigned: "If you had been of the world, the world would love its own: but because you are not of the world, but I have chosen you out of the world, therefore the world hateth you," (Jn. 15, 19). Likewise, the Lord promises a consolation, because it is *for my name's sake*. For this ought to be sweet to you, to suffer for My name, as it is written: "If you be reproached for the name of Christ, you shall be blessed" (I Pet. 4, 14). Similarly, He comforts them with another reason, that their tribulation should produce great fruit. For, because He foresaw that many would fall, for that reason He admonishes to perseverance; because ***he that shall persevere unto the end, he shall be saved.*** "I have fought a good fight, I have finished my course, I have kept the faith; as to the rest, there is laid up for me a crown of justice which the Lord the just judge will render to me in that day" (II Tim. 4, 7-8). Hence, in Leviticus it is said that the rump was being offered,[26] that is, the end of one's

---

26. "They shall offer thereof the rump and the fat that covereth the entrails" (Lev. 7, 3).

life. ***And when they shall persecute you in this city, flee into another***. Above, He taught them about their dangers, in which He explained what He had said, ***Behold I send you***, etc., but now He teaches how they ought to conduct themselves. And this part is divided: because, firstly, He teaches them to beware of evils, and of the danger regarding prudence; secondly, He teaches them to have equanimity in dangers, where it is said, ***Therefore fear not***. About the former, He firstly teaches them to avoid corporeal danger; secondly, He teaches them to avoid spiritual danger, where it is said, ***The disciple is not above the master***. About the first, He does two things. Firstly, He alludes to the evil of the dangers; secondly, He responds to a tacit objection, where it is said, ***Amen I say to you***, etc. He says, therefore: 'it was indeed said, that ***he that shall persevere unto the end, he shall be saved***. And it is not on account of this that you may expose yourselves to trials, nay, ***when they shall persecute you in this city, flee into another***': and this is expedient for weak men, lest, incautiously exposing themselves, they give up. "The discreet man considereth his steps: the fool leapeth over, and is confident" (Prov. 14, 15-16). Likewise, He is also teaching the perfect to avoid trials; and if they need not avoid trials for the sake of themselves, nevertheless, they ought to avoid them for the sake of the salvation of others, as it is stated: "But to abide still in the flesh is needful for you" (Phil. 1, 24). The Lord demonstrated this when, on account of Herod, He fled into Egypt, as stated above in chapter 2. Similarly, the disciples did this, as it is stated in Acts 8.[27]

But against this is brought forward what is written in John 10, that a hireling flees and leaves the sheep. Therefore, it is said that these words do not pertain to the Apostles, but to hirelings.

Augustine responds, that if persecution threatens a single person, then he ought to avoid the persecution and leave some other shepherds, through whom there may be salvation; but if persecution threatens the whole Church, it is necessary that either the whole Church flee to safer places, as it has happened in the past, or that some flee, and others who are firm remain, or else the pastor may remain with the flock.

He continues, ***Amen I say to you, you shall not finish all the cities of Israel, till the Son of man come***. He is responding to a tacit objection. They could say: 'You send us to Judea; if they cast us out, whither shall we go?' 'I say, given that they

---

[27]. "And at that time, there was raised a great persecution against the church which was at Jerusalem. And they were all dispersed through the countries of Judea, and Samaria, except the apostles" (Acts 8, 1).

expel you from one city, *flee into another*, and you will not able to travel through the cities of Judea, *till the Son of man come*, that is, until He rises again from the dead, and then He will send you to the Gentiles,' as it is stated below: "Going therefore, teach ye all nations" (28, 19). Hilary expounds this passage otherwise. For he says that Christ is speaking about a second mission, namely, when He says, *When they shall persecute you*; namely, flee from Judea to the Gentiles, as it is stated: "To you it behooved us first to speak the word of God: but because you reject it and judge yourselves unworthy of eternal life, behold we turn to the Gentiles" (Acts 13, 46). But they could say: 'Why do you wish that we would leave our own people?' 'It is because you will not be able to finish the cities of the children of Israel until your death, then the children of Israel shall be finished.' Mystically, this passage may be expounded thus: 'When the heretics will persecute you with their Scriptural passages, repel them with Scriptural passages; for they shall not be finished until the truth is manifested.' *The disciple is not above the master, nor the servant above his lord.* Here He admonishes them not to give up: and firstly, He admonishes them, by His example, not to give up; secondly, He admonishes them, by a benefit, not to give up, where it is said, *Therefore fear them not*; and thirdly, He admonishes them, on account of the divine judgment, not to give up, where it is said, *And fear ye not them that kill the body.* Firstly, He exhorts them, by His example, not to give up; and secondly, He sets forth a similitude; and thirdly, He applies it to the matter at hand. And firstly, He adduces what is unfitting; and secondly, He adduces what is perfect. He says, therefore, *The disciple is not above the master.* For they might say: 'You say that we will be hated by all men: how will we be able to withstand?' The Lord had given them great wisdom and great power: hence, to wisdom is due honor, and to power is due reverence: for that reason, the Lord sets Himself up as an example in respect to both: *The disciple is not above the master*, inasmuch as he is a disciple; hence, if they did not bestow honor to Me, which is due to a master, nor will they do so to you. Again, *The disciple is not above the master* may be expounded otherwise; and this inasmuch as it refers to mastership. Hence: "You call me Master and Lord. And you say well: for so I am," etc., (Jn. 13, 13). And now it ought to be a glory for anyone if he be like his master or teacher; for that reason, He adds, *It is enough for the disciple that he be as his master.* For just as it is in secular affairs, that everything is perfect when it is able to produce a thing similar to itself, so also a disciple is then perfect when he is very similar to his master; it is also similar regarding a servant. For that reason, it ought not to be burdensome to you if you are also as I am; hence, it is stated: "Christ also suffered for us, leaving you an example that you should follow his steps" (I Pet. 2, 21). And: "What is man, said I, that he can follow his master?" (Eccle. 2, 12). Then He calls them domestics: *If they have called the good man of the house Beelzebub, how much more them of his household?* And He calls them domestics for the sake of greater familiarity: hence, it is a great gift to suffer for Christ, as it is stated: "My brethren, count it all joy, when you shall fall into divers temptations, knowing that the trying of your faith worketh patience" (James 1, 2). And: "And they indeed went from the presence of the council, rejoicing that they were accounted worthy to suffer reproach for the name of Jesus" (Acts 5, 41). Hence, it is not a great matter that a domestic were to suffer for his friend. "You are fellow citizens with the saints and the domestics of God" (Eph. 2, 19). Hence, *if they have called the good man of the house Beelzebub*, it is not surprising if they say reproaches to you.

But what is that which is said, 'Beelzebub'? It ought to be known that Ninus[28] is said to be the son of Bel: hence, he made a statue of his father to be honored, and he called it 'Bel.' Then, afterwards, it was translated into another language, and it was called 'Beelzebub.' 'Zebub' means 'fly': sacrifice was made to this statue with much blood, whereas many flies gathered.

Therefore fear them not. Here He exhorts them not to give up in their tribulations on account of their benefit. And firstly, He comforts them; secondly, He gives a similitude; and thirdly, He applies it to the case at hand. He says, therefore: *They shall persecute you*; but fear not, because you ought to fear nothing except what is evil; but it is a great good to endure what the Lord endured. Hence, "I bear the marks of the Lord Jesus in my body" (Gal. 6, 17). *For nothing is covered that shall not be revealed.* This phrase can be referred to the preceding, or to the following, words. As referring to the preceding words, it is thus. These men will call you Beelzebub, but one ought not to be concerned, be-

---

28. "Under the office of king is also included the founding of the city or kingdom. For not a few kings founded the cities, in which they might reign, such as Ninus who founded Niniva, and Romulus who founded Rome" (*De Regimine Principum*, Bk. 1, chap. 14). "Augustine (*City of God*, bk. 16, chap. 17) says, that Ninus the son of Bel, when Abraham was born, was the king of the Assyrians, the head of which kingdom was the city of Babylon, and excepting India, he was the king of all Asia, which, according to him in the same place, is the middle part of the world" (*Postilla in Librum Geneseos*, chap. 14, line 26-31).

cause at the end of the world their malice will be made known to all. For that reason, do not fear, because ***nothing is covered that shall not be revealed***; as it is stated: "Therefore, judge not before the time: until the Lord come, who both will bring to light the hidden things of darkness and will make manifest the counsels of the hearts" (I Cor. 4, 5). ***Nor hid***. Something covered differs from something hid: because something not apparent is said to be covered, as is that which another has in his heart, according to the passage: "Why do you think evil in your hearts?" (above 9, 4). Something, however, is also said to be hid which, even if it is apparent, nevertheless is hid by something else. Or it can be expounded thus: 'Fear not, because if your truth does not appear immediately, nevertheless, afterwards it shall appear.' Then the Lord instructs them as an advocate is instructed: for, firstly, he is taught how he ought to argue before he speaks before others; so the Lord had chosen disciples for sowing His word to all the people; for that reason, He wished to teach them in secret, saying: ***That which I tell you in the dark, speak ye in the light***. There are two senses through which we learn: hearing and sight. What is said in the dark is hidden: likewise, what is said in the ears is hidden. ***That which I tell you in the dark, speak ye in the light***, because in the light all things are made manifest. Likewise, it is hidden, because it is heard in the ear; for that reason, He says, ***and that which you hear in the ear, preach ye upon the housetops***.

But the contrary seems to be said in John 18, 20: "In secret I have spoken nothing." But this ought to be understood thus: 'I have spoken nothing in secret which may not be said openly.' Or it is thus: ***That which I tell you in the dark***, that is to say, among the Jews, who are darkness. Hence: "You were heretofore darkness" (Eph. 5, 8). Or, what I say to you, who are darkness, ***speak ye in the light***; "Who both will bring to light the hidden things of darkness and will make manifest the counsels of the hearts" (I Cor. 4, 5).

And that which you hear in the ear, preach ye upon the housetops. "Wise men lay up knowledge" (Prov. 10, 14).[29] And: "Which thou having heard, consider it thoroughly in thy mind" (Job 5, 27). ***Preach upon the housetops***, because in some regions the custom is that roofs are flat; so that also there a presentation can be made to all. Mystically, one preaches upon the roof, who subjugating his flesh, preaches to others. ***And fear ye not them that kill the body***. Above, He showed that they were

---

[29]. Literally, "Wise men hide (*abscundunt*) knowledge."

obliged not to forsake the confession of the truth, both on account of His example, and on account of the benefit of tribulations; now He shows that they ought not to forsake the confession of the truth on account of the divine judgment, because their actions are subject to Divine justice. Or it can be joined together otherwise. He taught how persecutions are to be avoided; but now He teaches that on account of nothing may they cease from the execution of their office. For three things were able to impede the execution of their office: reproaches, the fear of death, and carnal affection. Therefore, He taught that they may not desist on account of reproaches; now, however, He teaches that they may not desist on account of the fear of death; thereafter, He teaches the they may not desist on account of carnal affection, where it is said, **Do not think that I came to send peace upon earth.** Hence, according to this, He firstly teaches that they are not to be feared, who kill the body, lest the preaching of the truth be abandoned; secondly, they are not to be feared, because they can do little harm, where it is said, **And are not able to kill the soul**; thirdly, He shows who are to be feared, namely, those who can do much harm. Firstly, therefore, He says, **fear ye not them that kill the body.** And why? Do not fear them, because the body in itself has the necessity of dying, hence, they do not cause anything which is not going to happen sometime; "And if Christ be in you, the body indeed is dead, because of sin: but the spirit liveth, because of justification" (Rom. 8, 10). Likewise, this is because the body's being slain for the sake of glory is desirable; hence: "Unhappy man that I am, who shall deliver me from the body of this death?" (Rom. 7, 24). Likewise, do not fear them, because the death of the body is brief and momentary; "For we who live are always delivered unto death" (II Cor. 4, 11). And, therefore, **fear ye not**; "Who art thou, that thou shouldst be afraid of a mortal man, and of the son of man, who shall wither away like grass?" (Is 51, 12). **And are not able to kill the soul.** Here He mentions what little harm they can do, namely, in that they are not able to kill the soul; hence, a spirit always lives; "Before man is life and death, good and evil, that which he shall choose shall be given him" (Eccli. 15, 18). For just as the body lives by the soul, so the soul lives by God: and in this way God is the life of the soul. Therefore, they are not to be feared, because they can do little. **And fear ye not them; but rather fear him that can destroy both soul and body in hell.** If you say they are to be feared who kill the body, I reply, rather he ought to be feared, who also can destroy the soul.

And it ought to be observed that this name of hell, 'gehenna,' is not found in Old Testament, nevertheless, it is derived by the Savior from Jeremias 19, 6, where it is said: "Therefore behold the days come, saith the Lord, that this place shall no more be called the valley of the sons of Hinnom, but the valley of slaughter." Hence, Hinnom is a valley at the foot of the mountain of Jerusalem, which was a rich valley, and was called the valley of Hinnom. Now it happened that, that place was consecrated to an idol;[30] and, for that reason, because the inhabitants were turned to pleasures, the Lord threatened that they would be killed, and that it would not be called the place of Hinnom, but Polyandrion,[31] that is, burial-place of the dead; for that reason He calls this place Gehenna. Hence, He says: Fear not those who only kill the body, *but rather fear him that can destroy both soul and body in hell*, because one ought not to be subject to God on account of fear of punishment, but on account of the love of justice, as is stated: "For you have not received the spirit of bondage again in fear: but you have received the spirit of adoption of sons of God" (Rom. 8, 15).

And it ought to be noted that here He excludes two errors. For some men were saying that the soul, when the body has died, perishes: and this He destroys, when He says: *Who can send the soul into hell*. Hence, it is evident that it remains after the body. Likewise, it was a position of certain men that there was no resurrection, as it is said in I Corintians 15. And He excludes this, because if the body and soul are sent into hell, it stands firm that there will be a resurrection: and this is stated in Apocolypse 20, 9: "They shall be cast into the pool of fire and brimstone."

Are not two sparrows sold for a farthing? So it was said, because these things ought not to be feared, because they can do little harm, etc. Likewise, they are not to be feared, because the little that they can do, they can only do by Divine Providence. And firstly, He sets forth the Divine Providence about the birds; secondly, He sets forth the Divine Providence about men, where it is said, *But the very hairs of your head are all numbered*; and thirdly, He proclaims to them their security: *Fear not therefore*, etc. He says, therefore, *Are not two sparrows*, by two sparrows He gives to understand all small birds, *sold for a farthing?* And in this He indicates a trifling value, because two are had for a farthing, because just as one is the least number, so a farthing[32]

---

30. i.e. Moloch (cf. "Hell," *The Catholic Encyclopedia* [1910 ed.]).

31. "Corriandrum" meaning coriander seed is given in the text, but the *Catena Aurea on St. Matthew* (p. 390) gives the more correct word of "Polyandrion."

32. In former British money, a farthing was worth a quarter of a penny.

is the least in weights. But note, according to Augustine, that something is said to have value in two ways: either according to the dignity of its nature; and so one sparrow is worth more than a penny: or it is referred according to our use, and in this way a penny is worth more.

But it is objected that Luke puts five sparrows and two farthings. It ought to be said that there is little difference: if two are had for a farthing, and five are had for two, there is not a great difference.

And not one of them shall fall on the ground without your Father, that is, without your Father's providence. And why does He say this? It is because this saying agrees with the saying of the Law (Lev. 14), because when someone was cured from leprosy, he offered two sparrows, and one was immolated, but the other was dipped with cedar wood and hyssop in the blood of the one killed, and the leper to be cleansed was sprinkled, and, in this way, the living sparrow was let go. Therefore, He wills that two be taken, and one not be killed: and this does not happen without God's providence. Hilary expounds the passage thus: "By two sparrows are understood the body and the soul, and they are given for a farthing, that is, for a little pleasure; 'behold you are sold for your iniquities, and for your wicked deeds have I put your mother away'" (Is. 50, 1). And of these only one falls to the ground, namely, the body; the soul, however, goes to judgment.

But it is objected: God does not care about oxen:[33] therefore, neither does He care about sparrows. It ought to be said that God takes care of all things, as it is stated: "There is no other God but thou, who hast care of all" (Wis. 12, 13). But it ought to be known that He provides for all things according to the manner of their natures. Now there is a diversity among created things, because certain things are naturally free, but others are not. That creature is said to be free, in whose power it is to do what it wants: that creature is not free, which does not have this power. Hence, He provides for rational creatures as being free; but He provides for others as servants: just as a the head of a family provides in one way for his children, and in another way for his servants; he provides for his children on account of themselves, but he provides for the servants according to what is useful for their masters, and also according to what each one is more suitable in serving: so the Divine Mercy divides His gifts to rational creatures on account of themselves, because all hap-

---

33. I Corinthians 9, 9: "Doth God take care for oxen?"

pens for the sake of their good, or for the sake of their punishment. Hence, to them, all things are either rewards or punishments of merits. The things which happen to irrational animals, either happen for the salvation of men or for the completion of the universe, as it is stated in III Kings, that a certain prophet was killed by a lion, and this was on account of a fault of his. A mouse is killed by a cat to keep the order of the universe. For this is the universal order, that one animal lives on another. For that reason, He afterwards shows Himself to have another care of both men and brutes, when He says: *But the very hairs of your head are all numbered.* He shows that there is a different kind of Divine Providence, according to the diverse ways it provides. For He had said, concerning sparrows, that one does not fall to the ground without the Father: but here He says that much less will you fall, nor even your hairs, without the Father: and here He indicates the providence about the least actions, because all things which are in the actions themselves, are ordained to them,[34] and concerning these God provides.

But it ought to be observed that He says, *are numbered.* And the reason is that it is customary, that what someone wishes to retain, he numbers; what he wishes, however, to bestow, he hands over to another. Hence, there is a difference between the providence for rational men and for other things, because the former are immediately ordained to God, because such a creature has a capacity for God, but the others do not. Likewise, the things which we number, we wish to keep for ourselves; and for that reason, He did not say, above, that the sparrows are numbered, because they do not continue to exist forever; but men so exist that they continue to exist forever, because the soul is everlasting.

But here there is a question: If the hairs are numbered, will not the entirety, which was cut from the hairs, be reintegrated at the resurrection? And if so, its length will be unbecoming.

Some say that matter does not perish; but what will be superfluous in one part, will belong to another part. But supposing that nothing will be diminished, what would happen as a result? For that reason, it ought to be understood that on this point there were three opinions. Some said that flesh will not rise again, except what is from true human nature. Others, however, said that flesh will not rise again, except what was taken from Adam, which was multiplied in this way into a great quantity. Others, however, said that flesh will not rise again, except what was not only taken

---

[34]. i.e. the actions. The meaning seems to be that the circumstances of the actions are arranged by Divine Providence such that the actions will be beneficial to men.

from Adam, but also what was taken from a near ancestor. Hence, whatever is added, that is, from true human nature, will rise again; but that which pertains to the quantity of the parts, will not rise again. But against this it seems that the heat acting upon the nutritive humor also acts upon the radical humor,[35] and in this way, man does not consume the one unless he consumes the other, since they are mixed together. For that reason, it seems that one ought to say otherwise, that whatever is from true human nature will remain, only inasmuch as it pertains to man's completeness. I call, however, that which is from true human nature, flesh according to the species; flesh according to the matter, however, is something else. The flesh, however, will rise again according to the species, not according to the matter.

But what is meant by the expression, 'flesh according to the species'? It ought to be said that the parts of man can be considered, either insofar as concerns the form, or insofar as concerns the matter. Insofar as concerns the form, they always remain. If, however, we consider the matter removed, something appears and disappears, as is evident in fire. And now, if wood be added to a fire, the fire remains the same according to its species; nevertheless, the matter disappears according to the removal of the wood. Hence, what is more perfect will rise again. Hence, He does not say: 'Your hairs are weighed'; but on the contrary, He says, *Your hairs are numbered*; hence, the parts of the body will not rise again in weight, but in form.

Fear not therefore, etc. Here He shows their security from the fact that their enemies can do but little: and that which they can do, they cannot do without God's providence. *Fear not therefore: better are you than many sparrows*. "Thou hast subjected all things under his feet, all sheep and oxen: moreover, the beasts also of the fields," as it is stated in Psalm 8, 8. And, "Let us make man to our image and likeness" (Gen. 1, 26); and it continues: "And let him have dominion over the fishes of the sea, and the fowls of the air, and the beasts, and the whole earth, and every creeping creature that moveth upon the earth." *Every one therefore that shall confess me before men, I will also confess him before my Father who is in heaven*. Here He touches upon the profit which ensues from the confession of Him; secondly, He touches

---

35. "The radical humor is said to comprise whatever the virtue of the species is founded on. If this be taken away it cannot be renewed; as when a man's hand or foot is amputated. But the nutritive humor is that which has not yet received perfectly the specific nature, but is on the way thereto; such is the blood, and the like. Wherefore if such be taken away, the virtue of the species remains in the root, which is not destroyed" (I, q. 119, a. 1 ad 4um).

upon the harm that ensues from the denial of Him, where it is said, ***But he that shall deny me before men, I will also deny him before my Father who is in heaven***. Hence, He says: 'Therefore I wish that you die and suffer.' And why? Certainly it is on account of your utility. Because ***Everyone therefore that shall confess me before men***, etc. And He crushes the error of a certain person, who was saying to confess the faith is necessary only before God in one's heart, not, however, with the mouth before men; which error is here proven manifestly false, because, "With the heart, we believe unto justice: but, with the mouth, confession is made unto salvation" (Rom. 10, 10). ***I will also confess him before my Father***, namely, when I shall have access to the Father, when it shall be said: "Come, ye blessed of my Father," etc., (below 25, 34). But they could say: 'You are on earth, for this reason confessing Thee can avail little'; for that reason, He adds, ***who is in heaven***, and He has power. ***He that shall deny*** by word, such as Peter, or by deed, as they of whom it is said: "They profess that they know God: but in their works they deny him" (Tit. 1, 16). ***I will also deny them***, when He will say, as it is stated above: "I never knew you" (7, 23), that is, I never approved of you. ***Do not think that I came to send peace upon earth***, etc.

Above, He admonished the disciples that they would not desist from preaching the truth, neither on account of reproaches, nor on account of the fear of death; now, however, He likewise admonishes that they do not desist on account of domestic affection. And firstly, He shows that separation from domestic affection is near at hand; secondly, how they ought to conduct themselves, where it is said, ***He that loveth father or mother more than me, is not worthy of me***. Firstly, He excludes what they might have assumed to be His intention; secondly, He sets forth His own plan; and thirdly, He explains it. The second part is where it is said, ***I came not to send peace***; the third is where it is said, ***For I came to set a man at variance against his father***, etc. He says, therefore: They might be able to think thus: 'Why is it, Lord, that so many things will happen to us? We believed that we would have peace at Your coming'; and for that reason, He says, ***Do not think***, etc. But what is it that He says? Is it not stated in Luke 2, 14, that when the Lord was born the angels sang, "Glory to God in the highest: and on earth peace to men of good will"? And the Bishop himself, when He first turns towards the people, says, "Peace be with you," and above, the Lord announced peace. For that reason, it ought to be said that there are two types of peace, namely, good and evil. By the name of peace is signified concord. There is an evil peace, about which it is spoken in Wisdom 14, 12: "But living in a great war of ignorance, they call so many and so great evils peace." This peace pertains to domestic affections. And it is as though He were to say, 'This peace I have not come to establish.' Hence: "It was given that he should take peace from the earth" (Apoc. 6, 4). And He is the good peace, about whom it is said: "He is our peace, who hath made both one" (Eph. 2, 14); and for that reason, the angels sang: "And on earth peace to men of good will" (Lk. 2, 14). Thus, *I came not to send peace, but the sword*. It belongs to the nature of a sword to divide. This sword is the word of God; "The word of God is living and effectual and more piercing than any two edged sword" (Heb. 4, 12). Hence, it is likewise said, "The sword of the Spirit (which is the word of God)" (Eph. 6, 17). And this word of God was sent to the earth. And some men believed, and some men did not. And for that reason, a war occurred, as it was stated: "How turn you again to the weak and needy elements which you desire to serve again?" etc., (Gal. 4, 9). Hence, He came to separate these two groups. He came, therefore, to send the sword, etc., namely, the word of God, but in part, because certain men believed, and this was due to Him; certain men, however, did not believe, and this was the due to their malice. This, nevertheless, was also caused by Him, because He permits this to happen, as it is stated: "For this cause, God delivered them up to shameful affections" (Rom. 1, 26).

But someone could say: 'You have come to set men at variance. Among whom did you come? Was it not among dissimilar people and strangers?' And He shows that it was not, but among those closely related. *For I came*, He said, *to set a man at variance against his father*, etc. For a close relationship is twofold; one kind of relationship is natural: another kind is called domestic, or household; and for that reason, He sends the sword against both. Natural amity is founded upon a natural act, and this is generation, or the union of man and woman: the domestic, or household, relationship is founded upon affinity. In opposition to the first, therefore, I have come to set a man at variance against his father.

But there is a question. It was said above: "I am not come to destroy, but to fulfill" (5, 17). But the Law commanded: Honor thy father and mother, etc. The solution is as follows. I say that you ought to obey him whenever he does not withdraw you from the love of God; but whenever he withdraws you, you are not held to obey.

36. i.e. the requirement of placing God before one's family.

And the daughter against her mother: and this refers to generation. *And the daughter in law against her mother in law*. And in this[36] the New Law agrees with the Old Law, as it is stated in Exodus 32, where it is said: "If any man be on the Lord's side, let him join with me. And all the sons of Levi gathered themselves together unto him, and he said to them: Put every man his sword upon his thigh." And it continues: "And let every man kill his brother, and friend" (verse 26-27). And that is accounted unto the praise of the Levites, as it is stated in Deuteronomy 33, 8, where it is said, "To Levi also he said: Thy perfection, and thy doctrine be to thy holy man." And it continues, "Who hath said to his father, and to his mother: I do not know you; and to his brethren: I know you not: and their own children they have not known" (verse 9).

But here there is a question, because here the Evangelist enumerates six persons; in Luke only three are enumerated. And it ought to be said that it is the same in either case, because a man's mother is the same thing as his wife's mother-in-law. Likewise, he sets forth those who pertain to the family circle, where He says, **And a man's enemies shall be they of his own household**, etc. And it is stated: "For I heard the reproaches of many, and terror on every side: Persecute him, and let us persecute him: from all the men that were my familiars" (Jer. 20, 10). And notice that the whole passage is found in Micheas 7, 6: "For the son dishonoureth the father, and the daughter riseth up against her mother, the daughter in law against her mother in law: and a man's enemies are they of his own household."

He that loveth father or mother more than me, is not worthy of me. Here He shows how in this separation they ought to conduct themselves. If you wish to receive the Lord's word, it is necessary that you be separated from the persons of whom I spoke. But someone might say: 'I do not want to be separated from my father,' or something of this kind; for that reason, He says, **He that loveth father or mother more than me, is not worthy of me**. The Lord exhorts that He be placed before any domestic affection. And firstly, He sets forth the exhortation; and secondly, He sets forth the utility following therefrom, where it is said, **He that receiveth you, receiveth me: and he that receiveth me**, etc. And He sets forth three degrees of domestic affection. For it is natural that a man love his father, but it is more natural that a father love his son: again, it is more natural that a man love himself. Why, therefore, does a father love his son more, rather than the contrary? Some men assign this reason, that the father has more knowledge about the son, if he is his, than the son about his father. Likewise, inasmuch as someone adheres longer to someone, so much the more is he rooted in the love of him. Similarly, another reason is that everyone loves himself more than another. But a son is what one might call a part of his father, the father, on the other hand, is not a part of the son; therefore, etc. Likewise, it is natural that everything loves what has been made by itself. But there is a different explanation, according to some men, because in a certain respect the son loves the father more: for, naturally, lineal descent occurs from the father to the son, nevertheless, the son is naturally subject to the father; for that reason, the father naturally loves the son, even a spiritual father, as it is stated: "I write not these things to confound you: but I admonish you as my dearest children" (I Cor. 4, 14). But sons are naturally subject to their fathers; for that reason, they naturally honor their father, and are more angered about an injury inflicted upon their father than about an injury inflicted upon themselves; "The glory of children are their fathers" (Prov. 17, 6). Hence, **He that loveth father or mother more than me, is not worthy of me**, because He Himself is God. And now, God is to be loved before all things; "I will not accept the person of man, and I will not level God with man" (Job 32, 21). For God is goodness itself; for that reason, He ought to be loved more. He is not, therefore, worthy of Me who loves his father or mother more than Me. **And he that loveth son or daughter**, etc. Why does a son love his father? It ought to be said, that whatever a son has, he has from his father: for he has from his father nourishment and teaching. And this a son cannot give to his father; but what things a son receives from his father, he receives more abundantly from God. For He Himself teaches us, as it is stated: "Who teacheth us more than the beasts of the earth, and instructeth us more than the fowls of the air," etc., (Job 35, 11). Likewise, He feeds us, as it is said in Genesis concerning Jacob.[37] Moreover, He preserves us in perpetuity. And this a man has more from God than a son has from his father. For that reason, God must always be loved more. "For I know that my Redeemer liveth, and in the last day I shall rise out of the earth. And I shall be clothed again with my skin, and in my flesh I shall see my God" (Job 19, 25-26). **And he that taketh not up his cross**. It was said that he who loveth

---

[37]. "And Jacob blessed the sons of Joseph, and said: God, in whose sight my fathers Abraham and Isaac walked, God that feedeth me from my youth until this day" (Gen. 48, 15).

his father, etc., nay, I say more: he who loves himself more than Me, is not worthy of Me. Because nothing can fill the whole heart except God. And therefore it is said: "Thou shalt love the Lord thy God with thy whole heart, and with thy whole soul, and with thy whole strength" (Deut. 6, 5). Hence, He says, *And he that taketh not up his cross, and followeth me, is not worthy of me.* He means that he who is not prepared to suffer even death on account of the truth, and the greatest death, namely, the death of the cross, *is not worthy of me*: nay, he ought to glory in the cross, as it is stated: "But God forbid that I should glory, save in the cross of the Lord" (Gal. 6, 14). And in saying this, He foretells His own death, and the manner of his death; "Christ suffered for us, leaving you an example that you should follow his steps" (I Pet. 2, 21). It is also expounded otherwise. It may be expounded that he accepts the cross, who afflicts his flesh, as it is stated: "They that are Christ's have crucified their flesh, with the vices and concupiscences," etc., (Gal. 5, 24). Likewise, the cross is carried in the heart, when one is saddened on account of sin, as the Apostle said: "Who is scandalized, and I am not on fire?" (II Cor. 11, 29). Likewise, that does not suffice except that the Lord be followed. Hence, *and followeth me.* If you fast, if you have compassion upon your neighbor, yet not for My sake, *you are not worthy of me.* For it is a great thing to follow the Lord, as it is stated: "It is great glory to follow the Lord"; but they could say, 'What will we have therefrom?' For that reason, He shows the punishment of the disobedient; hence, He says, *He that findeth his soul, shall lose it.* The soul denotes one's life: when someone is in danger of losing money, one is accustomed to say, 'I lost the money'; and if he is freed from the danger, he says that he found the money. Similarly, if someone is in bodily danger and is freed by some occasion, he says that he found his life. Therefore, he who finds his life, and will have been in danger for My sake, and denies Me, so that he may find life, *is not worthy of me. And he that shall lose his soul*, that is to say, his life, meaning if one will have exposed himself to death for My sake, *shall find it*; "He that shall find me, shall find life, and shall have salvation from the Lord" (Prov. 8, 35).

He that receiveth you, receiveth me. Here He sets forth a remedy. You say that we should make our living thus. Give to us an indulgence. Just as the Pope gives to his legates the power of granting an indulgence, so the Lord gives a reward to those receiving them. And He sets forth three things, of which two pertain to lesser matters. He says, therefore, *He that receiveth you, receiveth me*: because they will have God as a guest, because you are My members, because you are the body of Christ, members of member.[38] Hence, **He receiveth Me**. But they could say: 'You are a poor man: it is not a great thing to receive a poor man, such as yourself.' On the contrary, *he that receiveth me, receiveth him that sent me*: because, as it is stated, "He who honoureth the Son honoureth also My Father" (Jn. 5, 23). It is a great thing to have God as a guest, just as it was reputed unto the praise of Abraham, as it is stated in Hebrews 13.[39] Likewise, something else will be obtained, namely, the reward of a prophet. Hence, **He that receiveth a prophet in the name of a prophet, shall receive the reward of a prophet**. There are two excellent things in a prophet. The first, namely, is prophecy; "And it shall come to pass after this, that I will pour out my spirit upon all flesh: and your sons and your daughters shall prophesy" (Joel 2, 28); likewise, in them is the gift of justice; "But of him are you, who is made unto us wisdom and justice" (I Cor. 1, 30). This verse can also be understood thus: **He that receiveth a prophet in the name of a prophet**, that is, because he is a prophet, **shall receive the reward of a prophet**. You say that we ought to receive the Apostles. But some false prophets or false apostles will come; therefore, He says: 'I do not make a fuss about the truth, but about the name. Because he, who receives someone in the name of a prophet, will have a reward. And what reward? It will be the same which you would have if you would receive a true prophet. Hence, He says, **the reward of a prophet**, that is, which he would have for a prophet. Likewise, He does not make a fuss who he is, whether he be this or that prophet. For he who receives a prophet receives the reward of a prophet, because the prophet therefrom is more inclined to perform his work; because not only he, who does, receives a reward, "but they also that consent to them that do them," as it is stated at the end of Romans 1.[40] Hence, if you cooperate in a good work, from that good work you receive a reward; if you furnish what is needed to support a prophet's life, you will receive the reward of a prophet; because otherwise he could not fulfill his office. And what follows is similar: **He that receiveth a just man in the name of a just man, shall receive the reward of a just man**. But someone could say: 'If Peter or Elias were to

---

38. "Now you are the body of Christ and members of member" (I Cor. 12, 27).
39. "And hospitality do not forget: for by this some, being not aware of it, have entertained angels" (Heb. 13, 2).
40. Verse 32.

come, I would willingly receive him'; for that reason, He adds, ***And whosoever shall give to drink to one of these little ones***, that is, to the faithful, as it is stated below: "Amen I say to you, as long as you did it to one of these my least brethren, you did it to me," etc., (25, 40); it is as though He said: 'I do not care whether they are great or small.' Someone could say: 'I am poor; I do not have anything to give'; for that reason, He adds, ***A cup of cold water***: He does not say, ***of cold water***, on account of a scarcity of wood, lest one could thus excuse himself: hence, He wishes to say: 'Whatever least thing one shall have done, will have a reward.' And He confirms this, saying, ***Amen I say to you he shall not lose his reward***; "Behold the Lord shall come" (Is. 40, 10); and it continues, "And his reward is with him and his work is before him."

CHAPTER ELEVEN

1. And it came to pass, when Jesus had made an end of commanding his twelve disciples, he passed from thence, to teach and to preach in their cities.

2. Now when John had heard in prison the works of Christ: sending two of his disciples he said to him:

3. Art thou he that art to come, or look we for another?

4. And Jesus making answer said to them: Go and relate to John what you have heard and seen.

5. The blind see, the lame walk, the lepers are cleansed, the deaf hear, the dead rise again, the poor have the gospel preached to them.

6. And blessed is he that shall not be scandalized in me.

7. And when they went their way, Jesus began to say to the multitudes concerning John: What went you out into the desert to see? a reed shaken with the wind?

8. But what went you out to see? a man clothed in soft garments? Behold they that are clothed in soft garments, are in the houses of kings.

9. But what went you out to see? A prophet? Yea I tell you, and more than a prophet.

10. For this is he of whom it is written: Behold I send my angel before thy face, who shall prepare thy way before thee.

11. Amen I say to you, there hath not risen among them that are born of women a greater than John the Baptist: yet he that is the lesser in the kingdom of heaven is greater than he.

12. And from the days of John the Baptist until now, the kingdom of heaven suffereth violence, and the violent bear it away.

13. For all the prophets and the law prophesied until John:

14. And if you will receive it, he is Elias that is to come.

15. He that hath ears to hear, let him hear.

After saying these things, the Lord passed from thence in order to teach and preach; and this is on account of three things. One reason is so that what He had said by word, He might show by example; "Jesus began to do and to teach" (Acts 1, 1). Likewise, He did this to show that it is also necessary to preach to the unwise. Hence: "To the wise and to the unwise, I am a debtor" (Rom. 1, 14). Again, it was in order to give others a place of preaching, as it is stated: "But if anything be revealed to another sitting, let the first hold his peace" (I Cor. 14, 30). *Now when John had heard in prison the works of Christ.* Having set forth and confirmed Christ's doctrine, and the preachers having been instructed, here the rebellious are confuted. And firstly, He confutes John's disciples; and secondly, He confutes the scribes, where it is said, *And when they went their way*, etc. About the first, He does three things. Firstly, He confutes the doubtful; secondly, He accuses the crowds, where it is said, *But whereunto shall I esteem this generation to be like?*; and thirdly, He renders thanks for the Apostles' faith, where it is said, *At that time Jesus answered and said*, etc. About the first, to begin with, a question is put forth; and secondly, the solution of the question, where it is said, *And Jesus making answer*, etc. He says, therefore, *Now when John had heard in prison the works of Christ.* The occasion is related, why he sent these men. The same event is likewise found in Luke 7, nevertheless, it is in a different order. Therefore, the Evangelist says that John was in prison, as it was said above (chap. 4).[1] Then Jesus began to work miracles. And this was fitting, just as the sun does not appear when there are clouds. It is said below: "The prophets and the law were until John" (this chapter).[2] *Works*, that is, miracles, *of Christ: sending two of his disciples he said to him.*

Some men, on account of this passage, wish to condemn John, because he doubted whether Jesus was the Christ, and it is certain that a doubter of the faith is an infidel. Ambrose, on Luke, says that this question was not one of infidelity, but of piety: for he does not speak about His coming into the world, but of His coming to His Passion. Hence, he wonders if He had come to suffer, just as Peter said: "Be merciful to Thyself, O Lord" (below 16, 22).[3] But against this, Chrysostom says that John foreknew this from the beginning, since he said, "Behold the Lamb of God" (Jn. 1, 29). It is certain, therefore, that he knew that Christ was to be an immolated victim; hence, he is commended here by the Lord, that he is more than a prophet; but the prophets knew the future. Another reason is Gregory's, that it is not a question about His coming into the world, nor about His Passion, but about His descent into hell, because John was near to going to hell, for that reason he wished to be assured, *Art thou he that art to come*, etc.

But Chrysostom objects against this. Among those who are in hell, there is not a state of doing penance: hence, it seems that

---

1. "And when Jesus had heard that John was delivered up, he retired into Galilee" (above 4, 12).

2. Verse 13.

3. The verse literally reads, "Lord, be it far from thee."

this is said in vain. But this is not against Gregory, because John did not wish to make known the conversion of the world to the captives in hell, but to the just so that they might rejoice. There is another response. We read that the Lord would many times ask questions, not because He doubted, but in order to take away a calumny, as for instance, in John 11, 34, when He asked concerning Lazarus, "Where have you laid him?": not because He did not know, but so that those who showed to him the sepulcher would not be able to deny, nor calumniate Him: for that reason, John sent them, not because he doubted, but so that they would not calumniate, but instead confess Him. But why did he not send them before? It was because he was always with them, and, for that reason, he was assuring them; but when he willed to depart from them, he wanted them to be convinced by Christ.

He says, therefore, *Art thou he that art to come, or look we for another?* 'It is true that our Fathers awaited Thee,' as it is stated in Exodus 4.[4] *And Jesus making answer said to them*, etc. Here Christ's response is mentioned. Christ had many disciples, as is stated in John 4.[5] Therefore, there was a contention between them, because, seeing Christ's works, they preferred Christ to John. On the other hand, seeing John's abstinence, they preferred John to Christ. Hence, He firstly poses a question; secondly, He commends John. About the first, He responds according to His coming to His Passion. The time will come when God [as man] will suffer, and many will be scandalized, because He is a "stumblingblock unto the Jews" (I Cor. 1, 23). Hence, He responds when this will be. According to Chrysostom, He wishes to show that He came, whom the prophets foretold. Hence, three things were promised by the prophets. Sometimes, they were promising the coming of God, at other times, the coming of a new teacher, and at other times the coming of sanctification and redemption. 'How, therefore, will we know that God Himself will come?' And He answers in the way that it is answered in Isaias 35, 4: "God himself will come and will save us." Hence, 'you will see these miracles.' *Go and relate to John what you have heard*, in My teachings, *and seen*, in My miracles. Likewise, a teacher was being promised; "You, O children of Sion, rejoice," and it continues, "because he hath given you a teacher of justice" (Joel 2, 23). And this happened literally. It is answered likewise, if you ask, 'When

---

4. The Patriarchs showed their expectation of Christ by the practice of circumcision, a sign of their belief in the promise made to Abraham.

5. The text reads, "John had many disciples,' but this seems to be an error in the text. For John 4, 1 reads, "Jesus maketh more disciples and baptizeth more than John."

will He come?' "The spirit of the Lord is upon me: he hath sent me to preach to the meek (Isaias 61, 1)," or, in other words, to preach the Gospel; and this is signified when it is said, *the poor have the gospel preached to them*. He wished to signify something proper to Christ, as though He were to say: 'He will come to set forth a new doctrine.' *The poor have the gospel preached to them*, that is, poverty is preached; hence, it was said above: "Blessed are the poor in spirit: for theirs is the kingdom of heaven" (5, 3); and, "The spirit of the Lord is upon me. Wherefore he hath anointed me and hath sent me to preach the gospel to the poor" (Lk. 4, 18). Likewise, someone sanctified will come sanctifying sinners. Hence: "Sanctify the Lord of hosts himself" (Is. 8, 13). Hence, sanctification was being promised to some men, who, when they were sanctified, others were scandalized; hence, it is said, *And blessed is he that shall not be scandalized in me*. Hence: "Wherefore Jesus also, that he might sanctify the people by his own blood, suffered without the gate" (Heb. 13, 12). For that reason, He shows signs of His coming.

And if we speak morally, by this is signified the whole process of man's sanctification. For firstly, the sinner becomes blind when his reason is darkened; "Fire hath fallen on them, and they shall not see the sun" (Ps. 57, 9); and, "Bring forth the people that are blind, and have eyes" (Is. 43, 8). A man is said to be lame when his mind is drawn away to diverse things, as it is said: "How long do you halt between two sides?" (III Kings 18, 21). Likewise, he becomes full of sores in his deceits, and a leper, because then he cannot be drawn back, and infects others. And afterwards, he is made deaf, because he does not hear correction. Furthermore, he dies; "Rise, thou that sleepest, and arise from the dead" (Eph. 5, 14). And the Lord heals all these men, and, having been healed, they rise up to a certain firmness of mind, wherein there is true peace: "Much peace have they that love thy law, and to them there is no stumblingblock" (Ps. 118, 165).

And when they went their way, etc. Here He satisfies the doubt of the crowds. For the crowds had heard John's testimony concerning Christ; but now they seemed to be in doubt. For they could have three doubts in their hearts; because someone changes his word for three reasons: either on account of levity of mind, or for the sake of some benefit, or due to the human spirit, when he does not know the truth and afterwards learns it. "The Lord knoweth the thoughts of men, that they are vain" (Ps. 93, 11). For that reason, He firstly excludes levity from him; secondly, He excludes the desire of a benefit; and thirdly, He shows that he possesses the truth from prophetic knowledge. He says, therefore, *And when they went their way*, etc. The Lord teaches us great courteousness, because He did not wish to praise John with his disciples being present, just as neither did He wish to praise someone in his own presence, as it is stated: "Let another praise thee, and not thy own mouth: a stranger, and not thy own lips" (Prov. 27, 2). Because if he is good, he embarrasses him; if he is wicked, he flatters him. *What went you out into the desert to see?* Did you go out to see *a reed*? No. On the contrary, you went out to see a firm man. A reed, however, is easily moved with the wind; hence, a soul quickly changeable is reckoned a wind. "That henceforth we be no more children tossed to and fro and carried about with every wind" (Eph. 4, 14). Likewise, he is not light-minded for some benefit. *But what went you out to see?* For all riches pertain to some utility of the body, and this is either in food or in clothing: and it is clear that for none of these does he make a fuss. Therefore, it ought not to be believed that for some benefit would he give testimony to Christ; hence, He says, *What went you out to see? A man clothed in soft garments?* And why does He not make mention of food? It is because there could not be a doubt. He was clothed, however, of camel's hair. Hence, *they that are clothed in soft garments,* are not in the desert, but *in the houses of kings*. It is expounded differently by Chrysostom. Some men are made light-minded by nature, others are made light-minded by reason of their sins, as it is said: "Fornication, and wine, and drunkenness, take away the understanding" (Osee 4, 11). He eliminates the first possibility by His first words: He eliminates the second possibility by this which He says, *clothed in soft garments*, for that reason, he is not inconstant by reason of the sins of his life.

But here a question can arise concerning the pleasures derived from clothing, whether it is a sin; because if it is not a sin, it would not be charged to that rich man, who was daily clothed in purple and fine linen (Lk. 16, 19). Augustine responds that such things ought not to be considered, but the affection of the user: for every man ought to be clothed after the manner of those dwelling with him at the time, for that reason, the custom of clothing needs to be explained in more detail. For in some lands, all or many men are clothed with silk. Wherefore, some wear it sparingly, others wear it extensively, and in either manner it is distinguished: either it is worn on account of vainglory, and this is evil: or it is worn on account of its signification, as, for example, to designate a bishop or priest, and this is good.

Mystically, by men clothed in soft garments, adulators are signified: for he is clothed with soft garments, who makes great efforts with flattering words; for instance, proud men may seek glory in his mouth. And it is said: "A prince that gladly heareth lying words, hath all his servants wicked" (Prov. 29, 12).

But they might say: 'He is not inconstant, but he speaks by a human spirit,' and for that reason, He eliminates this possibility by saying, *But what went you out to see? A prophet?*, etc. Hence, He bears witness that John does not speak by a human spirit, but by a prophetic spirit. Hence, He first shows him to be a prophet; secondly, He shows him to be more than a prophet. For John was a prophet, as it is stated in Luke 1, 76: "And thou, child, shalt be called the prophet of the Highest," etc. Likewise, He extols him above the prophets saying, *Yea I tell you, and more than a prophet*: and this is true in regard to three things. Firstly, it is because it belongs to a prophet to foretell the future; he, however, shows not only the future, but also the present, saying: "Behold the Lamb of God. Behold him who taketh away the sin of the world." (Jn. 1, 29). Likewise, he is not only called a prophet, but also the Baptist, as said above (chap. 3).[6] Again, he is called the precursor, as it is stated: "For thou shalt, go before the face of the Lord to prepare his ways" (Lk. 1, 76). Moreover, he is more than a prophet so far as concerns his manner of prophesying: for he acted more miraculously than the prophets, because he prophesied from the womb, but the others did not, as it stated: "For behold as soon as the voice of thy salutation sounded in my ears, the infant in my womb leaped for joy" (Lk. 1, 44). *For this is he of whom it is written*. Here the Lord proves John's excellence. And firstly, He proves it by means of the authority of a prophet; secondly, He proves it by his special privileges, where it is said, *Amen I say to you*, etc. He says, therefore: 'I have said that he is more than a prophet, concerning whom it is written: *Behold I send my angel before thy face, who shall prepare thy way before thee*, etc.' (Mal. 3, 1). In this passage, John's points of excellence are set forth, because, firstly, He calls him an *angel*: for an angel is above a prophet, because just as a priest is in the middle between a prophet and the people, so a prophet is between the angels and the priests. An angel, however, is between God and the prophets; hence, Zacharias says, "The angel that spoke in me" (Zach. 1, 9). 'Angel' is the name of an office, not of a nature; hence, John is called an angel from his office: for

---

[6]. "And in those days cometh John the Baptist preaching in the desert of Judea" (Jn. 3, 1).

there is a difference between an angel and a prophet, because the angels see clearly, hence, it is stated below, where it is said: "For I say to you, that their angels in heaven always see the face of my Father who is in heaven" (18, 10). The angels always see the face of God, but the prophets do not. Hence, just as the angels always see the Father's face, so John specially saw Christ: and therefore, because he specially saw Him, for that reason He says, *my*. Again, He says, **Before my face**.[7] When a king walks in procession, many go before him, but those more intimately associated with him go before his face; so John is said to be more honorable, because he was sent before His face: for the nearer one is, the more honorable one is. Likewise, he was preparing the way, because he was baptizing; hence, He says, **Who shall prepare thy way before thee. Amen I say to you**, etc. Above, the Lord commended John by means of the authority of a prophet; now He intends to commend him by His own words, and He expounds the words of the prophet: and He does three things. Firstly, He commends him insofar as the difference of every order and state. And firstly, He commends him according to the difference of heavenly and earthly things; secondly, He commends him insofar as the difference of the Law and the Gospel; and thirdly, He commends him insofar as the difference of the present age and the future. And firstly, He shows him to be excellent among earthly things; secondly, He shows him to be the lesser among heavenly things, where it is said, **yet he that is the lesser in the kingdom of heaven is greater than he**. He says, therefore: 'It was said that John is an angel, and that I may briefly summarize, I say to you: **There hath not risen among them that are born of women a greater**.' He spoke in a strict sense when He said, **Hath risen**, because all men are born children of wrath, as it is written: "We were by nature children of wrath, even as the rest" (Eph. 2, 3).[8] Therefore, whosoever can arrive at the state of grace, rises. Hence, **Among them that are born of women**, etc. And He speaks significantly, such that Christ is excluded from this universality, because the word *mulier*[9] expresses corruption, but *femina*[10] expresses the sex; whence, if elsewhere 'son of a *mu-*

---

7. Here the words, "my face," seem to be taken from the passage cited by St. Matthew, namely, Malachias 3, 1.

8. All men born from Adam necessarily incur the debt of original sin (*de jure*) and thus are "children of wrath." But the Blessed Virgin Mary was exempted from actually contracting original sin (*de facto*) by her preventive redemption, Accordingly St. Thomas writes elsewhere, "Such was the purity of the Blessed Virgin Mary, who was exempt from both original and actual sin." (*Comm. in I Sent*, d. 44, q. 1, a. 3 ad 3um).

9. That is, "a married woman."

10. That is, "a woman."

lier' is found, such as in Jn. 19, 26: "Woman, behold thy son," it then names the sex, not the corruption.[11]

But what is it that He says: ***There hath not risen among them that are born of women a greater***? Is he on account of this statement, greater than all men? Jerome says that it does not follow that if a greater has not risen, then he is greater. Chrysostom, however, says that he is greater than all men. Therefore, according to the first exposition, I say that this argument is valid in reference to the angels, wherein exists a hierarchy, because that hierarchy, than which there is none greater, is the greatest; but among men it does not hold true, because among men there is not a hierarchy according to nature, only according to grace. Likewise, if it be said that he is greater than all the Old Testament Fathers, it is not unfitting: for a man is greater and more excellent, who is assumed to a greater office: for Abraham is greater among the Old Testament Fathers in regard to the trial of faith; but Moses is greater in regard to the office of a prophet, as it is stated: "There arose no more a prophet in Israel like unto Moses" (Deut. 34, 10). All these men were precursors of the Lord; no one, however, was in such excellence and favor; for that reason, John was assumed to the greater office; "He shall be great before the Lord" (Lk. 1, 15).

Yet he that is the lesser in the kingdom of heaven is greater than he. By the occasion of these words certain men have found an opportunity of calumniating: for they wish to condemn all the Old Testament Fathers: for if he is greater than the others, it follows that the others do not belong to the number of the saved: because by the kingdom of heaven the present Church is designated. If, therefore, John did not belong to the present Church, he was not belonging to the number of the elect, and therefore he was less than the others. And this opinion is erroneous, because it is clear that what the Lord says is said in praise of John.

Now this speech can be expounded in three ways. Firstly, it can be expounded such that by the kingdom of heaven the whole company of the blessed is understood: and he who is found among them as the lesser, is greater than any wayfarer. And for that reason, the Lord calls the present state of life a childhood. Hence: "When I became a man, I put away the things of a child" (I Cor. 13, 11), wherefore, He calls wayfarers children. And this is true

---

11. "He says women, not virgins. If the same word mulier, which denotes a married person, is anywhere in the Gospels applied to Mary, it should be known that the translator has there used 'mulier' for 'femina'; as in that, Woman, behold your son!" (*Catena Aurea on St. Matthew*, chap. 11, lect. 4)

by understanding the less in respect to actual excellence: for he who is already in possession of beatitude is actually excellent. It is otherwise concerning potential excellence, just as a small plant is said to be more excellent by its potential, although another is greater in size. It can be expounded otherwise, so that the kingdom of heaven designates the present Church: and the reason is, because the less is not said universally, but the less is said in relation to the time of His birth.[12] "He that shall come after me is preferred before me" (Jn. 1, 15 and above 3, 11).[13] Hence, He who is less in age, is greater than him. Or it can be expounded otherwise, that someone is said to be greater in two ways: either so far as concerns merit; and in this way many Patriarchs are greater than some men of the New Testament, just as Augustine says that the celibacy of John is not to be preferred to the wedlock of Abraham: or by comparing state to state, just as virgins are better than married persons; nevertheless, not every virgin is better than every married person: hence, John has this dignity, which is on a kind of a borderline, because he is greater than the wayfarers, but less than those actually possessing beatitude; hence, he holds a middle place.

And from the days of John the Baptist until now, etc. Here he is commended as to the division of the New and Old Testament. And John's excellence is pointed out, in that he is the beginning of the New Testament, and the end of the Old Testament. 'Therefore, I have said that *he that is the lesser in the kingdom of heaven is greater than he*': and this pertains to the fact that he is the beginning of the New Testament. But *from the days of John the Baptist*, that is, from John's preaching, *the kingdom of heaven suffereth violence*. This is expounded in three ways. You know that in robbery there is a certain violence and a certain effort; hence, it is necessary that for the sinner to come to the kingdom of heaven, he rise up to spiritual things, and make much effort. It is expounded otherwise. You know that the word robbery

---

12. "Aug; These words of the Lord may be understood in two ways. Either the kingdom of heaven is something which we have not yet received, that, namely, of which He speaks, *Come, you blessed of my Father, receive the kingdom*, because they in it are angels, therefore the least among them is greater than a righteous man who has a corruptible body. If we must understand the kingdom of heaven of the Church, whose children are all the righteous men from the beginning of the world until now, then the Lord speaks this of Himself, who was after John in the time of His birth, but greater in respect of His divine nature and supreme power. According then to the first interpretation it will be pointed, *He who is least in the kingdom of heaven, is greater than he*; according to the second, *He who is less than he, is in the kingdom of heaven greater than he*" (ibid).

13. "He that shall come after me, is mightier than I".

is employed in its proper sense when what belongs to another is taken by force against the will of the owner: the preaching of salvation was sent to the Jews, and by Christ it was sent everywhere. He says below, in chapter 15, 24: "I was not sent but to the sheep, that are lost of the house of Israel." And when He was being sent, they did not receive Him; nevertheless, those men to whom He was not sent, were taking salvation by force because of their humility. Hence: "Many shall come from the east and the west, and shall sit down with Abraham, and Isaac and Jacob in the kingdom of heaven; but the children of the kingdom shall be cast out into the exterior darkness" (above 8, 11-12). And it is said below: "The kingdom of God shall be taken from you and shall be given to a nation yielding the fruits thereof" (21, 43). Therefore, these men violently take salvation by force. And this is Hilary's exposition. There is a third exposition. That which is taken by force, is forcibly taken with haste; hence: "As the torrent that passeth swiftly in the valleys" (Job 6, 15); and this is on account of the speed of the movement. And because His preaching had so-moved the hearts of all men, it seemed to be a speedy occurrence. For that reason, He says, **Suffereth violence**, because they strive for the kingdom in a hasty manner; hence, the Gospel began from Him, and He Himself is the ending of the Law. Hence, Christ says, **For all the prophets and the law prophesied until John**: because all the prophets were on account of Christ; and they began to be fulfilled from the time of John's preaching. Hence: "All things must needs be fulfilled which are written concerning me" (Lk. 24, 44). And this prophesying of the prophets continued, **until John**.

But what is this? Were there not prophets after John? Do we not read below: "Behold I send to you prophets and wise men and scribes," etc., (23, 34)?

It ought to be said that a prophet is sent for two reasons: to confirm the faith, and to correct morals; "When prophecy shall fail, the people shall be scattered abroad," (Prov. 29, 18). A prophet is sent to confirm the faith, as it is stated: "Of which salvation the prophets have inquired and diligently searched, who prophesied of the grace to come in you, searching what or what manner of time the Spirit of Christ in them did signify" (I Pet. 1, 10). Hence, prophecy was serving these two purposes; but now the faith has been established, because the things promised with respect to Christ are fulfilled. But prophecy never fails, nor ever will fail for correcting morals. Therefore, John excels in that he is in the middle between the Old and New Law; hence, he was sent before His face almost at the same time as Christ.

And if you will receive it, he is Elias that is to come. Here He sets forth John's excellence as to the distinction of the present and the future Elias. For Elias was a precursor of the Lord, like John; hence: "Behold, I will send you Elias the prophet, before the coming of the great and dreadful day of the Lord," etc., (Mal. 4, 5). *And John is Elias.*

But what is that which the Lord is saying? Because when John was interrogated if he was Elias, he said that he was not. Now by this passage a certain heresy is extinguished, which put forward the transmigration of the soul, namely, that the soul went out from one body and entered into another body. For that reason, the soul of Elias entered John, as He was saying. But this opinion is false, because he himself denied that he was Elias. Christ, however, said that John was Elias on account of a threefold similarity. Firstly, John was Elias because, just as one angel is said to be similar to another angel, so John and Elias are equal in their office, because they both are precursors; "For he shalt go before the face of the Lord to prepare his ways," etc., (Lk. 1, 76). Likewise, John was Elias insofar as concerns his manner of life, because Elias led an austere life, as it is stated in III Kings 19. Likewise, John was Elias insofar as concerns persecution, because just as the latter was persecuted by Jezabel, so the former was persecuted by Herodias.[14] Hence, *if you will receive it*, as it ought to be received, *he is Elias*. And in order that they might understand that this was said mystically, He adds, *He that hath ears to hear,* that is, who spiritually has ears, *let him hear*, and understand.

16. But whereunto shall I esteem this generation to be like? It is like to children sitting in the market place.

17. Who crying to their companions say: We have piped to you, and you have not danced: we have lamented, and you have not mourned.

18. For John came neither eating nor drinking; and they say: He hath a devil.

19. The Son of man came eating and drinking, and they say: Behold a man that is a glutton and a wine drinker, a friend of publicans and sinners. And wisdom is justified by her children.

---

14. The text reads, "so the latter was persecuted by Herod" but "by Herodias" seems to fit the context better, namely, that both Elias and St. John the Baptist were persecuted by a woman. Accordingly, St. Ambrose wrote, "Why should I relate that Jezebel, also persecuted Elias after a bloodthirsty fashion (III Kings 19, 1 ff)? Or that Herodias caused John the Baptist to be slain (Mt. 14, 3 ff)?" (Letters 20, 18; MPL Vol. 16, n. 846).

Here He bursts out in a rebuke of the crowds. And firstly, He sets forth a question; secondly, He sets forth a kind of metaphor; and thirdly, He expounds it. He proceeds, therefore, thus: 'In this wise John is compared to Elias, but to what shall I compare this generation?' And why does He say this? He says this just as when someone did all the good he could do to another man, and that man is ungrateful, so that the benefactor does not know to whom he should be compared. So the Lord had done every good thing to this generation; hence: "What is there that I ought to do more to my vineyard, that I have not done to it?" (Is. 5, 4). 'To what shall I compare so great malice?'

It ought to be observed that sometimes a generation in Scriptures is taken for the congregation of the good, sometimes for the congregation of the wicked, and sometimes for the congregation of both. It is sometimes taken for the congregation of the good, as in Ps. 3, 2: "The generation of the righteous shall be blessed" (Ps. 111, 2). It is sometimes taken for the wicked congregation, where it is said above: "An evil and adulterous generation" (12, 39). It is sometimes taken for both, where it is said: "One generation passeth away, and another generation cometh: but the earth standeth forever" (Eccle. 1, 4).

It is like to children sitting in the market place, etc. Here He sets forth a kind of metaphor; and it can be explained according to the basic literal sense, or according to the mystical sense. Firstly, He sets forth the metaphor concerning the children; and secondly, He applies it, where it is said, **John came neither eating nor drinking**, etc.

For it ought to be observed that it is natural for man to seek pleasures, and he always seeks them, and unless he be detached by being very careful, he immediately falls into evil pleasures. But children are not very careful, for that reason they are unconcerned about the things which concern themselves, and this is why they play. Likewise, it ought to be observed that man is naturally social, and this is because one man naturally needs another, hence, he enjoys socializing. Hence, the Philosopher says in the first book of the *Politics*: "Every man who is a solitary, is either better than a man, and then he is a god; or he is worse than a man, and then is a beast." Hence, it is said, **sitting in the market place**, because no one wishes to play, except in a public place where a gathering of many men is made. Likewise, it ought to be observed that it is natural to man that his pleasure be in some representation: hence, if we were to see something sculpted well, which well represents what it ought, then we are delighted; for that reason, children, who delight in games, always make their games with some representation, either of war or of something else of this kind. Likewise, it ought to be observed that all the affections of the soul terminate in two passions, namely, either in joy or in sorrow.

Who crying, etc. This ought to be understood as follows. Let us suppose that there are children on one side, and others on the other, so that certain ones should sing, and others should dance; these children ought to do one thing, and the others ought to respond to them. If these were to sing, and those would not respond to them according to their plan, they would offend these children. Hence, they **say: We have piped to you, and you have not danced**. Likewise, nothing so transforms the spirit as singing; hence, Boethius reckons, in his *De Musica*, concerning a certain man who in the presence of Pythogoras was fighting with another man, and other men were singing a song. Then Pythogoras made the music to be changed, and the man stopped fighting; hence, all men were trained in music. For that reason, it ought to be noted that certain singing is for the sake of joy, as it is stated in Ecclesiasticus 40, 20: "Wine and music rejoice the heart"; for that reason, it is said: **We have piped**, that is, we have sung a song of joy, **and you have not danced**. Similarly, it is a common occurrence that just as some men are changed to joy by singing, so certain others are changed to weeping; hence: "Call for the mourning women, and let them take up a lamentation for us" (Jer. 9, 17-18). For that reason, they say, **We have lamented**, that is, we have made mournful songs, **and you have not mourned**. Mystically, by these children the people of the Old Testament are signified, among whom certain ones were motivators of spiritual joy, such as David: "Rejoice in the Lord, O ye just" (Ps. 32, 1). Certain others were motivators of sorrow, such as Joel: "Be converted to me with all your heart, in fasting, and in weeping, and mourning," etc., (2, 12). Hence, they can say, **We have piped**, that is, we have incited you to spiritual joy, and you did not take it up. **We have lamented**, that is, we invited to repentance, and you did not assent.

John came, etc. Here He applies the metaphor. And firstly, He applies it; and secondly, He gives the reasons. Men are doubly drawn to a good life; for some are drawn by the sight of holiness, others, however, are drawn by the way of friendliness. The Lord and John divided these two ways among themselves. John chose, rather the Lord chose for John, the way of austerity; He chose for Himself the way of leniency: and, nevertheless, by neither one were the Jews converted. Hence, He says, **John came neither eat-**

ing nor drinking: and this is said literally, because he was often abstaining. *And they say: He hath a devil*, just as hypocrites turn something good into something evil. *The Son of man came eating and drinking*, that is to say, He was using food differently, and it does not profit him, because you do not believe. On the contrary you say, *Behold a man that is a glutton and a wine drinker, a friend of publicans*; this is opposed to that which is written, "Be not in the feasts of great drinkers" (Prov. 23, 20).

Here it ought to be noted that he who heeds the sayings of men, never does anything well; "He that observeth the wind, shall not sow: and he that considereth the clouds, shall never reap" (Eccle. 11, 4).

But here there is a question. Why did the Lord choose for Himself the more lenient way, and demonstrate through John the more austere way? The reason for this is because the Lord was confirming His actions with miracles; John, however, was not performing miracles. For that reason, if he would have no excellence, his testimony would not be approved, just as we see in the Saints, that one has excellence in one thing, another in another thing; for instance, Augustine had excellence in doctrine, and Martin[15] had excellence in miracles. Likewise, another reason was that John was a pure man; for that reason, he was refraining himself from carnal desires. Christ, however, was God. For that reason, if He were to practice austerity, He would not be shown to be a man; for that reason, He assumed a more human life. Likewise, John was the end of the Old Testament, which imposed heavy burdens; but Christ was the beginning of the New Law, which employs the way of mildness.

And wisdom is justified by her children. This saying can be read in two ways. In one way, by referring it back to both things which were said concerning John and Christ; and then the sense is: when man does what he ought to do, and another man is not reformed, then he saves his own soul, and he is justified in his words. *Wisdom is justified*, namely, the Son of God, or Christ, that is to say, Wisdom, appeared just to her children, because He showed to the Jews what He ought to have shown them: He showed abstinence by John, and mildness by Christ. Or it can be meant in a different way. In this way, they might call His children devils, because *he is glutton and a wine drinker*; but the children of wisdom understand that life does not consist in food and drink, but in the evenness of mind, by

---

15. i.e. St. Martin of Tours.

using food and drink according to its place and time, and similarly, by abstaining when it is fitting, so that they do not exceed in a great amount or fall short in a small amount, as the Apostle says: "Every where and in all things I am instructed: both to be full and to be hungry: both to abound and to suffer need" (Phil. 4, 12). For that reason, He would not seem to show full justice if He would completely abstain, because it might be believed that the whole of justice consists in abstinence; but it does not consist in this, but in evenness of soul. And note that He says, **Wisdom**, because to use food, or to abstain from food, is according to the moderation of wisdom inasmuch as one abstains when one ought, and where one ought.

20. Then began he to upbraid the cities wherein were done the most of his miracles, for that they had not done penance.

21. Woe thee, Corozain, woe to thee, Bethsaida: for if in Tyre and Sidon had been wrought the miracles that have been wrought in you, they had long ago done penance in sackcloth and ashes.

22. But I say unto you, it shall be more tolerable for Tyre and Sidon in the day of judgment, than for you.

23. And thou Capharnaum, shalt thou be exalted up to heaven? thou shalt go down even unto hell. For if in Sodom had been wrought the miracles that have been wrought in thee, perhaps it had remained unto this day.

24. But I say unto you, that it shall be more tolerable for the land of Sodom in the day of judgment than for thee.

25. At that time Jesus answered and said: I confess to thee, O Father, Lord of Heaven and earth, because thou hast hid these things from the wise and prudent, and hast revealed them to little ones.

26. Yea, Father: for so hath it seemed good in thy sight.

27. All things are delivered to me by my Father. And no one knoweth the Son but the Father: neither doth any one know the Father, but the Son, and he to whom it shall please the Son to reveal him.

28. Come to me all you that labor and are burdened, and I will refresh you.

29. Take up my yoke upon you, and learn of me, because I am meek, and humble of heart: And you shall find rest to your souls.

30. For my yoke is sweet and my burden light

Above, He satisfied John's followers, now He upbraids the unbelievers: and He does two things. Firstly, what was done by the Lord is described; and secondly, His words are described, where it is said, ***Woe thee, Corozain***, etc. Upbraiding is in respect to benefits, and in respect to gifts. For the Lord had done a good deed, because He had enlightened them with His presence; hence, they were ungrateful, and for that reason they were deservedly upbraided; hence: "My people, what have I done to thee, or in what have I molested thee?" (Mic. 6, 3). It is as if He were to say, 'Nothing.' And He did not upbraid them because they had committed sins, but because they had not done penance: hence, what is said in Job 24, 23, befitted them: "God hath given him place for penance, and he abuseth it unto pride." And it is also said: "Knowest thou not that the benignity of God leadeth thee to penance?" (Rom. 2, 4)

But here there is a literal question, because Luke relates this in a different order. For he relates this at the time of the sending forth of the disciples;[16] Matthew relates it here. Augustine responds to this objection. It seems that Luke keeps more the chronological order: this Evangelist, however, follows the sequence of his memory.

But then it is objected that here it is said, ***Then***; therefore, it seems that here the historical sequence is followed. Augustine responds that ***then*** indicates an indefinite time. Or it can be said otherwise, that He said these words twice, and for that reason it could be that He said these words both at this time according to this Evangelist and at another time according to Luke.

Woe thee, Corozain, etc. Here the Lord's words are set forth. And firstly, a word is made about the suffragan cities, and secondly, about the metropolis, where it is said, ***And thou Capharnaum***, etc. And firstly, He compares guilt to guilt; secondly, He compares punishment to punishment, where it is said, ***But I say unto you***, etc. He says, therefore, ***Woe thee, Corozain***, etc. Now these are cities or towns in Galilee, where the Lord had performed many signs, and, nevertheless, they were not converted. For that reason, He says, ***Woe thee***, etc.

But what is it that the Lord is doing? On the contrary, it is written: "Curse not" (Rom. 12, 14). It ought to be pointed out that it is one thing to curse formally and it is another thing to curse materially. No one ought to curse formally, but one can curse materially. Hence, it should be observed that certain things are

---

16. cf. Luke 10, 13. In this chapter the 12 disciples are sent forth to preach.

joined together according to the sense, which, nevertheless, can be separated according to the intellect. For instance, in an apple there is the smell and the taste, which cannot be separated according to the senses, although they can be separated according to the intellect. Similarly, to want this man not to be punished, and to want the order of justice, cannot be at the same time, except according to the intellect. Hence, if I curse this man, because I delight in his harm, it is something evil. If, however, I delight not on account of his harm, but on account of the order of justice, in this way it is good. Hence, the Lord's words were not words of one delighting, but of one declaring the work of justice.

Woe thee, Corozain. Corozain is interpreted 'service to it.' Bethsaida is interpreted 'the house of fruits.' To whom more is entrusted, from him more is demanded. And why was more shown to it? It is because He fulfilled His ministry there: for that reason: "The wrath of God is revealed from heaven against all ungodliness and injustice of those men that detain the truth of God in injustice" (Rom. 1, 18). Bethsaida is 'the house of fruits.' If, therefore, the Lord bore fruit there, and they did not do penance, what will they deserve? "I looked that it should bring forth grapes, and it hath brought forth wild grapes" (Is. 5, 4). *Woe to thee... for if in Tyre and Sidon had been wrought the miracles that have been wrought in you, they had long ago done penance in sackcloth and ashes.* **Long ago**, that is, in the distant past.

And observe the manner of penance, because it was in ashes and sackcloth, because two things induce to penance. One is the remembrance of sins; and this is signified in the sackcloth, because it is made from the hairs of goats: for this animal was immolated for sin. The other is the consideration of death and the condition of human fragility; hence, it is said: "Dust thou art, and into dust thou shalt return" (Gen. 3, 19). And: "Therefore I reprehend myself, and do penance in dust and ashes" (Job. 42, 6).

But I say unto you, it shall be more tolerable for Tyre and Sidon in the day of judgment, than for you. Here He compares guilt to guilt, because if they are found more guilty, it will be worse for them: because what they heard, they did not do. For that reason, Corozain will have greater guilt, according to what is said: "If I had not come and spoken to them, they would not have sin" (Jn. 15, 22). It ought to be noted that from these words He excludes three errors. Certain men were saying all sins are equal, and similarly, all punishments are equal; He excludes this when He says that for these men it will be worse than for Tyre and Sidon. Likewise, certain men said that men could not be saved except those whom He foreknew: because if He preached to them, they would be converted. He excludes this when He says it will be bad for Tyre and Sidon, but, nevertheless, worse for these men, to whom the kingdom of God was announced. Hence, Augustine says in his *Book of Perseverance*: "The Lord does not remunerate for those things which one had done, but for those things which one does." Likewise, He removes a third error, because certain men were saying that the Lord sent the prophets and the preachers to the Jews, and not to other men: because He knew that others would not receive them. But He excludes this, because if He preached to them (Tyre and Sidon), they would have done penance.

But then a question remains: that if the Jews did not believe, it would seem that the Lord had not done well, since He did not send to the men in Tyre and Sidon, when they would have believed. Gregory says that to know God's secrets does not belong to man; nevertheless, according to what is seen, it was because it had been promised to the Old Testament Fathers, for that reason, to confirm the promises of the Fathers, He firstly preached to the Jews. Likewise, it was so that their condemnation might be shown to be more just, for that reason, He preached to them and afterwards sent His disciples to them. Remigius solves the question thus: it was because, although from Tyre and Sidon more men had believed in a greater numbers; nevertheless, among them were some perverse men, who were not yet prepared to believe; for that reason, He did not firstly send preachers to them. Augustine sets forth a third explanation, that the Lord foreknew that if they had believed, they would not have persevered in the time of the Passion; and for that reason, He did not send preachers to them. There is another explanation of Augustine, that predestination is the foreknowledge of God's benefits. Hence, whatever things pertain to salvation, are effects of predestination in the predestined: hence, the Lord distributes His gifts in different ways, because to certain men He gives a docile heart and an inclination to acting well; but this does not suffice unless there be an instructor. Likewise, sometimes there is an instructor, but the heart is hard: and just as for the former men a readiness to believe does not suffice, so a hard heart harms these men. Hence, to ask why He chooses this and not that man, is a foolish question; hence, Augustine says: "Why God draws this and not that man, do not judge if you do not wish to err." Hence, it is better that the whole matter be referred to God's ordinance than to human merits.

And thou Capharnaum, shalt thou be exalted up to heaven? In this part He upbraids the more important city. And firstly, He upbraids their pride, and this is because great men are more proud; secondly, He upbraids their impenitence, where it is said, **For if in Sodom had been wrought the miracles**, etc. About the former, He firstly upbraids their pride; and secondly, He threatens their punishment. He says, therefore, **And thou Capharnaum**, etc. And there is in this passage a double literal sense. One is interrogative. **Shalt thou be exalted up to heaven?** Another literal sense is, 'You are the city which has been exalted up to heaven.' For it was exalted by the Lord, both by the Lord's presence and His many good actions; "As great things as we have heard done in Capharnaum, do also here in thy own country" (Lk. 4, 23). Likewise, 'You exalted yourself: hence, were you exalted through pride, or by my doctrine? Howsoever much you were exalted, nevertheless, **thou shalt go down unto hell**'; "He shall be pulled down in the day of God's wrath; this is the portion of a wicked man from God" (Job 20, 28-29). Hence, you, who seemed to touch the sky, shall be pulled down to hell. Hence, the proper punishment of pride is casting down; in Isaias 14, 14 it is said against him who was saying, "I will ascend the stars of heaven," and it continues, "Thou shalt be brought down to hell." Afterwards, He accuses them of impenitence. And firstly, He compares them as to their guilt; and secondly, He compares them as to their punishment. He says, therefore, **For if in Sodom**, etc. And why does He say this? It is to signify the liberty of free will: because before man is life and death. No one warned them:[17] although Lot was among them, nevertheless, he did not perform miracles. But these men saw the Lord teaching and performing miracles, therefore, etc. Capharnaum is interpreted 'very pleasant village,' and Jerusalem has a similar meaning.[18] **But I say unto you**: 'On Judgment Day your punishment will be more severe than the punishment of that land, which was completely ruined.' Or it can be understood of its inhabitants; "And that servant, who knew the will of his lord and prepared not himself and did not according to his will, shall be beaten with many stripes" (Lk. 12, 47). **At that time Jesus answered and said: I confess to thee, O Father**, etc. Above, the Lord had upbraided the infidelity of the crowds; now He gives thanks for the faith of the disciples and of the other believers. And firstly, He renders thanks to the Father as the author; secondly, He shows Himself to have the same power, where it is said, **All things are delivered to me by my Father**. He says, therefore, **At that time**, namely, the

17. i.e. the inhabitants of Sodom.
18. 'Jerusalem' means 'vision of peace.'

time in which it occurred, etc., *Jesus answered*. But to whom does He answer? Does not what is said in Job 15, 2, apply to Him: "Will a wise man answer as if he were speaking in the wind?" It does not. Hence, He is answering to a tacit objection. For someone will say, 'These men to whom Thou has preached do not believe; other men, however, would have believed if it had been preached to them.' For that reason He answers, and by His answer He rebukes those who seek the reasons of the election, that is to say, why some are raised up into heaven, and others are cast down into hell. Take, for example, Origen, who asserted that a man's election was due to his merits. But here He reproves this opinion, showing that this ought to be attributed to the Divine will. He says, therefore, *I confess to thee, O Father*.

It ought to be observed that there are three kinds of confession. The first is, namely, the confession of faith; hence, in Romans 10, 10, it is said: "With the heart, we believe unto justice: but, with the mouth, confession is made unto salvation" (Rom. 10, 10). Likewise, there is the confession of sins; "Confess your sins one to another" (James 5, 16). Moreover, there is the confession of thanksgiving, about which it is said: "Give glory to the Lord, for he is good" (Ps. 105, 1). Of this latter kind is understood the Lord's words, *I confess to thee, O Father, Lord of Heaven and earth*. Two heresies are excluded, namely, the heresy of Sabellius, who did not distinguish the Son from the Father; hence, He says, *I confess to thee, O Father*, etc. Likewise, He excludes the heresy that the Father and the Son are not of the same nature. For that reason, He speaks of His own Father, which is against Arius. And He is truly the Lord, because He is the Father of Heaven and earth. And in Psalm 99, 3 it is said: "Know ye that the Lord he is God: he made us." And He is called His Father, not because He created Him, but because He begot Him; "He shall cry out to me: Thou art my father" (Ps. 88, 27). And why does He give thanks? He gives thanks concerning a certain differentiation, and He puts it thus, *Because thou hast hid these things from the wise and prudent, and hast revealed them to little ones*. Hence, one ought to consider here who are the little ones, and who are the wise, and who are the prudent. Some men are said to be little ones in three ways. Literally, the despised are called little ones; hence, in Abdias, verse 2, it is said: "Behold I have made thee small among the nations: thou art exceeding contemptible." Likewise, a man is said to be a little one by his humility, because he deems himself to have but few good qualities. Again, a man is said to be little by his simplicity: hence, the Apostle says: "In malice be children" (I

Cor. 14, 20). Hence, that passage can be understood to mean that 'Thou hast revealed these things to little ones and to despised fishermen.' And why is this? The Apostle gives the reason, saying, it is because "The foolish things of the world hath God chosen, that he may confound the wise" (I Cor. 1, 27). Augustine expounds this passage thus: "*To little ones*, that is, to the humble who do not presume about themselves: for where there is humility, there is wisdom." Hilary expounds this passage as concerning the simple. "Seek him in simplicity" (Wis. 1, 1). On the contrary, the wise and the prudent do not seek Him in simplicity, because they endeavor to seek Him in carnal wisdom; "Let not the wise man glory in his wisdom" (Jer. 9, 23). He did not reveal Himself to these men, but to rustic men not trusting in their own wisdom; "I have said: I will be wise: and it departed farther from me, much more than it was" (Eccle. 7, 24). For which reason the Apostle says: "For they, not knowing the justice of God and seeking to establish their own, have not submitted themselves to the justice of God" (Rom. 10, 3). Likewise, by the wise He understands proud men boasting about themselves; and He does not reveal Himself to such men. "Professing themselves to be wise, they became fools" (Rom. 1, 22). Similarly, He calls wise men those living according to the flesh, seeking the things which are of the flesh, but not the things which are of God (Phil. 2, 21). "They are wise to do evil, but to do good they have no knowledge" (Jer. 4, 22). *And thou hast revealed*. "That you walk not as also the Gentiles walk in the vanity of their mind" (Eph. 4, 17). Hence, *thou hast hid these things from the wise*, by revealing them to little ones. He hid wisdom from the wise, by not providing grace. Hence, it is said: "God delivered them up to a reprobate sense" (1, 28).

But does He give thanks because His Father hid these things from them? I say that He does not do this, to rejoice in their blindness, but to rejoice in the justice of God, who ordains so wisely. And why? Here the reason is not to be sought: for in such matters God's will is, as it were, the cause.

Yea, Father: for so hath it seemed good in thy sight. A builder can well give the reason why he placed certain stones in the foundation, and certain ones higher; but that he will have placed this one here and another one there, there is no other reason except his own will. Thus, that the Lord saves some men, this is due to His mercy, and that He damns others, this is due to His justice. But why He acts so mercifully about this man, rather than about another, this pertains solely to His Divine will. Hence: "He hath mercy on whom he will. And whom he will, he hardeneth" (Rom. 9, 18). Wherefore, He does so on account of His good pleasure. In Psalm 118, 108, it is said: "Do thy good pleasure, O Lord," etc. *All things are delivered to me by my Father.* He had given thanks to His Father, because He reveals His secrets to little ones: someone might believe that He Himself could not reveal these secrets. Hence, to do away with this opinion, He firstly mentions the greatness of His power; and secondly, He invites men to Himself; as though He were to say, 'Behold I am powerful; therefore come to Me,' etc. And firstly, He does two things. He firstly asserts the equality of the Son to the Father; and secondly, He applies this spiritually to the matter being discussed, where it is said, *And no one knoweth the Son but the Father.* He says, therefore: Someone could say, 'Can He do all things?' He answers, *All things are delivered to me.* And notice His equality, but nevertheless, His origin is from His Father, which is against Sabellius.

But what is it that He says, *All things*? It can be expounded in three ways. *All things*, this means He is over every creature. "All power is given to me in heaven and in earth" (Mt. 28, 18). Or, *All things are delivered to Me,* that is, the elect and the predestined, who are specially given to Him; "Thine they were: and to me thou gavest them" (Jn. 17, 5). Likewise, *All things*, namely, all things intrinsic to His nature are given to Him, that is, every perfection of the divinity; "As the Father hath life in himself, so he hath given to the Son also to have life in himself" (Jn. 5, 26). And we ought not to understand this corporeally, because, although He gave all things to the Son, He also retained them for Himself. And this explanation is Augustine's and Hilary's. But someone could say, 'How did He give all things?' For that reason, He adds the manner, when He says, *By my Father.* Hence, He receives these things through His generation.

And no one knoweth the Son but the Father. Now He specifically comes to the point, not only insofar as regards His equality to the Father, but also insofar as regards His consubstantiality. For the Father's substance is above all understanding, since the Father's essence itself is called unknowable, just like the Son's substance is called unknowable. Hence, here His equality may be observed, and Arius is confounded, who says the Father is invisible, but the Son is visible. *No one knoweth the Son but the Father.*

But what is this? Did not the Saints know the Son? I answer, saying that they know by coming in contact with Him, or by faith, but not by comprehending Him.

But what is this? Does not the Holy Ghost know Him? He does indeed. But it ought to be observed that exclusive expressions are sometimes added to the essential Divine names, and sometimes they are added to the personal names. And when they are adjoined to the personal names, they do not exclude that which is the same in the nature: wherefore, the names added to the Father do not exclude the Son. Hence, where it is said, "To the king of ages, immortal, invisible, the only God, be honour and glory" (I Tim. 1, 17), another Person is not excluded in His nature. Similarly, when He says here, **But the Son**, the Holy Ghost is not excluded, who is the same in the nature. But when He says, **No one knoweth**, etc., no human is understood except the Son. And in this way it is held that the Son knows the Father. But this is against Origen. For the Son knows the Father by comprehension. Therefore, because He knows the Father perfectly, and the Father is perfectly knowable, for that reason, He has the power of revealing the Father, just as the Father has; thus it is said, **And he to whom it shall please the Son to reveal him**. For the manifestation of the Father is through the Word; "I have manifested thy name to the men," etc., (Jn. 17, 6). And it is said, "No man hath seen God at any time," (ibid. 1, 18). But He knew the Father: therefore, He could manifest Him. Therefore, that which He had said about the Father, He attributed to Himself. For He had said, **Thou hast hid these things from the wise and prudent, and hast revealed them to little ones**; thus, the Son can reveal just as the Father can, from whom He has the same power.

Come to me all you, etc. 'Come to My benefits.' And firstly, the invitation is set forth; secondly, the necessity of the invitation is set forth; and thirdly, the usefulness of the invitation is set forth. He says, therefore: **Come to me**; which words are also found in a Sapiential book: "Come over to me, all ye that desire me, and be filled with my fruits" (Eccli. 24, 26). Hence, 'Draw near to Me ye unlearned,' because He wishes to give Himself. But what is the necessity of drawing near to Him? It is because, 'Without Me men labor too much'; **You that labor**. This particularly applies to the Jews, because they were laboring under the burdens of laws and commandments, as it is stated: "This is the burden which neither our fathers nor we have been able to bear" (Acts 15, 10). Likewise, this is said generally as referring to all men who labor on account of their human frailty; "I am poor, and in labors from my youth" (Ps. 87, 16). **And are burdened**, by the burden, namely, of their sins. "My iniquities as a heavy burden are become heavy upon me" (Ps. 37, 5). 'And what will we have if we would come to

Thee?' *I will refresh you.* "If any man thirst, let him come to me and drink" (Jn.7, 37). He afterwards explains the invitation. And firstly, He explains the invitation; and secondly, He assigns its reason, where it is said, *For my yoke is sweet*. About this first point it is as follows. He had put forth an invitation, and He had said to what purpose He had put it forth. Now He wishes to show what is the invitation, saying, *Take up my yoke upon you*. But what is this? 'Thou sayest that Thou dost want to refresh us, and to take labor away from us, and immediately Thou dost command us to bear a yoke? We believed that we would be without a yoke.' 'I say that it is true, you will be without the yoke of sin'; "For the yoke of their burden, and the rod of their shoulder, and the sceptre of their oppressor thou hast overcome" (Is. 9, 4). 'It is not that you may be without the law of God, but that you may be without the yoke of sin'; "Let us cast away their yoke from us" (Ps. 2, 3). "Return, O Israel, to the Lord thy God: for thou hast fallen down by thy iniquity," etc., (Osee 14, 2). "Being then freed from sin, we have been made servants of justice" (Rom. 6, 18). *Take up*, therefore, *my yoke*; namely, the teaching of the Gospel. And it is called a yoke, for just as a yoke joins and binds the necks of oxen for plowing, so the teaching of the Gospel binds both peoples[19] to its yoke. And what is that which is said: *Learn of me, because I am meek, and humble of heart*? For the whole New Law consists in two things: in meekness and humility. By meekness, a man is ordained to his neighbor. Hence: "O Lord, remember David, and all his meekness" (Ps. 131, 1). By humility, he is ordained to himself and to God. "Upon whom shall my spirit rest, but upon him that is quiet and humble" (Is. 66, 2). Hence, humility makes a man capable of being filled with God. Likewise, He had said, *I will refresh you*. What is this refreshment? *You shall find rest to your souls*. For the body is not refreshed as long as it is afflicted, and when it is no longer afflicted, then it is said to be refreshed. And just as hunger is in the body, so desire is in the mind: hence, the fulfillment of desires is refreshment; "Who satisfieth thy desire with good things," (Ps. 102, 5). And this rest is the rest of the soul; "I have laboured a little, and have found much rest" (Eccli. 51, 35). In this way, the meek are not quieted in the world: hence, *you shall find* everlasting *rest*, namely, the fulfillment of your desires. 'But do not be surprised if I invite you to take up My yoke, because My yoke is not a burden.' Why? *For*

---

19. i.e. the Jews and the Gentiles. "RABAN; The yoke of Christ is Christ's Gospel which joins and yokes together Jews and Gentiles in the unity of the faith" (*Catena Aurea on St. Matthew*, chap. 11, lect. 11).

my yoke is sweet and enjoyable; "How sweet are thy words to my palate!" (Ps. 118, 103). ***And my burden light.*** And these things can refer to two things. By a yoke oxen are held, but a burden is carried: hence, His yoke refers to the negative precepts, and His burden refers to the positive precepts.

But this seems to be false, because the burden of the New Law seems very heavy, as above it was said: "You have heard that it was said to them of old: Thou shalt not kill... But I say to you, that whosoever is angry with his brother, shall be in danger of the judgment" (5, 21): and so it seems to be a heavy burden. Likewise, it was said above: "Strait is the way that leadeth to life" (7, 14). Likewise, the Apostle says, "In many more labours" (II Cor. 11, 23). Hence, it seems to be a very heavy yoke.

For that reason, two things ought to be considered: the effect of the doctrine and the circumstances of the works; and, in all things, Christ's doctrine is light in practice, because it changes the heart in that it makes us not to love temporal things, but rather spiritual things. For a man who loves temporal things, to lose a little is more burdensome than for a man who loves spiritual things to lose much. The Old Law did not forbid those temporal things, and, for that reason, it was burdensome for those men to lose them. But now, even if, at the beginning, it is somewhat heavy, afterwards, nevertheless, it is light; "I will lead thee by the paths of equity, which when thou shalt have entered, thy steps shall not be straitened" (Prov. 4, 11-12). Furthermore, regarding the works, the Law burdened with exterior acts. Our Law, however, is only in the will; hence: "The kingdom of God is not meat and drink" (Rom. 15, 17). Similarly, Christ's Law gives joy; hence, the Apostle says, "But justice and peace and joy in the Holy Ghost" (Rom. 14, 17). Likewise, regarding the circumstances, it can be said that in the New Law there are many adversities, hence, "They that will live godly in Christ Jesus shall suffer persecution" (II Tim. 3, 12). But these are not heavy, because they are seasoned with the seasoning of love, because when someone loves another, whatever he suffers from him does not burden him: hence, love makes all weighty and impossible things light. Hence, if someone loves Christ well, nothing is heavy to him, and for that reason, the New Law does not burden.

CHAPTER TWELVE

1. At that time Jesus went through the corn on the sabbath: and his disciples being hungry, began to pluck the ears, and to eat.
2. And the Pharisees seeing them, said to him: Behold thy disciples do that which is not lawful to do on the sabbath days.
3. But he said to them: Have you not read what David did when he was hungry, and they that were with him:
4. How he entered into the house of God, and did eat the loaves of proposition, which it was not lawful for him to eat, nor for them that were with him, but for the priests only?
5. Or have ye not read in the law, that on the sabbath days the priests in the temple break the sabbath, and are without blame?
6. But I tell you that there is here a greater than the temple.
7. And if you knew what this meaneth: I will have mercy, and not sacrifice: you would never have condemned the innocent.
8. For the Son of man is Lord even of the sabbath.
9. And when he had passed from thence, he came into their synagogues.
10. And behold there was a man who had a withered hand, and they asked him, saying: Is it lawful to heal on the sabbath days? that they might accuse him.
11. But he said to them: What man shall there be among you, that hath one sheep: and if the same fall into a pit on the sabbath day, will he not take hold on it and lift it up?
12. How much better is a man than a sheep? Therefore it is lawful to do a good deed on the sabbath days.
13. Then he saith to the man: Stretch forth thy hand; and he stretched it forth, and it was restored to health even as the other.
14. And the Pharisees going out made a consultation against him, how they might destroy him.
15. But Jesus knowing it, retired from thence: and many followed him, and he healed them all.
16. And he charged them that they should not make him known.
17. That it might be fulfilled which was spoken by Isaias the prophet, saying:

18. Behold my servant whom I have chosen, my beloved in whom my soul hath been well pleased. I will put my spirit upon him, and he shall shew judgment to the Gentiles.

19. He shall not contend, nor cry out, neither shall any man hear his voice in the streets.

20. The bruised reed he shall not break: and smoking flax he shall not extinguish: till he send forth judgment unto victory.

21. And in his name the Gentiles shall hope.

Above, you have heard how the Lord satisfied John's disciples and rebuked those who did not believe in Him; here the Evangelist shows how the Pharisees are restrained. And he does two things. Firstly, he shows how Christ rebuked the Pharisees, and secondly, how the disciples are commended. And he does two things. Firstly, he shows how those criticizing the disciples are refuted; and secondly, how those criticizing Christ are refuted, where it is said, *And when He had passed from thence*, etc. About the first, the occasion of the reproving is related; secondly, the reproving is related, where it is said, *And the Pharisees seeing*, etc.; and thirdly, Christ's defense is related where it is said, *But he said to them*, etc. Now a twofold occasion is related; one is on the part of Christ, and the second is on the part of the disciples, where it is said, *And his disciples began to pluck the ears*. On the part of Christ, he says, *At that time Jesus went through the corn on the sabbath*. The Lord knew that the disciples were going to do this, and, nevertheless, the Lord let this happen, so that He might then begin to dissolve the Sabbath, as it is stated above: "The prophets and the law prophesied until John" (above 11, 13).

But it ought to be observed what is said, *At that time*; because the designation of time which is set forth here seems to pertain to the order of history; but Luke and Mark relate these events in a different order. Hence, all the preceding events seem to have occurred before John's death, but here they are after his death. And this is evident, for all the things that are said up until chapter 14, and, at that point, mention is made of John's death. Thus, it ought to be understood that, when his suffering was imminent, John sent his disciples, and then he was beheaded, and then these things occurred after his death.

Jesus went through the corn on the sabbath. By this corn, Holy Writ is understood. The sower is Christ; "He Himself is he who soweth" (below 13, 37). Similarly, the corn is the faithful people. *His disciples being hungry, began to pluck the ears.* Here two things ought to be considered. The first is their neediness, because they were hungry. And why was this? It is because they were poor; hence: "Even unto this hour we both hunger and thirst," etc., (I Cor. 4, 4). The second reason is that they were daily hindered from eating on account of the crowds; hence, they scarcely had time for eating, as it is stated in Mk. 6.[1] But how did they satisfy their hunger? An example of abstinence is given to us; hence, these men did not seek large plates of food, but ears of corn, according to the passage: "Having food and wherewith to be covered, with these we are content" (I Tim 6, 8). Mystically, in the plucking of the ears is understood the multiplicity of understanding of the Scriptures, or the conversion of sinners. Then he relates the reproving of the Pharisees; *And the Pharisees seeing them, said to him: Behold thy disciples do that which is not lawful to do on the sabbath days.* The disciples were doing two bad things: firstly, they were plucking another man's ears of corn, and secondly, they were violating the Sabbath. But the Pharisees were not reprehending them about the first, because that was permitted in the Law (Deut. 23).[2] For that reason, because it had been permitted, they were not blaming them unjustly about the first, but because they were plucking on the Sabbath, they were blaming them unjustly. And this overturns the heresy of the Hebrews, who were saying that the legal observances ought to be kept with the Gospel. And because Paul was opposed to this opinion, therefore they were reproving Paul. Against these men, Jerome argues that even the disciples were not keeping them. *But he said to them.* Here an excuse is given. And firstly, an excuse is given by certain examples, and secondly, by a passage from Scripture, where it is said, *And if you knew what this meaneth.* Regarding the first, He does two things. Firstly, He gives an example in which some men are excused on account of their neediness; secondly, He gives an excuse in which some men are excused on account of the holiness of the Temple, where it is said, *Or have ye not read in the law,* etc. He says, therefore, *But he said,* etc. In Leviticus 24 it is read that they used to make twelve loaves out of pure fine flour, and these were put on the table of proposition on the Sabbath. And on another Sabbath they were removed, and others were put in their place, and those first

---

[1]. "Come apart into a desert place, and rest a little. For there were many coming and going: and they had not so much as time to eat" (Mk. 6, 31).

[2]. "If thou go into thy friend's corn, thou mayst break the ears, and rub them in thy hand" (verse 25).

ones were eaten by the sons of Aaron. Likewise, it is found in I Kings 21 that when David fled from Saul, Abimelech shared those loaves with him and his men. And this is what He says, ***Have you not read what David did when he was hungry, and they that were with him?*** For this David was a good man, concerning whom the Lord said that He found a man according to His own heart (I Kings 13, 14). But someone will say: 'This David was a prophet, therefore, he was able to take the bread.' For that reason, He adds, ***And they that were with him.*** They were called 'loaves of proposition' which were offered on the Sabbath, to which men it was not lawful to use according to the precept, as it is stated in Leviticus 23.[3] But what does this have to do with the question in point? It is because when he did this, it was the Sabbath. And this is evident, because there it is said: "I do not have loaves of bread, except those I took from the Lord's table." And this he did not do, except on the Sabbath. Likewise, the feast of the new moon occurred on the day of the Calends:[4] for that reason, if it fell on the Sabbath, the Sabbath was necessarily broken.[5]

But still it seems that David did not break the Sabbath, because it is not a sin to eat on the Sabbath: hence, it seems that he did not break the Sabbath. But Chrysostom says that David broke the Sabbath more than Christ, because he took those loaves, which were not lawful for anyone to take, due to his neediness. It is found, however, that the Sabbath was broken by the Machabees on account of their necessity.

Likewise, it ought to be observed what Chrysostom says, that there are certain precepts that are prescribed on account of themselves, and these cannot be broken for any necessity. But there are certain others which are prescribed, not on account of themselves, but on account of their signification, and for that reason, such precepts can be broken in certain places and times, as, for instance, fasting can be omitted in necessity. Now that bread was a figure of another bread, namely, the bread of the altar, which is not only received by the priest, but also by other people; for that reason, David signifies in that passage the people. Hence: "Thou hast made us to our God a kingdom and priests" (Apoc. 5, 10).

Similarly, another example is set forth, namely, that it is related that some men were excused on account of the holiness of the Temple. And this passage is where it is said, ***Have ye not***

---

3. "And when the priest hath lifted them up with the loaves of the firstfruits before the Lord, they shall fall to his use" (verse 20).

4. i.e. the first day of the month.

5. "And on the first day of the month you shall offer a holocaust to the Lord, two calves of the herd, one ram, and seven lambs of a year old, without blemish" (Num. 28, 11).

read in the law, that on the sabbath days the priests in the temple break the sabbath, and are without blame? In Leviticus it had been prescribed that the oblation was doubled on the Sabbath, which was usually offered other days, and nevertheless, it was made on the Sabbath, because it was made for the service of the Temple and of God. Wherefore, the priests were excused. Hence, that example is used because the Apostles had completely dedicated themselves to one greater than the Temple, namely, to Christ. Hence, He says, *Have ye not read in the law, that on the sabbath days the priests in the temple were breaking the sabbath?* This killing of animals on the Sabbath would indeed violate the Sabbath if it were not done on account of the Temple. *But I tell you that there is here a greater than the temple.* The word *here*[6] is an adverb of place, and for the service of that place these men are acting. And what He insists to be something greater than the Temple is evident, for His own body is a Temple. Likewise, it ought to be seen that in the first example He did not assert that David was without fault. In the second, He asserts that if a man break the Sabbath on account of necessity, nevertheless, a man is not completely without fault; but if he break the Sabbath on account of God, he is entirely without fault. Then He concludes from the examples. And firstly, He concludes that one ought to act mercifully with His disciples. *Because if you knew what this meaneth: I will have mercy, and not sacrifice: you would never have condemned the innocent* (Osee 6).[7] And how this ought to be understood was said above.[8] "To do mercy and judgment, pleaseth the Lord more than victims," etc., (Prov. 21, 3). There is also another sign that shows their innocence, namely, their obedience. Hence, they can do these things, because I direct them. *For the Son of man* (He was accustomed to call Himself thus) *is Lord even of the sabbath*, and the lawgiver is not subject to the law; "He is our lawgiver" (Is. 33, 22). Therefore, He has power, because He has authority. *And when he had passed from thence, he came into their synagogues*, etc. Above, it was related how the Lord withstood the Pharisees criticizing His disciples. Here it is related how He withstood those attacking Himself. For they were opposing Him; firstly, by attempting to ensnare Him; secondly, by detracting Him; and thirdly, by tempting Him. And corresponding to this, He withstands them in three ways. The second

---

6. *Hic* in Latin.
7. "For I desired mercy, and not sacrifice" (verse 6).
8. cf. Mt. 9, 13.

is where it is said, ***Then was offered to him one possessed with a devil***; the third is where it is said, ***Then some of the scribes and Pharisees answered him***. About the first, the Evangelist does two things. Firstly, he shows how they were attempting to ensnare Christ in His doctrine; secondly, he shows how they were attempting to ensnare Him in His manner of life, where it is said, ***And the Pharisees going out made a consultation against him***. About the first, he does two things. Firstly, the insidious questioning is related; secondly, Christ's response is related, where it is said, ***But he said***, etc. About the first, he does three things. Firstly, the place is described; secondly, the occasion is described; and thirdly, the questioning is described. He says, therefore, ***And when he had passed from thence, he came into their synagogues***. According to the literal sense, the disciples were plucking the ears in this way, and Jesus excused them. Hence, when he says, ***And when he had passed***, it seems that He passed from thence on the same day. But this is excluded in Luke 6, because it is said there that He passed from thence on another Sabbath;[9] on account of this, it ought not to not be understood that He passed from thence immediately. Hence, he says, ***He came into their synagogues***, in order that He might preach salvation, as it is said in John 18, 20: "I have always taught in the synagogue and in the temple, whither all the Jews resort: and in secret I have spoken nothing." And in Psalm 39, 10, it is said: "I have declared thy justice in a great church." ***And behold there was a man who had a withered hand***. The occasion of the questioning follows: because ***they asked him***, etc. It is said that this man was a stonecutter, and he had a withered hand.[10] By this man, the human race is signified, whose hand withered through original sin: or he signifies all sinners, whose hand and operative power have withered; and at times their right hands are withered, because they are powerless for doing good, although they are powerful for doing evil. Then the questioning is related, and secondly, the response is related. He says, therefore, ***And they asked him, Is it lawful to heal on the sabbath***. They saw a mighty man, for that reason, they asked if it was lawful to heal on the Sabbath. And they asked this tempting Him, as it is

---

9. "And it came to pass also, on another sabbath, that he entered into the synagogue and taught" (verse 6).

10. "JEROME: In the Gospel which the Nazarenes and Ebionites use, and which we have lately translated into Greek out of the Hebrew, and which many regard as the genuine Matthew, this man who has the withered hand is described as a builder, and he makes his prayer in these words, 'I was a builder, and gained my living by the labor of my hands; I pray you, Jesus, to restore me to health, that I may not disgracefully beg my bread.'" (*Catena Aurea on St. Matthew*, chap. 12, lect. 2).

stated: "By much talk he will sift thee" (Eccli. 13, 14). For they asked not with the intention of learning, but rather of accusing, as it is stated in Psalm 27, 3: "Speaking peace with their neighbor, but evils are in their hearts."

But here there is a question, because in Mark 3 it is stated that the Lord asked; here, however, it is said that these men asked Him this question. Augustine answers that both happened, because when the man stood in the midst, and asked to be healed, they asked the question, and the Lord made him rise, and then He asked the question. Or it is otherwise, that these men observed him; hence, they were preparing themselves to ask the question, and then He asked it, because He knew that they were asking in order to accuse Him.

But he said to them, etc. Here His reply is related. And firstly, He replies by words; and secondly, by a deed, where it is said, **Then he saith to the man: Stretch forth thy hand.** In the first part, He does three things. Firstly, He cites a custom. Secondly, He makes a comparison, where it is said, **How much better is a man than a sheep?** And thirdly, He draws a conclusion, where it is said, **Therefore it is lawful to do a good deed on the sabbath days.** Therefore, He firstly says, **What man shall there be among you, that hath one sheep: and if the same fall into a pit on the sabbath day, will he not take hold on it and lift it up?** It was the custom among them, that if a sheep fell into a pit, that they would lift it out: for inasmuch as they were given to avarice, they considered a temporal loss to be worse than a spiritual loss. Hence, what is said in Ecclesiasticus 10, 9, applies to them, "Nothing is more wicked than the covetous man." And it continues a little after this: "Such a one setteth even his own soul to sale" (verse 10), namely, because he exposes himself to danger and eternal damnation for a small temporal gain. Secondly, a comparison is made, **How much better is a man than a sheep?** He is incomparably better than a sheep, because the universe is for the sake of man. For dominion over the universe was entrusted to man, as it is stated in Genesis 1, 26: "Let us make man to our image and likeness." And it continues, "that he may have dominion over the fishes of the sea, and the fowls of the air, and the beasts of the earth." And so, because man was made in God's image, he has dominion; for example, man has dominion over a sheep. He concludes from these things, **Therefore it is lawful to do a good deed on the sabbath days**, namely, it is lawful to do good to men on the Sabbath; "Cease to do perversely, learn to do well" (Is. 1, 16-17), because it is written: "Thou shalt do no work on it"[11] (Ex. 20, 10). Therefore, to do servile work on the Sabbath is a sin, but to do good on the Sabbath is lawful.

But then there is a question: Is it lawful to do all good deeds? It ought to be said that servile work can be understood literally: and, mystically, servile work signifies sin; "Whosoever committeth sin is the servant of sin" (Jn. 8, 31). Likewise, work is servile when the body is more exercised than the mind. For the soul has to rule the body. For that reason, to use one's mind is not servile work. Hence, we can see what things excuse from the Sabbath. For the Lord excuses the disciples by reason of their necessity, hence, necessity excuses. Likewise, it is lawful to do those things which are immediately ordained to God's worship, such as to burn incense, etc. Likewise, it is lawful to do those things which pertain to the health of the body, such as to prepare a medicine, or to prepare a plaster,[12] etc. Hence, these men are reprimanded, because they apply the precept of the Law with excessive strictness.

Then he saith to the man: Stretch forth thy hand. In this part, He responds by a deed, and this was to cure that man. For He would not cure unless it were lawful. The healing follows. **And it was restored to health even as the other.** Mystically, a man who has a withered hand, that is, a man who is weak in doing good actions, cannot be cured in a better way than by extending his hand in the relief of the poor. Hence, it is said, "Redeem thou thy sins with alms" (Dan. 4, 23). And it is said in Ecclesiaticus 3, 33, "Water quencheth a flaming fire, and alms resisteth sins." And in the same place, it is said, "Let not thy hand be stretched out to receive, and shut when thou shouldst give" (4, 36).

And observe that at first he had a healthy left hand and an infirm right hand, and it was restored even as the other, that is to say, the right hand was restored.[13] And this is the reason; because at first men are mighty to do evil, as it is stated, "Woe to you that are mighty for doing evil" (Is. 5, 22). But afterwards they are

---

11. "GLOSS: Thus He answers their question with a suitable example, so as to show that they profane the sabbath by works of covetousness who were charging Him with profaning it by works of charity; evil interpreters of the Law, who say that on the sabbath we ought to rest from good deeds, when it is only evil deeds from which we ought to rest. As it is said, you shall do no servile work therein, that is, no sin" (*Catena Aurea on St. Matthew*, chap. 12, lect. 2).

12. A plaster is a topical application of some substance harder than ointment, used to produce a local affect.

13. "And there was a man whose right hand was withered" (Lk. 6, 6). "This man is the Gentiles, who according to Luke had a withered hand: because he was not extending his right hand to the poor, and laboring in earthly things, he was not giving time to divine things" (Ven. Bede, *Expositio in Evang. S. Mt.*, chap. 12).

healed through grace, and then they are inclined to doing good deeds; "As you have yielded your members to serve uncleanness and iniquity, unto iniquity: so now yield to serve justice, unto sanctification," etc., (Rom. 6, 19).

And the Pharisees going out, etc. Here he shows how they were laying snares for him. And firstly, their snares are related; secondly, His evasion is related, where it is said, **But Jesus knowing it, retired from thence**; thirdly, a passage of Scripture is related, where it is said, **That it might be fulfilled which was spoken by Isaias the prophet, saying**. He says, therefore, **Going out**, namely, from the synagogue, so that it might be fulfilled which is stated in Psalm 53, 3, "The assembly of the mighty have sought my soul" (Ps. 85, 14). Therefore, they went out, so that they might act wickedly, as it is said, "Satan went forth from the presence of the Lord" (Job 1, 12). **They made a consultation**, that is, an assembly, how they might destroy and kill Him, because they had been unable to conquer Him with words; "Blessed is the man who hath not walked in the counsel of the ungodly" (Ps. 1, 1). **But Jesus knowing it, retired from thence**. Here it is related how He evaded their snares. And firstly, His evasion is mentioned; secondly, the fruits of His evasion are mentioned. Hence, He retired from thence, and why did He retire? It was because it was not yet the time of suffering. Likewise, He retired so that He might give a pretext of fleeing to His disciples, as it was said above (10, 23). Likewise, He retired to show that He is a man. Similarly, He left those men so that He would not incite them. For it is a characteristic of a good preacher that, when he sees that men are stirred up and incited, he leaves them, as it may be seen in Ecclesiasticus 8, 13, "Kindle not the coals of sinners by rebuking them, lest thou be burnt with the flame of the fire of their sins." **And many followed him**. Hence, He went to those who loved Him, who were hearing Him willingly. Hence, "My sheep hear my voice" (Jn. 10, 27). His healing of them is related; "Therefore it was neither herb, nor mollifying plaster that healed them, but thy word, O Lord, which healeth all things" (Wis. 16, 12). And in Psalm 106, 26, it is said, "He sent his word, and healed them." And how did He heal them? *He charged them that they should not make him known*. And why did He do this? It was so that He might give an example to us of avoiding human glory, as it was stated above (6, 1).[14] Moreover, He did this in order to spare the Pharisees, who were calumniating

---

14. "Take heed that you do not your justice before men, to be seen by them: otherwise you shall not have a reward of your Father who is in heaven," etc., (Mt. 6, 1).

Him concerning His deeds. *That it might be fulfilled which was spoken by Isaias the prophet.* Here the Evangelist cites a passage, which is found in Isaias 42, 1. And it ought to be known that some Apostles quote passages from the Hebrew original, others according to the Septuagint translation, and others were only expressing the sense of the words. And Isaias does three things. Firstly, he describes Christ's human nature, when he says, *Behold my child,*[15] because He was a child; "The child Jesus remained in the Temple" (Lk. 2, 43). Now, He is called 'a child' either from His purity, because "he did no sin, neither was guile found in his mouth," etc., (I Pet. 2, 22); or in that a servant is called 'a child.' Hence, when Isaias says, *Behold my servant*, Christ is called 'a servant' on account of His servile form; "He emptied himself, taking the form of a servant" (Phil. 2, 7). *My elect whom I have chosen.* Observe that in every holy man there are three things: a divine election, love, and an effect, which is grace. And this is one way in man and another way in God. In man, grace comes first; secondly, he loves; and thirdly, he chooses. And this is because man's will is not causative of this effect, which is grace, but God's love and will is the cause of grace; for that reason, He firstly chooses whom He wills to be good; secondly, He loves; and finally He bestows grace. Hence, according to this, the Prophet asserts three things. Firstly, he asserts His election, etc. In the Hebrew original there is not the word 'elect.' He says, therefore, *Behold my servant whom I have chosen*, etc. And this refers to His twofold election; which is entirely befitting to Christ, according to His human nature. For He was chosen for two reasons. He was chosen, namely, on account of the fact that He is the Son of God, as it is stated, "Who was predestinated the Son of God," etc. (Rom. 1, 4) and, "Blessed is he whom thou hast chosen and taken to thee" (Ps. 64, 5). Likewise, He was chosen for the work of human Redemption, as it is said, "For God so loved the world, as to give his only begotten Son," etc., (Jn. 3, 16). Similarly, He chose Him so that He might love Him; hence, it is said, *My beloved.* For if He loves some men, He loves His Only-Begotten Son much more. Hence, "The Spirit was not given to him by measure," (Jn. 3, 34). And if He loves other men, nevertheless, He loves this Man with a special love. Hence, He says, *In whom my soul hath been well pleased*, that is, 'My will hath been well pleased.' And this is a special love, because the will does not rest, except where it finds something acceptable. Now nothing is acceptable to God, except though grace, and

---

15. The Latin word used here for **servant** is *puer*, which can also mean 'a child.'

VER. 1-21   ACCORDING TO ST. MATTHEW   431

nothing pleasing was lacking in Christ. Hence, "This is my beloved Son, in whom I am well pleased" (above 3, 17). Then he relates the bestowal of grace, *I will put my spirit upon him*, as it is said in Joel 2, 28, "I will pour out my spirit upon all flesh." But He did not merely pour out some of His Spirit on Christ, but His whole Spirit, as it is stated, "The Spirit was not given to him by measure" (Jn. 3, 34); and, "The spirit of the Lord shall rest upon him" (Is. 11, 2). And this was insofar as He has the form of a servant. But what will He do? What office will He have? From ancient times, the Jews were boasting that they were God's chosen people; hence, they were saying, "He hath not done in like manner to every nation: and his judgments he hath not made manifest to them" (Ps. 147, 20). But that passage of Isaias was said to the Gentiles. Hence, **He shall shew judgment to the Gentiles**, materially, because He received the power of judging the Gentiles; "He who was appointed by God to be judge of the living and of the dead," (Acts 10, 42). And, "The Father hath given all judgment to the Son," (Jn. 5, 22). Also, is He worthy? He is, because two things are necessary in judgment; clemency and justice. And He shows both. And firstly, the Prophet shows that He has clemency. And He has it, because clemency can be in words, and secondly, it can be in deeds. For some men, even if they are unable to judge something, complain by word. For that reason, he excludes this from Him; hence, he says, **He shall not contend**; "Who, when he was reviled, did not revile" (I Pet. 2, 23). And what is said in Proverbs 20, 3, befits Him well, "It is an honour for a man to separate himself from quarrels." Similarly, some men do not contend, but they murmur. But He did not do this, because, **He shall not cry out**. Hence, "He shall be led as a sheep to the slaughter, and shall be dumb as a lamb before his shearer, and he shall not open his mouth" (Is. 53, 7). Clamor proceeds from inordinate affection. And so the Apostle commands, "Let all indignation and clamor be put away from you," (Eph. 4, 31). Some men do not shout, but they complain. And this is excluded from Him, where it is said, **Neither shall any man hear his voice in the streets**. They raise their voices in the streets, who walk in the way of sinners; "The stones of the sanctuary are scattered" (Lam. 4, 1); "Wisdom uttereth her voice in the streets" (Prov. 1, 20). Or, we take the streets to be the Gentiles, because they are outside the sanctuary. And although Christ tolerated the Gospel to be preached to the Gentiles, nevertheless, He did not preach to them in His own Person. Hence, He will not be heard in the streets, that is to say, among the Gentiles. Therefore, in this manner He was patient in word. Similarly, He was patient in His deeds: **The bruised reed he shall not**

break. And this can be understood in two ways; for, firstly, it can be read specifically in respect to the Jews; secondly, it can be read generally in respect to all men. In respect to the Jews, there were two things among them, namely, their royal power and their priestly dignity. Their royal power is signified by the reed, which had already been bruised, because they had been subjected to the Romans; for that reason, it was easy for Him, under these circumstances, to break the reed. And it is well signified by a reed, because a reed is movable, as it is stated above, "What went you out into the desert to see? a reed shaken with the wind?" (11, 7). ***And smoking flax he shall not extinguish.*** By smoking flax, the priesthood is signified. Whence, the priests wore linen[16] vestments. Likewise, ***smoking***: for smoke is extinguished by fire.[17] Again, smoke comes from a weak fire, which rather decomposes than consumes, and, due to this, an unpleasant odor is produced. These men, therefore, were like smoking flax, because they had not completely lost the faith. And, nevertheless, they did not have enough faith to keep themselves away from evils. Hence, although He could justly extinguish them, He shall not extinguish the smoking flax. Similarly, it can be expounded in another way in respect to all men such that, by the bruised reed, sinners are understood. By the smoking flax, which has little heat, those who are not in sin are understood, but they are tepid in respect to good deeds, and have some grace. Hence, the Prophet wishes to say, 'Nor does He preclude sinners from the way of salvation'. Hence, He says, "Is it my will that a sinner should die?" (Ez. 18, 23). Moreover, if someone has grace, He will not extinguish it. Hence, in this an example is given to us that we ought not to extinguish someone's grace, which the Lord gave him, but rather to foster it. Likewise, He will not do judgment, ***till he send forth judgment unto victory.*** This can be read as referring specifically to the Jews, namely, when He will have conquered all nations, because they were charging that He was casting out devils by Beelzebub; and He confuted them, and then He bestowed judgment upon them. And this was fulfilled by Titus and Vespasian.[18] And not only will this happen; but when

---

16. Linen is made from flax.
17. JEROME; The smoking flax He calls the people gathered out of the Gentiles, who, having extinguished the light of the natural law, were involved in the wandering mazes of thick darkness of smoke, bitter and hurtful to the eyes; this He not only did not extinguish, by reducing them to ashes, but on the contrary from a small spark and one almost dead He raised a mighty flame" (*Catena Aurea on St. Matthew* chap. 12, lect. 3).
18. Jerusalem fell before the Roman arms in August, A.D. 70, after a long and dreadful siege conducted by Titus, the son of the Emperor Vespasian and himself later emperor" ("Captivities of the Israelites," *The Catholic Encyclopedia*. (1908 ed.), Vol. 3, p. 319).

these men have been destroyed, *in his name the Gentiles shall hope*. Hence, "He shall be the expectation of nations" (Gen. 49, 10). Or it can be explained otherwise. As it has been said, He holds back His will and He judges no one; but when the enemy, death, shall be destroyed,[19] then all the Gentiles shall adhere to Him, and this will be on judgment day.

22. Then was offered to him one possessed with a devil, blind and dumb: and he healed him, so that he spoke and saw.

23. And all the multitudes were amazed, and said: Is not this the son of David?

24. But the Pharisees hearing it, said: This man casteth not out devils but by Beelzebub the prince of the devils.

25. And Jesus knowing their thoughts, said to them: Every kingdom divided against itself shall be made desolate: and every city or house divided against itself shall not stand.

26. And if Satan cast out Satan, he is divided against himself: how then shall his kingdom stand?

27. And if I by Beelzebub cast out devils, by whom do your children cast them out? Therefore they shall be your judges.

28. But if I by the Spirit of God cast out devils, then is the kingdom of God come upon you.

29. Or how can anyone enter into the house of the strong, and rifle his goods, unless he first bind the strong? and then he will rifle his house.

30. He that is not with me, is against me: and he that gathereth not with me, scattereth.

31. Therefore I say to you: Every sin and blasphemy shall be forgiven men, but the blasphemy of the Spirit shall not be forgiven.

32. And whosoever shall speak a word against the Son of man, it shall be forgiven him: but he that shall speak against the Holy Ghost, it shall not be forgiven him neither in this world, nor in the world to come.

33. Either make the tree good and its fruit good: or make the tree evil, and its fruit evil. For by the fruit the tree is known.

34. O generation of vipers, how can you speak good things, whereas you are evil? for out of the abundance of the heart the mouth speaketh.

---

19. cf. "And the enemy, death, shall be destroyed last" (I Cor. 15, 26).

35. A good man out of a good treasure bringeth forth good things: and an evil man out of an evil treasure bringeth forth evil things.

36. But I say unto you, that every idle word that men shall speak, they shall render an account for it in the day of judgment.

37. For by thy words thou shalt be justified, and by thy words thou shalt be condemned.

Above, the Lord refuted those who were calumniating both His doctrine and His life; here, however, He refutes those who detract from His miracles. And firstly, a miracle is related; secondly, the perversity of the detractors is related; and thirdly, their refutation is related. The second is where it is said, **And all the multitudes were amazed**; the third is where it is said, **And Jesus knowing their thoughts, said to them**, etc. About the miracle, two things are related. Firstly, a multiple sickness is related, and secondly, the perfect cure is related, where it is said, **And he healed him, so that he spoke and saw**. He says, therefore, **Then was offered to him one possessed with a devil**. Another account of the miracle is found in Luke 11 in different words. But it is not unfitting that what is told in one account is passed over in silence in another. The Gentiles are signified by this man, or the sinner is signified by him, who has a devil insofar as he is a servant of sin, because, "he who committeth sin is the servant of sin" (Jn. 8, 34). The sinner is blind, having been deprived of grace; hence, "We have groped for the wall, and like the blind we have groped as if we had no eyes," etc., (Is. 59, 10). Likewise, he is mute as to the confession of the faith. In Psalm 38, 3, it is said, "I was dumb, and was humbled, and kept silence from good things." And in a difference place it is said, "Because I was silent my bones grew old" (Ps. 31, 3). The perfect healing follows, **And he healed him**, by eliminating his muteness, so that **he spoke,** and He also healed him by eliminating his blindness, so that **he saw**. Hence, perfect healing was given; "Who forgiveth all thy iniquities: who healeth all thy diseases" (Ps. 102, 3). Hence, He did not send him away either blind or mute. The effect of the miracle follows. **And all the multitudes were amazed**, etc. Likewise, their praising follows; hence, **they said**, that is to say, they were praising Him, saying, **Is not this the son of David?** It had been promised in the prophets, that Christ would be born of the seed of David; "I will raise up to David a just branch" (Jer. 23, 5). And, moreover, what was said above seems to be fulfilled: "Because thou hast hid these things from the wise and prudent, and hast revealed them to little ones," etc., (11, 25). Hence, the crowds were praising Him. *But the Pharisees hearing it, said: This man casteth not out devils but by Beelzebub the prince of the devils*, who is the god of Accaron, as it is stated in IV Kings 1.[20] He is called the god of the flies on account of the very filthy ritual of the blood that was offered, by reason of which, many flies were gathered together. For that reason, they supposed him to be devil who was the chief of the devils, and for which reason, they supposed devils could be cast out by his power; "I will go therefore to the great men, and will speak to them" (Jer. 5, 5). And shortly afterwards, the verse continues, "And behold these have altogether broken the yoke more, and have burst the bonds." *And Jesus knowing their thoughts*, etc. In this part the Lord refutes those detracting His miracles. And firstly, He argues against the things which were said; secondly, He argues against those saying these things, where it is said, *Therefore I say to you: Every sin and blasphemy shall be forgiven men, but the blasphemy of the Spirit shall not be forgiven*. He disproves what was said by a fourfold argument. The second argument is where it is said, *And if Satan cast out Satan, he is divided against himself.* And the third is where it is said, *How then shall his kingdom stand?* The fourth is where it is said, *He that is not with me, is against me.* The first is stated very explicitly. Firstly, He states the major premise, when He says, *Every kingdom*, etc. There are three types of communities: the community of a household, of a city, and of a kingdom. A household is a community consisting of those by whom there is a common activity; for that reason, it consists in a triple bond: of the father and his children, of the husband and his wife, and of the master and his servant. The community of a city contains all things necessary for the life of man; hence, it is a perfect community in regard to the mere necessities of life. The third community is the community of a kingdom, which is a complete community. For where there is fear of enemies, a single city cannot subsist by itself; for that reason, on account of the fear of enemies, a community of many cities is necessary, which makes one kingdom. Hence, just as life is in every man, so peace is in every kingdom; and just as health is nothing other than the equilibrium of the humors, so peace occurs when everything keeps to its own place. And just as when health begins to fail, a man tends toward

---

20. "Is there not a God in Israel, that ye go to consult Beelzebub, the god of Accaron?" (verse 4).

destruction; the same is true of peace. For if peace leaves a kingdom, it tends toward destruction. Hence, the ultimate good to be pursued is peace. Hence, the Philosopher says, "Just as a doctor is for health, so the defender of a republic is for peace." For that reason, Christ says, ***Every kingdom divided against itself shall be made desolate***; "Their heart is divided: now they shall perish" (Osee 10, 2); "The child shall make a tumult against the ancient, and the base against the honorable" (Is. 3, 5). ***And if Satan cast out Satan, he is divided against himself.*** Expulsion involves a violent action; for that reason, it is necessary that where there is a disagreement, there is also a division, because, "Among the proud there are always contentions" (Prov. 13, 10).

But someone could say, 'It is not an expulsion, because he left voluntarily.' But this does not hold, because such a departure is not an expulsion, for it happens out of obedience to another person commanding; hence, here would be a voluntary departure. But the fact that they departed unwillingly appears from what was said above, namely, that they began to lament and cry out, "And behold they cried out, saying: "What have we to do with thee, Jesus Son of God? art thou come hither to torment us before the time?" (above 8, 29).

How then shall his kingdom stand? Jerome expounds this in reference to the question at hand as follows. ***How shall his kingdom stand?*** It is as though He were to say, 'The devil's kingdom stands in sinners until Judgment Day, because then all his power shall be reduced to nothing. Hence, if this would be the state of affairs, it would now be the end of the world.' Rabanus expounds this passage thus. '***How shall his kingdom stand?*** Because his kingdom fights against itself: therefore, it has collapsed; and so you ought to be on your guard against his kingdom.' Hilary explains this passage thus. ***How shall it stand?*** It is as though He were to say, 'It is from My power that I do what I do, namely, that one devil drives out another. Therefore, I destroy the devil's kingdom, and from this you ought to follow Me.' ***If I by Beelzebub.*** Here the second argument is related. If I cast out a devil, either I do this by the devil's power or by the power of the Holy Ghost. As to which of these it is, you ought not to detract Me. And firstly, He addresses the first possibility; secondly, He addresses the second possibility, where it is said, ***But if I by the Spirit of God cast out devils***, etc. He says, therefore, ***if I by Beelzebub cast out devils, by whom do your children cast them out?*** Jerome expounds this in two ways. In one way, he expounds this as referring to the exorcists, about whom it is stated in Acts 19, that certain exorcists were casting out devils in the name of Jesus Christ. Hence, *if I by Beelzebub cast out devils, by whom do your children cast them out?* It is as though He were to say, 'Your children cast out devils. If you do not calumniate them, neither should you calumniate Me. Therefore, you respect persons. Hence, **They shall be your judges**. Because I cast out devils by God's power, they themselves shall judge you, as it is said below about the Queen of the South, that she will judge.' Or it can be expounded as referring to the Apostles, and then *Your children* are the Apostles. Now he calls them their children, so that they might be touched with compassion towards them. Likewise, He is chiding them, because they are rebuking themselves. For if these men, who are your children, cast out devils, you could do likewise, if only you were disposed. For that reason, because these men are aware that I do this by the power given to Me, not by Beelzebub, *therefore they shall be your judges*, not only through comparison, but by their authority, as it is stated: "You also shall sit on twelve seats judging the twelve tribes of Israel," (below 19, 28). *But if I by the Spirit of God cast out devils, then is the kingdom of God come upon you.* It is as if He were to say, 'He is foolish who pushes away from himself what is for his own good; now this, namely, to expel demons, is for your good. From this, therefore, you can gather that I cast out devils by the Spirit of God, because the Holy Ghost is the finger of God, just as the Son is the hand of God. Nevertheless, it does not follow from this that there is some invocation of the Holy Ghost, but, on the contrary, this happens solely by My own power.' Hence, *if I by the Spirit of God cast out devils*, etc. But why then is the casting out of devils said to occur by the Holy Ghost? It is because love and goodness are appropriated to Him; for that reason, driving out the devil befits no Person so well as the Person of the Holy Ghost. *Is come upon you*; "The kingdom of God is within you" (Lk. 17, 21). And you can know that this driving out is effected by Christ, and that this is for your benefit, hence, He says, *upon you*. Or, *The kingdom of God*, that is God's dominion over men; "For he must reign, until he hath put all his enemies under his feet" (I Cor. 15, 25). If, therefore, the devils already begin to be trampled, God's kingdom and dominion has already come upon you. *Or how can anyone enter into the house of the strong*, etc.? Here the third argument is related, by which the Lord intends to refute the words of the Pharisees, and it is an argument from what commonly happens to men. Because when someone is powerful in his own house, he cannot be cast out of it, nor can his goods be rifled, unless someone stronger overcome him. But Christ despoiled the goods of the devil by expelling him from men, in whom he dwells as in his own goods. Therefore, Christ is stronger than him. And He gives this argument using these words: *The strong*. This is the devil, who is said to be strong from his power; "There is no power upon earth that can be compared with him" (Job 41, 24). And he is made stronger by a man's consent, because he who consents gives the devil power beyond his own; "They shall fight brother against brother, city against city, and I will deliver Egypt into the hand of cruel masters" (Is. 19, 2-4). This house is the world, or the congregation of sinners, not because the devil created the world, but because, by consenting to sin, it obeyed him; hence, he is called "The prince of this world" (Jn. 12, 31). His goods, or, more literally, his vessels, are men. A vessel can be taken in two ways. A vessel is called a vessel of something because it is full of that thing, as a vessel of water is so-called, because it is full of water, or a vessel of oil is so-called, because it is full of oil. In this way, some men are called vessels of the devil, because they are full of the devil, and this is regarding the body, as, for example, those obsessed by the devil. But regarding the soul, some men are full of the devil, whose hearts are full of the devil's will, as, for example, it is said of Judas. Sometimes certain instruments, appointed for some particular function, are called vessels. Hence, he is called a vessel of the devil, who gives an occasion of sin to others. And in whatever way it is taken, Christ plundered the vessels, or goods, of the devil; "Despoiling the principalities and powers, he hath exposed them confidently in open shew, triumphing over them in himself," etc., (Col. 2, 15). Nevertheless, this does not suffice unless He bind the strong; hence, it is said, *unless he first bind the strong*. What is this binding? It is that the power of harming, which the devil has from himself, is held back by God. Hence, by the power of his nature, the devil can do many things, but is held back by God's power, just as a man who is bound is held back from executing what he wills. Hence, it is said, "To bind their kings with fetters," (Ps. 149, 8). *And then he will rifle his house*, because once he has been bound, the men bound by him will be set free; "The captivity shall be taken away from the strong: and that which was taken by the mighty, shall be delivered" (Is. 49, 25). *He that is not with me, is against me*. Here the fourth argument is related, and here He reaffirms all the previous arguments. For some could say, 'If you take away the devil's goods by victory, your argument would be valid; but you do not triumph by might, but by suffering, and thus it is not a proof because you are bound.' For that reason, He states a fourth argument. The argument is this: those who agree in any one thing perform similar works: hence, those who do similar works, do not impede each other. But I do works opposed to them. Therefore, *He that is not with me, is against me.* Firstly, He puts forth the argument in general; secondly, He exemplifies the argument in particular. He says, therefore, *He that is not with me*, etc. 'And the devil is obviously not with Me, because he is opposed to My works'; "What concord hath Christ with Belial?" (II Cor. 6, 15). Now the fact that the devil is against Him is stated in Ecclesiasticus 33, 15: "Life is against death, so also is the sinner against a just man"; in this way, the devil, who is the father of sin, is against man. But in what is he opposed to Him? *And he that gathereth not with me, scattereth.* For the Lord gathers; "He shall gather together the lambs with his arm, and shall take them up in his bosom, and he himself shall carry them that are with young" (Is. 40, 11). The devil, on the other hand, scatters apart; hence, "The wolf casteth and scattereth the sheep" (Jn. 10, 12).

But in Luke 11, 50, it is stated, "He that is not against you is for you," etc. Here, however, He seems to say the contrary. Chrysostom says that both are said particularly. Hence, it is not understood universally, but in a particular instance, and specifically, that 'he who does not have a covenant with Me, is against Me.' Hence, there He was speaking in regard to His disciples, here, however, He is speaking in regard to the devils. Or we can say otherwise, that it can be understood in one way concerning God, and another way concerning men. It is undisputed that God is the natural end towards which all things tend; for that reason, he who is not with God must necessarily be separated from Him; hence, "Why do you halt between two sides? If the Lord be God, follow him" (III Kings 18, 21). But the relation of one man to another is not so, and thus, it follows that he who is not for Me [as man], is not on account of this against Me [as God]. *Therefore I say to you: Every sin and blasphemy shall be forgiven men*, etc. After refuting their words, here He inveighs against them. Firstly, He inveighs against them on account of the gravity of their sins; secondly, on account of their wicked intention; and thirdly, on account of their future judgment. The second is where it is said, *Either make the tree good*, etc. The third is where it is said, *But I say unto you.* About the first; He does two things. Firstly, He premises certain general statements, and secondly, He explains them, where it is said, *And whosoever shall speak a word against the Son of man*, etc. He says, therefore, 'You say that the miracle was performed in that manner, ***Therefore I say to you***, etc.' He makes two statements. Firstly, He makes a statement about the remission of sin in general: ***I say: Every sin***, namely; sins of deeds, ***and blasphemy***, namely, sins of words, ***shall be forgiven men***, namely, if they repent. Hence, it is said, "Who forgiveth all thy iniquities: who healeth all thy diseases" (Ps. 102, 3). And elsewhere it is said, "Blessed are they whose iniquities are forgiven, and whose sins are covered" (Ps. 31, 1). And in saying this, the opinion of Novatians, who said that not all sins are forgivable, is destroyed. Here, however, it is said that every sin is forgivable. Secondly, He presents a particular sin which is not forgiven, saying, ***But he that shall speak against the Holy Ghost, it shall not be forgiven***, that is, a willful sin of blasphemy, namely, when one blasphemes through certain malice. And these statements are said generally. Then He proceeds to the particular sin of blasphemy, and He explains the two general statements. And firstly, He explains the first statement. So it is said, that every sin, etc. 'And because this is true, I show this to be true of this instance, because a blasphemy against the Son is forgivable.' Hence, ***Whosoever shall speak a word against the Son of man, it shall be forgiven him***, namely, if he repent. ***But he that shall speak against the Holy Ghost, it shall not be forgiven him neither in this world, nor in the world to come***. And, as Augustine says, these words are difficult, because there are no stronger words in the Gospel. It ought to be said, therefore, that there are three manners of expounding this passage. Certain men expound it literally, namely, that these men were seeing the miracles that He was performing, and the works of the Holy Ghost, and they were saying that He had an unclean spirit; for that reason they were blaspheming against the Holy Ghost. Certain other men say that both statements ought to be referred to the Person of the Son. But in the Son there are two natures, the divine and the human natures; and, according to this, He is both a "Spirit"[21] and "Holy." Hence, the Son is called the "Holy Ghost," not according to the meaning of the words themselves, and Hilary expounds the passage thus. And there is another opinion. Whosoever shall say something out of weakness against the Son and against His human nature, has an excuse; but whosoever speaks against His divine nature, has no reason to be pardoned. Others expound the passage as referring to the Holy Ghost, in that He is the third Person in the Trinity. Hence, whosoever speaks against the Son

---

21. *Spiritus* means "Spirit" or "Ghost."

of man, that is, His human nature, shall be forgiven; but he who speaks against the Holy Ghost performing miracles, that man does not receive pardon. This seems to be the most complete explanation of the passage, and the context seems to support this.

But Augustine objects as follows. It is well-known that all pagans blaspheme, because they do not believe the Holy Ghost is in the Church. Likewise, many heretics blaspheme for the same reason, and, nevertheless, the way of pardon is not closed to them. Moreover, many Jews act in a similar manner, etc. But someone could say, 'This passage must be understood to apply after the faith has been accepted.' But I reply to this, 'If this were so, then should not forgiveness be refused to him if he repents?' Again, He does not say, 'Whatsoever Christian,' but instead He says more generally, **Whosoever.** Therefore, how can this question be solved? Augustine solves it in two ways. One explanation is given in *De Sermone Domini in Monte*, and he retracts that explanation. But He gives another explanation in His book, *De Verbis Domini*. Hence, you ought to understand that a blasphemy against the Holy Ghost is not called a sin against the Holy Ghost, but it is understood to be such from the manner of sinning. Goodness, charity and love are attributed to the Holy Ghost; goodness corresponds to malice, charity corresponds to envy. If someone, therefore, knowing the truth, out of malice detracts from the truth, he sins against the Holy Ghost. Likewise, if someone sees the deeds of holiness in someone, and out of envy detracts from them, he sins against the Holy Ghost. For envy of holiness, not of a person, is an unforgivable sin, not because it is not impossible that it be remitted, but because the stain of the sin is so great that by Divine justice it happens that the one who commits this sin does not repent. Hence, those who were saying that He was casting out devils by Beelzebub, were not sinning against the Holy Ghost, as Augustine says, because they had not come to the depths of malice, etc. But He began to say this, not because they did this, but so that they who had begun might take heed lest they come to this state. Augustine reproves and retracts this interpretation, because thus there would be someone in a state for whom one ought not to pray, which is not true for wayfarers. For that reason, he expounds it differently in His book *De Verbis Domini*, and it is this: Note that He did not say, 'Whosoever shall say a word of blasphemy,' but instead, **A word,** indeterminately. But such an expression, which is used indeterminately, is sometimes not meant universally, but particularly, as for example, "If I had not come and spoken to them, they would not have sin" (Jn. 15, 22).

"Sin" is not said simply or universally, but rather, they would not have the sin of infidelity. So, in like manner, He said *a word*; it is not any word whatsoever, but a particular type of word, which if it be said, is unforgivable. Now what kind of word it is, Augustine says. The Holy Ghost is charity, by which the members of the Church are united to their Head, Christ, and every sin is remitted by the Holy Ghost. Because, even if the whole Trinity remits every sin, it is appropriated to the Holy Ghost on account of love. Therefore, he who has an impenitent heart, speaks against the Holy Ghost. Hence, impenitence itself is opposed to the charity of the Holy Ghost. Hence, not whosoever shall speak any word whatsoever, but this word, namely, the word of impenitence, and that word is unforgivable. And He says, **Word**, not "words," because it is customary in Scripture to call many words one word; hence, in Isaias the Lord often says, 'Thou shalt say my word,' although He says many words to him.[22] Hence, He does not contradict that which was said above, where it was said, ***Therefore I say to you: Every sin and blasphemy***, etc., because he who shall speak this word against the Holy Ghost, blasphemes. Hence, when a certain teacher was asked what is the sin against the Holy Ghost, he said, "Impenitence treasures up to itself wrath."[23]

But what is it that He says, ***it shall not be forgiven neither in this world, nor in the world to come***? Are there not some sins forgiven in the world to come? Augustine says that there are not. Therefore, it is not said that some sins are forgiven in the present life and others in the future; it follows that sin is forgiven here in such a way that the forgiveness obtained here avails in the future life. Or it can be expounded otherwise. It is that certain sins, namely, mortal sins, are forgiven in the present life, but other sins, namely, venial sins, are forgiven in the future life; for example, if a man dies with some venial sin on his soul, it is certain that it is forgiven. Hence, some mercy will be in the future life, because then a man will still be a wayfarer.[24]

Chrysostom expounds this passage very clearly and he says that here He speaks about two types of blasphemy: blasphemy against the Son of man, and against the Holy Ghost. These men were blaspheming the Son of man because they were saying that

---

22. e.g. "And Isaias said to Ezechias: Hear the word of the Lord of hosts" (Is. 39, 5).

23. cf. "According to thy hardness and impenitent heart, thou treasurest up to thyself wrath" (Rom. 2, 5).

24. Wherefore, according to Chrysostom's commentary (Hom. xlii in Mt.), the Jews are said not to be forgiven this sin, neither in this world nor in the world to come, because they were punished for it, both in the present life, through the Romans, and in the life to come, in the pains of hell" (II II, q. 14, a. 3).

He was a wine drinker. Likewise, their other blasphemy was against the Holy Ghost, because they were saying that He was casting out devils by a demoniac spirit. About the first, they have an excuse, that they did not know the truth. But as to their speaking against the Holy Ghost, they did not have an excuse, because they should have known the Holy Ghost through the Scriptures, and, for that reason, their sin will not be forgiven.

But what is it that He says, *neither in this world, nor in the world to come*? This is said because some sins are punished in this world, others are punished in the world to come, still others are punished here and there. Certain sins are punished only in this world, as is evident in penitents. Certain sins are punished only in the world to come, such as those about which it is said, "They spend their days in wealth, and in a moment they go down to hell" (Job 21, 13). But a sin that is punished both here and in the world to come is the sin against the Holy Ghost. Hence, *it shall not be forgiven him neither in this world, nor in the world to come*. This is not because its forgiveness can occur in the world to come, but because its punishment will be in the world to come. Hence, the sense is that it will not be forgiven, moreover, one suffers its punishment in this world and in the world to come.[25] So speak the Saints concerning this sin.

It ought to be noted, however, that the Master[26] in the *Sentences* (ii, 43) makes a distinction, and assigns six kinds of sins against the Holy Ghost: despair, presumption, impenitence, obstinacy, resisting the known truth, and envy of our brother's spiritual good. Hence, they are said to sin against the Holy Ghost, who sin against the things appropriated to the Holy Ghost. To the Father is appropriated power; to the Son, wisdom; and to the Holy Ghost, goodness. Therefore, he is said to sin against the Father, who sins out of weakness; he is said to sin against the Son, who sins through ignorance; he is said to sin against the Holy Ghost, who sins through malice.

But it ought to be known that to sin through malice occurs when a man sins voluntarily, which is through certain malice. And this happens for one of two reasons. It is either because he has an inclination to sin, or he does not. For when some man commits many sins, a habit of sinning remains in him as a result, and in this way he sins by choice. Likewise, someone sins when what withdraws him from sin is removed. Now a man is with-

---

25. This can only be understood of souls who have not yet reached their final reward, namely, the souls in Purgatory.
26. i.e. Peter Lombard.

drawn from sin through the hope of eternal life. Hence, he who does not hope for eternal life, sins through certain malice; "Who despairing have given themselves up to lasciviousness" (Eph. 4, 19). Hence, he who sins through inclination, sins against the Holy Ghost, namely, from the fact that he departs from that which withdraws him from sin. Now this happens in six ways. For in God there is mercy and justice. From the contempt of His mercy arises despair; from the contempt of His justice arises presumption. Likewise, as regards the turning away from God, a man turns to a perishable good, which is obstinacy. Again, as regards the turning away from God, a man does not intend to return to God, and thus impenitence arises. Similarly, as regards the remedy, namely, faith[27] and charity, there arises resistance to the known truth, and envy of our brother's love. These are the sins against the Holy Ghost. If, therefore, there is actual impenitence, in these circumstances he is not forgiven, not because he cannot be forgiven in general, but because it is not easily forgiven, since he does not have any reason for being forgiven, but can only be forgiven by God's grace. It is as though someone who has a fever, namely, a tertian fever,[28] has sufficient strength that he can be cured; but one who has a semi-tertian fever,[29] does not have sufficient strength that he could be cured of himself, because he is not cured except by divine aid.

He continues, **Either make the tree good and its fruit good: or make the tree evil, and its fruit evil**. Above, the Lord refuted the Pharisees' manner of acting, in that they were speaking against His works, by showing the gravity of their sin; now He refutes their saying that His doctrine was perverse. And firstly, He gives a similitude; secondly, He applies it; and thirdly, He tells its meaning. The second is where it is said, **O generation of vipers**, etc.; the third is where it is said, **out of the abundance of the heart the mouth speaketh**. About the first, He does two things. Firstly, He puts forward a similitude; secondly, He brings forth evidence, where it is said, **For by the fruit the tree is known**. He says, therefore, **Either make the tree good**

---

27. The text here says, "namely, hope..." but this is opposed to what is found in II II, q. 14, a. 2, namely, "God's gifts whereby we are withdrawn from sin, are two: one is the acknowledgment of the truth, against which there is the resistance of the known truth, when, namely, a man resists the truth which he has acknowledged, in order to sin more freely." Since the acknowledgement of the truth pertains to faith, "faith" has been substituted for "hope" in this translation.

28. "The true tertian comes quickly to a crisis, and is not fatal" (Hippocrates, *Of the Epidemics*, Bk. 1, Sect. 2).

29. "In what is called the semi-tertian, other acute diseases are apt to occur, and it is the most fatal of all the other (intermittent fevers)" (ibid).

and its fruit good, etc. This passage is interpreted in two ways. One interpretation is according to Chrysostom and Jerome; another is according to Augustine. According to John Chrysostom, it is interpreted as follows. He wishes to show their reproof to be unreasonable; hence, He compares a man's actions to his life, as the fruits are to a tree. If someone sees a good fruit, he judges the tree to be good; similarly, if, on the contrary, he sees a bad fruit, he judges the tree to be bad. These men were seeing Christ's actions, for instance, He was expelling demons, and this was good; therefore, 'what you say is very unreasonable.' He proceeds very well from the effect to the cause, as the Apostle says, "For the invisible things of him from the creation of the world are clearly seen, being understood by the things that are made," etc., (Rom. 1, 20). Hence, He intends to say, 'Either you,' namely, the Pharisees, 'make,' that is, concede, 'that if the fruit is good, then the tree is good'; or, 'make,' that is, 'say', 'that if the fruit is bad, then the tree is bad. And you cannot say this.' Augustine, however, relates this passage to the question in point. They were saying that He was casting out devils by Beelzebub. Therefore, He wishes to show from what root this accusation originated; namely, from the malice of their hearts. For that reason, He says, **Either make**. Here, two admonitions are given. The first one pertains to merit, and it is said so that it might happen. **Make**, etc., and bestow labor and effort that you may be a good tree, and then there will be good fruit and good words. What follows is in order that they might take heed, namely, **or make the tree evil, and its fruit evil**. Otherwise, you are motivated by malice, and so you will be an evil tree, and then there will be evil fruit; "I planted thee a chosen vineyard, all true seed: how then art thou turned unto me into that which is good for nothing, O strange vineyard?" (Jer. 2, 21) The supporting evidence that follows, **For by the fruit the tree is known**, etc., is in accord with both of these interpretations, because by good fruit a good tree is known and by bad fruit a bad tree is known. **O generation of vipers**, etc. And these words are added in different ways according to the different interpretations. According to Augustine, it is a kind of application of the question in point as follows. It was said, **Either make**, etc. 'And you do evil. You are the evil tree, and because the tree is evil, you do evil, because you cannot say good things.' According to the interpretation of the others, He shows from what this malice originates, and He calls the Pharisees a generation of vipers, because they, who from their youth have malice, retain it more firmly; and so their malice is called the malice of a viper; "A young man according to his way, even when he is old, he will not depart from it" (Prov. 22, 6). For that reason, oftentimes men who have evil parents are more predisposed to evil; "We acknowledge, the iniquities of our fathers" (Jer. 14, 20). Hence, it is good that a man subjects and accustoms himself to good deeds. The nature of a serpent is similar, because they spew venom with their tongues, and evil men behave in this manner; "The viper's tongue shall kill him" (Job 20, 16). And in Psalm 139, 4, it is said, "They have sharpened their tongues like a serpent". For that reason, He says, *how can you speak good things?* He does not say 'do good things' but 'speak good things,' because you are children of a viper, which harms with its tongue. For that reason, since you are imitators of your fathers' crimes, how can you speak good things? It is as though He were to say, 'you cannot do so.' And then He gives the meaning of the similitude. And firstly, He gives the meaning in general; secondly, He does this in particular, where it is said, *A good man out of a good treasure bringeth forth good things*, etc. He says, therefore, 'You are unable to speak in this way.' Wherefore? *Because you are evil.* Why? *For out of the abundance of the heart the mouth speaketh*, because words are signs of ideas.[30] He says, *Out of the abundance of the heart*, because, according to Chrysostom, when someone speaks out of malice, it is a sign that greater malice is in his heart, because, in regard to that which he keeps to himself, he has nothing to fear, having little fear of God. Therefore, when someone utters something out of malice, it is a sign that there is more inside of him which he does not dare utter. For that reason, He says, *Out of the abundance of the heart the mouth speaketh*. And it is out of the abundance of malice, inwardly, that the mouth speaks, and this is in regard to something good or something evil. Hence, "The word of the Lord came in my heart as a burning fire," etc., (Jer. 20, 9). Likewise, in regard to something evil, a man acts similarly, because some men conceive something out of malice that they cannot keep to themselves; "The spirit of my bowels straiteneth me," etc., (Job 32, 18). *A good man out of a good treasure bringeth forth good things.* That which He had said, *Out of the abundance of the heart the mouth speaketh*, He expounds in detail. The word that goes out from the thought is like a gift that goes out from a treasure. Hence, if the thought is good, the word is good, and vice versa. The good treasure is knowledge of the truth and fear of the Lord; "Riches of salvation, wisdom and knowledge: the

---

30. "According to the Philosopher (Peri Hermenias I), words are signs of ideas" (I, q. 13, a. 1).

fear of the Lord is his treasure" (Is. 33, 6). Likewise, an evil treasure is an evil thought. And from this nothing comes forth except evil; "Treasures of wickedness shall profit nothing" (Prov. 10, 2). Note that what is said here about words can also be applied to actions. For just as a thought is the origin of a word, so an intention is the origin of an action; for that reason, if the intention is good, the deed is good. Hence, the Gloss says on the same passage, "You do as much as you intend to do."

In a regard to the good deed, it seems that an objection can be made. It may be asserted that someone may want to steal in order to give alms. The action is evil and the intention is good, therefore, etc. I reply: The intention and the act of the will are sometimes distinguished, namely, when in one and the same action the act of the will is different from the intention. The object of the act of the will is the object willed, and the object of an intention is the end. It is an act of the will, for instance, if I will to go to the window in order to see those passing by, the latter is the intention, as though 'stretching beyond';[31] wherefore, it is appropriate that the act of will and the intention be one. Hence, we can broadly consider the intention to also be the act of the will, and so it is this case. If the act of the will is evil, the action is evil; nevertheless, if the act of the will be excluded, and the intention is taken strictly, the saying is not true.

But given that the intention and the act of the will are one, what follows? It ought to be said that the principle of merit pertains to charity, and consequently, charity pertains to the merit of the other virtues. For merit regards the principle reward, governing which, charity is considered. Thus every work, which is performed with greater charity, has more merit. Charity alone has God for its object and end. Hence, the merit of charity corresponds to the substantial reward, while the merit of the other virtues corresponds to the accidental reward. Therefore, because charity informs the intention, inasmuch as a man intends to do something out of greater charity, so much does he do; but the same is not true as far as the accidental reward.

But I say unto you, etc. The Lord reprehended these men on account of the gravity of their sin, and on account of their malice; now, however, He reprehends them on account of the future judgment, which is a truth of our faith. For it is said, "Flee from the face of the sword, for the sword is the revenger of iniquities: and know ye that there is a judgment" (Job 19, 29); "All things that are

---

31. *Extra tentio.*

done, God will bring into judgment for every error, whether it be good or evil" (Eccle. 12, 14). Again it is written, "For we must all be manifested before the judgment seat of Christ, that every one may receive the proper things of the body, according as he hath done, whether it be good or evil," (II Cor. 5, 10). Hence, at that place there will be an examination, because everyone will render an account of his deeds. For that reason, He adds, concerning one's words, saying, **But I say unto you, that every idle word that men shall speak, they shall render an account for it in the day of judgment.** And this is also said in Wisdom 1, 8: "He that speaketh unjust things, cannot be hid." And this is added because a hidden idle word will not fall to the ground empty.

But what is it that He says concerning an *idle word*? A word is said to be idle in two ways. In one way, every evil word is said to be idle; because that is called idle which does not attain its end, just as if someone seeks a man, and does not find him, is said to have sought idly.[32] Now, a word is spoken for the sake of instruction. Therefore, when it accomplishes its purpose, it is not idle; "Let no evil speech proceed from your mouth: but that which is good, to the edification of faith: that it may administer grace to the hearers," etc., (Eph. 4, 29). And, according to Chrysostom, He is referring to the point at hand, because they had said that He casts out demons by Beelzebub, etc. That word was pernicious, and, for that reason, it was also idle, according to Jerome. Actually, a pernicious word differs from an idle word, because a pernicious word is that which inflicts harm, but an idle word brings no benefit, because it lacks all pious motive of utility or necessity. Hence, whatever word that is said lightly, is called idle, unless it has some pious utility or pious necessity.

But if it is clear that these men had spoken a pernicious word, why then does He only make mention of an idle word? It is because He wishes to accuse from the less; for if it is necessary to render an account for an idle word, much more for a pernicious word.

Then He shows the reason, **For by thy words thou shalt be justified**, etc. In the world's judgment, sometimes the innocent are punished and the wicked are set free, because the judgment is made according to the statements of witnesses; in God's judgment, it is from the man accusing himself, namely, by his own confession. Hence, so that you may not believe that you will be judged by the things which others will say about you, but by those things which you will say about yourself, for which reason, He

---

32. Or unprofitably.

says, *For by thy words thou shalt be justified, and by thy words thou shalt be condemned.* As it is said, "Out of thy own mouth I judge thee, thou wicked servant" (Lk. 19, 22).

38. Then some of the scribes and Pharisees answered him, saying: Master, we would see a sign from thee.

39. Who answering said to them: An evil and adulterous generation seeketh a sign: and a sign shall not be given it, but the sign of Jonas the prophet.

40. For as Jonas was in the whale's belly three days and three nights: so shall the Son of man be in the heart of the earth three days and three nights.

41. The men of Ninive shall rise in judgment with this generation, and shall condemn it: because they did penance at the preaching of Jonas. And behold a greater than Jonas here.

42. The queen of the south shall rise in judgment with this generation, and shall condemn it: because she came from the ends of the earth to hear the wisdom of Solomon, and behold a greater than Solomon here.

43. And when an unclean spirit is gone out of a man he walketh through dry places seeking rest, and findeth none.

44. Then he saith: I will return into my house from whence I came out. And coming he findeth it empty, swept, and garnished.

45. Then he goeth, and taketh with him seven other spirits more wicked than himself, and they enter in and dwell there: and the last state of that man is made worse than the first. So shall it be also to this wicked generation.

Above, the Lord refuted those detracting His miracles and doctrine; here He reproves those tempting Him; and here the Evangelist does two things. Firstly, their tempting request is related; secondly, their reproof, where it is said, *Who answering said to them*. It is said, therefore, *Then they answered*; this is after they had seen many miracles, and after they had heard many words of wisdom, so that it was fulfilled in Him what was said, "He speaketh with one that is asleep, who uttereth wisdom to a fool" (Eccli. 22, 9). *Master, we would see a sign from thee.* They say, *Master*, to tempt Him; "Who speak peace with their mouths, but evils are in their hearts," (Ps. 27, 3). *We would see a sign from thee.* Had they not seen many signs? Indeed; but a different Evangelist relates this as follows, saying, "We would see a sign from heaven" (Lk. 11, 16), as it is read that Samuel made thunder (I Kings, 12) and Elias made fire to come down from heaven (IV Kings 1). It is typical for the Jews to require a sign, as it is stated, "The Jews require signs" (I Cor. 1, 22). But although He had given earthly signs, they were not believing; even if He gave heavenly signs, they would not believe; "If I have spoken to you earthly things, and you believe not: how will you believe, if I shall speak to you heavenly things?" (Jn. 3, 12). *Who answering said to them*, etc. Consequently, He repulses them, and He does two things. Firstly, He refuses their request; secondly, He shows the unworthiness of the request, where it is said, *The men of Ninive*, etc. Firstly, He explains what they were requesting, and secondly, He refuses it. It is said, therefore, *Who answering said to them: An evil and adulterous generation seeketh a sign*. He calls them evil, because they were plotters. A man is said to be evil because he harms his neighbor. Therefore, they were an evil generation and wicked children. Their generation is called adulterous, as it is said, "But draw near hither, you sons of the sorceress, the seed of the adulterer, and of the harlot" (Is. 57, 3). In this manner, therefore, this generation subject to iniquity *seeketh a sign: and a sign shall not be given it, but the sign of Jonas the prophet*. "Ask thee a sign of the Lord thy God, either unto the depth of hell, or unto the height above," etc., (Is. 7, 11). Therefore, they were seeking a sign from the heavens, but they were not worthy to see it. For He gave this sign to His Apostles, who saw Him ascending into heaven, and who saw His glory on the mountain. But a sign will not be given to these men, except a sign in hell, in regard to His soul, and from the earth, in regard to His body. Hence, *a sign shall not be given it, but the sign of Jonas the prophet*. Hence, Christ's death was signified, and God's charity is shown, as the Apostle says, "Because when as yet we were sinners according to the time, Christ died for us," etc., (Rom. 5, 8-9). Likewise, His power to bring back to life is shown, as it is stated in I Corinthians 15. And these are signs of what things ought to be in us. By Christ's death is signified to us that we ought to die to sin; and, assuredly, by His Resurrection is signified that we ought to rise from sin. *For as Jonas was in the whale's belly three days and three nights*, really, in fact, *so shall the Son of man be in the heart of the earth*. And in this passage the error of Manichaeus is confuted, saying that He did not truly die. And He says, *in the heart of the earth*, because just as man's heart is deeply within him, so Christ was deeply within the earth. Or, *in the heart of the earth*, that is to say, in the heart of earthly men and His disciples, who were despairing of Him, as it is stated, "But we hoped that it was he that should have redeemed Israel" (Lk. 24, 21). *Three days and three nights.*

But here there is a literal question. It seems this was false, because He expired at the ninth hour, and He was buried in the evening, but He rose in the morning of the third day.

Augustine says that some men wish to affirm that the time is to be computed from the time when He was placed upon the Cross. Hence, they call that the first night, the darkness which then occurred; the second was Friday night, and the third was Saturday night. But, according to Augustine, this explanation is not valid. Nevertheless, we could permit this explanation if the Lord were in the tomb during all Sunday. For this reason it ought to be explained otherwise, that a natural day is taken for a day and night, for the space of twenty-four hours. But, as Augustine says, in Scripture a part is sometimes taken for the whole. Accordingly, therefore, it ought to be said that by the figure of synecdoche[33] Christ was three days and three nights in the tomb, because part of Friday is taken for the whole day and also for the preceding night. Of course there is no doubt about the second day; the third night in fact is taken for the subsequent night and day. Nevertheless, if we consider according to the reality, the time was two nights and one full day, to signify that His single death and Resurrection destroyed our double death. In us there was punishment and guilt, but in Him there was only punishment, therefore, etc.

The men of Ninive shall rise in judgment with this generation. Here He describes their unworthiness. Did He not do many miracles? Did He not raise Lazarus, and do many other signs? Why, therefore, is it said, *A sign shall not be given it, but the sign of Jonas the prophet*?

I reply: The kind of sign for which they were asking would not be given. Or a sign for their benefit shall not be given; for He knew that they would not return, because they were hardened. But He performed signs on account of the faithful and elect, of whom, afterwards, there were many.

The men of Ninive, etc. This passage shows their unworthiness. And firstly, the Gentiles are preferred before them; and secondly, the reason is related, where it is said, *And when an unclean spirit is gone out of a man,* etc. Take note. Someone is good either because he does not sin, or because he repents. Firstly, therefore, He places those who have repented before them,

---

33. A synecdoche is a figure of speech in which the one of the following (or its reverse) is expressed: A part stands for a whole; an individual stands for a class or a material stands for a thing.

namely, the Gentiles; and secondly, He places those who have not sinned, where it is said, ***The queen of the south***, etc. The Lord had compared His Resurrection to Jonas; for that reason, they might believe that what happened to the Ninivites, who were delivered,[34] might happen to them; but these men were not only not delivered, they were dispersed. Hence, ***the men of Ninive shall rise***. By these words, an error of the Jews is eliminated, that the resurrection will take place before the Judgment,[35] and that, in the intervening time, Jerusalem will be rebuilt. And they cite, in favor of their opinion, that which is said, "The Lord of hosts shall make in this mountain a feast of fat things" (Is. 25, 6). Others say that the just and the martyrs will rise before the others for a thousand years, and they cite, in favor of their opinion, that which is said, "I saw an angel coming down from heaven, having the key of the bottomless pit and a great chain in his hand" (Apoc. 20, 1-2); and it continues, "He laid hold on the dragon, the old serpent, who is called the devil, and bound him for a thousand years that he should no more seduce the nations" (Apoc. 20, 3). He excludes both opinions, when He says, those who are good and, simultaneously, those who are not good, ***shall rise in judgment with this generation***; ***and shall condemn***, by comparison, not by authority, because they will rise among the condemned; "This is Jerusalem, I have set her in the midst of the nations, and the countries round about her. And she hath despised my judgments, so as to be more wicked than the Gentiles; and my commandments, more than the countries that are round about her" (Ez. 5, 5-6). And in respect to what shall they condemn? ***Because they did penance***; but these men did not want to do penance. The Lord began His preaching by preaching penance: John did likewise, and they did not listen; "There is none that doth penance for his sin" (Jer. 8, 6). Moreover, those men did penance upon a single preaching of Jonas; Jesus, on the other hand, preached to the Jews many times, and nevertheless, they were not converted; "If I had not done among them the works that no other man hath done, they would not have sin" (Jn. 15, 24). Likewise, the Ninivites were converted upon the preaching of one prophet; but these men had not merely a prophet, but the Son of God. Hence, it is stated, "God, who, at sundry times and in divers manners, spoke in times past to the fathers by the prophets, last of all, in these

---

34. i.e. they were delivered from their impending chastisement.
35. "These words, likewise, overthrow that fable of the Jews, who used to say that the Resurrection shall be held a thousand years before the judgment" (*Catena Aurea on St. Matthew*, chap. 12, lect. 13).

days, hath spoken to us by his Son, whom he hath appointed heir of all things, by whom also he made the world" (Heb. 1, 1-2). And He continues, **And behold a greater than Jonas here**, as it is stated in Hebrews 3, 3: "For this man was counted worthy of greater glory than Moses." Therefore, the Ninivites are set before them, because they did penance. **The queen of the south shall rise in judgment with this generation, and shall condemn it**, namely, in regard to the wisdom that they did not wish to receive. Concerning this woman, it is stated in III Kings 10, 24, that she came to hear the wisdom of Solomon. By this woman, the Church is signified, on account of the faithful;[36] "The queen stood on thy right hand, in gilded clothing; surrounded with variety," etc., (Ps. 44, 10). The Church is called a queen because it ought to rule itself; "The king, that sitteth on the throne of judgment, scattereth away all evil with his look," etc., (Prov. 20, 8). And the Church is said to be *of the south*, by reason of the Holy Ghost; "Arise, O north wind, and come, O south wind, blow through my garden," etc., (Cant. 4, 16). This queen will rise in judgment with this generation. Observe that it is not said that she did not sin, but that she was not rebellious. Why? Because **she came from the ends of the earth to hear the wisdom of Solomon**, as it is stated in III Kings 10, 24.[37] And 'it is not necessary for you to come from the ends of the earth, because He is here.' Hence, **Behold a greater than Solomon here**, because Solomon was a temporal king and a sinner, but this King is innocent and eternal; "His power is an everlasting power that shall not be taken away: and his kingdom eternal that shall not be destroyed" (Dan. 7, 14). **And when an unclean spirit is gone out of a man**, etc. He showed above that the Gentiles were greater than the Jews; here He wishes to confirm this by an example. And so, firstly, He presents the example; and secondly, He applies it, where it is said, **So shall it be also to this wicked generation**. He presents the example of an unclean spirit.

You should note that an example is sometimes taken from a past event or sometimes from a parable. And when it is taken from a past event, it is fitting that every single thing be expounded separately so that both meanings require their own exposition, such as the example of Jonas presented here. Sometimes, an example is taken from a parable, as when it is said, "The kingdom of heaven is like," etc.

---

36. Of whom the Church is composed.

37. "All the earth desired to see Solomon's face, to hear his wisdom, which God had given in his heart."

In this case, it is not necessary to relate what is in the kingdom of heaven. We can, therefore, say, according to Jerome, that it is a similitude and a parable; and so there is one meaning. Or, it is an example taken from a past event, according to Augustine; and so there is a twofold meaning. An unclean spirit goes out from a man in two ways, because sometimes he tortures a man corporeally or sometimes spiritually. Hence, it ought to be seen how a man is filled with the unclean spirit; how he is filled corporeally and how spiritually; and thirdly, how this pertains to the point at hand. Therefore, four things are mentioned. Firstly, the liberation from the unclean spirit is mentioned; secondly, the repeated troubling; thirdly, the gravity; and fourthly, the occasion of the second troubling. He says, therefore, **If an unclean spirit is gone out of a man.** Everything that is mixed with a baser thing is said to be impure; but everything that is mixed with a purer thing is said to be more pure; for example, if silver is joined to lead, it becomes more base. In this manner, a created spirit, if it adheres to something lower, is said to be impure. And this kind of spirit sometimes goes out of a man whom it troubles corporeally, sometimes from a man whom it troubles spiritually, as, for instance, in Baptism. Next, the repeated troubling and the occasion are mentioned. And firstly, it is mentioned on the part of the demon; secondly, it is mentioned on the part of those who are troubled. On the part of the demon, firstly, his troubling is mentioned in regard to untroubled men; secondly, his troubling is mentioned in regard to the one troubled. For this is the manner of a demon, that it cannot rest unless it harms, because it loved sin from the beginning. Hence, when it is expelled from someone, it seeks where it may trouble. Hence, He says, **He walketh through dry places seeking rest, and findeth none.** Hence, sometimes he does not find rest. He does find rest, however, in certain men, as it is said, "He sleepeth under the shadow, in the covert of the reed, and in moist places" (Job 40, 16). The moist places are the hearts given to pleasures; the dry places are those who despise pleasures, who shun prosperity. And it is said concerning this, "Our bones are dried up, and our hope is lost" (Ez. 37, 11). He says, **He walketh**, and he searches for any man he may deceive. Hence, by the fact that it is said, **He walketh**, he shows his watchfulness; "Be sober and watch: because your adversary the devil, as a roaring lion, goeth about seeking whom he may devour" (I Pet. 5, 8). **Seeking rest, and findeth none**, except in moist places. So it was concerning the Jews, because going out from the Jews[38] he went to the Gentiles, who were dry by lacking the moisture of divine grace; but he did not find rest, because he was driven out, since they received the word of God. *Then he saith: I will return into my house from whence I came out.* From these words you can gather that if the devil is sometimes expelled by a man, because the man did penance, nevertheless, he does not completely depart from him; just as it is written of Christ (Luke 4, 13) that the devil departed from him for a time. Therefore, this ought to be understood, so that men might be always watchful lest he return. And this is what He says, *I will return*, etc. *And coming he findeth it empty.* Here is related the occasion on the part of him who is afflicted a second time. If we wish to apply this to the Jews, it is clear that when the devil was expelled from the Gentiles he returned to the Jews. Hence, a triple occasion is related. The first, namely, is idleness; hence, it is said, *Empty*; "Idleness hath taught much evil" (Eccli. 33, 29). For that reason, Jerome says, "Always do some good, so that the devil find you employed." Hence, *Empty*, means idle; "The enemies have seen her, and have mocked at her sabbaths" (Lam. 1, 7). *Swept*, because what is swept is only cleaned of the loose dirt. Hence, to sweep is the same as to clean lightly, and, wherefore, sweeping is imperfect cleaning. Likewise, *garnished*, and this means superficially adorned. Perfect cleansing ought to be made with fire, as it is stated in the Law, that a vessel ought to be cleansed with fire. Likewise, that which is garnished, has some beauty from itself, and only some from the garnishing, about which it is said in Psalm 143, 12: "Their daughters are decked out, adorned round about after the similitude of a temple," etc. But those who want to be secure ought to have interior beauty; "All the glory of the king's daughter is within in golden borders, clothed round about with varieties" (Ps. 44, 14). But when garnishing is made only in exterior things, one is not abandoned by the demons. It was thus in regard to the Jews, because they were observing the Sabbaths, in which they were resting more from good deeds than from evil deeds. Likewise, they were placing their whole concern in the smallest points of the Law. *Then he goeth, and taketh with him seven other spirits more wicked than himself.* Here is related the second, and worse, troubling, and it is shown to be more grave; firstly, in regard to its num-

---

38. "JEROME: The unclean spirit then went out from the Jews when they received the Law; and being cast out of the Jews, he walked through the wilderness of the Gentiles; as it follows, He walks through dry places seeking rest" (*Catena Aurea on St. Matthew*, chap. 12, lect. 14).

ber; secondly, in regard to its duration; and thirdly, in regard to its effect. It is more grave, in regard to its number, because **he taketh with him seven others**. According to Chrysostom, it is meant literally, because when someone falls, and he does not take heed, then something worse happens to him; "Behold thou art made whole: sin no more, lest some worse thing happen to thee," (Jn. 5, 14). According to Augustine, the passage, **he taketh seven others**, can be expounded in two ways. For, sometimes a penitent does penance, but is negligent, and then becomes more inclined to sin; "Wherefore God delivered them up to a reprobate sense" (Rom. 1, 28). And by the fact that He says, **seven**, the entirety of all vices is signified. It is expounded otherwise by Augustine as follows. Some men sin by a particular sin, and, in the state of penance, they add hypocrisy to their other sins. And just as there are seven gifts of the Holy Ghost, so there are seven hypocrisies. Hence, firstly there were simple vices, then there were added the false images of the virtues, which are the contraries of the vices, which are worse: and they are said to be seven, either on account of the universality of the vices, or on account of the Sabbath.[39] And those who sin in this manner become more persevering in evil. Hence, He says, **And they enter in and dwell there**, because they do not wish to recede from thence; "This people in Jerusalem is turned away with a stubborn revolting, they have laid hold on lying, and have refused to return" (Jer. 8, 5). And if it is expounded as pertaining to the Jews, it is evident that an evil spirit dwells in them and does not wish to leave them. **And the last state of that man is made worse than the first**. And here the heaviness of their sins is set forth in regard to the effect. Literally, a man is punished more who is more heavily laden with sins. Hence, "It had been better not to have known the way of justice than, after having known it, to turn back" (II Pet. 2, 21). Likewise, in regard to the Jews, they committed worse sins by blaspheming Christ than by worshipping idols. For that reason, He continues, **So shall it be also to this wicked generation**.

---

39. The Sabbath is the seventh day of the week and was the day of rest in the Jewish Law. Hence, the mentioning of it here seems to be a subtle reference to the hypocrisy of the Jews in fulfilling the Law. "AMBROSE: Seeing that in truth Israel has sacrilegiously profaned the seven weeks of the Law, (i.e. from Easter to Pentecost,) and the mystery of the eighth day. Therefore, as upon us is multiplied the sevenfold gifts of the Spirit, so upon them falls the whole accumulated attack of the unclean spirits. For the number seven is frequently taken to mean the whole. CHRYS: Now the evil spirits who dwell in the souls of the Jews, are worse than those in former times. For then the Jews raged against the Prophets, now they lift up their hands against the Lord of the Prophets" (*Catena Aurea on St. Luke*, chap. 11, lect. 7).

46. As he was yet speaking to the multitudes, behold his mother and his brethren stood without, seeking to speak to him.

47. And one said unto him: Behold thy mother and thy brethren stand without, seeking thee.

48. But he answering him that told him, said: Who is my mother, and who are my brethren?

49. And stretching forth his hand towards his disciples, he said: Behold my mother and my brethren.

50. For whosoever shall do the will of my Father, that is in heaven, he is my brother, and sister, and mother.

In the preceding part, the Lord confuted His adversaries; now He commends His believing disciples, etc., when the presence of His mother and brethren was acknowledged. Firstly, their presence is related; secondly, the announcement of their presence is related; and thirdly, the commendation of His disciples is related. He says, therefore, **As he was yet speaking**.

Here, however, there is a literal question: Why in Luke 11, where the same words which were said are related, the words which follow are not related, but instead the words are subjoined, "And it came to pass, as he spoke these things, a certain woman from the crowd, lifting up her voice," etc., (verse 29)? And so, it seems that there is an inconsistency.

Augustine solves the question thus: Without a doubt it was said as Matthew narrates, that it was as He was yet speaking, that is to say, it was at the same time as it was in his account, etc. But it could be that it happened as Luke says, and so it could be that Luke anticipates the event, or that he is recalling according to the order of his memory.

Behold thy mother and thy brethren stand without, seeking thee, etc. Concerning His mother, there is no doubt that it is she about whom it was spoken in chapter 1; about His brethren, however, there can be a question. And because mention is made of His brethren, it has been an occasion of a heresy, that when the Virgin had borne Jesus, Joseph knew Mary and had children of her; but that is heretical, because after giving birth the Virgin remained inviolate. There was also an opinion that these brethren were children of Joseph of another wife. But this is nonsense, because we believe that just as the mother of Jesus was a virgin, so was Joseph, because God entrusted the Virgin to a virgin: and as he was at the end, so he also was at the beginning. Who are, therefore, these brethren? Jerome said that men are called brethren in many ways. For some are brethren by nature, as it was said above, "Jacob begot Judas and his brethren" (above 1, 2). Sometimes brethren are of the same nation; "Thou mayst not make a man of another nation king, that is not thy brother" (Deut. 17, 15). Sometimes they are of the same religion, such as all Christians, as it will be said below (chap. 23, 8).[40] From this passage, the custom became established that men of the same religion are called brethren. Sometimes, men of one parentage are called brethren, as in Josue 2, 12: "And give me a true token that you will save my father and mother, and my brethren." Sometimes, all men are called brethren, who are of one Father, namely, God; "Have we not all one father? hath not one God created us? why then doth every one of us despise his brother?" (Mal. 2, 10) In none of these ways are these men here said to be the Lord's brethren; for that reason, in one way they are said to be brethren, namely, because they were blood-relations. Hence, Abraham said to Lot, "For we are brethren" (Gen. 13, 8), although Lot was Abraham's nephew. In this way, these men were His brethren, because they were His cousins. Afterwards, the announcement of their repentance is related, *And one said unto him: Behold thy mother and thy brethren stand without, seeking thee*. Why he said this, and why it was necessary, are explained in Luke. It was because there was such a great crowd that they could not get to Him. Mystically, by His Mother, the Church is signified; hence, it is said, "Go forth, ye daughters of Sion, and see king Solomon in the diadem, wherewith his mother crowned him" (Cant. 3, 11). *And thy brethren*, that is, the Jews, who stand without, abandoning Christ; "My brethren have abandoned me" (Job 6, 15). They seek, but they do not find, as it is stated, "But Israel, by following after the law of justice, is not come unto the law of justice" (Rom. 9, 31). *But he answering him*, etc. Christ's reply is related and He does two things. Firstly, He confutes the questioner; secondly, He commends His disciples where it is said, *And stretching forth his hand*, etc. Now, He says, *Who is my mother, and who are my brethren?* By reason of this passage, certain men denied that Christ had truly taken flesh, but merely the appearances of flesh. Hence, they were expounding this passage as follows: 'This woman is not My mother, nor are these men My brethren,' which is opposed to the Apostle saying, "God sent his Son, made of a woman," etc., (Gal. 4, 4). Again, he says, "Who was made

---

40. "For one is your master: and all you are brethren."

to him of the seed of David, according to the flesh" (Rom. 1, 3). Moreover, He recognized her on the Cross; "Woman, behold thy son," as it stated in John 19, 26.

Chrysostom asks, "Why does the Lord say, *Who is my mother, and who are my brethren?*" And Chrysostom says this for two reasons; of which one is sound, but the other is not. For he says that His mother and brethren succumbed to human frailty, because seeing Christ preaching, and the crowd following Him, they had vainglory. For that reason, they wanted to have some sort of glory; for that reason, the Lord wished to show that He was not doing these things by means of what He had assumed from His mother, but from His Father. This view is partly sound. For in respect to His brethren it is sound, for in like manner, it is stated in John 7, 5: "For neither did his brethren believe in him." But in respect to His Mother it is not sound, because it is believed that she never sinned, neither mortally nor venially. For, doubtlessly, it is said of her, "Thou art all fair, O my love, and there is not a spot in thee" (Cant. 4, 7). And Augustine says, "When the matter of sin is treated, it is my wish to exclude absolutely any mention concerning her." Therefore, Jerome solves the question otherwise, saying that he who announced them, had announced them insidiously. For he wanted to find out whether His attention was so attracted to spiritual things, that He would not be concerned about temporal things. For that reason, He gives advice on affections. Hence, He certainly would not have loved His Mother more unless she was more spiritual. Hence, He says, *Who is my mother?* He does not deny that she is His Mother, but He intends to forbid inordinate affection. Hence, "He that loveth father or mother more than me, is not worthy of me" (above 10, 37).

Afterwards, the commendation of his disciples is related. And firstly, He commends His disciples; and secondly, He commends all believers in general. He says, therefore, *And stretching forth his hand towards his disciples, he said: Behold my mother.* It is as though He were to say, 'I love these men more than the affection of My mother or My brethren.' For the affection of the Holy Ghost ought to be preferred. And He is not only referring to these men, but to all men. Hence, it is said, *For whosoever shall do the will of my Father, that is in heaven, he is my brother, and sister, and mother.* For He had a heavenly and an earthly begetting. Hence, He prefers the heavenly to the earthly. For those who do the will of My Father, they are related to Him by a heavenly begetting; hence, "If you be the children of Abraham, do the works of Abraham" (Jn. 8, 39). For He came to do the will of Him, as it is stated (Jn. 4, 34; 5, 30; 6, 38). He says, **brother**, with respect to the firmer believers, **and sister**,- with respect to weaker believers.

But what is it that He says, **And he is my mother**? It ought to be said that whosoever is faithful, who does the will of the Father, namely, he who obeys simply, he is His brother, because he is similar to Him, Who fulfilled the will of the Father. A man who not only does this, but also converts others, begets Christ in others, and so he becomes a mother. Just as, on the other hand, a man kills Christ in others, who provokes them to evil. "My little children, of whom I am in labor again, until Christ be formed in you" (Gal. 4, 10).

CHAPTER THIRTEEN

1. The same day Jesus going out of the house, sat by the sea side.

2. And great multitudes were gathered together unto him, so that he went up into a boat and sat: and all the multitude stood on the shore.

3. And he spoke to them many things in parables, saying: Behold the sower went forth to sow.

4. And whilst he soweth some fell by the way side, and the birds of the air came and ate them up.

5. And other some fell upon stony ground, where they had not much earth: and they sprung up immediately, because they had no deepness of earth.

6. And when the sun was up they were scorched: and because they had not root, they withered away.

7. And others fell among thorns: and the thorns grew up and choked them.

8. And others fell upon good ground: and they brought forth fruit, some an hundred fold, some sixty fold, and some thirty fold.

9. He that hath ears to hear, let him hear.

10. And his disciples came and said to him: Why speakest thou to them in parables?

11. Who answered and said to them: Because to you it is given to know the mysteries of the kingdom of heaven: but to them it is not given.

12. For he that hath, to him shall be given, and he shall abound: but he that hath not, from him shall be taken away that also which he hath.

13. Therefore do I speak to them in parables: because seeing they see not, and hearing they hear not, neither do they understand.

14. And the prophecy of Isaias is fulfilled in them, who saith: By hearing you shall hear, and shall not understand: and seeing you shall see, and shall not perceive.

15. For the heart of this people is grown gross, and with their ears they have been dull of hearing, and their eyes they have shut: lest at any time they should see with their eyes, and hear with their ears, and understand with their heart, and be converted, and I should heal them.

16. But blessed are your eyes, because they see, and your ears, because they hear.

17. For, amen, I say to you, many prophets and just men have desired to see the things that you see, and have not seen them: and to hear the things that you hear and have not heard them. 18. Hear you therefore the parable of the sower.
19. When any one heareth the word of the kingdom, and understandeth it not, there cometh the wicked one, and catcheth away that which was sown in his heart: this is he that received the seed by the way side.
20. And he that received the seed upon stony ground, is he that heareth the word, and immediately receiveth it with joy.
21. Yet hath he not root in himself, but is only for a time: and when there ariseth tribulation and persecution because of the word, he is presently scandalized.
22. And he that received the seed among thorns, is he that heareth the word, and the care of this world and the deceitfulness of riches choketh up the word, and he becometh fruitless.
23. But he that received the seed upon good ground, is he that heareth the word, and understandeth, and beareth fruit, and yieldeth the one an hundredfold, and another sixty, and another thirty.

Above, the Gospel teaching was set forth, and its adversaries were confuted; here He shows the power of the Gospel teaching; and firstly, He does this by words; and secondly, He does this by deeds in chapter 14. And about the first, the circumstances of the teaching are firstly related; secondly, Christ's teaching is related; and thirdly, the effect is related. The second is where it is said, **Behold the sower went forth to sow**; and the third is where it is said, **Have ye understood all these things?** And firstly, the Evangelist related four circumstances, namely, the place, the time, the position of the hearers, and the position of the speaker. He mentions the time when he says: **The same day**. From this, it is given to be understood that he mentions the order of what took place. For it can only be understood if the word ***day*** be taken as the time. Next, the circumstance of the place is mentioned, namely, **He sat by the sea side**, etc. And this can be explained according to a literal and to a mystical explanation. Chrysostom mentions the literal explanation. For it was because, above, he had said that a certain man said, when He was speaking to the crowd, "Behold thy mother," etc., whereupon Chrysostom had expounded that they had succumbed to human frailty, for that reason, the Lord wished to go out of the house to reprimand their, namely, His brethren's, wickedness. And He also went out to render honor to His Mother. Hence, it is said, "Honour thy father and thy mother" (Ex. 20, 12). Mystically, by the house, Judea is understood, going out from which on account of their unbelief, He came to the sea, namely, the Gentiles, who were stirred up by unbelief; "Behold, your house shall be left to you, desolate" (below 23, 38); as it is said, "I have forsaken my house, I have left my inheritance: I have given my dear soul into the hand of her enemies" (Jer. 12, 7). The world is called a sea; "So is this great sea, which stretcheth wide its arms: there are creeping things without number," etc., (Ps. 103, 25). Or, otherwise, by the house is understood the inner recesses of the mind; "When I go into my house, I shall repose myself with her" (Wis. 8, 16). Hence, sometimes, He went out from the secret place of contemplation to the public place of teaching. *And multitudes were gathered together unto him.* Here the Evangelist presents the hearers: for when the mind has gone out to the public place of teaching, then many can hear and profit; "Draw near to me, ye unlearned, and gather yourselves together into the house of discipline" (Eccli. 51, 31). Next, the position of the one teaching and those hearing are related; hence, it is said, *So that he went up into a boat and sat.* And why did He go into a boat? There could be a literal reason, namely, that there were many hearers, for that reason, He wanted to have them before His face, so that they might understand better. For all things are before Him; "Behold my eye hath seen all things" (Job 13, 1). Another reason is mystical, namely, that, by the boat, the Church gathered from the Gentiles is signified, wherein He sits by faith, and He teaches those who stand upon the shore, namely, the catechumens, who are ready for the faith. Or it may be expounded differently, that by the fact that Jesus is in the sea, and, on the other hand, the hearers stand on the shore, He gives an example to preachers, namely, that they do not expose their subjects to dangers. And this is signified in Exodus 13, that when Moses led out his people, he did not lead them out by the road to the land of the Philistines, thinking lest, perhaps, they might regret and return to Egypt. For that reason, Jesus sat in the rolling sea, but He left the others on the outside; for that reason, it is said, *And all the multitude stood on the shore.* The manner of the teaching follows, where it is said, *And he spoke to them many things in parables.* The reason is twofold. One reason is that, by parables of this kind, sacred things would be hidden from the unbelievers, lest they blaspheme: for it was said above, "Give not that which is holy to dogs" (7, 6). Therefore, because many men were blaspheming, for that reason, He wished to speak in parables. Hence, "To you it is given to know the mystery of the kingdom of God; but to the rest in parables" (Lk. 8, 10). The second reason is that uncultured men are taught better through parables of this kind. Hence, men, namely, the uncultured, when divine things are explained under similitudes, comprehend and retain them better. For that reason, the Lord wished to speak in parables, so that they might be better committed to memory. For because He had known that worthy men would receive His doctrine, He wished to give it to them in such a way that they might remember it better; "I will open my mouth in parables" (Ps. 77, 2). And why did He propose many parables? One reason is that, in a multitude of men, different men are affected in different ways; for that reason, He ought to diversify the parables, so that He might correspond with their different affections. Another reason is that spiritual things are hidden; for that reason, they cannot fully be made known through temporal things, hence, they have to be made known through different things; "I wish that God would speak with thee, and would open his lips to thee, that he might shew thee the secrets of wisdom" (Job 11, 5-6).

The sower went forth to sow, etc. Here the parabolic teaching is set forth. And He intends three things. Firstly, He relates the obstacles to the Gospel teaching; secondly, He relates its growth; and thirdly, He relates its dignity. The second is where it is said, *The kingdom of heaven is like to leaven*, etc.; the third is where it is said, *The kingdom of heaven is like to a merchant seeking good pearls*, etc. About the first, He begins by setting forth the interior obstacles; secondly, in the following parable, He sets forth those which are exterior. The first point is divided into three parts: for firstly, the parable is related; secondly, it is applied; and thirdly, it is explained. The second part is where it is said, *And his disciples came*, etc.; the third part is where it is said, *Hear you therefore the parable of the sower*. In the first part, He does three things. Firstly, the pursuit of the sower is described; secondly, the seed's obstacles are described; and thirdly, the seed's fruit is described. The second part is where it is said, *And whilst he soweth some fell by the way side*, etc.; the third is where it is said, *And others fell upon good ground*, etc. He says, therefore, *The sower went forth to sow*, namely, the seed of doctrine. Hence, Christ sows just as He baptizes, as it is stated in John 4, 1-2.[1] For a seed is the origin of a fruit. Hence,

---

1. "When Jesus therefore understood the Pharisees had heard that Jesus maketh more disciples and baptizeth more than John (Though Jesus himself did not baptize, but his disciples)..."

every good action is from God; "He who hath begun a good work in you will perfect it," etc., (Phil. 1, 6). And, in this passage, the error is abolished of those who say that the beginning of a good work is from us; which is false. Hence, Gregory says: "A preacher labors in vain, unless the Savior's grace is sown inwardly." Hence, He says: *The sower went forth to sow*, etc. It seems that He belabors these words; but He does not belabor them, because sometimes a sower goes forth in order to sow, and sometimes he goes to reap; in this way, Christ, in the beginning, went forth in order to sow; "To him that soweth justice, there is a faithful reward" (Prov. 11, 18). *The sower*, therefore, *went forth to sow*. And what did He sow? *His seed*. For certain men go forth to sow iniquity; "I have seen those who work iniquity, and sow sorrows, and reap them" (Prov. 4, 8). But He went forth to sow His seed. That seed is the Word of God, who proceeds essentially. Hence, He is the Word of the Father; "The word of God is the fountain of wisdom" (Eccli. 1, 5). But what does He do? He makes men similar to Him from whom He proceeds, because He makes them sons of God; "I have said: You are gods and all of you the sons of the most High" (Ps. 81, 6). "He called them gods to whom the word of God was spoken" (Jn. 10, 35). And in the same place it is said, "He gave them power to be made the sons of God" (1, 12). Therefore, *He went forth*, etc. But let us see about the seed's obstacles. For it is triply impeded, because three things are required. For it is required that the remembrance be preserved. Hence, "Bind them in thy heart continually" (Prov.6, 21). Secondly, it is required that it be rooted through love; "Thy word is exceedingly kindled: and thy servant hath loved it" (Ps. 118, 140). Thirdly, diligence is required; "Pursue justice, godliness, faith, charity, patience, mildness," etc., (I Tim. 6, 11). These three things are taken away by three things. Remembrance is taken away through vanity; love, or charity, is taken away through hardness; diligence is taken away through the springing up of vices. Hence, He says: *And whilst he soweth some fell by the way side*. As a road is open to every traveler, so the heart is exposed to any thought; "At every head of the way thou hast set up a sign of thy prostitution: and hast made thy beauty to be abominable" (Ez. 16, 25). Hence, when the word of God falls into a vain and unstable heart, it falls by the wayside and is subject to a double danger. But Matthew sets forth only one danger, namely, *The birds of the air ate them up*. But Luke sets forth two: namely, that it is trodden; and, likewise, that it is snatched up by the birds. It is in this way that vain men receive the word of God; it is trodden through vain thoughts, or wicked companionship. This is why the devil greatly rejoices whenever he can take away or tread upon this seed. "Why lookest thou upon scorners, and holdest thy peace when the wicked trod upon the man that is more just than himself?" (Hab. 1, 13). The second obstacle is hardness of heart; "His heart shall be as hard as a stone, and as firm as a smith's anvil" (Job 41, 15). And this is opposed to charity, because it belongs to love to melt; "My soul melted when the beloved spoke," etc., (Cant. 5, 6). For a thing is said to be hard that is constricted into itself and confined by its own boundaries. Love makes the lover to pass into the object of its love: hence, it is poured out. He says, therefore, **And other some fell upon stony ground**, etc. "I will take away the stony heart out of your flesh, and will give you a heart of flesh" (Ez. 36, 26). For there are some men who have a heart so deprived of all love, that they lack all flesh. However, some men have well-ordered affections, but have little of them: hence, they do not have a deep heart. One has a deep heart when its goal and affections are deep. Therefore, a man has a deep love who loves all things for the sake of God, and puts nothing before the love of God. Hence, some men correctly take delight in God, but take more delight in other things: and these men are not melted; and such men do not have much earth. And by earth is signified softness. Hence, this stony ground is taken for a hardened mind. It continues, **And they sprung up immediately**, etc. This is because they who think deeply, think for a long time; but those who do not think deeply, immediately rush into action. Hence, they go forth quickly; "For before the harvest it was all flourishing, and it shall bud without perfect ripeness" (Is. 18, 5). Hence, they hear quickly, but they are not rooted in Him, because they do not have the depth of the earth of love and charity. "Being rooted and founded in charity," etc., (Eph. 3, 17). The third obstacle is the destruction of the fruit, because if one loves riches more than God, when the time of tribulation comes, he assents to what he loves more. Hence, **When the sun was up they were scorched**, etc., namely, through their lack of self-control. "He that shall kill by the sword must be killed by the sword. Here is the patience of the saints" (Apoc. 13, 10). **And because they had not root, they withered away**, because God was not their root. "My strength is dried up like a potsherd" (Ps. 21, 16). Sometimes, in Scripture, a rock stands for something good, and, sometimes, for something bad. It is the same for the earth and the sun. Hence, there are some men who are well-affected, but, afterwards, conduct themselves negligently. It was not so of Paul, who was saying, "I chastise my body and bring it into subjection"

(I Cor. 9, 27). *And others fell among thorns.* Now the thorns are cares, wraths, quarrels, things of this kind; "Sow not upon thorns" (Jer. 4, 3); "I passed by the field of the slothful man"; and it continues, "And thorns had covered the face thereof" (Prov. 24, 20-31). *And the thorns grew up and choked them.*

But someone could say: 'The foolishness was on the part of the sower.' It can be said that if the discourse were about sensible ground, this would be true; but mention is made of spiritual ground, for that reason, the assertion does not hold, because it is referring to a completely different material.

Having set forth the obstacles, it is treated about the fruit of the seed. *And others fell upon good ground: and they brought forth fruit.* The ground, which is not by the wayside, which is not stony, which is not thorny, is good ground, that is to say, a good heart; and if the seed is sown there, it bears fruit; "For the Lord will give goodness: and our earth shall yield her fruit" (Ps. 84, 13). But what fruit? *Some an hundred fold, some sixty fold, and some thirty fold.* Certain men refer this to the reward that is in heaven, because they will indeed have a hundredfold, etc. "The fruit of good labors is glorious" (Wis. 3, 15). Others refer the thirtyfold fruit to belief in the Trinity, the sixtyfold fruit to the fruit of good works, and the hundredfold fruit to the contemplation of heavenly things. But this cannot be, because the hearer is he who produces the fruit. Likewise, the reward is received in the present time. Hence, it ought to be referred to the perfection of justice. The fruit, therefore, is properly the last thing that is awaited in the tree: so this refers to the fruit of justice that is had from preaching. And this is a hundredfold, etc., because perfection is threefold: lesser, greater, and middle, such that the hundredfold belongs to martyrs, the sixtyfold belongs to virgins, and the thirtyfold belongs to the married. And why is this? It is because, etc.[2] But the perfection of virgins is sixtyfold, because then they ought to rest from evil; and, for that reason, this perfection belongs to virgins and to those resting, who are separated from the world. By thirty, the perfection of those serving as soldiers in this life is signified, because such men are fit for war. Others give the reasons for these numbers by the counting on the hand, etc., as is

---

2. "AUG (*Questiones evangeliorum ex Matthaeo et Luca*, i, 9); There is fruit an hundredfold of the martyrs because of their sanctity of life or contempt of death; a sixtyfold fruit of virgins, because they rest not warring against the use of the flesh; for retirement is allowed to those of sixty years' age after service in war or in public business; and there is a thirtyfold fruit of the wedded, because theirs is the age of warfare, and their struggle is the more arduous that they should not be vanquished by their lusts" (*Catena Aurea on St. Matthew*, chap. 13, lect. 3).

stated in the Gloss.[3] You can expound these numbers, otherwise, according to the factors of the numbers. You see, therefore, that the seed is God's commandment: the number thirty is derived from the factors three and ten: sixty is derived from six and ten: a hundred is the product of ten multiplied by itself. The number three is a complete number, and it has an ordinary perfection: the number six, likewise, is a perfect number, because nothing is lacking to it, for it has the perfection of wholeness: ten is the perfect number, because it is the first numerical limit of the numbers,[4] hence, it has the perfection of an end. In this way, perfection is threefold. The first degree of perfection is common justice, and in this way there is the perfection of the number three, which is denoted by the number thirty; but when a man has a greater perfection beyond common justice, then he is said to produce sixtyfold fruit; but when a man is perfect, and already foretastes the sweetness of the fruit, then he attains to the hundredfold fruit. Or it is expounded otherwise, following Augustine, according to the three ways men bear temptations. For some men are severely tempted, but they resist strongly; and these have thirtyfold fruit. Others are little tempted, but they attack the temptations; and these have sixty fold fruit. But they have hundred fold fruit who already remain in undisturbed peace. And because this was said parabolically, therefore He adds, **He that hath ears to hear,** meaning ears of the heart, **let him hear** with his intellect. **And his disciples came**, etc. Above, the parable was set forth; here the meaning is told: and concerning this, two things are related here. Firstly, the question of the disciples is related; and secondly,

---

3. "The yield thirty fold signifies wedlock, for the joining together of the fingers to express that number, suggestive as it is of a loving gentle kiss or embracing, aptly represents the relation of husband and wife. The yield sixty fold refers to widows who are placed in a position of distress and tribulation. Accordingly, they are typified by that finger which is placed under the other to express the number sixty; for, as it is extremely trying when one has once tasted pleasure to abstain from its enticements, so the reward of doing this is proportionately great. Moreover, a hundred—I ask the reader to give me his best attention—necessitates a change from the left hand to the right; but while the hand is different the fingers are the same as those which on the left hand signify married women and widows; only in this instance the circle formed by them indicates the crown of virginity" (St. Jerome, Letter 48, n. 2) From this passage compared with Ep. cxxiii. 9, and Bede, *De Temporum Ratione*, c. 1. (*De Loquetâ Digitorum*), it appears that the number thirty was indicated by joining the tips of the thumb and forefinger of the left hand, sixty was indicated by curling up the forefinger of the same hand and then doubling the thumb over it, while one hundred was expressed by joining the tips of the thumb and forefinger of the right hand. See Professor Mayor's learned note on Juv. x. 249. (Noted in *Nicene and Post-Nicene Fathers*, (Second Series) vol. 6).

4. "For ten is, in a way, the perfect number (being the first numerical limit, since the figures do not go beyond ten but begin over again from one)" (II II, q. 87, a. 1).

the reply is related, where it is said, **Who answered**, etc. He says, therefore, **His disciples came and said to him.**

Here a literal question is provoked: Since He was in a boat, how, then, did they come to Him? It ought to be known that they were in the boat with Christ; they came to Him, however, through the attention of their minds, or they also came nearer corporeally, because they were a small distance apart away from Him: or, since they were out of the boat, they came to Him. In like manner, we, if we wish to come to Him, will be enlightened; "Come ye to him and be enlightened" (Ps. 33, 6). And two things are noticed. Firstly, an example is given of not asking importunately; hence, while He was teaching the crowds, they did not ask Him; "A time to keep silence, and a time to speak" (Eccle. 3, 7). **Why speakest thou to them in parables?** Likewise, here it ought to be considered, that what is for the salvation of souls should always be done; hence, the answer follows, **Who answered and said to them**. And firstly, God's ordinance is related; and secondly, a certain reason is given. He says: 'I speak in parables for this reason, because **to you it is given to know the mysteries of the kingdom of heaven: but to them it is not given**': in these words, three things are asserted. Firstly, it is asserted that certain men comprehend, but others do not. And this is not to be attributed to anyone, but to God ordaining; for this reason, it is given to you and not to others. And, therefore, it is a divine ordinance. Similarly, it is of great utility, because it is a sort of instruction about beatitude: hence, there is great utility, insofar as He gives you knowledge of divine mysteries; "Who is the wise man, that may understand this, and to whom the word of the mouth of the Lord may come that he may declare this" (Jer. 9, 12). Moreover, it is a sign of divine love; "But I have called you friends, because all things, whatsoever, I have heard of my Father, I have made known to you" (Jn. 15, 15). Again, this happens due to a gift, not due to your merit; "For unto you it is given for Christ, not only to believe in him, but also to suffer for him" (Phil. 1, 29). And this is "the mystery of the kingdom of heaven of God" (Lk. 8, 10), and the words "of God" mean 'from God'; "Or what hast thou that thou hast not received?" (I Cor. 4, 7). **For he that hath, to him shall be given, and he shall abound.** For a man has something that is given to him. And what is that? I answer, saying that four things are preparatory for a man to be given something. The first is his desire. Hence, if you wish to have knowledge, let your desire anticipate it, as it is stated: "The desire of wisdom bringeth to the everlasting kingdom" (Wis. 6, 21). And above it is stated: "Ask, and it shall be given you" (7, 7). Hence, **he that hath** a desire, **to** *him shall be given, and he shall abound*, because, "It is He who giveth to all men abundantly and upbraideth not" (James 1, 5). *But he that hath not*, and if it seems that he has some aptitude for wisdom, meaning justice, and is lukewarm, that which he seems to have but does not have *from him shall be taken away*. Hence, Chrysostom says: "If you see a lukewarm man, you ought to admonish him to cease being lukewarm, and if he does not want to cease, send him away." "I would thou wert cold or hot. But because thou art lukewarm and neither cold nor hot, I will begin to vomit thee out of my mouth" (Apoc. 3, 15-16). The second thing that is required is zeal; and this is the exposition of Remigius. Hence, he who has a good intelligence, and is not zealous, will not make progress. Hence, wisdom will be given to him who is zealous, and he will abound; "If thou shalt seek her as money, and shalt dig for her as for a treasure, then shalt thou understand the fear of the Lord, and shalt find the knowledge of God" (Prov. 2, 4). *But he that hath not* zeal, what he seems to have, namely, natural intelligence, will not make progress, but, on the contrary, it *from him shall be taken away*. The third thing that is required is charity: because charity is the root of all virtues and of all good works. The Apostle says: "Being rooted and founded in charity" (Eph. 3, 17). Hence, if you have, namely, charity, you will break forth into every good work; the Apostle says: "Charity is patient, is kind" (I Cor. 13, 4). Hence, if you do not have charity, all will dry up. Hence, whatever good a man has without charity is nothing, because, "He that loveth not abideth in death" (I Jn. 3, 14). The fourth thing that is required is faith, because the other goods of those who do not have faith avail little; "He sheweth himself to them that have faith in him" (Wis. 1, 2). And, "With the heart, we believe unto justice: but, with the mouth, confession is made unto salvation" (Rom. 10, 10). And he who does not have the justice of faith, that which he seems to have, whether natural or moral, shall be taken away from him. The Apostle says: "All that is not of faith is sin" (Rom. 14, 23). 'Therefore, I say that it was given to you, because you have faith, to those, however, it was not given.'

But here one ought to take heed of a certain error, because it seems that from zeal and from good natural qualities we can acquire eternal glory. But Paul says: "What hast thou that thou hast not received?" (I Cor. 4, 7). Hence, all these things; desire, zeal, charity and faith; are from God.

Therefore do I speak to them in parables, etc. Here He applies His words to the point at hand; and He does two things. Firstly, He applies His words, inasmuch as they pertain to the Jews;

and secondly, He applies them to the Apostles, where it is said, *But blessed are your eyes*, etc. And concerning the first point, He does two things. Firstly, He uses a similitude, lest He seem to speak out of hatred; and secondly, He invokes the authority of Scripture, where it is said, *And the prophecy of Isaias is fulfilled in them.* Notice that when He is showing the way to salvation He manifests His teaching by His actions. Hence: "Jesus began to do and to teach" (Acts 1, 1). And: "If I had not done among them the works that no other man hath done, they would not have sin" (Jn. 15, 24). Again it is said, "If I had not spoken to them, they would not have sin" (ibid. verse 22). Hence, at first He did not speak to them in parables, but after the working of the miracles, *I speak to them in parables: because seeing they see not.*[5] They see the miracles, but they do not see the consequences. Or it is thus: *Seeing*, that is to say, exteriorly, *they see not*, interiorly. "Bring forth the people that are blind, and have eyes: that are deaf, and have ears," etc., (Is. 43, 8). *And hearing they hear not, neither do they understand.* They hear the words by which they ought to be stirred up to do good; nevertheless, they do not hear them, meaning they do not have this effect; "If perhaps they will hear, and forbear" (Ez. 2, 7). And in the same place, it is said, "For they turn them into a song of their mouth" (33, 31). And why do they not see? It is because they do not understand; "They have not known nor understood: they walk on in darkness" (Ps. 81, 5). Afterwards, He invokes the authority of Isaias the prophet, *And the prophecy of Isaias is fulfilled in them, who saith: By hearing you shall hear, and shall not understand*, etc., which is written in Isaias 6, 9; and there it is said imperatively, but here it is said predictively. It is said there, "Hearing, hear, and understand not: and see the vision, and know it not." And three things are indicated. Firstly, the hardness of the Jews is indicated; secondly, the cause of their hardness; and thirdly, the effect of that cause. The second is where it is said, *For the heart of this people is grown gross*; the third is where it is said, *Lest they at any time they should see*, etc. And this is because the prophet had said two things, namely, about hearing and seeing; for that reason, He says two things, *You shall hear*, that is to say, you shall hear with an exterior hearing of Christ's teaching, *and shall not understand*, namely, the mysteries; "He would not

---

5. "CHRYS: Therefore because they spoke the very contrary to what they saw and heard, to see and to hear is taken from them; for they profit nothing, but rather fall under judgment. For this reason, He spoke to them at first not in parables, but with much clearness; but because they perverted all they saw and heard, He now speaks in parables" (*Catena Aurea on St. Matthew*, chap. 13, lect. 2). The text has been corrected according to this parallel passage.

understand that he might do well" (Ps. 35, 4); "Because thou hast rejected knowledge, I will reject thee, that thou shalt not do the office of priesthood to me" (Osee 4, 6). *And seeing you shall see, and shall not perceive.* You will see Christ's flesh with exterior vision, and you will not consider its power. "We have groped for the wall, and like the blind we have groped as if we had no eyes," etc., (Is. 59, 10). And the reason follows, *For the heart of this people is grown gross*, etc. For since He had made mention of hearing, and to understand properly belongs to the mind, for that reason, *the heart of this people*, i.e. their minds, *is grown gross*, i.e. are blinded. Why? It is because just as clarity is required for corporeal vision, so it is for spiritual vision. Hence, understanding is called the higher power, because it is the most spiritual. The intellect is grown gross when it is applied to dense and earthly things, but when it is drawn out of them, it is refined, as happened in the Apostles; "We look not at the things which are seen, but at the things which are not seen" (II Cor. 4, 18). Hence, these men were not considering anything except earthly things. As the Apostle says: "The sensual man perceiveth not these things that are of the Spirit of God" (I Cor. 2, 14). "The beloved grew fat, and kicked: he grew fat, and thick and gross, he forsook God who made him, and departed from God his saviour" (Deut. 32, 15). Likewise, it ought to be known that when a man hears things which do not please him, he cannot understand them easily: therefore, these men were understanding Him badly, because His words were not pleasing to them. Therefore, it is said: *And with their ears they have been dull of hearing*; "This saying is hard; and who can hear it?" (Jn. 6, 61). *And their eyes they have shut*, etc. It happens that someone has eyes, and he does not see, because he shuts his eyes: hence, he makes an obstacle for himself. But some things are so hidden that unless one fixes his glance for a long time, one cannot see them; but if a thing is out in the open, such as a wall, a man cannot fail to see it, unless he closes his eyes. For that reason, if the Lord had not performed evident miracles, it would not have been surprising if they did not believe; but He performed the most evident miracles, and, for that reason, these men would have acknowledged this fact, if they had not closed their eyes; "They turned away their eyes, that they might not look unto heaven" (Dan. 13, 9).

Hence, it ought to be observed that in this hardening, man is himself the cause, and that God does not harden anyone except by withholding grace. Therefore, God hardens because He does not give grace; but man puts an obstacle to the light before himself, thus, it is imputed to these men because they had closed their eyes.

Lest at any time they should see with their eyes. Here is related the harm which they incur. Hence, one can understand these words in two ways. It can be understood such that the words, *lest at any time*, are referring to all coming time, so that the sense is: 'They have closed their eyes in this manner, lest, etc.,' and, in this way, it is understood that it is through their malice: for some men sin through weakness, but some deliberately, or through certain malice: hence, these men not heeding this, have closed their eyes lest they understand; hence, their malice is implied. *Lest they be converted, and I should heal them*, meaning if they would convert; "Return, O ye revolting children," etc., (Jer. 3, 14). And this is Chrysostom's exposition. And three things are asserted: *lest they should see, lest they hear, and lest they understand with their heart*, and these correspond to the three things said before. Augustine expounds this passage otherwise, saying: *Lest they should see*, since now they do not see with their eyes, *and hear with their ears, and understand with their heart, and be converted, and I should heal them*. Hence, Augustine says[6] that these words can have a double meaning, because sometimes *lest they should* (*nequando*), stands for that which can happen, as it is stated: "If peradventure (*nequando*) God may give them repentance to know the truth" (II Tim. 2, 25). But other times it stands for that which cannot happen, meaning this would not happen unless we rebuke them, etc.

And what is it that He says: *is grown gross*? Augustine solves this question, saying that sometimes it happens that a man is proud, and it seems to him that he is very good; and God permits him to fall into some sins so that he might heal him from his pride. Such men are presumptuous, about whom it is said, "They, not knowing the justice of God and seeking to establish their own, have not submitted themselves to the justice of God" (Rom. 10, 3). Because, therefore, these men were proud, for that reason, I permitted that they be blinded, so that they might [not] see and hear, and so that I should heal them. And this exposition is taken from the text of Mark 4.[7] But the text of John 12, 39-40 contradicts this, because he says there, "Therefore they could not believe, because Isaias said again: He hath blinded their eyes and hardened their heart, that they should not see with their eyes, nor understand with their heart and be converted: and I should hear, and not understand; lest at any time they should be converted, and their sins should be forgiven them" (verse 12).

---

6. *Quaestionum septendecim in Evangelium secundum Matthaeum liber unus,* 13, 1.
7. "That seeing they may see, and not perceive; and hearing they may

heal them." Therefore, they are not blinded in order that they might believe, but in order that they might not believe.

But according to Augustine, this is an important question, because if they were blinded such that they may not believe, then it ought not to be imputed to them. Augustine solves the question thus: We can say that they merited the fact that they were blinded due to their past sins. "And their foolish heart was darkened. For, professing themselves to be wise, they became fools" (Rom. 1, 21). And it continues afterwards, "Wherefore, God gave them up," etc. Thus, He hardened them on account of their sins, not by hardening, but by withholding grace on account of their sins. And we can say otherwise, according to Augustine: *The heart of this people is grown gross*, such that they may not see and be converted, namely, immediately, but persisting, they crucify Christ, and afterwards, seeing His miracles, they convert. And Augustine says that this opinion seems far-fetched, if we do not see that it actually happened. For some men are not led back to humility unless they fall into a grave sin: the Lord acted in this way towards these men.

But blessed are your eyes which see, and your ears which hear, etc. Above, the Lord showed the Jews' misery, who seeing did not see; here, He shows the Apostles' blessedness who were seeing and hearing. And firstly, He shows their blessedness; and secondly, He shows an indication of their blessedness, where it is said, *For, amen, I say to you*. He says, therefore, that seeing they do not see, but *your eyes are blessed*. But if this were referred to the external eyes and ears, the eyes of the Jews would be made blessed as much as the eyes of the Apostles. For that reason, Jerome says that one ought to understand two kinds of eyes, namely, the exterior eyes, by which everyone saw Him; and He is not speaking about these eyes; or this may be referred to the internal eyes, by which only the Apostles saw Him. "That He may give unto you the spirit of wisdom and of revelation, in the knowledge of him: the eyes of your heart enlightened" (Eph. 1, 17-18). Hence, in like manner, a certain kind of eyes is exterior, and another kind of eyes is interior, concerning which it is said above: *He that hath ears to hear, let him hear.* "The Lord God hath opened my ear, and I do not resist: I have not gone back" (Is. 50, 5). He bestows beatitude in seeing, because this beatitude on earth consists solely in a participation of eternal beatitude, which consists in vision: for man's glory is in the vision of God. "Let not the wise man glory in his wisdom" (Jer. 9, 23); and it continues, "but let him that glorieth glory in this, that he understandeth and knoweth me" (verse 24). Then He sets forth the indication of their beatitude, *For, amen, I say to you*, etc. Augustine says: "Blessed is the man who has everything he wishes." Hence, they are blessed to whom were given all the things which the ancients, namely, the prophets and the just wished to have. For every just man is a king; hence, it is stated: "The king, that sitteth on the throne, scattereth away all evil" (Prov. 20, 8). Therefore, if what they desired, they did not possess, but you possess what you desire: then you already have obtained a participation of beatitude.

But what is that which He says: *And have not seen*? Is it not stated: "Abraham your father rejoiced that he might see my day: he saw it and was glad" (Jn. 8, 56)? Likewise, it is written: "I saw the Lord sitting upon a throne high and elevated" (Is. 6, 1). And it is likewise written concerning His Passion; hence: "We have seen him, and there was no sightliness" (ibid. 53, 2).

One solution is that some ancients saw these things, and others did not. But, as Jerome says, it is dangerous to say this. Or it can be explained otherwise, because they saw, but not as clearly as the Apostles did. "Which in other generations was not known to the sons of men, as it is now revealed to his holy apostles" (Eph. 3, 5). Or it is otherwise, that all these words refer to the vision and hearing of bodily presence, because to see in the flesh was desirable to the just. We have an example of this in Simeon (Lk. 2, 10). Hence, *blessed are your eyes which see*, etc.

And did not the Jews see? I say that concerning these things it is said that they do not see, because they only saw externally.

But the contrary is stated in John 20, 29, where it is said: "Blessed are they that have not seen and have believed." It ought to be replied that there is beatitude of possession, which is had through participation, and the beatitude of hope, which is had though meriting. Hence, they who do not see are blessed with the beatitude of hope or merit, and those who see are blessed with beatitude of possession or participation; hence, it is said of Abraham, "He rejoiced that he might see my day: he saw it and was glad" (Jn. 8, 56).

Hear you therefore the parable of the sower, etc. Here, the explanation is related. And firstly, He concludes that these men were worthy to hear the explanation, and secondly, He explains the parable. He says, therefore, *Hear you therefore*, etc., because, to wit, you are worthy to hear the explanation, and not only hear it, but to hear it from Myself; "A wise man shall hear, and shall be wiser" (Prov. 1, 5). *When any one heareth the word of the kingdom*, etc. Here He explains the parable; and because He had made mention of two kinds of ground, for that reason He firstly explains what He had said about the bad ground, and secondly, what He had said about the good ground, where it is said, *But he that received the seed upon good ground*, etc. Likewise, He had set forth three types of bad ground, for one type of ground was by the wayside, another type was upon stony ground, and another type was among thorns. And He now explains this.

And for the understanding of this, you ought to know that hearing God's word should have one effect, namely, that it be fixed in the heart; hence, it is written: "Blessed is the man who shall meditate on his law day and night" (Ps. 1, 1-2). Elsewhere in the Psalms it is written, "Thy words have I hidden in my heart, that I may not sin against thee" (118, 11). Similarly, another effect is that it be put into operation. For in certain men the first effect is impeded, and in certain other men the second effect is impeded. Here the first effect is considered: and it ought to be known that the text has an interjection, and it ought to be so understood. *When any one heareth the word of the kingdom, and understandeth it not, there cometh the wicked one, and catcheth away that which was sown in his heart.* And this is the man who is by the wayside. And why does he not understand? It is because his wicked fellow creature came, etc.; hence, *When any one heareth the word of the kingdom*, etc., that is to say, Christ preaching the kingdom of heaven, because Christ alone preached the kingdom of God: for Moses preached an earthly kingdom. Hence, Peter said, "Lord, to whom shall we go? Thou hast the words of eternal life" (Jn. 6, 69). Other men, such as unbelievers, do not hear; "I spoke, and you did not hear," etc., (Is. 65, 12); "Blessed are they who hear the word of God" (Lk. 11, 28). *But understandeth it not.* The Gloss reads, "Because a man hears words not in accordance with his affections, wherefore he does not lay them up in his heart." "He would not understand that he might do well" (Ps. 35, 4). And what will happen to this word? It is taken by robbers, because the mind is held back by its thoughts, and so it is carried off; and this is what He says, *There cometh the wicked one*, meaning the devil, not because he is wicked by nature, but by his perversity: *and catcheth away*, that is to say, secretly, by deceiving and presenting useless thoughts, *that which was sown in his heart*, namely, the seed: *this is the one that is sown by the way side.* 'The one that is sown' sometimes designates what is sown, other times it designates the field which is sown; Hence, when He says, *That which was sown*, the seed is understood; but when it is said, *the one that is sown*, the field is understood. For a man is called a field, concerning which field it is stated: "Diligently till thy ground," etc., (Prov. 24, 27). And how is it by the wayside? This is because it is not guarded, contrary to that which is said: "With all watchfulness keep thy heart, because life issueth out from it" (Prov. 4, 3). In this way, a man is said to be sown by the wayside, who receives the word, but does not guard it. The second effect is to put it into operation; hence, it is said: "Be ye doers of the word and not hearers only" (James 1, 22). Now this effect is impeded by prosperity and adversity. Concerning the man who is impeded by adversity, He says, *And he that received the seed upon stony ground*, etc. Firstly, therefore, He relates the cause of the good effect; secondly, He relates the occasion of the evil effect, where it is said, *Yet hath he not root in himself*; and thirdly, He relates the evil, where it is said, *When there ariseth tribulation*, etc. The stony ground is a bad heart, into which the word cannot penetrate, just as in stony ground, and where there is little soil; in this manner, some men do not open up their hearts so as to be penetrable. For a heart is called penetrable only when it prefers nothing to the word, such that it retains the word as its tap root. "I will take away the stony heart," etc., (Ez. 11, 19). *He heareth the word, and immediately receiveth it with joy*, therefore, he takes pleasure in justice, and becomes inclined towards what is good. "He who giveth to you the Spirit and worketh miracles among you" (Gal. 3, 5). And in this manner, he takes pleasure in the word; but it cannot be attached, because *He hath not root*, because it is sown upon rock. "Being rooted and founded in charity," etc., (Eph. 3, 17). *But is only for a time*, and he rejoices for a time; "There is a friend a companion at the table, and he will not abide in the day of distress" (Eccli. 6, 10). This is, therefore, the occasion, because it does not have root. And why is this? It is because it is badly attached. Hence, He says, *When there ariseth tribulation and persecution because of the word*, etc., for example, when those opposing the faith come upon him, and tribulations through interior or exterior adversities on account of the doctrine of the word, or on account of the faith, *he is presently scandalized*, because he recoils from the faith; "Much peace have they that love thy law, and to them there is no stumbling block" (Ps. 118, 165). He who perseveres is a friend. And He says, *Presently*: because even if they have charity, they can be scandalized by reason of a great tribulation. But when someone is presently scandalized by reason of a small tribulation, he was not rooted in charity; "God will not suffer you to be tempted above that which you are able: but will make also with temptation issue" (I Cor. 10, 13). And, "For you have not yet resisted unto blood" (Heb. 12, 4). And, according to Jerome, He says, *Presently*, because there is a great difference between the former and the latter cases. *And he that received the seed among thorns*, etc. Here is set forth the obstacles to bearing fruit well, because sometimes it comes about by reason of prosperity, and other times by reason of adversity; hence, He says, *And he that received the seed among thorns, is he that heareth the word of God.* These thorns are the cares of the world; for just as thorns sting, and do not allow a man to rest, so neither do these cares. *The care of this world and the deceitfulness of riches choketh up the word.* The care is about the future, *the deceitfulness of riches* is about the present: hence, when riches abound, they are deceitful; "Charge the rich of this world not to be highminded nor to trust in the uncertainty of riches" (I Tim. 6, 17). Likewise, when they are desired, they deceive in regard to their satisfaction, because they do not satisfy. Again, they cause anxiety for the future; and, for that reason, the Lord forbade His Apostles, "Be not solicitous therefore, saying: What shall we eat: or what shall we drink" (above, 6, 31). *Choketh up the word.* He had said above, *withered away*, here He says, *choketh up.* For you know that a candle can be extinguished either on account of a lack of fluid wax, and then it withers away: sometimes it is extinguished on account of an excess of fluid wax, and then it is choked up; so also natural life, which is based upon warmth and moisture,[8] can cease on account of an overabundance of moisture, or on account of a lack of moisture. Similarly, tribulations sometimes take away the fluid of consolation of the present life, and then it is made unstable, and so it withers away: sometimes it grows, and then it is choked up; for that reason, the seed is without fruit; hence, He says, *And he becometh fruitless.* "What fruit therefore had you then in those things of which you are now ashamed?" (Rom. 6, 21). And the Apostle continues, "But having become servants to God, you have your fruit unto sanctification" (verse 22); "For the fruit of the light is in all goodness and justice and truth" (Eph. 5, 9). *But he that received the seed upon good ground*, etc. Having explained the three types of bad receivers of the seed, He adds the good receiver, whom He distinguishes by his three effects, for *he heareth*, and more importantly, *he understandeth*; and furthermore, *he beareth fruit, and yieldeth the one an hundredfold, and another sixty, and another thirty.* This is expounded as was said above.

---

8. According to Aristotle in his *Book on Plants*.

It ought to be known, nevertheless, that Augustine (Book II, chapter 23 of his *City of God*) relates the exposition of certain men who wished to so interpret this verse that on the day when the Lord will come for judgment, many Saints will pray for many men; and inasmuch as they are better men, many more men will be given to them. Hence, to some men will be given thirtyfold, to others sixtyfold, and to some others a hundred. But this is against the faith: because mortal sins will not be forgiven, because they cannot be forgiven without charity; hence, mortal sins are contrary to charity, but venial sins are not: for that reason, etc.

24. Another parable he proposed to them, saying: The kingdom of heaven is likened to a man that sowed good seed in his field.
25. But while men were asleep, his enemy came and oversowed cockle among the wheat and went his way.
26. And when the blade was sprung up, and had brought forth fruit, then appeared also the cockle.
27. And the servants of the good man of the house coming said to him: Sir, didst thou not sow good seed in thy field? Whence then hath it cockle?
28. And he said to them: An enemy hath done this. And the servants said to him: Wilt thou that we go and gather it up?
29. And he said: No, lest perhaps gathering up the cockle, you root up the wheat also together with it.
30. Suffer both to grow until the harvest, and in the time of the harvest I will say to the reapers: Gather up first the cockle, and bind it into bundles to burn, but the wheat gather ye into my barn.

Above, he set forth the parable, in which the extrinsic obstacles to the Gospel teaching were shown; here, another parable is set forth, in which is set forth the obstacle to hearing the doctrine, which is intrinsic, because in this parable, things are portrayed to us concerning which our minds are wont to be seduced. Firstly, therefore, He teaches us about the origin of the good and the wicked; secondly, He teaches about their development; and thirdly, He teaches about their outcome. The second is where it is said, ***And when the blade was sprung up***, etc. The third is where it is said, ***And in the time of the harvest I will say to the reapers***, etc. About the first, two things are noted. Firstly, it is noted about the origin of the good seed; secondly, it is noted about the origin of the evil seed, where it is said, ***But while men were asleep***, etc. He says, therefore, *Another parable he proposed to them*. And to whom did He propose the parable? It was proposed to them. I say it was proposed not only to the Apostles, but also to the crowds. Hence, now that He had expounded the first parable to the Apostles, He turned to the crowds. He says, *another*, and not 'the other'; this is because He did not propose only two parables, but many; without a doubt one of two things is called 'the other.' Now He set forth many parables so that He might adapt himself to the needs of many different dispositions. For some men are affected in one way, others in another. *The kingdom of heaven is likened to a man that sowed good seed in his field.* The kingdom of heaven is composed of the king and those who are ruled: and these men are heavenly men, who are made equal to the angels; "He hath given his angels charge over thee; to keep thee in all thy ways," etc., (Ps. 90, 11). *It is likened to a man that sowed good seed in his field*. Three parables concerning seed are set forth one after the other. The first is about the sown seed; the second is about intermingled seed; and the third is about the multiplied seed. According to the intention of the text, the seed is to be taken in a different sense than it was above. For above, the seed which is sown is that which is sown in man, and this is the word of God, as is stated in Luke 8, 11.[9] Here, however, it is taken for man himself, in whom it is sown. And this is evident because below He says that this seed is the children of the kingdom; hence, a different exposition ought not to be made from that which the Lord has made. And man is called a seed because, just a seed is the principle of propagation, so good men are the foundation of the whole faith; hence, the whole Church sprouted forth from the Apostles. Hence, it is said: "Except the Lord of hosts had left us seed, we had been as Sodom" (Is. 1, 9). And this was the good seed, concerning which it is said: "That which shall stand therein, shall be a holy seed" (Is. 6, 13). Christ sowed this seed, but where did He sow it? It was *in his field*, that is to say, in the world. For the world is called a field, in which there are the good and the wicked, whom the Lord brought forth through creation; hence, it is said: "The world was made by him" (Jn. 1, 10). And in Psalms it is said: "With me is the beauty of the field," etc., (49, 11). Having treated the origin of the good seed, here He treats of the origin of the evil seed. And firstly, the occasion of the malicious deed is set forth; and secondly, the order of the deed is set forth. And firstly, a double occasion is set forth: one is on the part of the guards, and the second is on the part of the sower. On

---

[9] "Now the parable is this: The seed is the word of God."

the part of the guards, He says, *But while men were asleep*, etc., meaning the rulers of the human race who were appointed to guard, *were asleep*, namely, through the sleep of death. These rulers are holy men, namely, the Apostles, who knew that the heretics mixed themselves in with the wheat; hence, Paul says, "I know that after my departure ravening wolves will enter in among you, not sparing the flock" (Acts 20, 29). After that, another occasion is set forth; hence, He says, *His enemy came*, etc., meaning the devil; "The pride of them that hate thee ascendeth continually" (Ps. 73, 23): it is said, "of them that hate thee," meaning of the devils. This enmity is in accord with their perversity of will.

But there is a question. Is this true that something can hate God? It ought to be replied by saying that one can only love a thing which is known. Now God can be known in two ways: in Himself or in His effects: it is impossible that God be not loved in Himself: for whatever is loved, is loved under the aspect of a good. Since, therefore, He is the primal goodness, He cannot be hated. But in relation to His effect, this is not impossible. For the demons, insofar as they exist, love Him from whom they exist; but some effects displease them, for instance, that they are punished against their will, that men are not punished in accordance with their will, and similar things.

The parable continues concerning the order of the deed: *and oversowed cockle*. Each word has much meaning. Let us see, therefore, what it is that is sown, and how is the order. What is sown is cockle, which is similar to wheat, and is called darnel.[10] What is signified by the cockle? It signifies wicked children who love iniquity, especially heretics. There are three kinds of wicked men: bad Catholics, schismatics and heretics. Bad Catholics are signified by chaff, concerning whom it was said above: "The chaff he will burn with fire" (3, 12). Schismatics are signified by ears of grain that have rotted.[11] Heretics are signified by cockle. They are sown, therefore, in a field, meaning in this world. Similarly, cockle has a resemblance to wheat, and in this way, these men feign the appearance of good men, as it is stated: "Desiring to be teachers of the law: understanding neither the things they say, nor whereof they affirm" (I Tim. 1, 7).

10. Darnel is an annual grass, *Lolium temulentum*, found as a weed in grainfields.

11. "While schismatics again may be likened to ears that have rotted, or to straws that are broken, crushed down, and cast forth of the field. Indeed it is not necessary that every heretic or schismatic should be corporally severed from the Church; for the Church bears many who do not so publicly defend their false opinions as to attract the attention of the multitude, which when they do, then are they expelled" (*Catena Aurea on St. Matthew*, chap. 13, lect. 4).

And observe what is said above, **He sowed**, but here it is not said;[12] it is because the former seeds were Catholics, rather than heretics. For the devil, seeing the Church to have spread, was envious, and sowed destructive seed, and stirred up the hearts of the heretics, so that they might harm the Church more; hence, it is said, "They were from us," according to what is stated in I John 2, 19, "but they were not of us. For if they had been of us, they would no doubt have remained with us." Likewise, He says, **Among the wheat**. The devil does not care if there are heretics among the pagan nations, because he possesses them all; but he does care if they are among the wheat and the faithful. And this is what is said: "And in his angels he found wickedness" (Job 4, 18). And Augustine says, that no society is so good that there is not someone who is wicked: hence, in the society of the Apostles, one man was evil, namely, Judas. Likewise, He says, **And went his way**, meaning that he hid himself: for sometimes he instigates, but does not always put into effect: for if everything were always to succeed in accordance with his desires, he might be easily detected; for that reason, he sometimes forgoes his desires as a trick; "He lieth in wait, in secret, like a lion in his den" (Ps. 9, 30).[13]

Afterwards, it is treated concerning the development of the good and the wicked. **And when the blade was sprung up**. And in order that you may understand, three things are considered. Firstly, the manifesting of the good as distinct from the wicked is considered; secondly, the zeal of good men against the bad plants is considered; and thirdly, the tolerating of the wicked is considered. He says, therefore, **And when the blade was sprung up, and had brought forth fruit, then appeared also the cockle**, etc. For, at first, when a plant is sown it is not evident what it is, but when the plant grows it becomes evident. And this can be applied to both wheat and to cockle. Augustine expounds the parable as referring to the wheat, because when a man is young, he cannot judge; but when he grows up, and he bears fruit, and becomes spiritual, then he knows; "The spiritual man judgeth all things" (I Cor. 2, 15). Chrysostom expounds the parable in reference to the cockle, that firstly it is not evident what it is, because heretics initially hide their errors, because, firstly, they say some good things and preach to the laity, and afterwards, they insert some evil things about the clergy, which are willingly heard; and, in this way, they turn the people away from the love of the clergy,

---

12. Rather the word *oversowed* is used here instead of *sowed*.

13. The reference for the Douay translation is the second part of chapter 9, verse 9.

and so by consequence from the love of the Church. But after, when the people accept their doctrine, they show their malice. For firstly, they speak only of unimportant matters, but afterwards, they manifest themselves and their doctrine, which is symbolized by wine; about that wine it is said: "It goeth in pleasantly, however from behind, it will bite like a snake" (Prov. 23, 32).

And the servants of the good man of the house coming, etc. Here is set forth the zeal of good men against the bad plants. And firstly, it is inquired about the origin of the bad seed; secondly, they are moved with zeal to root up the bad plants, where it is said, **And the servants said**, etc. He says, **And the servants of the good man of the house coming**. First, it ought to be seen who are these servants. Below, He speaks of the reapers; but these reapers are not servants, but angels. These are the good men: and this is not unfitting, since the Lord is called both the gate and the gatekeeper. **And the servants coming**, by faith; "Come ye to him and be enlightened" (Ps. 33, 6). **Sir, didst thou not sow good seed in thy field?** Did not the Apostles sow good doctrine? They did indeed. "God saw all the things that he had made, and they were very good" (Gen. 1, 31). **Whence then hath it cockle?** A similar question is found in Jeremias 2, 21: "I planted a chosen vineyard, how then art thou turned unto me into that which is good for nothing, O strange vineyard?" The Lord responds, **and he said to them: A hostile man**[14] **hath done this**. And note that this evil is not from man's first origin, but the origin of the evil which is in man is from the devil; "By the envy of the devil, death came into the world" (Wis. 2, 24). The devil is called a man by falling away from the Deity; "Arise, O Lord, let not man be strengthened" (Ps. 9, 20). This man is called an enemy on account of his malice brought to the highest degree; "I will put enmities between thee and the woman, and thy seed and her seed" (Gen. 3, 15).

And the servants said. Here it is said that the servants are moved with zeal to root up the bad plants. **Wilt thou that we go and gather it up?** Two praiseworthy things are here said of these men; one is that they are moved to destroy the evil; "Put away the evil one from among yourselves" (I Cor. 5, 13). The other praiseworthy thing was that they do not wish to do this on their own initiative; hence, it is said: "Bless God at all times, that all thy counsels may abide in him" (Tob. 4, 20). **And he said to them**. Observe, this is a third praiseworthy thing, namely, the endurance of evils; about this it is said: "For because sentence is not

---

14. *Inimicus homo.*

speedily pronounced against the evil, the children of men commit evils without any fear" (Eccle. 8, 11). And firstly, He shows His plan; secondly, He gives the reason for His plan; and thirdly, He sets the limit of His endurance, because He will not always tolerate evil. Therefore, He says, *No*, meaning I do not wish that you gather them yet; "The Lord delayeth not his promise, as some imagine, but dealeth patiently" (II Pet. 3, 9). **Lest perhaps**. Here He gives the reason.

And you ought to immediately notice that good is great and victorious over evil, because good can exist without evil; evil, however, cannot exist without good; for that reason, the Lord endures many evils, so that many good things may come to be, or also that they may not perish. For that reason, He says, *No, lest perhaps gathering up the cockle*, to wit, the wicked, or the heretics, etc., *you root up the wheat also together with it*.

There can occur four good reasons why the wicked ought not to be rooted up for the sake of good men. One reason is that the good men are exercised by the wicked; "For there must be also heresies: that they also, who are approved may be made manifest among you" (I Cor. 11, 19); "The fool shall serve the wise" (Prov. 11, 29). If there had not been heretics, the knowledge of the holy men would not have shown forth, and this is the opinion of Augustine and others. Hence, he who wishes to root up the wicked, might also root up many good things. Likewise, it happens that he who is now evil, afterwards becomes good, such as Paul, for instance. Hence, if Paul had been killed, we would lack the teaching of so great a teacher, and far be that! For that reason, if you want to root up the cockle, you will root up the wheat together with it, namely, him who will be wheat; "I will turn them from Basan, I will turn them into the depth of the sea" (Ps. 67, 23). The third reason is that some men seem to be evil, and are not; for that reason, if you want to pluck up the wicked, you might immediately uproot many good men. And this is evident, because God does not will that they be gathered up until they arrive at complete maturity; hence: "Therefore, judge not before the time" (I Cor. 4, 5). The forth reason is that sometimes someone has great power; for that reason, if he be excluded, he draws many men with him, and, in this way, many will perish with that evil man. For that reason, a community is not excommunicated, nor is the prince of the people, lest many fall with him. What is said in Apocalypse 12, 4 applies to such a man, namely, that the dragon drew a third part of the stars with himself, etc. And it is said: "Far be it from thee to do this thing, and to slay the just with the wicked" (Gen. 18, 25). But will they always be spared? No, they will be spared only for a time; hence, He says, *Suffer both to grow until the harvest*, etc. A similar decree is found in Apocalypse 22, 11: "He that hurteth, let him hurt still: and he that is filthy, let him be filthy still."

Suffer both to grow until the harvest. Against this decree it is objected that it is said: "Take away the evil of your devices" (Is. 1, 16), etc. Likewise, it is said: "Purge out the old leaven, that you may be a new paste, as you are unleavened," etc., (I Cor. 5, 7). Why, therefore, does He say, *Suffer*, etc.?

Chrysostom says that what He says concerns killing. Hence, heretics are not to be killed, because many evils will follow therefrom. Augustine, in a certain letter, says that at one time it seemed to him that they ought not to be killed; but afterwards, he learned by experience that many men are converted through violence: for the Lord violently drew certain men, as for instance, He violently drew Paul. And Augustine has discussed this opinion (or question). Hence, this man, having been forcibly converted, made more progress than all others who believed voluntarily. Hence, according to Chrysostom's opinion, if a heretic cannot be killed without danger, it ought not to occur, but only where a greater danger is feared. And this is evident by bringing to mind the effect upon all men as a whole, for even if they are evil, they are useful for the exercising of the good. Nevertheless, because it is more to be feared that, through them, the Gospel teaching may perish in others, for that reason, etc. Likewise, it was said that those who are now evil, afterwards become good. It is true that the wicked ought not to be immediately killed, but, as it is stated, "A man that is a heretic, after the first and second admonition, avoid" (Titus, 3, 10). In reply to another objection, saying that the killing of heretics is opposed to the third reason, namely, that many men seem evil who are good, I answer that this is true, if the killing were to happen indiscriminately, as it is stated in I Timothy 4.[15] Similarly, it is objected that it was said that the prince of the people ought not to be excommunicated, and this is true, if you see that there would be a greater scandal if he were excommunicated than in him because he sins, he ought not to be excommunicated; but if someone had done something which endangered the faith, without a doubt he ought to be excommunicated, no matter what misfortune may happen as a result.

In the time of the harvest I will say to the reapers, etc. Above, the Lord expounded the origin of the good and wicked par-

---

15. "But avoid foolish and old wives fables" (verse 7).

abolically, and the development of both; here is treated about the likeness of both. And firstly, the time of the end of their development is related; secondly, the ministers are related; and thirdly, the manner and order, of which every single thing is ordained to the end. The time is mentioned, when it is said, *In the time of the harvest*, etc. The time of the harvest is the time of the collection of the fruits that are expected from the seeds. There is a twofold collection: one is in the Church in the present life, the other will be in heaven. And, for that reason, the harvest is twofold: there is a kind of harvest of the gathering of fruits in the present life, and concerning this it is said: "Lift up your eyes, and see the countries, for they are white already to harvest" (Jn. 4, 35). Likewise, there is a time of harvest in the Church triumphant; hence, it is said below in this chapter, that the harvest is the end of the world; therefore, it is deferred until that time. Who are the ministers? They are the reapers. Hence, *I will say to the reapers*. The reapers of the first harvest were the Apostles: for they gathered and converted the whole world, and about whom it is said: "I have sent you to reap that which you did not sow" (Jn. 4, 38). In the second harvest the reapers will be the angels; "Thrust in thy sickle and reap, because the hour is come to reap, for the harvest of the earth is ripe," etc., (Apoc. 14, 15). For things which happen through God's delegation, are believed to happen by the ministry of the angels; hence, it is said concerning the angels, "You ministers of his that do his will" (Ps. 102, 21). But let us see the order, and in what manner they obtain their end, and what end they obtain. And firstly, let us see concerning the wicked; and secondly, let us see concerning the good men. It ought to be known concerning the wicked that, firstly, they are gathered; secondly, they are bound; and thirdly, they are burned. At the beginning is the separation of the wicked from the good men. As long as the former time lasts, the wicked are with the good, the cockle with the wheat, the lily among the thorns, as it is stated in Canticles 2, 2; "When the Son of man shall come, he shall separate the good from the wicked, the goats from the sheep" (below 25, 31-32). Now good and bad things happen, as though indiscriminately, to the good and the wicked: and this is what is said in Ecclesiastes 9, that this is the worst of all the things that happen under heaven, namely, the same things happen to all men; but then good things shall be rendered upon the good, and evil things upon the wicked. Lest, therefore, they get mixed together, it is necessary that the wicked be separated and bound. Hence, He says, *And bind it*. In this binding the perpetuity of the punishment is signified; "To bind their kings with fetters," etc., (Ps. 149, 9); and "Bind his hands and feet, and cast him into the exterior darkness" (below 23, 13) which signifies the relentlessness and irrevocability of eternal damnation. *Into bundles.* All the wicked shall be separated from the vision of God: the pain of loss will be equal for all, for that reason, they are put into bundles. But in other respects their punishments will differ, as it is stated in Leviticus 13, where it is taught to distinguish between one disease and another, and between one leprosy and another; and likewise, in Isaias 27, 8, it is said, "In measure against measure." And why are they bound? *To burn,* that is to say, they shall be delivered to eternal fire. About this fire it is said: "For I am tormented in this flame" (Lk. 16, 24).

Then, when it is said, *But the wheat gather ye into my barn,* the outcome of the good is set forth. And, in contrast to the cockle, three things are set forth, namely, the wheat's purity, unity, and tranquility. Its purity is set forth when it is called *wheat.* But observe that the cockle was bound, and for that reason it was not thrashed, but the wheat was thrashed. And this signifies that the wicked shall be cast into hell with all their iniquities; but the good shall be completely cleansed from their iniquities; "It shall be called the holy way: the unclean shall not pass over it" (Is. 35, 8). Likewise, there shall be unity among them; hence, it is said, *Gather.* Among the wicked there is always strife, and, for that reason, they do not have unity; but, on the other hand, the good are gathered together; "Gather ye together his saints to him: who set his covenant before sacrifices," etc., (Ps. 49, 5); and "Wheresoever the body shall be, there shall the eagles also be gathered together" (below 24, 28). Similarly, there shall be tranquility among them; hence, He says, *Into my barn.* A barn is made for the preservation of the harvest; and so that heavenly country shall be the barn of the Saints, where they shall be with praise and everlasting joy, as it is stated in Isaias 35, 2.[16]

31. Another parable he proposed unto them, saying: The kingdom of heaven is like to a grain of mustard seed, which a man took and sowed in his field.

32. Which is the least indeed of all seeds; but when it is grown up, it is greater than all herbs, and becometh a tree, so that the birds of the air come, and dwell in the branches thereof.

---

[16]. "It shall bud forth and blossom, and shall rejoice with joy and praise: the glory of Libanus is given to it: the beauty of Carmel, and Saron, they shall see the glory of the Lord, and the beauty of our God."

33. *Another parable he spoke to them: The kingdom of heaven is like to leaven, which a woman took and hid in three measures of meal, until the whole was leavened.*
34. *All these things Jesus spoke in parables to the multitudes: and without parables he did not speak to them.*
35. *That it might be fulfilled which was spoken by the prophet, saying: I will open my mouth in parables, I will utter things hidden from the foundation of the world.*
36. *Then having sent away the multitudes, he came into the house, and his disciples came to him, saying: Expound to us the parable of the cockle of the field.*
37. *Who made answer and said to them: He that soweth the good seed is the Son of man.*
38. *And the field is the world. And the good seed are the children of the kingdom. And the cockle are the children of the wicked one.*
39. *And the enemy that sowed them, is the devil. But the harvest is the end of the world. And the reapers are the angels.*
40. *Even as cockle therefore is gathered up, and burnt with fire: so shall it be at the end of the world.*
41. *The Son of man shall send his angels, and they shall gather out of his kingdom all scandals, and them that work iniquity.*
42. *And shall cast them into the furnace of fire: there shall be weeping and gnashing of teeth.*
43. *Then shall the just shine as the sun, in the kingdom of their Father. He that hath ears to hear, let him hear.*

Above, the Lord showed the obstacles to the Gospel teaching by means of two parables. But because someone could say: 'If it is so that the teaching is impeded in these ways, namely, that some seed fell by the wayside, other seed fell upon stony ground, etc., it seems that it cannot flourish'; for that reason, He adds other parables about the marvelous growth of the seed, because, in fact, it flourished for two reasons. Firstly, its growth is marvelous on account of its apparent littleness; secondly, its growth is marvelous on account of its hiddenness. Hence, He sets forth two parables. The second is where it is said, *Another parable he spoke to them*. Thirdly, the Evangelist supports His way of preaching with the authority of a prophet, where it is said, *All these things Jesus spoke in parables*. About the first reason, He firstly treats of the sowing; secondly, He treats of the smallness of the seed; and thirdly, He speaks of the greatness of the fruit. The second point is where it is said, *Which is the least indeed of all seeds*; the third point is where it is said, *Which when it is grown up, it is greater than all herbs*. He says, therefore, *The kingdom of heaven is like to a grain of mustard seed*, etc. In a kingdom, there is a king, a prince, subjects, and also prisoners. Likewise, there are the rich, etc. Hence, we can liken a kingdom to all these things. Therefore, because He says that *the kingdom of heaven is like to a grain of mustard seed*, it can be expounded, as Jerome says, that by the grain of mustard seed the Gospel teaching is understood. And why is this? It is because this grain is hot; likewise, it protects against poisons. And this is signified, because the Gospel teaching makes one by the faith to be strong; "If you have faith as a grain of mustard seed, you shall say to this mountain: Remove from hence hither, and it shall remove: and nothing shall be impossible to you" (below 17, 19). Likewise, the Gospel teaching excludes errors; hence, it is useful for reproving, as it is stated in II Tim. 3, 16.[17]

Which a man took and sowed. This man is Christ, who sowed this seed; or he is anyone who sows the Gospel teaching. *In his field*, meaning in his heart, when he gives his assent to it. Christ sowed, because He gave the faith by which we are saved; "For by grace you are saved through faith: and that not of yourselves, for it is the gift of God" (Eph. 2, 8). Likewise, anyone who obeys, sows in his field, meaning in his heart; "Diligently till thy ground" (Prov. 24, 27). In this field there are various seeds, which are the various doctrines. The doctrines of Augustine and Jerome seem to be great, and are confirmed by powerful arguments: the same seems to be true for the doctrine of the Law. But the doctrine of the Evangelical law appears to be something little, because it preaches a God who suffered, was crucified, and things of this kind. And who can believe this? "The word of the cross, to them indeed that perish, is foolishness: but to them that are saved, that is, to us, it is the power of God" (I Cor. 1, 18). And, for that reason, He says, *Which is the least indeed of all seeds*; hence, at first a it appears to be the least. Its greatness follows. And firstly, its greatness is related; and secondly, its greatness is confirmed, where it is said, *But when it is grown up*, meaning when it sprouts forth, *it is greater than all herbs*, because the Gospel teaching bore more fruit than the doctrine of the Law, because the doctrine of the Law only bore fruit among the Jews;

---

[17]. "All scripture, inspired of God, is profitable to teach, to reprove, to correct, to instruct in justice."

hence, it was said: "He hath not done in like manner to every nation: and his judgments he hath not made manifest to them" (Ps. 147, 20). For there has not been any philosopher who convinced his whole country to follow his teaching: for if any philosopher, such as Plato, had said that such and such will happen, he would not be believed. "The wicked have told me fables: but not as thy law" (Ps. 118, 85). Therefore, the Gospel teaching is greater in solidity, in universality, and in utility. It is greater in solidity, because other teachings are soft herbs having no firmness, because they are subject to human reason; "For the thoughts of mortal men are fearful, and our counsels uncertain" (Wis. 9, 14); but this is a firm tree; "Forever, O Lord, thy word standeth firm" (Ps. 118, 89); "Heaven and earth shall pass away: but my words shall not pass away" (Lk. 21, 33). Thus, just as this tree compares to other trees, so this teaching compares to other teachings. *So that the birds of the air come, and dwell in the branches thereof.* Likewise, it is more excellent in the vastness of its teaching: for this science has many branches, and shows men what things are necessary for life. Hence, if they are married, they are informed through this teaching how they ought to govern themselves, and in like manner clerics are informed how they ought to live, and so on in regard to other men: for that reason, the various dogmas are the different branches. Similarly, it is more excellent in its usefulness, because the birds dwell in its branches, meaning all whose minds are in heaven; "our conversation is in heaven" (Phil. 3, 20). These men come, and meditate, and rest: for those who dwell on earth are not birds; "We look not at the things which are seen, but at the things which are not seen. For the things which are seen are temporal: but the things which are not seen, are eternal" (II Cor. 4, 18). Chrysostom expounds the parable as relating to the Apostles, whom Christ compared to a grain of a mustard seed, because they were fervent in spirit; and this grain *a man took*, meaning Christ, *in his field*, meaning in the Church, and from which grain the Church has all her fruitfulness: and they were small and abject; for no science has been spread among the people through such lowly men; hence, "Not many wise, not many mighty, not many noble; but the foolish things of the world hath God chosen, that he may confound the wise," etc., (I Cor. 1, 27). *But when it is grown up, it is greater* in its yield *than all herbs*, because the Apostles produced greater fruit. Alexander drew one part of the world to himself, and Rome similarly, but they never gained as much as these men, who did so much *that the birds of the air*, meaning good men, *dwell in the branch-*

es, meaning in their teaching; "They shall hold fast the skirt of one that is a Jew, saying: We will go with you: for we have heard that God is with you" (Zach. 8, 23). Hilary expounds the grain as referring to Christ, who was a grain of mustard seed on account of His fervor, because He was full of the Holy Ghost, which seed *he sowed* afterwards at His death, *in his field*, meaning, in His own people, which seed was the least on account of the contempt of the unbelievers; "We have seen him, and there was no sightliness, that we should be desirous of him, despised and the most abject of men, a man of sorrows, and acquainted with infirmity" (Is. 53, 2-3). *And it is greater than all herbs*, meaning He was greater than all perfect men were. "Gold cannot equal it" (Job 28, 17). And perfect men are compared to herbs, because herbs are given to the sick: for one who is sick eats herbs. But Christ's teaching is given to the perfect, and in this way He is reckoned to be a tree. And the latter is signified by a tree, concerning which tree it is stated in Dan. 4.[18]

Another parable he spoke to them. Here is set forth a parable about the growth of the Gospel teaching, and it is shown to be marvelous, because its growth is from a hidden seed; hence, He says, *The kingdom of heaven is like to leaven, which a woman took and hid in three measures of meal, until the whole was leavened.*

Note that it is not unfitting that sometimes the same thing is interpreted to be something good and other times it is interpreted to be something evil, as, for example, a rock is sometimes interpreted to be Christ, sometimes it is interpreted to be something contrary, such as hardness; "I will take away the stony heart out of your flesh" (Ez. 36, 26). Accordingly, leaven is sometimes interpreted to be a bad thing, insofar as it has putrefaction; "Purge out the old leaven," etc., (I Cor. 5, 7). Likewise, in the same place it is said, "Not with the old leaven, nor with the leaven of malice and wickedness: but with the unleavened bread of sincerity and truth" (v. 8). But in that it leavens and has the power of expanding, in this way, it expresses something good.

What, therefore, is signified by it? Four things are signified. Chrysostom says that the Apostles are this leaven. *A woman*, divine wisdom, *hid* them *in three measures of meal*, meaning it oppressed them with tribulations. But firstly it took them; hence: "I have chosen you out of the world that you should go forth" (Jn. 15, 16). Those whom He sent among the faithful, He placed *in*

---

[18]. "The tree which thou sawest is thou, O king, who art grown great, and become mighty" (Dan. 4, 17-19).

three measures of meal. The 'satum' is a measure,[19] and it has the value of a modius and a half; and so three 'sata' means three measures of meal.[20] And why is it said, *in three*? A finite number is put for the infinite, because the Apostles were put in the midst of many nations. Or it is on account of the three parts of the world, because they were sent to all parts of the world; or it is on account of the nations which arose from the sons of Noe. *Until the whole was leavened*, meaning until all were converted to God; "Their sound hath gone forth into all the earth: and their words unto the ends of the world" (Ps. 18, 5). Or otherwise, according to Augustine, by leaven is signified the fervor of charity, because leaven expands the meal, just as charity expands the heart; "I have run the way of thy commandments, when thou didst enlarge my heart" (Ps. 118, 32). The *woman*, meaning the reason or the soul, *hid in three measures*, that is, in the whole heart, in the whole soul, and in the whole strength. Or by the three measures is signified the three states, namely, of prelates, of contemplatives, and of active men, which are understood by Noe, Job, and Daniel.[21] Or they can be referred to the hundredfold, sixtyfold, and thirtyfold fruit. Jerome expounds this parable as referring to the Gospel teaching, which a woman, meaning wisdom, hid in three measures of meal, which are the spirit, soul, and body, or the rational, irascible and concupiscible appetites. Or otherwise, by the woman, faith is understood; by the three measures, the three Persons in the Divinity are understood. Hilary expounds the parable as referring to Christ, who is the leaven, which by the Father's providence was hidden in the world in the three laws: the natural law, the Mosaic law, and the law of the Gospel.

All these things Jesus spoke in parables, etc. Having set forth various parables to the multitudes, here the Evangelist confirms, or approves them by the authority of a prophet. And it is divided into three parts; namely, that firstly, Christ's custom of speaking in parables is related; secondly, the authority is cited; and thirdly, the explanation of the preceding parables is related. The second part is where it is said, *That it might be fulfilled which was spoken by the prophet*; and the third part is where it is said, *Then having sent away the multitudes, he came into the house*. He says, therefore, *All these things Jesus*

---

19. A 'satum' is 66 pounds according to Isidore of Seville in his *Etymologiae*, XVI, 26, 11. It was a type of measure of the province of Palestine.
20. Three measures of meal would be enough to produce about 27 one (Roman) pound loaves. The average Roman ate about two pound loaves a day.
21. cf. "And if these three men, Noe, Daniel, and Job, shall be in it: they shall deliver their own souls by their justice, saith the Lord of hosts" (Ez. 14, 14).

spoke in parables to the multitudes. Why, therefore, was He speaking to the multitudes in parables? There is a twofold reason: it was because some believers and some unbelievers were mixed in the crowd: likewise, some were of good will and some were of bad will: on account of the men of bad will and the unbelievers He was speaking in this manner, so that they might not understand, as it was said above, so that seeing, they may not see. And this is stated in Mark 4.[22] It was also on account of the believers, so that they might better grasp and retain what was said. "I could not speak to you as unto spiritual, but as unto carnal" (I Cor. 3, 1).

And without parables he did not speak to them. This seems to be false, because in the Lord's Sermon on the Mount and in many others He was not speaking in parables. Chrysostom solves this objection thus, saying that He preached this whole sermon parabolically to the multitudes. Augustine solves this objection thus, saying that the reason why it is said, without parables He did not speak to them, is because He did not deliver any discourse to the multitudes without inserting some parable into it. Hence, in the Sermon on the Mount He inserted a parable, where He said, "Let not thy left hand know what thy right hand doth" (above 6, 3). And He says that if sometimes a discourse is found without a parable, it ought to be said that the Evangelists did not relate them in order.[23] Hence, even if it was not written, a parable ought to be understood, on account of the fact that He says in this passage that without parables, He was not speaking to them, and so He did not speak without inserting parables.

That it might be fulfilled which was spoken by the prophet, saying (in Ps. 77, 2): *I will open my mouth in parables.* The Lord has spoken in two ways to the human race. Firstly, He spoke in prophets, and secondly, in Himself; "Behold it is I myself that spoke, behold I am here" (Is. 52, 6). In both He spoke parabolically, in the prophets many times, and through Himself similarly: for what was done in the prophets was a sign of that which would done by Christ; hence, He says, 'I the Lord, I who opened the mouths of the prophets in parables, will open My own mouth

---

22. That seeing they may see, and not perceive; and hearing they may hear, and not understand; lest at any time they should be converted, and their sins should be forgiven them" (Mk. 4, 12).

23. "AUG; We may indeed find discourses of His parabolic throughout, but none direct throughout. And by a complete discourse, I mean, the whole of what He says on any topic that may be brought before Him by circumstances, before He leaves it and passes to a new subject. For sometimes one Evangelist connects what another gives as spoken at different times; the writer having in such a case followed not the order of events, but the order of connection in his own memory" (*Catena Aurea on St. Matthew*, chap. 13, lect. 7).

in parables. *I will utter things hidden from the foundation of the world.'* In the opening of the mouth is the manifestation of secrets, as it was said above; an utterance is of intimate things. He is said to utter whenever He lets out secrets from the depth of His wisdom; "My heart hath uttered a good word" (Ps. 44, 2). The Lord's wisdom is hidden; "It is hid from the eyes of all living" (Job 28, 21); "No man hath seen God at any time: the only begotten Son who is in the bosom of the Father, he hath declared him," etc., (Jn. 1, 18). He uttered things hidden, and things which were hidden from the foundation of the world; "Which in other generations was not known to the sons of men, as it is now revealed to his holy apostles and prophets in the Spirit" (Eph. 3, 5). Or it is otherwise. I will utter those things that are from the foundation of the world, which are hidden. And why? It is because He Himself is from the foundation of the world, and He revealed Himself to us through those things which He made; "The invisible things of God are clearly seen, being understood by the things that are made" (Rom. 1, 20).

Then having sent away the multitudes, he came into the house. Here one of the previous parables is expounded. And firstly, the place is described; secondly, the questioning of the disciples is described; and thirdly, the exposition of the parable is described. He says, therefore, *Then having sent away the multitudes, he came into the house.* In doing which an example is given to us, that if we wish to investigate secrets, we ought to enter a secret place; "When I go into my house, I shall repose myself with her" (Wis. 8, 6); "Be first to run home to thy house, and there withdraw thyself, and there take thy pastime and do what thou hast a mind, but not in sin or proud speech," etc., (Eccli. 32, 15-16). *And his disciples came to him, saying: Expound to us the parable of the cockle of the field*, etc., because they were more in doubt about this parable. Sometimes they dared not come to Him out of reverence, as it is stated in John 4, 27, that no man said to Him, why was He speaking with the woman, etc. But here they took special courage, because they had heard, *To you it is given to know the mysteries of the kingdom of heaven.* In the same way, if we wish to get the meaning of some mystery, we ought to come to Him; "Come ye to him and be enlightened" (Ps. 33, 6). *Who made answer and said.* Here the exposition of the parable of the cockle is related. And firstly, the exposition regarding the first sowing is related; secondly, the exposition regarding the oversowing is related; and thirdly, the exposition regarding both is related. And firstly, He expounds what is the sower, what is the field, and what is the seed. ***He that soweth the good seed is the Son of man.*** He calls Himself the Son of man, both on account of humility, and so that He might refute future heretics: for certain men denied that He was God, but certain others denied that He was a man. Hence, He says that He is the Son of man, which pertains to a man; and He says that He sows a spiritual seed, which pertains to God. "The light of thy countenance, O Lord, is signed upon us," etc., (Ps. 4, 7). ***The field is the world***, which He created; hence, He said above, ***In his field***; "He came unto his own," etc., (Jn. 1, 11). Again, in the same place, it is said: "The world was made by him" (v. 10). ***And the good seed are the children of the kingdom***, from whom other men were propagated,[24] who were the good children; "Because if they are sons, they are heirs also" (Rom. 8, 17). Then He expounds what relates to the oversowing, and He says what is the seed. ***And the cockle are the children of the wicked one***; "Woe to the people laden with iniquity, a wicked seed, ungracious children" (Is. 1, 4). Then He says who is the sower, saying, ***And the enemy that sowed them, is the devil***, who brought sin into the world; "But by the envy of the devil, death came into the world" (Wis. 2, 24). Afterwards, it is treated concerning the separation; and He does three things. Firstly, the time of the separation is related; secondly, the ministers are related; and thirdly, the separation is related. He relates the time, saying, ***But the harvest is the end of the world***. As it was said, the first harvest was made by the Apostles, concerning which it is said, "Lift up your eyes, and see the countries, for they are white already to harvest" (Jn. 4, 35). But the other harvest is that in which there will be the harvest of the fruits, concerning which it is said: "What things a man shall sow, those also shall he reap" (Gal. 6, 8).[25] ***And the reapers are the angels***. For just as in the Church that is now, the good ministers are men; so then, the good ministers will be the angels. Afterwards, He relates the end of both kinds of men, where it is said, ***Even as cockle therefore is gathered up***, etc. And firstly, He speaks regarding the bad ministers; secondly, He speaks regarding the good ministers; and thirdly, He awakens the Apostles to the consideration of the spiritual meaning of the parable. He says, therefore: ***Even as cockle therefore is gathered up, and burnt with fire: so shall it be at the end of the world. The Son of man shall***

---

24. i.e. the Jews who believed had the Gentiles as their spiritual children.
25. "CHYR: The figure of harvest is thus applied to two different things. Speaking of first conviction and turning to the faith, He calls that the harvest, as that in which the whole is accomplished; but when He inquires into the fruits ensuing upon the hearing the word of God, then He calls the end of the world the harvest, as here" (*Catena Aurea on St. Matthew*, chap. 13, lect. 7).

send his angels (these words show that He is man and God), ***and they shall gather out of his kingdom all scandals.*** He is applying the words of the parable to sins committed against one's neighbor. What follows, however, ***And them that work iniquity***, refers to other sins. Now that which is said, ***kingdom***, is understood to mean the Church that is now, because there will not be scandals in the Church triumphant, and men will know the wicked through the tribulation preceding the final judgment. Augustine says that we do not read that the wicked are meant to remunerate the good, but the good are sometimes found to punish the wicked. That which He says, ***all scandals***, ought to be understood to mean the scandals which exist in the Church that is now, through tribulations inflicted by God, by which the wicked and even the good are punished. Chrysostom interprets the kingdom to be our heavenly home. And when He says, ***all scandals***, He does not mean that scandals exist there, but that scandals do not exist there; hence, they will gather, and will separate the wicked from the good, lest they be with them in heaven, ***and shall cast them into the furnace of fire.*** The pain of loss is the lack of the beatific vision. But the pain of sense is mentioned, when it is said, ***And shall cast them into the furnace of fire***; "There shall not enter into it any thing defiled" (Apoc. 21, 27). ***And He***, meaning the Son of man by His judicial power, ***shall cast them into the furnace of fire***; hence, it is said: "Depart from me, you cursed, into everlasting fire" (below 25, 41). This passage has been expounded; nevertheless, it can be affirmed, based upon these words, that the damned will be punished both in soul and in body; hence: "Fear him that can destroy both soul and body in hell" (above 10, 28). For weeping pertains to the eyes, gnashing pertains to the teeth; now the eyes and the teeth are bodily members, and in saying which the truth of the resurrection is indicated. Likewise, by weeping, which is quickly produced by smoke, the pain of fire is signified; by gnashing of teeth, coldness is signified. "Let him pass from the snow waters to excessive heat" (Job 24, 19). Or it may be expounded otherwise, saying that the weeping is from sadness, the gnashing is from anger; hence, it is said that "they gnashed with their teeth at him" (Acts 7, 54). "Behold my servants shall rejoice for joyfulness of heart, and you shall cry for sorrow of heart, and shall howl for grief of spirit" (Is. 65, 14). "Woe to you that now laugh: for you shall weep" (Lk. 6, 25). Similarly, impatience and strife are signified by this gnashing; "They gnawed their tongues on account of their impatience in withstanding pain" (Apoc. 16, 10). ***Then shall the just shine as the sun, in the kingdom of their Father.*** Here He expounds the parable in relation to the good; and in them there shall be a double splendor. The first, namely, will be in the soul, through which they shall see God; "In thy light we shall see light" (Ps. 35, 10), that is to say, an uncreated light; "He will fill thy soul with brightness" (Is. 58, 11). And it will flow on to the body; "He will reform the body of our lowness, made like to the body of his glory" (Phil. 3, 21). "The just shall shine, and shall run to and fro like sparks among the reeds," etc., (Wis. 3, 7). That which He says, *As the sun*, ought not to be understood absolutely as an equality in every way: for they will have a greater brightness than the sun; but this is said because among the sensible things of this world the sun shines the most. They will be like the sun, however, because just as the sun is not changed, so neither will the just be changed. "A holy man continueth in wisdom as the sun: but a fool is changed as the moon" (Eccli. 27, 12). Then He stimulates a spiritual understanding of the parable; **He that hath ears to hear,** meaning interior ears, **let him hear**, that is to say, by understanding. "The Lord God hath opened my ear" (Is. 50, 5).

44. The kingdom of heaven is like unto a treasure hidden in a field. Which a man having found, hid it, and for joy thereof goeth, and selleth all that he hath, and buyeth that field.
45. Again the kingdom of heaven is like to a merchant seeking good pearls.
46. Who when he had found one pearl of great price, went his way, and sold all that he had, and bought it.
47. Again the kingdom of heaven is like to a net cast into the sea, and gathering together of all kinds of fishes.
48. Which, when it was filled, they drew out, and sitting by the shore, they chose out the good into vessels, but the bad they cast forth.
49. So shall it be at the end of the world. The angels shall go out, and shall separate the wicked from among the just.
50. And shall cast them into the furnace of fire: there shall be weeping and gnashing of teeth.
51. Have ye understood all these things? They say to him: Yes.
52. He said unto them: Therefore every scribe instructed in the kingdom of heaven, is like to a man that is a householder, who bringeth forth out of his treasure new things and old.

53. *And it came to pass: when Jesus had finished these parables, he passed from thence.*

54. *And coming into his own country, he taught them in their synagogues, so that they wondered and said: How came this man by this wisdom and miracles?*

55. *Is not this the carpenter's son? Is not his mother called Mary, and his brethren James, and Joseph, and Simon, and Jude:*

56. *And his sisters, are they not all with us? Whence therefore hath he all these things?*

57. *And they were scandalized in his regard. But Jesus said to them: A prophet is not without honour, save in his own country, and in his own house.*

58. *And he wrought not many miracles there, because of their unbelief.*

Above, the Lord parabolically showed the both the obstacles and the growth of the Gospel teaching; now, however, He shows its dignity by way of some parables which He will explain to His disciples. The dignity of the Gospel teaching is shown in regard to three things: in regard to its abundance, its beauty, and its universality. The second is where it is said, **Again the kingdom of heaven is like to a merchant**, etc.; the third is where it is said, **Again the kingdom of heaven is like to a net cast into the sea**, etc. I say, therefore, that the abundance of the Gospel teaching is like a treasure, because just as a treasure is an abundance of riches, so the Gospel teaching is likewise; "Riches of salvation, wisdom and knowledge: the fear of the Lord is his treasure" (Is. 33, 6). As to this, He proceeds thus. Firstly, a hidden treasure is considered; secondly, the finding of the treasure is considered; and thirdly, the acquisition of the treasure, etc., is considered. The second point is where it is said, **Which a man having found**, etc.; the third point is where it is said, **And for joy thereof goeth**. This treasure can be expounded in multiple ways. According to Chrysostom, it is the Gospel teaching, concerning which it is said: "We have this treasure in earthen vessels" (II Cor. 4, 7), which was hidden in the field of this world, actually from the eyes of the unclean; "Thou hast hid these things from the wise and prudent" (above 11, 25). According to Gregory, the desire of heaven is said to be a treasure; "The fear of the Lord is his treasure" (Is. 33, 6). This is hidden in the field of spiritual discipline; because exterior things seem to be contemptible, but interior things have sweetness; "Diligently till thy ground" (Prov.

24, 27). According to Jerome, the treasure is the Word of God, concerning whom it is said: "In whom are hid all the treasures of wisdom and knowledge" (Col. 2, 3); which He hid in the field of His body, because it was hiding in His flesh. "There is no end of their treasures" (Is. 2, 7). Or, alternatively, it is understood to mean sacred doctrine, which is hidden in the field of the Church; "For she is an infinite treasure to men" (Wis. 7, 14). **Which a man having found, hid.** It is found in all men having faith. For it cannot be in any man who does not have faith; "He is found by them that tempt him not: and he sheweth himself to them that have faith in him" (Wis. 1, 2). But it is fitting that it be hidden, according to that which is said: "Thy words have I hidden in my heart" (Ps. 118, 11). However, it ought not to be hidden from envy, but from caution. Now there are multiple reasons why it ought to be hidden. One reason is that it bears more fruit and does more good, because it flames out more; for just as fire, when confined, gives more heat, so the word of the Lord gives more heat when it is hidden; "The word of the Lord became like a burning fire, shut up in my bones, and I was wearied, not being able to bear it" (Jer. 20, 9). And, "My heart grew hot: and in my meditation a fire shall flame out within me" (Ps. 38, 4). Likewise, it is hidden because of vainglory: for if it produces smoke externally, it is subject to danger. For that reason, the Lord said, "Pray to thy Father in secret" (above 6, 6). Similarly, it is hidden because, in this way, it is more safely kept; for when it is in public, then he who plunders finds it. "Who showed his treasures to the ambassadors of the king of Babylon." And it is added: "Behold the days shall come, that all that is in thy house shall be carried away" (Is. 39, 4).

But what is the meaning of this, because it was said above: "Let your good works shine forth" (5, 15). This objection is solved by distinguishing the times of the works: because when it is first found, it is good that it be hidden; but when a man has been strengthened, then it is good that it be manifested; "Wisdom that is hid, and a treasure that is not seen, what profit is there in them both?" (Eccli. 41, 17). Gregory says that a good work ought to be open in its effect, but hidden in one's heart. Hence, he speaks thus: "Let a work be in public, but let the intention remain in secret."

For joy thereof goeth, and selleth all that he hath. This is the third point, namely, concerning the acquisition of the treasure, because the man rejoices. "As they that dig for a treasure, and they rejoice exceedingly when they have found the grave"[26]

---

26. i.e. in which they hope to find some riches.

(Job 3, 21-22). When he found it by faith, *for joy thereof goeth*, and begins to prosper, *and selleth all that he hath*, meaning he despises all that he hath, so that he may have spiritual things, *buyeth that field*; the meaning is that either he seeks after good companionship for himself, or he buys for himself the rest which he does not have, namely, peace of soul. "I have counted all things to be but as dung, that I may gain Christ" (Phil. 3, 8); "If a man should give all the substance of his house for love, he shall despise it as nothing," etc., (Cant. 8, 7).

Again the kingdom of heaven is like to a merchant, etc. Here is shown the treasure's beauty and splendor. *The kingdom of heaven is like*. This parable is expounded in multiple ways. Chrysostom and Jerome expound it to be concerning the Gospel teaching. There are many false teachings. These are not pearls. A man, therefore, who seeks different teachings finds the one, namely, the Gospel teaching, which is one on account of its truth. For virtues are many but truth is one. Hence, Dionysius says that virtue divides, but truth gives unity. Hence, to designate the truth, He says one pearl. Likewise, one is said, on account of the various teachings of the prophets. *He goeth, and selleth*, that is to say, he left behind all the teachings both of the prophets and of the philosophers for this one. "As an earring of gold and a bright pearl, so is he that reproveth the wise, and the obedient ear," etc., (Prov. 25, 12). Gregory says that this pearl is heavenly glory, because what is good is naturally desirable, and a man always is willing to exchange what is less good for something better. Man's highest good is heavenly glory; when he has found this, he ought to leave all things behind for this glory; "One thing I have asked of the Lord, this will I seek after; that I may dwell in the house of the Lord all the days of my life" (Ps. 26, 4). Augustine expounds this in three ways. *The kingdom of heaven is like*, etc., that is to say, it is like to a man seeking good men by which his kingdom may be established, because one man is proficient in one virtue, another is proficient in another. And when he has found that pearl, namely, Christ, in whom all virtues exist in the highest degree, *he goeth*, etc. Similarly, it may be otherwise expounded such that the divine precepts and all the necessities of life are signified by the good pearls. And when a man has found the one pearl, meaning the one commandment, namely, of charity, *he goeth*, etc. "A new commandment I give unto you: That you love one another, as I have loved you, that you also love one another," etc., (Jn. 13, 34). And the Apostle says, "Love therefore is the fulfilling of the law" (Rom. 13, 10). Again, the pearls may be otherwise understood to mean distinct sciences, by investigating which, we find the source of all sciences, namely, the Word of God, about whom it is said: "The word of God is the fountain of wisdom" (Eccli. 1, 5). Hence, for this Word you ought to sell everything, both earthly things and also one's body and soul, because when you sell these things, you possess yourself, and you are master of yourself. "I have counted all things to be but as dung, that I may gain Christ" (Phil. 3, 8). Hence, you ought to give everything for this boon, just as Paul did: "One died for all, that they also who live may not now live to themselves, but unto him who died for them and rose again" (II Cor. 5, 14-15).

Again the kingdom of heaven is like to a net cast into the sea, etc. Here another parable is set forth. Secondly, the exposition, not of all but of part of the parable, is set forth, where it is said, *So shall it be at the end of the world*. And two things are done in this parable. Firstly, the universality of this teaching is set forth; secondly, a separation is set forth, where it is said, *when it was filled*, etc. This net is a type of apparatus that encloses a large portion of the sea; hence, by it, either the Gospel teaching or the Church can be signified: because the first teachers were fishermen; "For they were fishers" (above 4, 18). This net is put into the sea, that is to say, into the world; "This great sea, which stretcheth wide," etc., (Ps. 103, 25). *And gathering together of all kinds of fishes*. Take note of its universality. For the Law was only given to one nation; "He hath not done in like manner to every nation: and his judgments he hath not made manifest to them" (Ps. 147, 20). The Evangelical law, however, gathers all men together; "To the Greeks and to the barbarians, to the wise and to the unwise, I am a debtor" (Rom. 1, 14). And, "Go ye and preach the gospel to every creature" (Mk. 16, 15). But will the end of all men be the same? Now all men are together in the net, but at the end of the world they all will be separated; hence, He says: *Which, when it was filled*, that is, when all the elect will have entered so the number of the elect may be filled up, *they drew out, and sitting by the shore*, etc. By the shore, the end of the world is signified, because there shall not be upheavals among the Saints, but there shall be good things in their repose. And He says, *Sitting*, because such is suitable to judiciary power. "You who have followed me, in the regeneration, when the Son of man shall sit on the seat of his majesty, you also shall sit on twelve seats judging the twelve tribes of Israel" (below 19, 28). *They chose out the good into vessels*, meaning into the heavenly abodes; "In my Father's house there are many mansions"

(Jn. 14, 2). And He says, *vessels*, in the plural on account of the variety of recompenses; "They may receive you into everlasting dwellings" (Lk. 16, 9). *But the bad they cast forth*, because all the unclean shall be cast out. *So shall it be at the end of the world*. Here He expounds the parable. And it ought to be noted that He expounds the parable only in respect to the wicked.

But then there is a question, namely, why He expounds the parable concerning the wicked, rather than concerning the good. It ought to be replied that He made mention of a net, with which, when they capture the fish, the bad ones are cast forth and live; the good ones are killed and are eaten. For that reason, someone could say that this might be the correct perspective; hence, in order to exclude that possibility, He expounds the part of the parable relating to the wicked, saying, *The angels shall go out*, not because they abandon their interior contemplation, because wherever they go they contemplate God; rather it is because they go forth to an exterior ministry. And so is said concerning a certain angel: "I am now come forth to teach thee" (Dan. 9, 22).

And they shall separate the wicked from among the just. At present the wicked are among the good, the cockle is amidst the wheat, the lily is among the thorns, but they shall be separated from the company of the good; and because of this, there is a bad excommunication; yet this excommunication is a representation of that final separation, but it is, nevertheless, different from it, because the Church is often deceived, but then there shall be no deception. This is the final separation concerning which the Apostle says: "If any man love not our Lord Jesus Christ, let him be anathema, maranatha" (I Cor. 16, 22). The explanation continues regarding the pain of sense. *And shall cast them into the furnace of fire*. This is expounded as was said above.

But there is a question as to why the Lord repeated this, because it seems to be the same as what was said in the parable about the cockle. It ought to be answered that the parables are the same in a certain respect, because here both the good and the wicked are understood by the net; hence, it signifies those who have not been cut off from the Church. But by the cockle is signified those who have been cut off from the Church by their deviation from her dogmas, and these men are not in the Church.

Have ye understood all these things? They say to him: Yes. After the Lord finished His parabolic teaching and His explanation of the parables to His disciples, the Evangelist here specifies their effect; and he does this firstly in relation to the disciples, and secondly in relation to the crowds, where it is said, *And it came to pass*, etc. The effect upon the disciples was their understanding of the teaching: hence, three things are related. Firstly, an examination of their understanding is related; secondly, their affirmation of their understanding is related; and thirdly, their future office is related.

Now it ought to be observed that since He had spoken many things to the crowds and to the disciples, because the disciples were to be teachers, it follows that it was fitting that they would understand them. And observe that they were being examined concerning three things. Firstly, they were being examined concerning their comprehension, and so He says, *Have ye understood all these things?* Likewise, they were being examined concerning their love; "Simon, lovest thou me more than these?" (Jn. 21, 15). Again, they were being examined concerning the possibility of their suffering; "Can you drink the chalice that I shall drink?" (below 20, 22). "They shall suffer well, that they may preach"[27] (Ps. 91, 15-16). Granted, however, that it belongs to humility that a man does not extol himself; nevertheless, he is ungrateful if he were not to recognize a benefit received. "I will remember the tender mercies of the Lord" (Is. 63, 7). For that reason, they answer and say to Him, *Yes*. Herein is related their avowal of attributing their comprehension to Christ's word. "The declaration of thy words giveth light: and giveth understanding to little ones" (Ps. 118, 130).

Therefore every scribe instructed, etc. Here He shows the office that was forthcoming to them, as though they had now been examined. And this conclusion can follow from the aforesaid words in two ways. In the first way, it follows by relating this to what was said concerning a treasure. The sense, therefore, could be that the Lord wishes this to be expounded thus: 'You say that you understand. If you understand, you are able to know that the treasure is sacred doctrine. From this treasure you can bring forth new things and old.'

And it ought to be observed that these disciples are called scribes because they can converse on the kingdom of heaven and on sacred doctrine, wherein new and old things are contained. They are also called scribes on account of their worthiness, because they are scribes, meaning they are learned; "The learned shall understand" (Dan. 12, 10); "Behold I send to you wise men and scribes" (below 23, 34). Similarly, they are called scribes due to their office, because they are Christ's notaries, for they wrote

---

27. *Bene patientes erunt ut adnuntient* is translated in the Douay Bible as, "They shall be well treated, that they may shew."

Christ's commandments on the tablets of their hearts; "Bind them in thy heart continually" (Prov. 6, 21). Moreover, they wrote them on the hearts of others. Hence, the Apostle said, "You are our epistle, written in our hearts" (II Cor. 3, 2).

He is like to a man that is a householder, namely, Christ. For He is the Lord, **who bringeth forth out of his treasure new things and old** (this chapter, verse 52), namely, the obligations of the New Law. For the New Law adds new meanings to the Old Law, and Christ explained these meanings; and for that reason, it ought to be enough for us to be like Christ, as it is said above: "It is enough for the disciple that he be as his master" (10, 25). Or it can be said, 'He is similar to someone's father, because it is He who brings forth old and new things from the knowledge divinely bestowed upon Himself.' The Manichaeans were not like this, because they were not citing the old things.[28] "The new and the old I have kept for thee" (Cant. 7, 13). Therefore, this error can be answered from this exposition of the parable. According to Augustine, the parable can be expounded as follows: **Therefore every scribe instructed**, etc. 'You perceived how I spoke to the crowds parabolically, and you were instructed that you may understand what was said parabolically in a spiritual sense. Hence, you ought to know that you may explain those things which are read in the Old Law by the New Law.' Hence, the things which are said in the Old Testament are figures of the New Testament. Wherefore, the Apostle says, "All these things happened to them in figure" (I Cor. 10, 11). And these things were unveiled in the Passion. Hence, below it is said (27, 51) that when the Lord suffered, the veil of the Temple was rent. Hence, before the Passion, Christ spoke in parables so that when they heard them they would understand that those things which are said in the Old Testament are said in figure of other things, even if they were actual events. **Therefore every scribe instructed in the kingdom of heaven, is like to a man that is a householder, who bringeth forth out of his treasure new things and old.** Or, according to Gregory, it can be expounded

---

28. "The Manichaeans falsely... call the God of the Old Testament the God of darkness" (I, q. 66, a. 3) and "They said that the Old Testament was not from God" (*In Symb. Apost.*, a. 8). "They say that the patriarchs of the Old Testament, who were before Christ, were wicked and damned" (*Comm. On St. John's Gospel*, chap. 10, lect. 2). "Manichaeus objected, 'If the Old Law was given by Divine Providence, since that is immutable, the Law itself would also be immutable, and consequently it ought not to be changed. Therefore since it was changed, then it was not given by Divine Providence" (*Ad Hebr.*, chap. 7, lect. 3) But "It is against Manichaeus that the Apostle here (II Tim. 3, 15) calls the Old Testament 'holy scriptures,' which cannot be understood of the New Testament, because he (Timothy) was not taught the writings of the New Testament 'from His infancy'" (*Super ad Tim. II*, chap. 3, lect. 3).

that the old things refer to all those things which pertain to sin, and the new things refer to those things which pertain to the grace of Christ: hence, the rewards of eternal life are called the new things, and the punishments of hell are called the old things. That man, therefore, brings forth new things and old, who considers not only the rewards, but also the punishment of hell.

And it came to pass: when Jesus had finished these parables, etc. Here the twofold effect of the Gospel teaching upon the crowds is related, namely, both the effect of admiration and of scandal. And firstly, the place is described; secondly, their admiration is described; and thirdly, their reproof is described. He says, therefore, *It came to pass: when Jesus had finished these parables, he passed from thence*, etc. It ought to be observed that it seems that He did not depart immediately. Hence, the Evangelist does not keep to the historical order of events; and He departed, so that it would be understood that they were not worthy; for that reason, He went to other places, according to that which is said: "Where there is no hearing, pour not out words" (Eccli. 32, 6). And in the same place it is said, "He speaketh with one that is asleep, who uttereth wisdom to a fool" (22, 9). *And coming into his own country*. Nazareth is sometimes called his own country, where He was raised, and there He did a few miracles: sometimes Bethlehem, the place in which He was born, is called His own country: and sometimes Capharnaum is called His own country, because He performed miracles there. *He taught them in their synagogues*, etc. Their admiration follows. And firstly, their admiration is related; secondly, the effect caused by their admiration is related. He says, *So that they wondered*. It is not surprising that they were wondering; "Thy testimonies are wonderful" (118, 129). They were wondering from whence were those virtues: for admiration is caused for this reason, that the effect is seen but the cause is unknown. These men were seeing an evident effect, but they did not know its cause; hence, they were saying, *How came this man by this wisdom and miracles?* But this is a foolish admiration, because, as it is stated in I Corinthians 2, 5, He is the power and wisdom of God. But they did not know this, and so they wondered. And they state their admiration and their thoughts: hence, they were saying, *Is not this the carpenter's son?* For He was considered to be the son of Joseph, who was not a blacksmith, but a carpenter: although it could also be said that He was the son of the Craftsman, "Thou hast made the morning light and the sun" (Ps. 73, 16). *Is not his mother called Mary?* They knew everything that pertained to His humanity. Concerning this Mary, it was stated above, "When as his mother Mary was espoused to Joseph," etc., (1, 18). ***And his brethren James, and Joseph, and Simon, and Jude.*** Helvidius interpreted these men to be the sons of Mary. But this is false, but rather they were His cousins. Or they are called brothers, because they were kindred to Joseph, who was reputed to be the father of Jesus. "Let there be no quarrel between me and thee, and between my herdsmen and thy herdsmen: for we are brethren" (Gen. 13, 8) said Abraham to Lot, even though Lot was the son of Abraham's brother. And what follows ought to be understood in the same way: ***And his sisters, are they not all with us?*** Hence, on account of these women, who were His cousins according to the flesh, they were astonished, saying, ***Whence therefore hath he all these things?*** But it ought to be observed that astonishment sometimes has an appropriate effect, namely, the glorification of God, as it was said above in chapter 3;[29] but sometimes it has the effect of scandal; hence, he said, ***And they were scandalized in his regard.*** But what is the reason why astonishment sometimes brings forth glory, but at other times scandal? The reason is that certain men give a bad interpretation to the things that they hear, and, for that reason, such men are necessarily scandalized. "They blaspheme whatever things they know not" (Jude 1, 11). But some men who are well disposed always give a good interpretation to what they hear. These men were of the first category; and so He reprehends them, when he says, ***But Jesus said to them: A prophet is not without honour, save in his own country.*** The Lord calls Himself a prophet: and it is not surprising, because Moses also had called Him a prophet: "The Lord thy God will raise up to thee a prophet of thy nation and of thy brethren like unto me," etc., (Deut. 18, 15). And it can be said that a man is said to be a prophet who says something through revelation, which is above human understanding; and so Jesus is said to be a prophet because His mind was illumined by angels and by God. Or it can be said that someone is said to be a prophet from the words far [*procul*] and illumination [*phanos*]:[30] and, in this sense, Jesus cannot be called a prophet: "If there be among you a prophet of the Lord, I will appear to him in a vision" (Num. 12, 6). So the text reads. But if a man were a prophet, he would

---

29. "But John stayed him, saying: I ought to be baptized by thee, and comest thou to me?" (above 3, 14).

30. "Prophecy first and chiefly consists in knowledge, because, to wit, prophets know things that are far [*procul*] removed from man's knowledge. Wherefore they may be said to take their name from the Greek, apparition, because things appear to them from afar" (II II, q. 171, a. 1).

speak in enigmas: Christ was not a prophet in this way; "He that hath learned many things, shall shew forth understanding" (Eccli. 34, 9). In the prophets of the Old Testament we do not find any prophet honored by his own people, but, in fact, we find that he is honored more by other men, as, for instance, it is read in Jeremias, who was held captive by his own people, but when the city was captured, he was freed by strangers: so it was also concerning Christ, who was honored by foreigners, but was despised by his own people.

And what is the reason why no prophet is honored in his own country? One reason is that when he is in his own country, many who know his weaknesses remember the weaknesses: for this is from men's malice, that they think of his weakness rather than his perfections. Another reason can be given, namely, that the Philosopher says that the people reason incorrectly, because they suppose that because they are similar to a man in some way, they are similar to him in every way. Hence, when a man is in his own country, since they see that he is similar to themselves in some way, either in race or in other ways, they suppose that he cannot be greater than themselves; for that reason, He says well, *A prophet is not without honour, save in his own country.* Hence, the Evangelist continues, *And he wrought not many miracles there*; this was not because He could not do them there, since He was omnipotent, but He wrought not many miracles because the reason why He was working miracles was so that men would believe in Him. But these men were holding Him in contempt, because the miracles were being interpreted as being something bad, and, for that reason, they were not disposed to the faith: nevertheless, He worked some miracles, so that they might be rendered inexcusable; and, for that reason, he says, *Not many*, since He worked some miracles. And He did this on account of their incredulity.

CHAPTER FOURTEEN

1. At that time Herod the Tetrarch heard the fame of Jesus.
2. And he said to his servants: This is John the Baptist: he is risen from the dead, and therefore mighty works shew forth themselves in him.
3. For Herod had apprehended John and bound him, and put him into prison, because of Herodias, his brother's wife.
4. For John said to him: It is not lawful for thee to have her.
5. And having a mind to put him to death, he feared the people: because they esteemed him as a prophet.
6. But on Herod's birthday, the daughter of Herodias danced before them: and pleased Herod.
7. Whereupon he promised with an oath, to give her whatsoever she would ask of him.
8. But she being instructed before by her mother, said: Give me here in a dish the head of John the Baptist.
9. And the king was struck sad: yet because of his oath, and for them that sat with him at table, he commanded it to be given.
10. And he sent, and beheaded John in the prison.
11. And his head was brought in a dish: and it was given to the damsel, and she brought it to her mother.
12. And his disciples came and took the body, and buried it, and came and told Jesus.
13. Which when Jesus had heard, he retired from thence by a boat, into a desert place apart, and the multitudes having heard of it, followed him on foot out of the cities.
14. And he coming forth saw a great multitude, and had compassion on them, and healed their sick.

Above, the Lord showed the power of the Gospel teaching by way of some parables; here, He shows its power by deeds; and He does three things. Firstly, He shows to what effects it extends itself through an allegory of deeds; secondly, He shows the sufficiency of the Gospel teaching; and thirdly, He shows how it may be preserved in its purity. The second point is found in chapter 15 and the third is in chapter 16. Regarding the first point, a false opinion is firstly related; secondly, its occasion is related; and thirdly, the opinion is disproved. The second part is where it is said, **Herod had apprehended John**, etc.; the third part is where it is said, **Which when Jesus had heard, he retired from thence.** He says, therefore, **At that time Herod the Tet-**

rarch heard the fame of Jesus. And it ought not to be referred to that day, but to a time in general; because Mark and Luke do not recount this in the same order, for they recount this event after the sending of the disciples, as it found in Mark 6. Hence, it is uncertain which Evangelist is keeping the historical order. Nevertheless, that which is said, *At that time*, is said so that Herod's negligence may be indicated, because after the miracles, Herod had heard of the fame of Jesus: for this desire is frequently found in the rich, that they do not care about small matters.[1] "Charge the rich of this world not to be high-minded nor to trust in the uncertainty of riches," etc., (I Tim. 6, 17). He says, *Herod the Tetrarch*, to differentiate him from King Herod, under whom Christ was born, as it stated above in chapter 2. Hence, when that Herod died, Christ returned from Egypt. This Herod was his son, and was a tetrarch. His father was made a king by the Romans, and he had six sons, two of whom he killed during his lifetime,[2] at the time of his own death he killed another firstborn son,[3] although he had already appointed him to be made king, when his father was still living. The same Herod having died, Archelaus took the kingdom unto himself, and following his father's malice, he could not be tolerated by the Jews. They then approached the Romans, and the kingdom was divided into four parts: two parts were delivered to Archelaus, another was delivered to Herod, and another part was delivered to Phillip. Hence, this Herod was a tetrarch and the ruler over a fourth part of the kingdom. *Heard the fame of Jesus*. On account of this, he was reprehensible, because Christ has already been living for so long a time, and had performed miracles, and, nevertheless, he then heard for the first time; whence is fulfilled that which is written: "Destruction and death have said: With our ears we have heard his fame" (Job 28, 22). *And he said to his servants: This is John the Baptist*, etc. Some have said that he held the error of the transmigration of souls: for Plato and Pythagoras affirmed when the soul leaves one body, it enters into another body. Herod, holding this opinion, as

---

1. "CHRYS; It is not without reason that the Evangelist here specifies the time, but you may understand the pride and carelessness of the tyrant inasmuch as he had not at the first made himself acquainted with the things concerning Christ, but now only after a long time. Thus they, who in authority are fenced about with much pomp, learn these things slowly, because they do not much regard them" (*Catena Aurea on St. Matthew*, chap. 14, lect. 1).

2. Aristobulus and Alexander were the first and second sons of Herod by his wife, Mariamne, and were killed in 6 B.C. Antipater accused them of plotting against their father.

3. Antipater, the firstborn son of Herod by his second wife, Doris, was killed in 4 B.C. Antipater had been himself accused of preparing poison for his father.

they say, believed that John's soul passed into Christ's body.[4] But this cannot be, because he had killed him shortly before; now Jesus was thirty years old; hence, he did not believe this. Moreover, Christ had already performed miracles before John's beheading and imprisonment, as it is stated in John 3.[5] Nevertheless, Herod should be praised because he believed in the resurrection, concerning which it is written: "Shall man that is dead, thinkest thou, live again?" (Job 14, 14). Likewise, he had another good quality, namely, that he believed that the resurrection may bring about a better state of existence; for that reason, he believed that John might then work miracles which he had not performed before his resurrection; wherefore, he says, *And therefore mighty works shew forth themselves in him*, because he had reached a higher state of existence; hence, men will rise again in a better state of existence. Whence, the Apostle says: "It is sown in weakness: it shall rise in power" (I Cor. 15, 43).

But here there is a question, because Luke (9, 7) says that Herod heard and doubted; hence, he said, "John I have beheaded"; here, he speaks without hesitation when he says, *This is John*.

Augustine solves this question, saying that he was not saying what he believed, but what he heard from others. Hence, when he first heard he doubted, but when His fame spread he consented. Hence, Luke relates his first view, but Matthew relates his second view. Or it can be said otherwise, that Matthew is also mentioning Herod's doubting, so that it may be read interrogatively, *Is this John?*

For Herod had apprehended John. This was done previously; hence, he is not following the order of events, but is giving the reason for John's death from a past incident.

But there is a question: Why are the Evangelists giving the reason for John's death? And it is Chrysostom who asks this. He answers this, however, saying they are principally concerned with Christ's deeds, but also other deeds inasmuch as they relate to Christ.

Therefore, he here gives the reason for John's death from what follows. And firstly, he gives the reason for his imprisonment; secondly, he gives the reason for his death, where it is said, *But on Herod's birthday*, etc. About the first, he does three things. Firstly, he relates the imprisonment; secondly, he relates

---

4. The text here reads, "Christ's soul," but this has been changed based on St. Jerome 's explanation of the heresy of metempsychosis. cf. *Catena Aurea on St. Matthew*, chap. 14, lect. 1.

5. "This beginning of miracles did Jesus in Cana of Galilee and manifested his glory" (Jn. 2, 11). "For John was not yet cast into prison" (Jn. 3, 24).

its cause; thirdly, he relates the beheading. *For Herod had apprehended John and bound him, and put him into prison.* He mentions the order of events, namely, that Herod firstly apprehended him, bound him, and then imprisoned him; now the order of events concerning Christ was the same. He mentions the cause of the events when he says, *because of Herodias, his brother's wife.* Herod and Philip were brothers. Philip married Herodias, the daughter of Aretas, king of the Arabs. He had enmity with that king of the Arabs, and also with his brother Herod, so that the king of the Arabs, in hatred of Philip, took his daughter, and gave her to Herod.

Concerning this John, you ought to realize that he was a man of great virtue; hence, it is said of him: "He shall come in the spirit of Elias" (Lk. 1, 17). Likewise, you ought to observe that he is also called a martyr, because he died on account of defending the faith, since he died for the truth; and Christ is truth.

For John said to him: It is not lawful for thee to have her. It ought to be known that Antipater, the grandfather of King Herod, was a foreigner, but he was a proselyte,[6] hence, his children were Jews. But it was commanded in the Law that while a brother was still alive, another brother could not marry the brother's wife; for this reason, John, as though Herod were a zealous follower of the Law, was saying, *It is not lawful for thee to have her. And having a mind to put him to death, he feared the people.* It sometimes happens that when someone is unwilling to avoid a sin, he falls into a greater one. "Killing, and theft, and adultery, have overflowed, and blood hath touched blood" (Osee 4, 2). Hence, because he did not wish to avoid adultery, he committed murder. And though he wanted to commit murder, *he feared the people.* A disturbance of the people is to be greatly feared; "Of three things my heart hath been afraid: the accusation of a city, and the gathering together of the people, and a false calumny" (Eccli. 26, 6-7). Likewise, fear of the Lord takes away an evil will; but fear of man does not, although it may make one delay. Wherefore, because he could not kill him on account of his fear of the people, he delayed. *But on Herod's birthday*, etc. Here he does three things concerning the killing of John, because he was unable to kill him on account of his fear of the people. Firstly, the events preceding the killing are related; secondly, the killing itself is related; and thirdly, the events subsequent to the killing are related. About the first, three preceding events are re-

---

6. Antipater was an Idumaean (Jos., "Bel. Jud.", I, vi, 2).

lated, namely, the dancing, the promise, and the request. He says, therefore, **But on Herod's birthday**, etc. It was a custom among the ancients that they would celebrate the day of one's birth, contrary to that which is written: "The day of death than the day of one's birth" (Eccle. 7, 2). It is not read that anyone celebrated the day of his birth except this man and Pharaoh, the king of Egypt;[7] hence, **on Herod's birthday, the daughter of Herodias** (so she was called[8]) **danced before them**, that is to say, in the dining room (and in this he is rendered blameworthy, because in his lasciviousness he forgot his royal court, in which the occurrence of these things was inappropriate), **and pleased Herod**, contrary to that which is written: "Use not much the company of her that is a dancer" (Eccli. 9, 4). And he continues, **Whereupon he promised with an oath**, etc. Behold the thoughtless promise and the rash oath. "Let not thy mouth be accustomed to swearing: for in it there are many falls" (Eccli. 23, 9). **And she being instructed before by her mother, said: Give me here in a dish the head of John the Baptist**. Here the woman's request is related. Women are sometimes pious, and have a changeable disposition; hence, when they are pious, they are very pious, but when they are cruel, they are very cruel; "There is no head worse than the head of a serpent; and there is no anger above the anger of a woman" (Eccli. 25, 22-23). And it is said in the same place: "All malice is short to the malice of a woman" (verse 26). For a man would hardly ever think what an evil-minded woman thinks. Her mother, therefore, sought to satisfy her anger. Likewise, she feared that Herod might at some time be converted on account of John's words, and put her away. **And the king was struck sad because of his oath**. Here it is specified how he was killed. Chrysostom says: "An example is here given that honor is respected even by the wicked," as it is stated in Wisdom 5, 1 ff.

Jerome says that he is now sad who, before, wanted to kill him, but he feared the people. Why, therefore, does he say that he was sad? He solves the question thus. It is the custom of men to relate what is seen by men: as, for instance, they were saying

---

7. "The third day after this was the birthday of Pharaoh: and he made a great feast for his servants, and at the banquet remembered the chief butler, and the chief baker" (Gen. 40, 20).

8. According to Josephus, Herodias' daughter was named "Salome." "But Herodias... was married to Herod [Philip], the son of Herod the Great, who was born of Mariamne, the daughter of Simon the high priest, who had a daughter, Salome; after whose birth Herodias took upon her to confound the laws of our country, and divorced herself from her husband while he was still alive, and was married to Herod [Antipas], her husband's brother by the father's side, he who was tetrarch of Galilee" (Josephus, *Jewish Antiquities*, XVIII, 5:4).

that Christ was the son of Joseph, because they supposed this to be true, as is stated in Luke 3. Hence, he says, *He was struck sad*, because he seem to be so to men.

The execution follows. And firstly, the command is set forth; and secondly, the execution is set forth. *Because of his oath, and for them that sat with him at table.* In this he was foolish, because an oath concerning something dishonorable ought not to be respected, because by the very fact that I swear to something dishonorable, I have broken the oath; "Thou shalt swear in truth, and in judgment (meaning with discretion), and in justice" (Jer. 4, 2). Similarly, if he had sworn that he himself would do something, it should have been understood to be in relation to honorable things; "Love not a false oath" (Zach. 8, 17). He says, *And for them that sat with him at table*, to make them all accomplices of the homicide, for they all were asking him to heed the girl's request, *he commanded it to be given, and he sent, and beheaded John.* Here his execution is related. Herein is fulfilled what John had said: "He must increase: but I must decrease" (Jn. 3, 30) because Christ was stretched upon the Cross, and he was beheaded. Likewise, the beheading of John was a sign that, by the authority of the Law, they would lose Christ and the Law.

Afterwards, the events subsequent to the killing are related. And firstly, the fulfillment of the thing promised is related; and secondly, the burial is related. He says, therefore, *And his head was brought in a dish.* And in this, Herod was reprehensible because he used cruelty amidst pleasures: hence, it is said that a certain official[9] loved a certain mistress, and when she was sitting on his lap, she said that she had never seen a man killed. And when he was at dinner, he had some man brought forth who deserved death, and had him killed in front of her: the Romans knew what he did, and so he was exiled from Rome. So also this Herod was sent into exile.[10] *And his disciples came and took the body, and buried it.* Here it is treated concerning John's burial, and burial of the dead is numbered among the works of mercy: and, nevertheless, it seems that mercy does not pertain to the dead, because if it did pertain to them, it seems that what the Lord says would not be true: "Fear him that can destroy both soul and body in hell" (above 10, 28). Why, therefore, is it numbered among the works of mercy? It ought to be answered that even if it is not of use to him according to the effect, which it now has,

---

9. i.e. Flaminius, a Roman general. (*Catena Aurea on St. Matthew*, chap. 14, lect. 2).

10. He was exiled by Caligula in 39 A.D because Herod Agrippa had accused him of conspiring against the Romans.

it is, nevertheless, of use to him according to the affection which a man now has towards the dead; hence, **they took the body, and buried it**; it is said that they buried it in Sebastia,[11] since it was nearby. Afterwards, Julian the Apostate, seeing many men coming to John's relics, had him burned, except for his head. **And they came and told Jesus.** Hence, John's disciples, who at first were calumniating Jesus, returned to Him when John died, and were His companions: in this way, some men are converted to Christ in time of tribulation; "In their affliction they will rise early to me" (Osee 6, 1).

Which when Jesus had heard, he retired from thence by a boat, into a desert place apart. Above, Herod's opinion about Christ was related, and, by occasion of this the story of John, was introduced; now, however, Herod's opinion is shown to be false. He had said two things, namely, that Christ was John whom he had killed; and likewise, he had said that John, now risen, was working miracles. He says, therefore: **Which when Jesus had heard, he retired from thence by a boat**, etc.

Why did He retire? Jerome gives four reasons. The first was so that He might spare His enemies, lest they fall headlong from one murder to another murder; "Blood hath touched blood" (Osee 4, 2). Similarly, it was so that He might defer His Passion; hence, He Himself says: "My time is not yet come" (Jn. 7, 6). Again, it was so that He might give an example to us lest we bring torments upon ourselves: for it is not a virtue, but presumption, to bring torments upon ourselves. Hence, it is said above: "If they shall persecute you in one city, flee into another" (10, 23). Moreover, it was so that He might show with what great devotion the multitude was hearing the word of God; "The Lord your God trieth you, that it may appear whether you love him" (Deut. 13, 3).

Likewise, it ought to be observed that the Evangelist relates four things which should have deterred the multitude from following Christ. The first is that He retired into a boat; similarly, that He retired into the desert; again, that there were not any woods there because it was a desert; and moreover, that He did not retire along a road on which men readily travel; but, on the contrary, He retired apart. Now He did this so that the multitude's devotion would be commended more. Likewise, Chrysostom says that He retired so that He might commend a man; for that reason, He was unwilling to retire until John's death had been announced.

11. Sebastia is a town in Palestine.

He continues, *And the multitudes having heard*, etc. Here it is treated concerning His miracles. And firstly, the multitude's devotion is mentioned; and secondly, the miracles are mentioned. He says, therefore: *And the multitudes having heard of it, followed him on foot out of the cities*; it is this passage wherein the devotion of the multitudes and of the poor is treated, who follow the Lord because of their devotion. "In their affliction they will rise early to me" (Osee 6, 1). *And he coming forth saw a great multitude*, etc. Here he mentions the miracles which the Lord worked coming from the desert: and it was appropriate, because when He was in heaven, the multitudes were not seeking Him; "I came forth from the Father and am come into the world" (Jn. 16, 28). Hence, He is moved to compassion; wherefore it follows, *And He had compassion on them*; therefore, He immediately showed compassion on them: "Thou, O Lord, art a God of compassion, and merciful, patient, and of much mercy, and true" (Ps. 85, 15). The effect of this compassion follows, *And He healed their sick*, that is to say, gratuitously and not having been asked. "He sent his word, and healed them" (Ps. 106, 20).

15. And when it was evening, his disciples came to him, saying: This is a desert place, and the hour is now passed: send away the multitudes, that going into the towns, they may buy themselves victuals.

16. But Jesus said to them, They have no need to go: give you them to eat.

17. They answered him: We have not here, but five loaves, and two fishes.

18. Who said to them: Bring them hither to me.

19. And when he had commanded the multitude to sit down upon the grass, he took the five loaves and the two fishes, and looking up to heaven, he blessed, and brake, and gave the loaves to his disciples, and the disciples to the multitudes.

20. And they did all eat, and were filled. And they took up what remained, twelve full baskets of fragments.

21. And the number of them that did eat, was five thousand men, besides women and children.

22. And forthwith Jesus obliged his disciples to go up into the boat, and to go before him over the water, till he dismissed the people.

23. And having dismissed the multitude, he went into a mountain alone to pray. And when it was evening, he was there alone.

24. But the boat in the midst of the sea was tossed with the waves: for the wind was contrary.
25. And in the fourth watch of the night, he came to them walking upon the sea.
26. And they seeing him walking upon the sea, were troubled, saying: It is an apparition. And they cried out for fear.
27. And immediately Jesus spoke to them, saying: Be of good heart: it is I, fear ye not.
28. And Peter making answer, said: Lord, if it be thou, bid me come to thee upon the waters.
29. And he said: Come. And Peter going down out of the boat walked upon the water to come to Jesus.
30. But seeing the wind strong, he was afraid: and when he began to sink, he cried out, saying: Lord, save me.
31. And immediately Jesus stretching forth his hand took hold of him, and said to him: O thou of little faith, why didst thou doubt?
32. And when they were come up into the boat, the wind ceased.
33. And they that were in the boat came and adored him, saying: Indeed thou art the Son of God.
34. And having passed the water, they came into the country of Genesar.
35. And when the men of that place had knowledge of him, they sent into all that country, and brought to him all that were diseased.
36. And they besought him that they might touch but the hem of his garment. And as many as touched, were made whole.

After having excluded Herod's opinion, here the Evangelist mentions the power of Christ's doctrine. For its power is threefold: it feeds, it rescues, and it heals the sick. And so its first power is shown in that He feeds the multitudes; the second is shown in that He rescues the disciples from the perils of the sea; and the third power is shown in that He heals many men. The second is where it is said, **And forthwith Jesus obliged his disciples to go up into the boat**; and the third is where it is said, **And having passed the water**, etc. About the first, he does three things. For firstly, His decision to feed the multitudes is related, secondly, the distribution of food is related; and thirdly, the abundance of the food is related. The second thing is where it is said, **But Jesus said to them**, etc.

The third thing is where it is said, *And they did all eat*, etc. He says, therefore, *And when it was evening*, that is to say, at sunset, by which Christ's death is signified, because it was at that time that He delivered His body as food; hence, it is said: "This do for the commemoration of me" (I Cor. 11, 24). And, "You shall shew the death of the Lord, until he come" (verse 26). Then the disciples show the need of feeding the multitudes from the nature of the place, where they say, *This is a desert place*. Here that same question comes up which is found in Psalm 77, 19, namely, how could the Lord furnish a table in the wilderness? Similarly, if the place were near a town, one could supposed that He had food from there, but it was a desert place. Again, the need is set forth from the hour, for they say, *And the hour is now passed*, in which the multitudes could get food for themselves. *Send away the multitudes*. From this, it seems that the disciples were so intent upon the sweetness of Christ's words that they were finding more pleasure in hearing Christ than in procuring victuals for themselves: hence, they cared little for bodily refreshment. For it is stated in Luke 21, 37: "And in the daytime, he was teaching in the temple: but at night going out, he abode in the mount." Again, there was another reason to feed them, namely, that it was nightfall. Concerning this hunger, it is stated: "I will send forth a famine into the land: not a famine of bread, nor a thirst of water, but of hearing the word of the Lord" (Amos 8, 11). And in this, the multitude's devotion is indicated, as well as their love and respect for Christ, because they did not depart from him, although it was nightfall.

But here there is a literal question, namely, that it is stated in John that Jesus questioned Philip; here, however, it is stated that the disciples questioned Christ.

Augustine resolves the matter. This is not incongruous, because what one Evangelist leaves out, another may say. Hence, they firstly spoke to Christ; and secondly, Jesus lifting up His eyes asked the disciples.

But Jesus said to them. Here he relates the distribution of the food: and about this he does three things. Firstly, Christ's command is related; secondly, the quantity of the food is related; and thirdly, the manner and order of distributing the food is related. The second part is where it is said, *They answered him*, etc.; the third part is where it is said, *Bring them to me*, etc. They had said two things. Firstly, they had said that He should send away the multitudes; likewise, they had said that they should seek food for themselves: and Christ responds to these two things as follows. "You say, 'Send away the multitudes,' but *They have no need to go*, He is here 'who giveth food to all flesh' (Ps. 135, 25). Again, you say that they should look for food, but it is not necessary, because you can give them heavenly food"; hence, He says, *Give you them to eat.* Hence, an example is given that spiritual food ought to be preferred to bodily food. The quantity of the food follows where it is said, *They answered him: We have not here, but five loaves, and two fishes.* From this, we ought to observe that the Apostles were so given to the word of God that they did not even care about looking for food. "Make not provision for the flesh" (Rom. 13, 14). Mystically, the teaching of the Law is signified by the five loaves;[12] "With the bread of life and understanding, she shall feed him" (Eccli. 15, 3). By the two fishes, the teaching of the Psalms and the Prophets is implied; or, according to Hilary, the teaching of the Prophets and of John the Baptist are signified by the two fishes, just as there were two outstanding personages in the Law, namely, the royal and the priestly personages.[13] *Who said: Bring them hither to me.* Here, the manner of distribution is related; and firstly, the presentation is related; secondly, the arrangement of the multitudes is related; thirdly, the prayer is related; and fourthly, the distribution is related. Hence, he says, *Who said*. He, who was omnipotent, was able to create new loaves; but He willed to feed them from existing loaves.

But what is the reason? The literal reason, according to Chrysostom, is that it was to confute the heresy of the Manichaeans who said that these creatures were made by the devil, contrary to that which is written: "Every creature of God is good" (I Tim. 4, 4).[14] Hence, if they were from the devil, Christ would not have performed such great miracles with them. Likewise, it was to show that He is the Lord of the land and of the sea. For He, who in Genesis 1, 11, said: "Let the earth bring forth green herb", and who said: "Let the waters bring forth the creeping creature having life," etc., (ibid. verse 20), is the selfsame Person who multiplied the loaves. Similarly, this was to indicate that He did not reject the Old Law, but converted it into the New Law: for that reason, He says, *Bring them hither to me*, because the things which were written in the Old Law ought to be referred to the New Law. Hence, He said: "If you did believe Moses, you would perhaps believe me also: for he wrote of me" (Jn. 5, 46).

12. "HILARY: The five loaves, that is, the five books of the Law" (*Catena Aurea on St. Matthew*, chap. 14, lect. 4).
13. "The two fishes are either the two precepts of the love of God and our neighbour, or the two people of the circumcision and uncircumcision, or those two sacred personages of the king and the priest" (St. Augustine, Sermon LXXX, 1).
14. cf. *Reply to Faustus the Manichaean*, bk. 30, n. 5).

And when he had commanded the multitude to sit down upon the grass, etc. Here the arrangement of the men is related, namely, that He made them sit on the grass; "All flesh is grass" (Is. 40, 6). Therefore, to sit upon the grass is nothing other than to mortify the flesh. "Mortify therefore your members which are upon the earth" (Col. 3, 5). Similarly, by the grass, the Law is signified. Because these men were Jews, and they were elevated by the Law; for that reason, He did not want them to sit upon the soil. *He took the five loaves and the two fishes*, etc. It ought to be observed that when the Lord performs miracles, He sometimes prays, and sometimes does not pray. Sometimes He prays, as He does here, to show that He is a man: sometimes He performs even greater miracles and He does not pray, to show that He is God. *And looking up to heaven, he blessed.* He looks *up to heaven*, more precisely, to His Father. "I have lifted up my eyes to the mountains, from whence help shall come to me" (Ps. 120, 1). *He blessed*, because all things are blessed by God's word. Note that our act of blessing is not productive, but symbolic; God's act of blessing, however, is productive; hence, a blessing pertains to an increase by God's multiplication, hence, it is written: "He blessed them, saying: Increase and multiply, and fill the earth" (Gen. 1, 22). Afterwards, it is treated concerning the distribution: *He brake, and gave the loaves to his disciples*; in which words is indicated that the first distribution was made to the disciples by the head of the disciples, Christ; "The head of every man is Christ" (I Cor. 11, 3). But He broke the bread that He might make known His own distribution of bread. "Deal thy bread to the hungry" (Is. 58, 7). *He gave the loaves to his disciples*, as it were, to mediators. "Take ye and eat" (below 26, 26); "And let a man prove himself, so that he may eat of that bread and drink of the chalice," etc., (I Cor. 11, 28). *And the disciples gave to the multitudes*, as His distributors.

But how were the loaves multiplied? It ought to be said that the fragments were multiplied. And certain men say that this can occur naturally: just as matter could have any form whatsoever, so it could have any quantity. But this is foolishness, namely, to say that matter could have any material quantity: for this cannot happen except through rarefaction; now this rarefaction is determined in natural things. Certain others say that it multiplies, just as from a few grains much grain is produced; but in that example it happens through nature, here, however, it happens through Christ's action. Hence, Christ's hands were like the earth, and the fragments were like seeds: hence, just as seeds are multiplied, so were the fragments. But there was not only this matter of bread, but the bread was multiplied by conversion of different matter into itself, and so a miracle was performed.

He continues concerning the abundance of the food; and this was in respect to two things: as to its sufficiency, and as to its remains. Hence, it is said, *They did all eat, and were filled*, and this agrees with that which is written: "The poor shall eat and shall be filled," etc., (Ps. 21, 27). *And they took up what remained, twelve full baskets of fragments.* Here the abundance of the food is mentioned by way of the large amount of what remained.

But why did the Lord want the remains to be gathered? Chrysostom proposes a literal reason. He wished firstly that the disciples gather the remains, lest it seem to be an illusion, and, likewise, lest the miracle be forgotten by them. And that they took up twelve baskets, this was according to the number of the twelve Apostles, in order that each and every Apostle might take up his own, and thus, the number of the baskets would be impressed upon the memory of them all. Mystically, by the remains, the spiritual meanings are understood, which were not gathered by the multitude; but the remains were gathered in baskets, that is to say, in the wise; "For see your vocation, brethren, that there are not many wise according to the flesh, not many mighty, not many noble; but the foolish things of the world hath God chosen, that he may confound the wise: and the weak things of the world hath God chosen, that he may confound the strong," etc., (I Cor. 1, 26-27).

Then the number of those eating is related: *And the number of them that did eat, was five thousand men*; and so a thousand men ate from one loaf, according to Hilary. This also happened after the Ascension, when five thousand were converted in one day as a consequence of the Apostles' preaching. *Besides women and children*, who were unrecognized, and so did not merit to be counted. Something similar is found in the book of Machabees that the children and women are not counted for war.

Likewise, observe that this miracle was performed immediately after the killing of John, and it was near the feast of Passover, and Christ had already preached for a year, and Christ would suffer a year later.

And forthwith Jesus obliged his disciples. Here the power of Christ's teaching is portrayed, in that it delivers from dangers, for He delivered the disciples from dangers. Hence, Matthew does three things. Firstly, the occasion of undergoing danger is related; secondly, the danger itself is related; and thirdly, the deliverance from the danger is related. The second part is where it is said, *And having dismissed the multitude, he went into a mountain,* etc.; the third is where it is said, *And in the fourth watch of the night, he came to them walking upon the sea.* The occasion of the danger was Christ's command: for those willing to comply with God's will are frequently exposed to dangers, as the Apostle says: "In perils of waters, in perils of robbers, in perils from my own nation, in perils from the Gentiles, in perils in the cities, in perils in the wilderness, in perils in the sea, in perils from false brethren" (II Cor. 11, 26). *And forthwith Jesus obliged his disciples to go up into the boat.* Hence, immediately after having performed the miracle, He chose to go apart from the multitudes. And He did this for three reasons. It was firstly so that He might show the verity of the miracle, lest they say that it had happened on account of His presence:[15] for He is the truth, as it is stated in John 14, 6.[16] Secondly, it was so that He might teach us to avoid vainglory; for that reason, after having performed the miracle, He withdrew; "I seek not my own glory," etc., (Jn. 8, 50). Likewise, it was so that He might show the virtue of discretion: for it belongs to discretion to withdraw oneself, and to rest; "When I go into my house, I shall repose myself with her" (Wis. 8, 16). But it ought to be observed that He uses compulsion, because it was hard for them to part from Christ, just as Peter says: "Lord, to whom shall we go? Thou hast the words of eternal life" (Jn. 6, 69). Similarly, He makes known the affection of the multitude, namely, with what ardor they were following Him; "Thy name is as oil poured out: therefore young maidens have loved thee" (Cant. 1, 2).

And having dismissed the multitude, He went into a mountain alone to pray. He continues concerning the danger, and the danger is shown from the time, from the place, and from the wind. And firstly, Christ's absence is related, because when He had dismissed the disciples, *He went into a mountain alone to pray.* He had come to plant our faith, for that reason, He sometimes did something human, and other times He did something divine: for instance, that He multiplied the loaves, this is proper to God: that He prayed, this is proper to men, and this was not because He needed to pray, but to give an example: for every action of Christ is for our instruction. "For I have given you an example,

---

15. "For even if He had seemed, when in sight, to be presenting an illusion, and not to have wrought a truth; yet surely not in His absence also. For this cause then, submitting His proceedings to an exact test, He commanded those that had got the memorials, and the proof of the miracles, to depart from Him" (Chrysostom, *Homily XLIX*, 3).

16. "I am the way, and the truth, and the life."

that as I have done to you, so you do also" (Jn. 13, 15). And He gives us an example how to pray, and He shows that peace of soul, raising of the mind, and solitude are required for prayer. Peace of soul is indicated because it is said, *and having dismissed the multitude*, which denotes disturbing thoughts with which a man cannot pray, and, for that reason, He teaches us to close the door of our heart; "But thou when thou shalt pray, enter into thy chamber," etc., (above 6, 6). Likewise, raising of the mind is indicated; "He shall sit solitary, and will raise himself above himself" (Lam. 3, 28). Similarly, solitude is indicated. "I will lead her into the wilderness and I will speak to her heart" (Osee 2, 14). By the mountain, heaven is understood: for nothing is higher than heaven. And having dismissed the multitude means having left mortal things, He went to heaven, and He ascended alone and by His own power. "He shall go up that shall open the way before them" (Mic. 7, 23). Likewise, He ascended into heaven to pray; "He is able also to save for ever them that come to God by him; always living to make intercession for us" (Heb. 7, 25).

But here there seems to be a problem, because John seems to say that He feared the multitudes on the mountain, as it is stated in John 6;[17] here, however, it is said that He went up into the mountain after feeding the multitudes. But it is answered that that He fed them on the mountain, but afterwards He went up into a higher place on the mountain.

Likewise, there is another question, because in John 5 it is stated that He fled because they wanted to make Him king; here, however, it is said that He went up the mountain to pray. Augustine says that the same thing can be the reason for praying and for fleeing.

Afterwards, the danger from the time is described, for it was night, and there is greater danger from the sea at night; for that reason, he says: *And when it was evening*. And His Passion is signified, because in the Passion He ascended alone; "While they looked on, he was raised up: and a cloud received him out of their sight" (Acts 1, 9). *But the boat in the midst of the sea was tossed with the waves.* By the boat, the Church is signified; and by the sea, the world is signified; "So is this great sea, which stretcheth wide its arms" (Ps. 103, 25). And this Church, when Christ went into it, remained in the sea, and in the world's dangers. For when some great man attacks the Church, then it is agitated by the waves. "All thy waves thou hast brought in upon

---

17. "Jesus therefore, when he knew that they would come to take him by force and make him king, fled again into the mountains, himself alone" (verse 15).

me" (Ps. 87, 8). But because Christ prays, it cannot be submerged, even though it toss and be lifted up. "The waters lifted up the ark on high from the earth" (Gen. 7, 17). Likewise, it is agitated by the wind: and this wind is an assault instigated by the devil. "Because a wind came on a sudden from the side of the desert, and shook the four corners of the house" (Job 1, 19); "The blast of the mighty is like a whirlwind beating against a wall" (Is. 25, 4).

And in the fourth watch of the night, he came to them walking upon the sea. Having related the danger, the liberation from the danger is related: and about this he does two things. Firstly, the assistance is related; and secondly, the effect is related. The second point is where it is said, *And they that were in the boat came and adored him.* He had related three dangers. Firstly, he had related the darkness of the night, the danger of the sea, and the danger of the wind. In opposition to the first danger, he relates His visitation; in opposition to the second, he relates His certitude, where it is said, *And immediately Jesus spoke*, etc.; and in opposition to the third, He reaches out His hand: *And immediately Jesus stretching forth his hand took hold of him.* Likewise, in opposition to the third, he relates the calmness of the sea: *And when He was come up into the boat, the wind ceased.* About the first, His visitation is related; secondly, the effect of His visitation is related, where it is said, *And they seeing him walking upon the sea, were troubled.* He says, therefore: *In the fourth watch of the night, he came to them.* Here, both His arrival and the time are mentioned, because it is said, *In the fourth watch.* Jerome says that the ancients divided the night into four parts. Some men watched during the first part, others during the second part, others during the third, and others during the fourth; and those who had watched rested. Hence, he says that in the fourth watch, etc., because when they had been on the sea the whole night, *He came to them walking upon the sea.* And why was this? Chrysostom gives a literal reason, saying that He delayed so long so that He might be desired more. "My soul hath desired thee in the night" (Is. 26, 9). Likewise, it was in order that they might learn that if they do not immediately get assistance, they should not give up, because one ought to pray always. Mystically, by the four hours is signified the four states. Firstly, there was the state of the Law; secondly, there was the state of the prophets; thirdly, there was the time of grace; and fourthly, there was the time of His ascent into heaven, in which state the tempest ceased. Hence, He came at the fourth watch, that is to say, at the end of the night; hence, it is written: "Be you therefore also patient and strengthen your hearts: for the coming of the Lord is at hand" (James 5, 8). But how does He come? ***Walking upon the sea***. And why did He wish to come in this way? It was to show that He is the Lord of the sea: "Thou rulest the power of the sea: and appeasest the motion of the waves thereof" (Ps. 88, 10). Likewise, it was so that He might expose the abusers of the powers of the world: for the devil always abuses the powers of this world; "This sea dragon which thou hast formed to play therein" (Ps. 103, 26). But the Lord subdued these powers; "Thou hast broken the heads of the dragon" (Ps. 73, 14); and this means that the Church can only withstand tribulations, according to what He wills.

Here there was an opinion[18] that the Lord, during His life on earth, received four gifts: the gift of subtlety in His birth; the gift of impassibility, when He fasted forty days, or by transubstantiating the sacrament of the Eucharist; the gift of agility here; and the gift of brilliance in His transfiguration. But I do not believe this: for I believe that He performed these things miraculously.

And they seeing him. Here the effect of Christ's presence is related, namely, the troubling of the disciples; hence, their troubling is related, the cause of their troubling is related, and the sign of their being troubled is related. And he says, ***And they seeing him were troubled***, etc. You ought to know that when divine assistance is closer at hand, the Lord permits men to be more afflicted, so that then His assistance may be received with more devotion and thanksgiving. Likewise, then fear grows more because men are frequently converted through fear. And why were they troubled? It was because they believed that He was an apparition; hence, ***Saying: It is an apparition***, not believing what they saw to be His true body born of the Virgin. For, mystically, it is signified that before Christ comes, many men will affirm many imaginary things, as it is stated below.[19] ***And they cried out for fear***: for a cry is a sign of fear, so also in every tribulation we ought to cry out; "In my trouble I cried to the Lord: and he heard me" (Ps. 119, 1).

And immediately Jesus spoke to them, etc. Here His assistance is related. Because they were in darkness, for that reason, He gives them assurance: and He does three things. Firstly, He assures by His words; secondly, Peter asks for a sign in his actions; and thirdly, he is permitted. He had related three

---

18. cf. Innoc. III, *De sacro altaris mysterio*, l. 4, c. 2: ML 217, 864; III, q. 28, 2 ad 3ᵘᵐ.

19. "If therefore they shall say to you, Behold he is in the desert: go ye not out. Behold he is in the closets: believe it not" (24, 26).

things: their troubling from fear, the falsity of their opinion, and, likewise, their desperation: and in contrast to these, He does three things, because *immediately Jesus spoke to them.* And when someone cries to the Lord, if it is necessary, He comes immediately; "At the voice of thy cry, as soon as he shall hear, he will answer thee" (Is. 30, 19). Likewise, because they were despairing, He says to them, *Fear ye not.* Similarly, it is stated in John's Gospel: "In the world you shall have distress. But have confidence. I have overcome the world" (16, 33): that is to say, in Me you will have rest. Again, it was because they thought that He was an apparition, for that reason, He says, *It is I.*[20] And why does He speak in this manner? It is because they were assured by His manner of speaking; "My sheep hear My voice" (Jn. 10, 3). Moreover, it was so that He might show that He is God. Something similar is stated in Exodus 3, 13: "He who is, hath sent me to you," said Moses. Again, in opposition to the fact that they were troubled, He said, *Fear ye not;* "Who art thou, that thou shouldst be afraid of a mortal man, and of the son of man, who shall wither away like grass?" (Is. 51, 12). And, "The just, bold as a lion, shall be without dread" (Prov. 28, 1). *Peter making answer, said: Lord, if it be thou, bid me come to thee upon the waters.* Because He had given assistance by His words, for that reason, Peters asks for a sign in his actions. Now Peter asked confidently in the person of all the disciples, and he said, *If it be thou, bid me come to thee.* Here is Peter's great confidence. He did not say, 'Pray for me,' but he said, *bid me come to thee,* because he confessed: "Thou art Christ, the Son of the living God" (below 16, 16). Hence, by reason of the faith, which he had already conceived, he boldly trusts in His power. "O Lord, all things are in thy power, and there is none that can resist thy will" (Est. 13, 9). And he said this solely out of his desire to come to Him, and not to tempt Him, nor out of disbelief. "Being mindful of the work of your faith and labor and charity," etc., (I Thess. 1, 3). Then the sign is related; and so He said, *Come. And Peter going down out of the boat walked upon the water to come to Jesus.* And this is opposed to the Manichaeans who said that Christ did not have a true body: because if Christ did not have a true body, because He walked upon the water, then neither did Peter. By the fact that danger was still threatening after the fourth watch, it is signified by His coming at the fourth watch that what needs to be purged in the elect will

---

20. *Ego sum.*

be purged [at His second coming].[21] "A fire shall go before him, and shall burn his enemies round about" (Ps. 96, 3). ***But seeing the wind strong***, etc. Now here the third assistance is related, namely, that He saved Peter from submersion. And firstly, the cause is related; secondly, Peter's petition is related; and thirdly, Christ's assistance is related. ***But seeing the wind strong, he was afraid.*** On the sea, the wind does not have a constant force, just as it does not have a constant force on land; hence, it was interrupted when Peter first went upon the sea; but when he was on the sea it blew strongly, and then ***he was afraid***. And from this, what he tells ought to be considered, that it was more dangerous upon the sea than in the boat, and so the Lord permits strong men to be sunk in the sea's danger. Hence: "He that thinketh himself to stand, let him take heed lest he fall" (I Cor. 10, 12). But why did the Lord permit him to be in danger? Firstly, He commanded him to go upon the sea, so that His power might be shown, because both were walking upon the sea, and the disciples saw this. But that He permitted Peter to sink was done so that Peter might experience what he could do of himself. Hence, that Peter walked upon the sea was by Christ's power; that he began to sink, on the other hand, was owing to Peter's weakness, just as Paul says: "Lest the greatness of the revelations should exalt me, there was given me a sting of my flesh, an angel of Satan, to buffet me" (II Cor. 12, 7). The Lord also permitted Peter to sink because he was to be the pastor. Therefore, He wished to show to him his power and weakness. Likewise, He did this to suppress the jealousy of the disciples: for because they saw his danger, their jealousy ceased. ***And when he began to sink, he cried out, saying: Lord, save me.*** Something similar is stated in Psalm 68, 2: "Save me, O Lord: for the waters are come in even unto my soul." ***And immediately Jesus stretching forth his hand took hold of him.*** Christ does two things, namely, that He both gives assistance, and rebukes Peter's disbelief. He gives assistance, because He reaches out His hand; "Put forth thy hand from on high, take me out, and deliver me from many waters" (Ps. 143, 7). And it is said: "To the work of thy hands thou shalt reach out thy right hand" (Job 14, 15). Next, He rebukes him concerning his disbelief, and He says to Him: ***O thou of little faith, why didst thou doubt?*** In which words, it is indicated that if he had possessed a firm faith he could not

---

21. HILARY; The first watch was therefore of the Law, the second of the Prophets, the third His coming in the flesh, the fourth His return in glory" (*Catena Aurea on St. Matthew*, chap. 14, lect. 5).

have sunk, for that reason, we ought to be constant in our faith. Similarly, it is stated above: "Why are you fearful, O ye of little faith?" (8, 26). *And when they were come up into the boat, the wind ceased.* Here is related His fourth assistance, namely, against the wind. "He said the word, and there arose a storm of wind" (Ps. 106, 25). Hence, it is a sign, that when Christ is with His own disciples, they have no troubles; hence: "They shall no more hunger nor thirst" (Apoc. 7, 16).

The effect of their deliverance follows, *And they that were in the boat came and adored him*, namely, the disciples, or the sailors. "What manner of man is this, for the winds and the sea obey him?" (above 8, 27). *Indeed thou art the Son of God.* Now, by this is signified that when the Lord is with the faithful, then they truly believe; "And now, little children, abide in him, that when he shall appear we may have confidence and not be confounded by him at his coming" (I Jn. 2, 28).

And having passed the water, they came into the country of Genesar. Here Christ's power is set forth. And firstly, the place is described; then the devotion of the men is described; and afterwards, His operative power is described. He says, therefore, *And having passed the water, they came into the country of Genesar*, which place is on the other side of the sea, and is interpreted to mean "rise": hence, after the danger they came to rest.[19] Then he continues concerning the multitude's devotion: *And when the men of that place had knowledge of him, they sent into all that country, and brought to him all that were diseased*, etc., because they not only brought to Him their sick, but they sent for the sick who lived in other places. Hence, when they had knowledge of him through His fame and His teaching, they sent for the sick, and they brought them to Him; hence, they all believed in Him, because His word had such great power: and this is signified in Isaias: "I will send of them that shall be saved, to the Gentiles into the sea," etc., (66, 19). Likewise, their devotion is shown, because they were not only asking that He would lay His hands upon the sick, but they merely *besought him that they might touch but the hem of his garment.* By the hem, the smallest precepts are signified, or Christ's flesh is signified, or the sacrament of Baptism is signified. *And as many as touched, were made whole.* Hence: "He that believeth and is baptized shall be saved" (Mk. 16, 16).

22. "Rabanus: Genesar is interpreted, 'rise,' 'beginning.' For then will complete rest be given to us, when Christ shall have restored to us our inheritance of Paradise, and the joy of our first robe" (*Catena Aurea on St. Matthew*, chap. 14, lect. 6).

CHAPTER FIFTEEN

1. Then came to him from Jerusalem scribes and Pharisees, saying:

2. Why do thy disciples transgress the tradition of the ancients? For they wash not their hands when they eat bread.

3. But he answering, said to them: Why do you also transgress the commandment of God for your tradition? For God said:

4. Honour thy father and mother: And: He that shall curse father or mother, let him die the death.

5. But you say: Whosoever shall say to father or mother, The gift whatsoever proceedeth from me, shall profit thee.

6. And he shall not honour his father or his mother: and you have made void the commandment of God for your tradition.

7. Hypocrites, well hath Isaias prophesied of you, saying:

8. This people honoureth me with their lips: but their heart is far from me.

9. And in vain do they worship me, teaching doctrines and commandments of men.

10. And having called together the multitudes unto him, he said to them: Hear ye and understand.

11. Not that which goeth into the mouth defileth a man: but what cometh out of the mouth, this defileth a man.

12. Then came his disciples, and said to him: Dost thou know that the Pharisees, when they heard this word, were scandalized?

13. But he answering, said: Every plant which my heavenly Father hath not planted, shall be rooted up.

14. Let them alone: they are blind, and leaders of the blind. And if the blind lead the blind, both fall into the pit.

15. And Peter answering, said to him: Expound to us this parable.

16. But he said: Are you also yet without understanding?

17. Do you not understand, that whatsoever entereth into the mouth, goeth into the belly, and is cast out into the privy?

18. But the things which proceed out of the mouth, come forth from the heart, and those things defile a man.

19. For from the heart come forth evil thoughts, murders, adulteries, fornications, thefts, false testimonies, blasphemies.

20. These are the things that defile a man. But to eat with unwashed hands doth not defile a man.

Above, the Lord showed the power of His teaching under figures, now He shows its sufficiency. Now this is shown in two ways. Firstly, He shows that He does not require the observances of the Law; and secondly, He shows that His teaching may not only be given to the one nation of the Jews, but also to the Gentiles, where it is said, *Jesus went from thence, and retired into the coast of Tyre and Sidon.* About the first, the Evangelist does three things. Firstly, the circumstances of an accusation are mentioned; secondly, the accusation is mentioned; and thirdly, an explanation of the accusation is mentioned. The second is where it is said, *Why do thy disciples transgress the tradition of the ancients?* And the third is where it is said: *For they wash not their hands when they eat bread.* Now the Jews' bad behavior is worsened by three things. Firstly, it is worsened by the time, because at the time when He was performing these signs and miracles, they were giving proofs of their wickedness, whence they were maligning Him. "Thou hast hid these things from the wise and prudent," etc., (above 11, 25). Likewise, the worsening was compounded by the place, because although the Jews were spread throughout Judea, nevertheless, those who were in Jerusalem were the wise men, and yet, they were worse than the rest. "In the land of the saints he hath done wicked things, and he shall not see the glory of the Lord" (Is. 26, 10). Likewise, it was worsened by the condition of the persons, because from the great men came the Scribes, who were more learned, and the Pharisees, who were reckoned to be more holy. "I will go therefore to the great men, and will speak to them: for they have known the way of the Lord" (Jer. 5, 5). Then the matter about which they were accusing them is related, and so it is said, *Why do thy disciples transgress the tradition of the ancients?* It had been ordered, as it is stated in Deuteronomy 4, 2: "You shall not add to the word that I speak to you, neither shall you take away from it." Hence, by adding traditions, they were acting contrary to the Law; not because it was not allowed to make an ordinance, but because they were ordering that their decrees be observed just like Lord's Law. *For they wash not their hands*, etc. Here is explained what were their traditions. Yet this is explained more in Mark 7, 2: for there it is said that "When they had seen some of his disciples eat bread with common, that is, with unwashed hands, they found fault." And that they were not washing their hands can be explained in the literal sense. Why were they not washing their hands? It was because they were so preoccupied with the word of God that they did not even have time: hence, due to their preoccupation for spiritual things, they were not washing their hands in the manner that the Jews did, as it is stated in Mark 7, because all the Jews do not eat without often washing their hands: for that reason, the disciples were not washing their hands according to their ritual. Hence, the Jews themselves were thinking literally, washing what was exterior, and not what was interior. *But he answering, said to them.* The Lord does two things: namely, that He does not answer by excusing the disciples, but He shows that the men who were correcting them were themselves unworthy. "Thou hypocrite, cast out first the beam out of thy own eye" (above 7, 5). It is clear that to transgress God's commandment is worse than to transgress the traditions of men: and, for that reason, those who were transgressing God's Commandments, were sinning in greater matters. And so He firstly shows that they are the transgressors of the Law; and secondly, He shows which Commandment they are transgressing. He says, therefore, *Why do you transgress the commandment of God*, and you do not observe it, *for your tradition?* "They, not knowing the justice of God and seeking to establish their own, have not submitted themselves to the justice of God" (Rom. 10, 3). "Their tongue, and their devices are against the Lord, to provoke the eyes of his majesty" (Is. 3, 8). Then, when He says, *For God said*, etc., He relates which Commandment this is, namely, the Commandment concerning the honoring of one's parents. And firstly, He relates the Commandment; and secondly, He relates its penalty; hence, He says: *For God said* (Ex. 20, 12)*: Honour thy father and mother.* And it ought to observed that honor is nothing other than reverence shown as a testimony of virtue. For he shows reverence who furnishes the things which are needed: hence, a man is not only bound to stand up out of respect, but also to supply the necessities of his parents. "They that fear the Lord, keep his commandments" (Eccli. 2, 21). And it is evident that such honor is due, because Tobias loaned to Gabelus, which the Lord had commanded to be done.[1] Exodus 20, 12, immediately adds the reward:[2] "That thou mayest be long lived upon the land." Likewise, Leviticus 20, 9, adds the penalty to transgressors of this Commandment: "He that curseth his father, or mother, dying let him die." And so by the word "blessing" it ought not only be understood that you

---

1. "And when amongst a great multitude of his kindred, he saw Gabelus in want, who was one of his tribe, taking a note of his hand he gave him the aforesaid sum of money" (Tob. 1, 17). "I command thee to open thy hand to thy needy and poor brother, that liveth in the land" (Deut. 15, 11).

2. The text has "penalty" but this should more likely be "reward." Hence, the translation here includes this correction.

should bless with your mouth, but that you also pay out a blessing; "He that curseth his father, and mother, his lamp shall be put out in the midst of darkness" (Prov. 20, 20). But since He put forward an incentive by way of a punishment, why did He not put forward a reward of obedience? It was because men are more terrified by a punishment than by the desire for a reward; for a beast is also terrified by a punishment. For due to this, it is stated that if someone withholds the support of his father and mother, he is worthy of death, and so he who instigates others to withhold the support of them are worthy of death; wherefore, the disciples are not deserving of blame. Therefore, 'you are not worthy to accuse them.' *But you say*, etc. Here He mentions how they transgress God's Commandment. And firstly, He shows this; and secondly, He cites a passage of Scripture. And about the first, He depicts their custom; and secondly, He shows what is the consequence of their custom. He says: *You say: Whosoever shall say to father or mother*, etc. This is read in many ways. It may be read in one way as a complete sentence, and then it is understood as follows; *Whosoever*, meaning anyone at all, *shall say*, shall be able say. It may be read in another way as an incomplete sentence, and then it is understood as follows; when it is said, *Whosoever shall say*, etc., supply the words, 'he keeps the commandment, and so is immune from punishment.' What is the meaning of this verse? It is explained in three ways. Rabanus said that a spiritual good ought to be preferred to a temporal good; for that reason, they were speaking to those who had poor parents, so that they might say to them: 'Father, may it not displease you if I do not give you what you need, because the gift that I offer benefits you spiritually.' But this was not true, according to that which is written: "The most High approveth not the gifts of the wicked" (Eccli. 34, 23). And it is said: "He that stealeth anything from his father, or from his mother, and saith, This is no sin, is the partner of a murderer" (Prov. 28, 24). For that reason, if someone has a father or a mother, and they cannot live without him, then he who would say to him, 'Go beyond the sea,' or 'Enter religion,' falls under this sentence. There is another explanation. Now Jerome reads this sentence interrogatively, that is to say, "Shall it profit thee? No. Rather, it shall be unto your greater condemnation." Augustine expounds this as follows. The Jews were saying that children were bound to them while they were under their father's tutelage. Hence, when the children were small, the parents offer for their children and it benefits them; but when they are reckoned to be free, then another's devotion does not benefit them. Hence, they were saying that everyone who can attain to this state can also say to his father, *The gift whatsoever proceedeth from me, shall profit thee*; and he was not bound to support his father. But two difficulties follow from this teaching. One is contrary to one's neighbor, and the other is contrary to the Lord. One is contrary to one's neighbor because he who would speak in this manner and who is so instructed, does not honor his father. Hence: "Inventors of evil things, disobedient to parents" (Rom. 1, 30). And it continues: "They who do such things, are worthy of death" (verse 32). It is likewise contrary to God; hence, He says: *You have made void the commandment of God*; it is as though He were to say: 'You not only have done contrary to your neighbor, nay, you even *made void the commandment of God for your tradition. Hypocrites.* Men were called hypocrites in the strict sense, who entered into the theater, and had one personality and pretended to have another by using masks. Therefore, these men are hypocrites, who outwardly pretend to be something different than they are inwardly; hence, they were inwardly intending profit, and outwardly they were inducing men to offer gifts to God. "Dissemblers and crafty men prove the wrath of God, neither shall they cry when they are bound" (Job 36, 13). *Well hath Isaias prophesied of you.* This quotation is found in Isaias, 29.[3] He firstly sets forth their duplicity; and secondly, He sets forth the futilely of their religious practices, were it is said, *And in vain do they worship me.* He says, therefore, *This people honoureth me with their lips: but their heart is far from me.* And this was literally true, because they were honoring God with their lips, but their hearts were far from God; because they were not receiving Christ coming in God's name. Or it is thus: *This people honoureth me*, etc., for since they say that a man ought to offer gifts to God, it seems that they honor God, *but their heart is far from me*, because they were not striving after God's honor, but after their own gain: hence, the more greed there is, the less charity there is. This is stated in Jeremias 12, 2: "Thou art near in their mouth, and far from their reins." But did not this pretense benefit them? It did not, because it did not please the Lord; hence, He continues, *And in vain do they worship me.*

But what is the meaning of these words? To fast is a doctrine of men, and the canons are traditions of men; do those who teach these things worship God in vain? It ought to be understood that

---

3. "This people draw near me with their mouth, and with their lips glorify me, but their heart is far from me, and they have feared me with the commandment and doctrines of men" (verse 13).

their worship was vain in that it was prejudicial to God's Commandments. "I will not level God with man" (Job 32, 21). "We ought to obey God rather than men" (Acts 5, 29). Why is this? It is because God cannot be deceived. "Do not offer sacrifice in vain" (Is. 1, 13). From this, we maintain that a man ought to be more conscious of the transgression of a Commandment than of the transgression of an ecclesiastical ordinance.

And having called together the multitudes unto him, etc. Above, the Lord showed that the calumniating Pharisees were unworthy to reprehend the disciples because they were involved in greater sins; now, however, disregarding them, He instructs other men; this was to fulfill that which was said above: "Thou hast hid these things from the wise and prudent, and hast revealed them to little ones" (11, 25). And firstly, He instructs the multitudes; and secondly, He instructs the disciples, where it is said, *Then came his disciples*, etc. And about the first, He does two things. Firstly, He prepares them to listen; and secondly, He gives His teaching. The second is where it is said, *Not that which goeth into the mouth defileth a man.*

It ought to be observed that, to listen to someone else, attention is required, by which a man is recalled to interior things, and is gathered together into himself. And He does this when He says, *And having called together*, because it is fitting that we be gathered to Him; "Come ye to him and be enlightened" (Ps. 33, 6). Secondly, effort is necessary in listening: for that reason, He says, *Hear ye*; "A wise man shall hear, and shall be wiser" (Prov. 1, 5). Likewise, understanding is required; hence, He says, *And understand*; "Understand, ye senseless among the people: and, you fools, be wise at last" (Ps. 93, 8).

Afterwards, He sets forth the highest teaching, which is the perfection of a moral life: hence, it ought to be noted that some things are changed from without; for example, water is warmed by fire: other things are changed from within; for example, a man is changed by sin. For howsoever much a man is moved exteriorly, it is not a sin unless he interiorly consents; "Out of the inner parts shall a tempest come" (Prov. 37, 9). Hence, He firstly shows that a man is not changed by exterior things; and secondly, He shows that a man is changed by interior things. He says, therefore, *Not that which goeth into the mouth defileth a man.*

On the contrary, one may make an objection by quoting that which is stated in the Old Law; for it is stated in Leviticus that many foods are prohibited, and hence, the men who ate them were made unclean.

Augustine responds (*Contra Faustum*)[4] saying that something is said to be unclean in two ways. A thing is said to be unclean in one way on account of its nature: and, in this way, nothing is unclean, according to that which is written: "For every creature of God is good, and nothing to be rejected that is received with thanksgiving" (I Tim. 4, 4). Likewise, something can be unclean according to its signification; and, in this way, something can be a sign of uncleanness or of cleanliness; for example, if we consider a pig or a lamb in their natures, both are good; nevertheless, in respect to their signification, a pig signifies uncleanness, and a lamb signifies innocence: for that reason, in respect to their signification, one is clean and the other is unclean. And because, before the coming of Christ, there was a time in which men lived under figures, because the truth had not yet appeared; for that reason, those observances were to be retained, and they were matters of precept. But because the truth was manifested at Christ's coming, the figures ceased; therefore, etc.

But again another question remains, because it is stated in Acts 15 that the Apostles commanded that converts abstain from things strangled and from blood. Therefore, it seems that while maintaining the truth, those observances ought to be kept.

The ancients said that this passage ought to be understood literally, because one ought to still abstain from these things since they are unclean. But this is nonsense, because it contradicts the words of the Apostle: "All things are clean to the clean" (Tit. 1, 15). Some men said that this passage ought to be understood partly literally, and partly morally: for that which is said about fornication, that they forbade literally: that, however, which is said about abstaining from blood, this ought to be understood to mean that innocent blood ought not to be shed; but that which is said about a thing strangled ought to be so understood such that no one ought to calumniate another. But this passage ought not to be understood in this way, even though it is a true explanation. For the question revolves on whether converted Gentiles were held to not eat these things that the Apostle forbade. For that reason, it ought to be understood that these things were forbidden according to what was the custom of the Jews. Therefore, we must hold differently, that the Apostles were reflecting upon one thing and were forbidding something else, either because it was

---

4. "Faustus [Manichaean bishop of Mileve, (350-400 A.D.)] was an African by race, a citizen of Mileum; he was eloquent and clever, but had adopted the shocking tenets of the Manichaean heresy. He is mentioned in my *Confessions*, where there is an account of my acquaintance with him" (Augustine, *Contra Faustum Manichaeum*, lib. 1, n. 1). cf. *Confessions*, v. 3, 6.

in itself illicit, or because it was an occasion of scandal; hence, they forbade fornication as being illicit; they forbade eating blood lest they give scandal to others, and so that a scandal might be removed.[5] And the words of the Apostle convey the same sense: "But take heed lest this your liberty become a stumblingblock to the weak" (I Cor. 8, 9).

Likewise, it is objected: It may be claimed that someone may eat meat in Lent, and will they not be defiled? It ought to be said that they are not defiled from the food, but from the violation of the precept; "For the kingdom of God is not meat and drink" (Rom. 14, 17).

But what cometh out of the mouth, this defileth a man. Here He seems to treat only of sins which come out of the mouth, and these defile; "Out of thy own mouth I judge thee, thou wicked servant" (Lk. 19, 22). And, "Out of thy own mouth thou wilt be judged" (above 7, 2).[6] But it ought to be answered that the distinctive function of the mouth is to speak. Now to speak is twofold, exteriorly with the mouth of the body, and interiorly with the mouth of the mind, concerning which it is said: "The fool hath said in his heart: There is no God" (Ps. 13, 1). Accordingly, therefore, by the mouth, the heart's mouth may be understood, that is to say, a man's mind, and, in this way, every sin is from the mouth; because there never is a sin unless it is from the mind's intent. Consequently, *what cometh out of the mouth*, namely, the mouth of the heart, *this defileth*, because the sin is truly voluntary, because if it were not voluntary, it is not a sin.

Then came his disciples, etc. Here He instructs his disciples about avoiding scandal, and about the primary question, where it is said, *And Peter answering*. About the first, the Evangelist does two things. First, the disciples' question is related; and secondly, Christ's response is related. Here it ought to be understood that the Pharisees and the disciples heard this

---

5. "We must, therefore, follow the third opinion, and hold that these foods were forbidden literally, not with the purpose of enforcing compliance with the legal ceremonies, but in order to further the union of Gentiles and Jews living side by side. Because blood and things strangled were loathsome to the Jews by ancient custom; while the Jews might have suspected the Gentiles of relapse into idolatry if the latter had partaken of things offered to idols. Hence, these things were prohibited for the time being, during which the Gentiles and Jews were to become united together. But as time went on, with the lapse of the cause, the effect lapsed also, when the truth of the Gospel teaching was divulged, wherein Our Lord taught that "not that which entereth into the mouth defileth a man" (Matthew 15:11); and that "nothing is to be rejected that is received with thanksgiving" (I Timothy 4:4). With regard to fornication, a special prohibition was made, because the Gentiles did not hold it to be sinful" (I II, q. 103, a. 4 ad 3um).

6. The verse actually reads: "For with what judgment you judge, you shall be judged."

statement, in view of which, they were thinking that He was overthrowing all their traditions and not, however, the Lord's precepts; for that reason, while detesting this statement they said nothing, but they were disturbed: wherefore, the disciples said: ***Dost thou know that the Pharisees, when they heard this word, were scandalized?***

This word, 'scandal', is frequently found in the Scriptures; hence, one ought to see what it means. 'Scandal' in Greek is the same thing as a stumbling block, such as rock on a path; hence, something is called a stumbling block when it is an occasion of a spiritual downfall. But sometimes a man actively scandalizes, and other times he does so passively. A scandal is said to be active when it is some deed which is not only evil in itself, but is also a stumbling block to others: for that reason, something less than rightly said or done that occasions spiritual downfall is called a scandal. It is not said of thought because it needs to be exposed. Likewise, one does not say that a scandal is something evil, but something less right, because it is necessary that it have the appearance of evil; "From all appearance of evil refrain yourselves" (I Thess. 5, 22). Similarly, there is a passive scandal, for example, if someone were to say a good word, or were to pray, and another would be scandalized, and takes to himself an occasion of his spiritual downfall: hence, the Lord did not scandalize, but those men took an occasion of scandal. Hence, His disciples said that the Pharisees took scandal therefrom, and this was foretold by Isaias: "He shall be a sanctification to you. But for a stone of stumbling, and for a rock of offence" (Is. 9, 14).

But he answering, said. Here the Lord's reply is related, and He shows that their scandal ought to be condemned, firstly, because they are strangers to God; and secondly, because they are harmful to men, where it is said, ***Let them alone: they are blind, and leaders of the blind.*** He says, therefore, ***Every plant which my heavenly Father hath not planted, shall be rooted up.*** From these words, those who maintained that there are two kinds of nature wished to support their error, since they said that an evil nature was from an evil God, and a good nature from a good God; hence, they say: 'If a man originates from an evil creation, even if he seems to do good deeds, he is unable to persevere.' But this is not so: for, as Jerome says, the contrary is stated in Jeremias 2, 21: "Yet, I planted thee a chosen vineyard, all true seed: how then art thou turned into bitterness?" And so it is clear that this vineyard's bitterness is not from God. Therefore, it was turned into bitterness by its plants, and not from its nature; but something supervening is understood, and this is the perverse will; hence, nature always remains the same, but a perverse will is rooted up. Hence, these plants can be understood to represent traditions of men, which are to be rooted up, if they are opposed to God; but a tradition that is from God ought never to be rooted up. Hence, **Every plant**, that is, every tradition which is not from God My Father, **shall be rooted up**. And this is stated in Acts 5, 39, concerning Gamaliel who said: "If it be of God, you cannot contradict it." This is also apparent in all things. You will see someone who does good deeds that are founded in charity; "Being rooted and founded in charity" (Eph. 3, 17); and these cannot be rooted up. But other deeds which do not have a good foundation, such as to give alms on account of vanity, are rooted up; hence: "Every work that is corruptible shall fail in the end: and the worker thereof shall go with it" (Eph. 14, 20). Hence, that which is written ought to be understood in this manner: "Adulterous plants shall not take deep root" (Wis. 4, 3).

Contrary to this, is that stated in I Corinthians 3, 6, where Paul says: "I have planted, Apollo watered." Therefore, Paul will be rooted up. I say that Paul did not plant as the principal agent, but as a minister.

He continues, **Let them alone: they are blind**. Here He shows that their scandal ought to be condemned, because they are harmful to men. And firstly, He teaches that that their scandal ought to be condemned; secondly, their presumption ought to be condemned; and thirdly, their harm to men ought to be condemned. About the first, He says: 'You say that they are thus scandalized, but I say, **Let them alone**, and do not be concerned about them.'

But ought one never be concerned about scandal? Did not the Lord, to avoid scandal, send Peter to the sea, so that he might pay the tribute? It ought to be said that scandal sometimes arises from the truth; hence, it is said: Scandal must be avoided which can be avoided without prejudice to the truth or justice. Hence, a judge should not change his verdict if someone is scandalized therefrom. But, nevertheless, it ought to be distinguished, because some men are scandalized due to their weakness, and others are scandalized due to their certain malice. Scandal of the little ones ought to be avoided, while preserving the truth; and, even so, a man can delay or forego an action. But scandal does not need to be avoided if it is due to malice: and these men were scandalized in this way. Hence, if they were not scandalized due to malice, the Lord would not have said, **Let them alone**, but rather, 'Instruct them.' "A man that is a heretic, after the second admonition, avoid" (Tit. 3, 10); "We would have cured Babylon, but she is not healed" (Jer. 51, 9).

And why are they *blind*? The ignorant are spiritually blind; "His watchmen are all blind" (Is. 56, 10). And because they were scandalized due to certain malice, not only are they blind, but they are also *leaders of the blind*, and teachers of the blind. "If I have been ignorant, my ignorance shall be with me" (Job 19, 4). That they are leaders of the blind, this is something good; but because they themselves are blind, this is something bad. *If the blind lead the blind, both fall into the pit.* "Hide them in the dust" (Job 40, 8), namely, so far as concerns their body.[7]

And Peter answering. He is instructing them here concerning the main question; in which place, the Evangelist does three things: for firstly, Peter's request is related; secondly, the Lord's rebuke is related; and thirdly, His teaching is related. The second thing is where it is said, *Are you also yet without understanding?* The third thing is where it is said, *Do you not understand*, etc. He says, therefore: *And Peter answering, said to him: Expound to us this parable.* Peter was accustomed to hearing many parables from Him; for that reason, he supposed that He was speaking parabolically: or perhaps it was because Peter was brought up in the Legal observances, as he said in chapter 10 of the Acts of the Apostles: "Far be it from me. For I never did eat anything that is common and unclean" (verse 14): for that reason, he supposed that He was not speaking literally, but parabolically. "He shall understand a parable and the interpretation, the words of the wise, and their mysterious sayings" (Prov. 1, 6). *But he said: Are you also yet without understanding?* For the Lord answered all the disciples in Peter, who spoke for them all.[8] Here He rebukes them. But why? One reason, which Jerome gives, is that because His words were spoken publicly, they supposed that they were said parabolically. For just as a man ought to be rebuked who reveals secrets, so conversely, a man who hides things that have been revealed ought to be rebuked; "Do not become like the horse and the mule, who have no understanding," etc (Ps. 31, 9). Another reason is Chrysostom's, namely, that he seemed to be zealous for the Jews because he was raised in the teaching of the Law; for that reason, he seemed to be saddened by this. Afterwards, He expounds His words. And He expounds what He had

---

7. i.e. "Make the earth to swallow them up."

8. In the words, "Are you also yet without understanding," the word "you" is plural in the Latin text (*vos*).

said, namely, *That which goeth into the mouth*; secondly, He expounds that which follows that which He had said, *But what cometh out of the mouth, this defileth a man*; and thirdly, He concludes what He intended to prove. He says, therefore: *Do you not understand, that whatsoever entereth into the mouth, goeth into the belly, and is cast out into the privy?* And why does the Lord speak in this fashion? Chrysostom says that He speaks to them as to men accustomed to the observances of the Law. Now it was the intention of the Law that when food was undigested in the mouth, it was unclean; but when it was digested, it was clean. Hence, it was always said in the Law, "He shall be unclean until the evening."[9] For that reason, let us affirm that these observances were to be kept, nevertheless they did not make a man unclean, except for a time. Hence, a thing which passes cannot make them unclean. Or it may be understood otherwise. Nothing can make the soul unclean, which does not come in contact with it. Now food does not come in contact with the soul; and this is the proof, namely, that food *goeth into the belly, and is cast out into the privy.*

But as Jerome says, against this some men object, saying that the Lord was ignorant of natural science, because not all the food is transmitted into the privy. Hence, certain men wishing to understand His words such that all the food is cast out, want to believe that nothing is converted into the human nature, but that only what is derived from Adam is multiplied, and only this will rise again. Hence, workmen put lead with gold so that the lead may be consumed, and the gold preserved.[10] So the foods resist, lest the natural heat consume that which is derived from the power of the nature. But this seems impossible, because something cannot become larger except by rarefaction, because to be rarified is nothing else than to take on a greater quantity.[11] Likewise, man is like the animals in his sensitive nature, and he is like the plants in his nutritive and vegetative nature. But so it is that

---

9. "CHRYS; But the Lord in thus speaking answers His disciples after Jewish infirmity; He says that the food does not abide, but goes out; but if it did abide, yet would it not make a man unclean. But they could not yet hear these things. Thus Moses also pronounces that they continued unclean, so long as the food continued in them; for he bids them wash in the evening, and then they should be clean; calculating the time of digestion and egestion" (*Catena Aurea on St. Matthew*, chap. 15, lect. 4). cf. St. John Chrysostom, *Homily 51 on St. Matthew*.

10. "When one melts gold, lead is mixed with it, lest the gold be consumed (by the heat of the fire), but only the lead" (II Sent. Dist. 30, q. 2, a. 1).

11. "Now it is manifest that the multiplication of matter in the human body does not occur by rarefaction: for thus the body of a man of perfect age would be more imperfect than the body of a child" (I, q. 119, a. 1).

these things grow and are nourished from nutrition. Therefore, men also grow and are nourished in the same way. But what is it, therefore, that He says, *is cast out into the privy*? Jerome says that not only unclean feces are understood, in fact, this may occur in whatever way, whether by dung, or in another way.[12] And this is in accord with the Philosopher, who says that although a thing may remain according to its species, nevertheless, it flows away according to its matter, just as if fire would remain in species but the matter is consumed. It can also be said thus: ***Whatsoever entereth into the mouth, goeth into the belly***, can mean that something of whatever enters the mouth, goes into the belly: hence, sometimes in Scripture the whole is taken for the part.

But the things which proceed out of the mouth: it was already said that by the mouth the mind is understood, ***Come forth from the heart, and those things defile a man***: because the sins of the heart are the thoughts and affections; "Take away the evil of your thoughts from my eyes" (Is. 1, 16). Likewise, He sets forth the sins which are against the precepts of the Second Tablet, ***murders, adulteries, fornications, thefts***. Similarly, He sets forth the sins of the mouth against one's neighbor, ***false testimonies***; ***blasphemies***, these are the sins against the First Tablet. Hence, ***these are the things which defile a man***, because these things proceed from the mind. ***But to eat with unwashed hands doth not defile a man***. Here He concludes, and He makes this conclusion to answer the primary question. Likewise, it was because the disciples did not understand, and for that reason, He concludes that His statement was spoken merely against a tradition of the Pharisees.

21. And Jesus went from thence, and retired into the coast of Tyre and Sidon.

22. And behold a woman of Canaan who came out of those coasts, crying out, said to him: Have mercy on me, O Lord, thou son of David: my daughter is grievously troubled by a devil.

23. Who answered her not a word. And his disciples came and besought him, saying: Send her away, for she crieth after us:

24. And he answering, said: I was not sent but to the sheep, that are lost of the house of Israel.

---

12. "It may also be said that whatever is generated from food, can be dissolved by natural heat, and be cast aside through the pores, as Jerome expounds the passage" (I, q. 119, a. 1 ad 1um).

25. But she came and adored him, saying: Lord, help me.
26. Who answering, said: It is not good to take the bread of the children, and to cast it to the dogs.
27. But she said: Yea, Lord; for the whelps also eat of the crumbs that fall from the table of their masters.
28. Then Jesus answering, said to her: O woman, great is thy faith: be it done to thee as thou wilt: and her daughter was cured from that hour.

Above, the sufficiency of His teaching was shown, because it did not require the observance of the Law; here He shows that it is not restricted to one nation, but it also suffices for the salvation of the Gentiles. Now three effects of His teaching upon the Gentiles are shown. Firstly, an effect is shown in His delivering from the power of the devil; secondly, an effect is shown in His delivering from the infirmities of sins; and thirdly, an effect is shown in the spiritual refreshment. The second is where it is said, **And when Jesus had passed away from thence, he came nigh the sea of Galilee**; and the third is where it is said, **And Jesus called together his disciples, and said.** His delivering from the power of the devils is shown in that He delivered a woman possessed by the devil. Firstly, the place is described; secondly, the woman's request is described; and thirdly, the granting of her request is described. The second part is where it is said, **And behold a woman of Canaan**, etc. The third part is where it is said, **Then Jesus answering, said to her**, etc. He says, therefore, **And when He was gone out, He came into the coast of Tyre and Sidon**. Tyre and Sidon are cities of the Gentiles. Because He was being rejected by the Jews, He therefore retired to the Gentiles, according to that which is written: "To you it behoved us first to speak the word of God: but because you reject it and judge yourselves unworthy of eternal life, behold we turn to the Gentiles" (Acts 13, 46). And firstly, the Lord shows that the conversion of the observers of the Law is preeminent; secondly, He shows the turning to the Gentiles, which was signified in Acts 10, where it is said that when Peter was near by Cornelius, he saw a linen sheet, etc., and it was said to him: "What God cleanses, do not thou call unclean," etc. **And behold a woman.** Here the woman's request is related. Concerning whose petition, three things are denoted. Firstly, her piety is denoted; secondly, her faith is denoted; and thirdly, her humility is denoted: and these things are necessary to obtain one's petition. The second is where it is said, **But she came and adored him**; and the third is where it is said, **But** *she said: Yea, Lord*. Firstly, the interruption is related; and secondly, the disciples' help is related, where it is said, *And his disciples came and besought him*. About the first, the woman's piety is related; and secondly, Christ's silence is related, where it is said, *Who answered her not a word*. He says, therefore, *And behold a Canaanite woman*.

We can take note of six things. Firstly, the conversion of the one asking; "Before prayer prepare thy soul: and be not as a man that tempteth God" (Eccli. 18, 23). For a man prepares his soul when he cleanses himself from his vices; "When you multiply prayer, I will not hear: for your hands are full of blood" (Eccli. 1, 15). And this is designated by this name, *Canaanite*, which is the same as 'changed'; "This is the change of the right hand of the most High" (Ps. 76, 11). Likewise, a man who is converted ought not only to avoid sin, but also the occasion of sin; "Flee from sins as from the face of a serpent" (Eccli. 21, 2). Secondly, her devotion ought to be observed, because she was crying out. A cry indicates a great affection; "I cried to the Lord: and he heard me" (Ps. 119, 1). Thirdly, her piety is observed, because she considered the misery of another to be her own; hence, she says, *Have mercy on me*; and this is great compassion; "I wept heretofore for him that was afflicted, and my soul had compassion on the poor" (Job 30, 25). Similarly, her humility is mentioned, because she asked out of confidence in God's mercy; "Who keepest the covenant, and mercy to them that love thee, and keep thy commandments" (Job 9, 4). Fourthly, her faith is mentioned, which is necessary for a petition; "But let him ask in faith, nothing wavering" (James 1, 6). Moreover, she confesses His divine nature, in that she says, *Lord*; "Know ye that the Lord he is God" (Ps. 99, 3). Likewise, she confesses His human nature in that she says, *Thou son of David*, who was of the seed of David; "Who was made to him of the seed of David, according to the flesh" (Rom. 1, 3). Again, the telling of her need is mentioned, *My daughter is grievously*, that is greatly, *troubled by a devil*. And she can be a type of the whole church of the Gentiles, or a type representing anyone's conscience, which is troubled by the devil; "And they that were troubled with unclean spirits were cured" (Lk. 6, 18). And she says, *Grievously*, in which she associates a sin to the sickness; "I have sinned, O Lord, I have sinned, and I know my iniquity, take me not away together with my iniquities" (Ps. 25, 9 and 50,5-6; II Kings 12, 13).

Afterwards, Christ's silence is related. *Who answered her not a word*. But this seems surprising that the font of mercy was silent. And three reasons are assigned for this. The first is that it was so that He would not seem to go against that which He had said above, "Go ye not into the way of the Gentiles" (10, 5). For that reason, He did not wish to give her a favorable hearing right away; yet, nonetheless, because she was insistent, He granted what she asked. For that reason, it is given to be understood that on account of the insistence of the petition, what was above the Law was obtained: for it was part of the Law that only the Jews might be saved; but she, by her insistence, obtained what was above the Law. The second reason for His silence is that it was so that her devotion might grow more. "How long, O Lord, shall I cry, and thou wilt not hear? shall I cry out to thee suffering violence, and thou wilt not save? Why hast thou shewn me iniquity and grievance, to see rapine and injustice before me?" (Hab. 1, 2-3). The third reason is that it was so He might give an opportunity to His disciples, so that they might themselves intercede for her: because no matter how much someone is good, he still needs the prayers of others.

The intercession of the disciples immediately follows. And firstly, their request is related; and secondly, Christ's reply is related. He says, therefore, **And his disciples came and besought him**. And why did they come near Him? One reason is that they did not know why He was slowing down so much; and the second is that they were moved with compassion, and they likewise could not suffer the woman's importunity; "If he shall continue knocking, I say to you, although he will not rise and give him because he is his friend; yet, because of his importunity, he will rise and give him as many as he needeth" (Lk. 11, 8). The disciples, however, do not say, 'Heal her,' but **Send her away**; meaning, 'Tell her that You will have nothing to do with her.' And this is a manner of speech: because when we intend one thing, we say another.[13]

But it is objected that in Mark 7 it is said that she entered into the house,[14] and she asked there. Why then is it said here, **For she crieth after us**? Augustine says that without a doubt she firstly was in the house, and there she said, **Have mercy on me**, and then Jesus left the house and she followed Him.

---

[13]. "CHRYS; I judge that the disciples were sorry for the woman's affliction, yet dared not say, Grant her this mercy, but only Send her away as we, when we would persuade anyone, oftentimes say the very contrary to what we wish" (*Catena Aurea on St. Matthew*, chap. 15, lect. 5).

[14]. "And rising from thence he went into the coasts of Tyre and Sidon: and entering into a house, he would that no man should know it. And he could not be hid. For a woman as soon as she heard of him, whose daughter had an unclean spirit, came in and fell down at his feet" (verses 24-25).

Then Christ's response follows, *And he answering*, etc. The woman seemed to show enough piety, but this seemed to be natural, and so the Lord demanded a profession of faith; for that reason, He rebuffed her and said: *I was not sent but to the sheep, that are lost of the house of Israel*. The Hebrews were the chosen people, hence, they were saying, "We are the people of his pasture and the sheep of his hand" (Ps. 94, 7). And those sheep perished because they were led astray by various observances; hence, "Seeing the multitudes, he had compassion on them: because they were distressed, and lying like sheep that have no shepherd" (Mt. 9, 36); "I have gone astray like a sheep that is lost" (Ps. 118, 176).

But what is it that He says, *I was not sent but to the sheep, that are lost of the house of Israel*? Is it not written: "I have given thee to be the light of the Gentiles, that thou mayst be my salvation even to the farthest part of the earth" (Is. 49, 6)? Therefore, He was sent not only to the Jews, but also to the Gentiles.

It ought to be said that He was sent to all men, but He was sent firstly to the Jews, so that He might bring the Jews to the Gentiles; "For I say that Christ Jesus was minister of the circumcision for the truth of God, to confirm the promises made unto the fathers" (Rom. 15, 8).

But she came and adored, hence, she intrudes herself. And firstly, this woman's profession of faith is related; and second, His response is related. Her profession of faith is related in that she recognized that He is God, because she adored Him. For even though she might have been driven back by the Apostles, nevertheless, she intruded herself, and adored Him. And in doing this she recognized that He is God; "The Lord thy God shalt thou adore, and him only shalt thou serve" (Deut. 6, 13); "Let all the earth adore thee," etc., (Ps. 65, 4). *Who answering, said: It is not good to take the bread of the children, and to cast it to the dogs*. This is added to prove her humility, because she already was standing firm enough in the faith, showing the superiority of the Jews to the Gentiles: for then her humility is proved, when her nation is reproached; hence, He says, *It is not good*, etc. The Jews are called the children; hence, it is written: "I have brought up children, and exalted them: but they have despised me" (Is. 1, 2), and they are called the children because they were instructed in the commandments of God (Jn. 10).[15] The bread is doctrine; "With the bread of life and understand-

---

15. "He called them gods to whom the word of God was spoken" (verse 35).

ing, she shall feed him" (Eccli. 15, 3). This bread can be said to be the Lord's miracles, or the teachings of the Law. Therefore, this bread was due to the faithful, namely, to the Jews. *It is not good to take the bread of the children*, that is to say, of the Jews, who were still the children, *and to cast it to the dogs*, namely, to the Gentiles. Hence, is said above: "Give not that which is holy to dogs" (7, 6). Hence, they had not yet completely rejected Him, but, as Jerome says, it is fitting that the Jews be called dogs, according to that passage: "Many dogs have encompassed me" (Ps. 21, 17). And: "Now we, brethren are the children" (Gal. 4, 28).

But she said: Yea, Lord. Here the woman's marvelous humility and wisdom are mentioned. He seemed to despise her nation, but it is a mark of her humility that she overlooks the insult that was spoken. Hence, she says, *Yea, Lord.* Likewise, greater humility is shown, because the Lord had said, *dogs*, but this woman said *whelps*; hence, she says, *the whelps also eat of the crumbs.* Similarly, the Lord had called the Jews children, but she calls them masters: hence, she says, *That fall from the table of their masters.* And she knew how to humbly compel the Lord in this way; it is as though she were to say, 'I do not ask, Lord, that Thou confer so many benefits upon us as Thou didst confer upon the Jews, but only that you give to us of the crumbs'; "The prayer of him that humbleth himself, shall pierce the clouds" (Eccli. 35, 21). And, "He hath had regard to the prayer of the humble" (Ps. 101, 18). For that reason, the Lord granted her request, *Then Jesus answering, said to her*, etc. And He does three things. Firstly, her praise is related; secondly, the granting of her request is related; and thirdly, the effect is related. When she abases herself, He says, *Great is thy faith.* Her faith is great, because she believes great things. Likewise, it is great because of its steadfastness; "But let him ask in faith, nothing wavering" (James 1, 6). Moreover, it was great on account of its fervor. Hence: "If you have faith as a grain of mustard seed, you shall say to this mountain: Remove from hence hither, and it shall remove" (below 17, 19). Wherefore the granting of her request follows, *Be it done to thee as thou wilt*; "He will do the will of them that fear him" (Ps. 144, 19). The effect follows: *And her daughter was cured from that hour.* Hence, just as at the beginning of time He said, "Be light made. And light was made" (Gen. 1, 3): so He says here, *Be it done to thee*; for that word is the eternal Word; "His word is full of power" (Eccli. 8, 4).

29. And when Jesus had passed away from thence, he came nigh the sea of Galilee: and going up into a mountain, he sat there.

30. And there came to him great multitudes, having with them the dumb, the blind, the lame, the maimed, and many others: and they cast them down at his feet, and he healed them:

31. So that the multitudes marvelled seeing the dumb speak, the lame walk, the blind see: and they glorified the God of Israel.

32. And Jesus called together his disciples, and said: I have compassion on the multitudes, because they continue with me now three days, and have not what to eat, and I will not send them away fasting, lest they faint in the way.

33. And the disciples say unto him: Whence then should we have so many loaves in the desert, as to fill so great a multitude?

34. And Jesus said to them: How many loaves have you? But they said: Seven, and a few little fishes.

35. And he commanded the multitude to sit down upon the ground.

36. And taking the seven loaves and the fishes, and giving thanks, he brake, and gave to his disciples, and the disciples gave to the people.

37. And they did all eat, and had their fill. And they took up seven baskets full, of what remained of the fragments.

38. And they that did eat, were four thousand men, beside children and women.

39. And having dismissed the multitude, he went up into a boat, and came into the coasts of Magedan.

Above, the Gospel teaching was confirmed by the deliverance of the Gentiles from the power of the devil through Christ's might; now He confirms it through the deliverance from spiritual sicknesses, by this, that He cured many men: and the Evangelist does three things. Firstly, the place is related; secondly, the bringing forth of the sick is related; and thirdly, the deliverance is related. The second is where it is said, **And there came to him great multitudes**, etc.; and the third is where it is said, **And he healed them**. The place is firstly described in general, because **when he had passed**, namely, from the region of the Gentiles, **he came nigh the sea**, which was in Judea, which is sometimes called Genesareth, and sometimes it is called the Sea of Galilee. By this, that He returned to the Jews, it is signified that a remnant of Israel will be saved; "Even so then, at this present time also, there is a remnant saved according to the election of God's grace" (Rom. 11, 5). Then the place is described in particular, saying: *And going up into a mountain, he sat.* By the mountain, the loftiness of the Word is signified; "Thy justice is as the mountains of God" (Ps. 35, 7). Now Jesus did not stand, but sat, because unless He had descended, we would not have known Him, according to that which is written: "Lord, bow down thy heavens and descend" (Ps. 143, 5). Again, by the mountain the height of heavenly glory is signified, as it is stated: "Save thyself in the mountain," etc., (Gen. 19, 17), to signify that in that place there is true rest, and not here; "We have not here a lasting city: but we seek one that is to come" (Heb. 13, 14), meaning that we are waiting for the glory to come.

The bringing forth of the sick follows, *And there came to him great multitudes*, etc. And firstly, the great size of the crowds is depicted; secondly, the bringing forth of the sick is depicted; and thirdly, the manner is depicted. About the first, it is said, *Then came to him great multitudes*; "All the nations thou hast made shall come and adore before thee, O Lord" (Ps. 85, 9). And they did not come to Him aimlessly, because they came *having with them the dumb, the blind, the lame*, etc. And in this is signified that those who are converted to the Lord, ought to offer others to the Lord: and this is what he says, *having with them the dumb, the blind, the lame, the maimed.* 'Maimed' (*debiles*) in Latin means a lack of strength, but in Greek a man is said to be maimed who has a crippled hand: for just as a man is said to be lame who is injured in his feet, so a man is said to be maimed who has a withered hand. By these men, various kinds of spiritual sicknesses are signified. By the dumb are signified those who are unable to praise God, concerning whom it is written: "Dumb dogs not able to bark" (Is. 56, 10). They are said to be lame who never firmly walk to the good, but quickly are turned to evil; "How long do you halt between two sides? If the Lord be God, follow him" (III Kings 18, 21). By the blind are signified unbelievers, who are deprived of the light of faith; "We have groped in the dark" (Is. 59, 9-10). By the maimed are signified those who have a weak heart; "My strength is dried up like a potsherd" (Ps. 21, 16). *And many others.* In this they showed great faith, because they brought forth not only their own sick, but others also. Likewise, they show their devotion from their manner of acting: for sometimes they asked Him to impose His hand, as is said above in chapter 9;[16] while at another times, they asked to touch the hem of His garment, as it was said above in the same place, namely, in chapters 9 and 14.[17] But now it sufficed to place the sick at His feet. And by this, it is given to us to be mystically understood, that we ought not to make the sinners whom we convert subservient to ourselves, according to that which is found in I Corintheans 4, 1: "Let a man so account of us as of the ministers of Christ and the dispensers of the mysteries of God" (I Cor. 4, 1).

He continues concerning the healing. And firstly, the healing is related; secondly, the admiration is related; and thirdly, the effect is related. He says, therefore, **And he healed them**. "He sent his word, and healed them: and delivered them from their destructions" (Ps. 106, 20). And in another place it is said: "Who forgiveth all thy iniquities: who healeth all thy diseases" (Ps. 102, 3). And the admiration follows, **So that the multitudes marvelled seeing the dumb**, etc. Here the effect is related. This was foretold in Isaias 35, 5: "Then shall the eyes of the blind be opened, and the ears of the deaf shall be unstopped," etc.; and in Psalm 108, 3 it is said: "Wonderful are thy works."

But it is asked: Why does he not make mention of the maimed? It is because there was no opposite action, to which it could correspond.

But observe that some men, after they had seen miracles, blasphemed, as is stated above in chapter 14;[18] but these men were highly praising Him; hence, **they glorified the God of Israel**.

And Jesus called together his disciples, etc. Here it is shown that Christ's doctrine is praiseworthy through His feeding of good men. And firstly, His reason for acting is related; secondly, the food is related; thirdly, the arranging is related; and fourthly, the feeding is related. The second part is where it is said, **And the disciples say unto him**, etc.; the third is where it is said, **And he commanded the multitude to sit down**; and the fourth is where it is said, **And they did all eat, and had their fill**.

It ought to be observed that this reason for acting is set forth after the aforesaid events, because "Their soul abhorred all manner of meat" (Ps. 106, 18). For this reason, it was fitting that before they be fed, they were healed: so it is also in spiritual matters. Augustine says: "To a sick palate bread is a punishment, but to one that is healthy it is pleasant." And, therefore, the Lord feeds after healing.

16. "Lord, my daughter is even now dead; but come, lay thy hand upon her, and she shall live" (verse 18).
17. "For she said within herself: If I shall touch only his garment, I shall be healed" (9, 21) and "And they besought him that they might touch but the hem of his garment" (14, 39).
18. "Herod having heard the fame of Jesus [and His miracles] said to his servants: This is John the Baptist" (verses 1-2).

And one ought to note that firstly, He called together the disciples to make them attentive, so that they might remember the miracle. Likewise, it was to give us an example that no matter how great a man is, he ought to concern himself with his inferiors; "The greater thou art, the more humble thyself in all things" (Eccli. 3, 20).

Hence, **He called together his disciples, and said: I have compassion on the multitudes**, etc. This was His reason for acting; hence, He shows that compassion is befitting to the divinity. Mercy is a passion, because to be merciful is to have a compassionate heart, which looks upon another's unhappiness to be his own. But mercy is most befitting to God; "The Lord is compassionate and merciful" (Ps. 102, 8). And that which a man looks upon as his own, he ought to repel as his own. Hence, the Lord, insofar as He repels unhappiness, is said to be merciful. Now a threefold motivation for compassionating the multitudes is pointed out. Firstly, He points out their perseverance; secondly, He points out their neediness; and thirdly, He points out their imminent danger. Firstly, their perseverance is pointed out, when it is said, **Because they continue with me now three days**. From this, you may learn that those who persevere with Christ are refreshed with His bread: because "He that shall persevere to the end, he shall be saved" (Mt. 24, 13). By three days you may understand the confession of the Holy Trinity; "Going into the whole world, baptize in the name of the Father and of the Son and of the Holy Ghost" (below 28, 19). Or three actions may be understood; namely, the confession of the heart, of the mouth, and of deeds. Likewise, three ages of the world may be understood; namely, the time of the natural law, the time of the Mosaic law, and the time of the law of grace and the time of glory at the end of the world. "I shall be satisfied when thy glory shall appear" (Ps. 16, 15). Or by the three days may be understood the three days of Christ's death. Hence, those may be said to wait for the Lord three days who conform themselves to Christ's death; "He will revive us after two days: on the third day he will raise us up" (Os. 6, 3). Hence, as a result of Christ's death, we hope for justification. "We bear the marks of the Lord Jesus in our body" (Gal. 6, 17). The second motivation that is mentioned is their neediness; hence, He says, **They have not what to eat**. But why did He wait three days? He should not to be unjustly blamed, because they were fed for three days with the food that they had brought with them. The mystical meaning is that He has mercy upon those who know their own misery; "Knowest not that thou art wretched and miserable and poor and blind and naked" (Apoc. 3, 17). The third motivation is their danger, *I will not send them away fasting, lest they faint in the way*: for they faint on the way who are not refreshed with the word of God; "Not in bread alone doth man live, but in every word that proceedeth from the mouth of God" (Deut. 8, 3); "With the bread of life and understanding, she shall feed him" (Eccli. 15, 3).

And the disciples say unto him, etc. Here the food is related. And firstly, how He gave it is related; and secondly, how much was on hand is related; hence, he says, *Whence then should we have so many loaves in the desert?* Here the disciples' slowness of understanding and their forgetfulness is reproached, because, above, the Lord had filled five thousand men with five loaves. Hence, they are reproached for their slowness of understanding and forgetfulness. In a mystical sense, by this, God's grace and mercy are signified, who reveals His mysteries to the unworthy, and through them He administers the sacraments; "I cannot speak, for I am a child" (Jer. 1, 6). To whom the Lord said, "Say not: I am a child"; "I have more impediment and slowness of tongue," etc., (Ex. 4, 10). "I am no healer, and in my house there is no bread, nor clothing: make me not ruler of the people" (Is. 3, 7). Then it is related how much food was on hand; hence, *Jesus said to them: How many loaves have you?* And He did not ask as though He were unknowing, but so that the miracle might be shown. Wherefore, He also made the few fish in the other miracle to be called to mind.[19] And it is said that they had five loaves and two fish in that other miracle, in which the doctrine of the Law was signified; and those loaves were barley loaves:[20] here there are seven loaves, and they are not said to be barley loaves; in which is signified the New Law informed by God's sevenfold grace. Likewise, in the former miracle there were only two fish, in this miracle however there are many little fish. "Hath not God chosen the poor in this world, rich in

---

19. "We have not here, but five loaves, and two fishes" (Mt. 14, 17).
20. cf. John 6, 9: "AUG. The five barley loaves signify the old law; either because the law was given to men not as yet spiritual, but carnal, i.e. under the dominion of the five senses, (the multitude itself consisted of five thousand) or because the Law itself was given by Moses in five books. And the loaves being of barley is also an allusion to the Law, which concealed the soul's vital nourishment under carnal ceremonies. For in barley the corn itself is buried under the most tenacious husk. Or, it alludes to the people who were not yet freed from the husk of carnal appetite, which clung to their heart. BEDE. Barley is the food of cattle and slaves: and the old law was given to slaves and cattle, i.e. to carnal men. AUG. The two fishes, again, that gave the pleasant taste to the bread, seem to signify the two authorities by which the people were governed, the Royal, viz. and the Priestly; both of which prefigure our Lord, who sustained both characters. BEDE. Or, by the two fishes are meant the saying or writings of the Prophets, and the Psalmist" (*Catena Aurea on St. Matthew*, chap. 15, lect. 7).

faith" (James 2, 5). And in Psalm 8, 9 it is said: "The birds of the air, and the fishes of the sea, that pass through the paths of the sea," that is the sea of this world. *And he commanded the multitude to sit down upon the ground.* Here the arranging is related. And firstly, He arranges the multitude; secondly, He takes up the food; thirdly, He gives thanks, and breaks, and distributes the food. He says, therefore, *And he commanded.* In the other feeding of the multitude it is stated that He made them recline upon the grass. By the grass, temporal things are signified; hence, "All flesh is grass, and all the glory thereof as the flower of the field" (Is. 40, 6). Hence, in the Old Law the foundation was upon temporal things, in the New Law the foundation is solely upon the stability of glory; "The earth standeth for ever" (Eccle. 1, 4). Or by the grass is signified that we ought to sit upon temporal things. Hence, ownership of temporal things is not forbidden, but the love or the affection for them; "Love not the world, nor the things which are in the world" (I Jn. 2, 15). *And taking the seven loaves*: in which is signified that any spiritual thing administered to others was firstly in Christ; hence: "Jesus began to do and to teach" (Acts 1, 1). All spiritual things were in Him. Hence: "God doth not give the Spirit by measure" (Jn. 3, 34). *And giving thanks, he brake, and gave to his disciples*: hence, He gave us an example so that we would give thanks; "Giving thanks in all things" (I Thess. 5, 18). Then He gives an example that all things do not belong to everyone, as it is stated in I Corinthians 16.[21] Likewise, it is written: "There are diversities of graces" (I Cor. 12, 4).

Afterwards, the ordered distribution of the food follows, because he says, *and He gave to his disciples, and the disciples gave to the people.* He firstly gave to His disciples, who were mediators; "I was the mediator and stood between the Lord and you at that time, to shew you his words" (Deut. 5, 5). And: "Let a man so account of us as of the ministers of Christ and the dispensers of the mysteries of God" (I Cor. 4, 1).

Thereafter, he relates as to the plentitude of the feeding from the abundance of the remains, and from the number of those eating. *And they that did eat.* Someone might say that many men can partake from a small amount of bread, so that each man would have a little; but it was not so, on the contrary, *they had their fill*; hence, they ate until they were filled; "They did eat, and were all filled" (Ps. 77, 29). Likewise, many loaves were left over, because *they took up seven baskets.*

---

21. "Now concerning the collections that are made for the saints" (verse 1) may be what is referred to here since collections are made for those who are needy.

But why was it that when there were fewer loaves, that more left over loaves remained, namely, when He filled five thousand with five loaves? It can be said that the miracles were the same, or, what is more, the seven baskets of this miracle were of larger capacity than the twelve baskets of the former. Chrysostom says that He performed two different miracles, and He performed them in different ways, so that the disciples would remember them better. In the first miracle there were as many baskets left over as Apostles. Here, however, there were the same number as the initial number of loaves of bread, in which is signified that spiritual men ought to be refreshed with God's sevenfold grace; "For the sensual man perceiveth not these things that are of the Spirit of God" (I Cor. 2, 14).

The number of those eating follows, **And they that did eat, were four thousand men**. Above, there were five thousand, because they were open to follow their five senses; or this was on account of the five books of Moses; here, however, there are four thousand men on account of the four cardinal virtues or on account of the four Evangelists. **Beside children and women.**

But why are these excepted? It is because the imperfect and the weak are excluded from true doctrine; "Until we all meet unto a perfect man" (Eph. 4, 13).

CHAPTER SIXTEEN

1. And there came to him the Pharisees and Sadducees tempting: and they asked him to shew them a sign from heaven.
2. But he answered and said to them: When it is evening, you say, It will be fair weather, for the sky is red.
3. And in the morning: Today there will be a storm, for the sky is red and lowering. You know then how to discern the face of the sky: and can you not know the signs of the times?
4. A wicked and adulterous generation seeketh after a sign: and a sign shall not be given it, but the sign of Jonas the prophet. And he left them, and went away.
5. And when his disciples were come over the water, they had forgotten to take bread.
6. Who said to them: Take heed and beware of the leaven of the Pharisees and Sadducees.
7. But they thought within themselves, saying: Because we have taken no bread.
8. And Jesus knowing it, said: Why do you think within yourselves, O ye of little faith, for that you have no bread?
9. Do you not yet understand, neither do you remember the five loaves among five thousand men, and how many baskets you took up?
10. Nor the seven loaves, among four thousand men, and how many baskets you took up?
11. Why do you not understand that it was not concerning bread I said to you: Beware of the leaven of the Pharisees and Sadducees?
12. Then they understood that he said not that they should beware of the leaven of bread, but of the doctrine of the Pharisees and Sadducees.

Above, the Lord showed the sufficiency of the Gospel teaching, in that it is not in need of Legal observances, and, likewise, in that it is necessary not just for one people; here He shows its purity and excellence. Firstly, He shows that it must be kept pure from every tradition; secondly, by the loftiness of the faith, it flies above all human opinions, where it is said, *Jesus came into the quarters of Cesarea Philippi*. About the first, the calumnious temptation is firstly described; secondly, He refutes it; and thirdly, He teaches that one needs to be on one's guard against this. The second is where it is said, *But he answered and said to them*, etc.; the third is where it is said, *And when his disciples were come over the water*, etc. About the first, he begins by mentioning the place; and secondly, the tempting question is related.

It ought to be noted that, as above, when He had fed the multitudes from the five loaves, He dismissed them, and so it is here. In this, an example is firstly given to preachers of when they may not engage themselves, but withdraw; as it is said in Job 39, 5, concerning the wild ass: "Who hath sent out the wild ass free, and who hath loosed his bonds?" etc.

He went up into a boat, lest the multitude follow Him. Hence, an obstacle is placed whereby they could not follow Him. Hence, *He went up into a boat*, that is, into a mind that is agitated by the waves of this world; "For thou hast made a way even in the sea, and a path among the waves" (Wis. 14, 3); He is showing that He must enter there, in order that He may rest there. *And came into the coasts of Magedan*. Magedan is interpreted 'apple' and, by this place, Sacred Scripture is signified, where apples and other fruits grow; "I went down, to see the fruits of the valleys" (Cant. 6, 10).

The tempting question follows, *And there came to him the Pharisees and Sadducees tempting: and they asked him*. "There is one that humbleth himself wickedly, and his interior is full of deceit" (Eccli. 19, 23). *To shew them a sign from heaven*. And they asked for a sign from heaven. It is stated: "Your fathers did eat manna in the desert" (Jn. 6, 49), and hence, He gave them bread from heaven. "The Jews require signs" (I Cor. 1, 22). And in Psalm 73, 9, it is said: "Our signs we have not seen," etc. Then He reprehends them, and firstly, He reprehends them concerning their slothfulness in believing divine things. For if a man is defective due to the physical nature of his senses, he has an excuse; but when he has wisdom in earthly things, and ignorance in spiritual things, he ought to be reprehended; "All men are vain, in whom there is not the knowledge of God" (Wis. 13, 1). And firstly, He shows their diligence in regard to earthly things; and secondly, He shows their slothfulness in regard to spiritual things. He says, therefore: *But he answered and said to them: When it is evening*, etc. This has a literal and a mystical meaning. The literal meaning is that from some atmospheric condition they could recognize a sign of fair weather. *When it is evening, you say, It will be fair weather, for the sky is red.* Likewise, they could recognize a sign of stormy weather, because they say: *Today there will be a storm, for the sky is red and lowering*,[1]

---

1. Literally, "for the sky is sadly reddened (*rutilat enim triste caelum*)."

because a storm denotes sadness. For when the air is turbulent, men are not so happy. Evening redness is a sign of fair weather. The reason is, according to the Philosopher, that this is caused by the diffusion of the rays of the sun upon the water vapors. For when the vapors are many, then the rays cannot penetrate them, and then a dark color in the air occurs; but when the vapors are dispersed, the rays penetrate. But when that which is fiery dominates, then a red color appears, as appears in a flame, because when it is elevated more, more redness appears in it. For that reason, it is indicated that the vapors are not many, and fair weather is indicated. But if in the morning what is fiery[2] turns into dew, or into rain, it is a sign of a storm.[3] In a mystical sense, by the evening, Christ's Passion is signified. In the evening the sun sets, and so Christ suffered at the evening of the world; "And who shall be able to think of the day of his coming? And who shall stand to see him? For he is like a refining fire" (Mal. 3, 2): "In the evening weeping shall have place, and in the morning gladness" (Ps. 29, 6). Hence, when a red sky appears in the evening, it signifies fair weather; "After a storm thou makest a calm, and after tears and weeping thou pourest in joyfulness" (Ps. 3, 22). In the resurrection, which is signified by the morning, redness will appear in the martyrs, and it signifies a storm to the sinners. Or, by morning is signified the morning of the judgment day, which redness will precede; "A fire shall go before him" (Ps. 96, 3). Hence, you have been instructed in these earthly matters. *You know then how to discern the face of the sky: and can you not know the signs of the times?* There are two times: one corresponds to His first coming, the other to His second coming. Certain signs preceded His first coming; "Drop down dew, ye heavens, from above, and let the clouds rain the just: let the earth be opened, and bud forth a saviour," etc., (Is. 45, 8). And: "Verily thou art a hidden God" (ibid. 45, 15). But at the end of the world God will come manifestly, and signs will not appear in the heavens.[4] But it is

---

2. "According to Strabo, one heaven is called empyrean, that is, fiery, solely on account of its splendor" (I, q. 68, a. 2). Strabo (63 B.C.-after 21 A.D.) was a Greek geographer and historian.

3. "Now the fact that fire is in the air is evident by the words of the Philosopher in *I Meteororum*: for he says that the circular movement of fire is often scattered through the air, that is through the power of the heavenly motion, and it is violently carried downward. And, for that reason, there are some amounts of fire descending both in the dew and in the rain vapors, which receive the vapors in the region of the air. And, therefore, the rain waters are vaporous and heated." (*In De Gener. Et Corr. Continuatio*, Bk. 1, lc. 23, n. 7)."

4. "The day of the Lord is said to come as a thief, because the exact time is not known, since it will not be possible to know it from those signs: although, as we have already said, all these most manifest signs which will precede the judgment immediately may be comprised under the judgment day" (III, q. 73, a. 1 ad 2um).

not now the time of the Judgment Day. Or it is otherwise. *You know then how to discern the face of the sky*, etc., as though He were to say, 'You seek a sign of My coming. It is superfluous to ask for a sign, where there are many signs.' "The blind see, the lame walk, the lepers are cleansed," etc., (above 11, 5). This is the sign that Isaias gave: "God himself will come and will save you. Then shall the eyes of the blind be opened" (Is. 35, 4).

Certain men argue from this passage that we ought to try to know the time of His second coming. Augustine, however, expounds this passage as pertaining to His first coming. The first coming is most certain, because it is for our salvation, and salvation is through faith, and faith is through knowledge; for that reason, it is necessary that it be known. But the second is for rewarding us; for that reason, it is hidden, so that men might be more careful.

Then He denies the sign asked; hence, it is said, *A wicked and adulterous generation seeketh after a sign*. A generation is said to be wicked because it departs from God: for evil exists through departing from God. "He forsook God who made him, and departed from God his saviour," as it is stated in Deuteronomy 32, 15. But it is an adulterous generation, because they joined themselves to another. "If I shall have forsaken thee in my life" (Ps. 26).[5] "Let the wicked forsake his way, and the unjust man his thoughts" (Is. 55, 7). This generation *seeketh after a sign*, and it ought not to have a sign, because *a sign shall not be given it, but the sign of Jonas the prophet*, because just as Jonas was in the whale's belly three days and three nights: so, etc., as it was stated in chapter 12.[6]

But why does He mention the sign of the Resurrection rather than another sign? It ought to be said that salvation came to us through the Resurrection; "If thou believe in thy heart that Christ hath risen up from the dead, thou shalt be saved" (Rom. 10, 9), because, by rising, He restored our life, because we will rise through Christ's Resurrection. And, therefore, this sign was given to the faithful, and all other ones refer back to this one, such as, for example, that He raised Lazarus, etc. Hence, a sign was not given to these men. To His disciples, however, He gave a sign from heaven when He showed them His glory, as it is stated below in chapter 17. In this way, therefore, He shows their slothfulness.

---

5. This quotation is not found in Psalm 26, except perhaps by negation of verse 4: "This will I seek after; that I may dwell in the house of the Lord all the days of my life."

6. Matthew 12, 40.

The part follows in which He confutes them by His action of departing from them, *And he left them, and went away*; for He does not dwell with the malignant; "He separates Himself from the perverse" (Wis. 1, 3). After He confutes them, He teaches that they are to be avoided. And firstly, the occasion is set forth; secondly, His teaching is set forth; thirdly, the misunderstanding of the disciples is set forth; fourthly, the reprehension of the disciples is set forth; and fifthly, the effect of His reprehension is set forth. He says: *And when his disciples were come over the water*, etc. In this we ought to admire the interests of the disciples, because men are accustomed to forget only those things about which they care little: hence, since they forgot the loaves of bread, they cared little about them, and they cared only about spiritual things. *Who said to them: Take heed and beware*, etc. Here His teaching is set forth. By leaven, He means corrupt teachings; hence, He does not mean the teachings of the Law, but the traditions of the Pharisees, which are called leaven, because just as from a little leaven the whole is corrupted, so from a little error, one's whole life is corrupted, as, for instance, when a man departs a little from the path, he is afterwards separated from it: hence, the Philosopher in *Primo Coeli* says that a small error in the beginning becomes a big error in the end. Spiritual understanding is unleavened bread. Hence, by bread, true doctrine is understood; "With the bread of life and understanding, she shall feed him" (Eccli. 15, 3). Hence, it is said, *Take heed and beware*, because false doctrine is dangerous. For as long as faith remains in a man, there is no danger; but when the foundation is taken away, there is no hope. "Rase it, rase it, even to the foundation thereof" (Ps. 136, 7). Faith is the foundation; "A man that is a heretic, after the first and second admonition, avoid" (Tit. 3, 10). Because false doctrine, at first glance, seems to have a solid basis, for that reason, He says, *Take heed*, that is to say, examine carefully; "Let thy eyes look straight on, and let thy eyelids go before thy steps" (Prov. 4, 25).

Afterwards, the disciples' understanding of these words is related, *But they thought*, etc. For because they had previously taken up seven baskets of fragments and had not taken them with them, they supposed that He was saying, 'You did not take up the bread; but I do not want you to take bread from the Pharisees, because they are animals,' and, "The sensual man perceiveth not these things that are of the Spirit of God" (I Cor. 2, 14). In regard to this understanding, they could be reprehended on two grounds. Firstly, they could be reprehended because they did not understand;

and likewise, they could be reprehended because they lacked confidence in God's power. He did not reprehend them concerning the first point, but concerning the second. He says, therefore, *Why do you think within yourselves, O ye of little faith, for that you have no bread?* As though He were to say, 'You understand carnally what you ought to understand spiritually.' *Do you remember the five loaves among five thousand men, and how many baskets you took up?* 'Cannot I, who have fed so many men, feed you?' *Why do you not understand that it was not concerning bread I said to you*, that is to say, 'I did not speak to you concerning material bread, but rather concerning spiritual bread'; which bread is called doctrine in Jn. 6, 64: "The words that I have spoken to you are spirit and life." *Then they understood*, etc. Here the correction is set forth; "The declaration of thy words giveth light: and giveth understanding to little ones" (Ps. 118, 130).

13. *And Jesus came into the quarters of Cesarea Philippi: and he asked his disciples, saying: Whom do men say that the Son of man is?*
14. *But they said: Some John the Baptist, and other some Elias, and others Jeremias, or one of the prophets.*
15. *Jesus saith to them: But whom do you say that I am?*
16. *Simon Peter answered and said: Thou art Christ, the Son of the living God.*
17. *And Jesus answering said to him: Blessed art thou, Simon Bar-Jona: because flesh and blood hath not revealed it to thee, but my Father who is in heaven.*
18. *And I say to thee: That thou art Peter; and upon this rock I will build my church, and the gates of hell shall not prevail against it.*
19. *And I will give to thee the keys of the kingdom of heaven. And whatsoever thou shalt bind upon earth, it shall be bound also in heaven: and whatsoever thou shalt loose on earth, it shall be loosed also in heaven.*

Above, the Lord taught that the Gospel teaching ought to be kept pure from the leaven of the Jews; now here He teaches the loftiness of His doctrine. And firstly, He teaches this in regard to faith in His two natures, namely, His divine and human natures; secondly, He teaches this in regard to faith in His Passion, where it is said, *From that time Jesus began to shew to his disciples*, etc.; and thirdly, He teaches this in regard to His judiciary power, where it is said, *For the Son of man shall come in the glory of his Father.* About the first, the opinion of the multitudes about Christ is sought; and secondly, the disciples' faith is sought, where it is said, *But whom do you say that I am?* About the first, the place is firstly related; secondly, Christ's question is related, where it is said, *Whom do men say that the Son of man is?*; and thirdly, Peter's[7] reply is related, where it is said, *But they said*, etc. He says, therefore, *Jesus came into the quarters of Cesarea*; and he does not only say this, but he added *Philippi*, because there were two Cesareas, namely, Cesarea Palestinae,[8] where Peter was sent to Cornelius; another Cesarea is this one which is otherwise called Paneas. The first was established in honor of Caesar Augustus, and Philip[9] constructed the latter in honor of Tiberius Caesar.

But why did the Lord ask this question here? It ought to be said that this city was located beyond the borders of the Jews; for that reason, before He chose to question them concerning their faith, He brought them away from the Jews. Similarly, it is written that when the Lord led the Jews out of Egypt, He did not lead them out through the cornfields of the Philistines, as it is stated in Exodus 13.[10]

Afterwards, the questioning is related, *And he asked his disciples*, etc. Sometimes, when a wise man asks, he teaches, as Origen says.[11] Hence, we are instructed in many things, so that we may be mindful of what is said about ourselves: so that if any ill is said about us, we are careful to correct it: if any good is said about us, we are careful to keep and multiply it. Hence, "Take care of a good name: for this shall continue with thee, more than a thousand treasures precious and great" (Eccli. 41, 15). Hence, Christ asked what was being said about Himself. Likewise, those who know His divinity are called gods; "I have said: You are gods" (Ps. 81, 6); but those who know His humanity are called men;

---

7. "CHRYS; When the Lord inquires concerning the opinion of the multitudes, all the disciples answer; but when all the disciples are asked, Peter as the mouth and head of the Apostles answers for all" (*Catena Aurea on St. Matthew*, chap. 16, lect. 3).

8. Also known as *Cesarea Maritima*. The text actually reads, "Cesarea Trachonitis" (*Traconis*), but this seems erroneous because Cesarea Philippi was in Trachonitis.

9. i.e. the son of Herod the Great and brother of Archelaus and Herod Antipas.

10. "And when Pharao had sent out the people, the Lord led them not by the way of the land of the Philistines, which is near; thinking lest perhaps they would repent, if they should see wars arise against them, and would return into Egypt" (verse 17).

11. St. Jerome is mistakenly cited here, as is clear from the corresponding passage in the *Catena Aurea*: "ORIGEN; Christ puts this question to His disciples, that from their answer we may learn that there were at that time among the Jews various opinions concerning Christ; and to the end that we should always investigate what opinion men may form of us; that if any ill be said of us, we may cut off the occasions of it" (*Catena Aurea on St. Matthew*, chap. 16, lect. 3).

hence, it is said: ***Whom do men say that the Son of man is?*** But, as Hilary says, Christ seemed to be merely a man: for that reason, He wanted them to know that He is more than just a simple man. Hence, from this, He gives them to understand that there is something else in Him. Moreover, Christ's humility is shown, because He confesses that He is the Son of man, according to that which is written above: "Learn of me, because I am meek, and humble of heart" (11, 29).

Afterwards, the opinion of the multitudes is related, ***But they said: Some John the Baptist***, etc. Different men thought different things about Christ. The Pharisees were blaspheming Christ, but the multitudes were saying that He was a prophet; hence: "A great prophet is risen up among us," etc., (Lk. 7, 16). They were calling Him John by reason of His counsel, because John was preaching penance; "Do penance: for the kingdom of heaven is at hand" (Jn. 3, 2). Therefore, they thought that He was John, because Christ began in a similar way by saying, "Do penance, for the kingdom of heaven is at hand" (above 4, 17). Likewise, they held the prophet Elias in high esteem; "Behold, I will send you Elias the prophet, before the coming of the great and dreadful day" (Mal. 4, 5). Hence, they supposed that He was Elias on account of the power of His words and the force of His preaching; "And Elias the prophet stood up, as a fire, and his word burnt like a torch" (Eccli. 48, 1). And it was said concerning Christ that "He was teaching them as one having power" (above 7, 29). Similarly, on account of His preeminence of life, they supposed that He was Jeremias, concerning whom the Lord said: "Before I formed thee in the bowels of thy mother, I knew thee: and before thou camest forth out of the womb, I sanctified thee" (Jer. 1, 5). And in the same place, it is stated that he was honored by the Gentiles (chap. 40). In like manner, Christ was held in esteem by foreigners; however, He was being blasphemed by the Jews: for that reason, they compare Him to Jeremias.

But how is it that they were calling Him Elias? It was because it is stated in IV Kings 2 that Elias was taken up, and that he was still living, and that he was promised to the Jews for their salvation, as it is stated in Malachias 4.[12] It was also because certain men thought that there is a transmigration of souls: and so, according to this opinion, it was possible that the soul of Elias had entered into another body.

---

12. "Behold, I will send you Elias the prophet, before the coming of the great and dreadful day of the Lord. And he shall turn the heart of the fathers to the children, and the heart of the children to their fathers" (verses 5-6).

Jesus saith to them: But whom do you say that I am? Here the disciples' faith is investigated. And firstly, His question is related; secondly, the response is related; and thirdly, His approval is related. The second part is where it is said, *Simon Peter answered*; and the third part is where it is said, *And Jesus answering*, etc. *Jesus saith to them: But whom do you say that I am?* As though He were to say: 'So say the multitudes; but because more has been committed to you, therefore, more is required from you. You have seen miracles, for that reason, you ought to reckon Me to be more than this.'

But why did He ask? Did He not know? He did indeed know, but He wanted them to merit by their confession; "With the heart, we believe unto justice: but, with the mouth, confession is made unto salvation" (Rom. 10, 10). Hence, things are more meritorious inasmuch as they are more outstanding; and it is as though the multitudes, because they knew the least about Christ, do not give any better reply about Him, and for that reason, etc.

Peter answered and said: Thou art Christ, the Son of the living God. He replies for himself, and for the others; but he more frequently replies, and in this his perfect faith is touched upon, because his faith in Christ's humanity is mentioned. *Thou art Christ*, meaning 'the anointed.' And it is evident that He was anointed with the oil of the Holy Ghost. Anointing does not befit Him according to His divinity, because anointing proceeds from it, but it befits Him according to His humanity. Therefore, he says this, so that the disciples may esteem Christ's humanity to be different than the multitudes esteem it to be.

Now it is sought why they were saying that He was a prophet. A prophet was anointed, as it written concerning Eliseus. Kings were anointed, as it is written concerning Saul; likewise, priests were anointed, as it is written in Leviticus.[13] And all these things were inferred in the name 'Christ'; because He is also called a king, as it is written: "A king shall reign, and shall be wise" (Jer. 23, 5). Likewise, He is called a priest; "Thou art a priest for ever according to the order of Melchisedech" (Ps. 109, 4). Again, He is called a prophet; "The Lord thy God will raise up to thee a prophet of thy nation and of thy brethren," etc., (Deut. 18, 15).

Similarly, Peter not only confessed His humanity, but having penetrated the shell, he rises above it all the way to His divinity saying, *Thou art the Son of the living God.* For others were

---

13. "This is the anointing of Aaron and his sons, in the ceremonies of the Lord, in the day when Moses offered them, that they might do the office of priesthood" (Lev. 7, 35).

calling Him a blasphemer; hence: "For a good work we stone thee not, but for blasphemy: and because that thou, being a man, makest thyself God" (Jn. 10, 33). But he recognized the Son of God. And he says, *living,* to exclude the error of the Gentiles, who were calling dead men gods, such as Jupiter, etc., as it is stated in Wisdom 13.[14] Likewise, certain men called the elements and other dead things gods, such as the earth, fire, etc., as it is stated in Wisdom 13;[15] but he calls Him the Son of the living God. But it ought to be known that when it is said 'living God,' and 'living man,' this is said of man through a participation of life; but it is said of God not by participation, because He is the source of life; "For with thee is the fountain of life" (Ps. 35, 10). And in John 14, 6 it is said: "I am the way, and the truth, and the life."

Jesus answering, etc. Here He firstly approves his confession; secondly, He commands them to keep quiet, where it is said, **Then he commanded his disciples, that they should tell no one that he was Jesus the Christ.** About the first point, He firstly approves the confession by His praise of the one confessing; secondly, He approves it by His reward, where it is said, **And I say to thee: That thou art Peter,** etc. Hence, the Evangelist says, **Jesus answered: Blessed art thou, Simon Bar-Jona.** 'Bar' is the same thing as 'son of,' and, likewise, 'Jona' is the same thing as 'dove' according to its name. Hence, 'Bar-Jona' means 'son of the dove.' And Christ's reply seems to correspond to Peter's confession. This is because Peter had confessed Him to be the Son of God; now Jesus calls him son of the dove, namely, the Holy Ghost, because his confession could only be made by the Holy Ghost. But it is thought that firstly he was called 'Bar-Joannas,'[16] that is, the son of John, but he is so-called through an error in the text.

But what is this? Did not others confess that He is the Son of God? Indeed it is so-read of Nathanael in John 1.[17] Likewise, those who were in the boat also confessed this (above 14, 33).[18]

---

14. "For life prayeth to that which is dead" (verse 18). "JEROME; He calls Him the living God, in comparison of those gods who are esteemed gods, but are dead; such, I mean, as Saturn, Jupiter, Venus, Hercules, and the other monsters of idols" (*Catena Aurea on St. Matthew,* ibid.).

15. "But have imagined either the fire, or the wind, or the swift air, or the circle of the stars, or the great water, or the sun and moon, to be the gods that rule the world" (verse 2).

16. The text mistakenly has 'Jona' again here. cf. "Others take it in the simple sense, that Peter is the son of John, according to that question in another place, "Simon, son of John, do you love me?" affirming that it is an error of the copyists in writing here Bar-Jonas for Bar-Joannas, dropping one syllable" (*Catena Aurea on St. Matthew,* ibid.).

17. "Nathanael answered him and said: Rabbi: Thou art the Son of God. Thou art the King of Israel" (verse 49).

18. "And they that were in the boat came and adored him, saying: Indeed thou art the Son of God."

Why, then, is Peter here blessed, and the others were not? It is because the others confessed Him to be an adoptive son of God; here, however, he confesses Him to be the natural Son of God; for that reason, here he is blessed in preference to the others, because he was the first one to confess His divinity.

Origen says: "It seems that he did not confess Him to be the Son of God before." But how did He send them to preach? He answers that, at the beginning, they were not preaching that He was Christ, but they were merely preaching penance. Likewise, it may be that they were preaching that He is Christ; but this was the first time that Peter was confessing Him to be the Son of God. Therefore, He specially rewards him here.

Blessed art thou, Simon, etc., because beatitude is in knowledge; "Now this is eternal life: That they may know thee, the only true God" (Jn. 17, 3). But knowledge is twofold: there is one that is by natural reason, and there is another that is above reason. The first does not give beatitude, because it is doubtful; hence, it does not satisfy the mind; but beatitude ought to satisfy a natural desire, and this will be had in heaven; "Eye hath not seen, nor ear heard: what things God hath prepared for them that love him" (Is. 64, 4).[19] Therefore, in this life, inasmuch as a man can perceive more of this knowledge, he is more blessed; "Blessed is the man that findeth wisdom" (Prov. 3, 13). Hence, He says, **Blessed art thou**, because 'you begin to be blessed.' **Because flesh and blood hath not revealed it to thee.** This can be expounded such that flesh and blood are taken for one's carnal friends; "Immediately I condescended not to flesh and blood" (Gal. 1, 16). Hence: **Flesh and blood hath not revealed it to thee**; that is to say, you did not have this knowledge from the tradition the Jews, but from a revelation of God. Likewise, in Christ there were His flesh, blood, and divinity; wherefore, because Peter did not look to flesh and blood, it is said to Him, **Blessed art thou**, because you do not judge according to what flesh and blood reveal, but according to what My Father reveals. Or you do not have this knowledge from your natural industry, but from My Father. "For no one knoweth the Son, but the Father" (Lk. 10, 22). For it belongs to that man to make known, to whom it belongs to know. Hence, "No one knew the Son except he to whom the Father willed to reveal Him" (ibid). "There is a God in heaven that revealeth mysteries" (Dan. 2, 28).

---

19. This verse is taken from I Corinthians 2, 9. Isaias 64, 4 actually reads (in the Douay version), "From the beginning of the world they have not heard, nor perceived with the ears: the eye hath not seen, O God, besides thee, what things thou hast prepared for them that wait for thee."

And I say to thee: That thou art Peter, etc. Here He gives the reward for his confession. For he had confessed His humanity and divinity, and, for that reason, the Lord gives him a reward. Firstly, He gives him a name; and secondly, He gives him power. About the first, to begin with, He gives him the name; and secondly, He gives the reason for the name, where it is said, *And upon this rock I will build my church*. And for this He came into this world, that He would found His Church. "Behold I will lay a stone in the foundations of Sion, a tried stone, a corner stone, a precious stone, founded in the foundation" (Is. 28, 16). This was signified by the stone that Jacob put under his head, and anointed, as it is stated in Genesis 28. This stone is Christ, and from this anointing all Christians are called Christians; hence, we are not only called Christians from Christ, but also from the rock.[20] For that reason, He specially names him: *Thou art Peter*, from the rock which is Christ. Albeit, according to Augustine, it seems that this name was not given at this time, but was given at the beginning; "Thou shalt be called Cephas" (Jn. 1, 42). Or it can be said that it was then promised, and it was here given. As a sign of this, it is said, *upon this rock I will build my church*.[21] A distinctive characteristic of a rock is that it is placed in a foundation; likewise, another characteristic of a rock is that it gives firmness. "He is likened to a wise man that built his house upon a rock" (above 7, 24). Hence, it can be expounded of Christ. *And upon this rock*, that is, Christ, so that He may be its foundation, and having been placed as the foundation, the Church may gain firmness. Augustine, in his book of *Retractions,* says that this passage may be explained in multiple ways, and he left to his listeners to adopt the explanation that they prefer. For instance, this passage may be expounded such that the words *this rock* signify Christ; "And the rock was Christ" (I Cor. 10, 4). And elsewhere, it is written: "Another foundation no man can lay, but that which is laid: which is Christ Jesus" (ibid. 3, 11). There is another exposition: *Upon this rock*, meaning upon you who are a rock, because you yourself draw from me that you are a rock. And just as I am a rock, so upon you who are a rock I will build my Church, etc.

---

20. "'Pouring oil upon the top of it,' so as to be a sacred sign of the consecration of that rock. For by the oil he (Jacob) signified the abundance and presence of a divine anointing and grace, by which the worship of God is established and developed in the Church" (*Post. in Lib. Gen.,* chap. 28).

21. "JEROME; And pursuing the metaphor of the rock, it is rightly said to him as follows: And upon this rock I will build my Church" (*Catena Aurea on St. Matthew*, ibid.).

But what is this? Are both Christ and Peter the foundation? It must be answered that Christ, in and of Himself, is the foundation, but Peter is the foundation insofar as he confesses Christ, and insofar as he is His vicar. "Built upon the foundation of the apostles and prophets, Jesus Christ himself being the chief corner stone," etc., (Eph. 2, 20). "There are twelve foundations of the city: And in them, the twelve names of the twelve apostles of the Lamb" (Apoc. 21, 14). Christ, in and of Himself, is the foundation; but the Apostles, not in and of themselves but through Christ's delegation, and through the authority given them by Christ, are foundations as well; "The foundations thereof are the holy mountains" (Ps. 86, 1). But Peter's house especially, which was founded upon the rock, shall not be demolished, as said above in chapter 7.[22] Thus, this house can be assaulted, but it cannot be conquered.

And the gates of hell shall not prevail against it. "They shall fight against them, and shall not prevail" (Jer. 1, 19). And what are the gates of hell? They are the heretics: because just as through a gate one enters a house, so through these heretics one enters into hell. Likewise, they are tyrants, devils, and sins. And although other [local] Churches could be spoiled by heretics, nevertheless the Roman Church was not corrupted by the heretics, because it was founded upon a rock. Hence, in Constantinople, there were heretics, and the labor of the Apostles was lost; only the Church of Peter remained inviolate. Hence: "I have prayed for thee, Peter, that thy faith fail not" (Lk. 22, 32). And this is not only ascribed to the Church of Peter, but also to the faith of Peter, and also to the whole western Church. Hence, I believe that the western faithful ought to have more reverence to Peter than to the other Apostles.

And I will give to thee the keys of the kingdom of heaven. Here is related the second gift which Christ, according to His humanity, gave to Peter. For He founded the Church in the world, and He appointed Peter to be His Vicar, so that Peter might give the Church entrance into heaven, hence, He gave him that ministry, hence, He gave him the keys. For a key gives entrance; hence, Peter has the ministry of giving entrance. And Christ does two things. Firstly, He entrusts the keys; and secondly, He teaches their use, where it is said, **And whatsoever thou shalt bind**

---

22. "Everyone therefore that heareth these my words, and doth them, shall be likened to a wise man that built his house upon a rock, and the rain fell, and the floods came, and the winds blew, and they beat upon that house, and it fell not, for it was founded on a rock" (verses 25-26).

upon earth, it shall be bound also in heaven, etc. But let us see what the keys are. A house when it is locked prevents entrance; but a key removes this obstacle. The kingdom of heaven has an obstacle, but the obstacle is not on its own part; "I looked, and behold a door was opened" (Apoc. 4, 1); rather it is on our part, namely sin, because "nothing defiled shall enter into it."[23] Christ removed these obstacles through His Passion, because "He hath washed us from our sins in his own blood" (Apoc. 1, 5). And He shared this benefit with us so that, through Peter's ministry, our sins are taken away, which is accomplished through the power of Christ's blood: hence, the sacraments have power by virtue of Christ's Passion. Hence, I will give to you the ministry, etc. "I will lay the keys of David upon you" (Is. 22, 22). But He says, *I will give to thee*; for the keys were not made yet; now a thing cannot be given before it exists. Now these keys were to be made in His Passion; hence, their efficacy was in the Passion. Hence, here He promises to give the keys to Peter, but after the Passion He gave them to him, when He said: "Feed my sheep" (Jn. 21, 17).

But why does He say keys? It is because to absolve is to remove obstacles. For there are two obstacles, since two things are required, namely, power and knowledge.[24]

But what is this? Are there not some priests who do not have knowledge? You could understand this statement to mean that they have knowledge, because no one has the key of knowledge except a priest. But a habit of the intellect is not here called knowledge, etc., but instead the authority of discerning is here called knowledge. Hence, someone is a judge, who does not have knowledge in the first manner, and nevertheless, has knowledge in the second manner, when he has the authority of discerning; however, someone has knowledge in the first manner, and not in the second manner, when he does not have authority. Hence, the authority of discerning is here called knowledge, and any priest has this knowledge so that he may discern in absolving.

Afterwards, He sets forth the use of the keys, *Whatsoever thou shalt bind upon earth, it shall be bound also in heaven*. But it seems that their use is not suitably set forth, because the use of a key is not to bind but to open. I say that this is a fitting use of keys. For heaven was opened; "I saw a door opened" (Apoc. 4, 1). Hence, it is not necessary that heaven be opened; but

---

23. cf. Apocalypse 21, 27.
24. "RABAN; By the keys of the kingdom He means discernment and power; power, by which he binds and looses; discernment, by which he separates the worthy from the unworthy" " (*Catena Aurea on St. Matthew*, ibid.)

that a bound man who ought to enter heaven, should be loosed.

But here some errors ought to be avoided. The first is mentioned in the Gloss, namely, that certain men wrongly assumed that priests are able to absolve everyone that they choose to absolve, and take them into heaven. But this cannot stand, because to change wills belongs to God alone. Another error is that a priest does not absolve, but declares that a man is absolved. But this takes away the power of the sacrament, because the sacraments of the New Law produce what they signify; but the sacraments of the Old Law do not. Hence, if nothing were produced, it would not be a sacrament of the New Law. Thirdly, some men say that in sin there are three things: the guilt, the debt, and the punishment. A man is absolved from two of these through contrition; but when a man is absolved from these, he remains obliged to the temporal punishment, which a man is unable by himself to take away and avoid; for that reason, the keys are given, which lessen some of this punishment, and they bind to some punishment. Nevertheless, it seems to me that this is not well-said, because the sacraments of the New Law give grace, but grace is not ordained to be a remedy for punishment, but for guilt. Hence, I say that thus it is in this sacrament of Confession, even as it is in the sacrament of Baptism, which has a spiritual instrumental power, according to which it cleanses from guilt. Hence, Augustine says: "What is the power of water, that it washes the flesh, and takes away guilt?" So I say, that in the priest there is a spiritual instrumental power, by reason of which he is called a minister, and he ministerially effects the forgiveness of guilt, even as the water of Baptism does.

But the latter causes a difficulty, because now only children come to Baptism: and if an adult comes forward to be baptized, either he comes insincerely, or sincerely: he comes insincerely when he comes without a renewal of his soul, and then sin is not forgiven: he comes sincerely when he comes with the intention of confessing his sins;[25] hence, grace is required, or the intention of conversion, and this is from grace. Grace takes away guilt. Hence, in the sacrament of Baptism the adult coming forward, if he prepares himself, receives the forgiveness of guilt. So in the sacrament of Penance, to which only adults approach, one is not contrite unless he has the intention of subjecting himself to the discern-

---

25. "Confession of sins is twofold. One is made inwardly to God: and such confession of sins is required before Baptism: in other words, man should call his sins to mind and sorrow for them; since 'he cannot begin the new life, except he repent of his former life,' as Augustine says in his book on Penance (Sermone 351). The other is the outward confession of sins, which is made to a priest; and such confession is not required before Baptism" (III, q. 68, a. 6).

ment and judgment of the priest. If one is not contrite, the effect is not obtained, just as it would not be obtained in Baptism. But it can happen that someone not completely contrite approaches the sacrament of Penance, who by the power of the grace conferred in this sacrament, when it has been completed, is made contrite; for that reason, the words: **Whatsoever thou shalt loose** ought to be understood to mean, if you administer absolution. And He says, **Whatsoever**, because the priest not only absolves the guilt, but also the punishment. He says, **Shall be loosed in heaven**, meaning it will be accounted as absolved in heaven, just as it is concerning Baptism: hence, the priest ought to say, 'I absolve thee,' just as he says, 'I baptize thee.'

But someone could inquire how he binds. It ought to be known that a priest is God's minister, and an action of God's minister depends upon an act of the Lord: hence, in the same way by which the Lord binds and looses, so the priest binds and looses ministerially. God looses by infusing grace, He binds by not infusing grace: so the priest looses by the sacrament, by administering the sacrament, but he binds by not administering the sacrament. It is said, otherwise, that by heaven the present Church is designated; hence: **Whatsoever thou shalt bind or loose**, by excommunication, **shall be bound or loosed**, in regard to the administration of the sacraments of the Church. Hence, certain men maintain that this administration, this binding and loosing, is upon earth, such that it does not extend itself to the dead. But this is condemned, because it not only extends itself to the living, but also to the dead.[26] Hence, if the administration of the sacraments is ascribed to both binding and loosing, the meaning is: **Whatsoever thou shalt bind upon earth**, then I say while dwelling upon earth, **it shall be bound also in heaven**.

It ought to be said that He immediately gave this power to Peter; but the other disciples receive this power from Peter; for that reason, lest it be supposed that these things were only said to Peter, He says: "Whose sins you shall forgive," etc., (Jn. 20, 23).[27]

---

26. "SECOND COUNCIL OF CONSTANTINOPLE; How is it that some do presume to say that these things are said only of the living? Know they not that the sentence of anathema is nothing else but separation? They are to be avoided who are held of grievous faults, whether they are among the living, or not. For it is always necessary to fly from the wicked. Moreover there are diverse letters read of Augustine of religious memory, who was of great renown among the African bishops, which affirmed that heretics ought to be anathematized even after death. Such an ecclesiastical tradition other African Bishops also have preserved. And the Holy Roman Church also has anathematized some Bishops after death, although no accusation had been brought against their faith in their lifetimes" (*Catena Aurea on St. Matthew*, ibid.).

27. *Remiseritis* is in the second person plural.

And for this reason, the Pope, who is in St. Peter's place, has full power immediately from God, but the other Apostles[28] have their power from him.

20. Then he commanded his disciples, that they should tell no one that he was Jesus the Christ.
21. From that time Jesus began to shew to his disciples, that he must go to Jerusalem, and suffer many things from the ancients and scribes and chief priests, and be put to death, and the third day rise again.
22. And Peter taking him, began to rebuke him, saying: Lord, be it far from thee, this shall not be unto thee.
23. Who turning, said to Peter: Go behind me, Satan, thou art a scandal unto me: because thou savourest not the things that are of God, but the things that are of men.
24. Then Jesus said to his disciples: If any man will come after me, let him deny himself, and take up his cross, and follow me.
25. For he that will save his life, shall lose it: and he that shall lose his life for my sake, shall find it.
26. For what doth it profit a man, if he gain the whole world and suffer the loss of his own soul? Or what exchange shall a man give for his soul?
27. For the Son of man shall come in the glory of his Father with his angels: and then will he render to every man according to his works.
28. Amen I say to you, there are some of them that stand here, that shall not taste death, till they see the Son of man coming in his kingdom.

Above, Peter's confession of Christ's divinity was related; here, Christ commands silence for a time, namely, that they do not say that He is Christ.

But here there is a question. Because, above, the Lord had sent the disciples to preach the kingdom of God, how does He here forbid them to preach? According to a superficial literal sense, it can be said that above He did not command them to proclaim Christ, but the kingdom of God. But because the proclamation of the kingdom of God includes in itself the proclamation of Christ, therefore, it seems that here He forbids what He commanded above.

---

28. The Catholic bishops are in the place of the Apostles. This has been solemnly taught by the First Vatican Council."... the bishops, who, 'placed by the Holy Ghost,' [cf. Acts 20, 28] have succeeded to the places of the Apostles." (Dz. 1828).

Jerome says that He does not forbid what they had preached before, because before He had commanded that Jesus be preached, here He commands them not to call Him Christ: for Christ is a name of dignity: Jesus is the name of the Savior. Hence, it was said: "Thou shalt call his name Jesus" (above 1, 21). Origen answers that the Apostles were speaking about Christ as of a great man; but He wanted no mention to be made of Christ, so that, afterwards, He would seem greater to them; just as sometimes a teaching is presented beforehand, so that those being taught might have time to grasp it. Or it ought to be said that the previous passage: "And going, preach, saying" (above 10, 7), ought not to be associated with the time before the Passion, but with the time after the Passion. Hence, there it is mentioned that they will be dragged before kings and governors, etc., and this did not occur before the Passion.

But why did the Lord now command this to be kept silent? For it would be that the people would see Him suffering, and when some men are confused by a great man suffering, they are more inclined to scandal, for that reason, etc.

Chrysostom says: "If what is planted is uprooted, it cannot be so quickly planted." Hence, if the faith had been planted, and had been uprooted in the Passion, afterwards, it would not have been so quickly planted. Hence, many things must not be said for the sake of avoiding scandal. And it is clear that this is the reason why He commands this to be kept silent, because He immediately makes His Passion known; hence, it is added, *From that time Jesus began to shew to his disciples, that he must go to Jerusalem, and suffer many things.*

And about this, He does three things. Firstly, He foretells the Passion; secondly, He rebukes His disciple, where it is said, *Who turning, said to Peter*, etc.; and thirdly, He teaches the faith, where it is said, *Then Jesus said to his disciples*, etc. And about the first, He does two things. For He firstly foretells the Passion; and secondly, He foretells His Resurrection, where it is said, *And the third day rise again.* And about the first thing He mentions the place, the instigators, and its accomplishment. He says, therefore, *From that time Jesus began to shew to his disciples.* He spoke of His Passion here, in chapter 17, and in chapter 20.

But before this time He had not foretold this. So why did He begin to foretell this now? It is because He made Himself known to the Apostles. But why did He not foretell this before? It is because if He had foretold His Passion before the faith had been strengthened in them, they would have perhaps left Him: but now they believe in the true God, for that reason, etc.

And he says, *to shew*, not to tell; because things made visible to the eye are told, but things understood are shown; for that reason, He was telling things to the Jews, but He was showing things to the disciples; "Ought not Christ to have suffered these things and so, to enter into his glory?" (Lk. 24, 26). Thereafter, when He says, *He must go*, He mentions the place.

And why does He go to Jerusalem? He mentions the reason. But in that He says, *Jerusalem*, the first reason is that God's Temple was there, the place where sacrifices occurred. Now the sacrifices of the Old Law were figures of that sacrifice which was on the altar of the Cross; for that reason, He willed that in the place where the figure was, the truth would appear; "And He hath delivered himself for us, an oblation and a sacrifice to God for an odor of sweetness," etc., (Eph. 5, 2). Another reason is that the prophets suffered in Jerusalem, as it is written below: "Jerusalem, Jerusalem, thou that killest the prophets and stonest them that are sent unto thee" (23, 37). He wished, therefore, to suffer there to show that their death was a sign of Christ's Passion. Likewise, 'Jerusalem' means 'vision of peace'; but the Passion itself was making peace; "Making peace as to the things that are on earth and the things that are in heaven" (Col. 1, 20). Moreover, He wished to suffer there so that by this way there might be to us a way to the spiritual Jerusalem; "But that Jerusalem which is above is free: which is our mother" (Gal. 4, 26).

But from whom did He suffer? *From the ancients.* And this is because He suffered under their direction. He does the deed, by whose authority it happens; hence, they are more responsible for killing Him than the soldiers are. Hence, by this the people's malice is indicated, because those who seem better, are found to be worse. For some persons are withdrawn from sin on account of their age, others on account of their knowledge, and others on account of their dignity; nevertheless, age did not withdraw them, because He suffered *from the ancients*; nor were they withdrawn by their knowledge, because He suffered *from the scribes*; nor were they withdrawn by their dignity, because He suffered *from the chief priests*; "I will go therefore to the great men, and will speak to them: for they have known the way of the Lord, the judgment of their God: and behold these have altogether broken the yoke more" (Jer. 5, 5). Likewise, it was a sort of abasement and humiliation, because when a man suffers from the common people, it is not a great matter; but when a man suffers from the wise and from those who seem to be good men, it is a great abasement: hence, "Thy own nation and the chief priests have delivered thee up to me" (Jn. 18, 35). Similarly, He suffered unto death; for that reason He says, **And be put to death**; "Whom they killed, hanging him upon a tree" (Acts 10, 39); "Christ shall be slain: and the people that shall deny him shall not be his" (Dan. 9, 26). But the joy of the Resurrection is added, **And the third day rise again**; "On the third day he will raise us up" (Osee 6, 3).

And Peter taking him, began to rebuke him. Here He rebukes His objecting disciple. And firstly, his objection is related; and secondly Christ's response is related, where it is said, **Who turning, said to Peter**, etc. **And taking him**, either taking in his gaze, or taking Him near to himself, lest he seem presumptuous when he would reprehend the Lord before the others, he said, **Lord, be it far from thee, this shall not be unto thee.** The Lord had highly praised his confession, and had given him power because he had known that He is the Son of God, and, for this reason, he thought that if He were to be put to death, then his faith would be deceived, and that He would not be God; for that reason, he reproached Him. He maintained in his heart that He was the Son of God, and he did not take into consideration that God should not be reproached, as it is said: "Thou reprovest him by words, who is not equal to thee, and thou speakest that which is not good for thee" (Job 15, 3). But he still kept some faith in His divinity, because in Mark it is stated, "Have mercy upon thyself, O Lord, and do not deliver thyself up to death. Who turning about said: Go behind me, Satan" (Mk. 8, 33). Here His response is related. Hilary expounds this passage as follows: The devil, seeing that He had announced His Passion, and knowing the testimonies of the Prophets, incited Peter to say this so that he might dissuade Him. Therefore, the Lord seeing that he did not speak on his own initiative, rebuked him, and, for that reason, He said to Peter: **Go behind me**, so that a period could be put there. And He said to Satan: **Satan, thou art a scandal unto me.** Jerome says that he does not think that Peter spoke due to the suggestion of the devil, but from an affection of piety; hence, he spoke ignorantly. Hence, he does three things, for firstly, the admonition is related; secondly, the rebuke is related; and thirdly, the reason for the rebuke is given. There is an admonition because He says, **Go,** Peter. Hence, "Go behind me, Satan" has the same meaning as what was said above to the devil, (4, 10).[29] Or "Go behind me" means follow me. 'Satan' has the same

---

29. "Begone, Satan."

meaning as 'adversary.' Hence, he who contradicts the divine plan, is called a satan. *Thou art a scandal unto me*; that is to say, you wish to impede My plan.

But is there no scandal to those who love God? Origen says that to the perfect there is no scandal. Hence, they are not scandalized. Hence, Peter took scandal, but Christ did not. Or it is thus, namely, that He considers the scandal of His members to be His own. Hence, Paul says: "Who is scandalized, and I am not scandalized?" (II Cor. 11, 29). Because, therefore, he could be a scandal to the others, He said, *Thou art a scandal unto me*, and not on account of Me, but on account of My members.

But what is this? Above He had said, *Thou art Peter; and upon this rock I will build my church*; here, however, He calls him Satan.

Jerome says that the things that the Lord had promised, Peter did not yet have. But because he would have these things in the future, the Lord could call him Satan on account of these things. Chrysostom says that He wanted to show what man could do by himself, and what he could do by God's grace: because above, by God's grace, he recognized Christ's divinity; but when God withdrew His grace, Peter's humanity and weakness appeared, so much so that He called him Satan: so the Lord sometimes wishes perfect men to fall, so that they might know their humanity. And because this passage ought to be so understood, it sufficiently agrees with the passage which follows. Hence, He gives that reason: *Because thou savourest not the things that are of God*. For before, Peter had said, *Thou art the Son of God*, and there he understood in accord with the divinity; but here he understands what comes from man; "The sensual man perceiveth not these things that are of God" (I Cor. 2, 14); "He that is a fool, layeth open his folly" (Prov. 13, 16). Peter flees away from the death of the flesh, but the spirit of God does not; hence, it is said: "Greater love than this no man hath, that a man lay down his life for his friends" (Jn. 15, 13).

Then Jesus said to his disciples. Here He exhorts them to imitate His Passion. And firstly, the Evangelist relates the exhortation; secondly, he relates the reason for the exhortation; and thirdly, Christ confirms His exhortation. The second thing is where it is said, *He that will save his life, shall lose it*; the third thing is where it is said, *What doth it profit a man, if he gain the whole world*, etc. So Peter wished to impede the Passion, but He invites them saying: *If any man will come after me, let him deny himself, and take up his cross, and follow me*; it is as though He were to say: 'It is necessary that you be prepared to imitate Christ's Passion.' Martyrs corporally imitate the Passion in a special way, but spiritual men imitate it spiritually, by spiritually dying for Christ. Hence, this passage can be read as referring to a physical cross. Chrysostom says: "Therefore when He said, Peter, *Go behind me*, you may understand that He spoke only to Peter: but when He said, *If any man will come*, etc., He wants all men to come to Him." And He says, *will*, because a man is drawn more who is willingly drawn, than he who is drawn by compulsion; "I will freely sacrifice to thee" (Ps. 53, 8). Thus He says three things: that a man deny himself, that he take up his cross, and that He follow Me. Chrysostom says that he speaks by a similitude. If you had a son, and you see that he was behaving badly, and if you would not care, then you would disown him; so if you wish to follow the Lord's Passion, you ought to also deem yourself as nothing; "And I became as a man that heareth not: and that hath no reproofs in his mouth" (Ps. 37, 15). And it is written: "They have beaten me, but I was not sensible of pain: they drew me, and I felt not" (Prov. 23, 35). *And take up his cross, and follow me*: this means that he ought to be ready to suffer the cross, or die a most painful and a most shameful death; "Let us condemn him to a most shameful death" (Wis. 2, 20). Hence, a man ought to be ready to suffer whatsoever death on account of God. To suffer on account of one's own sins is shameful: but to suffer for God's sake is not shameful. Hence: "Let none of you suffer as a murderer, or a thief, or a railer, or coveter of other men's things. But, if as a Christian, let him not be ashamed: but let him glorify God in that name" (I Pet. 4, 15). According to Gregory, this passage is to be understood concerning spiritual mortification. For one practices self-denial in three ways. In the first way, a man denies himself when he gives up his prior state of sin; "Reckon that you are dead to sin" (Rom. 6, 11). Likewise, a man practices self-denial if he is not in sin, and transfers himself to the state of perfection; "If by any means I may attain to the resurrection which is from the dead. Not as though I had already attained, or were already perfect: but I follow after, if I may by any means apprehend, wherein I am also apprehended by Christ Jesus" (Phil. 3, 11-12). Similarly, a man practices self-denial who gives up his own will; "For I, through the law, am dead to the law, that I may live to God; with Christ I am nailed to the cross" (Rom. 2, 19). And: "If one died for all, then all were dead" (II Cor. 5, 14). The word 'cross'[30] is so called from the word 'torment.'[31] A

---

30. *Crux.*   31. *Cruciatus.*

man is spiritually tormented whose mind is tormented on account of his compassion for his neighbor, as the Apostle says: "Weep with them that weep" (Rom. 12, 15). A man is likewise tormented who is tormented through penance; "They that are Christ's have crucified their flesh, with the vices and concupiscences" (Gal. 5, 24). *And follow me.* Many feel compassion, but do not follow God. He who feels compassion, and is in sin, does not follow God, because Christ came to destroy sin. Likewise, if you afflict yourself on account of vainglory, you do not follow God; "When you fast, be not as the hypocrites, sad. For they disfigure their faces, that they may appear unto men to fast" (above 6, 16).

For he that will save his life, shall lose it. Here the reason is given for his admonition, and the reason is from the greatness of the reward. And this can be read in two ways. For there is a twofold well-being, namely, the well-being of the soul, and this belongs to the just; and there is the well-being of the body, and this belongs to all creatures, even the beasts; "Men and beasts thou wilt preserve, O Lord" (Ps. 35, 7). Hence, we may say: *He that will save his life*, by not giving up his corporal life, by not taking up his cross, *shall lose it.* Above He said, *If any man will*, and here He says, *he that will.* Hence, just as the former was able to be interpreted in two ways, so the latter also. *He that will save*, namely, because he would not be killed or because he would not feel compassion, *his life* (or rather *his soul*),[32] which is the principle of bodily life, *shall lose it.* "Thou hast destroyed all them that are disloyal to thee" (Ps. 72, 27). *And he that shall lose*, by giving himself up to death, by denying himself pleasures, *for my sake, shall find it*; "I have labored a little, and have found much rest" (Eccli. 51, 35). Or it is as follows. *He that will save his life*, also wills to lead it to everlasting salvation; "My salvation shall be forever" (Is. 51, 6); *shall lose it*, either by suffering death, or by abstaining from carnal delights. *He that shall lose his life for my sake*, namely, he that forsakes carnal desires, *shall find it*, namely life; "We also are weak in him: but we shall live with him" (II Cor. 13, 4).

For what doth it profit a man, if he gain the whole world and suffer the loss of his own soul? Here He confirms His exhortation by a reason. Someone could say: 'I do not care; I prefer the present life to the other one.' And He excludes this. He firstly excludes this by that inestimable life; and secondly, He excludes this by the irrecompensable harm to the soul. He says, therefore,

---

32. *Animus* in Latin means both life and soul.

What doth it profit, etc., what do these temporal things profit you, if you lose your soul? It is natural for man that he loves the end more than those things which are means to the end, such as the body rather than riches. Hence, it is natural that all things be abandoned for the health of the body. If the contrary occurs, it is the perversity of passion. So also it is natural to love the soul more than the body; hence, the wise man is the one who would prefer to suffer corporally, rather than to endure a great disgrace. If, then, it is so, a man ought rather to choose the salvation of his soul, than the health of his body, even if he could possess the whole world. But *what doth it profit a man, if he gain the whole world and suffer the loss of his own soul?* It is as though He were to say: 'The detriment of the soul is inestimable harm.' Likewise, someone could say: 'If I have my soul and I lose it, I will be able to recover it': for that reason the Lord excludes this, saying, *Or what exchange shall a man give for his soul?* It is as though He were to say, 'There is none.' "He will not accept for satisfaction ever so many gifts" (Prov. 6, 35).

But can he never be redeemed: "Redeem thou thy sins with alms" (Dan. 4, 24)? It ought to be said that here He speaks regarding the complete loss of one's soul, because a man would not be able to recover it, unless he had first found it; but when he is contrite he finds it again. Gregory expounds this differently: "There is a twofold time of the Church, the time of prosperity and the time of adversity: there are adverse things which ought to be embraced in adversity, and prosperous things which ought to be forsaken in prosperity."[33]

For the Son of man shall come in the glory of his Father. Here He treats of His judiciary power. And firstly, His judiciary power is related; secondly, He replies to a tacit objection. Perhaps you will say: 'For why will I follow Thee and take up my cross, etc.?' It is because there is the Son of Man's judgment and power. "He hath given him power to do judgment, because he is the Son of man" (Jn. 5, 27). Do not be sad from the fact that He will be condemned by the ancients, because *He shall come in the glory*

---

33. St. Gregory is here commenting on the previous verse, i.e. verse 25. "**For he that will save his life, shall lose it: and he that shall lose his life for my sake, shall find it.** This is said to a believer, as one might say to a farmer: 'If you save your grain, you lose it; if you sow it, you recover it.' Everyone knows that when you let go of grain, in the form of a seed, it disappears from sight, it falls into the ground. What makes it decay in the dirt is what makes it grow green again and be renewed. Since the Church has its times of persecution and its times of peace, our Redeemer has distinguished between these times in his precepts. We are to lay down our lives during times of persecution, but in times of peace we are to subdue the earthly desires which can so easily rule us." (Hom. In Ev. xxxii, 4).

of his Father: nor from the fact that He will be condemned before many men, because *He shall come with his angels*; "Every tongue should confess that the Lord Jesus Christ is in the glory of God the Father" (Phil. 2, 11). And: "And when the Son of Man shall come in his majesty, and all the angels with him, then shall he sit upon the seat of his majesty" (below 25, 31). Then He will render and compensate everyone according to their works. Afterwards, He replies to a tacit objection: *Amen I say to you*; it is as though He were to say: 'I have told you that the Son of Man will come, etc. But do not be surprised. Why? I want to show you, because *there are some of them that stand here, that shall not taste death.*' Sinners are swallowed by death, but the just taste death. Now these men were Peter, John and James.[34] *Till they see the Son of man coming in his kingdom*. This was a sign of their future glory. But He did not name them on account of the envy of the others. Now they might have been envious because more was given to them than to the others. Likewise, they might have been envious on account of an annoyance, because they would have been annoyed if He had shown them nothing. It can be said, otherwise, that the kingdom of God is the Church: for that reason, there is someone who will not taste death, such as John, *till he sees the Son of man coming in his kingdom*; that is, until the Church be expanded, because he lived so long that he saw the Church expanded, and many [local] Churches built.

---

34. "REMIG; What is here said, therefore, was fulfilled in the three disciples to whom the Lord, when transfigured in the mount, showed the joys of the eternal inheritance; these saw Him coming in His kingdom that is, shining in His effulgent radiance, in which, after the judgment passed, He shall be beheld by all the saints" (*Catena Aurea on St. Matthew*, chap. 16, lect. 8).

CHAPTER SEVENTEEN

1. And after six days Jesus taketh unto him Peter and James, and John his brother, and bringeth them up into a high mountain apart:
2. And he was transfigured before them. And his face did shine as the sun: and his garments became white as snow.
3. And behold there appeared to them Moses and Elias talking with him.
4. And Peter answering, said to Jesus: Lord, it is good for us to be here: if thou wilt, let us make here three tabernacles, one for thee, and one for Moses, and one for Elias.
5. And as he was yet speaking, behold a bright cloud overshadowed them. And lo a voice out of the cloud, saying: This is my beloved Son, in whom I am well pleased: hear ye him.
6. And the disciples hearing fell upon their face, and were very much afraid.
7. And Jesus came and touched them: and said to them: Arise, and fear not.
8. And they lifting up their eyes, saw no one, but only Jesus.
9. And as they came down from the mountain, Jesus charged them, saying: Tell the vision to no man, till the Son of man be risen from the dead.
10. And his disciples asked him, saying: Why then do the scribes say that Elias must come first?
11. But he answering, said to them: Elias indeed shall come, and restore all things.
12. But I say to you, that Elias is already come, and they knew him not, But have done unto him whatsoever they had a mind. So also the Son of man shall suffer from them.
13. Then the disciples understood, that he had spoken to them of John the Baptist.

In the preceding section, the Evangelist showed the power of the Gospel teaching, etc.; here is shown the purpose of the Gospel teaching, which is the glory to come: and about this, he does two things. Firstly, he shows how it was manifested in the transfiguration; secondly, he shows how one can arrive at it in chapter 18. This chapter begins with the words, "At that hour," etc. About the first, there are three things done.[1] Firstly, the glory to come is displayed; secondly, He commands secrecy; and thirdly, he sets forth a question. The second thing is where it is said, *And as they*

---

1. The text reads only "two things" but this seems to be a mistake in the text.

came down from the mountain; and the third thing is where it is said, *And his disciples asked him*, etc. About the first, he does three things. Firstly, the circumstances of the transfiguration are related; secondly, the transfiguration is related; and thirdly, the effect is related. The second part is where it is said, *And he was transfigured before them*; and the third part is where it is said, *And the disciples hearing fell upon their face*. Now, he relates three circumstances, namely, the time, the disciples, and the place. He relates the time when he says, *And after six days*.

But here, there is a literal question: Why was He not immediately transfigured as soon as he said, "There are some of them that stand here," etc.? Chrysostom solves the question. It was firstly to enkindle the desire of the Apostles; secondly, it was to lessen their envy, because, perhaps, they were troubled after these words.

But why is it stated here, *After six days*, and in Luke (9, 28) it is stated, "After eight days"?[2] It is apparent that Luke numbers the day on which He spoke these words, and also the day of the transfiguration; but Matthew numbers only the intermediate days; for that reason, when the first and the last days have been subtracted, there remain but six days. By six days are signified the six Ages, after which we hope to arrive at the glory to come. Likewise, in six days, the Lord finished His works; and so, the Lord chose to show Himself after six days, because, unless we are raised up to God above all the creatures that the Lord created, we cannot reach the kingdom of God.

Likewise, *He taketh unto him Peter and James, and John*. Why did He not take them all? It was to signify that not all who are called reach the kingdom of God; hence, it is said: "Many are called but few chosen" (below 20, 16). And why did He take only three disciples? It was to signify that no one can reach God's kingdom except in the faith of the Trinity. "He that believeth and is baptized shall be saved" (Mk. 16, 16). But why did He take these three rather than the others? The reason is that Peter was more fervent. John was taken because he was specially loved. Likewise, James was taken because he was the chief conqueror of the enemies of the faith; hence, Herod killed him first, because he wanted to do something great for the Jews, as it is said in the Acts: "And he killed James," etc., (12, 2). And the passage continues, "And seeing that it pleased the Jews" (verse 3).

2. The verse actually reads, "About eight days after these words"

And bringeth them up into a high mountain apart, etc. Why did He lead them up into a mountain? It was to signify that one is not led into contemplation unless he ascends into a mountain, as it is said concerning Lot: "Save thyself in the mountain" (Gen. 19, 17). And he says, *Very high*,[3] on account of the loftiness of contemplation. "It shall be exalted above the hills, and all nations shall flow unto it and people shall go, and say: Come and let us go up to the mountain of the Lord" (Is. 2, 2-3). And it was because that height of glory is above every height of knowledge and power. Likewise, He brought them apart, because they separated themselves from wicked men. "He shall separate them, as the sheep from the goats" (below 25, 32).

The transfiguration follows. *And he was transfigured before them.* And firstly, the transfiguration is related; and secondly, the testimony is related, where it is said, *As he was yet speaking*, etc. About the first, the transfiguration is related; secondly, the manner is related; and thirdly, Peter's admiration is related. He says, therefore, *And he was transfigured*, meaning He changed His figure,[4] *before them.* To be transfigured is the same thing as to be changed in one's own figure, as it is stated in II Corinthians 11, 14, that "Satan himself transformeth himself into an angel of light." For that reason, it is not surprising if the just are transfigured into a figure of glory; wherefore, He was transfigured because He put aside what was His own. Others have said that He assumed a different body, which is false; but if anyone is changed in his figure as to his exterior looks, it is said to be a transfiguration: for example, when someone who is normally healthy and ruddy is sick, he becomes pale, he is thus also said to be transfigured: so Christ, because He appeared in a different form than that in which He normally appeared, since His body was not luminous, but it received brilliance, for that reason, it is said to be transfigured. For that reason, he continues, *And his face did shine as the sun*; in this verse, the manner of the transfiguration is mentioned. And firstly, the manner is shown as to the brilliance of His face; secondly, it is shown as to the splendor of His garments; and thirdly, it is shown as to the testimony. He says, therefore, *And his face did shine as the sun.* Here He

---

3. The word "very" is added in Matthew 4, 8: "The devil took him up into a very high mountain."
4. "Figure is seen in the outline of a body, for it is 'that which is enclosed by one or more boundaries' (Euclid, Book 1, definition 14). Therefore, whatever has to do with the outline of a body seems to pertain to the figure. Now the brilliance, just as the color, of a non-transparent body is seen on its surface, and consequently the assumption of brilliance is called transfiguration" (III, q. 45, a. 1 ad 1um).

reveals the glory to come, wherein the bodies[5] will be bright and shining. And the brilliance was not from the essence of His body,[6] but from the interior brilliance of His soul, full of charity; "Then shall thy light break forth as the morning" (Is. 58, 8). And this quotation continues, "And the glory of the Lord shall gather thee up." Hence, there was a sort of refulgence of His soul in His body. For Christ's soul was seeing God, and had a brilliance above any other brilliance from the first moment of His conception; "We saw his glory" (Jn. 1, 14).

If, therefore, the brilliance in the other blessed overflows from their souls into their bodies, why is this not also the case for Christ who is both God and man? It ought to be said that because He is God, the order of human nature is in His power. Here, however, there is an ordination that the parts communicate with each other, such that when the body is tired, the suffering is shared by the soul, and from the soul the body is affected. But this order was subject to Christ. Hence, the joy that was in the higher part of His soul was so perfect that it was not going out beyond His soul: hence, He was both perfectly a wayfarer and perfectly a comprehensor.[7] Hence, when He wished, there was not an outpouring, and when He wished, there was an outpouring, and His splendor appeared.

But was not this gift in Christ? Some say[8] that it was, and that He received all the gifts on earth: the gift of subtlety in His birth, agility in walking on the waves, brilliance here, and impassibility in the administration of the sacrament of the altar. I, however, do not believe this, because a gift is a property of glory itself. Hence, that He walked upon the sea, that He shone with light, all this was by His Divine power, because a gift of glory is unsuited to a wayfarer, but He had some likeness to these gifts, because *His face did shine as the sun*; "His face was as the sun shineth in his power" (Apoc. 1, 16).

But it can be objected that the just will shine like the sun.[9] Therefore, Christ's splendor was not greater than that of the others.

---

5. cf. "Then shall the just shine as the sun, in the kingdom of their Father" (above 13, 43).

6. "But in Christ's transfiguration brilliance overflowed from His Godhead and from His soul into His body, not as an immanent quality affecting His very body, but rather after the manner of a transient passion, as when the air is lit up by the sun. Consequently the refulgence, which appeared in Christ's body then, was miraculous" (III, q. 45, a. 2).

7. "'Comprehension'... is opposed to 'non-attainment'; for he who attains to anyone is said to comprehend him when he attains to him. And in this sense God is comprehended by the blessed, according to the words, 'I held him, and I will not let him go' (Canticles 3:4)" (I, q. 12, a. 7 ad 1um).

8. Hugh of Saint Victor (Innocent III, De Myst. Miss. iv). cf. III, q. 45, a. 2.

9. "Then shall the just shine as the sun" (above 13, 43).

I say that this is correct. But this is because in the sensible things of this world there is nothing brighter to which it can be compared; for that reason, His brilliance is compared to the sun.

His garments became white as snow. Here it is treated regarding His garments. It is clear that this did not occur by Christ changing His garments, nor through a gift, because garments are incapable of receiving a gift.[10] By the garments, the Saints are signified; "I live, saith the Lord, thou shalt be clothed with all these as with an ornament" (Is. 49, 18). And He says: *Became white as snow.* Snow has brightness and coolness, just as the Saints have the brightness of glory; "The just shall shine, and shall run to and fro like sparks among the reeds," etc., (Wis. 3, 7). Likewise, they have refreshment from the heat of concupiscence; "They shall be whited with snow in Selmon"[11] (Ps. 67, 15). Or, by His garments, the words of Sacred Scripture are understood.

And behold there appeared to them Moses and Elias. And why did they appear? Chrysostom assigns three reasons. The first reason is that it was to strengthen the faith of the disciples. He had asked above, "Whom do men say that the Son of man is?" etc., (Chap. 16, 13). And they said: "Some Elias," etc. But in order that He might show the distinction between Himself and those men, He therefore willed to bring them forward; "There is none among the gods like unto thee, O Lord," etc., (Ps. 85, 8). The second reason is that it was to confute the Jews. For they were saying that He was a transgressor of the Law; likewise, they were saying that He was a blasphemer, as it is stated in John 10, 33: "For a good work we stone thee not, but for blasphemy." Wherefore, because Elias was holier than all the prophets and Moses was the lawgiver, He shows in the presence of Moses and Elias that He is not opposed to God, nor a transgressor of the Law. The third reason is that it was to show that He is the Judge of the living and the dead, because Elias was alive and Moses was dead. A fourth reason is that it was to be a confirmation to Peter; because Peter had rebuked the Lord concerning His death, for that reason, He shows, by summoning these two men, that men who expose themselves to death ought not to be rebuked; because Elias exposed himself to death before Jezabel,[12] and Moses exposed

---

10. Gift (*dos*) here means a preternatural endowment or quality.

11. Selmon is a very high mountain in Ephraim that is shaded with trees.

12. "And Elias went to shew himself to Achab, and there was a grievous famine in Samaria. And Achab called Abdias the governor of his house: now Abdias feared the Lord very much. For when Jezabel killed the prophets of the Lord, he took a hundred prophets, and hid them by fifty and fifty in caves, and fed them with bread and water. (III Kings 18, 2-4).

himself similarly on account of the Law.[13] A fifth reason is that it was because there were two things in Himself that He wanted to show forth in these two men, namely meekness, which He showed in Moses, and an example of zeal for God, which He showed in Elias, concerning whom it is said that "Elias the prophet stood up, as a fire, and his word burnt like a torch" (Eccli. 48, 1). A sixth reason is assigned in the Gloss, namely, that the whole Law and the Prophets bore testimony to Christ. Hence: "All things must needs be fulfilled which are written in the law of Moses and in the prophets" (Lk. 24, 44).

But then there is a question. Concerning Elias, it is not surprising that he was there, because he is living; but concerning Moses, there is the question how he was there. Some said that an angel was there in his place. But this opinion is worthless, because Moses was there in his soul only. But how was he seen? It ought to be said that it was just as the angels are seen.

Peter's reaction follows: *And Peter answering, said*, etc. And we can explain his words by attributing them to his carnality, or to his devotion. Chrysostom attributes them to his carnality. Above, Christ had said that He was about to suffer, and Peter had rebuked Him, wherefore Christ reprehended him. Hence, Moses and Elias appeared speaking about His Passion; and so, when Peter heard the prediction repeated, he could not accept it. Wherefore, he did not want to object; for that reason, he thought that if Christ would stay there, He would avoid death: therefore, lest they quickly depart, he said, *Let us make here three tabernacles.*

And why did he say, *One for Moses, and one for Elias*? It was because he saw that Christ desired His death, and he wanted these men to impede His death. Concerning Elias, it is read in IV Kings 1 that when the king sent fifty men, he made fire to come down from heaven. Likewise, it is read of Moses in Numbers 16, that when a quarrel occurred in the tabernacle, a cloud came down. For that reason, he thought that through Moses a cloud could be obtained, and through Elias fire could be obtained. Others, however, ascribe this to Peter's devotion. And, according to this, he does two things. Because he firstly mentions his reaction; and secondly, he mentions his suggestion, where it is said, *If thou wilt*, etc. He says, therefore, *Lord, it is good for us to be here.* Due to his exceedingly great fervor at seeing Christ's glory, he had been so affected that he wished never to be separated from

---

[13]. "The people were thirsty there for want of water, and murmured against Moses... And Moses cried to the Lord, saying: What shall I do to this people? Yet a little more and they will stone me" (Ex. 17, 3-4).

Him, if God so-willed. And what will it be in regard to those who shall be in perfect glory? Hence, those existing in that beatitude wish never to be separated from Him; "But it is good for me to adhere to my God" (Ps. 72, 28). Secondly, he makes a suggestion, and as it says in Luke 9, 23, he did so "not knowing what he said"; hence, he says, *If thou wilt, let us make here three tabernacles*: for we ought to submit our will to the divine will, as it was said above: "Thy will be done" (6, 10). Hence, in saying this, Peter spoke well; on the other hand, he spoke badly, because he imagined that glory can be had without death, which is contrary to that passage in II Corinthians 5, 1: "For we know, if our earthly house of this habitation be dissolved, that we have a building of God, a house not made with hands, eternal in heaven." Likewise, he spoke badly because he imagined that the glory of the Saints is in this world; which is not here on earth, but in heaven; "Be glad and rejoice for your reward is very great in heaven" (above 5, 12). Moreover, he spoke badly because he imagined that they would need houses, but they do not need them on earth, on the contrary, they have them in heaven, as it is written: "Behold the tabernacle of God with men" (Apoc. 21, 3). Again, he spoke badly because he wanted three tabernacles to be made: for one suffices for the Father, and the Son, and the Holy Ghost.[14] Similarly, he spoke badly because he put Christ on the same level as the others, but this ought not to be done in that way; "I will not level God with man" (Job 32, 21). O Peter, all men have one tabernacle, which is faith.

The testimony follows, *And as he was yet speaking, behold a bright cloud overshadowed them*, etc. Peter spoke foolishly, for that reason, he did not deserve a reply. He wanted a material tabernacle;[15] for that reason, the Lord willed to show that the Saints have no need of one. Likewise, by the cloud, He wished to show Himself;[16] "His magnificence is in the clouds" (Ps. 67, 35). But sometimes a bright cloud appears, and sometimes a dark cloud appears; in Exodus 19[17] it is said that a cloud of darkness appeared; but here a shining cloud appeared, because it

---

14. "JEROME; Make one tabernacle for the Father, Son, and Holy Spirit, that They whose divinity is one, may have but one tabernacle, in your bosom" (*Catena Aurea on St. Matthew*, chap. 17, lect. 1).

15. The text reads, *Volebat testimonium materiale* which seems incorrect. Rather *tabernaculum materiale* fits better with the following, corresponding, words of St. Jerome quoted in the *Catena Aurea*. "JEROME; While they thought only of an earthly tabernacle of boughs or tents, they are overshadowed by the covering of a bright cloud" (ibid., lect. 2).

16. "ORIGEN; I may also venture to call the Savior that bright cloud which overshadows the Gospel, the Law, and the Prophets, as they understand who can behold His light in all these three" (ibid).

17. "I come to thee in the darkness of a cloud" (verse 19).

signifies the consolation of glory; "God shall wipe away all tears from their eyes: and death shall be no more. Nor mourning, nor crying, nor sorrow shall be any more, for the former things are passed away" (Apoc. 21, 4). The testimony from the Father's voice follows; hence, *And a voice out of the cloud, saying*, etc. But why did the voice come from the cloud? It was to signify that it is the Father's voice. The Lord dwells in a cloud.[18] *This is my beloved Son, in whom I am well pleased.* Christ's dignity is indicated by the singularity of His filiation, by the perfection of His love, and by the likeness of His operation. Hence, the Father says: *This is*, as though in the singular, *my Son*. Others are sons by adoption; "I have said: You are gods and all of you the sons of the most High" (Ps. 81, 6); but this is the true Son, singularly so, in fact, as it is said: "The Son of God is come, and he hath given us understanding that we may know the true God" (I Jn. 5, 20). Likewise, He is *beloved*, but God's love is different from our love. Our love is based on a creature's goodness. For a thing is not good because I love it, but, rather, I love a thing because it is good. But God's love is the cause of the goodness in things. And just as God poured out goodness in creatures through creation, so in His Son through generation, since He communicates all goodness to His Son; hence, creatures are blessed by participation, but He gave all His goodness to His Son; "The Father loveth the Son: and he hath given all things into his hand" (Jn. 3, 35). Hence, Love itself proceeds from the Father loving the Son, and from the Son loving the Father. But it happens that a thing is given to someone, and he does not use well the things given to him, and, for that reason, he does not please the giver; but God gave to His Son a fullness of His gifts, and He used them well; for that reason, the Son pleases Him; hence, He says, *in whom I am well pleased*. Likewise, it is stated above: "In whom I am pleased and in whom my soul rests" (12, 18). Therefore, because this is so, *hear ye him*. Hence, He implies that He was given to be the teacher of all men; "The Lord thy God will raise up to thee a prophet of thy nation, listen to him just as you listened me" (Deut. 18, 15). Or, *hear ye Him*; not Moses, and not Elias, except inasmuch as they teach Christ, or rather Christ's doctrine.

Notice that Christ had the testimony of heaven by His Father, of hell by Moses,[19] of paradise by Elias, and of earth by the dis-

---

18. "Then Solomon said: The Lord said that he would dwell in a cloud" (III Kings 8, 12).

19. Moses was not in the hell of the damned but in the limbo of the Fathers which borders hell and for this reason shares its name in Sacred Scripture. cf. III, q. 69, a. 5.

ciples: "that in the name of Jesus every knee should bow, of those that are in heaven, on earth, and under the earth" (Phil. 2, 10). Likewise, one ought to notice that there is a twofold regeneration: one is in Baptism, and the other is when we will be cleansed from all defilement of the spirit. Hence, in His baptism, Jesus is pointed out by a dove, which is a simple animal, to point out the simplicity conferred by Baptism: it is also a fruitful animal, to signify the other regeneration.[20] He appeared in a bright cloud, to signify the clarity and the extinction of all concupiscence; "And the Lord will create upon every place of mount Sion, and where he is called upon, a cloud by day, and a smoke and the brightness of a flaming fire in the night" (Is. 4, 5).

And the disciples hearing fell upon their face, and were afraid. Having set forth the transfiguration, here the effect upon the disciples is set forth. And firstly, their fear is related; secondly, Christ's strengthening them against their fear is related; and thirdly, the effect of His strengthening is related. The second part is where it is said, **And Jesus came**, etc.; the third part is where it is said, **And they lifting up their eyes, saw no one**. He says, therefore, **And the disciples hearing**. They heard the Father's voice from the cloud, as it is said in II Peter 1, 18: "This voice we heard, when we were in the mount." And he relates the sign of their fear, namely, that *they fell upon their face*.

Their fear follows, **And they were very much afraid**. But why were they afraid? Jerome gives three reasons. The first reason is that they knew that they had erred, as it is said concerning Adam: "Lord, I heard thy voice in paradise; and I was afraid, because I was naked" (Gen. 3, 10). Likewise, it was because, being covered by the cloud, they recognized the presence of the Divine Majesty; "The Lord went before them to shew the way, by day in a pillar of a cloud," etc., (Ex. 13, 21). And it is natural that anybody is stunned by that to which he is unaccustomed. Moreover, they were afraid on account of the voice from the cloud; "What is all flesh, that it should hear the voice of the living God?" (Deut. 5, 26). And as a result of this, their strength failed, wherefore, *they fell upon their face*.

---

20. "Just as in the Baptism, where the mystery of the first regeneration was proclaimed, the operation of the whole Trinity was made manifest, because the Son Incarnate was there, the Holy Ghost appeared under the form of a dove, and the Father made Himself known in the voice; so also in the transfiguration, which is the mystery of the second regeneration, the whole Trinity appears—the Father in the voice, the Son in the man, the Holy Ghost in the bright cloud; for just as in baptism He confers innocence, signified by the simplicity of the dove, so in the resurrection will He give His elect the clarity of glory and refreshment from all sorts of evil, which are signified by the bright cloud" (III, q. 45, a. 4 ad 2um).

But it should be noted that the wicked fall differently than do the Saints. The wicked fall backwards, as it is stated in I Kings 4 of Heli, who, when he heard the news about the ark of the Lord, fell from his stool and having broken his neck, he breathed his last. But the Saints fall upon their faces; "Who fell down upon their faces" (Apoc. 7, 11). And the reason is that we do not see what is behind us.[21] "The eyes of a wise man are in his head" (Eccle. 2, 14).[22]

Afterwards, Christ's strengthening is related. And He strengthens them by deed and word: He strengthens them by deed against their fear and fall: He strengthens them against their fear by His presence, because *Jesus came*. "I will fear no evils, for thou art with me" (Ps. 22, 4). And above it was said: "It is I, fear ye not" (14, 27). Likewise, He strengthens them by His touch, because "He giveth strength to the weary" (Is. 40, 29); and in Daniel it is read, "A hand touched me, and lifted me up" (10, 10); hence, he says, *He touched them*. Similarly, He strengthened them as to their fall; hence, *He said to them: Arise*. "Rise, thou that sleepest, and arise from the dead: and Christ shall enlighten thee" (Eph. 5, 14). Likewise, He strengthened them against fear saying, *Fear not*. That fear was pusillanimity, and they who rise from sin, put away fear, because "perfect charity casteth out fear" (I Jn. 4, 18).

Afterwards follows the effect of His strengthening, *And they lifting up their eyes, saw no one, but only Jesus*. And this is the effect of divine strengthening, because, having been strengthened by Christ, they see nothing but Jesus, nor do they rejoice or are strengthened in anything except in Him; "For to me, to live is Christ: and to die is gain" (Phil. 1, 21). Likewise, *they saw no one, but only Jesus*, because once the shadow of the Law and the teaching of the Prophets, which are represented by Moses and Elias, receded, only Christ's teaching is held. Or, according to another literal interpretation, *He alone remained*, lest the voice seem to have been speaking about Moses or Elias. Hence, when they did not appear it was certain that the voice was speaking about Him.

---

21. "GREG. Why is this, that the Elect fall on their faces, but the reprobate backward? Because everyone who falls back, sees not where he falls, whereas he who falls forward, sees where he falls. The wicked when they suffer loss in invisible things, are said to fall backward, because they do not see what is behind them: but the righteous, who of their own accord cast themselves down in temporal things, in order that they may rise in spiritual, fall as it were upon their faces, when with fear and repentance they humble themselves with their eyes open" (*Catena Aurea on St. John*, chap. 18, lect. 2).

22. "Human works ought to be enlightened by the light of reason: "The eyes of a wise man are in his head" (*Super Ep. ad Romanos*, Chap. 13, lect. 3).

Afterwards, the command to delay the revelation of this vision is related; hence, he says, *And as they came down from the mountain, Jesus charged them, saying: Tell the vision to no man.* But what is the reason for this? There are three reasons. The first is that, as Jerome says, it was going to be that Christ would suffer and that the Jews would be scandalized; "Unto the Jews indeed a stumblingblock" (I Cor. 1, 23): wherefore, if they had heard this, they might have been more scandalized: hence, they would have reckoned Christ's suffering to have been unimportant. Remigius expounds this verse as follows: it was because if He had made this vision known, He would never have accomplished what He desired to happen, and so, He would have thwarted His desire; for it is stated in Luke 22, 15: "With desire I have desired to eat this pasch with you." Hilary expounds this passage as follows: He commanded silence because it was not fitting that spiritual glory be made known except through spiritual visions; but they were not yet spiritual; "As yet the Spirit was not given" (Jn. 7, 39).

And his disciples asked him, etc. In this part, He answers the disciples' question. And firstly, their question is related; secondly, the response is related; and thirdly, the effect is related. The second part is where it is said, *But he answering*, etc.; the third part is where it is said, *Then the disciples understood*, etc. The Apostles, seeing Him transfigured, were supposing that from then on He would begin to reign. For they had understood that Elias was due to come first (Mal. 4). And since they had seen him, they thought that he had already come, and His kingdom was drawing near, as it is written: "Behold the day shall come," etc., (Mal. 4, 1). And: "Behold, I will send you Elias the prophet, before the coming of the great and dreadful day of the Lord," etc., (ibid. verse 5). But they did not know this passage from Scripture, because they were simple men, but from the sayings of the Scribes. Hence, they say, *Why then do the scribes say that Elias must come first?* The Scribes, who had known this from the Law, were speaking thus, but they were perverting Scripture. For there is a twofold coming of Christ, namely, a coming of glory; and, in reference to this coming, Elias will precede Him; but there is another coming in the flesh: hence, those perverting Scribes were expounding the passage only[23] of the latter coming.

---

23. The text does not contain the word "only," but it may be supplied from the following quotation from the *Catena Aurea*: "CHRYS; The Scribes did not explain the coming of Christ and of Elias, as they ought to have done. For the Scriptures speak of two comings of Christ; that which has taken place, and that which is yet to be. But the Scribes, blinding the people, spoke to them only of His second coming" (*Catena Aurea on St. Matthew*, chap. 17, lect. 3)

The Lord clears up this difficulty. And firstly, He mentions the future coming of Elias; secondly, He mentions his past coming; hence, the Evangelist says: *But he answering, said to them: Elias indeed shall come.* Hence, He speaks of a twofold Elias, because He speaks of Elias coming in his own proper person: and he shall come in this world to proclaim the way of justice, *and restore all things*, and he will convert men's hearts to Christ, he will convert the Jews to the faith of the Patriarchs who had faith in Christ, because, as it is written, "Blindness in part has happened in Israel, until the fullness of the Gentiles should come in, and so all Israel should be saved" (Rom. 11, 25). Augustine expounds this passage differently: *He shall restore all things*, because, when Antichrist has come, all men will be seduced; but, when Antichrist has died, all will be restored to the faith through the preaching of Elias. Origen expounds this passage as follows: *He shall restore*, because if someone does not pay back what he owes, he is obliged to restore it. Every man is a debtor unto death; and because Elias had not yet died, when he shall come, he shall restore all things, and pay his debt unto death. It is added concerning the other Elias, *But I say to you, that Elias is already come.* Who is this? John the Baptist, not because he is Elias in his person, as it is stated in John 1, 21, when it was asked of him, "Art thou Elias? And he said: I am not." But he is Elias in his spirit and power: because just as Elias will be the precursor of the second coming of Christ, so John was the precursor of the first coming. Likewise, just as Elias was speaking against Jezabel, so John was speaking against Herodias: and just as Elias was an inhabitant of the desert, so John was also. Hence, it is said of him: "He shall go before him in the spirit and power of Elias" (Lk. 1, 17). In spirit, not because the spirit of Elias could change into John, as some have asserted, but, instead, he will have the same power. *And they knew him not*, meaning that they did not approve of him, as it is stated below (chap. 21), where the Lord asked if John's baptism was from heaven or from earth, because if they had said that it was from heaven, they would have been obliged to believe him. *But have done unto him whatsoever they had a mind*, for they treated him badly, not according to what justice required, but instead they imprisoned him. Something similar is written concerning Jeremias: "For they treated him evil, who was consecrated a prophet from his mother's womb" (Eccli. 49, 9). *So also the Son of man shall suffer from them.* John was Christ's precursor in respect to his birth, because just as John was born of an old and sterile woman above nature, so Christ was born of a virgin above nature. Likewise, He was His precursor in his preaching, because he began to preach saying, "Do penance,"[24] and so did Christ also.[25] Likewise, he was His precursor in respect to his baptism: for that reason, it was required that he would be His precursor in respect to his passion, because just as he was killed on account of justice, so also was Christ. Hence, *So also the Son of man shall suffer from them.*

But from which 'them' will He suffer? It seems that it is not from those by whom John suffered, because John suffered from Herod, and Christ suffered from the Scribes. But it can be said that they suffered from the same men, because John suffered from Herod and the Jews were consenting, but Christ suffered from the Scribes, and Herod was consenting. Hence, He was subject to those parties and was given up to them; "The kings of the earth stood up, and the princes met together, against the Lord, and against his Christ" (Ps. 2, 2). Or, *So also he shall suffer from them*, so that the word *them* indicates a simple relation, because all are in one generation, from whom John and Christ suffered.

Afterwards, the effect of this reply is related where it is said, *Then the disciples understood, that he had spoken to them of John the Baptist*; then is when the Lord spoke to them. "The declaration of thy words giveth light: and giveth understanding to little ones" (Ps. 118, 130).

14. And when he was come to the multitude, there came to him a man falling down on his knees before him saying: Lord, have pity on my son, for he is a lunatic, and suffereth much: for he falleth often into the fire, and often into the water.

15. And I brought him to thy disciples, and they could not cure him.

16. Then Jesus answered and said: O unbelieving and perverse generation, how long shall I be with you? How long shall I suffer you? Bring him hither to me.

17. And Jesus rebuked him, and the devil went out of him, and the child was cured from that hour.

18. Then came the disciples to Jesus secretly, and said: Why could not we cast him out?

19. Jesus said to them: Because of your unbelief. For, amen I say to you, if you have faith as a grain of mustard seed, you shall say to this mountain: Remove from hence hither, and it shall remove: and nothing shall be impossible to you.

---

24. Above 3, 2.   25. ibid., 4, 17.

20. But this kind is not cast out but by prayer and fasting.
21. And when they abode together in Galilee, Jesus said to them: The Son of man shall be betrayed into the hands of men:
22. And they shall kill him, and the third day he shall rise again. And they were troubled exceedingly.
23. And when they were come to Capharnaum, they that received the didrachmas, came to Peter, and said to him: Doth not your master pay the didrachma?
24. He said: Yes. And when he was come into the house, Jesus prevented him, saying: What is thy opinion, Simon? The kings of the earth, of whom do they receive tribute or custom, of their own children, or of strangers?
25. And he said: Of strangers. Jesus said to him: Then the children are free.
26. But that we may not scandalize them, go to the sea, and cast in a hook: and that fish which shall first come up, take: and when thou hast opened it's mouth, thou shalt find a stater: take that, and give it to them for me and thee.

Here, He foretells the tranquility of glory, which is assaulted by diabolical possession and the disturbance of men. And firstly, He foretells that the first ceases through the curing of a lunatic; secondly, He foretells the second. About the first, the curing of a lunatic is firstly related; secondly, He foretells His Passion, where it is said, *And when they abode together in Galilee*, etc.; and thirdly, it is treated concerning the paying of tribute, where it is said, *And when they were come to Capharnaum*, etc. About the first, He begins by healing; secondly, He clears up a difficulty, where it is said, *Jesus said to them*, etc. About the first, the Evangelist does two things. Firstly, the request of the father is related; secondly, the fulfillment of the request is related, where it is said, *Bring him hither to me*. About the first, he does three things. For firstly, the time is related; secondly, the pointing out of the sick man is related; and thirdly, the request is related. The time is related when he says, *And when he was come to the multitude*. Peter, having been allured by the sweetness of glory, wanted to be always on the mountain; but Christ, out of the charity which He had for the multitudes, because "Charity seeketh not her own" (I Cor. 13, 5), wanted to come down from the mountain, so that the multitudes might have access to Him. Hence, when He had come to the multitude, *there came to him a man falling down on his knees*. If He had not come down, that man would not have come to Him. And he approached humbly, because he was falling on his knees and because "He hath had regard to the prayer of the humble" (Ps. 101, 18). By this man the human race can be signified. "That in the name of Jesus every knee should bow, of those that are in heaven, on earth, and under the earth" (Phil. 2, 10). Then the father's request is related. He does not request the cure of his son, but merely declares his sickness. Firstly, he declares the sickness; secondly, he declares the incidents; and thirdly, he declares that he was not finding a remedy. He says, therefore, **Lord, have pity on my son, for he is a lunatic.** It ought to be observed that many men make requests for themselves, as it was said above concerning the woman having an issue of blood:[26] sometimes someone makes a request for another, as it is here: but sometimes He cures someone unasked, such as in a spiritual sickness, as it is stated concerning the Publican in Luke 18:[27] but sometimes someone is cured as a result of the request of another, as it is stated in James 5: "Pray one for another, that you may be saved";[28] sometimes someone is cured without prayer, as in the conversion of Paul (Acts 9).

But what does it mean when it is said that he is a lunatic? A lunatic is properly he who is made insane according to the phases of the moon. But it seems that this man was not a lunatic, but a man possessed by the devil, because, below, it is stated that the devil went out from him.

It can be said that these are not the words of the Evangelist but of the deceived father, who thought that he was a lunatic. Or it is because, above in chapter 4,[29] it was stated that He cured lunatics, and these were men possessed by the devil. Some say, such as some doctors, that they were not made insane by the devil, but from an evil temperament, or from the disposition of the body, and this is because when the moon is waxing everything wet enlarges. So, since the human brain is very wet, when the moon is eclipsed, the brain itself also shrinks: and so such men suffer shrinkage of the brain when the moon wanes. But this is opposed to the faith, because Scripture expressly calls them possessed: and this is evident that they are speaking out of arrogance, because many ignorant men suffer in this way and, nevertheless, they quote the Scriptures. For that reason, it must be said that proud spirits strive in many ways to ensnare men, and they wish to defame

---

26. Above 9, 20.
27. "And the publican... went down into his house justified" (verses 13-14). Might this reference more correctly refer to Zacheus in Luke 19?
28. Verse 16.

29. "They presented to him all sick people that were taken with divers diseases and torments, and such as were possessed by devils, and lunatics, and those that had the palsy, and he cured them" (verse 24).

them: for that reason, some demons bring about sicknesses and vexations according to the influences of the stars which they see to be suitable for this purpose, so that they may induce men into error, so that they might believe that, only due to the influence of the stars, it happens to them that they suffer much.

And suffereth much. Here the incidents are related. In any sickness there are various conditions; for some men have a higher fever, others have a lower fever, so also this man was grievously molested. *For he falleth often into the fire, and often into the water*; for that reason, he was in great danger. Hence, it ought to be observed that the Lord does not withdraw His hand in dangers. Wherefore, the man might have already been dead, if the Lord had not extended His hand, as it is read concerning Job (Chap. 1): although Satan was able to torment him much, nevertheless, the Lord commanded him not to lay hands upon his life. By this man, erratic reasoning is signified, concerning which it is said: "A fool is changed as the moon" (Eccli. 27, 12). *And he falleth often into the fire*, namely, the fire of anger; "A fire is kindled in my wrath, and shall burn even to the lowest hell" (Deut. 32, 22). *Often into the water*, namely, of concupiscence. "Thou art poured out as water, grow thou not" (Gen. 49, 4).[30] *I brought him to thy disciples, and they could not cure him.* Here the wickedness of this man is mentioned, because he wanted to accuse the disciples; hence: "On the elect he will lay a blot" (Eccli. 11, 33). Hence, the Lord rebukes him: *Jesus answered and said: O unbelieving and perverse generation.* Hence, His answer is related: and He does two things. Firstly, He rebukes the fault; and secondly, He shows an act of kindness. He says, therefore, *Jesus answered*, etc. This man wanted to defame the disciples to the multitudes, and even Jesus, that He did not have this power, and many were consenting in this matter; for that reason, Christ inveighs against the whole generation, and accuses them of unbelief, saying, *O unbelieving generation*, because this was not on account of an inability of the disciples, but on account of their unbelief. Likewise, He accuses them of perversity, *And perverse*, because they were laying their guilt on the Apostles; "They are a wicked and perverse generation. Is this the return thou makest to the Lord, O foolish and senseless people?" (Deut. 32, 5). *How long shall I be with you?* And Christ points out two things. Firstly, He points out their impenitence; and secondly, He points

---

30. Ruben, the eldest son of Jacob, forfeited his title to a double portion of inheritance by his sin of concupiscence; and so he was "poured out as water," that is, spilt and lost.

out the divine patience, because the association of the just with the unjust is not fitting; "If the wolf shall have fellowship with the lamb, so the sinner with the just" (Eccli. 13, 21); "What concord hath Christ with Belial?" (I Cor. 6, 15). Hence, He wishes to say: 'You have My fellowship, and nevertheless, you do not cease to detract Me and My disciples.' And, as Jerome says, the Lord does not say this as one who has been angered, but He speaks after the manner of a doctor, who comes to a sick man who does not want to follow his instructions, and who says: 'How long shall I visit you, who are not willing to follow my instructions?' For that reason, He gives an example to prelates, that although men are opposed to them, nevertheless, they may confer acts of kindness, just as He did, who cured the son of this man who was detracting Himself and His disciples. Hence, He says, **Bring him hither to me**. And firstly, His manner of curing is related; and secondly, the effect is related. Firstly, the performer of the cure is related, namely, Christ; hence, He says: **Bring him hither to me**. Men sin in many ways. Some sin through ignorance, some through weakness, and some through malice. Those who sin through ignorance, can be instructed by a man; those who sin through weakness, namely, he who sins by incontinence, who regrets his sin, and is led away by his passions, this man cannot be healed by anyone, but it is necessary to he be brought to Jesus, who heals all our weaknesses. And this is His manner of curing, for **He rebuked him**, because this happened to him by his own fault; "Thou art ensnared with the words of thy mouth, and caught with thy own words" (Prov. 6, 2). Or, **He rebuked him**, namely, the devil. The effect follows, **And the devil went out of him, and the child was cured from that hour**, because "He spoke, and they were made" (Ps. 148, 5).

Then came the disciples to Jesus secretly, etc. Above, the Lord cured the lunatic; here, He answers the disciples' question. And firstly, the question is set forth; and secondly, the answer is set forth, where it is said, **Jesus said to them**, etc. In order that you may understand the question, you ought to know that above (chap. 10) the Lord had given them the power of casting out devils; hence, they were wondering if they had lost that gift through their own fault; for that reason, they **came to Jesus**, etc. But why did they come secretly? It was not on account of shame, but because they were expecting to hear a great secret, and secret things ought not to be said to everyone; "To you it is given to know the mysteries of the kingdom of heaven: but to them it is not given" (above 13, 11). **Jesus said to them**. Here, He responds. And firstly, He answers their question; and secondly, He puts forward a general teaching, where it is said, *But this kind is not cast out but by prayer and fasting.* About the former, He firstly responds to the question, and secondly, He explains His answer, where it is said, *For, amen I say to you,* etc. They had asked, *Why could not we cast him out?* The Lord answers, *Because of your unbelief.* At which point it ought to be considered that this was before they had received the Holy Ghost in that great fullness with which they were all filled with the Holy Ghost; hence, the Lord rebuked them in Luke 24, 25: "O foolish and slow of heart to believe!" Nor is it surprising, because while the Lord was on the mountain, those who were foremost in the faith, namely, Peter, James and John, were absent: for weakness of faith is the cause of not performing miracles, for the working of miracles is derived from God's omnipotence, because faith relies upon God's omnipotence: hence, where there is weakness of faith, there is the failure of miracles. Hence, it is stated above (chap. 13) that he wrought only a few miracles in His own country because of their unbelief. Sometimes miracles occur on account of the need of the one asking, as it is stated above (chap. 15) concerning the woman of Canaan;[31] sometimes they occur to show the holiness of some saint: and this is stated in IV Kings 13, where it is said that when the rovers from Moab[32] had come into the land of Israel, they cast the body of a dead man near the body of Eliseus, and the man came back to life, not because the dead man deserved this, but rather it was to show the sanctity of Eliseus.

For, amen I say to you, if you have faith as a grain of mustard seed, etc. Here He explains His answer. And a sort of conditional proposition is set forth, the antecedent of which is, *If you have faith,* etc., the consequent is, *You shall say to this mountain: Remove from hence hither.* Some say that the faith which is compared to a grain of mustard seed is a little faith; it is as though He were to say: 'If you have some faith, you shall say,' etc. But Jerome disproves this, because the Apostle says: "If I should have all faith, so that I could remove mountains" (I Cor. 13, 2). Hence, perfect faith is required for the removal of mountains. By the fact that He says, *As a grain of mustard seed,* a threefold perfection of faith is indicated. For we find in a grain of mustard seed spiciness, fruitfulness, and littleness. Before a

---

[31]. "And behold a woman of Canaan who came out of those coasts, crying out, said to him: Have mercy on me, O Lord, thou son of David: my daughter is grievously troubled by a devil" (verse 22).

[32]. The text mistakenly reads "from Syria" but IV Kings 13, 20 says that they were from Moab.

grain of mustard seed is ground into powder, it seems to have no spiciness; when it is ground into powder it begins to be spicy: so a believer, before he is tried, seems despicable; but when he is worn down, then his holiness appears. "If now you must be for a little time made sorrowful in divers temptations: that the trial of your faith, much more precious than gold which is tried by the fire," (I Pet. 1, 6-7). Likewise, we find in a grain of mustard seed fruitfulness (above 13), because although it is small, it grows into a great tree, so that the birds of the air dwell there. This is said in Hebrews 11, where deeds of faith are told, and it continues: "The saints by faith conquered kingdoms," etc., (verse 33). Likewise, we find in a grain of mustard seed littleness, and the humility of faith can be designated by this. For then it is known who is humble in faith, when he consents to the words of God; "If any man consent not to the words of God, He is proud" (I Tim. 6, 4). So, on the contrary, he who consents to words of God is humble. Therefore, He wishes to say: *If you have faith*, and if you have a faith fervent, unfailing, fruitful in works, and if it be a small and humble faith, *you shall say to this mountain: Remove from hence, and it shall remove.*

Here there is a question, which unbelievers ponder. It is not found that the Apostles ever did this. Chrysostom replies: "And if it is not found to have been done by the Apostles, nevertheless, it is found to have been done by apostolic men." For it is read in the *Book of Dialogues of Blessed Gregory*, that when a certain man wanted to construct a church, not having a space to build, he commanded a mountain to make way for him, and it made way.[33] Or perhaps they did so, but it was not written. Or it can be said that if they did not do this, it was not on account of an impossibility, but because an opportunity did not present itself. Hence, miracles were sometimes performed for a need, and sometimes for utility: and because it was not necessary, for that reason, they

---

33. The miracle of the removal of a mountain was actually performed by S. Gregory Thaumaturgus, Bishop of NeoCaesarea (d. circa 270-275), as the Venerable Bede tells us in his Commentary upon St. Mark 11 (*Homil. Ad Matut.*): "This also could happen, that a mountain taken from the land be cast into the sea, if there were a need for it to happen. That such an event actually did happened we read by the prayers of the blessed Father Gregory of NeoCaesarea Bishop of Pontus, a man of exceptional mind and virtues, that a mountain made enough room as the inhabitants of a city needed. For when he wanted to build a church in a suitable place, they saw that it was narrower than the work required, in that they were constricted on one side by the seashore and on the other by a nearby mountain; he come by night to the place, and kneeling down he reminded the Lord of His promise, so that He would put the mountain farther away according to his faith. And when he returned in the morning he found that the mountain had left behind as much space as the builders of the church had needed."

did not perform this miracle. Or, the mountain represents the devil. *Remove from hence hither*, that is, from this body, *and it shall remove*. Or, according to Augustine, these words are to be applied to the spirit of pride.

And nothing shall be impossible to you. And what is this? Will they be omnipotent? No, because He alone is truly omnipotent, who by His own power is able to do all things; these men, however, act not by their own power, but just as a king commands differently than his servant commands, because a king commands in his own name, and the servant commands in the name of the king. *But this kind of devil* (the word *this* does not indicate the genus of lunatic, but every kind of devil) *is not cast out but by prayer and fasting*. Chrysostom says that inasmuch as the soul is more elevated, to that degree is it more of a terror to the devils; for Christ Himself was a terror to the devils: hence, they who are joined to Christ are a terror to them. Now, the lifting of the mind is impeded through heaviness of the flesh, it is impeded by surfeiting and drunkenness; hence, it is said: "Take heed to yourselves, lest perhaps your hearts be overcharged with surfeiting and drunkenness," etc., (Lk. 21, 34). Hence, one cannot have one's mind lifted up to God, who is made heavy with drunkenness; for that reason, fasting is required for the mind to be lifted up; hence, in Tobias it is said: "Prayer is good with fasting" (12, 8). Likewise: "I Daniel gave my heart to pray with fasting." For that reason, as Origen says, so that a spirit be expelled, one must not give oneself to feasting, but to prayers and fasting. Or, by the lunatic, the instability of the flesh is signified: or he who is led by various desires is signified. *Who falleth often into the fire and the water*, such are not cured except with fasting and prayer. "The flesh lusteth against the spirit: and the spirit against the flesh" (Gal. 5, 17). Therefore, it is necessary that the disciples be enfeebled in respect to the flesh, and strengthened in respect to the spirit. But the spirit is strengthened by prayer, because prayer is an elevation of the soul to God; the flesh, however, is enfeebled by fasting. Or because the spirit does not cease to war against the flesh, for that reason, in order that such a fight may cease, good actions are required, which are signified by prayer: and abstinence from evil is required, which is signified by fasting.

And when they abode together in Galilee, etc. Above, the tranquility of glory was figured by the deliverance of the lunatic from the power of the devils; this deliverance is accomplished through Christ's death; "That, through death, he might destroy him who had the empire of death, that is to say, the devil: and might deliver them, who through the fear of death were all their lifetime subject to servitude" (Heb. 2, 14). For that reason, the Evangelist immediately adds about the foretelling of the Passion. And firstly, the foretelling is related; and secondly, the effect is related, where it is said, *And they were troubled exceedingly.* Our Lord had foretold this before (chap. 16), and also now foretells it, and will again foretell it hereafter.[34] And why does He foretell it so many times? It is because things that are foreseen disturb less; for that reason, because it would come to be that the disciples might be scandalized at the Lord's death, He wished to foretell this often, so that they might be less scandalized. But He always adds something. Before He made mention of His death, but not of His betrayal; here, however, He makes mention of the betrayal, saying, *The Son of man shall be betrayed*. And He rightly says, *Son of man*, because even if He who is betrayed is the Lord of glory, nevertheless, He is betrayed insofar as He is the Son of man. Hence, Augustine says: "Although some things are said of the Son of God, and some things are said of the Son of man, nevertheless, a distinction is made, because weak things are said of His human nature, and firm things are said of His divine nature." But He does not say by whom He was delivered up, because He delivered up Himself; "Who delivered himself for me" (Gal. 2, 20). He was delivered up by His Father, "who spared not even his own Son, but delivered him up for us all" (Rom. 8, 32). Likewise, He was delivered up by Judas; "Who also betrayed him" (above 10, 4). Moreover, He was delivered up by the demons; in John 13 it is stated that the devil put into the heart of Judas to betray Him.[35] And in Wisdom 2, 12, it is said: "Come, let us kill the just one".[36] *And the third day he shall rise again*. "He will revive us after two days: on the third day he will raise us up, and we shall live in his sight" (Osee 6, 3). The effect follows, *And they were troubled*.[37] They were considering His death and Resurrection, but they did not see their utility. "Because I have spoken these things to you, sorrow hath filled your heart" (Jn. 16, 6).

And when they were come to Capharnaum. After the tranquility of glory was finished, he relates the paying of tribute; "The tribute hath ceased" (Is. 14, 4); "The servant is free from his master" (Job 3, 19). Hence, he does three things. Firstly, he relates the exaction of tribute; secondly, he relates the liberty of

---

34. Chap. 20, verse 18.
35. Verse 2.
36. This quotation is not literal but according to the sense of the passage.

Similar wording is found in Genesis 37, 20.
37. *Contristati sunt.* This can also be translated, "They were saddened."

the sons; and thirdly, he relates the payment of the tribute. He says, *And when he was come into the house, Jesus prevented him*, etc. Two denarii are called a didrachma. Hence, every Jew was obliged to pay two denarii.

But wherefore was that tribute? Some say that it was from the Law (Ex. 13).[38] It is, namely, that because the Lord had killed all the firstborns of Egypt, therefore, He decreed that the firstborn sons would be redeemed. Afterwards, He prescribed that the Levites be designated for God's service. And later He commanded that the Levites be numbered. And more firstborn sons were found than Levites. Then He prescribed that a price be paid for their redemption.[39] Jerome says that it is not from the Law of God, but of the emperor, and Judea was recently made tributary of the Romans, so that each person paid custom. And this seems more correct, because below it is said: *The kings of the earth, of whom do they receive tribute?* For that reason, He speaks of imperial tribute.

But why were they asked to pay tribute in Capharnaum? It is because tribute was received from everyone in his own city, but Capharnaum was the principal city of Galilee.

But because they held Christ in reverence, for that reason, they did not approach to Him, but to Peter; and they did not ask him except with kindness, *Doth not your master pay the didrachma?* Then Peter's response it related, *He said: Yes*; that is, it is true that He does not pay it. Chrysostom says that lest he be disquieted, he said, *Yes*, He pays it. Christ's question follows, and then Peter's reply. In His question two things are to be considered, namely, that Christ was not afraid of his warning, even though He had such dignity, that He was bound to be somewhat indignant; and some men as so disposed, that when they see a weakness in a great man, they are immediately scandalized. Therefore, lest they be scandalized, for that reason, *He prevented*, and, for that reason, He combined with His weakness something great, namely, that being absent He knew what was said to Peter. "All things are naked and open to his eyes" (Heb. 4, 13). Likewise, it ought to be noted that He commits the judgment to Peter, because He was more frequently speaking to him, saying: *What is thy opin-*

---

38. "And every firstborn of men thou shalt redeem with a price" (Ex. 13, 13).
39. Payment was required for the number of firstborn sons that exceeded the number of Levites. "CHRYS; For when God slew the firstborn of Egypt, He then accepted the tribe of Levi for them. But because the numbers of this tribe were less than the number of firstborn among the Jews, it was ordained that redemption money should be paid for the number that came short; and thence sprang the custom of paying this tax" (*Catena Aurea on St. Matthew*, chap. 17, lect. 7).

ion, Simon? "Doth not the ear discern words" (Job 12, 11) *The kings of the earth, of whom do they receive tribute or custom?* There is a difference between tribute and custom: for tribute is given for fields and vineyards; custom is given per head.[40] Hence, a man who is subject ought to give something as a sign of his subjection; and this is called custom. He wishes to argue from this that since the children of kings do not pay tribute, that He is not obliged to pay tribute: for He is the King of kings, through whom all kings reign. Likewise, according to the flesh, He was of royal seed. "Who was made to him of the seed of David, according to the flesh" (Rom. 1, 3). Chrysostom says that from this we can perceive that He is the natural Son of God, because before it is said who is the natural Son of God.[41] *And he said: Of strangers.* Then Christ's response is related, namely, that kings exempt their children. "Why do you consume my people, and grind the faces of the poor?" (Is. 3, 15). For it seems just. For he who presides, ought to have care of his subjects; for that reason, his subjects ought to serve him just as the members serve the body: for as the members of the body serve the whole body from what is their own, so every subject ought to serve his community from his own goods. For that reason, the Lord concludes, *Then the children are free.* Origen says: "This may be understood in one way as follows. 'Then the children of the kings of the earth are free,' but the children of God are free before God."

But what does this have to do with the point at hand? Either He is speaking according to the flesh concerning the sons of kings, and, in this way, He was not a son according to the flesh; or if He is speaking according to the spirit, then all Christians will be free. But this is contrary to the Apostle, "Render to all men their dues. Tribute, to whom tribute is due" (Rom. 13, 2).

I say that this passage was true for Him, who was, by nature, the Son of God. For He was truly free. But His children, according to the spirit, have freedom in that way by which they have sonship; through their likeness to Christ, who "is the Firstborn amongst many brethren" (Rom. 8, 29). Insofar as they are conformed to the Firstborn they are free. "Who will reform the body of our lowness, made like to the body of his glory" (Phil. 3, 2).

But that we may not scandalize them, etc. It is true that the Lord is free, but because He took the form of a servant, as is stated in Philippians 2, for that reason, He did not refuse to pay, and in this He gave an example of humility.

---

40. i.e. headmoney.   41. Matthew 16, 16.

And in this payment, three things to be praised and admired are observed. Firstly, His gentleness ought to be praised and admired, wherefore He is meek, according to what He Himself testified above: "Learn of me, because I am meek, and humble of heart" (11, 29). He is properly called meek, who wishes to offend no one; "Be without offence to the Jew, and to the Gentiles and to the church of God" (I Cor. 10, 32).

But, on the contrary, it is objected: Above it is stated that the disciples said: "Dost thou know that the Pharisees, when they heard this word, were scandalized?" (15, 12). And the Lord said: "Let them alone: they are blind, and leaders of the blind." He did not then care about scandal, but here He cares about it. Hence, it ought to be said that scandal sometimes arises from the truth; and then one ought not to be concerned: sometimes it arises from weakness and ignorance; and one must be concerned about this type of scandal. But if He had not paid, their scandal would have been due to their ignorance, because they did not know that He is God.

Likewise, Christ's poverty ought to be admired, because He was so poor that He did not have wherewithal to pay; "Who being rich became poor for your sakes: that through his poverty you might be rich" (II Cor. 8, 9).

Someone can object: Did He not have a purse? It is true, but everything in the purse had been given for the use the poor. He considered it to be robbery to spend what was for the use of the poor on other uses. Chrysostom says that He paid, so that when He pays tribute, on one hand, He shows His power, and, on the other hand, He shows a mystery.

Go to the sea, and cast in a hook: and that fish which shall first come up, take: and when thou hast opened its mouth, thou shalt find a stater. On that stater was Caesar's image: and he signifies the devil who had nothing in Him; "For the prince of this world: cometh: and in me he hath not anything" (Jn. 14, 30). And so, because He had nothing of His own, for that reason, He did not wish to pay out of His own possessions.[42]

Likewise, His providence ought to be admired; for that reason, Jerome[43] says that we ought to be amazed how He could know that a fish would immediately come to him that had a stater in its mouth. If, however, it was not so, but He created the fish

---

[42]. "GLOSS; Or because Jesus had not any image of Caesar, (for the prince of this world had nothing in Him,) therefore, He furnished an image of Caesar, not out of their own stock, but out of the sea. But He takes not the coin into His own possession, that there should never be found an image of Caesar upon the Image of the invisible God" (*Catena Aurea on St. Matthew*, chap. 17, lect. 7).

[43]. ibid.

anew, it is to be admired; but if He led it to the hook, it was an act of great providence. By this fish that first came to the hook, the first martyr, St. Stephen, is understood, who had a stater in his mouth which was worth a didrachma, and it is twofold; and it signifies Stephen himself, who saw His divinity itself and His humanity. Or it can be understood of Adam.[44] Likewise, observe that if someone often speaks of riches and of money, he has a stater in his mouth; hence, he who converts such a man, takes a fish who has a stater in his mouth. Likewise, the fish signifies humility: hence, **Take that, and give it to them for me and thee.** And by the fact that tribute was paid for Peter and for Himself, it is signified that by Christ's Passion, He acquired the glory of His Resurrection for Himself; "For which cause, God also hath exalted him" (Phil. 2, 9). Peter and other men were redeemed from their punishment and guilt. Or it is otherwise, namely, that He suffered for Himself, so that He might acquire the glory of His Resurrection; He suffered for the people, so that He might wash them from their sins. For He Himself "washed us from our sins in his own blood" (Apoc. 1, 5).

---

44. "JEROME; That fish which was first taken is the first Adam, who is set free by the second Adam; and that which is found in his mouth, that is, in his confession, is given for Peter and for the Lord" (*Catena Aurea on St. Matthew*, chap. 17, lect. 7).

CHAPTER EIGHTEEN

1. At that hour the disciples came to Jesus, saying: Who, thinkest thou, is the greater in the kingdom of heaven?
2. And Jesus, calling unto him a little child, set him in the midst of them.
3. And said: amen I say to you, unless you be converted, and become as little children, you shall not enter into the kingdom of heaven.
4. Whosoever therefore shall humble himself as this little child, he is the greater in the kingdom of heaven.
5. And he that shall receive one such little child in my name, receiveth me.
6. But he that shall scandalize one of these little ones that believe in me, it were better for him that a millstone should be hanged about his neck, and that he should be drowned in the depth of the sea.
7. Woe to the world because of scandals. For it must needs be that scandals come: but nevertheless woe to that man by whom the scandal cometh.
8. And if thy hand, or thy foot, scandalize thee, cut it off, and cast it from thee. It is better for thee to go into life maimed or lame, than having two hands or two feet, to be cast into everlasting fire.
9. And if thy eye scandalize thee, pluck it out, and cast it from thee. It is better for thee having one eye to enter into life, than having two eyes to be cast into hell fire.
10. See that you despise not one of these little ones: for I say to you, that their angels in heaven always see the face of my Father who is in heaven.
11. For the Son of man is come to save that which was lost.

Above, the Lord showed the glory to come in His transfiguration, here He treats of the route for attaining that glory. And it is divided into two parts: for firstly, He teaches what one must do to attain to it; and secondly, certain men inordinately seeking excellence in glory are reprehended, which begins in chapter 20. About the former, He firstly teaches how to attain it by the common way; and secondly, He teaches how to attain it by the way of perfection, which begins in chapter 19. Firstly, since one attains to glory through humility, He, therefore, firstly shows the manner of practicing humility; secondly, He forbids giving scandal, where it is said, *But he that shall scandalize one of these little ones*, etc.; and thirdly, He teaches that what has caused scandal ought to be discarded, where it is said, *And if thy hand, or thy foot, scandalize thee, cut it off, and cast it from thee.* About the first, a question of the disciples is related; secondly, Christ's reply is related. An occasion for the question is taken from the fact that He told Peter to go to the sea and pay the stater which he found in the fish for Himself and for Peter; hence, He seemed to have preferred him to the others. And because they were still weak, they consequently felt some jealousy and movement of envy. But see that when He brought the three alone into the mountain they were not so moved, as they are here when He prefers just one of them. Hence, they were asking, *Who, thinkest thou, is the greater in the kingdom of heaven?* Although, one does not attain this through greatness, but through the spirit of humility; "In humility, let each esteem others better than themselves," etc., (Phil. 2, 3).[1] In this request, there is this to be imitated; that they be not desirous of earthly things, but of heavenly things; "While we look not at the things which are seen, but at the things which are not seen," etc., (II Cor. 4, 18).

But what it this? Is not excellence in the kingdom of heaven to be sought? It ought to be said that to have eminence in the kingdom of heaven is twofold. Either it is sought such that we consider ourselves worthy; and this is pride and contrary to the Apostle saying: "In humility, let each esteem others better than themselves," etc., (Phil. 2, 3). But to desire greater grace, so that there will be more glory for us, is not evil, as it is said: "Be zealous for the better gifts" (I Cor. 12, 31). Likewise, the Apostles knew that in glory there are diverse mansions,[2] just as one star differs from another in brightness; for that reason, they were seeking eminence, because they believed that one thing is greater than another in glory, against certain heretics who affirmed the contrary.

Afterwards, Christ's response is related; and he relates Christ's action and words; hence, he says, *And calling unto him a little child.* Who this child is, is expounded in three ways. Chrysostom expounds him to truly be a child, because he was

---

[1] "Esteem others better than themselves." Saint Thomas (22, q. 162, a. 3) puts the question, how an innocent man can with truth think himself worse than the most wicked of men? He answers, that a man who has received very extraordinary gifts from God, cannot think these gifts less than what any other has received; but he may reflect that he has nothing, and is nothing of himself. And a man truly humble considers only his own sins and failings, and is persuaded that any other person would have made better use of the same graces; which agrees with what follows, (v. 4) in considering the things that are his own. "Each one not considering the things that are his own, but those that are other men's."

[2] "In my Father's house there are many mansions" (Jn. 14, 2).

free from passions, and would furnish an example of humility, as it is said below: "Suffer the little children to come to me" (19, 14). And it is said that this was blessed Martial.[3] It is expounded otherwise, that Christ, considering Himself to be a child, stood in their midst saying, *Unless you be converted, and become as little children, you shall not enter into the kingdom of heaven.* "I am in the midst of you, as he that serveth" (Lk. 22, 27). It is expounded otherwise, that, by the child, the Holy Ghost is understood, because He is the Spirit of humility; "I will put my spirit in the midst of you" (Ez. 36, 27). Likewise, the Lord's words ought to be noted. And firstly, He mentions the necessity of becoming as children; and secondly, He mentions its efficacy. He says, *Amen I say to you, unless you be converted*, namely, by becoming free from this vainglory; "Turn ye to me," etc., (Zach. 1, 3). *And become as this little child*, not in age, but in simplicity; "Do not become children in sense, but in malice be children" (I Cor. 14, 20). The qualities of children are many. They do not desire great things; "Not minding high things" (Rom. 12, 16). They are free from concupiscence; "Whosoever shall look on a woman to lust after her, hath already committed adultery with her in his heart" (above 5, 28). And children do not have this kind of concupiscence. Likewise, they do not hold grudges; hence, *Unless you become as this little child*, namely, unless you become imitators of the qualities of children, *you shall not enter into the kingdom of heaven*. For no one except the humble will enter heaven; "Glory shall uphold the humble of spirit" (Prov. 29, 23). Or, *you shall not enter into the kingdom of heaven*, meaning into the Gospel teaching, as it was said above: "The kingdom of God shall be taken from you and shall be given to a nation yielding the fruits thereof" (21, 43). Entrance into the Gospel teaching is through faith; hence, *unless you become*, and if you will not have believed, *as little children, you shall not enter into the kingdom of heaven*; "He that believeth not shall he condemned" (Mk. 16, 16). "Glory shall uphold the humble of spirit" (Prov. 29, 23). *And he that shall receive one such little child*, that is to say, whosoever is an imitator of childlike innocence, he is greater, because the more humble he is, so much the higher he will be: because "He that humbleth himself shall be exalted" (Lk. 18, 14).

---

3. This probably is taken from the *Life of St. Martial*, attributed to Bishop Aurelian, his successor, in reality, the work of an eleventh century forger who developed a legendary account of his life ("St. Martial," *The Catholic Encyclopedia*).

But there can be a question: for it seems that this is not true, because perfection consists in charity; therefore, where there is greater charity, there is greater perfection.

It ought to be said that humility necessarily accompanies charity. And you can see this if you would consider anyone who is humble. For as in pride there are two things, an inordinate affection and an inordinate opinion of oneself: such is the contrary in humility, because it does not care about its own superiority. Likewise, it does not consider itself worthy. This necessarily leads to charity. Every man desires an excellence that he loves. Therefore, the more humility a man has, so much the more does he love God, and the more he despises his own excellence, the less he attributes to himself: and so the more charity a man has, the more humility he has.

And he that shall receive one such little child in my name, receiveth me. Owing to the fact that they are children, to that extent they are worthy, and so they must not to be scandalized; hence, **And he that shall scandalize**, etc. And firstly, He shows that they ought not to be scandalized on account of the punishment; and secondly, they ought not to be scandalized on account of Divine Providence. The second part is where it is said, **See that you despise not one of these little ones.** Firstly, He says that scandal must not be given to little ones; and secondly, He says that scandal must not be avoided negligently, where it is said, **And if thy hand**, etc. And firstly, He relates the punishment in particular; and secondly, He relates the punishment in general, where it is said, **Woe to the world because of scandals**, etc. It ought to be seen that there is a twofold punishment, namely, a pain of loss and a pain of sense. He mentions both, **he that shall receive one such little child**, not for his sake but for My sake, **receiveth me**. He continues, **But he that shall scandalize one of these little ones**, etc.

If there be this kind of a person, it is evident that there be elders.[4] And how shall an elder be scandalized? For the perfect are not scandalized. Chrysostom says that to scandalize is the same thing as to inflict an injury, and this can be inflicted upon the perfect and the imperfect. Origen says that some men have become little, others are in the process of becoming little: those who have become little are they who have attained perfection, and these cannot be scandalized: those who are in the process

---

[4]. "Jerome, in commenting on Matthew 18:6, 'He that shall scandalize one of these little ones,' says: 'Observe that it is the little one that is scandalized, for the elders do not take scandal'" (II II, q. 43, a. 5 sed contra).

of becoming little, because they are imperfect, can be scandalized, as they are men who have recently converted. Jerome says that even though they are not scandalized, nevertheless, someone can scandalize them, because scandal is active and passive. The Lord seems to be referring to all the Apostles, but He is especially referring to Judas, as it is said below: "All you shall be scandalized," etc., (26, 31).

And what is this punishment? *It were better for him that a millstone should be hanged about his neck.* Once again, as Jerome says, the Lord is speaking according to the manner of the inhabitants of Palestine, who did not have mills powered by water, but, instead, had mills powered by horses. Hence, a millstone (*mola* a*sinaria*) is so called which a horse or an ass (*asinus*) can draw. *And that he should be drowned in the depth of the sea.* And this punishment was inflicted upon those who committed theft: because a millstone of this same type was hung about his neck, and he was cast into the sea; this was also done to blessed Clement, even though he was not a thief, etc. Hence, one who scandalizes a little one deserves an eternal punishment. Hence, it is better to undergo in the present life whatever kind of temporal punishment than to undergo eternal punishment; "It is a fearful thing to fall into the hands of the living God" (Heb. 10, 31); "It is better for me to fall into your hands without doing it, than to sin in the sight of the Lord" (Dan. 13, 23).

This passage can be otherwise expounded mystically; and this is done in three ways. In one way, by the millstone, the blindness of the Gentiles is understood, because the animals that are employed to draw this millstone are blind: in Judges 16 it is written that they pulled out the eyes of Samson, and made him grind. Hence, it would have been better for the Jews, to have never seen Christ, and to have been cast into the depths of the sea, meaning into the depths of infidelity.[5] Hence, it is said: "For it had been better for them not to have known the way of justice than, after they have known it, to turn back" (II Pet. 2, 21). Otherwise, by the millstone, the active life is understood. And it happens that someone passes on to the contemplative life, and when he is there, he makes contemplation

---

5. "HILARY; Mystically; The work of the mill is a toil of blindness, for the beasts having their eyes closed are driven round in a circle, and under the type of an ass we often find the Gentiles figured, who are held in the ignorance of blind labor; while the Jews have the path of knowledge set before them in the Law, who if they offend Christ's Apostles it were better for them, that having their necks made fast to a mill-stone, they should be drowned in the sea, that is, kept under labor and in the depths of ignorance, as the Gentiles; for it were better for them that they should have never known Christ, than not to have received the Lord of the Prophets" (*Catena Aurea on St. Matthew*, chap. 18, lect. 1).

a stumbling block, because it does not agree with him; therefore, it is better for him, *that a millstone should be hanged about his neck, and that he should be drowned in the depth of the sea,* that is to say, into the depths of temporal affairs.[6] Augustine expresses himself thus: *It were better,* that is to say, it is fitting, and it is a fitting punishment for him, *that a millstone,* that is, the desire for worldly things, because he who scandalizes is overly desirous, *should be hanged about his neck,* that is, in his affections, *and that he should be drowned in the depth of the sea,* namely, of inordinate desires.

Woe to the world because of scandals. Having set forth the punishment in particular, here it is set forth in general. And He does three things. Firstly, He foretells the punishment in general; secondly, He adds the necessity of the punishment; and thirdly, He removes all excuses, because to those who scandalize, it is better that a millstone be hung about their neck, etc. *Woe to the world because of scandals.* By the world, the lovers of the world are understood, because the more someone is attached to the world, so much the more does he suffer scandal; hence, the Lord says: "In me you may have peace, in the world you shall have distress" (Jn. 16, 33). *Woe to the world* and to lovers of the world. *For it must needs be that scandals come.* Certain heretics upheld that there was an absolute necessity that sins would occur, and this necessity could be drawn from the divine foreknowledge and from the nature of the stars. But this is false, because sin would be imputed to God, Who is the Author of nature. Chrysostom says that it is necessary that it so happen, in that the necessity of Divine Providence is a conditional necessity. Hence, it is necessary that if He foresees this man is going to sin, he will sin, but it does not follow that he will necessarily sin. Origin says that necessity presupposes the malice of the demons and the weakness of men; hence, *it must needs be that scandals come,* because it is necessary that the devil deceive men, and man give in to him, and thus, based on the supposition of the devil's malice and men's weakness, this necessity occurs. Others expound this passage as follows: *it must needs be,* that is, it is useful because by scandals men are proved; "For there must be also heresies: that they also, who are approved may be made manifest among you" (I Cor. 11, 19). Or, according

---

6. "He that is prone to yield to his passions on account of his impulse to action is simply more apt for the active life by reason of his restless spirit. Hence, Gregory says (*Moralium* vi,37) that 'there be some so restless that when they are free from labor they labor all the more, because the more leisure they have for thought, the worse interior turmoil they have to bear'" (I II, q. 182, a. 4 ad 3um).

to Haymo,[7] He is speaking about the scandal of the Cross; "We preach Christ crucified: unto the Jews indeed a stumblingblock, and unto the Gentiles foolishness" (I Cor. 1, 23).

But it is objected: If it be necessary that scandals come, therefore, those who scandalize are free from sin, since it is thus necessary that scandals come. I do not say that this is necessary by an absolute necessity; because He says, *woe to that man by whom the scandal cometh.* Hence, although demons instigate scandals, nevertheless, it is counted to them for punishment; "Neither yield ye your members as instruments of iniquity unto sin" (Rom. 6, 13). This is particularly said of Judas, who betrayed Him. You say, *woe to that man by whom the scandal cometh;* hence, scandal must not be given to little ones. And although it ought not to be given, nevertheless, they ought not to be negligent in avoiding scandal; nay, a man can avoid scandal by doing something useful in regard to his actions, or knowledge,[8] or support.

Hence, he puts this point forth under the similitude of the members of the body, *And if thy hand, or thy foot, scandalize thee, cut it off, and cast it from thee.* Nevertheless, you should not gather that the members of the body ought to be cut off, but by the members are understood one's friends and neighbors. For fellow men are necessary for a man's work, support, and instruction. The member that corrects the performance of our duties, is the hand: the one that which supports, is the foot; hence: "I was an eye to the blind, and a foot to the lame" (Job 19, 15). Hence, *if thy hand,* that is, he who directs your work, *or thy foot,* that is, he who supports you, *scandalize thee,* that is, is an occasion of sin to you, *cut it off, and cast it from thee.* And He gives the

---

7. Benedictine Bishop of Halberstadt during the ninth century. He was a fellow student of Rabanus Maurus and was taught by Alcuin.

8. "Observe that knowledge of false happiness is useful, because knowledge of evil is expedient for carefulness, according to Alain in his book *On the Complaint of Nature* (*De Planctu Naturae*), because evil is not avoided except when known, and because knowledge of evil leads to the knowledge of good through opposition" (In Boethii *De Consolatione Philosophiae,* lib. 3, ch. 17). "Alain de Lille (1128–1202), French scholastic philosopher, a Cistercian, honored by his contemporaries as the Universal Doctor. He was born in Lille; he taught at Paris and Montpellier before retiring to Cîteaux. Alain attempted to give rational support to the tenets of Christian faith in his writings. He held that the mind unaided by revelation can know the universe, but by faith alone can man know God. Although his thought was largely Neoplatonic, he made use of numerous Aristotelian and neo-Pythagorean elements. The mathematical and deductive method had an important place in the working out of his theology. One of his chief works, *De fide catholica contra haereticos,* was written in order to refute heretics and unbelievers. Alain de Lille was also one of the foremost didactic poets of his day; his chief poem *Anticlaudian* (tr. 1935) is a complicated allegory. He is also called *Alanus de Insulis,* the Latin form of his name" ("Alain de Lille," The Columbia Encyclopedia, 6th ed. New York: Columbia University Press, 2001–04).

reason, *It is better for thee*, etc., because it is better to suffer any temporal evil than to deserve eternal punishment. Likewise, someone is needed for teaching you, hence, he is an eye to you; hence, *And if thy eye scandalize thee, pluck it out*. And He gives the reason, *It is better for thee*, etc. Or the parable can refer to the whole Church, because the eyes are the prelates, the hands are the deacons, the feet are the laymen. Hence, it is better that a prelate be deposed, or a deacon cut off, than that the Church be scandalized. Or the eye stands for contemplation, the hand stands for activity, and the foot stands for advancement; hence, if you see that this contemplation, or activity, or promotion, be an occasion of sin for you, cut it off, and cast it from thee.

See that you despise not one of these little ones. Above, He had taught to avoid scandal on account of the punishment; here, however, He teaches to avoid it from the consideration of Divine Providence: and about this, He does two things. Firstly, He proposes the consideration; and secondly, He gives the reason, where it is said, *For I say to you*, etc. So I have said that *He that shall scandalize one of these little ones, it were better for him that a millstone should be hanged about his neck*, etc. *See that you despise not*: for littleness quickly fosters contempt. "Behold I have made thee a little one among the nations, despicable among men" (Jer. 49, 15).

But it is sought of which little ones does He speak here. It ought to be said that it is of the little ones who are little in respect to the estimation of men, but are great before God: these are the friends of God; "He that despiseth you despiseth me" (Lk. 10, 16).

But, against this, it is objected, that such are not scandalized, nor perish, and, nevertheless, it is stated below in this chapter that *the Son of man is come to save that which was lost*.

It ought to be said, and this is how Origen solves this objection, that by little ones are understood the humble, who are perfect; and such men are not scandalized, and, nevertheless, they sometimes perish. Or, although not all will be scandalized, some will be scandalized. According to Jerome, it is understood of the little ones in Christ, as, for instance, of those recently converted to Christ. And then it is continued with the preceding part.

It was thus said that the scandalizing part is to be cut off, and then the little ones, and the weak, and the sinners, although they are not to be scandalized, nevertheless, ought not to be contemned. *I say to you, that their angels in heaven always see the face of my Father who is in heaven*. Here the reason from Divine Providence is assigned. Firstly, as to the ministry of the angels; secondly, as to Christ's ministry, where it is said, *For the Son of man is come to save that which was lost.* So it was said that you may not despise the little ones, because they, of whom God has care, are not to be despised. *I say to you, that their angels.* Why are they theirs? It is because they have been assigned to be their guardians: because, as Jerome says, an angel was assigned to every man for his safekeeping. "He hath given his angels charge over thee; to keep thee in all thy ways" (Ps. 90, 11); "They are all ministering spirits, sent to minister for them who shall receive the inheritance of salvation" (Heb. 1, 14). These angels have a duty to bring down and announce divine things to us. Likewise, they convey and present our prayers to God; "The smoke of the incense of the prayers of the saints ascended up before God from the hand of the angel" (Apoc. 8, 4). Hence, if the Lord so bountifully provides for them, because He wants them to be served by angels, they are not to be despised; in Ecclesiasticus 35 it is said concerning a widow, that her tears ascend from her cheek all the way to heaven.[9] Or, *their angels*, because they are their fellow citizens, because the fellowship of the angels and men is one, hence, they are fellow citizens of the heavenly city. Hence, their dignity is so great that *they always see the face of my Father who is in heaven.*

And, herein, four things can be pointed out. Firstly, the continuity of their vision is indicated, because they always see God's face. Someone might say that they are sometimes sent on works of ministry, for which reason, they do not always see God's face, and so He says *always.*[10] Likewise, the sublimity of their vision is indicated. We ourselves see some of the highest things, but in some obscurity, and through creatures, as it is stated in Romans 1, 20: "The invisible things of him from the creation of the world are clearly seen, being understood by the things that are made." But the angels see from a sort of height; hence, He says, *In heaven.* Likewise, their clear vision is indicated; "We see now through a glass in a dark manner: but then face to face" (I Cor. 13, 12). It ought not to be said that God has a bodily face, but the clear vision of Him is called His face. For when someone is seen in a mirror, he is not seen with open vision; but when one looks at his face, then

---

9. "Do not the widow's tears run down the cheek, and her cry against him that causeth them to fall? For from the cheek they go up even to heaven" (Eccli. 35, 18-19).

10. "GREG: And therefore the angels always behold the face of the Father, and yet they come to us; for by a spiritual presence they come forth to us, and yet by internal contemplation keep themselves there whence they come forth; for they come not so forth from the divine vision, as to hinder the joys of inward contemplation" (*Catena Aurea on St. Matthew*, chap. 18, lect. 3).

he is openly seen. Thus, God is seen in a mirror, when He is seen through creatures; but when He is seen in Himself, and through Himself, then there will be face to face vision. Lastly, Chrysostom says that what one might call a superior joy is indicated, because these are perfect men: if the angels are their ministers, their joy denoted is in a certain respect greater than the joy of the angels. For they see that God is assisting them. Hence, not only the vision of God is a gift, possession of Him is also a gift; "But I follow after, if I may by any means apprehend" (Phil. 3, 12).

But why does He say, *My Father who is in heaven*? It is to exclude the error of those who were asserting *their Angels* means the demons. Hence, they were saying that the angels are in heaven, the demons are in a middle region, and, for that reason, they are intermediaries and our assistants. Therefore, to exclude this, He says, *They always see the face of my Father who is in heaven*. Likewise, another reason for His saying this is to foster our desire, because if they see, we ourselves will also see God's face, for we ought to hope for this. But lest it seem to be a small thing that the angels have been appointed to the guardianship of men, He also proves the above statement through Christ's ministry. And firstly, He proves this; and secondly, He puts forth a similitude. Therefore, He says that the little ones ought not to be despised, because *The Son of man is come to save that which was lost*. "Christ Jesus came into the world to save sinners" (I Tim. 1, 15). "He shall save his people from their sins" (above 1, 21).

12. What think you? If a man have an hundred sheep, and one of them should go astray: doth he not leave the ninety-nine in the mountains, and goeth to seek that which is gone astray?

13. And if it so be that he find it: Amen I say to you, he rejoiceth more for that, than for the ninety-nine that went not astray.

14. Even so it is not the will of your Father, who is in heaven, that one of these little ones should perish.

15. But if thy brother shall offend against thee, go, and rebuke him between thee and him alone. If he shall hear thee, thou shalt gain thy brother.

16. And if he will not hear thee, take with thee one or two more: that in the mouth of two or three witnesses every word may stand.

17. And if he will not hear them: tell the church. And if he will not hear the church, let him be to thee as the heathen and publican.

18. Amen I say to you, whatsoever you shall bind upon earth, shall be bound also in heaven: and whatsoever you shall loose upon earth, shall be loosed also in heaven.

19. Again I say to you, that if two of you shall consent upon earth, concerning anything whatsoever they shall ask, it shall be done to them by my Father who is in heaven.

20. For where there are two or three gathered together in my name, there am I in the midst of them.

21. Then came Peter unto him and said: Lord, how often shall my brother offend against me, and I forgive him? till seven times?

22. Jesus saith to him: I say not to thee, till seven times; but till seventy times seven times.

Here a similitude is set forth. And firstly, the careful search is set forth; and secondly, the joy of having found the sheep is set forth; hence, He says, **What think you?** It is said thus, because **The Son of man is come to save that which was lost**, for a pastor seeks lost sheep. **If a man have an hundred sheep.** By a hundred the totality of rational creatures is signified: ninety-nine is taken from the same number which is nine, but only when multiplied, because nine multiplied by ten makes ninety; which number, namely nine, falls short of ten by one; hence, by these sheep He signifies all rational creatures; "My sheep hear my voice" (Jn. 10, 27); "We are his people and the sheep of his pasture" (Ps. 99, 3). By the sheep that strayed, the human race is signified. And why is it signified by the sheep that strayed? It is because by one man all strayed; "For you were as sheep going astray" (I Pet. 2, 25). The passage is not, "in the desert," but *in the mountains*, as is found in the Greek.[11] And this is expounded in three ways. Firstly, it is expounded that these ninety-nine signify the angels who were left in the mountains, meaning in the heavenly places; "I will feed them in the mountains of Israel" (Ez. 34, 13). Or, by the ninety-nine, the just are signified, and by the lost sheep, sinners are signified; and so He left the ninety-nine in the mountains, meaning in the height of justice; "Thy justice is as the mountains of God" (Ps. 35, 7). Or, by the ninety-nine, the proud are signified, and by the sheep, the humble are signified: hence, **Doth he not leave the ninety-nine in the mountains**, meaning in their pride, **and goeth to seek that which is gone astray?** "I have gone astray like a sheep that is lost: seek thy servant, O Lord" (Ps. 118, 176).

11. "In the desert" is found in Luke 15, 4.

Afterwards, it is treated concerning the joy of having found the sheep, where it is said, *And if it so be that he find it*, etc. Here also a triple reason for this joy can be assigned. The first is that the Lord rejoices concerning the good, as it is stated: "He will rejoice over thee with gladness" (Soph. 3, 17). If, by the ninety-nine, the angels are signified, and by the sheep man is signified, the reason is apparent, namely, that man was worthy of restoration; "Nowhere doth he take hold of the angels: but of the seed of Abraham he taketh hold" (Heb. 2, 16). If by the ninety-nine we understand the just, the reason is likewise apparent, namely, that a leader loves a soldier more who falls in battle, and, afterwards, always fights manfully, than him who never fell, and always fights halfheartedly. So when a man has sinned, and, afterwards, rises again steadfastly, and always carries himself vigorously; He loves him more; "I am glad because you were made sorrowful unto penance" (II Cor. 7, 9); for that reason, the Lord rejoices more concerning him, etc., since he has greater zeal; nevertheless, this does not apply to all men, because a just man can have so much zeal, that God is more with him than with the penitent. According to the third explanation the reason is also apparent, namely, that God rejoices concerning him who recognizes his sin, as is evident from the parable of the Pharisee and the publican. He concludes, therefore, *Even so it is not the will of your Father, who is in heaven, that one of these little ones should perish*. He says little, and He means much, because His will is that they be saved; "Who will have all men to be saved" (I Tim. 2, 4). For if He did not want this, He would not send His angels. "Is it my will that a sinner should die, saith the Lord God" (Ez. 18, 23).

But if thy brother shall offend against thee, etc. Here it is treated concerning forgiving scandal. And firstly, the procedure of forgiving is related; secondly, the number of times one is to forgive is related, where it is said, *Then came Peter unto him*, etc. About the first point, He sets forth the secret admonition; and secondly, He sets forth the corroboration of the admonition by witnesses, where it is said, *And if he will not hear thee*, etc.; and thirdly, He sets forth the denunciation, where it is said, *And if he will not hear them: tell the church*, etc. About the first point, He firstly gives His teaching; and secondly, He gives the reason for the given teaching, where it is said, *And if he shall hear thee, thou shalt gain thy brother*. So I have said that the little ones are not to be despised. But what should be done if someone does scandalize them? Here He teaches, *But if thy brother shall offend against thee, go, and rebuke him between thee and him alone*. Notice, firstly, that He says, ***Shall offend***: hence, He speaks of a sin that has been committed. Hence, one ought to proceed in one way in regard to a sin that has been committed, and another way in regard to a sin that has yet to be committed, because a sin that has been committed cannot be uncommitted; hence, in regard to a sin has yet to be committed, one ought to strive that it does not occur; "Loose the bands of wickedness, undo the bundles that oppress," etc., (Is. 58, 6). Hence, the procedure that ought not to be followed in regard to a sin that has yet to be committed, ought to be followed in regard to a sin that has been committed. Likewise, He says, ***Against thee***; the Gloss says: "If he will have injured or insulted you." Hence, He wishes to say that an offense committed against us, we may forgive; but an offense that is made to God, we are unable to forgive, as the Gloss says on I Kings 2, 25: "If a man shall sin against the God, who shall pray for him?" Likewise, you ought to care about injuries made by him who is with you in the same society; concern ought to be had for other men also, but not as much. "What have I to do to judge them that are without?" (I Cor. 5, 12). ***Go, and rebuke him between thee and him alone.*** The Lord is leading His disciples to perfect diligence and correction. Above (chap. 7) the Lord had said that one might leave his gift before the altar, etc.; here, however, He goes further, because not only the one who injures, but the one who is injured ought to do this: hence, ***If thy brother shall offend against thee, go***, etc.; "With them that hated peace I was peaceable" (Ps. 119, 7). Should you forgive first? No; but first you ought to go and rebuke him: hence, He does not command us to forgive just anyone, but the repentant. Likewise, He says, ***Rebuke***, not 'scold' or 'exasperate': and show the offense briefly. If he acknowledges his offense, you ought to forgive him; hence, it is said, "Instruct such a one in the spirit of meekness" (Gal. 6, 1).

But does a man sin who omits to make this correction? Augustine says: "If you do not correct, you become worse by keeping silence, than he became by sinning."

But although this is true, because all are bound to correct, someone might say that it is only fitting for prelates who are bound by their office, but it is fitting for others out of charity. Sometimes, the Lord permits the good to be punished with the wicked. Why? It is because they did not correct the wicked. Nevertheless, Augustine says that sometimes we ought to refrain from correcting, "if you fear that they will not be emended by this correction, but will be made worse." Likewise, if you fear to correct lest it lead to a persecution of the Church, you do not sin if you do not correct. If, however, you abstain from correcting lest you be harmed in temporal goods, lest trouble come upon you, or some such thing, you sin; "Rebuke a wise man, and he will love thee" (Prov. 9, 8).

Rebuke him between thee and him alone. And why is this? It is because correction proceeds from charity; now charity is the love of God and neighbor. If you love your neighbor, you ought to love his salvation. But in this one ought to pay attention to two things, namely, his conscience and good reputation. If you wish, therefore, to save him, you ought to preserve his reputation; now you will do this by rebuking him between yourself and him: if you rebuke him before all, you take away his reputation, but his conscience ought to come before his reputation. For it frequently happens that when a man sees that his sin has been made public, he becomes so unrestrained that he exposes himself to every sin; "On every high hill, and under every green tree thou didst prostitute thyself"; "There is a shame that bringeth sin" (Eccli. 4, 25).

But, on the contrary, it is objected that it is stated in I Timothy 5, 20: "Him that sins reprove before all that the rest." And this is true if he sins publicly. For if someone sins publicly, then he must be publicly rebuked: and if someone sins in secret, then he ought to be rebuked secretly; and this is evident, because Augustine says that if you alone know that a man has sinned, **Rebuke him between thee and him alone.**

If he shall hear thee, thou shalt gain thy brother. Why does He say this? It is on account of three things: it is so that you may know for what purpose you ought to rebuke: because if you rebuke on account of yourself, you do nothing, because where one fails to seek his amendment, there is no meritorious correction;[12] but if it is done on account of God, then it is worthy of merit. Likewise, this is said so that you may know what you ought to intend, namely, to instill the correction and teaching into your brother's mind. Likewise, someone might say that to lose one's own brother would not be just. But if this were so, He would not have said, **Thou hast gained thy brother.** Likewise, **thou hast gained** him, because he is your fellow member: and just as one limb suffers with another limb, so also you suffer with your brother. Likewise, He says, **gained**, because you gain your own salvation; "He

---

12. "AUG; When anyone therefore offends against us, let us be very careful, not for ourselves, for it is glorious to forget an injury, forget, therefore, your own wrong, but not the wound your brother has sustained; and tell him of his fault between him and you alone, seeking his amendment and sparing his shame For it may be that out of shame he will seek to defend his fault, and thus you will only harden, while you sought to do him good" (ibid., lect. 4).

that judgeth his brother, detracteth the law and judgeth the law" (James 4, 11); "He who causeth a sinner to be converted from the error of his way shall save his soul from death and shall cover a multitude of sins" (ibid. 5, 20).

And if he will not hear thee, take with thee one or two. Here He calls for witnesses, *Take with thee one or two*, etc. "In the mouth of two or three witnesses every word shall stand" (Deut. 19, 15).

But here there is a question: Why does one not immediately call for witnesses? It ought to be said that his conscience ought to be cleansed in this way, because his reputation is not injured: hence, if the correction can be made in the first way and by itself, well indeed; if not, then call for witnesses. And Jerome says that one ought to call one firstly, and afterwards two. And why is this? It is so that they may be witnesses of the correction that was made, and then if he proceeds further with his sin, you cannot be blamed. Jerome says that the calling of witnesses serves another purpose, namely, it convicts a sinner of his sin: for some men are so pertinacious that they do not recognize their sins, and so you ought to call for witnesses, in order to convince him of the wrongfulness of his deed. Or perhaps he will repeat the injury. Or, according to Augustine, witnesses are called to prove him guilty.

But against this seems to be what Augustine says, namely, that before one present the guilty party to two witnesses, one ought to firstly present him to a ruler, and this is the same as to present him to the Church. Therefore, he seems to overthrow the order.

I say that he can be presented to a prelate, either by judicial process, or as a private person. Augustine means, therefore, that he ought to be presented to a ruler firstly as a private person, so that as a private person he may help make the correction; hence, He says, *If he will not hear them: tell the church.*

Here the denunciation is related. And firstly, one denounces; secondly, the sentence is related; and thirdly, the efficacy of the sentence is related. The second part is where it is said, *And if he will not hear the church*, etc.; and the third part is where it is said, *Amen I say to you*, etc. He says, *If he will not hear them: tell the church*, meaning to the whole community, so that he may be confounded, so that he, who was unwilling to be corrected without being made ashamed, may be corrected by being made ashamed. "For there is a shame that bringeth sin, and there is a shame that bringeth glory and grace" (Eccli. 4, 25). Or, *Tell the church*, that is to say, the judges, so that he may be rebuked; "If a man have a stubborn and unruly son, who will not hear the commandments of his father or mother, and being corrected, slighteth obedience: they shall take him and bring him to the ancients of the city, and to the gate of judgment," etc., (Deut. 21, 18-19). Then the punishment is added, *If he will not hear the church, let him be to thee as the heathen and publican.* Heathens are Gentiles and unbelievers; publicans are they who receive tribute, and who are public sinners. Hence, as though disjoined, they may be excommunicated by the sentence of the Church, because they would not listen to the Church. Hence, for contumacy alone may a man be excommunicated. *Amen I say to you*, etc. Here the efficacy of this sentence is related. Because someone could say: What do I care if it be told to the Church, and I be excommunicated? For that reason, He shows this efficacy when He says, *Amen I say to you, whatsoever you shall bind upon earth, shall be bound also in heaven: and whatsoever you shall loose upon earth.* Above, these things were said to Peter; here, however, it is said to the whole Church. And the Church is said to bind either because it does not loose, or because it excommunicates. Origen says that in this passage He says, *In heaven* (*in coelo*); however, when He spoke to Peter, He said, *In the heavens* (*in coelis*), to indicate that Peter has universal power. Here, however, He says, *In heaven*, because universal power does not belong to them, but they have power only in some particular place, because He gave universal power to Peter.

Again I say to you, etc. Here He sets forth the efficacy of prayer. And He firstly does this; and secondly, He gives the reason, where it is said, *For where there are two*, etc. And so He says, *Again I say to you.*

But against this you could object that we ask for many things which we do not obtain. This happens, firstly, on account of the unworthiness of those asking; hence, He says, *Two of you*, namely, you who live according to the Gospel. "You ask and receive not: because you ask amiss" (James 4, 3). Likewise, it is because they do not agree, because they do not have the bond of peace: for it is impossible for the prayers of many not to be heard, if out of many prayers is made, as it were, one prayer: "That for this gift obtained for us, by the means of the faces of many persons,[13] thanks may be given by many in our behalf" (II Cor. 1, 11). Likewise, it is because they ask for some things which are not expedient for their salvation: for a petition ought to be for a useful thing; "You know not what you ask" (below 20, 22).

---

13. "And he says 'of many faces', either in respect to the diversity of their age, their condition, or their race or morals" (*Super II ad Cor.*, Chap. 1, lect. 3).

It shall be done to them by my Father who is in heaven, meaning in the highest places: *in heaven*, meaning in us. *For where there are two or three gathered together in my name, there am I in the midst of them*; He is in the congregation of the Saints, not of the worldly. "In the council of the just, and in the congregation, great are the works of the Lord" (Ps. 110, 1-2). Therefore, *where there are two or three*. Charity is not in one, but in many; hence: "He that abideth in charity abideth in God, and God in him" (I Jn. 4, 16). For that reason, *I am in the midst of them*.

Then came Peter unto him and said: Lord, how often shall my brother offend against me, and I forgive him? Above, He taught by what procedure sin ought to be forgiven, namely, after correction and amendment; here He treats concerning the number of times one ought to forgive. Firstly, therefore, Peter's question is related; secondly, Christ's answer is related; and thirdly, a similitude is employed. The second part is where it is said, *Jesus saith to him*, etc.; and the third part is where it is said, *The kingdom of heaven likened to*. He says, therefore, *Then came*. *Then*, namely, when Peter had heard these words, *if thy brother shall offend against thee*, etc.; Peter then began to wonder whether he should forgive once or many times, and he said: How often shall my brother offend against me, etc., should I not forgive him till seven times? It is as though He were to say: Till seven times belongs to weakness, but more belongs to malice. For that reason, he asks if he should forgive till seven times. Likewise, he knew that which is said in IV Kings 5, namely, that Eliseus commanded Naaman to wash himself seven times in the Jordan; for that reason, he thought that he should forgive seven times. *Jesus saith to him: I say not to thee, till seven times; but till seventy times seven times*. This *seven times* that He says can be taken in one way as by addition, so that the sense is not seven times, but seven times and seventy times. Or it can be taken as by multiplication, so that the sense is seven times seventy: and Jerome explains this passage in that way. According to the first exposition, which is Augustine's, it is given to be understood that we ought to pardon all, because Christ pardoned all sins.[14] "Bearing with

---

14. "AUG; Yet not without reason did the Lord say, Seventy times seven; for the Law is set forth in ten precepts; and the Law is signified by the number ten, sin by eleven, because it is passing the denary line. Seven is used to be put for a whole, because time goes round in seven days. Take eleven seven times, and you have seventy-seven. He would therefore have all trespasses forgiven, for this is what He signifies by the number seventy-seven" (*Catena Aurea on St. Matthew*, chap. 18, lect. 6).

one another and forgiving one another, if any have a complaint against another. Even as the Lord hath forgiven you, so do you also" (Col. 3, 13). Or it can be said that the finite number stands for an infinite number, as in the Psalms, "The word which he commanded to a thousand generations" (104, 8). According to Jerome, the explanation is the same; nevertheless, the meaning of the number is added. For, by seven,[15] perfection is signified, and by a hundred, which is ten multiplied by ten, the Decalogue is signified. The first number that passes ten is eleven. And because by seven a totality is signified, for that reason, the totality of sins is signified; it is at though He were to say: Whatsoever sins your brother shall committed against you, forgive him. Hence, according to Jerome, it seems that He wishes to say, that a man can forgive more than he can offend.

23. Therefore is the kingdom of heaven likened to a king, who would take an account of his servants.

24. And when he had begun to take the account, one was brought to him, that owed him ten thousand talents.

25. And as he had not wherewith to pay it, his lord commanded that he should be sold, and his wife and children, and all that he had, and payment to be made.

26. But that servant falling down, besought him, saying: Have patience with me, and I will pay thee all.

27. And the lord of that servant being moved with pity, let him go and forgave him the debt.

28. But when that servant was gone out, he found one of his fellow-servants that owed him an hundred pence: and laying hold of him, he throttled him, saying: Pay what thou owest.

29. And his fellow-servant falling down, besought him, saying: Have patience with me, and I will pay thee all.

30. And he would not: but went and cast him into prison, till he paid the debt.

31. Now his fellow servants seeing what was done, were very much grieved, and they came, and told their lord all that was done.

32. Then his lord called him: and said to him: Thou wicked servant, I forgave thee all the debt, because thou besoughtest me:

33. Shouldst not thou then have had compassion also on thy fellow servant, even as I had compassion on thee?

---

15. The number six in the text should probably be seven according to the context. Hence, a change has been made in the translation.

34. And his lord being angry, delivered him to the torturers until he paid all the debt.
35. So also shall my heavenly Father do to you, if you forgive not everyone his brother from your hearts.

Here a similitude is related: and He does three things. Firstly, the divine mercy is suggested; secondly, ingratitude is mentioned, where it is said, *But when that servant was gone out*, etc.; thirdly, the punishment of ingratitude is mentioned, where it is said, *Now his fellow servants seeing*, etc. About the first, the assessment of the debts is related; secondly, the size of each debt is related, where it is said, *And when he had begun to take the account, one was brought to him, that owed him ten thousand talents*; thirdly, the exactor's justice is mentioned, where it is said, *And as he had not wherewith to pay it*, etc.; and fourthly, the remission of the debt is related, where it is said, *And the lord of that servant being moved with pity*, etc. He says, therefore: Because you ought to always be ready to forgive, wherefore, you ought to understand this similitude. *The kingdom of heaven* is the law of the kingdom; the Word of God Himself is justice and truth; "Who is made unto us wisdom and justice and sanctification and redemption" (I Cor. 1, 30). Therefore, this Word was likened to a king, when the Word was made flesh. Or, by the kingdom, the Church at the present time is designated, as was said above: "They shall gather out of his kingdom all scandals" (13, 41). And it is suitably called a kingdom, if we consider all the things that are in a kingdom. In a kingdom there is a king, servants, and suchlike things. *A king.* This king is God, and may be understood to be either the Father, or the Son, or the Holy Ghost. *Who would take an account of his servants.* By the servants of the Lord are understood the prelates of the Church, to whom was committed the care of souls. "The faithful and wise steward, whom his lord setteth over his family" (Lk. 12, 42). Therefore, what else does to take an account of things committed indicate, except that they are obliged to render an account? "They watch as being to render an account of your souls" (Heb. 13, 17). Also, since to everyone his own soul is committed, anyone whosoever can be called a servant; hence, "Hast thou considered my servant, Job," etc., (Job 1, 8). Hence, every single person is appointed to render an account of all the things committed to him: for it is necessary to render an account even for the least idle word, as it was said above.[16] *And*

---

16. "But I say unto you, that every idle word that men shall speak, they shall render an account for it in the day of judgment" (Mt. 12, 46).

when he had begun to take the account. The end of this account will be on Judgment Day; the beginning is when He brings upon us some tribulation. "Wherefore let them also that suffer according to the will of God commend their souls in good deeds to the faithful Creator" (I Pet. 4, 19). "Begin ye at my sanctuary" (Ez. 9, 6). Likewise, the careful examination of merits is mentioned. "Let us search our ways" (Lam. 3, 40), by which is understood the examination of consciences: and in this examination a servant was brought to the king who owed ten thousand talents. If we apply these talents to the prelates, we take the talents to be the sins of their subjects: because as many times a subject of theirs sins through their negligence, they are made debtors of talents. Hence, it is said: "Thy life shall be for his life" (III Kings 20, 39). Or, it can be said that a thousand is a perfect number, because it is cubic. Likewise, by ten the Decalogue is understood. Similarly, by the talents, the gravity of sin is understood. "And behold a talent of lead was carried" (Zach. 5, 7). Hence, by the talents is signified a man having a multitude of very great crimes; hence, when God wishes to take an account, and to examine a man's conscience, He finds a mass of crimes. "I have sinned above the sand of the sea".[17] Now, since this is an assessment of debts, three things are sought. Firstly, the reason for the assessment, or the reason for the punishment is sought; secondly, the punishment is described; and thirdly, the result of the punishment is described. A man is punished when he does not have, of himself, the wherewithal to recompense the debt; hence, He says, *And as he had not wherewith to pay it*, because all that he has does not suffice. Hence: "What shall I offer to the Lord that is worthy?" etc., (Mic. 6, 6). For that reason, *And as he had not wherewith to pay it, his lord commanded that he should be sold*, etc., because the Lord takes an account with man, and man does not have the wherewithal to pay and atone God's justice, or, more precisely, his punishment, He commands that he should be sold. When he is sold, the price of his sins is his punishment: for a price is that which someone accepts for a thing: and so a man is sold when his punishment is inflicted. "You are sold for your iniquities" (Is. 50, 1). *And his wife and children.* Of his wife, a man begets children. Now the children are his deeds, and the wife is concupiscence, or the root of sin. *And all that he had*, which

---

17. The reference given here in the text is I Paralipomenon 29, but this seems to be mistaken. In I Paralipomenon 21, 8 we do find a phrase with a similar meaning, namely, "I have sinned exceedingly." The actual phrase used by St. Thomas, "I have sinned above the sand of the sea," seems to have originated from the apocryphal "Prayer of Manasses" (verse 8) which was included in certain versions of the Septuagint but was rejected by the Council of Trent.

are God's gifts. "I gave her corn, and wine, and oil, and multiplied her silver, and gold," etc., (Osee 2, 8). Therefore, he is punished for his wife, and children, and the gifts given to him. "But to God the wicked and his wickedness are hateful alike" (Wis. 14, 9). "May his children be fatherless, and his wife a widow" (Ps. 108, 9).

But that servant falling down, besought him, saying. Here the Lord's mercy is related. And firstly, the stirring up of His mercy: for what greatly stirs up mercy is prayer. Hence, when man senses that he is in danger, he ought to have recourse to prayer. "My son, hast thou sinned? do so no more: but for thy former sins also pray that they may be forgiven thee" (Eccli. 21, 1). Now, the humility of this man is commended; likewise, his discretion is commended; and, moreover, his justice is commended. His humility is commended, because it is said, *falling down*. "The Lord hath had regard to the prayer of the humble" (Ps. 101, 18). Hence, *he besought him*. Origen writes that the words actually used here are, "He prayed to him."[18] Likewise, his discretion is mentioned, because he did not ask that the whole debt to be forgiven him, but instead he merely asked for time; hence, he says: *Have patience with me*: that is, give me time so that I can pay back the debt. He was asking in this manner: "Suffer me, therefore, that I may lament my sorrow a little" (Job 10, 20). Moreover, his justice is mentioned. *And I will pay thee.* "Then shall they lay calves upon thy altar" (Ps. 50, 21). Similarly, the pity of the remitting master is related, *And the lord of that servant being moved with pity, let him go and forgave him the debt.* Hence, the sorrow of the one repenting does not cause the remission, but the Lord's mercy; hence: "It is not of him that runneth, but of God that sheweth mercy" (Rom. 9, 16). *The lord being moved with pity*, etc. Observe that the Lord gives more things than man dares to ask: so that in that Collect it is said: "Who dost exceed both the merits and the desires of Thy suppliants."[19] Hence, *He let him go*, meaning he freed him, *and forgave him the debt* of sin. For contrition can be so great that the Lord forgives one's whole debt.

The servant's ingratitude follows, *But when that servant was gone out*, etc., and five things are related which aggravate his ingratitude. For firstly, it is aggravated from the time, because if it had happened after nine or ten years, it would not be surprising; but because he offends on the same day, he becomes ungrateful; he is like the sinner, who, when his sins are

18. Orabat.
19. This is taken from the Collect of the 11th Sunday after Pentecost.

forgiven, returns to his sins on the same day. Hence, it is said, ***Was gone out***. "For he beheld himself and went his way and presently forgot what manner of man he was" (James 1, 24). Likewise, his ingratitude is aggravated from his pretense, for in his master's opinion he was humble, but when he was gone out he immediately showed himself what kind of a man he was. "I will go forth, and be a lying spirit, in the mouth of all his prophets" (III Kings 22, 22). Again, that his ingratitude is aggravated is shown from his relationship to the one he offended, for ***He found one of his fellow-servants***. "Man to man reserveth anger, and doth he seek remedy of God?" (Eccli. 28, 3). Moreover, his ingratitude is aggravated from the smallness of the debt, because ***He owed him an hundred pence***; hence, in the number there was a difference, because he himself owed ten thousand; and in the amount there was a difference, that man owed pence, but he himself owed talents. Hence, the sins which are committed against God, are greater both in number and gravity than sins which are committed against a man, which are slight, because they are committed out of weakness; hence, the gravity is then different, as between talents and pence. For it is more serious to strike a king, than to strike a servant. Similarly, his cruelty in exacting the debt is indicated; for he was ***laying hold of him***, because he was dragging him into litigation, and he was bothering him, and ***he throttled him***, and he was not allowing him to breathe. And so his ingratitude is aggravated from his cruelty, in that he was unwilling to forgive. Hence, the supplication of the debtor is firstly related; and secondly, the cruelty of the former servant is related, where it is said, ***And he would not***, etc. It ought to be observed that all things that the former servant did to his master, this man did to him; hence, ***falling down, he besought him***. Above it is said, "He prayed to him," and here it is said, ***He besought him***, because, above, the first servant was rendering honor that is due to God; here, however, the second servant is dealing with honor that is due to a man: for that reason, He says, ***He besought him***. But nothing sufficed for him; hence, it is said, ***And he would not***. "The bowels of the wicked are cruel" (Prov. 12, 10). ***And he cast him into prison***, meaning into affliction, ***till he paid the debt***, meaning so that he would pay the debt. "The jealousy and rage of a man will not spare in the day of revenge" (Prov. 6, 34).

Now his fellow servants seeing. Here four things are mentioned. Firstly, his fellow servants' disapproval of this sin is related; secondly, the reproof of this sin on the part of God is related, where it is said, *Then his lord called him*; thirdly, the punishment is related, where it is said, *And his lord being angry, delivered him to the torturers*; and fourthly, the similitude is applied, where it is said, *So also shall my heavenly Father do to you*, etc. He says, therefore, *Now his fellow servants seeing*, etc. For we see that if one member suffers, the others suffer also; hence, seeing the man afflicted, they naturally suffer with him. "I beheld the transgressors, and pined away" (Ps. 118, 158). Hence, *they were grieved*. "Rejoice with them that rejoice: weep with them that weep" (Rom. 12, 15). *And they came, and told their lord*, meaning that they implored divine justice. "The Lord hath heard the desire of the poor: thy ear hath heard the preparation of their heart" (Ps. 9, 17).

Afterwards the reproof is related, *Then his lord called him*, etc. The Lord calls at the time of death. "Thou shalt call me, and I will answer thee" (Job 14, 15). Firstly, he upbraids his malice; secondly, he rebukes him regarding the favor done to him; and thirdly, he calls to mind what he should have done. He says, therefore, *Thou wicked servant*. Previously, when he owed him, he did not reproach him; but now when he ought not to have done what he did, he said, *Thou wicked servant*; because that a man sins, this is human; but if he persists, this is diabolical. *I forgave thee all the debt*. Here he upbraids him on account of the good deed, which he had not done as said above, *Shouldst not thou then have had compassion also on thy fellow servant?* It is as though he were to say: You received great things, and you did not want to bestow little things. *And his lord being angry*, etc. And firstly, He treats of the punishment by which one is separated from God. When the lord commanded him to be sold, He did not say that he was angry, because warnings are not from Divine justice, but from Divine mercy; but a reproach is from God's anger. "As the roaring of a lion, so also is the anger of a king" (Prov. 19, 12). Secondly, He treats of the punishment by which one is made subject to the demons; hence, *delivered him to the torturers*. "He will render to him according to his judgment" (Eccli. 33, 14). Likewise, the perpetuity of the punishment is mentioned, *Until he paid all the debt*; and this will be forever. For if the punishment ought not to cease until satisfaction of the debt be made, and no one can make satisfaction without grace; then he who dies without charity, will not be able to make satisfaction.

So also shall my heavenly Father do to you. Here He applies the similitude. His Father is God, as it is said above:

"Our Father who art in heaven" (6, 9). ***Shall do to you***, that is, He will not forgive your sins, ***if you forgive not everyone his brother from your hearts***. Here He seems to suggest that forgiven sins may return, as Origen maintains, because forgiven sins return to some people, as, for example, in the case of apostasy.[20] But this does not seem to be true, because the remission of sins has its efficacy from the sacraments: for that reason, both manifest and hidden sins are forgiven; however, they are said to return through ingratitude.

20. "OBJ 1: Augustine says (*De Baptismo contra Donatistas*, i,12): "Our Lord teaches most explicitly in the Gospel that sins which have been forgiven return, when fraternal charity ceases, in the example of the servant from whom his master exacted the payment of the debt already forgiven, because he had refused to forgive the debt of his fellow-servant"... Reply OBJ 1: This saying of Augustine seems to refer to the return of sins as to the debt of eternal punishment considered in itself, namely, that he who sins after doing penance incurs a debt of eternal punishment, just as before, but not altogether for the same reason. Wherefore Augustine, after saying (*Libri Responsionum Prosperi* i; Prosper, *Responsiones ad Capitula Gallorum* ii) that "he does not fall back into that which was forgiven, nor will he be condemned for original sin," adds: "Nevertheless, for these last sins he will be condemned to the same death, which he deserved to suffer for the former," because he incurs the punishment of eternal death which he deserved for his previous sins" (III, q. 88, a. 1 ad 1um).

CHAPTER NINETEEN

1. And it came to pass when Jesus had ended these words, he departed from Galilee and came into the coasts of Judea, beyond Jordan.
2. And great multitudes followed him: and he healed them there.
3. And there came to him the Pharisees tempting him, saying: Is it lawful for a man to put away his wife for every cause?
4. Who answering, said to them: Have ye not read, that he who made man from the beginning, made them male and female? And he said:
5. For this cause shall a man leave father and mother, and shall cleave to his wife, and they two shall be in one flesh.
6. Therefore now they are not two, but one flesh. What therefore God hath joined together, let no man put asunder.
7. They say to him: Why then did Moses command to give a bill of divorce, and to put away?
8. He saith to them: Because Moses by reason of the hardness of your heart permitted you to put away your wives: but from the beginning it was not so.
9. And I say to you, that whosoever shall put away his wife, except it be for fornication, and shall marry another, committeth adultery: and he that shall marry her that is put away, committeth adultery.
10. His disciples say unto him: If the case of a man with his wife be so, it is not expedient to marry.
11. Who said to them: All men take not this word, but they to whom it is given.
12. For there are eunuchs, who were born so from their mothers womb: and there are eunuchs, who were made so by men: and there are eunuchs, who have made themselves eunuchs for the kingdom of heaven. He that can take, let him take it.
13. Then were little children presented to him, that he should impose hands upon them and pray. And the disciples rebuked them.
14. But Jesus said to them: Suffer the little children, and forbid them not to come to me: for the kingdom of heaven is for such.
15. And when he had imposed hands upon them, he departed from thence.

16. *And behold one came and said to him: Good master, what good shall I do that I may have life everlasting?*

17. *Who said to him: Why askest thou me concerning good? One is good, God. But if thou wilt enter into life, keep the commandments.*

18. *He said to him: Which? And Jesus said: Thou shalt do no murder, Thou shalt not commit adultery, Thou shalt not steal, Thou shalt not bear false witness.*

19. *Honour thy father and thy mother: and, Thou shalt love thy neighbor as thyself.*

20. *The young man saith to him: All these have I kept from my youth, what is yet wanting to me?*

21. *Jesus saith to him: If thou wilt be perfect, go sell what thou hast, and give to the poor, and thou shalt have treasure in heaven: and come, follow me.*

22. *And when the young man had heard this word, he went away sad: for he had great possessions.*

23. *Then Jesus said to his disciples: Amen, I say to you, that a rich man shall hardly enter into the kingdom of heaven.*

24. *And again I say to you: It is easier for a camel to pass through the eye of a needle, than for a rich man to enter into the kingdom of heaven.*

25. *And when they had heard this, the disciples wondered much, saying: Who then can be saved?*

26. *And Jesus beholding, said to them: With men this is impossible: but with God all things are possible.*

27. *Then Peter answering, said to him: Behold we have left all things, and have followed thee: what therefore shall we have?*

28. *And Jesus said to them: Amen I say to you, that you who have followed me, in the regeneration, when the Son of man shall sit on the seat of his majesty, you also shall sit on twelve seats judging the twelve tribes of Israel.*

29. *And every one that hath left house, or brethren, or sisters, or father, or mother, or wife, or children, or lands for my name's sake, shall receive an hundredfold, and shall possess life everlasting.*

30. *And many that are first, shall be last: and the last shall be first.*

Above, it was shown how one comes to eternal life by the common way. Here, He teaches how one comes by the way of perfection, which is mentioned insofar as two things are alluded to: it is mentioned insofar as continence is touched upon, and insofar as voluntary poverty is touched upon. About the first, the Evangelist does two things. Firstly, he treats of His arrival: and secondly, he treats of continence, where it is said, *His disciples say unto him.* About the first, he does three things. Firstly, the temptation of the Pharisees is related; secondly, Christ's solution is related; and thirdly, an objection against His solution is related. The second part is where it is said, *Who answering, said to them*; and the third part is where it is said, *Why then did Moses command to give a bill of divorce?* About the first, he does three things: firstly, the place is described; secondly, the occasion for tempting is described; and thirdly, the temptation is described. He says, therefore, *And it came to pass,* because what He says comes to pass. "For he spoke and they were made" (Ps. 32, 9). *When Jesus had ended these words,* namely, His words about avoiding scandal, *he departed from Galilee and came into the coasts of Judea, beyond Jordan.* Judea is sometimes taken for the whole land that the Jews inhabit: sometimes it is taken for the land which fell to the tribe of Juda as an endowment, and so it is opposed to the other endowments; and here it is taken in this way: for a man had to pass through Judea, who wished to go to Jerusalem, which was in the tribe of Benjamin within the confines of Judea.

But why did He depart from Galilee? It was on account of three things. It was so that He might give an example to preachers, that one ought not to preach in just one place, but in many places; hence: "To other cities also I must preach the kingdom of God" (Lk. 4, 43). Likewise, it was because the time of the Passion was already imminent, and, for that reason, He wanted to approach the place where He was due to suffer. "He hath delivered himself for us, an oblation and a sacrifice to God for an odor of sweetness," etc., (Eph. 5, 2). Or, it was because He wanted to return to the Jews, to signify that at the end of time He will be disposed to convert the Jews.

And great multitudes followed him. It is a sign of the multitude's devotion that they followed him, just as children follow their father making a journey. "My sheep hear my voice" (Jn. 10, 27). *And he healed them.* "He will strike, and he will cure us" (Osee 6, 2). Sometimes the Lord was curing, and other times He was performing miracles. He was performing miracles to strengthen. "Jesus began to do and to teach" (Acts 1, 1). Someone might think that He went over to the Jews because He abandoned the Gentiles; for that reason, to show that He did not abandon them, he says, *Multitudes followed him,* meaning to salvation, "They, being a wild olive, are ingrafted and are made partakers of the olive tree" (Rom. 11, 17). Or, because they followed Him across the Jordan, it is signified that sins are forgiven through Baptism. *And there came to him the Pharisees tempting him.* And, in this, they are reprehensible: because, while the multitudes followed Him, the Pharisees were laying snares for Him. "I will go to the great men, and will speak to them" (Jer. 5, 5). Hence, they approached Him, saying: *Is it lawful for a man to put away his wife for every cause?* In these words, their malicious craftiness is firstly apparent, because they came to Christ in order to raise objections against Him; because [they thought that] either He would say that she ought or ought not to be put away. If He said yes, it would seem inappropriate for Him, because He Himself was a preacher of chastity. And if He said no, they would accuse Him, because this was contrary to Moses the Lawgiver. As Chrysostom says, they are rebuked concerning their incontinence, because if someone willingly listens to another speaking about separation from his wife, he is incontinent. Hence, because these men were speaking about divorce, they were showing themselves to be incontinent. The Lord had given the grounds on account of which a wife might be put away, namely, on account of her depravity; but these men were seeking divorce not only on these grounds, but seeking whether they might obtain divorce on any grounds. Hence, they wanted to have free power of putting away their wives. For that reason, His response follows, *Who answering, said to them.* The Lord gives the best way of responding: because when someone inquires in order to learn, the truth ought to be said immediately, but they who inquire in order to calumniate, ought not to be told the truth immediately, but ought firstly to be told some things which they cannot deny. For that reason, the Lord firstly interrogates them concerning the Law; hence, He firstly cites the words of Scripture; secondly, He says how they apply to the point under discussion; and thirdly, He concludes His main argument. And about the first, He does three things. Firstly, He shows the union of a man and a woman that God instituted; secondly, He shows the affection for each other that He intended; and thirdly, He shows that manner by which He united them. He intends to prove that the union of a man and a woman was instituted by God. *Have ye not read, that he who made man from the beginning, made them male and female?* For this is read in Genesis 1, 27: "And God created man to his own image and likeness".[1] This ought not

---

1. cf. Genesis 5, 1.

to be understood, as some have understood, that firstly He made a man and then a woman and, afterwards, He separated them; but firstly, He made one man, and, in making him, He made the one from whom the woman would come to be.

But why did God will this to be done in this way, namely, that a multitude of people would come into existence from one man and one woman? I answer that it was in order that it might be indicated that the form of matrimony was from God. Likewise, it was so that they might love each other more.

But then Chrysostom asks, why does He not always do so, namely, that a man and woman be born together. He answers that if it were so, it would seem necessary to be married. And because the Lord willed it to be lawful to be married, or not to be married, He firstly created a man and a woman to signify that marriage was lawful; but after creating man and woman together, He willed that a man would be born without a woman, and vice versa, so that they might have full liberty both of being married or not being married.[2]

According to this, a twofold error is excluded. For certain men were saying that matrimony was not from God; and He excludes this, because if He made them man and woman, and it is evident that He does nothing in vain, it follows that neither did He do any of those things, except for the union of marriage. Others said that if man had not sinned, God would not have made the woman, nay, men would have been multiplied in another way; but this is nonsense, because they were created before the sin. And He says man and woman, so that one man might have one woman.

For this cause shall a man leave father and mother. Here is related what affection He put into them. *And he said.* Who said? He who made them. But this does not seem true, because it seems that Adam said this. Augustine says that God cast a deep sleep upon Adam, and took one of his ribs. This deep sleep was an ecstasy; hence, He revealed many good things on that occasion; hence, the Lord also revealed to him that which is said

---

2. "PSEUDO-CHRYS; If, then, God created the male and female out of one, to this end that they should be one, why then, henceforth, were not they born man and wife at one birth, as it is with certain insects? Because God created male and female for the continuance of the species, yet is He ever a lover of chastity, and promoter of continence. Therefore, did He not follow this pattern in all kinds, to the end that, if any man choose to marry, he may know what is, according to the first disposition of the creation, the condition of man and wife; but if he choose not to marry, he shall not be under necessity to marry by the circumstances of his birth, lest he should by his continence be the destruction of the other who was not willing to be continent; for which same cause God forbids that after being joined in wedlock one should separate if the other be unwilling" (*Catena Aurea on St. Matthew*, chap. 19, lect. 1).

here; hence, it was said above: "For it is not you that speak, but the spirit of your Father that speaketh in you" (10, 20). Therefore, because Adam said this by God's inspiration, it is therefore stated that God said this; hence, a man leaves his father and mother, who nourished him, and cleaves to his wife.

What is the reason for this? A brother and sister are born of one set of parents, and they divide themselves; but a man and a woman are born of different parents, and, nevertheless, they do not divide themselves? Chrysostom says that this is from a divine ordination. Likewise, every cause seeks to produce its own effect, as the sap from the root to the branches. Hence, parents love their children more than vice versa; for that reason, a husband and wife, even though they are born of different parents, nevertheless, are united into one effect.

And they two shall be in one flesh. Jerome says: "Namely, in the flesh of their offspring." And this is the fruit of marriage. Chrysostom expounds this passage thus: In one flesh, that is, in one carnal affection, just as unity comes to be in one spiritual affection, as it is said: "The believers had but one heart and one soul" (Acts 4, 32). Or, *they two shall be in one flesh*, that is, in one carnal work. The Philosopher says that man and woman are always related to each other in that one work, because just as active and passive powers are always joined together into one effect, so, in that act, action and passion are joined together. *Therefore now they are not two, but one flesh.* Then He concludes His main point: *What therefore God hath joined together, let no man put asunder*, because it is an act coming from the will of God. If it is from God, man is not able to put it asunder; because if God has joined something together, only He can separate it. For a separation can occur either from God or from man: and the latter is either on account of his will, namely, that he wants to have some other woman, and this is not a sufficient reason: or it is on account of mutual consent, so that he might more freely serve God, and in this way it is from God.

They say to him: Why then did Moses command to give a bill of divorce, and to put away? Here their objection is related against the general law: for they disclose what was in their mind: *Why then did Moses command to give a bill of divorce, and to put away?* Moses did not command men to put away their wives, but rather, he indirectly wished to prohibit this, because Moses did not want a wife to be put away unless a bill of divorce be given; and this pertains more to a prohibition, because the bill of divorce was only given by the public authority; hence, one used to have recourse to the wise, so that they might see if the men had grounds to put away their wives.

He saith to them. Did not the Lord give the Law through Moses? Consider the following passage, namely, that the Apostle says: "Concerning virgins, I have no commandment of the Lord: but I give counsel" (I Cor. 7, 25). Hence, sometimes he was saying that he had acquired inspired teachings from the Lord, and sometimes he was saying that he had acquired them from his own efforts: so Moses did also. Now Moses permitted this bill of divorce, not because he heard it from the Lord, but it was from divine inspiration, yet, nevertheless, not confirmed by divine authority.

Moses by reason of the hardness of your heart permitted you to put away your wives. They had said that Moses commanded this; but he did not command, rather he permitted this to be done. Concerning the hardness of their hearts, it is stated: "You stiffnecked and uncircumcised in heart and ears, you always resist the Holy Ghost" (Acts 7, 51).

Here there is wont to be a question; whether those men sin mortally who put away their wives. Certain men said that those putting away their wives sin mortally. For permission is obtained in four ways. Something is said to be permitted when the contrary is not commanded, so that a lesser good is permitted, because a greater good is not commanded, as when the Apostle says: "I speak this by indulgence" (I Cor. 7, 6). Likewise, sometimes a thing is permitted through the lack of a prohibition; and, in this way, venial sins are permitted. Sometimes, however, a thing is permitted through lack of an obstacle; and, in this way, all the evils that occur in this life are sometimes said to be permitted, because a punishment is not imposed. For that reason, certain things were sometimes permitted to the Jews which were mortal sins, because punishments were not imposed for them. Now we find the same thing in the affairs of the world: for thus, we see that simple fornication is not punished according to human laws; hence, if the Old Law pertained only to the present life, it would follow that this solution is good. But although, according to its outer appearances, it seems to pertain to the present life, nevertheless, according to its inner core, it pertains also to eternal life; "I gave them my statutes" (Ez. 20, 11). The Lord said to the young man, below in this chapter: "If thou wilt enter into life, keep the commandments" (verse 17); for this reason, some say that the Jews were badly provided for, if it were that they were ignorant of sins, whereas it is written: "Shew my people their wicked doings" (Is. 58, 1). For that reason, Chrysostom says that the Lord took away the guilt of sin from sin. And although it was something inordinate, nevertheless, He did not want it to be imputed to them as their fault, just as the Lord had commanded Osee to beget children of fornication: hence, the permission did not derive from a precept, but rather it was permitted to avoid a greater evil.

But from the beginning it was not so. Hence, it was the existing practice, but it was not instituted from the beginning: hence, for many years, no one put away his wife. **And I say to you**, etc. Here He cites the Law. Firstly, He does so regarding the man; secondly, He does so regarding the woman. He says, therefore, **Whosoever shall put away his wife**, etc. But fornication is excepted.

But see that fornication is twofold, namely, carnal and spiritual. Hence, on account of both, a man may put away his wife, as it is stated in I Corinthians 7: If one spouse is faithful and the other is unfaithful, the faithful spouse may put away the unfaithful spouse. It ought to be observed that by no subsequent impediment can the bond of marriage be dissolved, because it signifies the union of Christ and the Church: hence, since the union of Christ and the Church cannot be dissolved, neither may the union of marriage. But, on account of fornication, a man can be separated from common life, and a man ought not to retain his spouse, lest he seem to be conscious of the shameful deed; but for other shameful deeds he cannot be separated, such as for drunkenness. Likewise, if she wishes to induce her husband into infidelity, he may put her away.

But why is there more mention of carnal fornication than of spiritual fornication? It is contrary to the fidelity of marriage: and fidelity should not be kept to one who is not faithful. Another reason is that which Origen proposes, namely, that the Lord said: "Whosoever shall put away his wife, excepting the cause of fornication, maketh her to commit adultery" (above 5, 32) and, for that reason, he gives her an occasion of committing adultery; but after she has sinned, he does not give her an occasion of committing adultery, and so he can put her away after her infidelity, but not before.

He that shall marry another, committeth adultery. But why does he only commit adultery if he marries another woman? It is because a thing is bound by the same things by which it is loosened. Hence, when a man has a wife that has been separated from himself, and not another woman, there is still hope that they can be reunited, either by sin just like her sin, or by mutual agreement; but when he has married another woman, then he has completely separated his heart, and withdrawn his marital consent from her. Another reason is that if a man could put away his wife for a reason other that fornication, it would sometimes happen that a man would charge his wife with a crime so that he might be separated from her, and she would be united to another; for that reason, the Lord willed that he might not have another wife. Hence, He expressly forbade that a man have different wives, because when he has put away one and accepted another, he commits adultery.

And he that shall marry her that is put away, committeth adultery. Here He gives the law regarding the woman: hence, he does not will that a wife that has been put away have another husband.

But why does He forbid the man from contracting marriage with her, and not the woman? I answer that women act more impetuously towards evil. "Thou hadst a harlot's forehead" (Jer. 3, 3). For that reason, by this prohibition, she might be hurled to greater evils. Hence, He commands the man not to contract marriage with her that is put away, but He does not forbid the woman.

But what is this? Was it not licit for her who had been repudiated to marry another man? Some say that it was not licit, because the bond of marriage remained: and they cite that which is stated in Deuteronomy 24, that he could not return to his previous spouse because she was defiled; but unless she had sinned, he could return to her. Others say that he could marry another woman, but not this one, because if he were able to return to her, he might more readily repudiate her.

Therefore, what is this you say, namely, that she was defiled? I say that she was defiled to this man, because she cannot return to him. Or it can be understood to mean legal uncleanness, because a priest cannot marry her.

His disciples say unto him: If the case of a man with his wife be so, it is not expedient to marry. The Lord, after having treated concerning the indissolubility of marriage, here treats of the perfection of those practicing continence; and about this, the Evangelist does two things. Firstly, he gives the disciples' opinion; and then he gives Christ's teaching, where it is said, *Who said to them,* etc. He says, therefore, *His disciples say: If the case of a man with his wife be so, it is not expedient to marry.* They were prompted to say this because they had heard that a wife could not be put away except for one ground, although many other grounds render marriage burdensome, as, for example, uncleanness, such as leprosy and the like; so that the passage in Ecclesiasticus 25, 23, is fulfilled which says: "It will be more agreeable to abide with a lion and a dragon, than to dwell with a wicked woman." Likewise, marriage brings many anxieties; "If a virgin marries, she thinketh on the things of the world" (I Cor. 7, 34). Hence, on this account, the disciples argue that it is not expedient for any man to marry; for that reason, the Lord tempers their opinion, because it happens that a thing is better in two ways; either simply or relatively: in this way, to be continent befits some men, but not other men: because, as the Apostle says, "It is better to marry than to be burnt" (I Cor. 7, 9). He approves the Apostles' opinion. And firstly, He does so by words; secondly, He does so by deeds, where it is said, **Then were little children presented to him**. And firstly, He approves continence; secondly, He points out the differences among those practicing continence, where it is said, **For there are eunuchs**, etc.; and thirdly, He points out the difficulty of practicing continence, where it is said, **He that can take, let him take it**. He says, therefore, **Who said to them: All men take not this word**. So you say that it is not expedient to marry: this is true for some men, but it is not true for all, because not all men have such great virtue that they may abstain; **but they to whom it is given**, but it is given to some not by their own doing, but by a gift of grace. "I knew that I could not otherwise be continent, except God gave it" (Wis. 8, 21). For it is not from man, but from God, that someone lives not according the flesh; "I would that all men were even as myself. But everyone hath his proper gift from God: one after this manner, and another after that" (I Cor. 7, 7). And since they might suppose that all could be continent, for that reason, He says, **For there are eunuchs**, etc. Hence, He distinguishes the continence that is in some men by nature, it is other times by compulsion, and other times by free choice. For that reason, He mentions three kinds of eunuchs: because certain men are eunuchs by nature, **who were born so from their mothers' womb**. Just as some men are abnormally born by lacking a hand, so also some are born without genital organs: and this is from God's providence, because if everything were to happen according to the usual course of nature, then all might be attributed to nature, and not to Divine Providence; hence: "She knoweth signs and wonders before they be done" (Wis. 8, 8). Likewise, certain men are eunuchs by compulsion, such as those who are castrated by tyrants or barbarians. Or, there are eunuchs who are castrated for the sake of the guardianship of women, **who were made so by men**, namely, whom men's cruelty or the protection of women castrated. And

Jerome says this, because he knows that boys were taken and castrated and placed in the house of Nabuchodonosor. But certain men are voluntarily castrated, as He says, *and there are eunuchs, who have made themselves eunuchs for the kingdom of heaven.* But this must be reproved, and men who have done this ought to be removed from the clergy, (Capit. *Ex parte,* et capitul. S*ignificavit, extra de corp. vit.*).[3] Hence, an occasion is given to the error of the Manicheans, who said that material creatures are the cause of evil. Likewise, an occasion is given to the error of the Gentiles, because some men are made eunuchs in their sacrifices. Moreover, this serves to no useful purpose, because such men, even if they do not have the act, nevertheless, are not immune from concupiscence. Hence: "The lust of a eunuch shall deflour a young maiden" (Eccli. 20, 2). For that reason, it is better that a man put a bridle upon himself than cut off a member of his body, so that he may refrain from evil thoughts and desires. "Take away the evil thoughts from your hearts" (Is. 1, 16).

Who have made themselves eunuchs, they have given themselves to continual chastity, and they have done this *for the kingdom of heaven.* For sometimes, a member of the body stands for an action, as for example: "If thy eye scandalize thee, pluck it out, and cast it from thee" (above 18, 9). So here the genital organs are taken for the act. Hence, he who castrates himself, is he who dedicates himself to chastity. Or, according to Jerome, men keeping continence are so born by frigidity, namely, of their nature, such that they are not moved to that act. Hence, they are called eunuchs on account of the behavior of eunuchs, which they have due to their natures which they have from the womb. Because some men are naturally inclined to certain virtues, such as Job, who was naturally inclined to mercy, and who says: "from my infancy mercy grew up with me" (31, 18). But some men are inclined to virtue due to their own will, or on account of a pretense; or a man has been taught by heretics, and consequently, has been made so by men. "Having an appearance indeed of godliness but denying the power thereof" (II Tim. 3, 5). But other men are so disposed on account of eternal life. The first two groups, namely,

---

3. cf. "If anyone in sickness has been subjected by physicians to a surgical operation, or if he has been castrated by barbarians, let him remain among the clergy; but, if any one in sound health has castrated himself, it behooves that such a one, if [already] enrolled among the clergy, should cease [from his ministry], and that from henceforth no such person should be promoted. But, as it is evident that this is said of those who willfully do the thing and presume to castrate themselves, so if any have been made eunuchs by barbarians, or by their masters, and should otherwise be found worthy, such men the Canon admits to the clergy" (Council of Nicea, Canon I).

they who are castrated by nature or by coercion, do not have the merit of eternal life, but only the third group.

But is it never true of the first group, that they do not merit eternal life? I say that they merit in respect to the will, although they do not merit in respect to the act; because although they cannot perform the act, nevertheless, they can will to be able to perform the act.

He that can take, let him take it. Having set forth the different types of continence, here an exhortation to continence is set forth, as Jerome says. The Lord is acting like the leader of an army, who, when a city is to be captured, says: 'this or that will be given to him who enters the city,' as David said to Joab.[4] So he that can take and be continent, let him take it and not withdraw himself. The Apostle says: "Be zealous for the better gifts" (I Cor. 12, 31).

But why does He say this? Is not everyone obliged to remain in the state of virginity? It seems so, because a man is obliged to do what is better. It ought to be answered that to remain in the state of virginity is not a commandment, but a counsel, as the Apostle says: "Concerning virgins, I have no commandment of the Lord: but I give counsel" (I Cor. 7, 25).

But why is this? Is not a man obliged to do the greater good? I say that one must distinguish the greater good in regard to the actual performance or in regard to the desire. One is not held to the greater good in regard to their actual performance, but to the desire to do them, because every rule and every action is determined to something defined and certain : but if one is bound to do every action that is better, one is bound to something uncertain. Hence, in regard to exterior actions, because one is not bound to do something uncertain, one is not bound to do the greater good; but in regard to the desire, one is held to desire the greater good. Hence, he who does not always wish to be better, cannot wish without contempt [of doing the greater good].[5]

But what is it that He says, **He that can take, let him take it**? For either one can remain in the state of virginity by one's natural power, and no one can do so in this way; or one does so by the power of grace; and everyone can do so in this way, because it is said: "Ask, and it shall be given you" (Lk. 11, 9). Likewise, God's grace can do all things.

---

4. "And (David) said: Whosoever shall first strike the Jebusites, shall be the head and chief captain. And Joab the son of Sarvia went up first, and was made the general" (1 Par. 11, 6).

5. "There is a way of fulfilling this precept, so as to avoid sin, namely, if one do what one can as required by the conditions of one's state of life: provided there be no contempt of doing better things, which contempt sets the mind against spiritual progress" (II II, q. 186, a. 2 ad 2um).

I say that the word *can* includes the power of the will: for there is a firm will and a weak will. Now it is evident that man, when he has a firm will, does not fear many sensual impulses; but when he does not have a firm will, he falls from an easily born sensual impulse. Hence, *he who* through firmness of will *can take, let him take it*, and it is not from nature, but from God. Hence, he who has this firmness of will from God, we counsel that he take this and be continent. Or, he who can, according to the opportuneness of the time or of the condition of the time, such as Abraham: hence, the celibacy of John is not preferred to the wedlock of Abraham. Likewise, this is according to the condition of the time; because he who is married, cannot be continent; hence, they are excluded, either by reason of the time or by the condition of the time.

Then were little children presented to him. Here He shows what He said by a deed. And firstly, the presentation of the children is related; secondly, the disciples' zeal is related; and thirdly, Christ's giving satisfaction is related. The second part is where it is said, *And the disciples rebuked them*; and the third part is where it is said, *But Jesus said to them*, etc. He says, therefore, *Then were little children presented to him*. The Lord had commended chastity: and because there is chastity and purity in children, for that reason, seeing that purity pleased Him. And they presented their children to Him, *that he should impose hands upon them and pray*. It ought to be noted that it was customary to present children to aged persons and they blessed and prayed over them to indicate that the blessing was from God. Similarly, they knew from experience that He had a salutary touch, because He had cured a leper and many others, for that reason, etc. Likewise, they presented the children because they believed that he who was touched by Him would not in the future be harassed by devils; for that reason, the Church adopted the custom that the sacraments of the Church be offered to children, so that they might be made stronger.

The disciples rebuked them. Here the disciples' zeal is treated. But why were they rebuked? It is because they supposed that He, being a true man, was tired due to the crowds of men; for that reason, they wanted to spare His labor, etc. Another reason is that they had a high opinion of Christ; for that reason, it seemed to them that it was inappropriate that children would approach Him. Origen says that by this it is signified that some uncultivated children are in the Church. By the disciples, the perfect are signified; hence, such men become indignant when they see the children, namely, these uncultivated men, come to Christ, being ignorant that He wants all men to be saved. The Apostle says: "To the Greeks and to the barbarians I am a debtor" (Rom. 1, 14).

Afterwards, He satisfies both. And firstly, He satisfies the disciples' zeal for justice; and secondly, He satisfies the devotion of those presenting the children. He says, therefore, **Suffer the little children to come to me**, meaning the humble or the poor; "In malice be children: and in sense be perfect" (I Cor. 14, 20). **And forbid them not**, namely, the poor, on account of their innocence. For the imperfect should not be forbidden to come to perfection. **For the kingdom of heaven is for such**. He says, **for such**, meaning the kingdom of God does not belong to these children as such, but to those who are as pure as children through innocence. "Unless you be converted, and become as little children, you shall not enter into the kingdom of heaven" (above 18, 3). "He that hath been humbled, shall be in glory" (Job 22, 29). Afterwards, He satisfies the devotion of those presenting the children, **When he had imposed hands upon them**. Whereby, He strengthened their virtues. "It is he that giveth strength to the weary" (Is. 40, 29). **He departed from thence**. Sometimes Christ employs His hands, and does not depart from thence: other times He employs His hands and departs, because some men are so strong that they do not regress. And so He called Peter and Andrew and remained with them (Jn. 1). Therefore, because these children were still imperfect, and were not skilled in following Him, for that reason, **He departed from thence**.

And behold one came, etc. Here, He treats of the perfection of poverty: and because the way is twofold, namely, the common way and the special way, just as the way of practicing continence is twofold: the first way is the way of salvation, and the second way is the way of perfection: for that reason, He begins by treating of the first way, and afterwards, of the second. And firstly, the asking of a question is related; and secondly, Christ's response is related; and thirdly, Christ's explanation of His response is related. The asking of a question is related, **And behold one came and said to him: Good master**. Concerning this man, there is a diversity of opinions, for Jerome says that the man had a wicked heart: and this is evident because he went away sad; hence, if he had approached with a good heart, he would not have gone away sad. Chrysostom says that he was held back by the passion of avarice; and, for that reason, he could not endure: and this is evident, because he did not come for the sake of tempting; because when some men were coming for the sake of tempting, the Lord always responded to their malice: 'Why do you tempt Me?' or He said something of this sort;

but the Evangelist does not relate any such answer here. Hence, it is evident that he was not a tempter, but that the man was imperfect; who was drawing near to God so that he might be made perfect; "Come ye to him and be enlightened" (Ps. 33, 6). *Good master*, etc. He calls Him 'master,' as though He was one having knowledge: for such a man, who has knowledge, ought to be a master. Likewise, he calls Him 'good': it belongs to the notion of goodness to communicate itself; hence, "Communicate without envy" (Wis. 7, 13). For He is truly good; "Thou art good; and in thy goodness teach me thy justifications" (Ps. 118, 68). **What good shall I do that I may have life everlasting?** He had heard many things about eternal life. He had heard well; "Decline from evil and do good" (Ps. 36, 27). But he had not heard eternal life promised in the Law, but only temporal goods were promised. "You shall eat the good things of the land" (Is. 1, 19).

Who said to him: Why askest thou me concerning good? Here, His response is related. Firstly, He answers, as it is stated in Mark: "Why callest thou me good?" (10, 8). Here, however, He says, **Why askest thou me?** And this is not open to misinterpretation; but, based upon what Mark says, the Arians adopted an error, saying that the Father is good essentially, but the Son is good by participation; and so they asserted that the Son was unequal to the Father. But it ought to be observed that He says: **One is good, God**. Now by the name of God, the Father, and the Son, and the Holy Ghost are understood: hence, by this statement, every creature is excluded, because they are not essentially good.

But why does He answer in this manner? Jerome says that He answers according to the mind of that man, who was praising the goodness that ought to be in man; because they were adhering more to the tradition of men than to the tradition of God, as it is said above: "You have made void the commandment of God for your tradition" (15, 6). And so, He reprehends him, because he was inquiring of Him as though He were just a good man, and not God.

But what is it that He says, **Why askest thou me concerning good?** He says this as one knowing the sentiments of the young man, because he did not have the will power to obey Him who is good, and because every temporal good is imperfect, and is a shadow of good in comparison to the Divine good; "All our justices [are become] as the rag of a menstruous woman" (Is. 64, 6). Hence, 'All these goods are from God; for that reason, if you wish to have them, ask from Him: for He alone is good'; "Praise the Lord, for he is good" (Ps. 135, 1). 'Wherefore, have recourse to God.'

But if thou wilt enter into life, keep the commandments. For some men have imperfect life, others have perfect life, still others are entirely without life, such as those who are in sin, or the infidels, because "The just man liveth by faith" (Heb. 10, 38). Therefore, some men have an initial and imperfect life, such as just men in this world; but those men have a perfect life, who are already in eternal life; hence, *If thou wilt enter into life, keep the commandments*, because a man is introduced to life through the Commandments. "I gave them my commandments, and I shewed them my judgments" (Ez. 20, 11).

But did the practice of the Commandments suffice for salvation? I say they did not, unless they were practiced out of faith and love of the Mediator; hence, the Apostle says: "If justice be by the law, then Christ died in vain" (Gal. 2, 21). Likewise: "Keep my commandments, and thou shalt live" (Prov. 7, 2).

He said to him: Which? An explanation of His response follows, in which He repeats the Commandments. And firstly, He puts forward the Commandments; secondly, He puts forward their root, where it is said, *Thou shalt love thy neighbor as thyself.* He says, therefore: *And Jesus said: Thou shalt do no murder*, etc. And why does He not make mention of the Commandments of the First Tablet? It is because He saw that he was inclined to the love of God, for that reason, it was not necessary. Likewise, the latter Commandments are conducive to the love of God. And firstly, He sets forth negative Commandments; and secondly, He sets forth an affirmative Commandment. He firstly begins from a greater Commandment, *Thou shalt do no murder*, which is opposed to actual life: *Thou shalt not commit adultery*, which is opposed to life in potency: *Thou shalt not steal*, which is against a person's possessions: *Thou shalt not bear false witness*, which is against a person himself. Likewise, He sets forth an affirmative Commandment: *Honour thy father and thy mother.* Thereafter, He sets forth the root of the Commandments: *Thou shalt love thy neighbor as thyself.* "He that loveth his neighbour hath fulfilled the law" (Rom. 13, 8).

The young man saith to him: All these have I kept from my youth. After the Lord laid down the doctrine of basic salvation, here He lays down the doctrine of perfection. And firstly, He lays down the doctrine of perfection; secondly, He lays down the necessity of this doctrine; and thirdly, He lays down the reward for the observance of this doctrine. The second part is where it is said, *Then Jesus said to his disciples*; and the third part is where it is said, *Peter answering*, etc. And firstly, the occasion of giving this teaching is related; secondly, the declaration of this teaching is related; and thirdly, the effect of this teaching is related. The second part is where it is said, *Jesus saith to him*, etc.; and the third part is where it is said, *When the young man had heard this word, he went away sad.* The occasion of declaring this teaching is the young man's question. And firstly, he declares that he is observant of the legal practices; secondly, he asks what the perfection is to which he could attain, where it is said, *What is yet wanting to me?* He says, therefore, *All these have I kept from my youth*; and he says, *All these*, because it does not suffice to do only one thing, unless all things be kept; "Whosoever shall offend in one point, is become guilty of all" (James 2, 10). Likewise, he says, *From my youth*; "A young man according to his way, even when he is old, he will not depart from it" (Prov. 22, 6). Hence, what is said in Job 23, 12, befitted him: "I have not departed from the way of his lips."

Now whether what he says is true, that is the question. Jerome says that he lied: and this is clear, because before this immediately precedes, *Thou shalt love thy neighbor as thyself.* If he had loved his neighbor in this way, he would not have gone away sad when the Lord said, *Go sell what thou hast, and give to the poor.* Chrysostom says that he spoke the truth, because he had kept the legal observances; and this is confirmed by that which is stated in Mark (10, 21), namely, that "When Jesus, looked on him, loved him"; because He would not have done this unless he were good. For the ways are twofold: one is sufficient for salvation; and this is the love of God and of neighbor with benefit to oneself without burdening oneself, according to that which is stated: "He who loves God, the same is known by him" (I Cor. 8, 3); and he had kept this way: another way is the way of perfection, namely, to love one's neighbor with loss to oneself; and he had not kept this way; for that reason, when it was told to him, *he went away sad.* He was not content with the first way; for that reason, he asked, *What is yet wanting to me?* Each and every man is bound to ask this question, according to that which is said: "O Lord, make me know my end. And what is the number of my days: that I may know what is wanting to me" (Ps. 38, 5). For He alone knows what is wanting to us. "Thy eyes did see my imperfect being" (Ps. 138, 16).

Jesus saith to him: If thou wilt be perfect, go, etc. Firstly, the desire is set forth; secondly, the way is set forth; thirdly, because the way is difficult, the reward is set forth; and fourthly, the consummation of perfection is set forth. He says, therefore:

If thou wilt be perfect, go sell what thou hast, and give to the poor. For we ought to strive for perfection; "Leaving the word of the beginning of Christ, let us go on to things more perfect" (Heb. 6, 1).

But Origen asks: The perfection of the Law is love; but He had said: *Thou shalt love thy neighbor as thyself.* Why, therefore, did He say: *If thou wilt be perfect,* since he was already perfect?

Some men say that the passage, *Thou shalt love thy neighbor as thyself,* is not found in certain books. And this is evident, because that passage is not stated in Mark. Alternatively, it can be said that He said these words, but not in this order, because in the Gospel of the Nazarenes[6] it is as follows, "The Lord said, Thou shalt not kill," etc., up until that which is said about love. And afterwards it continues, *All these,* etc. And then it continues, *Thou shalt love thy neighbor,* etc. Nevertheless, the solution is clear, because love of neighbor is twofold, namely, love of neighbor according to the common way, and love of neighbor according to the way of perfection. Hence, He says, *Go sell all,* etc., not just part, as Ananias and Saphira did, as it is stated in Acts 5. *And give to the poor,* and not to the rich. "If I should distribute all my goods to feed the poor" (I Cor. 13, 3). "He hath distributed, he hath given to the poor" (Ps. 111, 9). And do not give to one poor man, but to many.

And what is this? Would not such a man be perfect immediately? It seems that he is not, because there are still disordered passions in him; therefore, he is not perfect in virtue. Origen says that he was immediately perfect, just as they are perfect to whom he distributed his goods. "Let your abundance supply their want, that their abundance also may supply your want" (II Cor. 8, 14). Hence, the perfection of those men passed on to him, just as "he that receiveth a prophet in the name of a prophet, shall receive the reward of a prophet," etc., (above 10, 41). Hence, the way of perfection is not, *Go sell what thou hast;* but only that which follows, *and give to the poor.* Another response is: 'If thou wilt be perfect,' not that you will be perfect immediately, but you will have to some degree the beginning of perfection, because having been unburdened of these things, you will be able to contemplate heavenly things more easily.' Augustine says that vigils and things of this sort are instruments

---

6. "It seems most likely that this apocryphal Gospel was a revised edition of the canonical Gospel of St. Matthew, that it received various additions from the other canonical Gospels and other sources, and that it was used by the Nazarenes" (John Steinmuller, *A Companion to Scripture Studies* (New York, Joseph F. Wagner Inc., 1951), vol. 3, p. 57).

of perfection; but perfection consists in the words that follow, *And follow me.* Hence: "Peter and Andrew immediately leaving their nets, followed him" (above 4, 20). And Matthew did in like manner (above 9, 9). But when you relinquish all these things, a better use of them is to give them to the poor, and in doing this one's neighbor should be considered.[7] Hence, if perfection is not in these things, in what does it consist? It ought to be said that it consists in the perfection of charity; "But above all these things have charity, which is the bond of perfection" (Col. 3, 14). Hence, the love of God is perfection, but the relinquishment of things is the way to perfection. And how is this true? Augustine, in his book *Eighty-Three Different Questions,*[8] says that "As charity increases, cupidity diminishes; and that when charity becomes perfect, cupidity ceases to exist." A man, therefore, is perfect in charity, who loves God unto contempt of himself and unto contempt of his possessions. Hence, it is difficult and almost impossible that someone possess riches without being seduced by them: and this is evident concerning Gregory, about whom it is read,[9] that when he had considered that it would be better for him to serve Christ in secular garb, so many worldly cares began to arise against him, so that he was held back not only by his garb, but also by his mind; for that reason, there is nothing that makes the soul so free as to be unoccupied with riches: and this is the way of perfection. Hence, it is one thing to be perfect and another thing to have the state of perfection. Whosoever has perfect charity unto contempt of oneself and unto contempt of his possessions, has perfection. The state of perfection is twofold, it is the state of prelates and of religious; but this is equivocally so, because the state of religious is for acquiring perfection; hence, to this young man it was said, *If thou wilt be perfect*, and if you want to attain the state of perfection, etc. The state of prelates, however, is not for acquiring perfection for oneself, but for communicating perfection possessed: hence, the Lord said to Peter: "Peter, if lovest thou me, feed my sheep"; and He did not say, *If thou wilt be perfect*, etc. Hence, there is the same difference between the perfection of religious and of prelates, as there is between a student and a teacher: hence, it is said to students:

---

7. "REMIG; And He said not, Give to your neighbors, nor to the rich, but to the poor" (*Catena Aurea on St. Matthew,* chap. 19, lect. 5); "Ambrose says (*De Officiis ministorum* i,30): "It is a commendable liberality if you overlook not your kindred when you know them to be in want; yet not so as to wish to make them rich with what you can give to the poor'" (II II, q. 185, a. 7 ad 2um).

8. *De diversis quaestionibus octoginta tribus.*

9. This is found in the prologue to the *Moralia* (*Commentary on the Book of Blessed Job*) of St. Gregory the Great.

'If you want to learn more, go to school so that you might learn more.' To the teacher is said: 'Read, and bring to perfection.' Hence, the state of religious is more secure, because they are not held responsible for their ignorance as the prelates are. Hence, just as it would be laughable for a teacher to know nothing, so likewise, etc. But given that both do what they ought to do, and they use their position well, I say that there is no comparison, except between a teacher and a student: hence, a prelate is in a more perfect state, even if you bring forth a religious who is an Elias, or anyone else.

But there is a question. If a prelate be prefect, is he not bound to sell all his possessions? I say that this would follow if perfection consisted in the saying, **Go sell what thou hast**; but it does not, rather, it is the way and a preparation for acquiring perfection; for that reason, it is not necessary that he sell the things that he has. But because it rarely happens that someone have perfection with riches, all his possessions ought to be relinquished by him who comes to perfection; for that reason, the Lord gives what is easier. Hence, if a prelate were well-suited for his position, and fulfilled his duties well, I say that he would be more perfect than other men, just as someone can say: 'I want to go to school to learn more.' But it would be presumptuous to say, when a man knows nothing, that he wants to be a teacher. Hence, Augustine says in his *City of God*: "It is a higher state, without which the people cannot be ruled, even if they be managed properly, nevertheless, it is improperly desired." Likewise, it is one thing to be a prelate, and another thing to be in the state of a prelate.

Are priests having the cure of souls, or parish priests, in the state of perfection? I say that they are not in the state of perfection, because they do not qualify for the state of perfection. Every state is given with some solemnity, such as the episcopacy and religion. But when the common things are given, they are not given with solemnity: hence, parish priests do not have the state of perfection; which is evident, because a cure of souls and ministry is given to certain men,[10] and if such a man were not promoted, he could abandon his ministry and marry, and sometimes he is made a religious. A bishop, however, cannot abandon the episcopacy, unless by permission of his superior; a parish priest, on the other hand, can surrender the cure of souls by entering religion. But if he were in a more perfect state, he would at once fall from that state, and he would sin in doing so: hence, a parish priest

---

10. Presumably these men would not be in major Orders, but only in minor orders.

can have perfection according to the act, but not according to the state; because the state is only given with solemnity.[11]

Go, therefore, *and sell what thou hast, and give to the poor*, because by doing this you will have a great reward, because a reward corresponds with one's merit. *And thou shalt have treasure in heaven*. In a treasure there are two things, stability and abundance. You will have a treasure and an abundance of spiritual things. "Glory and wealth shall be in his house" (Ps. 111, 3). "And there shall be faith in thy times: riches of salvation, wisdom and knowledge" (Is. 33, 6). *And come, follow me*. This is the very highest perfection. Hence, they are perfect, who follow God with their whole heart. Hence: "Walk before me, and be perfect" (Gen. 17, 1). *And follow me*, that is to say, imitate Christ's life; hence: "If any man will come after me, let him deny himself" (above 16, 24). For the imitation of Christ's life consists in the diligence of preaching, of teaching, and of having the cure of souls. Hence, Chrysostom says: "It was said to Peter, 'Follow me,' namely, in accepting the cure of the whole world." "My foot hath followed his steps" (Job 23, 11).

And when the young man had heard this word, he went away sad. His disposition is shown, because *he went away sad*. This happens when we desire something, and we cannot have what we wish to have; hence, this man desired to have perfection, and he heard what he needed to do in order to have it. And because he was covetous, he went away sad. And why is this? *For he had great possessions*. Augustine says: "He who forsakes the desire of possessing, has great merit, because he gains merit for what he was able to have; but it is more meritorious to relinquish what one already has, because it is more difficult to detach things that are already united, than things that are not united." And this is evident, because this man, who had possessions, was unable to separate himself from them.

Then Jesus said to his disciples. Here the reason for the aforesaid teaching is related. Firstly, the reason is given; and secondly, He calms the astonishment of the disciples, where it is said, *And when they had heard this, the disciples wondered much*. He says, therefore, *Then Jesus said to his disciples*, etc. The occasion of saying these words was that the man went away sad, because He had said, *Go sell what thou hast*, etc. *That a rich man shall hardly enter into the kingdom of*

---

11. "The archdeacon or parish priest receives his cure by simple appointment; although they are consecrated by receiving orders before having a cure" (II II, q. 184, a. 6 ad 2um).

heaven: He does not say that it is impossible. And He says, *A rich man*, and not one who has riches: because some men have riches, and do not love them; but other men have them, and they love them, and trust in them. Those who have riches, and do not love them, can enter into the kingdom of heaven. For if this were not so, Paul would not have said: "Charge the rich of this world not to be highminded nor to trust in the uncertainty of riches" (I Tim. 6, 17). But those who have and love them, shall hardly enter, etc. "The care of this world and the deceitfulness of riches choketh up the word" (above 13, 22). "He that maketh haste to be rich, shall not be innocent" (Prov. 28, 20). "Blessed is the rich man that is found without blemish: and that hath not gone after gold," etc., (Eccli. 31, 8). But this is difficult; for that reason, the quotation continues: "Who is he, and we will praise him? for he hath done wonderful things in his life" (ibid., verse 9). He adds something which seems to be impossible; hence, He says: *And again I say to you: It is easier for a camel to pass through the eye of a needle, than for a rich man to enter into the kingdom of heaven*. Above, the Lord had said that a rich man shall hardly enter into the kingdom of heaven; here, He says that it is impossible, just as it is impossible for a camel to pass through the eye of a needle: hence, consider a rich man who has riches and does not love them, it is difficult for him to enter; but consider the rich man who loves riches and trusts in them, it is impossible for him to enter into the kingdom of heaven. For when it is said that a camel cannot enter through an eye of a needle, this is due to its nature; however, that a rich man who loves riches cannot enter into the kingdom of heaven, this is due to divine justice; but the whole world could be turned upside down before divine justice could be changed. Others say, such as Jerome: "Impossibility is not meant, but difficulty." In a certain Gloss it is found, the author of which is unknown, that in Jerusalem there was a gate which was called the eye of a needle, through which loaded camels could not pass: so a rich man cannot enter into the kingdom of heaven, except he unburden himself from his attachment to riches. But it is easier for a camel to be unloaded, than for a rich man to get rid of his attachment. Chrysostom expounds this passage mystically: By the camel are signified the Gentiles, who are burdened with the sin of idolatry, and by the rich man the Jews are signified; the needle is Christ, and the eye of the needle is the Passion. Hence, it was easier for the Gentiles to pass through Christ's Passion, than for the Jews, because they could not come except by abandoning the ceremonies of the Law, and this they would not do. Hence, a demon was once asked, "What sin is the gravest?"[12] And he answered, "To possess another's property"; to whom it was replied, "You lie." "Not so," he said, "because other sinners I often lose, but these sinners I never lose." Or it is as follows: *It is easier*, etc, ought to be expounded such that by the rich man we understand a proud man; by the camel we understand Christ; by the eye of the needle we understand Christ's Passion: for that reason, it is easier for a camel to pass through the eye of a needle than for a proud man to be humbled.

And when they had heard this, the disciples wondered much, saying: Who then can be saved? Above, the Lord gave the reason for His teaching; here, He calms the astonishment of the disciples. And firstly, their astonishment is related; and secondly, the calming is related, where it is said, *And Jesus beholding, said to them*. He says, therefore: *And when they had heard this, the disciples wondered much, saying: Who then can be saved?*

But here there is a literal question. Since there are more poor men than rich men, and it is difficult for the rich to be saved, why do they say, *Who then can be saved?* It is answered that they knew that He also meant the poor, who are rich by their desire; because there are many poor men who are rich men by their desire. Likewise, these men had already become solicitous for the whole world: for which reason, that solicitude came upon them, which is found in II Corinthians 11, as they were the solicitous rulers of all creatures.

And Jesus beholding, said to them: With men this is impossible, etc. Here, He calms their astonishment saying: *With men this is impossible: but with God all things are possible.*

But what is He saying? For it seems free will has been destroyed if it is impossible with men. It is true that man, of himself, has the power to sin; but to rise from sin, and perform works of salvation, this power he does not have of himself without God's grace; for God Himself is He who can do these things. "It is not of him that runneth, nor of him that willeth, but of God that sheweth mercy" (Rom. 9, 16). Hence: "I know that thou canst do all things, and with Thee nothing is impossible" (Job 42, 2). Hence, according to human power, it is impossible for man to be saved, because human power does not change the will; rather, it belongs to God alone to change it, as it stated: "Who worketh in you, both to will and to accomplish" (Phil. 2, 13).

---

12. The text reads, "*gravius peccatum*" (more grievous sin); but the superlative "*gravissimum peccatum*" (gravest sin) seems to fit the context better.

Afterwards, He specifies the reward of the perfect. Firstly, a question is related; and secondly, the response, where it is said, *And Jesus said to them*. Peter had heard poverty praised, and he had heard: *Go sell all what thou hast, and give to the poor*. He had also heard that it is difficult for the rich to enter the kingdom of heaven, and for that reason, Peter reckoned that he had done something great, because he had left all things; hence, the Evangelist says, *Peter answering, said to him: Behold we have left all things*. And because he had not only heard that saying, *Go, and sell*, but furthermore, *And follow me*, etc.; for that reason, Peter adds, *And we have followed thee*. To leave all things does not make perfection, but rather to leave all things and to follow Christ, for many philosophers left all things. But Peter had left his boat and net. He is praised, however, more for his affection than for that which he left, because he left these things with a prompt will, and also he would have left anything else if he had more things. Likewise, he knew that Christ knew his will, for that reason, he says, *Behold we*, etc. By this he gave an example that those who left what they had ought not to be judged to have left few things, even if they had few things. And Jerome says that to leave one's things does not constitute perfection, but rather to follow the Lord constitutes perfection. And someone follows God in multiple ways. One follows God with his mind by contemplation; "We shall know, and we shall follow on, that we may know the Lord" (Osee 6, 3). Hence, they follow God, who have God before their eyes, and know God by way of contemplation. Likewise, one follows the Lord through the observance of the Commandments; "My sheep hear my voice, and they follow me" (Jn. 10, 27). Likewise, one follows Him by imitation of His deeds; "My foot hath followed his steps" (Job 23, 11). Similarly, one follows Him through contempt of oneself and one's possessions; "If any man will come after me, let him deny himself, and take up his cross, and follow me" (above 16, 24). Again, one follows Him by purity of mind and body; "These are they who were not defiled with women: for they are virgins. These follow the Lamb whithersoever he goeth" (Apoc. 14, 4). Voluntary poverty disposes to this kind of following of the Lord.

And Jesus said to them: Amen I say to you. Here He treats of the reward of perfection. Firstly, He relates the reward of the Apostles' perfection; secondly, He relates the reward of the perfection of other men; and thirdly, He excludes a particular objection. The second part is where it is said, *And every one that hath left*, etc.; and the third part is where it is said, *And many that are first, shall be last.* He says, therefore, **Amen I say to you**, etc. Since He wanted what He said to be certain, for that reason, He declares that He is telling the truth by saying, **Amen**. And to show that perfection does not consist in: **Go sell all what thou hast**, but that it rather consists in: **Follow me**; He says, **That you who have followed me, in the regeneration... you also shall sit on twelve seats**, etc. Regeneration is twofold. One is that of the spirit, which happens by grace in Baptism, concerning which it is said: "He hath regenerated us unto a lively hope" (I Pet. 1, 3). Likewise, there is a regeneration of the body: for just as the spirit is regenerated by grace, so also will He raise up our bodies in the resurrection. "He will reform the body of our lowness, made like to the body of his glory" (Phil. 3, 21). Some expound these words of the first regeneration, and they read the passage thus: **you who have followed me, in the regeneration**, that is, you have been regenerated by grace, **you shall sit**, etc. Chrysostom expounds the passage in the same way, but he does not read it in the same way; hence, he says that Christ promised them a reward in the present life; thus: **you who have followed me... you shall sit**. The Church that is now is the faith in Christ. In this Church, there are various conditions of men. And although all virtues are necessary for salvation, nevertheless, one man is more praiseworthy in the act of one virtue than of another virtue, and so some are more praiseworthy in faith, others in chastity, and others in charity: and as it is in different faithful, so it is in different Apostles; for Peter was the most fervently zealous for the faith, but John was strong in chastity; and so those who are fervent in faith are the seat of Peter, those who are strong in chastity are the seat of John, and so on for the other Apostles. But all the Apostles are the seat of Christ, because all virtues were in Him; for that reason, He promised them that they would be the future pastors of the Church. Otherwise, according to Augustine, what is said here concerning the regeneration is taken, namely, for the resurrection: **Amen I say to you, in the regeneration**, that is in the resurrection, when men will be called back according to their body and soul, **you shall sit**, namely, in the seat of majesty, that is to say, you will have judiciary power, **judging the twelve tribes of Israel**, because just as God gave judgment to His Son, so also will it be given to those who have followed Him.

But what is this that He says, **The twelve tribes of Israel**? Will they not also judge other men? Why then does He say, **The twelve tribes of Israel**? The entire populace of the faithful of the whole world is understood, because the heathen nations entered into the fatness of the olive tree, and were made partakers of the promises made to the Patriarchs. Those, however, who are infidels, will not be judged: for Gregory says that certain men are damned, and are not judged, such as the infidels:[13] certain men, however, are damned and judged, such as those who believed and were perverted. And, as Jerome asserts, the enemies will be condemned in one way, and those who have kept the faith in another way;[14] because the enemies will be condemned while absent, but the others will be condemned while present. For that reason, it is said, **you shall judge the twelve tribes of Israel**. Because the Apostles were converted with the Jews; thus it is said that they will judge the twelve tribes. And how will they do this? They will do this by comparison, because they had warned them. They might say: 'How could we have believed that you are God, you who were living mortally among us, etc.?' But the Lord will say: 'You were wise men in the Law, and you did not believe; these men were fishermen, and they believed.'

Chrysostom inquires whether what was given to the Apostles was something great. Was this not also given to the Ninevites and to the Queen of the South? (above 12, 41). Chrysostom says, that the very manner of judging shows that the authority of judging was given to the Apostles, because those who judge with authority judge while sitting, lawyers and accusers judge while standing; for that reason, to designate that the Apostles will judge with authority, He says, **You shall sit**. But concerning the Ninevites, He says: "The men of Ninive shall rise in judgment with this generation, and shall condemn it" (loc. cit.).

But here there is a question, because some men will be damned and will not be judged: so some men will be saved and will not be judged, such as the Apostles and apostolic men; but others to be saved will be judged, and their merits will be discussed. And how will they judge?

---

13. St. Gregory (Moralium xxvi) wrote, "the Judge will not address Himself to unbelievers."

14. "The judgment as regards the sentencing to punishment for sin concerns all the wicked; whereas the judgment as regards the discussion of merits concerns only believers. Because in unbelievers the foundation of faith is lacking, without which all subsequent works are deprived of the perfection of a right intention, so that in them there is no admixture of good and evil works or merits requiring discussion. But believers in whom the foundation of faith remains, have at least a praiseworthy act of faith, which though it is not meritorious without charity, yet is in itself directed towards merit, and consequently they will be subjected to the discussion of merits. Consequently, believers who were at least counted as citizens of the City of God will be judged as citizens, and sentence of death will not be passed on them without a discussion of their merits; whereas unbelievers will be condemned as foes, who are wont among men to be exterminated without their merits being discussed" (Suppl. Q. 89, a. 7).

Some say they will judge by comparison. But this does not suffice, because the Queen of the South will also judge in this way. Some say that they will judge through Christ's judgment. But this does not suffice, because all the Saints approve His judgment. "The just shall rejoice when he shall see the revenge" (Ps. 57, 11). Likewise, some say that they will judge through a kind of exemplary justice, because the just will be lifted up to meet Christ into the air,[15] and they will be Christ's assessors.[16] But this also does not suffice, because He says: *You also shall sit judging.*[17] Some say that they will judge just as a book judges: for it judges, because there are written therein the laws which judge him; so, likewise, the hearts of the Apostles and of the just, who have kept God's Commandments, will be the book judging them. The dead were judged, when the books were opened (Apoc. 20, 12). But it is more than this, because they shall exercise something else. Hence, in Psalm 149, 6, it is said: "Two-edged swords in their hands." Therefore, how will they judge? Take note. There will be a mental judgment, because it will happen by the Divine power that each person will be reminded of all their sins. Hence, Lactantius[18] was deceived, who asserted that the resurrection would take place before the judgment which will take place during a thousand years. Therefore, this will be a mental judgment, because, by the Divine power, the deeds which each person has done will be recalled to memory. But it is not unfitting that someone receive some light from another, because the angels receive light from God, and men receive light from angels; for that reason, it is not surprising that men will be enlightened by the Apostles, who will be full of light; thus, they will not only judge, but also other just men will receive a sort of light from them. But Christ will judge differently than the Apostles, because Christ will judge with authority, but they will judge as promulgators: just as the Law was given by angels,[19] so also the execution of the Judgment will be made by 'angels,' because, behold, they are called 'angels' ("He giveth judgment to the poor"[20]) who have followed justice and have left all things.

And why will they judge? One reason is that sins come from the world. Hence, the men who ought to judge, ought to be outside the world, and such are the Apostles and apostolic men; hence:

---

15. I Thessalonians 4, 16.
17. "But this apparently does not suffice for the fulfillment of our Lord's promise (Matthew 19:28): 'You shall sit... judging,' for He would seem to make 'judging' something additional to 'sitting.'" (Suppl. Q. 89, a. 1).
19. Hebrews 2, 2.

16. An assessor is one who sits by the judge.
18. Lactantius was a Christian lay apologist of the fourth century and was a Latin tutor for Crispus, a son of Constantine.
20. Job 36, 6.

"I have chosen you out of the world" (Jn. 15, 19). Likewise, the Philosopher says that a virtuous man is the judge of all men, just the sense of taste is the judge of all things having taste. Therefore, just as he who wishes to know the taste of something gives it to him who has a correct sense of taste: for that reason, since a virtuous man has a correct sense of virtue, he is consequently a standard of all actions; and so it is fitting that perfect men will judge as a standard of all actions; for that reason, perfect men will judge as a standard. Similarly, there is another reason, namely, that they are estranged from the world, and so they follow Christ more fervently. Therefore, these men ought to judge rather than other men, because they grow fervent from contemplation; "My heart grew hot within me: and in my meditation a fire shall flame out" (Ps. 38, 4). Hence, because they are more accustomed to contemplate, they are more fervent. Again, these men ought to judge because they were poor and more abased, because the reward of abasement is exaltation; for that reason, they will be exalted. Hence, He says, **You also shall sit judging**, etc.

But will not Judas also judge? No, because these promises are always conditional; hence, the Lord says, **You who have followed me**, etc. Hence, he who will have followed Me, and will have persevered, will judge, etc.

But if these men judge, what will Paul do? If the seats are full, where then will Paul be? Augustine says that by the number twelve is signified all things, because all things revolve around the number seven.[21] Therefore, the number twelve is derived from the quantity of seven, because the number seven is the sum of three and four, and three times four is twelve, or four times three is twelve; for that reason, by this number all the elect are signified.

And every one that hath left house, or brethren, etc. Having set forth the Apostles' reward, here the reward of other men is related: and here there are questions.

The first question is why did He promise nothing temporal to the Apostles, but to others He did promise something temporal, because He says, **He shall receive an hundredfold**, etc.? And the answer to this is clear, because in Mark it is stated that one shall receive a hundredfold, now in this time, etc.[22] According to Chrysostom, something temporal was promised to the Apostles, because judgment in the Church was promised to them, as it was

---

21. "And seven signifies universality: because 'universal time is involved in seven days'" (III, q. 33, a. 3 ad 3ᵘᵐ). "Time is counted by periods of seven days" (*Catena Aurea on St. John*, chap. 21, lect. 1).
22. "Who shall not receive an hundred times as much, now in this time" (Mk. 10, 30)

said before. Or it is otherwise, because everyone is allured by that for which he has an affection. Hence, those who have left the world and the things that are in world, are not allured by the things that are in the world; but those who are attached to worldly things, are allured by them. For that reason, He did not promise anything temporal to the Apostles, because they had left everything; but He did promise temporal things to other men, because they have an affection for temporal things; therefore, He promised judgment to the Apostles. Or, according to Origen, referring to the words, *In the regeneration*, this is the reward of those who have abandoned all things for Christ's sake.

But someone could say: 'I do not want to leave all things for Thy sake, I will leave one house, or one field, etc.' I say that if you relinquish something you will have something; but if you relinquish all things, you will be a judge.

But there is another question. He said *House*, and about this there is no doubt; but He says, *Father, or mother*, etc. He who commands someone to leave his father or mother, commands a sin. Likewise, He prescribed that a wife ought not to be left for the sake of pleasing one's parents.[23]

It ought to be said that in these things two points ought to be considered. Firstly, natural affinity ought to be considered; and this ought not to be despised, but instead, one ought to do good to them if they be in need. Sometimes, however, they pull one away from the service of God: hence, then they are like a scandalizing member, and, hence, that member must be cut off; and, for that reason, He prescribed leaving these things. Likewise, there is another reason, namely, that the Lord foresaw the time of a future persecution, in which brothers would rise against their brothers; thus, He wishes men to be separated from them.

There is another question, when He says, *He shall receive an hundredfold*, etc., namely, how is this to be understood? Some have said that the Saints will rise before the Judgment for a thousand years, and then Christ will have a complete kingdom: and then he who has left his house will have a hundred houses. Jerome rejected this opinion, because one will not have a hundred fathers, etc. Likewise, a shameful crime is implied, for one will not have a hundred wives. For that reason, Augustine says that this passage ought to be understood as referring to spiritual things. Hence, the Lord chose us to be poor in this world and heirs of the kingdom: hence, God's grace is under-

---

23. "Wherefore a man shall leave father and mother, and shall cleave to his wife: and they shall be two in one flesh" (Gen. 2, 24).

stood, which outweighs whatever you forsake and infinitely so. Hence, **You shall receive an hundredfold**, that is to say, you shall receive what is worth a hundredfold. Origen says that this also ought to be understood literally. 'When you leave a field, it will be by God's providence that you will find many things for your use'; hence, these things agree with the passage: "As having nothing and possessing all things" (II Cor. 6, 10). Likewise, you will find brothers, that is to say, all spiritual men. Moreover, besides this, you will possess **life everlasting**; "My sheep hear my voice. And I know them: and they follow me. And I give them life everlasting" (Jn. 10, 27-28).

Afterwards, an incidental point is introduced, **And many that are first, shall be last: and the last shall be first.** They, who left something for Christ's sake, or all things, if they live negligently will they have this reward? I say that they will not, because they took up Christ's service imperfectly, and they will not be the first but the last. Or it is otherwise, because they could say: He said, **You who have left all things**, etc., therefore we will judge. Those who were puffed up through pride shall be the last. Origen says that this can be understood of those who come to Christ and live tepidly; afterwards, others who are fervent come, and they surpass the others by their fervor. Or, He calls the first those who were born as Christians, who were made the last in respect to others who were born of heathens or Jews. Or it can refer to men or angels; because those who were first in the order of angels were made the last through their fault; and the last, meaning men, will become the first and higher than the angels.

CHAPTER TWENTY

1. The kingdom of heaven is like to an householder, who went out early in the morning to hire labourers into his vineyard.
2. And having agreed with the labourers for a penny a day, he sent them into his vineyard.
3. And going out about the third hour, he saw others standing in the marketplace idle.
4. And he said to them: Go you also into my vineyard, and I will give you what shall be just.
5. And they went their way. And again he went out about the sixth and the ninth hour, and did in like manner.
6. But about the eleventh hour he went out and found others standing, and he saith to them: Why stand you here all the day idle?
7. They say to him: Because no man hath hired us. He saith to them: Go ye also into my vineyard.
8. And when evening was come, the lord of the vineyard saith to his steward: Call the labourers and pay them their hire, beginning from the last even to the first.
9. When therefore they were come that came about the eleventh hour, they received every man a penny.
10. But when the first also came, they thought that they should receive more: And they also received every man a penny.
11. And receiving it they murmured against the master of the house,
12. Saying: These last have worked but one hour. and thou hast made them equal to us, that have borne the burden of the day and the heats.
13. But he answering said to one of them: Friend, I do thee no wrong: didst thou not agree with me for a penny?
14. Take what is thine, and go thy way: I will also give to this last even as to thee.
15. Or, is it not lawful for me to do what I will? Is thy eye evil, because I am good?
16. So shall the last be first and the first last. For many are called but few chosen.

Above, the Lord treated concerning the attainment of the kingdom of heaven by the common way of salvation, and by the way of perfection; and because certain men suppose they can unduly attain to it, therefore, they are refuted. And firstly, those who intend to come to the kingdom of heaven on account of a long length of time are refuted; and secondly, those who intend to come to the kingdom of heaven on account of carnal origin are refuted. The second part is where it is said, *And Jesus going up to Jerusalem*, etc. Therefore, the first point is put forth by way of the parable of the householder and the hired laborers. Firstly, He sets forth the parable; and secondly, He concludes that which the parable denotes, where it is said, *So shall the last be first and the first last*. The parable has two parts. Firstly, it treats of the hiring; and secondly, it treats of the payment. The second part is where it is said, *And when evening was come*, etc. About the first part, four hirings are related, which are invitations for the workers to work. The second hiring is where it is said, *And going out about the third hour*, etc. The third hiring is where it is said, *And again he went out about the sixth and the ninth hour*, etc. The fourth hiring is where it is said, *But about the eleventh hour he went out*. About the first, He mentions three things. Firstly, He mentions the one hiring; secondly, the hired laborers are mentioned; and thirdly, the manner of the hiring is related. The second part is where it is said, *Who went out early in the morning to hire labourers*. The third part is where it is said, *And having agreed*, etc. This householder is God, whose family is the whole world, but especially rational creatures; and He is called a householder from the similarity of His governance; "But thy wisdom, O Father, governeth all things" (Wis. 14, 3). *Who went out early in the morning to hire labourers into his vineyard*. Here, He treats of the hired laborers. Firstly, it is sought what the vineyard is, who the hired laborers are, and why they were hired. What is this vineyard? According to Chrysostom, it is justice, and it produces as many virtues as a vineyard produces branches; "My vineyard is before me" (Cant. 8, 12). Gregory says: "By the vineyard the holy Church is signified." "The vineyard of the Lord of hosts is the house of Israel" (Is. 5, 7). And there are different branches. The workers, however, are those who are descended from Adam, hence, all mankind; "The Lord God took Adam, and put him into paradise, to dress it, and to keep it" (Gen. 2, 15). For everyone ought to work justice, and to cultivate it, and to have care of his neighbor; "God gave to every one of them commandment concerning his neighbour" (Eccli. 17, 12). Spiritually, prelates are the workers; "And they shall be called in it the mighty ones of justice, the planting of the Lord to glorify him" (Is. 61, 3). Now they are called workers, who work for merit, and as though they were hirelings; "The life of man upon earth is a warfare, and his days are like the days of a hireling" (Job 7, 1). For just as a hireling does not immediately receive his wages, but waits, so we also wait in this life. But in order to be a good hireling, one must work for his master's benefit: and so, if we labor in the vineyard of the Church, we ought to refer all to God. Hence; "Therefore, whether you eat or drink, or whatsoever else you do, do all to the glory of God" (I Cor. 10, 31). Likewise, one firstly cultivates, and afterwards eats: and so, let us cultivate and prepare the salvation of others, and afterwards let us seek temporal things; "Seek ye therefore first the kingdom of God, and his justice, and all these things shall be added unto you" (above 6, 33); "Gird thyself and serve me, whilst I eat and drink; and afterwards thou shalt eat and drink" (Lk. 17, 8). Similarly, it is thirdly required that one be occupied the whole day with labor: so the cultivator of the Lord's vineyard spends little time of things that pertain to himself; but it is necessary that we expend all our time in God's service; "Always abounding in the work of the Lord" (I Cor. 15, 58). Moreover, one is ashamed to appear before his master without good work; "Thou shalt not appear empty before me" (Ex. 23, 15 & 34, 20). Now let us see what is the morning. The whole time of this world is one day; "A thousand years in thy sight are as yesterday, which is past" (Ps. 89, 4). The various hours are the various ages of the world. The first age was from Adam until Noe, and, in that time, the Lord foretold through messengers and apparitions that He would go into the vineyard of justice. Or it can be said that the whole life of a man is one day. The morning of this day is childhood. For childhood is fresh like a plant; hence, some men are called from childhood, for example, Jeremias, Daniel and John the Baptist were called from childhood. For that reason, He says: *Who went out early in the morning*, etc.

Next, the manner of hiring is specified: hence, He says; *And having agreed with the labourers for a denarius[1] a day*. By this denarius, eternal life is signified, because that denarius is worth ten ases.[2] Likewise, it had the impressed likeness of the king. Hence, what is signified by this denarius, consists in the observance of the Decalogue; "If thou wilt enter into life, keep the commandments" (above 19, 17). Likewise, eternal life has the likeness of God; "When he shall appear we shall be like to him" (I Jn. 3, 2).

---

1. A denarius is called "a penny" in the Douay-Rheims translation. A denarius was a coin anciently equal to four sesterces or ten ases, both of which were small coins used by the Romans.

2. "ORIGEN; The denarius I suppose here to mean salvation... REMIG; Well, therefore, does the denarius represent the reward of the keeping of the Decalogue" (*Catena Aurea on St. Matthew*, chap. 20, lect. 1).

Afterwards, He treats of the second hiring, where it is said, *And going out about the third hour*, etc. If we take one day to mean the whole time of this world, then just as the first hour signifies the time from Adam to Noe, so the following hour is from Noe to Abraham. Before the promises were made concerning Christ, He informed many men about Christ through angels, and He also had many men who were informing other men. But if we take one day to mean the life of one man, then the third hour is adolescence, because just as at the third hour of the day the sun begins to get hot, so, in adolescence, the sun of intelligence begins to shine forth. Likewise, one then begins to get hot with passion; "The sun rose with a burning heat" (James 1, 11). And He found these men *in the marketplace idle*. This marketplace [*forum*], according to the latter interpretation of a day, is the present life. Now a place in which one litigates is called a forum; a place in which one buys and sells is also called a forum,[3] and it signifies the present life, which is full of litigations, buying and selling; "The whole world is seated in wickedness" (I Jn. 5, 19). And these men were idle, because they had already wasted part of their lives; for not only those who act badly are called idle, but also those who do not do good. And just as the idle do not attain their end, so neither will these men. For the end of man is life everlasting; therefore, he who works in the manner in which he ought, will have it, or in other words, if he be not idle; "Idleness hath taught much evil" (Eccli. 33, 29). *And he said to them: Go you also into my vineyard*. He says this because God rewards according to His justice; "God will reward every one according to his justice" (I Kings 26, 23). But he did not agree with them for a denarius a day. Why did He make this agreement with the first men, but not with these men? The reason is according to the interpretation that relates a day to the ages of the world. For Adam was about to sin, and, for that reason, he might have been excused if he had not known his reward; but he knew it, because he foretasted it. Likewise, he who has a better mind, knows the truth better. Therefore, since Adam had a better mind, he knew the truth better. But He did not make this agreement with the others, because He always rewards more than He promises to do. "Eye hath not seen, O God, besides thee, what things thou hast prepared for them that love thee" (Is. 64, 4 & I Cor. 2, 9). Likewise, the first men were hired for the whole day. Therefore, they ought to have the full pay; for that reason, a denarius per day,

---

3. A *forum* in an ancient Roman city was both the marketplace and also the central meeting place where litigations took place.

which will be the full pay, is promised them. But a worker of the third hour does not give the whole day to God; for that reason, a denarius per day is not appropriate for him, for it could be that he will work more ardently, and so he will be paid more: or it could be that he will do so more negligently, which will not deserve a denarius per day; and so He says, *And I will give you what shall be just*: because, if they make up for the lost time, they will have full pay; "Every man's work shall be manifest, the day of the Lord shall declare it" (I Cor. 3, 13). Likewise, He invited the first men to the same labor, but the latter men went of their own accord; because little children do not have discretion, and so, if they do something good, it seems to be more from the Holy Ghost than from discretion: but, in adolescence, a man is moved by his own counsel. Similarly, it is said of the first men that He sent them; of these, it is said that they went of their own accord.

And again he went out about the sixth and the ninth hour. Following the interpretation that the ages of the world are called a day, so the sixth hour was from Abraham until David and the ninth hour was from David until Christ. But why does He join together these two hours? It is because His people were diversified, namely, the Jews and the Gentiles.[4] Hence, it can be said that the sixth hour is youth, because in the middle of the day the sun is in its perfection, and such is man in youth. Now the ninth hour is old age: and He joins these two hours together because the same manner of living is in both.

But about the eleventh hour he went out. The fourth hiring is related here: and He does three things. Firstly, He reprehends; secondly, they excuse;[5] and thirdly, they are invited. The second part is where it is said, *Because no man hath hired us.* The third part is where it is said, *Go ye also into my vineyard.* He says, therefore, *But about the eleventh hour he went out.* The eleventh hour[6] is the time of Christ. Hence, it is said: "Little children, it is the last hour" (I Jn. 2, 18). And: "God spoke in times past to the fathers by the prophets, last of all in these days, hath spoken to us by his Son" (Heb. 1, 1). "Behold I myself that spoke, am here" (Is. 52, 6). Or elderliness, or a decrepit age, can be called

---

4. "PSEUDO-CHRYS; These two hours are coupled together, because in the sixth and ninth it was that He called the generation of the Jews, and had more frequent contact with men in order to make covenants, as if to indicate that the appointed time of salvation now drew nigh" (*Catena Aurea on St. Matthew*, ibid.).

5. The text reads, "he excuses" (*excusat*) but "they excuse" seems to fit the context better.

6. The text reads, "the ninth hour," but this has been corrected here and elsewhere in this paragraph according to the *Catena Aurea on St. Matthew*, chap. 20, lect. 1.

the eleventh hour, because certain men remain in sin until a decrepit age. "In the evening he shall fall, grow dry, and wither" (Ps. 89, 6). *And found others standing.* He found the other men in the marketplace, but He did not find these men there. The reason, according to the Philosopher, is because there is a difference between adolescents and the elderly, namely, that all adolescents are in hope, while the elderly are not in hope, but in their memories. Hence, those first men were found in the marketplace, as it were, seeking to gain; these men, however, are found standing, as though not wanting to gain, but to watch over what they have acquired. Likewise, He saw the first men and He did not rebuke them; He saw these men, however, and He rebuked them, because the first men were still weak and their passions ruled in them, and so they were to be excused for not using their time to serve God: but old men abound with understanding, and, for that reason, He rebukes them. *Why stand you here all the day idle?* "He that pursueth idleness is very foolish" (Prov. 12, 11); and, "He that followeth idleness, shall be filled with poverty" (ibid. 28, 19). Their excuse follows, *They say to him: Because no man hath hired us.* If we refer this verse to the ages of the world, in this way, these men signify the Gentile nations, who do not serve God, but idols. But they are excused, because they did not have the prophets as the Jews did; hence, "He hath not done in like manner to every nation: and his judgments he hath not made manifest to them" (Ps. 147, 20). Or, referring this to the age of man, it is signified that, to certain men, an occasion of returning to God is not given until their old age. And the reason is, because all things have their time. Or it can happen from a Divine dispensation, because "to them that love God all things work together unto good" (Rom. 8, 28). Hence, the Lord knew that if He had called them before, they would not have heeded. Therefore, they are then hired when they consent, and they more effectually rise back to life; hence, He says, *Go ye also into my vineyard.* Hence, although they are decrepit, nevertheless, He wants all to be saved (1 Tim. 2).[7] Likewise, He promised a reward to the first workers, but not to these, because a reward was due to the former, because they served Him from early in the morning; to these men, however, a reward is due only out of mercy. "Being made perfect in a short space, he fulfilled a long time" (Wis. 4, 13).

And when evening was come, etc. Here, He treats of the payment. And firstly, the payment is related; secondly, the mur-

---

7. "God... will have all men to be saved and to come to the knowledge of the truth" (verse 4).

muring is related; and thirdly, the response is related. About the first, He does three things. Firstly, the time is related; secondly, the person commissioning the payment of the workers is related; and thirdly, the person commissioned to pay the workers is related. The time is related when it is said, *And when evening was come*, etc. And it can be understood either of the end of life, or of the end of the world. "In the evening weeping shall have place" (Ps. 29, 6), because the world's light fails. And it is said, *Evening*, because the Judgment will be in this world. *The lord of the vineyard saith to his steward*. The lord is the whole Trinity; *saith to his steward*, that is to say, to Christ. And the power of raising to life and the power of judging are given to Him, and the order of the Judgment is mentioned. The power of raising to life is mentioned, where it is said, *Call the labourers*, that is to say, raise the dead; "All that are in the graves shall hear the voice of the Son of God" (Jn. 5, 28). The power of judging is mentioned, where it is said, *Pay them their hire*, that is to say, 'Be Thou the judge'; hence, He gives Him the power of judging; "He hath given him power to do judgment, because he is the Son of man" (Jn. 5, 27). Afterwards, the order of the Judgment is mentioned, *Beginning from the last even to the first*. And this can be referred to the ages of the world. *Beginning from the last*, namely, from these last men,[8] who have been admitted to the mysteries of the faith. Hence, a greater grace was given to them than was given to the first; "[The mystery of Christ] in other generations was not known to the sons of men, as it is now revealed to his holy apostles and prophets in the Spirit" (Eph. 3, 4). Hence, more abundant grace was given to them, although some particular person in the Old Testament may have had a greater grace in a certain respect; "As yet the Spirit was not given, because Jesus was not yet glorified" (Jn. 7, 39), not because the Holy Ghost was not given, but because He was not then given as abundantly. Or it can be referred to the age of man, because those who are of a decrepit age, die more quickly, and are paid more quickly. Or it can be that, due to their fervor, they recuperate what they had previously lost, as it is read of the good thief. In regard to both, Chrysostom says that a man does more liberally what he does out of mercy than what he does in any other way; for that reason, a certain showing of kindness and joy are designated; "There shall be joy before the angels of God upon one sinner doing penance" (Lk. 15, 10). Then the execution follows, *When they were come that came about the*

---

8. The Christians are the workers of the last age of the world.

eleventh hour, either the Christians or men in a decrepit age, *they received every man a penny.* "Every man shall receive his own reward, according to his own labour" (I Cor. 3, 8). *But when the first also came* (you ought not to apply this to the time of the world, because the Jews were not in the first age)[9] *they thought that they should receive more,* because they had more in another age. *And they also received every man a penny,* because they each received a robe.

But what is this? Will all men have equal glory? I say that in a certain respect there will be an equal reward, and in another respect there will not: because beatitude can be considered as to the object of beatitude, and, in this way, there is one beatitude of all the blessed: or, as it can be considered as to the participation of the object of beatitude, and, in this way, not all men will participate equally, because all will not see just as clearly as each other; "In my Father's house there are many mansions" (Jn. 14, 2). And a comparison is that it is just as if many men go to the water, and one man were to carry a larger container than another: the river lays completely exposed, nevertheless, not all carry water away equally: so he, who has a soul more dilated by charity, will receive more glory, etc. "The blessing of God maketh haste to reward the just, and in a swift hour his blessing beareth fruit" (Eccli. 11, 24).

And receiving it they murmured against the master of the house, saying: These last have worked but one hour, etc. Above, the payment was related; here, the murmuring of certain men is related.

But at this point, there is a twofold question, because He says that those receiving a single denarius were murmuring. By the denarius eternal life is understood. How can anyone imagine that a man who has received the reward of eternal life would murmur? For it seems not, because then sin would be there, as it is stated: "Neither do you murmur" (I Cor. 10, 10).

Chrysostom says that the meaning ought not to be determined from what is said, but why it is said. Hence, it ought to be understood that there was so great a reward, that, if it were possible, they would murmur. Or the murmuring can be understood to have occurred in this world. Gregory says that this murmuring is nothing else than that the reward was delayed, because the Saints who came last immediately received a reward, but

---

9. The first age was from Adam to Noe. "CHRYS; But we ought not to pursue through every particular the circumstances of a parable; but enter into its general scope, and seek nothing further" (*Catena Aurea on St. Matthew,* ibid).

the first Saints waited a long time; "But having the same recompense (I speak as to my children): be you also enlarged," etc., (II Cor. 6 13). Hence, the former men murmur; because they did not receive their reward immediately: the latter men, however, do not murmur, because they received their reward immediately. Hilary and Jerome declare the meaning as follows: Sometimes Scripture speaks of the whole entirety of the people, sometimes of the good people, and sometimes of the bad people, as it is said in Jeremias 26 that all the people rose up against Jeremias, and all the people delivered him.[10] Here, all the people is taken for part of the people. So, in the first time, some men were good, but not all; for that reason, something is attributed by reason of the good men, and something is attributed by reason of the bad men, not because they murmured then, but because they murmured before, because the Jews murmured against the Gentiles, because they were made equal to themselves.

There is also another question. What is it that He says, *That have borne the burden of the day and the heats*? Because they did not bear them, except insofar as they lived, but modern-day men have lived as well. What, therefore, is that which is said?

It is answered in three ways. The first response is: that "Hope that is deferred, afflicteth the soul".[11] But, in the beginning of the world, there were those who bore the burden, because they knew that their reward was delayed; for that reason, it is said that they have borne the burden of the day. Or it can be referred to the Jews, who bore the burden of the Law, about which burden Peter says: "This is the burden which neither our fathers nor we have been able to bear" (Prov. 15, 10). The Gentiles, on the other hand, did not bear such a burden, because they were not subject to the Law. Or, according to Gregory, it is because the first men lived for a longer time, hence, they were living nine hundred years, and so they carried a heavier burden.

But he answering said to one of them. Here, His response is related. And firstly, He shows His justice and His mercy: secondly, He shows the fairness of His payment. About the first point, He does three things. Firstly, He denies His injustice; secondly, He cites His agreement; and thirdly, He cites the payment made. He says, therefore, *But he answering said to one of them*; and add, 'and to them all,' because they all had one issue

---

10. "And all the people were gathered together against Jeremias in the house of the Lord... Then the princes, and all the people said to the priests, and to the prophets: There is no judgment of death for this man: for he hath spoken to us in the name of the Lord our God" (verse 9 & 22).
11. Prov. 13, 12.

to be decided; *He said, friend.* He calls him His friend because He had drawn him to Himself. "He chose their seed after them" (Deut. 4, 37). *I do thee no wrong,* because 'I give to this man what is mine, not what is yours, for that reason, I do thee no wrong.' "Doth God pervert judgment?" (Job 8, 3). Then He recalls the agreement, *Didst thou not agree with me for a penny?* that is, for attaining salvation. "I am thy reward exceeding great" (Gen. 15, 1). *Take what is thine,* that is, what you have from my promise, *and go thy way,* that is, into glory; "I know whom I have believed and I am certain that he is able to keep that which I have committed unto him, against that day" (II Tim. 1, 12). Some expound the verse as follows: *Take what is thine,* that is, damnation for your murmuring, *and go thy way,* into eternal fire. But this cannot be, because He said that they each received a denarius. Afterwards, He sets forth His conferred mercy saying, *I will also give to this last even as to thee.* And about this, He does two things. Firstly, He sets forth His mercy; and secondly, He sets forth His ability of having mercy: *I will also give to this last,* that is, to the Gentiles, *even as to thee.* "What then? Do we excel them? No, not so" (Rom. 3, 9). But they could say: 'You are unable to have mercy.' On the contrary, He says: *Or, is it not lawful for me to do what I will?* Because it is lawful for everyone to do what he wants with what he owns. For if a man were a debtor to another, it would not be lawful for him, likewise, if he were subject to another; but He is the Lord, hence, He can give more. For a bailiff cannot give anything, except according to someone's merits; therefore, God, who is the Lord of all, can give something not according to someone's merits; "He hath done all things whatsoever he would" (Ps. 113, 11);[12] "Who resisteth his will?" (Rom. 9, 19). Here, it ought to be noted that in what is given out of mercy, there is no acceptation of persons, because from what is purely mine, I am able to give to whom I will without an acceptation of person.[13] Hence, He says, *Is thy eye evil, because I am good?* It is clear that the preceding murmuring did not

---

12. This is verse 3 (second set of numbering) in the Douay-Rheims Bible. "It is difficult to determine whether Ps. 113 should be one or two psalms as in the Massoretic Text (i.e., 114+115)" (Steinmueller, *A Companion to Scripture Studies,* vol. II, p. 173).

13. "There is a twofold giving. One belongs to justice, and occurs when we give a man his due: in suchlike givings respect of persons takes place. The other giving belongs to liberality, when one gives freely that which is not a man's due: such is the bestowal of the gifts of grace, whereby sinners are chosen by God. In such a giving there is no place for respect of persons, because anyone may, without injustice, give of his own as much as he will, and to whom he will, according to Matthew 20:14,15, 'Is it not lawful for me to do what I will?... Take what is thine, and go thy way.'" (II II, q. 63, a. 1 ad 3um).

come from a fault of the Lord, but from His mercy bestowed upon another, therefore, it was on account of His mercy and goodness: for that reason, He says, *Is thy eye evil, because I am good?* Since, in your regard, I have shown justice, and in regard to another, I have shown mercy? Now it is clear that this murmuring resulted because of His goodness. And, above, it was said, "If thy eye be single, thy whole body shall be lightsome" (6, 22). Concerning the Lord's goodness, it is written: "How good is God to Israel, to them that are of a right heart!" (Ps. 72, 1).

So shall the last be first and the first last. Here, He concludes the main point on account of which the whole parable was delivered. Firstly, He gives the conclusion: and secondly, He does away with a false opinion. He says, *So shall the last be first.* According to Chrysostom, this can be read in two ways; namely, that the last will be made equal to the first, and so there will be no difference between them; and this corresponds to what was said, namely, that they each received a denarius: nor will there be a difference as to time. Or it is otherwise, namely, they who are last will be first; "The stranger shall be over thee, and he shall be as the head, and thou shalt be the tail" (Deut. 28, 43-44). Or some men who were first, on account of their negligence, will become last: and this corresponds to what was just said, namely, that they began from the last. But someone could say: 'Will not all the first men be saved?' He says: *Many are called but few chosen*, because they who believe the faith are all called; but those are chosen who do good works, and these are few, as it was said above: "Strait is the way that leadeth to life: and few there are that find it" (7, 14).

17. And Jesus going up to Jerusalem, took the twelve disciples apart and said to them:

18. Behold we go up to Jerusalem, and the Son of man shall be betrayed to the chief priests and the scribes: and they shall condemn him to death.

19. And shall deliver him to the Gentiles to be mocked and scourged and crucified: and the third day he shall rise again.

20. Then came to him the mother of the sons of Zebedee with her sons, adoring and asking something of him.

21. Who said to her: What wilt thou? She saith to him: say that these my two sons may sit, the one on thy right hand, and the other on thy left, in thy kingdom.

22. And Jesus answering, said: You know not what you ask. Can you drink the chalice that I shall drink? They say to him: We can.

23. *He saith to them: My chalice indeed you shall drink; but to sit on my right or left hand is not mine to give to you, but to them for whom it is prepared by my Father.*
24. *And the ten, hearing it, were moved with indignation against the two brethren.*
25. *But Jesus called them to him and said: You know that the princes of the Gentiles lord it over them; and that they that are the greater, exercise power upon them.*
26. *It shall not be so among you: but whosoever is the greater among you, let him be your minister.*
27. *And he that will be first among you shall be your servant.*
28. *Even as the Son of man is not come to be ministered unto, but to minister and to give his life a redemption for many.*
29. *And when they went out from Jericho, a great multitude followed him.*
30. *And behold two blind men sitting by the way side heard that Jesus passed by. And they cried out, saying: O Lord, thou son of David, have mercy on us.*
31. *And the multitude rebuked them that they should hold their peace. But they cried out the more, saying: O Lord, thou son of David, have mercy on us.*
32. *And Jesus stood and called them and said: What will ye that I do to you?*
33. *They say to him: Lord, that our eyes be opened.*
34. *And Jesus having compassion on them, touched their eyes. And immediately they saw and followed him.*

In the preceding section, the Lord refuted those who attempted to obtain glory on account of a long length of time; here, He refutes him who attempts to obtain glory on account of carnal origin. Firstly, therefore, the occasion of a request is related; secondly, the request is related; and thirdly, the response is related. The occasion was the announcement of Christ's Passion. Firstly, He announces the place; secondly, He announces the Passion; and thirdly, He announces His Resurrection. He says, **And Jesus going up to Jerusalem**, etc. Above, in chapter 19, it was said that, having left Galilee, He came into Judea, and He did not immediately go up to Jerusalem, but only afterwards when His Passion was imminent; hence, the Evangelist says; **And going up**, meaning when He was ready to go up. Jerusalem was a high place. **He took the twelve disciples apart**, etc. And why does he say, *apart*? It was for two reasons. Firstly, it was because He wanted to show them great things; therefore, they were not to be communicated to all men; "To you it is given to know the mysteries of the kingdom of heaven" (above 13, 11). Likewise, it was to avoid scandal, because the men who were not yet perfect would have turned away from Him if they had heard about His death; and the women would have been moved to tears. Similarly, one ought to know that Judas had not yet contrived his evil deed; for that reason, the Lord did not remove him from His society. *And said to them: Behold we go up to Jerusalem*, etc. Here, the firmness of His intention is indicated, hence: *Behold*, meaning, 'I have the same intention and the same will, because I do not change'; "A fool is changed as the moon, but a wise man continueth in wisdom as the sun" (Eccli. 27, 12). Likewise, He acts of His own volition; "He was offered because it was his own will" (Is. 53, 7). He mentions the place, namely, Jerusalem; "It cannot be that a prophet perish, out of Jerusalem" (Lk. 13, 33). And why is this? It is because it was the legal and sacerdotal place: and both correspond to Christ; because just as a true priest was obliged to offer sacrifice for the people, so also Christ offered Himself a victim for the world. Likewise, by His Passion, He acquired a kingdom. Moreover, Jerusalem is interpreted 'vision of peace'; "Making peace through the blood of his cross, both as to the things that are on earth and the things that are in heaven" (Col. 1, 20). Afterwards, the Passion is foretold. And He frequently mentions His Passion, so that He might call it to mind. And He mentions three things pertaining to the Passion. The first is that He suffered betrayal by a disciple, *The Son of man shall be betrayed*, namely, by a disciple. Concerning this betrayal, it is stated below (26, 15)[14] and in Psalm 40, 10: "He who ate my bread, hath greatly supplanted me." Likewise, He mentions His condemnation by the chief priests and scribes; hence, *And they shall condemn him to death*; "How dost thou so far condemn him that is just?" (Job 34, 17) "Let us condemn him to a most shameful death" (Wis. 2, 20). *And they shall deliver him to the Gentiles*, because the Jews delivered him into the hands of the Gentiles; hence, Pilate said: "Thy own nation and the chief priests have delivered thee up to me" (Jn. 18, 35). And He mentions three things which they did to Him, in opposition to three things which men desire the most, namely, honor, rest, and life. Opposed to honor, He was mocked; hence, He

---

14. "Judas Iscariot said to the chief priests: What will you give me, and I will deliver him unto you? But they appointed him thirty pieces of silver." The text gives as the reference, Mt. 27, 10, but this does not seem to be correct.

says, ***To be mocked***; "I am become a laughingstock all the day" (Jer. 20, 7); and in Psalm 37, 12, it is said: "My friends and my neighbors have drawn near, and stood against me." Opposed to rest, He was scourged; ***To be scourged***; "I have given my body to the strikers, and my cheeks to them that plucked them" (Is. 50, 6). Similarly, opposed to the third thing, He was killed; hence, ***To be crucified***; "He became obedient for us unto death, even to the death of the cross" (Phil. 2, 8). Then He treats of the Resurrection, ***And the third day he shall rise again***. Now God the Father did this; hence: "Whom God hath raised up, having loosed the sorrows of hell, as it was impossible that he should be holden by it" (Acts 2, 24). ***And the third day***. According to Augustine,[15] it is signified that His single [death] destroyed our double [death]; "He will revive us after two days: on the third day he will raise us up" (Osee 6, 3).

Then came to him the mother of the sons of Zebedee. Here the occasioned request is related. Firstly, the request is related in general; and secondly, it is specified, where it is said, ***Who said to her***, etc. He says, therefore: ***Then came to him the mother of the sons of Zebedee***. These sons were John and James, and their mother was Salome: hence, Salome is a woman's name. In Mark it is stated that the sons asked, but here it is stated that their mother asked; but it is true that the mother asked after having been prompted by her sons. ***Adoring***, because she asked with humility; for she knew that humble prayer always pleases God; "He hath had regard to the prayer of the humble" (Ps. 101, 18). And, "And falling down prostrate before the Lord, she cried to the Lord" (Judith 9, 1). ***And asking something***, to be given, ***by him***: that is to say, 'I ask Thee to give what I wish.' And this request is not to be heard, and he who grants this, grants it foolishly. It is read of Herod that he granted this to the daughter of Herodias, and he did not revoke it; Solomon, however, granted this to his mother; but because he was wise, he revoked what he had incautiously promised. Therefore, Christ, being wiser than these men, did not wish to grant something unless it were expressed; "And behold a greater than Solomon here" (above 12, 42). For that reason, the specification of the request follows, ***Say that these my***

---

15. "We certainly, as no Christian doubts, are dead both in soul and body: in soul, because of sin; in body, because of the punishment of sin, and through this also in body because of sin... The one death therefore of our Savior brought salvation to our double death, and His one Resurrection wrought for us two resurrections; since His body in both cases, that is, both in His death and in His Resurrection, was ministered to us by a kind of healing suitableness, both as a mystery of the inner man, and as a type of the outer" (*On the Trinity*, Bk. IV, chap. 3).

two sons may sit, the one on thy right hand, and the other on thy left, in thy kingdom.
But there is a question, namely, from whence this woman contrived this request. She had heard about the Passion and Resurrection, hence, she contrived something carnal, that He was due to be immediately surrounded by glory in Jerusalem; for that reason, she wished to request high places for her sons. Likewise, she had heard that the twelve were to judge; hence, she wanted to put her sons in the first places; hence, she understood literally what was said. And it ought to be known that James and John were honored the most after Peter; for that reason, they wanted to exclude Peter. Chrysostom says otherwise, that this woman asked for something spiritual, and in this she was to be praised, because mothers ask for what is temporal rather than for what is spiritual; hence, if a mother sees her son sinning, she is not as sad as she would be if she sees him sick. Hence, spiritual things are signified by the right hand, and earthly things by the left hand. Or, we can understand by the right and left hand, the active and contemplative lives; for that reason, she requests that these sons be perfected in both lives; "His left hand is under my head, and his right hand shall embrace me" (Cant. 2, 6).

And Jesus answering, said. Here the response is related; then the murmuring of the others is related, where it is said, *And the ten, hearing it, were moved with indignation against the two brethren.* And about the first, He does three things. Firstly, He rebukes their foolishness; secondly, He examines their readiness, where it is said, *Can you drink the chalice that I shall drink?*; and thirdly, He refuses their request, where it is said, *To sit on my right or left hand is not mine to give to you.*

But what is this? They were not asking, but the mother. The Lord knew that she was asking having been prompted by them, for that reason, He responds to them, as the Lord had said above (16, 23)[16] to Peter: *You know not what you ask.*

You know not what you ask; it is as though He were to say: 'You ought not to ask for temporal things, but rather for spiritual excellence.' Or, if they understood His right and left hand to be something spiritual, they were asking that they might have eminence over every creature, because to sit at His right hand is unseemly for any creature, as it is written: "To which of the angels said he at any time: Sit on my right hand?" (Heb. 1, 13).

---

16. "Who turning, said to Peter: Go behind me, Satan," etc.

Hence, to sit at His right hand surpasses every creature. Or it is to be understood otherwise, according to Hilary: *You know not what you ask*; because what you ask has already been granted to you, because it was said above: "You also shall sit on twelve seats," etc., (19, 28). Or it is otherwise: *You know not*, 'because I have called you to sit on My right hand, and you ask that one of you be on My left hand?' Or, just as the devil had drawn man by the woman to the left hand, so he wanted to bring back these men to the left hand by a woman; but he was unable to do this, due to the fact that salvation was won through a woman. Or, *You know not*, because you vie for a reward without the preceding merit. Therefore, you ought to consider that one does not receive a reward except by merit; for that reason, I want you to consider if you can suffer, etc. Hence, He says: *Can you drink the chalice that I shall drink?* Here, He examines them, and He gently rouses them to suffer, because He calls His suffering a chalice. Concerning this chalice, it is said in Psalm 115, 13: "I will take the chalice of salvation"; and it continues: "Precious in the sight of the Lord is the death of his saints" (verse 15). And His Passion is called a chalice, because it inebriates.[17] Likewise, He says, *That I shall drink*; "Christ also suffered for us, leaving you an example that you should follow his steps" (I Pet. 2, 21). *They say to him: We can*. And why do they answer in this way? It is on account of three things. Firstly, it was due to their love for Christ, because they were so united to Christ that death could not separated them from Him, as Peter said: "Yea, though I should die with thee, I will not deny thee" (below 26, 35).

Likewise, it was out of ignorance, because they did not consider their own strength, because sometimes one's strength fails in actually doing what before the fact seemed easy. Similarly, they spoke out of an excessive desire to get what they had requested. Hence, they thought that they would immediately obtain what they were requesting, thus, they immediately say out of cupidity, *We can* do this.

Afterwards, He rejects their request. Firstly, He foretells His Passion; and secondly, He replies to their request. He says, therefore, *My chalice indeed you shall drink*.

But what is this? It is true that James drank this chalice; hence, it is said: "And he killed James, the brother of John, with the sword" (Acts 12, 2). But John died without the chalice of suffering.

---

17. "Christ's Passion is understood by the chalice by way of comparison, because, like a cup, it inebriates, according to Lamentations 3:15: 'He hath filled me with bitterness, he hath inebriated me with wormwood'" (III, q. 78, a. 3 ad 3[um]).

But it ought to be said that he did not drink to the point of death, but he was scourged, put in oil, and exiled. Likewise, he suffered many punishments, and so he was not exempt from drinking this chalice.[18]

But to sit on my right hand. Here, He responds to the request for glory. If the Lord had said, 'I will give this to you,' the others would have been sad. If He had refused, these men would have been sad; and so He said, *But to sit on my right or left hand is not mine to give to you, but to them for whom it is prepared by my Father.* Based on this passage, the Arians argued that the greatness of the Father and the Son was not equal. Jerome and others expound this passage by saying that He gives with the Father. Hence, He wishes to say, *It is not mine to give to you*; it is as though He were to say, 'The dignity of greatness is not given to a person, but is merited; and this is done according to Divine predestination.' "Eye hath not seen, nor ear heard: neither hath it entered into the heart of man, what things God hath prepared for them that love him" (I Cor. 2, 9). "If I shall go and prepare a place for you," etc., (Jn. 14, 3). Hence, based upon these passages, the Father and He Himself prepare a place. Or, *'It is not mine to give to you*, without your merits. While other persons acquire greatness by merit, My dignity is from My predestination, which is Mine from My Father.' And Augustine expounds this passage as follows: Salome was the sister of Christ's mother:[19] and because they supposed that they were making their request though someone more closely joined to Him, they supposed that it ought to be given to them,

---

18. "In the second general persecution, in the year 95, St. John was apprehended by the proconsul of Asia, and sent to Rome, where he was miraculously preserved from death when thrown into a caldron of boiling oil. On account of this trial, the title of martyr is given him by the Fathers, who say that thus was fulfilled what Christ had foretold him, that he should drink of his cup" (*Butler's Lives of the Saints*, St. John the Evangelist).

19. "(1) Mary the mother of the Lord; (2) Mary the wife of Cleophas or Alphaeus, who was the mother of James the bishop and apostle, and of Simon and Thaddeus, and of one Joseph; (3) Mary Salome, wife of Zebedee, mother of John the evangelist and James; (4) Mary Magdalene. These four are found in the Gospel. James and Judas and Joseph were sons of an aunt (2) of the Lord's. James also and John were sons of another aunt (3) of the Lord's. Mary (2), mother of James the Less and Joseph, wife of Alphaeus was the sister of Mary the mother of the Lord, whom John names of Cleophas, either from her father or from the family of the clan, or for some other reason. Mary Salome (3) is called Salome either from her husband or her village. Some affirm that she is the same as Mary of Cleophas, because she had two husbands" (Fragments of Papias From the Exposition of the Oracles of the Lord, X). "Salome is otherwise called Mary, and was sister to the Blessed Virgin, which some take in the strict sense of the word; others understand by it only cousin-german, according to the Hebrew phrase, and think that the Blessed Virgin was an only daughter" (Butler, *Lives of the Saints*, "St. James the Greater").

because they were more closely joined to Him according to the flesh. But in Him there were two natures in one Person; hence, He says, *It is not mine*, namely, according to the power that I have from the Father, and, for that reason, I will give according to what My Father has appointed Me to give.[20]

The ten, hearing it, were moved with indignation against the two brethren. Above, the Lord had restrained the indiscrete request of the disciples; here, the Evangelist points out the indignation of the others. Firstly, their indignation is pointed out; secondly, they are restrained by words; and thirdly, they are restrained by a deed. The second part is where it is said, *But Jesus called them to him and said*; and the third part is where it is said, *Even as the Son of man is not come to be ministered unto, but to minister.* It ought to be considered that just as from a quasi-elation the two brothers wanted to be superior, so from a quasi-elation these others were indignant. "Among the proud there are always contentions" (Prov. 13, 10).

But why were they indignant concerning the two brothers? For they had not asked, but instead their mother asked. But the disciples understood from the Lord's words that the mother had asked at their instigation.

But why were they not indignant before? Chrysostom says that they were respecting their Master, hence, they waited for the Lord's judgment; but when they heard the Master reprehending, they then were indignant.

Afterwards, He reprehends them. Firstly, He puts before them the example of the Gentiles; secondly, He teaches that their example ought not to be followed, where it is said, *You know that the princes of the Gentiles lord it over them*; and thirdly, He proposes what example ought to be imitated, where it is said, *It shall not be so among you.* He says, therefore, *But Jesus called them to him*, to give them an example of humility. "Learn of me, because I am meek, and humble of heart" (above 11, 29). And He says: *You know that the princes of the Gentiles lord it over them.* Among the Jews, the Gentiles were abominable, as it is stated above: "Let him be to thee as the heathen and publican" (18, 17). Hence, He inspires them with horror, *The princes of the Gentiles lord it over them*; He says this so that they might know that this example ought not

---

20. "AUG; The Lord makes answer to His disciples in His character of servant; though whatever is prepared by the Father is also prepared by the Son, for He and the Father are one" (*Catena Aurea on St. Matthew*, chap. 20, lect. 3).

to be imitated. But it ought to be observed that preeminence is twofold, namely, of dignity and of power; and He mentions both when He says, *The princes of the Gentiles lord it over them*, etc. Princes are those who rule in virtue of their office.

But what is this? Is it evil to act lordly? Sometimes 'to lord' is said for 'to rule'; and it is not taken in this sense here: sometimes it is taken correlatively as having to do with a slave: hence, it is the same as to servilely subject a slave to oneself; and so it is taken here. For princes were appointed for the sake of procuring the good of their subjects; if, on the contrary, they wish to force them into servitude, then they abuse their subjects, because they use free men as slaves: for "what is free is cause of itself,"[21] a slave is a cause of another.[22] And because this was the custom among the Gentiles, and still is the custom among some men, so He says, *The princes of the Gentiles lord it over them*, meaning they force their subjects into servitude. "Her princes in the midst of her, are like ravening wolves" (Ez. 22, 27).

Likewise, some men have eminence not in dignity, but in power, as some nobles do. And it is common that those who have power do not use it for doing good, but *exercise power upon them*, in fact, to oppress them, and not according to justice. But the Lord does not want this practice to be in His Church; for that reason, He says, *It shall not be so among you*, meaning a man ought not to be among you as though domineering; "Neither as lording it over the clergy" (I Pet. 5, 3). *But whosoever*. But opposed to these two things, He says two things. *But whosoever is the greater among you*; and this refers to the second thing that was said, namely, *They that are the greater, exercise power upon them*; meaning he who so desires to have a position of authority in the Church of the Holy Ghost, ought to be as a minister; "As every man hath received grace, ministering the same one to another: as good stewards" (I Pet. 4, 10), such that so much the more will you have, the more you spend on useful things. For that reason, *he that will be greater among you*, meaning in the Church, *let him be your minister*, meaning

---

21. De Metaphysica i,2.
22. "It ought to be also known that a servant is properly one who is not a cause of himself: a freeman, on the other hand, is one who is the cause of himself: There is, therefore, a difference between the actions of a slave and a freeman: because a slave works as a cause of another; a freeman, however, works as a cause of himself, both in regard to the final cause of the work, and as to the moving cause. For a freeman works for himself, as for an end, and he works of himself, because he is moved to his work by his own will; but a slave works not for himself, but for his master, nor of himself but by his master's will, as though by compulsion" (St. Thomas, *Commentary of St. John*, chap. 20, lect. 3).

let him minister to the needs of others. Now as to that which is said, *The princes of the Gentiles lord it over them*; He says: *And he that will be first among you shall be your servant*; meaning, if anyone desires to have primacy in the Church, let him know that that is not to have dominion, but servitude. For it belongs to a slave that he expend himself entirely in the service of his master: so that prelates of the Church owe to their subjects everything whatsoever they have, everything they are; "Whereas I was free as to all, I made myself the servant of all" (I Cor. 4, 5). Hence, according to Chrysostom, it is something miserable. Therefore, it is so said because one ought not to act according to the custom of the Gentiles. Because, therefore, they could say: 'What custom will we follow?' He says, 'Follow Me': and He shows that He is a minister saying, *Even as the Son of man is not come to be ministered unto, but to minister.*

But it was on the contrary. Is it not stated above that "angels came and ministered to him" (4, 11)? Furthermore, in John 12, 2, it is said that "Martha served [Him]." I say that He was ministered unto, nevertheless, He did not come for that purpose. But why did He come? It was so that He might minister, meaning it was so that He might bestow the abundances of His glory upon others. "For I say that Christ Jesus was minister of the circumcision" (Rom. 15, 8). And in Luke 23, 27, it is said: "I am in the midst of you, as he that serveth."

But you will say: 'He certainly is not a servant, since He is a ruler.' Indeed. Yet a man is called a servant who is valued at a price: and He made Himself to be a price, and gave Himself as a redemption for many; hence, *He is come to minister and to give his life a redemption for many.* He does not say for all, because, as far as sufficiency, He came for all; but as far as efficiency, He came for many, namely, for the elect. Hence: "Greater love than this no man hath, that a man lay down his life for his friends" (Jn. 15, 13). "I have given my dear soul into the hand of her enemies" (Jer. 12, 7). *And when they went out from Jericho, a great multitude followed him.* After having repressed the indignation of the disciples with His words, here He represses it by a deed, namely, by ministering to others. Firstly, the devotion of other men is related; secondly, Christ's compassion is related, where it is said, *Behold two blind men*, etc. He says, therefore, *And when they went out from Jericho, a great multitude followed him*; because many followed Him, the Lord was solicitous about them, just as much corn is the solicitude of the harvester. But, according to a mystery, corruption is called Jericho,[23] and it signifies the corruption of the world. Hence, unless the Lord had come to these corruptions, men would not have come to Him. Hence, *A great multitude followed him*, as if they were His sheep; "My sheep hear my voice, and they follow me" (Jn. 10, 27). The devotion of the blind men follows, *And behold two blind men*, etc. Firstly, their devotion is related; and secondly, their constancy is related, where it is said, *And the multitude rebuked them that they should hold their peace*.

Augustine says that the blind man, about whom Luke writes, was different from these men, because he met Him before He entered Jericho. But Mark and Matthew say that He was coming out of Jericho;[24] but the reason why Mark did not say two men, as Matthew did, is because one was well-known and famous, and, on account of the miracle, he was more famous. And this is evident because he names him, when he is called Bartimeus, and only very well-known men are named in Scripture.

By these two men, two peoples are signified, namely, the people of the Jews and the people of the Gentiles, who were sitting along the way, which is Christ. "This is the way, walk ye in it" (Is. 30, 21). Or the converts from both peoples are signified, who were sitting along the way, meaning Christ; "I am the way, and the truth, and the life" (Jn. 14, 6). They heard through preaching, because Jesus passed through according to His human nature, so that He might undergo death, in order to cure the sick, and, for that reason, *they cried out, saying: O Lord, thou son of David, have mercy on us*. The reason for their being heard was not the loudness of their cry, but the fervor of their devotion. "In my trouble I cried to the Lord: and he heard me" (Ps. 119, 1). Likewise, they confessed Him to be God and man: God, because they say: *Lord*. "Know ye that the Lord he is God" (Ps. 99, 3). And they ask for what is proper to God, namely, to *Have mercy on us*. "His tender mercies are over all his works" (Ps. 144, 9). Likewise, they say He is of the seed of David: and in this they confess His humanity.

---

23. "RABAN; But Jericho, which is interpreted 'the moon,' denotes the infirmity of our changefulness" (*Catena Aurea* on *St. Matthew*, chap. 20, lect. 5).

24. "But since St. Luke's narrative agrees in all points with that of St. Matthew and St. Mark, we must suppose that it was one and the same blind man whose prayer to Christ for the restoration of his sight was not heard on account of the crowd, and Christ made as though He heard Him not, that He might quicken his faith and hope, and then on the following day he repeated his prayer as Christ went out and obtained it. So St. Ambrose, Madonatus, and others explain it" (Cornelius à Lapide, *The Great Commentary: St. Matthew's Gospel*, (John Hodges, 1893) vol. 2, pp. 391-392).

Afterwards, their constancy is related. Firstly, an obstacle is related; and secondly, their constancy is related. He says, therefore, **And the multitude rebuked them that they should hold their peace**, and this was possible, because, in this multitude, some men were venerating Christ, and these were rebuking them because they deemed it repugnant that vile persons would approach so great a man. On the other hand, those men who scorned Christ were rebuking these men because they were hearing what they did not want to hear: for they deplored that they were calling Him the son of David. "I will raise up David my servant" (Jer. 23, 5). Mystically, it is signified that some men, who have been blinded by sin, cry to the Lord, **Have mercy on us**. But the multitudes of carnal thoughts and of carnal men rebuke them for coming to Christ. "Therefore, various thoughts succeed one another in me, and my mind is hurried away to different things" (Job 20, 2). But a man ought to be constant against this and to fight and labor manfully, just as the Apostle teaches: "Labour as a good soldier of Christ Jesus" (II Tim. 2, 3). But the word of God is not hindered by the words of men; and so it follows, **But they cried out the more**.

And Jesus stood. Here, the Lord's mercy is related and shown, because He stood. And why did He stand still? It was because the way is rocky and full of pits; and so, He wished to stand, because if He were to go on, they might perhaps get hurt. There is a mystical meaning, namely, that, by coming into the world, He stirred up men to seek salvation, but by standing, He gave it. Hence, by the Incarnation, men are helped, but by His teaching and persevering they are healed. It continues, **He called them**. But why did He call them? It was so that others might make way for them; and it signifies those whom the Lord calls through predestination. "Whom he foreknew, he also predestinated" (Rom. 8, 29). Likewise, He examines their will, **What will ye that I do to you?** He does not ask so that He might know, but so that He might give us to understand that He satisfies the wishes of those who ask piously. "He will do the will of them that fear him" (Ps. 144, 19). **They say to him: Lord, that our eyes be opened**. And any sinner may justly ask for this. "Open thou my eyes: and I will consider the wondrous things" (Ps. 118, 18). And elsewhere, it is written: "Enlighten my eyes" (Ps. 12, 4). They were confessing Him to be God by saying, **Lord**, and man by calling Him the **son of David**; for that reason, He showed mercy to them. For He does everything out of mercy. "The mercies of the Lord that we are not consumed"

(Lam. 3, 22). *He touched their eyes, and immediately they saw.* By the fact that He touched their eyes, and they immediately saw, Christ's humanity and divinity are implied: for in that He touched, this was the work of His humanity; but that He immediately gave sight, this was the work of the divinity. The Lord Himself touches by grace, but He gives sight by glory; "Touch the mountains, and they shall smoke" (Ps. 143, 5). The passage continues, *And they followed him.* Hence, they were not ungrateful. For many men follow the Lord before they receive a favor, but once they have received it they leave Him, and this is contrary to that which is written: "It is great glory to follow the Lord" (Eccli. 23, 38).

CHAPTER TWENTY-ONE

1. And when they drew nigh to Jerusalem and were come to Bethphage, unto mount Olivet, then Jesus sent two disciples,

2. Saying to them: Go ye into the village that is over against you: and immediately you shall find an ass tied and a colt with her. Loose them and bring them to me.

3. And if any man shall say anything to you, say ye that the Lord hath need of them. And forthwith he will let them go.

4. Now all this was done that it might be fulfilled which was spoken by the prophet, saying:

5. Tell ye the daughter of Sion: Behold thy king cometh to thee, meek and sitting upon an ass and a colt, the foal of her that is used to the yoke.

6. And the disciples going, did as Jesus commanded them.

7. And they brought the ass and the colt and laid their garments upon them and made him sit thereon.

8. And a very great multitude spread their garments in the way: and others cut boughs from the trees and strewed them in the way.

9. And the multitudes that went before and that followed cried, saying: Hosanna to the son of David: Blessed is he that cometh in the name of the Lord: Hosanna in the highest.

10. And when he was come into Jerusalem, the whole city was moved, saying: Who is this?

11. And the people said: This is Jesus, the prophet from Nazareth of Galilee.

12. And Jesus went into the temple of God and cast out all them that sold and bought in the temple and overthrew the tables of the money changers and the chairs of them that sold doves.

13. And he saith to them: It is written, My house shall be called the house of prayer; but you have made it a den of thieves.

14. And there came to him the blind and the lame in the temple: and he healed them.

15. And the chief priests and scribes, seeing the wonderful things that he did and the children crying in the temple and saying: Hosanna to the son of David, were moved with indignation,

16. And said to him: Hearest thou what these say? And Jesus said to them: Yea, have you never read: Out of the mouth of infants and of sucklings thou hast perfected praise?

17. And leaving them, he went out of the city into Bethania and remained here.
18. And in the morning, returning into the city, he was hungry.
19. And seeing a certain fig tree by the way side, he came to it and found nothing on it but leaves only. And he saith to it: May no fruit grow on thee henceforward for ever. And immediately the fig tree withered away.
20. And the disciples seeing it wondered, saying: How is it presently withered away?
21. And Jesus answering, said to them: Amen, I say to you, if you shall have faith and stagger not, not only this of the fig tree shall you do, but also if you shall say to this mountain, Take up and cast thyself into the sea, it shall be done.
22. And all things whatsoever you shall ask in prayer believing, you shall receive.

Above, it was stated that Matthew's Gospel was divided into three parts: in the first part, he relates Christ's entrance into the world up until the third chapter; secondly, he treats of His course of life in the world; in the third part, he treats of His departure. Having completed, therefore, the first two parts, here is treated about the third. And it is divided as follows: firstly, he treats of what one might call preambles; secondly, he treats of the crucifixion, and this is in chapter 26. And firstly, the provocation of the persecutors is related; secondly, the strengthening of the disciples is related, and this is in chapter 24. He had strengthened the disciples by foretelling future events. Afterwards, some men were provoked by His glory, which they envied; this is treated in this chapter. Some men were provoked by His knowledge, and this is treated in chapter 22. The first part is divided into two parts. For firstly, Christ's glory is treated; and secondly, the persecutors' indignation is treated, where it is said, **And the chief priests and scribes, seeing**, etc. About the first, there are three things. Firstly, Christ's glory that was shown on the way is related; and secondly, His glory shown in the city is related; and thirdly, the glory which He received in the Temple by His powerful deeds is related. The second part is where it is said, **And when he was come into Jerusalem**, etc. The third part is where it is said, **And Jesus went into the temple of God**. On the way, glory was conferred upon Him by two things, namely, by His disciples and by the ministration of the multitudes. The second part is where it is said, **And a very great multitude spread**

their garments in the way. And about the first, there are three things. Firstly, orders about the ministration are related; secondly, the reason is related; and thirdly, the execution of the orders is related. The second part is where it is said, ***Now all this was done***, etc.; and the third part is where it is said, ***And the disciples going***, etc. About the first, there are three points. Firstly, the place is related; secondly, the persons to whom the orders are made are related; and thirdly, the orders are related. The place is related when he says, ***And when they drew nigh to Jerusalem***, etc. Gradually, the Evangelist set forth Christ's coming to Jerusalem. Firstly, he set forth how He had come from Galilee, and how through Jericho, and how He had given sight to blind men there, who were in the surrounding area. Afterwards, he says, ***When they drew nigh to Jerusalem and were come to Bethphage, unto mount Olivet.*** And it is so-called, because there were many olive trees there: and it is one mile distant from Jerusalem. Bethphage was a priestly town, because the priests were serving the Temple every week: now on the Sabbath day, the priest leaving came as far as that place, because they were not supposed to walk more than one mile on the Sabbath day. Also, those priests who were going to the Temple on the Sabbath day were departing from thence. Or, Bethphage has the same meaning as 'the house of jaw bones,' because the jaw bone of the victim was the portion of the priest.[1] According to the moral sense,[2] Jerusalem is interpreted to mean 'vision of peace,' and it

---

1. "Bethphage is a priestly place, the name of which means 'House of Jaw-bones.'" (Origen, *Commentary on the Gospel of John* Book X, 18). "After this, Paula visited the tomb of Lazarus and beheld the hospitable roof of Mary and Martha, as well as Bethphage, 'the town of the priestly jaws.'" (Jerome, Letter 108, 12). "But from the victims which are sacrificed away from the altar, in order to be eaten, it is commanded that three portions should be given to the priest, an arm, and a jaw-bone, and that which is called the paunch; the arm for the reason which has been mentioned a short time ago; the jawbone as a first fruit of that most important of all the members of the body, namely, the head, and also of uttered speech, for the stream of speech could not flow out without the motion of these jaws; for they being agitated ['*sei*'] (and it is very likely from this, that they have derived their name ['*siagon*']), when they are struck by the tongue, all the organization of the voice sounds simultaneously; and the paunch is a kind of excrescence of the belly" (A Treatise on the Question: *What the Rewards and Honors are Which Belong to the Priests* by Philo Judaeus). "They bring the animal to sacrifice, and this is the portion of the priest. And this shall be the priests' due from the people, from them that offer a sacrifice, whether it be ox or sheep, that they shall give unto the priest the shoulder, and the two cheeks, and the maw" (Masoretic text). Hence, the following passage of the *Catena Aurea* is incorrectly translated: "ORIGEN; Whence Bethphage is interpreted, The house of the Shoulder; for the shoulder was the priest's portion in the Law" (*Catena Aurea on St. Matthew*, chap. 21, lect. 1).

2. "...so far as the things done in Christ, or so far as the things which signify Christ, are types of what we ought to do, there is the moral sense" (I, q. 1, a. 10).

signifies the fellowship of good men. "Jerusalem, which is built as a city, which is compact together" (Ps. 121, 3). Hence, being willing to draw near to Jerusalem, He comes through Bethphage, and through the house of confession. "With the heart, we believe unto justice: but, with the mouth, confession is made unto salvation" (Rom. 10, 10). Bethphage is situated on Mount Olivet, where there is an abundance of olive oil. "A vineyard was planted in a horn of oil" (Is. 5, 1). Mercy is signified by oil, because it has the property of making people joyful. "That he may make the face cheerful with oil" (Ps. 103, 15). So also, mercy makes people cheerful: "For God loveth a cheerful giver" (II Cor. 9, 7). Likewise, oil avails for lighting lamps. The Lord commanded that the most clear oil be offered to Him.[3] Similarly, it is useful for healing sorrows; and it signifies the grace of the Holy Ghost which heals. Hence, it is said in Luke 10 that the Samaritan poured in oil and wine.[4] *Then Jesus sent two disciples saying to them*; and He signified the Apostles' mission into the world. "As the Father hath sent me, I also send you" (Jn. 20, 21). But He sent two disciples so that He might signify charity, which consists in at least two persons. Hence, elsewhere, it is said: "He sent them two and two" (Lk. 10, 1). Or, it signifies the active and contemplative life. Or, it signifies the two series of preachers, namely, the preachers of the Jews and the preachers of the Gentiles. Hence, the Apostle wrote: "He who wrought in Peter to the apostleship of the circumcision wrought in me also among the Gentiles" (Gal. 2, 8). Or, it signifies the two disciples who were sent to the Gentiles, namely, Peter and Philip. And He does three things. Firstly, He commands them to make a gainful journey; secondly, He gives a command about the thing gained; and thirdly, He gives a command about anyone contradicting His command. He says, therefore: *Go ye into the village that is over against you*. Literally, there was a certain town that was across from them, to signify the world into which the Lord sent them. "Go ye into the whole world and preach the gospel to every creature" (Mk. 16, 15). And this world will be against them. "I have chosen you out of the world, therefore the world hateth you" (Jn. 15, 19). He says, therefore, *Go ye into the village that is over against you*. He commands one thing and He foretells another. He commands by saying, *Go*, etc.; He foretells by saying, *And you shall find an ass tied and a colt with her*. The other Evangelists do not

---

3. "Command the children of Israel, that they bring unto thee the finest and clearest oil of olives, to furnish the lamps continually" (Lev. 24, 2).
4. Verse 34.

make mention of the ass. They found both. According to the moral sense, by the ass and colt, men living like beasts are signified, because, in this respect, they are like beasts; "Man when he was in honor did not understand; he is compared to senseless beasts, and is become like to them" (Ps. 48, 13). By the ass, Judea is signified; and by the colt, the Gentiles are signified. And why is the Jewish nation signified by the ass? It is because the characteristics of an ass are threefold. The first is that it is a stupid animal, hence, it is called an ass, that is to say, 'senseless'. Accordingly, a senseless man is one who abandons God's law. Likewise, an ass is deputed to burdens, so the Jewish nation was burdened with the works of the Law, as Peter said: "This is the burden which neither our fathers nor we have been able to bear" (Acts 15, 10). Likewise, the ass is a despicable animal; accordingly, those men are said to be despicable who scorn the Lord's Commandments. But also, the ass was tied, so the Jewish nation is tied with the bonds of ignorance. "For they were all bound with one chain of darkness" (Wis. 17, 2). Likewise, they were held by the bond of sin. "His own iniquities catch the wicked" (Prov. 5, 22). *Loose them and bring them to me.* Here, He begins to speak about the salvation of the nation. Loose them from the bonds of ignorance through doctrine. "He brought them out of darkness, and the shadow of death" (Ps. 106, 14). Similarly, loosen them from the bond of sin; hence, He said to Peter: "Whatsoever thou shalt loose on earth, it shall be loosed also in heaven" (above 16, 19). And in Psalm 31, 1, it is said: "Blessed are they whose iniquities are forgiven, and whose sins are covered." Hence, these disciples, when they were converting men, led them to Jesus. "Was Paul crucified?" (I Cor. 1, 13). "They shall declare my glory to the Gentiles" (Is. 66, 19). But, as the Apostle says in Titus 1, 9, it behooves a bishop to possess doctrine, "that he may be able to exhort in sound doctrine": hence, this word that He says, *Loose*, pertains to doctrine; but what follows, *And if any man shall say anything to you*, etc., pertains to power. Hence, *If any man shall say*, by contradicting, meaning if any man shall want to contradict, *You shall say that the Lord hath need of them. And forthwith he will let them go.* In this, Christ's power is shown, because they would not have let the animals go on account of the Apostles, but rather this happened by the action of Christ invisibly changing their hearts. Hence, He gave it to be understood that He is God, because it belongs to God alone to change the heart; hence, man's heart is in His hand. Likewise, because He says, *forthwith*, He makes known that just as those men were loosing immediately, so they themselves should immediately loose men. Or, according to the literal sense, because He will have them for a short time, and He will give them back immediately since He only needs them for a day.

But there is a question according to the mystical interpretation. Is it not said, "He does not need our goods?"[5] I say that He does not need them except for our necessity and for His glory. "Every one that shall call upon the name of the Lord, shall be saved" (Joel 2, 32). Every animal that calls upon My name shall be saved.

Now all this was done, etc. Here the reason for the command is set forth. Lest anyone think that this was done without reason, the Evangelist therefore, shows the reason: **That it might be fulfilled which was spoken by the prophet**, etc. He says this by Zacharias (chap. 9, 9). But the word *that* is not used causally but consecutively. For He does not do this because the prophet had said this, but rather vice versa: for the end of the prophecy is Christ. **Tell ye the daughter of Sion**, etc. Announce to the daughter of Sion, this name is given to the inhabitants of Jerusalem, which was located on Mount Sion. Likewise, it signifies the whole Church, because Sion is interpreted 'watchtower.'[6] "Declare his ways among the Gentiles" (Ps. 9, 12). His dignity is foretold, **Behold thy king**. These Jews had endured tyrants for a long time, hence, they were waiting for a king, as it was said: "A king shall reign, and shall be wise" (Jer. 23, 5). And he relates four things that acclaim a king's dignity; consequently, four things that are in tyrants are discovered. Firstly, His affinity is acclaimed, because a man has a greater rapport with those more closely united to himself. "Thou mayst not make a man of another nation king, that is not thy brother" (Deut. 17, 15). Hence, he says, **Behold thy king**, meaning of your own nation. But sometimes kings degenerate into being tyrants, because they seek after their own benefit, which is contrary to the custom of kings; for that reason, it is said, **cometh to thee**, meaning for your benefit. "Thou wentest forth for the salvation of thy people: for salvation with thy Christ" (Hab. 3, 13). **Meek**. Meekness pertains to a king, because

---

5. "I have said to the Lord, thou art my God, for thou hast no need of my goods" (Ps. 15, 2).

6. cf. Augustine's Exposition on Psalm 102: "But the Sion whose shadow was that Sion, which signifieth a watchtower; because when placed in the flesh, we see into the things before us, extending ourselves not to the present which is now, but to the future. Thus it is a watchtower: for every watcher gazes far. Places where guards are set, are termed watchtowers: these are set on rocks, on mountains, in trees, that a wider prospect may be commanded from a higher eminence. Sion, therefore, is a watchtower, the Church is a watchtower" (n. 21).

it belongs to fierceness to inflict punishment. "Mercy and truth preserve the king" (Prov. 20, 28). Thus, David was loved by his people because he was meek. Likewise, humility is required, because the Lord rejects the proud; for that reason, he says, *Sitting upon an ass*. "Learn of me, because I am meek, and humble of heart" (above 11, 29).

And the disciples going, did as Jesus commanded them. After having related His command, here the execution of the command is related. And firstly, the execution is related in general, *The disciples going*. Behold a commandment of obedience is given. "All that the Lord commanded, we shalt do" (Ex. 29, 35). Then the execution is related in detail, *And they brought the ass and the colt*. By this, it is signified that both the Jews and the Gentiles converted, as it is stated: "To the Greeks and to the barbarians, to the wise and to the unwise, I am a debtor" (Rom. 1, 14). *And they laid their garments upon them*. The garments are their virtues. "Put ye on therefore, as the elect of God, holy and beloved, the bowels of mercy" (Col. 3, 12). They laid their garments, because they were to be an example to others, as it is said: "Be ye followers of me, brethren: and observe them who walk so as you have our model" (Phil. 3, 17). *And they made him sit thereon*. According to the literal meaning, it is said upon both, because He was upon the hearts of the Jews and of the Gentiles.

And a very great multitude spread their garments in the way. After having described the glory conferred upon Him from the disciples' ministry, he describes the glory conferred upon Him from the multitude. Firstly, he describes the glory shown to Him by an action; and secondly, he describes the glory that they show to Him by words, where it is said, *And the multitudes... cried, saying: Hosanna to the son of David*. And firstly, *They spread their garments*; and secondly, they spread *boughs from the trees*. And why did they do these things? It was to render honor to Him, just as the way is strewn for great men who are coming. Likewise, it was because the way was stony, for that reason, lest He get injured, they were strewing the way. According to the mystical meaning, the disciples spread upon an ass their garments, which signify the virtues, which they received from God, and they communicated these virtues to the Gentiles and to the Jews. But the garments of the multitude are the legal observances which were scattered on account of Christ. "The things that were gain to me, the same I have counted loss for Christ" (Phil. 3, 7). Likewise, by the vestments, their bodies are signified. "Thou hast a few names in Sardis which have not defiled their garments"

(Apoc. 3, 4). Therefore, they who spread their garments in the way were the first martyrs. "Revenge not yourselves, my dearly beloved; but give place unto wrath" (Rom. 12, 19). *Others cut boughs from the trees.* These are the boughs that should bear fruit, by which are signified the holy Patriarchs. Therefore, he who cuts off the boughs is the one who converts them to Christ. "He shall be like a tree which is planted near the running waters" (Ps. 1, 3). *And the multitudes that went before and that followed cried.* Here the honor shown to Him by words is related. But by whom was He shown honor? By them that went before and that followed, namely, by the men who lived before and after His coming, and both seek salvation, and they obtain it from Christ. "But having the same recompense" (II Cor. 6, 13). Now the multitudes were seeking salvation; hence, *they cried, saying: Hosanna to the son of David*, etc. This salvation begins in the present life, and is perfected in the future life. "For he shall save his people from their sins" (above 1, 21). Hence, they were saying, *Hosanna*, etc. Many say that it signifies the redemption.[7] But it is the same as 'I beseech' and 'save':[8] *Anna* indicates the excitement of one entreating. "Save me, O Lord" (Ps. 11, 2). And they ask this from the son of David. So it is written: "I will raise up to David a just branch" (Jer. 23, 5). And it continues, "In those days shall Juda be saved" (verse 6). And will He be able to do this, because He is the son of David? No, but rather because *he cometh in the name of the Lord.* Why? It is because He comes confessing the Lord. "I am come in the name of my Father, and you receive me not" (Jn. 5, 43). There is, therefore, one salvation, the deliverance from sins. "He himself will come and will save us" (Is. 35, 4). Likewise, there is another salvation, by which we are delivered from all punishment. "My salvation shall be forever, and my justice shall not fail" (Is. 51, 8 & 6). And these words, *in the highest*, mean 'Thou wilt give salvation firstly on earth, and afterwards in heaven.'

---

7. "Hilary of Poitiers supposed the expression to signify 'redemption of the house of David'" (Jerome, Letter xx).

8. "JEROME; I shall shortly examine what is the meaning of this word Hosanna. In the hundred and seventeenth Psalm, which is clearly written of the Savior's coming, we read this among other things; Save me now, O Lord; O Lord, send now prosperity. Blessed you that are to come in the name of the Lord. For that which the LXX give, Save now, O Lord; we read in the Hebrew, 'Anna, adonai osianna,' which Symmachus renders more plainly, I pray you, O Lord, save, I pray you. Let none think that it is a word made up of two words, one Greek: and one Hebrew, for it is pure Hebrew. REMIG; And it is confounded of one perfect and one imperfect word. For 'Hosi' signifies 'save'; 'anna' is an interjection used in entreating" (*Catena Aurea on St. Matthew*, ibid.). According to *Catena Aurea on St. Mark*, chap. 11, lect. 1, *salve* in this text should read *salva*.

And when he was come into Jerusalem, etc. Here it is treated concerning the glory shown to Him in the city. And firstly, the admiration of the multitudes is related, *And the whole city was moved*, meaning the whole city marvelled. "Then shalt thou see, and abound, and thy heart shall wonder and be enlarged" (Is. 60, 5). "Thou hast moved the earth, and hast troubled it" (Ps. 59, 4). *Saying: Who is this?* And it is not surprising if these men marveled, because even the angels marveled at His Ascension saying: "Who is this that cometh from Edom, with dyed garments from Bosra?" (Is. 63, 1). The response is related. *This is Jesus, the prophet from Nazareth of Galilee*. The word 'prophet' signifies an act of declaration.[9] *From Nazareth*, because He was raised there, and hence, He was better known there, and for that reason, He is called a Nazarene.

And Jesus went into the temple of God and cast out them that sold and bought. Above, the Evangelist showed the glory that was rendered to Christ on the way, and that was rendered to Him in the city; but now he treats of the glory regarding those things that were done in the Temple. And three things were done in the Temple which pertain to Christ's glory. Namely, they are that He firstly cleansed the Temple; secondly, He cured the sick; and thirdly, He opened the mouths of the infants. The Evangelist describes these in order. About the first, the visitation of the Temple is related; secondly, the cleansing is related; and thirdly, the reproving of the Jews is related. The second part is where it is said, *And He cast out them that sold and bought*; and the third part is where it is said, *He saith to them*, etc. He says, therefore, *And Jesus went into the temple of God*, etc.

But why, upon entering the city, did He immediately come to the Temple? One reason is that He had come to offer victims; for that reason, He firstly came to the place of immolation, and this was the day appointed in which a lamb had to be presented, as it is read in Exodus 12, because on the tenth day of the moon a lamb had to be presented that was going to be killed on the fourteenth day of the moon. But the lamb was killed on Thursday in the afternoon. Therefore, His offering ought to have been made on Palm Sunday. The second reason is that He shows Himself to be the Son of His revered Father, inasmuch as He shows reverence to His Father by coming to His Father's house. "If I be a father, where is my honor?" (Mal. 1, 6). And in this, an example is given to us, namely, when we come into a city, that we firstly visit the house of God.

---

9. "Prophecy adds to the notion of vis-ion an act of exterior declaration, and a vision is the material content of a pro-phecy" (*Super Isaiam*, chap. 1, bk. 1).

"I will worship towards thy holy temple" (Ps. 5, 8). Likewise, He acted like a good doctor, who firstly eliminates the cause of illness. Hence, sickness and the cause of spiritual corruption proceed from the Temple, because if the priest is corrupt, the people will easily be corrupted; for that reason, He firstly visits the Temple, so that He might apply the remedy in the vicinity of the Temple.

For an understanding of these things you need to understand, as it is read in Exodus 23, that all the children of Israel had to appear before the Lord once a year, and they should not to appear empty, but they ought to make their offerings. And so it was that those who lived nearby brought their animals with them, so that they might thus be sold for profit. Likewise, because some men did not have money, therefore, they had money changers to loan to those not having money, such that, in this way, they could not excuse themselves from the offering. But because it was forbidden that they would loan for usury, for that reason, they did not take usury but instead they took little presents, called *collyba*,[10] namely, raisins, or things of this kind. Likewise, because some men were poor, who could not own big animals, nor were they loaned to them, for that reason, they had servants who sold turtledoves and doves, lest anyone lack an offering. Hence, the Lord did not reprove the offerings but their greed. He says, therefore, **He cast out all them that sold and bought**, literally. The sellers were the servants of the priests. Likewise, they had money changers: for that reason, **He overthrew the tables of the money changers**, meaning the seats on which they sat. In a mystical sense, in the Temple, meaning in the Church, there are those who covet temporal gains, and who are cast out of the Church because "They that will become rich fall into temptation and into the snare of the devil" (I Tim. 4, 9). The deacons can be called the money changers, to whom is given the administration of temporal goods, as it is stated in Acts 6. Hence, when the service of dispensing degenerates into profit seeking, they ought to be cast out of the Church. By the dove, the Holy Ghost is understood; hence, those selling the doves are prelates selling the spiritual gifts, such as Orders or suchlike things. "Keep thy money to thyself, to perish with thee" (Acts 8, 20). Similarly, it can be expounded that everyone is a temple of God. "Know you not that you are the temple of God" (I Cor. 3, 16). Hence, everyone ought to expel from

---

10. "*Collyba*, as St. Jerome says, means what we call sweet meats, or cheap little presents—for example, of parched peas, grapes, raisins, and apples of various kinds" (Cornelius à Lapide, *The Great Commentary: St. Matthew's Gospel*, (John Hodges, 1893) vol. 2, pp. 414).

himself the buyer and seller, so that they do not serve God for the sake of riches; likewise, everyone ought to expel greed, which is signified by the money changers; again, everyone ought to expel the depravity of simony, also signified by the money changers; and also, everyone ought to cast out the desire for simony, which is signified by the seats.

But here there is a literal question, namely, it is stated in John 2 that this miracle occurred before John's imprisonment: here, however, it is stated that it happened when Christ's Passion was near at hand. Augustine says that this miracle occurred twice; for that reason, they were more guilty, since they had been reprehended once before.

Likewise, since He was a lowly and humble man, how could He act against the will of the priests and powerful men? Jerome says that this is one of the greatest miracles that the Lord performed, and that a certain power radiated from His countenance, by which He terrified men when He wished.

And he saith to them: It is written, etc. Here He reprehends them. And firstly, He reprehends them in what relates to the dignity of the Temple; and secondly, He reprehends them in what pertains to its use. "My house is a house of prayer" (Is. 56, 7). The explanation of this passage is found in III Kings 8, 27, where it is said, "If heaven, and the heavens of heavens, cannot contain thee, how much less this house which I have built?" Hence, it is not called the Lord's house because He dwells there corporeally, but because the place is set apart for praying to God. Just as a master has a place where he receives and fulfills requests, so the Temple is the place where the Lord hears the prayers of the faithful. Our churches, in particular, are called houses, because Christ, who is God, dwells there corporeally in the Blessed Sacrament. "He hath not done in like manner to every nation" (Ps. 147, 20). Hence, Augustine, in his *Rule,* says: "In the Oratory nothing should be done other than that for which it was deputed."[11] Afterwards, He reprehends them in regard to the Temple's use saying, **But you have made it a den of thieves**: because those things that belong to religion they turn into gain, and thieves hide in dens so that they may rob passers by, and they acquire for themselves what is not theirs.

And there came to him the blind and the lame. Here is set forth what relates to Christ's glory in regard to His curing of the sick. Assuredly, the blind who are in the Temple, signify those who are blinded through ignorance. "We have groped for the wall,

---

11. *Regula Ad Servos Dei,* chap. II, n. 2.

like the blind" (Is. 59, 10). They are said to be lame, who walk in the ways of the wicked. "Why do you halt between two sides?" (III Kings 18, 21). And these men draw near to Christ in the Temple, and He heals them. And the place befits this deed, because by this miracle it is signified that spiritual maladies are cured only in the Church. He shows His glory by a deed, because the children cried out, **Blessed is he that cometh in the name of the Lord** (above). "Behold the Lord will come and will save us; then shall their eyes be opened" (Is. 35, 4-5).

The indignation of the priests follows; hence, he says, *And the chief priests and scribes, seeing... were moved with indignation.* Concerning such men, it is said: "Evil men shall always grow worse" (II Tim. 3, 13). And firstly, the reproof is related; secondly, a question is related; and thirdly, the response is related. About the first, three things are related. Firstly, the cause of their indignation is related; secondly, the indignation is related; and thirdly, the refutation is related. Hence, *Seeing the wonderful things that he did*, namely, giving sight to the blind, etc., and it was no less a miracle that He cast out the buyers and the sellers. For those seeing this miracle, and having been converted, were saying to Him, "Thy testimonies are wonderful: therefore my soul hath sought them" (Ps. 118, 129). Likewise, the chief priests and scribes, seeing *the children crying: Hosanna*, etc., should have been moved to reverence. "Thou hast hid these things from the wise and prudent, and hast revealed them to little ones" (above 11, 25). "That seeing they may see" (Mk. 4, 12). Hence, these children were praising, but these wise men were moved to indignation and they said to Him, *Hearest thou what these say?*, as though they were to say, 'It is not just that a mere man allow Himself to be praised as God.' In Acts 12 it is written that Herod allowed himself to be honored as God, for which reason, he was struck by an angel, and died being consumed by worms: in which event, an example is given to us that if we are praised more than we deserve, we ought not to allow it. But He could not be praised above what He deserves, because He is God. The reproof follows. And firstly, they are reproved in words; and secondly, they are reproved by actions. *And Jesus said to them: Yea.* The Lord replies very wisely. They figured that if He reprimanded the children, that they would achieve their goal: if not, they would have an accusation against Him. But the Lord replies so wisely, that He neither reproved those children, nor did they have anything whereby they might calumniate Him. Hence, He said, *Yea*; I hear, but they say nothing against Me. But David says: "Out of the mouth of infants and of sucklings thou hast perfected praise" (Ps. 8, 3). He does not say, 'said,' but 'perfected,' because that such children praise God is by divine inspiration, "because the works of God are perfect" (Deut. 32, 4). Hence, it was not from their own initiative but from the Holy Ghost. "Who made the tongues of infants eloquent" (Wis. 10, 21).

But why does He say infants? Since such are unable to speak: consequently, neither are they able to praise. I say that they are not called infants on account of their age, but on account of their simplicity, because they are free from malice. "Do not become children in sense, but in malice be children" (I Cor. 14, 20). Likewise, they are called sucklings, because they were stimulated by miracles: to be stimulated by miracles is indeed like drinking milk, because milk is drunk without difficulty, so these infants, by miracles, were brought with sweetness to the faith. "You are become such as have need of milk and not of strong meat" (Heb. 5, 12).

And leaving them, he went out of the city into Bethania. Here He confutes them by His actions. And firstly, He confutes by an action that happens pertaining to Himself; secondly, He confounds them by an action pertaining to a fig tree. He says, therefore, that *leaving them, he went out.* And that abandonment was a sign; that they had abandoned Him. "We would have cured Babylon, but she is not healed" (Jer. 51, 9). And He passed into Bethania, into the house of obedience: for Jesus dwells there (Rom. 6). *And He remained here*; because He remains in those who obey Him. "We ought to obey God rather than men" (Acts 5, 29). And He went not only into Bethania, but into whoever obeys Him. Hence: "If any one love me, he will keep my word" (Jn. 14, 23). And the passage continues: "We will make our abode with him." *And in the morning, returning into the city, he was hungry.* Here, the confutation is set forth under a certain figurative action. And firstly, the action is related; and secondly, the admiration of the disciples is related. About the first, the occasion for performing the miracle is related; secondly, the sterility of the tree is related; thirdly, the curse is related; and fourthly, the effect is related. He says, therefore, *In the morning, returning into the city.* By this is signified the attentiveness that He had for the salvation of the Jews. Hence, He came in the morning just as a workman is attentive concerning his food, as it was said above, namely, that "The kingdom of heaven is like to an householder, who went out early in the morning to hire labourers into his vineyard" (20, 1). *He was hungry*, both corporeally and spiritually; He was hungry spiritually because He always desires to do the will of the Father; "My meat is to do the will of him that sent me" (Jn. 4, 34). Likewise, He was hungry corporeally. But how was He hungry corporeally? Since He was God, He had all things in His power; wherefore, when He chose, He fasted; hence: "He fasted forty days and forty nights" (above 4, 2); but when He wished, *he was hungry. And seeing a certain fig tree.* But why did He perform this miracle on a fig tree rather than on another kind of tree? It was because it is a very moist tree. Hence, by the fact that it withered immediately, it was most evident that this was a miracle. And it signifies Judea on account of two reasons: both because it puts forth green figs which mature quickly,[12] and these were the Apostles, who were great men: and, likewise, this fruit under one skin has many seeds,[13] just as there were many men under one Law. And this tree was *by the way side*, and what is meant by 'the way' is Christ, because Judea was in expectation of Christ but did not want to come to the way: for He is the way; "I am the way, and the truth, and the life" (Jn. 14, 6); "This is the way, walk ye in it" (Is. 30, 21). In Mark, it is stated that He came to see if He could find something.

But what is this? It was not then the time for figs. It ought to be said that sometimes Scripture relates something, not because it is so, but on account of some effect: hence, He did not come to seek figs, but it is said that He came to seek figs because of the conjecture of the disciples; hence, He came in order to work a miracle. He came to it when He visited Judea. "The Orient from on high hath visited us" (Lk. 1, 78). This nation has leaves, namely, legal observances; but it does not have fruit. So also, some men have a certain appearance of godliness, even though they are inwardly evil and perverse.

The curse follows, *And he saith to it: May no fruit grow on thee henceforward.* It seems that He acted unjustly, because it was not the time for figs. Likewise, it seems that He inflicted an injury upon its owner: notice that just as the Lord's words are a sort of figure, so His deeds also. Sometimes, the Lord wishes to manifest His doctrine, and then He manifests it to men; sometimes, He wishes to manifest His power of punishment, and then He manifests it in other men. Hence, He exercised there His power of punishment, so that He might show that Judea was about to become sterile, as it is stated in Romans 9. So sometimes it happens that some men are inwardly

---

12. Ripe figs can be stored for no longer than two days.

13. Seeds may be large, medium, small or minute and range in number from 30 to 1,600 per fruit.

evil; however, outwardly they are flourishing, and they are dried up by the Lord lest they corrupt others. "Men corrupted in mind, reprobate concerning the faith, but they shall proceed no farther" (II Tim. 3, 8-9). "Behold, for these three years I come seeking fruit on this fig tree and I find none. Cut it down" (Lk. 13, 7). The effect follows: *And immediately the fig tree withered away.* "My strength is dried up like a potsherd" (Ps. 21, 16), because in the time of the disciples Judaism withered, and afterwards, when the Gospel grew, the legal ceremonies withered. "And became abominable" (Osee 9, 10); "A fruitful land was turned into barrenness, for the wickedness of them that dwell therein" (Ps. 106, 34). *And the disciples seeing it wondered.* Here, firstly, their admiration is related; and secondly, the satisfaction of their admiration is related. *And the disciples seeing it wondered.* Just as men wonder when a good soul is seen and quickly withers, so these men wonder how the fig tree withered so quickly. *And Jesus answering*, etc. Here He satisfies their admiration. And firstly, He does so by showing them the power of faith: hence, He says, *Amen, I say to you.* He related the same phrase above,[14] but here He explains it; hence, He says, *If you shall have faith and stagger not*; wherefore, faith ought to be firm and without hesitation; "Let him ask in faith, nothing wavering" (James 1, 6). *Not only this of the fig tree shall you do*: for He Himself dwells in man and works in man by faith, for that reason, just as He Himself performs miracles, so also he in whom He dwells will do the same. *If you shall say to this mountain, Take up and cast thyself into the sea, it shall be done.* Certain men say that it was never done. Jerome says that the Apostles did many things that were not written. Likewise, if it is not read that this was done by them, it is read that it was done by other apostolic men, for example, he relates that a certain Gregory did this, as was said above. Likewise, the Lord did not say that it would happen, but that it could happen if there were need; but the need did not present itself. Spiritually, by the mountain we understand the devil to be signified. Hence, if you were to say to the devil: *Cast thyself into the sea*, meaning into hell, *it shall be done.* Or if you were to say, *into the sea*, meaning into wicked men, *it shall be done.* Or by the sea, pride is signified. "Before the mountains were made, or the earth and the world was formed; from eternity and to eternity thou art God" (Ps. 89, 2). Hence, if you were to say to a proud man, *Take*

---

14. "Amen I say to you, if you have faith as a grain of mustard seed, you shall say to this mountain," etc., (17, 9).

up, or remove yourself from just men, *and cast thyself into the sea*, that is to say, into wicked men, *it shall be done*. Or, by the mountain, Christ is signified, hence, *If you shall say to this mountain*, meaning Christ, *Take up thyself*, namely, from the Jews, *and cast thyself into the sea*, meaning into the Gentiles, who are the sea by their violence, *it shall be done*. "Because you judge yourselves unworthy of eternal life, behold we turn to the Gentiles" (Acts 13, 46). Similarly, He mentions the power of faith in regard to prayer; because *all things whatsoever you shall ask in prayer believing, you shall receive*; "Ask, and you shall receive" (Jn. 16, 24).

23. And when he was come into the temple, there came to him, as he was teaching, the chief priests and ancients of the people, saying: By what authority dost thou these things? And who hath given thee this authority?

24. Jesus answering, said to them: I also will ask you one word, which if you shall tell me, I will also tell you by what authority I do these things.

25. The baptism of John, whence was it? From heaven or from men? But they thought within themselves, saying:

26. If we shall say, from heaven, he will say to us: Why then did you not believe him? But if we shall say, from men, we are afraid of the multitude: for all held John as a prophet.

27. And answering Jesus, they said: We know not. He also said to them: Neither do I tell you by what authority I do these things.

28. But what think you? A certain man had two sons: and coming to the first, he said: Son, go work today in my vineyard.

29. And he answering, said: I will not. But afterwards, being moved with repentance, he went.

30. And coming to the other, he said in like manner. And he answering said: I go, Sir. And he went not.

31. Which of the two did the father's will? They say to him: The first. Jesus saith to them: Amen I say to you that the publicans and the harlots shall go into the kingdom of God before you.

32. For John came to you in the way of justice: and you did not believe him. But the publicans and the harlots believed him: but you, seeing it, did not even afterwards repent, that you might believe him.

33. Hear ye another parable. There was a man, an householder, who planted a vineyard and made a hedge round about it and dug in it a press and built a tower and let it out to husbandmen and went into a strange country.

34. And when the time of the fruits drew nigh, he sent his servants to the husbandmen that they might receive the fruits thereof.

35. And the husbandmen laying hands on his servants, beat one and killed another and stoned another.

36. Again he sent other servants, more than the former; and they did to them in like manner.

37. And last of all he sent to them his son, saying: They will reverence my son.

38. But the husbandmen seeing the son, said among themselves: This is the heir: come, let us kill him, and we shall have his inheritance.

39. And taking him, they cast him forth out of the vineyard and killed him.

40. When therefore the lord of the vineyard shall come, what will he do to those husbandmen?

41. They say to him: He will bring those evil men to an evil end and let out his vineyard to other husbandmen that shall render him the fruit in due season.

42. Jesus saith to them: Have you never read in the Scriptures: The stone which the builders rejected, the same is become the head of the corner? By the Lord this has been done; and it is wonderful in our eyes.

43. Therefore I say to you that the kingdom of God shall be taken from you and shall be given to a nation yielding the fruits thereof.

44. And whosoever shall fall on this stone shall be broken: but on whomsoever it shall fall, it shall grind him to powder.

45. And when the chief priests and Pharisees had heard his parables, they knew that he spoke of them.

46. And seeking to lay hands on him, they feared the multitudes, because they held him as a prophet.

Here, they reprehend by questioning. And firstly, the questioning is related; and secondly, the refutation is related, where it is said, *Jesus answering, said to them*. About the first point, two things are related. And firstly, the questions are related; and secondly, Christ's answers are related. And firstly, a question of the Jews is related; and secondly, a question of Christ is related, where it is said, *Jesus answering, said to them: I also will ask you one word*, etc. They say, therefore: *By what authority dost thou these things?* He had cast out the buyers and the sellers from the Temple; likewise, He had performed miracles; for that reason, they ask by what authority He does these things. Chrysostom says that in the world there were two authorities, namely, the royal and the sacerdotal: hence, in regard to the first, they ask: Wherefore do you claim to have this power? Likewise, in regard to the second, they ask: Who gave this authority to you? Do you have authority from a priest or from God? For so it was that sons were succeeding the priests in authority. Who gave it to you? You do not have this from Caesar, nor from a priest. Hence, Chrysostom says: "Every man supposes a person to be like the opinion of him that is circulating." And so, because those men did not have a good opinion of Christ, therefore, etc. Or this may be referred to His performance of miracles. There is God's power and the devil's power. "There is no power upon earth that can be compared with this" (Job 41, 24). Hence, *by what authority dost thou these things?* God's or the devil's? But Origen objects that if He were performing miracles by the devil's authority, He would not say so. For that reason, He expounds this passage differently, namely, that God's authority is multiple, a certain general authority, and many particular authorities, such that one kind of authority is for one miracle, and another authority is for another miracle. Hence, they ask by what authority, meaning by which degree of authority, such as the authority coming from the prophets. For certain prophets had one power, others had another. According to Chrysostom, when someone asks in order to learn, then the truth ought to be answered to him; but when it is done to tempt, then he ought to be reprehended and confuted. So the Lord, because He knew that they were tempting Him, said, *I also will ask you one word, which if you shall tell me, I will also tell you by what authority I do these things. The baptism of John, whence was it? From heaven or from men?* Peter baptized and it is not said to be Peter's baptism, but John baptized and it is said to be John's baptism, because in John's baptism, all that was done was by a man's doing; but in Peter's baptism, sins are remitted, which cannot happen by a man's power. "He upon whom thou shalt see the Spirit descending and remaining upon him, he it is that baptizeth with the Holy Ghost" (Jn. 1, 33). For although John baptized, nevertheless, it did not originate from himself; hence, it is said: "He who sent me to baptize with water said to me," etc., (Jn. 1, 33).

Afterwards, it is treated concerning the replies. Firstly, it is treated concerning the Jews' reply; and secondly, it is treated concerning Christ's reply. It is true that the common people believed in John's baptism, but the Pharisees were indignant; for that reason, if they were to say that it was from men they would be put to shame. Likewise, all the common people held John to be a prophet; "What went you out into the desert to see, etc.?" (above 11, 7). *And answering, they said: We know not.* They are lying. "Iniquity hath lied to itself" (Ps. 26, 12). Afterwards, Christ's reply is related, *Neither do I tell you.* In which words we have an example, namely, of the Lord not wanting to say what He knows, because someone hid other things from Him; hence: "I have learned without guile, and communicate without envy" (Wis. 7, 13).[15]

But what think you? A certain man had two sons, etc. Above, the Lord repressed their questioning by His own questioning; here, He reproves the questioners. And firstly, He reproves them for their disobedience; and secondly, He reproves them for their malice, and He does this by way of two parables, the second of which explains and clarifies the first. About the first point, He does two things. Firstly, He presents a parable; and secondly, He presents the explanation, where it is said, *Jesus saith to them.* About the first, He does three things. Firstly, He leaves the judgment to His listeners; secondly, He tells the story; and thirdly, He demands their opinion. He says: *What think you?* It is a great testimony for His cause that He left its judgment to His adversaries. "Answer, I beseech you, without contention: and speaking that which is just, judge ye" (Job 6, 29). Then He puts forward the story, *A certain man had two sons.* This man is God; the two sons are two peoples. "Look upon all the works of the most High. Two and two, and one against another" (Eccli. 33, 15). Or there are two types of men, the just and the sinners. Not anyone is called just, but those who prove themselves to be just;[16] and not anyone is called a sinner, but those who do penance. Or these two sons are the clergy and the laity. Therefore, it is treated about obedience. And firstly, a command is related; secondly, the refusal of the command is related; and thirdly, the accomplishment of the command

---

15. The text has been corrected here. In the original text it is incorrectly said someone else is hiding what he knows from the Lord, whereas the Lord is actually the one who is hiding knowledge in this passage. cf. "BEDE; As if He had said, I will not tell you what I know, since you will not confess what you know" (*Catena Aurea on St. Mark*, chap. 11, lect. 5).

16. The text erroneously says that they are just "who declare themselves to be just." Hence, the text here has been modified.

is related. The first son is the Gentiles, who originated from Noe, just as the Jews originated from Abraham. Likewise, the first son is said to be the category of the laity, because the clergy exist for the sake of the laity, for informing them. Hence, He goes to the first people, meaning the Gentiles, through interior inspiration, or through the manifestation of angels. *Son, go work today in my vineyard.* God's vineyard is justice. To work in the vineyard is to do works of justice. And He says, *Today,* as it were, through the whole time of your life. And when did He say this? When He inspired you interiorly by giving you the light of reason. "Many say, Who sheweth us good things? The light of thy countenance, O Lord, is signed upon us" (Ps. 4, 6). Next, the refusal is related. *And he answering, said: I will not.* This is nothing other than to despise God's Commandments. "We desire not the knowledge of thy ways" (Job 21, 14). Afterwards, the accomplishment of the command is related. *But afterwards, being moved with repentance, he went.* "After thou didst convert me, I did penance" (Jer. 31, 19). The disobedience of the second son follows; and firstly, the commandment is related; and secondly, the transgression is related. *And coming to the other,* this is the Jewish people, or He is coming to the clergy, or He is coming to those who call themselves just, *he said in like manner. And he answering said: I go, Sir.* He declares that he will observe justice; hence, the Jewish people say: "We will do everything that the Lord hath commanded" (Ex. 24, 3). In like manner, also the clergy and every religious speak. Hence, he promised to go. *And he went not.* "But you have departed out of the way, and have caused many to stumble at the law: you have made void the covenant of Levi, saith the Lord of hosts" (Mal. 2, 8). Then He asks for their opinion: *Which of the two did the father's will?* The first son did not promise, but he did the father's will; the second promised, but he did not do the father's will. *Which of the two did the father's will?* They answer and say to Him: *The first*, because "It is much better not to vow, than after a vow not to perform the things promised" (Eccle. 5, 4). And, "It had been better for them not to have known the way of justice than, after they have known it, to turn back" (II Pet. 2, 21); for a double sin is therein: the sin of disobedience and the breaking of a vow. Afterwards, He applies the parable. And firstly, He sets forth the preeminence of the Gentiles over the Jews, or of the laity to the clergy; and secondly, He gives the reason. He says to them: *Amen I say to you that the publicans and the harlots shall go into the kingdom of God before you.* Something similar was said above: "The last shall be first and the first last" (20, 16).

Chrysostom asks, why does he choose to mention publicans and harlots rather than other men? He answers that by the publicans He means sinners. The sin of publicans is greed, because when they receive tribute, they acquire many things for themselves, and they take more than is assigned to themselves. But the sin of men is greed, while the sin of women is lust, since they are idle, and "Idleness hath taught many evils" (Eccli. 33, 29). "This was the iniquity of Sodom, the abundance of bread and idleness" (Ez. 16, 49).[17]

Shall go into the kingdom of God before you, meaning they draw closer to the kingdom of God; "The men of Ninive shall go before you" (above 12, 41). The reason follows. Firstly, He says that the Jews were disobedient; secondly, He says that the publicans obeyed; and thirdly, He says that the Jews did not follow Him. He says, *John came to you in the way of justice*, because he led you into the way of justice. Now John came *in the way of justice*, because he observed the way of justice, namely, a life of penance, *and you did not believe him*. For they were saying to him: "Art thou Elias?" (Jn. 1, 21). And when he had said, "No," they said: "Why then dost thou baptize?" *But the publicans and the harlots believed him*. And this was stated above in chapter 3, that they came to John in order to be baptized. *But you, seeing it*, namely, others converted and fulfilling what he had commanded, *Did not even repent, that you might afterwards believe him*. For the worst man is the one who does not repent of his deeds. "There is none that doth penance for his sin, saying: What have I done?" (Jer. 8, 6)

Hear ye another parable. The Lord had asked about John's baptism, and they did not want to answer: now, however, He asks subtly, so that they would not notice; and so, He presents a parable and does two things. Firstly, He relates the parable; and secondly, He demands their opinion, where it is said, *When therefore the lord of the vineyard shall come, what will he do to those husbandmen?* About the first, He does three things. Firstly, the favor bestowed is related; secondly, the seeking of the recompense is related, where it is said: *And when the time of the fruits drew nigh*, etc.; and thirdly, He sets forth their ingratitude, where it is said, *And the husbandmen laying hands on his servants*, etc. About the first point, He does three things. Firstly, the planting of the vineyard is related; secondly, its development

---

17. "PSEUDO-CHRYS; Avarice is found the most prevailing vice among men, and fornication among women. For a woman's life is passed in idleness and seclusion, which are great temptations to that sin, while a man, constantly occupied in various active duties, falls readily into the snare of covetousness, and not so commonly into fornication, as the anxieties of manly cares preclude thoughts of pleasure, which engage rather the young and idle" (*Catena Aurea on St. Matthew*, chap. 21, lect. 5).

is related; and thirdly, its leasing is related. He says, therefore, *There was a man, an householder, who planted a vineyard*, etc. Something similar is related in Isaias 5, 1, where it is said: "My beloved had a vineyard on a hill in a fruitful place." Here, however, He says that a householder plants a vineyard. Some say that in that passage He is inveighing against the vineyard; hence, He says: "What is there that I ought to do more to my vineyard" (verse 4). Here, however, He is inveighing against the husbandmen. For that reason, it is expounded in two ways following Jerome and Chrysostom. The Jewish people is called a vineyard; "The vineyard of the Lord of hosts is the house of Israel" (Is. 5, 7). That He inveighs against the husbandmen is because in regard to the existing malice of this nation it did not proceed from the people, but from their leaders; "Hath any one of the rulers believed in him, or of the Pharisees?" (Jn. 7, 48). Wherefore, He is not inveighing against the vineyard. This vineyard is not the house of Israel, but God's justice, which was subtly conveyed in Sacred Scripture; hence, He says, *There was a man, an householder, who planted a vineyard*, meaning the Jews; "Thou hast brought a vineyard out of Egypt" (Ps. 79, 9). Or, He put justice in the Law's doctrine. *And made a hedge round about it*, for the vineyard's protection, hence, the things that are placed for guarding are either the prayers of the Saints or the guardianship of the angels; they are called a hedge; hence, it is said: "I will hedge up thy way with thorns" (Osee 2, 6). If, however, justice be called a vineyard, the veiled words of Scripture are said to be a hedge. For according to the mystical meaning, the veiled words are not to be unveiled to just anyone, because something holy should not be given to dogs (above. 7, 6). *And dug in it a press.* A press is said to express the wine of charity. If the Jews are understood by the vineyard, the altar of holocausts is understood by the press. Likewise, the martyrs are understood, who poured out their blood for the faith: "I have trodden the winepress alone" (Is. 63, 3). Or the ranks of prophets can also be understood, in whom the wine of wisdom was expressed. Or the profundity of Sacred Scripture can be called a press. Similarly, all the fruits of the vineyard are gathered into the winepress: so whatever the soul is able to do, all ought to be gathered for God's praise. *And built a tower.* By the tower the Temple is understood. "And thou, O cloudy tower of the flock, unto thee shall it come the first power" (Mic. 4, 8).[18] Or it is

---

18. "HILARY; Or, The tower is the eminence of the Law, which ascended from earth to heaven, and from which, as from a watchtower, the coming of Christ might be spied" (ibid., lect. 5)

the knowledge of God. "The name of the Lord is a strong tower" (Is. 18, 10). Afterwards, He speaks of the leasing of the vineyard, *And let it out to husbandmen*, meaning He determined a reward for doing certain things. The husbandmen are Moses and Aaron, who held governance. "If I have afflicted the son of the tillers" (Job 31, 39). Gregory says: "The husbandmen are those who rule the people." *He went into a strange country*, namely, the Lord, not by changing place but by leaving man to his own free choice. "God made man from the beginning, and left him in the hand of his own counsel" (Eccli. 5, 14). Hence, it is said that He goes into a strange country, when He does not inflict punishment for each and every fault. Or, this is when He does not appear so manifestly as He previously did, namely, when He appeared in the bush (Ex. 3). *And when the time of the fruits drew nigh*. Everyone who produces something expects some benefit, and so the Lord expects a benefit to His glory to be given back to Himself. In regard to one man, the fruit is not in his childhood, but in his maturity, wherefore, when he reaches adolescence, then He seeks some fruit: so when the Jewish nation was founded, and the Law had been given, He sought some fruit, and they did not know Him. "The kite in the air hath known her time: but my people have not known the judgment of the Lord" (Jer. 8, 7). *He sent his servants*, that is, the prophets, *to the husbandmen*, that is, to the Jews, *that they might receive the fruits thereof*, that is, so that they might lead men to act well. "I sent to you prophets and wise men and scribes: and some of them you will put to death," etc., (below 23, 34). After this, it is treated concerning their malice. And firstly, it is treated regarding the first men sent; secondly, it is treated regarding the second men sent; and thirdly, it is treated regarding the son who was sent.[19] *The husbandmen laying hands on his servants, beat one*, for example, Micheas,[20] *and killed another*, for example, Isaias,[21] *and stoned another*, for example, Naboth.[22] "They were stoned, they were cut asunder, they were tempted, they were put to death by the sword" (Heb. 11, 37). *Again he sent other servants*; likewise, He sent

---

19. The text here reads, "thirdly regarding the third men sent" (*quantum ad tertios*) but this has been corrected according to the context.
20. "And Sedecias, the son of Chanaana, came, and struck Micheas on the cheek" (III Kings 22, 24).
21. Isaias was, according to the tradition of the Hebrews, of the blood royal of the kings of Juda: and after a most holy life, ended his days by a glorious martyrdom; being sawed in two, at the command of his wicked son in law, King Manasses, for reproving his evil ways.
22. "They, like men of the devil, bore witness against him before the people: saying: Naboth hath blasphemed God and the king. Wherefore they brought him forth without the city, and stoned him to death" (III Kings 21, 13).

the prophets one by one, such as Moses and Aaron, and the others; but afterwards, at the time of David, He sent many groups of prophets. For the Lord wished His mercy to contrast their malice. Hence, *And they did to them in like manner.* "You have always been rebellious against the Lord" (Deut. 31, 27). He continues with the third sending, *And last of all he sent to them his son*, etc., because the Jews were of consummate malice. And He does three things. Firstly, the Lord's mercy is set forth; secondly, their malice is set forth; and thirdly, the execution of their depraved plan is set forth. *And last of all he sent to them his son.* "God, who, at sundry times and in divers manners, spoke in times past to the fathers by the prophets, last of all, hath spoken to us by his Son" (Heb. 1, 1). *He sent to them his son, saying: It may be, they will reverence my son.*[23]

But what is it that He says, *It may be*? Was not the householder ignorant? Jerome says that this uncertain manner of speaking signifies the liberty of free will, to show what they were going to do, because he who does not honor a son, does not honor his father. Or He speaks in this manner, because some men respected Him.

Afterwards, their wicked plan is related. Firstly, the meeting is related; secondly, their plan is related; and thirdly, their wickedness is related. *But the husbandmen seeing the son, said among themselves: This is the heir: come, let us kill him, and we shall have his inheritance*; for that Son is the true heir of the Father, because what He asks He obtains. "Ask of me, and I will give thee the Gentiles for thy inheritance" (Ps. 2, 8). Likewise, He is the heir, because whatever the Father has, He also has: for He is not called the heir like someone who, when his father dies, has an inheritance, but because what belongs to His Father is always His own.

But on the contrary: "If they had known it, they would never have crucified the Lord of glory" (I Cor. 2, 8). It is true that they would not have killed Him if they had truly known Him, but they knew Him by conjecture.

Their plan follows, *Come, let us kill him.* "Let us condemn him to a most shameful death" (Wis. 2, 20). And what is their aim? *We shall have his inheritance*: for they knew from the Law that He should rule over the Jews. Hence, they feared that He would impose upon them the yoke of the Law and destroy their traditions: for that reason, they did not wish to bear Christ's

---

23. The words, "It may be" (*forsitan*), are probably taken by St. Thomas from the parallel verse in Luke 20, 13.

yoke: hence, they bore the Romans' yoke. Hence: "Lest perhaps the Romans come, and take away our place and nation" (Jn. 11, 48). Afterwards, the execution of their plan is related: ***And taking him, they cast him forth out of the vineyard and killed him***, because they crucified Him outside the city's gate and so they killed Him as though He were a stranger to the vineyard. "He shall be led as a sheep to the slaughter," etc., (Is. 53, 7). That they cast Him forth out of the vineyard is stated in John 9, because whoever confessed Christ's name should be put out of the synagogue.[24] Afterwards, He demands their opinion, ***When therefore the lord of the vineyard shall come, what will he do to those husbandmen?*** The Lord asks so subtly that they judge against themselves, just as Nathan did to David, when He sinned with Bethsabee. Their opinion is related, ***He will bring those evil men to an evil end***, that is, by destruction in the present life and in the future life. And they say, ***to an evil end***, meaning to a bitter end. "With what measure you mete, it shall be measured to you again" (above 7, 2). "The mighty shall be mightily tormented" (Wis. 6, 7). ***He will bring those evil men to an evil end and let out his vineyard***, meaning His own people, ***to other husbandmen***, meaning to the Apostles, ***that shall render him the fruit in due season***. "He shall be like a tree which is planted near the running waters, which shall bring forth its fruit, in due season" (Ps. 1, 3). "He shall break in pieces many and innumerable, and shall make others to stand in their stead" (Job 34, 24).

And here there is a question as to why, in Mark, the Lord answered: here, however, the Jews answered. Here is the solution. I say that the Lord spoke, and afterwards those men spoke. Likewise, in Luke 20 it is stated that when the Lord said this, they said, "God forbid."[25] The correct answer is that, firstly, they spoke, and once they understood that the judgment was against themselves, they said, "God forbid." Similarly, it is true that the rulers spoke. And although they perceived that the judgment was against them, they were not contradicting, but the people said, "God forbid."

Jesus saith to them. Here, the confirmation of the judgment is related. Firstly, a passage of Scripture is cited; and secondly, its explanation is related. He says, ***Have you never read in the Scriptures*** (this is found in Psalm 117, 22): ***The stone which the builders rejected, the same is become the head of the***

---

24. Verse 22   25. Verse 16.

corner? And He points out four things. Firstly, He points out their reprobation; secondly, He points out their dignity; thirdly, He points out the reason for their reprobation; and fourthly, He points out their admiration. He says, *The stone*, etc. The stone is Christ, who is called a stone based upon many similitudes. "Behold I will lay a stone in the foundations of Sion, a corner stone," etc., (Is. 28, 16). The builders are the Apostles. Let every man take heed how he builds.[26] Hence, that rock, *which they rejected*, meaning which they cast away, *the same is become*, meaning is constituted, *the head of the corner*, meaning the head of the Jews and the Gentiles. Hence, He was made the head of the Church. But they could say: He made Himself the head; for that reason, He says: *By the Lord this has been done*. "The right hand of the Lord hath wrought strength" (Ps. 117, 16). And what sort of exaltation is this? *And it is wonderful in our eyes*; "Behold ye among the nations, and see: wonder, and be astonished: for a work is done in your days, which no man will believe when it shall be told" (Hab. 1, 5). Their dignity was so great that it could only have been produced through the grace of God. "By grace you are saved through Christ" (Eph. 2, 8). Afterwards, He expounds the passage; and He makes two conclusions. Firstly, He expounds what was said in the parable; and secondly, He expounds what was said in the passage. It is said, therefore, *Therefore I say to you that the kingdom of God shall be taken from you*, meaning Sacred Scripture, because you will lose the understanding of Sacred Scripture. "He hath blinded their eyes and hardened their heart, that they should not see with their eyes, nor understand with their heart and be converted: and I should heal them" (Jn. 12, 40). Or, you will lose your authority over the Church of the faithful, because their glory has been transferred to others. *And shall be given to a nation yielding the fruits thereof.* "Behold I have given him for a witness to the people, for a leader and a master to the Gentiles. Behold thou shalt call a nation, which thou knewest not: and the nations that knew not thee shall run to thee" (Is. 55, 4-5). But how shall it be given to them? Above, it was said that He let it out, here, however, that it is given: because when it does not yield fruit, it is said to be let out, or rented; but when it is given, then it bears fruit. He indicates a twofold punishment, *And whosoever shall fall on this stone shall be broken*. It is expounded, according to Jerome, as follows: He falls upon a

---

26. I Cor. 3, 10.

rock, meaning Christ, who holds the faith from Him, that is to say, from Christ, but falls by sin because he acts against Him. The reason why sinners fall is because they do not have charity. *But on whomsoever it shall fall, it shall grind him to powder.* Christ, however, falls upon unbelievers. There is this difference, namely, that when a vessel falls upon a rock, the vessel is not broken because of the rock, but because of the way that it fell, inasmuch as it fell from a greater height; but when a rock falls upon a vessel, it breaks it according to the weight of the rock. So a man, when he falls upon a rock, which is Christ, then he is broken according to the greatness of the sin; but when he becomes an unbeliever, he is completely crushed. Or someone falls upon a rock when he perishes by his own free choice; but then a rock, in fact, falls upon him, when Christ punishes him, and then the whole man is crushed. "I shall beat them as small as the dust before the wind" (Ps. 17, 43). The time of wickedness follows, *And seeking to lay hands on him, they feared the multitudes, because they held him as a prophet.* And the meaning of these words is clear.

CHAPTER TWENTY-TWO

1. And Jesus answering, spoke again in parables to them, saying:
2. The kingdom of heaven is likened to a king who made a marriage for his son.
3. And he sent his servants to call them that were invited to the marriage: and they would not come.
4. Again he sent other servants, saying: Tell them that were invited, Behold, I have prepared my dinner: my beeves and fatlings are killed, and all things are ready. Come ye to the marriage.
5. But they neglected and went their ways, one to his farm and another to his merchandise.
6. And the rest laid hands on his servants and, having treated them contumeliously, put them to death.
7. But when the king had heard of it, he was angry: and sending his armies, he destroyed those murderers and burnt their city.
8. Then he saith to his servants: The marriage indeed is ready; but they that were invited were not worthy.
9. Go ye therefore into the highways; and as many as you shall find, call to the marriage.
10. And his servants going forth into the ways, gathered together all that they found, both bad and good: and the marriage was filled with guests.
11. And the king went in to see the guests: and he saw there a man who had not on a wedding garment.
12. And he saith to him: Friend, how camest thou in hither not having on a wedding garment? But he was silent.
13. Then the king said to the waiters: Bind his hands and feet, and cast him into the exterior darkness. There shall be weeping and gnashing of teeth.
14. For many are called, but few are chosen.

It was said above that Christ's persecutors were provoked to kill Him due to three causes: due to His glory, due to His wisdom, by which He was confounding them, and due to His justice, by which He was finding fault with them. Now it has been said in what way they were provoked by His glory; now, however, it ought to be said how they are provoked by His wisdom. And firstly, it is inasmuch as He predicts their damnation: secondly, it is inasmuch as He confutes them by disputing with them, where it is said, **Then** *the Pharisees going, consulted among themselves how to insnare him in his speech.* In this parable, in which the reprobation of the Jews and the calling of the Gentiles are set forth, the lesson of the marriage is firstly related; secondly, it is treated concerning the calling and the rejection of the Jews; and thirdly, it is treated concerning the calling of the Gentiles. The second part is where it is said, *And he sent his servants to call them that were invited*; and the third part is where it is said, *Then he saith to his servants*, etc. He says, therefore, *And Jesus answering, spoke*. Who was He answering? It is not said that He was speaking with anyone. But they wanted to seize him, for that reason, He answered not their words but their malice, and so He spoke *in parables to them, saying: The kingdom of heaven is likened to a king who made a marriage for his son*. Here, the parable about a marriage is related, and it is similar to the parable related in Luke 14, 16. And, according to Gregory, it does not seem to be the same parable, because in that account there is mention of a supper, here there is mention of a wedding feast. Likewise, no one was excluded from that supper, here, however, someone is excluded. Hence, it is a different parable. By that parable the heavenly feast is understood, by this parable a feast that occurs on earth is understood. And, for that reason, the former is called a supper, because no one is excluded from it, but from this feast someone is excluded. According to others, it is said that the parables are the same, because in ancient times the same thing was called a dinner and a supper, because men were not accustomed to eat until the ninth hour. Or it can be said that Luke says what Matthew omits. But I believe that the parable is a different one. About this parable, let us see who is the *man that is king*.[1] And it is said that this man is God. And the person of the Father is understood, because He says, *for His son*. But why does He say, *a man that is king*? The reason is, as Origen says, because a king (*rex*) is so-called from ruling (*regendo*). We, however, cannot be, nor are we capable of, His kingdom according to what it is, but according to our present condition.[2] "As the eagle enticing her young to fly, and hovering over them, he spread his wings" (Deut. 32, 11) and, therefore, He is called *a man that is king*, because

---

1. The Latin Vulgate uses the phrase, *homo rex*.
2. "ORIGEN; It is specified, *A man that is a king*, that what is spoken may be as by a man to men, and that a man may regulate men unwilling to be regulated by God. But the kingdom of heaven will then cease to be like a man, when zeal and contention and all other passions and sins having ceased, we shall cease to walk after men, and shall see Him as He is. For now we see Him not as He is, but as He has been made for us in our dispensation" (*Catena Aurea on St. Matthew*, chap. 22, lect. 1).

He rules us in a human manner. But when He will be seen as He is, then He will be a king, because then He will rule according to Himself. Hence, the Apostle says: "We see now through a glass in a dark manner: but then face to face" (I Cor. 13, 12). He says, ***The kingdom of heaven is likened to a king***. For as in an earthly kingdom there are many things, such as a king, a kingdom, and those who serve, so also in that kingdom; for that reason, it is ***likened to a king who made a marriage for his son***. The son is Christ, concerning whom it is said: "That we may be in his true Son. This is the true God and life eternal" (I Jn. 5, 20). What this marriage feast is can be expounded in four ways. Firstly, it can be expounded by the uniting of Christ's human nature to the divine nature, such that if the human nature be the spouse, the bridechamber was the womb of the virgin. "For he was as a bridegroom coming out of his bridechamber" (Ps. 18, 6). And this exposition contains some uncertainty, because it could be supposed that that the Person of the Father is not different from the Person of the Son. Hence, it can be said that this bridegroom is the Incarnate Word and the spouse is the Church; hence: "This is a great sacrament: but I speak in Christ and in the church" (Eph. 5, 32). Likewise, it can be expounded by the uniting of the Word Himself to our souls. For the soul becomes a sharer of God's glory by faith, and in this way, our wedding feast is made. "I will espouse thee in faith" (Osee 2, 20). Similarly, the wedding feast will be made in the general resurrection. Christ is the way of this resurrection; "I am the way" (Jn. 14, 6). Then will be the marriage feast, when our mortal bodies will be absorbed by life, as it is stated in II Cor. 5, 4. But if we speak according to Gregory, it ought to be expounded about present things, according to which the Church is espoused to Christ, and our soul to God through faith.

The parable continues, concerning the calling of the Jews. Firstly, a twofold calling is related; and secondly, the excusing is related, where it is said, ***But they neglected***, etc. About the first point, He does two things, in accordance with the two callings; hence, He says, ***And he sent his servants to call them that were invited***. And, according to what Origen says on this text, there are two texts of this passage, for one text has the words, ***He sent his servant***,[3] and another has, ***He sent his servants***. If the text is ***Servant***, then three things ought to be considered. Firstly, the invitation ought to be considered; secondly, the calling ought to be considered; and thirdly, the second invitation ought to

---

3. Lk. 14, 17.

be considered. Therefore, the Jews were invited in the Patriarchs; hence, it was said to Abraham: "In thy seed shall all the nations be blessed" (Gen. 22, 18). "To Abraham were the promises made and to his seed," etc., (Gal. 3, 16). Moses was firstly sent. "It is not so with my servant Moses who is most faithful in all my house" (Num. 12, 7). And the passage continues, "Why did you not fear him?" *And they would not come.* "While I am yet living, and going in with you, you have always been rebellious against the Lord" (Deut. 31, 27). The second calling is through the prophets, concerning whom it is written: "The Lord God doth nothing without revealing his secret to his servants the prophets" (Amos 3, 7). Or the text can be: *Servants*; and then, by the first servants, the prophets are signified, towards whom the Jews were always rebellious; "You always resist the Holy Ghost" (Acts 7, 51). By the second servants, the Apostles are signified, to whom it was said: "Go ye not into the way of the Gentiles" (above 10, 5). Or, by the first prophets, the Apostles are signified, and by the second prophets, the successors of the Apostles are signified.

Again he sent other servants. Here, the second invitation is related. And an added kindness is indicated on the part of the one inviting, and an added malice is indicated on the part of the ones excusing. In the first calling, the king promised nothing; but in this calling he promises something, because he says, *Tell them that were invited, Behold, I have prepared my dinner.* This dinner is spiritual refreshment; "She hath slain her victims, mingled her wine, and set forth her table, she hath sent her maids to invite to the tower" (Prov. 9, 2-3). *My beeves and fatlings are killed.* And this saying can be expounded, according to Origen, to mean the arrangement of God's wisdom. Strong reasons are called beeves; "He hath taught me, with a strong arm" (Is. 8, 11). Things well-fed, so to speak, are called fatlings. Fattened birds, which are fed and fattened, are especially called fatlings, and they signify the subtle meanings, and the subtle meanings become fattened when they are multiplied with holy meanings, by which the soul is fattened; "Let my soul be filled as with marrow and fatness" (Ps. 62, 6). For whatever is necessary is found in Sacred Scripture. For that reason, *All things are ready.* "The law of the Lord is unspotted, converting souls" (Ps. 18, 8). This is the invitation of Wisdom: "Come, eat my bread, and drink the wine which I have mingled for you" (Prov. 9, 5). Or it signifies spiritual refreshment. By the beeves the examples of the Saints are signified, which the Lord prepared as an example; "Take, my brethren, for example of suffering evil, of labour and patience, the prophets"

(James 5, 10). Hence, He puts forth the tribulations of the Saints as an example. According to Gregory, by the beeves, the Fathers of the Old Testament are signified, because a bull gores with its horns, and in the time of the Fathers vengeance was always being sought, and an eye was commanded to be given for an eye. By the fatlings, the Fathers of the New Testament are signified, who left all things for Christ, are fattened with God's wisdom, and were killed for God's sake, and both beeves and fatlings were killed for God's sake. *All things are ready. Come ye to the marriage*. Christ has suffered, He has opened heaven and He has sent the Apostles. Or, by the beeves, the priests of the Old Testament are understood; because a bull is an animal used in sacrifices; and by the fatlings, the prophets are understood, who were fattened with God's wisdom. *But they*, that is to say, those hardened in malice, *neglected*. Some men forego the feast out of negligence, others, however, do so out of malice, namely, those who persecute the preachers; hence, He says, *But they neglected*. And what was the reason? It was because *One went to his farm and another to his merchandise*. Outwardly, they seemed to have good reasons, but the Lord did not accept their reasons, because no temporal matters ought to detain one from coming to God. According to Hilary, by these words that He says, *To his farm*, He signifies the desire for human glory; "They loved the glory of men more than the glory of God" (Jn. 12, 43); "Perhaps these are poor and foolish, that know not the way of the Lord, the judgment of their God" (Jer. 5,4). By this that He says, *Another to his merchandise*, is indicated the desire of avarice; "From the least of them even to the greatest, all are given to covetousness" (Jer. 6, 13). According to Chrysostom, some men keep busy by laboring with their own hands, others keep busy with merchandise, meaning with their own employment. He continues: *And the rest laid hands on his servants*, meaning the Apostles, *and, having treated them contumeliously, put them to death*, because they killed many men of the Old and New Testament. Hence: "I send to you prophets and wise men and scribes: and some of them you will put to death," etc., (below 23, 34). And here He makes no mention of His death, but only of His disciples, because He had mentioned it sufficiently above.

Then their punishment follows: *But when the king had heard of it, he was angry*, etc. Above, He related the spiritual punishment, here He relates the temporal punishment; hence, above, He said, *A man that is king*; here, however, it is said, *The king*, because the title of man seems to pertain to kindness, but the title of king pertains to punishment; for that reason, He is here only called a king; "Those whom men could not honor in presence, because they dwelt far off, they brought their resemblance from afar, and made an express image of the king, whom they had a mind to honor: that by this their diligence, they might honor as present, him that was absent" (Wis. 14, 17).

The king was angry. It ought to be noted that when anger is attributed to God it does not signify a disturbance, but revenge; because the angered are accustomed to punish, hence, punishment is called anger. Which ought to be noted in opposition to the heretics, for they usually object, 'The God of the Old Testament was not good, because He ordered punishments,' etc.

Hence, **Sending his armies, he destroyed those murderers.** His armies are the angelic spirits, or the Roman citizens, who under Titus and Vespasian killed many Jews; "The earth is the Lord's and the fullness thereof" (Ps. 23, 1). *And burnt their city*, because their cities were burned; "He will burn your cities with fire" (Is. 1, 7). Or it can be understood mystically, namely, their bodies or the assemblies of the heretics.

The calling of the Gentiles follows, and the examination is related. And He does three things. Firstly, the command is related; secondly, the execution of the command is related; and thirdly, the effect of the command is related. The second part is where it is said, *And his servants going forth*, etc.; and the third part is where it is said, *And the marriage was filled with guests.* About the first, He does two things. Firstly, He gives the reason for the command; and secondly, He relates the command. He says, therefore, *Then he saith to his servants: The marriage indeed is ready; but they that were invited were not worthy. The marriage indeed is ready*, meaning the Son has taken flesh, according to that passage in Isaias 5, 4: "What is there that I ought to do more to my vineyard?" *But they that were invited were not worthy*, meaning, they rendered themselves unworthy. And how did they do so? As it is said: "They, not knowing the justice of God and seeking to establish their own, have not submitted themselves to the justice of God" (Rom. 10, 3); "Because you reject it and judge yourselves unworthy of eternal life, behold we turn to the Gentiles" (Acts 13, 46). Hence, by the sin of the Jews, salvation was effected to the Gentiles; "Hold fast that which thou hast, that no man take thy crown" (Apoc. 3, 11). The command follows, *Go ye therefore into the highways*, etc. By the highways are understood the various philosophies, because these are what one might call highways, which lead us to the truth. The Gentiles are at the ends of the highways.[4] Hence, *Go ye into the highways*, meaning to those who adhere to erroneous philosophies. Or it is understood differently, "The people that walked in darkness, have seen a great light" (Is. 9, 2). Hence, by the roads are understood good actions, concerning which it is said, "The Lord knoweth the ways that are on the right hand" (Prov. 4, 26); by the ends is understood whatever can concur to good actions. *As many as you shall find, call to the marriage*. Hence, it is said: "Go, teach ye all nations" (below 28, 19).

The execution of the command follows, *And his servants going forth into the ways, gathered together all*; "But they going forth preached everywhere: the Lord working withal, and confirming the word with signs that followed" (Mk. 16, 20).

But what is it that He says, *Both bad and good*? It can be said that the latter are they, who were firstly bad, and afterwards became good. Or it can be said, when He says, *Both bad and good*, that He speaks comparatively, because among the latter some are good in respect to the civil virtues.[5] Or, *Both bad and good*, because after they will have been gathered together, the good and the bad will be intermixed.

And the marriage was filled with guests, meaning the faithful. Above, something similar is related, "Which, when it was filled, they drew out, and sitting by the shore, they chose out the good into vessels, but the bad they cast forth" (13, 48). *And the king went in*, etc. Here the examination of those gathered together is related. Firstly, the one examining is set forth; secondly, the examination is set forth; and thirdly, the condemnation is set forth. The one examining entered: for He enters when He exercises judgment upon them; "I will go down and see" (Gen. 18, 21): likewise, He enters when tribulations threaten the Church. But who is the one examined? *He saw there a man who had not on a wedding garment*. What is this garment? It is Christ. Let us, who belong to Christ, put on Christ. "Put ye on the Lord Jesus Christ" (Rom. 13, 14). For some men put on Christ through the sacrament of Baptism; "As many of you as have been baptized

---

4. "Vulg. *the ends of the highways*; Gr. *the passages, the passages, the outlets of the ways*. The meaning is, Traverse and run through all the ways, and the turnings, and corners, and the bendings of the road. Let there be no nook which you do not traverse" (Cornelius à Lapide, *The Great Commentary: St. Matthew's Gospel*, (John Hodges, 1893) vol. 3, p. 6).

5. "Virtues are as oil to the machinery of government. Insofar as they are needed as an aid to government and social order, they are called 'civil virtues.' It must be confessed that the necessary standard of civil virtue is not very high. A man may be a good citizen, yet not a good man, still less a good Catholic" (Joseph Rickaby, S.J., *Four-Square or The Cardinal Virtues*, chap. XII: The Infused Virtues).

in Christ have put on Christ" (Gal. 3, 27). Others are in Christ through charity and love; "But above all these things have charity, which is the bond of perfection. And let the peace of Christ rejoice in your hearts, wherein also you are called in one body" (Col. 3, 14-15). Likewise, some men put on Christ through conformity of deeds; "Put ye on the Lord Jesus Christ" (Rom. 13, 14). Therefore, the wedding garment is to put on Christ through good actions, through a holy life, and through true charity; and if one of these is lacking, it is bad. Then the examination follows. He next says how he was at fault. He says, therefore, *Friend*. He calls him a friend by faith, or because He loved him. Or it can be said that wherever He calls someone a friend, He says this as a rebuke; hence, He rebukes the love by which He loved him. *How camest thou in hither not having on a wedding garment?*

But someone could say: 'On what grounds did He punish him since He called both the good and the bad?' But He wanted the bad to come only if they would prepare themselves, and dispose themselves, so that they would be good.

Then it follows how he was at fault. Hence, He continues, *But he was silent*, because the sinner is unable to have sufficient reason why he despised the wedding garment; "If he will contend with him, he cannot answer him" (Job 9, 3). And it is concluded with the parable's verdict. A twofold punishment is related, the pain of loss and the pain of sense: because in the world one is perfected in three ways: through the intellect, by thinking; through the affections, by tending to the highest good; and, likewise, through actions; wherefore he is punished in three ways. Hence, *the king said to the waiters: Bind his hands and feet, and cast him into the exterior darkness*. By his feet are understood his evil affections. In this world, men have feet, but they are not bound, because they can become good; but afterwards they will be bound, because, afterwards, they cannot change direction; "Whatsoever thy hand is able to do, do it earnestly: for neither work, nor reason, nor wisdom, nor knowledge shall be in hell, whither thou art hastening" (Eccle. 9, 10). Likewise, a man can now make progress in pondering truths, but then he cannot; for that reason, He says, *Cast him into the exterior darkness*. For now some sinners are not dark as to their exterior knowledge, although they are dark as to their interior knowledge; but then they will have exterior darkness. Or, according to the literal meaning, sinners will be cast into darkness not only as to their soul, but also as to their body, because they shall be separated from the company of the Saints. Then the pain of sense follows, *There shall be weeping and gnashing of teeth.* Weeping proceeds from sadness, gnashing proceeds from anger. In the Acts it is said: "They gnashed with their teeth at him" (7, 54). Some men weep for their sins, and they are humbled and cleansed. In that place there will be sadness, but not unto humility, but it will turn into anger. Likewise, there will be gnashing on account of impatience, because "the pride of them that hate thee ascendeth continually" (Ps. 73, 23). Or it can be said that there will be gnashing at the resurrection, because sinners will be punished not only in their souls, but also in their bodies; or it is because they will suffer heat and cold; "They will pass from the snow waters to excessive heat" (Job 24, 19). Then He concludes, *Many are called, but few are chosen,* because some men do not wish to come, and others do not have on a wedding garment. Hence: "Strait is the way that leadeth to life: and few there are that find it" (above 7, 14).

15. Then the Pharisees going, consulted among themselves how to insnare him in his speech.

16. And they sent to him their disciples with the Herodians, saying: Master, we know that thou art a true speaker and teachest the way of God in truth. Neither carest thou for any man: for thou dost not regard the person of men.

17. Tell us therefore what dost thou think? Is it lawful to give tribute to Caesar, or not?

18. But Jesus knowing their wickedness, said: Why do you tempt me, ye hypocrites?

19. Shew me the coin of the tribute. And they offered him a penny.

20. And Jesus saith to them: Whose image and inscription is this?

21. They say to him: Caesar's. Then he saith to them: Render therefore to Caesar the things that are Caesar's; and to God, the things that are God's.

22. And hearing this, they wondered and, leaving him, went their ways.

Above, the Lord confuted the Pharisees by a parable; here, He manifests His wisdom in a second way by disputing with them. And firstly, He does so by answering; and secondly, He does so by objecting, where it is said, *And the Pharisees being gathered together, Jesus asked them,* etc. And the Lord answers three questions. Firstly, He answers concerning the paying of tribute; secondly, He answers concerning the resurrection; and thirdly, He answers concerning the Law. The second part is where it is said, *That day there came to him the Sadducees*; and the third part is where it is said, *But the Pharisees, hearing*, etc. About the first point, the Evangelist does three things. Firstly, the question is related; secondly, the answer is related; and thirdly, the effect of His answer is related. The second part is where it is said, *But Jesus knowing their wickedness*; and the third part is where it is said, *And hearing this, they wondered*. In this question, three things are to be considered. Firstly, the intention of the questioners; secondly, the ministers of the questioners; and thirdly, the question of the questioners. The intention of the questioners is shown, when it is said, *the Pharisees going made*, meaning among themselves, *a plan*, actually, they made a foolish plan, *how to insnare him in his speech*. And this was foolish, because He was the Word of God, and the Word of God is not comprehensible; "We shall say much, and yet shall want words" (Eccli. 43, 29). Now, it was an ungodly plan; "Blessed is the man who hath not walked in the counsel of the ungodly" (Ps. 1, 1). And: "Let not my soul go into their counsel" (Gen. 49, 6). The ministers are described, when he says: *And they sent to him their disciples with the Herodians*. But why did they not go? The reason is that they wanted to question Him deceitfully: hence, had they gone, there would have been no room for deceit;[6] but the disciples themselves were also deceitful; "As the judge of the people is himself, so also are his ministers" (Eccli. 10, 2). *With the Herodians.*

Who are these Herodians? According to what is mentioned in Luke, Judea was made a tributary to the Romans under Herod. This son of Antipater, a foreigner, was made the king by the Romans; for that reason, He wanted to compel the Jews to pay tribute to the Romans. Hence, there were the Herodians, that is to say, his servants deputed to collect Herod's quota. But this Herod was dead at this time, and he had left three sons. One was Herod [Antipas], and this son was then ruling, as it is said in Luke 23, that he was also ruling at the time of the Lord's death: for that reason, it was easy for his servants to go with them.

But why did they did they go with the Herodians? One reason is that the Herodians were zealous for the Emperor. For that reason, the disciples of the Pharisees brought them with themselves, so that if He said that the tribute ought to be paid, they might accuse Him to the Pharisees: but if He said that it

---

6. "GLOSS. Who as unknown to Him, were more likely to ensnare Him, and so through them they might take Him" (*Catena Aurea on St. Matthew*, chap. 22, lect. 2).

ought not to be paid, then the Herodians would seize Him. Likewise, these men were unknown, wherefore, they supposed that He would not perceive their deceit; hence, they were acting contrary to that which is written: "I have not sat with the council of vanity: neither will I go in with the doers of unjust things" (Ps. 25, 4). Or it is otherwise, namely, that when Judea was made a tributary to the Romans, they were divided, because some men were saying that the people dedicated to God ought not to be a tributary to a man; but others were saying that because he was going to battle for the peace of all, all ought to give tribute to Caesar. Hence, those who were saying that tribute ought to be given to Caesar were called Herodians.

Having presented the ministers, the question is presented. Firstly, the flattery is related; and secondly, the question is related, where it is said, *Tell what dost thou think*. Wicked men begin with flattery. "Who speak good things, but evils are in their hearts" (Ps. 28, 3). And firstly, they praise His person; secondly, they praise His doctrine; and thirdly, they praise His constancy. They praise His person on account of His dignity and virtue; they praise Him on account of His dignity when they say, *Master*. And although they lie according to what is in their hearts, because they did not consider Him to be a master but a seducer, as it is stated below: "We have remembered, that that seducer said: After three days I will rise again," etc., (27, 63), nevertheless, He was truly a Master, as it is said: "One is your master," etc., (below 23, 8). Likewise, they praise Him when they say, *We know that thou art a true speaker*. A true speaker is he who speaks the truth; and this belongs to God and to Him who is joined to God; "I said in my excess: Every man is a liar" (Ps. 115, 11); "But God is true and every man a liar" (Rom. 3, 4). Christ is joined to God by union, and, therefore, He is a true speaker. And thus, He is praised for His dignity. Then He is praised for His virtue when they say, *And teachest the way of God in truth*. Firstly, it is necessary that one know what one teaches; "Which I have learned without guile, and communicate without envy" (Wis. 7, 13). Likewise, some men teach, but not profitable things; He, on the contrary, teaches profitable things, namely, the way of God; "I am the Lord thy God that teach thee profitable things" (Is. 48, 17). Again, some men teach the things which pertain to God, but not in truth, such as the heretics; He, however, teaches in truth. Concerning this, it is written: "Shew, O Lord, thy ways to me, and teach me thy paths," etc., (Ps. 24, 4). Likewise, they praise Him for His constancy; hence, they say,

Neither carest thou for any man, meaning you do not omit, for fear of any man, what you ought to say or do; "Who art thou, that thou shouldst be afraid of a mortal man?" (Is. 51, 12). And why is this? *For thou dost not regard the person of men*, namely, contrary to God. For he respects a person, who, for the sake of a man, omits to say the truth which he ought to say; "Neither shall you respect any man's person" (Deut. 1, 17). And see how malicious they were. The question has two parts; namely, whether they ought not to pay tribute, which pertains to God's honor, or that they ought to pay, which pertains to the favor of men. Hence, they wanted that He would seek God's favor, and teach the way of God: and so if He were to say that they ought not to pay, which they preferred, He would be immediately seized by the Herodians. The question follows, *Tell us therefore... Is it lawful to give tribute to Caesar, or not?* Tribute was money given per person. The answer follows, *But Jesus knowing their wickedness, said*. And He firstly answers their thoughts; secondly, He answers their words, where it is said, *Render therefore to Caesar the things that are Caesar's*. It belongs to a man to answer words, but to God to answer thoughts; therefore, since Christ is God and man, it follows that He answers both. "The searcher of hearts and reins is God" (Ps. 7, 10). *Ye hypocrites*. And well does He call them hypocrites, because hypocrites are properly those who have one thing in their mouth, and another thing in their heart. *Why do you tempt me?* For this was forbidden: "Thou shalt not tempt the Lord thy God" (Deut. 6, 16). Likewise, these men addressed Christ with smooth talk; Christ, however, answers harshly, because He is responding to their hearts, not to their words. Likewise, an example is given to us, that we ought not to believe flatterers; "A prince that gladly heareth lying words, hath all his servants wicked" (Prov. 29, 12). Similarly, when one wishes to answer something, one cannot better confute an opponent than according to his own words. Hence, He firstly puts forth a question; and secondly, He draws the truth from their answer. Firstly, He asks about a coin; and secondly, He asks about its appearance: for He wished to show clearly their intention; "The learning of the wise is easy" (Prov. 14, 6). He says: *Shew me the coin of the tribute*, namely, the denarius that is given for the tribute. This denarius is worth ten ases, and everyone paid one denarius.

Then He asks about its appearance, saying, *Whose image and inscription is this?* For writing is put on every type of State money, and so it was on this coin. They say, *Caesar's*: do not think that they are referring to Caesar Augustus, but to Tiberius Caesar. And you should know that the Lord was not asking due to ignorance, but rather due to the need to impart the truth gradually. He was certainly old enough, and had lived among men long enough, to know well the appearance of the denarius, but He asked in order to make an illustration. Afterwards, He concludes the truth, **Render therefore to Caesar the things that are Caesar's; and to God, the things that are God's**; it is as if He said: 'You belong to God and to Caesar, and you have for your use what belongs to God and to Caesar. You have natural riches from God, namely, bread and wine, and from these, give to God: you have these man-made things, such as the denarii, from Caesar, and render these to Caesar.' Mystically, it is as follows: 'We have a soul which is made to God's image, for that reason, we ought to render it to God; in regard to the things that we have from the world, we ought to have peace with the world.' Holy men, even in this life, have been raised up from the world, nevertheless, because they have social intercourse with others in the world, they ought to strive after Babylon's peace, as it is stated in Baruch 1.[7] And this is because all things that are of the flesh, which are of the world, or of the men with whom they live, they render to God. The effect follows, **And hearing this, they wondered and, leaving him, went their ways.** This was surprising, because when His wisdom was seen they should have been converted; but they could not catch him, and so they withdrew; "Thy knowledge is become wonderful to me: it is high, and I cannot reach to it" (Ps. 138, 6).

23. That day there came to him the Sadducees, who say there is no resurrection; and asked him,

24. Saying: Master, Moses said: If a man die having no son, his brother shall marry his wife and raise up issue to his brother.

25. Now there were with us seven brethren: and the first having married a wife, died; and not having issue, left his wife to his brother.

26. In like manner the second and the third and so on, to the seventh.

---

[7] "And pray ye for the life of Nabuchodonosor the king of Babylon, and for the life of Balthasar his son, that their days may be upon earth as the days of heaven and that the Lord may give us strength, and enlighten our eyes, that we may live under the shadow of Nabuchodonosor the king of Babylon, and under the shadow of Balthasar his son, and may serve them many days, and may find favor in their sight" (verses 11-12).

27. And last of all the woman died also.
28. At the resurrection therefore, whose wife of the seven shall she be? For they all had her.
29. And Jesus answering, said to them: You err, not knowing the Scriptures nor the power of God.
30. For in the resurrection they shall neither marry nor be married, but shall be as the angels of God in heaven.
31. And concerning the resurrection of the dead, have you not read that which was spoken by God, saying to you:
32. I am the God of Abraham and the God of Isaac and the God of Jacob? He is not the God of the dead but of the living.
33. And the multitudes hearing it were in admiration at his doctrine.

Here, the second question is related: and the Evangelist does three things. Firstly, the question is related; secondly, the response is related; and thirdly, the effect is related. The second part is where it is said, **And Jesus answering**, etc.; and the third part is where it is said, **And the multitudes hearing it were in admiration**. About the first point, to begin with, the disposition and condition of the ones asking are related; and secondly, the question is related. He says, therefore, **That day**. And why is it said on that day? It is not without reason, because when they had seen those men confounded, they sought Him and not without presumption. But, according to Chrysostom, they had agreed with each other to catch Him in His speech, and everyone wanted the honor of victory: for that reason, when those men were confounded, these wished to come forward; "His troops have come together, and have made themselves a way by me" (Job 19, 12). For there were two sects: the Pharisees, that is to say, the separate, and the Sadducees, that is, the just. And the latter erred in doctrine, because they did not accept the Prophets, nor did they believe in the resurrection. Likewise, they believed that when the body died that the entire man passed away: and this is what he says, **Who say there is no resurrection**. The question follows. And firstly, they cite the Law; secondly, they present a case; and thirdly, they put forth their question. He says, therefore, **And they asked him, saying: Master, Moses said: If a man die having no son**, etc. This is found in Deut. 25.[8] What was the reason for the law? The people were carnal. Hence, they were only seeking temporal things. For it is clear that a man is himself unable to remain on earth after he dies, and so it is a consolation for him that he remain in his own

---

[8] Verses 5-6.

likeness, namely, in his son; and nature desires this, such that what cannot be saved in itself, may be saved in its own likeness. Hence, it happens that someone would die without a son, and so Moses rendered assistance to this case by this law, namely, that a brother would marry his wife. A stranger, who was in no way related to him, was not chosen; moreover, a stranger would not have as great a care for his house and family as a brother would have: and this is what Moses says, **He shall raise up issue to his brother**, meaning he would beget a son who would have the inheritance of that brother. After citing the Law, they put forth the case, saying, **There were with us seven brethren: and the first having married a wife, died; and not having issue, left his wife to his brother**, etc. It may be that such a case occurred, or that they concocted it. Nevertheless, according to Augustine, by the seven brothers evil men are signified, who in the seven ages of the world die without fruit. The Apostle says: "What fruit therefore have (or had) you then in those things of which you are now ashamed?" (Rom. 6, 21). This woman is worldly living. "They shall perish but thou remainest: and all of them shall grow old like a garment" (Ps. 101, 27). Hence, they inquire: All died, and all had her: **at the resurrection therefore, whose wife of the seven shall she be**, who will not be able to be the wife of them all? This opinion is not good, and it is against the Pharisees, because they believed that the resurrection ought to be as far as concerns this life, namely, that everyone will take back his wife and his possessions, etc. Hence, they say, **Whose wife shall she be?**, because she cannot be the wife of them all. This opinion is rejected in Job: "Nor shall he return any more into his house" (7, 10). Hence, a man will not rise again to the same manner of life.

The response follows. And firstly, He shows the error and its cause; secondly, He insinuates the truth; hence, the Evangelist says, **Jesus answering, said: You err**, meaning you have an erroneous opinion; "They thought, and were deceived: for their own malice blinded them" (Wis. 2, 21). And what is the cause of the error? **Not knowing the Scriptures**. Hence, they were not meditating on God's commandments; "I have had understanding above ancients: because I have sought thy commandments" (Ps. 118, 100). Hence, he who meditates on God's Commandments can avoid errors; hence: "Search the scriptures" (Jn. 5, 39). These men, on the contrary, were not searching, and thus they erred, just as some men do who understand badly. Likewise, some men err, not knowing God's power, wishing to measure God's power according to lower powers; "The invisible things of God from the creation of the world are clearly seen, being understood by the things that are made" (Rom. 1, 20). *In the resurrection they shall neither marry nor be married.* He proves His assertion. And because He had said two things, namely, that they did not know Scripture nor God's power, wherefore, He firstly declares that they were ignorant of God's power; and secondly, that they were ignorant of the Scriptures.

And since He spoke about the Scriptures first, why is it addressed second? Chrysostom replies that when someone disputes with a man who errs out of malice, he ought to firstly cite an authority; when someone disputes with him who errs out of ignorance, he ought firstly to bring forth a reason, and, afterwards, an authority. So the Lord does here.

Firstly, He brings forth a reason; hence, He says: *In the resurrection they shall neither marry nor be married.* In the first place, according to the literal meaning, it is true, *They shall neither marry*, etc., because then it shall not be necessary as it is now. Jerome says: "*Nubere* is used in one way in Latin, and another in Greek, for in Latin 'to marry' is said only of women; hence, it is not said of either in the passive voice; but in Greek men marry, that is they take wives, while women are married, but do not marry." Therefore, He says, *They shall neither marry*, referring to men, *nor be married*, referring to women. For since marriage is for the procreation of children, such that a man is kept in existence in his own likeness, who cannot be kept in existence in himself, it follows that when the resurrection to immortality takes place, then marriages will not be necessary. For that reason, these men erred, and they did not know God's power. *But shall be as the angels of God in heaven.* That state is the state of reward, and the goal of this life. "Shall man that is dead, thinkest thou, live again? all the days in which I am now in warfare, I expect until my change come" (Job 14, 14). That life will be accompanied with the understanding of resplendent things.

But why will they be similar to the angels? It is because they shall be immune from the passions, for now a man has an intellect joined to the senses, and in this the angels are superior; but then he will be purified, wherefore, they will be similar to the angels; "For even as an angel of God, so is my lord the king, that he is neither moved with blessing nor cursing" (II Kings 14, 17). Hence, those who have a soul elevated above the passions are similar to the angels. Now the passions that especially make men brutish, are the passions of sexual intercourse, which are used in marriage; and so they will then neither marry nor be married.

Likewise certain men have said that not all will rise, but only men. But Augustine rejects this, saying that both sexes will rise; for gender will not be kept only in men. Christ refutes this opinion, when He says, they shall neither marry nor be married, from which words it is given to be understood that both sexes will rise, but they shall neither marry nor be married.[9]

And concerning the resurrection of the dead, etc. After having shown that they were ignorant of God's power; here, He shows that they were ignorant of the Scriptures. Hence, *have you not read that which was spoken by God, saying to you: I am the God of Abraham and the God of Isaac and the God of Jacob?* This is written in Exodus 3, 6.

But Jerome asks, since other passages are more explicit concerning the resurrection, such as those found in Isaias 6, Ezechiel 33, and Daniel 12,[10] why did He cite this passage which is ambiguous? He answers that they did not accept the Prophets, but only the five books of Moses.

And how does this passage serve His argument? He says: *I am the God of Abraham and the God of Isaac and the God of Jacob.* He is called the God of those who are worshipping Him. These, therefore, worship Him. But to worship God does not belong to the dead, but to the living. Therefore, Abraham, Isaac, and Jacob live: but not in respect to the body: therefore, they live in respect to the soul. But does this prove the resurrection? It does, because these men were saying that there is no soul; He, however, shows that the soul remains: and if the soul remains, therefore, there is also a resurrection, because the soul is naturally inclined to the body.

But what does He mean when He says that *He is not the God of the dead*? It is true in regard to the body. Nevertheless, He is also the God of the dead, because the dead live in regard to the spirit; "Whether we die, we die unto the Lord" (Rom. 14, 18). Likewise, the passage is against the heretics who damn the Patriarchs of the Old Testament, because here it says that they

---

9. "He even affirmed that the sex should exist, by saying, 'They shall not be given in marriage,' which can only apply to females; 'Neither shall they marry,' which applies to males" (Augustine, *City of God*, bk. 22, chap. 17).

10. "For behold the Lord will come out of his place, to visit the iniquity of the inhabitant of the earth against him: and the earth shall disclose her blood, and shall cover her slain no more" (Is. 26, 21); "The hand of the Lord was upon me, and brought me forth in the spirit of the Lord: and set me down in the midst of a plain that was full of bones... Behold I will open your graves, and will bring you out of your sepulchres, O my people" (Ez. 37, 1 & 12); "And many of those that sleep in the dust of the earth, shall awake: some unto life everlasting, and others unto reproach, to see it always" (Dan. 12, 2). The text seems to have mistaken references to Isaias 6 and Ezechiel 33.

live according to the soul. Similarly, the passage is in the singular, because in other nations everyone has his own God. "Hear, O Israel, the Lord our God is one Lord" (Deut. 6, 4).

The effect of His words follows, namely, that they were in admiration: "Thy testimonies are wonderful, O Lord," etc., (Ps. 118, 129).

34. But the Pharisees, hearing that he had silenced the Sadducees, came together.
35. And one of them, a doctor of the law, asked him, tempting him:
36. Master, which is the great commandment in the law?
37. Jesus said to him: Thou shalt love the Lord thy God with thy whole heart and with thy whole soul and with thy whole mind.
38. This is the greatest and the first commandment.
39. And the second is like to this: Thou shalt love thy neighbour as thyself.
40. On these two commandments dependeth the whole law and the prophets.
41. And the Pharisees being gathered together, Jesus asked them,
42. Saying: What think you of Christ? Whose son is he? They say to him: David's.
43. He saith to them: How then doth David in spirit call him Lord, saying:
44. The Lord said to my Lord: Sit on my right hand, until I make thy enemies thy footstool?
45. If David then call him Lord, how is he his son?
46. And no man was able to answer him a word: neither durst any man from that day forth ask him any more questions.

Above, the Lord answered the question made about the payment of tribute, and the question about the resurrection; here, however, He answers a question about the comparison of the Divine commandments: and Matthew does two things. For firstly, he describes the wickedness of the ones asking; secondly, he relates the question, where it is said, **Master, which is the great commandment in the law?** He describes their wickedness in regard to three things. Firstly, he describes their wickedness in regard to their shamelessness; secondly, he describes their wickedness in regard to their deliberate malice; and thirdly, he describes their wickedness in regard to their trickery. He describes their wickedness in regard to their shamelessness, when it is said, *Hearing that he had silenced*. He had just confuted the disciples of the Pharisees and the Sadducees, hence, from this, they had enough reason to believe Him and to be ashamed. Hence, Chrysostom says: "Envy and anger nourish and cause shamelessness." But these men do not give up on account of this, rather, they still interrogate Him; "Most impudent dogs, they never had enough" (Is. 56, 11). And it is indicated that, although they heard this, nevertheless, they were not silent. One man keeps silence spontaneously, and this is prudence. Likewise, another man keeps silence, because silence is imposed upon him, and this belongs to the impudent; "There is one that holdeth his peace, because he knoweth not what to say: and there is another that holdeth his peace, knowing the proper time" (Eccli. 20, 6); "A time to keep silence, and a time to speak" (Eccle. 3, 7). Likewise, their deliberate malice is mentioned, namely, so that they might better convict Him, they are gathered together at the same time; "The princes met together, against the Lord" (Ps. 2, 2). *They came together*. It can be said that the Pharisees and the Sadducees came together, because even though they were different sects, they were united in tempting the Lord. Or, the Pharisees came together against the Lord. Likewise, their trickery is indicated, because when they had been gathered together in a crowd, they did not want all to question Him, but only one of them; it was so that if he would be defeated, the others would not be confounded, and if he would triumph, they would all glory in him. *And one of them, a doctor of the law, asked him, tempting him*, for he did not have the intention of learning; "They have opened their mouths upon me, and reproaching me they have struck me on the cheek" (Job 16, 11).

Here an objection can be made concerning the literal meaning, namely, that Mark says that He said, "Thou art not far from the kingdom of God" (12, 34). And so, how it is said here that he was tempting Him?

Augustine solves this objection saying that he came firstly with the intention of tempting, but when Christ had satisfied him, he consented to Him. And, in this way, that he tempted Him ought to be referred to the beginning of the conversation; that he was not far from the kingdom of God ought to be referred to the end. And so it is not surprising if the Lord's words changed his motivation.

It ought to be known, however, that some men tempt from the fact that they are unsure, because, according to what the Wise Man says, "He that is hasty to give credit, is light of heart"

(Eccli. 19, 4). This man, when he had heard many things about Christ, wanted to see if such things were true: and this temptation was not bad; hence, he says, *Master, which is the great commandment in the law?* Nevertheless, this question seemed to be calumnious and presumptuous, because all of God's Commandments are great; "The commandment is a lamp, and the law a light" (Prov. 6, 23). Moreover, he asked indeterminately, since all are great, so that if He would answer concerning one, he would object about another. Similarly, his question was presumptuous, because one ought not to ask about a great commandment who has not fulfilled the least; "Why doth thy heart elevate thee, and why dost thou stare with thy eyes, as if they were thinking great things?" (Job 15, 12). And it could have been that there was a controversy among them about this question, for some were saying that salvation was in some exterior acts; hence, "This people honoreth me with their lips: but their heart is far from me" (Is. 29, 13).[11] But the Lord answers that it is only in the interior acts; hence, His answer follows, *Jesus said to him: Thou shalt love the Lord thy God*, etc. And He not only answers the proposed question, but He also teaches the truth. Firstly, He teaches which Commandment is the first; secondly, He teaches that the second Commandment is similar to it; and thirdly, He gives the reason. The second part is where it is said, *And the second is like to this*, etc. The third part is where it is said, *On these two commandments dependeth the whole law and the prophets.* He says, therefore, *Thou shalt love the Lord thy God*, etc. This passage is written in Deuteronomy 6, 5. Likewise, the Lord said through Moses: "What doth the Lord thy God require of thee, but that thou fear the Lord thy God?" (Deut. 10, 12). Therefore, the Lord commands two things; namely, fear and love.

And why does the Lord not answer concerning fear, as He does concerning love? It ought to be said that certain men fear God, who fear to suffer from Him, such as those who fear the punishment of hell, or who fear to lose something that they have from God; and this is servile fear, because he loves that in which he fears to be punished: there are others who fear God Himself on account of Himself, who fear to offend Him; and such fear is from love, and he fears due to the fact that he loves. Therefore, the beginning of fear is love; "God is charity: and he that abideth in charity abideth in God, and God in him" (I Jn. 4, 16). And, therefore, He says, *Thou shalt love the Lord*; He does not say, 'Thou

---

11. cf. Mt. 15, 8 and Mk. 7, 6 for this rendering of the quotation.

shalt fear,' because He is firstly loveable, because He is the first end, and everything else is loved on account of the end. Therefore, he who loves God as his end, loves Him with his whole heart; "Be converted to me with all your heart" (Joel 2, 12). And, however much you try, you will not be able to encompass Him, because God is greater than the whole heart.

But what is it that He says, **With thy whole heart and with thy whole soul and with thy whole mind**? Chrysostom expounds these words as follows: 'Because in love there are two things: one, which is the origin of love: and a second, which is the effect and consequence of love. The origin of love is twofold. For love can arise from passion and from the judgment of reason: it arises from passion when a man does not know how to live without that which he loves; it arises from reason, in that he loves as reason dictates. He says, therefore, that a man loves with his whole heart who loves physically; a man loves with his whole soul who loves from the judgment of reason. And we ought to love God in both ways: physically, so that our heart is physically inclined towards God; hence, in Psalm 83, 3, it is said: "My heart and my flesh have rejoiced in the living God." The second[12] thing is the consequence of love, because that which I love, I willingly see, I willingly think of it, and I willingly do what pleases it; "He who loves me, will keep my word" (Jn. 14, 23); and I refer everything to it; "How lovely are thy tabernacles, O Lord of hosts! my soul longeth and fainteth for the courts of the Lord" (Ps. 83, 2). And we can add that which Mark adds, "And with thy whole strength" (12, 33), because he who loves God, conveys himself unto Him, and expends his strength upon Him. In like manner, Augustine distinguishes between the heart, the soul, and the mind, according to the three things that proceed from them. From the heart comes forth thoughts, as it is stated above in chapter 15, from the soul proceeds life, and from the mind proceeds knowledge and understanding. Hence, in that He says, **With thy whole heart**, it is meant that we ought to direct all our thoughts to Him; in that He says, **with thy whole soul**, it is meant that we ought to direct our whole lives to Him; in that He says, **with thy whole mind**, it is meant that all our knowledge ought to be referred to Him, that is to say, taking our knowledge captive unto His service; "Bringing into captivity every understanding unto the obedience of Christ" (II Cor. 10, 5). A gloss of a certain master expounds that the soul is God's image according to its powers, according to its memory,

---

[12]. "Tertium" in the text seems to be mistaken here, and so is translated here not "third" but "second," according to the context.

understanding, and will; so that, that which is said, **With thy heart**, refers to the understanding; that which is said, **with thy soul**, refers to the will; and that which is said, **with thy mind**, refers to the memory, such that one live entirely for God. Origen expounds the passage thus: **Thou shalt love the Lord thy God with thy whole soul**, so that you ought to be prepared to lay down your life for Him if it be necessary; "I will lay down my life for thee" (Jn. 13, 37). But there is a difference between the mind and the heart. For the mind (*mens*) is so-called from measuring (*metiendo*); the heart is taken for simplicity of understanding; but the mind, however, is taken from its relationship to speaking, because, by words, the understanding or a thought is measured: hence, He wishes to say that in our speaking and in our meditations we ought to love God totally.

Having asserted this, He adds, **This is the greatest and the first commandment**. It is the greatest in its extension; for it is this Commandment in which all the Commandments are contained, because in this Commandment the love of neighbor is contained according to that which is said: "He who loveth God also loves his brother" (I Jn. 4, 21); and, for that reason, it is the greatest. Likewise, it is first in origin, the greatest in importance and extension. It is not the first in Scripture, because in Scripture the first Commandment was, "Hear, O Israel, the Lord our God is one" (Deut. 6, 4). And why? It is because every inclination of an appetitive power is directed towards love: for that reason, we have the Commandment that we worship God in love: "Love therefore is the fulfilling of the law" (Rom. 13, 10); "Being rooted and founded in charity" (Eph. 3, 17).

Secondly, He relates the second Commandment: **And the second is like to this: Thou shalt love thy neighbour as thyself.** He wished to indicate that in the Commandments there is an order. And what is the reason for this? It is evident that the Commandments pertain to acts of the virtues; now the virtues have an order, because one depends upon another, and so, just as the virtues have an order, so also do the Commandments have an order.

But why does He say that it is similar to the first? It is because when a man is loved, since man is made to God's likeness, God is loved in him; for that reason, it is similar to the first Commandment, because it pertains to the love of God.

But what does He understand by the name of neighbor, when He says, **Thou shalt love thy neighbour**? This point is sufficiently expressed in the parable, where it is asked, "Which, in thy opinion, was his neighbour?" (Lk. 10, 36), and it is answered, "He that showed mercy to him." Hence, he who ought to show mercy to us, or we ourselves to others, is included under the name of neighbor. But there is no rational creature to whom we ought not to show pity, and vice versa: and, for that reason, men and angels are included under the name of neighbor. And that which He says, *as thyself*, is not understood to mean as much as oneself, because this would be contrary to the order of charity; but *as thyself*, meaning for the same reason why you love yourself, or in the same manner that you love yourself. For the same reason, namely, that you ought not to love yourself on account of yourself, but on account of God, and also, in this way, you ought to love your neighbor. "Do all to the glory of God" (I Cor. 10, 31). Likewise, by the very fact that you love yourself, you love yourself in him, in whom you want something good for yourself, and such is good, because it is in accord with oneself and God's law, and this is the good of justice. So also, you ought to desire the good of justice for your neighbor; hence, you ought to love him either because he is just, or because he is becoming just. Likewise, you ought to love him in the same manner as yourself, because when I say, 'I love this thing,' I am saying 'I want its good.' Hence, the act of love refers to two things: either it refers to that which is good, or to a good which I want for it; hence, I love this thing, because I want it to be good for me: hence, a man loves temporal goods, because he knows that they are good for himself; but some men love a thing, because it is good in itself: in this manner, you ought to love yourself, and also your neighbor.

Afterwards, He gives the reason why these two are the greatest Commandments. **On these two commandments dependeth the whole law and the prophets.** The whole doctrine of the Law and the prophets depends on these Commandments. In morals, the end is what principles are in speculative science:[13] for science proceeds from principles to conclusions, and so all science is judged by its principles, just as in all operable things, all depends on the end; "The end of the commandment is charity" (I Tim. 1, 5); wherefore, all the others depend on these two, and this is Augustine's exposition. Origen expounds this as follows: 'On these, meaning on the observance of these, depends the understanding of the Law and of the prophets, because those who observe these things, merit the understanding of the Law and the prophets'; "Ye that fear the Lord, love him, and your hearts shall be enlightened" (Eccli. 2, 10); "By thy commandments I have had understanding: therefore have I hated every way of iniquity" (Ps. 118, 104).

13. cf. *Ethica Nicomachea* viii, 8.

And the Pharisees being gathered together, Jesus asked them. After He had responded to them, He wished to object: and the Evangelist does two things. Firstly, a question is related; and secondly, its effect is related, where it is said, *No man was able to answer him a word.* About the first thing, He firstly proposes a question; secondly, the answer is related; and thirdly, He objects against the answer. He says, therefore: *And the Pharisees being gathered together, Jesus asked them.* Now they had been gathered together to tempt Him; hence, He proposes the question, *What think you of Christ? Whose son is he?* This question was very difficult, and it was appropriate. It was very difficult, because it is found in Isaias 53, 8: "Who shall declare his generation?" It was also appropriate, because they held the opinion that He was only a man, and they did not believe that He was God, for then they would not have tempted Him, because it is written: "Thou shalt not tempt the Lord thy God" (Deut. 6, 16). Therefore, to show that He is God, He says, *What think you of Christ? Whose son is he?* The response follows: *They say to him: David's.* For there was a twofold begetting of Christ: one according to His flesh, and another according to His divinity, according to which, He is the Son of God the Father, concerning which it is said, "Thou art my son, this day have I begotten thee" (Ps. 2, 7). Hence, they reply concerning His generation according to the flesh, when they say, *David's.* "I will raise up to David a just branch" (Jer. 23, 5). And: "Who was made to him of the seed of David, according to the flesh" (Rom. 1, 3). And their answer was inadequate, because they did not know Him well enough. Then He objects so that they might gather that there is another generation: *How then doth David in spirit call him Lord, saying: The Lord said to my Lord: Sit on my right hand?* (Ps. 109, 1). It is stated in the Law that a father is greater than a son. A son is not, therefore, the lord of his father. Hence, either Christ is not the son of David, or there is something greater in Him than in David, since he calls Him Lord. But perhaps they might say that David was deceived: which objection He eliminates, because David is saying this in spirit; hence, "The men of God spoke, inspired by the Holy Ghost" (II Pet. 1, 21).

Now we can see three things in the passage from the Psalms. Firstly, we see His preeminence over the saints, His equality to the Father, and His dominion over the rebellious. We see His preeminence over the saints, when He says: *The Lord said to my Lord.* *The Lord*, namely, the Father, *to my Lord*, namely, to the

Son: for the Son Himself has dominion over all the saints: for no saint is illumined except by the true light: He, however, is the true light; "The life was the light of men" (Jn. 1, 4). Therefore, if He Himself is the light, by participation of which all the saints receive light, He has preeminence over all the saints as to that light, and so it is said, "With thee is the principality in the day of thy strength: in the brightness of the saints," etc., (Ps. 109, 3); hence, He is the source of the brightness of the saints. Likewise, His equality with the Father is mentioned, when it is said, *Sit on my right hand*: not that there are seats having a place, but metaphorically, because the honorable place is to sit at the right side. To say is to utter a word. That which the Lord said, *Sit on my right hand*, what else does it mean except that 'By begetting Me, the Word, He gave Me power, equality, and authority?' It can also be expounded regarding temporal things, meaning in the greater temporal goods, but that is not to the point: for the Lord is always seen on the right side, as, for example, in Mark 16, 5: "They saw a young man sitting on the right side" (Mk. 16, 5). And Stephen "saw Jesus standing on the right hand of God." And what will happen to His enemies? They will all be made subject to Him; hence, it is added, *Until I make thy enemies thy footstool*. These enemies are either those completely lacking the faith, or those who do not wish to obey and be subject to Him; hence, He makes these men *thy footstool*; for a footstool is something that is placed under a man's feet; now, that which is under a man, is completely subject to him; however, that which is in his hand is not subject to him. Some men are made to be a footstool as a punishment, others are made to be a footstool for their salvation: it is a punishment for those who do not wish to do His will; but it is for the salvation of those who do His will.

But the Arians object: 'Therefore, He is not equal to the Father.' I say that two things are read, both that He is subject to the Father, and that He is equal to the Father; "For he must reign, until he hath put all his enemies under his feet" (I Cor. 15, 25). Likewise, Christ will subject all things to Himself: "Who will reform the body of our lowness, made like to the body of his glory" (Phil. 3, 21). Hence, He says that to show His unity of power: wherefore, everything that the Father can do, the Son can also do.

But what is it that He says, *until I make thy enemies thy footstool?* These words seem to imply that after He shall have made His enemies subject, He will no longer sit on His right hand. It ought to be said that *until* sometimes implies a determined time, other times it implies an unlimited time. Here, it certainly implies an unlimited time.

But someone might say: 'Do not many men rebel against Christ?' Indeed, it is true that many rebel, and hence, there could have been a doubt regarding the time when many were rebelling against Christ: for that reason, Christ willed to express this.

If David then call him Lord, how is he his son? Therefore, the Son is also the Lord, because He is the son of David according to the flesh, since He derived His lineage from him, and He is the Lord according to His divinity.

And no man was able to answer him a word. Here, the effect is related, and it is twofold, because Christ was the answerer (*respondens*) and the questioner (*opponens*): because He was questioning, *no man was able to answer*; "If he will contend with him, he cannot answer him one for a thousand" (Job 9, 3). Likewise, because in answering He had confounded them, for that reason, it continues, *Neither durst any man from that day forth ask him any more questions.* Hence, you can see that these men were not asking questions so that He might teach them, but so that they might tempt Him; "Ask thy father, and he will declare to thee" (Deut. 32, 7).

CHAPTER TWENTY-THREE

1. Then Jesus spoke to the multitudes and to his disciples,
2. Saying: The scribes and the Pharisees have sitten on the chair of Moses.
3. All things therefore whatsoever they shall say to you, observe and do: but according to their works do ye not. For they say, and do not.
4. For they bind heavy and insupportable burdens and lay them on men's shoulders: but with a finger of their own they will not move them.
5. And all their works they do for to be seen of men. For they make their phylacteries broad and enlarge their fringes.
6. And they love the first places at feasts and the first chairs in the synagogues,
7. And salutations in the market place, and to be called by men, Rabbi.
8. But be not you called Rabbi. For one is your master: and all you are brethren.
9. And call none your father upon earth; for one is your father, who is in heaven.
10. Neither be ye called masters: for one is your master, Christ.
11. He that is the greatest among you shall be your servant.
12. And whosoever shall exalt himself shall be humbled: and he that shall humble himself shall be exalted.

Above, it was shown how the Pharisees and the Scribes were provoked by Christ's glory, and also by His wisdom, by which He had crushed them; now, however, he shows how they were provoked by His justice, by which He rebuked them: and He does two things. Firstly, He instructs some men; and secondly, He condemns them. The second part is where it is said, **Woe to you, scribes and Pharisees**. About the first thing, to begin with, He shows their dignity; and secondly, He exposes their intention in the use of their authority, where it is said, **All their works they do for to be seen of men**. About the first point, He does three things. Firstly, He commends their authority; secondly, He teaches that one ought to render obedience with caution; and thirdly, He gives the reason. The second part is where it is said, **All things therefore whatsoever they shall say to you, observe and do**; and the third part is where it is said, **They say, and do not**. He says, therefore, **Then Jesus spoke to the** *multitudes*, etc. So it is continued. The Lord confounded them to such an extent that they dared not to question Him, nor did they know how to respond. But, according to what Chrysostom says, words are useless that do not also instruct. Now it ought to be known that some men listen to Him like the disciples did, others listen like the multitudes did: they listen like disciples, who perceive the truth with their minds; "If you continue in my word, you shall be my disciples indeed" (Jn. 8, 31). Others listen like the multitudes, who are unable to grasp the truth with their minds; for that reason, sometimes He directs His words to the multitudes, sometimes to the disciples, and other times to them both. And He does so in different ways: for He speaks to the disciples about high things, as it is stated, "Whatsoever I have heard of my Father, I have made known to you" (Jn. 15, 15): but at other times, He speaks to the multitudes in parables, as it is stated above. He speaks to both, however, about the necessity of salvation, and these words are of this sort, **The scribes and the Pharisees have sitten on the chair of Moses.** A chair properly belongs to a teacher; and so they are said to sit upon his chair, who are the successors of Moses; "Moses commanded a law in the precepts of justices" (Eccle. 24, 33). Hence, they who were teaching the Law of Moses were sitting upon the chair of Moses. And in this Law are contained certain things pertaining to the end, and certain things pertaining to good morals. Those things, which were pertaining to the end, are those in which Christ was prefigured; hence, He Himself says, "If you did believe Moses, you would perhaps believe me also" (Jn. 5, 46). Likewise, the moral precepts were contained in the Law; "Moses commanded a law in the precepts of justices" (Eccle. 24, 33).

Then He admonishes them to obey with caution; and He does two things. Firstly, He exhorts to obedience; and secondly, He exhorts to being on guard: **Whatsoever they shall say to you, observe**, namely, in your heart, **and do**, in deed; "Thou shalt come to the priests of the Levitical race, and to the judge" (Deut. 17, 9); and afterwards, it is written: "and thou shalt do whatsoever they shall say"; and it continues: "and thou shalt follow their sentence." And the Apostle says: "Obey your prelates" (Heb. 13, 17). And this is opposed to the Manicheans, who said that the Old Law was not good. And it is evident that it is good, because the Lord commanded it to be observed.

But someone could object: 'Therefore, we ought to observe the prescriptions of the Law,' which is contrary to the teaching of the Apostles (Acts 15). It ought to be known that a decree of a legislator is always to be kept according to his intention; but a legislator decrees some things to be always observed, and such things ought to be always observed: he decrees other things, however, that are like a shadow, as it is stated: "Which are a shadow of things to come" (Col. 2, 17). Therefore, moral prescriptions are commandments according to the mind of the legislator, and they should always be kept; but the legal prescriptions are to be kept only for a time, namely, for the time before Christ. Hence, before that time they ought to be kept, but not afterwards: because he who would keep them does an injury to Christ. And Augustine gives an example: If someone were to say, 'I will eat tomorrow,' this statement is a prediction of the act: and if after he had eaten, he were to say the same thing again, he would not speak correctly. And so, since these legal prescriptions prefigured Christ's coming, therefore, after Christ came, he who would then observe them does not observe them well. Hence, **All things they shall say to you**, according to the intention of the legislator, **do**.

But according to their works do ye not. Here, He teaches caution. You ought to know that a prelate is given a position of authority so that he may teach not only by his doctrine, but also by his life. And we ourselves ought to be in agreement with him as to the things that he teaches, because, according to what is said, "If any one preach to you a gospel, besides that which you have received, let him be anathema" (Gal. 1, 9). Likewise, we also ought to conform our lives to his. For his life ought to be our model, just as the life of Christ is our model. Hence: "Be ye followers of me as I also am of Christ" (I Cor. 4, 16). These men, in fact, do not deviate from Christ's doctrine, but from His life; for that reason, we ought to pay heed to their teaching, but beware of their life.

For they say, and do not. Here, He assigns the reason. Firstly, He gives the reason; and secondly, He explains it, where it is said, **For they bind heavy burdens**, etc. You say: 'Do what they tell you to do,' because **they say**: 'You ought to do good actions,' **but they do not**; wherefore, you ought not to do according to their works, "Because thou, that teachest that men should not steal, stealest" (Rom. 2, 21). "But to the sinner God hath said: Why dost thou declare my justices, and take my covenant in thy mouth?" (Ps. 49, 16). **For they bind heavy and insupportable burdens**, etc. For the Lord wants to show their added malice, **because they say, and do not**. If they would simply say, and not do, this would still be tolerable: but this does not suffice for them, because they add very heavy burdens to God's precepts: and hence, their presumption is noted, because they bind other burdens in addition to the burdens imposed by God, for they make new observances, as it is stated in Mark 7,[1] namely, that they forbade men to eat bread, unless they frequently washed their hands; and this is contrary to Isaias 58, 6: "Loose the bands of wickedness, undo the bundles that oppress." Similarly, the cruelty is noted of them who impose such burdens contrary to that which is written: "Because his commandments are light" (I Jn. 5, 3). "For my yoke is sweet and my burden light" (above 11, 30). Again, their indiscretion is noted, because if they imposed something heavy upon a strong man, it would not be something great; but they impose insupportable burdens upon the weak: for a thing cannot be carried which is beyond the strength of the one carrying. In the Acts it is said: "This is a burden which neither our fathers nor we have been able to bear" (15, 10). Moreover, their excessive severity is noted, because if they would impose a burden, and show kindness, it would still suffice; but they command somewhat violently. **Lay them on men's shoulders**; hence, they are excessive in telling others what to do. Likewise, they are excessive in not doing what they tell others to do, for there are some men who do not want to accomplish all, nevertheless, they are willing to accomplish something. Similarly, there are some men who, even if they do not want to do what is difficult, nevertheless, are willing to do what is easy. Again, there are those who, even if they do not do anything, nevertheless, have the desire to do something; but he who is unwilling to do any of these things, overabounds in malice; hence, He says, **but with a finger of their own they will not move them**; hence, not only were they not doing them, but they do not even wish to even move them with their finger, meaning they do not wish to even begin doing them. Likewise, nor also do they do the easy things, which are signified by a finger: hence, you ought to do what they teach, but they are not to be followed in respect to their works because they do not the least thing. Chrysostom says: "Such are the men who say great things, but do little; such men are similar to tax collectors, who make others pay excessively large amounts, they themselves, however, pay nothing. I ought not see you teaching great things, but doing little. Hence, the Lord will spare you more if you incline to mercy, rather than to severity."

And all their works they do for to be seen of men. Here, He points out their intention: and He does two things. Firstly, He exposes their intention; secondly, He advises His disciples to

---

1. "Why do not thy disciples walk according to the tradition of the an-cients, but they eat bread with common hands?" (verse 5).

avoid them. And firstly, He points out their intention; and secondly, He explains His words where it is said, *For they make their phylacteries broad*, etc. What is the reason why they say and do not do? It is because they are incorrigible. The reason why a man is difficult to correct, or incorrigible, is the seeking of one's own glory; hence, Chrysostom says: "Take away vainglory from the clergy, and you will curtail all the other vices without labor." Hence, He begins from this vice, saying: *And all their works they do for to be seen of men*; "They loved the glory of men more than the glory of God" (Jn. 12, 43). Hence, He says, *All their works they do*, because they do not just one, but all their works, *for to be seen of men*, contrary to that which is said above, "Be not as the hypocrites" (6, 16). "Be not you therefore like to them" (ibid. 8). The explanation follows. *For they make their phylacteries broad*, etc. And He does two things. Firstly, He says what they do; and secondly, He says what they seek, *And they love the first places at feasts*, etc. What do they do? They do not do the things that are burdensome, but certain things that appear outwardly, they do well; hence, Bernard says: "They wear the garments of holiness, and this is not burdensome because they were showing off their phylacteries and fringes." For it is said: "Thou shalt bind them on thy hand and before thy eyes" (Deut. 6, 8). On thy hand, that is, in the fulfillment of your works, and before your eyes, that is, in your considerations;[2] hence, these glory seekers, in order to seem to be zealous advocates for God's Commandments, wrote the Commandments on sheets of paper and put them before their eyes, and they called them phylacteries, and they broadened them so that they could be better seen by men; hence, it is said, *They make their phylacteries broad*. Likewise, concerning the fringes it is read (Num. 15) that the Lord commanded that they make fringes, because He wanted the Jewish people to be distinguished from other peoples. And these men, that they might appear to be more religious, were enlarging the fringes, and they were attaching pins so that they might be seen to prick themselves, so that they might be reminded that they are Jews. Therefore, they were not showing zeal but only some outward appearances; "They come to you in the clothing of sheep" (above 7, 15). And what do they seek? *For to be seen of men*. This glory is shown in three things. In one's primacy, in the

---

2. "JEROME: You shall bind them for a sign upon your hand, and they shall be ever before your eyes; the meaning of which is, Let my precepts be in your hand so as to be fulfilled in your works; let them be before your eyes so as that you shall meditate upon them day and night" (*Catena Aurea on St. Matthew*, chap. 23, lect. 2).

reverence shown to oneself, and in the praise of one's name; for he who seeks glory, seeks one of these things or all of them. These men, however, were seeking primacy in the holy places and in the common places; hence, He says in regard to the common places, **And they love the first places at feasts**: for they wanted to sit at the head of the tables, contrary to the passage: "When thou art invited to a wedding, sit not down in the first place" (Lk. 14, 8); and He says, **they love**, because dignities are not reprehended, but the inordinate desire for them. For certain men are bodily in the first place, who, nevertheless, in their hearts sit in the last place; and, on the contrary, some sit in the last places, so that it may be said, 'See, he is humble and so, etc.'; but some men sit in the first place in their hearts, because from thence they seek glory. Likewise, some men seek glory in the holy places, because they seek it in the Church; hence, He says, **and the first chairs in the synagogues**, contrary to the passage, "Seek not of man a preeminence, nor of the king the seat of honor" (Eccli. 7, 4). Similarly, some men seek reverence; hence, He says, **And salutations in the market place**, meaning that they be saluted and honored by men, in that they remove their hoods in their presence, and genuflect before them, and they desire **to be called by men, Rabbi**, meaning that they be praised as masters. Origen applies this passage to those who seek dignities in the Churches: for there is a certain dignity of archdeacons, deacons, priests, and of bishops. It belongs to deacons to preside at tables (Acts 6). Hence, they who desire the first places at table desire the place of the deacons. Likewise, the chief seat in the church properly belongs to the priests; for that reason, they love the chief seats of the church who love the place of the priests. Those who ought to be teachers, are properly the bishops; hence, they wish to be called Rabbi, who love to be bishops.

But be not you called Rabbi. In this part, He restrains them from imitating the pursuers of glory; secondly, He invites them to humility, where it is said, **He that is the greatest among you shall be your servant**. It ought to be noted that they who hold the primacy have to instruct and to govern; the first of these properly belongs to teachers, and the second to fathers. And, for that reason, He firstly forbids vainglory in regard to both; and the second part is where it is said, **And call none your father upon earth**. About the first, He firstly sets forth His teaching; and secondly, He gives the reason for the teaching. He says, therefore, **But be not you called Rabbi**; this prohibition seems to be opposed to that which is written: "Let those that rule well be esteemed worthy of double honor: especially they who labour in the word and doctrine" (I Tim. 5, 17). It can be said in reply, *Be not*, meaning you should not seek after honors, and He gives the reason, *For one is your master*, etc., namely, God; "I will hear what the Lord God will speak in me" (Ps. 84, 9).[3]

But what does He wish to say? It ought to be said that a man is properly called a teacher, who has a doctrine from himself, and not he who spreads what has been passed down from another man to others: and, in this way, only one person is a teacher, namely, God, who strictly possesses His own doctrine; but many men are teachers by ministering His doctrine. But if you seek to have authority, you seek what is God's; but if you seek to be His servant, you seek what is humble; hence, He adds; *He that is the greatest among you shall be your servant*, meaning let him consider himself to be but a servant. Chrysostom says that just as God is one by nature, many men are one by participation: so also one is a teacher by nature, and many are teachers ministerially.

But how can a man know that he does not possess the doctrine from himself? It is obvious, because if it were so he would be free to give his teaching to whomever he wished, but he cannot; in fact, this belongs to God alone, who inwardly enlightens the heart: and there is a clear example in regard to health, namely, that a doctor heals, because he administers some things outwardly; but nature principally heals, while a doctor administers certain things exteriorly; and a doctor, like nature, heals by restoring a balance. So it is with knowledge, that the source is given to us by nature, namely, the intellect: one who teaches applies certain helps to the teaching, as a doctor does in regard to health, but only God operates in the intellect. Hence, *one is your master*; wherefore, you ought not to be called Rabbi.

Likewise, He shows that they ought not to love the authority of a father, *And all you are brethren*, and He demonstrates this from their equal condition. In teaching, He does not differentiate in the quality of condition, but in paternity He brings up one's condition; hence, He says, *All you are brethren*, that is, you are all from Me, your Father; "Behold, I will send you Elias the prophet," and afterwards it is said, "and he shall turn the heart of the fathers to the children, and the heart of the children to their fathers" (Mal. 4, 5-6). Likewise, you are My sons through regeneration; "Who hath regenerated us unto a lively

---

3. "PSEUDO-CHRYS: Be not you called Rabbi, that you take not to yourselves what belongs to God. And call not others Rabbi, that you pay not to men a divine honor" (ibid).

hope, by the resurrection of Jesus Christ" (I Pet. 1, 3). Hence, one man does not have authority over another.[4] And He continues: ***And call none your father upon earth***: for since you are sons of a heavenly Father, for that reason, you ought not to have a father on earth. A man is properly said to have a father on earth, who seeks his inheritance on earth; and he has a Father in heaven, who seeks his inheritance in heaven; "Who according to his great mercy hath regenerated us unto a lively hope, by the resurrection of Jesus Christ from the dead: unto an inheritance, incorruptible, and undefiled and that cannot fade, reserved in heaven" (I Pet. 1, 4).

Why then are the superiors in monasteries called "Father"? It ought to be answered that they are fathers in respect to their authority; "That you may understand my knowledge in the mystery of Christ," etc., (Eph. 3, 4).[5]

For one is your father. "Our Father who art in heaven" (above 6, 9). Likewise, ***Neither be ye called masters: for one is your master, Christ***: hence, Christ attributes His teaching to Himself, because Christ is the Word; and, for that reason, it belongs to Him to teach, for no one teaches except through words. Again, He is a teacher in respect to His human nature, because He was sent to teach; "No man hath seen God at any time: the only begotten Son who is in the Bosom of the Father, he hath declared him" (Jn. 1, 18). Likewise: "You call me Master and Lord" (ibid. 13, 13).

He that is the greatest among you shall be your servant. After withdrawing them from pride, He exhorts them to humility. Firstly, the Evangelist relates the exhortation; and secondly, he gives the reason. And this can be continued as follows. Chrysostom says: "You ought to neither be called fathers nor masters; hence, you ought not to desire these titles, but rather humility." Hence: "Let a man so account of us as of the ministers of Christ" (I Cor. 4, 1). Or, He had spoken otherwise as follows, ***Be not you called Rabbi***, wherefore, they might have said to Him: 'Do you wish there to be no authority on earth?'

---

4. Man of himself has no authority, but man can receive authority from God. "For if the power of rulers is from God and nothing is from God without order, it follows that the order whereby the lower are subjected to the higher powers is from God. *Therefore, he that acts against the order and resisteth the power resisteth the ordinance of God*: 'They have not rejected thee, but me' (I Kings 8, 7); 'He that despiseth you despiseth me' (Lk 10:16). (*Comm. on Romans*, chap. 13, lect. 1).

5. The Latin reads, "Potestis intellegere prudentiam meam in mysterio Christi," and in English means, "That you may understand my prudence in the mystery of Christ." Prudence is the principle virtue of those in authority. "It belongs to prudence to govern and command" (II II, q. 50, a. 1).

The Lord says: 'I do not want this, but I want that he who is greater among you be as your minister, meaning that he not esteem himself to be superior, but a servant'; "We ourselves your servants through Jesus" (II Cor. 4, 5). And this is what is said in Luke 22, 27: "Which is greater, he that sitteth at table or he that serveth?" etc. Then he gives the reason, *And whosoever shall exalt himself shall be humbled: and he that shall humble himself shall be exalted.* Hence, in the Virgin's canticle it is said: "He hath put down the mighty from their seat and hath exalted the humble" (Lk. 1, 52).

13. But woe to you, scribes and Pharisees, hypocrites, because you shut the kingdom of heaven against men: for you yourselves do not enter in and those that are going in, you suffer not to enter.

14. Woe to you scribes and Pharisees, hypocrites, because you devour the houses of widows, praying long prayers. For this you shall receive the greater judgment.

15. Woe to you, scribes and Pharisees, hypocrites, because you go round about the sea and the land to make one proselyte. And when he is made, you make him the child of hell twofold more than yourselves.

16. Woe to you, blind guides, that say, Whosoever shall swear by the temple, it is nothing; but he that shall swear by the gold of the temple is a debtor.

17. Ye foolish and blind: for whether is greater, the gold or the temple that sanctifieth the gold?

18. And whosoever shall swear by the altar, it is nothing; but whosoever shall swear by the gift that is upon it is a debtor.

19. Ye foolish and blind: for whether is greater, the gift or the altar that sanctifieth the gift?

20. He therefore that sweareth by the altar sweareth by it and by all things that are upon it.

21. And whosoever shall swear by the temple sweareth by it and by him that dwelleth in it.

22. And he that sweareth by heaven sweareth by the throne of God and by him that sitteth thereon.

23. Woe to you, scribes and Pharisees, hypocrites; because you tithe mint and anise and cummin and have left the weightier things of the law: judgment and mercy and faith. These things you ought to have done and not to leave those undone.

24. **Blind guides, who strain out a gnat and swallow a camel.**

25. **Woe to you, scribes and Pharisees, hypocrites; because you make clean the outside of the cup and of the dish, but within you are full of rapine and uncleanness.**

26. **Thou blind Pharisee, first make clean the inside of the cup and of the dish, that the outside may become clean.**

27. **Woe to you, scribes and Pharisees, hypocrites; because you are like to whited sepulchres, which outwardly appear to men beautiful but within are full of dead men's bones and of all filthiness.**

28. **So you also outwardly indeed appear to men just: but inwardly you are full of hypocrisy and iniquity.**

29. **Woe to you, scribes and Pharisees, hypocrites, that build the sepulchres of the prophets and adorn the monuments of the just,**

30. **And say: If we had been in the days of our fathers, we would not have been partakers with them in the blood of the prophets.**

31. **Wherefore you are witnesses against yourselves, that you are the sons of them that killed the prophets.**

32. **Fill ye up then the measure of your fathers.**

33. **You serpents, generation of vipers, how will you flee from the judgment of hell?**

After He instructed the disciples and the multitudes about the caution they ought to have concerning the Jew's doctrine, He here directs His words to the Scribes by rebuking them. Firstly, He rebukes them concerning their pretense of religion; secondly, He rebukes them concerning their pretense of purity, since they were impure; and thirdly, He rebukes them concerning their pretense of piety, since they were impious. The second part is where it is said, **Woe to you, scribes and Pharisees, hypocrites; because you make clean the outside of the cup**, etc.; the third part is where it is said, **Woe to you, scribes and Pharisees, hypocrites, that build the sepulchres of the prophets**, etc. In regard to religious matters, there are certain things that the priests owe to the people and vice versa. Therefore, He firstly points out their malice in those things that the priests owe to the people; secondly, He points out the malice in those things that the people owe to the priests, where it is said, **Woe to you that say, Whosoever shall swear**, etc. A priest owes something to those who are already converted, and something else to those who are not converted. To those who are not converted, he is obliged to convert them; and to those who are converted, he is obliged to give them doctrine; "The lips of the priests shall keep knowledge" (Mal. 2, 7). Likewise, he is bound to offer suffrages[6] for them; "For every high priest taken from among men is ordained for men in the things that appertain to God" (Heb. 5, 1). And these men were doing bad deeds in regard to both; hence, He firstly rebukes them about the first point; and secondly, He rebukes them about the second point, where it is said, *Woe to you who devour the houses of widows*, etc. In all these reproaches He shows Himself to be the Son of Him who gave the Old Law. In Deuteronomy 26 and 28 curses are bestowed upon those who will not continue in the Law, and, afterwards, blessings are bestowed upon those who continue in the Law. But because He had come to loosen the curses of the Law, it follows that the blessings are firstly given above, "Blessed are the poor... Blessed are the meek" (5, 3-4). But, towards the end of His teaching, He gives a curse. Hence, they wrongly find fault with the Old Law, who do so on the pretext that curses are contained therein, because what is found in the Old Law is also in the New. For as in the Old Law men were not cursed unless they violated the Law, so it is now; "Reject not the correction of the Lord" (Prov. 3, 11).

But what is it that He says, *You shut the kingdom of heaven against men*? The happiness of eternal life is called the kingdom of heaven; "Unless your justice abound more than that of the scribes and Pharisees, you shall not enter into the kingdom of heaven," (above 5, 20). Likewise, Sacred Scripture is called the kingdom of heaven; "The kingdom of God shall be taken from you," meaning the understanding of Sacred Scripture. Christ is the gate to both kingdoms; "I am the door. By me, if any man enter in, he shall be saved: and he shall go in and go out, and shall find pastures" (Jn. 10, 9). And so, what does it mean to close the kingdom of heaven, except that these men were closing it through their bad teachings and bad lives? Something is not closed unless it were opened. The teachings concerning Christ were opened: but these men were closing them, since they were making them obscure. It is written: "The Lord himself will come and will save you. Then shall the eyes of the blind be opened, and the ears of the deaf shall be unstopped" (Is. 35, 4-5). When the Lord was performing these miracles, this Scripture was opened, but they were closing it, saying, "He casteth out devils by Beelze-

---

[6]. "Suffrage by its very nature implies the giving of some assistance" (Supp. q. 71, a. 8).

bub, the prince of devils" (Lk. 11, 15). Likewise, they were closing it by their bad lives when, by their bad examples, they were inducing men to commit sin; "Blessed is the man who hath not walked in the counsel of the ungodly, nor stood in the way of sinners, nor sat in the chair of pestilence," (Ps. 1, 1). He is properly said to sit in the chair of pestilence, who receives the duty of teaching and, through his bad life, corrupts the people. Also, a judge destroys a man by an unjust sentence, yet he pronounces the unjust sentence in vain. For the power of binding and loosing is given for building, not for destroying. Hence, it can be said to them: *Woe to you... because you shut the kingdom of heaven against men.* Similarly, whosoever impedes entrance to the kingdom doubtless acts wickedly; hence, He continues, *For you yourselves do not enter in and those that are going in, you suffer not to enter*, meaning you do not allow others to be converted. Hence: "You have departed out of the way, and have caused many to stumble" (Mal. 2, 8).

Woe to you... who devour the houses of widows, praying long prayers. This is the second woe, in which is mentioned their pretense as to prayer. And firstly, He rebukes them concerning their voracity, when He says, *Who devour the houses of widows*, because whatever they did, all was related to their gluttony, such that the passage from II Machabees 6 applies to them, namely, that the whole Temple was full of lust and surfeiting. *The houses of widows*, meaning the possessions of widows. But why does He speak of the houses of widows rather than those of others? The reason is because they were more intent upon misleading widows, because men are wiser and more discerning, and are not so readily deceived. Likewise, women have a disposition more inclined to giving; "But, as it becometh women professing godliness, with good works" (I Tim. 2, 10). Likewise, He says, *the houses of widows*, because a woman who has a husband, has in him a head and a counselor and so she is not so easily deceived. Moreover, a married woman does not have control of her house, but a widow does; for that reason, a widow is able to give more than a married woman, and so they were making a greater profit from them than from other women, since they were more apt to give; hence, the passage well applies to them: "They have slain the widow and the stranger" (Ps. 93, 6). And they did this by way of prayer, *Praying long prayers*, on account of the pretense of sanctity: and so they turned prayer into profit, and profit to their glory. Hence, they could be reprehended since they were gluttons, since they were plunderers, and again, since they were pretenders of sanctity; and so, He continues, *For this you shall receive the greater judgment*, that is to say, for their greater sins. And why are their sins greater? It is because if someone robs using the arms of the devil, he sins: but if he robs using God's arms, he sins doubly, because he sins both against God and against his neighbor. Or He says, *greater*, etc., because 'You receive from those to whom you ought to give.' Or, *greater*, as it is stated: "The servant, who knew the will of his lord and prepared not himself and did not according to his will, shall be beaten with many stripes" (Lk. 12, 47).

Woe to you, scribes and Pharisees, hypocrites, because you go round about the sea and the land to make one proselyte. And this can be expounded in two ways, such that it refers to the time after Christ, or that it refers to the time before Christ. If it refers to the time after Christ, then He is speaking of the future and present time. For He foresaw that the Jews would be dispersed throughout the whole world, and that they would begin to follow their own law, and that they would draw away whoever they could from Christ. And, for that reason, it is said, *You go round about the sea and the land*, etc. Those who converted from the Gentiles or from the Christians to their faith are called proselytes, and, for that reason, He says this. And He says, *One*, because very few were converted. Therefore, they fell under that curse which is written: "I found Israel like grapes in the desert" (Osee 9, 10). *And when he is made*, namely, a Jew, *you make him the child of hell twofold more than yourselves*: because he was firstly a Gentile and then a Jew, and consequently he is guilty of double sins, namely, those of the Gentiles and those of the Jews, and he becomes a participant in the killing of Christ. If, however, he will have been a Christian and then became a Jew, he becomes worse in two ways, namely, he destroys the gifts of the Holy Ghost which he had received in the Sacraments. Likewise, he becomes a partaker in the sins of the Jews; "You are of your father the devil" (Jn. 8, 44). These words can also be referred to the time before Christ, because they converted some men to their faith before Christ. And this is evident, because everyone loves themselves more than others; therefore, if they would convert other men on account of the salvation of their souls, they ought to care more for their own salvation, but they did not care about their own salvation. Rather, they were doing everything for the sake of gain, more specifically, they wanted the oblations to be increased; hence, their teaching was useless. *And when he is made, you make him the child of hell twofold more than yourselves*; because he was firstly converted to Judaism and was scandalized, so, afterwards, he reverts to paganism. Hence: "It had been better for them not to have known the way of justice than, after they have known it, to turn back" (II Pet. 2, 21). Before he was a Jew, he was refraining from evil deeds, at least for the sake of men's praise, but afterwards, he did not refrain from evil: hence: "For when the Gentiles, who have not the law, do by nature those things that are of the law; these, having not the law, are a law to themselves" (Rom. 2, 14). Hence, they were following the example of the wicked.

Woe to you, blind guides. In saying this, He is showing that they are pretenders of holiness in relation to things owed to prelates. And firstly, they are pretenders as to oblations; and secondly, they are pretenders in regard to tithes, where it is said, *Woe to you... who tithe mint*, etc. Notice that He firstly cites their tradition; and secondly, He denounces it for three reasons. The first part, wherein their tradition and the reason for it are pointed out, has two parts. The second part is where it is said, *And whosoever shall swear by the altar*, etc. These men were turning all religion into gain, and so they encouraged men to make offerings. Much gold was put into the Temple: hence, they were saying that if someone swore by the Temple he owed nothing; but he who swore by its gold obliged himself for as much as he swore. Likewise, there was a second tradition, because there was an altar there and they were offering many things upon the altar; hence, they were saying that he who swore by the altar owed nothing; but he who swore by an oblation obliged himself to the value of the oblation. And why did they say this? It was so that they could profit from the penalties, and so, by exaggerating the holiness of the offering, they were inciting men to offer more. Firstly, he relates the first part; and secondly, he relates the second part. About the first, Matthew does two things. Firstly, he sets forth their tradition; and secondly he sets forth the reproof, where it is said, *Ye foolish and blind*, etc. He says, therefore: *Woe to you, blind guides*, etc. This is similar to what was said above: "They are blind, and leaders of the blind (15, 14); "His watchmen are all blind" (Is. 56, 10). *You that say, Whosoever shall swear by the temple of God, it is nothing*, because it is impossible that he would make another temple; *but he that shall swear by the gold of the temple*, that is by gold, *is a debtor*, namely, of that gold. Afterwards, he relates the reproof: *Ye foolish and blind: for whether is greater, the gold or the temple that sanctifieth the gold?* It is evident that what is in the Temple is holy by reason of the Temple: hence, he who steals something that is in the Temple, commits a sacrilege: hence, it is greater to swear by the Temple, than by the gold in the Temple. Chrysostom says: "This is contrary to those who say that to swear by God is nothing." Hence, some who swear by God, believe that they swear not at all; but when they swear by God's holy Gospels, they think that it is something great. Hence, it can be said to them: 'Which is greater, God or the Gospel?' It is clear that God is greater. And this is simply true; it is otherwise when some circumstance which aggravates the sin be added; for example, he who swears by God's holy Gospels, swears with a certain deliberation and solemnity and, for that reason, sins more grievously. Then he relates the second part of the tradition: *And whosoever shall swear by the altar, it is nothing; but whosoever shall swear by the gift that is upon it is a debtor.* Afterwards, he relates the reproof: *Ye blind: for whether is greater, the gift or the altar that sanctifieth the gift?* For a gift cannot be sanctified except by an altar. *He therefore that sweareth by the altar sweareth by it and by all things that are upon it.* Here, He gives another reason. The Temple contains the gold, and not vice versa. Hence, he who swears by the Temple, swears by the gold that is in the Temple; and he who swears on the altar, meaning by the altar, swears by that which is on it. Likewise, another reason follows: *And whosoever shall swear by the temple sweareth by it and by him that dwelleth in it.* These men were saying: 'He who swears by the Temple, swears nothing.' But He wants to show that he who swears by the Temple, swears by God, because he would not swear by the Temple unless it were sanctified, and it is not sanctified except by God. Therefore, he who swears by the Temple, swears by God. Then another reason is given: *And he that sweareth in heaven*, meaning by heaven, would not swear by it were it not God's throne and because God's power is manifested there; hence, *And he that sweareth by heaven sweareth by the throne of God and by him that sitteth thereon.* "God is in his holy temple, the Lord's throne is in heaven" (Ps. 10, 5). And this throne is said to be there by way of a similitude. But mystically, according to Origen, He makes mention of the Temple, of gold, and of the altar, by which the contemplative life and the life of glory are signified. By gold the contemplative life is signified, by which a derived subtle meaning of Scripture is signified: because no matter how much the meaning seems reasonable, it is worthless unless it be in the Temple, that is to say, unless it be confirmed in Holy Scripture. By the altar, the heart is signified, in which the fire of devotion ought to be; "The fire on the altar shall never cease" (Lev. 6, 12). By oblations, services and offerings are signified, which, unless they proceed from a pure heart, or from a holy altar, cannot have value; "If thy eye be single, thy whole body shall be lightsome" (above 6, 22). By the throne, the life of glory is signified: God who surpasses all things is there. Or by the altar and the Temple we understand Christ to be meant: for He calls Himself a temple; "Destroy this temple; and in three days I will raise it up" (Jn. 2, 19). Likewise, He is said to be an altar; "We have an altar whereof they have no power to eat who serve the tabernacle" (Heb. 13, 10). Hence, whatever good we do, unless it be in this temple, which is Christ, and sanctified, it is valueless; hence, all is contemptible unless it be referred to Christ.

Woe to you, scribes and Pharisees, hypocrites; because you tithe mint and anise and cummin. Here, He reprehends them concerning tithes; and He does three things. Firstly, He relates their practice; secondly, He introduces His teaching; and thirdly, He makes a sort of comparison. The second part is where it is said, **These things you ought to have done**; and the third part is where it is said, **Blind guides, who strain out a gnat**, etc. Hence, He says, **Woe to you, scribes and Pharisees**; and He adds, **hypocrites**, because their principle intention was a pretense, **because you tithe mint and anise and cummin**. It can be understood to be a tithe of things given or of things exacted; hence, there were very many priests and Levites who had the right to exact the tithes due them, as is stated in Numbers 18 and Deuteronomy 14; for that reason, they were very diligent in exacting tithes, therefore, they were exacting them even on the least things, such as cummin and anise. **And you have left the weightier things of the law: judgment and mercy and faith.** For certain things were due to the priests for themselves, such as the tithes on which they were to live; but there were other things to which they were obliged on account of God, such as to do judgment and mercy; hence, the Lord was demanding from them these things, namely, judgment and mercy; "Mercy and judgment I will sing to thee, O Lord" (Ps. 100, 1). Likewise, He wants faith on account of His glory: hence, they did not care about those things to which they were bound on account of God; hence, He says: **You have left the weightier things of the law: judgment and mercy and faith**. But concerning the tithes to which they were bound, on account of themselves, they cared very much, according to that which is written: "All seek the things that are their own not the things that are God's" (Phil. 2, 21). Charity does the contrary, namely, that it "does not seek the things that are its own," (I Cor. 13, 5) but the things "that are Jesus Christ's" (Phil. 2, 21). Likewise, it can be said: 'Woe to you who give tithes of the least things, of mint, of cummin, and of suchlike things, and you do this to appear religious; but about interior things you do not care, because you do not love mercy, or judgment, or faith'; "If you knew what this meaneth: I will have mercy, and not sacrifice: you would never have condemned the innocent" (above 12, 7). Origin says that by mint and cummin, etc., certain things can be understood which pertain to the godliness of religion: hence, mercy, judgment, and faith are like food, but the other things are like condiments. Hence, it is as if they were making a greater fuss in regard to the condiments in preparing the food than in regard to the food itself, so, likewise, these men were making more of a fuss in the fact that one genuflect before them, than in those things that pertained to God.

These things you ought to have done and not to leave those undone. Because He had said, *Woe to you, because you tithe*, someone could say that the Lord was forbidding the giving of tithes, and for that reason He says that indeed they ought to give tithes, when He says, *These things you ought to have done and not to leave those undone*; it is as though He were to say: "You do not sin in these things, but in omitting those things to which you are more obliged: for that reason, *these things you ought to have done*, meaning to exact tithes, *and those things*, judgment, justice, and faith, *not to leave undone.*

But here there can be a question about tithes. It seems that the Lord is asserting the necessity of paying tithes; so in the whole New Testament it is not as expressly mentioned as it is here. But is it stated as a precept of Law? No: because in the Law are contained some moral precepts, some ceremonial precepts, and some judicial precepts: the moral precepts are to be observed at every time and by all: the ceremonial precepts are to be observed by certain men and at certain times, such as circumcision, and these precepts were only figurative: similarly, some judicial precepts, for example, if someone were to steal a sheep, he ought to render fourfold; for that reason, it is sought regarding tithes, whether tithes are a moral precept. And it seems that it is not, because the moral precepts are of the natural law. Now a precept is only of the natural law because natural reason urges it. But it does not urge more to give a tithe, than a ninth or an eleventh, etc. Therefore, it is not of the natural law. Likewise, if tithes are ceremonial then they sin who pay them.

Regarding this question, those who were before us said that some precepts are purely moral, some are purely ceremonial, and some are partially moral and partially ceremonial. "Thou shalt not kill" is purely moral. Likewise, "The Lord thy God shalt thou adore," etc. If you say: "Thou shalt offer a lamb in the evening on the fourteenth day of the month," this is a purely ceremonial precept. But if it is said: "Remember that thou keep holy the sabbath day," the precept is partly ceremonial and partly moral: it is partly moral, namely, because natural reason suggests it, more particularly that one have a certain time during which one is free, or in which one is free to pray to God. But that the certain time be on Saturday or Sunday, etc., is a judicial precept. Hence, they say that the precept of tithes is partially ceremonial and partially moral. For tithes are meant for the support of the poor and of those who devote themselves to God's service, or to preaching: for to him who serves the community belongs the right to support from the community, and this is of the natural law; but that one be obliged to give a tenth part, this is a ceremonial precept.

But are men now never obliged to pay tithes? I say that the determination of this precept pertains to any ruler who has the power of making laws: hence, it is within the Church's power to establish an obligation to pay a tithe, or a ninth, or suchlike: hence, they are bound, not because it is from the natural law, but from the obligation established by the Church.

Blind guides, who strain out a gnat and swallow a camel. In this part, He makes a comparison: wherefore, He says, ***Strain out a gnat.*** He who strains out, swallows with difficulty. Hence, He wishes to say that they take great care in the least things, and little care in regard to important things. Or by the gnat, the smallest sins are understood, and by the camel, the greatest sins are understood: hence, they make a fuss in regard to small sins; and this is what He says, ***They swallow a camel.***

Woe to you, scribes and Pharisees, hypocrites; because you make clean the outside of the cup and of the dish. Above, the Lord rebuked the Pharisees concerning the simulation they were outwardly pretending, but did not have in their hearts, and instead were turning into profit; here, He rebukes them concerning the pretense of purity that they were outwardly displaying. And here, He firstly rebukes them in regard to their desire for temporal goods, or in regard to sins of the flesh; and secondly, He rebukes them in regard to spiritual sins. Firstly, He treats of the first point; and secondly, He treats of the second, where it is said, ***Woe to you... because you are like to whited***

sepulchres. About the first point, He does two things. For firstly, He rebukes their pretense; secondly, He puts forth His sacred teaching, where it is said, *Thou blind Pharisee*, etc. He says, therefore: *Woe to you, scribes and Pharisees, hypocrites; because you make clean the outside of the cup*, etc. Observe that this can be understood in two ways. In one way it is a proper form of speech; and He wishes to mention the Pharisees' custom of cleaning the external things, as it was stated above in chapter 7, namely, that they kept the cleanliness of pots and vessels; hence, *woe to you*, who impose great care in cleaning vessels, but not your hearts; hence, it follows: *but within*, meaning in the heart, *you are full of rapine and uncleanness*. Jerome maintains that it is figurative speech: hence, He wishes that all cleanliness that appears outwardly be understood. Meat is served on a dish; drink is served in a cup. Now man is called a dish; and the good works that he does are the meat that God enjoys; "My meat is to do the will of my Father" (Jn. 4, 34). 'It is clear that the outer surface of a cup and dish are not used, but the inner surface. Therefore, he cleans the cup outwardly, who prepares his body outwardly. You are of this sort': *But within you are full of rapine and uncleanness*. And He gives two kinds, rapine and uncleanness: because there are two kinds of sin: carnal sins which are consummated in pleasure of the flesh, namely, gluttony and lust; and the other kind of sin is consummated in pleasure of the spirit, namely, pride and avarice, because avarice in regard to its object belongs to the carnal sins: but in regard to its completion, because it is completed in the mind, namely, in the desire for money, it belongs to the spiritual sins; hence, He reprehends avarice when He says, *rapine*. Now rapine[7] properly exists when something belonging to another is taken; likewise, a man is properly avaricious who keeps what belongs to another: hence, it is opposed to justice; "The spoil of the poor is in your house" (Is. 3, 14). Similarly, they are *full of uncleanness*, as to gluttony and lust. The soul is made impure by passion: now no other passions so weigh down reason as gluttony and lust; "Fornication and all uncleanness or covetousness, let it not so much as be named among you" (Eph. 5, 3).

Then He returns to the sound doctrine: *Thou blind Pharisee, first make clean the inside of the cup and of the dish*. All exterior purity is from interior purity, as was stated above: "If thy eye be single, thy whole body shall be lightsome" (6, 22).

7. i.e. robbery.

For that reason, He teaches that if a man cleans his heart, then everything will be clean; hence, He says: *Thou blind Pharisee*, etc. "Their own malice blinded them" (Wis. 2, 21). *Make clean the inside*, because whatever happens exteriorly, as long as it happens from a good will, is all good; "With all watchfulness keep thy heart" (Prov. 4, 23). Likewise, the understanding of sacred Scripture can be understood; "With the bread of life and understanding, she fed him" (Eccli. 15, 3), in which wisdom is given. The bread of wisdom is the word of life: hence, some men wish to honor the word outwardly but do not care about its meaning. And these clean what is on the outside.

Woe to you,... because you are like to whited sepulchres. Here, He rebukes them in regard to their spiritual sins. Firstly, He makes a comparison; and secondly, He explains it. The place where a dead body rests is called a sepulchre. The dead bodies of the Saints are the temples of God, in whom God dwells. "The temple of God is holy, which you are" (I Cor. 3, 17). The body is the abode of the soul, and the soul is God's throne: so just as the body is the abode of the soul, so the soul is the dwelling place of God; "The Lord is in his holy temple," etc., (Ps. 10, 5). But the body of sin is a sepulchre, because it contains something dead, since the soul dies through sin, wherefore wicked men are called sepulchres; "Their throat is an open sepulchre" (Ps. 13, 3). In a sepulchre, there is a dead body inside, while sometimes on the outside there is a likeness which apparently seems to be alive; "Thou hast the name of being alive. And thou art dead" (Apoc. 3, 1). And, therefore, He says: *Which outwardly appear to men beautiful*, on account of the ornamentation put on the outside, *But within are full of dead men's bones and of all filthiness*, meaning with all rottenness and every uncleanness. Afterwards, He explains this: *So you also outwardly indeed appear to men just*, meaning that men judge you to be just, *but inwardly you are full of hypocrisy and iniquity*. He includes the carnal sins of avarice and gluttony, as was said above, under which vainglory is contained; "They loved the glory of men more than the glory of God" (Jn. 12, 43). Likewise, under iniquity all spiritual sins are included.

Then, when He says, *Woe to you, that build the sepulchres of the prophets*, He rebukes them concerning their simulation of piety. Firstly, He points out their simulation; and secondly, He points out their cruelty, where it is said, *Wherefore you are witnesses against yourselves*, etc. Likewise, they pretend in two ways, by deeds and by words. Hence, He firstly rebukes them concerning their deeds; and secondly, He rebukes them concerning their words. The second part is where it is said, *And say: If we had been*, etc. He says, therefore, *Woe to you, that build the sepulchres of the prophets.*

But what is this? Were they doing something bad? Do we not do this suitably, we who put the bodies of the Saints in silver and gold containers? Some say that they are not reprehended for their deed, but for their intention, because their intention was wicked: for they were doing this so that the memory of their fathers' crimes might be brought back to men's memories: hence, they want that the audacity of their parents, who dared to kill the prophets, might be in the memory of all. But this explanation is not consonant with the text. Therefore, it ought to be said otherwise, that they were not being rebuked on this account; but because they only did this to outwardly show signs of piety, as it is said above that they were tithing mint and cummin.

Moreover, *You adorn the monuments of the just.* They were adorning the monuments and, nevertheless, had the intention of killing on account of their simulation. "It is similar," says Chrysostom, "in our times, that if someone does many good things, for example, he may adorn the sepulchres, he may have an open hand and suchlike, but if he build with stones, and seeks after vainglory, he neither walks in the ways of the Lord, nor does it profit him." Again, they were showing piety in their words: *And say: If we had been in the days of our fathers, we would not have been partakers with them in the blood of the prophets.* It is common that in the doings of others all are severe judges: hence, if we see someone sinning, we judge it to be a big sin but we lessen our own sins; for that reason, these children knew their fathers' malice, but not their own; "Cast out first the beam out of thy own eye, and then shalt thou see to cast out the mote out of thy brother's eye" (above 7, 5).

Then He points out their cruelty. Firstly, He does so in general; and secondly, He does so in particular. And He declares their punishment during the time of this world, where it is said, *Behold I send to you prophets and wise men and scribes.* About the first part, He begins by describing their origin; secondly, He describes their imitation of their wicked fathers; and thirdly, He threatens their punishment. He says: *Wherefore you are witnesses against yourselves, that you are the sons of them that killed the prophets.*

But of what were they guilty, since it was not in their power? For that reason, it seems that the guilt ought not to be deputed to them. Note that sometimes a son does not imitate his father's sins, but sometimes he does imitate his father's wickedness. If he does not follow his father's wickedness, it is not imputed to him. Sometimes, it happens that someone has a good father and a bad mother, and vice versa, and he follows the goodness of his father or of his mother. But if both are wicked, it rarely happens that he does not imitate their malice. And the reason is that children of wicked parents are accustomed to evil deeds from the beginning; and to that which they are accustomed in their youth, they adhere to more strongly, and for that reason are more inclined to evil. Likewise, wicked parents, when they see their children do something bad, do not correct them; this is why their sins are made worse, such that the sins of parents redound unto their children; "I am the Lord thy God, jealous, visiting the iniquity of the fathers upon the children." For that reason, He says, *That you are the sons of them*, you who have their malice; "Their children wicked" (Wis. 3, 12). Hence, you are their children by imitation: and this is what follows, *Fill ye up then the measure of your fathers.* This is not imperative but declarative: *Fill ye up*, meaning you will fill, as though a man were speaking; that is to say, you will kill me; "That which thou dost, do quickly" (Jn. 13, 27). Or it can be permissive speech, meaning 'I will not stop you,' meaning, 'Sometimes you wanted to kill me but I did not permit it; but in the future, I will not stop you;' hence, *Fill ye up the measure of your fathers.*

But what is it that He says, *Fill ye up*? One ought to be aware that everything that occurs, happens by God's sure judgment. But in that judgment of God, punishment is not immediately imposed until the guilt is completely increased, and it may reach its height: hence, in regard to God's judgment, their guilt was not yet filled up. Hence, they killed the prophets, and their guilt is not yet filled up, but in killing Me it will be filled. Therefore, *fill ye up the measure of your fathers.* "In measure against measure, when it shall be cast off, thou shalt judge it" (Is. 27, 8). Or, *Fill ye up*, can be understood otherwise. Your fathers sinned, but you yourselves fill them up. Then it is that someone fills up when he reaches as much as his fathers. Thus, your fathers killed the prophets, and you yourselves fill them up. Or it can be said that they sinned by killing the servants of God; these men, however, sinned by killing the Son of God; hence, they filled up the iniquity of their fathers. But the Lord offered Himself up voluntarily, and did not stand in the way. Likewise, He did not reproach them for their sin against Himself, but only for their sins against others, because it is proper for a good pastor that he repute an injury to others as being done to himself.[8]

Then He subjoins about the punishment, *You serpents, generation of vipers,* etc. And it seems that He speaks suitably about their guilt. A serpent is a poisonous animal and it kills by its poison: so these men are called serpents, because they killed the prophets. Concerning vipers, it is said that they die when they give birth, hence, the offspring gnaws upon its mother's womb: so, since they themselves are evil, they were blaming their fathers. Hence, you being such, *how will you flee from the judgment of hell?* You escape punishment according to men's judgment, but according to God's judgment, how will you escape it? Hence, one ought to have a clean heart. "Flee then from the face of the sword" (Job 19, 29).

34. Therefore behold I send to you prophets and wise men and scribes: and some of them you will put to death and crucify: and some you will scourge in your synagogues and persecute from city to city.

35. That upon you may come all the just blood that hath been shed upon the earth, from the blood of Abel the just, even unto the blood of Zacharias the son of Barachias, whom you killed between the temple and the altar.

36. Amen I say to you, all these things shall come upon this generation.

37. Jerusalem, Jerusalem, thou that killest the prophets and stonest them that are sent unto thee, how often would I have gathered together thy children, as the hen doth gather her chickens under her wings, and thou wouldst not?

38. Behold, your house shall be left to you, desolate.

39. For I say to you, you shall not see me henceforth till you say: Blessed is he that cometh in the name of the Lord.

In this part, He relates their cruelty, and He adds their earthly punishment. To begin with, He does the first thing; and secondly, He adds their punishment. Firstly, He relates a benefit they have received; secondly, He relates their guilt; and thirdly, He relates the greatness of their punishment. Hence, He says, *Behold I send to you prophets and wise men and scribes,* etc. And it can be referred to that which immediately takes place,

---

8. "PSEUDO-CHRYS. But because He stooped to death of His own free choice, He does not lay on them the sin of His death, but only the death of the Apostles and other holy men. Whence, also He said, *Fill up,* and not *Fill over;* for a just and merciful Judge overlooks his own wrongs, and only punishes those done to others" (*Catena Aurea on St. Matthew,* chap. 23, lect. 11).

or to all that will take place. If it refers to what immediately will take place, in this way, it has a plainer meaning. 'So I say that you are about to fill up your fathers' sins, and that you are serpents, etc. *Hence I send to you prophets and wise men and scribes: and some of them you will put to death*, because you are the type of men who have become accustomed to kill.' Or it is otherwise, so that it may be referred to all that will take place. The Lord wants that judgment not only to be just, but also that it appear to be just, so that others can have examples. Hence, if someone has a good intention, the Lord rewards him for his good intention, and hence, He gives him the will of carrying out his good work: so, on the contrary, when someone has an evil intention, and is full of bad will, according to what is said: "I will hedge up thy way with thorns" (Osee 2, 6), he incites God's anger, and it is due to God's anger that his malice be manifested. Thus, *I send to you prophets and wise men and scribes: and some of them you will put to death*. And He says, *Behold*, because it would soon be that He would send the Apostles; hence: "You shall be witnesses unto me in Jerusalem, and in all Judea, and Samaria, and even to the uttermost part of the earth" (Acts 1, 8).

But observe in that He says, *I send to you prophets and wise men and scribes*, He indicates that there are diverse gifts of the Holy Ghost. "To one is given the gift of wisdom, diverse kinds of tongues" (I Cor. 12, 8-10). The Apostles had all these gifts. They had the gift of prophecy in foretelling the future; "I will pour out my spirit upon all flesh: and your sons and your daughters shall prophesy" (Joel 2, 28). Likewise, they had the gift of wisdom, because they knew all things; "I will give you a mouth and wisdom, which all your adversaries shall not be able to resist and gainsay" (Lk. 21, 15). Similarly, they were scribes, because they had the understanding of Scripture; "He opened their understanding, that they might understand the scriptures" (Lk. 24, 45).

And why does He foretell this? It is so that the disciples, recalling what they had heard, may more easily endure. Likewise, it is to prove the malice of the Jews, because just as their fathers killed the prophets, so these men will kill the Apostles; hence, *Some of them you will put to death*, as it is stated in the Acts, that "Herod killed James, the brother of John, with the sword, seeing that it pleased the Jews" (12, 2-3). Other Apostles were crucified; hence, *And you will crucify*. It was because this death was the most shameful that they killed Christ with this death, according to that which is written: "Let us condemn him to a most shameful death" (Wis. 2, 20). *And you will scourge.* In Acts 5 it is said that "after they had scourged them, they charged them that they should not speak at all in the name of Jesus" (verse 40). *And you will persecute.* This is evident in how they persecuted Paul. And: "If they shall persecute you in this city, flee into another" (above 10, 23).

Further on, the punishment is related, and, because it seemed to be severe, He confirms it, saying: *Amen I say to you, all these things shall come upon this generation.* He says: *That upon you may come all the just blood, from the blood of Abel the just, even unto the blood of Zacharias the son of Barachias.* It is known who Abel is, namely, he who was killed by his brother Cain. But this Zacharias, who he was, is not stated. It is read that there were three Zacharias'. A certain Zacharias was the son of Barachias, who was the eleventh among the prophets. But it cannot be understood of this man, because the altar did not exist yet. Another was the father of John, and of whom he was the son is not found; but Chrysostom says that he was killed on account of Christ, because in the Temple there was a place for virgins. And when the Virgin Mary sat in the place for virgins, the Jews wanted to expel her from that place; Zacharias, defending her, forbade this, and for this he was killed.[9] Another Zacharias is named the son of Joiada,[10] whom Joas killed in the court of the Temple; wherefore, he was killed between the Temple and the altar; hence, the place corresponds, but his name does not. But, nevertheless, Jerome says that "Barachias" is interpreted "blessed of the Lord," and the holiness of his father Joiada the priest is designated. And he says that he saw the Gospel of the Nazarenes,[11] and "the son of Joiada" was contained therein.

But why He ends with this Zacharias can be a literal question. Now the reason seems to be that even if the preceding killings of prophets were more frequent, nevertheless, these were

---

9. "ORIGEN; A tradition has come down to us, that there was one place in the temple in which virgins were allowed to worship God, married women being forbidden to stand there. And Mary, after the Savior's birth, going into the temple, stood to pray in this place of the virgins. And when they who knew that she had borne a Son were hindering her, Zacharias said, that forasmuch as she was still a virgin, she was worthy of the place of the Virgins. Whereupon, as though he manifestly were contravening the Law, he was slain there between the temple and the altar by the men of that generation; and thus this word of Christ is true which He spoke to those who were standing there, whom you slew. JEROME; But as this has no Scripture authority, it is as readily despised as offered" (*Catena Aurea on St. Matthew*, chap. 23, lect. 10).

10. "The spirit of God then came upon Zacharias the son of Joiada the priest" (II Par. 24, 20).

11. The Gospel of the Nazarenes is an Apocryphal book dating from before the end of the second century. It is no longer in existence and was never recognized by the Church as being canonical. It was an Aramaic translation of Matthew and a different work from the "Gospel according to the Hebrews."

found in Scripture. Or it is otherwise, that Abel was a shepherd and Joiada was a priest; for that reason, by these two, the laity and the clergy are signified. Hence, every punishment for the killing of men will come upon you. Or it is otherwise, that some men are active, others are contemplative; hence, both are signified by these two men.

Now He says, *Amen I say to you, all these things shall come upon this generation.* But how can it be that all these things can come upon this generation? Is one generation punished for another? "The son shall not bear the iniquity of the father" (Ez. 18, 20). Therefore, how can all these things come *upon this generation*?

Jerome solves the objection, saying that it is customary in Scripture that all the generations of good men are taken for one generation, and about which it is said: "The generation of the righteous shall be blessed" (Ps. 111, 2). Concerning the generation of the wicked it is said: "An evil generation seeketh a sign" (above 12, 39). Chrysostom says the following: 'Some men sin, but God does not immediately avenge'; hence: "Is he angry every day?" (Ps. 7, 12). 'But some men are never corrected when they sin, but become worse'; "But evil men and seducers shall grow worse" (II Tim. 3, 13); 'and then the Lord waits until their malice is filled up.' Hence, these men, in whom their malice will be filled up, carry the burden of all the generations as to the temporal punishment, nevertheless, as to the eternal punishment, every man carries his own burden. Hence, the punishment will be so great that it will seem to be for all the generations; hence, in Exodus 32 it is said that this sin will be kept until the day of vengeance.[12] Just as there was a fullness of good things to those who believe in Christ, so there was a fullness of bad things to those who killed Christ; for that reason, He says, *All these things shall come upon this generation.* But what is this punishment? It is the destruction of the city of Jerusalem. And because He intends to speak about the ruin of the city, He turns to the city, saying, *Jerusalem, Jerusalem.* Firstly, He points out their offense; secondly, He recalls the benefits they have received; and thirdly, He foretells their punishment. The second part is where it is said, *How often would I have gathered together thy children... and thou wouldst not?*; and the third part is where it is said, *Behold, your house shall be left to you, desolate.* He says, therefore, *Jerusalem, Jerusalem*; and this repetition indicates

---

12. "I in the day of revenge will visit this sin also of theirs" (verse 34).

the affection of one who sympathizes; hence, it is said in Luke 19, 41, that "seeing the city, he wept over it." *Thou that killest the prophets*; "Which of the prophets have not your fathers persecuted?" (Lk. 7, 52). And He says, *Thou that killest the prophets*, and not 'Thou that hast killed the prophets,' wherefore, they were yet persevering in their malice. This is that Jerusalem, about which it is said: "This is Jerusalem, I have set her in the midst of the nations, and the countries round about her. And she hath despised my judgments" (Ez. 5, 5-6). They might have excused themselves: 'We did not have someone to tell us'; for that reason, He says, *Thou stonest them that are sent unto thee*; hence, I sent prophets and many benefits, and you did not acknowledge them. *How often would I have gathered together thy children, as the hen doth gather her chickens under her wings, and thou wouldst not?* By these words, the perpetuity of His divinity is indicated, according to what He Himself says: "Before Abraham was made, I am" (Jn. 8, 58). Hence, Christ Himself sent the prophets, the Patriarchs, and the angels. Whenever He sent them, He wanted to *gather together their children*, etc. They are gathered who are converted to the Lord, because in Him all sinners are united: they are dispersed who are separated from this unity. Hence: *I have gathered together thy children, as the hen doth gather her chickens under her wings*. It is said that no animal cares for its offspring as the hen. A hen defends them against kites, and it exposes its life for them, and gathers them under its wings. In like manner, Christ cares for us, "Surely he hath borne our infirmities" (Is. 53, 4). Likewise, He exposes Himself to the kite, that is to say, to the devil; "While I am yet living, and going in with you, you have always been rebellious against the Lord" (Deut. 31, 27).

On the contrary, the Lord willed to gather them and these men did not want this: therefore, an evil will prevailed against God's will. Hence, it ought to be said: 'As often as I wished I did, but against your will, I did as often as I did; hence, your will prevented me as often as I did not do.'[13] Or the fact that He sent the prophets was a sign that He wanted to gather you, *and thou wouldst not*.

---

13. And where is that omnipotence which has done all that it pleased on earth and in heaven, if God willed to gather together the children of Jerusalem, and did not accomplish it? Or rather, Jerusalem was not willing that her children should be gathered together? But even though she was unwilling, He gathered together as many of her children as He wished: for He does not will some things and do them, and will others and do them not; but 'Whatsoever the Lord hath pleased he hath done, in heaven, in earth'(Ps. 134, 6)" (Augustine, *Enchiridion*, Bk. 1, n. 97).

Then the punishment follows: ***Behold, your house shall be left to you, desolate***. The whole nation was honored for the sake of Jerusalem, and Jerusalem, on account of the Temple; wherefore it is said, ***Your house shall be left***, meaning the Temple or their habitation. "Let their habitation be made desolate" (Ps. 68, 26). Or a house is said to be deserted when it lacks its due inhabitant; "The Lord is in his holy temple" (Ps. 10, 5). Hence, He is said to leave with respect to His habitation; for that reason, ***you shall not see me henceforth***, etc., because I was with you by the power of the divinity, and, afterwards, I was corporeally with you, but now I depart from you. But now ***your house shall be left to you, desolate***, and ***you shall not see me henceforth***, neither corporeally, namely, after the Passion, nor spiritually.

But would it always be true that no Jew would see Him, even though many Jews converted to Him? For that reason, He says, ***Till you say: Blessed is he that cometh in the name of the Lord***, because when we confess Him then we see Him by faith. Or, otherwise, He is subtly indicating His Second Coming: they were seeing Him corporeally, but they would not be able to see Him in this way until His Second Coming, 'When you will be able to say, and to recognize, that I am the ***Blessed one who cometh in the name of the Lord***.'

CHAPTER TWENTY-FOUR

1. And Jesus being come out of the temple, went away. And his disciples came to shew him the buildings of the temple.

2. And he answering, said to them: Do you see all these things? Amen I say to you, there shall not be left here a stone upon a stone that shall not be destroyed.

3. And when he was sitting on mount Olivet, the disciples came to him privately, saying: Tell us when shall these things be? And what shall be the sign of thy coming and of the consummation of the world?

4. And Jesus answering, said to them: Take heed that no man seduce you.

5. For many will come in my name saying, I am Christ. And they will seduce many.

6. And you shall hear of wars and rumors of wars. See that ye be not troubled. For these things must come to pass: but the end is not yet.

7. For nation shall rise against nation, and kingdom against kingdom: And there shall be pestilences and famines and earthquakes in places.

8. Now all these are the beginnings of sorrows.

9. Then shall they deliver you up to be afflicted and shall put you to death: and you shall be hated by all nations for my name's sake.

10. And then shall many be scandalized and shall betray one another and shall hate one another.

11. And many false prophets shall rise and shall seduce many.

12. And because iniquity hath abounded, the charity of many shall grow cold.

13. But he that shall persevere to the end, he shall be saved.

14. And this gospel of the kingdom shall be preached in the whole world, for a testimony to all nations: and then shall the consummation come.

Above, the multiple provocations of the Jews were related; now, the preparation for Christ's departure through the instruction of His disciples is related. Now they are instructed concerning dangers. And firstly, a question of the disciples is related; and secondly, Christ's answer is related, where it is said: ***And Jesus answering, said to them***. About the first point, there are two parts. Firstly, the occasion of the question is related, where it is said: *And when he was sitting on mount Olivet*, etc. The occasion was twofold. The occasion was His foretelling of the destruction of the Temple, which prediction He indeed made by deed and by word. Firstly, He predicted this by deed, because He went out of the Temple. Secondly, He predicted this by His words, "Behold, your house shall be left to you, desolate" (above 23, 38); and He shows this by the fact that He went out of the Temple; hence, by the fact that He went out from the Temple corporeally, He shows that He went out from there spiritually; "But Jesus hid himself and went out of the temple" (Jn. 8, 59). When a sinner does not want to be corrected, the Lord goes out from him; "From the daughter of Sion, all her beauty is departed" (Lam. 1, 6). Then the question is related, where it is said: *The disciples came to him privately, saying*; secondly, the answer is related, where it is said: *And he answering, said to them*, etc. So He *went away*. But then *his disciples came to shew him the buildings of the temple*, so that He might see how beautiful and how comely the house is: hence, elsewhere, namely, in Mark 13, 1, it is stated: "Behold what manner of stones and what buildings are here."

But Origen asks: Had He not been there other times, and did He not know the buildings well? He solves the matter, saying that they were not asking in order to teach Him, or as though He did not know, but so that He might find a remedy for the destruction. So a Christian is the temple of God, as is stated in I Corinthians 3; the disciples, however, are intercessors lest this temple be destroyed.

Then the Lord answers: 'These things seem to you to be great'; "The Lord of hosts hath designed it, to pull down the pride of all glory," etc., (Is. 23, 9). Hence, He adds: *Amen I say to you, there shall not be left here a stone upon a stone*.

Is this true? In the time of Chrysostom, it had not yet happened completely, but it was hoped that it would come to pass. Or it can be said that He only wishes to say that it will be destroyed. Or it can be said that, as according to God's foresight, at one time the Temple was restored: so, according to God's foresight, the confirmation of the New Law having begun, the Temple would be destroyed lest sacrifices be made in the Temple. Hence, if it had not been destroyed, many Jews, having become Christians, would perform the ceremonies and so return to the Temple: hence, by divine dispensation, it happened that the Temple was destroyed: and this is stated in Luke 21, 6, where it is said concerning the Temple: "The days will come in which there shall not be left a stone upon a stone that shall not be thrown down." So also it happens that someone builds through good virtues, but if he fall by some mortal sin, if he becomes negligent, and not careful, he falls completely and is destroyed; "Raze it, raze it, even to the foundation thereof" (Ps. 136, 7). Hence, He wishes to say that not only would the Temple be destroyed, but also the things pertaining to it, which were shadows, as it is stated: "The law, having a shadow of the good things to come" (Heb. 10, 1).

Having given the occasion, the question is related. And we ought to note that He went out and went to Mount Olivet, and this signifies the Church in which fruitful olive trees are planted; "I, as a fruitful olive tree" (Ps. 51, 10). And from there, He instructs His disciples. He had said that the Temple would be destroyed, wherefore, they ask three things. Firstly, they ask about the Temple; secondly, they ask about His Coming; and thirdly, they ask about the end of the world; hence, they say: ***Tell us when shall these things be?***, namely, the accomplishment of Your warning: and tell us about Your Coming, ***and what shall be the sign of thy coming***; likewise, they ask about the end of the world, ***and of the consummation of the world***. In Luke[1] only one question is mentioned, namely, about the destruction of the Temple, because they did not believe that it ought to be destroyed except after the Second Coming; hence, they said, "Wilt thou at this time restore again the kingdom of Israel?" (Acts 1, 6). In Mark 13, it is said that they sent only Peter, John, James and Andrew; for these were called first, and so had greater confidence in approaching Him. Wherein we have an example; that those who remain in contemplation longer are more familiar with God; "They that approach to his feet, shall receive of his doctrine" (Deut. 33, 3).

These disciples were asking about His Coming, and this is twofold. The Coming is the last, which is for judging; and this will be at the end of the world. You find this written: "So shall he come as you have seen him going into heaven" (Acts 1, 11). The other Coming was for comforting the minds of men, to whom He comes spiritually. "They shall see the Son of man coming in the clouds" (below in this chapter, verse 30), meaning in the preachers, because by preachers God comes into the minds of men. Hence, there is a doubt regarding to which Coming He refers. Nevertheless, Augustine says that it ought to be referred to His spiritual coming. But some say that it refers to His Second Coming. Others, however, expound this of both the destruction of Jerusalem, and the last Coming.

---

1. "And they asked him, saying: Master, when shall these things be?" (Lk. 21, 7).

Therefore, He firstly responds in regard to the destruction of Jerusalem; secondly, He responds in regard to the Second Coming, where it is said, *For as lightning cometh out of the east.* About the first part, He does two things. Firstly, He foretells the things that will precede the destruction of Jerusalem, where it is said: *When therefore you shall see the abomination of desolation*, etc. These preliminary events were on the part of those outside the Church, and on the part of those within the Church. Firstly, therefore, the events on the part of outsiders are related; secondly, events on the part of those who are within the Church are related, where it is said: *And many false prophets shall rise and shall seduce many.* About the first point, He does two things. Firstly, He premises the spiritual dangers; secondly, He premises the corporeal dangers, where it is said: *And you shall hear of wars and rumors of wars.* He says, therefore: 'You indeed ask about the end of the world, nevertheless, you ought to be solicitous about yourselves, that you be not deceived'; therefore, He says: *Take heed that no man seduce you.* "See therefore, brethren, how you walk circumspectly" (Eph. 5, 15). *For many will come in my name saying, I am Christ.* Some men come as being sent by Christ, and in such a way did the Apostles come. While others are said to come in Christ's name, but usurping His name, which is not given to another man, for themselves; "A name was given him which is above all names" (Phil. 2, 9). Hence, many seducers will come, who will come of themselves; Christ, on the other hand, did not come of Himself but from God; hence: "I am not come of myself" (Jn. 7, 28). However, even though this may be specifically said of the Antichrist, nevertheless, it can be said about many others. Hence, because they did not adhere to the truth, they were given over to errors. And this happened to Simon the magician, who wrote books and called himself the book of God, the great God, and everything of God, and he seduced many. For it is proper to those led astray, who are divided by their errors, to be many, because "The number of fools is infinite" (Eccle. 1, 15). Hence, the truth gathers, error, however, divides and this is its danger. This passage can also be referred to His Second Coming; for these things will happen close to Judgment Day.

And you shall hear of wars, etc. Here He firstly mentions wars; and secondly, He comforts them. He says, therefore: It was said: *Take heed that no man seduce you,... because you shall hear of wars*, etc. And this happened immediately after the Passion. For then, very bad tyrants were sent into Judea by the Emperor, who were burdening them such that they could scarcely bear it: hence, *And you shall hear of wars and rumors of wars*, because in wars rumors are powerful; hence, it often happens that a few men weaken many; "The snorting of his horses was heard from Dan, all the land was moved at the sound of the neighing of his warriors" (Jer. 8, 16). And *See*. Some might think that the end of the world was immediately at hand: hence, it is said that the tribulation was so great that they might have thought that it was the end of the world; wherefore, He says, *See that ye be not troubled. For these things must come to pass: but the end is not yet*, as though it were the destruction of Jerusalem, because its destruction was not until forty years after the Passion.

But someone could say: 'You say that we are going to hear of wars, but there have always been wars.' He answers: 'Never have you seen wars like this.' *For nation shall rise against nation*, namely, the Roman nation against the Jewish nation; *and kingdom*, namely, the Roman kingdom, *against kingdom*, namely, the Jewish kingdom. *And there shall be pestilences*, etc. One might say: 'These wars happen by chance and not by God's vengeance.' But it is evident that they happen by God's vengeance, because not only are these evils inflicted by a nation, but by God, because *there shall be pestilences*, which arise from the corruption of the air, *and famines and earthquakes in places*. And these things all happened before the destruction of Jerusalem. Someone might say: 'All these things happened by chance and were not indicative of an affliction,' but this is not so; hence, He says: *Now all these are the beginnings of sorrows*. "They shall be in pain as a woman in labour" (Is. 13, 8). So Chrysostom expounds the passage. But Origen so expounds the passage as referring to the end of time. So we ought to consider that the world is like a man, because when it approaches death, its vital forces begin to weaken. So, to demonstrate the universal change that will occur at the end of time, the Lord brings about some particular change such that the forces of nature do not have some power, and then there will be pestilences because the air, which serves us in two ways, will be corrupted.[2] Likewise, the earth will be corrupted, which serves us for food because it brings forth plants and grains, hence, food is produced, and this will be debilitated such

---

2. Air according to its nature is warm and moist, and it is so disposed as to receive the earth's vapor, in order to preserve its heat and humidity" (Aquinas, *On Meteorology*, Bk. 1, lect. 4, n. 6). "Then when he now says that nature uses breathed air for two operations... for the lessening of natural heat, which is necessary: and the cause of this is stated in the book on inhaling and exhaling: and it uses breathed air to make vocal sounds, which is for one's well being. (*In Libros de Anima II & III*, Bk. 2, lect. 18, n. 8).

that there will be a famine on earth. Likewise, the earth supports us, and against this, the earth will be disturbed, whence, earthquakes will occur. The first two afflictions will be universal, but the last one will be particular, because it will happen in certain places. And why will it not happen universally throughout the whole world? It will be so that men, upon seeing this, may consider within their hearts and be converted. Likewise, it happens that famines occur from a shortage of things, and then, due to the famine, nation shall rise against nation; and this could be near the end of the world. Otherwise, it could be that sometimes a nation will rise against a nation, not on account of a shortage, but on account of vainglory. Sometimes, it happens on account of the injustice of men. Sometimes, God is appeased and He restrains the bad angels by means of the good angels, as it is said: "You have not gone up to face the enemy, nor have you set up a wall for the house of Israel, to stand in battle in the day of the Lord" (Ez. 13, 5). Hence, the world continues through the prayer of good men. And then, namely, at the end of the world, **charity shall grow cold**, and then there will be many afflictions, because then the good angels will release the demons, who have power to harm the land and the sea; wherefore, since they have power over the land and the sea, they will move the whole earth. And that they can do this is found in Job 1. Jerome says that it can be said of the Lord's coming by which He comes daily to the Church. For in that heretics impede the very goods of the Church herself, then spiritual **pestilences** and **famines** occur, namely, the lack of good teaching (Amos 8, 11).[3] **and earthquakes**, meaning men who are firm will be moved.

Then shall they deliver you up to be afflicted. Then He mentions certain preliminary events which were to come in the Church. And to the Church would come favorable and unfavorable events. Firstly, He relates the unfavorable things; and secondly, He relates the favorable things, where it is said: **And this gospel of the kingdom shall be preached in the whole world.** He foretells the unfavorable things, however, in two ways; from those without and from those within the Church: "Without, the sword shall lay them waste, and terror within" (Deut. 32, 25). And He mentions three dangers: tribulation, killing and hatred. They could say: 'It is true that the world will suffer these things, but what is it to us?' He says the contrary, and it is for this reason that

---

3. "Behold the days come, saith the Lord, and I will send forth a famine into the land: not a famine of bread, nor a thirst of water, but of hearing the word of the Lord."

He says: *You*; it is as though He were to say, 'You will not be unaffected, but you will be troubled in the literal sense'; "in tribulation, in necessities," etc., (II Cor. 6, 4). Likewise, *they shall put you to death*; for example, He permitted that they kill Stephen and James: hence, it is said: "We are counted as sheep for the slaughter" (Ps. 43, 22). Similarly, *you shall be hated by all nations*, meaning the Jews. Or by all the Jews scattered throughout the world: "Blessed are they that suffer persecution for justice" (above 5, 10). And He gives a consolation, that although all men suffer, you will suffer *for my name's sake*. "Behold, them whom I have built, I do destroy" and it continues: "And dost thou seek great things?" (Jer. 45, 4-5). Origen says that what is said here refers to His Second Coming. Because there will be such a universal persecution that all evil men will persecute the good; and on account of this, He says: *Then*. For it was the custom that when afflictions happened they were saying that was because of the sins of the Christians. Hence, they rose up against them; hence: *Then shall they deliver you up to be afflicted. And then shall many be scandalized.* Here, He points out the dangers from those within the Church. For there is a threefold scandal that you will suffer, namely, of the weak, likewise, of mutual harm, and again, of debility; hence, He says: *Then shall many be scandalized*; because even the perfect will often be scandalized; hence: "It must needs be that scandals come" (above 18, 7). Hence, the elect are also afflicted when they see scandals, wherefore, Paul said: "Who is scandalized, and I am not on fire?" (II Cor. 11, 29). *And shall betray one another.* From this, the second affliction shall appear. "The brother also shall deliver up the brother to death," etc., (above 10, 21). And they shall betray one another, not only corporeally, but also spiritually; because some men are the source of an error and from this it will follow that *they shall hate one another. And many false prophets shall rise and shall seduce many.* Such are those who seduce many in the Church; "There were also false prophets among the people" (II Pet. 2, 1). Likewise: "There are become many Antichrists... They went out from us but they were not of us" (I Jn. 2, 18-19). Hence, these afflictions will take place because brethren will be corrupted, for *they shall seduce many.* Likewise, the third danger shall appear, because not only will they do this but they will also be corrupted; hence, they will falter: *Because iniquity hath abounded, the charity of many shall grow cold.* "But I have somewhat against thee, because thou hast left thy first charity" (Apoc. 2, 4). Charity can be said to grow cold because when men see others leaving charity, they themselves are made cold even though they may not completely perish: and this happened to many but not to all, because charity was always fervent in the Apostles; "Who then shall separate us from the love of Christ? Shall tribulation? Or distress? Or famine? Or nakedness? Or danger? Or persecution? Or the sword?" (Rom. 8, 35). Hence, such will happen to many but not to all, because *He that shall persevere to the end*, namely, the end of the present life, *he shall be saved*. The same saying is found above in chapter 10.[4]

And this gospel of the kingdom shall be preached in the whole world. Above, the Lord foretold the adversities that would happen within the Church; now, however, He predicts the favorable events, because the Apostles, who were born of the Jews, were zealous for their own race; "I have great sadness and continual sorrow in my heart" (Rom. 9, 2); for that reason, He says for their consolation that very many were being called to the faith: *This gospel of the kingdom shall be preached in the whole world*. For when He was beginning to preach He said: "Do penance, for the kingdom of heaven is at hand" (above 4, 17). This Gospel, however: *shall be preached in the whole world*: for the New Law was not meant for just one nation as was the Old Law; "Preach the gospel to every creature" (Mk. 16, 15). And Chrysostom says that this was fulfilled before the destruction of the city of Jerusalem, and He proves this by the Apostle's epistle to the Romans (10, 18), where the Apostle says: "Their sound hath gone forth into all the earth." For that reason, the evangelical teaching seems to have been diffused throughout the whole world. Likewise, He proves this by another passage, which is found in Colossians 1, 6: "The preaching of the gospel bringeth forth fruit."[5] And it is not surprising, because one Apostle, namely Paul, spread the evangelical teaching so far that He came to Rome and Spain: hence, was fulfilled that which was written: "Thou hast sent thy messengers far off" (Is. 57, 9). And, for that reason, Chrysostom says that, in this, Christ's power ought to be admired, because within the space of forty years His teaching grew so much that it filled the whole world; hence, He says well, *And this gospel of the kingdom shall be preached in the whole world*. But will all men believe? No; rather, some will and others will not. And the fact that some will believe will be in testimony against those who will not believe, as Jerome says. "We have received grace and apostleship for obedience to the faith,

---

4. Verse 22.
5. "...the word of the truth of the gospel, which is come unto you, as also it is in the whole world and bringeth forth fruit" (Col. 1, 5-6).

in all nations... so that they are inexcusable" (Rom. 1, 5 & 20). *And then*, namely, when all nations believe, **the consummation shall come**, meaning the destruction of Jerusalem: and concerning this, it can be understood what is said in Ezechiel 7, 3: "Now is an end come upon thee, and I will send my wrath upon thee." For He performed signs, He spread the Gospel among the people, and they did not want to believe; wherefore, what is said in Malachias 1, 10, happened to them: "I will not receive a gift of your hand." Augustine maintains that this passage be not referred to the consummation of Jerusalem, but of the world. Hence, Christ says, **Shall be preached**, namely, before the end of the world; hence, He says, **for a testimony to all nations**, because not all nations will believe; **and then shall the consummation come**, meaning the end of the world. And this is one sign, that until the preaching of the Gospel be spread throughout the whole world, the end of the world shall not come. And the preaching of the Gospel had not yet come, as Augustine says, to certain barbarians in Africa. And this is in accord with that which is written: "Their sound hath gone forth into all the earth" (Ps. 18, 5), which saying he put in the past tense for the future. And referring to that which is written to the Colossians, he says that it was not yet bringing forth fruit to the full but was still beginning. And it can be distinguished thus, that the spread of the Gospel can be understood in two ways: either as to its notoriety only, and so it was completed before the razing of the city; for even though some had not received it, nevertheless, there was no nation to which its fame had not reached; if, however, the spread of the Gospel with its effect be understood, then it is true what Augustine says, that it had not yet reached all nations.

15. When therefore you shall see the abomination of desolation, which was spoken of by Daniel the prophet, standing in the holy place: he that readeth let him understand.

16. Then they that are in Judea, let them flee to the mountains:

17. And he that is on the housetop, let him not come down to take anything out of his house:

18. And he that is in the field, let him not go back to take his coat.

19. And woe to them that are with child and that give suck in those days.

20. But pray that your flight be not in the winter or on the sabbath.

21. For there shall be then great tribulation, such as hath not been from the beginning of the world until now, neither shall be.

22. And unless those days had been shortened, no flesh should be saved: but for the sake of the elect those days shall be shortened.

Having already related the destruction, in this part He relates that the consummation will come: and He gives a sort of introduction. And firstly, He cites the prophecy; secondly, He gives a warning, where it is said: *Then they that are in Judea, let them flee to the mountains*; and thirdly, He gives the reason for the warning, where it is said: *For there shall be then great tribulation.* So He said: *The consummation shall come. When therefore you shall see the abomination of desolation*, etc. What is it that He calls the abomination? It can be said that the Roman army is the abomination, and they are called abominations of desolation because they were the destroyers of the land. Or, by abominations, the idols are understood: and it can be said of two idols. It is read that Pilate brought into the Temple the eagle, which was the Roman ensign which the Jews called an abomination.[6] Hence, when you see the placing of idols in the holy place, then you can recognize the fulfillment of Daniel's prophecy concerning the destruction of Jerusalem. Or it can be said that Jerusalem was destroyed twice. Firstly, it was destroyed by Titus and Vespasian, and on that occasion, the Temple was burned and yet some men were let go. Afterwards, still others rebelled, and then Hadrian, who succeeded Trajan, completely destroyed the city and made a law that no Jew could live there again, and he called the city by his own name. Moreover, he put an idol in the holy place: hence, the idol, which Hadrian placed, can be called the abomination; hence, 'When you see this,' etc. Concerning this expulsion, it is sufficiently found in Lamentations 2.[7] *He that*

---

[6]. "The Jews at the risk of their lives persuaded Pilate to remove the statues of Caesar set up among the standards of the army in Jerusalem ["Ant. Jud.", 1. XVIII, c. iii (iv), 1, *De bell. Jud.*, ix (xiv), 2-3]; they implored Vitellius not even to carry such statues through their land [ibid., c. v (vii), 3]. It is well known how fiercely they resisted various attempts to set up idols of false gods in the temple; though this would be an abomination to them even apart from their general horror of images of any kind. So it became the general conviction that Jews abhor any kind of statue or image. Tacitus says: 'The Jews worship one God in their minds only. They hold those to be profane who make images of the gods with corruptible materials in the likeness of man, for he is supreme and eternal, neither changeable nor mortal. Therefore, they allow no images (*simulacra*) in their cities or temples' (Hist., V, iv)" ("Veneration of Images," Catholic Encyclopedia (1910 ed.), vol. 7).

[7]. For example, "The Lord hath purposed to destroy the wall of the daughter of Sion: he hath stretched out his line, and hath not withdrawn his hand from destroying: and the bulwark hath mourned, and the wall hath been destroyed together" (verse 5).

readeth let him understand. And why does He say this? It is because in that prophecy of Daniel many things are said concerning Christ's Passion. For these words ought to be noticed; hence, it is said there: "Christ shall be slain... and there shall be in the temple the abomination of desolation: and the desolation shall continue even to the consummation, and to the end" (Dan. 9, 26-27). Hence, he who sees, let him understand that such things happened. ***Then they that are in Judea, let them flee to the mountains.*** He gives useful advice. Firstly, He gives it; and secondly, He rejects the obstacles to fleeing. For certain obstacles are avoidable, others are unavoidable. He says, ***Then they that are in Judea, let them flee to the mountains.*** *Then,* namely, in the time of Vespasian. At that time, a certain man called Agrippa ruled in the mountains, and this man obeyed the Romans and did not rebel against them: hence, when other nations were waging war, this man and his nation were at peace. Hence, by God's providence, the faithful who were in Judea were warned that they should depart and go to the kingdom of this Agrippa, and they did so: hence, ***Then they that are in Judea,*** namely, the faithful, ***let them flee to the mountains***; "O flee ye out of the land of the north," etc., (Zach. 2, 6).[8] Then, He rejects the obstacles to fleeing. And because certain obstacles are avoidable and others not, for that reason, He firstly points out the dangers that are avoidable; and secondly, He points out the unavoidable obstacles, where it is said, ***Woe to them that are with child,*** etc. The obstacles that are avoidable concern earthly affairs: and some of these occur in the city, others outside of the city; and so He points out both. The second type is where it is said: ***And he that is in the field, let him not go back to take his coat.*** He says, therefore: ***And he that is on the housetop, let him not come down to take any thing out of his house***; meaning whoever lives in the city, even if he be in his house, let him not go back to take, etc. Likewise: ***And he that is in the field, let him not go back*** into his house, ***to take his coat***, namely, anything that is necessary, because all that a man owns he will give for his life. And why does He say this? Because when the feast of the Pasch approached, many gathered in Jerusalem: for He knew that Titus would besiege the city when they were so gathered. Hence, He wishes to say: 'This

---

8. "REMIG. And this we know was so done when the fall of Jerusalem drew near; for on the approach of the Roman army, all the Christians in the province, warned, as ecclesiastical history tells us, miraculously from heaven, withdrew, and passing the Jordan, took refuge in the city of Pella; and under the protection of that King Agrippa, of whom we read in the Acts of the Apostles, they continued some time; but Agrippa himself, with the Jews whom he governed, was subjected to the dominion of the Romans" (*Catena Aurea on St. Matthew*, chap. 24, lect. 5).

affliction will happen so quickly that a man will not be able to be on his guard.' Similarly, He points out the unavoidable obstacles. And because certain obstacles are unavoidable by men's power and so are simply unavoidable, and other obstacles, although they are unavoidable, nevertheless by God's power are avoidable; and so He speaks, firstly, about the first type; and secondly, about the second type, where it is said, **But pray that your flight be not in the winter or on the sabbath.** The former which, when it exists, can in no way be avoided, is the burden of children: for although it can be said to someone, 'Save your life,' he could say, 'How can I abandon my child?' For that reason, He reveals this: **Woe to them that are with child and that give suck,** because such persons were unable to flee, for neither was it to be said that they should procure an abortion, nor to those giving suck that they kill their children; and so it was fulfilled what is said: "Blessed are the paps that have not given suck" (Lk. 23, 29). Likewise, there are other obstacles which man cannot remedy except by God. For a certain time is unsuitable either by nature or by law: a time is unsuitable by nature, such as winter time, because then a man is hindered from fleeing on account of the harshness of the season. Similarly, a time is unsuitable by law, for instance, if the adversity happens on a Sabbath, because the Lord commanded that they not travel more than one mile. 'And because this is not within your power, but within God's power, wherefore **pray that your flight be not in the winter or on the sabbath,** because in such matters recourse can be had only to God.' Hence: "Come, and let us return to the Lord. For he hath taken us, and he will heal us" (Osee 6, 1-2). **Pray that your flight be not in the winter,** because winter naturally impedes flight on account of perilous roads; **or on the sabbath,** because the Sabbath impedes travel on account of God's Law. Likewise, note that He says, **Sabbath,** whereby, He indicates that on the Sabbath they were appropriately killed. Whence the need of fleeing? It was on account of the greatness of the tribulation. Hence, He firstly relates the tribulation and the greatness of the tribulation; and secondly, He points out the cause, where it is said: **And unless those days had been shortened,** etc. He says, therefore: **For there shall be then great tribulation, such as hath not been from the beginning of the world.** And he who reads the historical account of Josephus can appreciate the extent of the tribulation, for many were killed by famine. Likewise, there were seditions in the city, such that they were killing each other: hence, when Titus, who was very gentle, wished to spare them, they did not want this. Moreover, there were thieves among them who killed many. And a certain woman ate her son.

Hence, there was so great a tribulation such as had never been seen. And Luke says this: "There shall be a tribulation and they shall fall by the edge of the sword" (Lk. 21, 23-24).

But will there not be a greater tribulation at the time of the Antichrist? Yes; but it will not be among the Jews. And Chrysostom asks on account of what sin did it happen, because the punishment of the Sodomites was not as severe, hence, there would not have been a greater punishment unless there was a greater sin.

And because they could say that this happened to them due to the sins of the Christians, wherefore, He says that this is not so; hence: *Unless those days had been shortened, no flesh should be saved.* Augustine says that some expound the passage as follows, namely, that the days were made shorter just as at the time of Josue they were made longer. But this is contrary to what the Psalms say: "By thy ordinance the day goeth on" (118, 91): and so this can have two meanings. Firstly, it can mean that the days of tribulation are shortened in number. Hence, if that time had lasted longer all would have been killed, for no one would have been left. And why was this? It was because the Romans ruled throughout the whole world; for that reason, if that time had lasted longer they would have been killed everywhere in the world. Or days are said to have been shortened when the afflictions are shortened. And why are they shortened? *For the sake of the elect*: and this was not because God's word failed to happen. For many were converted from that people, and they were asking for the people that seed would be left; "Except the Lord of hosts had left us seed, we had been as Sodom" (Is. 1, 9).

Then Chrysostom proposes two considerations; why this is said, namely, that there were some disciples there, and likewise, that John lived even after this time. For that reason, he says that John does not mention this in his Gospel because he wrote after this event: hence, he would have spoken about past events; but Matthew and Luke, who wrote before this event, mention it because then it was yet to occur; wherefore, he says that it was an evident miracle when the Romans fought the Jews and nearly the whole nation of the Jews was destroyed, that very few Jews were able to go throughout the world to convert nearly the whole world, and this was Christ's marvelous power.

Hilary explains that these words refer to the end of the world. *When therefore you shall see the abomination*, he names the abomination as the Antichrist. "That you be not terrified, neither by spirit nor by word, as if the day of the Lord were at hand. Let no man deceive you by any means" (II Thess. 2, 2).

Then they that are in Judea, let them flee to the mountains; because the Jews failed, they will flee the land of the Jews and be converted to the mountains of Christianity. *And he that is on the housetop, let him not come down to take any thing out of his house.* He means to say that the perfect ought not to be moved from their perfection. Hence, He touches upon the contemplative life which is signified by the roof; hence, such men ought not to recede from their contemplation. Likewise, when He says: *he that is in the field*, He treats of the active life. Such ought not to return to their original life but remain in their choice of life. And what is signified by those who are with child? They are men laden with sins. Those that give suck are imperfect men. Hence, He means to say, 'Woe to men burdened with sin, and are not strengthened.' According to Augustine, those who are with child are they who desire to do evil; those that give suck are those who have actually carried out an evil desire. And why does He say: *in the winter or on the sabbath*? By winter, sadness is signified; and by the Sabbath, joy is signified. Hence: *may your flight be not in the winter*, absorbing a man with sadness, *nor on the Sabbath*, lifting him up with joy.[9] Or, by the Sabbath, resting from good works is signified, and by winter, the growing cold of charity is signified. *And unless those days had been shortened*; for it shall last a short time, and if it would last longer, *no flesh should be saved*, meaning no man having flesh. Likewise, these words can be referred to Christ's coming through the Church; and so Origen says that as the word of the Gospel was spread by Christ's coming, so false doctrine will be spread by the coming of the Antichrist; and as Christ had his prophets, so the Antichrist also. Then He who is in the city let him flee into the mountains, that is, the mountains of perfect justice. They are said to be with child who are still perusing the word of salvation: those giving suck are they who have already done something. *But pray* that they be not impeded by slothfulness and inactivity. *For there shall be then great tribulation*, because there will be a perversion of Christian doctrine by false doctrine. *And unless those days had been shortened*, namely, by the teaching of doctrine, by an increase of true doctrine, *no flesh should be saved*, meaning all will be converted to the false teaching.

---

9. "AUG. That no one be found in that day in either joy or sorrow for temporal things" (ibid)

23. Then if any man shall say to you, Lo here is Christ, or there: do not believe him.

24. For there shall arise false Christs and false prophets and shall shew great signs and wonders, insomuch as to deceive (if possible) even the elect.

25. Behold I have told it to you, beforehand.

26. If therefore they shall say to you, Behold he is in the desert: go ye not out. Behold he is in the closets: believe it not.

27. For as lightning cometh out of the east and appeareth even into the west: so shall also the coming of the Son of man be.

28. Wheresoever the body shall be, there shall the eagles also be gathered together.

29. And immediately after the tribulation of those days, the sun shall be darkened and the moon shall not give her light and the stars shall fall from heaven and the powers of heaven shall be moved.

30. And then shall appear the sign of the Son of man in heaven. And then shall all tribes of the earth mourn: and they shall see the Son of man coming in the clouds of heaven with much power and majesty.

31. And he shall send his angels with a trumpet and a great voice: and they shall gather together his elect from the four winds, from the farthest parts of the heavens to the utmost bounds of them.

32. And from the fig tree learn a parable: When the branch thereof is now tender and the leaves come forth, you know that summer is nigh.

33. So you also, when you shall see all these things, know ye that it is nigh, even at the doors.

34. Amen I say to you that this generation shall not pass till all these things be done.

35. Heaven and earth shall pass: but my words shall not pass.

36. But of that day and hour no one knoweth: no, not the angels of heaven, but the Father alone.

37. And as in the days of Noe, so shall also the coming of the Son of man be.

38. For, as in the days before the flood they were eating and drinking, marrying and giving in marriage, even till that day in which Noe entered into the ark:

39. And they knew not till the flood came and took them all away: so also shall the coming of the Son of man be.

40. Then two shall be in the field. One shall be taken and one shall be left.
41. Two women shall be grinding at the mill. One shall be taken and one shall be left.

After the Lord answered the question of the disciples concerning the destruction of the city of Jerusalem, He begins here to answer them concerning His Second Coming. Now this Coming is a coming for judgment: wherefore, it is divided. For firstly, He relates the signs and the manner of His Coming; and secondly, He treats of the judgment: "The kingdom of heaven is like to ten virgins" (below 25, 1). About the first point, He does two things. Firstly, He foretells the signs preceding His Coming; and secondly, He treats about Himself, where it is said: *And they shall see the Son of man*, etc. About the first point, He says two things, namely, that there will be two signs preceding Christ's Coming; firstly, there will be a sign as to men and the elect; and secondly, there will be a sign as to the elements, where it is said, *And immediately after the tribulation of those days, the sun shall be darkened*, etc. About the first sign, He does two things. Firstly, He premises a certain warning; and secondly, He gives the reason for this warning, where it is said: *For there shall arise false Christs and false prophets*. He says, therefore: *Then if any man shall say to you, Lo here is Christ*, etc. It ought to be observed that the word, *Then*, does not indicate a determinate time but an indeterminate time, because this did not happen immediately after the destruction of Jerusalem but rather it is expected to occur at the end of the world. Something similar is stated above in chapter 2, where it is said that the Lord dwelt in Nazareth, hence, He is called a Nazarene, and the passage continues: "Then cometh John the Baptist preaching in the desert of Judea" (3, 1); it is not that he came then, because there were perhaps twenty years between the two times, hence, it is held to mean an indeterminate time. So it is here. For it shall happen that many seducers shall come, and say that the Antichrist is God. *Then if any man shall say to you, Lo here is Christ, or there: do not believe him.* "Be not easily moved from your sense nor be terrified, neither by spirit nor by word nor by epistle, as sent from us, as if the day of the Lord were at hand" (II Thess. 2, 2).

Then, when He says: *For there shall arise false Christs and false prophets*, He is giving the reason for the warning. And firstly, He gives the reason of necessity; and secondly, He gives the reason of the falsity of doctrine, where it is said, *For as lightning cometh out of the east*, etc. About the first, He does three things. Firstly, He points out the seducers; secondly, He shows the vehemence of the seduction; and thirdly, He gives a warning. He says, therefore, 'You say that there will be some men who will say that they are Christ: but will not there be others? Indeed. *For there shall arise false Christs*, meaning those who say that they are Christ, and this happened before the destruction of Jerusalem; "But you have heard that Antichrist cometh, wherefore there are become many Antichrists" (I Jn. 2, 18). *And false prophets*. For just as Christ had true prophets who foretold Him, so the Antichrist will have false prophets: and this is what is said in I John 4, 1: "Many false prophets are gone out into the world." But will these men perform miracles and effects? Hence, *They shall shew great signs and wonders*; "Whose coming is according to the working of Satan" (II Thess. 2, 9); "And I saw from the mouth of the dragon and from the mouth of the beast and from the mouth of the false prophet, three unclean spirits like frogs" (Apoc. 16, 13).

But there is a question: Can the devils perform miracles? It ought to be said that they cannot, if a miracle is to be taken in the strict sense: because what happens outside the order of a particular cause is not a miracle in the strict sense, but only when it is outside the order of the whole creation and this occurs by the Divine power alone. But it is quite possible that a higher creature be not restricted to an order of a lower creature; hence, something happens by a higher power which does not happen through the power of the elements: so in men someone does by skill something which seems marvelous to others: so it is regarding the demons, because they have a higher intelligence; for that reason, just as a skillful man does something that seems marvelous, so also the demons do some things naturally which seem to us marvels.

But how will this happen? Avicenna's opinion was that a corporeal nature obeys the command of the intellect,[10] hence, a body is

---

10. "Avicenna... agreed with Plato in supposing some spiritual substance to preside immediately in the sphere of active and passive elements; because, as Plato also said, he held that the forms of these sensible things are derived from immaterial substances. But he differed from Plato because he supposed only one immaterial substance to preside over all inferior bodies, which he called the active intelligence" (I, q. 110, a. 1 ad 3um). "Avicenna assigns the cause of bewitchment to the fact that corporeal matter has a natural tendency to obey spiritual substance rather than natural contrary agents. Therefore, when the soul is of strong imagination, it can change corporeal matter. This he says is the cause of the 'evil eye.' But it has been shown above (q. 110, a. 2) that corporeal matter does not obey spiritual substances at will, but the Creator alone. Therefore, it is better to say, that by a strong imagination the (corporeal) spirits of the body united to that soul are changed, which change in the spirits takes place especially in the eyes, to which the more subtle spir-

changed in consequence of its apprehension. But Augustine refutes this, because a body does not obey the command of any creature but only that of God. For that reason, it ought to be said that in natural things there are determinate powers for procreating certain things, such as frogs and suchlike things: the demons know these powers better than other creatures. And Augustine proves this, saying that the fire which descended upon Job's sheep was natural. For demons can raise up and gather bodies in order to perform such miracles.[11] But those miracles which do not proceed from the power of any natural thing, such they cannot do, namely, that the dead be raised. Hence, they do not do such things except by illusions, just as Simon the Magician made a head to move.[12] Hence, the demons are unable to do those things which cannot happen by the power of nature; hence, **they shall shew great signs**, meaning signs which men will consider to be great.

But what will be the effect? ***Insomuch as to deceive (if possible) even the elect.*** And Origen says that this statement is made by way of an exaggeration, because every living man, if considered in regard to himself, can be deceived; nevertheless, taking into consideration God's election, then the meaning is that it would be impossible for the elect to be seduced; for that reason, by hyperbole, He says that such will be the force, that unless they be preserved by Divine predestination they would be seduced. Or it can be said that they are not truly the elect, but are the elect in appearance only; "Which some rejecting have made shipwreck concerning the faith" (I Tim. 1, 19); "The Lord hath mingled in the midst thereof the spirit of giddiness: and they have caused Egypt

---

its can reach. And the eyes infect the air which is in contact with them to a certain distance: in the same way as a new and clear mirror contracts a tarnish from the look of a *menstruata*, as Aristotle says (*De Somno et Vigilia; De Insomniis* ii). So, therefore, when a soul is vehemently moved to wickedness, as occurs mostly in little old women, according to the above explanation, the countenance becomes venomous and hurtful, especially to children, who have a tender and most impressionable body. It is also possible that by God's permission, or from some hidden deed, the spiteful demons cooperate in this, as the witches may have some compact with them" (I, q. 117, a. 3 ad 2um).

11. Properly speaking... miracles are those things which are done outside the order of the whole created nature. But as we do not know all the power of created nature, it follows that when anything is done outside the order of created nature by a power unknown to us, it is called a miracle as regards ourselves. So when the demons do anything of their own natural power, these things are called miracles not in an absolute sense, but in reference to ourselves" (I, q. 110, a. 4 ad 2um).

12. "(Deceptions) firstly happen in illusions, when the appearances are deceptively changed by the demons, such that a thing seems to be something other than it actually is: for example Simon the magician had a ram beheaded, and afterwards it was shown to be alive; and a man was beheaded, and afterwards the man who was believed to be beheaded was shown to be alive, and it was believed that he was brought back to life" (*Super ad Thess.* II, chap. 2, lect. 2).

to err" (Is. 19, 14). ***Behold I have told it to you, beforehand***, because according to Gregory, darts which are foreseen do less harm; "The Lord God doth nothing without revealing his secret" (Amos 3, 7). Having asserted the necessity in general, He asserts the necessity more particularly: ***If therefore they shall say to you, Behold he is in the desert***, etc. It ought to be observed that true teaching is done in public; "That which you hear in secret, preach ye upon the housetops" (above 10, 27); but false teaching always seeks the dark corners; "Wisdom preacheth abroad" (Prov. 1, 20). Hence, the truth is light and it seeks to be seen in the light: but if there be a perverse teaching, it seeks hidden places: "Wisdom sits at the door" (Prov. 9, 14). And the passage continues: "Stolen waters are sweeter" (verse 17). Hence, a desert is a hiding place because there are no people there, or because it is a remote place; hence: ***if therefore they shall say to you, Behold he is in the desert: go ye not out***. And what does He wish to say? These unbelievers and heretics, when believers are in an association and a congregation where they cannot be deceived, strive that the believers be separated from the community, and then they deceive them; and this is what He wishes to say: ***If therefore they shall say to you, Behold he is in the desert: go ye not out***. Do not be separated from the fellowship and community. Likewise: ***If therefore they shall say to you, Behold he is in the closets***, because they always seek after a secret place and they do not dare to say their teaching in public; hence: "I have spoken openly to the world" (Jn. 18, 20). ***Believe it not***, because "He that is hasty to give credit, is light of heart." According to Jerome, it can refer to the time before the destruction of Jerusalem: but it is better if it is referred to the end of the world. Likewise, it can be understood of the seduction occurring in the Church. False Christs give the teaching of a lie, and it is called one teaching because all their teachings are united into one: every lie has its prophets; hence, they say: ***Here is Christ, or there***; "They have persisted to confirm what they have said" (Ez. 13, 6); and sometimes they want to confirm what they say by apocryphal scriptures, and other times by the hidden meanings of Scripture. When they confirm by apocryphal scriptures, they say that He is in the desert; when they confirm by the hidden meanings, they say that He is in the closets. Or, according to Augustine, true doctrine has two identifying characteristics, namely, the same doctrine is professed everywhere and it is professed publicly,[13] and heresy fails to be professed in these ways;

---

13. cf. Reply to Faustus the Manichaean, Bk. 13, n. 13.

hence, He says, **Here is Christ**, meaning in this world, and not in the other. Likewise, because their teaching is not public, wherefore, they say: **In the closets**; hence: **Believe it not**.

For as lightning cometh out of the east, etc. Here, He gives another reason, namely, that they say something false, that Christ will come secretly, but it is not true; on the contrary, He will come manifestly. And He puts forth two reasons. One is from Christ's manifestation, and the other is from the gathering of the saints. He says: **Believe it not**, that He would not come manifestly: *for as lightning cometh out of the east and appeareth even into the west: so shall also the coming of the Son of man be*; "God shall come manifestly" (Ps. 49, 3).

But will He come like lightning which is seen here now, and afterwards points to the East? For that reason, you should not understand that in this way He may be manifested in the East only, but in all directions. If we wish to refer to a mystery, the lightning is the coming of truth. Do not, therefore, seek secret teachings, because the truth is manifested through the whole world. Or the East is the beginning, and the West is the end. Hence, the truth of doctrine always has consistency from the beginning to the end: for the true doctrine accepts all Scripture. Some men do not accept the Old Testament: others do not accept the Prophets, and so they cannot be supported by the other Scriptures; but the true doctrine from the beginning of the early Church until the end time will have the support of the whole of Scripture; hence, it is said: "Behold I am with you all days, even to the consummation of the world" (below 28, 20).

Wheresoever the body shall be, there shall the eagles also be gathered together. For someone might say: 'These men say: **Here is Christ, or there**, and how will we know when He will come?' He shows, however, that they do not need to inquire because His coming will be manifest, in that other men will be gathered together. And it will be like to what happens when a man often asks his master, who is keeping secret his plan of moving the camp, saying: 'When will you move the camp? And he answers: 'Will you not hear the trumpet? Why do you ask?' So it is said here. You say that He will be here or there; I know that **Where the body shall be, there shall the eagles also be gathered together.** Note that in the Hebrew is found the word *Anathe*, which means a corpse: hence, He wished to signify Christ's Passion, because then Christ will come showing the signs of His Passion: and He speaks by way of a similitude: **Where the body shall be**, etc. "We shall meet Christ in the clouds" (I Thess. 4, 16). But some men are eagles, others are vultures and ravens. But He does not say vultures or ravens but eagles, by which the saints are signified. "They shall take wings as eagles, they shall fly and not faint" (Is. 40, 31). So, as Jerome says, wherever Christ's Passion is remembered, holy men ought to gather for a continual remembrance of His Passion. "Call to mind the former days, wherein, being illuminated, you endured a great fight of afflictions" (Heb. 10, 32).

And because these things will not only be manifested by tribulations, wherefore, He says: *And immediately after the tribulation of those days, the sun shall be darkened*, etc. And He treats concerning the signs taken from other things that are above us; and secondly, He treats of the effect. The second part is where it is said, *And then shall all tribes of the earth mourn*. Now in these things above us which He shows, there is a threefold order: heavenly bodies, angels and Christ. "He set him above all principality and power," etc., (Eph. 1, 21). Therefore, in regard to the first, He says: *And immediately after the tribulation of those days*, namely, when the Antichrist will come. *Immediately*, because it is not long afterwards, for the Antichrist was a danger for many; and this is opposed to those who assert the fable of the thousand years. *The sun shall be darkened and the moon shall not give her light*. And what is the meaning? This saying has a literal and a mystical meaning. In that it refers to His final Coming, it has a literal meaning; and in that it refers to the other, it has a mystical meaning.

But it seems that one can object to what He says, that the sun shall be darkened, because it is said, "And the light of the moon shall be as the light of the sun, and the light of the sun shall be sevenfold" (Is. 30, 26). Wherefore, in order to see this you ought to distinguish three times: the time before His Coming, the time at His Coming, and the time after His Coming. Before Christ's Coming, astrological observations of this kind will occur, concerning which it is said here, and in Joel 2, 31, it is said: "The sun shall be turned into darkness, and the moon into blood: before the great and dreadful day of the Lord doth come." At Christ's Coming, the sun and moon will not be changed as to their substance but by comparison, for the brightness of Christ and the saints will be so great that the brightness of the heavenly bodies will not be apparent; "And the moon shall blush, and the sun shall be ashamed" (Is. 24, 23). But, after Judgment Day, the brightness of the moon and the stars shall be increased. And then it shall true what is said in Isaias 30, 26, namely, that "the light of the sun shall be sevenfold, as the light of seven days."

But what is said seems false, namely, that the stars will fall from the sky, because one star is larger than the whole earth. Rabanus solves this objection by the passage of Mark 13, 25, that "the stars of heaven shall be falling down" in light, meaning they shall be lessened as to their light. But what will be able to cause this lessening of light? The light from a luminary is lessened by two things: either in itself, or due to something interposed, as, for example, if clouds are interposed or when the moon is eclipsed, its light is lessened; wherefore, Origen says that the passage can be understood in two ways. Firstly, it can be interpreted that what is interposed will be the fire that will precede Christ and consume all things up to the middle of that atmosphere, that is to say, as high as the waters of the flood rose, and much smoke will come from the fire so that the luminaries of the sky will darkened. Or it can be said, what certain men held, that these heavenly bodies are corruptible; and just as the elements will be changed, so these also. A quotation from the Apocalypse refers to these three things: "The sun became black as sackcloth of hair: and the whole moon became as blood. And the stars from heaven fell upon the earth" (Apoc. 6, 13).

The stars shall fall from heaven. The stars will be seen to fall from the sky when they are deprived of their light. Therefore, there will be a change in the heavenly bodies. Likewise, there will be a change in the angels; hence, He says: **And the powers of heaven shall be moved**, meaning the virtues[14] that serve God. And Augustine says that all corporeal bodies are ruled by the spirit of life;[15] hence, they are said to be moved in effect, because, at the Lord's Coming, the movement of the heavens will cease. Hence, those bodies are said to be moved when those things which pertain to their function are changed into a different state. Or the angels will be moved, not by a movement of fear, but of admiration, because they will admire Christ's power. Or they will be moved by a movement of joy upon the glorification of the saints. From this can be interpreted what is

---

14. "Virtue is twofold as applied to the angels, (Dionysius, *De Coelesti Hierarchia* xi). For sometimes the name of virtues is appropriated to one order, which according to him, is the middle order of the middle hierarchy, but according to Gregory (Hom. 34 *In Evangelia*) is the highest order of the lowest hierarchy. In another sense it is employed to denote all the angels" (III, q. 73, a. 3).

15. "A proof that the heavenly bodies are moved by the direct influence and contact of some spiritual substance, and not, like bodies of specific gravity, by nature, lies in the fact that whereas nature moves to one fixed end which having attained, it rests; this does not appear in the movement of heavenly bodies. Hence, it follows that they are moved by some intellectual substances. Augustine appears to be of the same opinion when he expresses his belief that all corporeal things are ruled by God through the spirit of life (*De Trinitate* iii,4)."

said in Job 26, 11, namely, that "The pillars of heaven tremble, and dread at his movement."[16]

And then shall appear the sign of the Son of man in heaven. Here, the sign of the Son of man, who is above the angels, is mentioned. The sign of the Son, meaning the sign of Christ's victory; for when the whole world is renewed, it will be indicated that He obtained the victory over all through His Passion, which does not now appear. Or the sign of the Cross will appear, so as to show that all this glory is through His Passion. Likewise, it is signified that He acquired all judicial power through His Passion. "If he will spread out clouds as his tent," etc., (Job 36, 29). And the citation continues: "For by these he judgeth people" (verse 31). Similarly, the sign of the Cross will appear to confound the wicked who did not want to follow Christ. Moreover, the sign of the Cross will be brighter than the sun.

But what will be the effect? *Then shall all tribes of the earth mourn*, seeing Christ's so great power which they had despised, and so great wisdom which they did not obey, and the so great brightness of the saints; hence, they will say what is written in Wisdom 5, 3-5: "These are they, whom we had sometime in derision, and for a parable of reproach. We fools esteemed their life madness, and their end without honour. Behold, how they are numbered among the children of God, and their lot is among the saints." Likewise, they despised the tribes of heaven, meaning they who bore the image of heaven. "To whom then have you likened God? or what image will you make for him?" (Is. 40, 18). They will pass judgment upon themselves to suffer such things; "Every eye shall see him: and they also that pierced him. And all the ends of the earth shall bewail themselves because of him" (Apoc. 1, 7). And: "They shall look upon me, whom they have pierced: and they shall mourn for him as one mourneth for an only son, and they shall grieve over him, as the manner is to grieve for the death of the firstborn" (Zach. 12, 10). This is the literal exposition. But if we refer this passage to Christ's Second Coming, then it will be expounded only mystically. Origen: "By the sun the devil is signified, by the moon the Antichrist is signified." Concerning these things it is said: "If I beheld the sun when it shined and the moon going in brightness: And my heart in secret hath rejoiced" (Job 31, 26-27). "If I saw," meaning if I approved, "the sun," meaning those things that seemed to have brightness and sanctity, and those who seemed to have power, then they shall appear as they

---

16. "At his beck" (*ad nutum eius*) is the original wording of this verse.

really are; "He will bring to light the hidden things of darkness and will make manifest the counsels of the hearts" (I Cor. 4, 5). Wherefore, all doctrine and all brightness will then appear, because the image of Christ will appear in all who bore His image. Or, by the sun, the Church is signified; hence, the Church, on account of its tribulations, will not seem to shine.

And why does He say, **After the tribulation**? Origen responds: "Both after and during."[17]

Likewise, **The stars shall fall from heaven**, meaning they who, after the tribulation, seemed to shine. **The powers of heaven**, meaning the saints, **shall be moved.**[18]

And they shall see the Son of man coming in the clouds of heaven, etc. Above, the Lord had foretold what things were to come before that Coming: now He foretells the Coming itself: and about this, He does three things. Firstly, He mentions His Coming; secondly, He mentions the certitude of His Coming; and thirdly, He mentions uncertainty of its hour and day. The second part is where it is said: **From the fig tree learn a parable**; and the third part is where it is said: **But of that day and hour no one knoweth.** About the first point, He does two things. Firstly, He mentions His Coming, or the appearance of the Son of man; secondly, He mentions the gathering of the saints to Him, where it is said: **And he shall send his angels**, etc. And observe that where He makes mention of His Coming, He relates two things, namely, that His Coming would be manifest, and that the saints would be gathered together; hence, He said: **For as lightning... so shall also the coming of the Son of man be.** And this is said regarding His manifestation. Likewise, He said: **Where the body shall be, there shall the eagles also be gathered together.** And He wishes to explain these two things more. And how will He come? **They shall see the Son of man coming in the clouds of heaven.** And who will see Him? All men: for He shall come to judge. For He has a human and a divine nature. In His divine nature He shall not be seen except by the clean of heart, etc., according to what was said above: "Blessed are the clean of heart: they shall see God" (5, 8); but in His human nature the wicked will also see Him; "All flesh shall see the salvation of

---

17. "AUG. And these things shall be after the tribulation of those days, not because they shall happen when the whole persecution is over, but because the tribulation shall be first, that the falling away may come after. And because it shall be so throughout all those days, it shall be after the tribulation of those days, yet on those very days" (*Catena Aurea on St. Matthew*, chap. 24, lect. 7).

18. "... many, who seemed to be shining in God's grace, shall give way to their persecutors, and shall fall, and even the stoutest believers shall be shaken"(ibid).

God" (Lk. 3, 6). Therefore, *they shall see the Son of man*, because the Son of man and the Son of God are the same Person; but they will not see Him as the Son of God, but as the Son of man; "He hath given him power to do judgment, because he is the Son of man" (Jn. 5, 27).

But there can be a question, whether both the good and the wicked shall see Him in His glorified appearance; and I answer that they shall. And the reason is given in Isaias 26, 10, where the Lord, discussing this with the prophet, says: "He shall not see the glory of the Lord." And the prophet replies: "Lord, let thy hand be exalted, and let them not see." To which the Lord responds: "Let the envious people see, and be confounded" (verse 11). Wherefore, the good will see Him for their joy, but the wicked for their torture and sadness: for when someone fears to be punished, the greater the judge's power against him appears to be, the more one is afflicted; so inasmuch as Christ will appear more glorious, so much more will the wicked be grieved. And this is indicated when it is said, *Coming in the clouds of heaven*. And this corresponds to that which He had said above, that *as lightning... so shall also the coming of the Son of man be*. In lightning there are two things, brilliance and terror. The brilliance betokens a certain pleasantness, the terror comes from the sound, and the clouds are made for refreshment; "And it will be as a cloud of dew in the day of harvest" (Is. 18, 4), which then is something pleasant.[19] Likewise, a cloud has darkness, and when it is dense it is terrible on account of the lightning and the rains which come from the clouds; and this is suitable for the terror of the wicked; "Clouds and darkness are round about him" (Ps. 96, 2). Similarly, it is suitable that He would come in the clouds to denote Christ's divinity, because God's majesty appeared in a cloud (Ex. 16, 10);[20] hence, it is said: "The Lord said that he would dwell in a cloud" (III Kings 8, 12): for that reason, He will come in the clouds. Likewise, it is suitable for showing His humanity; because, as it is stated: "While they looked on, he was raised up: and a cloud received him out of their sight, and they heard angels saying: As you have seen him

---

19. The "dew cloud" (*nubes rorida*) that is "something pleasant" during harvest time is not one bringing moisture which will spoil a crop, but a non-rain producing cloud that is a sign of fair weather and capable of producing rainbows. "For as light which is refracted by polished brass or iron, such as the arms of soldiers, has a clear and white color, and is shining, so light which is refracted by a cloud, or thick darkness and near to being converted into rain, although not yet converted into it (which is called a dew cloud (*nubes rorida*)) is white and clear" (*Meteor.* 3, lect. 8, n. 4). "A rainbow necessarily occurs on account of the opposition of the sun to a dew cloud (*nubes rorida*)" (*Quod-lib*, III, q. 14, art. 1, arg. 1).

20. "...behold the glory of the Lord appeared in a cloud."

going into heaven, so he shall come" (Acts 1, 9-11). Therefore, in order that it be shown that He is the same who was taken up on a cloud, He will appear on a cloud. It is also suitable for indicating His glorification. For when He was transfigured, a bright cloud appeared, and then there was one cloud; because He appeared to only three men, but at the end of the world there will be many, because He will appear to many men; "Behold, he cometh in the clouds, and every eye shall see him" (Apoc. 1, 7). And what will these clouds be? They shall be certain gleams of light coming from Christ's body and the bodies of the saints. Origen says that there will be angels taking Him up, not merely figuratively, but truly ministering to Him. For at His first Coming, He came as a humble man; "Behold thy king cometh to thee, meek" (Zach. 9, 9). But afterwards, He shall come *in the clouds of heaven with much power and majesty*. For at His first Coming, there were two things: for He had weakness and disgrace. He had weakness, since the Apostle said: "He was crucified through weakness" (II Cor. 13, 4). He had disgrace, according to what is written: "So shall his visage be inglorious among men, and his form among the sons of men" (Is. 52, 14). Corresponding to these two things, He says two things. Corresponding to weakness, He mentions His power; hence, concerning this, it is said, "All power is given to me in heaven and in earth" (below 28, 18); and this power is given to Him by His generation from the Father, insofar as He is the Son of God. But He merited insofar as He is man; and this is shown, when all the angels and all the elements minister to Him. Likewise, opposed to disgrace, He says that He will come in majesty, as the Judge of the living and the dead.

Then He will come, *and he shall send his angels with a trumpet and a great voice*. Here, He treats of the gathering of the saints; and He relates three things. Firstly, He speaks of the ministers; secondly, He speaks of those gathered together; and thirdly, He speaks of from whence they are gathered together. The ministers are the angels, as it is stated: "His angels: you that execute his word" (Ps. 102, 20). Now He says: *With a trumpet and a great voice*. In the Resurrection a threefold power will operate. Firstly, the divine power will operate; secondarily, the power of Christ's humanity will operate, for His Resurrection is the cause of our resurrection, as the Apostle says: "And as in Adam we all die, so also in Christ we all shall be made alive" (I Cor. 15, 22). Likewise, angelic power will operate for a certain preparation, namely, the gathering of the dust of the bodies of men. And He mentions these three things. He mentions the angelic power when He says, **He shall send his angels**; He mentions the power of God when He says, **With a trumpet**; and He mentions the power of His humanity by this which He says, **And a great voice**. Concerning this voice, it is written: "All who shall hear the voice of the Son of God, shall live" (Jn. 5, 25). And it will be appropriate that that voice be great, because "He will give to his voice the voice of power" (Ps. 67, 34). The divinity is well signified by the trumpet because the sound of a trumpet is greater than the human voice; "And they heard a great voice from heaven, saying to them: Come up hither" (Apoc. 11, 12). And a little further, it is written: "And the seventh angel sounded the trumpet: and there were great voices in heaven" (verse 15). And observe that a trumpet sufficiently befits Him, because the Lord commanded Moses that two trumpets be made; and they were sounding the trumpets for an assembly, for feasts, for fighting, and for moving the camp;[21] and so it will be at the Judgment; because then there will be an assembly, meaning a reuniting of all the saints, "The wicked shall not rise again in judgment: nor sinners in the council of the just" (Ps. 1, 5). Likewise, there will be an everlasting solemnity. Similarly, there will be a fight against the wicked, as it is written: "And even Juda shall fight against Jerusalem" (Zach. 14, 14). Again, there will then be a movement of camps, because the saints will be translated to the life of the saints; "And many nations shall be joined to the Lord in that day" (Zach. 2, 11). Likewise, some men are now gathered together but not all; but then all will be gathered; "All nations shall be gathered together before him" (below 25, 32). Only the elect will be gathered together at that place, for only they will be gathered together in order to reign with Him; "Gather ye together his saints to him" (Ps. 49, 5). Hence, He says: **And they shall gather together his elect**. But from where shall they be gathered together? *From the four winds, from the farthest parts of the heavens to the utmost bounds of them*. The winds of the sky are distinguished by the four parts of the world. From the East comes forth the *Subsolanus*; from the West comes the *Favonius*; form the North comes the *Boreas*; from South comes the *Auster*: and by these all the others are contained;[22] hence: *From*

---

21. "Make thee two trumpets of beaten silver, wherewith thou mayest call together the multitude when the camp is to be removed" (Num. 10, 2).

22. "The air, when it is stirred up, is wind. The wind has various names in books. The name is determined by where it blows from. There are four principal winds: the first is the Eastern wind, called *Subsolanus* because it blows from the place where the sun rises and is very temperate. The second principal wind is Southern and is called *Auster*; it stirs up clouds and flashes of lightning and blows various kinds of pestilence throughout

the four winds of heaven, meaning from all parts of the world. The passage continues: *From the farthest parts of the heavens to the utmost bounds of them.* These words can be expounded in two ways. Origen says that the meaning is as follows: *They shall be gathered.* Someone could say that this would be only a gathering of the living and not of the dead; which opinion He eliminates by making known that the dead shall also be gathered together; wherefore, He says: *From the farthest parts of the heavens*, etc. You know that the saints ascend into the heavens, and some heavens are lower, others are higher: because according to the measure of their merits will be the measure of their reward; hence, this is what Augustine says, namely, that *from the four winds*, He says this on account of the bodies: and, *to the utmost bounds of the heavens,* He says this on account of their souls. Remigius says the following, and it is in the Gloss: *I will gather together*, etc. Someone might suppose that the gathering would be only from the utmost bounds of the earth; but what will happen at the middle of the earth? Hence, He says: *to the utmost bounds of them.* And He wishes to say that not only will there be a gathering from the utmost bounds of the earth, but also from heaven, meaning from the middle of the universe.

And from the fig tree learn a parable. Here He teaches about the certitude of His Coming. He had said great things, unbelievable for some men; now, He certifies these things in three ways. Firstly, He certifies by a similitude; secondly, He does this by an assertion; and thirdly, He does this by a reason. The second part is where it is said, *I say to you that this generation shall not pass till all these things be done*; and the third part is where it is said, *Heaven and earth shall pass: but my words shall not pass.* He says, therefore: *From the fig tree learn a parable.* Chrysostom says: 'When God wills to show something, He always uses a natural similitude.' Trees in the winter have life, nevertheless, hiddenly; hence, they do then not produce leaves, nor do they produce fruit; but in the beginning of spring they sprout, and their life appears: so also the saints do not appear, as it is stated: "You are dead: and your life is hid with

the earth. The third principal wind is called *Zephyrus* in the Greek language and *Favonius* in Latin; it blows from the West and through its blowing all earthly plants revive and bloom, and that wind dissipates and thaws every winter. The fourth principal wind is called *Septemtrio*; it blows from the North, cold and snowy, and it makes dry clouds" (Aelfric, Abbot of Eynsham, *On the Seasons of the Year*). "[Aelfric] also known as 'the Grammarian,' the author of the homilies in Anglo-Saxon, a translator of Holy Scripture, and a writer upon many miscellaneous subjects. He seems to have been born about 955, and to have died about 1020" (Catholic Encyclopedia).

Christ in God" (Col. 3, 3); but then the life of the saints will appear, namely, the life of those who will not be seduced at the time of the Antichrist. The summer comes, meaning the eternal retribution; "Going they went and wept, casting their seeds"; and the passage continues: "But coming they shall come with joyfulness, carrying their sheaves" (Ps. 125, 6-7). Hence, He says: *From the fig tree learn a parable.* By the fig tree, the synagogue is signified, concerning which it is stated: "A certain man had a fig tree planted in his vineyard" (Lk. 13, 6).

When the branch thereof is now tender and the leaves come forth, you know that summer is nigh. And this can be expounded as follows: The tender branch is the Antichrist, whose power lasts for a short time, and, as it were, many leaves adhere to him, and then His power will be shown. Or it can be expounded as being something good. By the branch, the power and fortitude of the saints is signified. When the Church begins to come to an end, Christ's and the saints' power, which will sustain it, shall appear; "The fig tree hath put forth her green figs" (Cant. 2, 13). *So you also, when you shall see all these things*; that is to say, when you see the preceding signs occur, *know ye that He is nigh, even at the doors.* A thing is said to be near when it is at the doors; "Behold the hire of the laborers who have reaped down your fields, which by fraud has been kept back by you, crieth: and the cry of them hath entered into the ears of the Lord of Sabaoth" (James 5, 4).

Observe that Augustine stresses the fact that He says, *All*, when He says: *When you shall see all these things.* Above, He had said that the Lord is near; but what is this? Is not the Lord always near? For that reason, he says: "If we wish, we may say that nothing of what is said here pertains to the end of the world, but instead to Christ's coming through the Church; hence, what was said, *They shall see the Son of man coming in the clouds*, means in His preachers, *with much power*, for the Lord gives the word to the evangelizers with much power; and then He shall come with *majesty*, for they give Him veneration." Nevertheless, according to the exposition of others, we may refer this passage to the end of the world, and say otherwise. According to that which Augustine expounds, He is referring to something near at hand; hence, that which is said: *They shall see*, etc., refers to all that was said above, namely, regarding the signs, lightning, and earthquakes.

Therefore, He has shown the certitude of His coming by a similitude, and now He shows it by an assertion, namely, with an oath, saying: *Amen I say to you*, meaning that it is infallibly true, *that this generation shall not pass till all these things be done*. Origen says: "It is as though what you will hear were at hand." For someone might suppose that this was said concerning the destruction of Jerusalem, because many had remained until that time: hence, *this generation shall not pass*, meaning the men now living, *till all these things be done*. But it would be an exaggeration to maintain that everything said refers to the destruction of Jerusalem: for that reason, it ought to be affirmed otherwise, namely, that all the faithful are one generation; "This is the generation of them that seek the Lord" (Ps. 23, 6); and He had previously said, "The earth is the Lord's" (verse 1). Hence, He wants to say: *This generation shall not pass*, meaning the faith of the Church will not cease until the end of the world, against those who were saying that it would last until a certain time: because the Lord refuted this assertion, saying, "Behold I am with you all days, even to the consummation of the world" (below 28, 20). And then He states the reason why His coming is certain: *Heaven and earth shall pass: but my words shall not pass*; It is as if He would say: 'It is easier for heaven and earth to pass away, than for My words to pass away'; "But my word endureth for ever" (Is. 40, 8). Hence, His word is the cause of heaven, and the cause is always stronger than its effect, wherefore, etc. And it is not said that heaven and earth would pass, meaning that they would cease to exist, but instead it is meant that they shall pass into a different state of existence; "I saw a new heaven and a new earth" (Apoc. 21, 1). According to Origen, the good are signified by heaven and the wicked are signified by the earth; "Hear, O ye heavens, and give ear, O earth" (Is. 1, 2). Both will pass, the good into eternal life and the wicked into eternal fire. And when it is said that that the word of God shall not pass, it is not said that it will not pass as to the substance of the word, but as to whose it is: hence, this word of God, as Origen says, has the characteristic unlike other words that it will never pass away. The words of Moses, however, and of others passed away. Hence, the words are signs of the present day Church; but the words of Christ foretell the state of eternal life. Hence, Moses' words passed away, meaning that what Moses promised passed away: but what Christ promised will not pass away, because He promised the glory to come, which will not pass away. Likewise, Christ's word, as to its pertaining to earthly and temporal things, passes away.

But of that day and hour no one knoweth. Now, in this section, He tells of the uncertainty of the time of His Coming. And about this, He does two things. Firstly, He relates the uncertainty of the time; secondly, He exhorts by way of a similitude; and thirdly, He makes known the coming event. The second part is where it is said: *As in the days of Noe*, etc.; the third part is where it is said: *Then two shall be in the field*. He says that *they shall see the Son of man*. 'You are speaking vaguely about the time of Your coming; tell us exactly about the time if it is true.' *But of that day and hour no one knoweth: no, not the angels of heaven*. What He says about the angels of heaven is clear and does not have any significant uncertainty, because in them there is innate knowledge, and this knowledge extends only to those things which occur according to the course of nature; but the Judgment will occur only according to God's will. Likewise, there is another knowledge of glory, and by it they only know what things God wants to reveal, and this time of His Coming He has kept to Himself; "Behold, the Lord shall come, and who shall be able to know his coming?" (Mal. 3, 1-2). "The day of the Lord shall so come as a thief in the night" (I Thess. 5, 2).

But here there is a question, according to Jerome, because He says in Mark 13, 26: "Not even the Son of man"; from which words Arius seemed to confirm his heresy, because if the Father knows what the Son does not know then He is greater than Him. For that reason, it can be said that the Son knows and that Judgment Day is determined by some reason, and whatever is determined by God the Father is also determined by His eternal Son; wherefore, it is impossible that the Word would not know the time of the Judgment.

But why is it said that He does not know? Augustine and Jerome say that it is a customary manner of speaking, that a man say that he does not know, when he does not make it known; just as it is said: "Now I know that thou fearest God" (Gen. 22, 12), meaning, 'Now I have made thee know'; therefore, the Son is said not to know because He does not make it known. Origen states in another sense that Christ and the Church are like head and body, because just as the head and body are like one person, so Christ and the Church also. But Christ sometimes takes the form of the Church, as in the passage: "O God my God, look upon me" (Ps. 21, 2); hence, when it is said that Christ does not know, it is understood that the Church does not know: wherefore the Lord said: "It is not for you to know the time or moments" (Acts. 1, 7).

Note that Augustine says that He wanted to show that the coming of His Judgment cannot be known exactly from certain signs, because He does not fix any particular time. The proof says that it cannot be known, because just as it is in the ages of men, so it is in the ages of the world. Hence, as the final age of man does not have a definite limit, but sometimes is extended beyond some other age, so also it ought to be said concerning the final age of the world, that it does not have a definite limit and could last longer than all the other ages.

For, as in the times of Noe, so also shall the coming of the Son of man be. Above, the Lord related the uncertainty of the hour of His coming; now, however, He employs a comparison. And firstly, He puts it forward; and secondly, He explains it, where it is said, *For, as in the days before the flood*, etc. Now, He makes a fitting comparison, because while speaking about the end of the world, He stopped at the end of the world. Therefore, He put forward another comparison. For it is read that there is a twofold consummation of the world. One was by water; "And spared not the original world, but preserved Noe, the eighth person, the preacher of justice, bringing in the flood upon the world of the ungodly" (II Peter 2, 5). Hence, it is said well enough, because the first consummation was to cut off carnal sins; hence, it is said: "The sons of God seeing the daughters of men, that they were fair, took to themselves wives of all which they chose" (Gen. 6, 2). Therefore, against the burning of this concupiscence ought to be a consummation by water. At the end of the world, however, there will be sin because charity shall grow cold, as it was said above; thus, fire will fittingly be the punishment; hence, He says: *As in the times of Noe*, namely, that the end was uncertain, as it is stated: "The end of all flesh is come before me" (Gen. 6, 13). Wherefore, as they who adhered to Noe were saved, so, at the Coming of the Son of man, those who will adhere to Christ, the Son of man, will be saved. Secondly, He explains this comparison as to the uncertainty of the time of His Coming: *For, as in the days before the flood they were eating and drinking*, etc. In these words, it seems He mentions two things: one is, namely, the despair of His future coming and its cause. Now the cause why a man does not hope for His future Coming is that he is occupied with the cares of the flesh, for he walks according to his concupiscences; "You have feasted upon earth: and in riotousness you have nourished your hearts" (James 5, 5). For that reason, they will be occupied with wantonness, which has two parts, namely, "in rioting and drunkenness," and "in chambering and impurities" (Rom. 13, 13). Regarding the first part, He says: *Eating and drinking*: it is not that eating and drinking is a sin, but to fix them as one's end is a sin. As to the second part, He says: *Marrying and giving in marriage*, etc. And the passage continues,

And they knew not till the flood came and took them all away, namely, those who did not adhere to Noe, who was a figure of Christ. *So also shall the coming of the Son of man be.* But it is written: "Men withering away for fear" (Lk. 21, 26). And above, in this chapter, it is stated that *the sun shall be darkened* (verse 29). How, then, will men be secure such that they eat and have an easy life?

The answer is twofold. Jerome says that it is true that around the time of the Antichrist there will be many tribulations, and this will be to test the elect; and afterwards, they will be restored to tranquility, and in that tranquility, the wicked occupy themselves with joy.[23] Hence, Luke speaks regarding the state of tribulation; but Matthew speaks regarding the time immediately preceding the coming of God. Likewise, it may be said otherwise, that some men are good while others are wicked. And the Church will universally suffer tribulation and the good will be punished by the wicked: hence, it is said above: "You shall be hated by all men for my name's sake" (10, 22). Hence, they who will suffer will be the good; but those who will put into effect the tribulations of this kind will be the wicked. Therefore, that which is said here; *Eating and drinking*, etc., is understood in regard to the wicked; that, however, which is stated in Luke is said in regard to the good. Or it is as follows: Since it frequently happens that the good are corrected by tribulation but the wicked are not, therefore, the wicked shall wither but the good shall not.

Then two shall be in the field. One shall be taken and one shall be left. In this part, He relates the outcome of this incertitude of the time of His coming. And what will it be? Because it happens that of men put into one type of work, one will be taken up and the other left behind. And this can be expounded, according to Chrysostom, that He merely wishes to say that in every condition of man and in every type of work some will be reprobate and others will be elect: those who are good will be taken; and those who are wicked shall be left. How? As it was said above (chap. 13), the angels will come and take the elect, more precisely, to Christ. Likewise, some men are they who live delicately, on the other hand, others perform their duties. Likewise, there are

---

23. "JEROME; It is asked here, how it was said above, nation shall rise against nation, and kingdom against kingdom, &c. when here only tokens of peace are spoken of as what shall be then? We must suppose, that after the wars and the other miseries which shall waste the human race, shall follow a short peace, offering rest and quiet to approve the faith of the believers. CHRYS. Or, to such as are thoughtlessly disposed, it shall be a time of peace and enjoyment" (*Catena Aurea on St. Matthew*, chap. 24, lect. 11). Cf. Jerome, *Commentariorum In Evangelium Matthaei Libri Quattuor*, ML 26, n. 200.

certain occupations that pertain to men and others that pertain to women; the work of men is properly in the fields. *Then*, therefore, *two shall be in* one (understood literally) *field*, meaning two laboring men: *One shall be taken*, as the elect, *and one shall be left*, as the reprobate. Likewise, *two women shall be grinding at the mill. One shall be taken and one shall be left*. This is an occupation of women. It used to be customary that women would grind, and He speaks according to the custom of the region where there was no water; now one grinds with horses or with men, but then it was an occupation of women; "Take a millstone and grind meal" (Is. 47, 2).[24] Wherefore, when it is said that there will be two women grinding, the meaning is that there will be two women performing their duties. And then, *One shall be taken*, is expounded as before. Likewise, "There shall be two men in one bed. The one shall be taken and the other shall be left."[25] Chrysostom says that the rich do not labor but instead they rest; hence, they are designated by those who lie in bed; and of these two, *one shall be taken and one shall be left*. It can also be expounded allegorically, and this is Hilary's exposition. By the field, the world is signified, as it was said above.[26] By the two men, the faithful and the infidels are signified. Of these, one is taken, namely, the faithful; and the other is left, namely, the infidels. Likewise, the Old Law is signified by the millstone, which is heavy and burdensome; "This is a yoke which neither our fathers nor we have been able to bear," etc., (Acts 15, 10). And among those who receive the Old Law, some receive Christ, others do not. All those are said to grind at the mill who receive the Old Law; and those are indeed taken who receive the Old Law with the New; but those who do not are left. Likewise, they who receive Christ are like those lying in bed, because by the bed the remembrance of the Passion is signified, and of such men some are taken and others are left: for some conform themselves to the Passion by good works but others do not. It can be otherwise expounded, such that it refers to the three states of the faithful; for there are three kinds of men; some are contemplative, others are prelates, and others are active. No state is secure, nay, some may be damned in any state. The state of contemplation is signified by the bed. Concerning this it is said in Canticles 1, 15: "Our bed is flourishing"; and, nevertheless, some in this state are damned. The state of active men is signified by the millstone, because it is burdensome and they are solicitous; "Martha, Martha, thou art

---

24. This is addressed to the "virgin daughter of Babylon" (verse 1).
25. Lk. 17, 34.
26. Above chap. 13, lect. 2.

careful and art troubled about many things" (Lk. 10, 41). For they are involved in worldly affairs: and, for that reason, among them some are damned. By the field into which men go out to labor, the prelates are signified; "Come, my beloved, let us go forth into the field" (Cant. 7, 11). And among them, some are taken and others are left behind.

42. Watch ye therefore, because you know not what hour your Lord will come.
43. But this know ye, that, if the goodman of the house knew at what hour the thief would come, he would certainly watch and would not suffer his house to be broken open.
44. Wherefore be you also ready, because at what hour you know not the Son of man will come.
45. Who, thinkest thou, is a faithful and wise servant, whom his lord hath appointed over his family, to give them meat in season?
46. Blessed is that servant, whom when his lord shall come he shall find so doing.
47. Amen I say to you: he shall place him over all his goods.
48. But if that evil servant shall say in his heart: My lord is long a coming:
49. And shall begin to strike his fellow servants and shall eat and drink with drunkards:
50. The lord of that servant shall come in a day that he hopeth not and at an hour that he knoweth not:
51. And shall separate him and appoint his portion with the hypocrites. There shall be weeping and gnashing of teeth.

After the Lord affirmed the incertitude of the hour of His Coming, He advises vigilance. Firstly, He advises all men to be vigilant; and secondly, He advises prelates, where it is said, **Who, thinkest thou, is a faithful and wise servant**, etc.? About the first point, He does three things. Firstly, He makes the admonition; secondly, He makes a comparison; and thirdly, He draws the conclusion. The second part is where it is said: **But this know ye**, etc.; and the third part is where it is said: **Be you also ready**, etc. He says, therefore: 'So I say that the day is uncertain, and no one can rely upon his state of life, because one shall be taken from whatever state and another shall be left, wherefore, you ought to be diligent and solicitous. **Watch ye therefore**. And, as Jerome says, thus, the Lord wished to leave the time of the end of the world uncertain so that man might always wait. For man commits sins in three ways: He commits sins because his senses are unoccupied; similarly, because he ceases to move; and again, because he lies down; wherefore, *watch ye*, that your senses be elevated by contemplation; "I sleep, and my heart watcheth" (Cant. 5, 2). Likewise; *watch ye*, lest you become stiff in death: for a man watches who exercises himself with good works; "Be sober and watch: because your adversary the devil, as a roaring lion, goeth about seeking whom he may devour" (I Pet. 5, 8). Similarly, *watch ye*, lest you lie down through negligence; "How long wilt thou sleep, O sluggard?" (Prov. 6, 9). But what does He say? *Because you know not what hour your Lord will come*. He was saying this to the Apostles, and it is not found elsewhere that He so expressly calls Himself the Lord, as He says here, and He says in John 13, 13: "You call me Master and Lord. And you say well: for so I am."

But someone could say that the Lord was speaking to the Apostles; now the Apostles would not live until the end of the world. Therefore, why does He say: *Watch ye, because you know not what hour your Lord will come*?

Augustine says that these words were indeed necessary for the Apostles, and for those who were before us, and for us, because the Lord comes in two ways. At the end of the world, He will come to all men as a whole; likewise, He comes to each man at his end, that is to say, at death; "I will not leave you orphans: I will come to you" (Jn. 14, 18). Therefore, His Coming is twofold: at the end of the world, and also at death: and He wished both times to be uncertain. These comings are related to each other, because so a man will be found at His Second Coming, as he will be at His first. Augustine says: "The last day of the world will find him unprepared, whom the last day of his life finds unprepared." Similarly, this passage can be expounded as referring to another coming, namely, His invisible coming, when He comes to the mind: "If he come to me, I shall not see him" (Job 9, 11). Hence, He comes invisibly to many, and they do not perceive Him; wherefore: "I stand at the gate and knock. If any man shall hear my voice and open to me the door, I will come in to him and will sup with him" (Apoc. 3, 20).

But this know ye, that, if the goodman of the house knew at what hour the thief would come, he would certainly watch. But because he does not know at what hour he will come, he ought to watch the whole night. Who is this goodman? The house is the soul. In it a man ought to rest; "When I go into my house," meaning into my conscience, "I shall repose myself with her" (Wis. 8, 16). The good man is the mind; "The king, that sitteth on the throne, scattereth away all evil with his look" (Prov. 20, 8). Sometimes, a thief breaks open his house. A thief is some persuasion of a false doctrine or some temptation. And it is called a thief, as it is said in John 10, 1: "He that entereth not by the door into the sheepfold, the same is a thief and a robber." Natural knowledge or the Natural Law is properly called a door. Therefore, whoever enters through the mind enters through the door; but he who enters through the gate of concupiscence, or of anger, or of suchlike, is a thief. Thieves usually come in the night. "If thieves had gone in to thee, if robbers by night, how wouldst thou have held thy peace?" (Abdias 5). Hence, if they come in the daytime, they are not feared. So when a man is in the contemplation of divine things, temptation does not come then; but when a man behaves remissly, then temptation comes; wherefore, the Prophet David says well: "When my strength shall fail, do not thou forsake me" (Ps. 70, 9). Hence, we ought to watch because we do not know when the Lord will come, namely, for judgment. Or we can refer this passage to the day of death; "For when they shall say: Peace and security; then shall sudden destruction come upon them" (I Thess. 5, 3).

Wherefore be you also ready, because at what hour you know not the Son of man will come. Chrysostom says that men solicitous about temporal things watch during the night. And if they watch for the sake of temporal things, much more ought one to watch for the sake of spiritual things; "If thou shalt not watch, I will come to thee as a thief" (Apoc. 3, 3).

Who, thinkest thou, is a faithful and wise servant, whom his lord hath appointed over his family? Here, He specially admonishes prelates to watch. And He does this firstly by attracting them with rewards; and secondly, He does this by frightening them with punishments. About the first, He does three things. Firstly, He points out the qualifications of a good prelate; secondly, He points out the duties of a prelate; and thirdly, He points out the reward of a good prelate. The qualifications of a good prelate are that he be faithful and prudent. In every good work two things are necessary: that one's intention be fixed upon the due end, and likewise, that one take the appropriate means to that end; hence, in the duties of a prelate these things are necessary. Firstly, that he fix his intention upon the due end, which certain prelates place upon themselves, concerning whom it is said: "Woe to the shepherds of Israel, that fed themselves" (Ez. 34, 2); for they who fix their intention on the right end do not intend what is useful for themselves, but for many, so that many may be saved. And they rightly do all this for God's glory. But he who seeks what is his own does not act for God's glory. Hence, it behooves him to be faithful; "Now it is required among the dispensers that a man be found faithful" (I Cor. 4, 2). Likewise, he ought to be prudent, because it can be that someone is seeking God's glory but not according to knowledge: because it belongs to a prelate to reprove vices. Hence, He may reprove in such a manner that he incites to sin. Therefore, it is necessary that he be prudent. "Be ye therefore wise as serpents" (above 10, 16).

And observe that He calls him a servant, because there is a difference between a free man and a servant, namely, that every action of a servant redounds unto his master, but not those of a free man: so every action of a prelate ought to be referred to God. In this way, Paul was calling himself a servant, when he said: "And ourselves your servants through Jesus" (II Cor. 4, 5).

But why does He say: *Who, thinkest thou, is a faithful and wise servant*? It is because few are faithful; "For all seek the things that are their own not the things that are Jesus Christ's" (Phil. 2, 21); "But who shall find a faithful man?" (Prov. 20, 6). And if few are faithful, fewer are prudent; for that reason, the Lord says this noting their scarcity.

Then He mentions their duties: *Whom his lord hath appointed over his family*. And He does three things. Firstly, He treats of his appointment over his responsibilities, when He says: *Whom his lord hath appointed*, not that he procures his appointment by gifts or prayers; "Neither doth any man take the honor to himself, but he that is called by God, as Aaron was" (Heb. 5, 4). Then He mentions over what he has been appointed, namely, *over his family*, more precisely over His Church, not over temporal things, according to what the Apostle says, "No man, being a soldier to God, entangleth himself with secular businesses" (II Tim. 2, 4). Likewise, it behooves him to be prudent so that he may watch over the Church, and not over things outside the Church; "What have we to do concerning those things that are without?" (I Cor. 5, 12). Similarly, He mentions the responsibilities of a prelate: *To give them meat in season*. A prelate is to give meat, namely, the meat of doctrine, good example, and of temporal assistance; for that reason, the Lord says to Peter three times: "Feed... Feed... Feed my sheep" (Jn. 21, 15-17). Feed by word, feed by example, feed by temporal assistance; this is written in the last chapter, nevertheless, it is written. *In season*. "All things have their season" (Eccle. 3, 1). "I have yet many things to say to you: but you cannot bear them now" (Jn. 16, 12). For if you wish to speak words when it is not appropriate, you destroy.

He continues concerning their reward; and firstly, He says what it is; and secondly, He says in what it consists. What is the reward? It is beatitude; hence, He says: *Blessed*, either at his death or at the end of the world, *is that servant, whom when his lord shall come he shall find so doing*, namely, administering, as it said, "Blessed are the undefiled in the way, who walk in the law of the Lord" (Ps. 118, 1). And why are they blessed? *Amen I say to you: he shall place him over all his goods*. This passage is expounded in three ways. In one way, it is expounded such that it is shown in what consists all beatitude. For beatitude consists in some good; but all things belong to God. Therefore, is not beatitude in some one of these? Beatitude is in that good which is above all other goods: for a man is not blessed except in that good which is God; hence, *he shall place him over all his goods*, meaning he shall be made blessed in that, namely God, which is above all goods. In a second way, it can be expounded that He says this to show the preeminence which good prelates will have. In Luke 12, 37, it is stated that "he will make them sit down"; but here it is stated that *he shall place him over all his goods*; because among all rewards the greatest is the reward of a good prelate; "He that shall do and teach, he shall be called great" (Mt. 5, 19). "But they that are learned, shall shine as the brightness of the firmament: and they that instruct many to justice, as stars for all eternity" (Dan. 12, 3). And this is *over all his goods*, meaning above all the rewards of the saints. In a third way, it can be expounded by the union with Christ; because, as in this world, one will not arrive at the state of perfection except he follow Christ's footsteps, so neither, hereafter, will men arrive at the state of perfection except they shall have been joined to Christ: and they will have dominion over all things, inasmuch as their will is conformed to the divine will; "And I dispose to you, as my Father hath disposed to me, a kingdom" (Lk. 22, 29). And: "He that shall overcome, I will give him the morning star" (Apoc. 2, 26 & 28).

But if that evil servant shall say in his heart, etc. After He attracted them with rewards so that they might be vigilant, here, He frightens them with punishments. And firstly, He points out the guilt of an evil servant; and secondly, He points out the punishment, where it is said: *The lord shall come*, etc. In guilt there are two things, namely, the cause of guilt, and the guilt itself; and, nevertheless, both are guilt. The cause of guilt is despair of His Coming: *If he shall say: My lord is long a coming.* Augustine says that a man can say this due to a very great desire, and the one who was saying the following words was demonstrating this: "When shall I come and appear before the face of God?" (Ps. 41, 3). Sometimes, it is said on account of despair of His Coming quickly; "Son of man, what is this proverb that you have in the land of Israel? saying: The days shall be prolonged, and every vision shall fail" (Ez. 12, 22). "The Lord delayeth not his promise" (II Pet. 3, 9). Hence, this is the root of all guilt. But what are the things that follow from this? One is the guilt of cruelty and another is the guilt of pleasure. As to the first, He says: *And shall begin to strike his fellow servants*, because he shall deem others to be subject as servants to himself, contrary to that which is written: "But voluntarily, and not as lording it over the clergy" (I Pet. 5, 2-3). And this alone is not enough for him, but he also strikes and afflicts; "You that build up Sion with blood" (Mic. 3, 10). Or they strike their brothers, whom they consider to be their servants, by their bad example. Likewise, this is not enough for them, but they turn themselves to pleasures: *He shall eat and drink with drunkards*, meaning he shall associate with pleasure seekers if he is a pleasure seeker. And what follows from this? He sets forth the Judgment. For firstly, He relates their judgment as being unexpected; and secondly, He relates their punishment. He says, *The lord of that servant shall come in a day that he hopeth not*; because a man sometimes supposes that he is sure of having a long life and, nevertheless, suddenly passes away; "The day of the Lord shall come as a thief" (I Thess. 5, 2); "The destruction thereof shall come on a sudden, when it is not looked for" (Is. 30, 13). And what will happen as a result of this? Three punishments follow. *And he shall separate him*, not, as Jerome says, that he will divide him with a sword, but from the company of the good; "He shall separate them one from another, as the shepherd separateth the sheep from the goats" (below 25, 32). And this is the greatest punishment. Origen speaks as follows: 'In man there are three things: there is the soul, the body, and the spiritual gift. And these will not be divided in good prelates, but only in the bad prelates. The spiritual gift will be divided, because He will take the spiritual gift that He had given to them; the body and the soul, however, shall be cast into fire.' Likewise, there is another punishment that will be allotted to the wicked: hence, He says: *He shall appoint his portion with the hypocrites*. Hypocrites are pretenders who profess one thing and do another: hence, He will appoint His portion with such men. And so the following verse is understood: "Brimstone, and storms of winds, shall be the portion of their cup" (Ps. 10, 7). Likewise, these punishments will still not be sufficient, but there will be another punishment, for ***there shall be weeping and gnashing of teeth***. "They shall pass from the snow waters to excessive heat" (Job. 24, 19). Hence, weeping is caused by smoke, and gnashing of teeth is caused by cold. Origen says that from this we can consider that they speak incorrectly who say that bad prelates are not prelates.

Likewise, note the similitude which Augustine sets down. Let us remove from the eyes that servant concerning which the exhortation is made, and let us consider three servants who love the Lord's coming. One says: 'My Lord will come quickly, and, therefore, I will watch.' Another says: 'The Lord will delay, but I want to watch.' The last says: 'I do not know when He will come, and, therefore, I will watch.' Which of these speaks best? Augustine says the first is badly deceived, because if he thinks that He may come quickly, and later He delays, he is in danger lest he sleep out of weariness. The second can be deceived but he is not in danger. But the third does well, who out of doubt always waits; therefore, it is bad to fix some time of His Coming.

CHAPTER TWENTY-FIVE

1. Then shall the kingdom of heaven be like to ten virgins, who taking their lamps went out to meet the bridegroom and the bride.
2. And five of them were foolish and five wise.
3. But the five foolish, having taken their lamps, did not take oil with them.
4. But the wise took oil in their vessels with the lamps.
5. And the bridegroom tarrying, they all slumbered and slept.
6. And at midnight there was a cry made: Behold the bridegroom cometh. Go ye forth to meet him.
7. Then all those virgins arose and trimmed their lamps.
8. And the foolish said to the wise: Give us of your oil, for our lamps are gone out.
9. The wise answered, saying: Lest perhaps there be not enough for us and for you, go ye rather to them that sell and buy for yourselves.
10. Now whilst they went to buy the bridegroom came: and they that were ready went in with him to the marriage. And the door was shut.
11. But at last came also the other virgins, saying: Lord, Lord, open to us.
12. But he answering said: Amen I say to you, I know you not.
13. Watch ye therefore, because you know not the day nor the hour.

Above, it was treated concerning the Lord's Coming for the Judgment; here it is treated concerning the Judgment itself: hence, this chapter is divided into two parts. In the first part, He speaks about the Judgment by way of some parables; and in the second part, He openly and explicitly shows the form of the Judgment, where it is said, **And when the Son of man shall come in his majesty.** About the first point, He does two things. Firstly, a certain parable is related, in which some are excluded from the kingdom on account of an interior defect; and in the second parable, some are excluded on account of their negligence of exterior works, where it is said, **For even as a man going into a far country called his servants.** The first parable is about the virgins, and these parables are apt to exercise men's minds. And in this parable, three things ought to be considered. Firstly, the preparation of certain persons disposing themselves so that they might reign with Christ; secondly, the calling to the Judgment is related; and thirdly, the coming of the Judgment is related. The second part is where it is said, *And at midnight there was a cry made*; and the third part is where it is said, *Now whilst they went to buy behold the bridegroom came*. About the first point, He begins by mentioning the eagerness of those preparing; and secondly, He mentions their sleep, where it is said, *And the bridegroom tarrying, they all slumbered and slept*. About the first, He does two things. Firstly, He relates what is common to all those preparing themselves; and secondly, He relates the difference in these persons who are preparing themselves, where it is said, *And five of them were foolish and five wise*. About the first, four things common to all are considered: their number, state, duty, and intended goal.

Their number is mentioned, that they were ten: *The kingdom of heaven be like to ten virgins*. But why does He say ten? The reason is threefold. One reason is that ten is the number of universality; in counting we go up to ten, and, afterwards, we start from one: hence, by ten, by one, and by a hundred universality is signified. Or, according to Hilary, all men resist the Ten Commandments that ought to be observed, or all men are obliged to follow them. Or He says ten on account of the number of the five senses doubled. For they are doubled in one way, according to Gregory, in that five are in men and five are in women: and so there are ten. According to Jerome, they are doubled according to the fact that they refer to the different senses: for certain senses are interior and others are exterior. Concerning interior sight it is said: "No man hath seen God at any time" (Jn. 1, 18). Concerning interior taste it is said: "O taste, and see that the Lord is sweet" (Ps. 33, 9). Concerning interior smell it is said: "We will run after thee to the odor of thy ointments" (Cant. 1, 3). And so there are ten in all who come to the Judgment.

Their state is mentioned when it is said, *Virgins*. But why are they called virgins? The reason is threefold. According to Chrysostom, it is understood of those who keep the integrity of the flesh. But why does He mention of virgins rather than of others? He says what is written above concerning virgins, where He says that "there are indeed eunuchs, who have made themselves eunuchs for the kingdom of heaven. He that can take, let him take it" (19, 12). Wherefore, since virginity is so great a good that it does not fall under a precept, but under a counsel, according to what is written: "Concerning virgins, I have no commandment of the Lord: but I give counsel" (I Cor. 7, 25); if these are damned, all the more will others be also. Or they are called virgins who abstain from the allurements of the five senses. According to Jerome and Origen, the faithful who do not allow themselves to be corrupted are called virgins, according to what the Apostle says: "I have espoused you to one husband, that I may present you as a chaste virgin to Christ" (II Cor. 11, 2).

Now following we will see their state: *Who taking their lamps*. Lamps are vessels of light. Hence, according to Hilary, we can understand the lamps to be souls illumined with the light of faith which they received at Baptism; "Then shall thy light break forth as the morning" (Is. 58, 8). Or, by the lamps, works are signified, according to Augustine: for your works ought to be lamps; "So let your light shine before men, that they may see your good works, and glorify your Father who is in heaven" (above 5, 16). Therefore, to take lamps is to prepare the soul or to dispose it to do good works.

The fourth thing common to all that is related is that *they went out to meet the bridegroom and the bride*. Who is this bridegroom and who is this bride? It is expounded in two ways according to a twofold marriage. One marriage is that of the divinity to the flesh, which was celebrated in the womb of the Virgin; "He as a bridegroom coming out of his bridechamber" (Ps. 18, 6). The bridegroom is the Son Himself, and the bride is the human nature; hence, to go out to meet the bridegroom and the bride is nothing else than to serve Christ. Likewise, it is Christ's marriage with the Church; "He that hath the bride is the bridegroom" (Jn. 3, 29). Therefore, those preparing their lamps are endeavoring to please the bridegroom, meaning Christ, and His bride, meaning Mother Church. And so the virgins agree in these things. Two things are also related in which they differ, namely, in their inward discretion and in their outward diligence. Regarding the first thing, He says: *And five of them were foolish and five wise*; "Wisdom is prudence to a man" (Prov. 10, 23). That man is prudent, who does not want to lose in any way that which he does. Hence, it was said above: "Be ye wise as serpents" (10, 16). Or they are foolish as to their inward discretion, who turn away from God by their wicked intention, or by an intention that is inordinate, or by false doctrine; "A foolish woman and clamorous, and full of allurements, and knowing nothing at all, sat at the door of her house" (Prov. 9, 13-14). According to Origen, a man who has one virtue has them all: hence, one sense cannot be rightly ordered without the others being rightly ordered also. Likewise, as it is also said, "he who sins in one point, is become guilty of all" (James 2, 10). Similarly, they differ as to their outward diligence, because *the five foolish, having taken their lamps, did not take oil with them.* All these foolish virgins desired well to have lit lamps, because He who is the Light wants to be served with light; but light cannot be nourished without oil: for a man would be foolish to keep light in a lamp, without putting oil into it. By oil four things are signified, according to Jerome. By oil good works are signified. And why is this? Faith is the light of souls by which their lamps are lit. By good works faith is nourished; "This precept, I commend to thee, O son Timothy: according to the prophecies going before on thee, that thou war in them a good warfare, having faith and a good conscience, which some rejecting have made shipwreck concerning the faith" (I Tim. 1, 18-19). From this can be understood what is said in Proverbs 21, 20: "There is a treasure to be desired, and oil in the dwelling of the just: and the foolish man shall spend it." Taken in another way, by oil mercy is signified: and in this way Chrysostom speaks. Hence, it is stated in Luke 10, 34, that the Samaritan "poured in oil and wine." By wine severity is signified, and by oil the works of mercy are signified. Therefore, He wishes to say that he who intends to observe continency, and has not done mercy, is foolish. Hence, it says in James 2, 13: "Judgment without mercy to him that hath not done mercy." Again, by oil interior joy is signified, concerning which it is said: "That he may make the face cheerful with oil" (Ps. 103, 15). And, elsewhere, it is said: "God hath anointed thee with the oil of gladness" (Ps. 44, 8). There are many men who exteriorly fast and seek inward joy, namely, the joy of a good conscience, and there they have oil with themselves. But others do not seek joy of conscience but the glory of men, and these men do not have oil. According to Origen, by oil holy doctrine is signified: "Thy name is as oil poured out" (Cant. 1, 2). The oil of justice signifies right doctrine; "Thy words have I hidden in my heart" (Ps. 118, 11). Hence, they are called virgins who observe continency, who do mercy, who seek interior joy, and who accept right doctrine.

He continues concerning the short sleep. The reason for the sleeping is related and the sleep itself is related. For when some persons wait for someone, and especially at night, they quickly fall sleep. Hence, by this interval is signified the time between Christ's Coming in the flesh and His Coming for the Judgment; hence, He says: *And the bridegroom tarrying, they all slumbered and slept.* According to all expositors, this is expounded of their death.

And why is death called sleep? This is on account of the hope of the resurrection. For just as those who sleep intend to wake up, so those who sleep by death intend to rise again; "And we will not have you ignorant brethren, concerning them that are asleep, that you be not sorrowful, even as others who have no hope" (I Thess. 4, 12).

But what is slumbering and sleep? Gregory expounds them as follows: 'Slumber is properly the means to fall asleep; hence, by slumbering we can understand a long life, and by sleep, death.' According to Origen, this sleep is understood to refer to the sleep of laziness; "How long wilt thou sleep, O sluggard? when wilt thou arise out of thy sleep?" (Prov. 6, 9). Hence, *and the bridegroom tarrying*, either until the Judgment or until death, *they all slumbered and slept*; for there are scarcely any men who live for a long time without growing weary. Or those who are completely negligent sleep; but those who in some manner, to a certain degree, lose their first fervor, sleep.

Then the waking follows: secondly, the effect follows; thirdly, the request of the foolish virgins follows; and fourthly, the response of the wise virgins follows. He says, therefore: *At midnight there was a cry made*. Concerning this night, Origen expounds it differently than others and more literally. All others expound this waking as referring to the final Judgment; and according to this interpretation, this cry will be the trumpet or voice of Christ; "For the Lord himself shall come down from heaven with commandment and with the voice of an archangel and with the trumpet of God" (I Thess. 4, 15); "The trumpet shall sound..." (I Cor. 15, 52) "and the dead who are in Christ shall rise first" (I Thess. 4, 5).

And why does this happen at midnight? According to Jerome, the Hebrews say that just as an angel at midnight descended to kill the firstborn of Egypt, so the Lord shall come at midnight. Hence, there used to be a custom among them, that the people would not be sent away until midnight.[1] Augustine says that it is not on account of the reason of the time, but only on account of its concealment; "The day of the Lord shall so come as a thief in the night" (I Thess. 5, 2).

1. "JEROME; The Jews have a tradition that Christ will come at midnight, in like manner as in that visitation of Egypt, when the Paschal feast is celebrated, and the destroyer comes, and the Lord passes over our dwellings, and the door posts of each man's countenance are hallowed by the blood of the Lamb. Hence, I suppose, has continued among us that apostolic tradition, that on the vigil of Easter the people should not be dismissed before midnight, in expectation of Christ's coming; but when that hour has passed over, they may celebrate the feast in security; whence also the Psalmist says, 'At midnight did I rise to praise you' (Ps. 118, 62)" (*Catena Aurea on St. Matthew*, chap. 25, lect. 1).

But what is this that He says; ***Behold the bridegroom cometh. Go ye forth to meet him***? It is said because all men will rise to meet Him; "The hour cometh, wherein all that are in the graves, shall hear His voice" (Jn. 5, 28); "Be prepared to meet thy God, O Israel" (Amos 4, 2). Origen refers this to the present life. And this is when a man is held back by vainglory, and a shout is made by a preacher or by an interior inspiration; then he returns to Christ; "Lift up thy voice with strength, thou that bringest good tidings to Jerusalem" (Is. 40, 9).

Then the effect follows: ***Then all those virgins arose and trimmed their lamps.*** In the literal sense, when the cry is made by a trumpet or by Christ's voice, all will arise. Hence: "All that are in the graves, shall hear His voice" (Jn. 5, 28). But what did they do? ***They trimmed their lamps.*** And what is this? Will there really be time for this? It ought to be said that to trim lamps is nothing other than to count the works which they did so that they can render a fitting account. Hence, they will be concerned about their works when they will hear the voice of the Son of God, as it is said below: "When did we see thee hungry and fed thee: thirsty and gave thee drink, etc?" (below, verse 37). According to Origen, it is a more literal sense. For if it refers to the present life, when a shout is made by a preacher or by an internal inspiration then men rise from their negligence, and then they begin to rise to correct their deeds.

Then the request of the foolish virgins follows: ***And the foolish said to the wise: Give us of your oil, for our lamps are gone out.*** These virgins were foolish in one respect but not in another respect: because they had something of the light of faith; hence, they say: ***For our lamps are going out.***[2] For if they had no faith they might say, 'They have gone out' hence, they know that they cannot keep fire burning without oil. And what is the meaning of these words? Either the works of mercy or of justice may be understood by oil, and the meaning is the same, because those rising who do not have these works in abundance seek to supply their deficiencies with those who have more abundantly. But this will not be possible, because everyone will have what he needs; "Every one shall bear his own burden" (Gal. 6, 5). And because they shall see that the light of faith could not have value without the works of mercy, they were asking from the others who had done works of mercy. Augustine expounds this as follows: 'It is customary that when someone is preoccupied in some affair, he

---

2. Here the present tense, "going out (*extinguuntur*)" is used in the Latin text, but in the Douay-Rheims translation, the past tense is used, "are gone out."

is accustomed to have recourse to that in which he hopes: these virgins had an outward confidence, because they were seeking the praise of others';[3] hence, they say: *Give us of your oil*, meaning the oil of your praise, that is to say, 'praise us for our deeds.' But this will not avail them, according to what is written in Romans 2, 15: "Their conscience bearing witness to them"; "For behold my witness is in heaven, and he that knoweth my conscience is on high" (Job 16, 20). Hence, they trust in human favor which cannot benefit them. According to Origen, it happens that some men spend their lives in vain things: and when they recognize it, they run to others and they ask for their prayers and help. And in this they are not foolish if they begin to turn back to the Lord.

The wise answered, saying. Here the response of the wise virgins is related: and in this response two things are put forward. Firstly, the response of those rejecting the request is related; and, likewise, some advice is related, where it is said, *go ye rather to them that sell*. And what is the reason for the rejection? *Lest perhaps there be not enough for us*. Hence, *go ye*, because our oil of mercy, or interior joy, or exterior works is not enough for us and for you, as it is said: "If the just man shall scarcely be saved, where shall the ungodly and the sinner appear?" (I Pet. 4, 18). And the Apostle says: "The sufferings of this time are not worthy to be compared with the glory to come that shall be revealed in us" (Rom. 8, 18). And: "All our justices [are] as the rag of a menstruous woman," (Is. 64, 6). Therefore, because they are not enough for us and for you, *Go ye rather to them that sell and buy for yourselves*.

But will there be time for them to get oil? Wherefore, it ought to be understood that it is said more in the manner of a rebuke than in the manner of advice; it is as though they were to say, 'You should have gone before.' According to Chrysostom, these sellers are the poor, because they make merchandise of the kingdom; "Make unto you friends of the mammon of iniquity" (Lk. 16, 9); hence, they say, *Go ye*, meaning you ought to have gone, according to Augustine: for it is said in the manner of a rebuke. The sellers of oil are the flatterers: hence, seeing that these virgins ask for help, they say: *Go ye rather to them that sell and buy for yourselves*; as though they were to say: 'You sought nothing but oil,' meaning human praise: 'now you can go to the world and buy that testimony which you always sought.' According to Origen, it is merely literal, because he holds that all takes place in this world. Sometimes it happens that a sinner sees a just man, and asks

---

3. *Sermo* 93, n. 8.

what he should do. But some men are wise only to the extent that their wisdom suffices for themselves, but not both for themselves and for others. Hence, such men say to those who ask for their advice: 'We do not have so much spiritual doctrine that we can have enough both for us and for you; for that reason, go to the doctors of the Church, and to wise men who will sell to you.' Concerning this, it is written: "All you that thirst, come to the waters: and you that have no money make haste, buy, and eat" (Is. 55, 1).

But how can something be bought without money? I say that wisdom is sold without money. And what is its price? It is that a man willingly strive for it, and this is the price of wisdom; "If thou shalt seek her as money, and shalt dig for her as for a treasure, then shalt thou understand the fear of the Lord, and shalt find the knowledge of God" (Prov. 2, 4-5).

Now whilst they went to buy the bridegroom came. Augustine says that some refer this to the state of the present life; but it cannot be reconciled with that which is said, *And the door was shut.* For that reason, Origen expounds this as referring to the future life. And here, Christ does three things. Firstly, the coming of the judge is related; secondly, the receiving of the good virgins is related; and thirdly, the excluding of the bad virgins is related. He says, therefore, that while they went to buy the bridegroom came; that is to say, while they were worrying about how to excuse themselves at the Judgment, the Lord came to the Judgment. But Origen says that there are some men who will come for advice, for instance, to the priests, and with the intention of being converted, and then they die at the Lord's coming. Hence, the bridegroom comes when a man dies.

But what is this that He says, *The bridegroom came,* when above He said, *They went out to meet the bridegroom and the bride*? The reason is that at the Judgment the bridegroom, meaning Christ's flesh, will be taken up to be glorified. Or if we refer this to the Church, then it will be perfectly united to the Spouse Himself by assent. Hence, the Apostle says: "He who is joined to the Lord is one spirit with him" (I Cor. 6, 17). And the passage continues and those that were prepared entered with Him to the marriage. This marriage is the kingdom of heaven, about which it is said: "Because he is Lord of lords and King of kings: and they that are with him are called, and elect, and faithful" (Apoc. 17, 14). And immediately, *The door was shut,* because, afterwards, it will be opened to no one. Now, however, it is open; hence: "Lift up your gates, O ye princes" (Ps. 23, 7). And: "After these things I looked, and behold a door was opened in heaven" (Apoc. 4, 1). But then it will be closed.

Afterwards, the repulsion of the bad virgins is related: and three things are said. Firstly, their negligence is pointed out, in that they came late. Hence, He is designating those who do penance late: "Saying within themselves, repenting, and groaning for anguish of spirit" (Wis. 5, 3). Their desire is mentioned when they say: **Lord, Lord, open to us.** Hence, by this fact that they call Him Lord, they say the name through which they ought to pray. By this, however, that they groan, it is indicated that they ask out of anguish; hence, it is said above: "Not every one that saith to me, Lord, Lord, shall enter into the kingdom of heaven" (7, 21). Now their desire is touched upon when it is said, **Open to us.** The response follows: **But he answering said: Amen I say to you, I know you not**; that is to say, 'I do not approve of you.' For "The Lord knoweth who are his" (II Tim. 2, 19) just as an artist knows if a work does not accord with his art. Afterwards, He concludes: **Watch ye therefore, because you know not the day nor the hour.**

14. For even as a man going into a far country called his servants and delivered to them his goods;
15. And to one he gave five talents, and to another two, and to another one, to every one according to his proper ability: and immediately he took his journey.
16. And he that had received the five talents went his way and traded with the same and gained other five.
17. And in like manner he that had received the two gained other two.
18. But he that had received the one, going his way, digged into the earth and hid his lord's money.
19. But after a long time the lord of those servants came and reckoned with them.
20. And he that had received the five talents coming, brought other five talents, saying: Lord, thou didst deliver to me five talents. Behold I have gained other five over and above.
21. His lord said to him: Well done, good and faithful servant, because thou hast been faithful over a few things, I will place thee over many things. Enter thou into the joy of thy lord.
22. And he also that had received the two talents came and said: Lord, thou deliveredst two talents to me. Behold I have gained other two.
23. His lord said to him: Well done, good and faithful servant: because thou hast been faithful over a few things,

I will place thee over many things. Enter thou into the joy of thy lord.

24. But he that had received the one talent, came and said: Lord, I know that thou art a hard man; thou reapest where thou hast not sown and gatherest where thou hast not strewed.

25. And being afraid, I went and hid thy talent in the earth. Behold here thou hast that which is thine.

26. And his lord answering, said to him: Wicked and slothful servant, thou knewest that I reap where I sow not and gather where I have not strewed.

27. Thou oughtest therefore to have committed my money to the bankers: and at my coming I should have received my own with usury.

28. Take ye away therefore the talent from him and give it him that hath ten talents.

29. For to every one that hath shall be given, and he shall abound: but from him that hath not, that also which he seemeth to have shall be taken away.

30. And the unprofitable servant, cast ye out into the exterior darkness. There shall be weeping and gnashing of teeth.

Above, the Lord tells a parable about the Judgment, in which some are condemned for not keeping the interior spiritual good which they had received, but here He tells a parable in which some do not multiply the goods they have received: hence, the parables are different. More specifically, He firstly treats of the distribution of His gifts; secondly, He treats of their use; and thirdly, He treats of the judgment of those using His gifts. The second part is where it is said, **And he that had received the five talents went his way**, etc.; and the third part is where it is said, **But after a long time**, etc. In the first part, He does three things. Firstly, He relates the necessity of distributing His gifts; secondly, He relates their distribution; and thirdly, He relates the departure of the one distributing. He shows the necessity by the fact that He says, **For even as a man going into a far country called his servants and delivered to them his goods**. Wherein, you ought to note that this man is Christ. And we can say that He went ***into a far country*** in three ways: for He went to a place, and so, more specifically, He went to heaven, which, although it is a fitting place for Him in respect to His divinity, nevertheless, He was a stranger according to the flesh, because no man had ascended there. Hence: "No man hath ascended into heaven, but he that descended from heaven, the Son of man who is in heaven" (Jn. 3, 13). Likewise, He went because, being a stranger in the world, He departed to heaven; "Why wilt thou be as a stranger in the land, and as a wayfaring man turning in to lodge?" (Jer. 14, 8). Similarly, this can be understood spiritually: for now He is away from us, because we are away from Him; "While we are in the body we are absent from the Lord" (II Cor. 5, 6). However, when we will see him, then we will not be like strangers but like fellow citizens and the domestics of God.[4]

And it ought to be observed that, as Origen says, where the word "as" is said a thing ought to be associated unless it is said in a similitude as, for example, it is stated above: "For as lightning cometh out of the east, so shall also the coming of the Son of man" (above 24, 27). But here it is not said in a similitude, and afterwards, nothing else is said; wherefore, it ought to be read as follows: Someone goes into a far country as a man, because Christ is God and man. Hence, in that He is God, He does not go into a far country, because "all things are naked and open to his eyes" (Heb. 4, 13). However, He goes into a far country as man; "We saw his glory, the glory as it were of the only begotten of the Father" (Jn. 1, 14). And due to the fact that it was necessary that He go into a foreign country, it was necessary that He entrust the care of his possessions to others; and He does this when He says, *He called his servants and delivered to them his goods*. And firstly, the liberality of the one giving is mentioned; secondly, the diversity of the goods is mentioned; and similarly, the discretion of the one giving is mentioned. The liberality of the one giving is mentioned in two things: in that He anticipates those to whom He gave, and in that He gave to them abundantly. His liberality is mentioned by the fact that He anticipates, because he who waits to give, lessens his liberality; not so, however, does the Lord give; in Psalm 20, 4, it is said: Thou hast prevented him with blessings of sweetness." Hence, *He called His servants*, and they did not call Him; hence: "You have not chosen me: but I have chosen you" (Jn. 15, 16); "Those whom he foreknew, he also predestinated" (Rom. 8, 29). Likewise, His liberality is mentioned, because from His own possessions, *He gave His goods*, not the goods belonging to someone else. Some men are liberal well enough from the goods of another, but not from their own goods. Hence, concerning this, it can be understood what is said in Psalm 67, 19: "Thou

---

4. Eph. 2, 19.

hast ascended on high, thou hast led captivity captive; thou hast received gifts in men."

Afterwards, the differences of His gifts is related: *And to one he gave five talents, and to another two, and to another one.* He divided all these by three, into thirtyfold, into sixtyfold, and into one hundredfold fruit;[5] because every multitude is divided into the highest, and the lowest, and the middle. These talents are different gifts of graces: for just as a weight of metal is called a talent, so grace is a weight because it inclines the soul; hence, love is the weight of the soul. The Apostle says: "There are diversities of graces" (I Cor. 12, 4): hence, these gifts are different, such that they are not given equally to all; "To every one of us is given grace, according to the measure of the giving of Christ" (Eph. 4, 7). And that is what He says: *And to one he gave five talents, and to another two, and to another one.*

And what is the reason for these numbers? We can say that a man abounds in that he has a double measure; but a man abounds even more in that he has more than double. Hence, he who receives two, is related to him who has one, as by a double proportion: he, however, who receives five, has more than a double proportion. Hence, He wishes to say that a man receives five, who receives according to an incomparable measure. We can also say that these gifts are God's words and words of wisdom: for frequently wisdom is compared to riches; "Riches of salvation, wisdom" (Is. 33, 6).

What is that He says, that *He gave to one five talents, and to another two, and to another one*? Origen says that He gave five talents to him who refers everything which is said in Scripture to a spiritual understanding; hence, it was said above: just as there are five bodily senses, so there are five spiritual senses. In this manner, the Lord gave to the Apostles. In Luke 24, 45, it is said that "he opened their understanding, that they might understand the scriptures." And in Daniel 1, 17, it is said that "To the children God gave understanding in every book." Who are they who receive two talents? According to Origen, duality belongs to matter, hence, every number is derived from duality and unity; hence, to duality is attributed matter, and to unity is attributed form.[6] Hence, they are said to receive two who receive less, because they do not know how to conduct themselves in all affairs; but they have something in that they know how to conduct themselves in certain affairs, because they are good builders, or suchlike. Hence,

---

5. cf. above 13, 23.
6. "According to the Platonists, in numbers duality is attributed to matter, unity however to species: therefore only the unity is the species" (*Sententia Metaphysicae*, Bk. 7, lect. 11, n. 11).

according to Origen, a man receives more who receives one talent than he who receives two. According to Gregory and Jerome, it is the opposite, because by five talents is understood the five senses: hence, he receives five talents who receives grace from God about temporal things, about which the operation of the senses deal. By two talents, however, are understood the senses and the intellect. But by one is designated the intellect alone. Hence, a man receives one, who receives the grace of understanding but not the grace of doing. According to Hilary, he receives five who finds Christ in the five books of Moses; he, however, receives two who venerates the grace of the New and Old Testament and who venerates two natures in Christ, His human and divine nature; the Jews, who glory in the Laws, only receive one talent.

Then the reason follows: *To every one according to his proper ability.* If this refers to the interpretation that the talents are God's words, the exposition is clear, because they ought to be given according to a man's greater capacity; "I have yet many things to say to you" (Jn. 16, 12). And the Apostle says: "As unto little ones in Christ, I gave you milk to drink, not meat" (I Cor. 3, 2). Therefore, to the more discerning He gave more subtle truths.

However, if we refer this saying to the gifts of graces, it ought to be known that some men said that God gives His free gifts according to one's natural gifts. Hence, by the fact that a man has more natural gifts, he has more free gifts; and this was true for the angels but is not true for men. And what is the reason? It is because in the angels there is one spiritual nature; wherefore, towards whatever they are moved, they are completely moved. But man is composed of two contrary natures, of which one is drawn back from the other by its own body: hence, not as much is given to him, but only as much as a man has from his use of these natural gifts.

Likewise, there was another error, which asserted that the beginning of grace was from ourselves. And against this, Augustine objects using the words of the Apostle who says, "not that we are sufficient to think any thing of ourselves, as of ourselves" (II Cor. 3, 5). But what beginning is prior to thought? Therefore, if a thought is not from ourselves then neither is an action. Hence, he who strives harder has more grace; but that one strives more requires a higher cause; "Convert us, O Lord, to thee, and we shall be converted" (Lam. 5, 21).

If, however, you seek why one man has more grace than another, I say that of this thing there is a proximate cause and a first cause; the proximate cause is the greater effort of this man than of that man; the first cause is the divine election; "Why doth one day excel another, and one light another, and one year another year, when all come of the sun? By the knowledge of the Lord they were distinguished" (Eccli. 33, 7). And what is the reason for this? Observe that it is different with a universal and a particular agent. A particular agent presupposes something for itself; and, according to this, the agent acts in different ways, so that one worker gives one form to one matter, and other workers give another. But if one could make matter, it would be said that such a man made matter to be suchlike so that he might introduce a form according to his own will. Thus, the Lord, since He is the Creator of all things, created this thing so that He would make it in such a way; thus, the capacity of nature in connection with effort is understood, inasmuch as it may be understood.

Then the departure of the one giving is related when it is said: *And immediately he took his journey.* And it can be understood that this Man was taking His journey into a foreign country, because when He was with the Apostles He had said: "Receive ye the Holy Ghost" (Jn. 20, 22), and to Peter He had said: "Feed my sheep" (Jn. 21, 17). He immediately took His journey: hence, He said: "Little children, yet a little while I am with you" (Jn. 13, 33). And He immediately ascended. Or it can be said that He took His journey, not by departing but because He left them to their free will, because He did not compel them to use the gifts which they were given.

And he that had received the five talents went his way, etc. Here it is related concerning the use of the gifts, and this is in regard to the three servants. And firstly, it is related concerning the first servant; secondly, it is related concerning the second servant; and thirdly, it is related concerning the third servant; wherefore, He says: *And he that had received the five talents went his way.* Here the increase of virtue is designated; "They shall go from virtue to virtue" (Ps. 83, 8). And this is stated in Genesis 26, 13: "He went on prospering and increasing." For virtue increases through the exercise of use; for unless it is used, it grows weak; and, therefore, He says: *He traded.*[7] Hence, it is said: "The soul of them that work, shall be made fat" (Prov. 13, 4). *And He gained other five.* And why? A man profits in two ways: in one way he profits for himself, and in another way he profits for others. He profits for himself if he has the understanding of Scripture, and so he consequently profits; if he has charity he consequently profits

---

7. *Operatus est,* which in English means "He worked."

others. He profited so that he may profit others, and he receives so that he may share with others; "As every man hath received grace, ministering the same one to another" (I Pet. 4, 10).

Hence, if you share what you receive, that much do you gain. Hence, He says that *He gained other five*; for it rarely happens that a man gives to someone that which he does not possess. "For I have received of the Lord that which also I delivered unto you" (I Cor. 11, 23). But in that which one has, in that does one profit. The Apostle says: "His grace in me hath not been void" (I Cor. 15, 10). According to Hilary, he gains fivefold who profits in the five books of Moses, such that he gains Christ. *And in like manner he that had received the two*, namely, he profits by his understanding and actions, *gained other two*, meaning a rewarding as to both. Or he gained two because he not only profits by preaching to men but also to women, according to Gregory. According to Origen, he gained two because that which he had grasped according to knowledge of natural things, he refers to the understanding of the supernatural things. *But he that had received the one, going his way, digged into the earth*, etc. Now, what is meant by the words: "to dig in the earth"? According to Gregory, it can be expounded in three ways. A man hides a treasure who hides the gift given in sins of the flesh, or in temporal things: hence, he who can profit in spiritual things,[8] and turns to earthly things, hides his Lord's money in the earth: about such men it is said: "They have set their eyes bowing down to the earth" (Ps. 16, 11). According to Origen, when a man has the gift of understanding and wants to live religiously, yet he lives only for himself whereas he might have benefited many; this man hides his talent in the earth. "It is honorable to reveal and confess the works of God" (Tob. 12, 7). For such money ought to be multiplied and not hidden. Hilary says: "Who are they who receive one? It is the Jews, who accept only the literal sense. They hide the money in the earth, meaning in Christ's flesh, who on account of His flesh cannot believe that He is God." Hence, the Apostle says: "But we preach Christ crucified: unto the Jews indeed a stumblingblock, and unto the Gentiles foolishness" (I Cor. 1, 23).

But after a long time the lord of those servants came. Here it is treated concerning the Judgment. And first, the reason for the coming Judgment is related; and secondly, it is treated concerning the Judgment, where it is said, *He reckoned with them.* It ought to

---

8. The text here reads "temporal things," but this seems to be an error in the text, based on the words of St. Gregory the Great to which St. Thomas seems to refer here. It reads: "May no earthy care impede us from spiritual works, lest if one's talent be hidden in the earth, the lord of the talent be provoked to anger" (*XL Homiliarum in Evangelia*, lib. I, n. 7).

be observed that we are obliged to render an account of our actions and gifts; "About every idle word that men shall speak, they are obliged to render an account for it on Judgment Day" (above 12, 36). And: "The kingdom of heaven is likened to a man, who would take an account of his servants" (above 18, 23). And firstly, it is related in particular, *And He reckoned with them*, because everyone is held to render an account, firstly, at one's death; and secondly, everyone is held to render an account on Judgment Day, when Christ will oblige us to stand before His tribunal. Therefore, when He says, *But after a long time the lord came*, these words can be referred to both judgments: for if they be referred to Judgment Day, it is given to be understood that there is a long delay between Christ's Coming[9] and Judgment Day; this is contrary to what certain men believed at the time of the Apostles; "That you be not easily moved from your sense nor be terrified, neither by spirit nor by word nor by epistle. Be not terrified as if the day of the Lord were at hand" (II Thess. 2, 2). But if these words be referred to the day of one's death, Origen says: "You ought to consider the fact that a man shall rarely be useful for the Church who lives a short time." And He proves this in respect to Peter, to whom the Lord said: "When thou shalt be old, thou shalt stretch forth thy hands, and another shall gird thee" (Jn. 21, 18). Likewise, it was true in respect to Paul, who was a young man at the time of his conversion and afterwards became an old man; hence, it is said: "As Paul, an old man," etc., (Phil. v. 9). Hence, when it is said, *But after a long time*, it is given to be understood that the Lord gives a long time for doing well: and of this long time what is said in Prov. 3, 2, is understood: "They shall add to thee length of days, and years of life, and peace."

And he that had received the five talents coming, brought other five, etc. Here it is treated concerning the three servants. And firstly, it is treated concerning the first servant; secondly, it is treated concerning the second servant; and thirdly, it is treated concerning the third servant. In relation to the first, He does two things. Firstly, the account rendered is related; secondly, the due remuneration is related, where it is said, *His lord said to him*, etc. In respect to this man, He firstly relates his security,[10] fidelity, humility and strenuousness[11] or solicitude. He mentions the

---

9. i.e. Christ's first coming when He came to live on earth.
10. "Macrobius adds security, which banishes fear" (II II, q. 128, ad 6ᵘᵐ).
11. "Besides magnificence he mentions *andragathia* (ἀνδραγαθία), i.e. manly goodness which we may render strenuousness. For magnificence consists not only in being constant in the accomplishment of great deeds, which belongs to constancy, but also in bringing a certain manly prudence and solicitude to that accomplishment, and this belongs to the Greek, strenuousness" (ibid).

servant's security, because he did not wait for his master to call him but went of himself; hence, He says: **Coming**. Paul had this security through Christ's Blood: "Having therefore, brethren, a confidence in the entering into the holies by the blood of Christ" (Heb. 10, 19); "Having such hope, we use much confidence" (II Cor. 3, 12). Likewise, his fidelity is noted, because **He brought other five**. A man would be truly unfaithful, who took something for himself from his master's possessions: hence, he offered all to his master. Therefore, if you do something good, if you convert someone, and you attribute it to yourself and not to God, you are not faithful; "All things are thine: and we have given thee what we received of thy hand" (I Par. 29, 14). Likewise, the humility of his acknowledgement of the gift is noted, because he knew that he had received it from him; "What hast thou that thou hast not received?" (I Cor. 4, 7). Hence, this man acknowledges the gift, saying: **Lord, thou didst deliver to me five talents**, etc. Similarly, He mentions his strenuousness or solicitude: **Behold I have gained other five over and above**. Hence, he spoke well, like unto the Apostle, who said: "The grace of God in me hath not been void" (I Cor. 15, 10). The due remuneration follows: and in this He does four things. For firstly, the congratulations are related; secondly, the commendation of his merits is related; thirdly, the fairness of the judgment is related; and fourthly, the greatness of the reward is related. The congratulations are mentioned when He says: **Well done, good and faithful servant**, etc. Hence, it is said: "Behold the bridegroom shall rejoice over the bride, and thy God shall rejoice over thee" (Is. 62, 5). Hence, He receives him with a jubilant heart when He says, **Well done**.[12] **Well done** is an expression of jubilation. The commendation of his merits follows. And firstly, He commends the servant for his humility when He says, **Servant**, because he had acknowledged that he was a servant; "When you shall have done all these things that are commanded you, say: We are unprofitable servants" (Lk. 17, 10). Likewise, He commends him for his goodness in that He says, **Good**; because it is characteristic of goodness to share itself; hence, a good man multiplies goodness. Similarly, He commends him for his fidelity, because he did not keep anything for himself but offered it to his master; hence, it is said, **And faithful**; "Now it is required among the dispensers that a man be found faithful" (I Cor. 4, 2). And: "Who, thinkest thou, is a faithful and wise servant?" (above 24, 45). Hence, He approves him saying: **Faith-**

---

12. *Euge* in Latin.

ful. "For not he who commendeth himself is approved: but he, whom God commendeth" (II Cor. 10, 18). Then He points out the fairness of the judgment, in that He gives a fair judgment, saying: *Because thou hast been faithful over a few things, I will place thee over many things*. These few things are all the things which are in this life, because they are next to nothing in comparison to heavenly things. Hence, He wishes to say: 'Because you were faithful by reason of the goods which belong to the present life, *I will place thee over many things*, meaning I will give you spiritual things, which are above all these goods'; "He that is faithful in that which is least is faithful also in that which is greater" (Lk. 16, 10). The greatness of the reward follows: *Enter thou into the joy of thy lord*. For joy is the reward; "I will see you again and your heart shall rejoice" (Jn. 16, 22).

And someone could say: 'Is not vision the reward, or some other good?' I say that if another thing may be called the reward, nevertheless, joy is the final reward: just as I could say that the end of heavy things is a lower place; likewise, the end of heavy things is to rest in that place; but the former has a more primary importance.[13] So joy is nothing else than the rest of the soul in a good gained; hence, by reason of the end, joy is called a reward.

And why does He say: *Enter thou into the joy of thy lord*, and not 'Receive'? I answer, saying that joy is twofold: there is joy in exterior goods and in interior goods: he who rejoices in exterior goods, does not enter into the joy of the Lord but enters into joy in respect to himself; he, however, who rejoices in spiritual goods enters into the joy of the Lord; "The king hath brought me into his storerooms" (Cant. 1, 3). Or it is understood otherwise: What is in something is contained by it, and the container is bigger. Therefore, when joy is in something, which is smaller than your heart, then the joy enters into your heart. But God is bigger than the heart; wherefore, he who rejoices in God, enters into joy. Likewise, he enters *into the joy of thy lord*, meaning joy in the Lord, because the Lord is truth. Hence, beatitude is nothing other than the joy of the truth. Or it is as follows: *Enter thou into the joy of thy lord*, meaning a man rejoices in that joy in which your Lord rejoices, namely, in the enjoyment of Himself. Then, therefore, a man rejoices like the Lord when he enjoys like the Lord; hence, the Lord says to the Apostles: "I have appointed that you may eat and drink at my table, in my kingdom" (Lk. 22, 30), that is to say, that you may be happy in what I am happy.

---

13. cf. *Autographi Deleta*, G3, p. 10A.

And he also that had received the two talents came. Above, the action is of judgment as to the first servant, who had received five talents; here is treated about the judgment as to the second servant, who had received two talents. In relation to the literal sense nothing differs from the first judgment, nor is anything said except what was said concerning the first servant; and hence, it is not necessary to repeat it, because this servant also received the same commendation, and likewise, received the same reward as he who had received the five talents. In which is understood, according to Origen, that he who receives a small gift from God and uses it as well as he can, also receives as much as he who received a great gift. For the Lord only requires this from every man, that he serve Him with his whole heart, as it is stated in Deuteronomy 6.[14]

But about this, one can have a doubt. It might be maintained [from what was said above] that someone has a great amount of goods, and another a small amount; if the latter works according to the little charity that he has received, then he will merit as much as he who had received more: which seems that it cannot be, because in this way he who has less charity might merit as much or more than he who has more. And, therefore, it ought to be distinguished, that there are some goods which perfect, elicit and incline the act of the will; other goods, however, do not. A gift that inclines the will and elicits the act of the will is charity. Therefore, it cannot be that he who has more charity, and who uses great effort, is not also better. But there are other gifts which someone can use according to greater or lesser charity, such as knowledge and suchlike: in such things, he who uses greater effort merits more in respect to the reward; hence, it is said in Luke 21, that the poor woman cast into the treasury more than those who put in more, because she made use of her whole ability.[15]

But he that had received the one talent, came and said. Here the judgment of the wicked servant is settled. And firstly, his account is related; secondly, the condemnation which he receives is related, where it is said, *And his lord answering, said to him.* He proffers an astounding account. For firstly, he says a blasphemy; then he brings up his negligence; and thirdly, he concludes his innocence. And so his syllogism could not be valid. He says a blasphemy when he says: *Lord, I know that thou art a hard man.* He brings up his negligence when he says: *I went and*

---

14. "Thou shalt love the Lord thy God with thy whole heart, and with thy whole soul, and with thy whole strength" (verse 5).
15. Verses 2-3.

hid thy talent in the earth, etc. And let us consider what he says that happened. It was said above about him who had received five talents that he came, because he had confidence; but this man did not come with confidence, but by force. Or it can be understood otherwise, that some men, in regard to the things which they do badly, it seems to them that they do well. "The sluggard is wiser in his own conceit, than seven men that speak sentences" (Prov. 26, 16). Hence, it seemed to him that he had done well. According to Origen, the supposition about God as a hard man seems to belong to a man from whom someone withdraws himself on account of his hardness. "Keep thee far from the man that hath power to kill" (Eccli. 9, 18). And thus, as he who knows that a man is hard does not want to serve him; so some think about God, that He is a hard man. And according to this, that servant had three wrong opinions about God. Firstly, he had the opinion that God would not be merciful; secondly, he had the opinion that God would gain something from our goods; and thirdly, he had the opinion that not all things were from God; and all these opinions proceed from one evil root, namely, that he was thinking that God was, as it were, a man: and this is indicated when he says: ***I know that thou art a hard man***, meaning I consider you to be a hard man; and that is not true, as it is stated: "God is not a man" (Num. 23, 19); "As the heavens are exalted above the earth, so are my ways exalted above your ways" (Is. 55, 9). And he says, ***Hard***, because a hard man is inflexible. And it is said of such a man: "His heart shall be as hard as a stone, and as firm as a smith's anvil" (Job 41, 15). But God is not like this, for He is "a merciful and gracious Lord" (Ps. 110, 4); "A just king setteth up the land: a covetous man shall destroy it" (Prov. 29, 4); and so, he supposed that God was a hard man, and from this he supposed that He was covetous; hence, he attributes to Him things that are characteristic of a covetous person: ***Thou reapest where thou hast not sown and gatherest where thou hast not strewed***, meaning 'You are so hard that you do not cease to rob'; which, nevertheless, is false; "And if thou do justly, what shalt thou give him, or what shall he receive of thy hand?" (Job 35, 7). And it is said: "Thou hast no need of my goods" (Ps. 15, 2). Hence, in saying this, he was alleging that God needed our goods. The third thing he falsely supposed was that there are some things that are not from God; for example, there are some men who do not admit that they have from God the things that they have inherited or that they possess from their labor: and this is what he says, ***Where thou hast not sown***; this is contrary to the passage: "Every best gift and every perfect gift is from above, coming down from the Father of lights" (James 1, 17). Likewise, some men who suppose that God is a hard man, withdraw themselves from His service. Hence, some men, who can accomplish much, say: 'If I were to hear confessions and preach, perhaps something would not go well for me': such men repute God to be a hard man. Likewise, some men say: 'If I were to enter religion, perhaps I would sin, and it would be worse'; these men repute God to be hard, who believe that if they adhere to God, He would fail them. Such men are similar to those who despair of God's mercy. This servant was alleging these things. And, nevertheless, these things are true, and they have support from Scripture. For God is a hard man with sinners, and kindhearted to those having recourse to Him; "For thou didst admonish and try them as a father: but the others, as a severe king, thou didst examine and condemn" (Wis. 11, 11); "The Lord who is good will show mercy, to all them, who with their whole heart, seek the Lord the God of their fathers" (II Par. 30, 19). Therefore, He is hard with sinners and merciful to the good. And there is no doubt that He ought to be feared lest He be despised; hence, it is said: "It is a fearful thing to fall into the hands of the living God" (Heb. 10, 31). But insofar as He is merciful, we ought to hope that if someone gives himself to His service that he will not fall; and if he should fall, he shall rise again. Likewise, what he says, **Thou reapest where thou hast not sown**, although it is false, nevertheless, in a certain sense it can be true; because He does not demand for His own sake but for our utility; because He Himself reaps His glory which He has not sown. Similarly, **Thou gatherest where thou hast not strewed**. For he who reaps collects many things; he, however, who gathers, takes from many things. So the Lord wishes that His glory increase from various men. Hence, the Apostle says: "We are your glory: as you also are ours, in the day of our Lord Jesus Christ" (II Cor. 1, 14). Likewise, what he says, **Thou reapest where thou hast not sown**, is true in a certain respect, because man sows and God gathers; "It is one man that soweth, and it is another that reapeth. I have sent you to reap that in which you did not labor" (Jn. 4, 37-38). For man sows his works and God gathers them for His own glory; "What things a man shall sow, those also shall he reap" (Gal. 6, 8). And the Lord says: "I will come again and will take you to myself" (Jn. 14, 3). For if you give alms, you sow and the Lord reaps, perhaps because He considers it done to Himself. Hence, He says further on in this chapter: "What you did to one of these my least brethren, you did it to me" (verse 40). Moreover, as it was said above,

"The seed is the word of God" (chap. 13).[16] Hence, sometimes God gathers the fruits of a good work when preaching was not sown; "Men who do not have the law, are a law to themselves" (Heb. 2, 14). God gathers fruit in a third way, namely, certain evils come to be from man, such as evils of the flesh, from which an evil ought to be gathered. Concerning which it is said: "He that soweth in his flesh of the flesh also shall reap corruption" (Gal. 6, 8). Nevertheless, God turns it into something good, such as the good of justice, humility and suchlike; hence, this servant was firstly a blasphemer. Then his negligence is mentioned, where it is said, *Being afraid, I went*; "There have they trembled for fear, where there was no fear" (Ps. 13, 5). It is true that God ought to be feared, so that sin might be avoided, according to what is written: "For I have always feared God as waves swelling over me" (Job 31, 23). Hence, because a man fears God he does not sin, and this he ought to do out of love and not out of fear. Therefore, he continues: *I hid thy talent in the earth*, and he did this out of fear: for servile fear does many evil things. Then he concludes; *Behold here thou hast that which is thine.* Hence, he conserves his knowledge, but he does not multiply it. And this is not sufficient, because one ought to multiply it; "If I preach not the gospel, it is no glory to me" (I Cor. 9, 16).

And his lord answering, said to him. Here the condemnation of the servant is related. And just as with the other servants He firstly commended them, then He pointed out the fairness of the judgment, and, afterwards, He indicated the reward; so with this man, He firstly reproaches him; secondly, He points out the fairness of the judgment; and thirdly, He indicates the punishment. The second part is where it is said, *Thou knewest that I reap where I sow not*, etc.; the third part is where it is said, *Take ye away therefore the talent from him.* He says, therefore: *Wicked and slothful servant.* He calls him a servant because he deserted Him on account of fear, and it belongs to servants to serve servilely. And hence, it is said: "You have not received the spirit of bondage again in fear" (Rom. 8, 15). Likewise, He calls him a wicked servant, because he had said something wicked about his master; "An evil man out of an evil treasure bringeth forth evil things" (above 12, 35). Likewise, He calls him slothful, because he did not work; "Because of the cold the sluggard would not plough" (Prov. 20, 4), that is to say, on account of the cold of fear. *Thou knewest that I reap where I sow not*, etc. Now he rebukes him

---

16. cf. Lk. 8, 11.

concerning his guilt. And firstly, He points out that he knew; secondly, He points out what he ought to have done; and thirdly, He says what follows from this. He says, therefore: ***Thou knewest that I reap where I sow not***, and, nevertheless, you were not working, even though the passage may be cited: "The servant, who knows the will of his lord and does not do it, shall be beaten with many stripes" (Lk. 12, 47). Likewise, he had said that He was a hard man and that He gathered where He had not sown. The Lord admits that He gathers where He has not sown, but He does not admit that He is a hard man, because in regard to the fact that He requires something of the man, He does not do this on account of hardness but on account of His mercy, such that His good may be multiplied. ***Thou oughtest therefore to have committed my money to the bankers.*** And He continues: 'It is as you say, that I reap where I sow not, and I gather where I have not strewn. But because I do these things, all the more do I want that my money be multiplied.' And He is speaking according to a comparison with those men who exchange money to multiply it. This money is God's words: hence, in the Greek it is *argyreon*: for by *argentum*,[17] which is the metal of sounds, is signified God's word; "The words of the Lord are pure words: as silver tried by the fire" (Ps. 11, 7). Men can be called bankers in two ways on account of their twofold duties, namely, they have the responsibility to check whether the money is good: likewise, they are responsible that the money consigned to them yields a profit. In relation to the first duty, the bankers are hearers who ought to prove what they hear; "Doth not the ear discern words" (Job 12, 11). Likewise, they who multiply money are the men, such as the Apostles, who gave the gifts of the Holy Ghost by ordaining bishops, etc., "For this cause I left thee in Crete: that thou shouldest ordain priests in every city," etc., (Tit. 1, 5).

And at my coming I should have received my own. Hence, this good might result. But what is this good? This good is threefold. When the Lord gives you understanding, and you try to exercise it, you multiply it: "Be ye doers of the word and not hearers only" (James 1, 22). Likewise, when the Lord gives you virtue, and you try to use it well, you multiply it; "As newborn babes, desire the rational milk without guile, that thereby you may grow unto salvation" (I Pet. 2, 2). Similarly, when you try to give to others what you have in yourself, you multiply it.

Afterwards, He relates the punishment: and about this, He does two things. Firstly, He relates the pain of loss; and secondly,

---

17. *Argentum* means silver in Latin.

He relates the pain of sense. About the first pain, He firstly relates the pain of loss; and then makes a general declaration, where it is said, *For to every one that hath shall be given, and he shall abound.* He says, therefore: *Take ye away therefore the talent from him and give it him that hath ten talents.* As Gregory says, he who had received five talents is he who has knowledge of earthly things, which come under the five senses; he, however, who had received one talent, is he who has understanding without works. It happens, therefore, that he who has understanding, applies himself to it; "By thy commandments I have had understanding: therefore have I hated every way of iniquity" (Ps. 118, 104). On the other hand, it sometimes happens that a man has the gift of understanding and occupies himself with earthly things, and so loses everything; "Hold fast that which thou hast, that no man take thy crown" (Apoc. 3, 11). Or it can be said that he who receives five talents, receives more: and in that He labored more, he receives more. Hence, one man receives the talent of another, because a holy man not only rejoices over his own good deeds but over all good deeds which are done by anyone, and so he receives the crown of the latter servant and also he receives his talent.

Afterwards, the general declaration is related: *For to every one that hath shall be given, and he shall abound.* This passage can be expounded in four ways. Firstly, it can be expounded thus, according to Gregory: 'From a man who does not have, one cannot take something away from him; but it happens that a man has gratuitous gifts but does not have charity; hence, all his gifts will be taken away from him because he does not possess them for his utility; "If I speak with the tongues of men and of angels, and have not charity, I am become as sounding brass, or a tinkling cymbal" (I Cor. 13, 1). Hence, if a man has charity many good things are given to him, because he will receive the good of another man, because he will rejoice about the good of another man as about his own good.' Chrysostom expounds this passage as relating to doctrine: 'He who has the role of teaching and does not apply himself to it, loses it. On the other hand, he who does not have the role of teaching and applies himself to it, acquires it so that he becomes a teacher.' Jerome expounds this as follows: 'If a man has intelligence and gives himself to idleness, he is made ignorant and dull; however, a man who does not have intelligence, and applies himself, also acquires intelligence; and to the one who has a desire, knowledge and intelligence are given; and to the one who does not have a desire, also that which he has, namely, intelligence, will be taken away from him.' Likewise, according to Jerome, the passage may be expounded concerning faith, because to a man having faith, grace will be given; "By grace you are saved through faith" (Eph. 2, 8). Hence, he who does not have faith, even if he has other gifts, will avail nothing without faith. Hilary, however, expounds this passage as relating to the Jewish and Gentile nations, because the Jews seemed to have God's Law and did not want to obey, hence, they were made foreigners; the Gentile nations, however, received what they did not have, and they entered into the blessing of the olive tree.[18]

Subsequently, He treats of the pain of sense. Now there are two [primary] senses, namely, sight and touch.[19] Therefore, He relates firstly the punishment of sight, when He says; *And the unprofitable servant, cast ye out into the exterior darkness.* But note that He is not punished for the evil that he did, but on account of the good that he omitted; hence, it is written above: "Every tree that bringeth not forth good fruit, shall be cut down" (7, 19). And elsewhere it is written: "Every branch in me, that beareth not fruit, he will take away" (Jn. 15, 2). And he is called an unprofitable servant, because the good that he has, he does not use for others' benefit: for example, if he had understanding, he does not put it to good use by teaching others; and if he had money, he did not perform works of mercy. *Cast ye out into the exterior darkness.* Origen says that certain men before him had said that the damned will be cast out of the whole world. And they based their opinion upon what Job said: "He shall remove him out of the world" (Job 18, 18). *Into the darkness*, because he was ignorant; "They have not known nor understood: they walk on in darkness" (Ps. 81, 5). And the pain of touch follows: *There shall be weeping and gnashing of teeth.* This was expounded above in Chapter 24.[20]

31. And when the Son of man shall come in his majesty, and all the angels with him, then shall he sit upon the seat of his majesty.

32. And all nations shall be gathered together before him: and he shall separate them one from another, as the shepherd separateth the sheep from the goats:

33. And he shall set the sheep on his right hand, but the goats on his left.

---

18. cf. Rom. 11, 17: "And if some of the branches be broken and thou, being a wild olive, art ingrafted in them and art made partaker of the root and of the fatness of the olive tree."

19. These are the two most principal senses. "Sight... is the most spiritual, the most perfect, and the most universal of all the senses" (I, q. 78, a. 3). "The primary form of sense is touch, which belongs to all animals" (Aristotle, *De Anima* II, 2)

20. cf. verse 51.

34. Then shall the king say to them that shall be on his right hand: Come, ye blessed of my Father, possess you the kingdom prepared for you from the foundation of the world.

35. For I was hungry, and you gave me to eat: I was thirsty, and you gave me to drink: I was a stranger, and you took me in:

36. Naked, and you covered me: sick, and you visited me: I was in prison, and you came to me.

37. Then shall the just answer him, saying: Lord, when did we see thee hungry and fed thee: thirsty and gave thee drink?

38. Or when did we see thee a stranger and took thee in? Or naked and covered thee?

39. Or when did we see thee sick or in prison and came to thee?

40. And the king answering shall say to them: Amen I say to you, as long as you did it to one of these my least brethren, you did it to me.

41. Then he shall say to them also that shall be on his left hand: Depart from me, you cursed, into everlasting fire, which was prepared for the devil and his angels.

42. For I was hungry and you gave me not to eat: I was thirsty and you gave me not to drink.

43. I was a stranger and you took me not in: naked and you covered me not: sick and in prison and you did not visit me.

44. Then they also shall answer him, saying: Lord, when did we see thee hungry or thirsty or a stranger or naked or sick or in prison and did not minister to thee?

45. Then he shall answer them, saying: Amen: I say to you, as long as you did it not to one of these least, neither did you do it to me.

46. And these shall go into everlasting punishment: but the just, into life everlasting.

Above, the Lord premised different parables pertaining to the Judgment; here, however, He openly treats about His Judgment; and He does three things. Firstly, He treats of the coming of the Judge; secondly, He treats of the gathering of those to be judged; and thirdly, He treats of the Judgment itself. The second part is where it is said, *And all nations shall be gathered together before him*; and the third part is where it is said, *And the king shall say*, etc. About the first part, four things ought to be considered. Firstly, the condition of the coming Judge is mentioned; secondly, His dignity is considered; thirdly, His ministers are considered; and fourthly, His judicial authority is considered. When it is said, *When the Son of man shall come*, there is no doubt that this is none other than the Son of God.

But why does He call Him the Son of man rather than the Son of God? One reason is that He will judge insofar as He is the Son of man; "He hath given him power to do judgment, because he is the Son of man" (Jn. 5, 27). And He does this for three reasons. Firstly, He does this so that He might be seen by all men: for by an appearance of His divinity He would not be able to be seen except by the good. Hence, if He ought to be seen by all, He ought to be seen in the form of a man. "Every eye shall see him" (Apoc. 1, 7). Likewise, this will be done on account of Christ's merits: for He merited this by His Passion: "He humbled himself, becoming obedient unto death, even to the death of the cross. For which cause, God also hath exalted him" (Phil. 2, 8-9). Similarly, this will be done so that when He is about to judge He may appear in the same form in which He was judged; "O that a man might so be judged with God, as the son of man is judged with his companion" (Job 16, 22). Furthermore, He will judge as man due to God's clemency, so that men may be judged by a man; "We have not a high priest who cannot have compassion on our infirmities" (Heb. 4, 15). Therefore, He will be the Judge as the Son of man.

And of what dignity will He be? He will come *in his majesty*; "They shall see the Son of man coming in a cloud, with great power and majesty" (Lk. 21, 27). But what can be understood by His majesty? It ought to be said that it is His divinity, because even though He will appear in the form of a man, He will appear with His divinity. Hence, the Apostle says: "The Lord himself shall come down from heaven with commandment and with the voice of an archangel and with the trumpet of God" (I Thess. 4, 15). And this is also said in chapter 9 of the Acts of the Apostles.[21] Or 'in his majesty' means in His glory, because His body will be glorious; and He will come with glorious company; hence, it is said above, "The Son of man shall come in the glory" (15, 27). And hence, He adds; *And all the angels with him*. Here, He treats of His ministers. And it can be understood of the heavenly spirits: "Who makest thy

---

21. If the reference of Act 9 is correct, it seems to refer to the glorious appearance of Our Lord to St. Paul at his conversion. But in III, q. 90, a. 2, St. Thomas quotes: "Then they shall see the Son of man coming in a cloud with great power and majesty" (Luke 21:27) as a Scriptural proof of Christ's coming in His glorified humanity.

angels spirits" (Ps. 103, 4). And why will He come with them? It is because they are the guardians of men; "He hath given his angels charge over thee" (Ps. 90, 11). Therefore, they will come as witnesses, because the good men received their guardianship, the wicked, however, did not, but rather rejected it; "We would have cured Babylon, but she is not healed" (Jer. 51, 9). Or it is said, *all the angels*, meaning the preachers, or teachers of the truth; "The lips of the priests shall keep knowledge, and they shall seek the law at his mouth" (Mal. 2, 7). To them belongs judicial power, as Augustine says. "The Lord will enter into judgment and all his saints with him" (Is. 3, 14);[22] "Her husband is honorable in the gates, when he sitteth among the senators of the land" (Prov. 31, 23). Then His judicial power follows: *Then shall he sit upon the seat of his majesty.* We ought not to understand these words as referring to a physical seat; but rather men and angels are His seat. He will sit upon them, because He will exercise His Judgment through them. Concerning men, it is said above in chapter 19, that they will sit upon twelve seats, etc.[23] Concerning the angels, it is said: "Whether thrones, or dominations," etc.; and in Psalm 79 it is said: "Thou sittest upon the cherubims" (verse 2); and "Thou hast sat on the throne, who judgest justice" (Ps. 9, 5).

Afterwards, the gathering of those to be judged is related; and secondly, their division is related. He says, therefore: *And all nations shall be gathered together.* By nations, not only the nations are signified, but all men who were born from Adam until the end of the world; "We must all be manifested before the judgment seat of Christ, that every one may receive the proper things of the body, according as he hath done, whether it be good or evil" (II Cor. 5, 10). The little children who have been born are also among them, because even if they have nothing by their own merit, nevertheless, they have something, namely, the guilt from the first man or grace from Christ's sacraments.

Hence, it ought to be noted that not all these men will be gathered together to the same place; but there will be four categories of those who will be present at the Judgment. For some men will be present so that they may be judged by an evaluation of their merits; and of these some will be damned, others will be saved. But others will receive their sentence without any evaluation. For 'to be judged' can mean two things: namely, either to receive one's

---

22. The second part of this verse, instead of the words of Isaias: "with the ancients of his people, and its princes," is taken from the third antiphon of the Vespers of first Sunday of Advent.

23. "When the Son of man shall sit on the seat of his majesty, you also shall sit on twelve seats judging the twelve tribes of Israel" (verse28).

sentence, because all will either be rewarded or punished: or when it is said 'to be judged' it can mean a giving of the reason for one's sentence by an evaluation of one's merits. And this evaluation will not be needed for everyone, because the sins and merits will especially be evaluated of those who were joined to Christ through faith: for those who are completely unassociated with Christ will not need an evaluation, according to what is said in John 3, 18: "He that doth not believe is already judged." Gregory gives an example: 'He who welcomes his enemy during war does not expect a judgment, but is already judged: in like manner, etc.' Similarly, there are some men who have nothing in common with the world because they have left all things for Christ's sake, and these men will appear as judges; hence: "You who have followed me, shall sit on twelve seats judging the twelve tribes of Israel" (above 19, 28). Therefore, who are they who will be judged? It will be the faithful who were involved with temporal things, of whom some have used them well, as it is written: "Charge the rich to do good, to be rich in good work, to give easily, to communicate to others," etc., (I Tim. 6, 18). Those, however, who are held back, and entangled by them, will be damned.

But what is the need for the Judgment? Does not everyone receive what he deserves at his death? Why, then, will they be judged? It ought to be observed that the reward which is given to men according to God's just judgment is twofold: the first reward is the stole of the soul and the second is the stole of the body.[24] Regarding the stole of the soul, it is received at death, but later at the Judgment they shall also receive the glory of the body. Hence, regarding the soul, all the souls will receive their bodies at the same time, but as to the punishment of the bodies of the damned, their bodies shall all be damned at the same time; hence: "They shall be gathered together as in the gathering of one bundle" (Is. 24, 22), because they are one in sin. We can take this gathering to be a gathering in reference to place, because all will be gathered into one place; "I will gather together all nations and will bring them down into the valley of Josaphat" (Joel 3, 2); because those who are saved will be saved through Christ's Passion, those who are damned, are damned through contempt of His Passion; for that reason, the place where Christ's Passion occurred, there shall the Judgment take place. And it ought to be understood that

---

24. "'He shall be clothed,' as it is said, 'in white garments,' namely, the stole of the body. Note concerning the stole of the soul and of the body. The stole of the soul is woven out of three threads: namely, the direct vision, consummated love, and the secure apprehension of God. The stole of the body is woven out of four threads: namely, brilliance, agility, subtility, and impassibility." (Hugh of St-Cher, Exposition of Apocalypse, chap. 3).

the good will come to meet Him in the air; but some men will remain on earth, according to Origen. This gathering will not be in reference to a place, but they will be scattered, and gathered together in different places: and this corresponds with that which was said above, namely: "As lightning cometh out of the east and appeareth even into the west: so shall also the coming of the Son of man be" (24, 27), they shall be everywhere that they are located. Hence, He wants there to be a spiritual gathering, because now some are scattered away from Him, but others keep themselves with Him; but then all will be gathered together; "All flesh together shall see the salvation of our God" (Is. 40, 5).[25]

Then He treats of the separation of those judged: *And he shall separate them one from another, as the shepherd separateth the sheep from the goats.* Firstly, the separation is portrayed according to the names of those judged; and secondly, it is portrayed according to the places of those judged, where it is said, *And he shall set the sheep on his right hand*, etc. He says, therefore: *And he shall separate them one from another.*

Observe that while the world lasts, the wicked are mixed together with the good. There is hardly any group of men in which there are not some evil men; "As the lily among thorns, so is my love among the daughters" (Cant. 2, 2). But in that Judgment, the wicked will be in one place and the good in another; "He shall judge between the sheep and the goats."[26]

But why does He call the good men sheep? This is on account of four things. For we find in sheep innocence; "These that are the sheep, what have they done?" (II Kings 24, 17). Similarly, we find in sheep patience; "He shall be led as a sheep to the slaughter, and shall be dumb as a lamb before his shearer, and he shall not open his mouth" (Is. 53, 7). Likewise: "We are counted as sheep for the slaughter" (Ps. 43, 22). Moreover, we find in sheep obedience, because they are gathered by the shepherd's voice; "My sheep hear my voice" (Jn. 10, 27). Again, we find in sheep an abundance of products: as we perceive many products from sheep, so there are many fruits of good men; "You ate the milk, and you clothed yourselves with the wool" (Ez. 34, 3). Likewise, by goats He means sinners, because it is an animal that moves headlong, and, similarly, it is avid for intercourse; and it has the opposite properties of sheep; moreover, it was offered for sin.

---

25. This quotation has been combined with Is. 52:10: "All the ends of the earth shall see the salvation of our God."
26. The reference given for this passage is Eccli. 35, but Ez. 34, 17 seems more appropriate, "And as for you, O my flocks, thus saith the Lord God: Behold I judge between cattle and cattle, of rams and of he goats."

Afterwards, the division as to the position is related: *And he shall set the sheep on his right hand, but the goats on his left.* What is understood by the right hand, and what by the left? It can be said that it will literally take place in this manner, because the good will be placed on one side and the wicked on the other. Or it can be said that the right hand is more noble, wherefore, those who are good will have a more noble place, because they shall go to meet Christ in the air. Origen refers this to the final reward; because those who have directed their intention to God will be on the right hand, meaning they share in the eternal reward; "The heart of a wise man is in his right hand, and the heart of a fool is in his left hand" (Eccle. 10, 2). Likewise: "The Lord knoweth the ways that are on the right hand: but those are perverse which are on the left hand" (Prov. 4, 27).

Then shall the king say to them that shall be on his right hand, etc. Here it is treated concerning the Judgment. Firstly, the sentence in regard to the good is pronounced; secondly, the sentence in regard to the wicked is pronounced; and thirdly, He relates the completion of the Judgment. About the first part, He does three things. Firstly, the sentence is related; secondly, the astonishment of those saved is related; and thirdly, His explanation is related. The second part is where it is said, *Then shall the just answer him*; and the third part is where it is said, *The king answering shall say to them*. About the first, He does two things. Firstly, He invites the good to their reward; secondly, He compares their reward to their merit. He says, therefore: *Then shall the king say*. And He calls Himself a king, because it belongs to a king to judge; "The king, that sitteth on the throne of judgment, scattereth away all evil with his look" (Prov. 20, 8).

But there is a question. Will the Judgment occur by a vocal sentence? Some say that it will occur by a vocal sentence, just as the words of this passage indicate, and that the Judgment will take a long time; and Lactantius said that it will last for a thousand years.[27] But this is not true; but this ought to be referred to an interior speech; and He is putting before the minds of men that the good are deserving of glory, and the wicked are deserving of punishment. Hence, what these men say will not be vocal, but according to an interior prompting; and Augustine says this, namely, it will happen by Divine power that it will occur to everyone what he did. And this is evident from the words of the Apostle: "Their conscience bearing witness to them: and their

---

27. Lactantius was a Christian lay apologist of the fourth century and was a Latin tutor for Crispus, a son of Constantine

thoughts between themselves accusing or also defending one another, in the day when the Lord shall judge the secrets of men" (Rom. 2, 15-16). Therefore, these words ought to be referred to an interior speech.

And it is evident that He mentions three things, namely, the invitation is related, the reason for the sentence is related, and the reward itself is related. The invitation is related where it is said: *Come, ye blessed of my Father.*

But why does He say, *Blessed of my Father*? It is because the invitation will not be according to our merits, but according to the fact that we are strengthened by Christ's merits; hence: "To him that shall overcome, I will give to sit with me in my throne: as I also have overcome and am set down with my Father in his throne" (Apoc. 3, 21); "Behold I dispose to you, as my Father hath disposed to me, a kingdom" (Lk. 22, 29). 'I, inasmuch as I am a man, so much do I enjoy the Word.' It is likewise as regards the body; "Who will reform the body of our lowness, made like to the body of his glory" (Phil. 3, 21). *Come*, meaning 'be conformed'; "When he shall appear we shall be like to him" (I Jn. 3, 2).

But why are the good not now joined to God? I say that they are joined to God by an incomplete charity. Similarly, they are joined to God by a dark faith; but then they shall be gathered together in a full charity, and in a faith that is not dark;[28] because "The corruptible body is a load upon the soul, and the earthly habitation presseth down the mind that museth upon many things" (Wis. 9, 15).

The reason for this reward is twofold: the cause of damnation is from man, and the cause of salvation is from God; "Destruction is thy own, O Israel: thy help is only in me" (Osee 13, 9). Hence, we find the cause of temporal and eternal salvation: temporal salvation is the adding of glory; and this is mentioned when it is said, *Come, ye blessed of my Father.* When the Lord says one is His, He makes one His; hence: "He spoke and they were made" (Ps. 32, 9). Hence, His blessing is to infuse grace; hence, He says, *Of my Father*, because He is not from us but from God; "Every best gift and every perfect gift is from above, coming down from the Father of lights" (James 1, 17). Likewise, the other cause is Divine predestination; and this is indicated

---

28. The blessed in heaven no longer have any faith as it is replaced by the clear vision of God. The "faith that is not dark" mentioned here, is strictly not faith at all since faith necessarily is dark by its nature. For even Adam's faith was dark. "[Adam] did not have such clear knowledge that it sufficed to remove the darkness of faith, which is only removed by the fact that the first Truth becomes apparent" (*Qu. Disp. de Veritate*, q. 18, a. 3 ad 1um").

when He says, ***The kingdom prepared for you***. Hence, the Apostle says: "Whom he predestinated, them he also called" (Rom. 8, 30); "Eye hath not seen, nor ear heard: neither hath it entered into the heart of man, what things God hath prepared for them that love him" (I Cor. 2, 9).

And He says, ***From the foundation of the world***, but how is this? Has He not chosen them from eternity? "He chose us in him before the foundation of the world" (Eph. 1, 4). And it ought to be said that He chose them from eternity, but He manifested them from the foundation of the world.

But what is the reward that He mentions: ***Possess you the kingdom prepared for you***? This kingdom is the kingdom of heaven; "Thy kingdom is a kingdom of all ages" (Ps. 144, 13). He who possesses God possesses a kingdom; "And hast made us to our God a kingdom and priests" (Apoc. 5, 11).

And He says, ***Possess***, meaning 'enter into possession'. Now to enter into possession properly belongs to him who had a right to possess; now this right we have by divine ordination. Likewise, we have this right by Christ's acquisition, who acquired this for us. Likewise, we have this by His grace; "Who is the pledge of our inheritance" (Eph. 1, 14). Similarly, what is owned peacefully is called a possession; hence, full ownership is signified. Now we possess God but not tranquilly, because man is disquieted in many ways; but, hereafter, there will be the tranquil possession of God; "Unto this are you called, that you may inherit a blessing" (I Pet. 3, 9); "He shall possess life everlasting" (above 19, 29).

For I was hungry, and you gave me to eat, etc. Above, the sentence of the reward was related, and here it is related concerning the meriting of the reward. From which we ought to consider that there is a twofold cause of beatitude: one cause is on the part of God, that is to say, God's blessing; the other is on our part, meaning our merit which is from our free will: for men ought not to be lazy but cooperate with God's grace, as it is said: "By the grace of God, I am what I am. And his grace in me hath not been void" (I Cor. 15, 10).

But although there are many good and meritorious works, He only mentions the works of mercy. And on account of this, some men took occasion of erring, saying that they are saved only through works of mercy, or they are damned through their omission; so that if someone committed many sins and applied himself to the works of mercy, he will be saved, according to that which is written: "Redeem thou thy sins with alms, and thy iniquities with works of mercy to the poor" (Dan. 4, 24); and this is contrary to that which is stated: "They who do such things," namely sins, "are worthy of death" (Rom. 1, 32). And in Galatians 5, 6, the Apostle, after an enumeration of the sins of the flesh, says: "They who do such things shall not obtain the kingdom of God." Wherefore, this opinion ought not to be held. But it can be that someone abstains, repents, and in this way through alms, can be freed from his sins: for a man ought to begin from himself the almsdeeds; "Have pity on thy own soul, pleasing God" (Ps. 30, 24).

Then why is there more mention of these works than of the others? It ought to be said, according to Gregory, that He sets forth these as lesser works: for if they do not do these works, which nature suggests, nor will they do other, much greater, works. And this is consonant with the words of the Gospel, because these men say: *When did we see thee hungry and fed thee*, etc.?; as though they were to say: 'This work is very small.' And since they repute the work to be smaller than it is,[29] the Lord extols it more saying: *What you did to one of these my least brethren, you did it to me.* Augustine says that every man in the world sins, yet not all are damned; but he is damned who does not repent, and does not make satisfaction for his sins. But he who repents and promises to make satisfaction through works of mercy, is saved. Origen says that under the works of mercy all good works are said or they are omitted in order to omit works of the same kind. And it is signified that alms not only are done for one's neighbor, but also to oneself: for if someone feeds a hungry man, much more ought he feed himself when he is hungry, and, in like manner, concerning the other works. Likewise, not only are there corporal alms, but also spiritual alms; for that reason, whatever a man does either for his own benefit or for the benefit of his neighbor, all are included by the works of mercy. Hence, all works are included either under these works or under their contrary works. There are seven works of mercy, but only six are mentioned. These seven works are found in this verse:

Visito, poto, cibo, redimo, tego, colligo, condo.[30]

---

29. "ORIGEN; Mark how the righteous dwell upon each word, while the unrighteous answer summarily, and not going through the particular instances; for so it becomes the righteous out of humility to disclaim each individual generous action, when imputed to them publicly; whereas bad men excuse their sins, and endeavor to prove them few and venial. And Christ's answer conveys this. And to the righteous He says, In that you did it to my brethren, to show the greatness of their good deeds; to the sinners He says only, to one of the least of these, not aggravating their sin" (*Catena Aurea on St. Matthew*, chap. 25, lect. 3).

30. "To visit, to quench, to feed, to ransom, clothe, harbor or bury."

But there is no mention here of burial. Why? It is to exclude the error of those who said that souls do not obtain rest until their bodies are buried. But this is not true, because the soul receives nothing from the body when it is separated from the body. Therefore, He gives six works of mercy which are bestowed to remedy some need. And because certain needs are general, others are particular, firstly, He treats of the general needs, and secondly, of the particular needs. And because some general needs are from without and others from within, He firstly mentions interior needs; and secondly, He mentions exterior needs. He says, therefore: *I was hungry, and you gave me to eat*. This is stated in Isaias 58, 7: "Deal thy bread to the hungry."

I was thirsty, and you gave me to drink, because, on account of Me, you gave to your neighbor. Hence: "He who shall give to drink to one of these little ones a cup of cold water, he shall not lose his reward" (above 10, 42). Concerning these two works of mercy, it is said: "If thy enemy be hungry, give him to eat: if he thirst, give him water to drink" (Prov. 25, 21). Likewise, there are wants from without, and these are two, namely, one connected with clothing and another not connected with clothing. He says therefore: *I was a stranger, and you took me in*. "Hospitality do not forget: for by this some, being not aware of it, have entertained angels" (Heb. 13, 2). As to the work of mercy connected with clothing, He says: I was *naked, and you covered me*; "If I have despised him that was perishing for want of clothing": and the passage continues, "If his sides have not blessed me, and if he were not warmed with the fleece of my sheep" (Job 31, 19-20); "When thou shalt see one naked, cover him" (Is. 58, 7). Likewise, there are particular natural needs; and some of these are interior and others are exterior. A natural need that is also interior is sickness; hence, He says: I was *sick, and you visited me*. As to an exterior need, He says: *I was in prison, and you came to me*. And by prison any tribulation can be understood; "You also had compassion on them that were in bands" (Heb. 10, 34).

Then shall the just answer him, saying. Here a mental answer is related. It is characteristic of good souls to consider the things that they do for God to be little; "When you shall have done all these things that are commanded you, say: We are unprofitable servants" (Lk. 17, 10). And, "I reckon that the sufferings of this time are not worthy to be compared with the glory to come that shall be revealed in us" (Rom. 8, 18). Hence, they say that they acted unknowingly; and they, considering their works to be small, will say these things; hence: *When did we see thee hungry and thirsty*, etc.? Wherefore, being astonished, they will say these things.

And the king answering shall say to them. He appeases their astonishment, for when a man humbles himself, God also exalts this man; when a man belittles himself, God in turn praises him; hence: *As long as you did it to one of these my least brethren, you did it to me*; "He that receiveth you, receiveth me" (above 10, 40), because the head and the members are one body. And He says, *brethren*, because they are brothers who do God's will; hence, it is said above that stretching forth His hands He said: "These are my brethren" (above 12, 48).[31] And it ought to be observed that the alms are given to good men; "Give to the good, and receive not a sinner" (Eccli. 12, 5).

And should one never give to a sinner? Alms ought to be given to him, when he shall be in extreme need, but rather one ought to give firstly to just men; wherefore, He says, *my brethren*; for many come who are not God's brethren; hence: "Every spirit that dissolveth Jesus is not of God" (I Jn. 4, 3): hence, other things being equal, it is better that we give alms to the good; nevertheless, one ought to give to the wicked for their needs in a time of necessity, not on account of an alleviation of sin, but on account of an alleviation of nature. Are not all men God's brethren? Indeed; but some men are His brethren by nature, others by grace: by nature, all men, good and evil, are God's brethren; "Peril from false brethren" (II Cor. 11, 26); by grace, only good men are God's brethren; "He is the Firstborn amongst many brethren" (Rom. 8, 29). And one ought to primarily pity and help these men; hence, the Apostle says: "Let us work good to all men, but especially to those who are of the household of the faith" (Gal. 6, 10).

But why does He call them the least? He says this in relation to what people think. It is well known that men who are little for God's sake are considered to be the least of men; "Thou hast hid these things from the wise and prudent, and hast revealed them to little ones" (Mt. 11, 25). And He is speaking of the least because some men might say: 'If I had done this to someone equal to myself, or to some of the great men, I reckon that this would be done to Him.' For that reason, the Lord says that not only what is done to great men, but also to imperfect men, is done to Him; for that reason, He says, *To the least.*

Then he shall say to them also that shall be on his left hand. Here the condemnation of the wicked is related. And firstly, their condemnation is related; secondly, their excuse is related; and thirdly, the confounding of their excuse is related. And about

---

31. cf. Lk. 8, 21.

the first point, He begins by relating the sentence; and secondly, He relates their punishment. He says, therefore: *Depart from me, you cursed*. This sentence differs from the first, because He said in the first sentence: *Come, ye blessed of my Father*, etc.; here, however, He does not say: 'Ye cursed of My Father,' because our blessing is from God, our cursing, however, is from ourselves. And in Hebrews 6[32] and Deuteronomy 23[33] He turns a blessing into a curse. Likewise, a difference is that above He said: *Possess you the kingdom prepared for you*, etc., here, however, He says: *Depart into everlasting fire, which was prepared for the devil and his angels*. And what is the reason? Origen says that He did not make punishments for men, but instead He made men for something good; but they acquired death for themselves by their own hands; "In that day a man shall cast away his idols of silver, and his idols of gold, which your hands have made for you" (Is. 31, 7).

But someone might say: 'Did not the Lord make something good for the devil?' Note that the Lord speaks of preparation as it was shown from the beginning of the world. But the devil sinned from the beginning: hence, He did not prepare punishments for the angels, who, as to their nature, were created good, but for their sins.

I was hungry. Here nothing else is said but what is spoken in different ways to the good and to the wicked: for above, He explicitly said every single thing by itself, but here He joins many things together; hence, I was *sick and in prison*. And because He joins these two things together, it ought to be said that He proceeds after the manner of a good judge, who condemns unwillingly, and rewards abundantly: hence, He lengthens the words of rewarding, but shortens the words of condemnation.

Then they also shall answer him. And note that just as the good shortened their words about their good deeds, so the wicked shortened their words about their faults; hence, they say: *Lord, when did we see thee hungry or thirsty*, etc.? They say all these things together; in which it is given to be understood that they do not willingly examine their consciences, and this is opposed to that which is written: "Return, ye transgressors, to the heart" (Is. 46, 8). Hence, when they must return, they return to their hearts very briefly.

---

32. "For the earth, that drinketh in the rain which cometh often upon it and bringeth forth herbs meet for them by whom it is tilled, receiveth blessing from God. But that which bringeth forth thorns and briers is reprobate and very near unto a curse: whose end is to be burnt" (verses 7-8).

33. "The Lord thy God would not hear Balaam, and he turned his cursing into thy blessing, because he loved thee" (verse 5).

Then their confounding follows: *Amen: I say to you, as long as you did it not*, etc. Something similar is written: "He that despiseth you despiseth me" (Lk. 10, 16); "He that toucheth you, toucheth the apple of my eye" (Zach. 2, 8).

And these shall go into everlasting punishment, etc. After relating the sentence, the effect is now related. *And these shall go into everlasting punishment.* Above, He had said that they shall go into eternal fire, because one might uphold that the fire would be eternal; but, nevertheless, one would not be tormented eternally; for that reason, He says, *Into everlasting punishment. But the just, into life everlasting*; "This is eternal life: That they may know thee, the only true God, and Jesus Christ, whom thou hast sent" (Jn. 17, 3). Now that there be eternal punishment is stated in Daniel 12, 2: "Many of those that sleep in the dust of the earth, shall awake: some unto life everlasting, and others unto reproach, to see it always"; "He was cast into the pool of fire and brimstone, where both the beast and the false prophet shall be tormented day and night for ever and ever" (Apoc. 20, 9-10); "Their worm shall not die, and their fire shall not be quenched" (Is. 66, 24).

What is the cause of this eternal punishment? Some men, such as Origen, held that there was no eternal punishment. Hence, they assert that every punishment has an end. Wherefore, he says that what is said here, is said as an exaggeration. But Augustine argues: "If this is so, then what is said, namely, that the just will go into eternal life, might similarly be said to be an exaggeration. But this is said in regard to length of time, as even Origen admits. And this is detestable, that in the same Scripture there be such diversity. But that this cannot be is evident from the following: it is evident that justice requires that an equal punishment correspond to the guilt. "With what measure you mete, it shall be measured to you again" (above 7, 2).

But how will eternal punishment have, after death, so long duration? Gregory answers, saying that God is the judge of the will; hence, he who does not restrain his will from sin until death, sinned in his eternity; thus it is fitting that God punish in His eternity.[34] Augustine speaks thus: 'We see that a punishment

---

34. "GREGORY; They say that He held out empty terrors to deter them from sin. We answer, if He threatened falsely to check unrighteousness, then He promised falsely to promote good conduct. Thus while they go out of the way to prove God merciful, they are not afraid to charge Him with fraud. But, they urge, finite sin ought not to be visited with infinite punishment; we answer, that this argument would be just, if the righteous Judge considered men's actions, and not their hearts. Therefore it belongs to the righteousness of an impartial Judge, that those whose heart would never be without sin in this life, should never be without punishment" (*Catena Aurea on St. Matthew*, chap. 25, lect. 4).

ought to be equal, and such is also in human justice, because if someone sin against the society of a city, a judge does not intend to inflict death, except to separate him perpetually from the society of the city. But he who sins against God, intends to exclude himself from the society of the heavenly court.' According to Hilary, punishment is due to guilt; but guilt is not effaced except through charity. Therefore, as long as a man does not have charity, it is just that he always be in eternal punishment. Therefore, from the fact that he did not have charity in this life, it is necessary that he always remain in eternal punishment.

Likewise, it is objected that the Saints will pray, and they will be heard. Therefore, etc. Gregory says that while they are wayfarers, the Saints are heard for them, but not afterwards.

Moreover, it is objected: 'God does not delight in punishment; how, therefore, will He afflict without end?' It ought to be said that even if He does not delight in it, nevertheless, He does this to conserve His justice.

CHAPTER TWENTY-SIX

1. And it came to pass, when Jesus had ended all these words, he said to his disciples:
2. You know that after two days shall be the pasch: and the Son of man shall be delivered up to be crucified.
3. Then were gathered together the chief priests and ancients of the people, into the court of the high priest, who was called Caiphas:
4. And they consulted together that by subtilty they might apprehend Jesus and put him to death.
5. But they said: Not on the festival day, lest perhaps there should be a tumult among the people.
6. And when Jesus was in Bethania, in the house of Simon the leper,
7. There came to him a woman having an alabaster box of precious ointment and poured it on his head as he was at table.
8. And the disciples seeing it had indignation, saying: To what purpose is this waste?
9. For this might have been sold for much and given to the poor.
10. And Jesus knowing it, said to them: Why do you trouble this woman? For she hath wrought a good work upon me.
11. For the poor you have always with you: but me you have not always.
12. For she in pouring this ointment on my body hath done it for my burial.
13. Amen I say to you, wheresoever this gospel shall be preached in the whole world, that also which she hath done shall be told for a memory of her.
14. Then went one of the twelve, who was called Judas Iscariot, to the chief priests,
15. And said to them: What will you give me, and I will deliver him unto you? But they appointed him thirty pieces of silver.
16. And from thenceforth he sought opportunity to betray him.

The Evangelist, having related the preparatory things for the Passion, here enters upon Christ's Passion; and it is divided into two parts. For firstly, the Passion is recounted insofar as the things done by the Jews; and secondly, it is recounted as to the things done by the Gentiles: "And when morning was come," etc., (chap. 27, 1). About the first part, he does two things. Firstly, the foretelling of the Lord's Passion is related; and secondly, the Passion and the order of events are related, where it is said, ***Then went one of the twelve***. The Passion is foretold in three ways: by Christ's words, by the plotting of his enemies, and thirdly, by an action and homage. The second part is where it is said, ***Then were gathered together the chief priests and ancients of the people***; and the third part is where it is said, ***And when Jesus was in Bethania***. About the first point, he firstly relates the order of the foretelling, and then the foretelling itself. He relates the foretelling, where it is said: ***And it came to pass, when Jesus had ended all these words***. And the Evangelist speaks thus, because Christ is the only one who can complete them.[1] We ourselves can begin but not complete, according to that which is written: "We say much, and yet want words" (Eccli. 43, 29). Likewise, he says, ***These words***, namely, the words which Jesus had said from the beginning of His preaching, among which Jesus had said, "Do penance, for the kingdom of heaven is at hand" (above 4, 17). Or he is referring to the words which He had said concerning the foretelling of glory, because His Passion was an exaltation of glory;[2] "For which cause, God also hath exalted him and hath given him a name which is above all names, that in the name of Jesus every knee should bow, of those that are in heaven, on earth, and under the earth, and that every tongue should confess that the Lord Jesus Christ is in the glory of God the Father" (Phil. 2, 9-11). Similarly, he does not merely say that Christ completed 'all His words,' but instead, ***all these words***, because He spoke everything that would be useful for believers and for the faith. ***You know that after two days shall be the pasch***. In this prediction, He does not merely predict the Pasch, but instead He says: ***After two days shall be the pasch***: and this was done to designate that Christ's Passion is not just any suffering, but one signified by the Paschal sacrifice. And He says, ***After two days***. And by this, you ought to consider that these words were spoken on the thirteenth day of the lunar month, that is to say, on Tuesday,[3] because on the fifteenth day the Pasch is celebrated, but it is stated in John 12

---

1. An equivalent translation of the passage would be, "When Jesus had completed (*consummasset*) all these things."

2. "He merited a fourfold exaltation from His Passion. First of all, as to His glorious Resurrection... Secondly, as to His ascension into heaven... Thirdly, as to the sitting on the right hand of the Father and the showing forth of His Godhead... Fourthly, as to His judiciary power...' (III, q. 49, a. 6).

3. "*Ye know, & c., after two days.* He said, therefore, these things on the Tuesday evening, when, after the Hebrew custom, the fourth day of the week, or Wednesday, was about to be-

that the Lord came to Bethany, and this was Saturday; and the next day He came to Jerusalem, and He then cast out the buyers and the sellers: and on the following day, He returned to Bethany, and then on that day He delivered these parables. And on that day, when He had ended all these words, He said: ***You know that after two days shall be the pasch.*** This name *Pascha*, according to what Jerome says, is derived from the word for feeding,[4] but more properly it is derived from the Phase [*Pasach*], which means Passover. Now there is a fourfold Passover, in that the Pasch may be understood in four ways. Historically, the Pasch was celebrated when the destroyer slew the firstborn of Egypt; then the Lord commanded that they eat the Pasch (Ex. 12). Likewise, allegorically, it is understood as Christ's passing away by death; and concerning this it is written: "Jesus knowing that his hour was come, that he should pass out of this world to the Father," etc., (Jn. 13, 1). Moreover, in the moral or typical sense, it is understood that one has passed from a worldly way of life to a spiritual way of life; "Come over to me, all ye that desire me" (Eccli. 24, 26). Again, there is a general passage, in that it is said that heaven and earth shall pass away, etc. Hence, it is said, ***after two days***, namely, after the teaching of the Old Law and of the New Law. In Greek, the word Pasch is derived from the word *pasqui*, which means to be driven to pasture: hence, Christ, suitably knowing that He would pass from the world to His Father, said: ***And the Son of man shall be delivered up to be crucified.*** He does not say by whom He shall be delivered up, because He was delivered up by His Father; "He spared not his own Son, but delivered him up for us all" (Rom. 8, 32). Likewise, He was delivered up by Himself; "He hath loved us and hath delivered himself for us," etc., (Eph. 5, 2). Similarly, He was delivered up by Judas; "What will you give me, and I will deliver him unto you?" (below, verse 15). Moreover, He was delivered up by the Jews to Pilate; "Thy own nation and the chief priests have delivered thee up to me" (Jn. 18, 35). Again, He was delivered up by Pilate to the Gentiles; hence, it is said: "He delivered him to them to be crucified" (Jn. 19, 16).

---

gin. This was the reckoning employed with respect to festivals. For, as Pererius (+1610) says (*on Gen.* 1, 5, *on the words,* "The evening and the morning were one day"), "It is certain that the ancient Jews reckoned their days by a threefold method." First, the legal day from evening to evening. Secondly, the natural day from sunrise to sunrise. Thirdly, the common day from midnight to midnight. Wherefore Christ saith truly, After two days shall be the feast of the Passover, because after two days, that is to say, Wednesday and Thursday, on the evening of Thursday, when Friday is about to begin, is the Passover" (Cornelius à Lapide, *The Great Commentary: St. Matthew's Gospel,* on Chap. 26).

4. *Pascere* in Latin means to feed.

Then were gathered together the chief priests, etc. In this part, the perverse plan of the Pharisees is related. And firstly, their plan concerning Christ's Passion is related; and secondly, their plan concerning a delay is related, where it is said, ***But they said: Not on the festival day***. About the first point, we can observe that the Jews' sin is aggravated by the time of their sin, because their sin was ***then***, when the Paschal festival was at hand; "If thou turn away thy foot from the sabbath, from doing thy own will in my holy day" (Is. 58, 13). But, as I believe, the word ***then*** does not refer to that very day, but to about that time, because it is stated in John 11 that "They gathered a council and from that day therefore they devised to put him to death" (verses 47 & 53). And, thereafter, it is said that Jesus withdrew into a region near the desert. Hence, this was not done immediately. Likewise, the Jews' sin is aggravated by their numerosity;[5] hence, it is said: "My soul hateth your solemnities: for your hands are full of blood" (Is. 1, 14-15). Similarly, their sin is aggravated by the condition of those sinning, for they were the chief men; hence, it is said, ***chief priests***; "I will go to the great men, and will speak to them" and afterwards it continues; "These have altogether broken the yoke more, and have burst the bonds" (Jer. 5, 5). And: "The kings of the earth stood up, and the princes met together, against the Lord, and against his Christ" (Ps. 2, 2). Moreover, their sin is aggravated by the place where they sinned, because they met ***in the court of the high priest***. Hence, these men should have withheld others from evil, but they themselves were doing it; "Iniquity came out from the ancient judges" (Dan. 13, 5).

But were there many chief priests? For the Lord had commanded that there would be only one chief priest, but he was not enough for them. Hence, on account of cupidity, they divided the chief priesthood. Likewise, they had already had lost the chief priesthood, because they were buying the chief priesthood from the Romans. Or they call priests those who previously had been the high priests, and high priest the one who had held the office that year.

Likewise, what they were planning is mentioned: ***That by subtilty they might apprehend Jesus***. And this was foolish, namely, to believe that they could apprehend by subtilty Him who knew all things; "Their tongue is a piercing arrow, it hath spoken deceit" (Jer. 9, 8).

---

5. "REMIG. They are condemned both because they were gathered together, and because they were the Chief Priests; for the more the numbers, and the higher the rank and station of those who band together for any villainy, the greater the enormity of what they do, and the heavier the punishment stored up for them" (*Catena Aurea on St. Matthew*, chap. 26, lect. 2).

But they said: Not on the festival day. Here the delay is treated: and the plan and the reason for the plan are related. *But they said: Not on the festival day.* Someone could say that they said this out of devotion: for that reason, the Evangelist eliminates this interpretation, saying: *lest perhaps there should be a tumult among the people*; for they knew that many held Him to be a prophet, and some even held Him to be Christ: for that reason, there was a dissention among the people, as it is stated in John 7 and 10.[6] Therefore, they feared that they might take Him from their hands. These men were thinking this, but Christ thought something else: hence, they were thinking two things, namely, that they wanted to kill Him, and that He not be crucified on the feastday, which would signify that this immolation was superseding the immolation of the Paschal lamb.

And when Jesus was in Bethania. Here the foretelling is related by a woman's action. And firstly, the action is related; secondly, the reproach is related; and thirdly, the excusing of the action is related. The second part is where it is said, *And the disciples seeing it had indignation*; and the third part is where it is said, *And Jesus knowing it.* About the first part, the Evangelist does four things. Firstly, the place is described; secondly, the person is described; thirdly, the opportunity is related; and fourthly, the deed is related. Firstly, the place is related in two ways, namely, in general and in particular. The general area is related when he says: *And when Jesus was in Bethania*; the particular place is related when he says: *in the house of Simon the leper.*

Note that he was not then a leper, but had been cured by Christ: for if he were then a leper, Christ would not have stayed with him since that was forbidden in the Law: and, nevertheless, both the general and particular places pertain to a mystery. Bethany means 'house of obedience': hence, by this, His obedience is signified. "He became obedient unto death" (Phil. 2, 8). Thus, it befits Him to be in the house of a leper: "And we have thought him as it were a leper" (Is. 53, 4). And He came there especially on account of these passages. Another reason can be a literal one, namely, it was so that this woman would have the confidence of coming to Christ, because this leper was known to Mary, and his corporeal leprosy was cured by Him, and she was coming to be cured from her spiritual leprosy. And it ought to be noted that no one else is said to have come to Christ for spiritual health except this woman; for that reason, she deserved praise.

---

6. cf. Jn. 7, 43 & 10, 19.

There came to him a woman. Behold the person. Matthew and Mark say that this happened in the same place, but John and Luke say it was not the same place. For Luke speaks about this in chapter 7 and John in chapter 12. Therefore, this is an opinion of some men, such as Origen, that there were multiple women. Let us speak concerning the opinions of the two most prominent of these men. Jerome expressly says that this woman, about whom Luke speaks, was not the sister of Lazarus, because it is said of another woman that she anointed His feet, and of this woman that she anointed His head and feet. Ambrose, commenting on Luke's Gospel, says that both can be said, namely, that she is the same woman, or that there are different women: if we say that she is the same, then we can say: 'Even if she is the same woman, nevertheless, they do not have the same merit: but a sinner ought not dare to touch His head, but after gaining confidence she anointed His head.'[7] And Augustine proves that she is the same woman, because in John 11, 1-5, before she came to do this, he says: "Now there was Mary the sister of Lazarus, who anointed the Lord with ointment, and wiped his feet with her hair." Thus it seems that the woman of whom Luke speaks, is the same as she who is the sister of Lazarus. Origen says that that the women, the one of whom Luke speaks and another of whom John speaks, are not the same. And it can be proved by reason of the time, because that deed is read to have occurred before He went to Jerusalem; this was done when He says: *You know that after two days shall be the pasch.* Likewise, it can be proved from the place, because the former woman was in Martha's house, about whom it is written in John; the latter, however, was in the house of Simon. Likewise, it can be proved by the fact that there a woman anointed His feet, but here a woman anointed His head. The fourth proof is what Judas said: *To what purpose is this waste?* But elsewhere he said, "Why was not this ointment sold for three hundred pence and given to the poor?" (Jn. 12, 5). Augustine says that she is the same woman and he replies to Origen's reasons. To the first argument, he says that Matthew does not keep chronological order, but relates the event, because due to this incident, Judas took the occasion of sinning when he saw the ointment poured out. That to which Origen objects concerning the place, Augustine does not resolve. It can, nevertheless, be solved

---

7. "AMBROSE; It is possible therefore that they were different persons, and so all appearance of contradiction between the Evangelists is removed. Or it is possible that it was the same woman at two different times and two different stages of desert; first while yet a sinner, afterwards more advanced" (*Catena Aurea on St. Matthew*, chap. 26, lect. 3).

as follows: that this man was a high official and had authority, and the house belonged to them both because she was his relative. Otherwise, how else is it true what is said, namely, that "They made him a supper there... and Lazarus was one of them that were at table with him" (Jn. 12, 2).

There came to him a woman having an alabaster box of ointment. Alabaster is a type of marble that is translucent, and some windows are made of it. And certain boxes were made out of this rock, wherein ointments were stored, just as now they are made out of ground clay, because the ointments were preserved by its coolness; hence, the word *alabastrum* means an alabaster box full of ointment. And it is said here to be ***precious***, but elsewhere is said to be pistic nard. The word pistic is derived from the Greek word for 'faith,' whence pistic means 'faithful.' Hence, the word pistic means genuine or unadulterated. Afterwards, her action is related: ***And she poured it on his head as he was at table.***

But here there is a twofold question. Why did Christ allow this, since it seems extravagant? Augustine replies to this in his book, *On Christian Doctrine*. Christ can be considered in one way as an ordinary person, and in another way as a prophetical person: now considered as an ordinary person this was something done to Him, but as a prophetical person this was something done to Him as having a meaning. An allegorical exposition is that it signifies Christ's burial, because in ancient times it was customary that bodies would be anointed. In Mark 14 it is stated that she came beforehand to anoint His body for the burial. Likewise, the anointing mystically signifies any good deed. Now this deed can be done in two ways, since some deeds are not done for God's sake but for the sake of natural justice, such as a good deed of a Gentile, and this is an ointment but it is not precious. If one does a good deed for God's sake, it is precious ointment. Hence, one anoints His feet when one does a good deed for the sake of one's neighbor; but when one does a good deed for the glory of God, then one anoints His head.

But why does John say that she anointed His feet, but Matthew says that she anointed His head? Augustine says that she anointed both.

And why does Mark say that she broke the alabaster box? Augustine says that just as it sometimes happens that someone pours out a container such that nothing remains, and afterwards breaks the container: so, since nothing remained, she also broke it afterwards: and thus she did these things, she both poured out the ointment, and also broke the container. Or if someone wishes to misrepresent her actions, it can be said that she firstly anointed His feet, and then His head.

Then the rebuke of the woman follows: *And the disciples seeing it had indignation.* But here there is a conflict, because in John 12 it is said that only Judas said this, but this Evangelist says that they all spoke. There is a twofold answer, according to Jerome: for that which is said here, namely, that the disciples spoke, is said by way of a synecdoche.[8] The disciples means a disciple, and this manner of speech is common in Scripture; it is said, "They were cut asunder" (Heb. 11, 37), because one was cut asunder, namely, no one else but Isaias. Or it can be said that all spoke, because, according to what Augustine says, Judas instigated them all to speak. Likewise, it can be said that the others were motivated by the needs of the poor; but this man was motivated by greed; hence, they say: *To what purpose is this waste?*

But why did they say this? It is because they had heard the Lord often recommend works of mercy; "If thou wilt be perfect, go sell what thou hast, and give to the poor" (above 19, 21).

And Jesus knowing it, said to them. Here the excusing of the woman is related: and He does two things. Firstly, He excuses and commends her; and secondly, He mentions her reward. *Amen I say to you,* etc. And firstly, He excuses her; secondly, He answers the disciples' objection; and thirdly, He explains what He had said. He says, therefore: *Why do you trouble this woman?* The Lord is always the advocate of this woman. Because the Pharisee was accusing her of sin, hence, he said: "If he were if a prophet, would know surely who and what manner of woman this is that toucheth him, that she is a sinner," etc., (Lk. 7, 39), and the Lord excused her on the basis of her love. Likewise, in Luke 10, Martha also accused her of idleness, the Lord again excused her on the basis of her contemplation. Here, the disciples were accusing her for pouring out the ointment, and the Lord excuses her on the grounds of her devotion, saying: *Why do you trouble this woman?* "You rush in upon the fatherless, and you endeavor to overthrow your friend" (Job 6, 27). *She hath wrought a good work upon me*; "Do not withhold him from doing good, who is able: if thou art able, do good thyself" (Prov. 3, 27). Chrysostom says: It sometimes happens that someone does a good deed, generally speaking, and perhaps he could have done better; hence, one ought to act differently before the good deed and after the

---

8. A synecdoche is a figure of speech in which the one of the following (or its reverse) is expressed: A part stands for a whole; an individual stands for a class or a material stands for a thing.

deed was done. Hence, after it has been done, one ought to be commended for the deed; but if the person were to come before doing the deed, he ought to be advised to do what is better. Hence, one ought to suppose that if she had asked for His advice beforehand, He would have told her that she should give the ointment to the poor. *For the poor you have always with you*, etc. Here, His answer to their objection is related, because they were saying that she could have given it to the poor. *But me you have not always*. This is true in relation to His bodily presence, but it is not true in relation to His spiritual presence. Hence, He says below: "Behold I am with you all days, even to the consummation of the world" (Mt. 28, 20). And why did she do this? *For she in pouring this ointment on my body hath done it for my burial.*

And what is this? Did she intend to bury Christ? No. But, as Augustine says, just as the Holy Ghost moves someone to speak, so other times He moves someone to act; hence, it is written: "Whosoever are led by the Spirit of God, are not under the law" (Rom. 8, 14 & Gal. 5, 18). Hence, it happens that someone may be instructed by the Holy Ghost to act for some meaning which one does not intend. So this woman intended to do a good deed, but the Holy Ghost ordained it for His burial.

He says: *She hath wrought a good work upon me*. Someone could say that to give to one's neighbor would be a good work. That is true, but it would not be so good that it would be preached throughout the whole world. *Amen I say to you, wheresoever this gospel shall be preached in the whole world, that also which she hath done shall be told for a memory of her*, meaning in remembrance of her. Jerome says that He, being about to be crucified, foretells the spread of the Gospel in the whole world; and, nevertheless, it was not yet published, since Matthew had not yet written it. Likewise, observe that many men wanted to make known their own birth through the whole world, and the remembrance of them has been obliterated, nevertheless, the remembrance of this deed has not been obliterated; "The memory of the just is with praises" (Prov. 10, 7); "The just shall be in everlasting remembrance" (Ps. 111, 7).

Then went one of the twelve. Above, the Evangelist related the triple prediction of the Lord's Passion, here he intends to make a narration of the Passion: and he does two things. Firstly, he premises some preparatory events; and secondly, he treats of the Passion itself, where it is said, *As he yet spoke*, etc. Now there are three preparatory events. Firstly, an account of the betrayal is related; secondly, the institution of the Lord's Communion is related; and thirdly, an account of Christ's prayer is related. The second part is where it is said, *And on the first day of the Azymes*; and the third part is where it is said, *Then Jesus came with them into a country place which is called Gethsemani*. About the first part, he does three things. Firstly, the person of the betrayer is described; secondly, an account of the betrayal is related; and thirdly, the caution of the betrayer is related. He says, therefore, *Then*. You understand that he is not referring to what immediately preceded, because the account of this woman is said by a transposition; but it refers to that which was said, that *the chief priests and ancients of the people were gathered together... by subtilty they might apprehend Jesus and put him to death. Then went one of the twelve, who was called Judas Iscariot.* And his person is described by three things. He is described by his position, because he was one of the twelve, not merely one of the disciples, but one of the twelve specially called men; "Have not I chosen you twelve? And one of you is a devil?" (Jn. 6, 71)

But why did He choose a man who would be wicked and a traitor? The first reason can be to signify that He condemns no one because of his predestination, nor does He save anyone because of his predestination, but rather He saves on account of the present justice. Hence, if a man were to be condemned on account of his predestination, deeds would not be ascribed to anyone. Likewise, He chose him for the consolation of men: for He knew it would happen that many men would be deceived in their choices, for example, this happened to Philip, who chose Simon the Magician; therefore, the Lord permitted that there be a traitor among His disciples. Another reason could be that no one would be reproached if someone were wicked, since in the first College of the Apostles, there was a wicked man.

Similarly, the person of the traitor is described by his name: *Who was called Judas*. Among the disciples there were two men who were called by this name; nevertheless, one was wicked, by which it is indicated that some men who confess God are good while others are wicked. Concerning the good men it is said: "Judea was made his sanctuary," (Ps. 113, 2). Concerning the wicked it is said: "They profess that they know God: but in their works they deny him" (Tit. 1, 16). Moreover, he is described by his homeland, *Iscariot*. It is a certain village,[9] and it is interpreted to mean 'memorial of death,' because Judas' sin is held in

---

9. i.e. Scariotha.

remembrance. And it can refer to that which is said: "The sin of Juda is written with a pen of iron, with the point of a diamond" (Jer. 17, 1). ***Went to the chief priests***, who were intending to kill Christ, forgetting that which was said: "Blessed is the man who hath not walked in the counsel of the ungodly," etc., (Ps. 1, 1). And Jacob says in Genesis 49, 6: "Let not my soul go into their counsel." ***And said to them***. Here the account of his betrayal is related. And firstly, the account is related; and secondly, the perpetration of the betrayal is related. And firstly, his greed is considered; and secondly, his presumption is considered. His greed is considered when he says: ***What will you give me, and I will deliver him unto you?*** For the sake of money he despised all friendship; "There is not a more wicked thing than to love money: for such a one setteth even his own soul to sale" (Eccli. 10, 10). This man, because he did not refrain his cupidity, fell into perdition. For because he saw that he was defrauded of the price of the ointment, therefore, he wanted to recuperate it by betraying Christ. Similarly, his presumption is mentioned, when he says: ***I will deliver him unto you***. It was great presumption to betray Him who knows all things. Likewise, he speaks as one who knows God very poorly, because when someone wishes to sell something which he loves, he gives a price to it; but when he has something of which he wants to unburden himself, he says: Give me what seems right to you. In such a way does this man speak: ***What will you give me***? By this is meant, give me what you wish to give. "They set at naught the desirable land" (Ps. 105, 24). ***But they appointed him thirty pieces of silver***. Origen says that they act in like manner who send away God for some temporal good. For He dwells in us by faith; and then we send Him away when we adhere too much to temporal things; hence, he said: ***But they appointed him thirty pieces of silver***.

But why does he express himself thus? It is because it was signified by that which was written: "And they weighed for my wages thirty pieces of silver" (Zach. 11, 12). And it ought not to be said that Joseph was sold for thirty denarii, but Scripture maintains that he was sold for only twenty pieces of silver, meaning twenty denarii.[10]

But what does it mean to say that there were thirty? It ought to be understood as follows: This number is composed of five and six, hence, five times six is thirty. By the number five, the five books of Moses are signified, or temporal things are signified, which are

---

10. cf. Gen. 37, 28.

subject to the five senses; hence, it is signified that after the Law of Moses there will be salvation in the sixth age. *And from thenceforth he sought opportunity to betray him.* Here his caution is related. And why was he doing this? It was so that he might more easily and hiddenly perpetrate his crime, just as it is true of sinners, because "he that doth evil hateth the light" (Jn. 3, 20); and: "The eye of the adulterer observeth darkness" (Job 24, 15).

17. And on the first day of the Azymes, the disciples came to Jesus, saying: Where wilt thou that we prepare for thee to eat the pasch?
18. But Jesus said: Go ye into the city to a certain man and say to him: The master saith, My time is near at hand. With thee I make the pasch with my disciples.
19. And the disciples did as Jesus appointed to them: and they prepared the pasch.
20. But when it was evening, he sat down with his twelve disciples.
21. And whilst they were eating, he said: Amen I say to you that one of you is about to betray me.
22. And they being very much troubled began every one to say: Is it I, Lord?
23. But he answering said: He that dippeth his hand with me in the dish, he shall betray me.
24. The Son of man indeed goeth, as it is written of him. But woe to that man by whom the Son of man shall be betrayed. It were better for him, if that man had not been born.
25. And Judas that betrayed him answering, said: Is it I, Rabbi? He saith to him: Thou hast said it.

Next the Evangelist treats of the institution of the Blessed Sacrament, and because the new sacraments take the place of the old ones, as it is said: "The new coming on, you shall cast away the old" (Lev. 26, 10), he firstly treats of the old sacrament, and secondly, he treats of the new Sacrament. About the first part, he does two things. Firstly, the preparation of the Pasch is related; and secondly, the prediction of His betrayal is related, where it is said, *Whilst they were eating, he said*, etc. And about the first point, he firstly indicates the time; secondly, the preparation of the meal is related; and thirdly, the institution of the Sacrament is related. He says, therefore: *On the first day of the Azymes*.

And here there can be an objection, that this day was the first day of the Pasch. And it seems contrary to what is said in John 13, 1: "Before the festival day of the pasch," etc. The Greeks say that Matthew, Luke and Mark erred, and that John corrected them, because it happened before the day of the Pasch. Hence, they say that the Lord suffered on the fourteenth day of the lunar month, and that He made the supper on the thirteenth day. Hence, they say that the Lord confected the Sacrament not with unleavened bread, but with leavened bread. And they try to confirm this by many arguments. Firstly, they argue that it is said in John 18, 28 that "they went not into the hall, that they might not be defiled, but that they might eat the pasch": and so on the day of the Passion they were obliged to eat the Pasch. Likewise, another reason of theirs is that the women prepared spices, therefore, etc. But this cannot be upheld, because the Lord did not violate the ceremonies: for it is nowhere indicated that He anticipated the Pasch, yet it is indicated that He extended the Pasch. And if it would be conceded that the Pasch was anticipated, this does not benefit the Greeks, because it is written that the Pasch ought to be eaten with unleavened bread and wild lettuces. And so if they would have done otherwise, they would have acted contrary to the Law. Thus, according to that which the three Evangelists say, this was done on the fourteenth day of the lunar month, and then it was necessary to eat the Pasch.

What, therefore, ought to be replied to that which John says: "Before the festival day of the pasch"? It ought to be said that it was the custom that they begin the day from the evening, so the Paschal day began from the evening. And this stated in Exodus 12, 14: "On the fourteenth day of the month in the evening thou shalt celebrate the Pasch":[11] and from that time, nothing leaven was found in the Jews' houses until the twenty first day of the month. Hence, if we calculate from the evening of the fourteenth day of the month, the preparation was made before the day of the Pasch, yet it was the fourteenth day of the month. Therefore, John calls that day the day of the unleavened bread, and the day of the Pasch the fifteenth day of the month.[12]

That which the Greeks say secondly (from the cited passage of John), namely, that "they went not into the hall," etc., Chrysostom solves in this manner; and he says that the Lord does not omit any of the legal observances: hence, He ate the Pasch on the fourteenth day of the month. But these leading men began to kill Christ, on account of which, they delayed to eat the Pasch, and then they did not celebrate it at that time, and this was contrary to their Law. Or, by the Pasch, the unleavened bread is understood.

11. This is not a direct quotation but is based upon the context.

12. cf. III, q. 46, a. 9 ad 1um.

Regarding what they say concerning the women, Augustine says that they had many solemnities; but that Sabbath was a more solemn solemnity. Hence, one was not permitted to prepare food on the Sabbath. Thus, at that time, it so happened that the festival of the Pasch fell on a Friday, and the Sabbath was the following day; for that reason, at that time they prepared food on Friday and rested on the Sabbath day. Therefore, we can say that He celebrated the Pasch on the fourteenth day of the month.

The diligence of the disciples follows: *The disciples came to Jesus, saying: Where wilt thou that we prepare for thee to eat the pasch?* And firstly, a question is related; secondly, a command is related; and thirdly, the fulfillment of the command is related. He says: *His disciples came.* But which disciples came? Remigius says that Judas came out of obsequiousness, in order to hide his betrayal. Nevertheless, Pope Leo says that the others also came. *Where wilt thou that we prepare for thee to eat the pasch?* By this it is indicated that Christ did not have a house there, nor did anyone of His group; wherefore, His poverty is indicated; hence: "The Son of man hath not where to lay his head" (above 8, 20).

But He said. Here, His command is related. And firstly, He indicates the host; secondly, He mentions His Passion; and thirdly, He requests a place to eat. He says, therefore: *Go ye into the city to a certain man.* And you ought observe that He was not lodged in the city,[13] but in Bethania.

But what is that which He says, *A certain man*? Augustine says that the Lord named a particular man; but because it was not necessary to name him, Matthew omitted to do so. Chrysostom said that what He says, *Go ye to a certain man*,[14] meaning go to any man, because He wished to show His power so that they would not be troubled by His Passion. For His fame was so widespread that anyone who received Him would be put out of the synagogue. Hence, He wished to make understood that no one receives Him unless He changes his heart; "The heart of the king is in the hand of the Lord: whithersoever he will, he shall turn it" (Prov. 21, 1).

And say to him, etc. He predicts His Passion so that they will not be troubled; hence, He says, *My time*, and no time is said except the time determined by His Father. According to this manner of speaking, it is said: "My time is not yet come; but your

---

13. i.e. Jerusalem.
14. *Ite ad quemdam* can be translated either as: "Go to a certain man" or "Go to some man."

time is always ready" (Jn. 7, 6). *With thee I make the pasch*, meaning I will celebrate the Paschal meal with you. And He adds, *With my disciples*, to indicated that He will not celebrate it secretly, but publicly. According to Chrysostom, He said this because He wanted that enough food be prepared both for Himself and for His disciples.

But why is it that He celebrated the Paschal meal and we should not celebrate it? For it is said: "I have given you an example, that as I have done to you, so you do also" (Jn. 13, 15). To this, Augustine replies, that as Christ suffered to redeem us from death, so He willed to observe the Law to free us from the Law.

Then the execution of His command follows: *And the disciples did as Jesus appointed to them*, etc. Similarly, it is stated: "We will do all the words of the Lord, which he hath commanded" (Ex. 24, 3). Afterwards, the meal is treated: *But when it was evening, he sat down with his twelve disciples.* And it is said, *When it was evening*, because, as it is commanded in Exodus 12, 14: "On the fourteenth day of the month in the evening thou shalt celebrate the Pasch"[15] Or, *When it was evening*, because the time was getting close to sunset; "In the time of the evening there shall be light" (Zach. 7, 14). Or Christ's passage is signified, that is to say, the end of His life: for evening is the end of the day.

And whilst they were eating, he said, etc. Here, His prediction of His betrayal is related. And firstly, He indicates it by His dealings with His companions; secondly, it is indicated by Scripture; and thirdly, it is indicated by His own speech. The second part is where it is said, *But he answering*; and the third part is where it is said, *Thou hast said it*. And about the first point, firstly the prediction is related; and secondly, the effect is related, where it is said, *And they being very much troubled*. Hence, he says: *And whilst they were eating, he said: Amen I say to you that one of you is about to betray me. Amen I say*, He is affirming that He is saying something important, *that one of you*, whom I chose to be the columns of the Church; "There is a friend a companion at the table, and he will not abide in the day of distress" (Eccli. 6, 10) *is about to betray Me*. And in Jeremias 9, 4 it is said: "Do not trust in any brother of yours." Then the effect follows, and there is a twofold effect, namely, sadness and doubting. Regarding the sadness, the Evangelist says, *And they being troubled*. And why were they troubled? They were saddened concerning Christ's death, because it was bitter for them to

---

15. See footnote 11 above.

be without such a leader, such a patron. Likewise, they were saddened concerning so great a crime that would occur; "Who will give a fountain of tears to my eyes" (Jer. 9, 1). Then their doubting is related: ***Every one began to say.***

But why were they doubtful? Was not each one sure of himself? The answer is as follows. The disciples had been instructed that men are quickly prone to sin; hence, the Apostle says: "He that thinketh himself to stand, let him take heed lest he fall" (I Cor. 10, 12). Similarly, they were doubtful because they believed Him more than their own consciences. It is similar to that which is said: "I am not conscious to myself of anything. Yet am I not hereby justified" (I Cor. 4, 4).

But Christ, answering, says: ***He that dippeth his hand with me in the dish, he shall betray me.*** Here the prediction from a prophecy is related. And firstly, He relates the prophetic prediction; secondly, He relates the necessity of the Passion; and thirdly, He relates the punishment of the betrayer. He says, therefore: ***But he answering said.*** The passage can be understood to refer to this: "The man who ate my bread hath greatly supplanted me" (Ps. 40, 10). ***He that dippeth his hand with me in the dish*** [*paropsis*].[16] Mark says, "In the dish [*catinus*]." A square vessel is called a 'catinus', and it is so-called from its having almost equal sides. An earthen vessel for containing liquids is called a 'catinus': hence, liquids are put into a 'catino' and dry things are put into a 'paropsis'; hence, both could have been there. Or it was called a 'paropsis,' but it was called a 'catino' from its use.

And what is it that He says: ***He that dippeth his hand with me in the dish?*** It ought to be said that it was the custom among the ancients that many men would eat from one platter, and perhaps they were using a vessel. Hence, all being astonished withdrew their hands, except Judas, so that they might excuse themselves more: and thus was the saying doubtful, because He was dipping His hand with them all at the same time: for that reason, He did not wish to conceal the betrayer lest he become a greater sinner. Or it can be said that they were sitting two by two, and He had put him near Himself so that He might withdraw him from sin. But many men are not withdrawn by friendship.

The Son of man indeed goeth, as it is written of him. What is it that He says, that you will betray? He says: ***The Son of man indeed goeth***, that is to say, by His own will. Wherefore, His Passion was foretold by the Prophets, as it is stated: "And be-

---

16. The 'paropsis' is a serving bowl.

ginning at Moses and all the prophets, he expounded to them in all the scriptures the things that were concerning him" (Lk. 24, 27). And so nothing will harm the Son of man, because what He arranges happens.

But someone will say: 'If He goes by His own will, then it ought not to be imputed to Judas.' It ought to be said that it is on the contrary, because he did through bad will what the Son was doing spontaneously.

Wherefore, his punishment follows: *But woe to that man by whom the Son of man shall be betrayed.* As it was said above: "It must needs be that scandals come: but nevertheless woe to that man by whom the scandal cometh" (above 18, 7). And the greatness of the punishment is mentioned: *It were better for him, if that man had not been born.* From these words an occasion of error follows. For certain men say that to one who does not exist, no punishment is inflicted; thus they say that it is simply better not to have existed, which is contrary to the Apostle's words (Rom. 9).[17] Hence, according to Jerome, it ought to be said that He is speaking according to the common manner of speech, meaning there is less harm, that is to say, he feels greater torment than if he had not been born. And what is said in Ecclesiasticus 4, 2 seems to allude to this: "I praised the dead rather than the living" (Eccle. 4, 2). And this is opposed to Augustine in his book *De Libero Abitrio*. What is nothing cannot be chosen. Likewise, what we choose is closer to happiness. But what is not, is not nearer to happiness. Therefore, what is to be said? Can it be that someone choose not to be, rather than to be punished? Therefore, it ought to be said that to be can be taken in two ways: either in itself, or by comparison with something else. In itself, I say that it is not something chooseable, as Augustine says; but in comparison with something else it is chooseable, as Jerome says. Because this is not something in nature, but according to the apprehension in the soul it is taken as something, for example, not to sit. But a choice is taken of that which is apprehended: wherefore, to lack an evil is taken to be something good. When, therefore, one chooses something not in itself but as exclusive of evil, one chooses in this way, as the Philosopher says. By this, the answer to the second objec-

---

17. "Shall the thing formed say to him that formed it: Why hast thou made me thus? Or hath not the potter power over the clay, of the same lump, to make one vessel unto honor and another unto dishonor? What if God, willing to shew his wrath and to make his power known endured with much patience vessels of wrath, fitted for destruction, that he might shew the riches of his glory on the vessels of mercy which he hath prepared unto glory?" (Rom. 9, 20-22).

tion is evident. He says, therefore, that, that which withdraws more from evil, is taken as something nearer to happiness; hence, to a feverish man to be without the fever seems to be something good, because he seems to be without miseries; hence, it is better not to be than to be subject to miseries.

And Judas that betrayed him answering, said: Is it I, Rabbi? One ought to note that he did this in a pretended manner, hence, because he was slow to ask, he shows that he was sad, but he pretended. Likewise, the other Apostles call Him "Lord," but he calls Him "Master." Nevertheless, He was both; "You call me Master and Lord. And you say well: for so I am" (Jn. 13, 13). **He saith to him: Thou hast said it.** Notice the Lord's kindness. "Learn of me, because I am meek, and humble of heart" (above 11, 29); and He did this to give us an example of kindness; hence, He says, **Thou hast said it**, meaning you have acknowledged it. Or, you say this, and I do not declare it, but you say it. Hence, it is not the statement of one declaring. For He did not want to make him known; it is as though He said, 'I do not declare it, but you say it.'

26. And whilst they were at supper, Jesus took bread and blessed and broke and gave to his disciples and said: Take ye and eat. This is my body.

Above, the Evangelist related the celebration of the Pasch; here, the institution of the Sacrament of the altar is related. And firstly, the Sacrament is instituted; and secondly, the future scandalizing of the disciples is foretold, where it is said, **Then Jesus saith to them: All you shall be scandalized**. Firstly, He does two things. The paschal Sacrament is instituted; and secondly, a hymn of thanksgiving is sung, where it is said, **And a hymn being said, they went out unto mount Olivet**. And about the first point, the Evangelist does two things. Firstly, the institution of the Sacrament under the species of bread is related; secondly, the institution of the Sacrament under the species of wine is related, where it is said, **And taking the chalice, he gave thanks**, etc. About the first point, he firstly mentions Christ's actions; and secondly, he mentions Christ's words, where it is said, **Take ye and eat. This is my body.** Regarding His actions, five things ought to be noted. Firstly, the time is related; secondly, the matter is indicated; thirdly, the blessing is related; fourthly, the breaking is related; and fifthly, the communication, or distribution is related. The time is mentioned when he says, **And whilst they were at supper**, etc., meaning during their supper, meaning while they were eating.

And why did He institute this Sacrament during the meal itself and not before it? The reason is twofold. It is because the Lord wanted that this Sacrament would replace the Old Testament sacrament, just as the truth would replace a figure; wherefore, after the institution of the old sacrament, He instituted a new Sacrament; "The new coming on, you shall cast away the old" (Lev. 26, 10). Likewise, it was for another reason, namely, that He wanted that it be fixed in their memory: for the things that are lastly heard are deeply fixed in the memory; "Remember my poverty, and transgression, the wormwood and the gall" (Lam. 3, 19).

Then why did the Church determine that men should receive this Sacrament fasting? It ought to be said that this is for the reverence of the Sacrament; for it is fitting that it be received before food. And this is to be understood on the same day.[18] For since the day begins at midnight, one ought not to eat anything from midnight until the reception of this Sacrament.

But some men inquired whether if anything enter the mouth this prevents its reception, such as, if someone drinks water. One ought to know that there are two types of fasting, namely, the fasting of the Church and the fasting of nature. The drinking of water does not break the fasting of the Church, but it breaks the fasting of nature; because even if water does not nourish per se, it nourishes with other things. And you ought to know that one receives water and a drink if one rinses his mouth and swallows a drop accidentally. Nevertheless, one ought not to forgo the reception of this Sacrament; nay, it may be considered to be like saliva. Similarly, I say, concerning food, that if someone eats aniseed[19] late at night, and by chance some remains in the teeth, one ought not to forgo the reception of this Sacrament on account of this. Likewise, some make it a matter of conscience that if they do not sleep, they may not receive. But this does not hold, because it is not based upon a decision of the Church. Hence, it matters not whether someone sleeps or does not sleep.

Jesus took bread, etc. Here the matter of the Sacrament is mentioned. It ought to be noted that this Sacrament, inasmuch as it is related to something of the old sacrament, is related to it as the truth is to its figure. The former sacrament was eaten as food, because it was commanded that they eat a lamb: and the latter Sacrament, which takes its place, ought to be eaten as food. And as He is the true food, so also He is the true Lamb; "My flesh is

---

18. Formerly, the Church required that one fast from midnight before receiving Holy Communion.

19. Aniseed was used as a medicine, breath freshener, and teeth cleaner in the Middle Ages.

meat indeed" (Jn. 6, 51). Hence, that opinion is false which maintained that Christ was only symbolically present in the Sacrament, because if this were so, what more would the latter Sacrament have than the former? But the former sacrament was merely a symbol; while the latter is a figure and the truth.

But is it not an irreverence for someone to receive the Lord's Body? It ought to be said that this food differs from other foods, because other foods are converted into our body: hence, if Christ were to be so converted, it would be an irreverence. But it is not so, nay, on the contrary, as Augustine says: "You will not change Me into yourself, but you will be changed into Me." Hence, the latter Sacrament is the end and the perfection of all the sacraments: and the reason is, that a being that is by essence, is the end and perfection of those beings which are by participation: for the other sacraments contain Christ by participation; but in this Sacrament there is Christ according to His substance: thus Dionysius says that there is no sacrament which is not perfected by the Eucharist. Hence, if an adult is baptized, the Eucharist ought to be given to him. Therefore, this Sacrament is received as food, so that the truth may correspond to the figure.

And why is the Lord's Body not under its own species? One reason is for the sake of the merit of faith, because faith has no merit where human reason brings its own experience.[20] Similarly, it is so that those receiving it may be spared, because it is not customary that human flesh be eaten. Likewise, it is so that the Lord's Body may be defended from the derision of infidels.

And why is His Body under this species? It is because He wanted the Sacrament to be celebrated by all men everywhere in the world: hence, He wanted to give them a matter which is common to all men. Now a common food is bread, and a common drink of men is wine: hence, bread and wine are principal foods rather than other edibles. Likewise, in the other sacraments, in regard to the anointing, not just any oil is used, but the common oil, which is called olive oil, and is derived from many olives;[21] so the Church's unity is derived from many faithful. And so it is evident that our sacraments are older than the sacraments of the Old Law; because the sacraments of the Old Law had their beginning with Moses and Aaron; but the sacraments of the New

---

20. cf. St. Gregory (Hom. 26) quoted in I, q. 1, a. 8, obj. 2.
21. "Oil is, above all, the name of the liquid extract of olives, for other liquids are only called oil from their likeness to it, it follows that olive oil is the matter which should be employed in this sacrament" (Suppl. q. 29, a. 4). The word "oil" is derived from Latin *oleum*, meaning "olive oil," which is from the Greek *elaiwon*, *elaion*, further derived from *elaiw*, *elai*, meaning "olive."

Law began with Melchisedech, who offered bread and wine for Abraham. Thus, it is said that Christ was made "a priest for ever according to the order of Melchisedech" (Ps. 109, 4).

Afterwards, His blessing of the bread is treated; and this blessing relates to three things. It relates to the matter of the Sacrament, because He blessed the fruit of the earth, by which is signified that Adam's curse is revoked by Christ, which curse was pronounced when God said to him: "Cursed is the earth in thy work... thorns and thistles shall it bring forth to thee" (Gen. 3, 17-18). Likewise, it refers to what is contained in this Sacrament, namely, Christ; "Blessed is he that cometh in the name of the Lord" (above 21, 9). Similarly, it is related to the fruit of this Sacrament, because by this Sacrament the faithful are blessed, and the blessing passes from the Head to His members; "The blessing of the Lord is upon the head of the just" (Prov. 10, 6).

Then the breaking of the bread is treated, where it is said, *And he broke*: and this signifies three things. Firstly, it signifies the mystery of His future Passion, because in His Passion His members were pierced, according to that which is written: "They have dug my hands and feet. They have numbered all my bones" (Ps. 21, 17-18). And this was done because He Himself willed it. "He was offered because it was his own will" (Is. 53, 7). Likewise, it is signified that He was broken from unity into a multiplicity, hence, it signifies His Incarnation: because while the Word of God Himself is simple, He came into this multiplicity, but without losing His simplicity. Similarly, the effect which He produces upon various men is signified; because, according to the Apostle, "There are diversities of graces, but the same Spirit" (I Cor. 12, 4).

Likewise, the distribution of the bread is related: *He gave to his disciples*; "Give others to eat what thou hast in thy hand" (Eccli. 29, 32). And the Evangelist says, *to his disciples*, because a Sacrament of this type ought not to be given to one who is not baptized. Just as a priest cannot consecrate this Sacrament unless he be ordained, so this Sacrament ought not to be given to anyone unless he be baptized. Moreover, this Sacrament ought not to be given to anyone except the faithful; nay, unbelievers ought not to be allowed to even see this Sacrament: hence, in the primitive Church, when many men were catechumens, they were permitted to be in the church until the Gospel, and then they were put out of the church.

Similarly, since he says, *to his disciples*, it is inquired whether Judas was there. All say that Christ gave the Sacrament to all the disciples, and even to Judas, and this was so that He might call him back from sin. It was, likewise, to give a teaching to the Church that when there is a secret sinner, he not be forbidden from receiving this Sacrament; for men are not competent to judge concerning hidden matters. Hilary says that Judas was not there because he had already left. And he attempts to prove this by that which is said in John 10, 25, when the disciples asked: "Who is it that shall betray thee?" To whom He said: "He it is to whom I shall reach bread dipped" (verse 26). Thus, he shows that Judas had already left. But, rather, what the other Fathers say ought to be maintained.

And He said: Take ye and eat. This is my body. Here, His words are related: and, by these words, He does three things. Firstly, He exhorts the disciples to receive this Sacrament; secondly, He exhorts them to eat it; and thirdly, He indicates the truth. He says, **Take ye and eat**. And because He says, **take ye**, these words ought to be referred to a spiritual reception, because one only ought to receive this Sacrament with faith and charity; "He that eateth my flesh and drinketh my blood abideth in me: and I in him" (Jn. 6, 57). Likewise, He encourages them to eating, **Eat**, not only spiritually, but also sacramentally; "Eat, O friends, and drink" (Cant. 5, 1). Likewise, He indicates the truth, **This is my body**. The form of the Sacrament is contained in these words, which are the Lord's words, because, by these words of the Lord, the Sacrament was confected. Hence, if the words of Elias had so much power that they made fire to come down from the sky, much more shall God's word be able to change one body into another.

Then it is sought whether there is power in these words. And there is no doubt that this is so. Hence, it is said: "He will give to his voice the voice of power" (Ps. 67, 34); "And his word is full of power" (Eccle. 8, 4). Hence, the priest accomplishes this in the person of Christ, and he does not use these words in his own person, but in the person of Christ.

But what is this power? How great is this power? On this account, some say that there is no power there, except Christ's power, which assists there. And this does not seem to be correct, because the sacraments of the New Law effect what they signify.

But what power did the form acquire? It ought to be said that there is a principal agent cause, and this cause has power remaining in itself; likewise, there is an instrumental cause, and this cause does not operate by a power remaining in itself, but by a power passing from another cause: hence, the sacraments are causes, not as principal causes, but as instrumental causes having power passing from another.

But then it is inquired whether these words, ***Take ye and eat***, etc., actually belong to the form of the Sacrament. And it ought to be said that only the words, ***This is my body***, are the form of the Sacrament. Hence, it ought to be understood that this Sacrament differs from other sacraments; because the consecration of the matter is sometimes necessary, but other times it is not; for example, in Baptism, the consecration of the matter of Baptism is not necessary; but in anointings there is no anointing unless the olive oil be blessed. Also, in the other sacraments the sacrament is not received in the blessing, but in the application of the matter; because the olive oil and water, since they are inanimate, do not contain grace: hence, when grace is the end of the sacrament, grace cannot be transmitted except through the reception of the sacrament. But in this Sacrament, He who is the fullness of grace is contained; thus, the end of the Sacrament is not produced in us, but in the consecration of the matter. Hence, if it be supposed that no one were to receive the Sacrament, it would nonetheless be the Sacrament: hence, its use is consequential, and it is not of necessity. Wherefore, in the other sacraments, the words that belong to the form pertain to its use: these words do not pertain to the use of this Sacrament, but to the holiness of the matter. Hence, the words that are said, ***Take ye and eat***, which pertain to its use, do not belong to the form.

Likewise, the question is often asked whether the Lord confected the Sacrament using these words. And it seems that He did not: because it is said there, ***He took bread and blessed***. Therefore, it seems that He consecrated at the blessing. For this reason, some men said that He did not firstly consecrate by His words, but by His spiritual power. And He could do this on account of His power of excellence, because He was able to confer the truth of the Sacrament without the Sacrament, because He did not restrict His power by the sacraments: hence, He could do this by His power of excellence. Others say that He firstly spoke in secret and afterwards openly. It is better said that He spoke once, and not twice, and He consecrated the Sacrament by these words. Hence, it ought to be read such that those words that He spoke, ***Take ye and eat***, refer to His preceding words. Wherefore, while saying those words, He said: ***This is my body***.[22]

Here it is asked what does the pronoun ***this*** indicate? Some men have said that this word does not indicate to the senses but to the intellect, because the word points out merely the substance of the bread, and merely signifies it. Hence, the meaning is: ***This***

---

22. cf. III, q. 78, a. 1 ad 1um.

is my body, that is, what is signified by ***this*** is My Body. And this cannot stand, because the sacraments of the New Law effect what they signify; wherefore, the word does nothing else than what it signifies: and it signifies Christ's body, and so only Christ's body is present under this sign. Others say that the word ***this*** indicates the substance itself of Christ's body. But how is this? Is Christ's body immediately present when the priest says, ***This***? It is clear that it is not, because if the priest were to die, the bread would not be consecrated unless he complete the form. For this reason, others say that the word ***this*** delays its signification, and it indicates what will be present after the saying of the word ***my***.[23] This also is not suitable, because in this way it would seem that the priest is repeating the same thing, and it would be as though he were saying: 'My Body is My Body'; and this is unbefitting to God. Others say that the words are uttered materially, and not significatively. And this cannot stand, because Augustine says: "The word is added to the element, and this becomes a sacrament." What, therefore, does the pronoun ***this*** indicate? It ought to be said that it is uttered narratively, and at the same time that it is said narratively it is also said significatively. Why is this? It is because the priest is speaking in the person of Christ, and does this as if Christ were present: otherwise, the words would not resemble their proper matter. What, therefore, does the pronoun ***this*** indicate? It ought to be said that it is different with sacramental words than with human words: for human words are merely significative, while divine words are significative and productive. Hence, sacramental words have power from the divine power. Hence, at the same time that the priest says the sacramental words, he also produces something by divine power. For in material production, it so is that something common preexists in every change, and the common element, which is under one terminus of the change, is also at the end under the other terminus: take, for example, a body which changes from being black to white, in which change there was a body, but in the beginning it was black, and afterwards it was white. Hence, in one respect it is similar, namely, in that there is something common to both termini; but there is something dissimilar, because they are not in the same mode; therefore, this change differs from material changes, because in material changes there is a common subject and a different form; here, however, it is the opposite, because the common element is the accidents, and the different element is the substance. Hence, the substance is changed, and the accidents remain common.

23. In Latin, "my" is the last word said: "Hoc est enim Corpus *Meum*."

Therefore, what does the word *this* indicate? It ought to be said that the meaning is: ***This is my body***, that is to say, what is contained under the accidents is My Body. Or this becomes what is contained under the accidents, which is My Body. Hence, He put the noun at the end of the words, but He put the pronoun at the beginning, which signifies the indeterminate substance; but, by the noun, the determinate form is signified. Hence, the determinate form is not in the beginning, but at the end.

But how is Christ's Body present? One opinion was that the substance of the bread remained at the same time with Christ's Body. Hence, what He says, ***This is my body***, refers only to His Body. Others say that the substance of bread changes into its original matter, and Christ's Body becomes present, without the substance of bread changing into Christ's Body. This opinion is disproved as follows. For, according to this opinion, it would seem that something might begin to be where it was not at first, which cannot happen except either the thing be changed in respect to its place, or that something be converted into it. It is as if it were said: 'There is no fire here. Therefore, it cannot be there afterwards unless something which is there be changed into fire.' But, according to this opinion, the mode of conversion is taken away; therefore, Christ's Body is not present except by a change of place. But it is impossible for a body to be in different places at the same time; wherefore, etc. For that reason, it must be said otherwise, that Christ's Body becomes present not by local movement but by the conversion of something else into it; and in this conversion the form remains, and the subject changes. Hence, a subject is changed into a subject, which is the principle of individuation, and it is not on account of this that the bread is present at the same time with Christ's Body or that the substance of bread is annihilated; but it is by this principle that the bread is changed by conversion into Him.

But how can His Body be in such a small space? It ought to be said that something is there by the power of the Sacrament, and this is there principally; but something else is there by concomitance. His Body is there from the power of the Sacrament, into which the conversion is terminated. And because the bread is converted into Christ's Body, that which is signified is Christ's Body, and it is not without His soul, nor without His divinity: nevertheless, the bread is not converted into His soul, or into His divinity, but they are there by concomitance. Hence, if someone were to celebrate Mass during the three days when His soul was separated from His Body, His soul would not be there. For in the bread there are two things, substance and accidents: the accidents remain, but the substance changes. Therefore, that into which the transmutation terminates is there principally; but the transmutation terminates in the substance; therefore, the substance is there principally, but the accidents are there by concomitance; the dimensions, however, are accidents. Christ's Body in the Sacrament is not related to a place by its proper dimensions, but by the bread's preexisting dimensions.

Likewise, **He broke**. But is not His whole Body in each part? I say that this is so. And you ought to know that to be in a place is different than being located in a place; for being located is to be related to a place by its dimensions, but it is not so here. Hence, it ought to be noted, that wherever there is some difference of quantity, this does not always make a difference in substance; but if a thing is present according to its quantity, it is divided according to its quantity. But the soul does not have to get its totality from quantity, but it has its totality in every part: hence, Christ's Body is not related to the bread in relation to quantity, but only in relation to substance; therefore, just as the soul is in every part of the body, so Christ is in every part of the host.

But what happens to accidents of the host? It ought to be said that they remain without a subject by divine power. And how can this be, since the accidents depend upon the substance? It is replied that God is the principle of being; hence, He can produce an effect separated from its subject and without its principles; wherefore, since it is the principle of substance that keeps the accidents in existence, God can keep them in existence without His principles.

If you ask whether this be true for all the accidents of the host, it is said that all accidents are related to their substance by way of dimensions; hence, they are individuated in some way; hence, the dimensions of the host are without a subject, but the quality in the dimensions exist as in a subject. Hence, the meaning is: *This*, meaning what is contained under these accidents, which accidents remain in the dimensions, because the substance, which firstly underlies these accidents, is changed into Christ's Body.

27. And taking the chalice, he gave thanks and gave to them, saying: Drink ye all of this.

28. For this is my blood of the new testament, which shall be shed for many unto remission of sins.

29. And I say to you, I will not drink from henceforth of this fruit of the vine until that day when I shall drink it with you new in the kingdom of my Father.

Above, it was treated concerning the institution of a new Sacrament insofar as the Lord's Body; here it is treated concerning the institution of the same Sacrament, insofar as the Sacrament of the Lord's Blood: and about this, the Evangelist does two things. Firstly, Christ's actions are related; and secondly, His words are related, where it is said, *Drink ye all of this*. About the first part, three actions are related. Firstly, it is related that He took the chalice; secondly, it is related that He gave thanks; and thirdly, it is related that He gave to His disciples; hence, the Evangelist says: *And taking the chalice*, etc.; by which is signified that it was not instituted that the Sacrament be performed under one species, but under two species.

And what is the reason for this? One reason is that there are three things in this Sacrament. One is that which is the sacrament only, another is the reality only, and still another is the sacrament and the reality. The sacrament only is the species of bread and wine. The reality only is the spiritual effect; the reality and the sacrament is Christ's Body contained in this Sacrament. If, therefore, we consider the sacrament only, it is very fitting that the Body be signified by the species of bread, and that the Blood be signified by the species of wine, because they are signified as indicating spiritual refreshment; but refreshment properly consists in food and drink, wherefore, etc. Likewise, if the Sacrament be considered as a reality and a sacrament, it is fitting in that this Sacrament is rememorative of the Lord's Passion. And it cannot signify this better than in this way, as the Blood is signified as poured out and separated from the Body. Likewise, the Sacrament is very fitting when it be considered as the reality only, because blood pertains to soul, not because the blood is the soul, but that by blood life is preserved: hence, it is signified that although this Sacrament is for the salvation of the faithful, the Body[24] is offered for the health of the body, but the Blood is offered for the health of the soul. "Come, eat my bread, and drink the wine which I have mingled for you" (Prov. 9, 5), because this refreshment is in the bread and wine. Similarly, another reason is that the entire Christ is contained under the species of the bread.[25] What is, therefore, the necessity that the blood is by itself? Wherefore, what was said above must be taken in the sense that one thing is directly there by the power of the sacrament, and another thing

---

24. The word "bread" is used here in the text but has been replaced with "body" according to a parallel passage found in III, q. 74, a. 1.

25. Here the words of the text, "contained in the body," have been replaced with more precise wording, "contained under the species of the bread," found in III, q. 76, a. 3).

is there from natural concomitance. Christ's body is contained under the species of bread by the power of the sacrament, but the blood is there by concomitance. But as to the blood, it is the contrary, because Christ's blood is there directly by power of the sacrament, but His body is there by concomitance. Hence, if, at the time when Christ's blood was poured out on to the ground, the sacrament was celebrated, the blood would only have been there apart from the body. Thus, because certain men did not understand these things, they said that the forms of consecration of the bread and wine are connected. Hence, they say that when the body is consecrated, the blood is not there until the wine will have been consecrated. But this is not so, because if a priest were to die before he were to consecrate the wine, both Christ's body and blood would be in the host.

Likewise, the Evangelist says, ***Taking the chalice***, and he does not say, "Taking the wine"; for that reason, some have said that it ought to be done with water. And this is excluded, because Christ continues by saying: ***I will not drink of this fruit of the vine***, etc. Secondly, it is evident that there was wine mixed with water. And the reason for this is on the part of the Sacrament, because it must be celebrated as the Lord instituted it. But in hot climates it is customary that wine is not drunk except with water; wherefore, it must not be believed that He confected the Sacrament with pure wine. It is also fitting as to what is contained in the chalice, because this Sacrament is rememorative of the Lord's Passion; but from Christ's side went out blood and water, as it is stated in John 19.[26] Moreover, there is water and wine to signify the effect of the Sacrament, and this is done in two ways: therefore, it produces in us the effect of Christ's Passion. Now the effect of Christ's Passion is twofold, to wash and to redeem. He redeems us by His Blood; "Thou hast redeemed us to God, in thy blood" (Apoc. 5, 9). Likewise He washes away our stains of sin; "He washed us from our sins in his own blood" (Apoc. 1, 5). And these things were necessary so that He might wash and redeem us. And the washing is signified by the water, and the redemption is signified by wine. Likewise, by water the people are signified;[27] "Many waters, many people" (Apoc. 17, 1 & 15).[28] And by this

---

26. "But one of the soldiers with a spear opened his side: and immediately there came out blood and water" (verse 34).

27. "Pope Julius says (Concil. Bracarens iii, Canon 1): 'We see that the people are signified by the water, but Christ's blood by the wine. Therefore when water is mixed with the wine in the chalice, the people is made one with Christ.'" (III, q. 74, a. 6).

28. cf. St. Bernard of Clairvoux, *De consideratione*, chap. 8: "Many waters, many people."

Sacrament the people are united to Christ; therefore, by this admixture, the people being united to Christ is signified.

But what becomes of that water? Some say that it remains. Others say that it is converted into wine, because when a little is put in, the species of the water is changed, and so all the water is converted into wine; and in this way, it pertains to a mystery, because the unity of Church is contained in this mystery.

Likewise, in this that he says, **Taking**, it is signified that Christ underwent His Passion voluntarily; hence: "I will take the chalice of salvation; and I will call upon the name of the Lord" (Ps. 115, 13).

Similarly, *he gave thanks*. And for what did He give thanks? It was for two things, for a sign and for something signified. He gave thanks for a sign, because He gave thanks for the effect; He gave thanks for something signified, because He gave thanks for His Passion. In doing which, it is signified that we not only ought to give thanks for good things, but also for bad or adverse things; "Giving thanks in all things" (I Thess. 5, 18); "To them that love God all things work together unto good" (Rom. 8, 28). Moreover, He gave thanks for the institution of this Sacrament, because He was doing this by divine power; hence, it is said in John 5, 30: "I cannot of myself do any thing." Thus, He gave thanks to God the Father; "I give thee thanks that thou hast heard me" (Jn. 11, 41). In which an example is given to us that if Christ gave thanks, who is equal to the Father, then we ourselves ought to give thanks. Likewise, He gave thanks for the effect, because the effect is the salvation of the whole world. And He was only able to do this by His divinity; "It is the spirit that quickeneth: the flesh profiteth nothing" (Jn. 6, 64).

He continues, *And he gave to them*, so that they might receive the Sacrament. And by this, He signifies that the fruit of His Passion ought to be ministered by some men to others. Hence, the Apostles can be compared the offspring of an eagle, concerning whom it is said: "As the eagle enticing her young to fly, and hovering over them" (Deut. 32, 11). Then He enjoins the use of the Sacrament. Firstly, He relates its use; secondly, He relates the words of consecration; and thirdly, He foretells His Resurrection. He says, therefore: *Drink ye all of this*; "Drink, and be inebriated, my dearly beloved" (Cant. 5, 1). Hence, it is signified that Christians can communicate in the appropriate place and time.

This is my blood, etc. These are the words of consecration. And observe that in these words there is a difference with those that the Church uses. The Church adds: "This is the chalice."

Likewise, where He says, ***Of the new testament***, the Church adds, "Of the new and eternal testament." Moreover, where He says, ***Which shall be shed for many***, the Church adds, "Which shall be shed for you," etc. Whence, therefore, does the Church have this form? It ought to be said, as Dionysius says, that it was not the intention of the Evangelists to pass on the forms of the sacraments, but to guard them as secrets; hence, they only intended to tell the history. Whence, then, does the Church have them? She has them from the institution of the Apostles. Hence, Paul said: "The rest I will set in order, when I come" (I Cor. 11, 34).

But there is a question: Why does He say: ***This is my body***, or ***This is my blood***? Why does He not say: 'This is converted into My Body, or into My Blood,' etc.? But the reason is twofold. The first reason is that the forms of the sacraments ought to signify what they effect. That which they effect, is that the bread is converted into Christ's Body and the wine is converted into Christ's Blood, wherefore, the last effect ought to be signified; hence, it ought to be signified that this is His Body; not, however, that this is converted into His Body. In this form, however, there is something similar in the Old Testament, but also something different. It is similar in this, as it is stated in Exodus 24, 8, that when Moses read the Law, he immolated calves, and offered the blood, and said: "This is the blood of the covenant of the Lord." In this manner this blood was offered for the salvation of the people. In Hebrews 9 it is said, "The high priest alone, once a year: not without blood, which he offereth for his own and the people's ignorance."[29] He shows, however, the difference as to four things. Firstly, there is a difference in that the latter blood is of calves, but this Blood is Christ's; hence, this Blood is efficacious for remitting sin; "For if the blood of goats and of oxen, and the ashes of an heifer, being sprinkled, sanctify such as are defiled, to the cleansing of the flesh, how much more shall the blood of Christ, cleanse our conscience from dead works, to serve the living God?" (Heb. 9, 13). Likewise, the latter was called the blood of the testament, but this Blood is called the testament. Similarly, a testament may be taken in a broad sense or in a strict sense of the word. It is taken broadly for any testament made, because so it used to be that when any testament was made witnesses were summoned. A testament is said in a strict sense when a testament is read at death, according to what the Apostle says, that a testament is of force upon the death of the testator.[30] The word

---

29. Verse 7.   30. Hebrews 8, 17.

applies in both ways here, because there was a pact; and it was made with blood, because in ancient times they displayed blood when making an alliance of peace, and so it was called the blood of the covenant. Moreover, in that a testament is said to refer to the dead, in this way, there was a certain pact between God and men in the Old and New Law; but they were different; because the first pact pertained to temporal things, namely, the pact of the Old Testament, as it is evident that God promised them the land of the Amorrhites, wherefore, the testament was old, because men were not renewed but rather made older; the latter testament, however, pertained to heavenly things. Hence, it is said: "Do penance, for the kingdom of heaven is at hand" (above 4, 17). Wherefore, He says: *Of the new testament*; but in the Old Testament it was said: "This is the blood of the covenant, which the Lord hath made with you concerning all these words," etc., (Ex. 24, 8). "I will make a new covenant with the house of Israel, and with the house of Juda" (Jer. 31, 31). *For this is my blood of the new testament*, meaning it is dedicated to a new testament, in which we ought to have confidence; "We have a confidence by the blood of Christ" (Heb. 10, 19). Likewise, the testament befits a testament made at death; because by Christ's death the promise was confirmed. Similarly, there is another difference between the Old and New Testament, because this form adds, "Of the new and eternal testament," which can refer either to the eternal inheritance or to Christ, who is eternal. Another difference is that in the above passage (Ex. 24, 8) it is stated: "Which the Lord hath made with you"; hence, the former testament was limited to only the Jews; but this testament is also for the Gentiles; "He shall sprinkle," meaning with His Blood, "many nations" (Is. 52, 15). *For many*, and for all, because if its sufficiency be considered, "He is the propitiation for our sins: and not for ours only, but also for those of the whole world" (I Jn. 2, 2). But if we consider its effect, it only has its effect on those who are saved, and this is the fault of men. But the Church adds, "For you," meaning the Apostles, because they are the ministers of this Blood, and through them it is spread to the Gentiles. Likewise, it is said, *Unto remission of sins*, because the blood of the old testament could not remit sins.

And I say to you. Here their consolation is related, according to Chrysostom. Because He had made mention of the shedding of His Blood, whereby His Passion is signified, wherefore, He comforts them and He foretells His glory. Chrysostom expounds the passage in this way, namely, that the Lord had foretold His Passion, wherefore, He wishes to make them rejoice. *I will not drink from henceforth of this fruit of the vine*, meaning of this wine, *until that day*, etc. He calls this kingdom the kingdom of resurrection. At that time He receives a new kingdom, meaning in a new way. That He will drink with them appears in Acts 10.[31]

But why is it said that He will eat in a new way? It is because He ate in a different manner before than He did after His Resurrection; for before His Resurrection He ate out of necessity, but afterwards He did not eat due to necessity, but to show the truth of His Resurrection.

Jerome says the following, namely, that the nation of the Jews is signified by a vineyard; "The vineyard of the Lord of hosts is the house of Israel" (Is. 5, 7); "I planted thee a chosen vineyard, all true seed" (Jer. 2, 21).

And I say to you, I will not drink from henceforth of this fruit of the vine, meaning My soul will not rejoice concerning this nation, *until that day when I shall drink it with you new in the kingdom of my Father.* His kingdom signifies the existing Church; He says *new*, meaning renewed by faith, because when they will be converted, then I will rejoice with them. For many were converted and many will be converted. Remigius expounds this passage as follows, and he says that this ought to be referred to the Paschal ceremonies, meaning I will not celebrate again ceremonies of this kind until the establishment of the Church, when I will rejoice over the renewal of the Church. Augustine expounds the passage thus: "In that He says *new*, it is opposed to the old." Now oldness is twofold: there is the oldness of punishment and guilt, and these are derived from Adam, as it is stated in Romans 6.[32] Now Christ had the oldness of punishment but not the oldness of guilt. Hence, His single oldness undid our twofold oldness. He says, therefore: *I will not drink*, of the oldness of punishment, *until*, etc., He would put away that Body, and assume a glorified Body at His Resurrection; and He promises the Apostles that they also will assume glorified bodies; and He indicates that their bodies will not be of a different nature, because the Body that He will assume will be a Body the same in nature, but different in glory.

---

31. "Him God raised up the third day and gave him to be made manifest, not to all the people, but to witnesses preordained by God, even to us, who did eat and drink with him, after he arose again from the dead" (Acts 10, 40-41).

32. "For if we have been planted together in the likeness of his death, we shall be also in the likeness of his resurrection. Knowing this, that our old man is crucified with him, that the body of sin may be destroyed, to the end that we may serve sin no longer" (Rom. 6, 5-6).

30. And a hymn being said, they went out unto mount Olivet.
31. Then Jesus saith to them: All you shall be scandalized in me this night. For it is written: I will strike the shepherd: and the sheep of the flock shall be dispersed.
32. But after I shall be risen again, I will go before you into Galilee.
33. And Peter answering, said to him: Although all shall be scandalized in thee, I will never be scandalized.
34. Jesus said to him: Amen I say to thee that in this night before the cock crow, thou wilt deny me thrice.
35. Peter saith to him: Yea, though I should die with thee, I will not deny thee. And in like manner said all the disciples.
36. Then Jesus came with them into a country place which is called Gethsemani. And he said to his disciples: Sit you here, till I go yonder and pray.
37. And taking with him Peter and the two sons of Zebedee, he began to grow sorrowful and to be sad.
38. Then he saith to them: My soul is sorrowful even unto death. Stay you here and watch with me.
39. And going a little further, he fell upon his face, praying and saying: My Father, if it be possible, let this chalice pass from me. Nevertheless, not as I will but as thou wilt.
40. And he cometh to his disciples and findeth them asleep. And he saith to Peter: What? Could you not watch one hour with me?
41. Watch ye: and pray that ye enter not into temptation. The spirit indeed is willing, but the flesh is weak.
42. Again the second time, he went and prayed, saying: My Father, if this chalice may not pass away, but I must drink it, thy will be done.
43. And he cometh again and findeth them sleeping: for their eyes were heavy.
44. And leaving them, he went again: and he prayed the third time, saying the selfsame word.
45. Then he cometh to his disciples and said to them: Sleep ye now and take your rest. Behold the hour is at hand: and the Son of man shall be betrayed into the hands of sinners.
46. Rise: let us go. Behold he is at hand that will betray me.

After the institution of the new Sacrament has been related, here Christ foretells the future scandal of the disciples. And the Evangelist, firstly, premises the place where Christ foretells their scandal; and secondly, the prediction of their scandal is related, where it is said, **Then He saith to them.** And this place befits what preceded and what follows. Hence, the place can be associated with both.[33] He says, therefore: **And a hymn being said.** By this He gives us an example of two things; for firstly, it was a material supper and meal, after which, we ought to give thanks and to praise God; "The poor shall eat and shall be filled: and they shall praise the Lord that seek him" (Ps. 21, 27). Likewise, after this meal, there was a sacramental supper, after which we also ought to give thanks. Hence, after that meal, He said a hymn: hence, the hymn which is said in the Mass after Communion,[34] represents that hymn; for that reason, the faithful ought to wait until the end of Mass in order to hear this hymn. And this is what is said: "Father, glorify thy Son, that thy Son may glorify thee" (Jn. 17, 1). **And this being said, they went out unto mount Olivet.** For the Mount of Olives signifies fatness, because olives are full of fat; hence, it signifies spiritual fatness. "His bread shall be fat" (Gen. 49, 20). Hence, it signifies the fatness of grace and heavenly glory to which it impels; "The mountain of God is a fat mountain" (Ps. 67, 16). Oil assuages weary members, it mitigates sorrow, it gives fuel and brightness to fire. So it will be in that glory, because all labor and every sorrow will be eliminated; every glory will be there. Likewise, that which he says, **unto mount Olivet**, befits Christ's prediction of the future. By oil mercy is signified: for just as it floats above other liquids, so mercy is above the other virtues; "His mercies are over all his works" (Ps. 144, 9). Similarly, He is showing the scandal of the disciples in the Mount of Olives,[35] so that His foreseen mercy might be signified. "When he shall fall he shall not be bruised, for the Lord putteth his hand under him" (Ps. 36, 24).

Then He says, **All you shall be scandalized in me.** Here, the scandal in the Mount of Olives is signified. Firstly, it is signified in general; and secondly, it is signified in particular, where it is said, **And Peter answering.** About the first point, He does

---

[33] "BEDE; Beautifully after the disciples have been filled with the Sacraments of His Body and Blood, and commended to the Father in a hymn of pious intercession, does He lead them into the mount of Olives; thus by type teaching us how we ought, by the working of His Sacraments, and the aid of His intercession, mount up to the higher gifts of the virtues and the graces of the Holy Spirit, with which we are anointed in our hearts" (*Catena Aurea on St. Matthew*, chap. 26, lect. 9).

[34] The Communion antiphon sung in ancient times with a psalm seems to be the hymn mentioned here.

[35] "ORIGEN; Suitably also was the mount of mercy chosen whence to declare the offense of His disciples' weakness, by One even then prepared not to reject the disciples who forsook Him, but to receive them when they returned to Him" (*Catena Aurea on St. Matthew*, chap. 26, lect. 9).

two things. Firstly, He foretells their scandal; secondly, lest His prediction seem fortuitous, He cites a passage, *For it is written: I will strike the shepherd: and the sheep of the flock shall be dispersed.* And from these words it can be seen that the sin of the disciples was aggravated for many reasons. Firstly, it is aggravated by its universality, *All you*; "From the sole of the foot unto the top of the head, there is no soundness therein," etc., (Is. 1, 6). Likewise, the matter of the sin is mentioned, *All you shall be scandalized in me*; "We preach Christ crucified: unto the Jews indeed a stumblingblock" (I Cor. 1, 23). The Jews, because they sought nothing but the weakness of the flesh, suffered scandal. Moreover, the sin is aggravated by the nearness of the time, because it was after so many warnings, and after the reception of the Sacrament. Hence, they had already forgotten what He had done for them; wherefore, they are rightly compared to a man beholding his own countenance in a glass: "he beheld himself and went his way and presently forgot what manner of man he was" (James 1, 23-24). Furthermore, the sin was at night, because they who are drunk, and who sleep, sleep in the night (I Thess. 5, 7): so, likewise, those who are scandalized are scandalized at night. Then He adds the reference from Scripture: *For it is written: I will strike the shepherd: and the sheep shall be dispersed.* And it is written: "Strike the shepherd," namely Christ, "and the sheep shall be scattered" (Zach. 13, 6); now here it is said, *I will strike*, and it agrees sufficiently, because the prophet desired this to happen, wherefore, he said, "Strike the shepherd"; but Christ is speaking in His own person; and the prophet is for the first time foretelling Christ's Passion on that terrible day; secondly, He is foretelling the scandal, when He says, *I will strike the shepherd.* This shepherd is Christ; "I am the good shepherd" (Jn. 10, 11) And: "You are now converted to the shepherd and bishop of your souls" (I Pet. 2, 25). And He Himself was struck, because God delivered Him, because "He spared not His own Son" (Rom. 8, 32): and He did this on account of our sins: "For the wickedness of my people have I struck him" (Is. 53, 8). Likewise, He foretells the scandal and that the sheep will be dispersed. The sheep are the faithful; "My sheep hear my voice" (Jn. 10, 27). And so God suffered that they might be dispersed, and so that afterwards they might be gathered; "He will gather together the dispersed of Israel" (Ps. 146, 2). "Other sheep I have that are not of this fold: them also I must bring" (Jn. 10, 16).

Then He foretells the joy of the Resurrection, *But after I shall be risen again, I will go before you into Galilee*; because although the Father resurrected Him, as it is said elsewhere: "Whom God hath raised up, having loosed the sorrows of hell" (Acts 2, 24), nevertheless, He rose by His own power, because the Father's power is the Son's power; "Although he was crucified through weakness, yet he liveth by the power of God" (II Cor. 13, 4). Similarly, contrary to that which He had said, namely, that the sheep shall be dispersed, He says, *I will go before you into Galilee*. For the sheep follow the shepherd: hence, the shepherd gathers them by calling them by name; wherefore, He says: *I will go before you*. Or it can be referred to that which He says, *After I shall be risen again*. Because some might suppose that there would be much time until His Resurrection, wherefore, He said that there would not be much time, because *I will go before you into Galilee*. His custom was to stay a short time in Judea, and to quickly go over into Galilee. Therefore, He wished to say: 'I will rise again before you can come to Galilee, to show that He Himself will appear to them. For that reason, they could be sufficiently assured. Similarly, that which He says, that He will *go before*, gives security. Because they were suffering persecution in Judea, wherefore, He says that He will go before them into Galilee, to take away their fear.

And Chrysostom says that it ought not to be understood that He firstly appeared in Galilee: He did appear there, but not at first, for He appeared firstly in Jerusalem. Why then does He rather say, *into Galilee*? Galilee is interpreted to mean 'a passing': hence, it is signified that by the resurrection we will pass from mortal life to immortal life: and in this passing, He went before us, because Christ is "the firstfruits of them that sleep" (I Cor. 15, 20). Likewise, the passing of the disciples to the Gentiles is signified: and in this, Christ went before them by moving the hearts of the Gentiles.

And Peter answering. Here the prediction of Peter's scandal is related. And firstly, the occasion is related; secondly, the prediction is related; and thirdly, Peter's excusing is related. The second part is where it is said, *Jesus said to him*, etc.; and the third part is where it is said, *Peter saith to him*, etc.

Here there is a literal question; because it seems that Peter said this after they had left the supper-room; but Luke (22, 34-39) seems to say that He said this before they had left, and John (13, 36-38) is consonant with this.

Augustine solves the question by saying that Peter said this three times, and so all are in agreement, etc., because if we would consider the account, he said this for several reasons. Here, he was motivated by the fact that Christ had foretold the scandal.

The Lord had said: "But I have prayed for thee, that thy faith fail not" (Lk. 22, 32), and then Peter said: "Lord, I am ready to go with thee, both into prison and to death."[36] But in John it is said for another reason; for in John 13, 33 the Lord said: "Whither I go you cannot come; so I say to you now." Then Peter said: "I will lay down my life for thee."[37] Thus he spoke three times; wherefore, it can be that he spoke twice in the supper-room, but he spoke once outside, as it is said here. And it can be that he was speaking out of fervor, and he was not considering his own virtues. Nevertheless, he sinned in three ways. He sinned firstly because he did not believe the Lord more than himself, even though it is written: "Only God is true and every man a liar" (Rom. 3, 4). Likewise, he sinned because he preferred himself to the others; hence, he also said, **Although all shall be scandalized in thee, I will never be scandalized**. Hence, he considered himself to be more firm than the others; and he fell into that which is said: "I am not as the rest of men," etc., (Lk. 18, 11). Similarly, he was attributing to himself what he ought not, since it is written: "Without me you can do nothing" (Jn. 15, 5). Therefore, because he had spoken arrogantly, for that reason, God more readily permitted him to fall. And God does this, because He hates pride; "And beholding every arrogant man, he humbles him" (Job 40, 6).

Jesus says to him: **Amen I say to thee that in this night before the cock crow, thou wilt deny me thrice**. 'Because you might have thought that I was speaking comminatorily, wherefore I say to you, **Amen**, that is to say, I speak to you sincerely, *that in this night before the cock crow, thou wilt deny me thrice*.' And Peter's guilt is aggravated by the proximity of the time, because it happened *in this night*. Likewise, it is aggravated from the multiplicity of his denials, because he did this thrice: for just as he had presumed three times,[38] so also he denied Him three times after his presumption; "If my heart in secret hath rejoiced," (Job 31, 27).

But there is a question concerning these words, **Before the cock crow, thou wilt deny me thrice**; because in Mark 14, 30 it is stated: "before the cock crow twice." According to Augustine, the question can be resolved by saying that what Mark says is historically correct. And what Matthew says can be explained as

---

36. Verse 33.
37. Verse 37.
38. "AUG. Some would oblige us to understand that he thrice expressed his confidence, and the Lord thrice answered him that he would deny Him thrice before cock-crowing; as after His resurrection He thrice asked him if he loved Him, and as often gave him command to feed His sheep" (*Catena Aurea on St. Matthew*, chap. 26, lect. 9).

follows, that a man is said to do something when he intends to do it, as it was said above: "Whosoever shall look on a woman to lust after her, hath already committed adultery with her in his heart," (5, 28). So Peter was prepared to deny Him three times, or even more times; for what caused his fear sufficed for denying Him three or more times; wherefore, Matthew says that Peter denied Him three times before the cock crew because he was already prepared to deny Him three or more times. Hence, Matthew said what he was interiorly intending to do; but Mark said what he exteriorly did. Or it can be explained otherwise, as when I say: 'I will do this within such a time' then it is not necessary that it be done within that time, but it suffices that the action will have been started within that time. Hence, when Matthew said that Peter was going to deny Him three times before the crowing of the cock, it was not necessary that all his denials be completed before the crowing of the cock, but merely begun.

Peter's excusing follows, where it is said, **Peter saith to him**, etc. Peter excuses himself because he says, **Though I should die with thee, I will not deny thee**. And, nevertheless, he was afraid, because at the voice of a handmaid he denied Him. Jerome says that he did not know what he was saying, because only Christ was going to die, as only He was the Redeemer; "I have trodden the winepress alone" (Is. 63, 3).

Then he relates an affirmation, namely, of the others in like manner, and all the disciples said that they would not deny Him. Hence, they spoke as Peter did; nevertheless, the others had more reason than Peter for excusing themselves, because the others spoke without Peter's assertion.

Then Jesus came into a country place which is called Gethsemani. In this part, the preparation for the Lord's Passion is related, which is by prayer; and the Evangelist does three things. Firstly, Christ's intention of praying is related; secondly, the necessity of praying is related; and thirdly, the difference between the prayer of Christ and of the disciples is related. The second part is where it is said, **And taking Peter**, etc.; the third part is where it is said, **And going a little further, he fell upon his face**. About the first point, he does two things. Firstly, the place is related; and secondly, Christ makes known His intention of praying. He says, therefore: **Then Jesus came into a country place which is called Gethsemani**. The contrary seems to be said in John 18, 1, namely, that Jesus came across the brook Cedron. Hence, it ought to be observed that the country place was at the foot of Mount Olivet, wherefore, the places were the same;

and they came there after the supper as if for a walk. Then He announces His intention of praying and so He said to His disciples: *Sit you here, till I go yonder and pray.* Something similar is found in Genesis 22, 5: "Abraham said to his young men: 'Stay you here with the ass; I and the boy will go with speed as far as yonder, and after we have worshipped, will return to you.'"

But here Damascene raises a question. Prayer is the ascent to God, but Christ's intellect was joined to God, why, therefore, did God who was doing this need to do this? Hence, it may be said that He was praying not for His own sake, but for our benefit, and this benefit was twofold, for He prayed to give us an example, so that we might have recourse to Him in times of tribulation; "In my trouble I cried to the Lord" (Ps. 119, 1). Likewise, it was to show that He is from another Person, and what He possesses is from another Person; hence, He says: "The Son cannot do any thing of himself" (Jn. 5, 19) and "I do nothing of myself" (ibid. 8, 28). Moreover, it was to exclude an error, because some men said that the Father's and the Son's power were not the same; "I honor my Father" (Jn. 8, 49).[39] He, therefore, gives an example of praying, and how one ought to pray. For the first condition of prayer is that prayer ought to be humble: which is signified because He went to a valley; "The prayer of the humble and the meek hath always pleased thee" (Jud. 9, 15). Likewise, prayer ought to be devout; hence, He prayed in Gethsemani, namely, in a garden of fatness; "Let my soul be filled as with marrow and fatness" (Ps. 62, 6). Similarly, it ought to be solitary, as it was said above: "Enter into thy chamber, and having shut the door, pray to thy Father" (6, 6).

And taking with him Peter and the two sons of Zebedee, etc. Here, He proclaims the need of His prayer: and the need was His sadness. And firstly, the Evangelist relates the witnesses of His sadness; secondly, Christ shows His sadness; and thirdly, Christ repels His sadness. The second part is where it is said, *He began to grow sorrowful and to be sad*; the third part is where it is said, *Stay you here and watch with me.* He says, therefore: *And taking with him Peter and the two sons of Zebedee*, etc. He took three Apostles with Him. And why did He take these rather than the others? One reason is that these were more firm, and because His weakness scandalized them all, for that reason, He wished to show His weakness to these rather than to the others. Likewise, He had chosen these men to show them His glory; for that reason, as they had seen His glory, so

---

39. "ORIGEN. Christ alone honored the Father perfectly" (*Catena Aurea on St. Matthew*, chap. 26, lect. 12).

they would see His weakness, so that they might know that neither weakness absorbs glory, nor glory weakness.

The showing of His weakness follows. And firstly, He shows His weakness by an action; secondly, He shows it by His words. And according to this, the Evangelist does three things: for firstly, he says in what respect Christ was sad; secondly, he says why He was sad; and thirdly, he says how He was sad. In regard to the first point, **He began to grow sorrowful and to be sad**. Here one ought to beware of two errors; because certain men said that He was sad according to His divinity: and this cannot be, for He was sad because He was passible, but the divinity is not passible. Likewise, the opinion of the Arians, and also of Eunomius, was that there was no soul in Christ, but instead the Word took the place of His soul. And why was he saying this? It was so that everything that pertained to a defect was referred to the Word, so as to show that He was less than the Father, and this is false. For that reason, He suffered according to that which could suffer, meaning according to His soul.

Then he saith to them: My soul is sorrowful even unto death, etc. He does not say: 'I am sad,' because 'I' is ostensive of the person, but He was not sad insofar as the Word, but according to His soul, wherefore, the error of Arius and Apollinarius[40] is excluded; likewise, the error of Manichaeus is excluded, who asserted that He did not truly suffer. Hence, it is evident, according to what is said here, that He was sad.

But why was He sad? The Saints explain this in various ways. For Hilary and many others said that He was not sad for His own sake, nor on account of His death, but on account of the scandal of the disciples: and He tries to prove this by the fact that He took them with Him. Damascene says that He was sad for His own sake. And why? It is because sadness is within us due to the fact that we lack what we naturally love. The soul naturally wants to be united to the body, and this was in Christ's soul, because He ate, He drank, and He hungered. Therefore, the separation was against a natural desire: and so to be separated was something sad for Him. Nevertheless, we can understand that something was in the soul for its own sake and something was in the soul by comparison with something else: just as a bitter drink, considered in itself, is sorrowful; but related to the end of our health, it is a cause of joy. Just as one thing is the reason in respect to its

---

40. THEOPHYL. Apollinarius of Laodicea (+390) raised a heresy... saying, that Christ had flesh only, not a rational soul; in the place of which His divinity directed and controlled His body" (*Catena Aurea on St. John*, chap. 1, lect. 14).

nature and something else is the reason in another respect: so the death of Christ, considered in itself, was the reason for His sadness; but in that it was related to another reason, as referring to the purpose of His death, in this way He rejoiced. Wherefore, the words of Hilary and of Jerome are understood as referring to the purpose of His death.

Likewise, it is asked how sadness occurred in Christ. Wherefore, it ought to be observed that sometimes sadness occurs as a passion, sometimes it occurs as a propassion.[41] Sadness occurs as a passion when something is suffered and one is changed: but when something is suffered and one does not change, then one has a propassion. But sometimes passions of this kind are in us, such that reason is changed, and then the passions are complete: however, when reason is not changed, then it is a propassion. But in Christ His reason was never changed; for that reason, there was a propassion in Christ, and not a passion. Hence, the Evangelist significantly says: *He began to grow sorrowful*. Likewise, Augustine says that we have sadness as something contracted. Christ, however, had sadness as something assumed: for that is contracted, which is had by being born through origin; but Christ assumed our nature as He willed; wherefore, there was no need to take on passibility such as sadness, but He took it on by His will. Similarly, it ought to be observed what Damascene says, namely, that in us the movement of the passions forestalls reason, because sometimes there is passion in us, and other times there is propassion; in Christ, however, there was nothing except propassion, and it never was in Christ that a movement would arise in the lower powers of the soul, for on the contrary, the lower powers were completely subject to reason: and when He wished, He permitted the lower powers to act according to what was natural to them. Wherefore, another Evangelist said that He troubled Himself,[42] because these movements could not have occurred except to the degree that He wished.

Then he saith to them: My soul is sorrowful even unto death. Note what He says, *even unto death*, by which I will satisfy for this scandal and for others. Or, according to another exposition: 'You ought not to suppose that my passibility is bound to last forever; because as long as my body will be passible, and this is even unto death, my soul is sorrowful, but then it will be glorified.'

---

41. "[A passion] is a perfect passion when it dominates the soul, i.e. the reason; and a propassion when it has its beginning in the sensitive appetite, but goes no further" (III, q. 15, a. 4).

42. "Jesus, therefore, when he saw her weeping, and the Jews that were come with her weeping, groaned in the spirit and troubled himself" (Jn. 11, 33).

Then He excludes the other disciples: *Stay you here and watch with me. And going a little further, he fell upon his face, praying and saying*. Above, the Evangelist mentioned the cause of Christ's sadness; here, however, he treats of the order of Christ's prayer. And because He prayed three times, for that reason, this part is divided into three parts according to His three prayers. And about the first, he does two things. Firstly, he relates the prayer of the one praying; and secondly, he relates how Christ rebukes the failing of the disciples, where it is said, *And he cometh to his disciples*, etc. And in the first prayer, he relates the condition of the one praying; and secondly, he relates the tenor of the prayer. Now, His threefold condition is commended, because firstly, the Evangelist notes His earnestness; secondly, he notes His humility; and thirdly, he notes His devotion. He notes His solicitude, because he says, *going a little further*; because He even separated Himself from those He had chosen; "But thou when thou shalt pray, enter into thy chamber, and having shut the door, pray to thy Father in secret" (above 6, 6). But observe that He did not go very far but a short distance, to indicate that He is not far from those calling upon Him; "The Lord is nigh unto all them that call upon him" (Ps. 144, 18). Likewise, He went a little further so that His disciples might see Him praying, and they might have an example: for that reason, also His humility follows: *And he fell upon his face*; hence, He shows an example of humility. And firstly, He did this on account of humility in general, because humility is necessary for prayer; "The prayer of him that humbleth himself, shall pierce the clouds" (Eccli. 35, 21). Similarly, He did this for the humility of one individual, namely Peter, because he had said: *Though I should die with thee, I will not deny thee*. Wherefore, the Lord fell, to signify that one ought not to rely upon one's own strength; "Learn of me, because I am meek, and humble of heart" (above 11, 29). Moreover, the condition of piety or devotion is signified, when He says, *My Father*; for it is necessary for one praying that he pray with devotion; hence, it is said, *My Father*, because He is uniquely the Son; we, however, are sons by adoption; "I ascend to my Father and to your Father" (Jn. 20, 17); it is as though He is My Father in one way and yours in another.

Afterwards, he adds the tenor of His prayer: *If it be possible, let this chalice pass from me*. This prayer can be expounded in three ways; and in whatever way that it is expounded two things ought to be considered. Firstly, you ought to consider it generally in relation to every prayer, because, according to Damascene, prayer is the ascent of the mind to God: hence, prayer relates to the mind, or relates to the higher reason; and, nevertheless, prayer is constituted below God, yet above human nature, or prayer is under the divine will. Therefore, what ought to be understood? He prayed in such a way since His higher reason descended to these things, inasmuch as it was fitting, nevertheless, He willed that His will would always be subject to the Divine Reason; and this is noted when it is said, ***Nevertheless, not as I will but as thou wilt***; because His higher reason follows the will of nature, yet not simply, meaning, provided the will of nature does not conflict with the higher reason. Hence, He wishes to say: 'I will that what I want be fulfilled if it does not conflict with Thy justice, but on the contrary, I will that Thy justice be fulfilled.' And in this, He gives an example how we ought to order our affections, because we ought to order them in this manner, because they ought not to be discordant with the Divine rule. Hence, it is not a grave matter that someone shrinks from what is onerous, provided he order his will to the divine will. Likewise, it can be expounded, according to Chrysostom and Origen, such that, by the chalice, Christ's Passion is signified, concerning which it is said: "I will take the chalice of salvation," etc., (Ps. 115, 13). It is evident that Christ had a man's natural will; now this is what shrinks from death: wherefore, to show that He is a man, He asks that the chalice pass from Him. Wherefore, He said: ***If it be possible, let this chalice pass from me***, meaning His Passion, but it is as though He said: 'I do not speak absolutely, but if it be possible.' And because someone might suppose that He doubted whether it were possible for God, for that reason, He shows that it is possible, because He also said "all things are possible to thee" (Mk. 14, 36).[43]

Nevertheless, not as I will but as thou wilt, that is to say, if it is befitting to Thy justice, I will this; wherefore, He says: ***Not as I will***. Hence, He mentions two wills: He mentions one which He has from the Father insofar as He is God; for He had one will which He possesses with the Father; and in these words, the error of many men is confounded; likewise, He had another will insofar as He is a man: and He was submitting this will in all things to the Father; in this He is giving us an example, that we ought to submit our will to God's will; "I came down from heaven, not to do my own will but the will of my Father who sent me" (Jn. 6, 38). According to Jerome, He was not asking simply; but He was asking that this chalice would pass, because He saw that

[43]. The full verse is: "Abba, Father, all things are possible to thee: remove this chalice from me; but not what I will, but what thou wilt."

He would suffer from the Jews. Therefore, He wanted that this chalice would pass, meaning that He might redeem the world in such a way that it would not be the Jews' sin; "The offense of the Jews is the salvation of the Gentiles" (Rom. 11, 11). Hilary, however, speaks thus: The Lord does not ask to not die, but He asks that the chalice pass to other men; it is as though He were to say: 'I will take the chalice with confidence. I ask that My disciples will take it without hesitation.' But why does He say, *If it be possible*? It is because it would seem unnatural that they would accept death without sorrow. Hence, He means to say: 'I would want them not to suffer, if it were possible; but let it happen as Thou dost will,' meaning according to Thy ordination.

And he cometh to his disciples. Here He rebukes a fault of the disciples. And firstly, the fault is related; secondly, the rebuke is related; thirdly, the admonition is related; and fourthly, the reason for the admonition is related. When He had prayed, *He cometh to his disciples and findeth them asleep.* He states the literal reason, namely, part of the night had already passed and, for that reason, they were sleepy. Likewise, there was another reason, for they were sad men, and sleep easily creeps up upon such persons; "A sorrowful spirit drieth up the bones" (Prov. 17, 22). Similarly, it is signified that when Christ was going up to His Passion for us, many were sleeping, as it was said above, "They all slumbered and slept" (5, 5).

And he saith to Peter: What? Could you not watch one hour with me? But why does He speak to Peter rather than to the others? The reason is that Peter had boasted of himself, more than the others, that he would help Him in His necessities: for that reason, it was already a presage of his fall that would occur. *Could you not watch one hour with me?* And what is the reason why He later said this to them all? It was because all had promised with Peter; hence, it was said above: *And in like manner said all the disciples.*

Watch ye: and pray that ye enter not into temptation. In this part, the admonition is added. 'You trust in yourselves; but you ought to take refuge in the assistance of prayer: hence, *pray that ye enter not into temptation.*' Hence, in the general prayer He teaches us to ask this: "And lead us not into temptation" (above 6, 13). And He begins with vigilance as the preparation; "Before prayer prepare thy soul" (Eccli. 18, 23), meaning prudence is necessary; "Be ye wise as serpents" (above 10, 16).

The spirit indeed is willing, but the flesh is weak; it is as though He were to say: 'What you promise, from its promptitude is the spirit; yet, nevertheless, prayer is not necessary because of the spirit, but because of the flesh, which is weak; for that reason, vigilance is necessary. It is similar to what the Apostle says: "The body indeed is dead, because of sin: but the spirit liveth, because of justification" (Rom. 8, 10).

But it ought to be observed that of all things the flesh is the weakest, but not all men have a prompt spirit: in wicked men, in fact, as the flesh is weak, so also is the spirit: on the other hand, in good men, because they have a prompt spirit, for that reason, at the Resurrection the spirit will render the flesh prompt. Or there can be a twofold weakness. One weakness is evil which inclines to sin, according to what the Apostle says: "That which is good dwelleth not in my flesh" (Rom. 7, 18). The other weakness is good, in that the flesh is weak through promptness, according to that which is said: "Tell my beloved that I languish with love" (Can. 5, 8). And, for this reason, a man ought to watch, as Origen says, just like he who has a great treasure watches carefully to guard it.

Again the second time, he went and prayed. Here He prays a second time. According to Chrysostom, He prays a second time to more surely demonstrate His human nature: hence: "That thou didst see the second time, it is a token of the certainty" (Gen. 41, 32). Now, that which He says: *If this chalice may not pass away, but I must drink it, thy will be done*, can be explained in three ways. Firstly, it can be explained as follows. Above, He had asked conditionally; here, however, because it was certified that it could not be that He would not drink it, wherefore, He asks that His will be done; it is as though He would say: 'If it cannot be that I shall not pass over into the glory of immortality,' because His mortality was not contracted but assumed: for that reason, whether He suffer or not, He was to pass over into the glory of immortality. But the chalice could not pass from Him nor from His members; hence, if He would not drink, it would not pass from His members. He wishes, therefore, to say: 'If it cannot pass from Me and from My members, *thy will be done*; "That I should do thy will: O my God, I have desired it" (Ps. 39, 9). Secondly, Jerome explains it thus: 'If it cannot be that the truth can pass to the Gentiles, unless the Jews sin exceedingly, *thy will be done*: for their sin has become the salvation of the Gentiles.' Hilary explains it thus: 'If it cannot be that other saints drink the chalice of My Passion except by My example, *thy will be done*'; because other saints have taken an example from Christ's Passion. Therefore, He wishes to say: 'If this chalice cannot pass from Me to My disciples, unless I will drink it, so that they might be made stronger for drinking it, *thy will be done*.'

Afterwards, the second sleeping of the disciples is related: *And he cometh again and findeth them sleeping: for their eyes were heavy*, with sleep, meaning on account of sleep and on account of sadness; "My eye is troubled with wrath" (Ps. 30, 10).

And leaving them, he went again: and he prayed the third time. Here, the Evangelist treats of the third prayer: and he does two things. Firstly, he relates the order of the prayer; and secondly, he relates Christ's concession of sleep, where it is said, *Then he cometh to his disciples*, etc. He says: *And leaving them, he went again: and he prayed the third time, saying the selfsame word*. But what does it signify that He prayed three times? He prayed three times to free us from past, present, and future evils. Likewise, He did this to teach us to direct our prayer to the Father, Son and Holy Ghost; hence, in the prayers of the Church, it is always said: "Glory be to the Father, and to the Son, and to the Holy Ghost." Similarly, He did this to free Peter, by His threefold prayer, from his triple denial; "I have prayed for thee, Peter, that thy faith fail not" (Lk. 22, 32). Moreover, He prayed three times against three fears. For there is fear of a threefold concupiscence: of curiosity, of pride, and of the flesh. And these three concupiscences are mentioned in I John 2, 16: "All that is in the world is the concupiscence of the flesh and the concupiscence of the eyes and the pride of life." A threefold fear corresponds to this triple concupiscence, namely: the fear of pain corresponds to the concupiscence of the flesh; the fear of poverty corresponds to the concupiscence of the eyes; and the fear of shame and ignominy corresponds to the concupiscence of pride. And Christ suffered these things, not because He needed to do so, but for our sake.

Then he cometh to his disciples and said to them. And firstly, He is indulgent to their sleeping; and secondly He wakes them, where it is said, *Rise: let us go*. Firstly, He gives His allowance of their sleep; and secondly, He assigns the reason for waking them, where it is said, *Behold the hour is at hand: and the Son of man shall be betrayed*. Christ found them sleeping the first time and He rebuked them; He found them sleeping the second time, and He was silent; and the third time He found them sleeping, He permitted them to sleep. What is the reason? The literal reason is that to prelates is given a model of correction; because when a prelate comes to someone, and he finds him sleeping, he does not know if it happens to him due to negligence or due to weakness. And he can be indulgent. Likewise, it is because, after His Resurrection, He found the disciples sleeping, and he reproved them; "O foolish and slow of heart to believe"

(Lk. 24, 25). Likewise, He visited them after the receiving of the Holy Ghost, because they were still weak; because they were still observing the ceremonies of the Law, as it was said concerning Peter (Gal. 2). But He will lastly visit at His Coming, and He will leave them in a holy and peaceful sleep; "In peace in the self same I will sleep, and I will rest" (Ps. 4, 9). According to Augustine, He allowed them to sleep, and above He forbade them to sleep: but there is one kind of sleep here; and there is another kind above. For there is a sleep of weariness; and concerning this, He speaks above; and this sleep ought to be rebuked; here, however, the sleep is the sleep of rest; and this kind of sleep is permitted. Moreover, there is a sleep due to troubling; and this sleep is forbidden. Concerning this sleep it is said: "Rise, thou that sleepest, and arise from the dead" (Eph. 5, 14). For sometimes there is a sleep on account of the rest of the body, yet nevertheless the soul watches. "I sleep, and my heart watcheth" (Cant. 5, 2). Similarly, because they were about to labor, for that reason, it was fitting that they rest. Then He assigns the reason: *Behold the hour is at hand*. He did not have to do this by some necessity, but by the divine ordination; "They sought therefore to apprehend him: and no man laid hands on him, because his hour was not yet come" (Jn. 7, 30). But this hour had come; "Jesus knowing that his hour was come, that he should pass out of this world to the Father" (Jn. 13, 1). But some might say: If the hour is by divine ordination, then they did not sin in killing Him. Wherefore, when He relates this sin, He says: *the Son of man shall be betrayed into the hands of sinners*, meaning they do not do this such that it is by the divine ordination, but from the fulfilling of their own will. "I have given my dear soul into the hand of her enemies" (Jer. 12, 7). Then the Evangelist relates the waking up. And firstly, he relates it; and secondly, he relates the need for waking them, where it is said, *Behold the hour is at hand*. By the fact, however, that Christ says, *Rise*, He shows His promptness; hence, in John 18, it is said that He met them.[44] And why did He do this? *Behold he is at hand that will betray me*. He knew that he was near, not because He saw him with the eyes of His body, but rather He saw him with His spirit itself, namely, with the eye of His divinity.

But why did He say to them, *Rise*, since He had given them permission to sleep? Augustine solves this question, saying that He had said this rebuking them; it is as though He were to say: 'Sleep as much as you like: *Behold the hour is at hand*, etc.' And Augus-

[44]. "Jesus therefore, knowing all things that should come upon him, went forth and said to them: Whom seek ye?" (verse 4).

tine says that this explanation suffices, unless a better one comes along; for that reason, he says otherwise that these disciples slept a little, and when they had slept, He said: *Rise: let us go.*

47. As he yet spoke, behold Judas, one of the twelve, came, and with him a great multitude with swords and clubs, sent from the chief priests and the ancients of the people.
48. And he that betrayed him gave them a sign, saying: Whomsoever I shall kiss, that is he. Hold him fast.
49. And forthwith coming to Jesus, he said: Hail, Rabbi. And he kissed him.
50. And Jesus said to him: Friend, whereto art thou come? Then they came up and laid hands on Jesus and held him.
51. And behold one of them that were with Jesus, stretching forth his hand, drew out his sword: and striking the servant of the high priest, cut off his ear.
52. Then Jesus saith to him: Put up again thy sword into its place: for all that take the sword shall perish with the sword.
53. Thinkest thou that I cannot ask my Father, and he will give me presently more than twelve legions of angels?
54. How then shall the scriptures be fulfilled, that so it must be done?
55. In that same hour, Jesus said to the multitudes: You are come out, as it were to a robber, with swords and clubs to apprehend me. I sat daily with you, teaching in the temple: and you laid not hands on me.
56. Now all this was done that the scriptures of the prophets might be fulfilled. Then the disciples, all leaving him, fled.

Above, the events preparatory to the Passion were related, namely, the institution of the Sacrament and Christ's prayer; here, however, the Evangelist relates the Passion as to those things which were perpetrated by the Jews. And firstly, he shows how Christ was taken; secondly, he shows how He was examined; and thirdly, he shows how He was condemned. The second part is where it is said, *And the chief priests and the whole council sought false witness against Jesus*; and the third part is where it is said, *Then the high priest rent his garments.* About the first part, he does three things. Firstly, he treats of the betrayal; secondly, he treats of His arrest; and thirdly, he treats of how He was led away after His arrest. The second part is where it is said,

Then they came up and laid hands on Jesus; and the third part is where it is said, *But they holding Jesus led him to Caiphas the high priest.* About the first point, he does three things. Firstly, he describes the person of the betrayer; secondly, he describes the sign of the betrayal; and thirdly, he describes the perpetration of the betrayal. The second part is where it is said, *And he that betrayed him gave them a sign*; and the third part is where it is said, *And forthwith coming to Jesus, he said: Hail, Rabbi.* He describes the betrayer by three things. Firstly, he describes him by his name; secondly, he describes him by his dignity; and thirdly, he describes him by his companions. He describes him by his name, *As he yet spoke, behold Judas*, etc., more precisely, as Christ was speaking those words whereby He was boosting their confidence, *behold Judas*, whose name means "confessing." There were two Judas', of whom one was wicked, and the other good, to signify that certain men who were praising in the Church would be good; "With the mouth, confession is made unto salvation" (Rom. 10, 10); and others would be wicked; "They profess that they know God: but in their works they deny him" (Tit. 1, 16). Afterwards, he is described by his dignity, *One of the twelve*, because although he was appointed to such a great dignity, nevertheless, he fell into so great a sin. In which an example is given to us that no one ought to rely upon his rank. The Apostle says: "He that thinketh himself to stand, let him take heed lest he fall" (I Cor. 10, 12); "Have not I chosen you twelve? And one of you is a devil?" (Jn. 6, 71). And why did He choose him, since He knew that he would be wicked? One reason is that it was to give an example to prelates, so that they might not be desolated. Likewise, Judas is described by his companions, *And with him a great multitide*, etc. Just as he had a cruel soul, so he had cruel companions, because every soul seeks what is similar to itself. And this is described, because he says, *a great multitude.* In this it is observed that they were foolish, for foolish men are in a great multitude; "The number of fools is infinite" (Eccle. 1, 15). And those men were truly foolish, because they were contradicting Wisdom. Likewise, they were armed, for he says, *with swords and clubs.* And what is the reason for this? Origen says that many believed in Him, and, for that reason, they feared that a crowd would take Him from them. Similarly, because they were saying that He was casting out devils by Beelzebub (above 13);[45] wherefore, so that no power might protect Him, they came armed. Moreover, Judas

---

[45]. "But the Pharisees hearing it, said: This man casteth not out devils but by Beelzebub the prince of the devils" (verse 24).

is described by his authority, because *they were sent from the chief priests and the ancients of the people*; hence, they were invested with their authority, so that no one would contradict them, so that it might be fulfilled what is said in Psalm 2, 2: "The kings of the earth stood up, and the princes met together, against the Lord, and against his Christ."

Afterwards, the sign of the betrayal is treated: *And he that betrayed him gave them a sign, saying*, etc. But here there is a question. Since He was known in Judea, why were they asking for a sign? The reason can be twofold. One reason is that it was because Judas had heard that Christ was transfigured on the mountain, and he supposed that this was done by magical arts; wherefore, he wanted to anticipate this by the sign of a kiss before He could transfigure Himself. Jerome proposes this exposition. Origen, however, says that the reason is as follows, that just as the manna in the desert to each person had the taste of whatever they preferred, so Christ appeared to everyone according to the opinion each person had of Him; wherefore, it was necessary that he would give a sign. He gave a surprising sign, namely, *Whomsoever I shall kiss, that is he. Hold him fast*. He made a sign of friendship into a sign of betrayal; "Better are the wounds of a friend, than the deceitful kisses of an enemy" (Prov. 27, 6).

And forthwith coming to Jesus, he said: Hail, Rabbi. And he kissed him. Here the perpetration of the betrayal is related. Firstly, he showed the signs; and secondly, he began to act. And he firstly showed the signs by words, when he says, *Hail, Rabbi*; secondly, he showed the signs by an action, *And he kissed him*. Something similar is stated in II Kings 20, 9, namely, that Joab held the head of Amasa, and killed him.[46]

But why did he not come to Him immediately, but firstly greeted Him? One reason is that it was on account of his respect for the Master. Likewise, he firstly saluted Him, because he feared that before he might identify Him, He would be able to firstly transfigure Himself.

And Jesus said to him: Friend, whereto art thou come? And this verse can be read either as a question or as a forbearant statement. If it be read as a question, then it can be read that it was said as a reproach, as if He were to say: 'You show friendship by a kiss, and you have come to destroy me?' according to that which is written: "They speak peace with their neighbor, but evils are in their hearts" (Ps. 27, 3). And He said, *Friend*. As often as

---

46. "And he took Amasa by the chin with his right hand to kiss him."

He calls someone a friend, He is speaking as one reproaching. Hence, it was said above: "Friend, how camest thou in hither not having on a wedding garment?" (22, 12). And elsewhere above it is said: "Friend, I do thee no wrong," etc., (22, 12). "For we did not firstly love Him, but He first hath loved us" (I Jn. 4, 19).[47] Or it can be read as a forbearant statement, and it is not an expression of reprimand, but a permissive expression: ***Friend, whereto art thou come***, like to that which was said: "That which thou dost, do quickly" (Jn. 13, 27). And He calls him a friend in respect to Himself; since "With them that hated peace I was peaceable" (Ps. 119, 7). And although He knew that he would kiss Him, nevertheless, He met him.

Then they laid hands on Jesus holding him fast. Now His arrest is treated. Firstly, the severity of the arrest is related; secondly, a Scriptural reference is related; and thirdly, a rebuke of the disciples is related. About the first point, the Evangelist does three things. For firstly, he states how the servants of the high priest arrest Him; secondly, he states how a certain disciple tried to prevent His arrest; and thirdly, he states that Christ rebuked him. He says, therefore: ***Then they laid hands on Jesus holding him fast.*** "Your hands are full of blood" (Is. 1, 15). For He handed over Himself; "I have given my dear soul into the hand of her enemies" (Jer. 12, 7). Then it is related how one disciple attacked the attackers: ***And behold one of them that were with Jesus, stretching forth his hand, drew out his sword.*** Who was he? It must be said that it was Peter.[48] Hence, just as he wanted to prevent Christ's Passion above in chapter 16,[49] so also he wanted to prevent Him here. From what did he have the occasion of doing this? It was from that which is stated in Luke 22,[50] where the Lord commanded that they buy swords;[51] and knowing this, they supposed that the swords were needed; hence, they had a small knife for killing the lamb. Wherefore, Peter had one.

---

47. cf. St. Augustine, "Commentary on the First Letter of John", bk. 7, n. 9. "Not as though we had loved God, but because he hath first loved us" (I Jn. 4, 10).
48. "Then Simon Peter, having a sword, drew it and struck the servant of the high priest and cut off his right ear" (Jn. 18, 10).
49. "And Peter taking him, began to rebuke him, saying: Lord, be it far from thee, this shall not be unto thee" (verse 22).
50. "Then said he unto them: But now he that hath a purse, let him take it, and likewise a scrip: and he that hath not, let him sell his coat and buy a sword" (verse 36).
51. "BASIL; Or the Lord does not bid them... buy a sword, but predicts that it should come to pass, that in truth the Apostles, forgetful of the time of the Passion, of the gifts and law of their Lord, would dare to take up the sword. For often does the Scripture make use of the imperative form of speech in the place of prophecy. Still in many books we do not find, Let him take, or buy, but, he will take, he will buy" (*Catena Aurea on St. Luke*, chap. 22, lect. 10).

Striking the servant of the high priest, cut off his ear. Do not suppose that had he time for deliberation, he would have only cut off an ear; but he struck a blow, and when he wanted to deal a death blow, he happened to only cut off an ear. The name of this servant was Malchus,[52] which is interpreted, 'king.' And he signifies the cutting off of the kingdom from the Jewish people, because, although his name means 'king', nevertheless, he was made a servant of the high priests, that is to say, he was made a servant of the Romans: Peter cut off the ear of this man. By the ear hearing is signified; and this is twofold, namely, the right ear, by which eternal life is signified; the left ear, by which temporal life is signified. *He cut off his ear*, because he cut off the teaching of spiritual things from the people of the Jews; and this was done as an occasional cause, wherefore, the Gentiles received the right ear, because Peter was the first one to preach to the Gentiles; and so he cut off the ear, by drawing the Gentiles to the faith.

Then Jesus saith to him: Put up again thy sword into its place. Here the rebuking is related. And firstly, He rebukes Peter; and secondly, He rebukes the servants of the high priest, where it is said: *In that same hour, Jesus said to the multitudes*, etc. And firstly, He relates a warning, and secondly, He gives the reasons for the warning, where it is said: *For all that take the sword shall perish with the sword.* It is said, therefore: *Then Jesus saith to him: Put up again thy sword into its place.* He came voluntarily to suffer, wherefore, He did not wish to be defended. And in doing this, He was giving an example that martyrs suffering for Christ ought not to defend themselves. Then He gives the reasons why He does not wish them to take up the sword: and firstly, this is because of the punishment; secondly, this is because of Christ's will; and thirdly, this is because of a citation of Scripture. The second reason is where it is said, *Thinkest thou that I cannot ask my Father*, etc.; and the third reason is where it is said, *How then shall the scriptures be fulfilled?* Firstly, He calms them from fear of the punishment, saying: *All that take the sword shall perish with the sword.*

But this raises a question. Augustine considers this question, namely, that not all who carry a sword, perish by the sword, for sometimes they perish from fever; for that reason, this passage can be expounded in three ways, in that there are three types of

---

52. "And the name of the servant was Malchus" (Jn. 18, 10).

swords. There is the material sword, concerning which it is said: "The wicked have drawn out the sword" (Ps. 36, 14). Likewise, there is the sword of Divine sentence, concerning which it is said: "I will destroy them with the sword" (Jer. 19, 7). Moreover, there is the sword of the Divine word: "Take unto you the sword of the Spirit (which is the word of God)" (Eph. 6, 17). The sword in this passage can, therefore, be understood of all of these. It can be understood of a material sword, because he who kills with a sword, will perish by a sword, meaning he will perish by his own sword, and not with another's sword.[53] Hence: "Let their sword enter into their own hearts" (Ps. 36, 15). Likewise, it can be expounded of the sword of condemnation, concerning which it is stated in Genesis 3 that the Lord put a sword turning every way before the paradise.[54] Hence, those who condemn others will be condemned by the Divine sentence. Or some men take the sword by their own authority, which they do not have from another, and such men will perish by the sword.[55]

Thinkest thou that I cannot ask my Father, etc. Here He assigns the reason for calming Peter's motivation, giving him to understand that He was suffering voluntarily, and that He would be able to get away. And because He saw that Peter was presuming, for that reason, He says: *Can I not ask my Father?* And He does not say, 'Can I not call,' or 'Can I not bring,' but 'Can I not ask': for He speaks the words of a man, because it belongs to a man to pray. *And he will give me presently more than twelve legions of angels?* And this was said in accordance with the weakness of Peter's soul. Accordingly, Peter thought that he should defend Him, and that He needed the assistance of men; wherefore, He wished to say that if He could be defended by the assistance of men, so much more could He be defended by the assistance of angels. But it was not necessary, because the angels are rather sustained by Him.

But what is this that He says, *Twelve legions of angels*? It ought to be said that among the Greeks a group of soldiers is called a phalanx, among the Romans it is called a legion, and it has six thousand men: hence, twelve legions equal seventy-two thousand soldiers, and there are that many languages of men, as it is main-

---

53. "REMIG. Everyone who uses the sword to put man to death perishes first by the sword of his own wickedness" (*Catena Aurea on St. Matthew*, chap. 26, lect. 14).
54. Verse 24.
55. "AUG. That is, everyone who uses the sword. And he uses the sword, who, without the command or sanction of any superior, or legitimate authority, arms himself against man's life. For truly the Lord had given commandment to His disciples to take the sword, but not to smite with the sword" (*Catena Aurea on St. Matthew*, chap. 26, lect. 14).

tained based upon Genesis 11.[56] Hence, He means to say: 'If all men were to rise against Me, the Lord would be able to send a thousand angels against those speaking any one language: and if one angel destroyed so many thousand men, as shown it Isaias 37,[57] all the more could thousands of angels kill the men who speak one language; "Is there any numbering of his soldiers?" (Job 25, 3). And: "Thousands of thousands ministered to him, and ten thousand times a hundred thousand stood before him" (Dan. 7, 10). Remigius says the following: Whoever does God's will, can be called 'angels,' meaning 'messengers'; "Go, ye swift angels, to a nation rent and torn in pieces" (Is. 18, 2). For whosoever obeys God are called "angels"; "Who makest thy angels spirits: and thy ministers a burning fire" (Ps. 103, 4). Therefore, a legion of Roman soldiers can be understood by the word 'legion.' Hence, the Lord would be able to summon and rouse the Roman legions to destroy the Jews as was done later under Titus and Vespasian.[58] And by this passage, certain men refuted the opinion of those who said that the Lord was unable to do anything other than what He did; for if He was able to summon legions, which He did not summon, then it is evident that He can do many things which He does not do.

How then shall the scriptures be fulfilled? Here is the third reason why Peter ought not to impede His arrest: namely, it is because the Scriptures said that Christ would suffer; and, for that reason, so it must be done. And He does not say which Scriptures, because all the prophets said this either hiddenly or openly. Hence, it is said: "Ought not Christ to have suffered these things and so, to enter into his glory?" (Lk. 24, 26).

In that same hour, Jesus said to the multitudes. In this part, He rebukes the servants of the high priest; and He does two things. Firstly, He calls to mind their deed; and secondly, He calls

---

56. "There are several mediaeval historiographic accounts that attempt to make an enumeration of the languages scattered at the Tower of Babel. Because a count of all the descendants of Noah listed by name in chapter 10 of Genesis (LXX) provides 15 names for Japheth's descendants, 30 for Ham's, and 27 for Sem's, these figures became established as the 72 languages resulting from the confusion at Babel — although the exact listing of these languages tended to vary over time. Some of the earliest sources for 72 (sometimes 73) languages are the 2ND century Christian writers Clement of Alexandria (*Stromata* I, 21) and Hippolytus of Rome (*On the Psalms* 9); it is repeated in the Syriac book, *Cave of Treasures* (c. AD 350), Epiphanius of Salamis' *Panarion* (c. 375) and St. Augustine's *The City of God* 16.6 (c. 410). The chronicles attributed to Hippolytus (c. 234) contain one of the first attempts to list each of the 72 peoples who were believed to have spoken these languages" (Wikipedia, "Tower of Babel, *"http://en.wikipedia.org/wiki/Tower_of_Babel*).

57. "And the angel of the Lord went out and slew in the camp of the Assyrians a hundred and eighty-five thousand" (verse 36).

58. Titus was the commander of the Roman army and was the son of the Emperor Vespasian when Jerusalem was destroyed in 70 AD.

to mind the irrationality of their deed, when He says: *You are come out, as it were to a robber, with swords and clubs to apprehend me.* "He hath gnashed with his teeth upon me" (Job 16, 10), because they went out as if He were a robber; but they were rather coming like robbers. A robber hides so that he may not be arrested; but Christ offers Himself openly. And if robbers want to injure, they do not injure in public; but Christ was offering Himself; hence, He says; *I sat daily with you, teaching in the temple: and you laid not hands on me*; wherefore, 'you have come like thieves.' For in order to give them an opportunity of arresting Him, He went out of the city. *I sat daily with you, teaching in the temple.* Something similar is stated in John 18, 20: "In secret I have spoken nothing." And He says, *Teaching in the temple.* This was always His custom to teach in the Temple. *And you laid not hands on me.* Hence, it is evident that you have come like thieves.

Afterwards, the testimony of Scripture is related: *Now all this was done that the scriptures of the prophets might be fulfilled.* And the Evangelist does not say the books of which prophets, because it is as though it is found in them all; "They have dug my hands and feet. They have numbered all my bones" (Ps. 21, 17-18). And: "We reputed him the most abject of men, a man of sorrows" (Is. 53, 3). And he says, *That the scriptures of the prophets might be fulfilled.* The word 'that' can be used causatively, and here it is not used in this sense: or it can be used consecutively, and it is understood here in this sense. For this did not happen because the prophets said it; but rather, because it was going to happen, for that reason, they predicted it. Hence, the meaning is: 'That it might be fulfilled,' meaning that by this event happening, what the prophets had predicted has been fulfilled.

Then the disciples, all leaving him, fled; so that it might be fulfilled what is said in Psalm 37, 12: "My friends and my neighbors have left me."

But why did they not leave Him at first? Jerome replies: 'It is because it was written in John 7, 30, that "they sought therefore to apprehend him: and no man laid hands on him, because his hour was not yet come." Hence, at first, they believed that He could free Himself, and they would defend Him: but when they saw that He would be arrested, and that He did not wish to defend Himself, they fled and left Him.

57. But they holding Jesus led him to Caiphas the high priest, where the scribes and the ancients were assembled.

58. And Peter followed him afar off, even to the court of the high priest. And going in, he sat with the servants, that he might see the end.

59. And the chief priests and the whole council sought false witness against Jesus, that they might put him to death.

60. And they found not, whereas many false witnesses had come in. And last of all there came two false witnesses:

61. And they said: This man said, I am able to destroy the temple of God and after three days to rebuild it.

62. And the high priest rising up, said to him: Answerest thou nothing to the things which these witness against thee?

63. But Jesus held his peace. And the high priest said to him: I adjure thee by the living God, that thou tell us if thou be the Christ the Son of God.

64. Jesus saith to him: Thou hast said it. Nevertheless I say to you, hereafter you shall see the Son of man sitting on the right hand of the power of God and coming in the clouds of heaven.

65. Then the high priest rent his garments, saying: He hath blasphemed: What further need have we of witnesses? Behold, now you have heard the blasphemy.

66. What think you? But they answering, said: He is guilty of death.

67. Then did they spit in his face and buffeted him. And others struck his face with the palms of their hands,

68. Saying: Prophesy unto us, O Christ. Who is he that struck thee?

69. But Peter sat without in the court. And there came to him a servant maid, saying: Thou also wast with Jesus the Galilean.

70. But he denied before them all, saying: I know not what thou sayest.

71. And as he went out of the gate, another maid saw him; and she saith to them that were there: This man also was with Jesus of Nazareth.

72. And again he denied with an oath: I know not the man.

73. And after a little while, they came that stood by and said to Peter: Surely thou also art one of them. For even thy speech doth discover thee.

74. Then he began to curse and to swear that he knew not the man. And immediately the cock crew.

75. And Peter remembered the word of Jesus which he had said: Before the cock crow, thou wilt deny me thrice. And going forth, he wept bitterly.

Above, it was treated concerning Christ's arrest; now, it is treated wither He would be led; and the place and those gathering at the place are described. He says, therefore: *But they*, namely, those who held Him, *led him to Caiphas*. This Caiphas was the priest of that year, according to Jerome, and according to that which is stated: "Being the high priest that year" (Jn. 11, 49). For, at that time, the priesthood was not being treated according to the precepts of the Law. The Lord had commanded that Aaron and his sons would be priests by a hereditary right, such that when one died another priest would replace him. But afterwards, when the Jews' ambition grew, they were unable to bear the Law, and when Judea became subject to the Romans, this Caiphas bought the priesthood from the Jews and he bought it from Pilate; wherefore, the leader was wicked.[59] And it is not surprising that a wicked judge or leader makes a wicked judgment. And this relates to a mystery; because just as Christ's Passion was the offering of a true sacrifice, so also the place ought to befit a true sacrifice, such that Christ, who is a priest forever, should be offered in the house of the priest. 'Caiphas' is interpreted 'investigator,'[60] and this can refer to the malice with which he condemned Christ.

But here there is a question, because in John 18 it is said that He was firstly led to Annas.[61] And this is understood to be true; and in this their malice appears, because although they ought to have been intent upon the solemn feast, they were intent upon doing evil, such that what is said in Isaias 1, 14 applies well to them: "My soul hateth your solemnities." Hence, what is said in Psalm 2, 2 was fulfilled: "They met together, against God, and against his Christ."

And Peter followed him afar off. Above, it was treated concerning the place of Christ's arrest, here it is treated concerning Peter's coming to Him. Firstly, Christ is led away, and then Peter arrives. And the Evangelist does three things: for firstly, he mentions the manner in which Peter came to Christ; secondly, he

---

59. "Caiphas was appointed High-Priest of the Jews by the Roman procurator Valerius Gratus, the predecessor of Pontius Pilate, about A.D. 18 (Ant., XVIII, ii, 2), and removed from that office by the procurator Vitellius, shortly after he took charge of affairs in Palestine, A.D. 36 (Ant., XVIII, iv, 3). During this period the famous Annas, father-in-law of Caiphas (John 18:13), who had been high-priest from A.D. 6 to 15, continued to exercise a controlling influence over Jewish affairs, as he did when his own sons held the position" ("Joseph Caiphas," *Catholic Encyclopedia (1907 ed.)*, vol. 3, p. 143).

60. "The name 'Caiphas' is interpreted to mean 'investigator,' or 'prophetic,' or 'vomiting from his mouth.' For he unjustly condemned the Just One with his mouth although he had foretold this by a prophetic mystery." (St. Isidore of Seville, *Etymologies* (or *Origins*), bk. 7, par. 10, n. 7)

61. "And they led him away to Annas first" (verse 13).

mentions how the place where he came to Christ;[62] and thirdly, he mentions how Peter, following Christ, came to Him. In that he came, this was due to his fervor; in that he was afar off, this was due to his fear; hence, the Church, founded upon Peter's faith, would follow Christ, yet afar off; because Christ suffered for the Church, not for Himself; however, Peter and the Church suffered for themselves. Likewise, the place where Peter comes to Christ is mentioned, for he says, **Even to the court of the high priest**: for Peter did not dare to enter the house, lest he be seen to be a disciple of Jesus. Now regarding how he entered, Matthew is silent, but John recounts that "a certain disciple therefore, who was known to the high priest brought in Peter" (18, 15).

His company follows: **And going in, he sat with the servants, that he might see the end**; and he was doing this either out of curiosity or out of piety. And there were three things at this point that were somewhat dispositive to Peter's fall: that he was following afar off was disposing to this, because it indicated that he was not firm: for he who is firm ought to draw near. Hence, it is said: "Draw nigh to God: and he will draw nigh to you" (James 4, 8). For in God's house there is the throne of God and of the Lamb, as it is stated in Apocalypse 22, 3.[63] For in Christ's house there is perfect charity. Hence, Peter did not draw near to Christ's charity.

Similarly, he had not become as malicious as the Jews, for that reason, he was tepid; wherefore, there happened to him what is said: "Because thou art lukewarm, I will begin to vomit thee out of my mouth" (Apoc. 3, 16). Likewise, he was disposed to fall because there were wicked servants. "As the judge of the people is himself, so also are his ministers" (Eccli. 10, 2). And, for that reason, it was not surprising that he fell, because he remained in bad company. This is why it is said: "With the holy thou wilt be holy... and with the perverse thou wilt be perverted" (Ps. 17, 26-27).

Then Christ's trial follows. And firstly, He is tried by witnesses; and secondly, He is tried by His own confession, where it is said, **And the high priest rising up, said to him**, etc. About the first part, the Evangelist does three things. Firstly, the evil intention of the chief priests is made manifest; secondly, the lack of proof is pointed out; and thirdly, the false testimony is shown. He says, therefore: **And the chief priests and the whole council sought false witness against Jesus, that they might put him to death**.

---

62. This second point is missing in the text but has been interpolated from the context.

63. "The throne of God and of the Lamb shall be in it."

But there is a question, why did they not put Him to death without testimony? One reason is that hypocrites seek what appears to be good, but they do not seek the truth: so these men sought to appear as not acting of themselves; hence, they were acting against the Law: "Thou shalt not bear false witness against thy neighbor" (Ex. 20, 16). If it be not lawful to speak false testimony, it is also not lawful to seek it. Another reason was that they did not possess the authority to kill, and for that reason, they were seeking false testimony so that they could hand Him over to the Roman leader.

And they found not, whereas many false witnesses had come in. Behold, the lack of testimony, in which Christ's innocence is shown, such that He could say: "I have walked in my innocence" (Ps. 25, 1). For they were always lying in wait for Christ, but they found nothing evil. Hence, He fulfilled that which is stated: "By doing well you may put to silence the ignorance of foolish men" (I Pet. 2, 15). Then the false testimony follows: *And last of all there came two false witnesses, and they said.*

But here there is a question, why are they called false witnesses: because it is clear that Christ had said what is found in John 2.[64] According to Jerome, not only one may be called a false witness, who says what he does not know, but also one who gives a false interpretation to what has been said. *This man said, I am able to destroy the temple of God and after three days to rebuild it.* But He did not mean the material temple, but the temple of His own Body. Likewise, not only is there false witness as to the meaning, but also as to the words, because He had said: "Destroy this temple" (Jn. 2, 19); and He had not said: 'I can destroy God's Temple'; and it was as though He said: 'You Jews destroy the temple, meaning Christ, and after three days I will raise it up'; because to rebuild pertains more to a material temple, but to raise it up pertains rather to a body: hence, they were false witnesses both in respect to the words, and in respect to the meaning.

Likewise, there is a question. Why do they not accuse Him of violating the Sabbath? Chrysostom answers that it is because they often accused Him of this, and He had always excused Himself, and He had confirmed His excuse with miracles; wherefore, they thought that it would not avail them. Moreover, the judge was not Jewish,[65] and, for that reason, they knew that he would not accept this accusation.

64. "Destroy this temple; and in three days I will raise it up" (verse 19).
65. i.e. Pontius Pilate, the Roman Procurator.

Then the trial by His own confession follows. And firstly, a question regarding the testimony of the witnesses is related; secondly, a question of the chief priest is related. The second part is where it is said, *And the high priest said to him*, etc. He says, therefore: *And the high priest rising up, said to him: Answerest thou nothing to the things which these witness against thee?* The fact that he rose up was due to his impatience and fury, hearing that Christ was not being convicted: and what he says: *Answerest thou nothing*, etc., he does not say this to excuse Him, but to catch Him in His words; "The fool will speak foolish things, and his heart will work iniquity" (Is. 32, 6).

But Jesus held his peace. But why was He silent? It was for three reasons. It was to teach us caution: for He knew that whatever He would say, they would turn it all into a calumny; and in this case, one ought to be silent before those laying snares; "I have set a guard to my mouth, when the sinner stood against me" (Ps. 38, 2). Another reason was that it was not then the time for teaching, but for having patience: and so was fulfilled that which is said: "He shall be led as a sheep to the slaughter, and shall be dumb as a lamb before his shearer, and he shall not open his mouth" (Is. 53, 7). The third reason is to teach us constancy when someone accuses us unjustly; "Fear ye not the reproach of men" (Is. 51, 7).

Then the question of the chief priest follows: *And the high priest said to him: I adjure thee by the living God, that thou tell us if thou be the Christ the Son of God.* And firstly, the question is related; and secondly, the Lord's reply is related. The high priest, seeing that he could not ensnare Him, adjured Him: and he did this to catch Him in His words. And this is stated in John 10, 21: "How long dost thou hold our souls in suspense? If thou be the Christ, tell us plainly." For among the Jews it was considered to be a great matter to adjure: for to adjure is to pressure someone to take an oath. For just as Christians ought not to swear except out of necessity, so they ought not to use adjurations, but instead of adjurations they ought to use words of request. Then the reply follows: *Jesus saith to him: Thou hast said it*. Observe, that when there was something said against Himself, He kept silent: but immediately when God's power is adjured, He answers. Hence, He always sought the glory of His Father; "I seek not my own glory" (Jn. 8, 50). And concerning this, the Evangelist firstly relates His response; and secondly, he relates His manifestation. He says, therefore: *Jesus saith to him: Thou hast said it*. This can be expounded such that Christ is not asserting anything, but left the matter in doubt. "Give not that which is holy to dogs" (above 7, 6). Or it can be understood as an assertion: ***Thou hast said it***, meaning that what was said is true; and this is evident, because it is said in Mark 14, 62: "I am." Then He shows the proof of what He said: ***Nevertheless I say to you, hereafter you shall see the Son of man sitting on the right hand of the power of God.*** And He evidently wishes to show that He is the Son of God, according to two passages. One is in Psalm 109, 1: "The Lord said to my Lord: Sit thou at my right hand." And by this passage He had shown (above 22),[66] that Christ is the Son of God. Another passage is: "I beheld in the vision of the night, and lo, one like the Son of man came with the clouds of heaven," etc., (Dan. 7, 7). I say that He is speaking in this way, namely, ***Thou hast said it***; 'but you have not known the truth.' Observe, that the Truth shall be manifested, because ***You shall see the Son of man sitting on the right hand of the power of God.*** Because He said, 'sitting on the right hand,' Chrysostom expounds that sitting at the right hand signifies a royal dignity; "He shall sit upon the throne of David, and upon his kingdom" (Is. 9, 7). Or, to sit on the right hand is to be in the full beatitude of power, or to be in goods of greater consequence: for the right hand is the more noble one; wherefore, it signifies a greater dignity, not that He has greater power, but equal power; "All power is given to me in heaven and in earth" (below 28, 18). Likewise, concerning His power He says: ***Coming in the clouds of heaven.***

But what is it that He says, ***Hereafter you shall see***, etc.? It ought to be observed that what He says, ***In the clouds***, can be referred to His last Coming, or to His daily coming. His last Coming will be in a cloud; "As you have seen him going into heaven" (Acts 1, 11). This phrase can be expounded in another way concerning His daily coming, about which it is said: "If he come to me, I shall not see him" (Job 11, 11). And this coming is in the clouds, meaning in the Apostles and in holy teachers. Concerning these men, it is said: "Who are these, that fly as clouds?" (Is. 60,8). These men are called 'clouds,' because they ascend upon high. Likewise, clouds are fruitful. The first point pertains to the loftiness of their lives, and the second point pertains to the fruitfulness of their teaching. And they are 'the clouds of heaven,' meaning they are heavenly men, because they carried the heavenly image. But what is the meaning of the words, ***Hereafter you shall see***? The meaning is that, immediately after the Passion, He converted

---

[66] "If David then call him Lord, how is he his son?" (verse 45).

some men to the faith, and He converted others through the evidence of their deeds. Similarly, some were converted on account of their faith, and others on account of their good deeds. Moreover, if this passage be referred to His last Coming, Origen says: "All the world's time compared to eternity is nothing, and is like one moment." "A thousand years in thy sight are as yesterday, which is past" (Ps. 89, 4). Wherefore, He says, **Hereafter**, because the time until the Judgment, in respect to eternity, is nothing. 'Nevertheless, after you have departed from Me, nothing remains to be done except that you will know me clearly, because I will come in the clouds of heaven. And then you will know that I am the Son of man.' A similar manner of speech is found above: "You shall not see me henceforth till you say: Blessed is he that cometh in the name of the Lord" (23, 39).

Then the high priest rent his garments. Here His condemnation is related. And firstly, how He was condemned is related; and secondly, how He was denied by His disciple is related. And firstly, the Evangelist treats of His condemnation; and secondly, he treats of the mockery. For firstly, the high priest condemns Him; and secondly, asks for a verdict. The condemning high priest lays blame both by an action and by words; he does this by an action, in that he rends his garments. He rends his garments with the same fury with which, shortly before, he rose from his seat: for it was the custom that those who heard a blasphemy rent their garments as a sign that they could not bear to listen. But the fact that He did these two things signified something: the fact that he rose from his seat signified that he lost the priesthood; and that he rent his garments, signified that the priesthood was due to be transferred; "The priesthood being translated, it is necessary that a translation also be made of the law" (Heb. 7, 12). Christ's garment was not rent; "Let us not cut it but let us cast lots for it, whose it shall be" (Jn. 19, 24). Hence, it signified an abolition. And this is signified in I Kings 15, 28: "The Lord hath rent the kingdom of Israel from thee this day" (I Kings 15, 28). In this way, the priesthood was rent from the Jews, and given to Christ's members. Then the high priest lays blame, saying, **He hath blasphemed**. Because Christ had said this, he considers Him to be a blasphemer; hence: "For a good work we stone thee not, but for blasphemy: and because that thou, being a man, makest thyself the Son God" (Jn. 10, 33); and such a man deserves death. Then he lays blame: **What further need have we of witnesses?** Then he asks for a verdict: **What think you? But they answering, said: He is guilty of death**, according to the judgment of the

Law. And this would have been true, if He were a blasphemer; but He was not, wherefore, they judged Him badly, because they condemn the Author of life to death; "As death is through Adam unto all men, so also is life through Jesus" (I Cor. 15, 22).

Then did they spit in his face, etc. After Christ's condemnation, the mockery is treated. And this is very fitting, because Christ bore our sins, as it is said in Isaias 53.[67] Now man, by sin, was handed over to death, when it was said to him: "In what day soever thou shalt eat of it, thou shalt die the death" (Gen. 2, 17). Likewise, he lost his own honor, because "man when he was in honor did not understand; he is compared to senseless beasts" (Ps. 48, 13). And, for that reason, Christ the Redeemer firstly undergoes death and reproaches by an action; and secondly, He undergoes these by words, where it is said, *Prophesy unto us, O Christ*. In the first part, He is spit upon, and beaten; in the second part, He is struck in the face. As to the first point, it is said: *Then did they spit in his face and buffeted him*; according to the words given in Holy Writ, this used to be done as a sign of contempt of God's commandment: hence, it is stated in Deuteronomy 25, that if someone did not want to take the wife of his brother, that they spat upon his face.[68] Similarly, this was done as a sign of contempt of a father's commandment: so it was said concerning Mary the sister of Moses.[69] Wherefore, they spat in His face, because they considered Him to be a blasphemer; "I have not turned away my face from them that rebuked me, and spit upon me" (Is. 50, 6). Likewise, *they buffeted him*, as would be done to a drunkard or a fool; "We have seen him the most abject of men" (Is. 53, 2), meaning that He seemed so despised as if He were the most abject of men. *And others struck his face with the palms of their hands*, as an irreverence; "He shall give his cheek to him that striketh him" (Is. 3, 30). Mystically, according to Augustine, some still do this: for to spit in the face is nothing other than to contemn the presence of Christ's grace; "How much more, do you think he deserveth worse punishments, who hath trodden under foot the Son of God and hath esteemed the blood of the testament unclean, by which he was sanctified, and hath offered an affront to the Spirit of grace?" (Heb. 10, 29). Now properly, they beat, who esteem the head less than the hands: and such are they who seek

---

[67] "He hath borne our infirmities" (verse 4).
[68] "The woman shall come to him before the ancients, and shall take off his shoe from his foot, and spit in his face" (verse 9).
[69] "If her father had spitten upon her face, ought she not to have been ashamed for seven days at least?" (Num. 12, 14).

rather their own dignity than Christ's honor. Concerning such men, it is said that "Men loved darkness rather than the light" (Jn. 3, 19). Now they who strike the face, are they who, in a certain way, strive to destroy His presence, such do the Jews. Concerning them it is said: "Let the Holy One of Israel cease from before us" (Is. 30, 11). Then they mock Him with words: *Prophesy unto us, O Christ. Who is he that struck thee?* And they said this mockingly, because none of them held Him to be a prophet; and it was not necessary to say anything: for their bad conduct was manifest. Hence, He did not wish to speak; "Reproaching me they have struck me on the cheek" (Job 16, 11).

But Peter sat without in the court. Here Peter's denial is treated. Now Luke recounts these events in a different order, because, firstly, he relates Peter's denial, and afterwards the mocking of Christ; Matthew, however, does the contrary. And there is no contradiction, because when He was being mocked, the denial happened at the same time; hence, it does not matter if the denial be related before or afterwards. And it ought to be observed that when He was being led away, Peter did not deny Him; but when He was being mocked, he denied Him, to signify that some men fear reproaches more than beatings, contrary to that which is written: "Fear ye not the reproach of men, and be not afraid of their blasphemies" (Is. 51, 7). And concerning this, the denial is firstly related; and secondly, Peter's repentance when both the cock crowed and he recalled the words of Jesus. The first part is divided into three parts, according to his three denials. The second part is where it is said, *And as he went out of the gate*; and the third part is where it is said, *And after a little while, they came that stood by*, etc. And firstly, the place is related; secondly, the occasion of his denial is related; and thirdly, the denial is related. He says, therefore: *But Peter sat without*, namely, outside of the place where Christ was suffering: "O Lord, all that forsake thee shall be confounded" (Jer. 17, 13). On the contrary, it is written: "Come ye to him and be enlightened: and your faces shall not be confounded" (Ps. 33, 6). For he who is outside of Christ's Passion, easily falls.

Then what prompted him to deny Christ is related, *And there came to him a servant maid, saying: Thou also wast with Jesus the Galilean.* And Peter's fall corresponds to the fall of the first man; "From the woman came the beginning of sin" (Eccli. 25, 33). In like manner, Peter denied Christ upon the words of a woman; in which the Lord wished to humble his presumption, because he fell not upon the words of a man, but upon the words of a woman. *This man also was with Jesus of Nazareth.* And this should have been something glorious to him, but now it was something terrifying to him, and, for that reason, he denied Him, and he denied Him before others, saying: *I know not what thou sayest.* If we wish to increase Peter's guilt, we can increase it due to three things. It is increased in that he immediately denied Him from a little fear; "The sound of a flying leaf shall terrify them" (Lev. 26, 36). Likewise, his guilt is increased because he was not ashamed to deny Him in front of others. Moreover, his guilt is increased by his lie, because he said: *I know not what thou sayest,* and *I know not the man*; and this is opposed to what is written: "Be not ashamed to say the truth" (Lev. 4, 24).

And as he went out of the gate, another maid saw him; and she saith to them that were there: This man also was with Jesus of Nazareth. And firstly, the place is mentioned; secondly, his motivation is mentioned; and thirdly, his denial is mentioned. As to the historical account, according to Mark, the cock crew after a first denial, and then Peter went out of the gate, and the maid saw him, and he denied Him a second time.[70] But this seems opposed to the other Evangelists, because it seems that the others say that they spoke sitting down; and Luke says that one of those sitting spoke.[71] Why, therefore, is it said here that the maid spoke as he went out of the gate? It ought to be observed, according to Augustine, that Peter went out after he had denied Him: and when he was going out, the maid spoke to him, etc.; and then he denied Him again; and because Peter heard the maid speaking to others, he came back in.[72] Then those who had heard the maid, asked him again. And it can be that one man, who knew him, was

70. "When [the maid] had seen Peter warming himself looking on him, she saith: Thou also wast with Jesus of Nazareth. But he denied, saying: I neither know nor understand what thou sayest. And he went forth before the court; and the cock crew" (Mk. 14, 67-68).

71. "And when they had kindled a fire in the midst of the hall and were sitting about it, Peter was in the midst of them. Whom when a certain servant maid had seen sitting at the light and earnestly beheld him, she said: This man also was with him" (Lk. 22, 55-56).

72. "AUG. This maid is not the same, but another, as Matthew says. Indeed we must also understand, that in this second denial he was addressed by two persons, that is, by the maid whom Matthew and Mark mention, and by another person, of whom Luke takes notice. It goes on: And he denied it again. Peter had now returned, for John says that he denied Him again standing at the fire; wherefore the maid said what has been mentioned above, not to him, that is, Peter, but to those who, when he went out, had remained, in such a way however that he heard it; wherefore coming back and standing again at the fire, he contradicted them, and denied their words. For it is evident, if we compare the accounts of all the Evangelists on this matter, that Peter did not the second time deny him before the porch, but within the palace at the fire, whilst Matthew, and Mark who mention his having gone out are silent, for the sake of brevity, as to his return" (*Catena Aurea on St. Mark,* chap. 14, lect. 12).

inciting him more: *And again he denied with an oath: I know not the man*; and this is contrary to that which is written: "Let not thy mouth be accustomed to swearing" (Eccli. 23, 9). Then, the third denial follows. And firstly, the time is told; secondly, the motivation is told; and thirdly, the denial is related. He says, therefore: *And after a little while*. Luke says that it was "after the space, as it were of one hour" (22, 59). And the devil was controlling this, so that Peter would not have time to catch his breath. Hence, they say to him: *Thou also art one of them*; and they were proving this: *For even thy speech doth discover thee*.

But it is evident that they were all Jews: how then does he say: *For even thy speech doth discover thee*? Jerome resolves this question, saying, that in the same language there are often different manners of speaking, as it appears in France, there are different manners of speaking in Picardy and in Burgundy, and, nevertheless, there is one language. So the Galileans have a different manner of speaking from the Jerusalemites. So also it can be said to anyone: *For even thy speech doth discover thee*; because, as it is said: "Out of the abundance of the heart the mouth speaketh" (Lk. 6, 45); because when a man is carnal, he quickly bursts out in carnal words; and when a man is spiritual he bursts out in spiritual words.

Then he began to curse and to swear, etc. There are some men who try to excuse Peter, namely, that he did not sin; hence, when he said, *I know not the man*, it is true that that he did not know him as just a man, but as man and God. And this is not good, because it ascribes a lie to Christ: because Christ had said: *Thou wilt deny me*. For that reason, it is better to say that Peter lied, rather than Christ. Likewise, it ought to be observed that he not only denied Christ, but he also denied that he was a Christian. Hence, he said in one denial, *I do not know him*, that is to say, I am not a Christian. Similarly, it ought to be observed that he who does not quickly remove himself from evil, quickly goes from bad to worse; "He that contemneth small things, shall fall by little and little" (Eccli. 19, 1). Hence, he added perjury to his denial, and blasphemy to perjury. Hence, Gregory says: "The sin which is not remitted by penance soon draws man into another sin."[73] Moreover, it ought to be noted that the threefold temptations by which man is tempted are signified. For man is tempted by the concupiscence of the flesh; "Every man is tempted by his own concupiscence" (James 1, 14). Like-

---

73. Super Ezech. 11.

wise, man is tempted by the concupiscence for earthly things; "This the desire of gain devised" (Wis. 14, 2). Similarly, man is tempted by the demons, and this is signified by that denial, in which it is said: *After a little while, they came that stood by.* "Our wrestling is not against flesh and blood; but against principalities and powers, against the rulers of the world of this darkness, against the spirits of wickedness in the high places" (Eph. 6, 12). Concerning these three temptations, it is stated: "All that is in the world is the concupiscence of the flesh and the concupiscence of the eyes and the pride of life" (I Jn. 2, 16). Or it ought to be said otherwise, according to Augustine, that the errors of all the heretics are signified by these three denials. For some men denied Christ's divinity, such as Photinus; others denied His humanity, such as Eunomius;[74] certain other men denied both Christ's humanity and divinity, such as Arius, who said that the Son was not equal to the Father. Similarly, according to Origen, three persecutions are signified, which the Church was about to have. The first persecution was by the Jews, in which many men died; the second was by the Gentiles, in which many men were made martyrs; and the third was by the heretics, who seduced many, and some men also died.

Likewise, it ought to be observed that certain writings are found which seem to excuse Peter, saying that he did not sin mortally, because Bernard says: "Charity in him was not quenched, but cooled." It ought to be said, however, that Peter sinned mortally, nevertheless, it was not due to malice, but to fear of death. And Bernard wished to say this, in saying that his charity was cooled, etc.

And immediately the cock crew. Here, Peter's repentance is treated. And firstly, the motive or stimulus of his repentance is treated; and secondly, his repentance is treated, where it is said, *And going forth, he wept bitterly.* Two things are mentioned, by which the incitement occurred. Firstly, there was the cock's crowing; hence: *And immediately the cock crew.* By the cock, preachers are signified, who rouse sinners to repentance; hence: "Awake, ye just, and sin not" (I Cor. 15, 34); and: "Rise, thou that sleepest, and arise from the dead: and Christ shall enlighten thee" (Eph. 5, 14). The second stimulus of his repentance was Peter's remembering: *And Peter remembered the word of Jesus which he had said*, etc. "All the ends of the earth shall remember, and shall be converted to the Lord" (Ps. 21, 28). And

---

74. Eunomius died about 395.

these two things often happen as a consequence of a preacher's words, because those who forget God through their sins, return to Him by the preacher's words. Concerning that cock, it is said: "Who gave the cock understanding?" (Job 38, 36). Likewise, Luke relates a third stimulus, namely, that "The Lord looked on Peter" (22, 61). The Apostle says: "Being justified freely by his grace" (Rom. 3, 24). "Convert us, O Lord, to thee, and we shall be converted" (Lam. 5, 21). Afterwards, Peter's repentance is treated: *And going forth, he wept bitterly.* And his repentance is commendable for three reasons. And it is commendable, firstly, because it was quick, since he went out immediately: "Delay not to be converted to the Lord" (Eccli. 5, 8). Likewise, it was prudent, because he withdrew from the company of those who had led him to deny the Lord; so also penitents ought to avoid occasions of sin: "Go out from among them and be ye separate, saith the Lord, and touch not the unclean thing, and I will receive you" (II Cor. 6, 17-18). Moreover, his repentance was efficacious and true; "Make thee mourning as for an only son, a bitter lamentation" (Jer. 6, 26); "I will recount to thee all my years in the bitterness of my soul" (Is. 38, 15).

CHAPTER TWENTY-SEVEN

1. And when morning was come, all the chief priests and ancients of the people took counsel against Jesus, that they might put him to death.
2. And they brought him bound and delivered him to Pontius Pilate the governor.
3. Then Judas, who betrayed him, seeing that he was condemned, repenting himself, brought back the thirty pieces of silver to the chief priests and ancients,
4. Saying: I have sinned in betraying innocent blood. But they said: What is that to us? Look thou to it.
5. And casting down the pieces of silver in the temple, he departed and went and hanged himself with an halter.
6. But the chief priests having taken the pieces of silver, said: It is not lawful to put them into the corbona, because it is the price of blood.
7. And after they had consulted together, they bought with them the potter's field, to be a burying place for strangers.
8. For this cause that field was called Haceldama, that is, the field of blood, even to this day.
9. Then was fulfilled that which was spoken by Jeremias the prophet, saying: And they took the thirty pieces of silver, the price of him that was prized, whom they prized of the children of Israel.
10. And they gave them unto the potter's field, as the Lord appointed to me.
11. And Jesus stood before the governor, and the governor asked him, saying: Art thou the king of the Jews? Jesus saith to him: Thou sayest it.
12. And when he was accused by the chief priests and ancients, he answered nothing.
13. Then Pilate saith to him: Dost not thou hear how great testimonies they allege against thee?
14. And he answered him to never a word, so that the governor wondered exceedingly.
15. Now upon the solemn day the governor was accustomed to release to the people one prisoner, whom they would.
16. And he had then a notorious prisoner that was called Barabbas.
17. They therefore being gathered together, Pilate said: Whom will you that I release to you: Barabbas, or Jesus that is called Christ?

18. *For he knew that for envy they had delivered him.*
19. *And as he was sitting in the place of judgment, his wife sent to him, saying: Have thou nothing to do with that just man; for I have suffered many things this day in a dream because of him.*
20. *But the chief priests and ancients persuaded the people that they should ask Barabbas and make Jesus away.*
21. *And the governor answering, said to them: Whether will you of the two to be released unto you? But they said: Barabbas.*
22. *Pilate saith to them: What shall I do then with Jesus that is called Christ? They say all: Let him be crucified.*
23. *The governor said to them: Why, what evil hath he done? But they cried out the more, saying: Let him be crucified.*
24. *And Pilate seeing that he prevailed nothing, but that rather a tumult was made, taking water washed his hands before the people, saying: I am innocent of the blood of this just man. Look you to it.*
25. *And the whole people answering, said: His blood be upon us and upon our children.*
26. *Then he released to them Barabbas: and having scourged Jesus, delivered him unto them to be crucified.*

Above, the Evangelist recounted what Christ suffered from the Jews; here, he recounts what He suffered from the Gentiles: and he does four things. Firstly, he treats how He was handed over to the Gentiles; secondly, he treats how He was examined; thirdly, he treats how He was condemned; and fourthly, he treats how He suffered. The second part is where it is said, **And Jesus stood before the governor**; the third part is where it is said, **Upon the solemn day the governor was accustomed**; and the fourth part is where it is said, **Then the soldiers of the governor, taking Jesus into the hall**, etc. About the first part, he does two things. Firstly, he recounts the decision by which Christ is handed over to the Gentiles; secondly, he recounts the death and sin of the betrayer, where it is said, **Then Judas, who betrayed him, seeing that he was condemned**. About the first point, he does three things. Firstly, he states the motive for handing Christ over to the Gentiles; secondly, he states the manner; and thirdly, he states the events. The cause of His condemnation was the proposal made concerning His death: and regarding this, he mentions three things, due to which, their sin was aggravated. Firstly, their sin was aggravated by their evil zeal to put Him to death; and he mentions this when he says: ***And when morning was come, they took counsel***; because although they had been mocking Him the whole night, nevertheless, in the morning they took counsel. Hence, they were very eager to put Him to death; "The murderer riseth at the very break of day" (Job 24, 14). Likewise, their sin is aggravated by their pervasiveness, because ***all the chief priests took counsel***. For if one or two had gathered together, they would have been excusable; but they all gathered together; "From the sole of the foot unto the top of the head, there is no soundness therein" (Is. 1, 6); wherefore, he says, ***All the chief priests***; "Son of man, these are the men that study iniquity, and frame a wicked counsel in this city" (Ez. 11, 2). Similarly, their sin is aggravated by their cruelty, because they could have been thinking about many other things, but they were thinking about ***how they might put him to death***; "Their feet run to evil, and make haste to shed blood" (Prov. 1, 16). But how will they do this? ***They brought him bound***. This was the custom that condemned men were brought bound and, thereby, it was indicated that they were condemned to death. And this signified that just as He destroyed our death by His death, so He destroyed the bonds of our sins by His bonds. ***And they delivered him to Pontius Pilate***. And why did they do this? There were three reasons. One reason is historical, that Pilate was the representative of the Emperor, and the Jews did not have the authority to inflict capital punishment. On account of which, it is said: "It is not lawful for us to put any man to death" (Jn. 18, 31). Likewise, they delivered Him to Pilate due to their intention: for they did not want to kill Him secretly, but publicly, so that the news might be spread, according to that which is stated: "Let us condemn him to a most shameful death" (Wis. 2, 20). The third reason why they delivered Him to Pilate was that He wanted to die for all men, wherefore, He wanted that all men be gathered together, both Jews and Gentiles, so that which is written was fulfilled: "The kings of the earth stood up, and the princes met together" (Ps. 2, 2). ***Then Judas, who betrayed him, seeing that he was condemned***, etc. Here, Judas' repentance and death are treated. And about this, the Evangelist does two things. Firstly, he speaks about the betrayal; and secondly, he speaks about what happened to the wages of Judas, where it is said, ***But the chief priests having taken the pieces of silver, said***. Regarding the first thing, Judas' repentance is firstly treated; and secondly, his despair is treated, where it is said, ***And casting down the pieces of silver in the temple, he departed***. Regarding the first point, he does three things. Firstly,

Judas' motive is related; secondly, his repentance is related; and thirdly, the effect of his repentance is related. His motive is related where it is said: ***Then Judas seeing that he was condemned, repenting himself, brought back the thirty pieces of silver.*** It could be that Judas supposed when he sold Him that He would not be killed, but that He would only be scourged; wherefore, seeing that He was condemned, he repented.

But there is a question, namely, when He was handed over to the governor, how could Judas have seen that Christ had been condemned? Jerome says that he saw this with his mind's eye, because by the fact that he saw that He had been condemned by the Jews, and delivered to Pilate, he thought that Pilate would judge according to their will, that is to say, according to the Jews' will. Origen wrote that some men said: 'Judas seeing that he was condemned, means that, due to this, Judas himself was moved to repent.' Hence, it is said, ***repenting himself, brought back the thirty pieces of silver.*** And this repentance was not a true repentance; nevertheless, it had some characteristic of repentance, because repentance ought to be in the middle between hope and fear; Judas, however, indeed had fear and sorrow, since he was sorry for his past sin, but he did not have hope. And such is the repentance of the wicked; "Repenting, and groaning for anguish of spirit" (Wis. 5, 3).

And why was he repenting? It ought to be noted what Origen says, namely, that sometimes it happens that the devil impels a man to sin, and sometimes a man sins of himself; but this happens in different ways, for man sins in order to satisfy his lust, but the devil impels man to sin in order to destroy man. And if the devil incites man to sin, then man is not bound to sin due to his creation, and, for that reason, he is able to repent. And this is contrary to the Manicheans, who say that there is a twofold creation, good and evil, and those who are from the evil creation are unable to behave well, and vice versa. And, according to them, Judas was from the bad creation. Therefore, how could he repent? Origen says, therefore, that the fact that he despaired was only due to his being negligent.

The effect of his repentance follows. The effect of repentance is that the sinner strives to amend. He had sinned because he had sold Christ, for he had done all he could do to Christ: wherefore, ***he brought back the thirty pieces of silver.*** And firstly, his retraction is related; and secondly, his repentance is related, where it is said, ***I have sinned in betraying innocent blood.*** Therefore, ***he brought back the thirty pieces of silver***; and in this, he retracted by saying, ***I have sinned***, meaning I have truly offended. Now in that he says, ***Betraying innocent blood***, even if he speaks well, nevertheless, he does not speak entirely, because such words can be referred to a just man. Hence: "If you put me to death, you will shed innocent blood against your own selves" (Jer. 26, 15). Hence, Jerome says that if he had possessed a right faith, he would not have despaired. For he ought to have said, 'Betraying God.' In this that he said, ***Betraying innocent blood***, he depreciated His power, and showed that he did not have a right faith.

Then the obstinacy of the Jews is related, where it is said: ***But they said: What is that to us?*** Judas was acknowledging that Christ was a just man, and, nevertheless, they say, ***What is that to us?*** "My people have not known the judgment of the Lord" (Jer. 8, 7). ***Look thou to it***, meaning we will not follow your conscience. Remigius says: ***What is that to us?*** You firstly sold Him, and, afterwards, you acknowledge that He is a just man. Who do you seem to be to us, you who so change your mind? For to change from evil to good, is good: but to change from evil to evil, is bad; "A just man stands firm for ever: but a fool is changed as the moon" (Eccli. 27, 12).

Then his despair is related. For one who has despaired cares nothing about temporal goods; and so this man acts, because ***casting down the pieces of silver in the temple, he departed*** (he did not care about the money) ***and went and hanged himself with an halter***. Hence, it is stated in Acts 1, 18, that "he hung himself and burst asunder in the midst."

And why did he hang himself? Origen says that it happens that the devil casts a man down into sin, and although he leaves him alone for a time, nevertheless, he wants to cast him down into another sin. And the Apostle wishes to caution against this, saying: "Lest perhaps such a one be swallowed up with overmuch sorrow" (II Cor. 2, 7). So Judas became so swallowed up with sorrow, that ***he went and hanged himself with an halter***. "And let not the deep water swallow me up" (Ps. 68, 16). Origen relates the opinion of certain men, saying that because Judas had heard Christ speaking about the Resurrection, for that reason, he supposed he would meet Christ, and, therefore, he hung himself.[1]

Augustine asked when this took place. For if we consider this, we scarcely find time before the Passion during which this might

---

1. "ORIGEN; Or, perhaps, he desired to die before his Master on His way to death, and to meet Him with a disembodied spirit, that by confession and deprecation he might obtain mercy; and did not see that it is not fitting that a servant of God should dismiss himself from life, but should wait God's sentence" (*Catena Aurea on St. Matthew*, chap. 27, lect. 1).

have happened, because the chief priests were busy the whole day with Christ's death. Likewise, the next day was the Sabbath, and they would not have accepted money on that day: wherefore, Augustine seems to hold that this happened after the Resurrection. Yet, it can be said that even if some chief priests had gone to Pilate and were attending to Christ's death, still some stayed in the Temple and Judas handed over to them the thirty pieces of silver.[2]

But the chief priests having taken the pieces of silver, said, etc. He shows what would be done with Judas' money. And firstly, it is said how his money is excluded from the corbona;[3] and secondly, it is said on what it was spent. He says, therefore: **But the chief priests having taken the pieces of silver, said: It is not lawful to put them into the corbona**, etc. It ought to be noted that free offerings or voluntary donations were placed into the corbona. Hence, there were some offerings that were offered voluntarily, other offerings were offered from a duty; voluntary offerings were put into the corbona, but the others were put elsewhere; "The most High approveth not the gifts of the wicked" (Eccli. 34, 23). **It is not lawful to put them into the corbona, because it is the price of blood**. And in saying this, the Lord's words are verified: "They are swallowing a camel and straining out a gnat" (above 23, 24). They did not want to put this money into the corbona, but they were quite willing to deal with the death of the Son of God. Then, he recounts what happened thereafter. And firstly, he says what happened; and secondly, he says what happened thereafter. He says, **And after they had consulted together**, etc. Why did they do this? It ought to be said that God thus made sure that this event would always be remembered. Hence, **they bought with them the potter's field, to be a burying place for strangers**, not for those who were from their country, but for foreigners. It was fitting in a mystical sense, because by Christ's death, not only justification was hastened, but also the repose of death; "From henceforth now, saith the Spirit, that they may rest from their labors" (Apoc. 14, 13). Or it can be that pilgrims are they who do not have their home in this world; "Woe is me, that my sojourning is prolonged" (Ps. 119, 5). Now these men are buried with Christ. The Apostle says: "You are buried together with him" (Rom. 6, 4). This field is holy Church. Hence: "The kingdom of heaven is like unto a treasure hidden in a field" (above 13, 44).

---

[2]. "CHRYS. All those then who had been Chief Priests, are here called Chief Priests" (*Catena Aurea on St. Matthew*, chap. 26, lect. 2).

[3]. The *corbona* (Latin: treasure chambers) was the treasury of the Temple wherein the monetary offerings were deposited.

This field is Christ. Hence, it is said: "As clay is in the hand of the potter, so are you in my hand, O house of Israel" (Jer. 18, 6). Then a confirmation of the event is related. And firstly, there is a confirmation from the name of the field: *For this cause that field was called Haceldama, that is, the field of blood, even to this day*; more precisely, the field was so named until the time when this Gospel was written. Then he confirms the name of the field by a passage of Scripture: *Then was fulfilled that which was spoken by Jeremias the prophet.*

But there is a question, why does he say: *Was spoken by Jeremias the prophet*, because these words, according to the words quoted here, are not written anywhere in Scripture. Nevertheless, something similar is found in Zacharias 11, 12: "They weighed for my wages thirty pieces of silver." Therefore, there is a question why it is asserted that this was said by Jeremias, since it was said by Zacharias. Augustine says that it is found written somewhere that this was said by 'the Prophet,' and not by Jeremias, nevertheless it seems that he is Jeremias, as is stated in this text.[4] Jerome mentions as a solution that the prophets wrote some books which were canonized by the Jews. Hence, there are some books of the prophets which are not in the canon of the Bible, for example Jude refers to certain things in his epistle, and the other Apostles also accepted all of them. Hence, he says that certain men brought to him a book of Jeremias wherein these words had been written word for word, and the Evangelist wrote according to what he found in an apocryphal text. Augustine solves the question as follows: Sometimes it happens that when someone wishes to state the name of one author, the name of someone else comes to mind; wherefore, it can be that when the Evangelist wished to write Zacharias, he wrote Jeremias. But there were many Jews then who knew the Law; why did they not correct this? It is because they thought that it was said divinely, because all the prophets spoke by the Holy Ghost, and the words of a prophet do not have efficacy except by the Holy Ghost; wherefore, so that they might insinuate this mystery, they did not correct these words. Another solution which he states is that although they are not the words of Jeremias, nevertheless, there is there a similar event, as it is found in Jeremias 32, that he received a command that he should

---

[4]. "AUG. But if anyone thinks this lowers the historian's credit, first let him know that not all the copies of the Gospels have the name Jeremias, but some simply by the Prophet. But I do not like this defense, because more copies, and more ancient ones, have Jeremias, and there could be no reason for adding the name, and thus making an error" (*Catena Aurea on St. Matthew*, chap. 26, lect. 2).

buy a field.[5] Or the Holy Ghost so moved Matthew in regard to the same event, as he moved Jeremias.[6] But if we wish, we can accept the words of Jerome in his book, *On the Best Method of Translating*,[7] who says that a follower of Christ does not imply any mark of falsity: for it is the duty of a good interpreter not to consider the words, but the meaning. For this reason, he cited the meaning of certain passages of Jeremias and other passages of Zacharias, just as it is found in Mark that he cites a passage of Isaias, of which one part belongs to Malachias and another to Isaias.[8] So also Matthew joined together two sentences, one of which is taken from Zacharias and the other is taken from Jeremias (chapter 32). For what is in Zacharias (11, 12), namely, that "they weighed" (meaning they took) "thirty pieces of silver," and these words are not found in Jeremias; but that he bought a field, which made known the event to the whole nation. *As the Lord appointed to me.* This was expressly stated from that which the Lord commanded Jeremias, where it was said above, that he should buy a

5. "And Hanameel my uncle's son came to me, according to the word of the Lord, to the entry of the prison, and said to me: Buy my field, which is in Anathoth in the land of Benjamin: for the right of inheritance is thine, and thou art next of kin to possess it. And I understood that this was the word of the Lord" (verse 8).

6. "AUG. For what Matthew adds to the prophecy, *Whom they of the children of Israel did value, and gave them for the potter's field, as the Lord appointed me* this [part of the phase], *as the Lord appointed me,* is found neither in Zacharias nor Jeremias. It must then be taken in the person of the Evangelist as inserted with a mystic meaning, that he had learned by revelation that the prophecy referred to this matter of the price for which Christ was betrayed" (*Catena Aurea on St. Matthew,* chap. 26, lect. 2).

7. "It is evident that the rendering of the Septuagint differs widely from the quotation of the evangelist. In the Hebrew also, though the sense is the same, the words are quite different and differently arranged. It says: 'And I said to them: If it be good in your eyes, bring hither my wages: and if not, be quiet. And they weighed for my wages thirty pieces of silver. And the Lord said to me: Cast it to the statuary, a handsome price, that I was prized at by them. And I took the thirty pieces of silver, and I cast them into the house of the Lord to the statuary.' (Zach. 11, 12-13) They may accuse the apostle of falsifying his version seeing that it agrees neither with the Hebrew nor with the translators of the Septuagint: and worse than this, they may say that he has mistaken the author's name putting down Jeremias when it should be Zacharias. Far be it from us to speak thus of a follower (*Pedissequus*) of Christ, who made it his care to formulate dogmas rather than to hunt for words and syllables." (*Liber de optimo genere interpretandi* Letter LVII. (*To Pammachius*)).

8. "As it is written in Isaias the prophet: Behold I send my angel before thy face, who shall prepare the way before thee. A voice of one crying in the desert: Prepare ye the way of the Lord; make straight his paths" (Mk. 1, 2-3). "JEROME; But this is not written in Isaias, but in Malachias, the last of the twelve prophets. PSEUDO-CHRYS. But it may be said that it is a mistake of the writer. Otherwise it may be said, that he has compressed into one, two prophecies delivered in different places by two prophets; for in the prophet Isaias (40, 3) it is written after the story of Ezechias, *The voice of one crying in the wilderness*; but in Malachias (3, 1), *Behold, I send mine angel.* The Evangelist therefore, taking parts of two prophecies, has put them down as spoken by Isaias, and refers then here to one passage, without mentioning, however, by whom it is said, *Behold, I send mine angel*" (*Catena Aurea on St. Mark*, chap. 1, lect. 2).

field. Wherefore, the first part of these words is found in Zacharias, and the second part is found in Jeremias.

And Jesus stood before the governor, and the governor asked him. Above, the Evangelist recounted how the Lord was put into the hands of the Gentiles; here, however, he treats of His trial: and about this, he does three things. Firstly, he recounts how He is present before an earthly judge; secondly, he recounts how He is examined; and thirdly, he recounts how He is accused. He says, therefore: 'Thus it was said concerning Judas when he had betrayed Jesus to the governor.' Jesus, therefore, stood before the governor, meaning as one who is guilty and accused; "Thy cause hath been judged as that of the wicked, cause and judgment thou shalt recover" (Job 36, 17). For by this He merited to become the judge of the living and the dead. Then the examination follows; and firstly, a question is related; and secondly, His reply is related, where it is said, *Jesus saith to him.* The chief priests were accusing Him of many things, namely, of overthrowing the Law, and that He was calling Himself a king. Hence, Pilate was not interested in questioning Him about the Law, but rather about what seemed to touch upon the crime of treason, namely, He asked: **Art thou the king of the Jews?** Because it is stated in John 19, 12: "Whosoever maketh himself a king speaketh against Caesar." Then, His reply follows: **Jesus saith to him: Thou sayest it.** Jerome says that Christ so moderated His words that He neither affirmed nor denied, but says: **Thou sayest it.** "He that setteth bounds to his words, is wise" (Prov. 17, 27). Likewise observe, according to Hilary, that above (26, 63), when He was asked by the high priest of the Jews, "If thou be the Christ the Son of God," He said: "Thou hast said it": and He replied in the past tense; but when He replies to a Gentile, He answers in the present tense. And by this is indicated that the confession of Christ by the Jews is in the past, because it was done by the prophets; "A king shall reign, and shall be wise" (Jer. 23, 5) But speaking to a Gentile He says, **Thou sayest it**, because the Gentiles were now confessing Christ.

Afterwards, the accusation of Christ is related. And firstly, the accusation is related; and secondly, the inducement to respond is related, where it is said, **Then Pilate saith to him.** He says, therefore, **And when he was accused by the chief priests and ancients, he answered nothing.** About what things He was being accused, Matthew is silent, but Luke says this in chapter 23.[9]

---

[9] "And they began to accuse him, saying: We have found this man perverting our nation and forbidding to give tribute to Caesar and saying that he is Christ the king" (verse 2).

This is the custom of the Evangelists, namely, that what one omits to say, another tells. Hence, it is said there that He was seducing the people, etc., and that He was forbidding to give tribute to Caesar, and, moreover, that He was saying that He was a king. And this is false as to His intention, because they were seeking after a temporal kingdom; but He says: "My kingdom is not from hence" (Jn. 18, 36). But Christ answers nothing. Then was fulfilled what was said by Isaias: "He shall be dumb as a lamb before his shearer, and he shall not open his mouth" (Is. 53, 7). "Neither shall his voice be heard abroad" (Is. 42, 2). **Then Pilate saith to him.** From that time, Pilate was trying to free Him, wherefore, He was trying to make Him respond; hence, he said: **Dost not thou hear how great testimonies they allege against thee?** And firstly, his prodding is related, **Dost not thou hear**, etc. Now he was saying this because he wanted to release Him: for those who were His accusers, were witnesses, and, for that reason, Pilate did not wish to respond. But a reason on Christ's part why He did not respond was because He did not wish to free Himself from His Passion: for He could free Himself from it by speaking: wherefore, He did not wish to speak: "He was offered because it was his own will" (Is. 53, 7). Likewise, this was to give us an example, because "when he was reviled, did not revile."[10] Similarly, because the Jews had seen so many signs, they could have converted, and for that reason, He deemed them unworthy; "Where there is no hearing, pour not out words" (Eccli. 32, 6).

And it ought to be observed that He speaks many times and He is silent many times, because if He were to always speak, He would excuse Himself: likewise, if He would always keep silent, He would seem pertinacious. Now He sometimes answers Pilate, because Pilate was ignorant, wherefore, sometimes He made the truth known to him, but the Jews were obstinate and to them He was silent.

Then Pilate's marveling is related: **So that the governor wondered exceedingly.** And why does he wonder? It is because he heard Him speaking very eloquently: and this is what David says: "But I, as a deaf man, heard not: and as a dumb man not opening his mouth" (Ps. 37, 14), meaning it was as though I were ignorant.

And note what he says, **Exceedingly**: for that someone who is wise answers nothing is something wondrous; but that a man would answer nothing in such a trial, wherein he is being sentenced to death, is exceedingly wondrous. Likewise, he wondered because he saw that He was not terrified: for in such a case men are certainly terrified

---

10. I Pet. 2, 23.

Then His condemnation is treated. And firstly, the various efforts of those wishing to exonerate Him are related; secondly, the efforts of those wishing to condemn Him are related, where it is said, *But the chief priests and ancients persuaded the people that they should ask Barabbas*; and thirdly, His condemnation is related, where it is said, *Then he released to them Barabbas*. About the first point, Pilate's efforts to free Him are firstly related; secondly, the efforts of the chief priests to condemn Him are related. About the first part, he firstly relates some opportunities of releasing Christ; secondly, he treats of Pilate's efforts to release Christ; and thirdly, he gives the reason for his efforts to release Christ. The second part is where it is said, *They therefore being gathered together, Pilate said*; and the third part is where it is said, *For he knew that for envy they had delivered him*. In the first part, he relates two opportunities. He says, therefore: *Now upon the solemn day the governor was accustomed to release to the people one prisoner*. This custom was not from the Emperor's law, but from Pilate's will to make the people more loyal to himself: because on the solemn day they should be more agreeable, he did not want that on this day there would be a reason for sadness. So also, in Rome, on that day in which the Emperor entered no one was sentenced to death. Likewise, Pilate had recently acquired the prefecture and, for that reason, he wanted them to be loyal to himself. Nevertheless, something similar is read in the Old Testament, namely, that Saul freed Jonathan, who was sentenced to death (I Kings 14).[11] Then he relates an opportunity of releasing Him by way of a certain thief, who was called Barabbas, which is interpreted 'son of his father,' namely the devil; "You are of your father the devil" (Jn. 8, 44).

They therefore being gathered together, Pilate said: Whom will you that I release to you? Here Pilate acts contrary to the custom of the Jews, because he would not customarily ask them but they would be asking him. But he does this because he wanted to release Jesus, and it seemed that this would persuade them, because it seemed to him that they ought to prefer Christ to Barabbas; for the latter was guilty of treason and he had harmed many men. Moreover, he seemed persuasive by the fact that he calls Him Christ, saying: *Or Jesus that is called Christ?* For 'the anointed one' is called 'Christ.' Hence, he was calling Him a

---

[11] "And the people said to Saul: Shall Jonathan then die, who hath wrought this great salvation in Israel? this must not be: As the Lord liveth, there shall not one hair of his head fall to the ground, for he hath wrought with God this day. So the people delivered Jonathan, that he should not die" (verse 45).

king, wherefore, he supposed that they ought to choose Christ; "Before man is life and death" (Eccli. 15, 18). Thus, Pilate placed before them a good man and an evil man; and they chose the evil one, for that reason, evil always follows them. Then he relates his reason for trying to release Christ: *For he knew that for envy they had delivered him*. From whence did he know this? He had heard many good things about Him, and he saw that He was standing firm; hence, *he knew that for envy they had delivered him*. For just as envy was adverse to the first man, so the envy of these men ought to be adverse to Christ. For, in this way, Joseph was handed over out of envy by his brothers (Gen. 37).[12]

And as he was sitting in the place of judgment, his wife sent to him. Above, the Evangelist related one reason why Pilate was trying to release Him; here likewise he relates another reason, namely, the warning of his wife. And firstly, the warning is related; and secondly, the reason for the warning is related, where it is said, *For I have suffered many things this day in a dream because of him. And as he was sitting in the place of judgment*. As a certain gloss says, 'the place of judgment' (*tribunal*) is a judgment seat. "The king, that sitteth on the throne of judgment, scattereth away all evil with his look" (Prov. 20, 8). A seat properly belongs to teachers; "The scribes and the Pharisees have sitten on the chair of Moses" (above 23, 2). The place of judgment (*tribunal*) is so called from the tribunes, because firstly, tribunes were elected by the Romans to make judgments; and he says, *In the place of judgment* (*pro tribunali*): and this is a Greek manner of speech. For sometimes *pro* means 'before'; as, for example, 'the army is before (*pro*) the camp,' meaning 'in front of (*ante*) the camp.' And other times *pro* means 'in the place of'; hence, *pro tribunali*, meaning 'in the place of judgment.' *His wife sent to him, saying*. This woman was a Gentile and she represents the Church of the Gentiles, which received Christ, as it is said in I Corinthians 1. *Have thou nothing to do with that just man*, meaning it does not belong to you to judge Him; nay, He ought to be your judge; "He who was appointed by God to be judge of the living and of the dead" (Acts 10, 42). *For I have suffered many things this day in a dream because of him*. Here, the reason is related. For such is a manner of speech: for when someone is withdrawn from their sense, some things appear in his imagination: and it was customary that sight be referred to the things which appear,

---

12. "And when the Madianite merchants passed by, they drew him out of the pit, and sold him to the Ismaelites, for twenty pieces of silver: and they led him into Egypt" (verse 28).

although there be an alienation from one's senses: now this sometimes happens when one is awake, and other times in a dream. When this happens when one is awake, it is called a 'vision'; hence, "If there be among you a prophet of the Lord, I will appear to him in a vision, or I will speak to him in a dream" (Num. 12, 6). Here, however, a prophetic "vision" is put for both.

It ought to be observed that the intrinsic reason for this is sometimes bodily, as when blood is superabounding, an apparition of red bodies appears, and, in like manner, concerning other apparitions. Other times an apparition is due to an extrinsic cause, such as when from coldness someone dreams that they are in the snow. Sometimes, however, an apparition occurs by a spiritual cause, and this is either by God through a good angel; and concerning this, it is said: "By a dream in a vision by night he openeth the ears of men" (Job 33, 15-16); And these apparitions are true, and contain truths; yet, one ought not to trust them very much; "Set not thy heart upon them, for dreams have deceived many" (Eccli. 34, 6-7). Other times they occur by the devils, who can affect the imagination because it is a corporeal power; hence, divinations and the like are forbidden in the Law; "Let there not be found among you any one that consulteth soothsayers, or observeth dreams and omens," etc., (Deut. 18, 10).

Concerning this vision, we can say that it was done by God through the good angels; or by the devil, because it was meant to impede the Passion: because in the Passion there was the sin of killing, and so the vision was happening through the good angels to impede sin; but from the Passion fruit was produced, wherefore, the devil already perceiving Christ to be God and fearing to lose his power through the Passion, just as he had put it into Judas' mind to betray Him, so also now he wanted to impede Pilate by this vision, not because he wanted to impede his sin, but rather, to impede the fruit of the Passion.

Then the efforts of the Jews wanting to kill Christ are related: *But the chief priests and ancients persuaded the people that they should ask Barabbas.* For the Jews in both groups show themselves to be abominable, because the chief priests are they who ought to correct others; "He that justifieth the wicked is abominable" (Prov. 17, 15). Similarly, they are abominable in that they are the ancients; "Iniquity came out from the ancient judges" (Dan. 13, 5).

And the governor answering, said to them. Here, he relates an attempt, by which Pilate was attempting to release Christ. And firstly, he shows what words he spoke to free Christ; and secondly, he shows what actions he did, where it is said, *And Pilate seeing that he prevailed nothing*. He tried to release Him, to free Him. Firstly, he tried to free Him on account of a comparison; secondly, he tried to free Him on account of His dignity; and thirdly, he tried to release Him on account of His innocence. He tried to free Him on account of a comparison, for he compared Him to an evil doer, namely, when he was answering the petition of the people, or more precisely, when answering these chief priests who were instigating them: *Whom will you that I release to you? But they said: Barabbas*. For doing which Peter also reproached the people, saying concerning Christ: "Whom you indeed delivered up and denied before the face of Pilate, when he judged he should be released. But you denied the Holy One and the Just: and desired a murderer to be granted unto you," etc., (Acts 3, 13-14). Pilate, therefore, says: *What shall I do then with Jesus that is called Christ?* Here he asserts His dignity saying, *What shall I do then with Jesus*, as though he were to say: 'It will be harmful to you if you kill him, *that is called Christ*.' But they could not be frightened: on the contrary, they all said, *Let him be crucified*: for this was the most shameful death. Wherefore, what was said is fulfilled: "Let us condemn him to a most shameful death" (Wis. 2, 20); "Their tongue, and their devices are against the Lord" (Is. 3, 8). *The governor said to them: Why, what evil hath he done?* He alleges His innocence, intending to free Him, as though using those words which are said: "What iniquity have your fathers found in me?" (Jer. 2, 5). And: "Which of you shall convince me of sin?" (Jn. 8, 46). *But they cried out the more, saying: Let him be crucified*. Hence, they could not be deterred, according to that which is written: "They have laid hold on lying, and have refused to return" (Jer. 8, 5). Therefore, they were pertinacious in malice.

And Pilate seeing that he prevailed nothing. Here, Pilate seeks His liberation by an action; and firstly, the action is related; and secondly, the people's demand for punishment is related. He says: *And Pilate seeing that he prevailed nothing*. By this he gives to understand that he had said many other things, and that he prevailed nothing. *Taking water washed his hands*. This was the custom, that when someone wished to show that he was innocent he would wash his hands, and so he acted here in like manner; he said: *I am innocent of the blood of this just man*, etc. In accordance with this manner of acting, it is stated: "I will wash my hands among the innocent" (Ps. 25, 6). And he would have truly been innocent if he had remained steadfast in his judgment, wherefore, he calls Him a just man. *Look you to it*, meaning it belongs to you to decide what should happen. Hence, it is said: "Take him you, and judge him according to your law" (Jn. 18, 31). Then the obligation to punishment follows: *"**His blood be upon us and upon our children**.* And so it will happen that Christ's Blood is required from them until today; and what was said applies well to them: "The blood of thy brother Abel crieth to me from the earth" (Gen. 4, 10). But Christ's Blood is more efficacious than Abel's blood. "We have blood which speaketh better than that of Abel" (Heb. 12, 24); "But if you put me to death, you will shed innocent blood against your own selves" (Jer. 26, 15). ***Then he released to them Barabbas. He released***, meaning he pardoned him from his sentence of death. ***And having scourged Jesus, delivered him unto them to be crucified.*** And why was He scourged? Jerome says that it was because there was a custom of the Romans that one who was condemned to death would firstly be scourged. And, as it is said in John 19, he scourged Him; hence, is fulfilled in Him that which is stated: "I am ready for scourges" (Ps. 37, 18). Some men say that he scourged Him so that the Jews might be moved to pity, and, in this way, after He was scourged, they might release Him.

27. Then the soldiers of the governor, taking Jesus into the hall, gathered together unto him the whole band.

28. And stripping him, they put a scarlet cloak about him.

29. And platting a crown of thorns, they put it upon his head, and a reed in his right hand. And bowing the knee before him, they mocked him, saying: Hail, King of the Jews.

30. And spitting upon him, they took the reed and struck his head.

31. And after they had mocked him, they took off the cloak from him and put on him his own garments and led him away to crucify him.

32. And going out, they found a man of Cyrene, named Simon: him they forced to take up his cross.

33. And they came to the place that is called Golgotha, which is the place of Calvary.

34. And they gave him wine to drink mingled with gall. And when he had tasted, he would not drink.

35. And after they had crucified him, they divided his garments, casting lots; that it might be fulfilled which was spoken by the prophet, saying: They divided my garments among them; and upon my vesture they cast lots.

36. And they sat and watched him.

37. And they put over his head his cause written: THIS IS JESUS THE KING OF THE JEWS.

38. Then were crucified with him two thieves: one on the right hand and one on the left.

39. And they that passed by blasphemed him, wagging their heads,

40. And saying: Vah, thou that destroyest the temple of God and in three days dost rebuild it: save thy own self. If thou be the Son of God, come down from the cross.

41. In like manner also the chief priests, with the scribes and ancients, mocking said:

42. He saved others: himself he cannot save. If he be the king of Israel, let him now come down from the cross: and we will believe him.

43. He trusted in God: let him now deliver him if he will have him. For he said: I am the Son of God.

44. And the selfsame thing the thieves also that were crucified with him reproached him with.

45. Now from the sixth hour, there was darkness over the whole earth, until the ninth hour.

46. And about the ninth hour, Jesus cried with a loud voice, saying: Eli, Eli, lamma sabacthani? That is, My God, My God, why hast thou forsaken me?

47. And some that stood there and heard said: This man calleth Elias.

48. And immediately one of them running took a sponge and filled it with vinegar and put it on a reed and gave him to drink.

49. And the others said: Let be. Let us see whether Elias will come to deliver him.

50. And Jesus again crying with a loud voice, yielded up the ghost.

51. And behold the veil of the temple was rent in two from the top even to the bottom: and the earth quaked and the rocks were rent.

52. And the graves were opened: and many bodies of the saints that had slept arose,

53. And coming out of the tombs after his resurrection, came into the holy city and appeared to many.

54. Now the centurion and they that were with him watching Jesus, having seen the earthquake and the things that were done, were sore afraid, saying: Indeed this was the Son of God.

55. And there were there many women afar off, who had followed Jesus from Galilee, ministering unto him:

56. Among whom was Mary Magdalen and Mary the mother of James and Joseph and the mother of the sons of Zebedee.

57. And when it was evening, there came a certain rich man of Arimathea, named Joseph, who also himself was a disciple of Jesus.

58. He went to Pilate and asked the body of Jesus. Then Pilate commanded that the body should be delivered.

59. And Joseph taking the body wrapped it up in a clean linen cloth:

60. And laid it in his own new monument, which he had hewed out in a rock. And he rolled a great stone to the door of the monument and went his way.

61. And there was there Mary Magdalen and the other Mary, sitting over against the sepulcher.

62. And the next day, which followed the day of preparation, the chief priests and the Pharisees came together to Pilate,

63. Saying: Sir, we have remembered, that that seducer said, while he was yet alive: After three days I will rise again.

64. Command therefore the sepulcher to be guarded until the third day: lest perhaps his disciples come and steal him away and say to the people: He is risen from the dead. And the last error shall be worse than the first.

65. Pilate saith to them: You have a guard. Go, guard it as you know.

66. And they departing, made the sepulcher sure, sealing the stone and setting guards.

After relating His condemnation, here, His Passion and death are treated; and secondly, His burial is treated, where it is said, **And when it was evening**, etc. About the first part, the Evangelist does two things. For firstly, he recounts what things Christ undeservedly bore; and secondly, he recounts what things He magnificently did, where it is said, **Now from the sixth hour, there was darkness**. The first part is divided into three parts. In the first part, he treats of the mocking by the soldiers; in the second part, he treats of the crucifixion; in the third part, he treats of the derision made by the Jews. The second part is where it is said, **And after they had mocked him**; and the third part is where it is said, **And they that passed by blasphemed him**. About the first part, the mockers are firstly described, and secondly, the mockery is described. He says, therefore: *Then the soldiers of the governor gathered together unto him the whole band.* A group of soldiers is called a band (cohort): and anyone who had judicial power had a band of soldiers for executing justice. The place where judgments were exercised is called a hall (*praetorium*). Hence, both Gentiles and Jews gathered to Him, so that no one would be guiltless, because all had to be redeemed.[13] Wherefore, what is stated is befitting: "God hath concluded all in unbelief, that he may have mercy on all" (Rom. 11, 32). And: "They came around me like bees" (Ps. 117, 12). *And stripping him, they put a scarlet cloak about him.* Here, His mockery is described. And it is described firstly as to His clothing; secondly, it is described as to His honor; and thirdly, it is described as to His disgrace. The second part is where it is said, *And bowing the knee before him, they mocked him*; and the third part is where it is said, *And going out, they found a man of Cyrene, named Simon*, etc.

It ought to be observed that although they had accused Him of many things, nevertheless, He suffered for no other reason than that He said He was a King, as it stated: "If thou release this man, thou art not Caesar's friend" (Jn 19, 12). Hence, on this account, Pilate feared more. Hence, wishing to mock Him, the soldiers put on Him the insignia of a king. For it was the custom that kings would be clothed in purple: and these men, in place of this color, clothed Him with a scarlet garment. Likewise, kings customarily had a crown; and, in place of this, they made a crown of thorns. Moreover, they customarily had a scepter; and, in place of this, they gave Him a staff of a reed.[14] He says, therefore, *And they put a scarlet cloak about him*, meaning a red cloak.

But what is that which Mark says (15, 17), namely, that they clothed Him with purple? Augustine explained that Mark said this due to the similarity of the color. It can be said that, although it was scarlet, nevertheless, it did contain some amount of purple.

By the fact that He was stripped of His own clothes, and clothed with other clothes, the heretics are reprehended who were saying that He was not a true man. This cloak can signify Christ's flesh stained with His own blood: "He was wounded for our iniquities,

---

13. The Blessed Virgin Mary alone was guiltless and exempted from actually contracting Original Sin by her preventive redemption, though she still incurred the debt of original sin as she was born from Adam. cf. above in chapter 11, footnote no. 8.

14. "This, which represented His scepter as King of the Jews, was a fragile, worthless, mean, and ridiculous thing" " (Cornelius à Lapide, *The Great Commentary: St. Matthew's Gospel*, (John Hodges, 1891) vol. 3, pp. 276).

he was bruised for our sins" (Is. 53, 5).[15] Or it signifies the blood of the martyrs, who washed their stoles in the Blood of the Lamb. Or it signifies the sins of the Gentiles.[16] *And platting a crown of thorns, they put it upon his head.* Hence, instead of a crown of glory they put upon Him a crown of contumely; "Crown him with a crown of tribulation" (Is. 22, 18). By these thorns are signified the pricks of sins, by which the conscience is wounded: and Christ accepted these for us, because He died for our sins. Or it can be referred to Adam's curse, where it was said: "Thorns and thistles shall it bring forth to thee" (Gen. 3, 18). Hence, it was signified that this curse was removed. And instead of a scepter, *they put a reed in his right hand.* And the power of the devils is signified, according to Origen, which Christ snatched out of their hands: "Do not trust in a staff of a reed" (IV Kings 18, 21). The frailty of the Gentiles can be signified by the reed, which, nevertheless, Christ assumed; "Ask of me, and I will give thee the Gentiles for thy inheritance" (Ps. 2, 8). And the Gentiles are fittingly compared to a reed, because just as a reed is swayed by every wind, so the Gentiles were swayed into every error. Likewise, they used a reed for writing errors. Furthermore, they used a poisoned reed for killing. In this way, by using a reed, Christ draws the faithful to Himself and enrolls them, but His persecutors, by using a reed, put the faithful to death.

Then the mock-honor is treated, and they show this by an action; hence, it is said, *And bowing the knee before him, they mocked him.* And although they did this mockingly, nevertheless, it signifies that every knee is obliged to bend before Him; "In the name of Jesus every knee should bow" (Phil. 2, 10). Hence, they were mocking with words, saying to Him: *Hail, King of the Jews.* And by these words are signified those who "profess that they know God: but in their works they deny him" (Tit. 1, 16). Likewise, they offered various insults, for they spat in His face; "I have not turned away my face from them that spit upon me" (Is. 50, 6). Similarly, *They took the reed and struck his head* as though He were a fool. And who are they who strike Christ's head? Christ's head is God, as it is stated in I Corinthians 11.[17]

---

15. "REMIG. By the scarlet robe is denoted the Lord's flesh, which is spoken of as red by reason of shedding of His blood" (*Catena Aurea on St. Matthew*, chap. 27, lect. 5).
16. "Symbolically: 'In the scarlet robe,' says St. Jerome, 'the Lord bears the blood-stained works of the Gentiles.' 'He bore,' says St. Athanasius, 'in the scarlet garment a resemblance to the blood wherewith the earth had been polluted.' And Origen says, 'The Lord, by taking on Him the scarlet robe, took on Himself the blood, that is, the sins of the world, which are bloody and red as scarlet; for the Lord hath laid on Him the iniquity of us all.'" (Cornelius à Lapide, vol. 3, pp. 273).
17. "The head of Christ is God" (verse 3).

Therefore, they strike Christ who blaspheme Christ's divinity. By the reed, Sacred Scripture is signified. Such men confirm their errors with Sacred Scripture.[18]

And going out, they found a man of Cyrene. After His mocking, the crucifixion is treated; and about this, the Evangelist does two things. Firstly, he indicates the place of the crucifixion; and secondly, he indicates His clothing, and what things happened in that place. And firstly, he recounts how Christ was led to that place; secondly, he recounts how the Cross was carried; and thirdly, he relates how they came to His Passion. ***And after they had mocked him, they took off the cloak***, namely, the cloak which they had put on Him.

Observe that He is mocked in another's garments, but led away in His own garments; by this is signified that it did not belong to Him to be mocked, but to be killed; because, as it is stated, "He humbled himself, becoming obedient unto death, even to the death of the cross" (Phil. 2, 8). For His strength appeared therein: "The right hand of the Lord hath wrought strength" (Ps. 117, 16); "He shall be led as a sheep to the slaughter" (Is. 53, 7).

And going out, they found a man of Cyrene. Here, the carrying of the Cross is treated. And by this is signified that He did not wish to suffer in the city, but outside the city. And the reason is given in Hebrews 13, 12, where it is said: "Wherefore Jesus also, that he might sanctify the people by his own blood, suffered without the gate." It also befits a figure, because, as it is stated in Leviticus 16, a goat, which was due to be immolated for sin, was brought outside the camp; so also Christ was immolated outside the camp, because He was the victim for the people. Likewise, He was brought outside the city for our edification, namely, to give us to understand that we ought to go forth to Him outside our social relationships; "Let us go forth therefore to him without the camp, bearing his reproach" (Heb. 13, 13). Similarly, He suffered outside the camp so that the power of His Passion would not be limited to one nation; as it is said in John 11, He died to gather together all nations.

Him they forced to take up his cross. Here there seems to be a discrepancy, because in John 19, 17 it is stated that "he went forth bearing his own cross." Here is a solution according to Jerome, namely, that He firstly carried the cross, but afterwards going along they met Simon, and they forced Him to carry the cross,

---

18. "RABAN. They smite the head of Christ with a reed, who speak against His divinity, and endeavor to maintain their error by the authority of Holy Scripture, which is written by a reed" (*Catena Aurea on St. Matthew, chap.* 27, lect. 5).

etc. Origen says that it was the opposite, such that Simon firstly carried the cross and Christ afterwards. And there is a mystical reason why Christ carried it first. For it is said above: "If any man will come after me, let him deny himself, and take up his cross, and follow me," etc., (16, 24). And it ought to be observed that this Simon was a foreigner: and he signifies the Gentiles, who bore Christ's cross; "The word of the cross, to them indeed that perish, is foolishness: but to them that are saved, that is, to us, it is the power of God" (I Cor. 1, 18). And Simon is interpreted to mean 'obedient': and the Gentiles obeyed; "A people which I knew not, hath served me: at the hearing of the ear they have obeyed me" (Ps. 17, 45). And he was coming from a country place.[19] A country place in Latin (*pagus*) is called a 'pagos' in Greek. Hence, he came from a country place who came from paganism. It is also fitting that he is called a Cyrenian, because Cyrenian is interpreted to mean 'the inheritance of a reward'; "Ask of me, and I will give thee the Gentiles for thy inheritance" (Ps. 2, 8). And that which he says, namely, that they forced him, signifies those who outwardly bear their cross; inwardly, however, they bear it by force, because they do not bear it for God's sake but for the world's sake. "They that are Christ's have crucified their flesh, with the vices and concupiscences" (Gal. 5, 24).

Afterwards, the place is related: ***And they came to the place that is called Golgotha, which is the place of Calvary.*** Calvary means 'a bare skull' in common speech, as is found in cemeteries. Hence, it is called in Greek *Kranion*. And some say that Adam was buried in that place. Jerome refutes this, saying that Adam was buried in Hebron, as it is stated in Josue 14.[20]

And why did He suffer there? It ought to be observed that in every city there is some place where the condemned are customarily tortured: hence, the place of the condemned was there.

Then it is told what happened during His crucifixion. And firstly, His drinking is related; secondly, His crucifixion is related; and thirdly, other things which happened are related. And about the first point, what is offered to be drunk is firstly related; and secondly, how He reacted to what was offered is related. He says, therefore: ***And they gave him wine to drink mingled with gall.*** They wanted that all His senses would suffer: His sight suffered by the spittle and the watchings: His hearing suffered by the blasphe-

---

19. "And they forced one Simon a Cyrenian, who passed by coming out of the country" (Mk. 15, 21).

20. "The name of Hebron before was called Cariath-Arbe: Adam the greatest among the Enacims was laid there and the land rested from wars" (verse 15).

mies and words of mockery: His sense of touch suffered, because He was scourged: wherefore they wanted that His sense of taste would suffer. And what is said was fulfilled: "And they gave me gall for my food, and in my thirst they gave me vinegar to drink" (Ps. 68, 22): and: "How then art thou turned unto me into that which is good for nothing, O strange vineyard?" (Jer. 2, 21).

But there is a question: why is it that in Mark 15 it is stated that they gave Him wine mingled with myrrh.[21] It ought to be said that myrrh is very bitter, and wine mixed with gall is bitter. But it is the custom that every bitter thing be named under the classification of gall. Hence, in reality there was wine mingled with myrrh, but, nevertheless, it is named for its likeness to gall. And, by this, it was signified that He bore the bitterness of our sins.

Afterwards it is related how He reacted, for it is said, **And when he had tasted, he would not drink.**

But why is it that Mark says that He did not take it, but here Matthew says that He tasted it? It can be said that He did not take it, except to taste it, and this signifies that He tasted death: for since He rose quickly from the dead, He was scarcely seen to be dead, because He was "free among the dead" (Ps. 87, 6).

And after they had crucified him, etc. But it can be asked why He preferred to die this kind of death. One reason is on the part of those crucifying Him, because they wished that He would be defamed by this kind of death, according to that which is written: "Let us condemn him to a most shameful death," etc., (Wis. 2, 20), and this is the death of the cross. Likewise, another reason is on the part of God's ordination, because Christ wanted to be our teacher by giving us an example of suffering death. Hence, He suffered death to free us by His death, as it is stated in Hebrews 2.[22] Now there are many who wish to suffer death well, but shrink from a shameful death; wherefore, the Lord gave an example, lest they would shrink from any kind of death. Moreover, it was befitting the redemption, because it befitted the satisfaction for the sin of the first man. Now the first man sinned in relation to wood; for that reason, the Lord willed to suffer on wood; "Blessed is the wood, by which justice cometh" (Wis. 14, 7). Furthermore, Christ was exalted by His Passion, wherefore, He willed to be raised up by His Passion on the Cross. Similarly, He wanted to draw our hearts to Him: "If I be lifted up from the earth, will draw all

---

21. "And they gave him to drink wine mingled with myrrh" (verse 23).
22. "He also himself in like manner hath been partaker of the same: that, through death, he might destroy him who had the empire of death, that is to say, the devil: And might deliver them, who through the fear of death were all their lifetime subject to servitude" (verses 14-15).

things to myself" (Jn. 12, 32). Again, He was elevated upon the Cross so that our hearts might be elevated.

They divided his garments. Here is related the things that happened unto the dishonor of the One crucified. And firstly, the division of His garments is related; secondly, the posting of His cause is related; and thirdly, His fellowship is related. About the first part, the Evangelist firstly relates the deed; and secondly, he cites a prophecy. He says, therefore, ***They divided.*** Chrysostom says that this was done as a great insult. For it was the custom that the condemned was not stripped unless he were a man of very little worth: wherefore, in order that they might greatly insult Him, they stripped him, so that we might be instructed that we ought to strip ourselves of every affection for carnal acts. Matthew passes over when this was done, but John tells when it was done in chapter 19, where he says that each soldier took his part from another garment;[23] but for His seamless coat they cast lots. Then a prophecy is cited: ***That it might be fulfilled which was spoken by the prophet.*** The word *that* is not used causatively but consecutively, because when Christ suffered, it happened that what was said was fulfilled. ***And they sat and watched him***, etc., so that He might not be buried; "And they have looked and stared upon me" (Ps. 21, 19).[24]

Then the superscription follows: ***And they put over his head his cause written***, etc. And it ought to be noted that this superscription, which they made from an intention to dishonor Him, turned to His honor. Hence, ***they put his cause***, meaning the reason why He was suffering; in the Apocalypse the writing is found: "King of kings and Lord of lords" (19, 16). Therefore, what it says, ***King of the Jews***, pertains to His honor, because He was about to be the King over all nations; "But I am appointed king by him over Sion, his holy mountain" (Ps. 2, 6).

Then His companionship is related: ***Then were crucified with him two thieves.*** This was His companionship, because He was in the middle of two thieves as a malefactor; hence: "He was reputed with the wicked" (Is. 53, 12). He received His Cross as a judge: for as in a judgment some are on the right hand and others are on the left hand, so it is here. Hence, by this is signified that

---

23. "The soldiers therefore, when they had crucified him, took his garments, (and they made four parts, to every soldier a part) and also his coat. Now the coat was without seam, woven from the top throughout" (verse 23).

24. The Roman custom was to let the bodies of those executed by crucifixion hang until they were destroyed by decay or by predatory animals; according to the Romans this was a way for crucifixion to achieve its salutary effect of preserving the existing social order. "People sentenced to death forfeited their property and were forbidden burial" (Tacitus, *Annals* 6.29).

He is the Judge of the living and the dead; "For which cause, God also hath exalted him and hath given him a name which is above all names: that in the name of Jesus every knee should bow, of those that are in heaven, on earth, and under the earth" (Phil. 2, 9-10); "Thy cause hath been judged as that of the wicked, cause and judgment thou shalt recover" (Job 36, 17). Likewise, by the fact that one thief was on His right and the other on His left side, is signified that Christ suffered for all men; but, nevertheless, some believe, and others do not; "But we preach Christ crucified: unto the Jews indeed a stumblingblock, and unto the Gentiles foolishness" (I Cor. 1, 23). Or it can be said that some men endure the cross for God's sake, and these are on His right side; others, however, endure the cross not for God's sake, but for the world's sake, and these are on His left.

Then it is treated concerning the mockery of Him crucified; **And they that passed by blasphemed him**. And firstly, the mockery that He received from the people is treated; secondly, that which He received from the chief priests; and thirdly, the mockery that He received from the thieves is treated. About the first part, he firstly describes the blasphemers; and secondly, he describes the blasphemies. Therefore, he firstly describes the blasphemers by the fact that he says, **they that passed by**, meaning going off the road: about such men it is said: "Turn away the path from me, let the Holy One of Israel cease from before us" (Is. 30, 11). Likewise, they are described in that **they were wagging their heads**: and they were doing this to make fun of Him. By the head, reason is signified, and by the feet, one's affections are signified; hence, firstly they moved their affections to evil, and afterwards, they moved their heads, because they were made senseless in their sins. They mocked Him in three ways. Firstly, they mocked Him concerning His words; secondly, they mocked Him concerning the works that He performed; and thirdly, they mocked Him concerning the dignity which He appropriated to Himself. Concerning the first point, he relates their mockery concerning His words: **Vah, thou that destroyest the temple of God**, etc. 'Vah' is an interjection of derision. His words were already well-known and they did not want to believe; hence, it is said concerning these men: "They have laid hold on lying, and have refused to return" (Jer. 8, 5). It is as though they said: 'If you want to rebuild the Temple, rebuild yourself'; but He could not rebuild it unless it be firstly destroyed: wherefore, He firstly wished that it be destroyed, because He had said this about the temple of His Body. Next, they mock Him concerning His works; **Save thy own self**; it is as though they were to say:

'You saved others, save yourself. But you did not truly save others, and neither can you save yourself.' Likewise, they mocked Him on account of His dignity, because they said, *If thou be the Son of God, come down from the cross.* This conditional statement is not good; nay, rather, if He be the Son of God, He ought to be obedient to His Father. For "He became obedient unto death" (Phil. 2, 8). Moreover, they ought to have said instead: 'If you are the Son of God, ascend, and do not come down'; "No man hath ascended into heaven, but he that descended from heaven , the Son of man who is in heaven" (Jn. 3, 13). They use the same words which the devil used when he was tempting Him: "If thou be the Son of God, cast thyself down" (above 4, 6). For it does not belong to the Son of God to come down: hence, they were speaking by diabolical persuasion, the devils being willing to impede His Passion.

Then the Evangelist continues concerning the mockery of the chief priests: *In like manner also the chief priests, with the scribes and ancients, mocking*, etc. Hence, not only the people, but the leading men, were mocking Him. A person does not make a fuss if he be condemned by the lowliest men, but is unable to bear the derision of more important men; for a man naturally desires to be honored; now honor occurs in recognition of virtue. Hence, mockery occurs on account of reproach. And these men are described by their authority, for some were chief priests. Likewise, they are described by their teaching, for some were scribes. Similarly, they are described by their manner of life, for some were Pharisees, who were preeminent in their manner of life; "I will go therefore to the great men, and will speak to them: for they have known the way of the Lord, the judgment of their God: and behold these have altogether broken the yoke more, and have burst the bonds" (Jer. 5, 5). And they say three things. Firstly, they reproach the miracles that He performed; secondly, they reproach His royal dignity; and thirdly, they reproach the fact that He made Himself the Son of God. Regarding the first point, they say: *He saved others: himself he cannot save*. They wished to say: 'If He saved others, He would be able to save Himself; but He is unable to save Himself: therefore, neither did He save others.' But we, on the contrary, ought to argue: 'He saved others, therefore He can save Himself; but He was able to save Himself by rising from the dead: therefore, He will be able to save us.' "He became, to all that obey him, the cause of eternal salvation" (Heb. 5, 9). Hence, these men merely sought temporal salvation; Christ, however, wished to show that one ought to prefer eternal salvation; hence, they say: *If he be the king of Israel, let him now come down from the cross.*

Here, they reproach His royal dignity, and they make a false promise, and they draw a false conclusion, because if He is the king of Israel, He ought not to come down, because He ought to ascend by the cross; "The Lord hath reigned from a tree," (Ps. 95, 10)[25] and "The government (meaning the Cross) is upon his shoulder" (Is. 9, 6). Likewise, He did something that is greater, namely, that He rose from the sepulcher, and they still did not believe, hence, they were liars; "Hearken not to the words of the prophets that prophesy to you, and deceive you" (Jer. 23, 16): and the verse continues: "For they speak a vision of their own heart." Likewise, they reproach the fact that He said that He is the Son of God: *He trusted in God: let him now deliver him if he will have him*: "He hoped in the Lord, let him deliver him: let him save him, seeing he delighteth in him" (Ps. 21, 9). He was able to deliver Himself, if He so willed; but He did not wish to do so, because God wanted Him to expose Himself at the time of His death, in order to procure salvation for us and honor for Himself. Hence, it was fulfilled what was said : "All curse me" (Jer. 15, 10).

And the selfsame thing the thieves reproached him with. But why is it said here that both reproached Him? In Luke 23, on the other hand, it is said that only one reproached Him.[26] Augustine solves the question, saying that sometimes it is the custom in Scripture that the plural is used for the singular, as in Hebrews 2, 33: "They stopped the mouths of lions," meaning, he stopped the mouths of lions, namely, Daniel: and it is a manner of speaking, as it is said: 'The rustics were hostile to me,' even if only one rustic attacked him. Matthew is speaking in this manner here. Or it is otherwise, according to Jerome, that at the beginning both thieves reproached Him; but one, seeing the miracles that He was working, repented. And this, as Chrysostom says, happened by a divine dispensation. Hence, those are signified, who after many heinous crimes, return to Christ.

Now from the sixth hour, there was darkness over the whole earth. Above, the Evangelist told how the Lord suffered on the Cross; here, he tells how He performed marvelous works. And firstly, he relates the works that He performed before His death; and

---

25. In this verse where the Vulgate reads *Dicite in gentibus, quia Dominus regnavit* ("Say ye among the Gentiles, the Lord hath reigned"), the Old Latin reads, *dicite in gentibus, Dominus regnavit a ligno* ("Say ye among the Gentiles, the Lord hath reigned from a tree"), apparently following an early Septuagint reading. The hymn *Vexilla regis prodeunt,* by Venantius Fortunatus in line 16: *Regnavit a ligno Deus* ("God ruling [the nations] from a Tree") is based upon this variation.

26. "And one of those robbers who were hanged blasphemed him, saying: If thou be Christ, save thyself and us" (verse 39).

secondly, he relates the works that he performed after His death, where it is said, *And Jesus again crying with a loud voice, yielded up the ghost.* About the first point, he does two things. Firstly, he tells of the darkening that occurred; and secondly, he tells of the cry, where it is said, *And about the ninth hour, Jesus cried.* He says, therefore: *Now from the sixth hour, there was darkness over the whole earth.* As Origen relates, the Gentiles, hearing this Gospel being recited as supporting a miracle, scoffed at it and they said that this had happened naturally; wherefore, they supposed what an ignorant man would say, namely, that this happened since the sun naturally underwent an eclipse. But this eclipse was not natural, but miraculous. But if you wish to see that this is so, listen to what Dionysius says, who was twenty-five years old and was studying the stars in the city of Heliopolis. And while he was looking, he and Apollonius were astonished; and it seemed to them that the eclipse was not natural, and they considered four miraculous things. The first is from the time, because it was the day on which the Pasch ought to occur, it was the fifteenth day of the month, when the moon is in opposition to the sun: but a natural eclipse happens due to the conjunction of the moon with the sun. The second miracle was that when the sun is in the west, the moon ought to be in the east; but here the course of the moon was changed. Likewise, the third sign is that the darkening always begins from the western part, because all planets have a double motion, proper and common. The moon, regarding its proper movement, is faster, and when it comes to the body of the sun, it comes from the west; but it was not so in this case, because it came from the east. There was a fourth miracle, because from the same direction the darkness begins, the illumination also returns; but this was not then the case, because that portion which it first occupied, it left last, because the moon came from the east towards the body of the sun, and then went backwards, hence, the portion last occupied was firstly illuminated. And, therefore, Dionysius, considering these things, at the coming of Paul, converted and, afterwards, he converted his companion. The fifth miracle, which is greater, as [Chrysostom] says,[27] is that when there is a natural eclipse it lasts a short duration: for the sun itself is not darkened, but it becomes dark by the interposition of the moon; but the body of the moon is not larger than the body of the sun, wherefore, an eclipse does not last long; but this eclipse lasted three hours, and, therefore, it was a great miracle.

27. This fifth reason comes from St. John Chrysostom. cf. III, q. 44, a. 2 ad 2um.

But Origen asks: 'If this were such a great miracle, why did no astrologist record it? He answers, and he said that this darkness was not universal, but near the land of the Judea. Or it is said that it was *over the whole earth*, namely, over Judea. There is a similar manner of speech when it is said: "There is no nation or kingdom," etc.,[28] for these words ought to be understood as concerning that nation, so also here. But Chrysostom says that *over the whole earth* is understood as meaning over the whole world, because He was dying for the whole world; therefore, He wanted to become known by a sign of the Passion. But Dionysius says that he was in Egypt and he saw this sign, and in this way, he was able to understand that it extended up to Asia: hence, he is to be believed more. A certain astronomer tells of a particular eclipse, that happened during the time of Tiberius, but he does not say when, or how long it lasted, or why it happened; yet, it can be said that because it was not then time for an eclipse, they did not consider its manner carefully. Hence, some men said that many clouds were interposed between us and the sun; others, however, said that the sun withdrew its rays; hence: "The sun went down at midday" (Amos 8, 9).

But there is a question, because here it is said that He was crucified at the sixth hour, but Mark says that it was at the third hour (chapter 15).[29] It ought to be said that Matthew recounts the history, in that Christ was crucified at the sixth hour, and that He died at the ninth hour: and this befits a mystery, because, at the sixth hour, the sun is in the middle of the sky; wherefore, it befits the Son of God, who is the true Sun; "Unto you that fear my name, the Sun of justice shall arise" (Mal. 4, 2). Likewise, it befits the transgression of the first man; because Adam sinned in the afternoon (Gen. 3),[30] wherefore, Christ wished to satisfy for this transgression at the same hour.

Why, therefore, does Mark say that it was at the third hour? It ought to be said that He was crucified at the third hour by the tongues of the Jews, but at the sixth hour He was crucified by the hands of the soldiers.[31] Likewise, there were three hours of dark-

---

28. Abdias said to Elias, "As the Lord thy God liveth, there is no nation or kingdom, whither my lord hath not sent to seek thee" (III Kings 18, 10).
29. "And it was the third hour: and they crucified him" (verse 25).
30. "And when they heard the voice of the Lord God walking in paradise at the afternoon air, Adam and his wife hid themselves" (verse 8).
31. *"The third hour.* The ancient account divided the day into four parts, which were named from the hour from which they began: the first, third, sixth, and ninth hour. Our Lord was crucified a little before noon; before the third hour had quite expired; but when the sixth hour was near at hand" (Challoner).

ness, and this was prefigured by that which is written in Exodus 10, 22, namely, "And Moses stretched forth his hand towards heaven: and there came horrible darkness in all the land of Egypt for three days." So Christ extended His hands on the Cross, and there was darkness for three hours, to signify that they were deprived of the light of the Trinity.

And about the ninth hour, Jesus cried with a loud voice. Here he relates Christ's cry. And firstly, His cry is related; and secondly, its effect is related, where it is said, *And some that stood there*, etc. He says, therefore: *And about the ninth hour, Jesus cried with a loud voice.* According to Origen, Christ cried with a loud voice and it signifies many mysteries. "The seraphims cried one to another, and said: Holy, holy, holy, the Lord God of hosts" (Is. 6, 3). Hence, he who wishes to interpret this such that He cried due to the weariness of death, does not understand the mystery; wherefore, it ought not to be so interpreted, and because He wanted to make it understood that He is equal to His Father, He said with a loud voice in the Hebrew language, *Eli, Eli, lamma sabacthani?*[32] Similarly, by this, it ought to be understood that He wanted to signify that this was foretold by the prophets, wherefore, He said the words, "My God, look upon me: why hast thou forsaken me?" (Ps. 21, 2). Hence, Jerome says that they are wicked who wish to expound this psalm otherwise than relating to Christ's Passion.

Observe that some have misunderstood these words. Hence, you ought to know that there were two heresies. There was one that did not affirm that in Christ the Word was united to the soul, but instead asserted that the Word took the place of the soul, and Arius asserted this.[33] Others, however, held that the Word was not naturally united to the soul, except by grace, as in a just man, as in the prophets, and Nestorius spoke thus. Hence, they were expounding the words: *My God, My God, why hast thou forsaken me?* as follows. They say that the Word of God said this because Christ is His creature, and it follows that this Word made Christ to be united to Himself, and, afterwards, forsook Him. But this is an impious explanation, because God is always with

---

32. "CHRYS. Also for this reason He cried out with a loud voice to show that this is done by His own power. For by crying out with a loud voice when dying, He showed incontestably that He was the true God; because a man in dying can scarcely utter even a feeble sound" (*Catena Aurea on St. Matthew*, chap. 27, lect. 9).

33. "As Augustine says (*De Haeresibus* 69,55), it was first of all the opinion of Arius and then of Apollinaris that the Son of God assumed only flesh, without a soul, holding that the Word took the place of a soul to the body" (III, q. 5, a. 3).

Him; hence, His Divinity did not leave His flesh, nor did it leave His soul: hence, it is said in John 8, 29: "He that sent me is with me." What then do these words mean? It ought to be said that by this manner of speech, it is clear what ought to be understood concerning Christ: for it is said concerning Him: "I ascend to my Father and to your Father, to my God and to your God" (Jn. 20, 17). He calls Him His Father, in that He is God; He calls Him His God, in that He is man: wherefore, when He says, *My God, My God*, etc., it is clear that He is speaking insofar as He is a man; hence, He groans, to express the greatness of His human suffering. And that which is said, *Thou hast forsaken me*, is said as a similitude, because what we possess, we possess from God; hence, just as when someone is exposed to some evil, he is said to be abandoned: so when the Lord abandons a man to fall into the evil of pain, or the evil of guilt, he is said to be abandoned; wherefore, Christ is said to be abandoned, not in regard to His union with God, nor in regard to His grace, but in regard to His suffering; "For a small moment have I forsaken thee" (Is. 54, 7). And He says, *Why?*, not as from weariness, but it can indicate His compassion toward the Jews; hence, He did not speak except after it became dark; hence, He wishes to say: 'Why did you want Me to be handed over to suffering, and these Jews to be darkened?' Likewise, He said this to indicate His admiration, for God's charity is admirable. "God commendeth his charity towards us: because when as yet we were sinners according to the time Christ died for us" (Rom. 5, 8-9).

Then the effect of His cry follows, where it is said: *And some that stood there*, etc. And firstly, the common effect upon all is related; and secondly, the effect upon one of them is related, where it is said, *And immediately one of them running*. He says, therefore: *And some that stood there and heard said: This man calleth Elias.*

Who were these men? Jerome says that they were the soldiers, who did not know the Hebrew language and, on account of this, they supposed that He was calling Elias, because Elias was very famous, since he was taken into heaven as it is stated in IV Kings 2.[34] Or it can be said that they were Jews, and they wished by this to show that Christ was a man, and not God, who was asking the help of another.

Then the effect of his cry upon one man is related: and firstly, what he did is told; and secondly, what others did is told. He says,

---

34. "Elias went up by a whirlwind into heaven" (verse 11).

therefore: *And one of them took a sponge and filled it with vinegar*. Why he did this is not said here, but in John 19, 28, namely, that Christ, seeing that all things were accomplished, said, "I thirst": wherefore, this man, wishing to satisfy him, gave him the drink of the condemned. Hence, it was fulfilled what is said: "And they gave me gall for my food, and in my thirst they gave me vinegar to drink" (Ps. 68, 22). It ought to be observed that it was wine mixed with myrrh, but it is called gall and vinegar, because it had a bitter taste. Mystically, by wine mixed with myrrh is signified those who have no faith. Or by vinegar, which is produced by the corruption of wine, is signified the corruption of human nature. Now Christ drank this bitterness. Or, by vinegar, the Jew's malice is signified. And it is put into a sponge, which is hollow, and it signifies the deceits and hypocrisies of the Jews. But they put it on a reed. By the reed Sacred Scripture is signified;[35] hence, they wanted to confirm their malice by Scripture. And it can be that this man was motivated by compassion; hence, this man wanted to help Him but the others were unwilling, hence, they said: *Let be. Let us see whether Elias will come to deliver him.*

And Jesus again crying with a loud voice, yielded up the ghost. Here it is treated concerning those things that happened after His death. And firstly, Christ's death is related; secondly, the things that happened after His death are related; and thirdly, the effect of the events is related. The second part is where it is said, *And behold the veil of the temple was rent*; and the third part is where it is said, *Now the centurion*, etc. About the first point, His death and the manner of His death are treated. Three reasons for His death are given: one reason was to show how much He loved us. Augustine says: "There is no greater reason for love than to be loved first." "God commendeth his charity towards us: because when as yet we were sinners according to the time, Christ died for us" (Rom. 5, 8-9). Likewise, He died to teach us to disregard death. By His death, He destroyed all sin. Similarly, He died to take away the punishment of Adam's sin, namely, so that He might free us from Adam's sin. For it was said to him: "In what hour soever thou shalt eat of it, thou shalt die the death" (Gen. 2, 17): from this death, He delivered us. Moreover, He died because the devil, who is the author of death, had assaulted Him who did not deserve to die, wherefore, the devil lost his power over other men; hence, "He delivered His own soul

---

35. Scripture was written with a reed as a writing instrument.

unto death,"[36] to free our souls. Again, by His death, His mortal condition is indicated: *And crying with a loud voice, He yielded up the ghost*.

Some have said that the divinity had died; but this is false, because life cannot die, but God is not merely living, but is even life itself. Others said that His soul died with His body: which cannot be, because death would not have been able to lay hold of immortality. Likewise, it ought to be noted that all men die due to necessity; Christ, however, died by His own will. Hence, the Evangelist does not say, 'He died,' but, **He yielded up**, because it was from His will; and this indicates His power, as it is said elsewhere: "I have power to lay it down: and I have power to take it up again" (Jn. 10, 18).

And He willed to die with a loud voice, to indicate that He died by His own power, and not due to necessity: hence, He laid down His life when He willed, and He took it up again when He willed. Hence, it was easier for Christ to lay down His life, and to take it up again, than it is for a man to fall asleep and to wake up. But why, then, was His death imputed to them? It is because they did all that they could do to cause Him to die.

And behold the veil of the temple was rent, etc. In this part, the effects of His death are treated. Firstly, those things that happened in respect to the Temple are treated; secondly, those things that happened in the elements are treated; and thirdly, those things that happened in men are treated. And it ought to be seen that Matthew recounts these events in a different order than Luke. Augustine says that Matthew recounts them in the historical order: and this is evident, because he says: *And behold the veil of the temple was rent*. In Luke, however, nothing about this is found.

And it ought to be observed that in the Temple there were two veils, namely, in the tabernacle, because there was the veil within the Holy of Holies, and there was another one, which was not in the Holy of Holies.[37] And these two veils signify a twofold veiling, because the inside veil signifies the veiling of heavenly mysteries, which will be revealed to us: for then we shall be like to Him, when His glory shall have appeared. The other veil, which was outside, signifies the veiling of mysteries which pertain to the Church. Hence, the outer veil was rent, but the other one was not, to signify that mysteries which pertain to the Church were

---

36. Is. 53, 12.
37. "ORIGEN; It is understood that there were two veils; one veiling the Holy of Holies, the other, the outer part of the tabernacle or temple" (*Catena Aurea on St. Matthew*, chap. 27, lect. 10).

made known by Christ's death; but the other veil was not rent, because heavenly secrets still remain veiled. Hence, the Apostle says: "But when Israel shall be converted to the Lord, the veil shall be taken away" (II Cor. 3, 16). Hence, by the Passion, all mysteries, which were written in the Law and the prophets, were opened, as it is stated: "Beginning at Moses and all the prophets, he expounded to them in all the scriptures the things that were concerning him" (Lk. 24, 27). Or the rending of the veil signifies the dispersion of the Jews. And because their glory was in the veil that was rent at the Lord's Passion, it was signified that all glory was divided from them.

And the earth quaked and the rocks were rent, etc. Above, a miracle was related, which happened in respect to the Temple; here, the Evangelist relates a miracle that happened in respect to the elements. And these events are found to be fitting, firstly in relation to the power of the Passion; secondly, they are fitting in relation to the effect of salvation; and thirdly, they are fitting in relation to the judiciary power that Christ merited by suffering. It is fitting that the earth quaked, etc., because one is unable to sustain the presence of such majesty without trembling; hence: "He looketh upon the earth, and maketh it tremble" (Ps. 103, 32); by which earthquake, it is signified that no power can resist Him; "The Lord passeth overthrowing the mountains, and breaking the rocks in pieces" (III Kings 19, 11). The monuments are tombs of dead bodies. Hence, it is signified that He burst the bonds of death; "O death, I will be thy death" (Os. 13, 14). Likewise: "Death is swallowed up in victory" (I Cor. 15, 54). Similarly, it is fitting in relation to the effect of His Passion. The earth is moved when anything earthly is cast away. "Thou hast moved the earth, and hast troubled it: heal thou the breaches thereof, for it has been moved" (Ps. 59, 4). Similarly, the rocks are rent when the hardness of hearts is moved to compassion; "My words are as a fire, saith the Lord: and as a hammer that breaketh the rock in pieces" (Jer. 23, 29). Moreover, that the monuments were opened signifies that those dead in their sins ought to rise; "Rise, thou that sleepest, and arise from the dead" (Eph. 5, 14). Again, it befits the Person coming to judgment, that when He comes, the earth will be moved; "Yet one little while, and I will move the heaven and the earth" (Ag. 2, 7). Furthermore, the rocks are rent, because all haughtiness of men will be brought down. Likewise, the monuments will be opened, because the dead will come to judgment; "The hour cometh wherein all that are in the graves shall hear the voice of the Son of God" (Jn. 5, 28).

Afterwards, a miracle in relation to men is related. And firstly, he mentions the Resurrection; and secondly, he mentions the appearance of those resurrected. He says, therefore: ***And many bodies of the saints that had slept arose.***

Concerning these bodies of the saints, the question is usually raised, whether or not they were going to die again. It is undisputed that some men rose again, after they had died, such as Lazarus. But concerning these men it can be said that they rose so as not to die again, because they rose for the showing of Christ's Resurrection. Now it is certain that Christ rising from the dead will now die no more. Likewise, if they had risen, it would not have been beneficial for them, but rather detrimental; wherefore, they rose as being about to go with Christ into heaven.[38]

And coming out of the tombs after his resurrection, came into the holy city. And note that although this was said at Christ's death, nevertheless, it is understood to be said by anticipation, because it happened after Christ's Resurrection; because Christ is "the first begotten of the dead" (Apoc. 1, 5). ***And they came into the holy city***, not because it was then holy, but because it had been holy before; "How is the faithful city, that was full of judgment, become a harlot?" (Is. 1, 21). Or it is called holy because holy things were conducted there. Or, according to Jerome, it is said ***into the holy city***, namely, the heavenly city, because they came with Christ in glory, ***and appeared to many***. For as Christ has the power to show Himself to whom He will, so it is understood concerning glorified bodies.

Now the centurion, etc. Here the effects of the miracles are treated. And firstly, the effect on the Gentiles is treated; and secondly, the effect on the women is treated, where it is said, ***And there were there many women***. About the first point, he does three things. Firstly, the centurion's careful consideration is related; secondly, his fear is related; and thirdly, his true confession of the faith, arising from his fear, is related. He says, therefore: ***Now the centurion and they that were with him watching Jesus, having seen the earthquake and the things that were done, were sore afraid.***

---

38. In III, q. 53, a. 3 ad 2um, St. Thomas wrote, "There are two opinions regarding them who rose with Christ" but he prefers the opinion of St. Augustine (Ep. 164 *ad Evodius*) that the saints who rose with Christ would have to die again. Yet in Supp. q. 77, a. 1 ad 3um, which was written by his disciples, it is stated that these saints "really rose again to immortal life, to live forever in the body, and to ascend bodily into heaven with Christ, as a gloss says on Matthew 27:52. The latter seems more probable, because, as Jerome says, in order that they might bear true witness to Christ's true Resurrection, it was fitting that they should truly rise again."

In Luke it is said that this fear was due to the fact that Christ died crying out; here, however, it is said that *having seen the earthquake* they were afraid. And Augustine says that it would not be easy to solve this question except that he said, *And the things that were done.* Now this centurion represents the Gentile nations, which confessed Christ with a salutary fear; hence: "I will say to that which is not my people: Thou art my people: and they shall say: Thou art my God." (Os. 2, 24). "I will call a nation, not my nation" (Rom. 9.25). "In thy presence, O Lord, we have conceived," (Is. 26, 17-18) "and have brought forth the spirit of salvation."[39]

Then the centurion's true confession is related, where it is said, *Indeed this was the Son of God.* By these words, Arius is confounded, who did not confess Him who exists in heaven to be the Son of God, whom the centurion confessed at His death; "This is the true God and life eternal" (I Jn. 5, 20).

The devotion of the women follows: *And there were there many women*, etc. And they are described by past events, and then in regard to present events. In which it ought to be considered that, when the crowd left, the women held fast, so that it was fulfilled what was said: "No man remained with me" (Is. 50, 2).[40]

But it ought to be considered that here it is said that they stood afar off. John, however, says that "they stood by the cross," etc., (Jn. 19, 25). Augustine says that it could be said that some women were nearby, and others were far away; unless it be said that they were in both places, because Mary Magdalene was one woman who was in both places.[41] Wherefore, it ought to be said otherwise, that just as many and few are said relatively, so near and far also: and just as the same thing can be said, many and few, in respect to different things, so also near and far. In this way, it ought to be considered that the centurion and the Gentiles were near the Cross; but the women were behind them, but the crowds were farther away. Hence, according to different comparisons, they were far and near: far in comparison to the centurion and the Gentiles; and they were near in comparison to the crowds. Or it can be said that firstly they stood near, but when He yielded up the ghost, they stood far off.

Likewise, observe what he says, that *they had followed Jesus from Galilee, ministering unto him.* For He, unto whom

---

39. From the Septuagint (LXX) version of the same verse.
40. The actual text in Is. 50, 2 is: "There was not a man."
41. "And there were also women looking on afar off: among whom was Mary Magdalen" (Mk. 15, 40). "Now there stood by the cross of Jesus, his mother and... Mary Magdalen" (Jn. 19, 25).

the angels minister, permitted that He be ministered unto by women. In this He gave a lesson to the Apostles following Him, that they would receive temporal things from those to whom they would minister spiritual things. And this was the ancient custom, that teachers of spiritual things received what they needed from good men, whom they taught. But Paul, because He was preaching to the Gentiles, among whom this custom did not exist, lest he seem to preach for money, did not wish to receive anything.

Among whom was Mary Magdalen and Mary the mother of James, etc. From these words, Helvidius took occasion of an error, which was that Jesus was born of the seed of Joseph. To this, Jerome says that there were two James': there was James the Greater, who was the brother of John, and James the Less, who was the son of Alpheus, whose mother was also the mother of Joseph.[42] Hence, the former Mary who was the mother of James the Greater, was not the mother of James the Less: because it is immediately added: *And the mother of the sons of Zebedee*.

But what is it that is said: "Mary of Cleophas"[43] and Mary "of Alpheus"?[44] Jerome resolves the question, saying that it could have been that that Mary had a husband, who had two names; hence, he was called both Cleophas and Alpheus. Or it can be said that firstly she married Cleophas, and when he had died she married Alpheus. Or it can be said that Cleophas was James' father and his mother was called Salome, because he says "Mary and Salome" (Mk. 15, 40): hence, Salome is the name of a woman.[45] Hence, the error of the Master[46] appears in his gloss on the second chapter of the Galatians, namely, that Salome was the name of a man. And the *Magister Historiarum*[47] says that in Greek the name is *Solomei*, which has a feminine ending that is never found in a masculine name.

And when it was evening, etc. In this part, the burial of Christ is treated; secondly, the great respect shown to His body is treated; and thirdly, the guarding of His body is treated. The second part is where it is said, *And taking the body wrapped it*

---

42. The Joseph mentioned here is not the foster father of our Lord, but rather the Joseph mentioned in this passage: **and Mary the mother of James and Joseph.**
43. Jn. 19 25.
44. cf. Mt., 10, 3; Mark, 3, 18; Luke, 6, 15; Acts, 1, 13.
45. "And there were also women looking on afar off: among whom was Mary Magdalen and Mary the mother of James the Less and of Joseph and Salome" (Mk. 15, 40). "ORIGEN; But it seems to me, that here three women are chiefly named, by Matthew and Mark. Two indeed are set down by each Evangelist, Mary Magdalene, and Mary the mother of James; the third is called by Matthew, the mother of the sons of Zebedee, but by Mark she is called Salome" (*Catena Aurea on St. Mark*, chap. 15, lect. 7).
46. i.e. Peter Lombard.
47. i.e. Peter Comestor (d. about 1178), the author of *Historia Scholastica*.

up in a clean linen cloth; and the third part is treated where it is said, *And the next day*, etc. About the first part, the traits of the one burying are related; and secondly, his request is related. Four traits of the one burying are set forth; hence, **When it was evening** (because it was fitting that He be taken down, lest He remain there on the Sabbath), *there came a certain rich man of Arimathea*. And he is described by his resources, that he was rich; "Blessed is the rich man that is found without blemish: and that hath not gone after gold, nor put his trust in money nor in treasures" (Eccli. 31, 8).

But why does he say that he is rich? I reply that he does not say this for his praise or for flattery; but due to the fact that he could make a request to Pilate, which a poor man would have been unable to do.

Likewise, he is described by his place of origin, for he was *of Arimathea*, which is the same place as Ramatha, which was Samuel's place of origin. And it means 'exalted,' and this man was exalted. Likewise, he is described by his name, for his name, *Joseph*, is said, which means 'growing.' Likewise, he is described by his religion, for it is said, *who also himself was a disciple of Jesus*, because he had not fallen away from the faith; "If you continue in my word, you shall be my disciples indeed" (Jn. 8, 31). Then it is treated concerning the granting of his request; and firstly, his request is related; and secondly, the granting is related: *He went to Pilate and asked the body of Jesus*. And he is praised in that he went to Pilate. And the granting of his request follows: *Then Pilate commanded that the body should be delivered*. The burial follows: *And Joseph taking the body wrapped it up in a clean linen cloth*. And it is treated concerning the veneration of the body and its burial. Concerning the signs of respect shown to the body, it was a simple sign of respect, because His body was wrapped in a simple linen cloth. And, therefore, according to Jerome, excessive signs of respect are to be disapproved. By this linen cloth, three things are mystically signified. Firstly, Christ's pure flesh is signified; for the cloth is made from flax, which is made white by much labor: in like manner, Christ's flesh by much labor arrived at the brilliance of the Resurrection; "It behoved Christ to suffer and to rise again from the dead, the third day" (Lk. 24, 46). Or it signifies the Church having no stain or wrinkle: and this is signified by this linen, which is woven from diverse threads. Likewise, a clean conscience is signified by the place wherein Christ rests. *And laid it in his own new monument*. And the Evangelist says four things about this monument.

Firstly, he says that it was Joseph's own. And this was very fitting, that He who had died for the sins of others, would be buried in another's tomb. Likewise, he says, *new*, because if other bodies had been put there, it could not have been known who had arisen. Similarly, he says that Christ's body was laid in a monument hewn out *in a rock*, and not in a monument constructed out of various stones, so that all calumny might be avoided.[48]

But why was He not buried beneath the earth? The reason was so that it would not be supposed that the disciples had taken Him out through tunnels in the earth. Likewise, he says that *he rolled a great stone*. And, therefore, because it was large, it could not have been rolled back by a few men, and especially since there were guards there.

Then the women's devotion follows. Hence, the women, who loved Him more ardently, followed Him to the tomb: wherefore it is said: *There was there Mary Magdalen and the other Mary*: Mary, the wife of Zebedee is not named, who was not there because she did not love Him so ardently.

And the next day, etc. Here, the guarding of the tomb is treated: and he does three things. Firstly, the request is related; secondly, the granting of the request is related; and thirdly, the execution of what was requested is related. About the first point, the time, the reason, the request, and the imminent danger are related. The time is related where it is said: *And the next day, which followed the day of preparation*. The Parasceve is interpreted 'preparation.' Hence, the Jews, because they used to do nothing on the Sabbath, prepared for the Sabbath on the previous day, and, therefore, it was called the Parasceve; hence, although they had some solemnity on the day of preparation, nevertheless, the Sabbath was of greater observance, wherefore, they prepared nothing on the Sabbath due to a commandment, whereby the Lord commanded that on Friday they should collect enough manna for two days (Ex. 16).[49] *Then the chief priests came together*, hence, they were very intent upon persecuting Him, because it was not enough for them to persecute Him until His death, but they persecuted Him even after His death; hence, they wanted to impede His Resurrection. But why did they come together? The

---

48. "JEROME; He was laid in a tomb hewn out of the rock, lest had it been one raised of many stones, it might have been said that He was stolen away by undermining the foundations of the pile" (*Catena Aurea on St. Matthew*, chap. 27, lect. 11).

49. "But the sixth day let them provide for to bring in: and let it be double to that they were wont to gather every day" (Ex. 16, 5).

reason follows: ***Sir, we have remembered, that that seducer said.*** They call Him a seducer; hence, it is said "For some said: He is a good man. And others said: No, but he seduceth the people" (Jn. 7, 12). ***After three days I will rise again.*** They knew this by the fact that He had said, "As Jonas was in the whale's belly three days and three nights: so shall the Son of man be in the heart of the earth three days and three nights" (above 12, 40). And part of a day is put for a whole day in these words, as it was explained above. Similarly, their request is related: ***Command therefore the sepulcher to be guarded.*** The very efforts of the Jews help us to be more certain; hence, the more they tried to do harm, the more did they assist the salvation of believers; "He catcheth the wise in their craftiness" (Job 5, 13), because what they intend to do, the Lord changes to something else. Then the reason for their request is related: ***Lest perhaps his disciples come and steal him away and say to the people: He is risen from the dead***: and in saying this, they prophesied, and, therefore, they sinned the more, because they saw miracles and yet they did not believe that He could rise from the dead.

The granting of their petition follows: ***Pilate saith to them: You have a guard***; meaning you may have a guard, and it is as though he were saying: 'It is up to you to guard him.'

The execution of what they requested follows: ***And they departing, made the sepulcher sure, sealing the stone and setting guards.*** Hence, it was not sufficient for them to station guards, but they also sealed the tomb. Nor was it sufficient for them that the soldiers would do this, but they also, themselves, sealed the tomb; "The council of the malignant hath besieged me" (Ps. 21, 17).

CHAPTER TWENTY-EIGHT

1. And in the end of the sabbath, when it began to dawn towards the first day of the week, came Mary Magdalen and the other Mary, to see the sepulchre.
2. And behold there was a great earthquake. For an angel of the Lord descended from heaven and coming rolled back the stone and sat upon it.
3. And his countenance was as lightning and his raiment as snow.
4. And for fear of him, the guards were struck with terror and became as dead men.
5. And the angel answering, said to the women: Fear not you: for I know that you seek Jesus who was crucified.
6. He is not here. For he is risen, as he said. Come, and see the place where the Lord was laid.
7. And going quickly, tell ye his disciples that he is risen. And behold he will go before you into Galilee. There you shall see him. Lo, I have foretold it to you.
8. And they went out quickly from the sepulchre with fear and great joy, running to tell his disciples.
9. And behold, Jesus met them, saying: All hail. But they came up and took hold of his feet and adored him.
10. Then Jesus said to them: Fear not. Go, tell my brethren that they go into Galilee. There they shall see me.
11. Who when they were departed, behold, some of the guards came into the city and told the chief priests all things that had been done.
12. And they being assembled together with the ancients, taking counsel, gave a great sum of money to the soldiers,
13. Saying: Say you, His disciples came by night and stole him away when we were asleep.
14. And if the governor shall hear of this, we will persuade him and secure you.
15. So they taking the money, did as they were taught: and this word was spread abroad among the Jews even unto this day.
16. And the eleven disciples went into Galilee, unto the mountain where Jesus had appointed them.
17. And seeing him they adored: but some doubted.
18. And Jesus coming, spoke to them, saying: All power is given to me in heaven and in earth.

19. Going therefore, teach ye all nations: baptizing them in the name of the Father and of the Son and of the Holy Ghost.

20. Teaching them to observe all things whatsoever I have commanded you. And behold I am with you all days, even to the consummation of the world.

After the Evangelist finished the mysteries of the Lord's Passion, he treats of the triumph of the Lord's Resurrection: and it is divided as follows. For firstly, it is shown how the disciples knew Christ's Resurrection by hearing; secondly, it is shown how they knew it by seeing, so that by hearing and seeing, their testimony would be certain. About the first part, it is firstly related how they knew the Resurrection from the women; secondly, it is related how they knew it from the guards. The second part is where it is said, *Who when they were departed, behold, some of the guards came into the city.* About the first point, he does two things. Firstly, he says how the women knew the Resurrection by an angel; secondly, he says how the women knew this by seeing Christ, where it is said, *And they went out quickly from the sepulchre.* About the first part, he does three things. Firstly, the persons to whom the revelation was made are related; secondly, the angel revealing is related; and thirdly, the revelation is related. The second part is where it is said, *And behold there was a great earthquake*; and the third part is where it is said, *And the angel answering, said.* In the first part, he does three things. Firstly, he indicates the time; secondly, he indicates the persons; and thirdly, he indicates their eagerness. He indicates the time where it is said, *And in the end of the sabbath.*

And about this, there is a twofold question. The first is about that which he says, *In the end*;[1] and the second is about that which he says, *it began to dawn.* About the first phrase, there is a question, because Matthew seems contrary to John, because John says that it was still dark (20, 1).[2] Why then does he say here: *And in the end of the sabbath*?

There are three solutions. The first is Jerome's, namely, that they came in the evening and in the morning. And the fact that he says here, *In the end*, is not an inconsistency, but rather, *When it began to dawn*, indicates the diligence of the holy women. Bede resolves the matter thus, namely, that they started to come in the evening but they arrived in the morning. But was there

---

1. *Vespere.* i.e. "in the evening."
2. "And on the first day of the week, Mary Magdalen cometh early, when it was yet dark, unto the sepulchre."

really that length of time? He says that there was not; but rather someone is said to do something when he is prepared to do it. And this is stated in Luke 23, 55 that "having seen the sepulchre and how his body was laid and returning, they prepared spices." They bought spices on the day of preparation and they rested on the Sabbath, and in the end of the Sabbath they prepared themselves to go to the tomb. The third solution is Augustine's, who says that the usual manner in Sacred Scripture is that a part is taken for the whole; hence, the evening is understood for the whole night of the Sabbath; hence, **In the end of the sabbath**, means that it was after the Sabbath; hence, the end of the Sabbath is the beginning of the first day of the week. Something similar is found in Genesis 1, 5 in the recounting of God's works: "And there was evening and morning one day." Hence, they came in the evening, because they came at the last part of the night. And this is **when it began to dawn towards the first day of the week.** In the evening it did not begin to dawn, because it got dark in the evening. Hence, they came when it began to dawn, meaning at the first hour of the day. Notice that the Jews begin all the days of the week after the Sabbath; hence, the first day of the week is called the "Lord's Day." And if you inquire from Augustine why Mark uses such a manner of speaking, he will say that in the evening they prepared spices and in the morning they came; hence, he reverts to the same thing that Bede says. But how is what he says, **it began to dawn,** to be understood according to Jerome? Because, in the evening it gets dark. And the reason is, that they were determining the day from the moon; now the moon begins to shine in the evening; hence, for them the day began in the evening, but it began to dawn at the first hour of the week. A similar manner of speaking is found in Luke 23, 54: "And it was the day of the Parasceve: and the Sabbath drew on." And this manner of speaking is fitting according to a mystical sense. Firstly, it befits the solemnity of the Lord's Resurrection, because that night was illuminated; "And night shall be light all the day" (Ps. 138, 12). Likewise, it befits the human restoration, which was made through Christ: for in the first man there was a change from day into night, namely, the night of sin; so also in the second Man there was a change of the human state, namely, from night into day; "You were heretofore darkness, but now light in the Lord" (Eph. 5, 8). Similarly, it is signified that whatever was darkness in the Law and the prophets, all began to dawn through Christ's Resurrection. "Dark waters in the clouds of the air" (Ps. 17, 12). Now this darkness in the Law and the prophets was illuminated upon Christ's Resurrection, as it is stated: "Beginning at Moses and all the prophets, he expounded to them in all the scriptures the things that were concerning him" (Lk. 24, 27).

Afterwards, he treats of the persons to whom the revelation was made when he says, ***Came Mary Magdalen and the other Mary***; and Mark adds a third, saying, "And Salome": hence, Salome is the name of a woman. But this is not without a mystical meaning, that there came two women having the same name; hence, He wished to firstly appear to a woman, because by doing this the female sex is, in a certain way, repaired: because, just as a woman firstly, in a place of life, listened to death, so in the place of death, by the divine ordination, a woman firstly saw life; "From the woman came the beginning of sin" (Eccle. 25, 33). Likewise, they had the same name because by them the unity of the Church is signified: for firstly, one congregation was composed of the Gentiles and another of the Jews, but now all are one Church; "One is my dove" (Cant. 6, 8). Similarly, they are called 'Mary': for as Mary gave birth from a closed womb, so these Marys going out from the tomb merited to see Him. Hence, these women came to see the tomb; and, in this, their devotion is indicated because they could not be satisfied, wherefore, since they were unable to see Him, they wanted to at least see His tomb. "Where thy treasure is, there is thy heart also" (above 6, 21).

And behold there was a great earthquake. Here the revealing angel is treated. And firstly, the angel's coming is related; secondly, his action is related; thirdly, his position is related; and fourthly, his effect is related. The second part is where it is said, ***And coming rolled back the stone***; the third part is where it is said, ***And sat upon it***; and the fourth part is where it is said, ***And for fear of him, the guards were struck with terror***. And about the first part, the angel's coming is denoted; secondly, the reason for his coming is mentioned, where it is said, ***For an angel of the Lord descended***. He says, therefore, ***And behold there was a great earthquake***. This was fitting, and it has a literal reason. One reason, according to Chrysostom, is that these women came at night, and, therefore, it could have been that the guards were sleeping; wherefore, in order that they might be aroused, there was an earthquake to awaken them. Jerome says that something was mentioned concerning Christ's humanity, for that reason, it was needful that something be mentioned concerning His divinity; wherefore, when the tomb is treated, which pertains to His humanity, it is said that an earthquake occurred, to indicate that such a Man who had died could not be held beneath the earth. "For

He was free among the dead" (Ps. 87, 6). Mystically, the earthquake occurred twice, so that by one earthquake the movement of hearts is signified, because by His death we are freed from sin; by the second earthquake His transference to glory is signified; "He was delivered up for our sins and rose again for our justification" (Rom. 4, 25). And in Psalm 59, 4 it is said: "Thou hast moved the earth, and hast troubled it." Likewise, His Resurrection in the present age is a certain prefigure of the future resurrection: now in the future resurrection there will be an earthquake; "The earth trembled and was still, when God arose in judgment" (Ps. 75, 9-10). And why did the earthquake occur? The reason follows, *An angel of the Lord descended from heaven.* If the earth could not withstand an angel, much less will it be able to withstand Christ's coming for the Judgment: and he says, *descended*; for although an angel is not circumscribed by place, nevertheless, he is associated to a place according to his operation; and, therefore, some kind of movement belongs to him. Likewise, it is fitting that Christ's Resurrection be announced by an angel, both on account of the glory of Him through whom Christ's Resurrection takes place, as Paul says: "God raised him up from the dead" (Acts 13, 30). Now, His ministers are the angels. Likewise, it is fitting that Christ's Resurrection be announced by an angel, to indicate the dignity of the one resurrecting. Of Him it is said, that "angels came and ministered to him" (above 4, 11). Similarly, this was fitting because by the Resurrection heavenly things are joined to earthly things. Afterwards, the angel's action is related: *And coming rolled back the stone*, etc. And in the literal meaning this was done so that the entrance might be opened to the women, because, in fact, Christ had already risen: for as He went out from a closed womb, so He went out from the sealed tomb. Hence, this was done so that the tomb might be shown to the women: hence, *He rolled back*, meaning he rolled it back to show the glory of the one rising; and this rolling back of the stone signifies the exposition of the Law which was written on stone tablets. Afterwards, the posture of the angel is related. And firstly, he is described as to his position; secondly, he is described as to his appearance; and thirdly, he is described as to his clothing. As to his position, it is said that *He sat*, not as one who is tired, but to indicate that he is a teacher of the divine Resurrection. Likewise, to sit belongs to those resting: and by this is signified the rest which Christ now has in the state of glory after His Resurrection; "Christ, rising again from the dead, dieth now no more. Death shall no more have dominion over him" (Rom. 6, 9). Likewise, to sit belongs to a ruler;

"The Lord said to my Lord: Sit thou at my right hand" (Ps. 109, 1). And this angel sits *upon a stone*, namely the devil, to show that Christ now has dominion over death and the devil. *And his countenance was as lightning.* Here he is described by his appearance; and in this it is evident that he appeared in an assumed body. And why was his countenance *as lightning*? It is because as lightning has brightness, so also the angels have knowledge; "His eyes as a burning lamp" (Dan. 10, 6). But Christ is He who "enlighteneth every man that cometh into this world" (Jn. 1, 9). Likewise, lightning is terrifying, and so also the appearance of an angel is terrifying; hence, in Luke 1, 12, it is said that Zachary was frightened by the voice of an angel. Similarly, the angel is described by his clothing, *His raiment as snow*, by which the splendor of the just is signified. Mystically, however, the glory of the Resurrection is signified; "He that shall overcome shall be clothed in white garments" (Apoc. 3, 5). Moreover, purity of life is signified; "At all times let thy garments be white" (Eccle. 9, 8). Furthermore, note that he says that *his countenance was as lightning and his raiment as snow*, because at the Judgment Christ will be terrifying to the wicked and will comfort the good; "I will see you again and your heart shall rejoice" (Jn. 16, 22).

And for fear of him, the guards were struck with terror. Here the effect of the apparition is related, namely, that fear was in their hearts; and rightly so, because the wicked were serving Him with a bad conscience and "wickedness is always fearful" (Wis. 17, 10). *And became as dead men*, signifying those, who as far as lies in them, want to keep Christ dead; "At the voice of the angel the people fled" (Is. 33, 3).

And the angel answering, said to the women, etc. Here the announcement of the Resurrection is related. And firstly, he comforts the women; secondly, he commends their intention; thirdly, he makes known the joyful news; and fourthly, he enjoins upon them the duty of announcing the good news. He says, therefore: *And the angel answering*, etc. But to what is he answering? He is answering the thoughts of the women. It is not read that they had said anything due to their fear: for it is always the case that men are troubled upon an apparition of an angel, whether a good or a bad angel appears; because human nature is weak. But, as Blessed Anthony says, if it is a good angel, he always leaves one consoled, as appears in the apparition of Zachary and the Virgin, etc., (Lk. 1): and, in this manner, he comforted them. And if an angel were to leave a man in desolation, it is evident that he was not a good angel; wherefore, he said, *Fear not you*; it is as though he were saying: 'You have no reason to fear, because you love Christ.' "For you have not received the spirit of bondage in fear" (Rom. 8, 15). But he did not comfort the guards because they were unworthy. Then he commends their intention: *For I know that you seek Jesus who was crucified.*

But do the angels know our thoughts? It seems that they do not; "The heart is perverse above all things, who can know it? I am the Lord who search the heart, and prove the reins" (Jer. 17, 9-10). It ought to be responded that they do not know our thoughts, except by divine revelation; or by a sign, because, frequently, by gestures of the body indications of the will are known.

You seek Jesus. He names Him, in order to indicate that He is the same man after His Resurrection as before. Likewise, he says 'crucified': and in saying this he is insinuating their little faith, because they were seeking Him in a place of death, and they supposed that He could be held by death.

Then he announces the Resurrection: *He is risen*, more precisely, by His own power; "I have slept and have taken my rest: and I have risen up, because the Lord hath protected me" (Ps. 3, 6). And he proves this by recalling God's word: *As he said*; because He had said: "And the third day he shall rise again" (above 20, 19). For God's word cannot fail. Likewise, he indicates Christ's Resurrection by what they could see: *Come, and see the place where the Lord was laid.* Hence, they saw the stone rolled back, and now they saw that Christ had risen, because He rose when the tomb was closed. Then he makes known to them their duty of announcing the Resurrection: *And going quickly, tell ye his disciples that he is risen.* And he makes known three things. Firstly, he states that they will announce the Resurrection; secondly, he states the place where they would see Him; and thirdly, he promises them that they would see Him. And as the first woman firstly spoke with the devil, so here the first women speak with an angel, so that all things might be restored. Secondly, the place is mentioned: *He will go before you into Galilee.*

But why does he firstly speak of Galilee? For Christ was not firstly seen in Galilee, but rather in Jerusalem. Why then does he rather speak of Galilee? It is to indicate that He who arose is the same person who used to live in Galilee. Likewise, the angel said this to free them from fear, because He dwelt more safely in Galilee than in Judea. Or mystically, Galilee means 'a passing,' and it can signify His passing to the Gentiles. Hence, *you shall see Him* in Galilee, meaning you will announce His name to the Gentiles. Now they would not do this, unless He went before them.

There you shall see him. Lo, I have foretold it to you. Hence, the Lord's word is of such power that it cannot happen otherwise.

But here there is a literal question, namely, that here it is said that they saw the angel sitting upon the stone; and in another Gospel it is said, "entering into the sepulchre, they saw a young man sitting on the right side" (Mk. 16, 5). Augustine solves the question, saying that they twice saw a vision of angels: hence, it was possible that they saw one angel outside the tomb and another inside the tomb. Or it can be said that not only the cut rock is called the tomb, but there was there some substance whereby the monument was enclosed; hence, what Mark says, "entering into the sepulchre" ought not to be understood of that rock, but of the space in which it was enclosed: and this is evident, because it is said here that *they went out quickly from the sepulchre with fear and great joy*, etc.

Above, the Resurrection was announced to the women; here, they are made certain about it by Christ: and the Evangelist does three things. Firstly, the women are described; secondly, their meeting of Christ is described; and thirdly, the duty of announcing His Resurrection is enjoined. The second part is where it is said, *And behold, Jesus met them*; and the third part is where it is said, *Fear not you*, etc. In the first part, three noteworthy things ought to be considered. Firstly, the state of the women ought to be considered; secondly, their emotions ought to be considered; and thirdly, their intention ought to be considered. Their state is mentioned when it is said, *They went out quickly from the sepulchre*. As to the literal meaning, the cut stone is not called the sepulchre, but that space which was protected by some barrier. According to the mystical meaning, a tomb is a place for the dead: and by this tomb the state of sin is signified; "Like the slain sleeping in the sepulchres" (Ps. 87, 6). Hence, to go out from the tomb is to go out from sin: "Wherefore: Go out from among them," etc., (II Cor. 6, 17). And observe that he says, *quickly*, because one ought to go out from sin quickly; "Delay not to be converted to the Lord, and defer it not from day to day" (Eccli. 5, 8). Likewise, their twofold emotions are mentioned, namely, of fear and of joy. Their fear was from seeing an angel, and their joy was from Christ's Resurrection: their fear was due to their human frailty, and their joy was from the divine vision; "In the evening weeping shall have place, and in the morning gladness" (Ps. 19, 6). "Be not without fear about sin forgiven" (Eccli. 5, 5). But one ought to rejoice from the hope of the Resurrection; "Serve ye the Lord with fear: and rejoice unto him with trembling" (Ps. 2, 11). Then he mentions their intention: *Running, tell ye his disciples*, etc. And this belongs to penitents, because they ought to run and make haste to make progress in doing good; "So run that you may obtain" (I Cor. 9, 24). And, as it is also said: "Let us hasten to enter into that rest" (Heb. 4, 11). Likewise, the Evangelist mentions the angel's good proposal, namely, that he wanted that they would communicate what they had received to others; "As every man hath received grace, ministering the same one to another" (I Pet. 4, 10).

And behold, Jesus met them. Here, their meeting of Christ is related. And firstly, the meeting is related; secondly, His greeting is related; and thirdly, the reverence shown by the women is related. He says, therefore: *And behold, Jesus met them*. And he says rightly that Jesus met them, because He met them unexpectedly, giving them a favor; "She preventeth them that covet her, so that she first sheweth herself unto them" (Wis. 6, 14); "Thou hast met him that rejoiceth, and doth justice" (Is. 64, 5). Likewise, He greeted them, saying, *All hail*. 'Hail' in Greek means 'joy'; hence, it was said above that they went with joy. Hence, spiritual joy always increases in the just, and this happens through spiritual speech; "I will hear what the Lord God will speak in me" (Ps. 84, 9). And these words are words of consolation, because just as the first woman heard a curse, so these women heard a blessing; the blessing corresponds to the curse. And then, *they came up and took hold of his feet and adored him*. Hence, they come up, take hold of his feet, and adore him. So the souls of sinners ought not to receive the grace of God in vain: and this is indicated, because *they came up*; "Come ye to him and be enlightened:" (Ps. 33, 6). Likewise, they ought to adhere firmly to Him: and this is signified in that which is said, *they took hold of his feet and adored him*. "They that approach to his feet, shall receive of his doctrine" (Deut. 33, 3). Similarly, he mentions their showing reverence in that which he says, *And they adored him*, for they acknowledged him to be God; "We will adore in the place where his feet stood" (Ps. 131, 7).

But there can be a question, namely, that in John 20, 17, it is said to her: "Do not touch me"; here, however, it is said that *they took hold of his feet*. Wherefore, it ought to be understood that they saw angels twice, and one time they saw one angel, as Augustine says, and another time they saw two angels, but they also saw Christ twice. Firstly, Mary Magdalene, weeping, saw Him, as it is stated in John 20. But afterwards, others having joined her,

He met them, and then they held His feet; but Mary Magdalene, at first, could not hold Him, and the reason for this, according to Augustine, is that she firstly doubted and therefore, she was not worthy; but once she became certain, she was made worthy to touch Christ, so that the outward touch agrees with her interior.

Afterwards, He enjoins the duty of announcing the Resurrection. And when He does this, He firstly expels their fear; and secondly He enjoins this duty, where it is said, *Go, tell my brethren*. He says, therefore: *Then Jesus said to them: Fear not*. And this was fittingly done, because those who are given the office of preaching ought not to fear; hence, the Lord sending the disciples said, "Fear not."[3] Now fear is twofold, namely, servile and initial, and the latter is good. "Pierce thou my flesh with thy fear" (Ps. 118, 120). Hence, He said, *All hail*, to increase the charity in them. But because "perfect charity casteth out fear" (I Jn. 4, 18), wherefore, He says, *Fear not*. And firstly, He gives them the duty of announcing His Resurrection; and secondly, He shows them His perfect charity. Now He enjoins the duty of announcing His Resurrection to women, so that as a woman brought the words of death to a man, so, contrariwise, it was fitting for a woman have been the herald of salvation. And firstly, the announcement is mentioned; and secondly, the place of the apparition is mentioned.

And why does He say, *my*? It is to prove the reality of His human nature. For since He had gone out of the tomb, and was appearing glorious, someone might suppose that He had not taken true flesh, wherefore, He says: *My brethren*. Likewise, He says, *my*, on account of a likeness by grace, because He willed to become our Brother for our justification; "That he might be the Firstborn amongst many brethren" (Rom. 8, 29). Similarly, He says, *brethren*, meaning coheirs. "Heirs indeed of God and joint heirs with Christ" (Rom. 8, 17). Hence, the inheritance already having been acquired, He calls us His brethren.

That they go into Galilee. These words seem to say that He firstly appeared in Galilee. He does not make mention of the other apparitions; but Augustine[4] says that He appeared ten times. He appeared five times on the day of His Resurrection. Firstly, He appeared to Mary Magdalene, as it is said in John 20. Secondly, He appeared to the two women of whom Matthew makes mention here. Thirdly, He appeared to Peter; yet how and when it is

---

3. cf. Lk. 5, 10.
4. Venerable Bede is cited here but since the listing of these apparitions is given by St. Augustine in the Catena Aurea on St. Matthew (chap. 28, lect. 4), his name has been inserted here. Cf. Augustine, De Consensu Evangelistarum iii, 83 quoted in III, q. 55, a. 3.

not said, but that it happened is not passed over in silence in the Gospel of St. Luke. Fourthly, He appeared to the two disciples going to Emmaus. Fifthly, He appeared to all the disciples, except Thomas. Still, after these apparitions, it is read that He appeared five other times.[5] The first apparition after the ones here mentioned, was when, on the eighth day, He appeared to all the disciples, Thomas included.[6] The second was when He appeared while the disciples were fishing, when Peter said, "I go a fishing" (Jn. 21, 3). Another apparition is that which is related here.[7] Another is when He rebuked their unbelief.[8] The last apparition was when He was on Mount Olivet, when He ascended into heaven (Mk. 16, 19).[9] Nevertheless, there were other apparitions, as St. Paul says. (I Cor. 15).[10]

But what is it that both Christ and the angel say, that 'He will go before you into Galilee?' Chrysostom says that the reason why He says this is because they used to live there. Likewise, He says this because they would have been safe there, and they could safely wait for Him there. Nevertheless, Augustine says that, in the mystical sense, Galilee means 'passing': hence, it signifies the passing to the Gentiles, or the passing from this world into glory. "While we are in the body we are absent from the Lord" (II Cor. 5, 6).

Who when they were departed, behold, some, etc. Here it is treated concerning the announcing of His Resurrection, which was made by the guards. And firstly, the Evangelist relates their announcing; and secondly, he relates the obstacle, where it is said, **And they being assembled together with the ancients**, etc., He says, therefore: **And when they were departed**, etc. And why did they wait so long? It ought to be answered by what was said, namely, that **the guards were struck with terror**. And perhaps the Lord did this so that they would not bother the women. **Behold, some of the guards came into the city and told the chief priests**. And why did they tell the chief priests? It is because they were associated with them; likewise, it was because they had received their pay from them. Nevertheless, they told

---

5. The listing of these apparitions is given by St. Augustine (*De Consensu Evangelistarum iii*) in III, q. 55, a. 3.

6. "And after eight days, again his disciples were within, and Thomas with them. Jesus cometh, the doors being shut" (Jn. 20, 26).

7. "And the eleven disciples went into Galilee, unto the mountain where Jesus had appointed them. And seeing him they adored" (verse 16-17).

8. "At length he appeared to the eleven as they were at table: and he upbraided them with their incredulity and hardness of heart, because they did not believe them who had seen him after he was risen again" (Mk. 16, 14).

9. "Although the place of the Ascension is not distinctly stated, it would appear from the Acts that it was Mount Olivet" ("Ascension," *Catholic Encyclopedia* (1907 ed.), vol. 1).

10. "After that, he was seen by James: then by all the apostles" (verse 7).

Christ's Resurrection to Pilate; hence, in a letter, which Pilate sent to Tiberius, it is written how the guards told this to Pilate, etc. *And they told.* Already, it was signified that by the mouths of the Gentiles, Christ's Resurrection would be made known.

Then the malice of those impeding the announcing of Christ's Resurrection is related. And firstly, the malice of the chief priests is related; secondly, the corrupting of the guards is related; and thirdly, the corrupting of the people is related. About the first point, four things work together to increase their malice. Firstly, the assembling of the chief priests is related; hence, he says: *And they being assembled together with the ancients*, etc. because not just one of the chief priests was malicious; "Iniquity came out from Babylon, from the ancients of the people" (Dan. 12, 5). Likewise, their iniquity is increased by the fact that they did not do this out of weakness, but out of malice, that is to say, from a malicious plan; and this is the counsel of the wicked, about which is said: "Blessed is the man who hath not walked in the counsel of the ungodly" (Ps. 1, 1). Similarly, they committed fraud, because they paid money that was offered to be used for a lie; hence, they knew that "all things obey money" (Eccle. 10, 19); as Jerome says, they were like those who spend what belongs to the Church to do what they wish. Moreover, they increase their malice by the fact that they persuade others to lie. And firstly, they persuade; and secondly, they promise impunity. They persuade others to lie, where it is said: *Say you, His disciples came by night and stole him away.* "They have taught their tongue to speak lies" (Jer. 9, 5). And in Psalm 26, 12 it is said: "Iniquity hath lied to itself." And, as Jerome says, it is truly a lie, because the disciples were so stunned that they would not have dared to go to the tomb. Likewise, if they had needed to go to the tomb, they would have gone on the first day, when the guards were not there. Similarly, this is evident, because the linen cloth remained, whereas, if they had taken His body, they would not have left the linen cloth. Furthermore, it is certain that He was buried with spices, hence, the linen cloth was stuck like glue;[11] hence, they would have been hardly able to move it. Again, the stone was large; hence, they would not have been able to turn it without much help and much noise. Likewise, Augustine argues as follows: 'Either they came to you when you were awake or asleep. If you were awake, why did you not expel them? If you were asleep, how did you see them?' And so it is evident that it was a lie. Then they promise impunity:

11. Here the vulgar Latin word *colla*, coming from the Greek *kolla*, is used. In English it means "glue."

hence, the guards could say: 'We will be punished, if the governor were to hear'; wherefore, they say: *If the governor shall hear of this, we will persuade him and secure you.* And how could they do that? It ought to be said that the governor did not care much about this. Likewise, they knew that he would not punish the guards, unless by their request; therefore, they knew that, etc. In this, the devil's precaution is indicated. *So they taking the money, did as they were taught.* It is not surprising that the soldiers were corrupted by money, because one of Christ's disciples was also corrupted by money. "Nothing is more wicked than the covetous man" (Eccli. 10, 9). *And this word was spread abroad.* And this word was spread not only until the time when this was written, but even until now.

And the eleven disciples went into Galilee, etc. Above, it was heard how the news of the Resurrection reached the disciples by the women's revelation; here, it is heard how they learned of the Resurrection by seeing Him. And it is divided: for firstly, Christ's apparition is related; and secondly, His instruction when He appeared is related. The second part is where it is said, *And Jesus coming, spoke to them.* About the first point, the Evangelist does three things. Firstly, the place of the apparition is described; secondly, the apparition is described; and thirdly, a work to be done is described. He says, therefore, *And the eleven disciples went into Galilee*; because they, obeying Christ, went to Galilee. That which he says, *The eleven*, ought to be understood, because Judas had left: "Have not I chosen you twelve? And one of you is a devil" (Jn. 6, 71). But two things ought to be noticed, one is that Christ is seen in Galilee, and that He is seen on a mountain. Galilee is interpreted, 'passing.' By this is signified that no one can see God, unless one be transferred by a twofold passing, namely, from vice to virtue; "Blessed are the clean of heart: they shall see God" (Mt. 5, 8); likewise, one must pass from mortality to immortality; hence, the Apostle says: "But I am straitened between two: having a desire to be dissolved and to be with Christ" (Phil. 1, 23). Similarly, He was seen on a mountain to signify that one who wishes to see God ought to tend to the heights of justice; "They shall go from virtue to virtue" (Ps. 83, 8). Likewise, the fact that He was seen on a mountain signifies that loftiness to which He was exalted by the Resurrection: because, when He was in the world, He was in the valley of mortality, and He ascended unto the mountain of immortality by His Resurrection. "He shall be exalted above the hills, and all nations shall flow unto Him" (Is. 2, 2).

And notice that He appears to them *in the place where Jesus had appointed them*, in which obedience is signified, because only those who obey come to the divine vision; "If you love me, keep my commandments" (Jn. 14, 15): the passage continues: "I will love him and will manifest myself to him" (verse 21). "By thy commandments I have had understanding" (Ps. 118, 104); that is to say, by observing the Commandments I have had understanding; hence, in the Old Law no one could go up into the mountain;[12] the New Law, however, supplies what was lacking in the Old Law. And it was necessary that He would have appeared to them, because witnesses ought to be given for such a great work. But He provided witnesses not only through hearing, but through sight; "That which we have seen and have heard, we declare" (I Jn. 1, 2).

But the question is, when did this apparition take place: and according to what Augustine says, it was not on the first day of the Resurrection, because it happened in the evening when Thomas was not present. Likewise, it was not within the octave, and it was not on the octave day, because they were in Jerusalem for eight days. Nor can we say that it was immediately after the eight days: because we would then contradict John, who says that when He showed Himself at the sea of Tiberius, Jesus had been seen three times; and the apparition here was not the third, but after the third had occurred.

And seeing him. It ought to be observed that among those who consider the great works of God there are two kinds of people, for some hold those things in reverence: hence, Abraham said: "I will speak to my Lord, whereas I am dust and ashes" (Gen. 18, 27); and "What am I then, that I should answer him, and have words with him?" (Job 9, 14). Likewise, we find this reverence among the angels. "All the angels stood round about the throne and the ancients and the four living creatures. And they fell down before the throne upon their faces and adored God" (Apoc. 7, 11). And the reason for this is that the more one knows Him, so much the more does one revere Him. But some are turned into infidelity: for they want to put everything on the level of their understanding; hence, whatever they do not understand, they blaspheme. The former was the case of the disciples, because it is said, *And seeing him they adored*. "We will adore in the place where his feet stood" (Ps. 131, 7). Wherefore, the Lord let Himself to be touched, as it is said in Luke 24.[13]

---

12. "And Moses said to the Lord: The people cannot come up to Mount Sinai: for thou didst charge, and command, saying: Set limits about the mount, and sanctify it" (Ex. 12, 23).

13. "Handle, and see: for a spirit hath not flesh and bones, as you see me to have" (Lk. 24, 39).

And Jesus coming, spoke to them. Here the instructions given by Christ are related. And three things ought to be considered. Firstly, He tells them of His power; secondly, He enjoins a duty; and thirdly, He promises help in the future. The second part is where it is said, **Going therefore, teach ye all nations**; and the third part is where it is said, **Behold I am with you all days.** He says, therefore: *And Jesus coming, spoke to them.* The disciples were divided, for some held Him in reverence, but others doubted; wherefore, both groups were in need, namely, they needed that He would show Himself, and that He would comfort them. In this way, He comes to all people; "The people (the Gentiles) that walked in darkness, have seen a great light" (Is. 9, 2). Similarly, He told them of His power: *All power is given to me in heaven and in earth.* And, as Jerome says, power was given to Him who previously was crucified by the people. God's power is nothing other than omnipotence; and this was not given to Christ, because it does not befit His humanity. However, it somewhat befits Him, both in that He is man, and in that He is God: hence, in Christ as man, there is knowledge, will, and free choice; and, similarly, as God. Thus, in Christ there are two wills, namely, a created and an uncreated will. Therefore, it can be argued that there are two powers, and two types of knowledge, etc.

Therefore, there is a question: Why is it that, just as all science was communicated to Him, all power was not communicated to Him? The reason is this. Science and knowledge are according to the assimilation of the knower to the thing known, because it suffices that the species of the things known in some way be in the knower, either in such a way that one knows through the essence, in other words, that there would be infused species, or in such a way that the species be received from things: however, the species may be in the knower, this suffices for knowledge: hence, it is not necessary that the essence of all things be in the knower, but that the knower be capable of all things. Now this is to be of infinite receptibility, like prime matter. But an active potency follows the act, because to the extent that a thing is in act, to that extent it has the power to act; wherefore, one who has active omnipotence, has the power to do all things. But this would not be this case, unless one have infinite power, which does not befit Christ insofar as He is a man, but only insofar as He is God.

Why then does He say that *all power is given to me in heaven and in earth*? It ought to be observed, according to Hilary, that the giving can be understood either as referring to His divinity, because the Father from eternity communicated His essence to the Son; and because His essence is His power, it follows that, from eternity, He gave His power to the Son; or it can also be referred to His humanity. But it must be understood that Christ's humanity received some things by the grace of union, and these are all things that are proper to God; now, He received some things as a consequence of the grace of union, such as the fullness of grace and so forth, and these things are, as it were, effects of the union; "We saw him as it were of the only begotten of the Father, full of grace and truth" (Jn. 1, 14). Therefore, in all these things which are in Christ by the grace of union, it is not necessary that all things be attributed to both natures, but in the other things which follow, it is necessary that they be attributed to both natures. Hence, I say that His power was given, not because another power was not given, but it was given in that it is united to the Word, meaning it was to the Son of God by His nature, but it was given to Christ by the grace of union.

But why, after the Resurrection, does He say, *All power is given to me*, rather than before the Resurrection? It ought to be said, that in Scripture, something is said to happen, when it is firstly made known: accordingly, therefore, before the Resurrection, His omnipotence was not so clearly manifested, although He had it; but it was manifested the most at this time, when He was able to convert the whole world. We can also say otherwise, that power signifies the honor of authority, as we say men have power; and power is so understood here. It is evident that Christ, who from eternity had possessed the rulership of the world as the Son of God, received the execution of His rulership from the time of the Resurrection: it is as though He were to say: 'I now have possession of my kingdom.' Concerning this, it is stated: "A judgment shall sit, that his power may be taken away, and be broken in pieces, and perish even to the end. And that the kingdom, and power, and the greatness of the kingdom may be given to the people of the saints of the most High, whose kingdom is an everlasting kingdom, and all kings shall serve him, and shall obey him" (Dan. 7, 26-27). Hence, a certain actual preeminence is understood: it is as though the Son were to be elevated to the exercise of the power which He naturally had; "The Lamb that was slain is worthy to receive power and divinity" (Apoc. 5, 12).

Going therefore, teach ye all nations. Here He enjoins their duty; and He enjoins a threefold duty. Firstly, He enjoins the duty of teaching; secondly, He enjoins the duty of baptizing; and thirdly, He enjoins the duty of instructing regarding morals. He says, therefore: *Going therefore, teach all nations*. And it follows in this way; it is as though He were to say: 'All power is given to Me by God, so that not only the Jews but also the Gentiles may be converted to Me; wherefore, because it is the time, He says, **going, teach all nations**.' "As the Father hath sent me, I also send you" (Jn. 20, 21). And, as it is also said: "I dispose to you, as my Father hath disposed to me, a kingdom" (Lk. 22, 29). And He says, **Going therefore, teach**; He says this because this is the first thing, that we ought to instruct, namely the faith, because "without faith it is impossible to please God" (Heb. 11, 6). And from this arose the custom in the Church that firstly one catechizes those to be baptized, meaning that one instructs them in the faith. And, having received power, He sends them to all nations; and this is what He says: **Teach all nations**. "I have given thee to be the light of the Gentiles, that thou mayst be my salvation even to the farthest part of the earth" (Is. 49, 6).

And after they are taught concerning the faith, He gives the duty of baptizing them. **Baptizing them**, etc. It is as though He were to say: 'He who is promoted to some dignity, ought firstly to be notified of the dignity, so that reverence may be had for it.' "As many of you as have been baptized in Christ have put on Christ" (Gal. 3, 27). But what is the form of baptism? **In the name of the Father and of the Son and of the Holy Ghost**.

In Christ there are two things, His humanity and His divinity. His humanity is the way, not the end; "I am the way, and the truth, and the life" (Jn. 14, 6): He is the truth, as the end of the contemplative way: He is the life, as the end of the active way. I do wish that you remain in the way, namely, in My humanity, but that you may pass on to My divinity. Wherefore, it was fitting that two things be signified, His humanity and His divinity. By baptism, His humanity is signified; "We are buried together with him by baptism into death" (Rom. 6, 4). And by the form of the words, His divinity is signified such that sanctification is through the divinity. And, therefore, He says, **In the name of the Father and of the Son and of the Holy Ghost**. And the reason is that by baptism a regeneration takes place, and in this regeneration three things are required. Firstly, it is required that there be someone for whom the regeneration takes place; secondly, it is required that there be someone through whom the regeneration takes place; and thirdly, it is required that there be someone by whom it takes place. For whom is said, namely, for God the Father, as the Apostle says: "Whom he foreknew, he also predestinated to be made conformable to the image of his Son" (Rom. 8, 29). And: "He gave them power to be made the sons of God, to them that believe in his name" (Jn. 1, 12). Through whom is said, because it occurs through the Son; "God sent his Son... that we might receive the adoption of sons" (Gal. 4-5), because by our adoption in relation to His natural Son we are His sons. Likewise, by whom is said, because we receive the gift of the Holy Ghost at baptism; "You have not received the spirit of bondage again in fear: but you have received the spirit of adoption of sons" (Rom. 8, 15). Wherefore, it was fitting that there be mention made of the Father, Son and Holy Ghost. And these three were involved with Christ's baptism, for the Son was the one through whom He was baptized, the Father was the one for whom He was baptized, and the Holy Ghost, by whom He was baptized, was in the form of a dove. And it is said, *In the name*, meaning in the invocation of the name, or in the power of the name, because the name has power; "But thou O Lord, art among us, and thy name is called upon by us, forsake us not" (Jer. 14, 9). Likewise, He says, *In the name*, not "in the names," and heresies are confounded, which do not make a distinction of the Persons, in that He says, *In the name of the Father and of the Son*. Now, Arius is also confounded by the fact that He says, in the singular, *In the name*.

It ought to be observed that in the primitive Church, one was baptized in the name of Christ, and this was done so that His name would be made venerable. But would it be sufficient to baptize in this manner? I believe that it would not be sufficient, because an express invocation of the Trinity is required. The Trinity is implicitly contained in Christ: thus, He introduces Baptism in this manner to instruct them on how to baptize. But, contrary to this, the Apostle says that God did not send him to baptize, but to preach the gospel,[14] and to baptize through others, as Christ did not baptize, but His disciples baptized.[15]

Teaching them to observe all things whatsoever I have commanded you. But is it not sufficient for salvation to believe and to be baptized? It is not; nay, instruction on morals is also required; wherefore, He says: *Teaching them to observe all things whatsoever I have commanded you*. "Thou hast commanded thy commandments to be kept most diligently" (Ps. 118, 4). And He says, *Which I have commanded you*, not which I have advised. Hence: "What I say to you, I say to all" (Mk. 13, 37).

Then he relates the third point of His instruction: *And behold I am with you all days, even to the consummation of the world*. Here He promises help; the reason why He says this is

---

14. "For Christ sent me not to baptize, but to preach the gospel" (I Cor. 1, 17).

15. "Jesus himself did not baptize, but his disciples" (Jn. 4, 2).

that He is answering those who say: 'You command that we teach all men, but we are not sufficient for this.' 'Do not fear, because *I am with you.*' And note that, just as the command is related to go forth to all nations, so also His help to go to all nations is related; because He promises similar help both to the Apostles and to others after them: hence, when He is praying to the Father, He says: "Not for them only (namely, the disciples) do I pray, but for them also who through their word shall believe in me" (Jn. 17, 20). Hence, He commonly promises help to all; "He that believeth in me, the works that I do, he also shall do: and greater than these shall he do" (Jn. 14, 12). Similarly, He says for all time; hence, He says: **All days, even to the consummation of the world.** He does not so speak as though He would not be with us afterwards, and only until the consummation of the world, but that then, by the consummation, we will be in glory; "Behold the tabernacle of God with men: and he will dwell with them. And they shall be his people: and God himself with them shall be their God" (Apoc. 21, 3). Hence, it is also said in Isaias 7 that His name shall be called Emmanuel[16] which being interpreted is, God with us.[17] **Even to the consummation of the world**; it is as though He were to say: 'The generation of believers is stronger than the world. For the world shall not perish until all things take place,' meaning the Church of the faithful be consummated, and the number be filled up of those chosen by God unto everlasting life, to Whom be honor, glory, and power for endless ages upon ages. Amen.[18]

---

16. "Behold a virgin shall conceive, and bear a son and his name shall be called Emmanuel" (Is. 7, 14).

17. Above 1, 23.

18. I Tim. 4, 11.

APPENDIX

Transcription of Basel Manuscript B.V. 12

Made by Dr. Hans Kraml of the University of Innsbruck
Edited by Fr. Paul Kimball of the Society of St. Pius X

Chapter 6, v. 1-8 (Lectures 1-2) 47rb

"Attendite ne iustitiam". Supra dominus adimplevit legem quantum ad praecepta, nunc incipit adimplere quantum ad promissa. In veteri enim lege promittebantur temporalia sicut dicit Augustinus,[i] quae erant maxima duo desiderabilia, scilicet gloria mundana et affluentia divitiarum, Deut. 28(1): "Si audieris vocem domini" etc.[ii] Dominus autem docet in hoc capitulo non facere iustitiae opera propter temporalia neque propter gloriam mundi neque propter affluentiam divitiarum.

Dividitur autem hoc capitulum in partes duas. In prima parte docet non esse facienda opera iustitiae propter gloriam mundi, secundo non esse facienda propter divitias ibi: "Nolite thesaurizare" (19).

Circa primum duo facit, primo ponit doctrinam in generali, secundo exsequitur per partes ibi: "Cum ergo facis" (2). Circa primum duo facit, primo ponit documentum, secundo documenti rationem assignat ibi: "Alioquin" (1).

Dicit ergo: "Attendite". Signanter dicit "attendite" propter tres rationes.

Primo quia ibi est opus attentione ubi[1] aliquid occulte subintelligitur. Ita est de appetitu humanae laudis. Unde Chrysostomus:[iii] Occulte intrat et omnia quae intus sunt insensibiliter aufert. Psalmus (90,6): "A sagitta volante".

Secundo opus est attentione contra ea quibus difficile resistitur. /47va/ Augustinus [Presbyter] in [Ep. ad] *Aurelium* [*Episcopum*]:[iv] Quas virtutes ad volendum habeat humanae gloriae cupido non facile noverunt nisi illi qui eis bellum indixerint quia etsi facile non quaeritur cum negatur, difficile tamen[2] relinquitur cum offertur. Ioh. 3(12, 39), propterea credere non poterant, tertio quia quam opera sunt maiora, tam[3] minus potest homo praecavere. Chrysostomus:[v] <omne malum> vexat filios diaboli, hoc autem filios Dei, Zach. 3(1): Sathan sedebat a dextris, id est diabolus insidians bonis operibus.

Et non dixit "attendite" (6.1) nisi postquam removit iram animi et concupiscentiam et odium. Animus enim subiectus passionibus non potest attendere quid in corde geratur, Prov. 4(23): "Omni custodia serva" et post (Prov. 4,25) "oculi videant recta".

1. ubi] *mg.*, nisi
2. *alterum* quaeritur cum *delevi*
3. tam] tamen

"Ne iustitiam", id est opus iustitiae. Iustitia quandoque sonat in vicium, quandoque scilicet praesumitur ex propriis viribus, Rom. 10(3): "Ignorantes Dei iustitiam" etc., aliquando sonat in virtutem sicut hic "ne iustitiam", quae scilicet a nobis exigitur. Dixerat enim dominus: "Nisi abundaverit" (5.20) etc., et determinat quomodo poterat observari, et si totum referretur[4] ad laudem hominum, non valeret, et ideo necessaria est recta intentio et hoc est "ne iustitia" etc.

Sed quaerit Chrysostomus:[vi] Quid si traham pauperem in partem? Dicendum quod si gloriam habeat in corde et ad gloriam habeat intentionem non valet, et ideo Gregorius dicit:[vii] Ita opus fiat in[5] publico ut intentio maneat in occulto et hoc est "ne /47vb/ videamini" (1). Sed numquid semper quaerimus gloriam quando volumus videri ab hominibus? Augustinus dicit[viii] quod dupliciter aliquid quaeritur, uno modo ut finis ultimus, alio ut necessarium ad finem. Illud autem proprie quaerimus quod volumus ut finem ultimum, aliud autem non proprie quaerimus quod volumus ut necessarium ad finem sicut aliquis quaerit navem <ut> vadat in patriam. Hic non proprie quaerit navem, sed patriam. Unde si ergo vis videri ab hominibus ut des eis exemplum et propter gloriam Dei, non prohiberis quia supra dixit: "Sic luceat lux vestra" (5,16) etc. Prohibetur autem ne intentio feratur sicut in principalem finem et hoc est "ut videamini ab eis" tantum, scilicet sicut etiam placere hominibus aliquando vituperatur: Gal. (1,10): "Si adhuc hominibus placerem", Aliqando laudatur: Cor. 10(33).

Consequenter assignat rationem sui documenti, unde "alioquin mercedem". Nullus meretur aliquid apud aliquem cui nihil dat. Unde qui facit aliquid propter homines et non propter Deum, dicitur nihil dare. Chrysostomus:[ix] Quae sapientia elemosynam dare et mercedem Dei perdere. De hac mercede loquitur de qua Gen. 15(1): "Ego Deus merces" et supra (5,12) "merces vestra copiosa est" etc.

Consequenter exequitur per partes cum dicit: "Cum ergo facis"[6] (2) et hoc quantum ad elemosynam, orationem et ieiunium.

Secundum ibi: "Cum oratis" (5), tertium "cum ieiunatis" (16). Et ponit ista tria quia secundum Chrysostomum[x] dominus voluit instruere /48ra/ contra illa quibus sint temptatus, scilicet de gula, de avaritia et de inani gloria, sicut patet supra 4., et est contra gulam ieiunium, contra avaritiam elemosyna, contra inanem gloriam oratio. Nihil enim eam vincere potest cum etiam de bonis operibus amplietur.

    4. referretur] referritur   6. facis] facit
    5. populo *add. et exl.*

Considerandum quod ista tria sunt partes iustitiae dupliciter. Satisfactoriae[7] enim iustitiae est ut qui peccat satisfaciat. Peccatum autem est triplex. Vel contra Deum, vel conra se ipsum, vel contra proximum. Contra Deum peccatur per superbiam et huic opponitur humilitas orationis. Eccli. (Sir 35,21): "Oratio humiliantis se". Contra proximum per avaritiam et ideo satisfacit per elemosynam. Contra se per carnis concupiscentiam et ideo satisfacit per ieiunium.[xi] Hieronymus:[xii] Oratione sanantur pestes cunctae mentis,[8] ieiunio pestis corporis.

Item ista tria sunt partes iustitiae quae est religionis proprius actus. Religiosi enim debent offerre sacrificium Deo. Est autem triplex bonum: Exterius, scilicet res, interius corpus et anima.[xiii] Per elemosynam ergo offerunt exteriora bona. Hebr. ultimo (13,16): "Beneficientiae et communionis". Per ieiunium corpora propria. Rom. 12(1): "Exhibeatis corpora vestra hostiam".[9] Per orationem animam, est enim oratio[10] "assensus[11] mentis in Deum."[xiv] Psalmus (141,2): "Dirigatur oratio mea".

Circa elemosynam ergo quae prima est duo facit. Primo excludit modum indebitum, secundo ponit debitum ibi: "Te autem" (3). Circa primum excludit modum indebitum, /48rb/ secundo assignat rationem ibi: "Amen dico" (2). Modum indebitum excludit ex tribus: Ex signo, loco et fine. Quantum ad primum dicit: "Cum ergo facies" (2). Continuatio: "Attendite ne iustitiam" (1) etc. Unde cum elemosyna sit pars iustitiae "cum facis[12] elemosynam noli" etc. Consuetudo erat apud Iudaeos quod quando faciebant publicas elemosynas clangebant tubis ad hoc quod pauperes congregarentur. Istud ergo quod ex quadam necessitate inductum fuit, malitia hominum pervertit ad gloriam inanem. Et ideo dominus prohibet et secundum Chrysostomum[xv] idem est quasi tuba clangens quando de quocumque[13] bono appetis apparere etiam si in occulto fiat. Is. 24 (40,9): "Exalta in fortitudine vocem". "Sicut hypocritae". (2) Hic primo ponitur de hypocritis. Unde videndum quid est hoc nomen 'hypocrita' (mg.) proprie. Derivatum est et productum a repraesentatione quae fiebat in ludis theatralibus ubi inducebant homines habentes facies larvatas[14] ad repraesentandum homines quibus gesta repraesentabant. Unde dicebatur 'hypocrita' ab 'hypo' quod est 'sub' et 'crisio' quod est 'iudicium'.[xvi] Alius enim erat et alius videbatur et talis est hypocrita qui exterius habet speciem sanctitatis et interius non implet quae ostendit. Gregorius[xvii] dicit quod non si aliquando cadit

---

7. satisfactoriae] *mg.*, satisfactione
8. mentis *mg.*
9. vestra] *add. et exl.*, domino
10. oratio] elevatio *exp.*
11. assensus] *mg., forte corrigendum* ascensus; elevatio *exp.*
12. facis] facit *txt.* facies Vulg.
13. quocumque] quodamcumque
14. larvatas] lamatas

propter infirmitatem, illi enim proprie sunt hypocritae qui tantum ut videantur speciem sanctitatis habent.

Consequenter excludit quantum ad locum et hoc etiam reprehenditur si simulatorie fiat, non autem si propter exemplum. /48va/

"In synagogis" (2) sicut modo in ecclesia, "et in angulis" (5) sicut in loco publico. "Ut videantur" (5) et hoc est quod supra[15] dixit "coram[16] ut honorificentur" (2) etc. Io. 5(44): "Quomodo potestis" etc.

Consequenter assignat rationem: "Amen dico vobis mercedem" (5). Illud est enim merces uniuscuiusque propter quid operatur, Ioh. (Mat. 20,13) "Nonne ex denario convenisti"[17] etc.

Consequenter assignat modum debitum et convenientem et postea assignat rationem ibi: "ut sit elemosyna" (4). Dicit ergo: "Te autem faciente" (3). Istud multipliciter exponitur.

Chrysostomus[xviii] enim dicit quod in libro Canonum apostolorum sic exponitur quod per sinistram intelligitur populus infidelis, per dexteram fidelis. Unde vult quod nihil fiat coram infidelibus.

Contra hoc Augustinus:[xix] Quia cum facit elemosynam propter gloriam et tunc etiam neque a fidelibus debet videri, vel propter utilitatem, et tunc debet fieri coram infidelibus: [hoc] "proprie [utilis] est « ut videntes" etc. Matt. (5, 16).

Alii autem exponunt quod per sinistram intelligit uxorem quae solet impedire aliquando virum ab operibus misericordiae. Unde vult quod etiam uxor nescia et similiter intelligendum de quocumque alio. Et similiter obicit contra hoc Augustinus[xx] quia hoc praeceptum datur etiam, nullus ergo deberet dicere "nesciat dextera tua" (3) etc.[xxi] Unde Augustinus[xxii] aliter exponit et etiam Chrysostomus[xxiii] et quasi in idem reducitur: Dicunt quod in scriptura per sinistram intelliguntur temporalia bona, per dexteram spiritualia, Prov. 4(3,16): "In dextera illius longitudo" etc. Unde /48vb/ voluit dominus quod non fieret per gloriam terrenam. Vel aliter et quasi in idem redit, per dexteram aliquando intelliguntur opera virtutis, per sinistram peccata quasi quando fit opus virtutis non fiat cum aliquo peccato.[xxiv] Chrysostomus[xxv] tamen ponit litteralem et dicit quod dominus loquitur per excessum sicut si aliquis dicat si posset fieri nollet quod hoc sciret pes meus.

Ponitur ratio "ut sit elemosyna in abscondito" (4) et in conscientia tua quae occulta est,[xxvi] Cor. 3(2,11): "Quae sunt hominis nemo" et iterum Cor. (2, 1,12): "Gloria nostra haec est, testimonium". Sic enim accipitur illud Rom. 2(28): "Non enim qui in manifesto Iudaeus"[18] etc.

15. supra] su- *corr.s.l.*
16. coram] coranti
17. convenisti] convenistis
18. Iudaeus] videmus

"Et pater tuus reddet tibi": Hebr. 4(13): "Omnia nuda et aperta"[19] etc. Jer. (17, 9): « Pravum est cor hominis." Augustinus[xxvii] dicit quod in quibusdam exemplaribus invenitur "reddet tibi palam" quia sicut diabolus conatur aperire et publicare quae in conscientia sunt ut scandalum faciat, ita Deus ad maiorem utilitatem et etiam ad exemplum malorum adducet bona. Unde etiam sancti multi non potuerunt latere.[xxviii] Psalmus (37,6): "Edducet[20] quasi lumen iustitiam" quam scilicet in occulto tenebas. Hoc tamen non videtur esse de textu.

"Et cum oratis" (5). Supra dominus ostendit de opere elemosynae quod non est faciendum per humanam gloriam, hic ostendit idem de oratione et circa hoc duo facit. Primo docet modum orandi, secundo docet quid sit in oratione petendum /49ra/, [ibi:]"Sic ergo orabitis" (9).

Circa primum duo facit, primo docet vitare in oratione vanitates[21] hypocritarum, secundo vanitatem gentilium ibi: "Orantes" (7). Circa primum duo facit, primo excludit modum inconvenientem orandi, secundo assignat convenientem ibi: "Tu autem" (6). Excludit modum orandi exemplo hypocritarum. Unde primo excludit exemplum istud, secundo exponit, tertio rationem assignat. Secundum ibi: "Qui amant" (5), tertium: "Amen dico" (5).

Satis convenienter post elemosynam agit hic <de> oratione quia sicut Eccli. 18(23), "ante orationem" etc. Per bona enim opera inter quae prima est elemosyna anima praeparatur ad orationem.[xxix] Treni 3(41): "Levemus corda nostra" etc., quod fit quando bona opera consonant.

Et notandum quod dominus non inducit ad orandum sed docet modum orandi[xxx] et hoc est « cum oratis non eritis sicut hypocritae qui amant in synagogis et in "angulis"[22] (5). Per 'hypocritae' intelliguntur simulatores qui faciunt[23] totum propter laudem humanam et quamvis hoc vicium[24] sit in omni opere vitandum,[25] tamen in oratione specialiter secundum Chrysostomum,[xxxi] quia oratio est quoddam sacrificium quod offerimus Deo ex intimis cordis. Psalmus (141,2): "dirigatur oratio" etc. Sacrificium non licet offerri nisi Deo, offertur autem hominibus si fiat propter humanam gloriam. Unde tales sunt idolatrae. Describitur autem hypocrita quantum ad affectandum[26] locum supra et infra[27] totum. Quantum ad primum dicit "qui amant". (5) Contingit enim aliquando fieri /49rb/

---

19. etc] Hieronymus *mg.* =Ieremias (17, 9), ubi lectio varians est „Pravum est cor hominis." Cf. I, q. 57, a. 4 sc.; III, q. 59, a. 2 obj. 3; *De Veritate* q. 8, a. 4 sc. 8?
20. adducet] educet Vulg.
21. vanitates] vanitatis
22. oratis non eritis sicut hypocritae qui amant in synagogis et in *txt.*
23. faciunt] fatuum
24. vicium] *mg.*, videatur
25. vitandum] *mg.*, videndum
26. affectum] affectatandum
27. infrascriptus] infra

aliqua titillatio in viris sanctis inanis gloriae, sed non sunt propter hoc in numero hypocritarum nisi[28] ex proposito hoc agant, Ier. 2(24) "In desiderio animae suae."

Et nota duo genera hypocritarum qui manifeste[29] gloriam humanam quaerunt, scilicet qui in locis publicis orant. Unde dicit "In synagogis" (5) ubi erat congregatio populorum. Psalmus (7,8): "Synagoga". Aliqui orant in locis privatis et ex ipsa vitatione gloriae gloriam quaerunt.[xxxii] Volunt enim videri quaerere occultum cum tamen ament publicum[30] et hoc est "in synagogis et angulis" (5). Si enim occultum in rei veritate quaererent, non angulum platearum, sed camerae locum quaererent. Vel possumus dicere quod quaerunt apertum publicum. Sed duplex est publicum, quoddam deputatum[31] orationi, scilicet "synagoga", aliud non deputatum orationi, scilicet "angulum", et est proprie angulus ubi duae lineae sese intersecant.[32] [xxxiii] Unde "anguli platearum" enim duae plateae se intersecant ita quod fit ibi quadrivium et hoc est valde publicum nec orationi deputatatum, Treni 4(1): "Dispersi sunt lapides".

Notandum etiam quod unum de rebus facientibus ad orationem est humilitas, Iudith 9 (16): Humilium et mansuetorum. . Psalmus (31,8): "Respexisti humilitatem meam",[33] sed isti stant quasi superbi. Sed videtur quod in nullo loco sit prohibitum orare[34] ante Tim. 2(8): "Volo omnes viri etc.". Psalmus (68,27): "in ecclesiis[35] benedicite". Sed dicendum quod non est peccatum nisi sub hac intentione "ut videantur ab hominibus" (5) et sicut dicit Chrysostomus[xxxiv] etsi velle videri ab hominibus /49va/ noceat in aliis operibus, tamen specialiter in oratione quia nocet et quantum ad finem et quantum ad substantiam quia etsi fiat in bona intentione, vix potest homo[36] tenere animum quin evagetur per diversa, multo magis ergo quando fit propter gloriam hominum[xxxv] et hoc est "ut videantur". Numquid ergo non est orandum in loco publico?

Sciendum quod Deus intendit prohibere modum orandi per quem tollitur inanis gloria quae numquam quaeritur nisi de aliquo singulari quia quando sunt multi qui servant unum ibi non quaeritur gloria ab alio. Unde dominus tollit singularem modum orandi ut scilicet nullus oret in loco non deputando orationi nisi aliquis sit tantae auctoritatis quod etiam aliis ad orandum inducat. Unde secundum Chrysostomum[xxxvi] hoc quod dicit "in angulis" referendum est ad omne illud per quod videris discretus esse ab aliis cum quibus conversaris.[xxxvii]

28. nisi] *mg.*, ubi
29. *male leg.*
30. publicum] privatum
31. deputatum] deputant
32. intercecant] intersecant
33. humilitatem meam] in omnem
34. orare] *mg.*
35. ecclesiis] *male leg.*
36. homo] potest *add.*

"Amen dico" (5). Hic assequat rationem et dicit duo: "merces" et "suam" (2). Merces uniuscuiusque est per quam pascitur de opere suo.[xxxviii] Unde quando nos facimus aliquid propter gloriam hominum, gloria hominum est merces nostra, cum tamen debemus expectare gloriam Dei veram, et hoc est "[receperunt mercedem suam]» ratione" quia usurpaverunt,[xxxix] Gal. ultimo (6,8): "Quae seminaverit homo". "Tu autem" (6). Hic ponit debitum[37] modum, et primo ponit eum, secundo assignat rationem: "Et pater" (6). Dicit ergo: "Tu cum orabis" (86), id est orare disponeris.[xl] /49vb/

"Intra in cubiculum" (6). Hoc tripliciter exponitur. Intelligitur primo ad litteram de secreto[38] camerae.[39] Sed numquid contrarium faciunt qui ad ecclesiam vadunt?[xli] Sed dicendum quod loquitur de oratione privata quae non est facienda nisi in loco privato et hoc propter tria, primo quia concordat fidei quia tunc confiteris Deum ubique esse praesentem.[xlii] Psalmus (38,10): "Domine ante te omne". Ieremias 23 (24): "Caelum et terram". Secundo quia quamvis[40] cum multis impeditur oratio quae in secreto quieta est,[xliii] Osee 2(14).: "Ducam eam in solitudinem". Tertio quia vitatur inanis gloria,[xliv] Reg. 14 (4 Reg. 4,33): "Ingressus". Tamen dicendum ut oraret coram domino, solus, scilicet "et clauso" (6) ad litteram, ut etiam excludas possibilitatem adeundi.[xlv] Secundo per cubiculum potest intelligi interius secretum cordis. [xlvi] Psalmus (4,5): "Quae dicitis in cordibus". "Cluso[41] ostio" Eccles. (Sir) 28(28): "Ori tuo facito ostia",[42] quasi dicat: Ora silenter, et hoc propter tria, primo quia attestantur fidei quia tunc confiteris quod Deus cogitationes cordium sciat.[xlvii] Reg. 16 (1 Sam 16,7): "Homo videt ea quae parent".[43] Secundo quia non debet[44] quod alii sciant petitiones tuas,[xlviii] Isaia 4 (24,16): "Secretum meum mihi". Tertio quia si voce loqueris alios impedires,[xlix] Reg. 6 (3 Reg. 6,7): "Malleus et securis non sunt auditae" etc.

Sed quid[45] dicemus de oratione publica? Dicendum quod dominus loquitur de privata in qua quaeritur utilitas unius. Sed etiam in publica quaeritur /50ra/ utilitas multitudinis, et quia per huiusmodi clamores ad devotionem excitantur aliqui, ideo instituti sunt cantus. Unde Augustinus dicit in libro de Confessionibus[l] quod beatus Athanasius ne nimis delectaretur in cantu volebat quod omnia legerentur submisse. Sed quia beatus Augustinus antequam[46] converteretur multum profuerunt sibi huiusmodi cantus, non ausus est contradicere sed approbat.

37. debitum] *mg.pr.m.*, dubium.
38. secreto] ad *add. et exp.*
39. camerae] *corr.s.l.*, cameram
40. quando] quamvis est *add. et exl.*
41. ostio] cluso
42. ostia] hostium
43. homines vident ea quae paret *txt.*
44. debet] decet
45. quid] quod
46. antequam] *mg.*, numquam

Sed quaestio utrum aliquis in loco privato orans debeat dicere verba vel non. Sed distinguendum est hic quia aliquando verba proveniunt ex intentione, aliquando ex impulsione cordis quia sicut dicitur Iob (4.2): "Conceptum sermonem". Unde ex ipso impetu spiritus aliqui proferuntur ad aliqua verba dicenda, et hoc est omnis[47] effectus.

Verba autem dupliciter possunt considerari: Vel ut debita et tunc reddenda.[li] Sic sunt horae.[48] Psalmus (141,2): "Voce mea ad dominum". Vel ut utilia ad orandum et tunc distinguendum de principio et fine quia melior est finis orationis etc. ecclesiae. Si enim in principio orationis affectus excitatur per verba ad devote orandum, tunc utile est proferre verba, quando autem non excitatur affectus,[49] tunc non sunt proferenda verba et operi(endus) [affectus]quia sicut calidum evaporando diminuitur, ita affectus evacuatur per verba sicut etiam patet de dolore expresso[50] aliis. Psalmus (39,4): "Concaluit cor meum intra me". Ieremias (20,9): "Dixi non loquar in nomine domini /50rb/ et factus est ignis" etc. Hoc sic exponit Augustinus.[51] [lii] Sed "clauso ostio"[52] tertio modo sic exponit Augustinus[liii] quod per "cubiculum" intelligitur cor, per "ostium"[53] exteriores sensus et etiam imaginatio quasi quia talis debet intrare cor suum et claudere sensus et imaginationem ut nihil interius intret nisi quod pertinet ad orationem. Et Cyprianus[liv] assignat duas rationes. Primo quia vituperabile[54] est quod non attendis quae dicis cum loqueris cum rege aliquo. Secundo quia Deus quomodo[55] intelligit te si tu te ipsum non intelligis.[lv] Hoc est ostium[56] de quo Apoc.2 (3,20): "Ecce (ego txt.) sto ad ostium[57] et pulso".

"Et pater tuus" (6) hic assignat rationem. Nullus enim orat nisi illum quem videt. Deus autem "omnia nuda et aperta" etc. Hebr. 4 (13). "In abscondito" (6) vel cordis vel loci "reddet tibi". "Orantes" (7) etc. Hic docet vitare secundum vicium, scilicet multiloquium gentilium, et circa hoc tria facit. Primo docet vitare exemplum gentilium, secundo ponit intentionem, tertio assignat rationem. Secundum ibi: "Putant enim" (7). Tertium ibi: " Nolite ". Dicit ergo "Orantes" (7), et nota quod non dicit "nolite multum orare" quia hoc est contra illud Rom. 12(12): "Orationi instantes" et Luc. 22(43): "Factus in agonia", 26 (Luc. 6,12): Orabat "pernoctans in oratione", sed dicit "nolite". Augustinus[lvi] in libro *De orando*: Non sit mul-

---

47. omnis] omnes
48. horae] *corr.s.l.*, orae
49. affectus] effectus*
50. expresse] expresso
51. Chrysostomus] Augustinus *ex. ad Probam.* Ep. 130, ix, 18 (PL 33, 501)).
52. ostio] hostio
53. ostium] hostium
54. vituperabile] *mg.*, incurabile
55. quomodo *mg.*
56. ostium] hostium
57. ostium] hostium

ta locutio sed sit multa precatio si non desit fervens intentio. Sed multum et paucum,[58] magnum et parvum relativa sunt, multum enim potest dici dupliciter, in comparatione ad orationem quae est /50va/ "assensus ad Deum,"[lvii] vel multum loquuntur quando verba excedunt orationem et hoc potest esse dupliciter, si scilicet verba sunt de illicitis et haec sunt nociva, et quando non adest devotio, tunc magis homo redditur taediosus et orare redditur odiosum, et ideo dicit Augustinus[lviii] quod monachi[59] in Aegypto habebant crebras orationes sed breves. Videbant enim quod devotio erat oranti necessaria quae evacuabatur per multitudinem verborum, et ideo in ecclesia statutum est quod diversis horis diversa dicantur, Eccle. 5(1): "Ne temere quid loquaris". Augustinus:[lix] "Hoc negotium, scilicet orationis, plus gemitibus quam verbis" etc.

"Sicut ethnici" (7). Gentiles colebant daemonia pro diis.[lx] Psalmus (96,5): "Omnes dii gentium". In daemonibus scilicet considerandum, scilicet quod nesciunt futura vel occulta cordium nisi inquantum eis revelantur.[lxi] Unde necessarium erat gentilibus quod totum diceretur per verba.[lxii] Reg. 14 (3, 18,27): "Clamate" altius etc.

Item daemones habent affectum mutabilem. Unde per verba mutari possunt. Unde dicit Augustinus[lxiii] quod Plato dixit quod verbis mutabantur.[60] Deus autem et omnia scit nec verbis flectitur. Mal (3,6). "Ego deus et non mutor".[61] Numeri 23 (19): "Non est Deus ut homo". Iob 14 (41, 3): "Non parcet ei et"[62] verbis potentibus et ad deprecandum[63] compositis.[64][lxiv]» "Putant enim" (7) etc. "Nolite ergo" (8) etc. et quare: "scit enim" etc. Psalmus (38,10): Dominus "ante te omne". Ergo si scit non debemus verba multiplicare. Sed dicetur: Deus scit quae nobis sunt /50vb/ necessaria. Quare ergo oramus? Et respondet Hieronymus[lxv] quod non petimus[65] verbis ut[66] significemus, sed ut postulemus. Et iterum posset dici: Quare proferimus verba? Respondet Augustinus[lxvi] quod aliter est in oratione quam facimus homini et[67] Deo quia in homine multum valent verba ad hoc quod flectemus eum, in Deo ad hoc ut cor nostrum ad eum levemus, et ideo dicit Augustinus[lxvii] quod cum semper sit habendus affectus ad Deum, tamen oportet aliquando verbis orare ut non deficiat. Et sicut dicit Chrysostomus,[lxviii] ex frequenti oratione provenit quod homo redditur Deo familiaris et Deus ei. Exo. 33(9): "Loquebatur Moyses" etc.

---

58. Paucum] parvum *cf. Quodlibeta IV, q. 12. a. 1. ad 9ᵘᵐ*: "Magnum et parvum, multum et paucum, secundum Philosphum, dicuntur relative."
59. monachi] *mg.*,manichei
60. multabantur] mutabantur
61. mutor] muter
62. eis] ei et *txt*.
63. condemnandum] deprecandum *txt*.
64. componi] compositis *txt*.
65. petimus] *mg.*, petas
66. ut *s.l.*
67. et] homi *add. et exp.*

Item ex hoc provenit humilitas quia consideratur altitudo Dei et infirmitas propria,[lxix] Gen. 14(18,27): "Loquar ad dominum meum".

Item homo ex hoc in actibus suis dirigitur et auxilium a Deo petit.[lxx] Psalmus (121,1): "Levavi oculos meos in montes"[68] etc. Col. 3(17): "Omne quodcumque facitis" etc.

Text of Corpus Thomisticum (Previously Transcribed)

Chapter 6, 9-15 (Lecture 3)

"Sic ergo orabitis". Supra dominus docuit modum orandi... ut scilicet malum non frequentetur, et sic non peccat.

End of Text of Corpus Thomisticum

Chapter 6, 16-34 (Lectures 4-5)

"Cum ieiunatis" (16). Postquam determinavit modum orandi et elemosynam faciendi hic determinat modum ieiunandi, et primo excludit modum inconvenientem, secundo astruit verum ibi: "Tu autem" (17).

Circa primum tria facit. Primo docet vitare hypocritarum modi exemplum, secundo manifestat illud, tertio rationem[69] sui documenti assignat. Secundum ibi: "Exterminant" (1b), tertium ibi "Amen" (1c).

Satis convenienter post orationem de ieiunio tractat quia gracilis est oratio quam non concomitatur /55vb/ ieiunium,[lxxi] et non est quia oratio est "levatio mentis in Deum."[lxxii] Quanto[70] autem caro magis roboratur tanto magis debilitatur, Tob. 12(8): "Bona est oratio cum ieiunio", et ubicumque[71] legitur aliqua oratio solemnis facta, ibi[72] sit mentio de ieiunio.[lxxiii] Dan. 9(3) et Joel 2(15): "Sanctificate".

Dicit ergo "cum ieiunatis". Chrysostomus:[lxxiv] Non dicit "nolite esse" quia impossibile est quod ieiunantes non incidant[73] in passiones tristitiae sicut e converso illi qui ieiunant ex comestione et potatione redduntur[74] laeti. Sed dicit "nolite fieri", id est non detis operam ut tristes fiamini exterius, sed interius dolendo de peccatis, Cor. 8 (2 Cor. 7,10): tristitiam "saeculi". Eccles. (Sir) 30(22): "Tristitiam non des animae tuae et ne affligas temet ipsum in consilio tuo." "Sicut hypocritae", id est ea intentione. "Hypocritae" dicuntur simulatores qui simulant[75] personam iusti sicut supra exposi-

---

68. in montes] ad manus
69. rationem] *mg.*, removet
70. quanto *corr.s.l.*
71. ubicumque] *mg.*, uterque.
72. ibi] *mg.* nisi

73. incidant] in temptationes *add. et exl.*
74. redduntur] *corr. s.l.* ,reducuntur
75. simulant] simulat

tum est. Quando autem fiant tristes subiungit "exterminant" (1b). Hieronymus:[lxxv] Hoc, scilicet "exterminant" improprie positum est ut metaphorice quia exterminare proprie dicitur 'extra terminos ponere'. Unde sumptum est ab exulibus civitatum. Unde dicitur quod Saul (1 Sam. 28,3.9) exterminavit magos et ariolos de terra. Hic autem proprie ponitur quod demoliuntur.[76] [lxxvi] Vel dicendum quod "exterminant facies" ponendo extra modum communem. "Ut videantur" (5). Ista est oratio Eccles. (Sir) 19(26): "Ex visu cognoscitur vir et ab occursu faciei."

Hic nota secundum Augustinum[lxxvii] quod non solum gloria quaeritur de pompa vestium sed etiam de vilitate vestium et secundum eum /56ra/ hoc est magis periculosum quia quod alii fallant de pompa vestium et huiusmodi, non potest nocere cum cognoscatur, sed quando quaeritur de scalore corporis potest esse periculum quia si non est spiritualis homo potest de facili inducere in errorem. Dicit tamen Augustinus quod talis potest discerni ex aliis actibus quia si ex una parte sequitur abiectionem mundi et ex alia acquirit lucra, simulator est. Sed numquid propter quod quod aliqui hypocritae usurpant sibi vilitatem vestium ad malitiam occultandam, debent demittere illi qui faciunt propter Deum? Dicendum quod non quia sicut dicit Glossa,[lxxviii] non debet dimittere pellem suam ovis quamvis lupus aliquando ea se contegat.

"Amen" assignat rationem sui documenti. Stultum enim est pro laude hominum amittere praemium aeternum.[lxxix] Gen. (15,1): "Ego Deus merces tua magna".

"Tu autem" (17). Hic ponitur modus conveniens ieiunandi et circa hoc tria facit. Primo ponit modum, secundo assignat rationem, tertio utilitatem. Dicit ergo "tu autem", simile Ecl. 9(8): "Omni tempore sint vestimenta tua candida et oleum de capite tuo non deficiat", et movet hic Augustinus[lxxx] quaestionem quod quamvis consuetudo sit apud multos quod cotidie faciem suam lavent, tamen quod caput ungant ad lasciviam[77] reputatur. Numquid ergo hoc dominus vult?

Item dicit Chrysostomus[lxxxi] quod ieiunium occulte debet fieri. Sed quandocumque videmus aliquem unctum dicemus quod ieiuniat.

Istis obiec- /56rb/ -tionibus tripliciter respondent. Hieronymus[lxxxii] ita dicit, et credo quod sit magis litteralis, quod consuetudo erat apud palaestinos tempore illo quod homines cotidie ungebant caput oleo et lavabant faciem. Unde illa dixit Regum (4,4,2): "Non habeo nisi modicum oleo quo ungar". Unde consuetudo ista inter

---

76. demoliti] demoliuntur *ex Catena Aurea in Matthaeum*, c. 6, lect. 12.

77. lasciviam] *corr.s.l.*, laxiviam

necessaria computabatur. Vult ergo dominus dicere quod ille qui ieiunat non debet mutare modum vivendi qui est quod caput ungat et faciem lavet.[lxxxiii] Vel aliter secundum Chrysostomum:[lxxxiv] Dominus loquitur per excessum sicut etiam supra "te autem faciendo elemosynam" quare si conveniens esset, deberes facere communia[78] hypocritis. Tertio secundum Augustinum et etiam Chrysostomum,[lxxxv] dominus loquitur similitudine, et ista expositio est mystica. Per caput duo intelliguntur, Cor. 11(3): "Caput viri Christus." Tunc autem ungis caput quando misericordiam proximo impendis. Infra 25 (40): "Quod "uni ex minimis" etc.[lxxxvi] Vel caput hominis ratio est vel spiritus secundum Augustinum[lxxxvii] qui est vir, quasi: Sic debes carnem affligere ut spiritus interius reticetur per devotionem. Cor. 5 (2 Cor. 4,16), "licet is qui foris est noster homo corrumpitur, tamen is qui intus est renovatur de die in diem". "Noster homo", id est caro, "qui foris est", id est expositus malis, "corrumpitur", "is qui intus est", id est anima[79] munita[80] spe futuri cui[81] non accedit humanus furor.[82] [lxxxviii] "Renovatur de die in diem" id est assidue purior a viciis efficitur per ignem "tribulationis", Cor. 11 (2 Cor. 11), "licet is qui foris[83] homo noster" (2 Cor 4,16).[lxxxix] Dicit autem "faciem tuam lava" (17) id est conscientiam. Sicut enim homo redditur gratiosus propter faciem honestam[84] /56va/ hominibus, ita per conscientiam puram Deo.[xc] Prov. (22,11) "Qui diligunt cordis munditiam". Ies. 58(6): "Nonne hoc est ieiunium quod elegi" et dicit "unge caput" et non 'lava' quia Christus non indiget lotione, sic conscientia nostra.[xci] "Ne videaris". Haec est ratio. Intelligendum est de ieiunio singulari, non de communi. "Sed patri qui est in abscondito" (18) aeternitatis. Iob 28(21): "Abscondita est ab oculis" vel "in abscondito conscientiae"[xcii] quia Deus habitat in nobis per fidem (Eph. 3, 17).[xciii] "Reddet". Cor. (Rom. 2,6): "Reddet unicuique secundum opera sua", "sic scrutans corda et renes" Psalmus (7,10).

"Nolite thesaurizare". Supra dominus determinavit ne opera propter gloriam faceremus. Hic docet quod non debemus in bonis operibus ponere divitiarum finem. Duo enim mala sunt, cupiditas et inanis gloria quae se invicem consequuntur. Multi enim quaerunt divitias non ad necessitatem sed ad pompam,[xciv] vel potest sic continuari:[xcv] Dominus supra non docuit nec ammonuit ut elemosynas vel orationes faceremus, sed docuit modum faciendi. Nunc vult inducere ad hoc quod ista opera faciamus, et primo quod elmosynas,

---

78. *Vel lege*: convivia (?)
79. anima] alia
80. munita] *male leg.*
81. cui] enim *ex* Petrus Lombardus, *Collectanea in Epist. D. Pauli* (PL 192, 34D)

82. humanus] habens *Locus corruptus ut videtur.*
83. foris] *mg.*
84. honestam] honustam

secundo quod orationes ibi: "Petite", tertio quod ieiunium ibi: "Arta" est "via" (7,14).[85] [xcvi] Vel aliter: Supra docuit quod elemosynas et ieiunium faceremus[86] non propter gloriam, hic vult ultra ostendere quod "nullus [homo potest duobus dominis servire]" (24).[xcvii] Sed prima est magis consona litterae et est Chrysostomus.[xcviii] Secundum ergo hunc sensuum quia /56vb/ omnes quasi idem sint, duo facit: Primo docet vitare superfluam curam divitiarum, secundo sollicitudinem[87] necessariorum ibi: "Ideo[88] dico vobis" (25).

Circa primum duo facit. Primo monet non congregare superfluas divitias et probat ex ratione instabilitatis, secundo ex damno quod inde provenit ibi: "Ubi est thesaurus" (21).

Circa primum duo facit. Primo ponit instabilitatem divitiarum terrenarum, secundo ponit stabilitatem divitiarum caelestium quas congregare debemus ibi: "Thesaurizate" (20).

Dicit ergo primo ita: Dico quod non debemus facere bona opera propter gloriam terrenam sed etiam nec divitias congregare, et hoc est: "Nolite" etc., "in terra", id est in quacumque re terrena. Sed secundum hoc videtur quod reges et episcopi faciant contra istud praeceptum. Sed dicendum quod in thesauro duo intelligere, scilicet "abundantiam" quae est duplex, scilicet necessaria et superflua. Homini enim privato superfluum est congregare divitias regias, regi autem non quia indiget ad regni custodiam et defensionem. Unde hoc prohibetur, scilicet congregare divitias ultra necessitatem personae vel officii. Aliud quod in thesauro intelligitur est fiducia quae habetur in eis et hoc etiam prohibetur et hoc est "nolite thesaurizare" (19). Tim ultimo (1, 6,17): "Divitibus huius saeculi", Baruch 4(3,18): "Argentum thesaurizant et aurum".

Consequenter ostendit instabilitatem: "Ubi erugo" (19) /57ra/ et ponit tria genera quibus ad litteram divitiae destruuntur, divitiae enim aut habentur in metallis aut in vestibus aut in lapidibus et huiusmodi. Metalla consumuntur rubigine, vestes tinea, fures autem asportant lapides. Vel aliter: Alia littera habet: "ubi tinea" et comeduntur "et comestura exterminant,"[xcix] et istam exponit Chrysostomus:[c] Temporalia enim tripliciter destruuntur, ex parte rerum quia de vestimento procedit tinea, ex luxuria possidentis, unde dicit "comeduntur", ab extraneis, unde dicit "fures". Sed posset dici quia hoc non semper contingit, et dicit Chrysostomus[ci] quod si non semper fiat, tamen frequenter contingit et si non frequenter contingat, tamen possibile est fieri et hoc dominus vult argumentari quia docet ponere spem in perpetuis et stabilibus,

---

85. cf. *Super Isaiam*, cap. 30: "Arta est via."
86. *alteram* elemosyna(+)s *delevi*.
87. sollicitudinem] solemnitatem
88. ideo] iam

Joel 1(4): "Residuum comedet locusta". Mystice erugo apparet, sed tinea latet, unde per 'erugo' possunt intelligi peccata carnalia, per 'tinea' spiritualia. Quaedam enim peccata committunt in se ipsum et hoc intelligitur per eruginem et tineam, quaedam in scandalum alterius et hoc per fures. Vel[89] aliter: Rubigo efuscat decora, unde potest intelligi superbia quae bonis operibus insidiatur ut pereant,[90] Eccles. 12, 10. Quasi aeramentum tinea corrodit vestimenta quae sunt exteriora /57rb/ opera quae consumuntur per invidiam: Prov. 25 (20): "Sicut vermis" ligno"[91] etc. Daemones autem quando non possunt decipere furtive trahunt ad inanem gloriam et hoc "ubi fures". Posita instabilitate terrena ponit stabilitatem thesauri caelestis. Unde "thesaurizant", id est congregant multitudinem praemiorum in caelestibus.

Et notandum secundum Augustinum[cii] quod non est intelligendum de caelo corporeo quia in mala re corporali cor nostrum figere [non] debemus nec thesaurum ibi habere. Unde intelligendum "in caelo", id est in spiritualibus bonis, id est in ipso Deo: Psalmus (115,16): "Caelum caeli domino". Et dicit "thesaurum" quia si homo carnalis vult magis et magis congregare in terra, non debet ei sufficere quod qualemcumque statum habeat in re caelorum, sed quod habeat maiorem mercedem, et ideo dicit "thesaurum", id est abundant praemiis, et dicit "vobis" quia sicut[92] dicitur Iob 35(7), "porro si iuste egeris." Quomodo autem thesaurizandum sit ostendit Luc. 19 (Mat.19,21): "Si vis perfectus esse". Ergo per elemosynam thesaurizatur et ideo dicit Chrysostomus[ciii] quod hic inducit ad elemosynam. Hic "thesuarus incorruptibilis" est quia nec ex se habet corruptionem quia nec aerugo ex parte corporis, Cor. 15(53), "corruptibile hoc induet," nec ex parte animae, Ies. (60,21): "Populus tuus omnes iusti", nec ab exterioribus, hoc est ab insidiatoribus, id est daemonibus, et hoc est "ubi[93] fures", nec occulte nec manifeste, Ies. 11(9): "Non occident nec nocebunt. "Ubi est" /57va/ thesaurus". Hic vult ostendere quod[94] debemus in caelo et non primum[95] propter nocumentum quod inde provenit et est duplex. Primum distractio cordis,[96] secundum alienatio a Deo ibi: "Nemo potest duobus" (24). Circa primum duo facit. Primo ponit nocumentum distractionis cordis, secundo ostendit huius damni magnitudinem ibi: "Lucerna" (22). Dicit ergo: Dixi quod "fures effodiunt" (20) etc. Sed restat aliud inconveniens. Unde "ubi est thesaurus" (22). Ubi enim est amor, ibi oculus, Cor. 4(2, 4,18): "Non

---

89. vel *mg.*
90. pereant] efuscat decora *add. et sign.* va- -cat *s.l.*
91. ligno] *mg.*, homo *exl.*
92. sicut *s.l.*
93. ubi] nisi
94. quod] vult *add. et exl.*
95. primum] thesaurizare *add. et exp.*
96. cordis] *s.l.*, corporis

contemplantibus nobis" sed isti e converso. Prov. 17(24): "Oculi stultorum". Et quia hoc damnum, scilicet distractio[97] cordis pauci considerant, ideo dominus ostendit quantum sit hoc periculum quodam exemplo. Unde "Lucerna" per sensibilia instruit de intelligentibus, et potest hoc dupliciter legi. Primo ut dominus proponat similitudinem de caelo corporali et post adaptet similitudinem ad spiritualia ibi: "Si ergo lumen", (23) et haec expositio plana est. Et circa hoc tria facit, primo demonstrat officium oculi,[98] secundo utilitatem boni et tertio damnum mali occulti. Dicit ergo: "Lucerna corporis est oculus"[99] (22) corporalis qui sicut lucerna dirigit. "Si oculus tuus fuerit simplex" (22), id est fortis ad videndum /secundum Hieronymum,[civ] alias non posset intelligi de oculo corporali. Unde simplex, id est fortis ad videndum.[100] Homo enim quando habet oculum debile, una res videntur duae. Unde si oculus in uno figere potest propter fortitudinem, "totum "corpus tuum lucidum erit" (22) per lumen enim oculi lux capitur ad dirigenda omnia membra in suis actibus.[101] /57vb/ "Si autem nequam fuerit" (23), id est turbatus, scilicet lippus, etiam "corpus" (23), id est membra omnia ita agent sicut in tenebris.

Consequenter adaptat: "Si ergo lumen quod in tenebris in te est"[102] scilicet lumen rationis, "tenebrae sunt, ipsae tenebrae" (23). De hoc lumine Psalmus (4,7): "Signatum est super nos". Vult ergo dicere quod si cor quod est oculus animae obtenebratur applicando se terrenis alii oculi qui secundum suam naturam sunt tenebrae quia non possunt cognoscere nisi corporalia, erunt maximae tenebrae. Unde si[103] ratio quae potest in spiritualia, dirigitur ad terrena, tunc omnes sensus ad terrena dirigentur, et hoc est: "si ergo" (23) etc. Vel aliter. Dominus vult hic loqui de oculo spirituali et hoc "si ergo lumen" (23) etc. inducere[104] ad probandum praemissa per locum a minori, et dicuntur sic prius. Dicit ergo "lucerna corporis tui oculus tuuus" (22). Hic 'oculus' potest quattuor modis exponi, scilicet de ratione sicut dictum est, et hoc secundum Chrysostomum[cv] et Hilarium.[cvi] Sicut enim per lucernam illuminantur ad videndum, ita per rationem ad operandum, Prov. 30(20,27): "Lucerna <domini>"[105] "spiraculum". "Si oculus tuus fuerit simplex", id est si ratio tua tota dirigatur in unum, scilicet in Deum, "totum" etc. et "si nequam", id est applicatur ad terrena, "totum corpus" etc., et potest hoc intelligi dupliciter. Erit enim lucidum vel tenebrosum quantum ad praesentia opera, "lucidum" si omnia exteriora membra propter

---

97. distractio] destructio
99. oculus] *correxi sec.* Mt, e *txt.*
101. actibus] agent sicut in tenebris *add. et sign.* va- -cat
104. Inducere] induere
98. oculi] occulti
100. /secundum ... videndum] *mg.*
102. in te est] intus
103. si] scilicet
105. domini] quam

Deum operantur, et hoc fit ratio dirigatur /58ra/ in Deum quia tunc membra pura conservantur a peccato cum peccatum non procedat nisi ex consensu mentis. "Tenebrosum autem". Si ratio fuit occupata terrenis quia tunc membra occupabuntur operibus tenebrosis, Rom. 13(12): "Abiciamus opera tenebrarum."

Vel aliter secundum Hilarium: Si oculus, id est si ratio simpliciter dirigatur in Deum, "totum corpus tuum lucidum" quia ex claritate animae redundat claritas ad corpus. Ita (dicitur Mt. 13, 43): "fulgebunt iusti." "Si autem nequam" etc. Aliter secundum Augustinum[cvii] per oculum intelligitur intentio. Sicut enim homo primo respicit distantia ad terminum, postea procedit. Ita in operando primo determinat finem et ex fine intentio procedit ad operandum, ergo oculus dirigit, Prov. ultimo (31,18): "Non extinguetur in nocte lucerna". Unde si intentio fuerit pura et opus sive congeries operum ex illa intentione procedens erit purum et hoc intelligendum est de his quae secundum se bona quia sicut dicitur Rom. (3, 8), "damnatio iusta est" illorum qui dixerant: "Faciamus mala" etc. Si autem intentio fuerit perversa, tota operatio redditur tenebrosa, nec debet videri extraneum si per opera corpus significatur quia sicut dicitur Col. 3(5), "mortificate membra vestra" etc. Tertio [Chromatius][cviii] ponit: Oculus[106] animae est fides quae /58rb/ dirigit totum opus. Psalmus (119,105): "Lucerna pedibus" simplex est quando non vacillat. Sed (Gal. 5, 6): "per dilectionem operatur". Si autem fides fuerit depravata, totum corpus, id est opus, est tenebrosum, Rom. 14(23): "Omne quod non est ex fide". Vel aliter: Oculus praelatus qui est visibilium secundum Reges (?) 32. (2 Sam. 21,17): "Dixerunt viri" etc., "ne extinguas lucernam Israel", etc. Eccles. 11 (10, 2): "secundum iudicem populi." Quod autem dicit: "Si ergo lumen", secundum primam expositionem syllogizat ex praecedentibus, sed secundum istas probat praecedens quasi: Tu dicis: si oculus tuus etc., probatio: "Si ergo lumen" de quo minus providetur "ipsae tenebrae" etc., si lumen rationis tenebra / et opus et quantum ad hoc non mutatur expositio sed ad alia sic quia sicut dicit[107] Augustinus[108] [cix] quilibet potest scire ex intentione qualis sit, sed quales effectus habeat opus non potest, unde lucerna est intentio, sed opus est tenebra, Eph. 5(13): "Omne quod manifestatur", opus autem non manifestatur. Vel aliter secundum Augustinum,[109] [cx] duplicia sunt opera lucis et tenebrae.

Rom. (13,12): Opera lucis sunt opera iustitiae. Si ergo opus iustitiae in te sit tenebrosum, id est fiat propter malam intentionem, "ipsae tenebrae", id est actiones malae "quantae erunt". Vel

---

106. Oculus] osculus
107. et ... dicit *mg.*
108. Augustinus] *corr.*
109. Augustinum] Chrysostomum

aliter: Si fides mala omnia alia mala quae per fidem dirigantur et similiter si praelatus malus, multo magis subditi.

"Nemo potest" (24). Supra dominus posuit unum documentum quod non (s.l.) debemus congregare thesauros in terra quia distrahitur ex hoc cor, nunc /57va/ ponit aliud quia scilicet facit alienum a Deo, et hoc est "nemo potest". Vel aliter potest continuari: Supra monuit quod non debemus thesauros congregare in terra, sed in caelo, posset autem aliquis dicere: Volo in caelo et in terra congregare, et ideo dominus hic ostendit esse impossibile dicens "nemo potest". Sed prima melior est et est Chrysostomi.[cxi] Potest autem haec littera legi dupliciter, primo ut hoc "nemo potest" intelligatur conclusivum vel illative, et tunc dominus secundum expositionem Chrysostomi[cxii] et Hieronymi[cxiii] procedit a communibus opinionibus ad propositum ostendendum. Alio modo potest intelligi legi ut dominus primo proponit quod intendit et postea procedat et hoc secundum Augustinum.[cxiv] Prosequamur autem utrumque. Secundum ergo primam expositionem duo facit, primo ponit communem hominum opinionem et consuetudinem, secundo rationem assignat ibi: "Aut enim unum" (24). Dicit ergo "nemo potest". Ratio autem huius apparet si accipiamus quid[110] sit proprie servus et quid dominus. Servi enim ratio consistit in hoc quod est alterius, scilicet domini. Unde finis eius est dominus. Impossibile autem est quod unum feratur in duo tamquam in ultimos fines. Si ergo hoc est esse servi ordinare actus suos in dominum tamquam in ultimum finem, impossibile est quod servat duobus dominis. Ies. 34 (28,20): "Angustatum est stratum" etc. Posset tamen servus /57vb/ habere duos, quorum unus sit sub alio sicut finis sub fine est, vel secundum Glossam: "Nemo potest duobus dominis servire" contrariis, quia si consentiunt, sunt unum.

Assignat rationem "aut unum odio habebit". Et sciendum quod duplex est dominium. Quidam enim dominantur hoc modo quod a subditis diliguntur et hoc est dominium regale, quidam dominantur ut timeantur, et hoc est tyrannorum. Si ergo servus servat[111] dominum amore et ita oportet quod odiat contrarium, si autem timore servus, tunc oporet quod "sustineas", id est toleres[112] "et alterum", et hoc est "aut unum" etc., de hoc dominio quod magis sit sustinendum quam diligendum habetur Proverb. 29(2): "Cum impii sumpserint" fingere etc., id est "sustinebit" patientur tollerando, "nemo ergo potest duobus", sed Deus et diabolus sunt contrarii quia ad contraria inclinant, ergo "non potestis" etc. "Mammona",[113] id est divitiis, persica lingua, secundum Hieronymum.[cxv]

110. quid] quod
111. servat] amat
112. toleres] tolleres
113. mammonae *ill.*

Sciendum tamen quod aliud est abundare divitiis et servire. Aliqui enim[114] abundant et tamen ad bonum ordinatum et isti non serviunt divitiis, aliqui habent et tamen ex eis fructum non capiunt nec corporalem nec spiritualem, et isti serviunt quia se affligunt ut divitias congregent. Ecl. 6(1): "Est et aliud malum" etc. In quacumque enim re homo constituit[115] /59ra/ ultimam[116] finem, illa res est Deus suus, Phil. 3(19), "quorum Deus venter est", vel per "mammonem" intelligitur diabolus qui praeest divitiis, non quod eas dare possit sed quia utitur eis ad decipiendum. Singulis enim viciis aliquis spiritus praeest. Unde spiritus avaritiae[117] dicitur per avaritiam homines allicit ad peccandum. Haec est una expositio huius. "Nemo potest" ut scilicet legatur illative et generaliter. Augustinus[cxvi] autem intelligit spiritualiter, scilicet de Deo et diabolo qui sunt contrarii, Cor. 6(2, 6,15): "Quae conventio Christi" et quod non potestis simul esse participes. Reges 18 (3 Reg. 18,21): "Usquequo claudicatis". "Aut unum", id est diabolum, "et alterum diliget", id est Deum.

Et nota quod non dixit e converso, sed dixit "aut unum sustinebit" quia quaelibet creatura naturaliter convertitur ad diligendum Deum. Sed diabolus quia habet naturam depravatam statim est in horrore cum nullus diligat malum et ideo dixit "aut unum sustinebit" quia diabolus sustinetur sicut tyrannus opprimens sicut aliquis sustineret dominum ancillae cui coniungitur non quia diligat dominum sed propter ancillam. Ita cupidus sustinet diabolum propter cupiditatem quae est ancilla diaboli. Unde quando aliquis vult frui quocumque peccato ad hoc quod eo fruatur patitur servitutem diaboli et hoc est "aut unum sustinebit" et inquantum[118] sustinet recedet a man- /59rb/ -datis Dei et recedendo contemnit et hoc est "et alterum contemnet". Sed obicitur hic de hoc quod dicitur quod Deus non habetur odio quia Psalmus (74,23) dicit: "Superbia eorum qui te oderunt" etc., ergo aliquis Deum habet odio. Propter istam auctoritatem Augustinus[cxvii] in libro Retractationum retractat quod prius dixerat quod Deus non habetur odio, sed tamen utrumque verum est quia si consideretur id quod est Deus, scilicet ipsa bonitas, non potest haberi odio quia bonum semper diligitur secundum se, potest autem haberi odio quantum ad effectum[119] qui est contrarius voluntati. Sic ergo patet quod non potest duobus dominis serviri. Eccli. (Sir) 2 (14): V(a)e peccatori terram ingredienti.

"Ideo dico vobis". (25) Postquam dominus ostenderat quod non debemus ponere finem in thesauris terrenis et superfluis,

---

114. enim] *mg.*, tamen
115. constituit] constituitur
116. ultimam] ultra
117. avaritiae] *corr.mg.*
118. inquantum] *mg.corr.*, inquimus
119. effectum] effectus

vult etiam ostendere quod in[120] necessariis acquirendis[121] et hoc est "ideo dico vobis", et circa hoc duo facit, primo prohibet sollicitudinem necessariorum quantum ad (necessaria exp.) praesentia, secundo quantum ad futura ibi: "nolite" (31). Circa primum duo facit, primo proponit quod intendit, secundo probat propositum ibi: "Nonne anima" (25). Dicit ergo "ideo dico vobis" quasi quia non potestis Deo servire et mammone, ideo nullus debet servire divitiis (mg.)[122] ad hoc quod Deo serviatis.

"Neque animae". Sed videtur quod anima non indiget cibo. Sed dicendum quod quamvis non indigeat secundum se, tamen indiget inquantum coniuncta corpori quia aliter ibi esse non posset /59va/ vel vocetur ibi anima absque vita, Ioh. 12(25): "Qui amat animam".

"Neque corpori vestro" (25). Nota quod ex hoc verbo sumpserunt exordium haereses. Secundum Augustinum[cxviii] (est exl.) enim fuerunt quidam dicentes non licere homini contemplativo operari, et contra istos fecit Augustinus[cxix] librum *De opere monachorum*. Sed qualiter sit intelligendum hoc quod dominus dicit debemus investigare a sanctis. Dicitur autem Cor. (2 Thess 3,10): "Qui non vult operari non manducet", et intelliget de opere manuum sicut patet per ea quae praemittit. Unde etiam in exemplum ipse Apostolus operatus est manibus.

Sed numquid omnes tenentur? Si omnes, aut est praeceptum aut consilium. Si praeceptum, nullus debet praemittere, si consilium: Cui dabatur hoc consilium? Constat quod plebi illi quia tunc non erant religiosi. Ad consilium autem nullus tenetur nisi ex voto, ergo possent omnes desistere (mg.corr destruere). Dicendum quod hoc est praeceptum et ad hoc omnes tenentur quia omnibus datur. Apostolus enim toti ecclesiae loquitur. Sed est aliquid praeceptum dupliciter, per se ipsum et propter aliud. Verbi gratia: Si accepistis crucem ad eundum ultra mare, praeceptum est quod vadat et praeceptum per se ipsum, sed quod quaeras navem hoc non propter se sed propter aliud est praeceptum quia quicumque tenetur ad aliquem finem et ad omnia quae sunt ad finem tenetur. Quilibet autem tenetur ad conservationem vitae /59vb/ suae lege naturae, et ideo tenentur ad omnia alia quibus vita conservatur. Si ergo aliquis habeat unde vivere possit, non tenetur laborare manibus et ideo Apostolus non dicit[123] "manibus", sed "qui non vult operari" etc. quasi: Eo modo tenemini laborare quo manducare. Qui autem teneantur laborare manibus, hoc ad praesens dimittatur. Quod autem dicit "solliciti" sciendum quod sollicitudo

---

120. in] *add. et exp.*, terrenis
121. acquirendis] appetendis *exl.*
122. *delevi* duobus.
123. dicit] *add. et exp.*, mandamus

pertinet ad providentiam, sed non quaelibet providentia est sollicitudo, sed 'sollicitudo' proprie nominat providentiam cum studio quod est vehemens applicatio animi. Unde hic importat sollicitudo vehementem animi applicationem. In ista autem vehementi applicatione quattuor modis potest esse peccatum. Primo quando est ad temporalia sicut ad ultimum finem, et secundum hoc[124] reprehenditur Prov. 11 (7): "Expectatio sollicita ducet in perditionem". Secundo quando superflue intendit ad temporalia conquirenda, et sic accipitur Ecl. 2(26): "Peccatori[125] autem dedit" Deus etc. et post "et hoc vanitas[126] et cassa sollicitudo". Tertio quando animus nimis se occupabit circa cogitationem temporalium. Unde Hieronymus:[cxx] "Sollicitudo vitanda est, sed labor exercendus" et sic accipitur 1. Cor. 7(33): "Qui coniunctus est uxori sollicitus est" quia cor /60ra/ distrahitur ad diversa. Quarto quando sollicitudo est cum quodam timore et desperatione. Videtur enim quibusdam quod numquam tantum acquirere possunt quod possit eis sufficere et omnia ista hic prohibentur sicut patet per sequentia. Et sic isto ultimo modo accipitur Reg. 9 (1 Sam. 9,20): "Ne sis sollicitus" quaerere asinos, id est ne desperes de inventione.

"Nonne anima". (25) Supra docuit dominus ut non essemus solliciti de necessariis, hic inducit huius admonitionis rationem et ponit tres rationes. Prima sumitur a maiori, secunda a minori, tertia ex opposito. Secundum ibi: "Respicite volatilia" (26). Tertium ibi: "Nolite" (31). Prima talis: qui dedit maiora dabit minora. Sed dominus dedit animam et corpus, ergo dabit cibum. Et hoc est "nonne anima", id est vita, non enim vivimus ut manducemus sed econverso. Esca enim ordinatur ad vitam et ideo simpliciter vita melior est sicut finis melior est his quae sunt ad finem, et similiter vestimentum propter corpus et non e converso. Quod autem Deus dederit animam et corpus habetur quando primo « formavit Deus » materiam ad corpus (Gen. 2,7), inspiravit materiam ad animam. Sed qui dedit conservabit dando ea quae necessaria sunt. Sap. 5 (1,14): "Creavit Deus ut essent". Hilarius[cxxi] hoc exponit aliter quia enim sollicitudo importat quamdam dubitatem[127] dominus vult /60rb/ removere dubietatem futurae resurrexionis animi. "ne solliciti" (25), id est non velitis discredere de resurrexione quia ille qui reformabit corpus in resurrexione conservabit absque indumento et cibo. Sed hoc non est litteralis.

Consequenter ponitur secunda ratio a minori et est talis: Ille qui providit minoribus de quibus minus videtur, et maioribus providebit. Sed Deus providet plantis et avibus etc. et circa hanc duo

---

124. hoc] *add. et exp.*, impeditur (?) 126. vanitas] nam est
125. peccatori] peccatum 127. dubitatem] *corr.*, dubitationem

facit. Primo deducit rationem quantum ad cibum, secundo quantum ad vestitum ibi: "Et de vestimento" (28). Circa primum duo facit, primo docet abicere sollicitudinem exemplo animalium, secundo propter inefficaciam ejus[128] ibi: "Quis autem vestrum" (27).

Circa primum quattuor facit, primo inducit ad considerandum bruta animalia, secundo ponit defectum consequentem ea, tertio divinam providentiam, quarto ex hoc argumentatur. Ergo "respicite" (26), id est considerate Iob 12(7): "Interroga iumenta". Ex consideratione enim istorum homo aliqando addiscit. Prov. 5 (6,6): "Vade ad formicam". "Quoniam non serunt". (26)

Cibus cottidianus panis est. Ad eius acquisitionem triplici opere pervenitur, per seminationem, per metitionem et per reconditionem. Unde haec tria excludit ab avibus. "Non serunt" etc. Est autem seminatio etiam spiritualis doctrinae (ita licet excludit exl.) infra 13(3): "Exiit qui seminat" bonorum operum, Prov. 11(18): "Seminanti" elementarum.[129] Cor. 9(2, 9,6): "Qui parce seminat, parce" etc. Est et mala seminatio carnalium peccatorum. Gal. ultimo (6,8): "Qui seminat in carne" spiritualium /60va/ peccatorum, Iob 5(4,8): "Quin immo vidi eos qui seminant". Metuunt autem sancti praedicatores quando rapiunt aliquos ad fidem, Ioh. 4(38): "Ego misi vos metere".

Consequenter ponitur[130] auxilium divinae providentiae, "et pater" dicit, "vester". Non[131] illorum quia proprie Deus pater est creaturae rationalis quae ad imaginem eius est, Gen. 1(25). Dicit: "etiam "caelestis" quia nos habemus aliquid ad caelum attinens, scilicet animam quae pertinet ad similitudinem substantiarum. Unde pater noster pascit illa quorum est Deus tantum, multo magis nos quorum est pater. Psalmus (147,9): Qui "dat iumentis".

Consequenter argumentatur: "Nonne plus", id est maioris valoris ordinatione, scilicet Gen. 1(26), "ut praesit piscibus". Aliquando enim plus venditur equus quam homo quia duplex est aestimatio rerum. Quantum ad ordinem naturae et sic homo melior omnium rerum, vel quantum ad aestimationem sive delectationem, et sic aliquando animal plus venditur.

Circa istam litteram considerandum quod[132] quidam, et credo quod Origenes, exponit aliter et dicunt quod per "volatilia" intelliguntur sancti angeli qui non exercent labores carnales et tamen Deus pascit eos cibo spirituali de quo Psalmus (78,25): Panem angelorum. Sed sicut dicit Hieronymus,[cxxii] hoc non potest stare quia Deus subiungit "nonne[133] plus". Hilarius[cxxiii] autem per vola-

---

128. ejus] eorum
129. elementarum]? *forte lege* clementia (Prov. 11,19)
130. *alterum* divinum *delevi*
131. non] *exl.* verborum
132. quod *s.l.*
133. nonne] deus *add. et exp.*

tilia intelligit daemones itaque aves caeli qui pascuntur inquantum conservantur /60vb/ in esse naturae et homines sunt pluris illis quia dominus argumentatur quia si illi qui sunt praedestinati ad mortem sustentantur a Deo multo magis nos. Sed secundum Augustinum[cxxiv] ista quae dominus dicit non allegorice accipienda quia dominus vult trahere argumentum ab istis sensibilibus ad propositum ostendendum.

Sed sciendum quod hic fuit error quorundam dicentium non licere spiritualibus viris laborare corporaliter propter similitudinem avium, contra quos Augustinus[cxxv] in libro *De operibus monachorum* dicit quod impossibile est quod homines in omnibus vitam imitari. Unde aliqui perfecti qui iverunt in desertum et raro ibant ad civitatem unde oportebat eos multum congregare de victualibus, apostoli autem secundum Augustinum operati sunt manibus, unde non[134] laborare non pertinet ad perfectionem et ponit exemplum Augustinus quia Deus sperantes in se in tribulatione liberat sicut patet de Daniele et pueris in fornace. Numquid ergo constitutus in tribulationibus nihil debet agere ad hoc quod liberetur? Immo quod dominus dixit[135] "si vos persecuti fuerint in una civitate, fugite in aliam" et ideo dicendum quod dominus vult quod in omnibus homo faciat quod in se est et sperando in Deum. Deus dabit ei quae viderit expedire /61ra/ quod autem aliter faceret temptator esset et stultus. Habet igitur Deus providentiam de factis hominum, ita tamen quod unicuique providet secundum modum suum quia aliter hominibus et avibus quia avibus non dedit rationem qua[136] procuret sibi necessaria, sed totum ei inditum est a natura, homini vero[137] dedit rationem qua sibi necessaria procuraret. Unde omnia dedit homini dando rationem qua sibi necessaria procuraret. Unde omnia dedit homini dando rationem et ideo si fecerimus quod in nobis est et ipse faciet quod in se est.

"Quis vestrum" (27) trahit argumentum ex experimento. Manifestum est enim quod sicut Deus animalibus providet in operibus naturae ita hominibus. In homine enim est quaedam pars quae subiacet rationi sicut pars in motiva et appetitiva, quaedam quae non, sicut nutritiva et augmentativa. Sed homo secundum[138] ea quae subiacent rationi differt a brutis et ideo aliter providetur ei quia sibi per rationem, aliis per naturam. Sed quantum ad ea in quibus cum brutis communicat aequaliter providetur omnibus. Omnia enim augentur per opus naturae et quia augmentum[139] corporis est ex divina providentia non debemus prae mi-

---

134. non *s.l.*
135. dixit] *add. et exp.* quod
136. qua] *corr.*
137. vero] non
138. secundum *s.l.*
139. augmentum] argumentum

nima sollicitudine temporalium opera spiritualia dimittere. Sap. 13 (6,8): "Pusillum et magnum" et hoc est: "Quis autem vestrum". Hilarius[cxxvi] exponit de statu futurae resurrexionis et dicit /61rb/ quod in resurrexione omnes erunt aequales in quantitate et ideo aliquibus addetur de quantitate et hoc est "quis autem vestrum". Sed hoc improbat Augustinus[cxxvii] in libro *De civitate Dei*, et credo quod melius dicit. Dicitur enim Phil 3(21): quod "reformabit corpus""[humilitatis] nostrae configuratum corpori claritatis", ergo ea quae in Christo resurgente apparuerunt et manifestata sunt discipulis,[140] haec debemus sperare in nobis. Sed Christus in eadem quantitate resurrexit in qua prius fuit, ergo nihil ei accrevit vel item alicui subtrahitur quia dominus dicit capillus de capite nostro non peribit. Unde dicendum quod in resurrexione[141] omnes conformabuntur Christo[142] quantum ad aetatem et unusquisque resurget in quantitate in qua habiturus fuisset in illa aetate. Quod autem est de defectu naturae sicut in nanis, tolletur. Unde resurgent in tali quantitate in quali pervenissent[143] si natura non defecisset usque ad talem aetatem, scilicet Christi.

"Et de vestimento" (28). Hic deducit rationem quantum ad vestimentum, et primo ponit quod intendit, secundo inducit similitudinem, tertio ex illis argumentatur. Secundum ibi: "Considerate" (28), tertium ibi: "Si enim faenum" (30). Convenienter post sollicitudinem cibi et potus de sollicitudine[144] vestimenti agitur quia sicut cibus et potus pervenirent ad necessitatem vitae ita et vestimentum, Tim. ultimo (1 Tim 6,8): "Habentes vestimentum". Et Iacob dixit Gen. 18(28,20): Si fuerit mecum dominus. "Considerate" (28). Inducit exemplum et proponit duo, comparationem /61va/ et auxilium divinae promissionis ibi: "Dico autem" (29). Dicit "considerate". Consideratio autem divinorum operum valet ad hoc quod animus prorumpit in laudem creatoris: "Meditabor in omnibus" (Ps 77,13), "quomodo crescunt" (28), Cor. 3(6): "Deus" enim "incrementum". "Non laborant" (28). Ad vestimentum necessarium est opus viri et mulieris et hoc est "non laborant neque nent" vel "non laborant" ad colorandum "neque nent" ad praeparandum, unde nec propter colorem nec propter substantiam vestimenti laborant.

"Dico autem" (29). Hic ponitur beneficium divinae promissionis. Ita enim providet quod totum studium humanum non posset ei adaequari quia quae fiunt secundum artem non possunt adaequari eis quae fiunt secundum naturam et hoc est quod "nec Salomon" (29) qui gloriosior omnibus regibus notis a Iudaeis,

---

140. discipulis] *mg.*, diabolis *exl.*
141. resurrexione *corr.*
142. Christo] *mg.*, primo
143. pervenissent] pervenisset
144. sollicitudine] similitudine

Par. 1 (2,1,1), et dicit "in omni" quia nec per unum diem habere potuit vestimentum sicut habent flores et hoc est expositio Chrysostomi[cxxviii] et litteralis. Aliter "nec Salomon" etc. quia ista corporalia habent vestimentum sine sollicitudine quod non Salomon. Hilarius:[cxxix] Anagogice per lilium sancti angeli. Canticum (2,16): "Dilectus meus mihi et ego", et vult dominus amovere sollicitudinem de resurrexione de vestimentis in resurrexione. Sicut enim angeli induuntur claritate[145] ita et corpora nostra induentur. "Si enim faenum". Hic ex exemplo argumentatur. Supra dominus fecerat /61vb/ mentionem de liliis, hic commutat in faenum quia intendit argumentari a minori. Unde ponit defectum ex una parte ut ostendit praeeminentiam, ex alia unde ostendit praeeminentiam quantum ad dignitatem substantiae quia nos homines, flos faenum: Ies. 11 (40,7): "Exsiccatum est". Durationem quia nos perpetui quantum ad animam, flos quasi momentaneum "quia "hodie est" etc. Et ponit futurum indeterminatum pro determinato sicut Gen. 20 (30,33): "Respondebit mihi cras." Psalmus (129,6): "Fiant sicut faenum tectorum". Finem quia homo factus est propter beatitudinem, huiusmodi autem ut in hominis usum veniant. Psalmus (147,8): "Qui producit in montibus[146] faenum". Vel ideo dixit supra "lilia" et postea "faenum" quia flores[147] ad herbas sicut vestimenta ad homines. Est enim usus vestimentorum, scilicet ad protegendum et ornandum, et si Deus minoribus providet ad ornatum, multo magis maioribus ad necessitatem, et hoc est "si faenum" etc. "Modicae fidei,"" qui nec minora a Deo sperata, infra 14 (31): "modicae fidei". quare [dubitasti]?" Hilarius[cxxx] autem non continuat cum praecedenti, sed sicut per 'lilia' sancti angeli, ita per 'faenum' infideles intelligantur, Ies. 40(7): "Vere faenum est populus" quia si Deus providet infidelibus praescitis ad poenam quanto magis nobis praescitis ad vitam aeternam.

"Nolite ergo" (31). Hic argumentatur /62ra/ et circa hoc duo facit, primo infert unam conclusionem, secundo ad eandem conclusionem inducit aliam ibi: "Haec enim omnia" (32). Seorsum determinat de sollicitudine cibi et potus et de vestimentis, hic concludit de utroque. "Unde « Nolite." (34) Et recitanda sunt ea quae supra dicta sunt quia sollicitudo temporalium prohibetur quantum ad quattuor, ut scilicet non ponamus in eis finem, ut non superflue quaeramus, ut non nimis occupemus mentem in eis, ut non desperemus de providentia Dei. Hic ponuntur quaedam alia et ponit unum alium sensum. Unde dicit "Nolite ergo" etc., id est quando vivitis in aliqua societate nunc sitis solliciti

---

145. claritate] claritatem
146. montibus] mentibus
147. flores] fluunt

habere aliquid speciale in cibis, potibus et vestimentorum. Eccles. (Sir) 32(1): "Esto in eis quasi unus". "Haec enim omnia" (32), quasi non debent facere infideles, unde infideles vituperantur,[148] sed gentiles de hoc vituperantur, ergo etc. Et primo ponit errorem infidelium, secundo improbat, tertio ostendit quid sit faciendum fidelibus. Secundum ibi: "Scit" (32), tertio ibi "quaerite ergo" (33). Dicit ergo ita:[149] Dico quod vos non debetis circa hoc esse solliciti quia non debetis "conformari huic saeculo", Rom. 12(2).

"Haec enim omnia inquirunt" (32) et hoc propter duo secundum quod inquirere dupliciter potest sumi quia potest importare in principio rationem finis et sic gentes non credunt aeterna qui ista inquirunt /62rb/ ut finem, vel si non quaerunt ut finem ultimum, tamen quaerunt tota sollicitudine quia non credunt divinam providentiam et per consequens nec Deum, Eph. 5 (1 Thess 4,5): "Sicut et gentes quae ignorant".

Consequenter asserat providentiam divinam, et sciendum quod providentia duo praesupponit, cognitionem et voluntatem, et ideo utrumque ostendit.[150] Nihil est enim aliud providentia nisi ordinatio aliquorum in finem, scilicet praefixo fine eligere vias per quas perveniatur in finem. Unde primo oportet quod cognoscat et velit finem, secundo quod cognoscat ordinem in proportionem eorum quae sunt ad finem sicut aedificator cognoscit ordinem lapidum ponendorum in domo. Unde oportet ad hoc quod Deus, ad hoc quod habeat providentiam de rebus humanis, requiritur quod sciat et cognoscat ea et quod velit dirigere in finem et ideo dicit "scit enim", Eccles. (Sir) 23(29): "Domino Deo nostro" etc. Hebraeos 4(13): "Omnia nuda". "Pater ergo" vult administrare. Sap. 11(14,3): "Tua autem pater gubernat". Non enim esset pater nisi esset provisor, infra: "Si vos cum sitis mali" (7,11). "Quaerite ergo". Tria hic ponit, regnum tamquam finem quia in regno Dei intelligitur beatitudo aeterna. Tunc enim proprie aliquid regitur quando subditur regulae gubernantis. Sed in vita ista non subduntur totaliter Deo quia non sumus sine peccatis et haec erunt in gloria ubi perfecte faciemus voluntatem /62va/ divinam: Lucas 9 (14,15): "Beatus qui manducabit". Secundo viam rectam. In regnum enim itur per iustitiam. Unde si vis ire ad regnum Dei oportet quod serves iustitiam regni. Et dicit "iustitiam" non simpliciter, sed "eius" quia duplex est iustitia, hominis qua suis viribus praesumit posse Dei mandata implere, et "Dei" quae per auxilium gratiae credit homo se posse salvari. Rom . 10(3): "Ignorantes Dei iustitiam". Tertium est quod ponit "et haec omnia adicientur". Liberalis venditor possessorum

---

148. vituperantur] vitaperantur
149. ita] *corr.* ibi
150. ostendit *mg.*

aliquid dat et adicit, nos convenimus cum Deo « ex denario diurno », infra (Rom exp.) 20"qui est vita aeterna". Unde quicquid superaddit totum est quaedam adiectio et non computatio et hic[151] est "et haec omnia adicientur". Non dicit 'dabuntur', Prov. 10(3): "Non affliget".[152] Prov. 3 (30,8): "tantum victui meo".

Et nota quod 'quaerere primo' intelligitur dupliciter, sicut finem aut mercedem et sic dicit: "Quaerite primum regnum Dei" et non temporalia. Non enim debemus evangelizare ut manducemus, sed e converso. Si[153] non primo quaeras regnum Dei pervertis[154] ordinem.

Et sciendum quod dominus idem docet in oratione sua ubi[155] ponuntur septem petitiones quia primo debemus quaerere ipsum bonum Dei, scilicet gloriam eius. In aliis autem primo regnum Dei, secundo iustitiam, tertio "fiat voluntas tua", [quarto][156] quae sunt adicienda, "Panem nostrum" etc.

Sed contra hoc, « et "haec omnia adicientur", (33) obicit Augustinus[cxxxi] quia Apostolus dicit "in fame et siti", Cor. 4(11), /62vb/ et 2. Cor 11, 26(27), et respondet quod Deus sicut medicus sapiens scit[157] quod expediat. Unde sicut medicus aliquando subtrahit cibum propter salutem corporis, ita Deus propter salutem animae subtrahit temporalia quia propter bonum nostrum,[158] ut scilicet puniantur peccata praeterita et caveamus[159] de futuris vel propter bonum aliorum ut videndo patientiam proficiant in bonum.

"Nolite" (34). Hic prohibet sollicitudinem futurorum, et primo ponit suam[160] admonitionem, secundo exponit ibi: "Crastinus". Dicit ergo: "nolite solliciti".

Et nota quod et non[161] intendit dominus prohibere quod homo non sit aliquid[162] sollicitus quid comedere debeat in crastinum. Non enim docet servare maiorem perfectionem quam ipsi apostoli servaverunt, sed ipse habebat loculos ut dicitur Ioh. de Iuda qui portabat pecuniam domini. Unde non docuit quod non fecit qui coepit facere et docere, et iterum apostoli congregaverunt victualia sicut dicitur Acta 11(28-30). Unde hic ponuntur quattuor expositiones quarum ultima est magis litteralis. Prima Augustini[cxxxii] qui sic dicit: "Nolite solliciti in crastinum", id est de temporalibus. Crastinus enim ponitur pro futuro in scriptura, temporalia autem variantur per heri et cras, Cor. 4 (2, 4,18), "non contemplantibus

---

151. hic] *s.l.*, non *exp.*
152. adfliget in *Biblia S. Vulgatæ Ed., Sixti V Pont. Max. Jussu*
153. Si] similiter ?
154. pervertis *mg.corr.*
155. ubi] nisi
156. cf. *In Oratione Dominica*, art. 7
157. scit] *mg.corr.* fit
158. nostrum] suum. *cf. De serm. Dom. II, xvii, 58 (PL 34, 1296):* „... *quando detrahat, sicut **nobis** judicat expedire" et infra ",... vel propter bonum **aliorum**».*
159. caveant] caveamus
160. suam *mg.*
161. non] ideo ?
162. aliquid] quid

(cogitantibus txt.) nobis", sed ista temporalia quae pertinent ad tempus habent suam sollicitudinem /63ra/ annexam et ideo dicit "crastinus enim".[163] "Sufficit diei", id est praesenti vitae, "malitia", id est necessitas qua cogimur ad providendum de temporalibus et dicitur 'malitia' quia ex culpa primi parentis derivata est. Chrysostomus:[cxxxiii] Quae congregantur semper congregantur ut sufficiant ad multum tempus. Unde "nolite sollicitati" id est ad congregandum superflua. "Crastinus enim", id est superfluitas rerum temporalium invenit sibi sollicitudinem quia homines sunt solliciti quomodo[164] eripiant tibi istas divitias. "Sufficit diei", id est sufficit ut accipias necessaria. Hilarius:[cxxxiv] In qualibet actione duo sunt consideranda, scilicet ipsa actio et eventus actionis. Quod enim homo seminet hoc est actio quaedam, sed quid invenire debeat, hoc eventus quidam est. Vult ergo dominus quod de his quae non sunt in nobis non debeamus solliciti esse et hoc est magis litteralis et subtilior. Quarta etiam est Hieronymi et plana: "Nolite solliciti" non est intelligendum de tempore futuro, sed vult quod sollicitudo quae debet incumbere in futurum non sit in praesenti. Tempore enim messis quaerendi sunt messores et non tempore vindemiarum et e converso, et hoc consona litterae. "Crastinus", id est futurum tempus, habebit suam sollicitudinem. "Sufficit diei malitia", id est poena afflictio, sic Eccles. (Sir) 11(29): "Ma- /63rb/ -litia unius".

---

163. enim] id est superfluitas rerum temporalium *add et sign.* va- -cat   **164.** quomodo] *mg.*, quando

ENDNOTES

[i] *Contra Faustum Manichaeum* iv, 2 (PL 42, 217).
[ii] cf. I II, q. 108, a. 3 ad 4um.
[iii] *In Matth*, hom. 19, 1. (PG 57, 273).
[iv] Ep. 22, c.. 2, n. 8 (ML 33, 93); cf. II II, q. 132, a. 3 obj. 3.
[v] *Opus imperf.*, hom. 13, ibid. (PG 56, 704).
[vi] ibid.
[vii] *Homiliarum in Evangelia Libri Duo*, lib. 1, hom. 11, n. 1 (PL 76, 1115 B).
[viii] Augustinus, *De serm. Dom.* II, 1, 3 (PL 34, 1271).
[ix] *Opus imperf.* hom. 13 (PG 56, 706).
[x] *Opus imperf.* hom. 15, Hom. 15 (PG 56, 715).
[xi] Suppl., q. 15, a. 3.
[xii] Pseudo-Hieronymus, *Catena Aurea super Marcum*, ix, lect. 3.
[xiii] II II, q. 85, a. 3 ad 2um.
[xiv] Damascenus, De Fide Orthodoxa, iii, 24 (PG 94, 1090 D); cf. III, q. 21, a. 1, Obj. 3
[xv] *Opus imperf.*, hom. 13.PG 56, 707.
[xvi] Isidorus, *Etymologiarum* x ad litt. H (ML 82, 379); II II, q. 111, a. 2 sc.
[xvii] *Moralia*, xxxi, 13, 5 (PL 75, 586 C-D).
[xviii] *Opus imperf.*, hom. 13.(PG 56, 707).
[xix] *De serm. Dom.*, II, 6 (PL 34, 1272).
[xx] ibid.
[xxi] *Glossa Ordinaria*.
[xxii] *De serm. Dom.*, II, 8 (PL 34, 1273).
[xxiii] *Opus imperf.*, hom. 19, 2 (PG 57, 275).
[xxiv] *Glossa Ordinaria*.
[xxv] *Opus imperf.*, hom. 19, 1 (PG 57, 273).
[xxvi] *Glossa Interlinearis*.
[xxvii] *De serm. Dom.* II, 2, 9 (PL 34, 1274).
[xxviii] *Catena Aurea super Matthaeum*, 6, lect. 2; *Op. imp. in Matth.*, Hom. xiii (PG 56, 708).
[xxix] *Catena Aurea super Matthaeum*, 6, lect. 3; *Op. imp. in Matth.*, Hom. xv (PG 56, 715).
[xxx] Augustinus, *De serm. Dom.* II, 3, 11 (PL 34, 1274).
[xxxi] *Opus imperf.*, hom. 13, (PG 56,708 s.).
[xxxii] Chrysostomus, *In Matth.*, hom. XIX, 3 (PG 57, 276).
[xxxiii] *Glossa Ordinaria*.
[xxxiv] *Op. imp. in Matth.*, hom. XIV (PG 57, 710).
[xxxv] *In Matth.*, hom. XIX, 3 (PG 57, 276).
[xxxvi] *Opus imperf.*, hom. 13, (PG 56, 709).

xxxvii ibid, 709.
xxxviii ibid. 709.
xxxix Hieronymus, *Comm. in Matth.*, I (PL 26, 42 B).
xl Pseudo-Chrysostom, *Op. imp. in Matth.*, Hom. xiv (PG 56, 709).
xli *In Matth.*, hom. XIX, 3 (PG 57, 276).
xlii Cyprianus, *De oratione Dominica*, iv (PL 4, 521 C).
xliii Augustinus, *De serm. Dom.* II, 3, 11 (PL 34, 1274).
xliv Hieronymus, *Comm. in Matth.*, I (PL 26, 42B).
xlv Pseudo-Chrysostomus, *Op. imp. in Matth.*, Hom. xiv (PG 56, 709).
xlvi *Glossa Ordinaria* (PL 114, 875D).
xlvii Pseudo-Chrysostom, *Op. imp. in Matth.*, Hom. xiv (PG 56, 710).
xlviii ibid.
xlix ibid.
l August., *Conf.* X, cap. 33, n. 50 (PL 32, 800).
li II II, q. 83, a. 12.
lii Augustinus, *ad Probam.* Ep. 130, ix, 18 (PL 33, 501).
liii *De serm. Dom.* II, 1, 11 (PL 34, 1274).
liv *De oratione Dom.*, iv (PL 4, 539 C).
lv ibid.
lvi *Ad Probam, de orando Deum*, Ep. 130, x, 20 (PL 33, 502).
lvii Damascenus, *De Fide Orth.* iii, 24 (PG 94, 1089 C).
lviii *Ad Probam*, Ep. 130, x, 20 (PL 33, 501).
lix ibid. (PL 33, 502).
lx *Glossa Ordinaria*.
lxi *Qu. Disp. de Veritate*, q. 18, a. 4, arg. 14.
lxii ibid.
lxiii *De Civitate Dei*, bk. 8, xxi (PL 41, 245).
lxiv Gregorius, *Moralia* xxxiii, 23 (in Job 41, 3) (PL 76, 701); *Catena Aurea* vi, lect. 3.
lxv *Comm. in Matth.*, I (PL 26, 42 C).
lxvi *De serm. Dom.* II, 3, 12 (PL 34, 1274-1275).
lxvii *De serm. Dom.* II, 3, 14 (PL 34, 1275).
lxviii *In Matth.*, hom. 19, 5 (PL 57, 278).
lxix *In Matth.*, hom. 19, 4 (PL 57, 277).
lxx ibid.
lxxi *Opus imperf.*, hom. 15 (PG 56, 715).
lxxii Damascenus, *De Fide Orth.* iii, 24 (PG 94, 1089 C).
lxxiii *Op. imp. in Matth.*, hom. xv (PG 56, 716-717).
lxxiv ibid. (PG 56, 716 s.).
lxxv *Comm. in Matth.*, I (PL 26, 44 A).
lxxvi Hieronymus, *Comm. in Matth.*, I (PL 26, 44 A).

lxxvii Augustinus, *De serm. Dom.* II, xii, 41 (PL 34, 1287).
lxxviii *Glossa Ordinaria* (ML 114, 103C).
lxxix *Op. imp. in Matth.*, hom. xv (PG 56, 718).
lxxx Augustinus, *De serm. Dom.* II, xii, 42 (PL 34, 1288).
lxxxi *Opus imperf.* Hom. 15 (PG 56, 718).
lxxxii Hieronymus, *Comm. in Matth.*, I (PL 26, 44 B).
lxxxiii *Comm. in Matth.*, I (PL 26, 44 B).
lxxxiv *Opus imperf.*, hom. xv (PG 56, 718).
lxxxv ibid.
lxxxvi cf. II II q. 188, a. 2: "secundum illud Matth. XXV: ‚quod uni ex minimis meis fecistis, mihi fecistis.'"
lxxxvii *De serm. Dom.* II, xii, 42 (PL 34, 1288).
lxxxviii cf. *Glossa Interlinearis in II Cor. 4, 16* : « Anima munita spe futuri, cui non accedit humanus furor (*Glossa Interlinearis, Bibliorum Sacrorum cum Glossa Ordinaria* (1603), pg. 388D)» et *Glossa Ordinaria*: «*Renovatur de diem* id est, assidue purior efficitur per ignem tribulationis » (ibid.). cf. Petrus Lombardus, *Collectanea in Epist. D. Pauli* (PL 192, 34D); Ambrosius, *In Epistolam Beati Pauli Ad Corinthios Secundam* (PL 17, 309 A-B).
lxxxix cf. Super II ad Cor., cp. 4, lc. 5.
xc ibid. (PG 56,717).
xci ibid (PG 56, 718).
xcii Glossa Interlinearis, *Bibliorum Sacrorum cum Glossa Ordinaria* (1603), p. 135A.
xciii Glossa Ordinaria (*Catena Aurea on St. Matthew*, ch. 6, lec. 13); ‚Eph. 3, 17' *ex* III, q. 62, a. 5.
xciv Chrysostomus, *In Matth*, hom. xx, 2 (PG 57, 288-289).
xcv ibid. (PG 56, 718-719).
xcvi ibid. (PG 56, 733).
xcvii *Catena Aurea in Matthaeum*, chap. 6, lect. 14; Augustinus, *De serm. Dom.* II, xiii, 44 (PL 34, 1288-1289).
xcviii *In Matth*, hom. xx, 2 (PG 57, 288-289).
xcix Verba haec sic citantur ab Augustino (*De serm. Dom.* II, xliv, (PL 34, 1288)) et Cypriano (*Testimoniorum Libri Tres Adversus Judaeos*, lib. 3 (PL 4, 730 B)).
c *Opus imperf.*, hom. 15 (PG 56, 719).
ci ibid.
cii *De serm. Dom.* II, xiii, 44 (PL 44, 1289).
ciii *Opus imperf.*, hom. 15, (PG 56, 720).
civ *Comm. in Matth.*, I (PL 26, 44 C).
cv *Opus imperf.*, hom. 15, (PG 56, 720).
cvi *In Evangelium Matthaei Commentarius*, v, 4 (PL 9, 944A).
cvii *De serm. Dom.* II, xiii, 45 (PL 34, 1289).

cviii *In Evangelium Sancti Matthaei*, tract. xvii PL 20, 366C; cf. *Glossa Interlinearis, Bibliorum Sacrorum cum Glossa Ordinaria* (1603), p. 137.

cix *De serm. Dom.* II, xiii, 46 (PL 34, 1289-1290).

cx *Contra Mendacium Ad Consentium* vii, 18 (PL 40, 528-529).

cxi *In Matth*, Hom. xxi, 1 PG 57, 295.

cxii *Op. imp. in Matt.*, hom. xvi (PG 56, 722).

cxiii *Comm. in Matth.*, I (PL 26, 45 A).

cxiv *De serm. Dom.* II, xiii-xiv, 46-47 (PL 34, 1290).

cxv *Comm. in Matth.*, I (PL 26, 44 D): "sermone Syriaco" cf. Johannes Chrysostomus, *Opus imperf.*, Hom. 16 (PG 56, 722).

cxvi *De serm. Dom.* II, xiv, 47 (PL 34, 1290).

cxvii *Retractationum* I, xix, 8 PL 32, 617.

cxviii *De Haeresibus*, 57 (PL 42, 41).

cxix *De Opere Monachorum* chap. 1, n. 2 (PL 40, 549).

cxx *Comm. in Matth.*, I (PL 26, 45 A).

cxxi Hilarius, *Comm. in Matth.*, c. 5, n.8 (PL 9, 946).

cxxii *Comm. in Matth.*, I (PL 26, 45 C).

cxxiii Hilarius, *Comm. in Matth.*, c. 5, n.9 (PL 9, 947 A).

cxxiv *De serm. Dom.* II, xv, 52 (PL 34, 1291-1292).

cxxv *De Opere Monachorum* chap. 26-30, n. 35-39. (PL 40, 574-578).

cxxvi ibid. n. 10 (PL 9, 947 B-C).

cxxvii *De Civitate Dei*, lib. xxii, c. 12 & 16 (PL 41, 775 & 778).

cxxviii *In Matth.*, hom. xxii, 1 (PG 57, 300).

cxxix Hilarius, *Comm. in Matth.*, c. 5, n. 11 (PL 9, 948 A).

cxxx Hilarius, *Comm. in Matth.*, c. 5, n. 12 (PL 9, 949 A)

cxxxi *De serm. Dom.* II, xvii, 58 (PL 34, 1296).

cxxxii *De serm. Dom.* II, xvii, 56 (PL 34, 1294).

cxxxiii *Opus imperf.*, hom. 16 (PG 56, 724).

cxxxiv Hilarius, *Comm. in Matth.* c. 5, n. 13 (PL 9, 950A).